COMPUTER CONCEPTS +

MICROSOFT® OFFICE 365™

OFFICE 2016

For Microsoft® Office updates, go to sam.cengage.com

PARSONS + BESKEEN
CRAM + DUFFY
FRIEDRICHSEN + REDING

CENGAGE
Learning·

Australia • Brazil • Mexico • Singapore • United Kingdom • United States

Illustrated Computer Concepts &
Microsoft® Office 365™ & Office 2016
Parsons/Beskeen/Cram/Duffy/Friedrichsen/Reding

SVP, GM Skills & Global Product Management:
 Dawn Gerrain

Product Director: Kathleen McMahon

Senior Product Team Manager: Lauren Murphy

Product Team Manager: Andrea Topping

Associate Product Managers: Reed Curry,
 William Guiliani, Melissa Stehler

Senior Director, Development: Marah Bellegarde

Product Development Manager: Leigh Hefferon

Senior Content Developer: Christina Kling-Garrett

Contributing Author: Rachel Biheller Bunin

Developmental Editors: Rachel Biheller Bunin,
 Barbara Clemens, Pam Conrad, MT Cozzola,
 Lisa Ruffolo

Product Assistant: Erica Chapman

Marketing Director: Michele McTighe

Marketing Manager: Stephanie Albracht

Senior Production Director: Wendy Troeger

Production Director: Patty Stephan

Senior Content Project Manager: Stacey Lamodi

Designer: Diana Graham

Composition: GEX Publishing Services

For product information and technology assistance, contact us at
Cengage Learning Customer & Sales Support, 1-800-354-9706

For permission to use material from this text or product, submit all requests online at **www.cengage.com/permissions**
Further permissions questions can be emailed to
permissionrequest@cengage.com

Mac users: If you're working through this product using a Mac, some of the steps may vary. Additional information for Mac users is included with the Data Files for this product.

Some of the product names and company names used in this book have been used for identification purposes only and may be trademarks or registered trademarks of their respective manufacturers and sellers.

Windows® is a registered trademark of Microsoft Corporation.
© 2012 Microsoft. Microsoft and the Office logo are either registered trademarks or trademarks of Microsoft Corporation in the United States and/or other countries. Cengage Learning is an independent entity from Microsoft Corporation and not affiliated with Microsoft in any manner.

Disclaimer: Any fictional data related to persons or companies or URLs used throughout this text is intended for instructional purposes only. At the time this text was published, any such data was fictional and not belonging to any real persons or companies.

Disclaimer: The material in this text was written using Microsoft Windows 10 Professional and Office 365 Professional Plus and was Quality Assurance tested before the publication date. As Microsoft continually updates the Windows 10 operating system and Office 365, your software experience may vary slightly from what is presented in the printed text.

Library of Congress Control Number: 2015959036
ISBN: 978-1-305-87904-1

Cengage Learning
20 Channel Center Street
Boston, MA 02210
USA

Cengage Learning is a leading provider of customized learning solutions with employees residing in nearly 40 different countries and sales in more than 125 countries around the world. Find your local representative at **www.cengage.com**

Cengage Learning products are represented in Canada by Nelson Education, Ltd.

For your course and learning solutions, visit **www.cengage.com**

Purchase any of our products at your local college store or at our preferred online store **www.cengagebrain.com**

Printed in the United States of America
Print Number: 03   Print Year: 2017

Contents

Productivity App

Productivity Apps for School and Work PA-1
   Introduction to OneNote 2016 ....PA-2
   Introduction to Sway.....................................PA-6
   Introduction to Office Mix...............................PA-10
   Introduction to Microsoft Edge..........................PA-14

Concepts

Module 1: Computer and Internet Basics .... Concepts 1
   Computers in Your World ....Concepts 2
   How Computers Work................................Concepts 4
     Understanding the importance of stored programs
   Types of Computers..................................Concepts 6
     Video game consoles
   Personal Computers ....Concepts 8
   Computer Software ....Concepts 10
   The Internet and the Web ....Concepts 12
     Working in the cloud and using web apps
   How to Communicate Using Digital Devices..Concepts 14
     What is spam?
   How to Protect Your Privacy, Data, and Devices..Concepts 16
   Key Terms & Module Review.....................Concepts 18
   Concepts Review ....Concepts 19
   Independent Challenges ....Concepts 20
   Visual Workshop ....Concepts 22

Module 2: Computer Hardware....... Concepts 23
   Input Devices...Concepts 24
     Dedicated mobile digital devices
   Display Devices......................................Concepts 26
   Printers..Concepts 28
     Options for printing your photos
   Data Storage—An Overview ....Concepts 30
     Maintaining your hardware
   Data Storage Systems Features.................Concepts 32
     Non-technical words used to describe using a data storage system
   Optical Data Storage Systems..................Concepts 34
     Understanding hard drive partitions
     Viewing your data storage systems using File Explorer

   Solid-State Data Storage Systems.............Concepts 36
   How to Add Devices to Your Computer ....Concepts 38
   Key Terms & Module Review....................Concepts 40
   Concepts Review ....Concepts 41
   Independent Challenges ....Concepts 42
   Visual Workshop ....Concepts 44

Module 3: Computer Software......... Concepts 45
   Computer Software..................................Concepts 46
     Installed software that comes with new personal computers
   Licenses and Copyrights..........................Concepts 48
     How does digital technology affect intellectual property laws?
   How To Install and Uninstall Software......Concepts 50
   Operating Systems—An Overview............Concepts 52
   Operating Systems—A Comparison..........Concepts 54
     Comparing types of operating systems
   Utility Software.....................................Concepts 56
   Office Productivity Software ....Concepts 58
     Software suites
     Other productivity software
   Graphics Software ....Concepts 60
     Using data responsibly
   Other Application Software......................Concepts 62
   Key Terms & Module Review....................Concepts 64
   Concepts Review ....Concepts 65
   Independent Challenges ....Concepts 66
   Visual Workshop ....Concepts 68

Module 4: File Management and Digital Electronics .... Concepts 69
   File Management Tools ....Concepts 70
   Computer Folder Basics ....Concepts 72
     Folders and subfolders vs. directories and subdirectories
   Computer File Basics ....Concepts 74
   How to Manage Computer Files.............Concepts 76
     Deleting folders and files
   How Computers Represent Data ....Concepts 78
     More about bits and bytes
   Integrated Circuits—An Overview ....Concepts 80
   Processors—An Overview.......................Concepts 82
     How the processor gets instructions

Computer Memory: RAM ....Concepts 84
Other Types of Computer Memory ....Concepts 86
   Understanding remote vs. cloud storage?
Key Terms & Module Review ....Concepts 88
Concepts Review ....Concepts 89
Independent Challenges ....Concepts 90
Visual Workshop ....Concepts 92
Talking Points....................................Concepts 93

Windows 10

Module 1: Getting Started with Windows 10 .... Windows 1

Start Windows 10 ....Windows 2
   Using a touch screen with Windows
Navigate the Desktop and Start Menu ......Windows 4
Point, Click, and Drag ....Windows 6
   Selecting and moving items using touch-screen devices
Start an App ....Windows 8
   Using the Windows Store
Work with a Window ....Windows 10
   Using the Quick Access toolbar
Manage Multiple Windows ....Windows 12
Use Buttons, Menus, and
Dialog Boxes ....Windows 14
Get Help..Windows 16
   Using Cortana
Exit Windows 10 ....Windows 18
   Installing updates when you exit Windows
Practice ....Windows 20

Module 2: Understanding File Management .... Windows 25

Understand Files and Folders ....Windows 26
   Plan your file organization
Create and Save a File.............................Windows 28
Explore the Files and Folders on Your
Computer ....Windows 30
   Using and disabling Quick Access view
Change File and Folder Views ....Windows 32
   Using the Windows Action Center
   Customizing Details view
Open, Edit, and Save Files ....Windows 34
   Comparing Save and Save As
   Using Microsoft OneDrive
Copy Files ....Windows 36
   Copying files using Send to
Move and Rename Files ....Windows 38
   Using Task View to create multiple desktops

Search for Files and Folders ....Windows 40
   Using the Search Tools tab in File Explorer
   Using Microsoft Edge
Delete and Restore Files..........................Windows 42
   More techniques for selecting and moving files
Practice ....Windows 44

Office 2016

Module 1: Getting Started with Microsoft Office 2016 ....Office 1

Understand the Office 2016 Suite .... Office 2
   What is Office 365?
Start an Office App .... Office 4
   Enabling touch mode
   Using shortcut keys to move between Office programs
   Using the Office Clipboard
Identify Office 2016 Screen Elements .... Office 6
   Using Backstage view
Create and Save a File.................................... Office 8
   Saving files to OneDrive
Open a File and Save It with a New Name... Office 10
   Exploring File Open options
   Working in Compatibility Mode
View and Print Your Work............................ Office 12
   Customizing the Quick Access toolbar
   Creating a screen capture
Get Help, Close a File, and Exit an App .... Office 14
   Using Sharing features and Co-authoring capabilities
   Recovering a document
Practice .... Office 16

Word 2016

Module 1: Creating Documents with Word 2016 .... Word 1

Understand Word Processing Software .... Word 2
   Planning a document
Explore the Word Window............................. Word 4
Start a Document... Word 6
Save a Document .... Word 8
Select Text.. Word 10
Format Text Using the Mini Toolbar and
the Ribbon .... Word 12
Use a Document Template .... Word 14
   Using the Undo, Redo, and Repeat commands
Navigate a Document................................... Word 16
   Using Word document views
Practice .... Word 18

Module 2: Editing Documents............. Word 25
Cut and Paste Text................................... Word 26
   Using keyboard shortcuts
Copy and Paste Text............................... Word 28
   Splitting the document window to copy and
   move items in a long document
Use the Office Clipboard............................ Word 30
   Copying and moving items between documents
Find and Replace Text .... Word 32
   Navigating a document using the Navigation
   pane and the Go To command
Check Spelling and Grammar .... Word 34
   Using Smart Lookup
   Inserting text with AutoCorrect
Research Information .... Word 36
   Publishing a blog directly from Word
   Using a dictionary and other add-ins for Word
Add Hyperlinks... Word 38
   Sharing documents directly from Word,
   including e-mailing
Work with Document Properties.................. Word 40
   Viewing and modifying advanced document
   properties
Practice .... Word 42

**Module 3: Formatting Text and
    Paragraphs.............................. Word 49**
Format with Fonts .... Word 50
   Adding a drop cap
Use the Format Painter............................... Word 52
   Underlining text
Change Line and Paragraph Spacing .... Word 54
   Formatting with Quick Styles
Align Paragraphs... Word 56
   Formatting a document using themes
Work with Tabs... Word 58
Work with Indents....................................... Word 60
   Applying text effects and clearing formatting
Add Bullets and Numbering......................... Word 62
   Creating multilevel lists
Add Borders and Shading............................ Word 64
   Highlighting text in a document
Insert Online Pictures................................. Word 66
Practice .... Word 68

Module 4: Formatting Documents .... Word 77
Set Document Margins................................ Word 78
   Changing orientation, margin settings, and
   paper size
Create Sections and Columns .... Word 80
   Changing page layout settings for a section

Insert Page Breaks...................................... Word 82
   Controlling automatic pagination
Insert Page Numbers................................... Word 84
   Moving around in a long document
   Inserting Quick Parts
Add Headers and Footers............................ Word 86
   Adding a custom header or footer to the gallery
Insert a Table .... Word 88
Add Footnotes and Endnotes .... Word 90
   Customizing the layout and formatting of
   footnotes and endnotes
Insert Citations.. Word 92
Manage Sources and Create a Bibliography..... Word 94
   Working with Web sources
Practice .... Word 96

Excel 2016

**Module 1: Getting Started with
    Excel 2016................................... Excel 1**
Understand Spreadsheet Software................... Excel 2
Identify Excel 2016 Window Components...... Excel 4
   Using OneDrive and Office Online
Understand Formulas .... Excel 6
Enter Labels and Values and Use the AutoSum
Button.. Excel 8
   Navigating a worksheet
Edit Cell Entries... Excel 10
   Recovering unsaved changes to a workbook file
Enter and Edit a Simple Formula .... Excel 12
   Understanding named ranges
Switch Worksheet Views................................ Excel 14
Choose Print Options..................................... Excel 16
   Printing worksheet formulas
   Scaling to fit
Practice .... Excel 18

**Module 2: Working with Formulas and
    Functions .... Excel 25**
Create a Complex Formula .... Excel 26
   Using Add-ins to improve worksheet functionality
   Reviewing the order of precedence
Insert a Function .... Excel 28
Type a Function... Excel 30
   Using the COUNT and COUNTA functions
Copy and Move Cell Entries .... Excel 32
   Inserting and deleting selected cells
Understand Relative and Absolute Cell
References... Excel 34
   Using a mixed reference

Copy Formulas with Relative Cell
References..Excel 36
   Using Paste Preview
Copy Formulas with Absolute Cell
References..Excel 38
   Using the fill handle for sequential text
   or values
Round a Value with a Function......................Excel 40
   Using Auto Fill options
   Creating a new workbook using a template
Practice ....Excel 42

Module 3: Formatting a Worksheet ...... Excel 51

Format Values..Excel 52
   Formatting as a table
Change Font and Font Size ....Excel 54
   Inserting and adjusting online pictures and
   other images
Change Font Styles and Alignment ....Excel 56
   Rotating and indenting cell entries
Adjust Column Width..................................Excel 58
   Changing row height
Insert and Delete Rows and Columns...........Excel 60
   Hiding and unhiding columns and rows
   Adding and editing comments
Apply Colors, Patterns, and Borders ....Excel 62
   Working with themes and cell styles
Apply Conditional Formatting......................Excel 64
   Managing conditional formatting rules
Rename and Move a Worksheet.....................Excel 66
   Copying, adding, and deleting worksheets
Check Spelling..Excel 68
   Emailing a workbook
Practice ....Excel 70

Module 4: Working with Charts .... Excel 79

Plan a Chart..Excel 80
Create a Chart..Excel 82
   Creating sparklines
Move and Resize a Chart ....Excel 84
   Moving an embedded chart to a sheet
Change the Chart Design ....Excel 86
   Creating a combo chart
   Working with a 3-D chart
Change the Chart Format ....Excel 88
   Adding data labels to a chart
Format a Chart ....Excel 90
   Previewing a chart
   Changing alignment and angle in axis labels
   and titles

Annotate and Draw on a Chart ....Excel 92
   Adding SmartArt graphics
Create a Pie Chart......................................Excel 94
   Using the Insert Chart dialog box to discover
   new chart types
Practice ....Excel 96

Integration

Module 1: Integrating Word and Excel...........................Integration 1

Integrate Data Between Word and
Excel..Integration 2
   Understanding object linking and embedding
   (OLE)
Copy Data from Excel to Word ....Integration 4
Copy a Chart from Excel to Word..........Integration 6
Create Linked Objects ....Integration 8
   Opening linked files and reestablishing links to
   charts
Embed a Word File in Excel..................Integration 10
Practice ....Integration 12

Access 2016

Module 1: Getting Started with Access 2016 ....Access 1

Understand Relational Databases..................Access 2
Explore a Database ....Access 4
Create a Database ....Access 6
Create a Table ....Access 8
   Creating a table in Datasheet View
Create Primary Keys ....Access 10
   Object views
   Learning about field properties
Relate Two Tables......................................Access 12
Enter Data...Access 14
   Changing from Navigation mode to Edit mode
   Cloud computing
Edit Data...Access 16
   Resizing and moving datasheet columns
Practice ....Access 18

Module 2: Building and Using Queries....................................Access 27

Use the Query Wizard ....Access 28
   Simple Query Wizard
Work with Data in a Query ....Access 30
   Hiding and unhiding fields in a datasheet
   Freezing and unfreezing fields in a datasheet

Use Query Design View .... Access 32
    Adding or deleting a table in a query
Sort and Find Data .... Access 34
Filter Data .... Access 36
    Using wildcard characters
Apply AND Criteria .... Access 38
    Searching for blank fields
Apply OR Criteria .... Access 40
Format a Datasheet .... Access 42
Practice .... Access 44

Module 3: Using Forms .... Access 53
Use the Form Wizard .... Access 54
Create a Split Form .... Access 56
Use Form Layout View .... Access 58
    Table layouts
Add Fields to a Form .... Access 60
    Bound versus unbound controls
Modify Form Controls .... Access 62
Create Calculations .... Access 64
Modify Tab Order .... Access 66
    Form layouts
Insert an Image .... Access 68
    Applying a background image
Practice .... Access 70

Module 4: Using Reports .... Access 79
Use the Report Wizard .... Access 80
    Changing page orientation
Use Report Layout View .... Access 82
Review Report Sections .... Access 84
Apply Group and Sort Orders .... Access 86
    Record Source Property
Add Subtotals and Counts .... Access 88
Resize and Align Controls .... Access 90
    Precisely moving and resizing controls
Format a Report .... Access 92
Create Mailing Labels .... Access 94
Practice .... Access 96

Integration

Module 2: Integrating Word, Excel, and Access .... Integration 17
Integrate Data Among Word, Excel, and Access .... Integration 18
Import an Excel Worksheet into Access .... Integration 20

Copy a Word Table to Access .... Integration 22
Link an Access Table to Excel and Word .... Integration 24
Link an Access Table to Word .... Integration 26
    Opening linked files and enabling content
Practice .... Integration 28

Powerpoint 2016

Module 1: Creating a Presentation in PowerPoint 2016 .... Powerpoint 1
Define Presentation Software .... Powerpoint 2
    Using PowerPoint on a touch screen
Plan an Effective Presentation .... Powerpoint 4
    Understanding copyright
Examine the PowerPoint Window .... Powerpoint 6
    Viewing your presentation in gray scale or black and white
Enter Slide Text .... Powerpoint 8
    Inking a slide
Add a New Slide .... Powerpoint 10
    Entering and printing notes
Apply a Design Theme .... Powerpoint 12
    Customizing themes
Compare Presentation Views .... Powerpoint 14
Print a PowerPoint Presentation .... Powerpoint 16
    Microsoft Office Online Apps
Practice .... Powerpoint 18

Module 2: Modifying a Presentation .... Powerpoint 25
Enter Text in Outline View .... Powerpoint 26
    Using proofing tools for other languages
Format Text .... Powerpoint 28
    Replacing text and fonts
Convert Text to SmartArt .... Powerpoint 30
    Choosing SmartArt graphics
Insert and Modify Shapes .... Powerpoint 32
    Using the Eyedropper to match colors
Rearrange and Merge Shapes .... Powerpoint 34
    Changing the size and position of shapes
Edit and Duplicate Shapes .... Powerpoint 36
    Editing points of a shape
Align and Group Objects .... Powerpoint 38
    Distributing objects
Add Slide Footers .... Powerpoint 40
    Creating superscript and subscript text
Practice .... Powerpoint 42

Module 3: Inserting Objects into a Presentation .... Powerpoint 49

Insert Text from Microsoft Word......... Powerpoint 50
   Sending a presentation using email
Insert and Style a Picture..................... Powerpoint 52
   Inserting a screen recording
Insert a Text Box................................... Powerpoint 54
   Changing text box defaults
Insert a Chart.. Powerpoint 56
Enter and Edit Chart Data.................... Powerpoint 58
   Adding a hyperlink to a chart
Insert Slides from Other Presentations .... Powerpoint 60
   Working with multiple windows
Insert a Table .... Powerpoint 62
   Setting permissions
Insert and Format WordArt................. Powerpoint 64
   Saving a presentation as a video
Practice .... Powerpoint 66

Module 4: Finishing a Presentation .... Powerpoint 73

Modify Masters.................................... Powerpoint 74
   Create custom slide layouts
Customize the Background and Theme... Powerpoint 76
Use Slide Show Commands.................. Powerpoint 78
Set Slide Transitions and Timings .... Powerpoint 80
   Rehearsing slide show timings
Animate Objects .... Powerpoint 82
   Attaching a sound to an animation
Use Proofing and Language Tools .... Powerpoint 84
   Checking spelling as you type
Inspect a Presentation .... Powerpoint 86
   Digitally sign a presentation
Create an Office Mix .... Powerpoint 88
   Inserting an interactive quiz
Practice .... Powerpoint 90

Integration

Module 3: Integrating Word, Excel, Access, and PowerPoint .... Integration 33

Integrate Data Among Word, Excel, Access, and PowerPoint ....Integration 34
Import a Word Outline into PowerPoint ....Integration 36

Embed an Excel Worksheet in PowerPoint ....Integration 38
Link Access and Excel Objects to PowerPoint ....Integration 40
Manage Links.....................................Integration 42
Practice ....Integration 44

Outlook 2016

Module 1: Getting Started with Email .... Outlook 1

Communicate with Email ....Outlook 2
Use Email Addresses ....Outlook 4
Create and Send Emails..............................Outlook 6
   Understanding message headers in emails you receive
Understand Email Folders ....Outlook 8
   Managing your email
Receive and Reply to Emails.....................Outlook 10
   Setting up vacation responses
Forward Emails ....Outlook 12
   Controlling your message Flagging or labeling messages
Send Email Attachments ....Outlook 14
   Reviewing options when sending messages
Employ Good Email Practices ....Outlook 16
   Creating distribution lists
Practice ....Outlook 18

Module 2: Managing Information Using Outlook .... Outlook 25

Describe Outlook.......................................Outlook 26
   Weather in Calendar view
Organize Email ....Outlook 28
Manage Your Contacts ....Outlook 30
Manage Your Calendar ....Outlook 32
   Sending electronic business cards
Manage Tasks...Outlook 34
Create Notes ....Outlook 36
Connect Mail to Contacts ....Outlook 38
Apply Categories......................................Outlook 40
   Coordinating calendars
Practice ....Outlook 42

Glossary... **Glossary 1**

Index .... **Index 26**

Productivity Apps for School and Work

Corinne Hoisington

Lochlan keeps track of his class notes, football plays, and internship meetings with OneNote.

Zoe is using the annotation features of Microsoft Edge to take and save web notes for her research paper.

Nori is creating a Sway site to highlight this year's activities for the Student Government Association.

Hunter is adding interactive videos and screen recordings to his PowerPoint resume.

© Rawpixel/Shutterstock.com

Being computer literate no longer means mastery of only Word, Excel, PowerPoint, Outlook, and Access. To become technology power users, Hunter, Nori, Zoe, and Lochlan are exploring Microsoft OneNote, Sway, Mix, and Edge in Office 2016 and Windows 10.

In this Module

Introduction to OneNote 2016 2

Introduction to Sway 6

Introduction to Office Mix 10

Introduction to Microsoft Edge............. 14

Learn to use productivity apps!
Links to companion **Sways**, featuring **videos** with hands-on instructions, are located on www.cengagebrain.com.

Introduction to OneNote 2016

notebook | section tab | To Do tag | screen clipping | note | template | Microsoft OneNote Mobile app | sync | drawing canvas | inked handwriting | Ink to Text

As you glance around any classroom, you invariably see paper notebooks and notepads on each desk. Because deciphering and sharing handwritten notes can be a challenge, Microsoft OneNote 2016 replaces physical notebooks, binders, and paper notes with a searchable, digital notebook. OneNote captures your ideas and schoolwork on any device so you can stay organized, share notes, and work with others on projects. Whether you are a student taking class notes as shown in **Figure 1** or an employee taking notes in company meetings, OneNote is the one place to keep notes for all of your projects.

Figure 1: OneNote 2016 notebook

Each **notebook** is divided into sections, also called **section tabs**, by subject or topic.

Use **To Do tags**, icons that help you keep track of your assignments and other tasks.

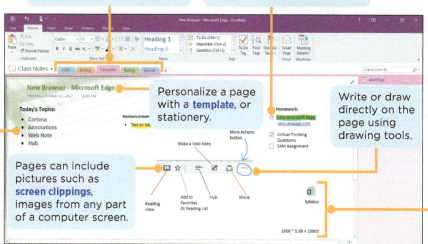

Type on a page to add a **note**, a small window that contains text or other types of information.

Personalize a page with a **template**, or stationery.

Write or draw directly on the page using drawing tools.

Pages can include pictures such as **screen clippings**, images from any part of a computer screen.

Attach files and enter equations so you have everything you need in one place.

Creating a OneNote Notebook

OneNote is divided into sections similar to those in a spiral-bound notebook. Each OneNote notebook contains sections, pages, and other notebooks. You can use OneNote for school, business, and personal projects. Store information for each type of project in different notebooks to keep your tasks separate, or use any other organization that suits you. OneNote is flexible enough to adapt to the way you want to work.

When you create a notebook, it contains a blank page with a plain white background by default, though you can use templates, or stationery, to apply designs in categories such as Academic, Business, Decorative, and Planners. Start typing or use the buttons on the Insert tab to insert notes, which are small resizable windows that can contain text, equations, tables, on-screen writing, images, audio and video recordings, to-do lists, file attachments, and file printouts. Add as many notes as you need to each page.

Syncing a Notebook to the Cloud

OneNote saves your notes every time you make a change in a notebook. To make sure you can access your notebooks with a laptop, tablet, or smartphone wherever you are, OneNote uses cloud-based storage, such as OneDrive or SharePoint. **Microsoft OneNote Mobile app**, a lightweight version of OneNote 2016 shown in **Figure 2**, is available for free in the Windows Store, Google Play for Android devices, and the AppStore for iOS devices.

If you have a Microsoft account, OneNote saves your notes on OneDrive automatically for all your mobile devices and computers, which is called **syncing**. For example, you can use OneNote to take notes on your laptop during class, and then open OneNote on your phone to study later. To use a notebook stored on your computer with your OneNote Mobile app, move the notebook to OneDrive. You can quickly share notebook content with other people using OneDrive.

Figure 2: Microsoft OneNote Mobile app

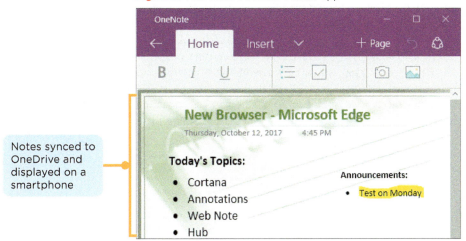

Notes synced to OneDrive and displayed on a smartphone

Taking Notes

Use OneNote pages to organize your notes by class and topic or lecture. Beyond simple typed notes, OneNote stores drawings, converts handwriting to searchable text and mathematical sketches to equations, and records audio and video.

OneNote includes drawing tools that let you sketch freehand drawings such as biological cell diagrams and financial supply-and-demand charts. As shown in **Figure 3**, the Draw tab on the ribbon provides these drawing tools along with shapes so you can insert diagrams and other illustrations to represent your ideas. When you draw on a page, OneNote creates a **drawing canvas**, which is a container for shapes and lines.

On the Job Now

OneNote is ideal for taking notes during meetings, whether you are recording minutes, documenting a discussion, sketching product diagrams, or listing follow-up items. Use a meeting template to add pages with content appropriate for meetings.

Figure 3: Tools on the Draw tab

Draw tab

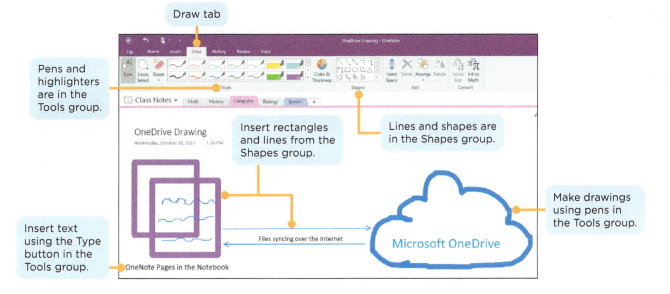

Pens and highlighters are in the Tools group.

Insert rectangles and lines from the Shapes group.

Lines and shapes are in the Shapes group.

Make drawings using pens in the Tools group.

Insert text using the Type button in the Tools group.

Converting Handwriting to Text

When you use a pen tool to write on a notebook page, the text you enter is called **inked handwriting**. OneNote can convert inked handwriting to typed text when you use the **Ink to Text** button in the Convert group on the Draw tab, as shown in **Figure 4**. After OneNote converts the handwriting to text, you can use the Search box to find terms in the converted text or any other note in your notebooks.

Figure 4: Converting handwriting to text

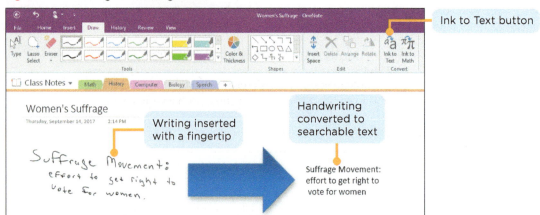

Ink to Text button

Writing inserted with a fingertip

Handwriting converted to searchable text

Women's Suffrage
Thursday, September 14, 2017   2:14 PM

Suffrage Movement: effort to get right to vote for women.

Suffrage Movement: effort to get right to vote for women

On the Job Now

Use OneNote as a place to brainstorm ongoing work projects. If a notebook contains sensitive material, you can password-protect some or all of the notebook so that only certain people can open it.

Recording a Lecture

If your computer or mobile device has a microphone or camera, OneNote can record the audio or video from a lecture or business meeting as shown in **Figure 5**. When you record a lecture (with your instructor's permission), you can follow along, take regular notes at your own pace, and review the video recording later. You can control the start, pause, and stop motions of the recording when you play back the recording of your notes.

Figure 5: Video inserted in a notebook

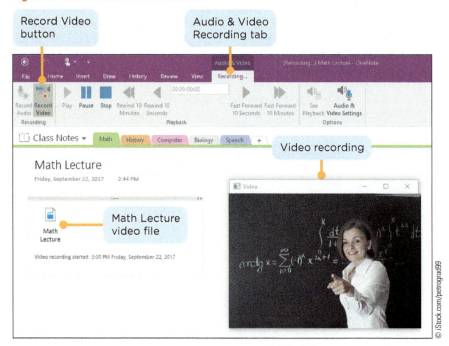

Record Video button

Audio & Video Recording tab

Video recording

Math Lecture
Friday, September 22, 2017   2:44 PM

Math Lecture video file

Video recording started: 3:00 PM Friday, September 22, 2017

© iStock.com/petrograd99

Try This Now

Learn to use OneNote!
Links to companion **Sways**, featuring **videos** with hands-on instructions, are located on www.cengagebrain.com.

1: Taking Notes for a Week

As a student, you can get organized by using OneNote to take detailed notes in your classes. Perform the following tasks:

a. Create a new OneNote notebook on your Microsoft OneDrive account (the default location for new notebooks). Name the notebook with your first name followed by "Notes," as in **Caleb Notes**.

b. Create four section tabs, each with a different class name.

c. Take detailed notes in those classes for one week. Be sure to include notes, drawings, and other types of content.

d. Sync your notes with your OneDrive. Submit your assignment in the format specified by your instructor.

2: Using OneNote to Organize a Research Paper

You have a research paper due on the topic of three habits of successful students. Use OneNote to organize your research. Perform the following tasks:

a. Create a new OneNote notebook on your Microsoft OneDrive account. Name the notebook **Success Research**.

b. Create three section tabs with the following names:

   - **Take Detailed Notes**
   - **Be Respectful in Class**
   - **Come to Class Prepared**

c. On the web, research the topics and find three sources for each section. Copy a sentence from each source and paste the sentence into the appropriate section. When you paste the sentence, OneNote inserts it in a note with a link to the source.

d. Sync your notes with your OneDrive. Submit your assignment in the format specified by your instructor.

3: Planning Your Career

Note: This activity requires a webcam or built-in video camera on any type of device.

Consider an occupation that interests you. Using OneNote, examine the responsibilities, education requirements, potential salary, and employment outlook of a specific career. Perform the following tasks:

a. Create a new OneNote notebook on your Microsoft OneDrive account. Name the notebook with your first name followed by a career title, such as **Kara - App Developer**.

b. Create four section tabs with the names **Responsibilities, Education Requirements, Median Salary**, and **Employment Outlook**.

c. Research the responsibilities of your career path. Using OneNote, record a short video (approximately 30 seconds) of yourself explaining the responsibilities of your career path. Place the video in the Responsibilities section.

d. On the web, research the educational requirements for your career path and find two appropriate sources. Copy a paragraph from each source and paste them into the appropriate section. When you paste a paragraph, OneNote inserts it in a note with a link to the source.

e. Research the median salary for a single year for this career. Create a mathematical equation in the Median Salary section that multiplies the amount of the median salary times 20 years to calculate how much you will possibly earn.

f. For the Employment Outlook section, research the outlook for your career path. Take at least four notes about what you find when researching the topic.

g. Sync your notes with your OneDrive. Submit your assignment in the format specified by your instructor.

Introduction to Sway

Sway site | responsive design | Storyline | card | Creative Commons license | animation emphasis effects | Docs.com

Expressing your ideas in a presentation typically means creating PowerPoint slides or a Word document. Microsoft Sway gives you another way to engage an audience. Sway is a free Microsoft tool available at Sway.com or as an app in Office 365. Using Sway, you can combine text, images, videos, and social media in a website called a **Sway site** that you can share and display on any device. To get started, you create a digital story on a web-based canvas without borders, slides, cells, or page breaks. A Sway site organizes the text, images, and video into a **responsive design**, which means your content adapts perfectly to any screen size as shown in **Figure 6**. You store a Sway site in the cloud on OneDrive using a free Microsoft account.

Figure 6: Sway site with responsive design

You can display a Sway presentation in a web browser.

Sway uses responsive design to make sure pages fit perfectly on any device.

© iStock.com/marinello, © iStock.com/mariekoliasz

Creating a Sway Presentation

You can use Sway to build a digital flyer, a club newsletter, a vacation blog, an informational site, a digital art portfolio, or a new product rollout. After you select your topic and sign into Sway with your Microsoft account, a **Storyline** opens, providing tools and a work area for composing your digital story. See **Figure 7**. Each story can include text, images, and videos. You create a Sway by adding text and media content into a Storyline section, or **card**. To add pictures, videos, or documents, select a card in the left pane and then select the Insert Content button. The first card in a Sway presentation contains a title and background image.

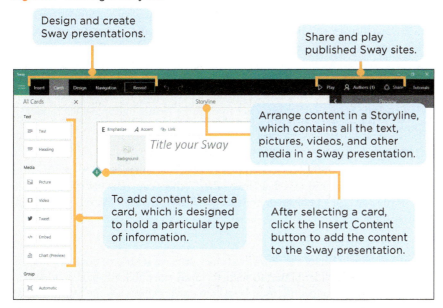

Design and create Sway presentations.

Share and play published Sway sites.

Arrange content in a Storyline, which contains all the text, pictures, videos, and other media in a Sway presentation.

To add content, select a card, which is designed to hold a particular type of information.

After selecting a card, click the Insert Content button to add the content to the Sway presentation.

Adding Content to Build a Story

As you work, Sway searches the Internet to help you find relevant images, videos, tweets, and other content from online sources such as Bing, YouTube, Twitter, and Facebook. You can drag content from the search results right into the Storyline. In addition, you can upload your own images and videos directly in the presentation. For example, if you are creating a Sway presentation about the market for commercial drones, Sway suggests content to incorporate into the presentation by displaying it in the left pane as search results. The search results include drone images tagged with a **Creative Commons license** at online sources as shown in **Figure 8**. A Creative Commons license is a public copyright license that allows the free distribution of an otherwise copyrighted work. In addition, you can specify the source of the media. For example, you can add your own Facebook or OneNote pictures and videos in Sway without leaving the app.

On the Job Now

If you have a Microsoft Word document containing an outline of your business content, drag the outline into Sway to create a card for each topic.

Figure 8: Images in Sway search results

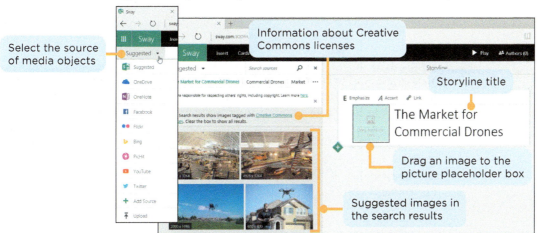

Select the source of media objects

Information about Creative Commons licenses

Storyline title

The Market for Commercial Drones

Drag an image to the picture placeholder box

Suggested images in the search results

Designing a Sway

Sway professionally designs your Storyline content by resizing background images and fonts to fit your display, and by floating text, animating media, embedding video, and removing images as a page scrolls out of view. Sway also evaluates the images in your Storyline and suggests a color palette based on colors that appear in your photos. Use the Design button to display tools including color palettes, font choices, **animation emphasis effects**, and style templates to provide a personality for a Sway presentation. Instead of creating your own design, you can click the Remix button, which randomly selects unique designs for your Sway site.

Publishing a Sway

Use the Play button to display your finished Sway presentation as a website. The Address bar includes a unique web address where others can view your Sway site. As the author, you can edit a published Sway site by clicking the Edit button (pencil icon) on the Sway toolbar.

Sharing a Sway

When you are ready to share your Sway website, you have several options as shown in **Figure 9**. Use the Share slider button to share the Sway site publically or keep it private. If you add the Sway site to the Microsoft **Docs.com** public gallery, anyone worldwide can use Bing, Google, or other search engines to find, view, and share your Sway site. You can also share your Sway site using Facebook, Twitter, Google+, Yammer, and other social media sites. Link your presentation to any webpage or email the link to your audience. Sway can also generate a code for embedding the link within another webpage.

Figure 9: Sharing a Sway site

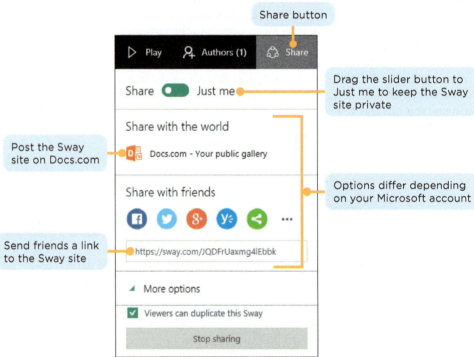

Try This Now

Learn to use Sway!
Links to companion **Sways**, featuring **videos** with hands-on instructions, are located on www.cengagebrain.com.

1: Creating a Sway Resume

Sway is a digital storytelling app. Create a Sway resume to share the skills, job experiences, and achievements you have that match the requirements of a future job interest. Perform the following tasks:

a. Create a new presentation in Sway to use as a digital resume. Title the Sway Storyline with your full name and then select a background image.
b. Create three separate sections titled **Academic Background, Work Experience**, and **Skills**, and insert text, a picture, and a paragraph or bulleted points in each section. Be sure to include your own picture.
c. Add a fourth section that includes a video about your school that you find online.
d. Customize the design of your presentation.
e. Submit your assignment link in the format specified by your instructor.

2: Creating an Online Sway Newsletter

Newsletters are designed to capture the attention of their target audience. Using Sway, create a newsletter for a club, organization, or your favorite music group. Perform the following tasks:

a. Create a new presentation in Sway to use as a digital newsletter for a club, organization, or your favorite music group. Provide a title for the Sway Storyline and select an appropriate background image.
b. Select three separate sections with appropriate titles, such as Upcoming Events. In each section, insert text, a picture, and a paragraph or bulleted points.
c. Add a fourth section that includes a video about your selected topic.
d. Customize the design of your presentation.
e. Submit your assignment link in the format specified by your instructor.

3: Creating and Sharing a Technology Presentation

To place a Sway presentation in the hands of your entire audience, you can share a link to the Sway presentation. Create a Sway presentation on a new technology and share it with your class. Perform the following tasks:

a. Create a new presentation in Sway about a cutting-edge technology topic. Provide a title for the Sway Storyline and select a background image.
b. Create four separate sections about your topic, and include text, a picture, and a paragraph in each section.
c. Add a fifth section that includes a video about your topic.
d. Customize the design of your presentation.
e. Share the link to your Sway with your classmates and submit your assignment link in the format specified by your instructor.

Introduction to Office Mix

add-in | clip | slide recording | Slide Notes | screen recording | free-response quiz

To enliven business meetings and lectures, Microsoft adds a new dimension to presentations with a powerful toolset called Office Mix, a free add-in for PowerPoint. (An **add-in** is software that works with an installed app to extend its features.) Using Office Mix, you can record yourself on video, capture still and moving images on your desktop, and insert interactive elements such as quizzes and live webpages directly into PowerPoint slides. When you post the finished presentation to OneDrive, Office Mix provides a link you can share with friends and colleagues. Anyone with an Internet connection and a web browser can watch a published Office Mix presentation, such as the one in **Figure 10**, on a computer or mobile device.

Figure 10: Office Mix presentation

Adding Office Mix to PowerPoint

To get started, you create an Office Mix account at the website mix.office.com using an email address or a Facebook or Google account. Next, you download and install the Office Mix add-in (see **Figure 11**). Office Mix appears as a new tab named Mix on the PowerPoint ribbon in versions of Office 2013 and Office 2016 running on personal computers (PCs).

Figure 11: Getting started with Office Mix

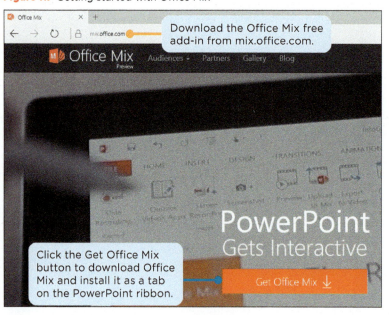

Capturing Video Clips

A **clip** is a short segment of audio, such as music, or video. After finishing the content on a PowerPoint slide, you can use Office Mix to add a video clip to animate or illustrate the content. Office Mix creates video clips in two ways: by recording live action on a webcam and by capturing screen images and movements. If your computer has a webcam, you can record yourself and annotate the slide to create a **slide recording** as shown in **Figure 12**.

Figure 12: Making a slide recording

Record your voice; also record video if your computer has a camera.

Use the Slide Notes button to display notes for your narration.

For best results, look directly at your webcam while recording video.

Choose a video and audio device to record images and sound.

Use inking tools to write and draw on the slide as you record.

When you are making a slide recording, you can record your spoken narration at the same time. The **Slide Notes** feature works like a teleprompter to help you focus on your presentation content instead of memorizing your narration. Use the Inking tools to make annotations or add highlighting using different pen types and colors. After finishing a recording, edit the video in PowerPoint to trim the length or set playback options.

The second way to create a video is to capture on-screen images and actions with or without a voiceover. This method is ideal if you want to show how to use your favorite website or demonstrate an app such as OneNote. To share your screen with an audience, select the part of the screen you want to show in the video. Office Mix captures everything that happens in that area to create a **screen recording**, as shown in **Figure 13**. Office Mix inserts the screen recording as a video in the slide.

Figure 13: Making a screen recording

Record the action on the screen within the red dashed outline.

Record audio while capturing your on-screen actions.

Select Area button

Inserting Quizzes, Live Webpages, and Apps

To enhance and assess audience understanding, make your slides interactive by adding quizzes, live webpages, and apps. Quizzes give immediate feedback to the user as shown in Figure 14. Office Mix supports several quiz formats, including a **free-response quiz** similar to a short answer quiz, and true/false, multiple-choice, and multiple-response formats.

Figure 14: Creating an interactive quiz

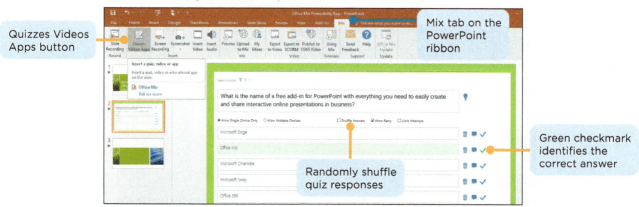

Sharing an Office Mix Presentation

When you complete your work with Office Mix, upload the presentation to your personal Office Mix dashboard as shown in Figure 15. Users of PCs, Macs, iOS devices, and Android devices can access and play Office Mix presentations. The Office Mix dashboard displays built-in analytics that include the quiz results and how much time viewers spent on each slide. You can play completed Office Mix presentations online or download them as movies.

Figure 15: Sharing an Office Mix presentation

Try This Now

Learn to use Office Mix!
Links to companion **Sways**, featuring **videos** with hands-on instructions, are located on www.cengagebrain.com.

1: Creating an Office Mix Tutorial for OneNote

Note: This activity requires a microphone on your computer.

Office Mix makes it easy to record screens and their contents. Create PowerPoint slides with an Office Mix screen recording to show OneNote 2016 features. Perform the following tasks:

    a. Create a PowerPoint presentation with the Ion Boardroom template. Create an opening slide with the title **My Favorite OneNote Features** and enter your name in the subtitle.

    b. Create three additional slides, each titled with a new feature of OneNote. Open OneNote and use the Mix tab in PowerPoint to capture three separate screen recordings that teach your favorite features.

    c. Add a fifth slide that quizzes the user with a multiple-choice question about OneNote and includes four responses. Be sure to insert a checkmark indicating the correct response.

    d. Upload the completed presentation to your Office Mix dashboard and share the link with your instructor.

    e. Submit your assignment link in the format specified by your instructor.

2: Teaching Augmented Reality with Office Mix

Note: This activity requires a webcam or built-in video camera on your computer.

A local elementary school has asked you to teach augmented reality to its students using Office Mix. Perform the following tasks:

    a. Research augmented reality using your favorite online search tools.

    b. Create a PowerPoint presentation with the Frame template. Create an opening slide with the title **Augmented Reality** and enter your name in the subtitle.

    c. Create a slide with four bullets summarizing your research of augmented reality. Create a 20-second slide recording of yourself providing a quick overview of augmented reality.

    d. Create another slide with a 30-second screen recording of a video about augmented reality from a site such as YouTube or another video-sharing site.

    e. Add a final slide that quizzes the user with a true/false question about augmented reality. Be sure to insert a checkmark indicating the correct response.

    f. Upload the completed presentation to your Office Mix dashboard and share the link with your instructor.

    g. Submit your assignment link in the format specified by your instructor.

3: Marketing a Travel Destination with Office Mix

Note: This activity requires a webcam or built-in video camera on your computer.

To convince your audience to travel to a particular city, create a slide presentation marketing any city in the world using a slide recording, screen recording, and a quiz. Perform the following tasks:

    a. Create a PowerPoint presentation with any template. Create an opening slide with the title of the city you are marketing as a travel destination and your name in the subtitle.

    b. Create a slide with four bullets about the featured city. Create a 30-second slide recording of yourself explaining why this city is the perfect vacation destination.

    c. Create another slide with a 20-second screen recording of a travel video about the city from a site such as YouTube or another video-sharing site.

    d. Add a final slide that quizzes the user with a multiple-choice question about the featured city with five responses. Be sure to include a checkmark indicating the correct response.

    e. Upload the completed presentation to your Office Mix dashboard and share your link with your instructor.

    f. Submit your assignment link in the format specified by your instructor.

Introduction to Microsoft Edge

Reading view | Hub | Cortana | Web Note | Inking | sandbox

Microsoft Edge is the default web browser developed for the Windows 10 operating system as a replacement for Internet Explorer. Unlike its predecessor, Edge lets you write on webpages, read webpages without advertisements and other distractions, and search for information using a virtual personal assistant. The Edge interface is clean and basic, as shown in **Figure 16**, meaning you can pay more attention to the webpage content.

Figure 16: Microsoft Edge tools

Forward button
New tab button
Web address in the Address bar
Add to favorites or reading list button
Back button
Reading view button
More button
Share Web Note button
Refresh (F5) button
Hub (Favorites, reading list, history, and downloads) button
Make a Web Note button

Browsing the Web with Microsoft Edge

One of the fastest browsers available, Edge allows you to type search text directly in the Address bar. As you view the resulting webpage, you can switch to **Reading view**, which is available for most news and research sites, to eliminate distracting advertisements. For example, if you are catching up on technology news online, the webpage might be difficult to read due to a busy layout cluttered with ads. Switch to Reading view to refresh the page and remove the original page formatting, ads, and menu sidebars to read the article distraction-free.

Consider the **Hub** in Microsoft Edge as providing one-stop access to all the things you collect on the web, such as your favorite websites, reading list, surfing history, and downloaded files.

Locating Information with Cortana

Cortana, the Windows 10 virtual assistant, plays an important role in Microsoft Edge. After you turn on Cortana, it appears as an animated circle in the Address bar when you might need assistance, as shown in the restaurant website in **Figure 17**. When you click the Cortana icon, a pane slides in from the right of the browser window to display detailed information about the restaurant, including maps and reviews. Cortana can also assist you in defining words, finding the weather, suggesting coupons for shopping, updating stock market information, and calculating math.

Figure 17: Cortana providing restaurant information

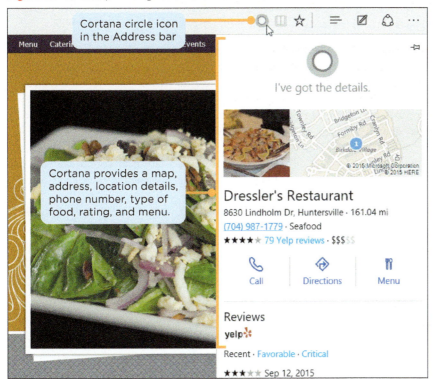

Cortana circle icon in the Address bar

I've got the details.

Cortana provides a map, address, location details, phone number, type of food, rating, and menu.

Dressler's Restaurant

8630 Lindholm Dr, Huntersville · 161.04 mi

(704) 987-1779 · Seafood

★★★★☆ 79 Yelp reviews · $$$$$

Call   Directions   Menu

Reviews

yelp

Recent · Favorable · Critical

★★★☆☆ Sep 12, 2015

Annotating Webpages

One of the most impressive Microsoft Edge features are the **Web Note** tools, which you use to write on a webpage or to highlight text. When you click the Make a Web Note button, an **Inking** toolbar appears, as shown in **Figure 18**, that provides writing and drawing tools. These tools include an eraser, a pen, and a highlighter with different colors. You can also insert a typed note and copy a screen image (called a screen clipping). You can draw with a pointing device, fingertip, or stylus using different pen colors. Whether you add notes to a recipe, annotate sources for a research paper, or select a product while shopping online, the Web Note tools can enhance your productivity. After you complete your notes, click the Save button to save the annotations to OneNote, your Favorites list, or your Reading list. You can share the inked page with others using the Share Web Note button.

On the Job Now

To enhance security, Microsoft Edge runs in a partial sandbox, an arrangement that prevents attackers from gaining control of your computer. Browsing within the **sandbox** protects computer resources and information from hackers.

Figure 18: Web Note tools in Microsoft Edge

Inking toolbar with Web Note tools for making annotations

Writing and drawing created with the Pen tool

Highlighted text

Surface Pro

Work anywhere

Save a copy of the webpage with annotations

Typed note

Try This Now

1: Using Cortana in Microsoft Edge

Note: This activity requires using Microsoft Edge on a Windows 10 computer.

Cortana can assist you in finding information on a webpage in Microsoft Edge. Perform the following tasks:

a. Create a Word document using the Word Screen Clipping tool to capture the following screenshots.

- Screenshot A—Using Microsoft Edge, open a webpage with a technology news article. Right-click a term in the article and ask Cortana to define it.
- Screenshot B—Using Microsoft Edge, open the website of a fancy restaurant in a city near you. Make sure the Cortana circle icon is displayed in the Address bar. (If it's not displayed, find a different restaurant website.) Click the Cortana circle icon to display a pane with information about the restaurant.
- Screenshot C—Using Microsoft Edge, type **10 USD to Euros** in the Address bar without pressing the Enter key. Cortana converts the U.S. dollars to Euros.
- Screenshot D—Using Microsoft Edge, type **Apple stock** in the Address bar without pressing the Enter key. Cortana displays the current stock quote.

b. Submit your assignment in the format specified by your instructor.

2: Viewing Online News with Reading View

Note: This activity requires using Microsoft Edge on a Windows 10 computer.

Reading view in Microsoft Edge can make a webpage less cluttered with ads and other distractions. Perform the following tasks:

a. Create a Word document using the Word Screen Clipping tool to capture the following screenshots.

- Screenshot A—Using Microsoft Edge, open the website **mashable.com**. Open a technology article. Click the Reading view button to display an ad-free page that uses only basic text formatting.
- Screenshot B—Using Microsoft Edge, open the website **bbc.com**. Open any news article. Click the Reading view button to display an ad-free page that uses only basic text formatting.
- Screenshot C—Make three types of annotations (Pen, Highlighter, and Add a typed note) on the BBC article page displayed in Reading view.

b. Submit your assignment in the format specified by your instructor.

3: Inking with Microsoft Edge

Note: This activity requires using Microsoft Edge on a Windows 10 computer.

Microsoft Edge provides many annotation options to record your ideas. Perform the following tasks:

a. Open the website **wolframalpha.com** in the Microsoft Edge browser. Wolfram Alpha is a well-respected academic search engine. Type **US$100 1965 dollars in 2015** in the Wolfram Alpha search text box and press the Enter key.

b. Click the Make a Web Note button to display the Web Note tools. Using the Pen tool, draw a circle around the result on the webpage. Save the page to OneNote.

c. In the Wolfram Alpha search text box, type the name of the city closest to where you live and press the Enter key. Using the Highlighter tool, highlight at least three interesting results. Add a note and then type a sentence about what you learned about this city. Save the page to OneNote. Share your OneNote notebook with your instructor.

d. Submit your assignment link in the format specified by your instructor.

Computer and Internet Basics

Learning Outcomes

1. Define a personal computer and describe computer use in daily life

2. Explain the four basic functions of a computer system

3. Identify the main computer categories

4. Describe digital devices that can be part of a personal computer

5. Define software and give examples of operating systems

6. Define the Internet and explain how to navigate webpages

7. Explain ways to use the Internet and digital devices to communicate with others

8. Explain how to protect your digital data and devices

LESSON TOPICS

- Computers in Your World
- How Computers Work
- Types of Computers
- Personal Computers
- Computer Software
- The Internet and the Web
- How to Communicate Using Digital Devices
- How to Protect Your Privacy, Data, and Devices

Computers in Your World

Whether you realize it or not, you already know a lot about personal computers and other digital devices. You've picked up information from advertisements and magazine articles, from books and movies, from conversations, and perhaps even from using a computer, smartphone, or other digital device. The digital revolution and the expansion of the Internet into daily life are the reasons computers are all around you. See FIGURE 1-1. This lesson helps you start organizing what you know about the digital revolution and computers.

Learning Outcome 1:
Define a personal computer and describe computer use in daily life

● **What is the digital revolution and how does it affect me?** The **digital revolution** is an ongoing process of social, political, and economic change brought about by **digital technology**. Digital technology includes digital devices such as computers, portable media players, cameras, mobile phones, smartphones, tablet computers, global positioning systems (GPSs), DVD and CD players, e-book readers, digital voice recorders, and video games. Even cars and home appliances, such as microwave ovens, refrigerators, and washing machines, use digital electronics. Many of these everyday objects can send and receive data over the Internet, a phenomenon known as The **Internet of Things**. The digital revolution influences the tools you use to work, play, teach, and govern, especially when you use a computer.

● **What is a computer?** A **computer** is an electronic device that accepts input, processes data, stores data, and produces output as information. If a machine performs these four basic functions, it is a computer.

● **Why would I use a computer?** You might use a computer to access information on the web, create documents, calculate a budget, edit and share digital photographs, create music, and produce original graphics. Most likely, you use a computer to communicate through the Internet.

● **Do all computers look alike?** Computers come in many styles and sizes. The way a computer looks depends on how the computer system is set up and what it will be used for. Usually, when people talk about computers, they are talking about a **personal computer (PC)**. A **computer system** includes hardware and software.

● **What is hardware?** **Hardware** refers to the electronic and mechanical parts of the computer. The **system unit** is the box that houses the most important parts of a computer system. The term hardware refers not only to the internal parts of the computer but also to its external parts, which are called peripheral devices.

FIGURE 1-1: Computers are a part of daily life

- **What is a peripheral device?** A **peripheral device** is hardware that can be added to a computer system to expand what the computer can do. Popular peripheral devices include printers, media players, digital cameras, external drives, scanners, and graphics tablets. Once your computer system is set up with its hardware and peripheral devices, it needs software in order to work as a computer.

- **What is software?** **Software** is a computer program that tells the computer how to perform tasks. You may have heard the terms word processing software, antivirus software, apps, or web applications. These terms refer to some of the software that runs on your computer and other digital devices, such as your smartphone. There are many categories of software available for computers.

- **How do I use a computer?** To use a computer, you must input data or information. You use an **input device** (such as a keyboard, mouse, or touch screen) to input information. The input device and the computer work together to change the information into a series of electronic signals the computer can understand. Once the computer has the input, it processes the information and sends the processed information to an **output device**. Common output devices include display devices (screens), printers, or speakers. As you work, you continue to input information and to use the output.

- **What is digitization, and why is it important in my daily life?** **Digitization** is the process of converting text, numbers, sound, photos, and video into data that can be processed by a computer. Digital images and sounds can be easily stored, copied, and shared. Digitization creates versatility. You can take a photo, instantly post it to social media online, store it on a hard drive, or copy it to a flash drive. You can email it to a friend, add it to a report, print it, combine it with other photos to make a slide show, burn the slide show to a DVD, watch the slide show on your home theater system, and put it on the web. Digital video is responsible for special effects in movies, trends in 3D animation, portable video, and affordable home video. Digital sound has transformed the way music is marketed, sold, purchased, and played. Human speech can also be digitized. For example, when you call a business for help or information, digitized voice telephone systems understand and respond to your spoken words. GPS devices tell you the directions as your drive.

- **Is my smartphone a computer?** Yes, because a smartphone performs the four basic functions of a computer, it can be considered a computer. For example, it accepts input—the phone numbers you type in. It processes the input—calling the number. It stores data—keeping phone numbers. It outputs data—the conversation. When you think of a smartphone this way, it is a computer.

  Other digital devices, such as tablet computers, video game consoles, and media players, also perform the four basic functions of a computer. These devices accept input, process data, store data, and output information in the form of text, spoken words, music, video, and images. These digital devices share other computer characteristics. For example, many tablets feature a keyboard, accept handwriting input, and work with touch screen icons. These digital devices today are the result of digital convergence.

- **What is digital convergence?** **Digital convergence** is the trend to blend several technologies that have distinct functions into a single product. An example of digital convergence is the office machine that has Internet and communications features and works as a fax, printer, and scanner. Today many devices, such as mobile phones, portable media players, cameras, and GPSs, include features that overlap each other. Most mobile phones are smartphones. See **FIGURE 1-2**. Smartphones include voice communication and other features such as text messaging, email, web access, removable storage, camera, radio, music player, games, financial management tools, personal organizers, and navigation tools.

FIGURE 1-2: Smartphones blend several technologies

Speakers (for output)
Clock and calendar
GPS software for navigation
Send and receive email
Send and receive phone calls
Internet browser

Camera for input
Processor inside unit (for processing)
Touch screen (for input and for output)
Microphone (for input)

© photomaker.kiev.ua/Shutterstock.com

How Computers Work

The parts of a computer system work together to accomplish these basic computer tasks—accept input, process data, store data, and produce output as information you can use. Most computers also are able to communicate to share information with other computers. Refer to FIGURE 1-3 as you read more about how computers work.

Learning Outcome 2:
Explain the four basic functions of a computer system

FIGURE 1-3: Basic computer parts and functions

Camera for input

System unit for processing and storing data

Speaker for output

Keyboard for typing input

Display device for output

10:49
Friday, July 31

Connections to the Internet and local networks for input and output

CD/DVD drive for storing and getting data

Mouse for input

Printer for producing hard copy output

External hard drive for backup

Flash drive for storage

Right Center: © S.Dashkevych/Shutterstock.com; Right Bottom: © You can more/Shutterstock.com

● **How do I turn on my computer?** A computer is often a computer system. You may need to press more than one switch or button to turn on the monitor, printer, speakers, and finally the computer. However, some computers, such as notebook or tablet computers, have one button or switch that turns on the entire computer system, including the computer, the monitor or display, and the speakers. Most computers take a few minutes to power up, and then you may be prompted to enter your **user ID** and **password**.

● **Why do I need a user ID and password?** You are assigned a user ID and password for security reasons. In a public setting, such as a school lab, you will usually be assigned a user ID and a password by the system administrator. If your personal computer asks for a user ID and password, you can create your own the first time you start the computer. You use that user ID and password every time you sign on to that computer and access the programs you have permission to use. Never share your user ID or password with anyone.

● **What does "run a program" mean?** It means to start a program. The instructions that tell a computer how to carry out the processing tasks are referred to as a **computer program**, or simply a **program**. Programs, especially smaller programs on tablets and smartphones, are also called apps—short for applications. Once the program is running, it is ready for you to use.

● **How do I tell a computer what I want it to do?** You tell a computer what to do by interacting with it. You use a keyboard to type commands and other text. You use a mouse to access menus, as well as to click buttons and icons. On a computer with a touch screen, such as a tablet or smartphone, you touch and drag icons. Many digital devices today have on-screen keyboards. When you tell a computer what to do, you are providing input. Computer **input** is whatever is put into a computer system. Input can be supplied by a person, by the environment, or by another computer. Once information is input into a computer, it becomes data.

- **What do computers do with data?** Computers process—that is, they work with—data in many ways. In the context of computing, data refers to the symbols that represent facts, objects, and ideas. In a computer, most **processing** takes place in a **processor** (also known as a **microprocessor**). The main processor in a computer is called the **central processing unit (CPU)**, which is sometimes described as the brain of the computer. A computer does two things with processed data. It stores the data and it outputs the data as information.

- **Is there a difference between computer memory and computer storage?** Yes. **Memory** temporarily holds computer data waiting to be processed, stored, or output. **Storage** holds computer data on a permanent basis when it is not immediately needed for processing. While you are working on a document, it is in memory; it is not in storage until you save it for the first time. After you save the document as a computer file, it is stored on the hard drive or some other storage medium, such as a flash drive. It is also still in memory until you close the document, exit the program, or turn off the computer.

- **What are computer files?** A computer file, or **file**, is a named collection of data that exists on a **storage medium**, such as a disk drive, CD, DVD, or flash drive. Every file has a **filename**, which should provide meaningful information about the file contents. The filename has two parts: the filename and the file extension. An example of a filename for a photo is Bridge.jpg. The name that you give the file is to the left of the period. The **file extension** is the period and two or more characters to the right of the period.

- **What is output and how do I use it?** **Output** is the processed results produced by a computer. It is the information you want, such as reports, documents, music, graphs, and pictures. An output device (such as a monitor, a printer, or speakers) displays, prints, says, or otherwise transmits the results of processing.

- **Do all computers have network and Internet access?** Many personal computer systems include built-in technology for wired or wireless connections to a computer network. Networking technology is useful for constructing a home network, connecting one or more computers to share devices, or connecting to public networks such as the Internet.

- **Do I have to turn off my computer?** If you aren't going to use your computer for a while, you can turn the power off. Computers have different ways to power down. Typically, you do so by issuing a command to the operating system. You will need to press the power button to turn the computer back on (see **FIGURE 1-4**). However, for most computers, there's no need to turn the power off. Instead, you can put your computer to sleep. Most notebooks and tablets "go to sleep" if you don't use them for a while or when you close the lid. Some devices require you to press the power button. Sleep mode uses very little battery power, and your computer will start up faster. Most computers save unsaved work and turn off the computer if the battery is too low. For privacy and security, most computers can be set up to enter your password when you resume working.

FIGURE 1-4: Power buttons

Common symbol for the Power button on many computers

Power button

Understanding the importance of stored programs

Computers use stored programs, that is, the instructions for a computing task are stored on the computer so they can be loaded quickly into a computer's memory when needed. These instructions can easily be replaced by different instructions when it is time for the computer to perform a different task. So you can use your computer for one task, such as writing a letter, and then easily switch to a different task, such as editing a photo, looking at a webpage, or sending an email message.

An emerging trend is to store data and use programs stored in the cloud. The **cloud** is mass storage on remote computers. **Cloud computing** refers to working in the cloud. When you use a program that is stored in the cloud, parts of the programs you use are downloaded to your computer for efficiency.

Types of Computers

Computers are electronic devices that perform many tasks. Some types of computers are better for certain jobs than others. Computers are categorized according to how they are used, what they cost, their physical size, and their processing capability. Knowing about computer categories can help you buy the computer that best meets your needs.

Learning Outcome 3:
Identify the main computer categories

● **Which type of computer is right for me?** You will most likely use a personal computer. A personal computer meets the needs of an individual for home, school, or small business use. It typically provides access to a wide variety of software, such as word processing, photo editing, financial management, email, and Internet access. Personal computers include **desktop computers** and portable computers.

● **Will a desktop computer fit on my desk**? Probably, yes. A desktop computer's system unit can be housed in a vertical case or a horizontal case. Most horizontal cases are placed under the display device to save desk space. A vertical case can be placed on the desk, or in a space beneath the desk. The case for a vertical system unit is often referred to as a tower. Tower units are the system unit of choice for those who want to upgrade their system, such as by adding additional storage devices or a more powerful graphics card. It is easy to get inside a tower case and swap parts. Some manufacturers of desktop computers create an all-in-one unit. These computers build the computer technology into the back of a flat-panel screen or into a keyboard. See **FIGURE 1-5**.

FIGURE 1-5: Examples of personal desktop computers

Tower unit   All-in-one unit

Left: © Oleksiy Mark/Shutterstock.com

● **What if I need to use my computer in different locations?** You will want to consider a portable computer.

Portable computers include **notebook computers** (sometimes called **laptop computers**), **netbooks**, **tablet computers**, slate tablets, and handheld computers. Examples of portable computers are shown in **FIGURE 1-6**.

FIGURE 1-6: Examples of portable personal computers

Notebook

Tablet

2-in-1 tablet

● **What are the advantages of a notebook computer?** You might consider buying a notebook computer if you want to be able to move the computer from place to place, such as from home to school. Notebook computers have a clamshell design, which means they open and close on a hinge. When the computer is closed, the screen, pointing device, and keyboard are protected inside the case.

● **Why should I consider a tablet computer?** A tablet computer is a portable computer that features a touch screen, circuitry, and battery in a single unit. You use the screen for entering text, or as drawing pad. A tablet computer is slightly smaller than a notebook computer. Most tablet computers can access the Internet or wireless networks. Tablet computers often have built-in web cams and are also configured to accept voice input.

● **What is a netbook?** A netbook computer offers more portability than a standard notebook computer. These small computers are scaled-down versions of standard clamshell-style notebook computers. They are typically only seven or eight inches wide and weigh about two pounds.

● **What if I just need a small portable computer that fits in my pocket?** Then, a **handheld computer** is just the answer. A handheld computer is one type of handheld digital device. Other types include mobile phones, cameras, e-readers, or portable media players. The most popular handheld digital device is the smartphone.

Handheld digital devices usually have features such as removable storage, email, web access, voice communications, built-in camera, and GPS. Handheld digital devices run computer programs, but they usually run special scaled-down versions of these programs. With its slow processing speed and small screen, a handheld computer is not powerful enough to handle many of the tasks that can be accomplished using desktop, notebook, tablet, or even netbook computers.

● **What are some other categories of computers I should know about?** There are three more general categories of computers you might hear people talk about.

■ **Workstations** are usually powerful desktop computers designed for specialized tasks that require a lot of processing speed, such as medical imaging, full-motion video graphics, and computer-aided design. Most are designed for creating and displaying three-dimensional and animated graphics.

■ A **mainframe computer** is a large and expensive computer capable of simultaneously processing data for hundreds or thousands of users. Mainframes are generally used by businesses, universities, or governments to provide centralized storage, processing, and management of large amounts of data where reliability, data security, and centralized control are necessary. See **FIGURE 1-7**.

FIGURE 1-7: IBM Mainframe computer

© senticus/Shutterstock.com

■ A computer is categorized as a **supercomputer** if, at the time it is built, it is one of the fastest computers in the world. Supercomputers can tackle tasks that would not be practical for other computers such as breaking codes and modeling worldwide weather systems.

● **What does it mean when I hear, "The server is down?" Is a server another type of computer?** The purpose of a **server** is to serve computers on a network (such as the Internet or a home network) by supplying them with data. Just about any personal computer, workstation, mainframe, or supercomputer can be configured to perform the work of a server. When you hear that a server is down, it means a computer connected to that server can't access the programs and files on that server.

Video game consoles

A video game console, such as Nintendo's Wii, Sony's PlayStation, or Microsoft's Xbox, is not generally referred to as a personal computer. Video game consoles originated as simple digital devices that connected to a TV set and provided only a pair of joysticks for input. Today's video game consoles contain processors and storage that are equivalent to any processor found in a personal computer.

They produce graphics, including 3D graphics, that rival those on sophisticated workstations. Many consoles include built-in Wi-Fi for easy connection to the Internet. Consoles can be used to watch movies, send and receive email, and participate in online activities such as multiplayer games. Despite these features, video game consoles are not considered a replacement for a personal computer.

Personal Computers

The term computer system usually refers to a computer and all of the input, output, and storage devices that are connected to it. Despite differences in the size and dimensions of components (often called a computer's **form factor**), a personal computer system includes standard equipment or devices. Each computer type is suited for a particular purpose. See TABLE 1-1.

Learning Outcome 4:
Describe digital devices that can be part of a personal computer

● **What are the basic parts of a desktop personal computer system?** FIGURE 1-8 shows the basic parts of a typical desktop personal computer system. Refer to the figure as you read about each part.

■ **System unit:** The system unit is the case that holds the power supply, storage devices, and the circuit boards. It houses the main circuit board (also called the motherboard), which contains the processor.

■ **Display device**: Most computers have a **display device** called a **monitor**. The monitor screen is the primary output device. The monitor for a desktop computer is a separate part connected to the system unit.

■ **Keyboard**: Most computers are equipped with a **keyboard** as the primary input device. It is used to enter text and numbers.

■ **Mouse**: A **mouse** is a input device designed to move and select on-screen graphical objects and controls.

■ **Storage devices**: A **storage device** is used to store data on a computer or to share data among computers. Storage devices are both input and output devices. Data is read from a storage medium and often can be written to a storage medium. Most personal computers have more than one type of storage device. Each storage device uses a different storage medium. The primary storage device is the **hard drive** (also called **hard disk drive**). The hard drive is usually mounted inside the system unit.

   Other storage devices can be used with a personal computer. A **USB flash drive** plugs directly into a USB port on the computer system unit. An external hard drive also plugs directly into a USB port. A CD drive, a

FIGURE 1-8: Typical desktop computer system

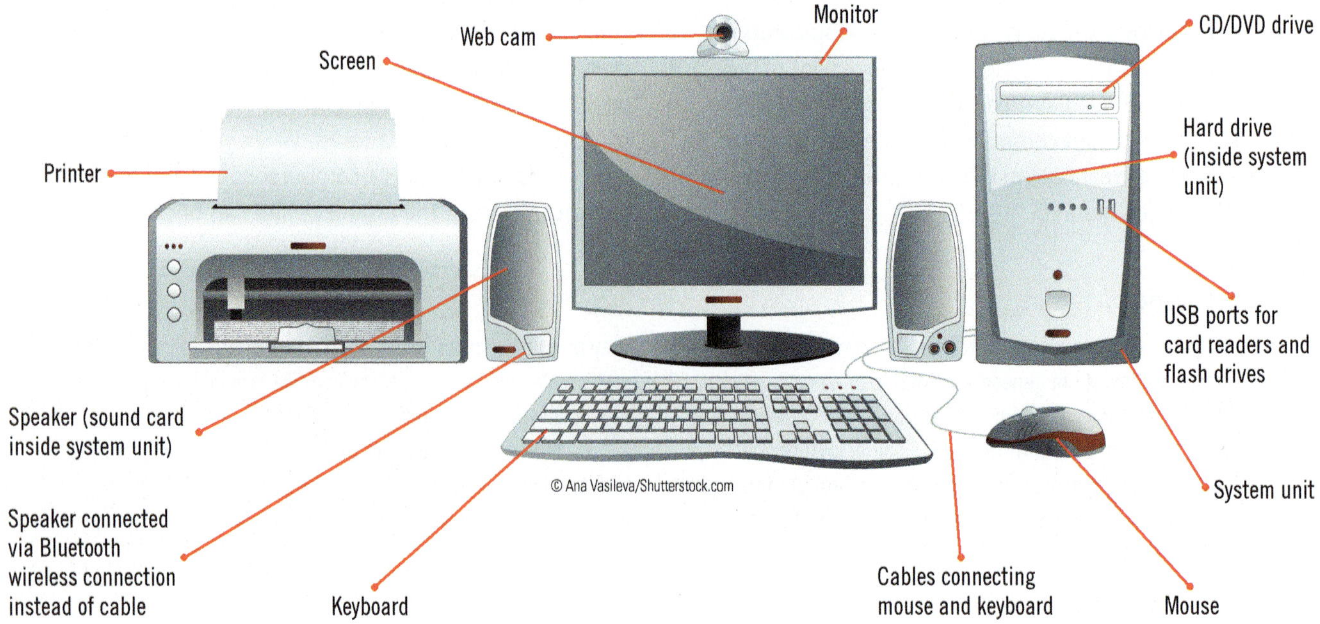

© Ana Vasileva/Shutterstock.com

Web cam
Screen
Monitor
CD/DVD drive
Printer
Hard drive (inside system unit)
Speaker (sound card inside system unit)
USB ports for card readers and flash drives
Speaker connected via Bluetooth wireless connection instead of cable
Keyboard
Cables connecting mouse and keyboard
System unit
Mouse

DVD drive, a Blue-ray Disc (BD) drive, or a combination drive is usually mounted inside the system unit. These **optical drives** are storage devices that work with storage media such as CDs, DVDs, and BDs. Optical drives are used to store computer data and also handy for playing audio and movies.

- **Sound system**: A **sound system** is made up of speakers and a small circuit board called a **sound card**, required for high-quality music, narration, and sound effects. A desktop computer's sound card sends signals to external speakers. The sound card is an input and an output device, while speakers are output devices only.
- **Printer**: A **printer** is an output device that produces computer-generated text, photographs, or graphic images on paper velum, fabric, or some other surface.
- **Web cam:** A **web cam** allows you to capture video images using your computer. Software makes it possible to send and receive video in real time with another person to communicate with voice as well as images.
- **Peripheral devices**: There are many other peripheral devices that can be connected to a computer. For example, you can connect a portable **digital media player** and a **digital camera** in order to transfer music and photos between the devices and the computer system. Peripheral devices can be connected via cables or a short range network called **Bluetooth**.

- **Does a portable computer have all these parts?** Yes, but a portable computer, such as a notebook computer, is a single unit that includes the system unit, a built-in flat-panel monitor, a built-in keyboard, and built-in speakers. Many new portable computers include a built-in web cam. Other devices, such as a printer, can be connected to a portable computer in the same way they can be connected to a desktop computer. Portable computers can also be part of a network and can have Internet access.

- **How do I know if my computer has network and Internet access?** Many personal computer systems include built-in technology for wired or wireless connections to a computer network. Networking is useful for connecting to a home network or to public networks, such as the Internet. Internet connections require a **modem**. Modems can be built into portable computers. For tablets you can use an aircard or portable modem, which works like a mobile phone. For Internet access using a smartphone, the modem is built into the device. Modems for cable, satellite, and other types of Internet access from your home or office are usually separate devices.

- **What is a computer network?** A **computer network** consists of two or more computers and other devices that are connected for the purpose of sharing data and programs. For example, a **LAN (local area network)** is simply a computer network that is located within a limited geographical area, such as your home, a school computer lab, or a small business. If your computer is on a network, you can easily access files on other computers that are on the same network.

- **What parts of a computer system do I absolutely need?** You need a system unit for processing and storage, a monitor for output, and a keyboard and pointing device for input. Many people also want a printer and a portable storage device, such as a flash drive.

TABLE 1-1: Comparing categories of computers

Type of computer / Features and Drawbacks		
Desktop	**Notebook**	**Mobile Device (Tablet or Smartphone)**
• Most power per dollar • Can make repairs and upgrade components yourself (except for all-in-one units) • Full-size keyboard with numeric keypad • Large screen for multiple windows and detail work • Adjustable placement of components means less strain on eyes, back, and wrists • The choice for dedicated gamers, serious designers, desktop publishers, and video editors • Can place components for less strain on eyes, back, and wrists • Not portable; needs power outlet	• All components in one unit, so portable • Battery powered for portability • Connects to Wi-Fi networks for Internet access • May not have a CD/DVD drive • Great for most tasks that are not dependent on cellular connections • The choice for students and on-the-go professionals • Lightweight models have higher price tags	• Small and easy to carry; battery powered for portability • Small screen limits multitasking • Connects to Wi-Fi networks; cellular data plans available for mobile Internet access • Convertible units with keyboards available for writing long documents • Does not use software designed for desktops and laptops • Tablets great for ebooks, music, and videos, as well as the web and social media • Smartphones great for voice calls, texting, web browsing, and mobile apps, but not for creating content • Smartphones have longer battery life than tablets and laptops

Computer Software

A computer needs software to work. Software provides the instructions that tell a computer how to perform tasks. There are two main categories of software: operating system software and application software. Every computer has an operating system. But, as a computer user, you are probably most familiar with application software. You use application software to look at webpages on the Internet, write reports, create budgets, view and edit photographs, play games, as well as other tasks you do using your computer. The operating system you have on your computer determines the software you can run on your computer.

Learning Outcome 5:
Define software and give examples of operating systems

● **What is an operating system?** An **operating system (OS)** is the master controller for all the activities that take place within a computer system. An operating system is classified as **system software**. Its primary purpose is to help the computer system monitor itself in order to function efficiently. Most people have only one operating system running on their computer and most personal computers can run only one operating system at one time. There are several different operating systems available for personal computers, such as Windows, Mac OS, and Linux. The two most popular operating systems, Windows and Mac OS, look and even work in a similar way, but they are different. See **FIGURE 1-9**. Each is designed to run on different computer platforms.

FIGURE 1-9: Windows and Mac operating systems

Windows 10

Mac OS

● **What is a computer platform?** A **computer platform** determines the hardware and software of the computer system. Two of the most important factors that define a computer's platform are the processor and the OS. The Windows operating system was designed specifically for PCs. The PC platform is sometimes called the Windows platform. The Macintosh OS was designed specifically for Macintosh computers, which are based on a proprietary design and manufactured almost exclusively by Apple Computer, Inc. The Linux OS is usually used as an alternative to the Windows OS.

Today, many Mac computers use the same processors as PCs. If you have a Mac computer with an Intel processor (sometimes called an Intel Mac), you can install the Windows OS on that machine and run Windows software.

● **What is Windows software?** Windows software is software designed to run on a PC platform. Generally, software designed to run on a PC platform will not run on a Mac platform, and software designed to run on a Mac platform will not run on a PC platform. When shopping for new software, it is important to read the package to make sure that the software is designed to work with your computer platform.

● **How do I use the operating system?** Most of the time, you use the operating system without realizing it. See **FIGURE 1-10**. You interact with the operating system for certain tasks, such as starting programs and finding data files. How you use the operating system depends on its user interface. Operating systems use a **graphical user interface (GUI)**.

FIGURE 1-10: All computers have an operating system

Top: © Stanislaw Mikulski/Shutterstock.com; Bottom: © mama_mia/Shutterstock.com

© Alexey Boldin/Shutterstock.com

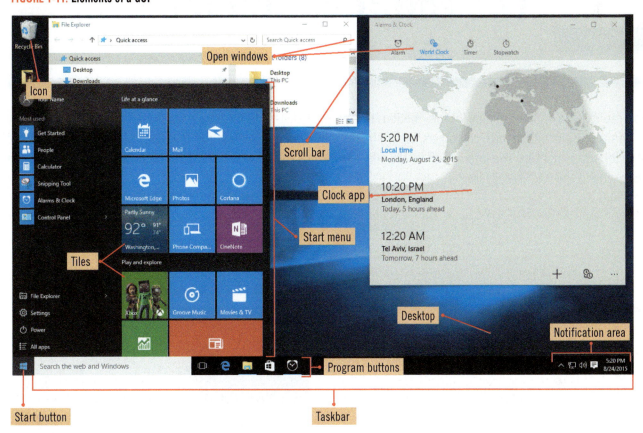

FIGURE 1-11: Elements of a GUI

Icon · Open windows · Scroll bar · Clock app · Start menu · Tiles · Desktop · Notification area · Program buttons · Start button · Taskbar

See **FIGURE 1-11**. A GUI displays on-screen icons, menus, buttons, and other graphical controls. These controls are manipulated by a mouse or other pointing device. For example, you might click a tile to start an application program, or drag time slots on a calendar to create appointments. If you are using a touch screen, you touch, tap, and drag icons with your fingers.

● **Does my mobile phone use the same OS as my personal computer?** No, mobile devices use an OS designed specifically for mobile devices, such as Android or iOS for iPhones. OSs are also known as mobile software platforms or handheld operating systems.

● **What are apps?** **Apps**, sometimes called **mobile apps**, are programs that often have a single purpose, such as weather forecasting, health monitoring, or ticket searching programs, designed to run on mobile devices, such as your tablet or smartphone as well as your computer. Apps are available for download from online stores. Mobile apps range from simple utilities that turn the device into a flash-light, to more sophisticated apps for communication, entertainment, and learning. See **FIGURE 1-12**. Most are available for free or a small fee.

● **How does the operating system help me do my work?** The operating system runs the software on your computer. **Application software** is a general term used

to classify the programs that help you use the computer to carry out tasks. Word processing software, for example, helps you create, edit, and print documents. Browser software helps you view webpages on the Internet. Each application software program has its own name, such as Microsoft Word, Chrome, or Skype. Your computer can run more than one application program at one time.

FIGURE 1-12: Mobile apps have many useful features

© Denys Prykhodov/Shutterstock.com

● **Can my Windows PC and my friend's Mac share files?** For the most part, yes. However, some files depend on system compatibility. Some application software has been created so one version exists for the Windows plat-form and another for the Macintosh platform.

The Internet and the Web

You can use the Internet to look for information, to learn new skills, and to share photos and videos. You can use it to communicate with friends, coworkers, or family. You can even use the Internet to buy products and services, look for a job, or plan a trip. The Internet offers abundant resources. This lesson will help you understand how to use the Internet and the web in daily life.

Learning Outcome 6:
Define the Internet and explain how to navigate webpages

- **What is the Internet?** The **Internet** is the largest computer network in the world. It is a collection of local, regional, national, and international computer networks. These networks are linked together to exchange data and share processing tasks.

- **How do I access the Internet?** To access the Internet your computer must have special hardware and software. You need equipment called a router. The **router** connects to your computer and to the Internet. Computers connect to the Internet either with wires or wirelessly. To connect to the Internet you also need an **Internet Service Provider**. This is a company that provides the service of connecting the router to the Internet, usually for a monthly fee.

- **Is the web the same as the Internet?** The **web** (short for **World Wide Web**) is a collection of **webpages** that are interconnected through the use of **hypertext** or links. The Internet is the network that carries webpages to computers. Webpages can include text, photos, videos, animations, and sounds. The web is the part of the Internet you will probably use most often.

- **Why would I use the Internet?** You might use the Internet to research and then buy products and services. For example, you can buy airline tickets through the Internet. If you want to sell a product or service, you can use the Internet to help you run your own small business. You might use the Internet to share photographs and videos with family and friends. At a job, you can use the Internet to work on documents with coworkers. Most banks have websites that customers use for bill paying and online banking. You can use the Internet to communicate with others. See **FIGURE 1-13**.

- **How do I view a webpage?** To view webpages on your computer, you need a software program called a web browser. Popular **web browsers** include Microsoft Edge,

FIGURE 1-13: Using the Internet to communicate

© ArtFamily/Shutterstock.com

Google Chrome, Mozilla FireFox, and Apple Safari. You enter a URL in the Address box of the browser window. If you are viewing a webpage, you can also click a link to view another webpage.

- **What is a link?** A **link** (also called a hyperlink) is text, a graphic, or other object on a webpage that is "linked" to another webpage or another area on the current webpage. You click a link to "jump" to another webpage, website, or place on the same webpage. Links are the main tool you will use to navigate among webpages.

- **What is a URL?** Every webpage has a unique address called a **URL (Uniform Resource Locator)**. The URL for a webpage indicates the computer on which it is stored, its location on the web server, the folder name or names indicating where it is stored, its filename, and its file extension. Most browsers provide a space near the top of the window for entering URLs. **FIGURE 1-14** identifies the parts of the URL for a National Park Service webpage. A URL never contains a space, even after a punctuation mark. An underline character is sometimes used to give the appearance of a space between words.

FIGURE 1-14: Parts of a URL

http://www.nps.gov/yose/index.htm

| Web protocol standard | Web server name | Folder name | Document name and file extension |

● **What is http:// in the Address box?** Most URLs begin with http://. **HTTP (Hypertext Transfer Protocol)** is the technology used to transport webpages over the Internet. You might also see https://, which is used for additional security at websites such as those that offer banking and shopping. When typing a URL, you do not have to type the http://. If you do type it, be sure to use the correct type of slash—always a forward slash (/).

● **How do I navigate a website?** Webpages on a related topic are often grouped together to create a **website**. Most websites have a main page, the **home page**, which acts as a doorway to the rest of the website pages. Usually, the webpages have a navigation bar that contains

links you click to move to other pages in the website. See **FIGURE 1-15**. In addition, your browser has buttons to help you navigate the web. For example, the browser's Back button lets you retrace your steps to view pages that you've seen previously.

● **How do I find information on the web?** The term **search site** refers to a website that provides a variety of tools to help you find information on the web. A **keyword** is any word or phrase that you type to describe the information that you are trying to find. Based on the keyword you input, the search site uses its **search engine** to provide a list of links to websites that may have the information you are looking for. So you can click each link to see if any website in the list has what you are looking for. You should try different variations on your keyword to improve your results. Also, search sites have different ways of ranking the search results. As a result, if you use two different search sites to search for the same keyword, you will probably get different results.

FIGURE 1-15: Navigating a webpage

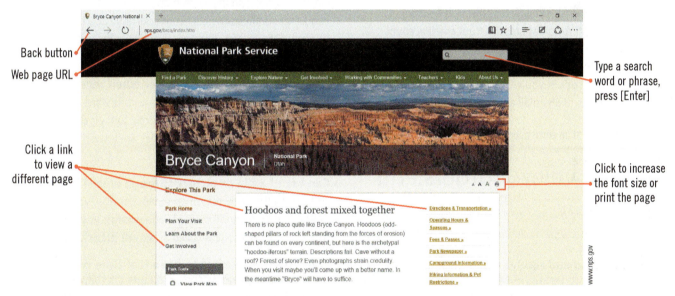

Back button
Web page URL

Click a link to view a different page

Type a search word or phrase, press [Enter]

Click to increase the font size or print the page

Working in the cloud and using web apps

Cloud computing provides access to information, applications, communications, and storage over the Internet. With cloud computing, you use a **browser** to access applications that run from the Internet, instead of software that you have installed on your hard disk.

A **web application** (**web app**) is software that you access through a web browser. Instead of running on your computer, the software runs on a distant computer, in the **cloud**, connected to the Internet or other network. Web apps are available for many tasks, such as email, calendars, photo sharing, games, and even word processing. Web apps allow you to work on projects with people in

multiple locations. When you use cloud storage, you can access your files from any computer that has a browser and Internet access.

Mobile web apps are designed to work on mobile devices. Mobile web apps have features designed for portability and a small screen.

Working in the cloud has risks. A security breach of a cloud provider could expose the data of all its users. Outages at the cloud provider, on the Internet in general, or locally at your computer can mean that you cannot get to your programs and files. If a cloud provider goes out of business without notice (and there are no regulations to prevent this from happening), all your data could become unavailable.

How to Communicate Using Digital Devices

Each year, countless email, text, and instant messages are sent around the world over the Internet. Social networks are universally used to share ideas, photos, and information around the world as well as among groups of friends. This lesson will help you understand the many ways you can communicate digitally with coworkers, family, and friends.

Learning Outcome 7:

Explain ways to use the Internet and digital devices to communicate with others

- **What is email?** Email (short for electronic mail) is a message sent electronically over the Internet. To send an email message, you must have an email account.

- **How do I get an email account?** You get an email account through an email provider. There are many providers, such as your Internet service provider or university. Web-based email includes Gmail (through Google) or Outlook.com (through Microsoft). Your email account includes a storage area, often called a mailbox. Depending on your provider, you will either be assigned an email address or you will create one. FIGURE 1-16 shows the parts of an email address.

FIGURE 1-16: Parts of an email address

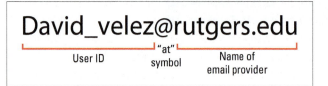

- **How do I send and receive email?** Your computer or smartphone must be able to connect to the Internet and if you are not using web-based email, it must have email software installed. Email software usually includes an address book to help you maintain the email addresses of people you contact frequently.

- **What does an email message look like?** An email message has several parts, including the recipient's email address, the address of anyone who is receiving a copy of the message, the message subject, the body, and the name of any file attachments. The body of the email contains your message. An email message is created in a form, which includes options for formatting text, attaching files, or adding additional recipients as courtesy (Cc), or blind courtesy (Bcc) copies. Basic email activities include writing, reading, replying to, and forwarding messages.

- **Do I need to be at my computer when sent an email?** No. Email is based on store-and-forward technology. Emails that cannot be sent directly to their destinations are temporarily stored until they are forwarded to the email mailbox.

- **Can I send a file or picture through email?** Yes. In addition to the body text of an email message, you can send documents, photos, video, and sounds. Any file sent with an email message is called an email attachment.

- **Can I use the Internet to have real-time conversations with people?** Yes. One popular way you can do this is participating in a chat group, which consists of several people who connect to the Internet and communicate in real time by typing notes or using audio and video to talk to each other. A version of chat is called

What is spam?

Spam is unwanted junk email. Most spam is generated by marketing firms that harvest email addresses from mailing lists, membership applications, and websites. Some spam messages advertise illegal products. Others are outright scams to try to get you to download a virus, divulge your bank account numbers, or send in money for products you will never receive. If offers seem just too good to be true—these offers are probably spam.

A **spam filter** automatically routes junk mail to the Deleted Items or a spam folder maintained by your email provider. However, they sometimes block email messages you want. Be sure to examine your Deleted Items folder periodically to make sure the spam filters are not blocking emails that you want. If they are, reset your filters.

instant messaging (IM). IM allows you to send text messages, images, and hyperlinks back and forth to another person instantly. If you are online at the same time as the person you want to chat or instant message, you can type messages back and forth in real time.

You can also use the Internet to talk to people in real-time thanks to **Internet telephony**, also called **Voice Over IP (VoIP)**. VoIP allows voice conversations to travel over the Internet. VoIP requires special software at both ends of the conversation. Instead of using a telephone, you have to use speakers and a microphone connected to a computer. A headset can provide both functions. VoIP providers, such as Google Hangouts or Skype, also offer video conversations. If you and the person you are talking with both have a web cam connected to your computers, you can see each other while you are talking. Other popular ways of communicating are through forums, wikis, blogs, and social networking.

● **What are forums, wikis, and blogs?** The Internet is a forum for personal expression using personal websites, blogs, chat groups, social media, and collaborative wikis. An **Internet forum** is a website where you can post comments to discussion threads. Threads are a chain of connected messages on the same topic. Comments can be read at any time by others who visit the forum. Most forums have a moderator who monitors the discussions, weeds out troublesome participants, and handles membership requests.

A **wiki** is a collaborative website that allows people to add to and modify material posted by others. Participants can post content on a topic, and others can change it. Wikis can also include discussion pages where people just comment on topic material. The best known is Wikipedia.

The term **blog** is derived from the phrase web log. It refers to a personal journal focusing on a single topic or a variety of topics. The information in a blog is usually available to the public. Some blog sites allow you to restrict access to those you invite to read your blog. People often create blogs to share travel adventures, political views, or important events in their lives.

● **What is social networking?** **Social networking** is an online networking activity that allows registered members to communicate with others in the network. You can use online social networks, such as Google+, LinkedIn, Instagram, Pinterest, and Facebook. Twitter, another social networking option, limits messages to 140 characters. See **FIGURE 1-17**.

To become a member of an online social network, you fill out a questionnaire to create your profile and to identify a list of friends. You can then interact with your friends or with friends of friends who are members of the same social network. This networking technique offers a level of security because members are interacting with friends or with friends of friends, rather than with strangers. Social networking sites provide private messaging options.

Social networking sites all have mobile apps to make it easy to follow and network from smartphones. In addition to using your mobile phone to social network, you can use it to send text messages.

● **What are text messages?** **Text messages** are typed messages you send using your smartphone or mobile device. You can send text messages by using the websites of mobile providers, but it is more common to use your mobile device to send text messages. If your mobile phone service has Multimedia Messaging Service (MMS), you can send pictures and video in addition to text. You do not need the added features of a smartphone to send text messages from a mobile phone.

The line between when to use your computer and when to use your smartphone to communicate is blurring. Computers and smartphones are allowing you to communicate in new and exciting ways with your circle of family, friends, and coworkers.

FIGURE 1-17: Social networking using Twitter

Source: 2015 Twitter

How to Protect Your Privacy, Data, and Devices

Computers and digital communication have built-in dangers. Whether you are using the web for finding a recipe, or shopping, or clicking to purchase airline tickets online, security and safety should always be your primary concern. You have to safeguard your health, safety, and personal data. You also need to take care of your digital devices so they work properly when you need them. This lesson will help you avoid potential pitfalls in the digital world so you can enjoy safe computing.

Learning Outcome 8:
Explain how to protect your digital data and devices

● **What can go wrong?** Many things can happen. Someone might steal your computer, or you might misplace it. Your data might get damaged or stolen. A thief might steal your credit card numbers or, worse, your identity. You might drop your computer or spill a drink on it. See FIGURE 1-18. Fortunately, there are simple steps you can take to prevent things from going wrong.

FIGURE 1-18: Spills can ruin a computer

© Milkovasa/Shutterstock.com

● **How can I prevent things from going wrong?** Use common sense and tools to protect yourself, your data, and your digital devices. To protect yourself, you must safeguard your personal data. To protect your data, you must install an antivirus program, a firewall, and other programs that help keep your data safe.

● **What if my computer is stolen?** Your identity is at risk if your computer is stolen. Why? Because your computer contains data about you. This may include your bank account information and credit card numbers, and PINs. A thief can use stolen data to assume your identity, empty your checking and savings accounts, get into legal difficulties, ruin your credit rating, and cause you no end of trouble.

● **How can I keep my computer from being stolen?** You should never leave your computer unattended in a

public place. Do not leave your computer visible in a car, even in a locked car. If you live in a group situation, anchor your computer to your desk with a specially designed lock.

In addition to these precautions, be sure to password-protect your computer. Then, if a thief steals your computer, he or she will need the password to access your data. So, even if a thief is able to turn on the computer, he or she will not be able to get at the information on it.

● **What should I use for a password?** Use a **password** you can remember but that others cannot guess. Here are some tips for creating a unique password.
  ■ Use at least eight characters, mixing numbers with letters, as in m3p1e8.
  ■ Do not use your name, birthday, the name of a family member, or your pet's name.
  ■ Do not use a word that can be found in the dictionary.
  ■ Do not keep a written copy of your password near your computer.

While passwords keep your data safe from unwanted visitors, they do not keep your data safe from malware.

● **What is malware?** **Malware**, also known as **malicious software**, is a type of software that can do harm to your computer data. There are different types of malware, such as viruses, worms, Trojan horses, and spyware. On a personal level, malware can steal data or destroy files. On a larger scale, malware can create network traffic jams that affect websites or corporate computer systems. Malware is often installed on your computer without your knowledge. For example, malware can be installed behind the scenes while you download software. See FIGURE 1-19. Malware is created by **hackers**, people that want to steal or damage your data or assume your identity.

FIGURE 1-19: Know that your downloads are safe

© cherezoff/Shutterstock.com

● **How can I protect my computer from malware?**
You should install programs, such as an antivirus program, a firewall, or a malware detection program, that can stop malware from being installed. These programs can also find and delete any malware that slipped through the safety net and got installed. Use these programs to scan files to be sure they are safe to download and keep your computer malware free and your data safe.

Not only computers but all digital devices, including smartphones, can get malware. It is also important to keep the anti-malware software on all your digital devices up to date.

● **Do I need to protect my privacy when using digital communication?** Yes. When you are social networking, posting to webpages, chatting, IMing, sending email messages, or communicating in any way over the Internet, you have to protect your personal information.

TABLE 1-2 provides some guidelines to help you protect your personal information and your privacy.

● **How can I limit who sees my digital communications?** Anything you write, or any photo you upload, can be copied, posted, or forwarded around the Internet with just a few clicks. Anyone can read or see your digital communications unless you take some precautions. Here are some tips on how to limit who has access to your electronic messages.

When emailing…

- Click Reply to reply only to the person who sent an email message. Clicking Reply limits who sees your response. Click Reply All if you want your response sent to everyone who received the original email message (except the Bcc recipients).
- Use Cc: to include people you want to read your email but that don't need to respond to the message.
- Use Bcc: to blind copy your email to people without revealing to the Send to and Cc: recipients.
- Create a group if you have people you send messages to regularly. This will ensure all the people in the group get the same message. It will also save time because you only have to enter the group name and not type the address of each person in the group.

When posting…

- Check the options to identify those people or groups you want to see a message you post on a blog or wall of a social networking site. Some sites post to the general public if you don't specify otherwise.
- Be sure you have permission from anyone in a picture when you post or tag the photo; only post your own photos and graphics.
- Regard wall messages, posted photos, and chat messages as postcards that can be read and seen by anyone. Do not say or share anything you would not want repeated or broadcast to the world!

TABLE 1-2: Ways to protect your privacy

Tips	Tips
Do not publish or post personal information, such as your home address, passwords, Social Security number, phone number, or account numbers.	Do not submit data to a social networking site until you've read its privacy policy and have made sure that you can remove your data when you no longer want to participate.
If asked for personal information, verify the website is legitimate, or call to confirm that you have to submit the information, and then confirm that the information will be securely transmitted and stored.	Avoid financial transactions when using a public computer. Never click the save my password box and make sure you log out from password-protected sites. Disable autocomplete for sensitive sites.
Be wary of contacts you make in public chat rooms and on social networking sites.	Never use a password-protected website on a public computer that doesn't give you the option to save the password.

Key Terms & Module Review

Key Terms

App
Application software
Blog
Bluetooth
Browser
Central processing unit
(CPU)
Chat group
Cloud
Cloud computing
Computer
Computer network
Computer platform
Computer program
Computer system
Desktop computer
Digital camera
Digital convergence
Digital media player
Digital revolution
Digital technology
Digitization
Display device
Email (electronic mail)
Email account
Email address
Email attachment
Email message

File
File extension
Filename
Form factor
Graphical User Interface
(GUI)
Hacker
Handheld computer
Hard disk drive
Hard drive
Hardware
Home page
HTTP (Hypertext Transfer
Protocol)
Hypertext
Input
Input device
Instant messaging (IM)
Internet
Internet forum
Internet service provider
(ISP)
Internet telephony
Keyboard
Keyword
LAN (local area network)
Laptop computer
Link

Mailbox
Mainframe computer
Malicious software
Malware
Memory
Microprocessor
Mobile app
Modem
Monitor
Mouse
Netbook
Notebook computer
Operating system
Optical drive
Output
Output device
Password
Peripheral device
Personal computer (PC)
Portable computer
Printer
Processing
Processor
Program
Router
Search engine
Search site
Server

Social networking
Software
Sound card
Sound system
Spam
Spam filter
Storage
Storage device
Storage medium
Supercomputer
System software
System unit
Tablet computer
Text message
URL (Uniform Resource
Locator)
USB flash drive
User ID
Voice Over IP (VoIP)
Web (World Wide Web)
Web app (Web application)
Web browser
Web cam
Webpage
Website
Wiki
Workstation

Module Review

1. Make sure that you can define each of the key terms in this module in your own words. Select 10 of the terms with which you are unfamiliar and write a sentence for each of them.

2. Explain how you use computers in your daily life.

3. Explain the basic functions of a computer: input, processing, storing, and output.

4. Identify and describe the purpose of each of the components of a basic personal computer system.

5. Describe the difference between an operating system and application software.

6. Explain why stored programs are important to computers.

7. List at least three activities that are not communications related and that you can accomplish using the Internet. If you have used the Internet, write a brief paragraph explaining how you benefitted from using it.

8. Make a list of at least three different ways you can use the Internet to communicate with other people.

9. Name the parts of a URL.

10. List the advantages and disadvantages of at least three types of computers as described in this module and why you might choose one over the other.

Concepts Review

Select the best answer.

1. Which of the following is not a type of personal computer?
   a. notebook
   b. mainframe
   c. desktop
   d. tablet

2. The part that is considered the brain of the computer is called the _____ processing unit.
   a. main
   b. computer
   c. central
   d. local

3. The idea of stored programs means that instructions for a computing task can be loaded into a computer's _____ .
   a. flash drive
   b. memory
   c. operating system
   d. software

4. The system _____ houses important parts such as the circuit boards, processor, power supply, and storage devices.
   a. unit
   b. memory
   c. drive
   d. processor

5. A device that expands a computer's capability is called a(n) _____ device.
   a. input
   b. peripheral
   c. output
   d. processing

6. A(n) _____ is a peripheral device that makes it possible to capture video.
   a. flash drive
   b. web cam
   c. mp3 player
   d. scanner

7. A(n) _____ system is the software that acts as the master controller for all computer activities.
   a. application
   b. processor
   c. digital
   d. operating

8. A computer _____ consists of two or more computers and other devices that are connected for the purpose of sharing data and programs.
   a. system
   b. network
   c. web
   d. hardware

9. Android is a type of _____ .
   a. power supply
   b. wiki
   c. operating system
   d. network

10. A _____ is the system unit of choice for computer owners who want to upgrade because it is easy to get inside and swap parts.
    a. tower unit
    b. notebook
    c. smartphone
    d. tablet

11. Every file must have a _____ .
    a. connection
    b. application
    c. filename
    d. operating system

12. Of the four options below, the _____ is the most portable computer.
    a. desktop unit
    b. notebook
    c. tower unit
    d. tablet

13. A(n) _____ is a personal journal posted on the web for access by the public.
    a. chat
    b. email
    c. instant message
    d. blog

14. An email account has a unique address that typically consists of a user ID, the _____ symbol, and the name of the computer that maintains the mailbox.
    a. X
    b. *
    c. @
    d. #

15. Every webpage has a unique address called a(n) _____ .
    a. ARL
    b. URL
    c. RUL
    d. LUR

16. Of the four services listed below, which website is not an example of social networking?
    a. Facebook
    b. Skype
    c. LinkedIn
    d. Twitter

17. To find information on the web, it is best to use a(n) _____ engine.
    a. information
    b. search
    c. VOIP
    d. program

18. A _____ is a series of webpages on a specific topic.
    a. blog
    b. group
    c. website
    d. URL

19. _____ is unwanted email that can result in scams.
    a. Spam
    b. Chat
    c. Blog
    d. Wiki

20. A(n) _____ is any word or phrase that you type in a search engine to describe the information that you are trying to find.
    a. email
    b. keyword
    c. app
    d. blog

Independent Challenges

Independent Challenge 1

When discussing computers and computer concepts, it is important to use proper terminology. You learned many computer terms that describe computer equipment and how computers are used in the world today. If you would like to explore any of the terms in more detail, there are online sources that can help you expand your understanding of these terms. You can use Google to help you better learn about specific computer terms, for example, a tablet computer. Be sure to check when the material was posted or updated to determine if it is current. You might also consider the information source. Blogs, social media sites such as Facebook, and YouTube videos often express opinions rather than facts. See FIGURE 1-20.

FIGURE 1-20: **Getting information from the web**

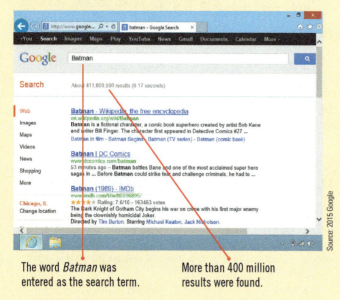

The word *Batman* was entered as the search term.

More than 400 million results were found.

Source: 2015 Google

For this Independent Challenge:

1. Write a one-page paper that describes the way you are most likely to use computers and what is the reason you want to learn more about computers.

2. Write a short paragraph that describes the computer or digital electronic device you use most frequently. Refer to the key terms used in this module and use terms from it to describe the parts of your computer, including their functions.

3. Underline each key term that you used in your paper.

4. Follow your instructor's directions for submitting your paper either as an email attachment or as a printed document.

Independent Challenge 2

Imagine that the producers for a television game show ask you to help them write computer-related questions for the next show. They want to know the impact of social networking. Part of the mission is to find out how computer literate people have become over the years. To help the producers, you will compose a set of 10 questions based on the information provided in this module. Each question should be in multiple-choice format with four possible answers.

For this Independent Challenge:

1. Write 10 questions that test a person's knowledge of the concepts covered in this module: two very simple questions, five questions of medium difficulty, and three difficult questions. Each question should be on an index card.

2. For each question, indicate the correct answer on the back of each card and the page in this book on which the answer can be found.

3. Gather in small groups and take turns asking each other the questions.

4. Get 10 additional index cards. On each card write the name of a social networking app or website. These can include Facebook, LinkedIn, Twitter, Instagram, SnapChat, and others. On the flip side write two unique features that define the term on the other side. Pass the cards around to see who can correctly match the definition with the term.

Independent Challenge 3

As a busy student, you are constantly on the go. When you are away from your home, you still need access to the Internet, your calendar, and contacts. For this independent challenge, assume that you have a basic mobile phone. You are considering upgrading to a smartphone. You are unsure if it makes sense to get a new smartphone or to invest in a tablet computer and keep your current mobile phone. See **FIGURE 1-21**. You have heard about great apps for smartphones as well as tablet computers. It is time for you to start researching your options.

You can buy your digital device from a brick-and-mortar store, or from an online computer company. Each type of vendor has its advantages and disadvantages based on the kind of shopping experience you prefer. A brick-and-mortar store provides

FIGURE 1-21: Smartphones and tablet computers

© Eugenio Marongiu/Shutterstock.com

face-to-face service. A communications store provides the most up-to-date devices for its cellular service. A computer company often provides a wide selection of devices that are compatible with different cellular services.

In addition to purchasing the digital device, you will also need cellular service for the device. You will need to determine the network your digital device can access in order to receive and send data, as well as the price of the data service.

For this Independent Challenge:

1. Use the Internet to research the latest offerings in smartphones and tablets.

2. Based on your research, list three different smartphones that you like. Be sure to compare the apps and features that come with each smartphone or that are available for each smartphone.

3. Based on your research, list three different tablets that you like. Be sure to compare the apps and features that come with each tablet or that are available for each tablet.

4. List the type of network required for each digital device, for example, Wi-Fi, 4G, LTE. You do not have to understand the differences at this point, just list the type based on your findings.

5. Fill in the table below to help organize your findings.

6. Based on your research, write a concluding paragraph explaining your decision to purchase either a smartphone or a tablet. Support your decision based on your findings.

	Price	Operating system	Display size	Network carrier (Verizon/AT&T/Sprint? Other?)	Memory	Weight	Features/Apps included	Connectivity (Wi-Fi? Bluetooth? 3G? 4G? LTE? Other?)	Camera
Smartphones									
Tablets									

Visual Workshop

Today, more and more people use email to communicate. See **FIGURE 1-22** for one example of an email message.

To send and receive email, you need an Internet connection, an email account, and software that enables you to compose, read, and delete email messages. An email account consists of an email address, a password, and a mailbox. You can usually obtain an email account from your Internet service provider, your school, or a web-based email provider, such as Outlook.com, Yahoo! Mail, or Gmail.

To access your mail, you need a computer that has an Internet connection. Since web mail can be accessed from any computer, you can send and receive email from public computers (such as those at a library or in a school lab). You do not need to own a computer. Once you are sure the computer is connected to the Internet, you simply open a browser and type the URL of the website that supports the email you signed up for (outlook.com, yahoo.com, or gmail.com). As soon as you are logged in to your email account, you can begin sending and receiving email.

FIGURE 1-22: Using email to communicate

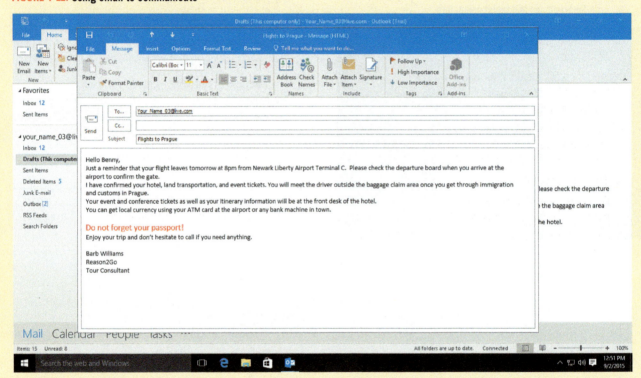

To get a web-based Gmail account using your own computer, or a public computer if you do not own a computer, just follow these steps.

1. In the Address bar of your browser, enter www.gmail.com.

2. When the Gmail window appears, follow the directions to Create an account.

3. Follow the directions to enter your first name, last name, and login name.

4. You will be offered a chance to check the availability of a name you are selecting. If the login name you want is already in use, you'll have to try a different one, and recheck the availability.

5. When you've selected a valid login name, continue down the page to create a password. Try not to use a name, date, or any dictionary word as your password.

6. Continue down the page to complete the rest of the registration form.

7. Before finalizing your registration, review the information you've entered and jot down your login name and password.

8. Read the Terms of Service, and if you agree, click the I Accept button. That's it! You now have a Gmail account.

Computer Hardware

Learning Outcomes

1. Identify and describe how to use input devices
2. Name different types of display devices, and explain their key features
3. Describe different types of printers, and the advantages and disadvantages of each
4. Identify and explain the different storage devices and their corresponding storage media
5. Explain the advantages and disadvantages of magnetic, optical, and solid-state storage
6. Explain optical storage options
7. Describe the different types of solid-state cards and drives
8. Identify expansion ports and expansion cards, and explain how to use them

LESSON TOPICS

- Input Devices
- Display Devices
- Printers
- Data Storage—An Overview
- Data Storage Systems Features
- Optical Data Storage Systems
- Solid-State Data Storage Systems
- How to Add Devices to Your Computer

Input Devices

When you use a computer or any digital device, you need to tell it what you want by inputting information. To input the information, you use an input device. An **input device** is computer hardware that you use to communicate with the computer. Most computer systems include a keyboard and a pointing device.

Learning Outcome 1:
Identify and describe how to use input devices

● **Are all keyboards the same?** Most keyboards are similar. In addition to standard keyboards, you might use on-screen keyboards on smartphones or tablets. See **FIGURE 2-1**. A computer keyboard includes keys with letters, numbers, and keys with characters and special words to control computer-specific tasks. You use the keyboards to input commands, respond to prompts, and type text.

FIGURE 2-1: Keyboard examples

On-screen keyboard   Standalone keyboard

Built-in keyboard

You use the navigation keypad, which includes keys such as the Home, End, and arrow keys, to move the **insertion point** (also called the **cursor**) around the screen. The insertion point typically looks like a flashing vertical bar. The insertion point indicates where the characters you type will appear. You can change the location of the insertion point by pressing the navigation keys or by clicking or tapping a **pointing device**, such as a mouse.

● **Why do I need a mouse?** Often, you will find that it is easier to use a mouse to give some commands to a computer than it is to use a keyboard. A **mouse** allows you to control an on-screen pointer. A desktop computer uses a mouse as its primary pointing device. You can also use a mouse with notebook computers. A typical mouse, shown

in **FIGURE 2-2**, includes one or more buttons and a scroll wheel on top.

FIGURE 2-2: Typical mouse

Scroll wheel button
Left mouse button
Additional buttons
Right mouse button

Openclipart.org

● **How do I use a mouse?** You use a mouse by sliding a mouse along a hard surface. Some people use a mouse pad for ease of use. As you move the mouse, a pointer on the screen moves. If you move the mouse to the left, the pointer on the screen moves to the left. In addition, you click the buttons on the mouse to give commands to the computer. Some mice have extra buttons for additional actions. For example, a scroll wheel can be used to scroll up or down a window. Some mice have an extra button in the left side of the mouse that can be pressed to undo a command.

● **How do mice communicate with the computer?** Wired mice communicate with the computer through the cable. Other mice are wireless. Wireless mice communicate with the computer using radio signals. Many people prefer wireless mice because there is no cable to get tangled when they move the mouse.

For both wired and wireless mice, you have several choices. An **optical mouse** uses an LED (an electronic light) and computer chip to track your mouse movements as a light beam bounces off a hard surface, such as a desk or mouse pad. A **laser mouse** uses a laser as the light source to track mouse movement.

- **What other pointing devices can I use?** Other pointing devices include touchpads and trackballs. These devices are typically used with notebook computers and other mobile devices as an alternative to a mouse. A **touchpad**, also called a **trackpad**, is a touch-sensitive surface on which you can slide your fingers to move the on-screen pointer. See FIGURE 2-3. A **trackball** is a roller ball on the top of a mouse. You use your fingers or the palm of your hand to roll the ball and move the pointer.

FIGURE 2-3: Touchpad on a notebook

- **Why do some computers have touch screens?** Many smartphones, tablet computers, and information kiosks use a touch screen. See FIGURE 2-4. **Touch screen technology** can interpret a single touch or more complex input, such as handwriting. You cycle through screens by swiping the display. You zoom in and out by pinching and expanding two fingers. You rotate objects by twisting two fingers. Be sure to use fingers or the stylus intended for your touch screen because touch screens can be damaged by sharp objects.

- **How does a touch screen work?** Touch screens display a **virtual keyboard** for devices that are not connected to a physical keyboard. Touch events, such as taps, drags, and pinches, are sometimes called **gestures**. The coordinates for a touch event are processed in the same way as a mouse click. For example, if you touch your iPad screen

at the location of a button labeled Calendar, the area you touch generates coordinates and sends them to the processor. The processor compares the coordinates to the image displayed on the screen to find out what is at the coordinates, and then responds—in this case, by opening your appointment calendar.

FIGURE 2-4: Touch screens

- **What if I want to input text or a drawing that is on paper?** If you have data that exists on paper, you can use a **scanner**. The scanner captures the image or text and creates a digital graphics file.

- **Can I enter data by speaking?** Yes, a microphone is an input device that converts spoken words or sound information to digital format. There are speech-to-text programs that can accept sound as input, which creates a text file from the spoken words. Also, if you use your computer as an Internet telephone or to video chat, you speak into a microphone and the program sends it through the computer to the person you are speaking with.

- **Are digital cameras input devices?** Yes, a digital camera, even those on smartphones, create images as files. A web cam and a digital video camera capture moving images with sound as files. Image and video files can be transferred from a camera to any computer. Once these images or videos are on a computer, you can view, play, or change the images.

Dedicated mobile digital devices

Devices, such as fitness trackers, cameras, ebook readers, media players, game consoles, and handheld GPS devices, are dedicated to specific tasks. Devices such as smartwatches, smartglasses, and fitness trackers, can be classified as **wearable computers**. These devices all contain a processor and input and output data. See FIGURE 2-5.

FIGURE 2-5: Examples of mobile digital devices

Kindle

Smartglasses

Smartwatch

Fitness tracker

Display Devices

While working on a computer, you will want to see what's going on. You need to look at the data as you input it. You also want to look at the output. A display system is the main output device for a computer. Two key components of a computer display system are a display device or screen and a graphics card.

- **What is a display device?** A **display device** is the computer hardware that shows, or displays, the data. It shows the input as you enter data. It shows the output once the data has been processed. The main display device for a computer is either a monitor or a screen. Smartphones, tablets, and other mobile devices have screens.

- **Are a monitor and a screen the same thing?** Many people use the terms *monitor* and *screen* interchangeably, but they are not technically the same thing. A monitor is a stand-alone display device that connects to a computer. A screen is the area where output is displayed. A desktop computer has a monitor with a screen. A notebook, netbook, and tablet, as well as other mobile devices such as a smartphone, each have a screen.

- **What are my choices for a display device?** Two technologies are commonly used for computer display devices: LCD and LED. Your computer monitor will most likely have an **LCD (liquid crystal display)** screen. See **FIGURE 2-6**.

LCD monitors are also called flat-panel displays. LCD monitors produce an image by manipulating light within a layer of liquid crystal cells. The advantages of an LCD monitor include display clarity, low radiation emission, portability, and compactness. LCD screens are standard equipment for notebook computers. An **LED (light emitting diodes)** screen looks similar to an LCD screen, but it uses light emitting diodes for the backlighting.

- **What is a graphics card?** A graphics card is another important component of your display system. A **graphics card** contains the technology used to display images on the screen. See **FIGURE 2-7**. It also contains special memory, which stores images as they are processed but before they are displayed. The amount of available memory is the key to the overall performance, including response rate, of the display system. A graphics card can be built into a computer's motherboard or plugged into the motherboard. For a notebook, tablet, or mobile device, the graphics card is a chip built into the motherboard.

FIGURE 2-6: An LCD monitor

Each dot, or pixel, on the screen contains three liquid crystal cells: one red, one green, and one blue.

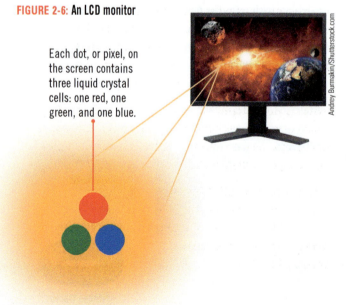

Andrey Burmakin/Shutterstock.com

FIGURE 2-7: A graphics card

- **What does a graphics card do?** Think of the computer screen as a grid. The rows and columns make cells in the grid. A graphics card sends an image to the screen to fill the grid. The graphics card sends the image at a specific resolution. **Resolution** is the maximum number of horizontal and vertical pixels displayed on the screen. A **pixel (picture element)** is a single point or the smallest unit in a graphic image. Each pixel fills one cell of the grid. As resolutions increase, the computer displays a larger work area on the screen with text and other objects appearing smaller. See **FIGURE 2-8**. You can set the resolution on a Windows PC using options in the Control Panel. Higher resolutions are possible if your graphics card has enough memory to support those resolutions and if your display device is capable of displaying those resolutions.

FIGURE 2-8: Comparing screen resolutions

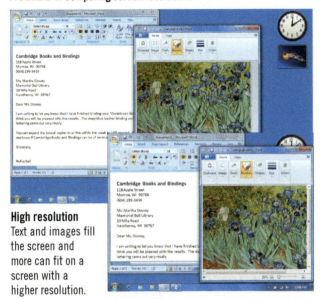

High resolution
Text and images fill the screen and more can fit on a screen with a higher resolution.

Low resolution
Text and images appear larger but less content can fit on a lower resolution screen.

● **What is response rate? Response rate** is how fast a screen updates the information being displayed. Display devices with fast response rates display a crisp image with minimal blurring or "ghosting" of moving objects. Response rate is an important factor for fast action games, 3D modeling, and graphics-intensive desktop publishing.

● **Does it matter if my display device is square or rectangular?** No, but you should use a resolution that works best for your display device. **Aspect ratio** is the proportional relation between the width and height of an image or video frame. The 4:3 was the standard aspect ratio for television and screens on the first generation of personal computers. Today's widescreen devices, such as notebooks and smartphones, are designed for the 16:9 aspect ratio, which is recommended for most modern videos. When 4:3 videos are displayed in a widescreen player, they are bordered by the black bars. See **FIGURE 2-9**. Some older monitors look square. For these monitors, a resolution based on a 4:3 aspect ratio works best. The 4:3 ratio matches the monitor since the width is slightly larger than the height. Most new monitors have a rectangle

FIGURE 2-9: Comparing aspect ratios

4:3 aspect ratio

16:9 aspect ratio

shape. For these widescreen monitors, a resolution based on a 16:9 aspect ratios works best.

● **What other factors besides resolution affect image quality?** In addition to resolution, image quality is determined by screen size, dot pitch, and color depth. These factors are all controlled by the graphics card.

● **What is screen size? Screen size** is the measurement in inches from one corner of the screen diagonally across to the opposite corner. Screen sizes range from 3" on smartphones to 60" or more for home entertainment systems. Typical computer monitor screen sizes range from 15" to more than 26". In addition to screen size, you should also consider a monitor's **viewing angle width**, which indicates how far to the side you can still clearly see the screen image. A wide viewing angle indicates that you can view the screen from various positions without compromising image quality.

● **What is dot pitch? Dot pitch (dp)** is a measure of image clarity. A smaller dot pitch means a crisper image. Unlike resolution, dot pitch is not customizable. A display device's specifications include dot pitch.

● **What is color depth?** The number of colors that a monitor and graphics card can display is referred to as **color depth** or **bit depth**. Most PCs are capable of displaying millions of colors and photographic-quality images. On a Windows PC, you can change the color setting to customize the color depth by using options in the Control Panel.

Printers

Most output is viewed using a display device. This output is called **soft copy**. Sometimes, you want the output on paper. To create printed copy, you use a printer. Printed output is called **hard copy**. You can print hard copy on different media, such as paper, labels, or transparencies. Printers differ in resolution and speed, both of which affect the print quality and price. To find a printer that meets your needs, it is important to understand the different types of printers and their features.

Learning Outcome 3:
Describe different types of printers, and the advantages and disadvantages of each

● **What are the most common types of printers in use today?** The most common types of printers in use today are either ink-jet printers or laser printers. Both ink-jet printers and laser printers are available as black and white or color printers. Both have trays for different paper sizes. You can print on 8½" × 11" paper, 8½" × 14" paper, envelopes, postcards, transparencies, and more. Both types of printers also have drawbacks to consider, for example, cost over the life of the printer, as well as the speed at which the printer produces hard copy.

● **How does an ink-jet printer work?** An **ink-jet printer** has a print head that sprays ink onto paper to form characters and graphics. Ink-jet printers usually use two cartridges: a black ink cartridge and a color cartridge that holds colored inks. Most ink-jet printers use CMYK color, which requires only cyan (blue), magenta (pink), yellow, and black inks to create a printout that appears to contain thousands of colors. See **FIGURE 2-10**. Most ink-jet printers are small, lightweight, and inexpensive, yet produce very good-quality color output. However, the ink cartridges can be expensive and can add to the overall cost of printing.

FIGURE 2-10: An ink-jet printer uses color ink cartridges

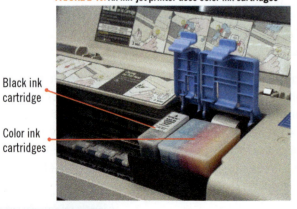

Black ink cartridge

Color ink cartridges

● **How does a laser printer work?** A **laser printer** uses a technology that produces dots of light on a light-sensitive drum. Instead of ink cartridges, laser printers use toner cartridges. See **FIGURE 2-11**. **Toner** is the fine powder that is applied to the drum, and then creates the image on the paper. Laser printers are popular for situations that require high-volume output or good-quality printouts. Laser printers are generally more expensive than ink-jet printers.

FIGURE 2-11: **A laser printer**

Toner cartridge

Paper tray

● **What determines the quality of the printed images?** **Printer resolution** determines the quality or sharpness of printed images and text. Resolution is measured by the number of dots printed per linear inch, or **dots per inch (dpi)**. At normal reading distance, a resolution of about 900 dots per inch appears solid to the human eye. At 900 dpi, if you look closely, a dot pattern will be evident. Good-quality printers are rated from 2400 to 4800 dpi. If you want the printed images to have the quality of professionally printed books, use a printer with a resolution of 2400 dpi or higher.

● **How can I know if a printer is fast?** You can look at the pages per minute (ppm) and memory specifications provided by the manufacturer. Printer speed is measured by the number of **pages per minute (ppm)** output. Color printouts typically take longer to print than black-and-white printouts. Pages that contain mostly text tend to print faster than pages that contain graphics. Most printers for personal or small business use are rated from 15 to 30 ppm.

Memory capacity is another factor to consider when evaluating printer speed. Printers often work in the background while you work on other computer tasks. If your printer has lots of memory, you can send many print jobs to the printer. The print jobs will be in the printer's memory and not in your computer's memory. More memory is required to print color images and documents with graphics. You can work more efficiently if your printer has more memory.

● **Can a printer print on both sides of a page in one pass?** Yes, a **duplex printer** can print on both sides of the paper. This environment-friendly option saves paper. However, duplex printing slows down the print process on ink-jet printers because they have to pause to let the ink dry before printing the second side.

● **Does the number of pages I print affect the life of my printer? Duty cycle** determines how many pages a printer is able to print in a specified time period. For example, on average, a personal laser printer's duty cycle is about 3,000 pages per month—roughly 100 pages per day. However, you wouldn't want to produce 3,000 pages on one day. You can print more pages than the specified duty cycle, but this could shorten the useful life of your printer. Also, a printer with a higher duty cycle will have a shorter useful life.

● **How does a printer connect to my computer?** A printer connects to your computer using one of the following connection options: USB port, serial port, parallel port, or network port. Usually a cable is used to connect a printer to a computer. However, a printer can also connect to a computer wirelessly if the printer and computer both have the wireless technology needed to connect. You can connect a printer directly to your personal computer and use it only with that computer. But, sometimes, you might want to use a printer with more than one computer.

● **How do I use a printer with more than one computer?** If your computers are part of a LAN (local area network), you can share your printer with the other computers. In this situation, each computer on the network sends its print jobs to your computer's printer for output. This allows many computers to share one resource, the printer.

Another way to configure network printing for multiple users is to purchase a **network-enabled printer** that connects directly to the network, rather than to one of the computers on a network. The network connection can be wired or wireless.

● **Do I need a different printer to print lots of photographs?** Yes, for more professional output, you want to use a **photo printer**. These printers have slower output speeds when compared to ink-jet or laser printers, but they do produce professional-quality images on specialized papers.

● **Is it possible to print objects?** Yes! The type of printer you need is a 3D printer. Once just available for industry, personal **3D printers** are now available that allow you to print objects such as a toy or replacement part based on a design. There are several different technologies used in 3D printers that use different substances to create or print the objects layer by layer. See **FIGURE 2-12**.

FIGURE 2-12: A 3D printer

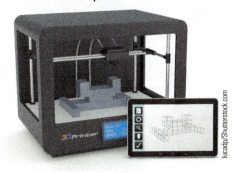

lucadp/Shutterstock.com

Options for printing your photos

Do you print a lot of photographs? For photos on paper, compare the cost of printing the photographs using your printer to the cost of using a professional printer. If you consider the cost of paper and ink to print large quantities of photographs, these services often are more economical. But for occasional use, a photo-printer provides quality images at a reasonable cost. You can have digital images printed over the web using online services. There are apps on smartphones that take your photos directly to an online site. The printed photos are then mailed to you. Many companies offer printing on canvases, shirts, mugs, and other items. You can also take the digital image files on a disc or flash drive to a self-service station in a store to print the photographs immediately. Some stores allow you to upload images to their web site, where you specify your printing preferences, and then pick up the photos at your local store. Many printing services usually allow you to edit your digital images, for example, to remove red-eye or to crop an unwanted object out of the image.

Data Storage—An Overview

As you use a computer, you will want to store or save your work using storage technology. Once your work is stored, you can use it again or share it with other people. **Storage technology** refers to data storage systems that make it possible for a computer or digital device to store and retrieve data.

Learning Outcome 4:
Identify and explain the different storage devices and their corresponding storage media

● **What is a data storage system?** A data storage system is made up of two main parts: a storage device and a storage medium. A **storage device** is the equipment that stores and retrieves data from its storage medium. Storage devices include hard drives, card readers, flash drives, optical drives, and solid-state card readers. A **storage medium** is the technology that holds data. Storage media include hard drives, memory cards, flash drives, CDs, DVDs, and Blue-ray discs. Refer to **FIGURE 2-13** for examples of a data storage system.

FIGURE 2-13: Example of a data storage system

Source: Lexar

Memory cards are available in several formats and capacities.

Card reader

Many digital devices are equipped with a card reader for transferring data to and from solid-state memory cards.

● **Are the storage medium and the storage device always two separate parts?** No. Some data storage systems are self-contained, while others are two distinct parts. For example, a hard drive is both the storage device and the storage medium. A USB flash drive is both a storage device and the storage medium. But, a CD/DVD drive is a storage device and it uses CDs or DVDs as the storage media. And, a flash card reader is a storage device and it uses solid-state cards as its storage media.

● **What is the main data storage system for a personal computer system?** The main storage system for a personal computer is a **hard drive**. Hard drives can be internal (permanently installed inside the system unit), removable, or external. Hard drives can be mechanical or use **solid-state technology**. Mechanical drives have moving parts. **Solid-state drives (SSD)** have no moving parts. The terms hard drive and hard disk drive are often used interchangeably.

● **Why are hard drives so popular?** Hard drives are the preferred type of main storage for most computer systems. They provide lots of storage, fast access to data, and are inexpensive. Most computers come with an internal hard drive that is installed in the computer and cannot be moved easily from one computer to another. See **FIGURE 2-14**. You may not know what a hard drive looks like because it is usually found inside the system unit. Personal computer hard drive platters are typically 3½" in diameter with storage capacities ranging from 60 GB to over 2 TB. Tablet computers, mobile devices, and some notebooks use a solid-state non-removable internal hard drive.

FIGURE 2-14: The inside of a mechanical hard drive

Read-write head   Spindle   Platter

● **What other storage devices can I use with my personal computer?** In addition to a hard drive, you can use additional storage devices such as CD/DVD/BD drives, USB flash drives, solid-state drives (see FIGURE 2-15), and solid-state card readers.

FIGURE 2-15: Solid-state drive (SSD)

● **Why would I want to use different storage devices?** Storage devices, such as hard drives, provide fast access to data. Some storage devices, such as CDs, DVDs, and BDs, are more dependable than others. Some storage devices, such as solid-state storage **USB flash drives** and external hard drives, are portable and can be moved easily from one computer to another computer.

● **How do these storage devices connect to my computer?** The system unit case for a desktop computer contains several storage device "parking spaces" called **drive bays** or **expansion bays**. Storage devices are installed in these drive bays. These bays are typically hidden from view with a faceplate. When you buy a computer, you will need to find out how many drive bays the computer has and what type of storage devices can be connected to the computer using the drive bay(s). Any drive that is mounted inside the system unit and that uses removable media or that has to be controlled manually by pushing a button or inserting the media into a slot, such as a CD/DVD/BD drive, must be able to be accessed from outside the system unit.

● **What if my computer doesn't have any empty drive bays?** In this case, you will want to add an external storage device. Some storage devices such as an external hard drive, a USB flash drive, or a card reader connect to your computer using a USB port. If you do not have enough USB ports for all the devices you want to connect, then you can use a USB hub. A **USB hub** adds ports to your computer to add devices easily.

● **How do I connect storage devices to my notebook and tablet computers?** These computers do not have drive bays. You will want to connect storage devices to these computers using an available USB port or a USB hub. See FIGURE 2-16.

FIGURE 2-16: Using a USB hub

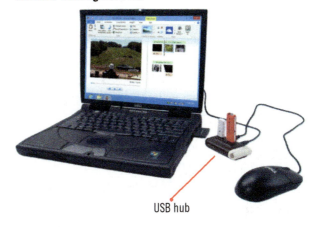

USB hub

● **How can I increase my storage capacity?** You can increase the storage capacity of your computer by adding a second internal hard drive to an empty drive bay. You can also add an external hard drive that connects via a USB port.

● **Is my data safe on the hard drive?** In general, yes. But keep in mind that the read-write heads in a mechanical hard drive hover a microscopic distance above the disk surface. If a read-write head runs into dirt on the disk, or if the hard drive is jarred while in use, a "head crash" may occur, which will damage some or all of the data on the disk. To help prevent dirt from contacting the platters and causing head crashes, a hard drive is sealed in its case. Although hard drives have become considerably more rugged in recent years, you should still handle and transport them with care.

Maintaining your hardware

There are four components of digital devices that require maintenance: the system unit, keyboard, screen, and battery. Touchscreens collect fingerprints and are a breeding ground for bacteria, so it is a good idea to clean them periodically. Before you undertake any maintenance, turn the device off—not just asleep—and disconnect any power cables. The products you can use depend on the component you are cleaning. Always follow the manufacturer's advice for cleaning procedures and products. Never immerse a device in liquid; water and electronics don't mix. Dust with a clean microfiber cloth and disinfect with antibacterial wipes. Use a low vacuum setting to remove dust from fan vents. Do not spray cleaning agents directly on the device; spray them onto a cleaning cloth, then wipe. Handle storage media and devices carefully and do not attempt to open sealed units.

Data Storage Systems Features

Data storage systems for personal computers use magnetic, optical, or solid-state technology. Data storage systems can be compared based on their versatility, cost, durability, capacity, and speed.

Learning Outcome 5:
Explain the advantages and disadvantages of magnetic, optical, and solid-state storage

- **Why do I need versatility in a data storage system?** Most likely you will be working with other people. You will want to be able to store data on your storage medium and then give that storage medium to another person. That person can then use the storage medium to access the data. Or, you may have to use different computers. To move data among different computers, you will want data storage systems that are versatile. Some storage devices can access data from only one type of medium. More versatile storage devices can access data from several different media. For example, a DVD drive can access data on these storage media: DVDs, DVD movies, audio CDs, data CDs, and CD-Rs. A USB flash drive can plug into any USB port. Both a DVD and a flash drive are versatile.

- **Why do I need a data storage system that is durable?** Do you travel or carry your data files with you? If so, then you need a storage system that is durable. Most data storage systems can be damaged by mishandling or by extreme heat or cold, dust, and moisture. Optical and solid-state technologies are more durable than magnetic technologies. They do not damage easily. This helps you prevent data loss. Solid-state storage devices are the most durable at this time.

- **Why is storage capacity important?** Different data storage systems hold different amounts of data. **Storage capacity** is the maximum amount of data (documents, photographs, songs, video) that can be stored on a storage medium. Storage capacity is measured in kilobytes (KB), megabytes (MB), gigabytes (GB), or terabytes (TB). On average, larger capacity systems cost more. Graphics and video require more storage capacity than text. You need more storage for photographs and video than you need for your school reports or letters. Before deciding on a data storage system, you need to be sure the data storage systems you use can hold all the data you need to store.

- **Do different data storage systems access and transfer data at different speeds?** Yes. There are two factors to take into account when considering access speed: access time and data transfer rate. **Access time** is the average time it takes a computer to locate data on the storage medium and read it. Access time is measured in **milliseconds** (thousandths of a second, abbreviated as **ms**). **Data transfer rate** is the amount of data that a storage device can move from the storage medium to the computer per second. So, if you are watching a movie on your computer, you want the fastest data transfer rate possible.

- **What does random access mean?** **Random access** (also called **direct access**) is the ability of a device to jump directly to the requested data. Hard drives, solid-state drives, CD drives, DVD drives, and BD drives are random-access devices.

- **Which data storage systems use magnetic storage technology?** Hard drives use magnetic storage. **Magnetic storage** stores data by magnetizing microscopic particles on the disk surface. The particles retain their magnetic orientation until that orientation is changed. Patterns of magnetized particles are interpreted as the 0s and 1s that represent data. Data stored magnetically can be changed or deleted simply by altering the magnetic orientation of the appropriate particles on the disk surface. Refer to **FIGURE 2-17**.

FIGURE 2-17: Magnetic storage

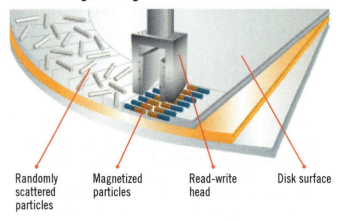

Randomly scattered particles   Magnetized particles   Read-write head   Disk surface

● **Which storage systems use optical storage technology?** CDs, DVDs, and BDs use optical storage technologies. **Optical storage** stores data as microscopic light and dark spots on the disc surface. Low-power laser light is used to read the data stored on an optical disc. Patterns of light and dark are interpreted as the 1s and 0s that represent data. **FIGURE 2-18** shows the layers that make up an optical disc. You use an optical storage system because its storage media (CDs, DVDs, and BDs) are easy to transport and fairly durable. However, CDs, DVDs, and BDs do still require some special handling in order to be sure that data stored on these optical media is not lost or damaged due to environmental conditions or poor handling.

FIGURE 2-18: **Optical storage**

Polycarbonate substrate
Reflective layer
Recording layer 1
Spacer layer
Semitransparent reflective layer

Laser beams
Recording layer 0
Polycarbonate substrate

● **Which data storage systems use solid-state storage technology?** Some hard drives, a variety of compact storage cards (also called memory cards or memory sticks), and flash drives (also called thumb drives or jump sticks) use solid-state technology. **Solid-state storage** technology stores data in a durable, erasable, low-power chip. Solid-state storage technology provides faster access to data than magnetic or optical storage technology because it includes no moving parts. Little power is required, which makes solid-state storage ideal for battery-operated devices, such as a digital camera. Solid-state storage is very durable—it is usually not affected by vibrations, magnetic fields, or extreme temperature fluctuations—and very portable. Flash drives have become trendy stylish items that are easy to carry. They can even be worn as a fashion accessory. See **FIGURE 2-19**.

FIGURE 2-19: **Examples of flash drives**

ekler/Shutterstock.com

stefanolunardi/Shutterstock.com

Non-technical words used to describe using a data storage system

You use certain words to describe what happens when you use a data storage system. When you want to retrieve data, you say the storage device is "reading," "loading," or "opening" a file. The storage device reads the file on the storage medium and loads the information into RAM. Once the file is loaded, it is open and ready for you to use. "Ripping" is the term used to describe copying files from CDs, DVDs, and BDs onto your hard drive. For CDs, DVDs, and BDs, you often use the term "burning" to describe when files are copied to a disc.

Optical Data Storage Systems

You may have used a CD to listen to music. You may have used a DVD or a Blu-ray Disc (BD) to watch a movie. But did you know you can also use these media to store computer data? **CDs (compact discs)**, **DVDs (digital video disc or digital versatile disc)**, and **BDs (Blu-ray Discs)** use optical storage technologies. Optical storage media use one of three technologies: read-only (ROM), recordable (R), or rewritable (RW).

Learning Outcome 6:
Explain optical storage options

- **What are the parts of an optical storage system?** An optical storage system consists of a drive and the storage media used in that drive. This lesson provides more information about the types of optical drives available, as well as the type of storage media each drive can use.

- **What is the main difference between CD, DVD, and BD?** Today, most computers come equipped with one or more drives designed to work with CD, DVD, or BD discs. The basic difference between these technologies is the amount of data each disc can store. Current CD standards have the capacity to store 80 minutes of music or 700 MB of data. DVD standards offer 4.7 GB (4,700 MB) of data storage, about seven times as much capacity as a CD. A double layer DVD has two recordable layers on the same side and can store 8.5 GB of data. Currently, BDs have the highest storage capacity for optical storage media. They offer 25 GB capacity per layer. A double layer BD disc holds 50 GB of data.

- **What do the extra letters after CD, DVD, and BD mean?** The extra letters associated with a CD, DVD, or BD help you recognize how you can use the disc. Using CD as an example:
  - CD-ROM means read-only technology. A computer CD-ROM, DVD-ROM, or BD-ROM disc contains data that was stamped on the disc surface when it was manufactured, such as commercial software, music, and movies. Data cannot be added, changed, or deleted from CD-ROM, DVD-ROM, or BD-ROM discs.
  - CD-R means CD **recordable technology**. If you need to write data to the storage media, then you need to purchase recordable discs. You can usually write to a CD-R disc in multiple sessions. For example, you can store two files on a CD-R disc today, and add data for a few more files to the disc at a later time. This is also true for DVD-R/DVD+R and BD-R discs.
  - CD-RW means CD **rewritable technology**. If you need to write to the disc and rewrite to the disc, then you need to purchase the rewritable (multiple session use) discs. When you use these discs, you can record and erase stored data multiple times, which makes this a flexible storage option. This is also true for DVD-RW/DVD+RW. For Blu-ray Discs, you would look for BD-RE discs. BD-RE can be erased and re-recorded multiple times.

- **What type of optical disc should I buy?** When you purchase optical discs, be sure to purchase the type that works in your computer system's optical drive and meets your storage needs. To be able to write to the disc, you would need either the R or RW/RE format.

Understanding hard drive partitions

A hard drive partition is a section of a hard drive that is treated as a separate storage device. Many computers are configured with a single hard drive partition that contains the operating system, programs, and data. Some new computers come with two partitions. It is even possible to partition external hard drives. Partitions appear as independent hard drives, but they are one physical drive in your computer. When you look at the single drive using File Explorer, each partition is labeled separately (such as C drive and D drive). These are sometimes called logical drives. The main partition is often labeled OS (C:), and it contains the operating system and other program and data files. The default folders for Windows are on the C drive. The second partition is often labeled Recovery (D):. This partition contains files that can be used to help restore the computer if drive C malfunctions. Partitions are not the same as folders. Partitions are more permanent, and a special utility is required to create, modify, or delete them.

- **Should my computer system have a CD, DVD, or BD drive?** Yes, it is a good idea to have a **CD drive**, a **DVD drive**, or a **BD drive**. You need to know your storage needs to know which type of optical disc drive is best for you. The most versatile, and at the moment the most expensive, optical storage device is a Blu-ray Disc writer/DVD writer. Optical drives can be built into your computer or you can use external optical drives that connect through USB ports. External optical drives can be moved as needed among your computers.

- **How do I insert a disc into an optical drive?** First, you must open the drive. Usually there is button that you push. When you push the button the drawer slides out. See **FIGURE 2-20**. You hold the disc on the sides and place it in the drawer so the label or printed description of the disc is facing up. After the disc is set in the drawer, gently push the drawer or press the button and the drawer will close.

- **Can I use a CD, DVD, or BD drive instead of a hard drive?** No. A rewritable CD, DVD, or BD drive is a

fine addition to a computer system, but it is not a replacement for a hard drive. Unfortunately, the process of reading data from and writing data to a rewritable disc is relatively slow compared to hard drive access speed. In addition, the storage capacity of CDs and DVDs is much less than the storage capacity of hard drives.

- **How does the optical drive work?** **FIGURE 2-21** illustrates how a CD drive works. Optical drives contain a spindle that rotates the disc over a laser lens. The laser directs a beam of light toward the underside of the disc. As the drive reads the disc, the light's reflections are translated into the 0s and 1s that represent data. Blu-ray disc technology uses blue-violet colored lasers to read data. DVD technology uses a red laser. CD technology uses a near infrared laser.

FIGURE 2-20: Inserting a DVD in an optical drive

sattahipbeach/Shutterstock.com

FIGURE 2-21: How an optical drive works

Tracking mechanism positions a disc track over the laser lens

Laser lens directs a beam of light to the underside of the CD-ROM disc

Laser pickup assembly senses the reflections and translates the information into 1s and 0s

Drive spindle spins disc

Viewing your data storage systems using File Explorer

All of the data storage systems connected to your computer are named. You can view the data storage systems connected to your computer using a file management system, such as File Explorer. You can see how much space is used on any or all of the storage devices connected to your computer, including any external hard drives, any optical drives such as CD, DVD, or BD drives, any solid-state drives such as flash drives, and even cameras that you connect through a USB cable. See **FIGURE 2-22**.

FIGURE 2-22: Checking storage space used

Courtesy: Apple Inc. All rights reserved

Solid-State Data Storage Systems

Have you ever used a cell phone or smartphone? A digital camera? An MP3, digital audio, or portable music player? If you have, then you have also used solid-state data storage. Solid-state data storage is portable and durable. It provides fast access to data, offers high-capacity storage, and uses very little power. It is an ideal solution for storing data on mobile devices and transporting data from one device to another.

Learning Outcome 7:
Describe the different types of solid-state cards and drives

● **When would I use solid-state storage?** Solid-state storage systems are suitable for many storage needs. Solid-state memory cards are used mainly in mobile electronics, such as GPS devices, media players, and cameras. Memory cards come in many sizes, speeds, and capacities. See **FIGURE 2-23**. Flash drives are used for storage through a USB connection. SSDs can be installed inside a computer for permanent storage. External SSDs are good for portable storage through a USB connection; they have a larger storage capacity than a flash drive.

FIGURE 2-23: Memory cards are available in several formats and capacities

Source: Lexar

You might use a solid-state memory card in your digital camera. See **FIGURE 2-24**. A solid-state memory card in a digital camera can store hundreds of pictures. You can remove the card from the camera and insert it into a card reader that is connected to a computer. Once the card is connected to your computer, you can transfer the files to your hard drive so the photos can be edited using the computer's graphics software and transmitted via the computer's Internet connection.

FIGURE 2-24: Solid-state storage media is used in cameras

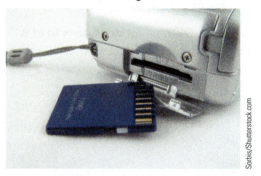

Sorbis/Shutterstock.com

You might use a solid-state memory card in your portable or digital audio player or even your smartphone. See **FIGURE 2-25**. You can download MP3 music files or podcasts using your computer and then store the files on a solid-state memory card so you can hear your favorite tunes or podcasts while you are on the go.

You might use solid-state storage, such as a flash drive or an external solid-state drive, for your portable computing needs, that is, for transporting data from one computer to another.

FIGURE 2-25: Micro solid-state cards add storage to a smartphone

ExaMedia Photography/Shutterstock.com

● **Why is solid-state storage so popular?** Solid-state storage uses a technology that stores data in a nonvolatile, erasable, low-power chip. A **chip** (FIGURE 2-26) is an electronic circuit. Very little power is required to store the data. Solid-state storage is ideal for battery-operated devices, such as digital cameras or smartphones. Once the data is stored, the chip retains the data without the need for an external power source.

FIGURE 2-26: **Chips are electronic circuits**

Chip etched with circuits

Chip ready for packaging

© 2011 Intel-Vintage A

● **How do I know which solid-state cards to buy?** The type of card you buy depends on the device it will be used with. The device you buy should indicate the cards you can use with that device. Solid-state cards are small and can easily be misplaced if you are not careful. The formats for these small, flat cards include CompactFlash (CF), Secure Digital (SD), Secure Digital High Capacity (SDHC), Micro SD, Micro SDHC, and Secure Digital Extended Capacity (SDXC). The micro cards are used in smartphones and portable media players.

■ **CompactFlash (CF) cards** are about the size of a book of matches and provide high storage capacities and access speeds. CompactFlash cards include a built-in controller that reads data from and writes data to the card. CompactFlash cards use a card reader to transfer data from the card to your computer; the built-in controller tells the card reader what to do. With their high storage capacities and access speeds, CompactFlash cards are ideal for use on high-end digital cameras that require megabytes of storage for each photo.

■ **SecureDigital (SD) cards** are popular for digital images and MP3 storage. They use a card reader to copy data from the card to a computer.

● **Will my computer be able to read my solid-state storage cards?** Solid-state storage cards require a device called a **card reader** to transfer data to or from a computer. A card reader can be built into a computer's system unit or into a laptop. Refer to FIGURE 2-27. Sometimes card readers are referred to as 5-in-1, 7-in-1, or all-in-one card readers; these combination devices work with multiple types of solid-state storage formats. If your computer has one of these readers, it will be able to read your solid-state storage cards.

FIGURE 2-27: **Card reader built into a laptop**

Card reader

Many digital devices are equipped with a card reader for transferring data to and from solid-state memory cards.

● **What if my computer system does not have a built-in card reader?** If you are able to get into your computer, you can buy a card reader and add it to the system unit. You can also use a stand-alone card reader. A stand-alone card reader usually connects to a computer via USB. See FIGURE 2-28. To connect the stand-alone card reader to your computer, simply plug the USB cable into an available USB port.

FIGURE 2-28: **USB card reader**

ipixs/Shutterstock.com

● **Do I always need a card reader to read solid-state storage?** No. USB flash drives and solid-state drives (SSDs) incorporate the memory and the reader into one device. Each has a built-in connector that plugs directly into a computer's port. USB flash drives plug into a USB port and internal solid-state drives plug into the motherboard. External USB solid-state flash drives that connect via a USB port are also available. SSDs have no moving parts so they are more durable than mechanical hard drives.

● **What is the best choice for portability?** USB flash drives are easy to take from one computer to another. When connected to your computer's USB port, you can open, edit, delete, and run files stored on a USB flash drive just as if though those files were stored on your computer's hard drive. USB flash drives are about the size of a large paperclip and so durable that you can carry them on your key ring. They are usually called flash drives, thumb drives, or jump sticks. They are also nicknamed pen drives, keychain drives, or UFDs (Universal Flash Drive). They come in a variety of shapes and sizes.

How to Add Devices to Your Computer

You can expand or improve the capability of your computer by adding computer peripherals. Some peripherals you might want to add include a scanner, a different mouse, a joystick, a digital camera, a web cam, a graphics tablet, and more. You typically plug the device into an expansion port on your computer. You can also expand or improve the capability of your computer by adding or upgrading expansion cards, such as sound cards, video cards, and so on.

Learning Outcome 8:
Identify expansion ports and expansion cards, and explain how to use them

- **What is an expansion card?** An **expansion card** is a small circuit board that makes it possible for the computer to communicate with a peripheral device, such as a scanner, a joystick, or a digital camera. Expansion cards are also called expansion boards, controller cards, or adapters.

- **How are expansion cards connected to the computer?** An expansion card is plugged into an expansion slot on the motherboard. An **expansion slot** is a long, narrow socket on the motherboard into which you can plug an expansion card. Once an expansion card is plugged into the expansion slot, a peripheral device can be attached to the expansion card via the expansion port.

- **What is an expansion port?** An **expansion port** is a connector that passes data between a computer and a peripheral device. An expansion port is part of an expansion card. System units are designed with openings that make these ports accessible from outside the case. Common built-in expansion ports that come with a computer are shown in **FIGURE 2-29**.

FIGURE 2-29: Expansion ports

Thunderbolt	USB	USB 3.0	FireWire
VGA	DVI	HDMI	Mini DisplayPort
Audio In	Audio Out	Ethernet	Wireless antenna

- Graphics ports: connect display devices
- FireWire ports: connect peripheral devices such as digital cameras and high-speed external data storage devices
- Ethernet network ports: connect the computer to a wired network
- eSATA ports: connect high-speed external data storage devices
- USB ports: connect peripheral devices such as mice, keyboards, flash drives, external drives, and cameras
- HDMI ports: connect high-definition video cables
- Audio ports: connect speakers, a headset, and/or a microphone

- **Why would I want to add more expansion cards and ports?** You might want to add more cards and ports to upgrade existing expansion cards or to install new expansion cards to enhance sound or communications functionality. For example, you can install a high-end graphics card (sometimes called a video card) if you want to use the computer for advanced graphics or gaming.

- **How does an expansion card work?** The computer controls the peripheral device by sending data over circuits called a **data bus**. One part of the data bus runs between **RAM (Random Access Memory)** and the processor; the other part runs between RAM and various peripheral devices. RAM is volatile storage used by a computer. The segment of the data bus between RAM and the peripheral devices is called the **expansion bus**. As data moves along the expansion bus, it may travel through expansion slots, cards, ports, and cables. See **FIGURE 2-30**.

- **How do I install an expansion card?** Usually, installing an expansion card requires you to open the system unit. Be sure to turn off the power to the system unit before opening a computer. An expansion card is inserted into an expansion slot in the motherboard. Expansion cards are built for only

FIGURE 2-30: Expansion bus

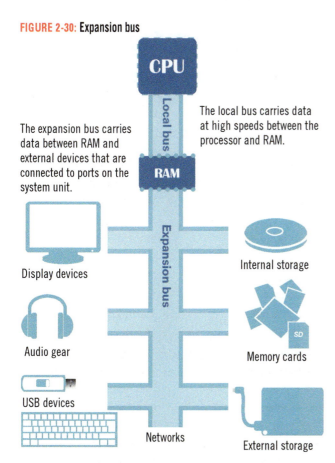

The local bus carries data at high speeds between the processor and RAM.

The expansion bus carries data between RAM and external devices that are connected to ports on the system unit.

Display devices

Audio gear

USB devices

Networks

Internal storage

Memory cards

External storage

one type of slot. If you plan to add or upgrade a card in your computer, you must make sure the right type of slot is available on the motherboard.

● **Once I install the peripheral device or expansion card, will it work automatically?** PCs include a feature called Autodetect, sometimes called "plug and play," works well for most popular peripheral devices. This means that once you plug a peripheral device into its port, the device is ready to use. Each peripheral device or expansion card requires software called a **device driver**. This software program sets up communication between your computer and the device

or card. The directions supplied with your new peripheral device or card will include instructions on how to install the device driver if it does not happen automatically when you start the computer.

● **How do I connect most peripherals to my computer?** Today, many peripheral devices connect to your computer using an external **USB (universal serial bus) port**. See FIGURE 2-31. USB is currently the most popular technology for connecting peripherals. A USB connector is shaped like a flat rectangle. Make sure you know which side of the plug is up; the top is usually labeled with the USB logo. USB ports are conveniently located on the front or sides of the system unit for easy access. Notebook computers often have USB ports on the sides and back of the computer case. Several types of storage devices, such as USB flash drives, also use USB connections.

● **Can I just unplug the peripheral device when I am done using it?** When you connect a peripheral device while the computer is operating, you are hot-plugging. You can only do this with USB and FireWire devices. Before you unplug a device, such as a USB flash drive, however, your computer might require that you issue a command.

FIGURE 2-31: Plugging in a portable hard drive

Photographee.eu/Shutterstock.com

Key Terms & Module Review

Key Terms

3D printer
Access time
Aspect ratio
BD (Blu-ray Disc)
BD drive
Bit depth
Card reader
CD (compact disc)
CD drive
Chip
Color depth
CompactFlash (CF) card
Cursor
Data bus
Data transfer rate
Device driver
Direct access
Display device
Dot pitch
Dots per inch (dpi)
Drive bay

Duplex printer
Duty cycle
DVD (digital video disc or
    digital versatile disc)
DVD drive
Expansion bay
Expansion bus
Expansion card
Expansion port
Expansion slot
Gesture
Graphics card
Hard copy
Hard drive
Ink-jet printer
Input device
Insertion point
Laser mouse
Laser printer
LCD (liquid crystal display)
LED (light emitting diode)

Magnetic storage
Millisecond (ms)
Mouse
Network-enabled printer
Optical mouse
Optical storage
Pages per minute (ppm)
Photo printer
Pixel (picture element)
Pointing device
Printer resolution
RAM (random
    access memory)
Random access
Recordable technology
Resolution
Response rate
Rewritable technology
Scanner
Screen size
SecureDigital (SD) card

Soft copy
Solid-state drive (SSD)
Solid-state storage
Solid-state technology
Storage capacity
Storage device
Storage medium
Storage technology
Toner
Touch screen technology
Touchpad
Trackball
Trackpad
USB flash drive
USB hub
USB (universal serial
    bus) port
Viewing angle width
Virtual keyboard
Wearable computers

Module Review

1. Make sure that you can use your own words to define the bold terms that appear throughout the module.

2. Create a table to summarize what you know about different input devices discussed in this module.

3. Create a table to summarize what you know about different printer technologies discussed in this module.

4. Describe the advantages and disadvantages of magnetic storage, optical storage, and solid-state storage. Give an example of each type of storage. Summarize important uses for each type of storage technology.

5. List three facts that explain why a hard drive is the main storage device for a computer.

6. Describe the differences between the various optical storage technologies and why you would use one over the other.

7. Summarize the different technologies available for display devices. Be sure to include advantages and disadvantages.

8. List any peripheral devices that are attached to your computer. Describe what each one does. Be sure to identify each one as input, output, or storage. Identify how it is connected to your system unit.

9. If possible, identify USB ports on your computer and list any devices you have connected through USB ports. Are the ports on the front or back of the system unit?

10. Think about your storage needs. What storage media are you using for your photos? podcasts? music files? document files? How do you transfer them between devices?

Concepts Review

Select the best answer.

1. A(n) _____ storage system uses lasers to read data.
   a. optical
   b. magnetic
   c. solid state
   d. light

2. The _____ keys include the Home, End, and arrow keys.
   a. navigation
   b. numeric
   c. movement
   d. function

3. A laser printer uses a(n) _____ cartridge to store ink.
   a. ink
   b. color
   c. laser
   d. toner

4. A standard desktop computer uses a _____ as its primary pointing device.
   a. navigation pad
   b. tablet
   c. mouse
   d. keyboard

5. You should use a _____ disc, which has the most storage capacity, if you want to store a full-length feature movie.
   a. USB
   b. CD
   c. DVD
   d. flash

6. Most USB flash drives are _____ .
   a. for storing movies
   b. not durable
   c. portable
   d. only for tablets

7. If you want to input data that currently exists in print format, you need to use a _____ .
   a. scanner
   b. network
   c. digital camera
   d. web cam

8. A variety of memory cards and flash drives can be classified as _____ storage, which stores data in a nonvolatile, erasable, low-power chip.
   a. magnetic
   b. optical
   c. solid-state
   d. digital

9. The light technologies on the bottom of many mice is used to _____ .
   a. clean the pad
   b. track motion
   c. light the desktop
   d. store data

10. A USB _____ drive is a portable storage device featuring a built-in connector that plugs directly into a computer's USB port and requires no card reader.
   a. compact
   b. Blu-ray
   c. optical
   d. flash

11. A _____ and a monitor are the two main output devices for a computer system.
   a. mouse
   b. printer
   c. keyboard
   d. hard drive

12. _____ displays have a brighter image, better viewing angle, and faster response rate than standard LCD screens.
   a. LED
   b. DVD
   c. CRT
   d. PPM

13. Change display settings to a higher _____ to be able to see more content on a screen.
   a. pitch
   b. resolution
   c. viewing angle
   d. color depth

14. Tablet computers and smartphones typically use a(n) _____ to enter text.
   a. LCD
   b. laser mouse
   c. flash drive
   d. touch screen

15. If your computer and others are connected to a(n) _____, you can share a printer.
   a. network
   b. Internet
   c. flash drive
   d. USB hub

16. Popular inexpensive printers for personal computers that produce quality color printouts are _____ printers.
   a. ink jet
   b. thermal
   c. plasma
   d. duplex

17. The best way to quickly add additional storage to your computer is to use a(n) _____ .
   a. CD player
   b. internet drive
   c. external hard drive
   d. USB drives

18. An expansion _____, often located on the back of a desktop computer, is a connector that passes data between a computer and a peripheral device.
   a. port
   b. bus
   c. drive
   d. bay

19. CD/DVD drives connect to a computer through a drive _____ .
   a. belt
   b. bed
   c. bay
   d. bus

20. A(n) _____ card is a small circuit board with a port that makes it possible for a computer to communicate with a peripheral device, such as a storage device.
   a. expansion
   b. add-on
   c. peripheral
   d. graphic

Independent Challenges

Independent Challenge 1

Storage technology has a fascinating history. Engineers and scientists have developed many ways to retain and store data. From the ancient days when Egyptians were writing on papyrus to modern day and futuristic technologies, societies have found ways to retain more and more information in permanent and safe ways.

For this Independent Challenge:

1. Research the history of storage technologies and create a timeline that shows the developments. Be sure to include such items as 78-rpm records, 8-track tapes, floppy disks (all formats including 8", 5.25", and 3.5"). Your research should yield some interesting technologies and systems. See **FIGURE 2-32** for some examples.

FIGURE 2-32: Old storage media

strelov/Shutterstock.com

2. For each technology, list the media, the device used to retrieve the information, two significant facts about the technology, the era in which it was used or was popular, and explain either what led to its demise or why it is still popular.

3. You can create the timeline using images or just words. This is a creative project. Your best research, artistic, and communication skills should come together to create this timeline.

Independent Challenge 2

It is important that you are familiar with the type of computer you use daily. If you do not own your own computer, use a typical computer in the lab at your school or use a friend's computer to complete this exercise. You may need to consult your technical resource person to help you complete this independent challenge.

For this Independent Challenge:

1. Identify the parts on your computer. What type of computer are you using? What kind of system unit do you have?

2. What display device is attached to the computer? What type of technology does it use? What is the screen size? Do you know the resolution?

3. Is there a printer attached to the computer? Is it a network printer? What type of printer is it (laser, ink-jet)? What is the brand, model?

4. What storage devices are part of the computer? Are there removable devices in use for the computer? What type are they? How much storage is available in the hard drive on the computer?

5. What peripheral devices are attached to your computer? List the name, manufacturer, and function of each device, if available. How are these devices attached or connected to your system unit?

6. Draw a sketch of your computer. Label each component and identify what it does.

Independent Challenge 3

Technology is ever-changing so it can be impossible to predict all the ways you might use your computer in the future. But if you purchase a computer that is expandable, you will increase the possibility of using your computer for a long time.

For this Independent Challenge:

1. Refer to the ad in FIGURE 2-33. Use one color marker to highlight all the components that come with this computer system that would make it possible for you to use this computer for video chatting, listening to music, and creating and editing photographs.

2. Refer again to the ad in FIGURE 2-33. Use a second color marker to highlight all the parts of this system that are part of data storage systems.

3. Review the information in this ad and make a short list of any additional equipment you would need if this was your computer.

4. Use the Internet to research three peripheral devices you would like to add to any computer system (such as the scanner shown in FIGURE 2-34), then explain the following for each component:

   a. Why would you like to add this peripheral device?

   b. What is the cost to add this peripheral device?

   c. What technology would you use to attach this device to your computer?

FIGURE 2-34: A scanner is a useful peripheral device

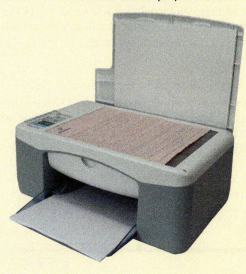

FIGURE 2-33: Computer ad for laptop PC

Nimbus 2000 Series
DO EVERYTHING YOU LOVE.

- 4th Generation Intel Core i7 processor 3.1 GHz 1066 MHz FSB
- 4 MB cache
- 8 GB DDR3-1600 MHz 2 DIMM memory
- 750 GB SATA HD (7200 rpm)
- 8x CD/DVD burner (Dual Layer DVD+/–R)
- 15.6" High FHD (1080p) LCD display screen
- 1 GB NVIDIA GeForce graphics card
- Integrated speakers
- Integrated 1.3 megapixel web cam
- 4 USB 3.0 ports
- 1 IEEE 1394 port
- 1 HDMI graphics port
- 5-in-1 media card reader
- Wireless networking 802.11 BGN
- 1 GB Ethernet
- 58 WHr, 4-cell battery
- Windows 10 64-bit operating system
- Home/small business software bundle
- 1-year limited warranty

Visual Workshop

The Internet has many websites focused on the environmental impact of improperly discarded computers and other electronic devices. Some manufacturers are doing what they can to reduce the toxicity of components. Others are encouraging recycling. For this Visual Workshop, you will write a short paper about recycling computers based on information that you gather from the Internet. You will use the information you gather to create a poster for a campaign to promote Green Computing or responsible recycling in your community. FIGURE 2-35 shows a possible theme for a poster.

1. Connect to the Internet and use your favorite search engine to search for and find web pages to get an in-depth overview of the environmental impact and issues relating to the use and disposal of electronic devices and computers.

2. Determine the specific aspect of the issue that you will present in your paper. You might, for example, decide to focus on the toxic materials contained in computers that end up in landfills. You might investigate labor laws that protect those who dismantle computer parts for scrap. Current laws for shipping electronic devices such as monitors, printers, and computer parts to developing nations depend on the plan for the e-trash. If the plan is to use the computers, laws are more lenient. If the plan is to scrap the devices for their copper, lead, and gold, then the laws are more strict. Often people are hired to work in deplorable conditions without regard to the toxicity of the materials they are touching and breathing. You can investigate the government regulations that help to discourage the shipment of old computers across national borders or try to protect those who work in the scrapping industry.

3. Whatever aspect of the issue you decide to present, make sure that you can back up your discussion with facts and references to authoritative articles and web pages. Place citations to your references (include the author's name, article title, date of publication, and URL) according to your instructor's directions, such as at the end of your paper as endnotes, on each page as footnotes, or in parentheses following the appropriate paragraphs. Follow your instructor's directions for submitting your paper via email or as a printed document.

4. After completing the paper, consider the main points that you want to convey in a poster to your community. Use paper to sketch out your ideas. Complete the poster using poster board. Follow your instructor's directions for submitting the poster.

FIGURE 2-35: Recycling poster

Huguette Roe/Shutterstock.com

Computer Software

Learning Outcomes

1. List and describe computer software categories
2. Explain copyright law and define the different software licenses
3. Explain how to install and uninstall software
4. Identify the basic functions and features of operating systems
5. Compare operating systems
6. Describe utility software, including device drivers
7. Define office productivity software, and name examples in each major category
8. Define graphics software, and name examples in each major category
9. Name other categories of application software, and give examples in each major category

LESSON TOPICS

- Computer Software
- Licenses and Copyrights
- How to Install and Uninstall Software
- Operating Systems—An Overview
- Operating Systems—A Comparison
- Utility Software
- Office Productivity Software
- Graphics Software
- Other Application Software

lightpoet/Shutterstock.com

Computer Software

Software, also called **computer programs**, gives computers the instructions and data necessary to carry out tasks. Software is used to create documents or graphics. Software is used to help schedule classes or to listen to music. Software makes it possible to communicate using computers. Most software uses a **graphical user interface (GUI)**. This allows you to give the computer commands using pointing devices and graphics such as menus, buttons, icons, links, and more.

Learning Outcome 1:
List and describe computer software categories

● **When do I use software?** You use software every time you use your desktop, notebook, or tablet computer. In addition, you use software when you use your mobile phone, digital camera, retail and banking machines, some home appliances, cars, some medical devices, and much more. Software carries out your commands anytime you press buttons or touch a screen to tell a machine what to do.

● **Are there different types of software?** Yes. Software is usually categorized as either system software or application software. **System software** is used by the computer for tasks that help the computer work. For example, you use system software to run your computer and all the programs on it. It can diagnose a problem with your hard drive, printer, or Internet connection. **Application software** helps you carry out tasks such as sending an email, getting you street-by-street driving directions, editing a photo, or writing a report.

Software can be grouped in subcategories according to how the software is used. System software can be grouped into subcategories for operating systems—for controlling a digital device's internal operations; utilities—for file management, security, communications, backup, network management, and system monitoring; and device drivers so that devices can communicate with each other. Application software can be grouped according to tasks, such as producing documents, creating spreadsheets, or communicating with others. **Development software** includes programming and scripting languages for writing scripts, creating webpages, and querying databases and testing software. FIGURE 3-1 shows common ways to categorize system software, development software, and application software. Some software can be in more than one category, so use these categories as a general guideline.

FIGURE 3-1: Examples of software categories

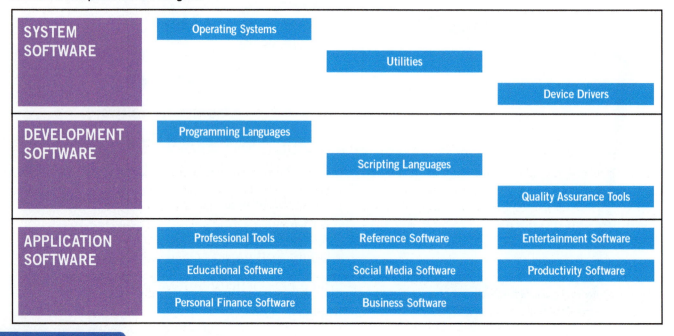

SYSTEM SOFTWARE	Operating Systems		
		Utilities	
			Device Drivers

DEVELOPMENT SOFTWARE	Programming Languages		
		Scripting Languages	
			Quality Assurance Tools

APPLICATION SOFTWARE	Professional Tools	Reference Software	Entertainment Software
	Educational Software	Social Media Software	Productivity Software
	Personal Finance Software	Business Software	

- **Are there other ways to group software?** Yes. Software applications (often called apps) can also be categorized according to their accessibility and where they are installed. These categories include local applications, web applications, portable applications, or mobile applications.

- **What is a local application?** A **local application** is software that is installed on a computer. When you install a local application, the program files are placed in the appropriate folders on the computer's hard drive. After the software is installed, the computer makes sure the program is ready to run.

- **What is a web application?** A **web application** (also called **web app** or **cloudware**) is software that is accessed with a web browser. Instead of running locally on a computer, much of the program code for the software runs on a remote computer connected to the Internet or other computer network. Web apps are available for many of the same applications that run locally. These include email, calendars, databases, photo sharing, project management, maps, games, and even word processing. Web apps make it possible for groups of people to collaborate on projects in multiple locations.

  The advantage of a web app is that you can use it anywhere you have access to a computer connected to the web. However, there are also disadvantages when using web apps. For example, you don't have access to the web app if you lose power to your computer or if you lose your Internet connection. And, you don't have access if the Internet server hosting the web app goes down.

- **What is a portable application?** A **portable application** is designed to run from a removable storage device, such as a USB flash drive. Program files are not installed on the hard drive, and no configuration data is stored on the computer. When the media containing the portable software is removed from the computer, no trace of the portable application is left on the computer. Portable software can only be used when the removable storage device is connected to a computer.

- **What is a mobile application?** A **mobile application** (or **app**) is designed to run on mobile devices such as smartphones and tablet computers. Mobile apps include games, calendars, stock market trackers, tour guides, highway traffic monitors, news feeds, and more.

- **How do I know if a software program will work on my computer?** The **system requirements**, which specify the operating system and minimum hardware capacities, give you the information you need to know if a software program will work on a computer. You can find the system requirements on the software manufacturer's website or on the software packaging. See **FIGURE 3-2**.

FIGURE 3-2: System requirements

eCourse Internet LearnItQuick	
Information	
Seller	eCourseWare Corp.
Category	Education
Updated	July 1, 2017
Version	2.2
Size	31.6 MB
Rating	4+
Compatibility	Requires iOS 8.0 or later, compatible with iPhone, iPad, and iPod Touch, optimized for iPhone 6.

123 ★★★★★
90 ★★★★
18 ★★★
5 ★★
0 ★
Read Reviews

Installed software that comes with new personal computers

Most computers are sold with the operating system installed so you can turn on the machine and use it right away. The operating system Windows 10, for example, typically includes a web browser, media player, and several simple programs. These include a simple text editor, a few games, and some apps. Some computers come with application software that you can use to create documents, manage budgets, and produce presentations. Your computer may come with antivirus software. Be sure to check the terms of the application software that is installed.

Some developers and manufacturers install trial software that you can use free for a few months. To continue using the software beyond the trial period, however, you have to pay for it. If you're purchasing a computer to do a task that requires specialized software, you should factor its cost into the cost of your computer system. Check the specifications listed on the software box or on the software developer's website to make sure your new computer has enough memory and processing speed to run it.

Licenses and Copyrights

Just because it is easy to copy and share **digital content** such as other people's documents, photographs, and music though email or post it on your website, doesn't mean it's legal to do so. Copyright and intellectual property laws, as well as the software license, govern how you can use digital content. This includes digital content you buy at a brick-and-mortar store or download from the web using a computer. Understanding copyright law and software licenses for digital content will help you avoid legal troubles.

Learning Outcome 2:
Explain copyright law and define the different software licenses

- **What is copyright?** **Copyright** is a legal protection that grants the author of an original work an exclusive right to copy, distribute, sell, and modify that work, except under special circumstances described by copyright laws. Exceptions include the purchaser's right to copy software from a distribution disc or website to a computer's hard drive in order to install it.

- **If I don't see the © symbol, does it mean the software is not protected?** Most software displays a **copyright notice**, such as "© 2017 Microsoft Corporation. All Rights reserved," on one of its starting screens. However, this notice is not required by law. As a result, even programs without a copyright notice are protected by copyright law. People who go around copyright law and illegally copy, distribute, or modify software are sometimes called **software pirates**. Their illegal copies are referred to as **pirated software**.

- **What is a software license?** A **software license**, or **license agreement**, is a legal contract that lets you know the ways in which you may use or share that computer program. Once you purchase software, or even if you get software for free, you can only use the software as defined by the software license. The type of license determines how the software is classified legally.

- **How is software classified legally?** Software is legally classified in two categories: public domain and proprietary. **Public domain software** is not protected by copyright because the copyright has expired, or the author has placed the program in the public domain making it available without restriction. Public domain software may be freely copied, distributed, and even resold. The primary restriction on public domain software is that you are not allowed to apply for a copyright on it. Creative Commons is an organization committed to freely

sharing content on the Internet. See **FIGURE 3-3**. Their website explains licensing options for distributing software.

FIGURE 3-3: Creative Commons website

creativecommons.org

Proprietary software has restrictions on its use that are delineated by copyright, patents, or license agreements. Some proprietary software is distributed commercially, whereas some of it is free. Depending on the licensing rights, proprietary software is distributed as commercial software, demoware, shareware, freeware, or open source software. These classifications determine the software license.

- **What is commercial software?** **Commercial software** is typically sold in stores or on websites. Although you buy this software, you actually purchase only the right to use it under the terms of the software license. Some commercial software is available as a trial version, called **demoware**. Demoware is distributed free and often comes preinstalled on new computers. Demoware is often limited in some way until you pay for it. Demoware publishers usually take steps to prevent users from overriding time limitations.

- **What is shareware?** Shareware is copyrighted software marketed under a try-before-you-buy policy. It typically includes a license that permits you to use the software for a trial period. To use it beyond the trial period, you must send in a registration fee. A shareware license usually allows you to make copies of the software and distribute it to others. If they choose to use the software, they must send in a registration fee. Registration fee payment relies on the honor system.

- **What is freeware?** Freeware is copyrighted software that is available without a fee. Because the software is protected by copyright, you cannot do anything with it that is not expressly allowed by copyright law or by the author. Typically, the license for freeware permits you to use the software, copy it, and give it away, but does not permit you to alter it or sell it. Many utility programs, device drivers, and some games are available as freeware.

- **What is open source software?** Open source software makes the program instructions available to programmers who want to modify and improve the software. Open source software may be sold or distributed free of charge, but it must, in every case, include the source code. Despite the lack of restrictions on distribution and use, open source software is copyrighted and is not in the public domain. The Firefox browser is open source software. The Open Source Initiative is a non-profit corporation that advocates for open source software. See FIGURE 3-4. Two of the most common open source and free software licenses are BSD and GPL. The BSD license originated as the Berkeley Software Distribution license for a server operating system. GPL (General Public License) was developed for a free operating system called GNU.

FIGURE 3-4: Open Source Initiative

Source: opensource.org The OSI logo trademark is the trademark of Open Source Initiative.

- **Do I have to accept the license agreement to run the software?** Yes, usually before you install and run a program, you have to agree to the terms as stated in the EULA (end-user license agreement). The EULA opens on the screen when you install the software. You can indicate that you accept the terms by clicking a designated button or check box labeled OK, I agree, or I accept. See FIGURE 3-5.

FIGURE 3-5: A software license

- **Since I didn't actually sign anything, am I still legally bound to this license?** Yes, while most legal contracts require signatures before the terms take effect, software publishers typically use two techniques to validate a software license. A shrink-wrap license goes into effect as soon as you open the packaging. Downloaded software has an installation agreement that goes into effect as soon as you click the option to accept the terms of the agreement.

- **What software licenses are available?** A single-user license limits use of the software to one person at a time. A site license is generally priced at a flat rate and allows software to be used on all computers at a specific location. A multiple-user license is priced per user and allows the allocated number of people to use the software at any time. A concurrent-use license is priced per copy and allows a specific number of copies to be used at the same time.

How does digital technology affect intellectual property laws?

Intellectual property refers to the ownership of certain types of information, ideas, or representations. It includes patents, trademarks, and copyrighted material, such as music, photos, software, books, and films. In the past, such works were difficult and expensive to copy. However, digital technology has made it easy to produce copies with no loss in quality from the original. Pirating software is simple and inexpensive. It has caused significant revenue loss for software publishers, as well as

recording studios and film producers. The fight against piracy takes many forms. Governments have passed strict anti-piracy laws. Technology is available that scrambles and encrypts content. Several companies use digital rights management technology that physically prevents copying. Organizations such as the Software & Information Industry Association have committed to consumer education and created anti-piracy videos that are shown to the public.

How To Install and Uninstall Software

You often want to add application software or apps to your digital device. Software can be obtained in many ways, such as on distribution media (CD, DVD, or BD) or downloaded from the web. Unless you are using web apps, you must install software before you can use it. Installation procedures depend on your computer's operating system and whether the software is a local, portable, or mobile application. In addition to installing software, you should also know how to upgrade your software and how to uninstall software you no longer need.

Learning Outcome 3:
Explain how to install and uninstall software

● **What does it mean to install software?** When you install software, you are copying the software from a distribution media, such as from a CD, DVD, BD or the web, to your hard drive so you can use the program. You generally won't install the OS. It usually comes installed on the computer or mobile device when you buy it.

● **How do I start the installation process?** To install software from a CD or a DVD, place the disc in the CD or DVD drive. Once the disc is in the drive, you will see blinking lights on the drive and information will appear on your screen as a setup program starts.

To install software from the web, read any information on the website about installing the software, then click the download link. See FIGURE 3-6. The files you need will be downloaded and copied to a folder on your computer. Downloaded software files are usually transferred as one large compressed file to your computer's Downloads folder. Compressed files are smaller so they download faster than uncompressed files. Some compressed files are zip files, others are executable files. Once the files are downloaded, a setup program starts.

FIGURE 3-6: Download link

1. At the distribution website, read the installation instructions, then select the Download link.

2. If you are downloading from a trusted site and have antivirus software running, select the Run button.

Courtesy of Inkscape Inc.

● **What is a setup program?** A **setup program** is a series of steps designed to guide you through the installation process. You follow directions as prompted on the screen to complete the installation process. If you are

installing software from the web, the downloaded file is unzipped into the original collection of files. See FIGURE 3-7.

FIGURE 3-7: Downloading and installing software

1. Wait for the download to finish. The setup program included in the download starts automatically.

3. Select a folder to hold the new application.

2. Read the license agreement and accept its terms to continue with the installation.

4. Wait for the setup program to uncompress the downloaded file and install the software in the selected directory.

Courtesy of Inkscape

● **How do I know where the software is installed?** During the installation process, you will be prompted to specify the location where you want to store the program files. You can use the default folder specified by the setup program or a folder of your own choosing. You can also create a new folder during the setup process. Generally, when you install software, the new software files are placed in the appropriate folders on your computer's hard drive.

● **How do I install software on a Mac?** Mac software downloads are typically supplied as a **DMG** or a "disk image" package which has a .dmg extension. It contains the main APP file for the software, and it may also contain a Read Me file or other data files used by the application. Once the download is complete, open the DMG file from the Downloads folder, and then drag the APP file to your Applications folder as shown in **FIGURE 3-8**.

FIGURE 3-8: Installing Mac software

1. Select the DMG file from the downloads dock. 2. Drag the program file to the Applications folder.

● **What else happens during the installation process?** As part of the installation process, your computer performs any software or hardware configurations necessary to make sure the program is ready to run.

● **How do I start the program?** When the installation is complete, you should start the program you just installed to make sure it works. Techniques for running programs depend on your computer's operating system. See **FIGURE 3-9**.

FIGURE 3-9: Several ways to start a program on a PC

Double-click or double-tap a desktop icon

Click or tap an app on the Start menu   Click or tap a taskbar icon   Click or tap a tile

On a Mac, you can access most software from the Launchpad at the bottom of the screen. Clicking an icon tells the computer to start the APP executable file. Drag an icon from the Launchpad to the Dock if you use it frequently. See **FIGURE 3-10**.

● **Do I have to activate the software?** Yes. Although you may be allowed to run a program for a set number of times before activation, generally you need to activate the program for long-term use. To combat piracy, many software publishers require users to type in a validation

code to complete an installation and activate the software. A **validation code** is a long sequence of numbers and letters that is typically supplied separately from the software itself. Validation codes can usually be found on distribution media packaging. If you download the software, the validation code is sent to you via email.

FIGURE 3-10: Starting a program on a Mac

1. Open the Launchpad to display application icons. 2. Select the icon for the application you want to run.

● **What is software registration?** Software registration collects your personal information, such as your email address. Generally, product activation is not the same as registration. A few software publishers tie activation and registration together. Activation is required but registration is voluntary.

● **Why would I want to register my software?** You register your software in order to receive product information and updates.

● **What are software updates?** After you install your software, several types of updates are usually available. These updates are patches, service packs, and software upgrades. **Patches** are small programs designed to correct, secure, or enhance an existing program. **Service packs** are a collection of updates, fixes, and/or enhancements to a software program delivered in the form of a single installable package. They are usually distributed over the Internet. Patches and service packs automatically install themselves when you download them. **Software upgrades** are available to consumers who already have a software program installed.

● **How do I remove software I don't need anymore?** Most software programs come with an uninstall program. In addition, most operating systems, such as Windows and Mac OS, provide access to an uninstall program. Uninstall programs are designed to delete all the related program files from your computer's program and system folders on the hard drive and from the desktop.

Operating Systems— An Overview

An **operating system (OS)** is system software. It is the master controller for all of the activities that take place in any computer system, including desktop, notebook, and tablet computers as well as smartphones and other mobile devices. The operating system determines how people interact with a digital device. It also controls how a digital device communicates with other computers on a network or peripheral devices such as printers and scanners.

Learning Outcome 4:
Identify the basic functions and features of an operating system

● **How do I start the operating system?** The operating system starts each time you turn on your computer or digital device. The first task of the operating system when you turn on a computer is to start the **boot process**. This is why turning on a computer is also called "booting a computer." Six major events happen during the boot process. Refer to **TABLE 3-1**.

TABLE 3-1: Six steps in the boot process

Step	Description
1. Power up	When you turn on the power switch, the power light is illuminated and power is distributed to the computer circuitry.
2. Start bootstrap program	The processor begins to execute the bootstrap program that is stored in permanent memory called ROM.
3. Power-on self-test (POST)	The operating system performs diagnostic tests of several crucial system parts.
4. Identify peripheral devices	The operating system identifies the peripheral devices that are connected to the computer and checks their settings.
5. Load operating system	The operating system is copied from the hard drive to Random Access Memory (RAM).
6. Check configuration and customization	The operating system reads configuration data and the processor executes any customized startup routines.

● **What does the operating system do?** Your computer's operating system ensures that input and output proceed in an orderly manner. It provides buffers to hold data while the computer is busy with other tasks. A **buffer** is an area of memory that holds data from one device while it is waiting to be transferred to another device. By using a keyboard buffer, for example, your computer never misses one of your keystrokes, regardless of how fast you type. In addition, the operating system manages a computer's resources by interacting with your computer's software and hardware. See **FIGURE 3-11**.

FIGURE 3-11: Example of how the operating system works

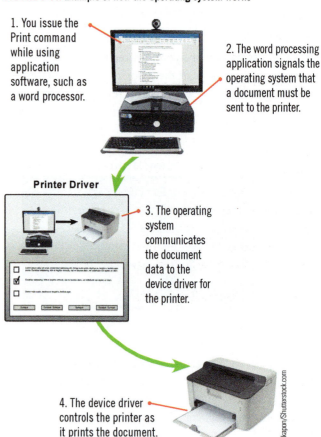

1. You issue the Print command while using application software, such as a word processor.

2. The word processing application signals the operating system that a document must be sent to the printer.

Printer Driver

3. The operating system communicates the document data to the device driver for the printer.

4. The device driver controls the printer as it prints the document.

ekkapon/Shutterstock.com

● **What is a computer's resource?** The term **resource** refers to any computer component that is required to perform work. For example, computer resources include the CPU (central processing unit), RAM, storage devices, and peripherals. While you interact with application software, your computer's operating system is busy behind the scenes with resource management tasks such as those listed in FIGURE 3-12.

FIGURE 3-12: Resource management tasks

Manage processor resources to handle simultaneous input, output, and processing tasks

Manage memory by allocating space for all the programs and data that are in use during a computing session

Keep track of storage resources so that files and programs can be found

Ensure that input and output proceed in an orderly manner by communicating with peripheral devices

Establish basic elements of the user interface such as the appearance of the desktop, menus, and toolbars

Source: Intel Corporation. All rights reserved; Ekkapon/Shutterstock.com

● **How does the operating system let you know there is a problem?** The operating system displays messages on the device screen if it encounters a problem. For example, if a device driver or a peripheral device is not performing correctly, the operating system displays an on-screen warning about the problem.

● **How do I know what programs are currently running on my computer?** When using Windows, you can open the Task Manager to see a list of programs. See FIGURE 3-13. The operating system is **multitasking** when more than one program is running at one time. In addition to programs, many activities—called **processes**—compete for the attention of your computer's processor. Most processes are programs that run in the background to carry out tasks for the operating system, device drivers, and applications. You can see the list of processes that are running by clicking the Processes tab in the Task Manager.

FIGURE 3-13: Windows 10 Task Manager

Task Manager					
File Options View					
Processes Performance App history Startup Users Details Services					
		5%	37%	0%	0%
Name	Status	CPU	Memory	Disk	Network
Apps (6)					
Microsoft Edge		0%	9.0 MB	0 MB/s	0 Mbps
Microsoft Outlook (2)		0%	36.1 MB	0 MB/s	0 Mbps
Settings		0.7%	16.4 MB	0 MB/s	0 Mbps
Snagit 8		0.8%	11.4 MB	0.1 MB/s	0 Mbps
Task Manager		0.5%	6.9 MB	0 MB/s	0 Mbps
Windows Explorer (2)		0.2%	28.6 MB	0 MB/s	0 Mbps
Background processes (43)					
AcroTray		0%	0.3 MB	0 MB/s	0 Mbps
Adobe Acrobat Update Service		0%	0.3 MB	0 MB/s	0 Mbps
Application Frame Host		0%	7.8 MB	0 MB/s	0 Mbps
avast! Antivirus		0%	9.2 MB	0 MB/s	0 Mbps
avast! Service		0%	18.3 MB	0 MB/s	0 Mbps
AvastVirtualBox Interface		0%	3.5 MB	0 MB/s	0 Mbps
Fewer details					End task

● **How do I use the operating system?** Although its main purpose is to control what happens behind the scenes of a computer system, many operating systems provide tools to make computing easier or more fun for you. You can use these operating system utilities to control and customize your computer equipment and work environment. The Windows 10 Settings app lets you personalize many features. See FIGURE 3-14. For example, using options in the Settings app, you can change your display properties, uninstall a program, change the default program for a file type, and other system tasks. The Windows Control panel lets you set more advanced system options. TABLE 3-2 lists some ways you interact with your computer's OS.

FIGURE 3-14: Windows Settings app

TABLE 3-2: Ways you use an operating system

You can	Most operating systems
Launch programs	display graphical objects such as icons, a Start button, and the Programs menu that you can use to start programs
Manage files	include programs, such as Windows Explorer, that allow you to view a list of folders and files, move them to different storage devices, copy them, rename them, and delete them
Get help	offers a online Help system that you can use to find out more about the OS, such as how various commands work
Customize the user interface environment	provide utilities that help you customize your screen display, system sounds, security and access
Configure equipment and install and uninstall programs	provide access to utilities that help you set up and configure your hardware and peripheral devices, install and uninstall software

Operating Systems—
A Comparison

When you purchase a personal computer or a mobile device, it generally comes with the operating system already installed. The operating system you use depends on the type of personal computer or digital device you use, as well as the type of processor running your personal computer or digital device. The operating system determines the user interface on your digital device.

Learning Outcome 5:
Compare operating systems

● **What is a user interface?** A **user interface** is the combination of hardware and software that helps you communicate with a computer. Your computer's user interface includes a display device, mouse, and keyboard as well as software elements, such as icons, toolbars, menus, and command buttons. This combination of hardware and software determines how you interact with your computer. When a user interface has graphical elements, it is called a **graphical user interface (GUI)**.

● **What are the main operating systems in use today for personal computers?** The three main operating systems for personal computers in use today are **Windows**, **Mac OS**, and **Linux**. The Windows operating system is installed on PCs. The Mac OS is installed on Apple computers. Linux can be installed on PCs. Each operating system has different versions, such as home or professional.

● **Why are there different versions of an operating system?** There are different versions to meet the wide range of consumer needs. For example, your home personal computer probably doesn't need as powerful an operating system as a computer used in a large business. You need your computer to perform basic tasks. A business may need its computers to perform basic tasks as well as network with other computers in the company. Different versions allow users to buy the operating system to best meet their needs. For example, Microsoft offers several versions, called editions, of the Windows operating system for various markets. As a consumer, you can choose from among these editions of Windows. Each edition has features that meet specific markets or needs.

In addition to the desktop version, there are also server and embedded versions of Microsoft Windows. Server editions are designed for LAN, Internet, and web servers.

Embedded editions are designed for handheld devices, such as tablets and mobile phones.

● **Which version of Windows will probably be on my computer?** If you purchase a PC, it will be running the most current version of Windows for personal computers. FIGURE 3-15 shows the Windows 10 operating system. Since its introduction in 1985, Windows has evolved through several versions. The latest version boasts easy personalization, enhanced security, flexible file management, and powerful search capabilities.

FIGURE 3-15: Windows 10 user interface

● **What operating system is available for the Macintosh computer?** Mac OS X (the X can be pronounced either as ten or the letter X) is the operating system used on Apple Macintosh computers. Like Windows, Mac OS X has also been through a number of versions. Previous version of Mac OS X were named after big cats; the current version is named El Capitan, for the iconic landmark in Yosemite National Park. Previous versions include Lion, Snow Leopard, Cheetah, Puma, Jaguar, Panther, Tiger, and Leopard. The Apple logo at the top of the screen on the menu bar and the Dock at the bottom of the desktop help you recognize that the computer is running Mac OS.

● **What are Linux and Chrome OS?** Linux is an operating system that is available as a free download. Linux was developed by Linus Torvalds in 1991. The Linux operating system is distributed under the terms of a General Public License (GPL), which allows everyone to make copies for his or her own use, to give it to others, or to sell it. This licensing policy has encouraged programmers to develop Linux utilities, software, and enhancements. A Linux OS called Ubuntu is installed on various types of hardware and can be installed on Macs and PCs. Google launched the Chrome operating system in 2009. The Chrome OS kernel is based on Linux. It powers inexpensive clamshell-style Chromebooks that are popular in educational settings. See **FIGURE 3-16**.

FIGURE 3-16: The Chrome user interface

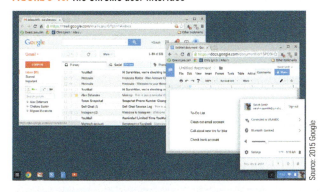

Source: 2015 Google

● **What operating systems run on tablet computers?** Leading tablet operating systems include Windows, Android, and iOS. **Android** is a mobile operating system that is a popular platform for tablet computers, smartphones, and ebook readers. Tablets running Android are made by many manufacturers. Many Android devices have a screen-based home button rather than a physical button. Touching the on-screen home button recalls the

home screen. Apple tablets run the proprietary iOS Apple operating systems. See **FIGURE 3-17**.

FIGURE 3-17: Windows and Android run on tablet computers

Source: 2015 Google

Windows   Android

● **What operating systems run on smartphones?** Smartphones are essentially communications devices, so their operating systems need to accommodate voice as well as data on very small screens. These special requirements are met by several operating systems. Some manufactures produce smartphone models that use different mobile operating systems. iOS for mobile devices is shown in **FIGURE 3-18**. However, you can buy one Sony smartphone that runs Android and a different Sony smartphone that runs Windows Mobile.

FIGURE 3-18: iOS for mobile devices

iOS on iPhone   iOS on iPad

Comparing types of operating systems

Operating systems for computers, notebooks, and mobile devices provide many similar services, such as scheduling processor resources, managing memory, loading programs, managing input and output, and creating the user interface. But because mobile devices, such as smartphones and tablets, tend to be used for less sophisticated tasks, their operating systems are simpler and significantly smaller. By keeping the operating system small, it can be stored in ROM. Because operating systems for these mobile devices do not need to load the OS from the disk into RAM, these mobile devices are ready almost instantly when they are turned on.

Operating systems for mobile devices often provide built-in support for touch screens, handwriting input, wireless networking, and cellular communications. Touch-screen input makes it possible to use fingers to press, pinch, swipe, squeeze, and expand content in order to control the size and placement of objects on the screen.

Utility Software

As you use your computer, you will find it is important to keep it in good working order. Utility software can help you do just that. **Utility software** (also referred to as **utilities**) is a type of system software designed to perform a specialized task. Examples of utility software include diagnostic and maintenance tools, setup wizards, communications programs, security software, device drivers, and apps.

Learning Outcome 6:
Describe utility software, including device drivers

● **Why do I need utility software?** You need utility software to help maintain your computer and safeguard your files. Utility software helps you monitor and configure settings for your computer system hardware, the operating system, and application software. Utilities are used for backing up, securing, permanently deleting, and cleaning up files on hard drives. These utilities include security features for shredding files so they cannot be recovered. Other utilities can help you recover files deleted (but not shredded) by mistake. Utility software includes diagnostics that track down file errors and other problems that prevent computers from running at peak efficiency. These utilities can also give your PC a performance-enhancing tune-up. See **FIGURE 3-19**.

FIGURE 3-19: Utility to protect your computer system

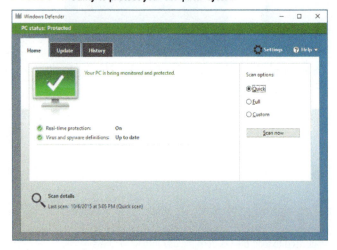

● **Do any utilities come with the operating system?**
Yes. A variety of utilities are included with your operating system. For example, **FIGURE 3-20** shows an uninstall utility

to remove programs. System and Security utilities provide access to the many Windows operating system utilities. You use the Control Panel to access the System and Security utilities.

FIGURE 3-20: Uninstall utility

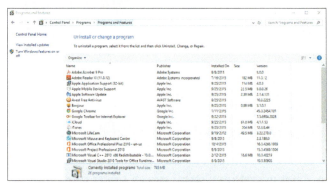

● **Do I always have to run the utilities or are some automatic?** There are operating system utilities that run in the background. For example, one Windows utility periodically sets a **restore point**, which is a snapshot of your computer settings. Restore points are created automatically every week, and just before significant system events, such as the installation of a program or device driver. If a hard drive problem causes system instability, you might be able to roll back your system to a restore point when your computer was operational. You can manually set restore points, too. For example, you might want to set a restore point before setting up a network. You do this so you can restore your system to the way it was before the installation if unexpected problems are created when you set up a network. This can save you a lot of time and aggravation.

- **Do I have to use the utilities that come with my operating system or do I have other choices?** You have choices. In addition to utilities that come with your operating system, other third-party utilities are available. You will typically use utilities from third-party vendors because operating system utilities are often not as comprehensive or do not provide as many features as third-party utilities. Third-party utilities are designed by companies that specialize in system maintenance or security.

- **What are some utility programs I should know about?** If you work with large files, you might use a **compression utility** to reduce file size for quick transmission or efficient storage. The Windows operating system comes with a file compression utility. Many computer owners prefer to use a third-party utility, such as WinZip, IZArc, Quick Zip, or PKZIP.

   You will also want to use **security utilities**. These utilities can scan incoming and outgoing files to be sure they are safe. They can scan your applications to see if any are missing security patches. They can also help you control nuisance ads, intrusion attempts, and spam. Other security-related utilities include file-encryption software that scrambles file content for storage or transmission. You can also buy utilities that remove Internet history lists, files, and graphics from disk storage locations that can be scattered in many parts of the hard drive.

- **Can utilities help me customize my desktop?** Yes, for example, you can use utilities to customize your desktop with screen savers that display clever graphics when the machine is idle. Different themes can change the way fonts are displayed in menus and icons in programs. Themes can also customize sounds that are played when operating system events occur. For example, when an action doesn't work, you might hear a buzzer.

- **What is PDF?** PDF stands for **Portable Document File**. The **PDF** file format is used so that a document can be read by people regardless of what type of computers they are using or the software they have installed on their computers. To read a PDF file, you need a document reader utility, such as the popular and free Adobe Reader. See **FIGURE 3-21**. Links to download Adobe Reader are available on many websites.

FIGURE 3-21: Adobe Reader is a free utility to read PDF files

Source: adobe.com

- **What is a device driver?** A **device driver** is a type of utility software that helps a peripheral device to establish communication with a computer. Device drivers are used by printers, monitors, graphics cards, sound cards, network cards, modems, storage devices, mice, and scanners. Once installed, a device driver starts automatically when it is needed. Device drivers usually run in the background, without opening a window on the screen. On a PC, the Windows Device Manager offers access to device drivers so you can check if they are working, change settings, and check the device driver's version number to compare it with the most recent version posted online. Device drivers, updates, and instructions for installing them are either supplied on CDs by the device manufacturer or can be downloaded from the manufacturer's website. See **FIGURE 3-22**.

FIGURE 3-22: Checking device driver updates

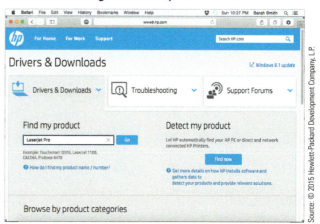

Source: © 2015 Hewlett-Packard Development Company, L.P.

Office Productivity Software

If you work in an office, you will use a computer to create documents, schedule meetings, send email, manage numbers, make presentations, and organize data. **Office productivity software** (also called **productivity software**) is generally defined as the software that allows you to be productive in an office setting. It integrates these major software categories: word processing, spreadsheet, presentation, database, and scheduling.

Learning Outcome 7:
Define office productivity software, and name examples in each major category

● **What is word processing software?** **Word processing software** is used to produce documents, such as reports, letters, books, blogs, and manuscripts. If you are writing a paper, writing a blog, or organizing your résumé, you will probably use a word processor. Word processors allow you to apply a theme and styles to create a unified look across documents using the same word processing program. They give you the ability to create, check the spelling of, edit, and format a document on the screen before you commit it to paper. See **FIGURE 3-23**. Microsoft Word and OpenOffice Writer are examples of word processors.

● **What is spreadsheet software?** **Spreadsheet software** is ideal for projects that require repetitive calculations, such as budgeting, maintaining a grade book, balancing a checkbook, tracking investments, and calculating loan payments. Because it is so easy to experiment with different numbers, spreadsheet software is useful for what-if analysis. Spreadsheet software can generate colorful graphs and charts based on the data in the spreadsheet. Spreadsheet software provides the tools to create electronic worksheets. A **worksheet** is a grid of columns and rows. See **FIGURE 3-24**. Microsoft Excel and OpenOffice Calc are examples of spreadsheet programs.

FIGURE 3-23: A new document in Microsoft Word

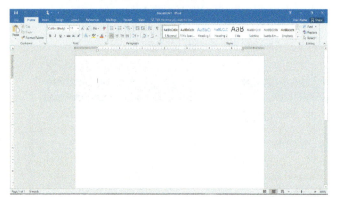

FIGURE 3-24: A spreadsheet in Microsoft Excel

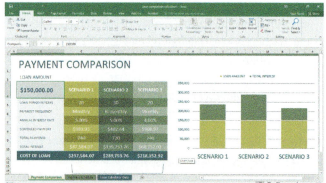

Software suites

A **software suite** is a collection of application software sold as a single package. Popular office suites include Google Docs, iWork, LibreOffice, Microsoft Office, Microsoft Office Online, and Zoho Office Suite. The applications often include the following: Word processing, spreadsheet, presentation, database, mail, and calendar programs. Purchasing a software suite is usually much less expensive than purchasing each application in the suite separately.

Because all the applications in a suite are produced by the same software publisher, they tend to have similar user interfaces and provide an easy way to transport data from one application to another. The disadvantage of a software suite is that it might include applications you do not need. You should calculate the price of the applications you do need and compare that to the cost of the suite.

● **What is database software?** Database software provides the tools needed to create a database. A database is a collection of data that is stored electronically as a series of records in tables. See FIGURE 3-25. Database software can help you print reports, export data to other programs (such as to a spreadsheet, where you can graph the data), and transmit data to other computers. A database can contain any sort of data, such as your music collection, a university's student records, or a company's customer information. Microsoft Access, FileMaker Pro, and OpenOffice Base are examples of database programs for personal computers.

FIGURE 3-25: Microsoft Access

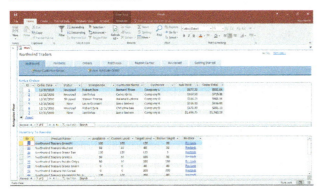

● **What is presentation software?** Presentation software provides the tools you need for combining text, graphics, graphs, animations, video, and sound into a series of electronic slides. See FIGURE 3-26. You can display the electronic slides on a monitor for a one-on-one presentation, or you can use a computer projection device for group presentations. On-screen tools such as the highlighter or pen make it possible for you to annotate the slide during the presentation. How the slides advance is up to you. You can have the slides display automatically at set intervals, or you can advance the slides manually. Transitions between slides, such as checkerboard or wipes, create dramatic effect. You can output the presentation as a video or paper copies of the slides with or without notes. You can share presentations over email, online, or publish them to a website. Microsoft PowerPoint, iWork Keynote, and OpenOffice Impress are examples of presentation software programs.

FIGURE 3-26: Microsoft PowerPoint

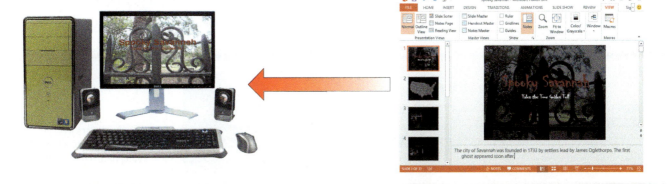

Other productivity software

Word processing, spreadsheet, database, presentation, and scheduling software are the five main types of office productivity software. Scheduling and contact management software such as Microsoft Outlook includes an email program. Two other office productivity software include web authoring and desktop publishing software.

Web authoring software helps you design and develop webpages that can be published on the web. Web authoring software provides tools for generating HTML tags, which is the code used to display a document on the web.

Desktop publishing (DTP) software provides both word processing and graphic design tools. Many of today's word processing programs offer page layout and design features. However, desktop publishing programs, such as Microsoft Publisher, provide more sophisticated features to help you produce professional-quality publications. Most word processing software is page-oriented, meaning that it treats each page as a rectangle that can be filled with text and graphics. Text automatically flows from one page to the next. In contrast, most DTP software is frame-oriented, allowing you to divide each page into several rectangular-shaped frames that you can fill with text or graphics. Text flows from one frame to the next. You will want to use DTP to create complex documents, such as marketing brochures or magazines.

Graphics Software

You may want to include images, such as digital photos or pictures you draw using the computer, in your work. These images are called graphics. The term **graphics** refers to any picture, drawing, sketch, photograph, image, or icon that appears on your computer screen or on your printed output. **Graphics software** is designed to help you create, display, modify, manipulate, and print graphics. Many kinds of graphics software are available, and each one is typically used with a particular type of graphic. Individuals who work with graphics will undoubtedly use more than one graphics program.

Learning Outcome 8:
Define graphics software, and name examples in each major category

● **Can I use my computer to draw or create graphic images?** Yes. You can use **paint software** (sometimes called **image editing software**) to create more sophisticated images. Paint software provides a set of electronic pens, brushes, and paints for painting images on the screen. You can create these images from scratch, or you can use an existing image or photograph and add your own touches. See FIGURE 3-27. A simple program called Microsoft Paint is included with Windows. More sophisticated paint programs include Corel Paint Shop Pro and Adobe Photoshop.

● **Can I use my computer to edit my digital photographs?** Yes. You can use **photo editing software**, such as Adobe Photoshop and Corel PaintShop Pro, to improve the quality of your photos. For example, using photo editing software, you can modify an image's contrast and brightness, crop unwanted objects, and remove "red eye." Programs include editing tools such as those that correct image distortions or "clone" parts of an image by pulling pixels from one area of an image and applying them to another. See FIGURE 3-28. You can even reconstruct lost or deteriorated areas in a photo.

FIGURE 3-27: Microsoft Paint

FIGURE 3-28: Photo editing software

Photo editing software lets you remove unwanted objects and fill in appropriate replacement images

You can also use **drawing software**, which provides tools, such as a set of lines, shapes, and colors. You can use these tools to create simple images, such as diagrams and corporate logos. The drawings created with drawing software, such as Adobe Illustrator and CorelDraw, tend to have a flat cartoonlike quality, but they are easy to modify and look good at almost any size.

● **Is there a quick way to include art in my document?** You have several options. First, you can use clip art in your document, presentation, spreadsheet, or even database table. **Clip art** is a collection of graphic images. These images might be drawn images or they might be photographs. These images are readily available. You can purchase collections of clip art focused on a particular theme at a store or download them from a website. You can use your favorite search engine to find a wide variety of clip art that is ready to be inserted into your document. Before using any clip art, be sure to review its acceptable use statement to ensure you do not violate its copyrights. When using one of the Microsoft Office productivity programs, you search using a key-word to find an image online that meets your needs. See **FIGURE 3-29**.

FIGURE 3-29: Inserting clip art in a presentation

In addition to clip art, you can scan images, such as photographs, using a scanner. Once the image is scanned and saved, you have an electronic file of that image. You can insert that image and manipulate it in your document in the same way you would insert any picture in a document.

● **What software can I use to create three-dimensional graphics?** You can use 3D graphics software to create 3D graphics. **3D graphics software** provides a set of tools for creating wire-frame models that represent three-dimensional objects. A wire-frame model is similar to the frame for a pop-up tent. In much the same way that you would construct the frame for the tent and then cover it with nylon fabric, you can use a 3D graphics program to cover a wire-frame model with

surface texture and color to create a graphic of a 3D object. See **FIGURE 3-30**.

FIGURE 3-30: 3D wireframe drawing

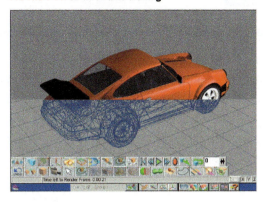

● **What software is used to create technical drawings or blueprints? CAD (computer-aided design)** is a special type of 3D graphics software. It is used by architects, engineers, and others who use computers to create blueprints and product specifications. You can purchase scaled-down versions of professional CAD programs. These programs provide simplified tools you can use for tasks such as redesigning your kitchen or drawing up new landscaping options. You may have used a CAD program at a home improvement store, where CAD is used to help customers visualize home improvement designs.

● **Do movie studios use computers to create graphics in films?** Computers and 3D graphics software are used extensively in the movie industry. Feature-length 3D animated films are responsible for stunning technology breakthroughs, such as the ability to realistically depict the movement of clothing on a moving animated character and animate individual strands of hair or fur. Graphics design companies such as Pixar Animation Studios and DreamWorks use 3D animation techniques to produce animated feature films as well as special effects.

Module 3

Other Application Software

In addition to office productivity and graphics software, there are many other categories of application software. Some of the major categories are entertainment, gaming, music and video, education, business, and science. Application software in these categories can help you use your computer for entertainment, such as listening to music, playing games, and watching videos. They can help you use your computer for number-crunching tasks such as money management, mathematical modeling, or statistical analysis. This lesson looks at just a few of the many other types of application software.

Learning Outcome 9:

Name other categories of application software, and give examples in each major category

● **Can I use my computer to play games?** Yes. Computer games are the most popular type of entertainment software. Computer games are generally classified into subcategories, such as simulations, multiplayer, role-playing, action, adventure, puzzles, and strategy/war games. Some games can be played using the keyboard. See **FIGURE 3-31**. Other games use game controllers that simulate musical intruments to interact with a computer. For example, you can use a guitar game controller to play lead guitar, bass guitar, and rhythm guitar across numerous rock

FIGURE 3-31: Playing a computer game

Georgejmclittle/Shutterstock.com

music songs. Multiplayer games provide an environment in which two or more players can participate in the same game. Players can use Internet technology to band together in sophisticated virtual environments. Large-scale multiplayer games operate on multiple Internet servers, each one with the capacity to handle thousands of players at peak times.

● **Can I use my computer to create music and sound?** You can use **audio editing software** to make digital voice and music recordings. You can store these files on your computer. Audio editing software typically includes playback as well as recording capabilities so you can preview your work and make changes as needed. Your operating system might supply audio editing software, such as Sound Recorder, or you can download open source software, such as Audacity.

Ear training software targets musicians and music students who want to learn to play by ear, develop tuning skills, recognize notes and keys, and develop other musical

skills. Notation software is the musician's equivalent of a word processor. It helps musicians compose, edit, and print the notes for their compositions. For non-musicians, **computer-aided music software** is designed to generate unique musical compositions simply by selecting the musical style, instruments, key, and tempo. MIDI sequencing software and software synthesizers are great for sound effects and for controlling keyboards and other digital instruments. Music composition software with MIDI support makes it easy to place notes on a screen-based music staff, then play back the composition on a MIDI keyboard or through the speakers of a digital device. See **FIGURE 3-32**.

FIGURE 3-32: Music composition software

Source: Software © MakeMusic, Inc. Music
© Media Technics

● **Can I use my computer to edit and create videos?** Yes. You can use **video editing software** and **DVD authoring software**. These programs provide tools for transferring video footage from a camcorder to a computer, deleting unwanted footage, assembling video segments in any sequence, adding special visual effects, and adding a sound track. See **FIGURE 3-33**. Video editing software allows desktop video authors to share their movies on social networking sites or to transfer their productions to DVDs and watch them on standard DVD players connected to television sets or projectors. Just like commercial movies, desktop videos can now include menu selections, such as Play Movie, Scene Selection, and Special Features.

FIGURE 3-33: Video editing software

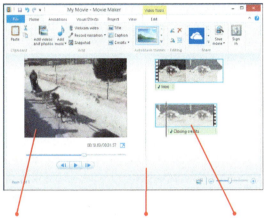

Preview your video to see how the clips, transitions, and soundtrack all work together

Add titles and transitions, import video clips, crop the footage, and arrange it in any order

Arrange the audio tracks to synchronize with each video clip

● **How can I use my computer to learn new skills?** You can use **educational software** to learn and practice new skills. For the youngest students, this software can be used to reinforce basic skills. Instruction is presented in game format, and the level of play is adapted to the player's age and ability. When educational software is also entertaining, it is called **edutainment software.** For older students and adults, software is available to teach new skills, such as a foreign language, or to improve existing skills, such as keyboarding skills. **Reference software** spans a wide range of applications from encyclopedias and medical references to map software, trip planners, cookbooks, and telephone books. To find information in a reference program, you can search using keywords or you can click hyperlinks to access related articles.

● **What software is used to track business projects?** **Project management software**, such as Microsoft Project, is an important tool for planning and managing large or small projects. The software helps you with scheduling the project, assigning project tasks, tracking and allocating resources, and keeping an eye on project costs. See **FIGURE 3-34**. Project management software is used to report progress and an overview of the project at any point to the main stakeholders and managers of a project.

FIGURE 3-34: Project management software

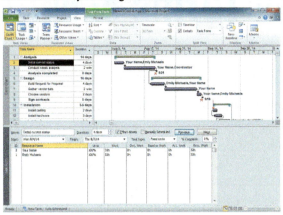

● **What software is used to manage business finances?** **Accounting software** and **finance software** is used to keep a record of monetary transactions and investments. See **FIGURE 3-35**. These programs do not require more than a basic understanding of accounting and finance principles. This software helps you invoice customers, track what they owe, and store customer data, such as contact information and purchasing history. Inventory functions track the products that you carry. Payroll capabilities calculate wages and deduct federal, state, and local taxes. **Tax preparation software** is a specialized type of **personal finance software** designed to help organize your annual income and expense data, identify deductions, and calculate your tax payment.

FIGURE 3-35: Finance software

Oleksiy Mark/Shutterstock.com

● **Is there software specifically designed to analyze data?** Yes. **Mathematical modeling software**, such as MathCAD and Mathematica, provides tools for solving a wide range of math, science, and engineering problems. Students, teachers, mathematicians, and engineers like how this software helps them see patterns that can be difficult to identify in columns of numbers.

You can use **statistical software** to analyze large sets of data in order to discover relationships and patterns. Statistical software is a helpful tool for summarizing survey results, test scores, experiment results, or population data. Most statistical software includes graphing capability so that data can be displayed and explored visually.

Key Terms & Module Review

Key Terms

3D graphics software
Accounting software
Android
App
Application software
Audio editing software
Boot process
BSD License
Buffer
CAD (computer-aided design) software
Clip art
Cloudware
Commercial software
Compression utility
Computer-aided music software
Computer program
Concurrent-use license
Copyright
Copyright notice
Digital content
Database
Database software
Demoware
Desktop publishing software

Development software
Device driver
DMG (Disk image)
Drawing software
DVD authoring software
Educational software
Edutainment software
EULA (end-user license agreement)
Finance software
Freeware
General Public License (GPL)
Graphical user interface (GUI)
Graphics
Graphics software
Image editing software
Installation agreement
Intellectual property
License agreement
Linux
Local application
Mac OS
Mathematical modeling software
Mobile application
Multiple-user license

Multitasking
Office productivity software
Open source software
Operating system (OS)
Paint software
Patch
Personal finance software
Photo editing software
Pirated software
Portable application
Portable Document File (PDF)
Presentation software
Processes
Productivity software
Project management software
Proprietary software
Public domain software
Reference software
Resource
Restore point
Security utility
Service pack
Setup program
Shareware

Shrink-wrap license
Single-user license
Site license
Software
Software license
Software pirate
Software suite
Software upgrade
Spreadsheet software
Statistical software
System requirements
System software
Tax preparation software
User interface
Utility software (utilities)
Validation code
Video editing software
Web app
Web application
Web authoring software
Windows
Word processing software
Worksheet

Module Review

1. Use your own words to define each of the bold terms that appear throughout the module. List ten terms that are the least familiar to you and write a sentence for each of them.

2. List at least five categories of application software and give an example of how you might use each type.

3. Explain the single-user, site license, multiple-user, and concurrent-user software licenses described in this module.

4. In your own words, explain shareware, freeware, demoware, and open source software.

5. Describe the main activities you must perform when you install software on your computer. Explain the differences between downloaded software and software you buy in a store.

6. List and summarize three features of the Windows operating system discussed in this module.

7. Name three resources managed by an operating system.

8. List three types of office productivity software that you might use, and describe how you might use each one.

9. List three types of software that you might use for creating and editing graphics, and describe how you might use each one.

10. Create a list of three utilities described in this module and give an example of why you would use each one on the list.

Concepts Review

Select the best answer.

1. You use _____ software when you create a document.
   a. system
   b. application
   c. utility
   d. security

2. You should use _____ software for writing a letter.
   a. spreadsheet
   b. word processing
   c. database
   d. utility

3. A _____ is a legal protection that grants the author of an original work an exclusive right to copy, distribute, sell, and modify that work.
   a. copyright
   b. GUI
   c. suite
   d. license

4. A(n) _____ is utility software that helps a peripheral device communicate with a computer.
   a. device driver
   b. Linux
   c. connector
   d. operating system

5. To run more than one program at a time, the _____ must allocate specific areas of memory for each program.
   a. RAM
   b. PDF
   c. OS
   d. ROM

6. When _____ software is used, no program files and no configuration data is stored on the hard drive.
   a. demoware
   b. portable
   c. web app
   d. freeware

7. _____ is distributed under the terms of a General Public License (GPL), which allows everyone to make copies for his or her own use, to give it to others, or to sell it.
   a. IOs
   b. Windows
   c. Mac OS
   d. Linux

8. The _____ is the combination of hardware and software that helps you communicate with a computer.
   a. operating system
   b. program
   c. user interface
   d. Task Manager

9. The first task of the operating system when you turn on a computer is to start the _____ process.
   a. boot
   b. Windows
   c. buffer
   d. power up

10. You can use _____ software to help organize information, such as library books and contacts.
    a. database
    b. spreadsheet
    c. document production
    d. finance and accounting

11. Which of the following describes a collection of graphic images that you can purchase or download for use in your document?
    a. Icon
    b. Clip art
    c. CAD file
    d. Logo

12. _____ software is a special type of 3D graphics software designed for architects and engineers who use computers to create blueprints and product specifications.
    a. DTP
    b. EULA
    c. CAD
    d. PDF

13. To create a wire-frame model, use a _____ program.
    a. web app
    b. 3D graphics
    c. finance
    d. utility

14. To read a Portable Document File (PDF), you need to use _____ software.
    a. Microsoft Excel
    b. Microsoft Word
    c. CAD
    d. Adobe Reader

15. To combat piracy, many software publishers require users to type in a(n) _____ code, a sequence of numbers and letters in order to complete an installation.
    a. validation
    b. PIN
    c. private
    d. pass

16. Snow Leopard, Cheetah, Puma, Jaguar, Panther, Tiger, and Leopard are all examples of _____.
    a. Windows programs
    b. Android OSs
    c. license agreements
    d. Apple OSs

17. _____ laws provide software authors with the exclusive right to copy, distribute, sell, and modify their work, except under special circumstances.
    a. Copyright
    b. Software
    c. Shareware
    d. Piracy

18. _____ software is not application software.
    a. Notation
    b. CAD
    c. Paint
    d. Device driver

19. A(n) _____ is a Mac software download that contains the main APP file for the software and other data files used by the application.
    a. Zip file
    b. DMG package
    c. EULA agreement
    d. Apple OS

20. _____ software is not copyrighted, making it available for use without restriction, except that you cannot apply for a copyright on it.
    a. Demoware
    b. Productivity
    c. Public Domain
    d. Commercial

Independent Challenges

Independent Challenge 1

Software is often dictated by the computer or device you are using and the installed operating system. Operating systems are updated every few years, giving you more options for newer features and new software.

Application software is also updated regularly. In addition, new programs come on the market frequently. In fact, the amount of software available in each category can be overwhelming, and no two packages offer all the same features. How can you make a decision about which software you need? Which software to buy? Do you follow recommendations received by word of mouth? Do you read reviewer comments in professional magazines? Do you simply try it out? Do you go to the web and read all the reviews and descriptions?

For this Independent Challenge:

Write a short summary answering each of the questions that follow.

1. Which operating system do you use?

2. What software is installed on your computer? How did you acquire the software? How would you categorize each program?

3. There is no universal standard for categorizing software, but various categorization schemes have many similarities. For example, Google Play uses a different set of categories from Apple's App Store and Amazon, and yet there are similarities. Look for similarities and differences in the software categories shown for these three online merchants. Write a brief summary of your findings.

4. Identify one software program you want to download to your computer, such as an office productivity, a graphics, a web development, an email, or a utility program. Locate vendor ads either on the Internet or in local papers or trade magazines that sell or discuss that program. Find two competitive products for the program you want to buy. Read comparison reviews of the products. Create a chart detailing the features and prepare a competitive analysis of the two products.

5. What kind of software license is required by each program? Do you have to pay for using it? Can you try it first, then pay after a trial period? Do you understand the licensing agreement? Write a short summary of your findings, indicating which program you would buy and why.

Independent Challenge 2

Copyrights and software piracy are relevant issues for software users, developers, businesspeople, and educators. There is constant debate among all stakeholders as to the best models for software distribution, as well as how developers, publishers, or programmers should be compensated.

For this Independent Challenge:

1. Use your favorite search engine to search for websites that discuss software piracy. Using information you have gathered through your research, select one of the following viewpoints and argue for or against it.

Discuss the topic of software piracy from the perspective of one of the following: a.) an advocate who believes in free software for all, b.) a person who believes that copyright laws, go too far in their efforts to protect the rights of software authors and publishers, c.) a person who believes all software is protected by copyright law and the consumer should purchase all software and abide by the EULA.

2. Select one of the perspectives listed above or state your own perspective, then write a two- to five-page paper about this issue, based on information you gather from the Internet.

3. Be sure to cite your sources and list them as part of the paper.

4. Follow your instructor's directions for formatting and submitting your paper.

Independent Challenge 3

Smartphones and tablet computers are becoming the digital devices of choice. As a result, more and more mobile apps are being developed to meet the growing consumer demand. See FIGURE 3-36. Currently, there are apps that exist for fun and games. There are apps to help people navigate through their day, or around the world. And, there are apps that are just for fun or silly. Whether or not you own a smartphone or a tablet now, you probably know at least one person who does. Learning about smartphones and tablets, as well as the mobile apps becoming so popular today, provides insight into the world of mobile computing.

For this Independent Challenge:

1. Log onto the Internet and search for information on the following mobile operating systems: Windows Mobile, Android, and iOS.

Complete the chart shown in TABLE 3-3 to learn more about each of the operating systems.

2. Go to a website that features Android apps. Explore the offerings and the different categories, then answer the following questions:
  a. What is the most interesting free app that you can find to download? Why would you want this app? What made you select this app?
  b. What is the most interesting app that you have to pay for? Why would you want this app? Why do you think it is worth paying for this app rather than getting a different free app?

FIGURE 3-36: Smartphone apps

iQoncept/Shutterstock.com

3. Go to a website that features apps for Apple tablets or smartphones. Explore the offerings, then answer the following questions:
  a. What is the most interesting free app that you can find to download? Why would you want this app?
  b. What is the most interesting app that you have to pay for? Why would you want this app? Why do you think it is worth paying for this app rather than getting a different free app?

TABLE 3-3: Comparison chart

	Windows Mobile	Android	iOS
Current version			
Latest features mentioned most in the marketing			
Three digital devices that can be purchased with this OS preinstalled			
Two game apps			
Two productivity apps			
One surprising fact			

Visual Workshop

Mobile devices, such as tablet computers and smartphones now have the ability, through software and the different networks, to allow you to video chat or conference with other people directly from your device. Popular video chatting services include Tango, Fring, FaceTime, Google Hangouts, and Skype. See **FIGURE 3-37**. Video chats can be used for business or fun, in a casual atmosphere or an office environment. You will compare and contrast each option on its basic features.

FIGURE 3-37: Video chatting

Andrey_Popov/Shutterstock.com

Log onto the Internet. Find websites that discuss each of the video chatting services listed above.

1. In your research, find three facts about each of the competing services.

2. What are the purchasing options, fees, and licensing options for each?

3. What operating systems are required for each? Are there limitations?

4. Which devices are supported by each of these video chatting services?

5. Are any interesting features built into these video chatting services?

MODULE 4
Concepts

File Management and Digital Electronics

Learning Outcomes

1. Explain how file management programs help you manage your computer files

2. Explain how to create and use folders to store files

3. Identify the key elements of a computer file

4. Describe the file management steps for working with files

5. Describe how digital data representation produces numbers, text, images, video, and sound

6. Define integrated circuits and explain the role they play inside a computer

7. Explain how CPU factors affect computer performance

8. Define RAM and explain its importance to computers

9. Explain how a computer uses virtual memory and ROM

LESSON TOPICS

- File Management Tools
- Computer Folder Basics
- Computer File Basics
- How to Manage Computer Files
- How Computers Represent Data
- Integrated Circuits—An Overview
- Processors—An Overview
- Computer Memory: RAM
- Other Types of Computer Memory

File Management Tools

A typical personal computer stores thousands of computer files, usually in folders. You use file management tools to manage your files and folders. To organize your computer files and folders, you need to practice good **file management**. Good file management practices include how you create, open, save, delete, and rename files.

Learning Outcome 1:
Explain how file management programs help you manage your computer files

● **What is a computer file?** A computer file, or simply file, is defined as a named collection of data that exists on a storage medium. The storage medium can be a hard drive, solid-state storage device, CD, DVD, BD, or tape. The content of the file is determined by the software program used to create the file and the data you enter. For example, you can use a word processing program to create a document file for your résumé.

● **What is a folder?** A **folder** is a logical representation of where you store your files on a computer. Folders help you organize your computer files.

● **How do folders help me organize my files?** By storing files in folders, you assign each file a place in a hierarchy of folders. Think of a data storage system as a filing cabinet. See **FIGURE 4-1**. Each storage device is a drawer in a filing cabinet. Just like the drawers in a filing cabinet, a storage device is made up of folders and the folders hold files. Folders within folders are called subfolders.

FIGURE 4-1: Files are stored in folders

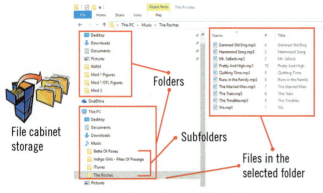

File cabinet storage · Folders · Subfolders · Files in the selected folder

Computer file storage

The file cabinet is a useful way to visualize how files and folders are organized on a storage device. The drive, folder names, and filename all work together to identify the file path.

● **What is a file path?** The location of a file on a storage device is defined by its **file path** (also called **file specification**). The

file path begins with the drive letter and is followed by the folder(s), filename, and file extension. A folder name is separated from a drive letter and other folder names by a special symbol. In Windows, this symbol is often represented on screen as an arrow head and written as the backslash (\ ). For example, the path to the folder Sarah uses to store Elvis music would be C:\Users\Sarah\My Music\Elvis\Hound Dog. mp3. This path tells you that Sarah stored an MP3 file called Hound Dog in the Elvis folder in the My Music folder on her hard drive. Its file path is shown in **FIGURE 4-2**.

FIGURE 4-2: A file path

C:\Users\Sarah\	My Music\	Elvis\	Hound Dog	.mp3
Primary folder	Subfolder	Subfolder	Subfolder	Filename	File extension

● **Who decides where my files are stored?** You decide where your files are stored. But to help you, Windows supplies a series of default locations. These locations include default folders such as Documents, Downloads, Music, Pictures, and Videos. See **FIGURE 4-3**.

FIGURE 4-3: Windows default folders

● **What are Quick Access and OneDrive?** When you open **File Explorer**, you'll see folders and devices listed in the **Navigation pane** on the left side of the window. At the top, a special listing called **Quick Access** is selected, and below it is a list of frequently used folders. The right pane has links to folders that you use most frequently and files that you've used recently. You can add or **pin** folders that you create to Quick Access. The Navigation pane also contains a link to **OneDrive**, a cloud storage area that you can use if you have a Microsoft account. You can access OneDrive directly using File Explorer to save and access your files.

- **Where are my files stored?** Your files are stored at the location you specify. For example, when you save a data file, you specify the location where you want to save the file. The default location for a file such as a letter or spreadsheet is the Documents folder. You can save your file to a default folder, or you can create a new folder and save your file to the new folder. Right-click a folder to see all the options, including the command to create a new folder. See **FIGURE 4-4**. However, avoid storing files in the root directory of your hard drive. Files should be stored in subfolders in the root directory.

FIGURE 4-4: Right-click a folder for shortcut menu options

When you install a program, the installation process usually creates a new folder within the default Programs folder. Although you can change the suggested location when you install a software program, it is recommended that you don't.

- **What is the root directory?** The **root directory** is the main directory of the hard drive or other storage medium. So for a hard drive named C:, the root directory is also C:. A device letter is usually followed by a colon. The main hard drive is usually referred to as as Local Disk (C:).

- **Do I name the root directory?** No, the root directory is the name of your storage device and it is assigned by your operating system. For example, the Windows operating system labels storage devices with letters, such as A: and C:. See **FIGURE 4-5**. Additional storage devices can be assigned letters from D through Z.

The device letters for additional storage devices are not standardized. As a result, the file path for a file can change. For example, if you store a data file on a flash drive, the file path for the file will include the drive letter for the flash drive. The drive letter is based on which computer the flash drive is connected to. If you remove the flash drive and insert it in a new computer, the flash drive is assigned a new drive letter based on that computer. So, the file specification for a file might be F:\Cards\Birthday1.docx on a flash drive connected to one computer, but the file path for that same file might be H:\Cards\Birthday1.docx on the same flash drive connected to a different computer.

- **What should I use to manage the files on my computer?** Most operating systems provide a **file management program**. These programs contain the tools you need to organize your files. For computers running Windows, the file management program is File Explorer. Using File Explorer, you can see the storage devices and a list of files and folders on those storage devices or on your network. You can find files, move files, make copies of files, delete files, view file properties, and rename files.

In addition, a file management program makes it easy to find the file or folder you are looking for by using the program's search capabilities.

FIGURE 4-5: Storage devices shown in File Explorer

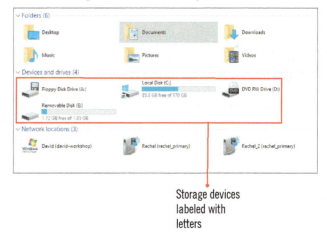

Storage devices labeled with letters

Computer Folder Basics

A folder is a logical representation of where you store your files on a computer. For example, you can use a folder called My Documents to hold reports, budgets, letters, and so on. If you understand how to use and manage folders, you will be able to organize the files on your computer successfully.

Learning Outcome 2:
Explain how to create and use folders to store files

● **Why should I use folders to organize my files?** You can store thousands of files on one storage device. Without folders, it would be difficult to find the file you want. You create folders to hold folders and files. Folders within folders are **nested folders**, also called **subfolders**. You give folders descriptive names to help you remember what is in the folders.

● **How do I know which folder to use?** Windows supplies default folders. When you save a file, you can use a default folder, you can create a new folder at the same level as the default folder, or you can create subfolders in any folder. You create folders and subfolders to meet your needs. For example, you might create a subfolder named TownProject in the default Documents folder to hold documents related to a project in town. Within that folder you might create another subfolder named Budgets for all the spreadsheets containing budget data.

● **How do I create new folders?** To create a new folder, you can use File Explorer. With File Explorer open, you can navigate to the location on the storage device where you want to create the folder. Once you have selected the drive and folder location for the new folder, you click the New Folder button on the Ribbon or Quick Access toolbar to create a new folder. Then, when it is created, a text box appears to the right of the folder. You type the folder name in the text box. See **FIGURE 4-6**. Be sure to give the folder a meaningful name that will help you remember what files are stored in that folder. File and folder naming rules restrict you from using special characters such as a colon or a slash in folder names.

● **Can I copy or move a folder?** In addition to finding folders, File Explorer provides a set of file management tools that help you organize your folders. To work with a folder, you must select it. Once a folder is selected, you can copy, move, rename, or delete it as needed. See **FIGURE 4-7**.

FIGURE 4-6: Creating a new folder

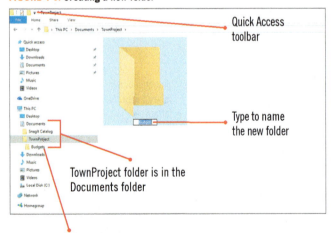

Quick Access toolbar

Type to name the new folder

TownProject folder is in the Documents folder

Budgets folder is in TownProject folder

FIGURE 4-7: Moving a folder

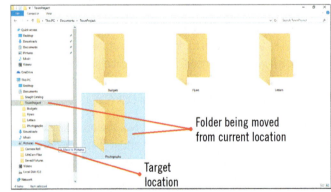

Folder being moved from current location

Target location

● **Can I copy or move more than one folder at a time?** Yes, to copy or move more than one folder, you can select more than one folder and then perform the action. To select more than one folder, you press and hold the [Ctrl] while you click each folder you want to copy or move. Once selected, you can work with the selected folders just as you would work with a single folder. If the folders are right next to each other in the list, you can click the first folder, hold [Shift] and then click the last folder in the list to select the first folder, the last folder, and all the folders between the two selected folders.

● **What are folder properties?** Folder properties include the size of the folder, the date it was created, the number of files and folders contained in the folder, and the location or path to the folder. Folder properties also carry security and sharing information to determine who can access the folder and whether or not they can make changes to the folder.

● **Is there a way to see or change folder properties?** File Explorer lets you work with a folder's properties. With File Explorer open, you can right-click any folder, and then click Properties to open the Properties dialog box for the selected folder. See **FIGURE 4-8**. For example, the General tab in the Properties dialog box provides general information about the files and folders that are stored in that folder.

Each tab in the Properties dialog box includes additional information about the selected folder. You will see different tabs depending on the location and properties of the selected folder.

● **What are folder options?** When you work with folders you have options for how you can open and view the folders. These options are features of the operating system that can be customized to meet your needs. For example, you can see different icons depending on the contents of a folder. You can also decide if you have to double or single click to open a folder.

● **How do I change folder options?** Sometimes you might want to change the way you view and search for files and folders in File Explorer. For example, you might want to display file icons representing file types in a folder as folder thumbnails. You may also choose to include hidden files and folders in a search of the folder. To view or change a folder's options, open the File Explorer Options dialog box. To open the File Explorer Options dialog box, you open the Control Panel, click Appearance and Personalization, and then click the File Explorer Options link. In the File Explorer Options dialog box, you select one of the three tabs, General, View, and Search. Refer to **FIGURE 4-9**.

FIGURE 4-8: Properties dialog box for Documents folder

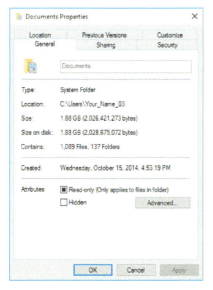

FIGURE 4-9: File Explorer Options dialog box

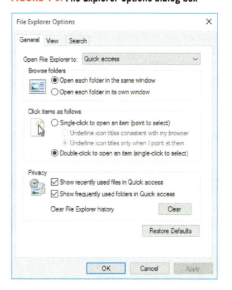

Folders and subfolders vs. directories and subdirectories

Directories and subdirectories mean the same thing as folders and subfolders when talking about file management. The operating system on your computer maintains a list of files called a **directory**. There is a directory for each storage device. The main directory of a drive is the root directory. A root directory is often subdivided into smaller **subdirectories**. When you use Windows, Mac OS, or a Linux graphical file manager, these subdirectories are depicted using icons that look like folders because subdirectories work like the folders in a filing cabinet to store related files.

Computer File Basics

There are several important elements that define a computer file. These include the contents of the file, the software that was used to create it, and the way the computer uses it. There are several categories of files, such as data files, executable files, configuration files, and drivers. Most of the files you create on your computer are data files. Although files can contain different data, they have several key elements, including filename, format, location, size, and date.

Learning Outcome 3:
Identify the key elements of a computer file

● **What is a filename?** A **filename** is a set of letters, symbols, or numbers that identifies a file. A filename consists of a name followed by a period, followed by a file extension. Every saved file has a filename.

● **Are there rules I need to know for naming files?** Yes, the filename must follow specific rules, called **filenaming conventions**. Each operating system has a unique set of filenaming conventions. When you use the Windows operating system, you cannot use the symbols : * \ < > | " / and ? as part of a filename. If you try to save the file using one of the restricted symbols, you will receive a message telling you there is a problem with the filename. When you name a file, you should give it a meaningful name that can help you remember the contents of the file.

● **What are file extensions?** A **file extension** (or **filename extension**) is a set of letters and/or numbers added to the end of filename following a period that helps to identify the file contents or file type. A file extension helps describe the file contents. For example, the music files you listen to on your portable media player probably have the .mp3 file extension. A file extension is separated from the main filename by a period, as in BornToRun.mp3. In this example, the file extension .mp3 indicates that this is a music file.

You will also recognize that some file extensions are associated with a particular application program. See **TABLE 4-1** for a list of some common file extensions. Knowing the file extension can help you identify which application program was used to create the data file. Once you know the file format, you will know which application to use if you want to open the file. A software program can typically open a file that exists in its **native file format**, set when the file was created, plus several additional **file formats**.

TABLE 4-1: Common file extensions

File extensions	Application
xls, xlsx	Microsoft Excel
doc, docx	Microsoft Word
txt, rtf	Text editor (WordPad, Notepad)
ppt, pptx	Microsoft PowerPoint
mdb, accdb	Microsoft Access
gif, tif, jpg, bmp, raw, png	Graphic or photo viewer or editor
wav, mid, mp3	Music and sound player or editor
zip	Compressed file
pdf	Adobe Acrobat or Reader

As you work with files, you will begin to recognize that some file extensions, such as .txt (text file) or .jpg (graphics file), indicate a file type (such as a document or a photograph). They are not specific to any one program. Understanding file extensions can help you if you receive a file but they don't tell you much about the file's contents.

● **Do I decide the file extensions?** Generally, no. As a user, you do not decide the extension. The software program assigns an extension to the file automatically when you save it. Some programs give you several options. For example, when you save a graphic you can decide if you want a jpg, tif, or some other graphic format.

● **Can I change the file extension?** Technically, yes, but you really shouldn't change file extensions because a file extension is usually related to the file format. Sometimes, a file extension is changed in error when you try to rename a file. Be careful to change only the name to the left of the period when you change a filename. If you change a file extension while renaming a file, the file will not be able to be opened.

- **Why can't I see the file extensions when I look at my files using File Explorer?** File extensions should be shown by default. You can always change the settings to show them. It is a good idea to show file extensions because they help you identify the file type. To view file extensions, be sure the Hide extensions for known file types check box in the File Explorer Options dialog box on the View tab does not have a check mark.

- **When do I name a file?** You name a file the first time you save it. You can rename a file any time after it has been saved. One way you can rename a file is to use the Save As command.

- **How do I know when to use Save and when to use Save As?** The flowchart in FIGURE 4-10 can help you decide whether to use the Save or the Save As command. When you try to use the Save command for a file that has not been saved, the program will open the Save As dialog box, even though you selected the Save command.

FIGURE 4-10: Save or Save As?

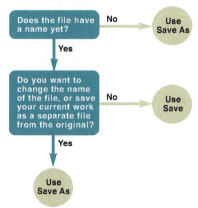

- **Why can't I open some files?** If you can't open a file because the file extension is not recognized, you might see a warning message like the one shown in FIGURE 4-11 and Windows will try to identify and open it using the application you select as the best one to use.

FIGURE 4-11: Unrecognized file type

You might not be able to open a file for one of the following reasons:

- You do not have the software application needed to open the file.
- The file might have been damaged—or corrupted—by a transmission or disk error.
- The file extension might have been changed, perhaps while renaming the file, and so the file is no longer associated with its application program. In this situation, if you think you know the correct file extension, you can change the file extension again and try to open the file.
- The file might use a file format for a newer version of the software than you have.

Several websites provide lists of file extensions and their corresponding software. By looking up a file extension in one of these lists, you can find out what application software you'll need to open a file based on its file extension.

- **What other information is stored with each of my files?** The File Properties dialog box is a good way to find out information about a file. See FIGURE 4-12. General information such as file size and file date can be helpful as you manage your files. **File size** is usually measured in bytes, kilobytes, or megabytes. Knowing the size of a file can be important, especially when you are sending a file as an email attachment. Your computer's operating system keeps track of file sizes. Your computer also keeps track of the date on which a file was created or last modified. The **file date** is useful if you have saved a file using slightly different filenames each time and you want to know which is the most recent.

FIGURE 4-12: Properties dialog box for a file

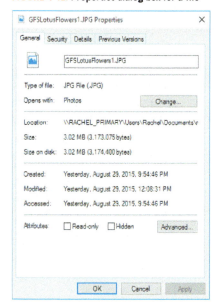

How to Manage Computer Files

To manage files, you use the same file management tools you used to copy, move, rename, or delete a folder. As you work with programs, you will need to open and save files. You can open files while working with an application program or by using a file management program. You can also save files from within an application program such as a word processor.

Learning Outcome 4:
Describe the file management steps for working with files

● **Do I have to remember all the information about where my files are stored?** No, you don't have to remember the details, but it is helpful to create a system for naming files and folders that is easy for you to use. Although file management programs, like File Explorer, help you locate your files, knowing the basics (the drive, the folder name(s), and the filename) will help you find your files faster.

Most application software provides access to file management tasks through the Save, Save As, and Open dialog boxes. **TABLE 4-2** lists additional file management tasks you will do when working with files and folders.

TABLE 4-2: Additional file management tasks

File or folder command	Description and examples
Rename	Change the name of a file or folder to describe its contents better. When renaming a file, be careful to keep the same file extension so that you can open it with the correct software.
Copy	Create a copy of a file or folder; the file or folder remains in the original location and a duplicate is added to a different location. For example, copy a document file to a new folder so that you can revise the content in the copy and leave the original content intact.
Move	Move a file or folder from one folder to another, or from one storage device to another. For example, move a file to a new folder to organize your hard drive. When you move a file or folder, it is erased from its original location.
Delete	Remove the file from the folder and place it in the Recycle Bin. For example, delete a file or folder with files when you no longer need it. Note: most file management programs delete all the files (and subfolders) in a folder when you delete a folder.

● **What is a file tag?** Some applications also allow you to add tags to a file. A **file tag** is a short word or phrase that describes a file. It is useful when you search for a file. Tags appear in the Details pane in File Explorer. Add tags using the Details tab of the Properties dialog box. See **FIGURE 4-13**. For example, tags help you describe the location, camera settings, and subject pictured in a photograph.

FIGURE 4-13: Tags appear in the Details pane

● **Is it possible to convert a file from one format to another?** Yes. The easiest way to convert a file from one format to another is to find a program that works with both file formats. Graphics programs can often handle most of the major file formats for graphics. For example, you can use a program such as Paint to convert a file from the .tif file format to the .bmp file format: Open the file using Paint, click the File tab, then click the Save As command to see other formats. If you need a format not listed, click Other formats to open the Save As dialog box. Then select a new file format, assign the file a new name if you want, and save it. See **FIGURE 4-14**.

FIGURE 4-14: Converting a file to another file format

- Do not mix data files and program files, that is, do not store data files in the folders that hold your software. On computers running Windows, most software programs are stored in subfolders of the Program Files folder.
- Do not store programs or data files in the root directory (C:\) of your computer's hard drive. It is better to create folders and store your files in those folders.
- Be aware of storage locations. When you save files, make sure the drive letter and folder name specify the correct storage location.
- Organize your folders from the top down. When creating a hierarchy of folders, consider how you want to access and back up files. A **backup** is a copy of your files made for safekeeping. You should back up your folders regularly. For example, if your files are stored in one folder, such as the Documents folder, then it is easy to backup that folder and all nested subfolders. If your important data is scattered in a variety of folders, however, making backups is more time consuming.
- Access files from the hard drive. For best performance, copy files from portable storage media to your computer's hard drive before accessing them.
- Follow copyright rules. When copying files, make sure you do not violate copyright and license restrictions.
- Delete or archive files you no longer need. Deleting unneeded files and folders helps keep your list of files from growing to an unmanageable size. One way to delete a file is to right-click the file name in File Explorer, and then click Delete on the shortcut menu. File archiving utility programs combine a number of files together into one archive file, or a series of archive files, for long-term storage.

● **Are there rules and guidelines I should follow when managing files?** Yes. The following tips will help you manage your files:

- Use descriptive names. Give your files and folders descriptive names when you save or create them, and avoid using cryptic abbreviations.
- Maintain file extensions. When renaming a file, keep the original file extension so that you can open it with the correct application software.
- Group similar files and consider using the default folders in Windows, such as Documents, Pictures, Music, and so on. Separate files into folders based on subject matter. For example, store your creative writing assignments in one appropriately named folder and your music files in another appropriately named folder.

Deleting folders and files

The Windows Recycle Bin and similar utilities in other operating systems protect you from accidentally deleting folders and files from your hard drive. When you give the command to delete a folder or file, the operating system moves the folder or file to the Recycle Bin folder. See **FIGURE 4-15**. The deleted folder or file still takes up space on the hard drive, but it does not appear in the usual directory listing. The folder file does, however, appear in the directory listing for the Recycle Bin folder. You can undelete any folders or files in this listing. It is important to remember that only folders or files you delete from your hard drive are sent to the Recycle

Bin. Folders or files you delete from a removable storage medium, such as a USB device, CD, or DVD, are not sent to the Recycle Bin and are permanently deleted.

FIGURE 4-15: Recycle Bin

No items | At least one item

How Computers Represent Data

Data representation refers to the way in which data is created, stored, processed, output, and transmitted. It is the technology that makes it possible for you to use digital electronic devices such as iPods, GPS devices, mobile phones, and computers. Data representation makes it possible to input, store, process, and display text, numbers, graphics, photos, or play music and videos. Digital data is represented using the binary number system.

> ### Learning Outcome 5:
> Describe how digital data representation produces numbers, text, images, video, and sound

- **What is the binary number system?** The **binary number system** makes it possible for computers to represent data simply by using 0s and 1s. The 0s and 1s are translated into electrical on and off signals that the computer can understand. **TABLE 4-3** compares the decimal number system with the binary number system. Notice that the decimal system, base 10, uses ten symbols (0, 1, 2, 3, 4, 5, 6, 7, 8, and 9) to represent numbers. The binary number system has only two digits: 0 and 1.

TABLE 4-3: Comparing the decimal and binary number systems

Decimal	Binary	Decimal	Binary
0	0	7	111
1	1	8	1000
2	10	9	1001
3	11	10	1010
4	100	11	1011
5	101	1000	1111101000
6	110	1001	1111101001

- **What is digital data?** **Digital data** is text, numbers, graphics, sound, and video that has been converted into the digits 0 and 1. All digital data is created from 0s and 1s. The 0s and 1s are electronic signals that represent on and off, or yes and no, respectively. The computer interprets these electronic signals as data.

- **How does the computer interpret these electronic signals?** The electronic signals are coded as a series of 0s and 1s. Each 0 or 1 is one **binary digit**, or **bit**. A series of eight bits is referred to as a **byte**. Each byte represents one piece of data, such as the letter g, the number 5, or one dot

in a picture. Bytes are coded using different coding schemes. Most computer coding schemes use eight bits to represent each number, letter, or symbol. Digital computers use many different coding schemes to represent data. The coding scheme used by a computer depends on whether the data is numeric or character data. **Numeric data** includes numbers that might be used in arithmetic operations such as your annual income, your age, or the cost of dinner.

- **How can my computer process character data?** **Character data** is composed of letters, symbols, and numerals that will not be used in arithmetic operations. Examples of character data include your name, address, and telephone number. Character data is represented by coding schemes, which use a series of 1s and 0s. For example, when you type the word dog, you press the key that represents each letter. As you press each key, an electronic signal is sent to the processor. The signal is the code for the letter you typed. See **FIGURE 4-16**.

FIGURE 4-16: Coding data

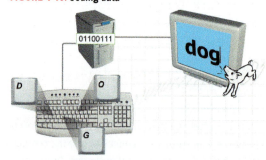

The most common coding schemes for coding character data are ASCII, EBCDIC, and Unicode. Unicode is the most flexible, and currently provides code for characters from all written languages, including languages such as Chinese, Russian, and Hebrew. Modern personal computers use the Extended ASCII (American Standard Code for Information Interchange) coding scheme.

- **How can my computer process numbers to be used in calculations?** Computers use the binary number system to represent numeric data. So, when you type the number you want to use in a calculation, such as 3, the number is converted to its binary representation, 11. The computer recognizes this digital data as the number 3.

- **How can my computer process images, such as the photos from my camera?** Images, such as photos, pictures, line art, and graphs, are not discrete objects like a number or letter of the alphabet. A computer must **digitize** the information that makes up the picture (such as the colors) into 1s and 0s. Digitized images are a series of colored dots, also called **pixels** (picture elements). See **FIGURE 4-17**. Each pixel is assigned a binary number based on the color of that pixel. A digital image is simply a list of binary numbers for all the dots it contains. Each binary number in the list is associated with one pixel. The computer interprets the list of numbers to recreate the image.

FIGURE 4-17: Pixels in an image

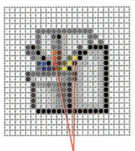

Each pixel is assigned a binary number based on its color.

- **How are digital sound files created?** Sounds are continuous analog sound waves. In order for a computer to understand a sound, it must digitize the information that makes up the sound. Sound, such as music and speech, is characterized by the properties of a sound wave. An analog sound wave is digitized by sampling it at various points, and then converting those points into digital numbers. The more samples your computer takes, the closer the points come to approximating the full wave pattern. This process of sampling, as shown in **FIGURE 4-18**, is how digital recordings, such as the music files on your portable media player, are made.

FIGURE 4-18: Digitizing sound

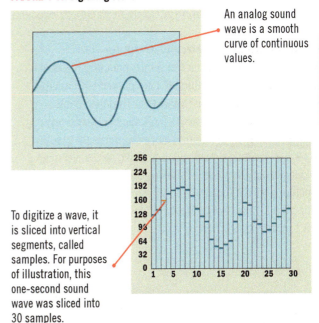

An analog sound wave is a smooth curve of continuous values.

To digitize a wave, it is sliced into vertical segments, called samples. For purposes of illustration, this one-second sound wave was sliced into 30 samples.

More about bits and bytes

As discussed, a bit is one binary digit, and a byte is eight bits. The word bit can be abbreviated as a lowercase b, and the word byte can be abbreviated as an uppercase B. The terms used to quantify computer data are summarized in **TABLE 4-4**. The prefixes **kilo-** (thousands), **mega-** (millions), **giga-** (billions), **tera-** (trillion), **peta-** (thousand trillion), **exa-** (quintillion), and **zetta-** (sextillion) are used for large amounts of data.

Bits and bytes are used in different ways. Data transmission speeds are usually expressed in bits, whereas storage space is usually expressed in bytes. Typically, kilobytes (KB) are used to refer to most common documents, megabytes (MB) are used to refer to RAM, and gigabytes (GB) are used to refer to hard drive, optical storage media, and solid-state drive capacities. In a smartphone ad, you might notice that it can store up to 64 GB. The Internet data transfer speed for your computer might be listed as 50/50 Mbps to 500/500 Mbps or megabits per second.

TABLE 4-4: Terms used to describe digital data

Term	Value	Term	Value
Bit	1 binary digit	**Byte**	8 bits
Kilobit (Kb)	1,000 bits (exactly 1,024)	**Kilobyte (KB)**	1,000 bytes (exactly 1,024)
Megabit (Mb)	1 million bits	**Megabyte (MB)**	1 million bytes
Gigabit (Gb)	1 billion bits	**Gigabyte (GB)**	1 billion bytes
Terabyte (TB)	1 trillion bytes	**Petabyte (PB)**	1,000 terabytes (2^{50} bytes)
Exabyte (EB)	1,000 petabytes (2^{60} bytes)	**Zettabyte (ZB)**	1,000 exabytes (2^{70} bytes)

(Note: All values are approximate unless noted otherwise.)

Integrated Circuits—
An Overview

Computers and digital devices are electronic devices that use electrical signals to process data. The electronic parts of a personal computer store, process, and transfer the data. In the beginning, the electronic parts were large and bulky. Over time, the electronic parts have become smaller and more efficient. The most significant technology that made the miniaturization of electronics parts possible is the integrated circuit.

Learning Outcome 6:
Define integrated circuits and explain the role they play inside a computer

● **What is an integrated circuit?** An **integrated circuit (IC)** is a very thin slice of semiconducting material, such as silicon and germanium. ICs are packed with microscopic circuit elements. See **FIGURE 4-19**. These elements include wires, transistors, capacitors, logic gates, and resistors, and are used to create miniature electronic parts and pathways. Electronic signals, the bits and bytes, travel over these electronic pathways. The terms **computer chip**, microchip, and **chip** are all synonymous with the term integrated circuit. Chips are manufactured in sterile environments to protect their parts.

FIGURE 4-19: How an integrated circuit is made

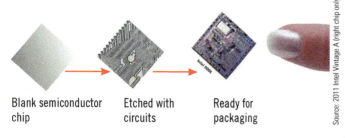

Source: 2011 Intel Vintage A (right chip only)

Blank semiconductor chip   Etched with circuits   Ready for packaging

● **Are there chips in all electronic devices?** Yes, chips are not only in a computer's system unit but also in other electronic devices, such as tablets, cameras, smartphones, and GPS devices. Chips are also embedded in household devices such as refrigerators, microwaves, and cars. In fact, electronic devices use integrated circuits for processors, memory, and support circuitry.

● **What protects chips from possibly being damaged?** Each chip is packaged in a protective carrier or chip package. Chip packages vary in shape and size, including the **DIP (dual inline package)** chip package, the **LGA (land-grid array)** chip package, and the **DIMM (dual inline memory module)** chip package. See **FIGURE 4-20**.

FIGURE 4-20: Packaging for integrated circuits

DIPs have two rows of pins that connect the chip to a circuit board.

An LGA is a square chip package, typically used for microprocessors, with pins arranged in concentric squares.

● **How are all these chip packages connected to the computer?** Chip packages are connected to the computer's motherboard. The **motherboard** is the computer's main circuit board. See **FIGURE 4-21**. The DIP and PGA chip packages are plugged into sockets and connectors on the motherboard. DIMM chip packages and small circuit boards are plugged into slots on the motherboard. Some chips are soldered permanently in place. The motherboard contains the electronic circuitry that connects all these parts. Expansion cards attach to the motherboard through expansion slots.

Because some chips can be inserted and removed easily, they can be replaced if they become damaged or need to be upgraded. Sometimes, multiple chips are required for a single function, such as generating stereo-quality sound. In this case, the chips might be housed on a separate small circuit board, such as an expansion card.

FIGURE 4-21: **Chips on a motherboard**

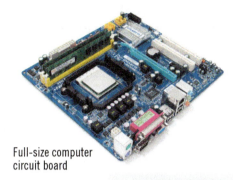

Full-size computer circuit board

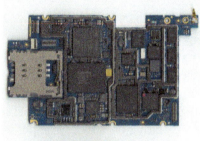

iPhone circuit board (enlarged)

Source: iFixit (right fig only)

● **What is a processor?** A **processor** (also called a **microprocessor**) is one type of chip or integrated circuit. The main processor in a personal computer is the **CPU (central processing unit).** It is designed to process instructions. A processor is a very complex integrated circuit, containing hundreds of millions of miniaturized electronic parts. See FIGURE 4-22. It is the most important and usually the most expensive single part of a computer. Looking inside a computer, you can usually identify the processor because it is the largest chip on the motherboard. Most of today's processors are housed in a PGA chip package. All digital devices have processors. As you might

FIGURE 4-22: **Every digital device has a processor**

thanmano/Shutterstock.com

suspect, processors for mobile devices such as smartphones, cameras, and tablet computers are smaller than processors for desktop computers.

● **Which companies produce most of today's popular PC processors?** Intel is the world's largest chip-maker and supplies a sizeable percentage of the processors that power PCs. AMD (Advanced Micro Devices) is Intel's chief rival in the PC chip market. Whereas processors based on x86 Intel technology are inside just about all desktop and laptop computers, processors based on ARM technology dominate tablets and smartphones. ARM technology was originally designed by a British company and are now designed and manufactured by many companies. ARM-based processors are energy efficient—necessary for devices that run primarily on battery power.

● **How can I tell what CPU my computer uses?** A typical personal computer ad contains a long list of specifications describing a computer's parts and technical details, often beginning with the processor brand, type, and speed. You can use software to identify your computer's CPU and its specifications. If you are running Windows, you can access this information through the Windows Control Panel. See FIGURE 4-23. If you have a Mac, click About This Mac from the Apple menu in the upper-left menu bar, and then click More Info to view the name of the processor.

FIGURE 4-23: **Installed processor specs**

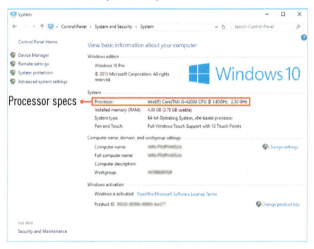

Processor specs

● **Can I replace my computer's processor with a faster or better one?** Yes, it is possible to upgrade your computer's processor, but computer owners rarely do. A processor can cost almost half as much as an entirely new computer system. Technical factors also discourage processor upgrades. A processor operates at full efficiency only if all parts in the computer can handle the faster speeds.

Processors—An Overview

The central processing unit (CPU) contains all the circuitry that performs the central processing tasks of the computer on a single chip. Different personal computers come with different processors. Processors have certain factors in common. Knowing how each of the processor's factors affects the performance of a computer can help you make an informed decision when buying a computer.

Learning Outcome 7:
Explain how CPU factors affect computer performance

● **What factors affect processor performance?** A processor's performance is affected by several factors, including number of cores, clock speed, bus speed, word size, and cache memory size. These factors combine to affect the processing speed, which determines the computer's performance. A processor's factors are described as part of a processor's specs (specifications). A processor's specs are available on the manufacturer's website.

● **What do processor specs tell me about the processor?** A processor that contains circuitry for more than one processing unit on a single chip is called a **multi-core processor**. Multi-core processors are faster than processors with a single core. To gain maximum speed, however, your computer's operating system and software should be optimized for multi-core processing. Most operating systems support multi-core processing. The 2.4 GHz Intel i5 processor has two cores, giving it the equivalent of 4.8 GHz performance (2.4 x 2). The 1.6 GHz Intel i7 processor has four cores, giving it the equivalent of 6.4 GHz performance (1.6 x 4). The thin wafer of silicon and the microscopic circuitry it contains is called a die. See **FIGURE 4-24**.

FIGURE 4-24: Microscopic view of a processor with multiple cores

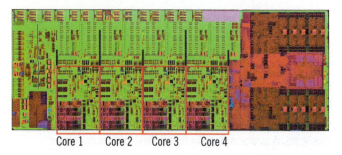

Core 1   Core 2   Core 3   Core 4

Computer ads typically include specs that determine a processor's performance. **FIGURE 4-25** shows the specs for an Intel Core i7 quad-core processor in part of a sample computer ad.

FIGURE 4-25: Processor specs in an ad

Intel Core i7 2860QM processor 2.50 GHz 1600 MHz FSB 8 MB L2 cache

● **What is clock speed?** The **processor clock** is a timing device that sets the pace (the clock speed) for executing instructions. The **clock speed** is specified in megahertz (MHz), which is millions of cycles per second, or gigahertz (GHz), which is billions of cycles per second. A **cycle** is the smallest unit of time a processor can recognize. The faster the clock, the more instructions the processor can execute per second. For the processor in the sample ad shown in **FIGURE 4-26**, the clock speed is 2.50 GHz. This means the processor's clock operates at 2.5 billion cycles per second.

FIGURE 4-26: Clock speed specs in an ad

Intel Core i7 2860QM processor 2.50 GHz 1600 MHz FSB 8 MB L2 cache

● **What is bus speed?** A **bus** is an electronic pathway that carries the electronic signals between the electronic parts of a computer. Bus speed identifies how fast the electronic signals move along the bus pathway. **FSB** stands for **front side bus**. The **data bus** refers to the main circuits that carry data at lightning speeds as pulses of electrical voltages. The part of the data bus that runs between the processor and RAM is called the local bus or internal bus. This is the fastest part of the data bus because it has to keep up with the data demands of the processor. See **FIGURE 4-27**.

FIGURE 4-27: Local bus

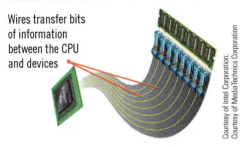

Wires transfer bits of information between the CPU and devices

Courtesy of Intel Corporation;
Courtesy of MediaTechnics Corporation

Bus speed is measured in megahertz (MHz). In the sample ad in **FIGURE 4-28**, the speed is 1600 MHz. When comparing processors, larger numbers indicate faster speeds.

FIGURE 4-28: Bus specs in an ad

Intel Core i7 2860QM processor 2.50 GHz 1600 MHz FSB 8 MB L2 cache

● **What is word size?** Word size refers to the number of bits that a processor can manipulate at one time. A processor with a 32-bit word size, for example, has 32-bit registers, processes 32 bits at one time, and is referred to as a 32-bit processor. Processors with a larger word size can process more data during each processor cycle. Today's personal computers typically contain 32-bit or 64-bit processors.

● **What is cache?** Cache, also called RAM cache or cache memory, is high-speed memory that a processor can access more rapidly than memory elsewhere on the motherboard. The amount of cache memory, as well as its location, affects performance. A Level 1 (L1) cache is built into the processor chip, whereas a Level 2 (L2) cache is located on a separate chip, and so it takes a processor more time to get data from the L2 cache to the processor. Usually, cache capacity is expressed in megabytes (MB). The processor in the sample ad in **FIGURE 4-29** has 8 MB L2 cache.

FIGURE 4-29: Cache specs in an ad

Intel Core i7 2860QM processor 2.50 GHz 1600 MHz FSB 8 MB L2 cache

● **How can I tell which processor best meets my needs?** Benchmarking is a technique used across many industries to compare and measure performance. Testing laboratories run a series of tests called benchmarks to gauge the overall speed of a processor. The results of benchmark tests are usually available on the web.

All things being equal, a computer with a 3.8 GHz processor is faster than a computer with a 2.4 GHz processor—and a computer with a processor that has a larger word size can process more data during each processor cycle than a computer with a processor that has a smaller word size. Furthermore, all things being equal, a computer with Level 1 cache is faster than a computer with the same amount of Level 2 cache.

● **What happens inside a computer chip?** A processor contains circuitry and components divided into different kinds of operational units, such as the ALU and the control unit. The ALU (arithmetic logic unit) is the part of the processor that performs arithmetic operations, such as addition and subtraction. It also performs logical operations, such as comparing two numbers to see if they are the same. The ALU uses registers to hold data that is being processed. The processor's control unit fetches each instruction. Data is loaded into the ALU's registers. Finally, the control unit gives the ALU the signal to begin processing. **FIGURE 4-30** illustrates a processor control unit and its ALU preparing to add 5 + 4.

FIGURE 4-30: How a processor adds two numbers

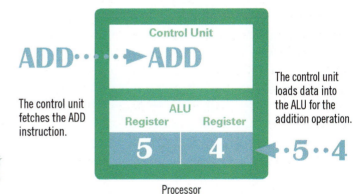

The control unit fetches the ADD instruction.

The control unit loads data into the ALU for the addition operation.

Processor

How the processor gets instructions

Computer programmers write programs that control computers. These programs include the instructions that tell a processor what to do. These programs are usually written in a high-level programming language. The human-readable version of a program is called **source code**. Source code has to be converted into a digital format before the processor can use it. The procedure for translating source code into 0s and 1s is done by a compiler or an interpreter. A **compiler** converts all the statements in a program in a single batch. The resulting collection of instructions, called **object code**, is placed in a new file. Most of the program files distributed as software contain object code that is ready for the processor to execute. An **interpreter** converts and executes one statement at a time while the program is running.

Computer Memory: RAM

Memory is the electronic circuitry that holds data and instructions so it is available when needed by a computer. Computers use three categories of memory: random access memory (RAM), virtual memory, and read-only memory (ROM). Each type of memory is characterized by the type of data it contains and the technology it uses to hold the data. This lesson discusses random access memory, commonly called RAM.

Learning Outcome 8:
Define RAM and explain its importance to computers

- **What is RAM?** In a personal computer, **RAM (random access memory)** is the waiting room for the computer's processor. RAM is usually several chips or small circuit boards that plug into the motherboard. RAM holds operating system instructions that control the basic functions of a computer system. These instructions are loaded into RAM every time you start your computer. These instructions are stored in RAM until you turn off your computer. RAM is also a temporary holding area for program instructions, as well as for data waiting to be processed, displayed, or printed. In addition, RAM holds the results of processing until they can be stored more permanently using a storage system. Refer to **FIGURE 4-31**.

FIGURE 4-31: RAM is a a temporary holding area

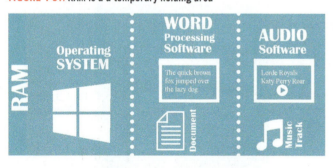

- **Does RAM matter?** Yes. The amount of RAM your computer has makes a difference in how well your computer can perform. Usually the more RAM your computer has, the better the performance. In fact, along with processor speed, RAM capacity is the other most important factor in determining and comparing the power of a computer system. The performance of your computer is directly related to how much RAM is available for your applications, data, and operating system. RAM is made by different manufacturers. Be sure to read reviews about a RAM product before purchasing it because quality can affect performance.

- **How does RAM work?** In RAM, electronic parts called **capacitors** hold the bits that represent data. You can visualize the capacitors as microscopic lights that can be turned on or off. A charged capacitor is turned on and represents a 1 bit. A discharged capacitor is turned off and represents a 0 bit. You can visualize the capacitors as being arranged in banks of eight. Refer to **FIGURE 4-32**. Each bank holds eight bits, or one byte, of data. Each RAM location has an address and holds one byte of data. A RAM address at each location helps the computer locate data as needed for processing. The content of RAM is changed by changing the charge of each capacitor. The capacitor charge is changed when you input data and the computer processes that data.

FIGURE 4-32: How RAM works

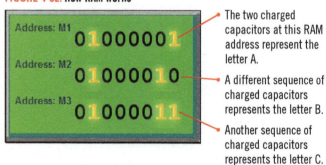

The two charged capacitors at this RAM address represent the letter A.

A different sequence of charged capacitors represents the letter B.

Another sequence of charged capacitors represents the letter C.

- **How does RAM differ from hard drive storage on my computer?** RAM holds data temporarily in circuitry that's directly connected to the motherboard. In contrast, the hard drive stores data on magnetic or solid-state media. Data in RAM is temporary storage. Data stored on the hard drive storage is more permanent. In some respects, RAM is similar to a whiteboard. You can use a whiteboard to write formulas, erase them, and then write an outline for a report. In a similar way,

RAM can hold the numbers and formulas when you use spreadsheet software to manage a budget, and RAM can hold the text of your essay when you use word processing software. Unlike a whiteboard, however, RAM is volatile, which means that it requires electrical power to hold data. If the computer is turned off or if the power goes out, all data in RAM instantly and permanently disappears.

● **How much RAM should my personal computer have?** The amount of RAM your computer needs depends on the software that you use. The capacity of RAM is expressed in gigabytes (GB). Today's personal computers typically feature 2–8 GB of RAM. Handheld devices usually have 1–2 GB of RAM. If you are using a Windows computer, you can view information about your computer, including how much RAM is currently installed, using the Control Panel. See FIGURE 4-33.

FIGURE 4-33: Installed RAM specs

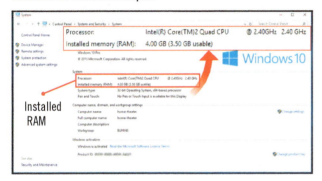

RAM requirements are routinely specified on the outside of a software package. If you want to buy a new program that needs more RAM than is installed on your computer, you can purchase and install additional RAM. However, the amount of RAM is limited by the computer's motherboard, such as by the number of slots the motherboard has to hold RAM. The manufacturer of the motherboard sets the limits. Also, if you plan to upgrade, contact the manufacturer of the computer or motherboard so you can be sure to buy the correct type of RAM.

● **Why is it important to have the most RAM possible?** RAM capacity makes a difference you can notice. For example, if you are working on a spreadsheet, the program instructions and the worksheet are stored in RAM. See FIGURE 4-34. With lots of RAM, you will notice that calculations happen faster and that many graphics operations take less time than with a computer that has less RAM capacity.

FIGURE 4-34: RAM influences performance

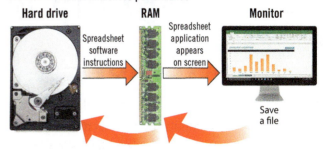

Mauro Rodrigues/Shutterstock.com
Radu Bercan/Shutterstock.com
antpkr/Shutterstock.com

● **Does RAM speed make a difference?** Yes. The amount of time that RAM takes to write or to read data once the request has been received from the processor is called the access time. So, faster RAM generally means faster performance. RAM speed is often expressed in **nanoseconds (ns)**, which are billionths of a second. Whenever referring to nanoseconds, lower numbers mean faster transmission and processing of data. For example, 8 ns RAM is faster than 10 ns RAM. RAM speed can also be expressed in MHz (millions of cycles per second). This measurement is used so RAM speed can be compared to clock speed. The way you interpret MHz rates is just the opposite of the way you interpret nanosecond rates. Higher MHz ratings mean faster speeds. For example, 1066 MHz RAM is faster than 800 MHz RAM.

● **What does the 64 GB mean for my smartphone?** The specifications for smartphones don't typically list RAM, although all smartphones have RAM. The 64 GB specs describe storage capacity, therefore 64 GB helps you know how many apps, photos, videos, and other data you can store on the phone. See FIGURE 4-35.

FIGURE 4-35: Smartphone RAM

Oleksandr Lysenko/Shutterstock.com

Other Types of Computer Memory

In addition to RAM, a computer uses virtual memory and read-only memory (ROM). These other main categories of memory are commonly used in computers. This lesson looks at these types of computer memory and how all computer memory types work together.

Learning Outcome 9:
Explain how a computer uses virtual memory and ROM

● **What is virtual memory?** When RAM nears capacity if you open several application programs and several large graphics or videos at the same time, you can push RAM to its limit. When this occurs, the computer slows down. You might notice that it takes longer to load a screen or respond to a command. To help solve this problem, the operating system uses an area of the hard drive to temporarily store data from RAM. This area of the hard drive is called **virtual memory**. The data that has been moved from RAM to virtual memory is called a **swap file**. See **FIGURE 4-36**. Virtual memory stores parts of a program or data file until needed. By exchanging the data in RAM with the data in virtual memory, your computer gains almost unlimited memory capacity.

FIGURE 4-36: How virtual memory works

Data is copied from RAM to the virtual memory area of the hard drive and back again as needed for processing.

RAM

Hard drive

Radu Bercan/Shutterstock.com
Mauro Rodrigues/Shutterstock.com

Too much dependence on virtual memory can have a negative effect on your computer's performance. Getting data from a mechanical device, such as a hard drive, is much slower than getting data from an electronic device, such as RAM. Installing as much RAM as your computer system allows will help your computer improve its performance.

● **What is ROM?** **ROM (read-only memory)** is a type of memory that holds the computer's startup routine and other basic system information. ROM is housed in a single integrated circuit and is usually a large chip that is plugged into the motherboard. Unlike RAM, which is temporary and volatile, ROM is permanent and nonvolatile. The instructions in ROM are permanent and are not lost even when the computer power is turned off. The only way to change the instructions in ROM is to replace the ROM chip. To overcome this limitation, some newer computers use flash memory chips instead of ROM for storing the startup routine and other system information. Flash memory chips can be changed and they do not lose data when the power is turned off.

● **Does ROM control the boot process?** Yes. When you turn on a computer, the ROM circuitry receives power and begins the boot process by executing the bootstrap program. The boot process has six major events, including the power-on self-test (POST). During the boot process, the bootstrap program in ROM instructs the core operating system programs to load into RAM.

Understanding remote vs. cloud storage?

Storage devices that are built into a digital device or that can be plugged directly into a device are classified as local storage. In contrast, **remote storage** is housed on an external device that can be accessed from a network. Remote storage may be available on a home, school, or work network. It can also be available as an Internet service, in which case it is called **cloud storage**. Cloud storage is provided to individuals by services such as Apple iCloud, Microsoft OneDrive, Google Drive, and Dropbox. The basic concept is that files can be stored in a subscriber's cloud-based storage area and accessed by logging in from any device. In a simple implementation, cloud storage functions just like a local drive—it appears in File Explore, Save As, and Open dialog boxes.

- **When I boot my computer, sometimes I see a message about BIOS. What is that?** When you turn on your computer, the processor receives electrical power and is ready to begin executing instructions. But, because the power was off, RAM is empty and contains no instructions for the processor to execute. Your computer needs to know how much memory is available so that it can allocate space for all of the programs that you want to run. This configuration information cannot be stored in RAM because no information is in RAM when the computer power is turned off. Instead, this configuration information is stored in ROM.

ROM contains a small set of instructions called the **ROM BIOS (basic input/output system)**. When the computer is turned on, the BIOS message tells you that the operating system is reading the configuration settings. While ROM BIOS instructions are accomplished mainly without user intervention, the computer will not function without the ROM chip and the BIOS instructions. You know the boot process is complete when the operating system is loaded into RAM and your computer is ready to accept commands. See **FIGURE 4-37**.

FIGURE 4-37: ROM and the boot process

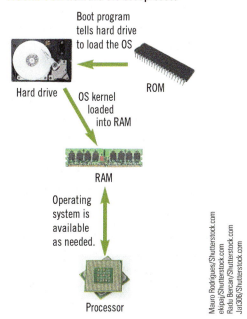

Boot program tells hard drive to load the OS

Hard drive

ROM

OS kernel loaded into RAM

RAM

Operating system is available as needed.

Processor

Mauro Rodrigues/Shutterstock.com
ekipaj/Shutterstock.com
Radu Bercan/Shutterstock.com
Jaiz306/Shutterstock.com

- **How does the computer recognize the devices connected to my computer?** When you turn on your computer, the boot program checks the configuration settings to see what hardware and which devices are connected to your computer. When you add new hardware, the computer needs information about the hardware in

order to recognize the hardware you added. This information is stored in the configurations settings. Computer configuration settings include the date and time, hard drive capacity, number of CD/DVD/BD drives, and RAM capacity.

- **Can I change the contents of ROM?** The process of changing the contents of ROM is sometimes called flashing. There are several reasons that you might want to change the contents of ROM and boot loader instructions.
  - **Repair.** Electrical surges and other hardware problems might corrupt the contents of ROM, which would prevent the device from powering on properly. Flashing the ROM to restore the boot loader instructions might correct the problem.
  - **User modification.** The boot loader may limit the programs that can be downloaded and run on a device. Flashing the ROM with a modified boot loader can bypass these limitations. The process is sometimes called "jailbreaking" on iOS devices and "rooting" on Android devices. This is not advisable as these ROM modifications may cause more problems than they solve and may void the device's warranty.
  - **Updates.** Device manufacturers offer updates to the boot loader as necessary to patch security weaknesses. Such updates are performed by running a program supplied by the manufacturer. Be sure to back up your device before flashing, and carefully follow instructions for this procedure. If the flash fails, your device will not start until you get the ROM chip replaced. After a successful update, your device should boot normally.

Most users will never change the contents of ROM or follow the steps of a boot program. For most users, you push the power button, log into your computer with a password, if it's set up securely, and begin to enjoy what your computer can offer you for work or entertainment. See **FIGURE 4-38**.

FIGURE 4-38: Computer is ready to go!

Kaesler Media/Shutterstock.com

Key Terms & Module Review

Key Terms

ALU (Arithmatic Logic Unit)
Backup
Benchmark
Binary digit
Binary number system
Bit
Bus
Byte
Cache
Cache memory
Capacitor
Character data
Chip
Clock speed
Cloud storage
Compiler
Computer chip
Computer programmer
CPU (Central processing unit)
Control Unit
Cycle
Data bus
Data representation
Digital data

Digitize
DIMM (dual inline memory module)
DIP (dual inline package)
Directory
DRAM
Exa-
Exabyte (EB)
File date
File Explorer
File extension
File format
File management
File management program
File path
File size
File specification
File tag
Filename
Filenaming conventions
Filename extension
Folder
FSB (front side bus)
Giga-
Gigabit (Gb)

Gigabyte (GB)
Integrated circuit (IC)
Interpreter
Kilo-
Kilobit (Kb)
Kilobyte (KB)
LGA (land grid array)
Mega-
Megabit (Mb)
Megabyte (MB)
Microprocessor
Motherboard
Multi-core processor
Nanosecond
Native file format
Navigation pane
Nested folder
Numeric data
Object code
OneDrive
Path
Peta-
Petabyte (PB)
Pin
Pixel

Processor
Processor clock
Quick Access
RAM (Random Access Memory)
RAM cache
Register
Remote storage
ROM (Read Only Memory)
ROM BIOS (basic input/ output system)
Root directory
Source code
Subdirectory
Subfolder
Swap file
Tera-
Terabyte (TB)
Virtual memory
Word size
Zetta-
Zettabyte (ZB)

Module Review

1. Review the bold terms in this module. Then pick 10 terms that are the least familiar to you. Be sure that you can use your own words to define the terms you have selected.

2. Describe how the binary number system uses only 1s and 0s to represent numbers.

3. Describe three types of information that are stored with a file and the importance of a file extension.

4. Describe the difference between the Save and the Save As commands.

5. Describe three file management tasks that might best be accomplished using a file management program, such as File Explorer.

6. Using a sample file path from your own computer, describe a file path and how it describes the location of a file on the storage medium.

7. List five tips to follow when organizing files on your hard drive.

8. Explain the difference between bits and bytes, and the technical meaning of common prefixes, such as kilo, mega, giga, peta, and tera. What aspect of a computer system does each measure?

9. Make sure that you understand the meaning of the following measurement terms: KB, Kb, MB, Mb, GB, Gb, PB, TB, ZB, MHz, GHz, and ns.

10. List three different types of memory and briefly describe how each one works as you use your computer.

Concepts Review

Select the best answer.

1. The _____ is a unique set of characters that identifies a file and should describe its contents.
   a. folder
   b. file size
   c. file path
   d. filename

2. If a program exceeds the allocated RAM, _____ stores parts of a program or data file until they are needed.
   a. flash
   b. virtual memory
   c. ROM
   d. RAM

3. The terms computer chip, microchip, and chip are all synonymous with the term _____ circuit.
   a. digital
   b. integrated
   c. web
   d. silicon

4. A file _____ often lets you know which application can be used to open the file.
   a. extension
   b. folder
   c. letter
   d. map

5. When you delete a file from a folder on the hard drive, it goes into the _____.
   a. Delete Pail
   b. Trash Bin
   c. OneDrive folder
   d. Recycle Bin

6. Use the _____ command to specify a name and storage device for a file and then store it.
   a. Open
   b. New folder
   c. Save As
   d. Select

7. Which of the following is not a component of a processor chip?
   a. ALU
   b. RAM
   c. Register
   d. Control Unit

8. The _____ message tells you that the operating system is reading the configuration settings.
   a. CHIP
   b. BIOS
   c. RAM
   d. CPU

9. The _____ number system represents numeric data as a series of 0s and 1s.
   a. integrated
   b. decimal
   c. binary
   d. singular

10. _____ data is text, numbers, graphics, sound, and video that has been converted into discrete digits, such as 0s and 1s.
    a. RAM
    b. CPU
    c. Digital
    d. ROM

11. Which of the following is not a valid term?
    a. Bigabyte
    b. Petabyte
    c. Exabyte
    d. Terabyte

12. A series of eight _____ is referred to as byte.
    a. words
    b. RAMs
    c. megabytes
    d. bits

13. A file's location is defined by a file path, which includes the drive _____, folder(s), filename, and extension.
    a. number
    b. extension
    c. name
    d. letter

14. The word size refers to the number of _____ that a processor can manipulate at one time.
    a. CPUs
    b. bits
    c. cycles
    d. words

15. The chips are placed on the _____ in a computer.
    a. silicon
    b. packaging
    c. motherboard
    d. circuitry

16. A single processor that contains circuitry for more than one processing unit is called a _____ processor.
    a. digital
    b. semiconducting
    c. full-core
    d. multi-core

17. _____ is a temporary holding area for data, application program instructions, and the operating system.
    a. CPU
    b. ROM
    c. Virtual memory
    d. RAM

18. _____ is not a binary number.
    a. 401
    b. 1010
    c. 1
    d. 100

19. RAM speed is often expressed in terms of _____.
    a. gigabytes
    b. megahertz
    c. nanoseconds
    d. seconds

20. The root directory of a disk is the _____ directory.
    a. first
    b. sub
    c. main
    d. virtual

Independent Challenges

Independent Challenge 1

How will you organize the information that you store on your hard drive? Your hard drive or other storage medium is your electronic filing cabinet for all your work and papers. You can create many different filing systems. The way you set up your folders guides your work and helps you keep your ideas and projects organized so that you can work efficiently with your computer. Take some time to think about the work that you do, the types of documents or files you will be creating, and then decide how you will organize your files and folders.

Windows provides a feature that allows you to customize the icons for your folder shortcuts. You can use these custom icons to help you organize your folders even more. Start File Explorer and be sure you are viewing the folders listed under a user name and not the folders shown in the libraries. You must click the user name, and then continue to open each nested subfolder from there. Once you get to the folder, right-click it in the left pane of File Explorer, and then click Properties. In the Properties dialog box, click the Customize tab, then click Change Icon. See FIGURE 4-39. *Note*: In Windows 7 you cannot change the folder icon if you access the folder through a library.

FIGURE 4-39: Changing folder icons

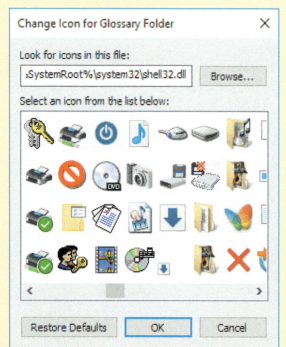

If you are using a Mac, you can also customize the icons. Every volume (disk), application, file, and folder on your Mac appears as an icon. For example, your internal hard drive looks like a hard drive, removable drives look like removable drives, and optical discs such as CDs and DVDs look like discs. File icons generally show a document with an application logo that lets you know what application was used to create it or what can be used to open it, such as a graphic editor or Word. To make changes to the icons, you use the File menu and use the Get Info command.

For this Independent Challenge:

1. Read each of the following plans for organizing files and folders on a hard drive or other storage medium and comment on the advantages and disadvantages of each plan.
   a. Create a folder for each file you create.
   b. Store all the files in the root directory.
   c. Store all files in the Documents folder.
   d. Create a folder for each application you plan to use and store only documents you generate with that application in each folder.
   e. Create folders for broad types of documents such as memos, flyers, letters, budgets, art, photographs, and data, then store all related files within the folders.
   f. Create folders based on specific topics such as business, personal, household, and school, then store all related documents and files within the respective folders.
   g. Create a new folder for each month and store all files or documents created in that month in the appropriate folder.

2. Write a summary of how you plan to organize the folders and files on your hard drive or other storage medium, and explain why you chose the method you did.

3. Describe how you might use icons to help you identify the types of files in the folders.

Independent Challenge 2

You can use File Explorer or any file management program on your computer to explore and find specific files and folders on your hard drive. File Explorer lets you organize and view applications, files, folders, discs, and memory cards located on the hard drive of your PC, and on shared drives on your network.

For this Independent Challenge:

1a. Start File Explorer. List the devices under Computer or This PC. Identify each device as a Network Device, Hard Drive, or Removable Storage.

1b. If you are using a Mac, use the Finder program. The Finder is the blue smiling face icon on the Dock. Finder lets you organize and view applications, files, folders, discs, and memory cards located on the hard drive of your Mac, and on shared drives on your network.

2. Pick any five files on the computer that you typically use and write the full path for each one. Refer to **FIGURE 4-40**. Identify the programs that were used to create each of the files you found.

FIGURE 4-40: Path to a file

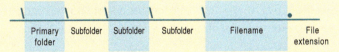

Primary folder | Subfolder | Subfolder | Subfolder | Filename | File extension

3. Open the Documents folder on the Local Disk C: (if not available, find the folder that has your documents). List how many folders are in the Documents folder (or alternate folder if you selected one) on your hard drive.

4. Open one of the folders in the Documents folder (or an alternate folder), click the View tab, then display the Details view. Are file extensions showing? If so, list them and identify which programs would open those files. Look at the folder using at least two views. Explain the differences between the views.

5. How many different types of files can you find on your hard drive? List up to 10.

Independent Challenge 3

How powerful is your computer? Some computers are more powerful than others because they can store more data and process data faster. To find out how your home, work, or lab computer compares to others, you'll need to know a few of its specifications.

For this Independent Challenge:

Check your computer's specifications by doing the following:

1. Start your computer.

2a. If you are using a Windows computer: open the Control Panel. Click the System icon or click the System link to open the System Properties dialog box. Depending on your version of Windows, you may have slightly different commands to open the System Properties dialog box or System and Security window. You might have to click System and Maintenance or System and Security to view this page. If you see a dialog box with tabs, make sure the General tab is displayed. If you see a page, be sure you are looking at the System page. You will see basic information about your computer system, including the operating system, the manufacturer and model, the processor, and the installed RAM.

2b. If your computer is a Mac running MAC OS X: click the Apple icon on the menu bar located at the top of the desktop, then select About This Mac. In the About This Mac window that opens, you will see the Mac OS version as well as the processor speed (in GHz) and the processor series (G4, G5) for your Macintosh. Additionally, it will list the amount of memory (RAM) installed. Click System Report, and on the right side of the window that opens, click the arrow next to Hardware to view the list of devices.

3. Record information about your computer similar to the information listed in **TABLE 4-5**.

TABLE 4-5: Computer specifications

	Your computer	Notes
Computer model and manufacturer:		
Processor manufacturer and model:		
Processor speed:		
Number of cores in the processor:		
Installed RAM:		
RAM capacity:		
System type:		
Operating system:		
Operating system version:		

4a. Just to get an idea of other hardware you have attached to your Windows computer, click the link or icon for Device Manager. You can access the Device Manager through the Control Panel.

4b. If you are using a Mac, open Finder. Expand the icons to see the display adapters, the disk drives, keyboard, pointing devices, ports, and processors.

5. List five of the devices. Tell why each device is connected to the computer.

_____

_____

_____

_____

6. When you're done, close all open dialog boxes.

Visual Workshop

Understanding the specifications listed for processors often seems overwhelming. Advertisements for computers are often filled with confusing specs similar to the sample ad in FIGURE 4-41. You can find processors by manufacturer (Intel or AMD), by brand (Atom and Xeon, or Phenom and Opteron), and by model names. You can choose from processor families, such as the latest generation Intel Core processor. More often than not, you will buy a computer, rather than buy only a processor. It is important to know about processors, however, so you can make an informed decision about the processor in each computer you are considering buying. Go to the Intel.com website advertising high-end processors and also go to the AMD.com website advertising their most recent processors. If you go to these websites, you can see that these two processor manufacturers have a very large selection of processors for many different applications. See FIGURE 4-42.

FIGURE 4-41: Example of a computer ad

Nimbus 2000 Series
DO EVERYTHING YOU LOVE.

- 4th Generation Intel Core i7 processor 3.1 GHz 1066 MHz FSB
- 4 MB cache
- 8 GB DDR3-1600 MHz 2 DIMM memory
- 750 GB SATA HD (7200 rpm)
- 8x CD/DVD burner (Dual Layer DVD+/-R)
- 15.6" High FHD (1080p) LCD display screen
- 1 GB NVIDIA GeForce graphics card
- Integrated speakers
- Integrated 1.3 megapixel webcam
- 4 USB 3.0 ports
- 1 IEEE 1394 port
- 1 HDMI graphics port
- 5-in-1 media card reader
- Wireless networking 802.11 BGN
- 1 GB Ethernet
- 58 WHr, 4-cell battery
- Windows 10 64-bit operating system
- Home/small business software bundle
- 1-year limited warranty

FIGURE 4-42: Processor purchases can be overwhelming

Jiri Vaclavek/Shutterstock.com

1. Log on to the Internet or use any resource available to find these or similar web pages describing current processors available for desktop and laptop computers. Find two featured processors at each site and list four key specifications for each. Write a brief statement, using the terms you learned in this module, to explain each feature.

2. Find two computer ads on the Internet. Identify the processors for those computers. Can you find the processors on the Intel or AMD website? Explain your findings.

3. Both Intel and AMD also sell personal computer systems from their website. Each has a "Help me find the right PC" feature (although the exact name may be different). Use this tool to find two computers from each manufacturer. Write a brief description of your search results and include the specifications for each computer.

Talking Points: Is Your Computer Making You Sick?

More and more workers spend their entire eight-hour day in front of a computer screen. Many work longer than the typical 40-hour workweek of eight-hour days for five days a week. Road warriors are lugging notebook computers through airports and trying to get work done in the cramped confines of economy seats. As computers and other digital devices continue to infiltrate the workplace, worker advocates are concerned about health risks associated with computer use. They raise questions about how the use of digital devices affect ordinary consumers too. The general population in most developed countries own more digital gadgets and spend more time using them than ever before. Studies have shown that the average American spends about two hours a day using a computer. The popularity of LAN parties has spawned intensive daylong competitions, and many serious gamers are still hunched over their keyboards in the wee hours of the morning. It is rare to go anywhere and not see someone talking on a cell phone or plugged into a portable music player. How does this digital lifestyle affect the health of our nation and world?

Radiation Risks

Although we tend to associate radiation with the fallout from nuclear blasts and debilitating cancer treatments, the term refers simply to any energy that is emitted in the form of waves or particles. Radiation streams out of the sun in the form of heat and out of your stereo system as sound waves. Even more radiation pulses out from electrical appliances, wireless networks, cell phone towers, and electrical power lines. Most of the radiation in your everyday world is considered safe, especially in moderation. A few types of radiation can be harmful. Gamma rays and X-rays, for example, contain enough electromagnetic energy to alter chemical reactions in the body and disrupt molecules in human tissue. Shielding against these types of radiation is an important safety factor.

Every electronic device emits some type of radiation; otherwise, they would not be functional. The light emitted by computer, mobile phone, smartphone, and portable music player screens is essential for their use. Cell phones emit sound waves so we can listen to the person at the other end of the connection. Wireless routers emit radio waves to carry data from one workstation to another. Although the radiation from most digital gadgets is considered harmless, researchers have raised concerns about radiation from cell phones and computer display devices.

> **The available scientific evidence does not allow us to conclude that mobile phones are absolutely safe, or that they are unsafe.**
>
> *U.S. Food and Drug Administration (FDA)*

LCD, LED, and OLED display devices generate an image by illuminating a matrix of tiny lights. LCD, LED, and OLED technologies have no tubes, no electron sprays, and generate no X-rays. LCD and OLED devices do, however, emit low levels of radiation. Emission levels vary depending on manufacturer, brand, and model. Various devices designed to block radiation are on the market, but their effectiveness is questionable. Regardless of the type of display device you use, do not sit too close to it. Your exposure to radiation is reduced the farther away you sit from it.

The easiest way to reduce your exposure to mobile phone radiation is to use a hands-free headset. For drivers, many new cars have Bluetooth for hands-free driving while talking. Headsets offer the additional benefit of reducing your chance of becoming involved in a traffic accident. Today, many states require hands-free cell phone usage while driving. See FIGURE 4-43.

FIGURE 4-43: Use a headset for mobile phone calls

Africa Studio/Shutterstock.com

Repetitive Stress Injuries

Most of the health risks associated with computer use are not caused by the equipment itself, but by how the equipment is set up and used. Improper positioning of your keyboard and mouse can cause repetitive stress injuries to wrists, arms, neck, back, and shoulders. A repetitive stress injury is not a specific disease. Instead, it is a group of similar overuse disorders that affect the tendons, muscles, and nerves. Symptoms include stiffness and minor pain in your hands, wrists, arms, or shoulders. See **FIGURE 4-44**. Your symptoms might appear while you're working, or they might appear several hours or days later. With rest, these injuries tend to heal. Although there are some problems, such as carpal tunnel syndrome, that might require medical intervention.

FIGURE 4-44: Carpal tunnel syndrome

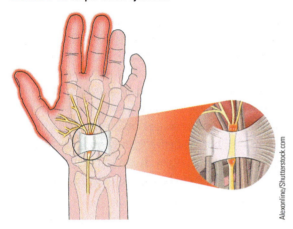

Alexonline/Shutterstock.com

Your wrist contains eight carpal bones surrounding a large nerve that controls your thumb, index, and ring fingers. How you place your hands on the keyboard can affect the pressure on that nerve. Anything that compresses this nerve, such as arthritis or thickened tendons, can cause numbness, pain, or tingling in your fingers. This condition is called carpal tunnel syndrome. At one time, it was generally accepted that keyboarding was a major cause of carpal tunnel syndrome. A Mayo Clinic study, however, concluded that keyboarding does not cause carpal tunnel syndrome. Although the study did find that keyboarding can make the condition worse.

Most computer-related hand and arm injuries are repetitive stress injuries, which can be avoided by following ergonomic guidelines. Ergonomics is the study of safe and efficient environments, particularly working environments. Ergonomics provides guidelines for making work environments safer and healthier. In the United States, the Occupational Safety and Health Administration (OSHA) sets and enforces standards for the safety and health of American workers. Although a federal law to enforce ergonomic standards in the workplace was repealed in 2001, many states have regulations designed to protect workers from repetitive stress injuries.

> **Most computer-related hand and arm injuries are repetitive stress injuries, which can be avoided by following ergonomic guidelines.**

To avoid future computer-related stress injuries, keep ergonomic principles in mind wherever you work. The key to avoiding uncomfortable stress injuries is in the placement and use of your keyboard, mouse, monitor, desk, and chair. **FIGURE 4-45** provides an overview of ergonomic workstation

FIGURE 4-45: Correct posture for using a computer

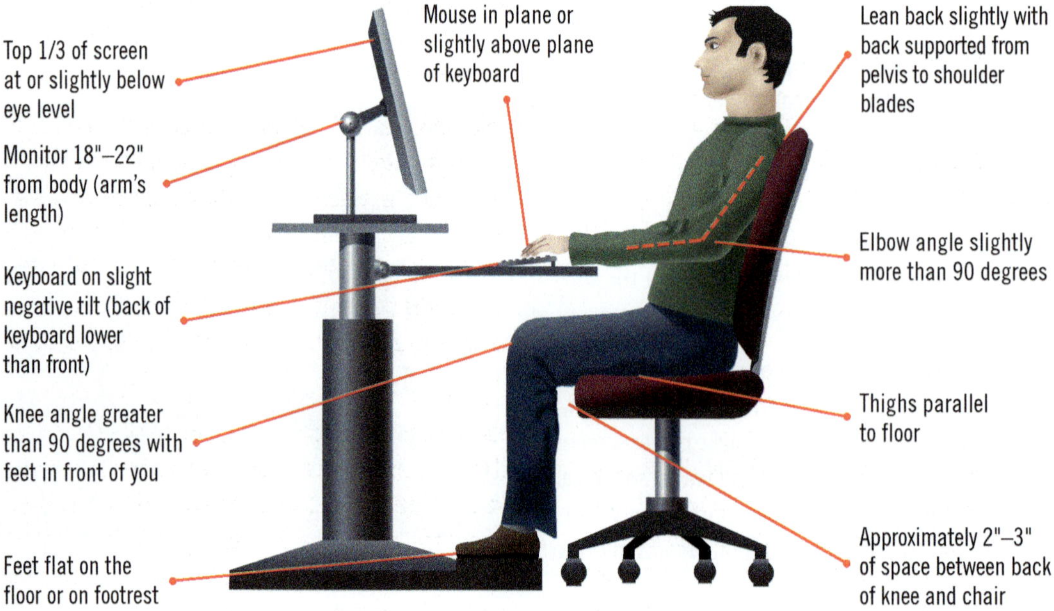

Top 1/3 of screen at or slightly below eye level

Monitor 18"–22" from body (arm's length)

Keyboard on slight negative tilt (back of keyboard lower than front)

Knee angle greater than 90 degrees with feet in front of you

Feet flat on the floor or on footrest

Mouse in plane or slightly above plane of keyboard

Lean back slightly with back supported from pelvis to shoulder blades

Elbow angle slightly more than 90 degrees

Thighs parallel to floor

Approximately 2"–3" of space between back of knee and chair

Talking Points: Is Your Computer Making You Sick?

guidelines. Some specific tips for setting up your keyboard and mouse follow:

- Position the keyboard so that it is just above your lap and your elbows are able to extend past the 90-degree angle when you type.

- When shopping for a computer desk, make sure it has a keyboard tray. The tray should be adjustable if possible. Also, look for one with a small lip that reduces the distance between the tray and your thighs.

- Angle the keyboard so that your wrists are straight when typing.

- If you have a wrist rest, use it only when you are not typing. Resting your wrist or arm on a wrist rest while typing causes your wrist to be at an angle that is not efficient.

- Use a keyboard that fits the size of your hands and fingers. When you rest your fingers on the home keys (asdf and jkl;), there should be 1/8 to 1/4 inch of space between them. When you type, your fingers should not be cramped together or overextended.

- Make sure your mouse is positioned close by so that you don't have to reach for it.

- Keep the mouse at the same height as your keyboard to minimize arm movements.

- Use your mouse with a relaxed arm and wrist.

- When working at mouse-intensive activities, you should change mouse hands occasionally. You might also consider using an air mouse or trackball, each of which requires a different set of muscles.

Eye Strain

Studies have found links between computer use and eye problems. The most common symptoms are sore, tired, burning, or itching eyes; watery eyes; dry eyes; blurred or double vision; headaches; difficulty shifting focus between the screen display and printed documents; and increased sensitivity to light. For many computer users, eye problems can be avoided by proper monitor placement and adjustment.

"Studies have found links between computer use and eye problems."

To position your monitor correctly, sit back slightly in your chair and stretch your right arm out straight ahead of you. Your middle finger should almost touch the center of your screen. See FIGURE 4-46. Once the screen is set at the proper height, tilt it backwards just a bit. You should feel like you

are looking down slightly at the screen. Your screen should be directly in front of you and parallel to your shoulders. A monitor that is tilted to one side or another makes your eyes focus at different distances, which is tiring.

FIGURE 4-46: Positioning a monitor

If you use two monitors, place your second monitor as close to the first monitor as possible, but angled so that when you turn your head slightly, you face it straight on. You might also consider moving it to the other side of your primary monitor periodically. When positioning your monitor, try to minimize the amount of glare from lights or windows that is reflected on the screen. Angle the screen away from windows. It is best not to end up facing a window where bright outdoor light can interfere with the way your pupils need to dilate for the brightness of your computer screen. If glare is a problem in your work area, you can purchase an antiglare screen that fits over your monitor. Keeping the surface of your monitor free of dust can also cut down on glare. Notebook computers present an ergonomic problem because the screen and keyboard are typically attached to each other. Placement becomes a compromise between the best viewing angle and the best typing height. When possible, use an external keyboard and mouse with your notebook computer to achieve a more ergonomic work area.

People who wear bifocal and trifocal lenses tend to focus on the computer screen through the bottom of the lens. In order to do this, wearers raise their chins to view the screen. This puts stress on neck muscles and causes headaches. To avoid this situation, bifocal and trifocal wearers might have to lower their screens or ask their optometrist for eyewear dedicated to viewing the computer screen.

One of the most effective steps you can take to avoid eyestrain is to adjust the resolution of your monitor so that you can easily read the text displayed on your screen. Remember that you can make two types of adjustments. You can adjust the resolution of your monitor through the operating system. Selecting a resolution lower than a screen's native resolution forces the display device to interpolate pixels. This results in a slightly fuzzy display.

Once your monitor is set to its native resolution, you might find that the text on webpages and in documents is too small to view comfortably. In that situation, you can adjust the zoom level within various applications. For example, you might set your browser to display larger text, and set your word processor to display text at 125 percent or 150 percent.

Back Pain

Back pain can be caused by many factors, including poor posture and careless lifting of heavy objects. Doctors and physical therapists more commonly use the term *flex-forward position* to describe the sitting posture shared by many computer users. The layman's term *computer slump* refers to the posture of sitting hunched over a computer keyboard with your neck craned forward. See FIGURE 4-47. Habitual slouching can lead to stiffness and muscle tenderness. Left uncorrected, the problem can cause nerve irritation that spreads down the arms and back. Back problems caused by habitual flex-forward posture are sometimes referred to as T4 syndrome, after the fourth cervical vertebra that is most affected.

FIGURE 4-47: Incorrect posture

The key to comfort while working on a computer is keeping your shoulders relaxed so that tense muscles don't generate headaches and stiffness. If the arm rests on your chair make your shoulders rise, you should remove the armrests or get another chair. Conventional wisdom about sitting straight has been challenged recently by a body of evidence that indicates the best position for computer work is with your upper torso leaning back slightly. With your torso at a 100-110 degree angle, the back of your chair helps to support your spine.

> **The key to comfort while working on a computer is keeping your shoulders relaxed so that tense muscles don't generate headaches and stiffness.**

Carrying a heavy notebook computer can also contribute to back problems. To lighten your load, try to reduce the number of peripheral devices you carry. Consider toting your notebook computer in a backpack instead of a shoulder bag. Be sure the backpack provides the proper protection for your notebook computer. When traveling, place your notebook computer in a wheeled carrier.

Sedentary Lifestyle

People who live and work in digital cultures tend to spend many hours each day in sedentary pursuits, such as watching television and using computers. Many researchers believe that there is a link between our increasingly sedentary lifestyle and a steady climb in obesity and cardiovascular disease. To counteract the effects of a sedentary lifestyle, it is important to exercise and eat right. A good balance of stretching and cardiovascular exercise can help you keep physically fit and has the additional benefit of helping to prevent repetitive stress injuries and back pain.

Sitting still for long periods of time, especially in positions that limit blood circulation, can be a health risk, similar to the risk of long-haul air travel. A condition called deep vein thrombosis is the formation of blood clots that commonly affect veins in the legs. Symptoms include pain, swelling, and redness in the affected area. Deep vein thrombosis requires treatment to prevent life-threatening complications if the clot moves to the heart. Although the condition is not common in young people, good work habits can help you maintain healthy circulation. For example, your chair should allow for good circulation to your legs. Make sure there are at least two inches of clearance between your calf and the front of your chair. Your thighs should be parallel to the ground to allow for good blood flow; if necessary, use a footrest to raise your feet and reduce the pressure on the backs of your thighs.

To combat potential health hazards associated with computer use, you should try to take breaks periodically, say, every 20 minutes or at least once every hour. At minimum, try the 20/20/20 break: Every 20 minutes, take 20 seconds and look 20 feet away. Longer breaks of two to five minutes are more effective. During a longer break, stand up to change your circulation. Rest your eyes by focusing on distant objects. Gently rotate and stretch your wrists, shoulders, and neck. Break reminder software, such as RSIGuard and open source Workrave, can help you remember when it is time to take a break from your work.

In conclusion, computer use can be hazardous to your health if you do not follow the guidelines set forth by health experts and common sense. But if you take proper care, you can work to improve your health and avoid computer-related health problems.

Getting Started with Windows 10

CASE You are about to start a new job, and your employer has asked you to get familiar with Windows 10 to help boost your productivity. You'll need to start Windows 10 and Windows apps, work with on-screen windows and commands, get help, and exit Windows. *Note: With the release of Windows 10, Microsoft now provides ongoing updates to Windows instead of releasing new versions periodically. This means that Windows features might change over time, including how they look and how you interact with them. The information provided in this text was accurate at the time this book was published.*

Module Objectives

After completing this module, you will be able to:

- Start Windows 10
- Navigate the desktop and Start menu
- Point, click, and drag
- Start an app
- Work with a window
- Manage multiple windows
- Use buttons, menus, and dialog boxes
- Get help
- Exit Windows 10

Files You Will Need

No files needed.

Start Windows 10

Windows 10 is an **operating system**, a type of program that runs your computer and lets you interact with it. A **program** is a set of instructions written for a computer. If your computer did not have an operating system, you wouldn't see anything on the screen after you turned it on. Windows 10 reserves a special area called a **Microsoft account** where each user can keep his or her files. In addition, a Microsoft account lets you use various devices and services such as a Windows Phone or Outlook.com. You may have more than one Microsoft account. When the computer and Windows 10 start, you need to **sign in**, or select your Microsoft account name and enter a password, also called **logging in**. If your computer has only one Microsoft account, you won't need to select an account name. But all users need to enter a **password**, a special sequence of numbers and letters. Users cannot see each other's account areas or services without the other person's password, so passwords help keep your computer information secure. After you sign in, you see the Windows 10 desktop, which you learn about in the next lesson. **CASE** ▸ *You're about to start a new job, so you decide to learn more about Windows 10, the operating system used at your new company.*

STEPS

1. **Press your computer's** power button, **which might look like** 🔘 **or** ▭🔵▭ **, then if the monitor is not turned on, press its** power button

   On a desktop computer, the power button is probably on the front panel. On a laptop computer it's likely at the top of the keys on your keyboard. After a few moments, a **lock screen**, showing the date, time, and an image, appears. See **FIGURE 1-1**. The lock screen appears when you first start your computer and also if you leave it unattended for a period of time.

2. **Press [Spacebar], or click once to display the sign-in screen**

   The **sign-in screen** shows your Windows account picture, name, and e-mail address, as well as a space to enter your Microsoft account password. The account may have your name assigned to it, or it might have a general name like "Student" or "Lab User."

3. **Type your** password, **as shown in** FIGURE 1-2, **using uppercase and lowercase letters as necessary**

   If necessary, ask your instructor or technical support person what password you should use. Passwords are **case sensitive**, which means that if you type any letter using capital letters when lowercase letters are needed, or vice versa, Windows will not let you use your account. For example, if your password is "booklet43+", typing "Booklet43+" or "BOOKLET43+" will not let you enter your account. For security, Windows substitutes bullets for the password characters you type.

4. **Click or tap the** Submit button ➡

   The Windows 10 desktop appears. See **FIGURE 1-3**.

Using a touch screen with Windows

Windows 10 was developed to work with touch-screen computers, including tablets and smartphones. See **FIGURE 1-4**. So if you have a touch-screen device, you'll find that you can accomplish many tasks with gestures instead of a mouse. A **gesture** is an action you take with your fingertip directly on the screen, such as tapping or swiping. For example, when you sign into Windows 10, you can tap the Submit button on the screen, instead of clicking it.

FIGURE 1-4: Touch-screen device

© vovan/Shutterstock.com

FIGURE 1-1: Lock screen with time and date

Your lock
screen contents
may differ

10:49
Friday, July 31

FIGURE 1-2: Typing your password

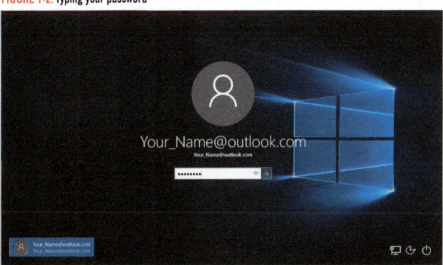

Your_Name@outlook.com
Your_Name@outlook.com

Your_Name@outlook.com
Your_Name@outlook.com

FIGURE 1-3: Windows 10 desktop

Recycle Bin

Navigate the Desktop and Start Menu

Learning
Outcomes
• Examine the
desktop
• Open the Start
menu
• View Start menu
apps
• Close the Start
menu

Every time you start your computer and sign in, the Windows 10 desktop appears. The **Windows 10 desktop** is an electronic work area that lets you organize and manage your information, much like your own physical desktop. The desktop contains controls that let you interact with the Windows 10 operating system. These controls are called its **user interface (UI)**. The Windows 10 user interface is called the **Windows 10 UI.** CASE ▶ *To become better acquainted with Windows 10, you decide to explore the desktop and Start menu.*

STEPS

1. **Examine the Windows 10 desktop**

   As shown in **FIGURE 1-5**, the desktop currently contains one item, an icon representing the **Recycle Bin**, an electronic wastepaper basket. You might see other icons, files, and folders placed there by previous users or by your school lab. The desktop lets you manage the files and folders on your computer. A **file** is a collection of stored information, such as a letter, video, or program. A **folder** is a container that helps you organize your files. A file, folder, or program opens in a window. You can open multiple windows on the desktop at once, and you can move them around so you can easily go back and forth between them. You work with windows later in this module. At the bottom of the screen is a bar called the **taskbar**, with buttons representing commonly used programs and tools. In a default Windows installation, the taskbar contains four buttons, described in **TABLE 1-1**. Also on the taskbar is the search box, which you can use to find an item on your computer or the Internet. On the right side of the status bar you see the **Notification area**, containing the time and date as well as icons that tell you the status of your computer. At the left side of the taskbar, you see the Start button. You click the **Start button** to display the **Start menu**, which lets you start the programs on your computer.

2. **Move the pointer to the left side of the taskbar, then click or tap the Start button** ⊞

   The Start menu appears, as shown in **FIGURE 1-6**. Your user account name and an optional picture appear at the top. The menu shows a list of often-used programs and other controls on the left, and variously-sized shaded rectangles called **tiles** on the right. Each tile represents an **app**, short for **application program**. Some tiles show updated content using a feature called **live tile**; for example, the Weather app can show the current weather for any city you choose. (Your screen color and tiles may differ from the figures shown here. Note that the screens in this book do not show live tiles.)

3. **Move the pointer near the bottom of the Start menu, then click or tap the All apps button**

   You see an alphabetical listing of all the apps on your computer. Only some of the apps are visible.

4. **Move the pointer into the list, until the gray scroll bar appears on the right side of the list, place the pointer over the scroll box, press and hold down the mouse button, then drag to display the remaining programs; on a touch screen, swipe the list to scroll**

5. **Click or tap the Back button at the bottom of the Start menu**

   The previous listing reappears.

6. **Move the pointer back up over the desktop, then click or tap once to close the Start menu**

FIGURE 1-5: Windows 10 desktop

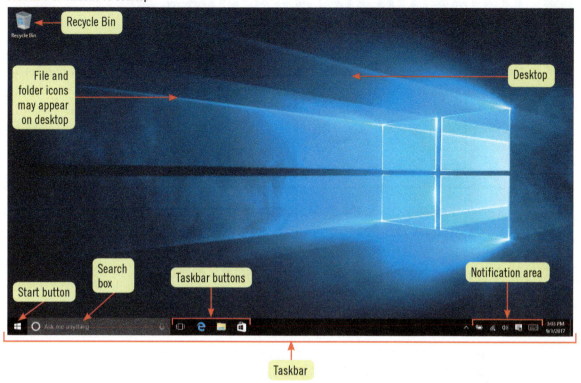

Recycle Bin

File and folder icons may appear on desktop

Desktop

Search box

Taskbar buttons

Notification area

Start button

Taskbar

FIGURE 1-6: Start menu

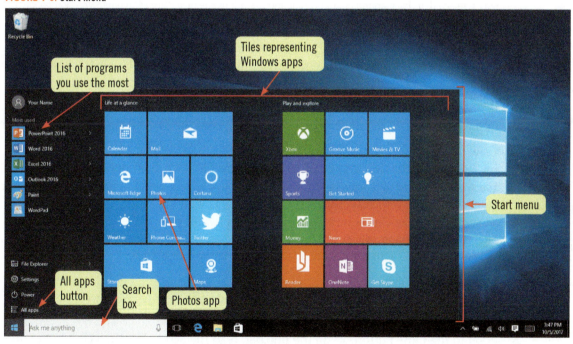

List of programs you use the most

Tiles representing Windows apps

Start menu

All apps button

Search box

Photos app

TABLE 1-1: Windows taskbar buttons

button	looks like	what it does
Task View		Shows miniatures of all open windows and lets you create multiple desktops, so you can switch from one to another
Microsoft Edge		Opens the Microsoft Edge web browser
File Explorer		Lets you explore the files in your storage locations
Store		Opens the Windows Store featuring downloadable apps, games, music, movies, and TV

Point, Click, and Drag

Learning Outcomes
• Point to, select, and deselect a desktop icon
• Move a desktop icon

You communicate with Windows 10 using a variety of pointing devices (or, with a touch-screen device, your finger). A **pointing device** controls the movement of the **pointer**, a small arrow or other symbol that moves on the screen. Your pointing device could be a mouse, trackball, graphics tablet, or touchpad. There are five basic **pointing device actions** you use to communicate with your computer; see **TABLE 1-2**. Touch-screen users can tap, press, and tap and hold. **CASE** *You practice the basic pointing device actions.*

STEPS

1. **Locate the pointer ☊ on the desktop, then move your pointing device left, right, up, and down (or move your finger across a touch pad or screen)**

   The pointer shape ☊ is the **Select pointer**. The pointer moves in the same direction as your device.

2. **Move your pointing device so the Select pointer is over the Recycle Bin (if you are using a touch screen, skip this step)**

   You are **pointing to** the Recycle Bin icon. The icon becomes **highlighted**, looking as though it is framed in a box with a lighter color background. (Note that touch-screen users cannot point to items.)

3. **While pointing to the Recycle Bin icon, press and quickly release the left mouse button once (or tap the icon once), then move the pointer away from the Recycle Bin icon**

   You click or tap a desktop icon once to **select** it, which signals that you intend to perform an action. When an icon is selected, its background changes color and maintains the new color even when you point away from it.

4. **With a pointing device, point to (don't click) the Microsoft Edge button 🄴 on the taskbar**

   The button becomes highlighted and an informational message called a **ScreenTip** identifies the program the button represents. ScreenTips are useful because they help you to learn about the tools available to you. **Microsoft Edge** is the new Microsoft web browser that lets you display and interact with webpages.

5. **If you are using a pointing device, move the pointer over the time and date in the notification area on the right side of the taskbar, read the ScreenTip, then click or tap once**

   A pop-up window appears, containing the current time and date and a calendar.

6. **Click or tap on the desktop, point to the Recycle Bin icon, then quickly click or tap twice**

   You **double-clicked** (or double-tapped) the icon. You need to double-click or double-tap quickly, without moving the pointer. A window opens, showing the contents of the Recycle Bin, as shown in **FIGURE 1-7**. The area at the top of the window is the title bar, which displays the name of the window. The area below the title bar is the **Ribbon**, which contains tabs, commands, and the Address bar. **Tabs** are groupings of **buttons** and other controls you use to interact with an object or a program.

7. **Click or tap the View tab**

   The buttons on that tab appear. Buttons act as **commands**, which instruct Windows to perform tasks. The **Address bar** shows the name and location of the item you have opened.

8. **Point to the Close button ☒ on the title bar, read the ScreenTip, then click or tap once**

9. **Point to the Recycle Bin icon, hold down the left mouse button, or press and hold the Recycle Bin image with your finger, move the mouse or drag so the object moves right as shown in FIGURE 1-8, release the mouse button or lift your finger, then drag the Recycle Bin back to its original location**

FIGURE 1-7: Recycle Bin window

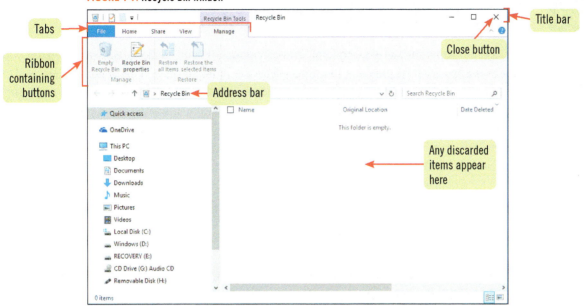

Tabs

Ribbon containing buttons

Address bar

Title bar

Close button

Any discarded items appear here

FIGURE 1-8: Dragging the Recycle Bin icon

Releasing mouse button moves object to this location

Recycle Bin → Recycle Bin

TABLE 1-2: Basic pointing device actions

action	with a mouse	with a touch pad	use to
Point	Move mouse to position tip of pointer over an item	Move your finger over touch pad to position tip of pointer over an item	Highlight items or display small informational boxes called ScreenTips
Click	Press and release left mouse button once	Tap touch pad once	Select objects or commands, open menus or items on the taskbar
Double-click	Quickly press and release left mouse button twice	Tap touch pad twice in quick succession	Open programs, folders, or files represented by desktop icons
Drag	Point to an object, press and hold down left mouse button, move object to a new location, then release mouse button	Slide finger across touch pad to point to an object, press and hold left touch pad button, drag across touch pad to move object to new location, then release button	Move objects, such as icons, on the desktop
Right-click	Point to an object, then press and release right mouse button	Point to an object, then press and release right touchpad button	Display a shortcut menu containing options specific to the object

Selecting and moving items using touch-screen devices

If you use a touch-screen computer, a tablet, or a smartphone, you click desktop items by tapping them once on the screen. Tap an icon twice quickly to double-click and open its window. Press and hold an icon, then drag to move it. A touch-screen device does not let you point to an object without selecting it, however, as mice and touchpads do.

Start an App

Apps are programs that let you perform tasks. Windows 10 runs Windows apps and desktop apps. **Windows apps** are small programs that are available free or for purchase in the Windows Store, and can run on Windows desktops, laptops, tablets, and phones. Windows apps are also called **universal apps**. They are specially designed so they can stay open as you work without slowing down your computer, and often have a single purpose. Examples include the Photos app, which lets you view your photographs, and the OneDrive app, which lets you connect to files and programs you have stored on the Microsoft OneDrive website. **Desktop apps** are fully-featured programs; they may be available at an online store or on disk. For example, Microsoft Word allows you to create and edit letters, reports, and other text-based documents. Some smaller desktop apps called **Windows accessories**, such as Paint and Notepad, come already installed in Windows 10. **CASE** ▶ *To prepare for your new job, you start three apps.*

STEPS

1. **Click or tap the Start button ⊞, then click or tap the Weather tile, shown in FIGURE 1-9**

   The Weather app opens, letting you find the current weather in various locations.

2. **If you are asked to choose a location, begin typing your city or town, then click the full name if it appears in the drop-down list**

   The current weather for your selected city appears in Summary view. **FIGURE 1-10** shows a forecast for Boston, MA.

3. **Click or tap the Weather app window's Close button ✕**

4. **Click or tap ⊞, then type onenote**

   Typing an app name is another way to locate an app. At the top of the Start menu, you see the OneNote Trusted Windows Store app listed, as shown in **FIGURE 1-11**. OneNote is a popular app that lets you create tabbed notebooks where you can store text, images, files, and media such as audio and video.

5. **Click or tap the OneNote Trusted Windows Store app name**

   The OneNote app opens, showing a blank notebook (or a notebook you have previously created).

6. **Click or tap the Close button ✕ in the upper right corner of the OneNote app window**

   You have opened two Windows apps, Weather and OneNote.

7. **Click or tap ⊞, then type paint**

   The top of the Start menu lists the Paint Desktop app, shown in **FIGURE 1-12**. Paint is a simple accessory that comes installed with Windows and lets you create simple illustrations.

8. **Click or tap the Paint Desktop app name at the top of the Start menu**

   Other accessories besides Paint and Notepad include the Snipping Tool, which lets you capture an image of any screen area, and Sticky Notes, that let you create short notes.

Using the Windows Store

The Windows Store is an app that lets you find all kinds of apps for use on Windows personal computers, tablets, and phones. You can open it by clicking or tapping its tile on the Start menu or by clicking or tapping the Store button on the taskbar. To use the Windows Store, you need to be signed in to your Microsoft account. You can browse lists of popular apps, games, music, movies, and TV including new releases; you can browse the top paid or free apps. Browse app categories to find a specific type of app, such as Business or Entertainment. To locate a specific app, type its name in the Search box. If an app is free, you can go to its page and click the Free button to install it on your computer. If it's a paid app, you can click or tap the Free trial button to try it out, or click or tap its price button to purchase it. Any apps you've added recently appear in the Recently added category of the Start menu.

FIGURE 1-9: Weather tile on the Start menu

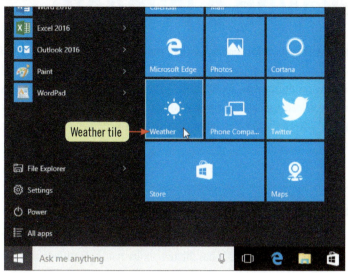

Weather tile

FIGURE 1-10: Weather app

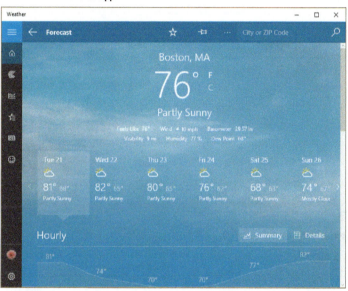

FIGURE 1-11: OneNote Windows app name on Start menu

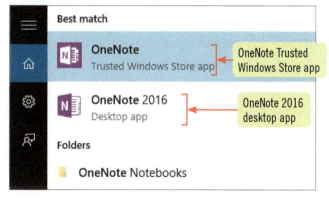

OneNote Trusted Windows Store app

OneNote 2016 desktop app

FIGURE 1-12: Paint Desktop app name on Start menu

Paint Desktop app

Work with a Window

Learning Outcomes
- Minimize, restore, and maximize a window
- Scroll a window
- Move a window

When you start an app, its **window**, a frame displaying the app's tools, opens. In many apps, a blank file also opens so you can start creating a new document. For example, in Paint, a blank document opens so you can start drawing right away. All windows in the Windows 10 operating system have similar window elements. Once you can use a window in one app, you will know how to work with windows in many other apps. **CASE** ▶ *To become more familiar with the Windows 10 user interface, you explore elements in the Paint window.*

DETAILS

Many windows have the following common elements. Refer to FIGURE 1-13:

- At the top of the window, you see a **title bar**, a strip that contains the name of the document and app. This document has not been saved, so it has the temporary name "Untitled" and the app name is "Paint."

- On the right side of the title bar, the **Window control buttons** let you control the app window. The **Minimize button** — temporarily hides the window, making it a button on the taskbar. The app is still running, but its window is temporarily hidden until you click its taskbar button or its miniature window in Task view to reopen it. The **Maximize button** ☐ enlarges the window to fill the entire screen. If a window is already maximized, the Maximize button changes to the **Restore Down button** ❐, which reduces it to the last non-maximized size. Clicking or tapping the **Close button** ✕ closes the app.

- Many windows have a **scroll bar** on the right side and/or the bottom of the window. You click (or press) and drag scroll bar elements to show additional parts of your document. See **TABLE 1-3**.

- Just below the title bar is the Ribbon, a bar containing tabs as well as a Help icon. The Paint window has three tabs: File, Home, and View. Tabs are divided into **groups** of buttons and tool palettes. The Home tab has five groups: Clipboard, Image, Tools, Shapes, and Colors. Many apps also include **menus** you click to show lists of commands, as well as **toolbars** containing buttons.

- The **Quick Access toolbar** lets you quickly perform common actions such as saving a file.

STEPS

1. **Click or tap the Paint window Minimize button** —
   The app is reduced to a taskbar button, as shown in **FIGURE 1-14**. The contrasting line indicates the app is still open.

2. **Click or tap the taskbar button representing the Paint app** 🎨 **to redisplay the app**

3. **Drag the gray scroll box down, notice the lower edge of the work area that appears, then click or tap the Up scroll arrow** ⏶ **until you see the top edge of the work area**

4. **Point to the View tab, then click or tap the View tab once**
   Clicking or tapping the View tab moved it in front of the Home tab. This tab has three groups containing buttons that let you change your view of the document window.

5. **Click the Home tab, then click or tap the Paint window Maximize button** ☐
   The window fills the screen, and the Maximize button becomes the Restore Down button ❐.

6. **Click the window's Restore Down button** ❐ **to return it to its previous size**

7. **Point to the Paint window title bar (if you are using a pointing device), then drag about an inch to the right to move it so it's centered on the screen**

FIGURE 1-13: Typical app window elements

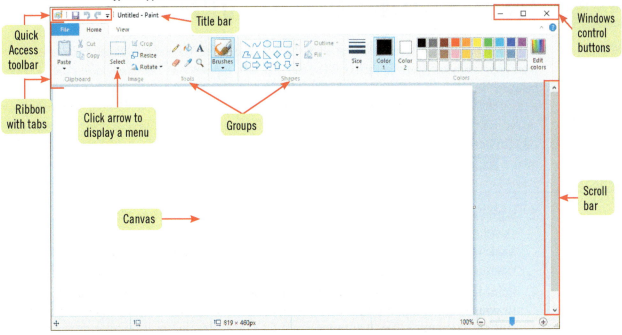

Quick Access toolbar

Ribbon with tabs

Click arrow to display a menu

Groups

Title bar

Windows control buttons

Scroll bar

Canvas

FIGURE 1-14: Taskbar with minimized Paint program button

Buttons without contrasting lines represent programs that are not open

Your buttons may differ

Paint program button with contrasting line indicating program is open

Windows 10

TABLE 1-3: Parts of a scroll bar

name	looks like	to use
Scroll box	☐ (Size may vary)	Drag to scroll quickly through a long document
Scroll arrows	⋀ ⋁	Click or tap to scroll up, down, left, or right in small amounts
Shaded area	(Above, below, or to either side of scroll box)	Click or tap to move up or down by one screen

Using the Quick Access toolbar

On the left side of the title bar, the Quick Access toolbar lets you perform common tasks with just one click. The Save button 💾 saves the changes you have made to a document. The Undo button ↩ lets you reverse (undo) the last action you performed.

The Redo button ↪ reinstates the change you just undid. Use the Customize Quick Access Toolbar button ▼ to add other frequently used buttons to the toolbar, move the toolbar below the Ribbon, or minimize the Ribbon to show only tabs.

Manage Multiple Windows

Learning Outcomes
- Open a second app
- Activate a window
- Resize, snap, and close a window

You can work with more than one app at a time by switching among open app windows. If you open two or more apps, a window opens for each one. You can work with app windows individually, going back and forth between them. The window in front is called the **active window**. Any open window behind the active window is called an **inactive window**. For ease in working with multiple windows, you can move, arrange, make them smaller or larger, minimize, or restore them so they're not in the way. To resize a window, drag a window's edge, called its **border**. You can use the taskbar to switch between windows. See **TABLE 1-4** for a summary of taskbar actions. **CASE** ▶ *Keeping the Paint app open, you open the OneNote app and then work with both app windows.*

STEPS

1. **With Paint open, click or tap the** Start button ⊞, **then the** OneNote tile

   The OneNote window appears as a second window on the desktop, as shown in **FIGURE 1-15**. The OneNote window is in front, indicating that it is the active window. The Paint window is the inactive window. On the taskbar, the contrasting line under the OneNote and Paint app buttons tell you both apps are open.

2. **Point to a blank part of the** OneNote window title bar **on either side of the app name (if you are using a pointing device), then drag the** OneNote window **down slightly so you can see more of the Paint window**

3. **Click or tap once on the Paint window's** title bar

   The Paint window is now the active window and appears in front of the OneNote window. You can make any window active by clicking or tapping it, or by clicking or tapping an app's icon in the taskbar.

4. **Point to the** taskbar **if you are using a pointing device, then click or tap the** OneNote window button

   The OneNote window becomes active. When you open multiple windows on the desktop, you may need to resize windows so they don't get in the way of other open windows.

5. **Point to the lower-right corner of the** OneNote window **until the pointer changes to** ⤡, **if you are using a pointing device, or tap and press the corner, then drag down and to the right about an inch to make the window larger**

   You can also point to any edge of a window until you see the ↔ or ↕ pointer, or tap and press any edge, then drag to make it larger or smaller in one direction only.

6. **Click or tap the** Task View button ▢ **on the taskbar, click or tap the** Paint window, **click or tap** ▢ **again, then click or tap the** OneNote window

   The **Task View button** is another convenient way to switch among open windows.

7. **Point to the** OneNote window title bar **if you are using a pointing device, drag the window to the left side of the screen until the pointer or your finger reaches the screen edge and you see a vertical line down the middle of the screen, then release the mouse button or lift your finger from the screen**

   The OneNote window instantly fills the left side of the screen, and any inactive windows appear on the right side of the screen. This is called the **Snap Assist** feature. You can also drag to any screen corner to snap open app windows to quarter-screen windows.

8. **Click or tap anywhere on the reduced-size version of the** Paint window

   The Paint window fills the right side of the screen. Snapping makes it easy to view the contents of two windows at the same time. See **FIGURE 1-16**.

9. **Click or tap the OneNote window** Close button ✕, **then click or tap the** Maximize button ▢ **in the Paint window's title bar**

   The OneNote app closes. The Paint app window remains open.

FIGURE 1-15: Working with multiple windows

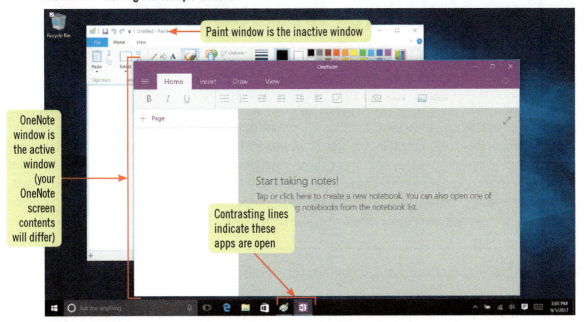

Paint window is the inactive window

OneNote window is the active window (your OneNote screen contents will differ)

Contrasting lines indicate these apps are open

FIGURE 1-16: OneNote and Paint windows snapped to each side of the screen

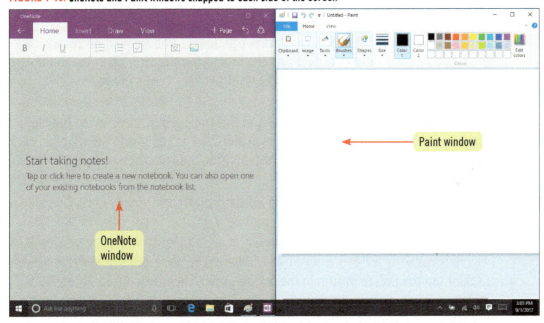

Paint window

OneNote window

TABLE 1-4: Using the taskbar

to	do this
Add buttons to taskbar	Open an app, right-click or press its icon on the taskbar, then click or tap Pin this program to taskbar
Change order of taskbar buttons	Drag any icon to a new taskbar location
See a list of recent documents opened	Right-click or press taskbar app button
Close a document using the taskbar	Point to taskbar button, point to document image, then click its Close button
Minimize/Redisplay all open windows	Click or press Show desktop button (the thin bar) to the right of taskbar date and time
See preview of documents in taskbar	With a pointing device, point to taskbar button for open app
Bring a minimized window to the front	Click or press the Task View button, then click or tap the window or desktop you want in front
Rearrange windows on the desktop	Right-click taskbar, click Cascade Windows, Show windows stacked, or Show windows side by side

Getting Started with Windows 10

Use Buttons, Menus, and Dialog Boxes

Learning Outcomes
- Use a button and a menu
- Work in a dialog box

When you work in an app, you communicate with it using buttons, menus, and dialog boxes. **Buttons** let you issue instructions to modify app objects. Buttons are often organized on a Ribbon into tabs, and then into groups like those in the Paint window. Some buttons have text on them, and others show only an icon that represents what they do. Other buttons reveal **menus**, lists of commands you can choose. And some buttons open up a **dialog box**, a window with controls that lets you tell Windows what you want. **TABLE 1-5** lists the common types of controls you find in dialog boxes. **CASE** *You practice using buttons, menus, and dialog boxes to create some simple graphics in the Paint app.*

STEPS

1. **In the Shapes group, click or tap the More button ⤓ just to the right of the shapes, then click the Triangle button △**

2. **Click or tap the Turquoise button ▣ in the Colors group, move the pointer or your finger over the white drawing area, then drag down and to the right, to draw a triangle similar to the one in FIGURE 1-17**

   The white drawing area is called the **canvas**.

3. **In the Shapes group, click or tap ⤓, click the down scroll arrow if necessary, click or tap the Five-point star button, click or tap the Indigo color button ▣ in the Colors group, then drag a star shape near the triangle, using FIGURE 1-17 as a guide**

   Don't be concerned if your object isn't exactly like the one in the figure, or in exactly the same place.

4. **Click or tap the Fill with color button ▨ in the Tools group, click or tap the Light turquoise color button ▣ in the Colors group, click or tap inside the triangle, click or tap the Purple color button ▣, click or tap inside the star, then compare your drawing to FIGURE 1-17**

5. **Click or tap the Select list arrow in the Image group, then click or tap Select all, as shown in FIGURE 1-18**

   The Select all command selects the entire drawing, as indicated by the dotted line surrounding the white drawing area. Other commands on this menu let you select individual elements or change your selection.

6. **Click or tap the Rotate button in the Image group, then click or tap Rotate 180°**

   You often need to use multiple commands to perform an action—in this case, you used one command to select the items you wanted to work with, and another command to rotate them.

7. **Click or tap the File tab, then click or tap Print**

   The Print dialog box opens, as shown in FIGURE 1-19. This dialog box lets you choose a printer, specify which part of your document or drawing you want to print, and choose how many copies you want to print. The **default**, or automatically selected, number of copies is 1, which is what you want.

8. **Click or tap Print, or if you prefer not to print, click or tap Cancel**

   The drawing prints on your printer. You decide to close the app without saving your drawing.

9. **Click or tap the File tab, click or tap Exit, then click or tap Don't Save**

   You closed the file without saving your changes, then exited the app. Most apps include a command for closing a document without exiting the program. However, Paint allows you to open only one document at a time, so it does not include a Close command.

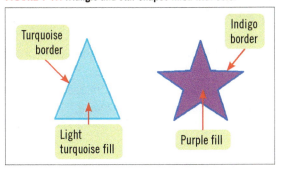

FIGURE 1-17: Triangle and star shapes filled with color

Turquoise border

Indigo border

Light turquoise fill

Purple fill

FIGURE 1-18: Select menu options

Select list arrow

Select menu

Select all command

FIGURE 1-19: Print dialog box

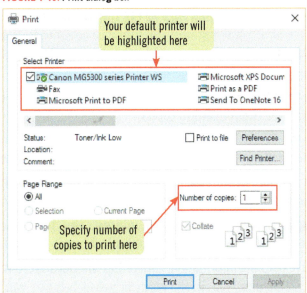

Your default printer will be highlighted here

Specify number of copies to print here

TABLE 1-5: Common dialog box controls

element	example	description
Text box	1 - 27	A box in which you type text or numbers
Spin box	1	A box with up and down arrows; you can click or tap arrows or type to increase or decrease value
Option button	◉	A small circle you click or tap to select the option; only one in a set can be selected at once
Check box	☐ ☑	A small box that turns an option on when checked or off when unchecked; more than one in a set can be selected at once
List box		A box that lets you select from a list of options
Button	Save	A button you click or tap to issue a command

Get Help

Learning Outcomes
- Explore the Getting Started app
- Search for Windows help using Cortana

As you use Windows 10, you might feel ready to learn more about it, or you might have a problem and need some advice. You can use the Windows 10 Getting Started app to learn more about help options. You can also search for help using Cortana, which you activate by using the search box on the taskbar. **CASE** ▷ *You explore Windows 10 help using the Get Started app and Cortana.*

STEPS

Note: Because Help in an online resource, topics and information are liable to change over time. If your screen choices do not match the steps below exactly, be flexible by exploring the options that are available to you and searching for the information you need.

1. Click or tap the Start button ⊞, then in the Explore Windows section click or tap the Get Started tile; if the Explore Windows section does not appear on your Start menu, begin typing Get Started, then click or tap Get Started Trusted Windows Store app in the list

   The Get Started app window opens. The window contains a menu expand button ☰ in the upper left and a bar containing buttons on the left side.

2. Click or tap the Menu Expand button ☰, move the pointer over the list of topics, then scroll down to see the remaining topics

3. Click or tap the Search and help topic, click the Search for anything, anywhere tile, then read the information, as shown in **FIGURE 1-20**, scrolling as necessary

4. Click or tap the Back button ← in the top-left corner of the window, click the Search for help tile, then read the Search for help topic and watch any available videos

5. Click or tap ☰, click or tap a topic that interests you, then read the information or click or tap one of the tiles representing a subtopic if one is available

QUICK TIP
Depending on your current settings, the prompt text in the search box reads, "Ask me anything" or "Search the web and Windows."

6. After you have read the information, click or tap the Get started window's Close button ☒

   As the Help topic explained, you can also search the web for help with Windows using Cortana.

7. Click in the search box on the taskbar, then type windows help

   As you type, Cortana begins a search, and shows results on the Start menu. See **FIGURE 1-21**. Your results may also include topics from the Microsoft Store, the web, Store apps, and OneDrive, your online storage location.

QUICK TIP
You learn more about OneDrive in Module 2.

8. Click any web option that interests you

9. When you are finished, click or tap the window's Close button ☒ to return to the desktop

FIGURE 1-20: Get Started Search and Help topic

Menu Expand button →

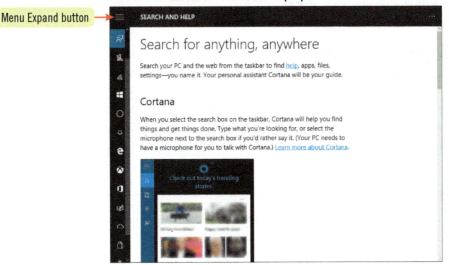

FIGURE 1-21: Search results information

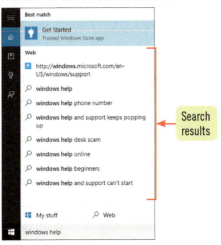

Search results

Using Cortana

Cortana is the digital personal assistant that comes with Windows 10 and Windows phones. You can interact with Cortana typing or using your voice. Use Cortana to search the web, remind you of events or appointments, set alarms, change computer settings, get directions, get current news and weather, track airline flights, play, and even identify music. **FIGURE 1-22** shows Cortana's response to "What's the weather in New York?" which may also give a voice response. You call Cortana by saying, "Hey Cortana," or by clicking or tapping the microphone icon on the right side of the taskbar search box, and then asking a question or saying a command. Depending on your request, Cortana may reply out loud, display results in the Start menu, or display results in a Microsoft Edge web browser window. You may need to set up Cortana on your computer and answer security questions before you use it. The first time you use Cortana, you may be asked to answer questions to help the assistant recognize your voice or solve issues with your computer's microphone.

FIGURE 1-22: Using Cortana to check the weather

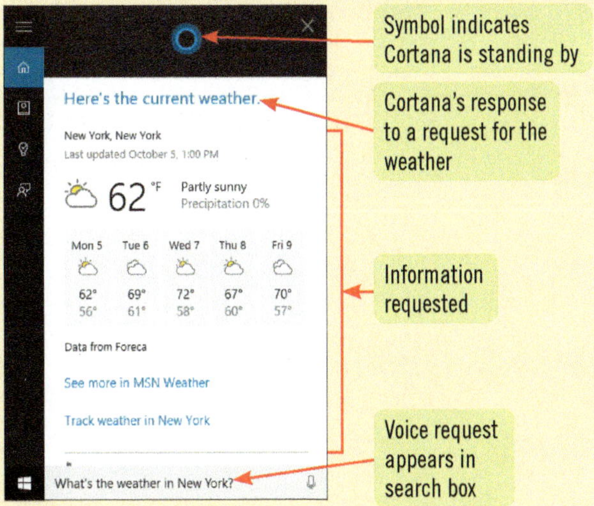

Symbol indicates Cortana is standing by

Cortana's response to a request for the weather

Information requested

Voice request appears in search box

Exit Windows 10

Learning Outcomes
- Exit Windows and shut down

When you finish working on your computer, you should close any open files, exit any open apps, close any open windows, and exit (or **shut down**) Windows 10. TABLE 1-6 shows options for ending your Windows 10 sessions. Whichever option you choose, it's important to shut down your computer in an orderly way. If you turn off or unplug the computer while Windows 10 is running, you could lose data or damage Windows 10 and your computer. If you are working in a computer lab, follow your instructor's directions and your lab's policies for ending your Windows 10 session. **CASE** *You have examined the basic ways you can use Windows 10, so you are ready to end your Windows 10 session.*

STEPS

QUICK TIP
Instead of shutting down, you may be instructed to sign out, or log out, of your Microsoft account. Click or tap Start, click or tap your account name, then click or tap Sign out.

QUICK TIP
If you are using a Windows 10 tablet, press the lock button on your tablet to bring up the lock screen, swipe the lock screen, then click or tap the Shut down button to power off your computer.

1. **Click or tap the Start button ⊞, then click or tap Power**

   The Power button menu lists shut down options, as shown in FIGURE 1-23.

2. **If you are working in a computer lab, follow the instructions provided by your instructor or technical support person for ending your Windows 10 session; if you are working on your own computer, click or tap Shut down or the option you prefer for ending your Windows 10 session**

3. **After you shut down your computer, you may also need to turn off your monitor and other hardware devices, such as a printer, to conserve energy**

FIGURE 1-23: Shutting down your computer

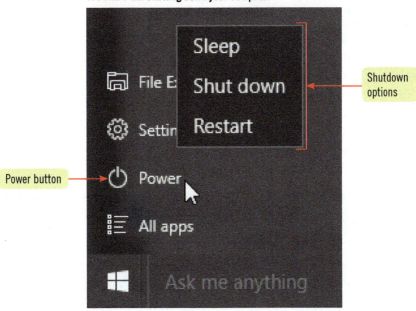

Shutdown options

Power button

TABLE 1-6: Power options

option	description
Sleep	Puts computer in a low-power state while keeping any open apps open so you can return immediately to where you left off
Shut down	Closes any open apps and completely turns off the computer
Restart	Closes any open apps, shuts down the computer, then restarts it

Installing updates when you exit Windows

Sometimes, after you shut down your machine, you might find that your machine does not shut down immediately. Instead, Windows might install software updates. If you see an option on your Power menu that lets you update, you can click or tap it to update your software. If you see a window indicating that updates are being installed, do not unplug or press the power switch to turn off your machine. Let the updates install completely. After the updates are installed, your computer will shut down, as you originally requested.

Practice

Concepts Review

Label the elements of the Windows 10 window shown in FIGURE 1-24.

FIGURE 1-24

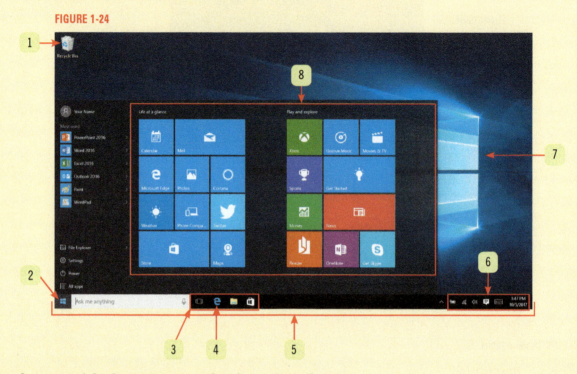

Match each term with the statement that best describes it.

9. Cortana
10. Snap Assist
11. Desktop app
12. Microsoft account
13. User interface
14. Operating system
15. Windows app

a. A special area of the operating system where your files and settings are stored
b. Controls that let you interact with an operating system
c. The personal digital assistant in Windows 10
d. Full-featured program that is installed on a personal computer
e. Feature that displays windows at full height next to each other on the screen
f. Available from the Windows store, it runs on Windows laptops, tablets, and phones
g. A program necessary to run your computer

Select the best answer from the list of choices.

16. The bar containing buttons and other elements at the bottom of the Windows 10 desktop is called the _____.
    a. title bar
    b. address bar
    c. scroll bar
    d. taskbar

17. Paint is an example of a(n) _____.
    a. group
    b. accessory
    c. active window
    d. operating system

18. **Which of the following is in the upper-left corner of a program window, and lets you perform common actions?**

   a. Application program

   b. Quick Access toolbar

   c. Operating system

   d. Accessory program

19. **The new Microsoft web browser is called Microsoft _____.**

   a. Paint

   b. WordPad

   c. Edge

   d. File Explorer

Skills Review

1. **Start Windows 10.**
   a. If your computer and monitor are not running, press your computer's and (if necessary) your monitor's power buttons.
   b. If necessary, select the user name that represents your user account.
   c. Enter your password, using correct uppercase and lowercase letters.

2. **Navigate the desktop and Start menu.**
   a. Examine the Windows 10 desktop.
   b. Open the Start menu.
   c. Display all the apps using a command on the Start menu, and scroll the list.
   d. Return to the Start menu.
   e. Close the Start menu.

3. **Point, click, and drag.**
   a. On the Windows 10 desktop, click or tap to select the Recycle Bin.
   b. Point to display the ScreenTip for Microsoft Edge in the taskbar, and then display the ScreenTip for each of the other icons on the taskbar.
   c. Double-click or double-tap to open the Recycle Bin window, then close it.
   d. Drag the Recycle Bin to a different corner of the screen, then drag it back to its original location.
   e. Click or tap the Date and Time area to display the calendar and clock, then click or tap it again to close it.

4. **Start an app.**
   a. Open the Start menu, then start the Maps app. (If asked to allow Windows to access your location, do so if you like.)
   b. Click or tap the icons on the left side of the Maps app window and observe the effect of each one.
   c. Close the Maps app.
   d. Reopen the Start menu, then type and click or tap to locate and open the Sticky Notes accessory.
   e. Click or tap the Sticky Notes Close button, clicking or tapping Yes to delete the note.
   f. Open the Weather Windows app.

5. **Work with a window.**
   a. Minimize the Weather window, then use its taskbar button to redisplay the window.
   b. Use the Weather app window's scroll bar or swiping to view the information in the lower part of the window, and then scroll or swipe up to display the top of it. (*Hint*: You need to move the pointer over the Weather app window, or swipe it, in order to display the scroll bar.)
   c. Click or tap the menu expand button, then click Historical Weather.
   d. Read the contents of the window, then click or tap two other menu buttons and read the contents.
   e. Maximize the Weather window, then restore it down.

6. **Manage multiple windows.**
   a. Leaving the Weather app open, go to the Start menu and type to locate the Paint app, open Paint, then restore down the Paint window if necessary.
   b. Click or tap to make the Weather app window the active window.
   c. Click or tap to make the Paint window the active window.
   d. Minimize the Paint window.

Skills Review (continued)

e. Drag the Weather app window so it's in the middle of the screen.

f. Redisplay the Paint window.

g. Drag the Paint window so it automatically fills the right side of the screen.

FIGURE 1-25

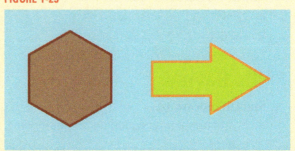

h. Click or tap the Weather app window image so it snaps to the left side of the screen.

i. Close the Weather app window, maximize the Paint window, then restore down the Paint window.

7. Use buttons, menus, and dialog boxes.

a. In the Paint window, draw a Dark red Hexagon shape, similar to the one shown in **FIGURE 1-25**.

b. Use the Fill with color button to fill the hexagon with a brown color.

c. Draw an Orange right arrow to the right of the hexagon shape, using the figure as a guide.

d. Use the Fill with color button to fill the orange arrow with a lime color.

e. Fill the drawing background with Light turquoise color, as shown in the figure.

f. Use the Select list arrow and menu to select the entire drawing, then use the Rotate command to rotate the drawing 180°.

g. Open the Print dialog box, print a copy of the picture if you wish, then close the Paint app without saving the drawing.

8. Get help.

a. Open the Get Started app, then use the menu expand button to display the available help topics.

b. Use the Menu button to display help for Cortana.

c. Click or tap a tile representing a Cortana help topic that interests you, read the help text, scrolling or swiping as necessary.

d. Display the Search and Help topic, then close the Get Started window.

e. In the search box on the taskbar, type Help Microsoft Account, then click the help Microsoft account result to search the web.

f. In the Microsoft Edge browser window, select a help topic that interests you, read the information (ignore any commercial offers), then click or tap the Microsoft Edge window's Close button.

9. Exit Windows 10.

a. Sign out of your account, or shut down your computer using the Shut down command in the Start menu's Power command or the preferred command for your work or school setting.

b. Turn off your monitor if necessary.

Independent Challenge 1

You work for Chicago Instruments, a manufacturer of brass instruments. The company ships instruments and supplies to music stores and musicians in the United States and Canada. The owner, Emerson, wants to know an easy way for his employees to learn about the new features of Windows 10, and he has asked you to help.

a. Start your computer if necessary, sign in to Windows 10, then use the search text box to search for **what's new in Windows 10**.

b. Click or tap the Search the web link in the Best match section at the top of the Help menu, then in the Microsoft Edge browser window, click or tap a search result that interests you.

c. Open the Getting Started app and review the new features listed there.

d. Using pencil and paper, or the Notepad accessory if you wish, write a short memo to Emerson summarizing, in your own words, three important new features in Windows 10. If you use Notepad to write the memo, use the Print button to print the document, then use the Exit command on the File tab to close Notepad without saving your changes to the document.

Independent Challenge 1 (continued)

e. Close the browser window, then sign out of your account, or shut down your computer using the preferred command for your work or school setting. Turn off your monitor if necessary.

Independent Challenge 2

You are the new manager of Katharine Anne's Garden Supplies, a business that supplies garden tools to San Diego businesses. Some of their tools are from Europe and show metric sizes. For her American customers, Katharine Anne wants to do a simple calculation and then convert the result to inches.

a. Start your computer and log on to Windows 10 if necessary, then type to locate the Windows app called Calculator, and start it.

b. Click or tap to enter the number 96 on the Calculator.

c. Click or tap the division sign (÷) button.

d. Click or tap the number 4.

e. Click or tap the equals sign button (=), and write down the result shown in the Calculator window. (*Hint*: The result should be 24.)

f. Select the menu expand button in the Calculator window, then under CONVERTER, select Length.

g. Enter 24 centimeters, and observe the equivalent length in inches.

h. Start Notepad, write a short memo about how Calculator can help you convert metric measurements to inches and feet, print the document using the Print command on the File tab, then exit Notepad without saving.

i. Close the Calculator, then sign out of your account, or shut down your computer using the preferred command for your work or school setting. Turn off your monitor if necessary.

Independent Challenge 3

You are the office manager for Erica's Pet Shipping, a service business in Dallas, Texas, that specializes in air shipping of cats and dogs across the United States and Canada. It's important to know the temperature in the destination city, so the animals won't be in danger from extreme temperatures when they are unloaded from the aircraft. Erica has asked you to find a way to easily monitor temperatures in destination cities. You decide to use a Windows app so you can see current temperatures in Celsius on your desktop. (Note: To complete the steps below, your computer must be connected to the Internet.)

a. Start your computer and sign in to Windows 10 if necessary, then on the Start menu, click or tap the Weather tile.

b. Click or tap the Search icon in the location text box, then type **Toronto**.

c. Select Toronto, Ontario, Canada, in the drop-down list to view the weather for Toronto.

d. Search on and select another location that interests you.

e. Close the app.

f. Open Notepad, write Erica a memo outlining how you can use the Windows Weather app to help keep pets safe, print the memo if you wish, close Notepad, then sign out, or shut down your computer.

Independent Challenge 4: Explore

Cortana, the Windows 10 personal digital assistant, can help you with everyday tasks. In this Independent Challenge, you explore one of the ways you can use Cortana.

a. Click or tap the microphone icon, to the right of the search box in the Windows 10 taskbar, to activate Cortana and display its menu. (*Note*: If you have not used Cortana before, you will not see the microphone icon until you answer some preliminary questions and verify your user account; you may also need to first help Cortana to understand your speaking voice.) Cortana displays a pulsating circle, indicating that she is listening for speech, and then shows you a greeting and some general information.

Independent Challenge 4: Explore (continued)

FIGURE 1-26

b. In the list of icons on the left side of the menu, click the menu expand button to show the names of each one, as shown in **FIGURE 1-26**.

c. Click or tap the Reminders button, then click the plus sign at the bottom of the menu. Click or tap Remember to…, then enter information for a to-do item, such as "Walk the dog." Click or tap the time box and use the spin boxes to set the time for one or two minutes from now. Click or tap the check mark, then click Remind to set the reminder. Click or tap the Reminders icon again to see your reminder listed, then click the desktop. When the reminder appears, click Complete.

d. Click or tap the microphone icon again, and when you see the pulsating circle, speak into your computer microphone and tell Cortana to remind you to do something in one minute. Click or tap Remind, then close the Cortana window. When the reminder appears, click or tap Complete.

e. Click or tap the Close button on the Cortana menu, then sign out of your account, or shut down your computer.

Visual Workshop

Using the skills you've learned in this module, open and arrange elements on your screen so it looks similar to **FIGURE 1-27**. Note the position of the Recycle Bin, and the size and location of the Notepad and Weather app windows, as well as the city shown. In Notepad, write a paragraph summarizing how you used pointing, clicking (or tapping), and dragging to make your screen look like the figure. Print your work if you wish, close Notepad and the Weather app without saving changes, then sign out or shut down your computer.

FIGURE 1-27

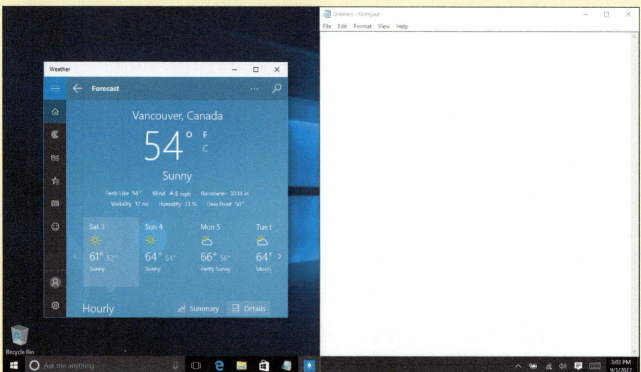

Understanding File Management

CASE ▸ Now that you are familiar with the Windows 10 operating system, your new employer has asked you to become familiar with **file management**, or how to create, save, locate and delete the files you create with Windows apps. You begin by reviewing how files are organized on your computer, and then begin working with files you create in the WordPad app. *Note: With the release of Windows 10, Microsoft now provides ongoing updates to Windows instead of releasing new versions periodically. This means that Windows features might change over time, including how they look and how you interact with them. The information provided in this text was accurate at the time this book was published.*

Module Objectives

After completing this module, you will be able to:

- Understand files and folders
- Create and save a file
- Explore the files and folders on your computer
- Change file and folder views

- Open, edit, and save files
- Copy files
- Move and rename files
- Search for files and folders
- Delete and restore files

Files You Will Need

No files needed.

Understand Files and Folders

Learning Outcomes
- Analyze a file hierarchy
- Examine files and folders

As you work with apps, you create and save files, such as letters, drawings, or budgets. When you save files, you usually save them inside folders to help keep them organized. The files and folders on your computer are organized in a **file hierarchy**, a system that arranges files and folders in different levels, like the branches of a tree. FIGURE 2-1 shows a sample file hierarchy. **CASE** ⟩ *You decide to use folders and files to organize the information on your computer.*

DETAILS

Use the following guidelines as you organize files using your computer's file hierarchy:

- ### Use folders and subfolders to organize files

  As you work with your computer, you can add folders to your hierarchy and name them to help you organize your work. As you've learned, folders are storage areas in which you can group related files. You should give folders unique names that help you easily identify them. You can also create **subfolders**, which are folders that are inside other folders. Windows 10 comes with several existing folders, such as Documents, Music, Pictures, and Videos, that you can use as a starting point.

QUICK TIP

When you open File Explorer, you see a list of recently opened files and frequently used folders in the Quick Access area that helps you go directly to files and locations.

- ### View and manage files in File Explorer

  You can view and manage your computer contents using a built-in program called **File Explorer**, shown in FIGURE 2-2. A File Explorer window is divided into **panes**, or sections. The **Navigation pane** on the left side of the window shows the folder structure on your computer. When you click a folder in the Navigation pane, you see its contents in the **File list** on the right side of the window. To open File Explorer from the desktop, click the File Explorer button 📁 on the taskbar. To open it from the Start menu, click the File Explorer shortcut.

QUICK TIP

The name "File Explorer" only appears in the title bar when you first open it. As you navigate, you'll see the current folder name instead.

- ### Understand file addresses

  A window also contains an **Address bar**, an area just below the Ribbon that shows the address, or location, of the files that appear in the File list. An **address** is a sequence of folder names, separated by the ⟩ symbol, which describes a file's location in the file hierarchy. An address shows the folder with the highest hierarchy level on the left and steps through each hierarchy level toward the right; this is sometimes called a **path**. For example, the Documents folder might contain subfolders named Work and Personal. If you clicked the Personal folder in the File list, the Address bar would show Documents ⟩ Personal. Each location between the ⟩ symbols represents a level in the file hierarchy. If you see a file path written out, you'll most likely see it with backslashes. For example, in FIGURE 2-1, if you wanted to write the path to the Brochure file, you would write "Documents\Reason2Go\Marketing\Brochure.xlsx. File addresses might look complicated if they may have many levels, but they are helpful because they always describe the exact location of a file or folder in a file hierarchy.

QUICK TIP

Remember that in the Address bar and Navigation pane you single-click a folder or subfolder to show its contents, but in the File list you double-click it.

- ### Navigate up and down using the Address bar and File list

  You can use the Address bar and the File list to move up or down in the hierarchy one or more levels at a time. To **navigate up** in your computer's hierarchy, you can click a folder or subfolder name to the left of the current folder name in the Address bar. For example, in FIGURE 2-2, you can move up in the hierarchy three levels by clicking once on This PC in the Address bar. Then the File list would show the subfolders and files inside the This PC folder. To **navigate down** in the hierarchy, double-click a subfolder in the File list. The path in the Address bar then shows the path to that subfolder.

- ### Navigate up and down using the Navigation pane

  You can also use the Navigation pane to navigate among folders. Move the mouse pointer over the Navigation pane, then click the small arrows to the left of a folder name to show ⟩ or hide ⌄ the folder's contents under the folder name. Subfolders appear indented under the folders that contain them, showing that they are inside that folder.

FIGURE 2-1: Sample folder and file hierarchy

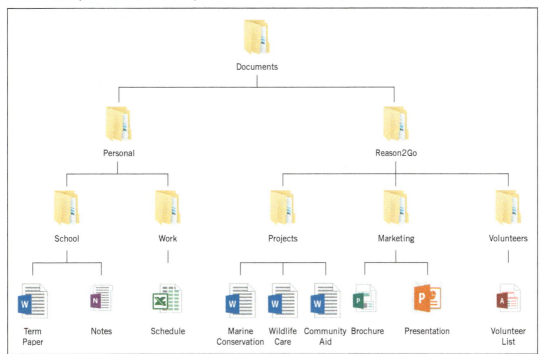

FIGURE 2-2: File Explorer window

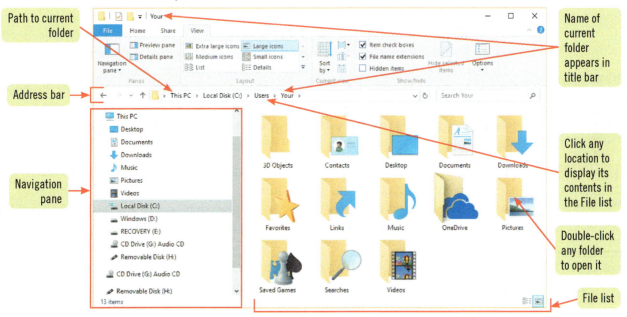

Plan your file organization

As you manage your files, you should plan how you want to organize them. First, identify the types of files you work with, such as images, music, and documents. Think about the content, such as personal, business, clients, or projects. Then think of a folder organization that will help you find them later. For example, you can use subfolders in the Pictures folder to separate family photos from business photos or to group them by location or by month. In the Documents folder, you might group personal files in one subfolder and business files in another subfolder. Then create additional subfolders to further separate sets of files. You can always move files among folders and rename folders. You should periodically reevaluate your folder structure to make sure it continues to meet your needs.

Create and Save a File

After you start a program and create a new file, the file exists only in your computer's **random access memory (RAM)**, a temporary storage location. RAM contains information only when your computer is on. When you turn off your computer, it automatically clears the contents of RAM. So you need to save a new file onto a storage device that permanently stores the file so you can open, change, and use it later. One important storage device is your computer's hard drive built into your computer. You might want to store your files online in an online storage location like Microsoft OneDrive. Or you might use a **USB flash drive**, a small, portable storage device that you plug into a USB port on your computer. **CASE** *You create a document, then save it.*

STEPS

1. **Click or tap the Start button, then type** word
   Available apps with "word" in their names are listed. See **FIGURE 2-3**.

2. **Click the** WordPad Desktop app listing**, then maximize the WordPad window if necessary**
   Near the top of the WordPad window you see the Ribbon containing buttons, similar to those you used in Paint in Module 1. The Home tab appears in front. A new, blank document appears in the document window. The blinking insertion point shows you where the next character you type will appear.

3. **Type** Company Overview**, then press** [Enter] **twice, type** Conservation**, press** [Enter]**, type** Community Work**, press** [Enter]**, type** Research**, press** [Enter] **twice, then type your name**
   See **FIGURE 2-4**.

4. **Click the** File tab**, then click** Save
   The first time you save a file using the Save button, the Save As dialog box opens. You use this dialog box to name the file and choose a storage location for it. The Save As dialog box has many of the same elements as a File Explorer window, including an Address bar, a Navigation pane, and a File list. Below the Address bar, the **toolbar** contains buttons you can click to perform actions. In the Address bar, you can see the Documents folder, which is the **default**, or automatically selected, storage location. But you can easily change it.

5. **If you are saving to a USB flash drive, plug the drive into a USB port on your computer, if necessary**

6. **In the Navigation pane scroll bar, click the** down scroll arrow ✔ **as needed to see This PC and any storage devices listed under it**
   Under This PC, you see the storage locations available on your computer, such as Local Disk (C:) (your hard drive) and Removable Disk (H:) (your USB drive name and letter might differ). Above This PC, you might see your OneDrive listed. These storage locations are like folders in that you can open them and store files in them.

7. **Click the name of your USB flash drive, or the folder where you store your Data Files**
   The files and folders in the location you chose, if any, appear in the File list. The Address bar shows the location where the file will be saved, which is now Removable Disk (H:) or the name of the location you clicked. You need to give your document a meaningful name so you can find it later.

8. **Click in the** File name text box **to select the default name** Document.rtf**, type** Company Overview**, compare your screen to** FIGURE 2-5**, then click** Save
   The document is saved as a file on your USB flash drive. The filename Company Overview.rtf appears in the title bar. The ".rtf" at the end of the filename is the file extension that Windows added automatically. A **file extension** is a three- or four-letter sequence, preceded by a period, which identifies a file to your computer, in this case **Rich Text Format**. The WordPad program creates files in RTF format.

9. **Click the** Close button ✕ **on the WordPad window**
   The WordPad program closes. Your Company Overview document is now saved in the location you specified.

FIGURE 2-3: Results at top of Start menu

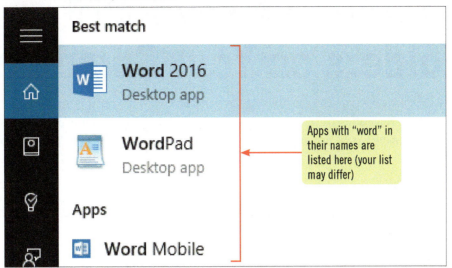

Apps with "word" in their names are listed here (your list may differ)

FIGURE 2-4: WordPad document

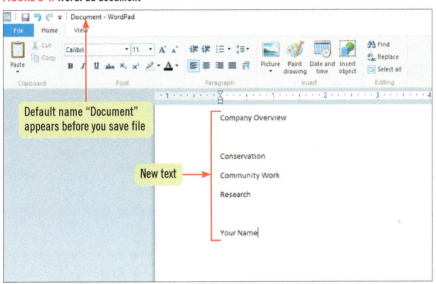

Default name "Document" appears before you save file

New text

Company Overview

Conservation

Community Work

Research

Your Name

FIGURE 2-5: Save As dialog box

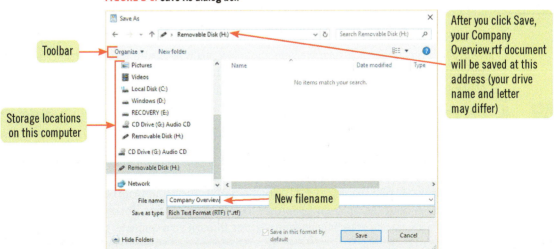

Toolbar

Storage locations on this computer

New filename

After you click Save, your Company Overview.rtf document will be saved at this address (your drive name and letter may differ)

Explore the Files and Folders on Your Computer

In a File Explorer window, you can navigate through your computer contents using the File list, the Address bar, and the Navigation pane. Examining your computer and its existing folder and file structure helps you decide where to save files as you work with Windows 10 apps. **CASE** *In preparation for organizing documents at your new job, you look at the files and folders on your computer.*

STEPS

1. **At the Windows desktop, click the File Explorer button** 📁 **on the taskbar, then in the File Explorer Navigation pane, click This PC**

TROUBLE

If you don't see the colored bars, click the View tab, click Tiles in the Layout group.

2. **If you do not see a band of buttons near the top of the window, double-click the View tab**

The band containing buttons is called the **Ribbon**. Your computer's storage devices appear in a window, as shown in **FIGURE 2-6**. These include hard drives; devices with removable storage, such as CD and DVD drives or USB flash drives; portable devices such as smartphones or tablets; and any network storage locations. Colored bars shows you how much space has been taken up on your drives. You decide to move down a level in your computer's hierarchy and see what is on your USB flash drive.

3. **In the File list, double-click Removable Disk (H:) (or the drive name and letter for your USB flash drive)**

You see the contents of your USB flash drive, including the Company Overview.rtf file you saved in the last lesson. You decide to navigate one level up in the file hierarchy.

TROUBLE

If you do not have a USB flash drive, click the Documents folder instead.

4. **In the Address bar, click This PC, or if This PC does not appear, click the far-left address bar arrow** ⟩ **in the Address bar, then click This PC**

You return to the This PC window showing your storage locations.

5. **In the File list, double-click Local Disk (C:)**

The contents of your hard drive appear in the File list.

6. **In the File list, double-click the Users folder**

The Users folder contains a subfolder for each user account on this computer. You might see a folder with your user account name on it. Each user's folder contains that person's documents. User folder names are the names that were used to log in when your computer was set up. When a user logs in, the computer allows that user access to the folder with the same user name. If you are using a computer with more than one user, you might not have permission to view other users' folders. There is also a Public folder that any user can open.

7. **Double-click the folder with your user name on it**

Depending on how your computer is set up, this folder might be labeled with your name; however, if you are using a computer in a lab or a public location, your folder might be called Student or Computer User or something similar. You see a list of folders, such as Documents, Music, and OneDrive. See **FIGURE 2-7**.

QUICK TIP

In the Address bar, you can click ⟩ to the right of a folder name to see a list of its subfolders; if the folder is open, its name appears in bold in the list.

8. **Double-click Documents in the File list**

In the Address bar, the path to the Documents folder is This PC ⟩ Local Disk (C:) ⟩ Users ⟩ *Your User Name* ⟩ Documents.

9. **In the Navigation pane, click This PC**

You once again see your computer's storage locations. You can also move up one level at a time in your file hierarchy by clicking the Up arrow ⬆ on the toolbar, or by pressing [Backspace] on your keyboard. See **TABLE 2-1** for a summary of techniques for navigating through your computer's file hierarchy.

FIGURE 2-6: File Explorer window showing storage locations

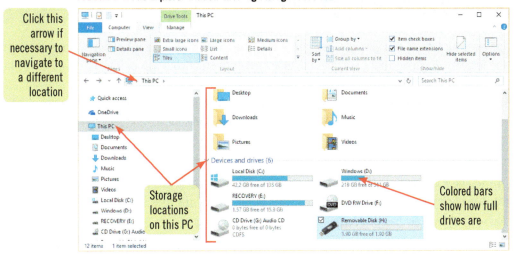

Click this arrow if necessary to navigate to a different location

Storage locations on this PC

Colored bars show how full drives are

FIGURE 2-7: Your user name folder

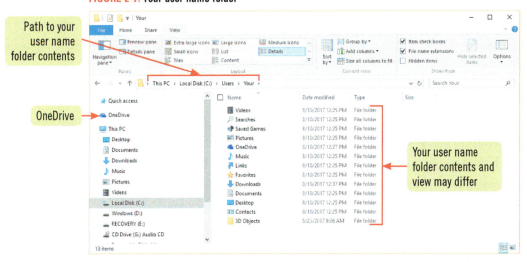

Path to your user name folder contents

OneDrive

Your user name folder contents and view may differ

TABLE 2-1: Navigating your computer's file hierarchy

to do this	Navigation pane	Address bar	File list	keyboard
Move up in hierarchy	Click a drive or folder name	Click an item to the left of ▸ or Click the **Up to** button ↑		Press [**Backspace**]
Move down in hierarchy	Click a drive or folder name that is indented from the left	Click an item to the right of ▸	Double-click a folder	Press ↑ or ↓ to select a folder, then press [**Enter**] to open the selected folder
Return to previously viewed location		Click the **Back to** button ← or **Forward** button →		

Using and disabling Quick Access view

When you first open File Explorer, you see a list of frequently-used folders and recently used files, called Quick access view. Quick Access view can save you time by giving you one-click access to files and folders you use a lot. If you want File Explorer to open instead to This PC, you can disable Quick Access View. To do this, open a File Explorer window, click the View tab, click the Options button on the right side of the Ribbon, then click Change folder and search options. On the General tab of the Folder Options dialog box, click the Open File Explorer to list arrow, click This PC, then click OK.

Windows 10
Module 2

Change File and Folder Views

Learning Outcomes

- View files as large icons
- Sort files
- Preview files

As you view your folders and files, you can customize your **view**, which is a set of appearance choices for files and folders. Changing your view does not affect the content of your files or folders, only the way they appear. You can choose from eight different **layouts** to display your folders and files as different sized icons, or as a list. You can change the order in which the folders and files appear, and you can also show a preview of a file in the window. **CASE** *You experiment with different views of your folders and files.*

STEPS

QUICK TIP
To expand your view of a location in the Navigation pane, click the Expand button [>] next to that location.

1. **In the File Explorer window's Navigation pane, click Local Disk (C:); in the File list double-click Users, then double-click the folder with your user name**
   You opened your user name folder, which is inside the Users folder.
2. **Click the View tab on the Ribbon if necessary, then if you don't see eight icons in the Layout list, click the More button [▼] in the Layout group**
   The list of available layouts appears, as shown in FIGURE 2-8.
3. **Click Extra large icons in the Layout list**
   In this view, the folder items appear as very large icons in the File list. This layout is especially helpful for image files, because you can see what the pictures are without opening each one.

QUICK TIP
You can scroll up and down in the Layout group to see views that are not currently visible.

4. **On the View tab, in the Layout list, point to the other layouts while watching the appearance of the File list, then click Details**
   In Details view, shown in FIGURE 2-9, you can see each item's name, the date it was modified, and its file type. It shows the size of any files in the current folder, but it does not show sizes for folders.
5. **Click the Sort by button in the Current view group**
   The Sort by menu lets you **sort**, or reorder, your files and folders according to several criteria.
6. **Click Descending if it is not already selected with a check mark**
   Now the folders are sorted in reverse alphabetical order.

QUICK TIP
Clicking Quick Access in the Navigation pane displays folders you use frequently; to add a folder or location to Quick Access, display it in the File list, then drag it to the Quick Access list.

7. **Click Removable Disk (H:) (or the location where you store your Data Files) in the Navigation pane, then click Company Overview.rtf in the File list**
8. **Click the Preview pane button in the Panes group on the View tab if necessary**
   A preview of the selected Company Overview.rtf file you created earlier appears in the Preview pane on the right side of the screen. The WordPad file is not open, but you can still see the file's contents. See FIGURE 2-10.
9. **Click the Preview pane button again to close the pane, then click the window's Close button [X]**

Using the Windows Action Center

The Windows Action Center lets you quickly view system notifications and selected computer settings. To open the Action Center, click the Notifications button on the right side of the taskbar. The Action Center pane opens on the right side of the screen. Any new notifications appear in the upper part of the pane, including messages about apps, Windows tips, and any reminders you may have set. In the lower part of the pane, you see Quick Action buttons, shown in FIGURE 2-11, for some commonly-used Windows settings. For example, click Note to open the OneNote app; click the Brightness button repeatedly to cycle though four brightness settings; click the Airplane mode button to place your computer in airplane mode, which turns off your computer's wireless transmission; click Quiet hours to silence your computer's notification sounds. Clicking the All settings button opens the Settings windows, where you can access all Windows settings categories. Note that the buttons available will vary depending on your hardware and software configuration.

FIGURE 2-11: Quick Action buttons

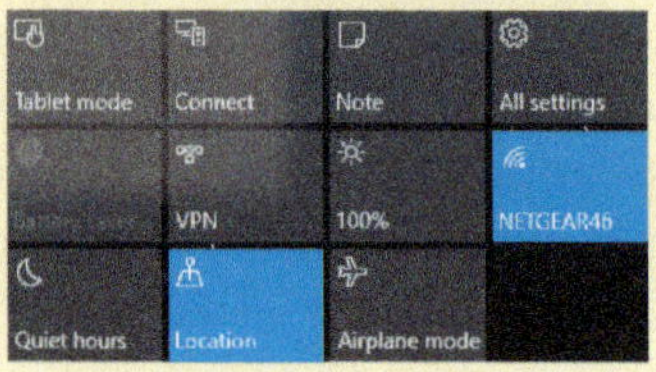

FIGURE 2-8: Layout options for viewing folders and files

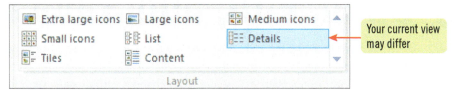

FIGURE 2-9: Your user name folder contents in Details view

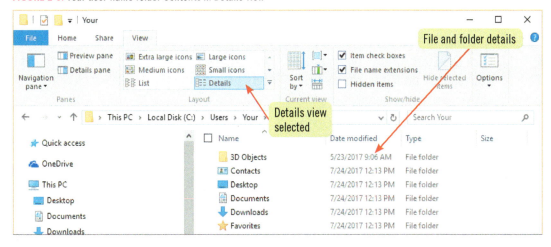

FIGURE 2-10: Preview of selected Company Overview.rtf file

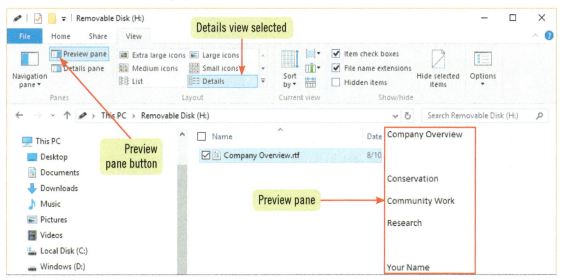

Customizing Details view

When you use File Explorer to view your computer contents in Details view, you see a list of the files and folders in that location. At the top of the list you see each item's Name, Size, Type, and Date Modified. If the list of file and folder details doesn't show what you need, you can customize it. To change a column's location, drag a column heading to move it quickly to a new position. To change the order of, or **sort**, your files and folders, click any column header to sort the list by that detail; click it a second time to reverse the order. To show only a selected group of, or **filter**, files, click the ☑ icon to the right of the Name, Size, Type, or Date Modified, column headers, and select the check boxes for the type of items you want to include. To change the kind of details you see, right-click or tap-hold a column heading in Details view, then click or tap the detail you want to show or hide. To see more details or to change the list order, right-click or tap-hold a column title, then click or tap More.

Open, Edit, and Save Files

Learning
Outcomes
• Open a file
• Edit a file
• Save a file

Once you have created a file and saved it with a name to a storage location, you can easily open it and **edit** (make changes to) it. For example, you might want to add or delete text or add a picture. Then you save the file again so the file contains your latest changes. Usually you save a file with the same filename and in the same location as the original, which replaces the existing file with the most up-to-date version. To save a file you have changed, you use the Save command. **CASE** ▶ *You need to complete the company overview list, so you need to open the new Company Overview file you created earlier.*

STEPS

QUICK TIP

When you double-click a file in a File Explorer window, the program currently associated with that file type opens the file; to change the program, right-click a file, click Open with, click Choose another app, click the program name, select the Always use this app to open [file type] files check box, then click OK.

1. **Click the Start button, begin typing wordpad, then click the WordPad program if it is not selected or, if it is, simply press [Enter]**

   The WordPad program opens on the desktop.

2. **Click the File tab, then click Open**

   The Open dialog box opens. It contains a Navigation pane and a File list like the Save As dialog box and the File Explorer window.

3. **Scroll down in the Navigation pane if necessary until you see This PC and the list of computer locations, then click Removable Disk (H:) (or the location where you store your Data Files)**

   The contents of your USB flash drive (or the file storage location you chose) appear in the File list, as shown in **FIGURE 2-12**.

QUICK TIP

You can also double-click a file in the File list to open it.

4. **Click Company Overview.rtf in the File list, then click Open**

   The document you created earlier opens.

5. **Click to the right of the "h" in Research, press [Enter], then type Outreach**

   The edited document includes the text you just typed. See **FIGURE 2-13**.

QUICK TIP

To save changes to a file, you can also click the Save button 💾 on the Quick Access toolbar (on the left side of the title bar).

6. **Click the File tab, then click Save, as shown in FIGURE 2-14**

   WordPad saves the document with your most recent changes, using the filename and location you specified when you previously saved it. When you save changes to an existing file, the Save As dialog box does not open.

7. **Click the File tab, then click Exit**

   The Company Overview document and the WordPad program close.

Comparing Save and Save As

Many apps, including Wordpad, include two save command options—Save and Save As. The first time you save a file, the Save As dialog box opens (whether you choose Save or Save As). Here you can select the drive and folder where you want to save the file and enter its filename. If you edit a previously saved file, you can save the file to the same location with the same file-name using the Save command. The Save command updates the stored file using the same location and filename without opening the Save As dialog box. In some situations, you might want to save a copy of the existing document using a different filename or in a different storage location. To do this, open the document, click the Save As command on the File tab, navigate to the location where you want to save the copy if necessary, and/or edit the name of the file.

Understanding File Management

FIGURE 2-12: Navigating in the Open dialog box

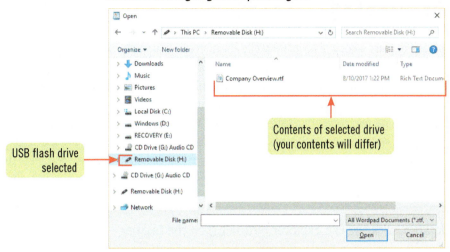

USB flash drive selected

Contents of selected drive (your contents will differ)

FIGURE 2-13: Edited document

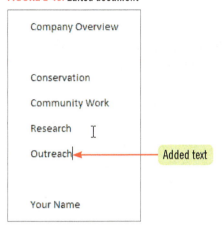

Added text

FIGURE 2-14: Saving the updated document

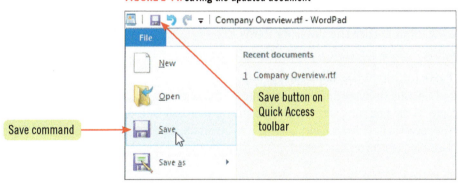

Save command

Save button on Quick Access toolbar

Using Microsoft OneDrive

Microsoft OneDrive is a location on the World Wide Web where you can store your files. Because OneDrive is an online location instead of a disk or USB device, it's often called a **cloud storage location**. When you store your files on OneDrive, you can access them from different devices, including laptops, tablets, and smartphones. Any changes you make to a file stored "in the cloud" are automatically made on OneDrive; this is known as **file syncing**. For example, if you make changes to a file from your laptop, and then open it on your tablet, you will see the changes. You can share OneDrive folders with others so they can view or edit files using a web browser such as Microsoft Edge or Internet Explorer. You can even have multiple users edit a document simultaneously. In Windows 10, OneDrive appears as a storage location in the navigation bar in File Explorer, and in the Open and Save As dialog boxes in Windows apps, so you can easily open, modify, and save files stored there. You can also download the free OneDrive Windows app from the Windows Store to help manage your OneDrive files from all your devices.

Understanding File Management

Copy Files

Sometimes you need to make a copy of an existing file. For example, you might want to put a copy on a USB flash drive so you can open the file on another machine or share it with a friend or colleague. Or you might want to create a copy as a **backup**, or replacement, in case something happens to your original file. You can copy files and folders using the Copy command and then place the copy in another location using the Paste command. You cannot have two copies of a file with the same name in the same folder. If you try to do this, Windows asks you if you want to replace the first one, and then gives you a chance to give the second copy a different name. **CASE** *You want to create a backup copy of the Company Overview document that you can store in a folder for company publicity items. First you need to create the folder, then you can copy the file.*

STEPS

1. **On the desktop, click the File Explorer button** 🖿 **on the taskbar**

2. **In the Navigation pane, click Removable Disk (H:) (or the location where you store your Data Files)**

   First you create the new folder you plan to use for storing publicity-related files.

3. **In the New group on the Home tab, click the New folder button**

   A new folder appears in the File list, with its default name, New folder, selected.

4. **Type Publicity Items, then press [Enter]**

   Because the folder name was selected, the text you typed, Publicity Items, replaced it. Pressing [Enter] confirmed your entry, and the folder is now named Publicity Items.

5. **In the File list, click the Company Overview.rtf document you saved earlier, then click the Copy button in the Clipboard group, as shown in FIGURE 2-15**

   After you select the file, its check box becomes selected (the check box appears only if the Item check boxes option in the Show/Hide group on the View tab is selected). When you use the Copy command, Windows places a duplicate copy of the file in an area of your computer's random access memory called the **clipboard**, ready to paste, or place, in a new location. Copying and pasting a file leaves the file in its original location.

6. **In the File list, double-click the Publicity Items folder**

   The folder opens. Nothing appears in the File list because the folder currently is empty.

7. **Click the Paste button in the Clipboard group**

   A copy of the Company Overview.rtf file is pasted into the Publicity Items folder. See **FIGURE 2-16**. You now have two copies of the Company Overview.rtf file: one on your USB flash drive in the main folder, and another in your new Publicity Items folder. The file remains on the clipboard until you end your Windows session or place another item on the clipboard.

Copying files using Send to

You can also copy and paste a file using the Send to command. In File Explorer, right-click the file you want to copy, point to Send to, then in the shortcut menu, click the name of the device you want to send a copy of the file to. This leaves the original file on your hard drive and creates a copy in that location. You can send a file to a compressed file, the desktop, your Documents folder, a mail recipient, or a drive on your computer. See **TABLE 2-2**.

FIGURE 2-15: Copying a file

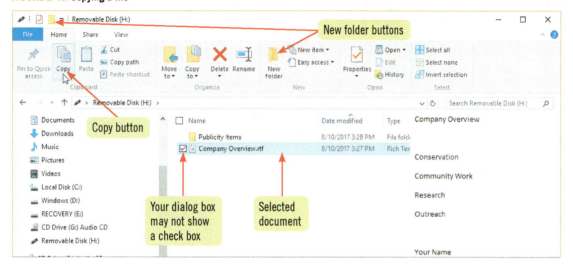

New folder buttons

Copy button

Your dialog box may not show a check box

Selected document

FIGURE 2-16: Duplicate file pasted into Publicity items folder

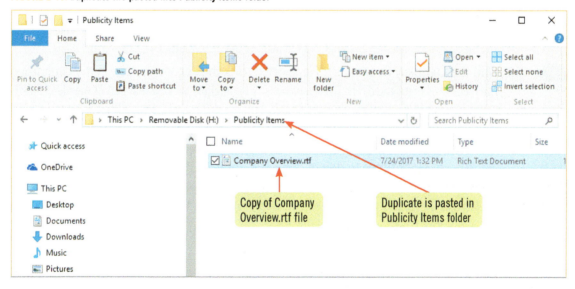

Copy of Company Overview.rtf file

Duplicate is pasted in Publicity Items folder

TABLE 2-2: Selected Send to menu commands

menu option	use to
Compressed (zipped) folder	Create a new, compressed (smaller) file with a .zip file extension
Desktop (create shortcut)	Create a shortcut (link) for the file on the desktop
Documents	Copy the file to the Documents library
Fax recipient	Send a file to a fax recipient
Mail recipient	Create an e-mail with the file attached to it (only if you have an e-mail program on your computer)
DVD RW Drive (D:)	Copy the file to your computer's DVD drive (your drive letter may differ)
CD Drive (G:) audio CD	Copy the file to your computer's CD drive (your drive letter may differ)
Removable Disk (H:)	Copy the file to a removable disk drive (your drive letter may differ)

Understanding File Management

Move and Rename Files

Learning Outcomes
• Cut and paste a file
• Rename a file

As you work with files, you might need to move files or folders to another location. You can move one or more files or folders at a time, and you can move them to a different folder on the same drive or to a different drive. When you **move** a file, the file is transferred to the new location, and unlike copying, it no longer exists in its original location. You can move a file using the Cut and Paste commands. Before or after you move a file, you might find that you want to change its name. You can easily rename it to make the name more descriptive or accurate. **CASE** *You decide to move your original Company Overview.rtf document to your Documents folder. After you move it, you edit the filename so it better describes the file contents.*

STEPS

1. **In the Address bar, click Removable Disk (H:) (or the name of the location where you store your Data Files) if necessary**

2. **Click the Company Overview.rtf document to select it**

3. **Click the Cut button in the Clipboard group on the Ribbon, as shown in FIGURE 2-17**

4. **In the Navigation Pane, under This PC, click Documents**
   You navigated to your Documents folder.

5. **Click the Paste button in the Clipboard group**
   The Company Overview.rtf document appears in your Documents folder and remains selected. See FIGURE 2-18. The filename could be clearer, to help you remember that it contains a list of company goals.

6. **With the Company Overview.rtf file selected, click the Rename button in the Organize group**
   The filename is highlighted. The file extension isn't highlighted because that part of the filename identifies the file to WordPad and should not be changed. If you deleted or changed the file extension, WordPad would be unable to open the file. You decide to change the word "Overview" to "Goals."

7. **Move the I pointer after the "w" in "Overview", click to place the insertion point, press [Backspace] eight times to delete Overview, type Goals as shown in FIGURE 2-19, then press [Enter]**
   You changed the name of the pasted file in the Documents folder. The filename now reads Company Goals.rtf.

8. **Close the File Explorer window**

Using Task View to create multiple desktops

As you have learned in Module 1, you can have multiple app windows open on your desktop, such as WordPad, Paint, and OneNote. But you might need to have a different set of apps available for a different project. Instead of closing all the apps and opening different ones, you can use Task View to work with multiple desktops, each containing its own set of apps. Then, when you need to work on another project, you can switch to another desktop to quickly access those apps. To open Task View, click the **Task View** button ▭ on the taskbar. The current desktop becomes smaller and a New desktop button appears in the lower-right corner of the screen. Click the New desktop button. A new desktop appears in a bar at the bottom of the screen, which you can click to activate and work with its

apps. See FIGURE 2-20. To switch to another desktop, click the Task View button and click its icon.

FIGURE 2-20: Working with multiple desktops in Task view

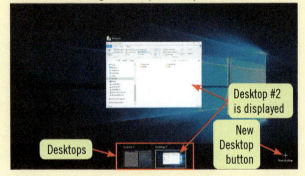

Desktop #2 is displayed

New Desktop button

Desktops

FIGURE 2-17: Cutting a file

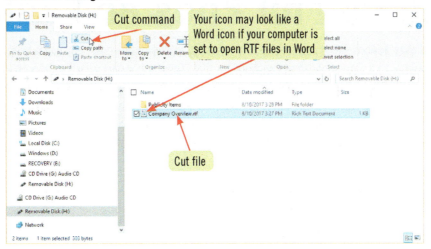

FIGURE 2-18: Pasted file in Documents folder

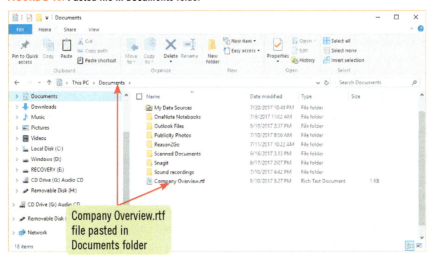

FIGURE 2-19: Renaming a file

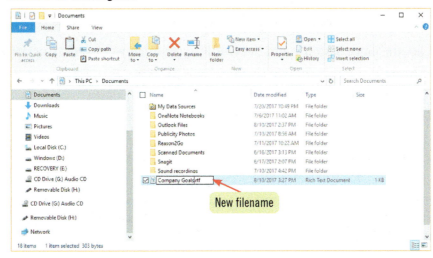

Windows 10

Search for Files and Folders

Learning Outcomes
• Search for a file
• Open a found file

Windows Search helps you quickly find any app, folder, or file. You can search from the Search box on the taskbar to locate applications, settings, or files. To search a particular location on your computer, you can use the Search box in File Explorer. You enter search text by typing one or more letter sequences or words that help Windows identify the item you want. The search text you type is called your **search criteria**. Your search criteria can be a folder name, a filename, or part of a filename. **CASE** *You want to locate the Company Overview.rtf document so you can print it for a colleague.*

STEPS

1. **Click in the search box on the taskbar**
   The Cortana menu opens.

2. **Type company**
   The Search menu opens with a possible match for your search at the top, and some other possible matches below it. You may see results from The Windows Store, the Internet, or your computer settings.

3. **Click My stuff, near the bottom of the menu**
   This limits your search to the files and folders in your storage locations on this device. It includes documents with the text "company" in the title or in the document text.

4. **Scroll down if necessary to display search results under This Device, including the Company Goals.rtf file you stored in your Documents folder**
   See **FIGURE 2-21**. It does not find the Company Overview.rtf file stored on your Flash drive because it's searching only the items on this device. To open the found file, you could click its listing. You can also search using File Explorer.

5. **Click the File Explorer button 🗂 on the taskbar, then click This PC in the Navigation pane**

6. **Click in the Search This PC box to the right of the Address bar, type company, then press [Enter]**
   Windows searches your computer for files that contain the word "company" in their title. A green bar in the Address bar indicates the progress of your search. After a few moments, the search results, shown in **FIGURE 2-22**, appear. Windows found the renamed file, Company Goals.rtf, in your Documents folder, and the original Company Overview.rtf document on your removable drive, in the Publicity Items folder. It may also locate shortcuts to the file in your Recent folder. It's good to verify the location of the found files, so you can select the right one.

7. **Click the View tab, click Details in the Layout group then look in the Folder column to view the path to each file, dragging the edge of the Folder column header with the ⇔ pointer to widen it if necessary**

8. **Double-click the Company Overview.rtf document in your file storage location**
   The file opens in WordPad or in another word-processing program on your computer that reads RTF files.

9. **Click the Close button ⊠ on the WordPad (or other word-processor) window**

Using the Search Tools tab in File Explorer

The **Search Tools tab** appears in the Ribbon as soon as you click the Search text box, and it lets you narrow your search criteria. Use the commands in the Location group to specify a particular search location. The Refine group lets you limit the search to files modified after a certain date, or to files of a particular kind, size, type, or other property. The Options group lets you repeat previous searches, save searches, and open the folder containing a found file.

FIGURE 2-21: Found file

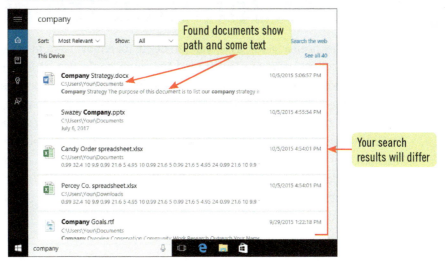

FIGURE 2-22: Apps screen and Search pane

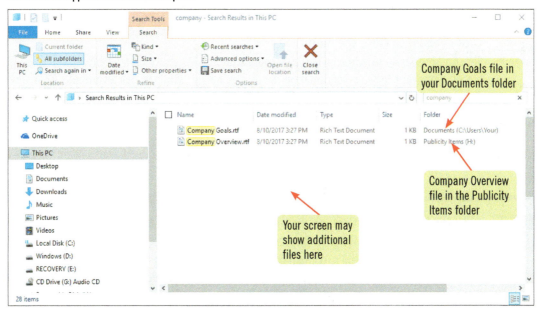

Using Microsoft Edge

When you search for files using the search box on the Windows taskbar and click Web, the new web browser called **Microsoft Edge** opens. You can also open Edge by clicking its icon  on the taskbar. Created to replace the older Internet Explorer browser, Edge is a Windows app that runs on personal computers, tablets, and smartphones. Edge features a reading mode that lets you read a webpage without ads. It also lets you annotate pages with markup tools such as a pen or highlighter, and add typed notes, as shown in **FIGURE 2-23**. You can also add pages to a Reading list or share them with OneNote or a social networking site.

FIGURE 2-23: Web page annotated in Microsoft Edge

Understanding File Management

Delete and Restore Files

Learning Outcomes
• Delete a file
• Restore a file
• Empty the Recycle Bin

If you no longer need a folder or file, you can delete (or remove) it from the storage device. By regularly deleting files and folders you no longer need and emptying the Recycle Bin, you free up valuable storage space on your computer. Windows places folders and files you delete from your hard drive in the Recycle Bin. If you delete a folder, Windows removes the folder as well as all files and subfolders stored in it. If you later discover that you need a deleted file or folder, you can restore it to its original location, as long as you have not yet emptied the Recycle Bin. Emptying the Recycle Bin permanently removes deleted folders and files from your computer. However, files and folders you delete from a removable drive, such as a USB flash drive, do not go to the Recycle Bin. They are immediately and permanently deleted and cannot be restored. **CASE** ▶ *You decide to delete the Company Goals document that you stored in your Documents folder.*

STEPS

1. **Click the Documents folder in the File Explorer Navigation pane**
   Your Documents folder opens.

2. **Click Company Goals.rtf to select it, click the Home tab, then click the Delete list arrow ✕ in the Organize group; if the Show recycle confirmation command does not have a check mark next to it, click Show recycle confirmation (or if it does have a check mark, click ✕ again to close the menu)**
   Selecting the Show recycle confirmation command tells Windows that whenever you click the Delete button, you want to see a confirmation dialog box before Windows deletes the file. That way you can change your mind if you want, before deleting the file.

3. **Click the Delete button ✕ in the Organize group**
   The Delete File dialog box opens so you can confirm the deletion, as shown in **FIGURE 2-24**.

4. **Click Yes**
   You deleted the file. Because the file was stored on your computer and not on a removable drive, it was moved to the Recycle Bin.

5. **Click the Minimize button — on the window's title bar, examine the Recycle Bin icon, then double-click the Recycle Bin icon on the desktop**
   The Recycle Bin icon appears to contain crumpled paper, indicating that it contains deleted folders and/or files. The Recycle Bin window displays any previously deleted folders and files, including the Company Goals.rtf file.

6. **Click the Company Goals.rtf file to select it, then click the Restore the selected items button in the Restore group on the Recycle Bin Tools Manage tab, as shown in FIGURE 2-25**
   The file returns to its original location and no longer appears in the Recycle Bin window.

7. **In the Navigation pane, click the Documents folder**
   The Documents folder window contains the restored file. You decide to permanently delete this file after all.

8. **Click the file Company Goals.rtf, click ✕ in the Organize group on the Home tab, click Permanently delete, then click Yes in the Delete File dialog box**

9. **Minimize the window, double-click the Recycle Bin, notice that the Company Goals.rtf file is no longer there, then close all open windows**

FIGURE 2-24: Delete File dialog box

FIGURE 2-25: Restoring a file from the Recycle Bin

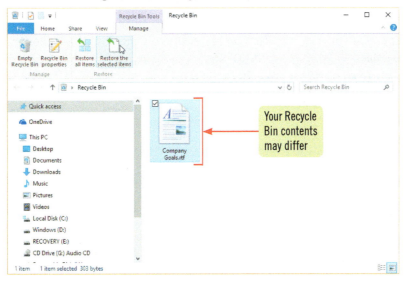

Your Recycle Bin contents may differ

More techniques for selecting and moving files

To select a group of items that are next to each other in a window, click the first item in the group, press and hold [Shift], then click the last item in the group. Both items you click and all the items between them become selected. To select files that are not next to each other, click the first file, press and hold [Ctrl], then click the other items you want to select as a group. Then you can copy, cut, or delete the group of files or folders you selected. **Drag and drop** is a technique in which you use your pointing device to drag a file or folder into a different folder and then drop it, or let go of the mouse button, to place it in that folder. Using drag and drop does not copy your file to the clipboard. If you drag and drop a file to a folder on a different drive, Windows *copies* the file. However, if you drag and drop a file to a folder on the same drive, Windows *moves* the file into that folder

instead. See **FIGURE 2-26**. If you want to move a file to another drive, hold down [Shift] while you drag and drop. If you want to copy a file to another folder on the same drive, hold down [Ctrl] while you drag and drop.

FIGURE 2-26: Moving a file using drag and drop

ScreenTip confirms action

Image of file appears as you drag

Practice

Concepts Review

Label the elements of the Windows 10 window shown in FIGURE 2-27.

FIGURE 2-27

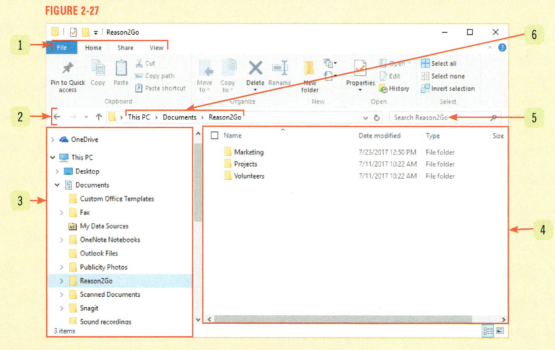

Match each term with the statement that best describes it.

7. **View**

8. **File extension**

9. **Address bar**

10. **Path**

11. **Clipboard**

12. **Snap Assist**

a. A series of locations separated by small triangles or backslashes that describes a file's location in the file hierarchy

b. A feature that helps you arrange windows on the screen

c. An area above the Files list that contains a path

d. A three- or four-letter sequence, preceded by a period, that identifies the type of file

e. A set of appearance choices for files and folders

f. An area of a computer's RAM used for temporary storage

Select the best answer from the list of choices.

13. **Which part of a window lets you see a file's contents without opening the file?**

   a. File list

   b. Address bar

   c. Navigation pane

   d. Preview pane

14. **The new Microsoft web browser is called Microsoft _____.**

   a. View

   b. Task

   c. Edge

   d. Desktop

15. **The text you type in a Search text box is called:**

   a. Sorting.

   b. RAM.

   c. Search criteria.

   d. Clipboard.

16. **Which of the following is not a visible section in a File Explorer window?**

   a. Clipboard

   b. Navigation pane

   c. File list

   d. Address bar

Skills Review

1. Understand files and folders.

    a. Create a file hierarchy for an ice cream manufacturing business, using a name that you create. The business has departments for Product Development, Manufacturing, and Personnel. Product development activities include research and testing; manufacturing has facilities for ice cream and frozen yogurt; and Personnel handles hiring and payroll. How would you organize your folders and files using a file hierarchy of three levels? How would you use folders and subfolders to keep the documents related to these activities distinct and easy to navigate? Draw a diagram and write a short paragraph explaining your answer.

    b. Use tools in the File Explorer window to create the folder hierarchy in the Documents folder on your computer.

    c. Open NotePad and write the path of the Hiring folder, using backslashes to indicate levels in the hierarchy. Do the same for the Testing folder.

2. Create and save a file.

    a. Connect your USB flash drive to a USB port on your computer, then open WordPad from the Start menu.

    b. Type **Advertising Campaign** as the title, then start a new line.

    c. Type your name, press [Enter] twice, then create the following list:

        Menu ads

        Email customers

        Web page specials

        Local TV spots

    d. Save the WordPad file with the filename **Advertising Campaign.rtf** in the location where you store your Data Files, view the filename in the WordPad title bar, then close WordPad.

3. Explore the files and folders on your computer.

    a. Open a File Explorer window.

    b. Use the Navigation pane to navigate to your USB flash drive or the location where you store your Data Files.

    c. Use the Address bar to navigate to This PC.

    d. Use the File list to navigate to your local hard drive (C:).

    e. Use the File list to open the Users folder, and then open the folder that represents your user name.

    f. Open the Documents folder. (*Hint*: The path is This PC\Local Disk (C:) \Users\Your User Name\Documents.)

    g. Use the Navigation pane to navigate back to This PC.

4. Change file and folder views.

    a. Navigate to your Documents folder or the location of your Data Files using the method of your choice.

    b. Use the View tab to view its contents as large icons.

    c. View the folder's contents in the seven other views.

    d. Sort the items in this location by date modified in ascending order.

    e. Open the Preview pane, view a selected item's preview, then close the Preview pane.

5. Open, edit, and save files.

    a. Start WordPad, then use the Open dialog box to open the Advertising Campaign.rtf document you created.

    b. After the text "Local TV spots," add a line with the text **Social media**.

    c. Save the document and close WordPad.

6. Copy files.

    a. In the File Explorer window, navigate to the location where you store your Data Files if necessary.

    b. Copy the Advertising Campaign.rtf document.

    c. Create a new folder named **Advertising** on your USB flash drive or the location where you store your Data Files (*Hint*: Use the Home tab), then open the folder.

    d. Paste the document copy in the new folder.

7. Move and rename files.

    a. Navigate to your USB flash drive or the location where you store your Data Files.

    b. Select the Advertising Campaign.rtf document located there, then cut it.

Skills Review (continued)

  c. Navigate to your Documents folder, then paste the file there.

  d. Rename the file **Advertising Campaign - Backup.rtf**.

8. Search for files and folders.

  a. Use the search box on the taskbar to search for a file using the search text **backup**. (*Hint*: Remember to select My stuff.)

  b. If necessary, scroll to the found file, and notice its path.

  c. Open the Advertising Campaign - Backup document from the search results, then close WordPad. (*Hint*: Closing the program automatically closes any open documents.)

  d. Open a File Explorer window, click in the search box, search your USB flash drive using the search text **overview**.

  e. Open the found document from the File list, then close WordPad.

9. Delete and restore files.

  a. Navigate to your Documents folder.

  b. Verify that your Delete preference is Show recycle confirmation, then delete the Advertising Campaign - Backup.rtf file.

  c. Open the Recycle Bin, and restore the document to its original location.

  d. Navigate to your Documents folder, then move the Advertising Campaign - Backup.rtf file to the Advertising folder on your USB flash drive (or the location where you store your Data Files).

Independent Challenge 1

To meet the needs of gardeners in your town, you have opened a vacation garden care business named GreenerInc. Customers hire you to care for their gardens when they go on vacation. To promote your new business, your website designer asks you to give her selling points to include in a web ad.

  a. Connect your USB flash drive to your computer, if necessary.

  b. Create a new folder named **GreenerInc** on your USB flash drive or the location where you store your Data Files.

  c. In the GreenerInc folder, create two subfolders named **Handouts** and **Website**.

  d. Use WordPad to create a short paragraph or list that describes three advantages of your business. Use **GreenerInc Selling Points** as the first line, followed by the paragraph or list. Include your name and email address after the text.

  e. Save the WordPad document with the filename **Selling Points.rtf** in the Website folder, then close the document and exit WordPad.

  f. Open a File Explorer window, then navigate to the Website folder.

  g. View the contents in at least three different views, then choose the view option that you prefer.

  h. Copy the Selling Points.rtf file, then paste a copy in the Documents folder.

  i. Rename the copied file **Selling Points Backup.rtf**.

  j. Cut the Selling Points Backup.rtf file from the Documents folder, and paste it in the GreenerInc\Website folder in the location where you store your Data Files, then close the File Explorer window.

Independent Challenge 2

As a freelance webpage designer for nonprofit businesses, you depend on your computer to meet critical deadlines. Whenever you encounter a computer problem, you contact a computer consultant who helps you resolve the problem. This consultant has asked you to document, or keep records of, your computer's available drives.

  a. Connect your USB flash drive to your computer, if necessary.

  b. Open File Explorer and go to This PC so you can view information on your drives and other installed hardware.

  c. View the window contents using three different views, then choose the one you prefer.

  d. Open WordPad and create a document with the text **My Drives** and your name on separate lines. Save the document as **My Drives.rtf**.

Independent Challenge 2 (continued)

e. Use Snap Assist to view the WordPad and File Explorer windows next to each other on the screen. (*Hint*: Drag the title bar of one of the windows to the left side of the screen.)

f. In WordPad, list the names of the hard drive (or drives), devices with removable storage, and any other hardware devices installed on the computer as shown in the Devices and Drives section of the window.

g. Switch to a view that displays the total size and amount of free space on your hard drive(s) and removable storage drive(s), and edit each WordPad list item to include the amount of free space for each one (for example, 22.1 GB free of 95.5 GB).

h. Save the WordPad document with the filename **My Drives** on your USB flash drive or the location where you store your Data Files.

i. Close WordPad, then maximize the File Explorer window. Navigate to your file storage location, then preview your document in the Preview pane, and close the window.

Independent Challenge 3

You are an attorney at Garcia and Chu, a large accounting firm. You participate in the company's community outreach program by speaking at career days in area schools. You teach students about career opportunities available in the field of accounting. You want to create a folder structure to store the files for each session.

a. Connect your USB flash drive to your computer (if necessary), then open the window for your USB flash drive or the location where you store your Data Files.

b. Create a folder named **Career Days**.

c. In the Career Days folder, create a subfolder named **Valley Intermediate**. Open this folder, then close it.

d. Use WordPad to create a document with the title **Accounting Jobs** at the top of the page and your name on separate lines, and the following list of items:
Current Opportunities:
Bookkeeper
Accounting Clerk
Accountant
Certified Public Accountant (CPA)

e. Save the WordPad document with the filename **Accounting Jobs.rtf** in the Valley Intermediate folder. (*Hint*: After you switch to your USB flash drive in the Save As dialog box, open the Career Days folder, then open the Valley Intermediate folder before saving the file.) Close WordPad.

f. Open WordPad and the Accounting Jobs document again, add **Senior Accountant** after Accountant, then save the file and close WordPad.

g. Store a copy of the file using the Save As command to your Documents folder, renaming it **Accounting Jobs - Copy.rtf**, then close WordPad.

h. In File Explorer, delete the document copy in your Documents folder so it is placed in the Recycle Bin, then restore it.

i. Open the Recycle Bin window, snap the File Explorer to the left side of the screen and the Recycle in to the right side, then verify that the file has been restored to the correct location.

j. Cut the file from the Documents folder and paste it in the Career Days\Valley Intermediate folder in your Data File storage location, then close all windows.

Independent Challenge 4: Explore

Think of a hobby or volunteer activity that you do now, or one that you would like to start. You will use your computer to help you manage your plans or ideas for this activity.

a. Using paper and pencil, sketch a folder structure with at least two subfolders to contain your documents for this activity.

b. Connect your USB flash drive to your computer, then open the window for your USB flash drive.

Independent Challenge 4: Explore (continued)

c. In File Explorer, create the folder structure for your activity, using your sketch as a reference.

d. Think of at least three tasks that you can do to further your work in your chosen activity.

e. Start a new WordPad document. Add the title **Next Steps** at the top of the page and your name on the next line.

f. Below your name, list the three tasks. Save the file in one of the folders created on your USB flash drive, with the title **To Do.rtf**.

g. Close WordPad, then open a File Explorer window and navigate to the folder where you stored the document.

h. Create a copy of the file, place the copied file in your Documents folder, then rename this file with a name you choose.

i. Delete the copied file from your Documents folder, restore it, then cut and paste the file into the folder that contains your To Do.rtf file, ensuring that the filename of the copy is different so it doesn't overwirte the To Do.rtf file.

j. Open Microsoft Edge using its button on the taskbar, click in the search text box, then search for information about others doing your desired hobby or volunteer activity.

k. Click the Make a Web Note button ✎ at the top of the window, click the Highlighter tool, then highlight an item that interests you.

l. Click the Share button ⬡, click Mail, choose your desired email account, then send the annotated page to yourself. You will receive an email with an attachment showing the annotated page.

m. Close Edge, your email program, and any open windows.

Visual Workshop

Create the folder structure shown in **FIGURE 2-28** on your USB flash drive (or in the location where you store your Data Files). Create a WordPad document containing your name and today's date, type the path to the Midsize folder, and save it with the filename **Midsize.rtf** in a Midsize folder on your USB Flash drive or the location where you store your Data Files.

FIGURE 2-28

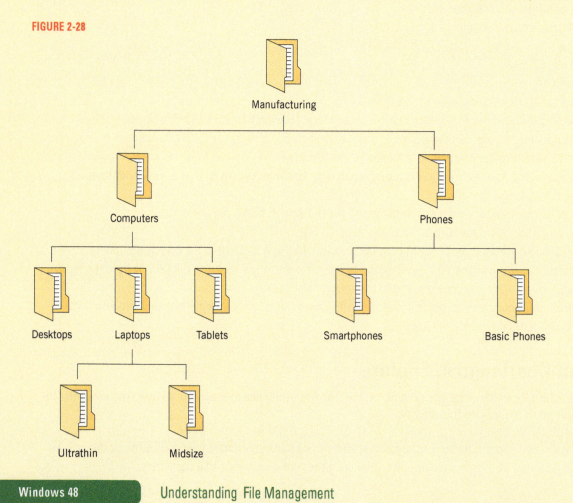

Getting Started with Microsoft Office 2016

CASE This module introduces you to the most frequently used programs in Office, as well as common features they all share.

Module Objectives

After completing this module, you will be able to:

- Understand the Office 2016 suite
- Start an Office app
- Identify Office 2016 screen elements
- Create and save a file
- Open a file and save it with a new name
- View and print your work
- Get Help, close a file, and exit an app

Files You Will Need

OF 1-1.xlsx

Understand the Office 2016 Suite

Learning Outcomes
- Identify Office suite components
- Describe the features of each app

Microsoft Office 2016 is a group of programs—which are also called applications or apps—designed to help you create documents, collaborate with coworkers, and track and analyze information. You use different Office programs to accomplish specific tasks, such as writing a letter or producing a presentation, yet all the programs have a similar look and feel. Microsoft Office 2016 apps feature a common, context-sensitive user interface, so you can get up to speed faster and use advanced features with greater ease. The Office apps are bundled together in a group called a **suite**. The Office suite is available in several configurations, but all include Word, Excel, PowerPoint, and OneNote. Some configurations include Access, Outlook, Publisher, Skype, and OneDrive. **CASE** *As part of your job, you need to understand how each Office app is best used to complete specific tasks.*

DETAILS

The Office apps covered in this book include:

QUICK TIP

In this book, the terms "program" and "app" are used interchangeably.

- #### Microsoft Word 2016

  When you need to create any kind of text-based document, such as a memo, newsletter, or multipage report, Word is the program to use. You can easily make your documents look great by using formatting tools and inserting eye-catching graphics. The Word document shown in **FIGURE 1-1** contains a company logo and simple formatting.

- #### Microsoft Excel 2016

  Excel is the perfect solution when you need to work with numeric values and make calculations. It puts the power of formulas, functions, charts, and other analytical tools into the hands of every user, so you can analyze sales projections, calculate loan payments, and present your findings in a professional manner. The Excel worksheet shown in **FIGURE 1-1** tracks checkbook transactions. Because Excel automatically recalculates results whenever a value changes, the information is always up to date. A chart illustrates how the monthly expenses are broken down.

- #### Microsoft PowerPoint 2016

  Using PowerPoint, it's easy to create powerful presentations complete with graphics, transitions, and even a soundtrack. Using professionally designed themes and clip art, you can quickly and easily create dynamic slide shows such as the one shown in **FIGURE 1-1**.

- #### Microsoft Access 2016

  Access is a relational database program that helps you keep track of large amounts of quantitative data, such as product inventories or employee records. The form shown in **FIGURE 1-1** can be used to generate reports on customer invoices and tours.

Microsoft Office has benefits beyond the power of each program, including:

- #### Note-taking made simple; available on all devices

  Use OneNote to take notes (organized in tabbed pages) on information that can be accessed on your computer, tablet, or phone. Share the editable results with others. Contents can include text, web page clips (using OneNote Clipper), email contents (directly inserted into a default section), photos (using Office Lens), and web pages.

- #### Common user interface: Improving business processes

  Because the Office suite apps have a similar **interface**, your experience using one app's tools makes it easy to learn those in the other apps. Office documents are **compatible** with one another, so you can easily **integrate**, or combine, elements—for example, you can add an Excel chart to a PowerPoint slide, or an Access table to a Word document.

  Most Office programs include the capability to incorporate feedback—called **online collaboration**—across the Internet or a company network.

FIGURE 1-1: Microsoft Office 2016 documents

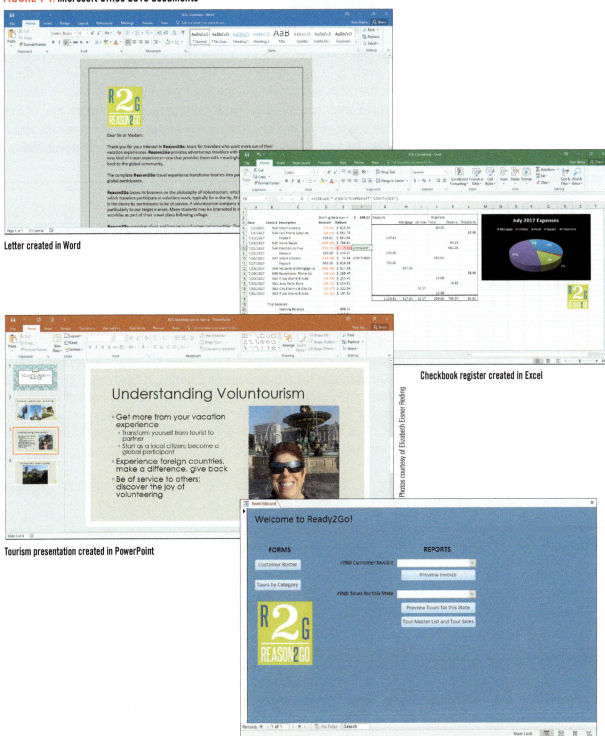

Letter created in Word

Checkbook register created in Excel

Tourism presentation created in PowerPoint

Form created in Access

Photos courtesy of Elizabeth Eisner Reding

What is Office 365?

Until recently, most consumers purchased Microsoft Office in a traditional way: by buying a retail package from a store or downloading it from Microsoft.com. You can still purchase Microsoft Office 2016 in this traditional way—but you can also now purchase it as a subscription service called Microsoft Office 365, which is available in a wide variety of configurations.

Depending on which configuration you purchase, you will always have access to the most up-to-date versions of the apps in your package and, in many cases, can install these apps on multiple computers, tablets, and phones. And if you change computers or devices, you can easily uninstall the apps from an old device and install them on a new one.

Start an Office App

Learning Outcomes
- Start an Office app
- Explain the purpose of a template
- Start a new blank document

To get started using Microsoft Office, you need to start, or **launch**, the Office app you want to use. An easy way to start the app you want is to press the Windows key, type the first few characters of the app name you want to search for, then click the app name In the Best match list. You will discover that there are many ways to accomplish just about any Windows task; for example, you can also see a list of all the apps on your computer by pressing the Windows key, then clicking All Apps. When you see the app you want, click its name. **CASE** *You decide to familiarize yourself with Office by starting Microsoft Word.*

STEPS

1. **Click the Start button ⊞ on the Windows taskbar**

   The Start menu opens, listing the most used apps on your computer. You can locate the app you want to open by clicking the app name if you see it, or you can type the app name to search for it.

2. **Type word**

   Your screen now displays "Word 2016" under "Best match", along with any other app that has "word" as part of its name (such as WordPad). See **FIGURE 1-2**.

3. **Click Word 2016**

   Word 2016 launches, and the Word **start screen** appears, as shown in **FIGURE 1-3**. The start screen is a landing page that appears when you first start an Office app. The left side of this screen displays recent files you have opened. (If you have never opened any files, then there will be no files listed under Recent.) The right side displays images depicting different templates you can use to create different types of documents. A **template** is a file containing professionally designed content and formatting that you can easily customize for your own needs. You can also start from scratch using the Blank Document template, which contains only minimal formatting settings.

Enabling touch mode

If you are using a touch screen with any of the Office 2016 apps, you can enable the touch mode to give the user interface a more spacious look, making it easier to navigate with your fingertips. Enable touch mode by clicking the Quick Access toolbar list arrow, then clicking Touch/Mouse Mode to select it. Then you'll see the Touch Mode button 🖐 in the Quick Access toolbar. Click 🖐, and you'll see the interface spread out.

Using shortcut keys to move between Office programs

You can switch between open apps using a keyboard shortcut. The [Alt][Tab] keyboard combination lets you either switch quickly to the next open program or file or choose one from a gallery. To switch immediately to the next open program or file, press [Alt][Tab]. To choose from all open programs and files, press and hold [Alt], then press and release [Tab] without releasing [Alt]. A gallery opens on screen, displaying the filename and a thumbnail image of each open program and file, as well as of the desktop. Each time you press [Tab] while holding [Alt], the selection cycles to the next open file or location. Release [Alt] when the program, file, or location you want to activate is selected.

FIGURE 1-2: Searching for the Word app

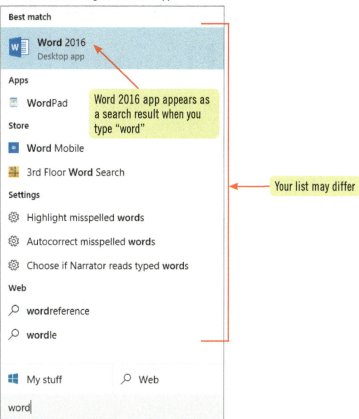

Word 2016 app appears as a search result when you type "word"

Your list may differ

FIGURE 1-3: Word start screen

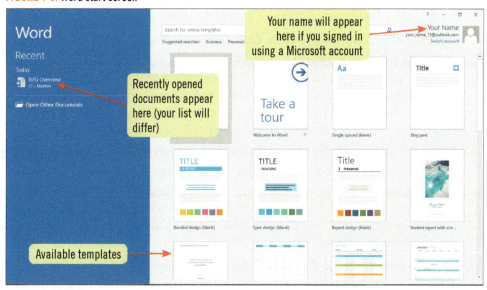

Your name will appear here if you signed in using a Microsoft account

Recently opened documents appear here (your list will differ)

Available templates

Using the Office Clipboard

You can use the Office Clipboard to cut and copy items from one Office program and paste them into others. The Office Clipboard can store a maximum of 24 items. To access it, open the Office Clipboard task pane by clicking the dialog box launcher 🔲 in the Clipboard group on the Home tab. Each time you copy a selection, it is saved in the Office Clipboard. Each entry in the Office Clipboard includes an icon that tells you the program it was created in. To paste an entry, click in the document where you want it to appear, then click the item in the Office Clipboard. To delete an item from the Office Clipboard, right-click the item, then click Delete.

Identify Office 2016 Screen Elements

Learning Outcomes
- Identify basic components of the user interface
- Display and use Backstage view
- Adjust the zoom level

One of the benefits of using Office is that its apps have much in common, making them easy to learn and making it simple to move from one to another. All Office 2016 apps share a similar user interface, so you can use your knowledge of one to get up to speed in another. A **user interface** is a collective term for all the ways you interact with a software program. The user interface in Office 2016 provides intuitive ways to choose commands, work with files, and navigate in the program window. **CASE** *Familiarize yourself with some of the common interface elements in Office by examining the PowerPoint program window.*

STEPS

1. **Click the Start button ⊞ on the Windows taskbar, type pow, click PowerPoint 2016, then click Blank Presentation**

   PowerPoint starts and opens a new file, which contains a blank slide. Refer to **FIGURE 1-4** to identify common elements of the Office user interface. The **document window** occupies most of the screen. At the top of every Office program window is a **title bar** that displays the document name and program name. Below the title bar is the **Ribbon**, which displays commands you're likely to need for the current task. Commands are organized onto **tabs**. The tab names appear at the top of the Ribbon, and the active tab appears in front. The **Share button** in the upper-right corner lets you invite other users to view your cloud-stored Word, Excel, or Powerpoint file.

2. **Click the File tab**

   The File tab opens, displaying **Backstage view**. It is called Backstage view because the commands available here are for working with the files "behind the scenes." The navigation bar on the left side of Backstage view contains commands to perform actions common to most Office programs.

3. **Click the Back button ⬅ to close Backstage view and return to the document window, then click the Design tab on the Ribbon**

   To display a different tab, click its name. Each tab contains related commands arranged into **groups** to make features easy to find. On the Design tab, the Themes group displays available design themes in a **gallery**, or visual collection of choices you can browse. Many groups contain a **launcher**, which you can click to open a dialog box or pane from which to choose related commands.

4. **Move the mouse pointer ⬚ over the Ion Boardroom theme in the Themes group as shown in FIGURE 1-5, but *do not click* the mouse button**

   The Ion Boardroom theme is temporarily applied to the slide in the document window. However, because you did not click the theme, you did not permanently change the slide. With the **Live Preview** feature, you can point to a choice, see the results, then decide if you want to make the change. Live Preview is available throughout Office.

5. **Move ⬚ away from the Ribbon and towards the slide**

   If you had clicked the Ion theme, it would be applied to this slide. Instead, the slide remains unchanged.

6. **Point to the Zoom slider ⊟———▮——⊞ 100% on the status bar, then drag to the right until the Zoom level reads 166%**

   The slide display is enlarged. Zoom tools are located on the status bar. You can drag the slider or click the Zoom In or Zoom Out buttons to zoom in or out on an area of interest. **Zooming in** (a higher percentage), makes a document appear bigger on screen but less of it fits on the screen at once; **zooming out** (a lower percentage) lets you see more of the document at a reduced size.

7. **Click the Zoom Out button ⊟ on the status bar to the left of the Zoom slider until the Zoom level reads 120%**

FIGURE 1-4: PowerPoint program window

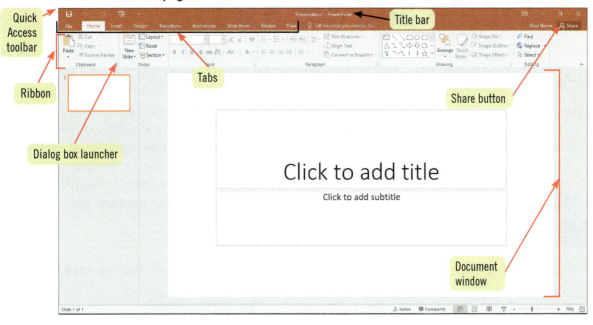

Quick Access toolbar

Ribbon

Dialog box launcher

Tabs

Title bar

Share button

Document window

FIGURE 1-5: Viewing a theme with Live Preview

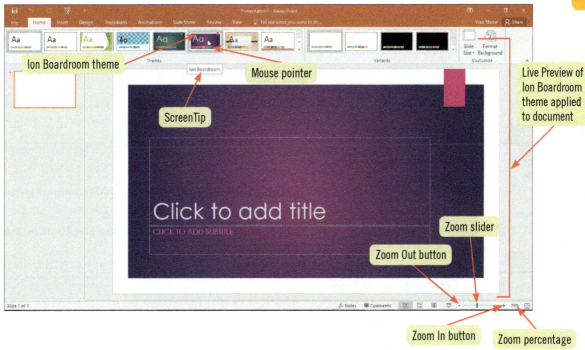

Ion Boardroom theme

ScreenTip

Mouse pointer

Live Preview of Ion Boardroom theme applied to document

Zoom slider

Zoom Out button

Zoom In button

Zoom percentage

Office 2016

Using Backstage view

Backstage view in each Microsoft Office app offers "one stop shopping" for many commonly performed tasks, such as opening and saving a file, printing and previewing a document, defining document properties, sharing information, and exiting a program. Backstage view opens when you click the File tab in any Office app, and while features such as the Ribbon, Mini toolbar, and Live Preview all help you work *in* your documents, the File tab and Backstage view help you work *with* your documents. You can click commands in the navigation pane to open different places for working with your documents, such as the Open place, the Save place, and so on. You can return to your active document by clicking the Back button.

Create and Save a File

Learning Outcomes
• Create a file
• Save a file
• Explain OneDrive

When working in an Office app, one of the first things you need to do is to create and save a file. A **file** is a stored collection of data. Saving a file enables you to work on a project now, then put it away and work on it again later. In some Office programs, including Word, Excel, and PowerPoint, you can open a new file when you start the app, then all you have to do is enter some data and save it. In Access, you must create a file before you enter any data. You should give your files meaningful names and save them in an appropriate location, such as a folder on your hard drive or OneDrive so they're easy to find. **OneDrive** is a Microsoft cloud storage system that lets you easily save, share, and access your files from anywhere you have Internet access. **CASE** *Use Word to familiarize yourself with creating and saving a document. First you'll type some notes about a possible location for a corporate meeting, then you'll save the information for later use.*

STEPS

1. **Click the** Word button [W] **on the taskbar, click** Blank document, **then click the** Zoom In button [+] **until the level is** 120%, **if necessary**

2. **Type** Locations for Corporate Meeting, **then press [Enter] twice**

   The text appears in the document window, and the **insertion point** blinks on a new blank line. The insertion point indicates where the next typed text will appear.

3. **Type** Las Vegas, NV, **press [Enter], type** Chicago, IL, **press [Enter], type** Seattle, WA, **press [Enter] twice, then type your name**

4. **Click the** Save button [💾] **on the Quick Access toolbar**

   Because this is the first time you are saving this new file, the Save place in Backstage view opens, showing various options for saving the file. See **FIGURE 1-6**. Once you save a file for the first time, clicking [💾] saves any changes to the file *without* opening the Save As dialog box.

5. **Click** Browse

   The Save As dialog box opens, as shown in **FIGURE 1-7**, where you can browse to the location where you want to save the file. The Address bar in the Save As dialog box displays the default location for saving the file, but you can change it to any location. The File name field contains a suggested name for the document based on text in the file, but you can enter a different name.

6. **Type** OF 1-Possible Corporate Meeting Locations

   The text you type replaces the highlighted text. (The "OF 1-" in the filename indicates that the file is created in Office Module 1. You will see similar designations throughout this book when files are named.)

7. **In the Save As dialog box, use the Address bar or Navigation Pane to navigate to the location where you store your Data Files**

   You can store files on your computer, a network drive, your OneDrive, or any acceptable storage device.

8. **Click** Save

   The Save As dialog box closes, the new file is saved to the location you specified, and the name of the document appears in the title bar, as shown in **FIGURE 1-8**. (You may or may not see the file extension ".docx" after the filename.) See **TABLE 1-1** for a description of the different types of files you create in Office, and the file extensions associated with each.

QUICK TIP

A filename can be up to 255 characters, including a file extension, and can include upper- or lowercase characters and spaces, but not ?, ", /, \, <, >, *, |, or :.

QUICK TIP

Saving a file to the Desktop creates a desktop icon that you can double-click to both launch a program and open a document.

QUICK TIP

To create a new blank file when a file is open, click the File tab, click New on the navigation bar, then choose a template.

TABLE 1-1: Common filenames and default file extensions

file created in	is called a	and has the default extension
Word	document	.docx
Excel	workbook	.xlsx
PowerPoint	presentation	.pptx
Access	database	.accdb

FIGURE 1-6: Save place in Backstage view

Saves to your OneDrive account

Click to display a list of recently accessed locations on this PC

Click to open the Save As dialog box

FIGURE 1-7: Save As dialog box

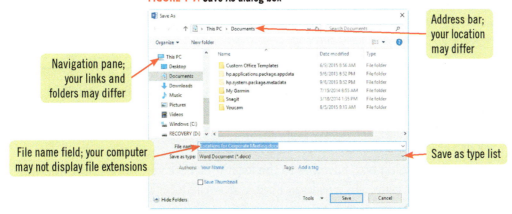

Navigation pane; your links and folders may differ

File name field; your computer may not display file extensions

Address bar; your location may differ

Save as type list

FIGURE 1-8: Saved and named Word document

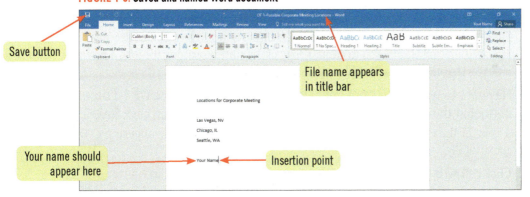

Save button

File name appears in title bar

Your name should appear here

Insertion point

Learning
Outcomes
• Open an existing
file
• Save a file with a
new name

Open a File and Save It with a New Name

In many cases as you work in Office, you need to use an existing file. It might be a file you or a coworker created earlier as a work in progress, or it could be a complete document that you want to use as the basis for another. For example, you might want to create a budget for this year using the budget you created last year; instead of typing in all the categories and information from scratch, you could open last year's budget, save it with a new name, and just make changes to update it for the current year. By opening the existing file and saving it with the Save As command, you create a duplicate that you can modify to suit your needs, while the original file remains intact. **CASE** ▶ *Use Excel to open an existing workbook file, and save it with a new name so the original remains unchanged.*

STEPS

1. **Click the Start button ⊞ on the Windows taskbar, type exc, click Excel 2016, click Open Other Workbooks, This PC, then click Browse**

    The Open dialog box opens, where you can navigate to any drive or folder accessible to your computer to locate a file.

2. **In the Open dialog box, navigate to the location where you store your Data Files**

    The files available in the current folder are listed, as shown in **FIGURE 1-9**. This folder displays one file.

3. **Click OF 1-1.xlsx, then click Open**

    The dialog box closes, and the file opens in Excel. An Excel file is an electronic spreadsheet, so the new file displays a grid of rows and columns you can use to enter and organize data.

4. **Click the File tab, click Save As on the navigation bar, then click Browse**

    The Save As dialog box opens, and the current filename is highlighted in the File name text box. Using the Save As command enables you to create a copy of the current, existing file with a new name. This action preserves the original file and creates a new file that you can modify.

5. **Navigate to where you store your Data Files if necessary, type OF 1-Corporate Meeting Budget in the File name text box, as shown in FIGURE 1-10, then click Save**

    A copy of the existing workbook is created with the new name. The original file, OF 1-1.xlsx, closes automatically.

6. **Click cell A18, type your name, then press [Enter], as shown in FIGURE 1-11**

    In Excel, you enter data in cells, which are formed by the intersection of a row and a column. Cell A18 is at the intersection of column A and row 18. When you press [Enter], the cell pointer moves to cell A19.

7. **Click the Save button 🖫 on the Quick Access toolbar**

    Your name appears in the workbook, and your changes to the file are saved.

Exploring File Open options

You might have noticed that the Open button in the Open dialog box includes a list arrow to the right of the button. In a dialog box, if a button includes a list arrow you can click the button to invoke the command, or you can click the list arrow to see a list of related commands that you can apply to the currently selected file. The Open list arrow includes several related commands, including Open Read-Only and Open as Copy.

Clicking Open Read-Only opens a file that you can only save with a new name; you cannot make changes to the original file. Clicking Open as Copy creates and opens a copy of the selected file and inserts the word "Copy" in the file's title. Like the Save As command, these commands provide additional ways to use copies of existing files while ensuring that original files do not get changed by mistake.

FIGURE 1-9: Open dialog box

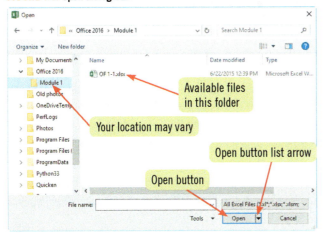

FIGURE 1-10: Save As dialog box

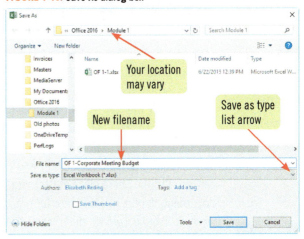

FIGURE 1-11: Your name added to the workbook

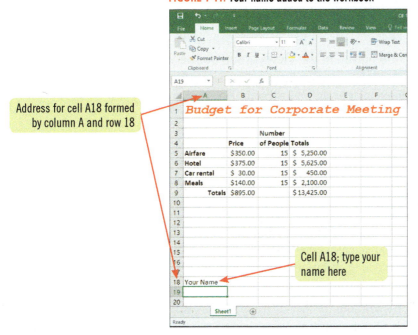

Working in Compatibility Mode

Not everyone upgrades to the newest version of Office. As a general rule, new software versions are **backward compatible**, meaning that documents saved by an older version can be read by newer software. To open documents created in older Office versions, Office 2016 includes a feature called Compatibility Mode. When you use Office 2016 to open a file created in an earlier version of Office, "Compatibility Mode" appears in the title bar, letting you know the file was created in an earlier but usable version of the program. If you are working with someone who may not be using the newest version of the software, you can avoid possible incompatibility problems by saving your file in another, earlier format. To do this in an Office program, click the File tab, click Save As on the navigation bar, then click Browse. In the Save As dialog box, click the Save as type list arrow in the Save As dialog box, then click an option in the list. For example, if you're working in Excel, click Excel 97-2003 Workbook format in the Save as type list to save an Excel file so it can be opened in Excel 97 or Excel 2003.

Office 2016

View and Print Your Work

Each Microsoft Office program lets you switch among various **views** of the document window to show more or fewer details or a different combination of elements that make it easier to complete certain tasks, such as formatting or reading text. Changing your view of a document does not affect the file in any way, it affects only the way it looks on screen. If your computer is connected to a printer or a print server, you can easily print any Office document using the Print button in the Print place in Backstage view. Printing can be as simple as **previewing** the document to see exactly what the printed version will look like and then clicking the Print button. Or, you can customize the print job by printing only selected pages. You can also use the Share place in Backstage view or the Share button on the Ribbon (if available) to share a document, export to a different format, or save it to the cloud. **CASE** ▸ *Experiment with changing your view of a Word document, and then preview and print your work.*

STEPS

1. **Click the Word program button ▨ on the taskbar**

   Word becomes active, and the program window fills the screen.

2. **Click the View tab on the Ribbon**

   In most Office programs, the View tab on the Ribbon includes groups and commands for changing your view of the current document. You can also change views using the View buttons on the status bar.

3. **Click the Read Mode button in the Views group on the View tab**

   The view changes to Read Mode view, as shown in **FIGURE 1-12**. This view shows the document in an easy-to-read, distraction-free reading mode. Notice that the Ribbon is no longer visible on screen.

4. **Click the Print Layout button ▦ on the Status bar**

   You return to Print Layout view, the default view in Word.

5. **Click the File tab, then click Print on the navigation bar**

   The Print place opens. The preview pane on the right displays a preview of how your document will look when printed. Compare your screen to **FIGURE 1-13**. Options in the Settings section enable you to change margins, orientation, and related options before printing. To change a setting, click it, and then click a new setting. For instance, to change from Letter paper size to Legal, click Letter in the Settings section, then click Legal on the menu that opens. The document preview updates as you change the settings. You also can use the Settings section to change which pages to print. If your computer is connected to multiple printers, you can click the current printer in the Printer section, then click the one you want to use. The Print section contains the Print button and also enables you to select the number of copies of the document to print.

6. **If your school allows printing, click the Print button in the Print place (otherwise, click the Back button ⊙)**

   If you chose to print, a copy of the document prints, and Backstage view closes.

Customizing the Quick Access toolbar

You can customize the Quick Access toolbar to display your favorite commands. To do so, click the Customize Quick Access Toolbar button ▾ in the title bar, then click the command you want to add. If you don't see the command in the list, click More Commands to open the Quick Access Toolbar tab of the current program's Options dialog box. In the Options dialog box, use the Choose commands from list to choose a category, click the desired command in the list on the left, click Add to add it to the Quick Access toolbar, then click OK. To remove a button from the toolbar, click the name in the list on the right in the Options dialog box, then click Remove. To add a command to the Quick Access toolbar as you work, simply right-click the button on the Ribbon, then click Add to Quick Access Toolbar on the shortcut menu. To move the Quick Access toolbar below the Ribbon, click the Customize Quick Access Toolbar button, and then click Show Below the Ribbon.

FIGURE 1-12: Read Mode view

Print Layout button

View buttons on status bar

FIGURE 1-13: Print settings on the File tab

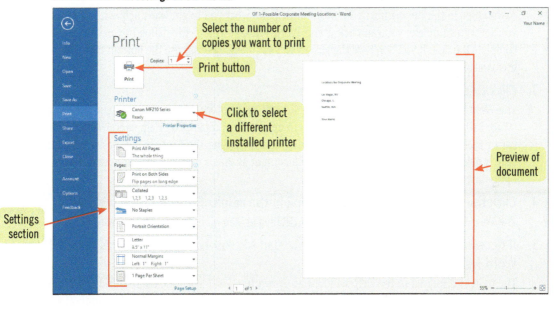

Select the number of copies you want to print

Print button

Click to select a different installed printer

Preview of document

Settings section

Creating a screen capture

A **screen capture** is a digital image of your screen, as if you took a picture of it with a camera. For instance, you might want to take a screen capture if an error message occurs and you want a Technical Support person to see exactly what's on the screen. You can create a screen capture using the Snipping Tool, an accessory designed to capture whole screens or portions of screens. To open the Snipping Tool, click the Start button on the Windows taskbar, type "sni", then click the Snipping Tool when it appears in the left panel. On the Snipping Tool toolbar, click New, then drag the pointer on the screen to select the area of the screen you want to capture. When you release the mouse button, the screen capture opens in the Snipping Tool window, and you can

save, copy, or send it in an email. In Word, Excel, and PowerPoint 2016, you can capture screens or portions of screens and insert them in the current document using the Screenshot button in the Illustrations group on the Insert tab. Alternatively, you can create a screen capture by pressing [PrtScn]. (Keyboards differ, but you may find the [PrtScn] button in or near your keyboard's function keys.) Pressing this key places a digital image of your screen in the Windows temporary storage area known as the **Clipboard**. Open the document where you want the screen capture to appear, click the Home tab on the Ribbon (if necessary), then click the Paste button in the Clipboard group on the Home tab. The screen capture is pasted into the document.

Get Help, Close a File, and Exit an App

Learning Outcomes
• Display a ScreenTip
• Use Help
• Close a file
• Exit an app

You can get comprehensive help at any time by pressing [F1] in an Office app or clicking the Help button on the title bar. You can also get help in the form of a ScreenTip by pointing to almost any icon in the program window. When you're finished working in an Office document, you have a few choices for ending your work session. You close a file by clicking the File tab, then clicking Close; you exit a program by clicking the Close button on the title bar. Closing a file leaves a program running, while exiting a program closes all the open files in that program as well as the program itself. In all cases, Office reminds you if you try to close a file or exit a program and your document contains unsaved changes. **CASE** ▶ *Explore the Help system in Microsoft Office, and then close your documents and exit any open programs.*

STEPS

1. **Point to the Zoom button in the Zoom group on the View tab of the Ribbon**

   A ScreenTip appears that describes how the Zoom button works and explains where to find other zoom controls.

2. **Click the Tell me box above the Ribbon, then type Choose a template**

   As you type in the Tell me box, a Smart list anticipates what you might want help with. If you see the task you want to complete, you can click it and Word will take you to the dialog box or options you need to complete the task. If you don't see the answer to your query, you can use the bottom two options to search the database.

3. **Click Get Help on "choose a template"**

   The Word Help window opens, as shown in **FIGURE 1-14**, displaying help results for choosing a template in Word. Each entry is a hyperlink you can click to open a list of topics. The Help window also includes a toolbar of useful Help commands such as printing and increasing the font size for easier readability, and a Search field. Office.com supplements the help content available on your computer with a wide variety of up-to-date topics, templates, and training.

4. **Click the Where do I find templates link in the results list Word Help window**

   The Word Help window changes, and a more detailed explanation appears below the topic.

5. **If necessary, scroll down until the Download Microsoft Office templates topic fills the Word Help window**

   The topic is displayed in the Help window, as shown in **FIGURE 1-15**. The content in the window explains that you can create a wide variety of documents using a template (a pre-formatted document) and that you can get many templates free of charge.

6. **Click the Keep Help on Top button ⊡ in the lower-right corner of the window**

   The Pin Help button rotates so the pin point is pointed towards the bottom of the screen: this allows you to read the Help window while you work on your document.

7. **Click the Word document window, notice the Help window remains visible**

8. **Click a blank area of the Help window, click ⊥ to Unpin Help, click the Close button ☒ in the Help window, then click the Close button ☒ in the Word program window**

   Word closes, and the Excel program window is active.

9. **Click the Close button ☒ in the Excel program window, click the PowerPoint app button 📊 on the taskbar if necessary, then click the Close button ☒ to exit PowerPoint**

   Excel and PowerPoint both close.

FIGURE 1-14: Word Help window

Search field

Help toolbar

Click to learn how to find templates

Help topics are updated frequently; your list may differ

FIGURE 1-15: Create a document Help topic

Print button

Drag scroll bar to read more

Keep Help on Top button

Using sharing features and co-authoring capabilities

If you are using Word, Excel, or PowerPoint, you can take advantage of the Share feature, which makes it easy to share your files that have been saved to OneDrive. When you click the Share button, you will be asked to invite others to share the file. To do this, type in the name or email addresses in the Invite people text box. When you invite others, you have the opportunity to give them different levels of permission. You might want some people to have read-only privileges; you might want others to be able to make edits. Also available in Word, Excel, and PowerPoint is real-time co-authoring capabilities for files stored on OneDrive. Once a file on OneDrive is opened and all the users have been given editing privileges, all the users can make edits simultaneously. On first use, each user will be prompted to automatically share their changes.

Recovering a document

Each Office program has a built-in recovery feature that allows you to open and save files that were open at the time of an interruption such as a power failure. When you restart the program(s) after an interruption, the Document Recovery task pane opens on the left side of your screen displaying both original and recovered versions of the files that were open. If you're not sure which file to open (original or recovered), it's usually better to open the recovered file because it will contain the latest information. You can, however, open and review all versions of the file that were recovered and save the best one. Each file listed in the Document Recovery task pane displays a list arrow with options that allow you to open the file, save it as is, delete it, or show repairs made to it during recovery.

Practice

Concepts Review

Label the elements of the program window shown in FIGURE 1-16.

FIGURE 1-16

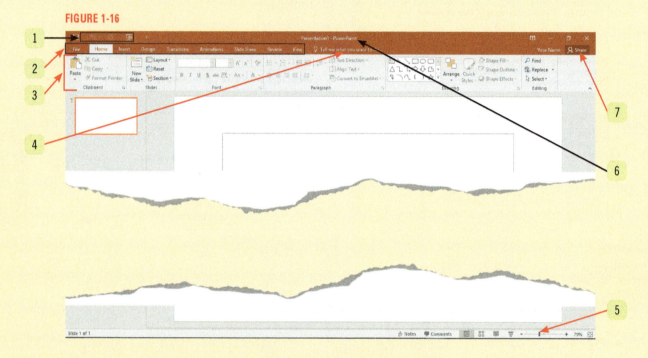

Match each project with the program for which it is best suited.

8. Microsoft PowerPoint   a. Corporate convention budget with expense projections

9. Microsoft Word   b. Presentation for city council meeting

10. Microsoft Excel   c. Business cover letter for a job application

11. Microsoft Access   d. Department store inventory

Independent Challenge 1

You just accepted an administrative position with a local independently owned insurance agent who has recently invested in computers and is now considering purchasing a subscription to Office 365. You have been asked to think of uses for the apps and you put your ideas in a Word document.

  a. Start Word, create a new Blank document, then save the document as **OF 1-Microsoft Office Apps Uses** in the location where you store your Data Files.

  b. Change the zoom factor to 120%, type **Microsoft Access**, press [Enter] twice, type **Microsoft Excel**, press [Enter] twice, type **Microsoft PowerPoint**, press [Enter] twice, type **Microsoft Word**, press [Enter] twice, then type your name.

  c. Click the line beneath each program name, type at least two tasks you can perform using that program (each separated by a comma), then press [Enter].

  d. Save the document, then submit your work to your instructor as directed.

  e. Exit Word.

Creating Documents with Word 2016

CASE ▸ You have been hired to work in the Marketing Department at Reason2Go (R2G), a company that provides adventurous travelers with meaningful project options for giving back to the global community. Shortly after reporting to your new office, Mary Watson, the vice president of sales and marketing, asks you to use Word to create a memo to the marketing staff and a letter to one of the project hosts.

Module Objectives

After completing this module, you will be able to:

- Understand word processing software
- Explore the Word window
- Start a document
- Save a document
- Select text
- Format text using the Mini toolbar and the Ribbon
- Use a document template
- Navigate a document

Files You Will Need

WD 1-1.docx

Understand Word Processing Software

Learning Outcomes
• Identify the features of Word
• State the benefits of using a word processing program

A **word processing program** is a software program that includes tools for entering, editing, and formatting text and graphics. Microsoft Word is a powerful word processing program that allows you to create and enhance a wide range of documents quickly and easily. FIGURE 1-1 shows the first page of a report created using Word and illustrates some of the Word features you can use to enhance your documents. The electronic files you create using Word are called **documents**. One of the benefits of using Word is that document files can be stored on a hard disk, flash drive, or other physical storage device, or to OneDrive or another Cloud storage place, making them easy to transport, share, and revise. **CASE** *Before beginning your memo to the marketing staff, you explore the editing and formatting features available in Word.*

DETAILS

You can use Word to accomplish the following tasks:

- **Type and edit text**

  The Word editing tools make it simple to insert and delete text in a document. You can add text to the middle of an existing paragraph, replace text with other text, undo an editing change, and correct typing, spelling, and grammatical errors with ease.

- **Copy and move text from one location to another**

  Using the more advanced editing features of Word, you can copy or move text from one location and insert it in a different location in a document. You also can copy and move text between documents. This means you don't have to retype text that is already entered in a document.

- **Format text and paragraphs with fonts, colors, and other elements**

  The sophisticated formatting tools in Word allow you to make the text in your documents come alive. You can change the size, style, and color of text, add lines and shading to paragraphs, and enhance lists with bullets and numbers. Creatively formatting text helps to highlight important ideas in your documents.

- **Format and design pages**

  The page-formatting features in Word give you power to design attractive newsletters, create powerful résumés, and produce documents such as research papers, business cards, brochures, and reports. You can change paper size, organize text in columns, and control the layout of text and graphics on each page of a document. For quick results, Word includes preformatted cover pages, pull quotes, and headers and footers, as well as galleries of coordinated text, table, and graphic styles. If you are writing a research paper, Word makes it easy to manage reference sources and create footnotes, endnotes, and bibliographies.

- **Enhance documents with tables, charts, graphics, screenshots, and videos**

  Using the powerful graphics tools in Word, you can spice up your documents with pictures, videos, photographs, screenshots, lines, preset quick shapes, and diagrams. You also can illustrate your documents with tables and charts to help convey your message in a visually interesting way.

- **Use Mail Merge to create form letters and mailing labels**

  The Word Mail Merge feature allows you to send personalized form letters to many different people. You can also use Mail Merge to create mailing labels, directories, e-mail messages, and other types of documents.

- **Share documents securely**

  The security features in Word make it quick and easy to remove comments, tracked changes, and unwanted personal information from your files before you share them with others. You can also add a password or a digital signature to a document and convert a file to a format suitable for publishing on the web.

FIGURE 1-1: A report created using Word

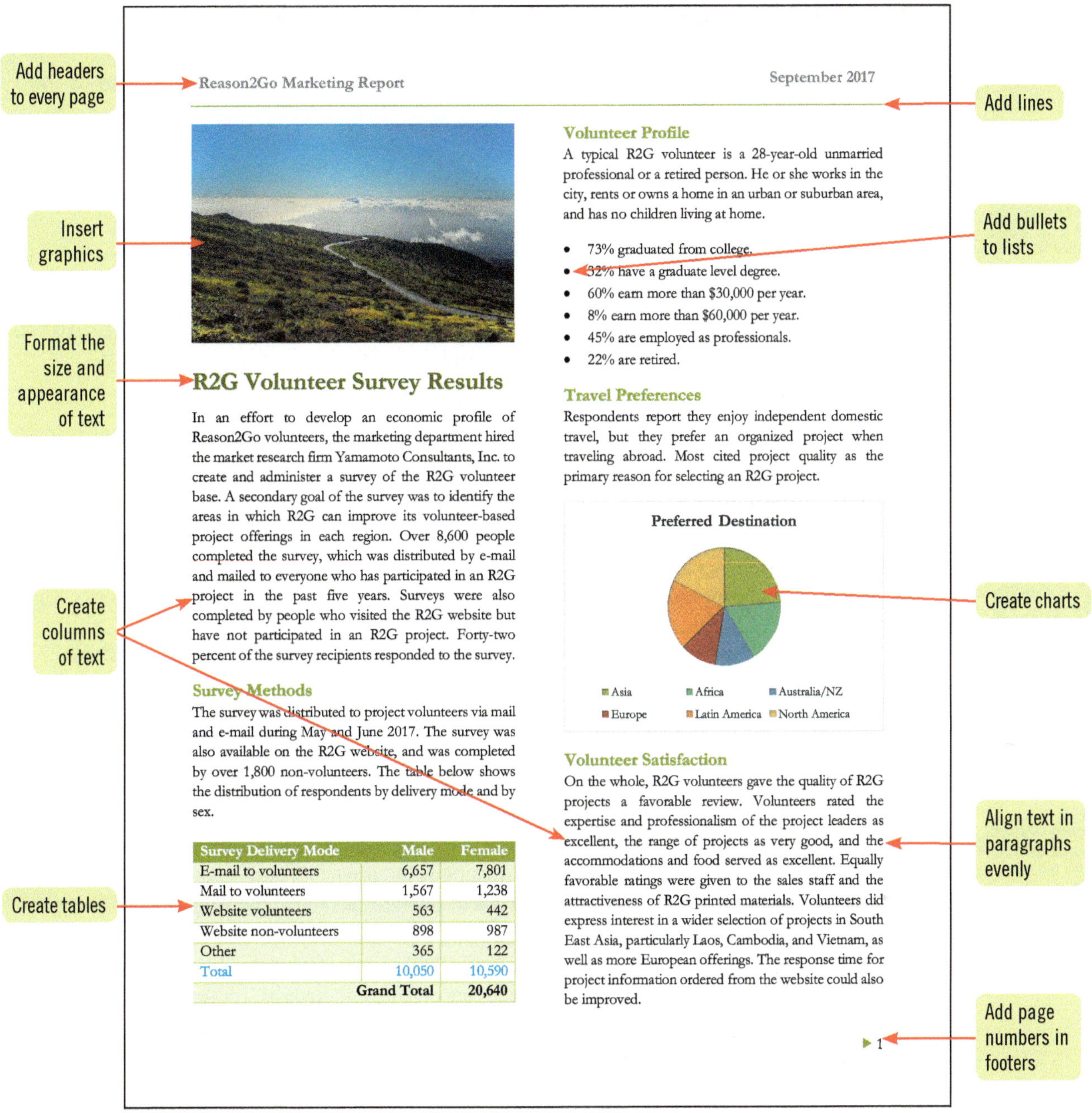
Add headers to every page
Insert graphics
Format the size and appearance of text
Create columns of text
Create tables
Add lines
Add bullets to lists
Create charts
Align text in paragraphs evenly
Add page numbers in footers
Preferred Destination
Asia
Africa
Australia/NZ
Europe
Latin America
North America

Reason2Go Marketing Report

September 2017

R2G Volunteer Survey Results

In an effort to develop an economic profile of Reason2Go volunteers, the marketing department hired the market research firm Yamamoto Consultants, Inc. to create and administer a survey of the R2G volunteer base. A secondary goal of the survey was to identify the areas in which R2G can improve its volunteer-based project offerings in each region. Over 8,600 people completed the survey, which was distributed by e-mail and mailed to everyone who has participated in an R2G project in the past five years. Surveys were also completed by people who visited the R2G website but have not participated in an R2G project. Forty-two percent of the survey recipients responded to the survey.

Survey Methods

The survey was distributed to project volunteers via mail and e-mail during May and June 2017. The survey was also available on the R2G website, and was completed by over 1,800 non-volunteers. The table below shows the distribution of respondents by delivery mode and by sex.

Survey Delivery Mode	Male	Female
E-mail to volunteers	6,657	7,801
Mail to volunteers	1,567	1,238
Website volunteers	563	442
Website non-volunteers	898	987
Other	365	122
Total	10,050	10,590
	Grand Total	20,640

Volunteer Profile

A typical R2G volunteer is a 28-year-old unmarried professional or a retired person. He or she works in the city, rents or owns a home in an urban or suburban area, and has no children living at home.

- 73% graduated from college.
- 32% have a graduate level degree.
- 60% earn more than $30,000 per year.
- 8% earn more than $60,000 per year.
- 45% are employed as professionals.
- 22% are retired.

Travel Preferences

Respondents report they enjoy independent domestic travel, but they prefer an organized project when traveling abroad. Most cited project quality as the primary reason for selecting an R2G project.

Volunteer Satisfaction

On the whole, R2G volunteers gave the quality of R2G projects a favorable review. Volunteers rated the expertise and professionalism of the project leaders as excellent, the range of projects as very good, and the accommodations and food served as excellent. Equally favorable ratings were given to the sales staff and the attractiveness of R2G printed materials. Volunteers did express interest in a wider selection of projects in South East Asia, particularly Laos, Cambodia, and Vietnam, as well as more European offerings. The response time for project information ordered from the website could also be improved.

1

Source: Unsplash.com

Planning a document

Before you create a new document, it's a good idea to spend time planning it. Identify the message you want to convey, the audience for your document, and the elements, such as tables or charts, you want to include. You should also think about the tone and look of your document—are you writing a business letter, which should be written in a pleasant, but serious, tone and have a formal appearance, or are you creating a flyer that must be colorful, eye-catching, and fun to read? The purpose and audience for your document determine the appropriate design. Planning the layout and design of a document involves deciding how to organize the text, selecting the fonts to use, identifying the graphics to include, and selecting the formatting elements that will enhance the message and appeal of the document. For longer documents, such as newsletters, it can be useful to sketch the layout and design of each page before you begin.

Explore the Word Window

When you start Word, the Word start screen opens. It includes a list of recently opened documents and a gallery of templates for creating a new document. **CASE** ▶ *You open a blank document and examine the elements of the Word program window.*

STEPS

1. **Start Word, then click Blank document**

   A blank document opens in the **Word program window**, as shown in **FIGURE 1-2**. The blinking vertical line in the document window is the **insertion point**. It indicates where text appears as you type.

2. **Move the mouse pointer around the Word program window**

   The mouse pointer changes shape depending on where it is in the Word program window. You use pointers to move the insertion point or to select text to edit. **TABLE 1-1** describes common pointers in Word.

3. **Place the mouse pointer over a button on the Ribbon**

   When you place the mouse pointer over a button or some other elements of the Word program window, a ScreenTip appears. A **ScreenTip** is a label that identifies the name of the button or feature, briefly describes its function, conveys any keyboard shortcut for the command, and includes a link to associated help topics, if any.

DETAILS

Using FIGURE 1-2 as a guide, find the elements described below in your program window:

- The **title bar** displays the name of the document and the name of the program. Until you give a new document a different name, its temporary name is Document1. The left side of the title bar contains the **Quick Access toolbar**, which includes buttons for saving a document and for undoing, redoing, and repeating a change. The right side of the title bar contains the **Ribbon Display Options button**, which you use to hide or show the Ribbon and tabs, the resizing buttons, and the program Close button.

- The **File tab** provides access to **Backstage view** where you manage files and the information about them. Backstage view includes commands related to working with documents, such as opening, printing, and saving a document. The File tab also provides access to your account and to the Word Options dialog box, which is used to customize the way you use Word.

- The **Ribbon** contains the Word tabs. Each **tab** on the Ribbon includes buttons for commands related to editing and formatting documents. The commands are organized in **groups**. For example, the Home tab includes the Clipboard, Font, Paragraph, Styles, and Editing groups. The Ribbon also includes the **Tell Me box**, which you can use to find a command or access the Word Help system, and the **Share button**, which you can use to save a document to the Cloud.

- The **document window** displays the current document. You enter text and format your document in the document window.

- The rulers appear in the document window in Print Layout view. The **horizontal ruler** displays left and right document margins as well as the tab settings and paragraph indents, if any, for the paragraph in which the insertion point is located. The **vertical ruler** displays the top and bottom document margins.

- The **vertical** and **horizontal scroll bars** are used to display different parts of the document in the document window. The scroll bars include **scroll boxes** and **scroll arrows**, which you use to scroll.

- The **status bar** displays the page number of the current page, the total number of pages and words in the document, and the status of spelling and grammar checking. It also includes the view buttons, the Zoom slider, and the Zoom level button. You can customize the status bar to display other information.

- The **view buttons** on the status bar allow you to display the document in Read Mode, Print Layout, or Web Layout view. The **Zoom slider** and the **Zoom level button** provide quick ways to enlarge and decrease the size of the document in the document window, making it easy to zoom in on a detail of a document or to view the layout of the document as a whole.

FIGURE 1-2: Elements of the Word program window

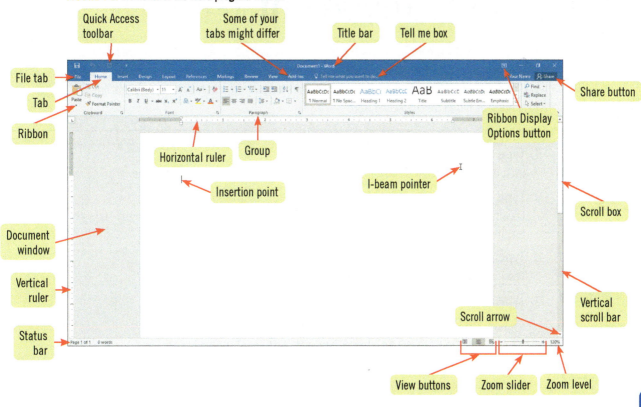

TABLE 1-1: Common mouse pointers in Word

name	pointer	use to
I-beam pointer	I	Move the insertion point in a document or to select text
Click and Type pointers, including left-align and center-align	I≣ I	Move the insertion point to a blank area of a document in Print Layout or Web Layout view; double-clicking with a Click and Type pointer automatically applies the paragraph formatting (alignment and indentation) required to position text or a graphic at that location in the document
Selection pointer	⌖	Click a button or other element of the Word program window; appears when you point to elements of the Word program window
Right-pointing arrow pointer	⇖	Select a line or lines of text; appears when you point to the left edge of a line of text in the document window
Hand pointer	☝	Open a hyperlink; appears when you point to a hyperlink in a task pane or when you press [Ctrl] and point to a hyperlink in a document
Hide white space pointer	⊣⊢	Hide the white space in the top and bottom margins of a document in Print Layout view
Show white space pointer	≑	Show the white space in the top and bottom margins of a document in Print Layout view

Word 2016

Start a Document

You begin a new document by simply typing text in a blank document in the document window. Word uses **word wrap**, a feature that automatically moves the insertion point to the next line of the document as you type. You only press [Enter] when you want to start a new paragraph or insert a blank line. **CASE** ▶ *You type a quick memo to the marketing staff.*

STEPS

1. **Type Reason2Go, then press [Enter] twice**
   Each time you press [Enter] the insertion point moves to the start of the next line.

2. **Type TO:, then press [Tab] twice**
   Pressing [Tab] moves the insertion point several spaces to the right. You can use the [Tab] key to align the text in a memo header or to indent the first line of a paragraph.

3. **Type R2G Managers, then press [Enter]**
   The insertion point moves to the start of the next line.

4. **Type:** **FROM: [Tab] [Tab] Mary Watson [Enter]**
   DATE: [Tab] [Tab] March 13, 2017 [Enter]
   RE: [Tab] [Tab] Marketing Meeting [Enter] [Enter]
   Red or blue wavy lines may appear under the words you typed, indicating a possible spelling or grammar error. Spelling and grammar checking is one of the many automatic features you will encounter as you type. **TABLE 1-2** describes several of these automatic features. You can correct any typing errors you make later.

5. **Type The next marketing staff meeting will be held on the 17th of March at 2 p.m. in the conference room on the ground floor., then press [Spacebar]**
   As you type, notice that the insertion point moves automatically to the next line of the document. You also might notice that Word automatically changed "17th" to "17th" in the memo. This feature is called **AutoCorrect**. AutoCorrect automatically makes typographical adjustments and detects and adjusts typing errors, certain misspelled words (such as "taht" for "that"), and incorrect capitalization as you type.

6. **Type Heading the agenda will be the launch of our new Sea Turtle Conservation Project, a rewarding opportunity to supervise hatcheries, count and release baby turtles, and patrol the nighttime shores of Costa Rica. The project is scheduled for September 2017.**
   When you type the first few characters of "September," the Word AutoComplete feature displays the complete word in a ScreenTip. **AutoComplete** suggests text to insert quickly into your documents. You can ignore AutoComplete for now. Your memo should resemble **FIGURE 1-3**.

7. **Press [Enter], then type Sam Roiphe is in Tamarindo hammering out the details. A preliminary draft of the project brochure is attached. Bring your creative ideas to the meeting.**
   When you press [Enter] and type the new paragraph, notice that Word adds more space between the paragraphs than it does between the lines in each paragraph. This is part of the default style for paragraphs in Word, called the **Normal style**.

8. **Position the I pointer after for (but before the space) in the last sentence of the first paragraph, then click to move the insertion point after "for"**

9. **Press [Backspace] three times, then type to begin in**
   Pressing [Backspace] removes the character before the insertion point.

10. **Move the insertion point before staff in the first sentence, then press [Delete] six times to remove the word "staff" and the space after it**
    Pressing [Delete] removes the character after the insertion point. **FIGURE 1-4** shows the revised memo.

FIGURE 1-3: Memo text in the document window

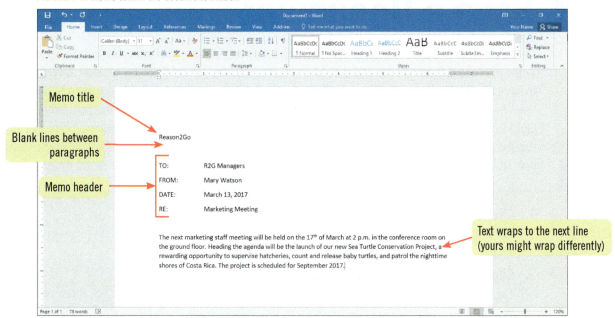

Memo title

Blank lines between paragraphs

Memo header

Text wraps to the next line (yours might wrap differently)

FIGURE 1-4: Edited memo text

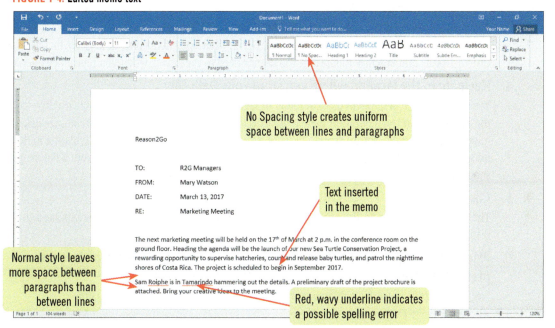

No Spacing style creates uniform space between lines and paragraphs

Text inserted in the memo

Normal style leaves more space between paragraphs than between lines

Red, wavy underline indicates a possible spelling error

TABLE 1-2: Automatic features that appear as you type in Word

feature	what appears	to use
AutoComplete	A ScreenTip suggesting text to insert appears as you type	Press [Enter] to insert the text suggested by the ScreenTip; continue typing to reject the suggestion
AutoCorrect	A small blue box appears when you place the pointer over text corrected by AutoCorrect; an AutoCorrect Options button appears when you point to the blue box	Word automatically corrects typos, minor spelling errors, and capitalization, and adds typographical symbols (such as © and ™) as you type; to reverse an AutoCorrect adjustment, click the AutoCorrect Options list arrow, then click the option that will undo the action
Spelling and Grammar	A red wavy line under a word indicates a possible misspelling or a repeated word; a blue wavy line under text indicates a possible grammar error	Right-click red- or blue-underlined text to display a shortcut menu of correction options; click a correction option to accept it and remove the wavy underline

Save a Document

Learning Outcomes
- Save a file using a descriptive filename
- Use the Save As dialog box

To store a document permanently so you can open it and edit it at another time, you must save it as a **file**. When you **save** a document you give it a name, called a **filename**, and indicate the location where you want to store the file. Files created in Word 2016 are automatically assigned the .docx file extension to distinguish them from files created in other software programs. You can save a document using the Save button on the Quick Access toolbar or the Save command on the File tab. Once you have saved a document for the first time, you should save it again every few minutes and always before printing so that the saved file is updated to reflect your latest changes. **CASE** *You save your memo using a descriptive filename and the default file extension.*

STEPS

1. **Click the Save button 🖫 on the Quick Access toolbar**

   The first time you save a document, the Save As screen opens. The screen displays all the places you can save a file to, including OneDrive, your PC, or a different location.

TROUBLE

If you don't see the extension .docx as part of the filename, the setting in Windows to display file extensions is not active.

2. **Click Browse in the Save As screen**

   The Save As dialog box opens, similar to **FIGURE 1-5**. The default filename, Reason2Go, appears in the File name text box. The default filename is based on the first few words of the document. The default file type, Word Document, appears in the Save as type list box. **TABLE 1-3** describes the functions of some of the buttons in the Save As dialog box.

3. **Type WD 1-Sea Turtle Memo in the File name text box**

   The new filename replaces the default filename. Giving your documents brief descriptive filenames makes it easier to locate and organize them later. You do not need to type .docx when you type a new filename.

4. **Navigate to the location where you store your Data Files**

   You can navigate to a different drive or folder in several ways. For example, you can click a drive or folder in the Address bar or the navigation pane to go directly to that location. You can also double-click a drive or folder in the folder window to change the active location. When you are finished navigating to the drive or folder where you store your Data Files, that location appears in the Address bar. Your Save As dialog box should resemble **FIGURE 1-6**.

5. **Click Save**

   The document is saved to the drive and folder you specified in the Save As dialog box, and the title bar displays the new filename, WD 1-Sea Turtles Memo.docx.

6. **Place the insertion point before conference in the first sentence, type large, then press [Spacebar]**

   You can continue to work on a document after you have saved it with a new filename.

7. **Click 🖫**

   Your change to the memo is saved. After you save a document for the first time, you must continue to save the changes you make to the document. You also can press [Ctrl][S] to save a document.

FIGURE 1-5: Save As dialog box

Active folder or drive (yours might differ)

Folders and files in the active folder or drive (yours might differ)

Default filename and file extension are selected

Click to change the file type

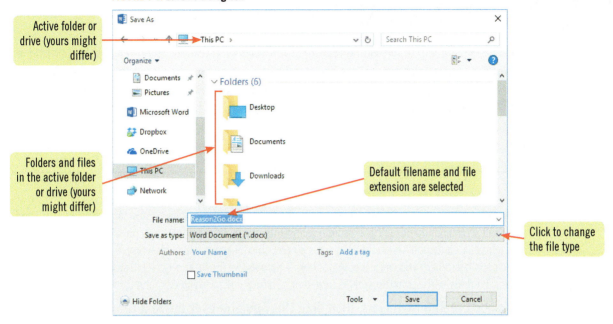

FIGURE 1-6: File to be saved to the Mod 1 folder

Click to create a new folder in the active folder or drive

Save location (yours might differ)

Your dialog box might list the files and folders in the active drive or folder here

New filename

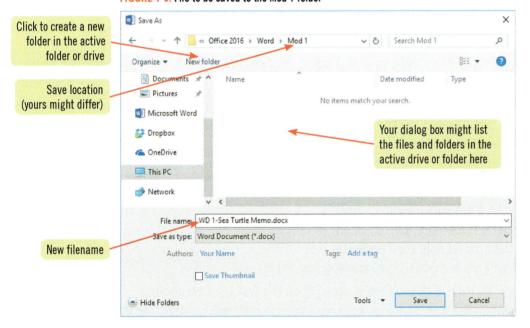

TABLE 1-3: Save As dialog box buttons

button	use to
Back	Navigate back to the last location shown in the Address bar
Forward	Navigate to the location that was previously shown in the Address bar
Up to	Navigate to the location above the current location in the folder hierarchy
Organize	Open a menu of commands related to organizing the selected file or folder, including Cut, Copy, Delete, Rename, and Properties
New folder	Create a new folder in the current folder or drive
Change your view	Change the way folder and file information is shown in the folder window in the Save As dialog box; click the Change your view button to toggle between views, or click the list arrow to open a menu of view options

Select Text

Learning Outcomes
- Select text using the mouse
- Use formatting marks

Before deleting, editing, or formatting text, you must **select** the text. Selecting text involves clicking and dragging the I-beam pointer across the text to highlight it. You also can click in the margin to the left of text with the ⇗ pointer to select whole lines or paragraphs. **TABLE 1-4** describes the many ways to select text. **CASE** ▶ *You revise the memo by selecting text and replacing it with new text.*

STEPS

1. **Click the Show/Hide ¶ button 🔳 in the Paragraph group**

   Formatting marks appear in the document window. **Formatting marks** are special characters that appear on your screen but do not print. Common formatting marks include the paragraph symbol (¶), which shows the end of a paragraph—wherever you press [Enter]; the dot symbol (·), which represents a space—wherever you press [Spacebar]; and the arrow symbol (▲), which shows the location of a tab stop—wherever you press [Tab]. Working with formatting marks turned on can help you to select, edit, and format text with precision.

QUICK TIP
You deselect text by clicking anywhere in the document window.

2. **Click before R2G Managers, then drag the Ⅰ pointer over the text to select it**

   The words are selected, as shown in **FIGURE 1-7**. For now, you can ignore the floating toolbar that appears over text when you first select it.

3. **Type Marketing Staff**

   The text you type replaces the selected text.

4. **Double-click Mary, type your first name, double-click Watson, then type your last name**

   Double-clicking a word selects the entire word.

TROUBLE
If you delete text by mistake, immediately click the Undo button on the Quick Access toolbar to restore the deleted text to the document.

5. **Place the pointer in the margin to the left of the RE: line so that the pointer changes to ⇗, click to select the line, then type RE: [Tab] [Tab] Launch of new Sea Turtle Conservation Project**

   Clicking to the left of a line of text with the ⇗ pointer selects the entire line.

6. **Select supervise in the third line of the first paragraph, type build, select nighttime shores, then type moon-lit beaches**

7. **Select the sentence Sam Roiphe is in Tamarindo hammering out the details. in the second paragraph, then press [Delete]**

   Selecting text and pressing [Delete] removes the text from the document.

QUICK TIP
Always save before and after editing text.

8. **Click 🔳, then click the Save button 🔲 on the Quick Access toolbar**

   Formatting marks are turned off, and your changes to the memo are saved. The Show/Hide ¶ button is a **toggle button**, which means you can use it to turn formatting marks on and off. The edited memo is shown in **FIGURE 1-8**.

FIGURE 1-7: Text selected in the memo

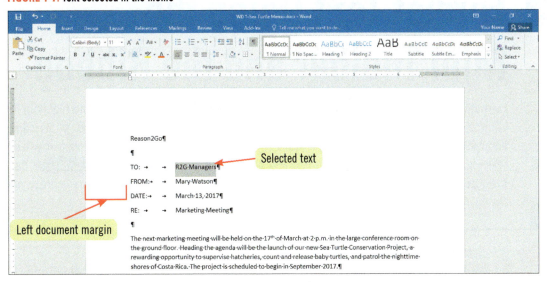

FIGURE 1-8: Edited memo with replacement text

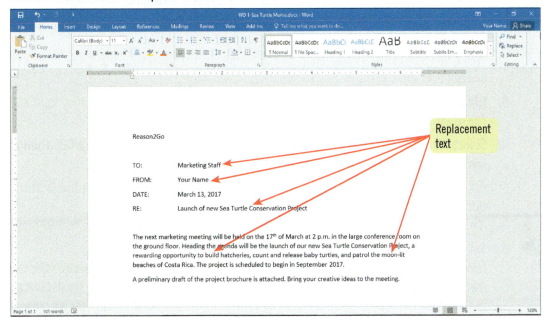

TABLE 1-4: Methods for selecting text

to select	use the pointer to
Any amount of text	Drag over the text
A word	Double-click the word
A line of text	Move the pointer to the left of the line, then click
A sentence	Press and hold [Ctrl], then click the sentence
A paragraph	Triple-click the paragraph or double-click with the pointer to the left of the paragraph
A large block of text	Click at the beginning of the selection, press and hold [Shift], then click at the end of the selection
Multiple nonconsecutive selections	Select the first selection, then press and hold [Ctrl] as you select each additional selection
An entire document	Triple-click with the pointer to the left of any text; press [Ctrl][A]; or click the Select button in the Editing group on the Home tab, and then click Select All

Format Text Using the Mini Toolbar and the Ribbon

Learning Outcomes
• Apply bold to text
• Increase the font size of text
• Print a document

Formatting text is a fast and fun way to spruce up the appearance of a document and highlight important information. You can easily change the font, color, size, style, and other attributes of text by selecting the text and clicking a command on the Home tab. The **Mini toolbar**, which appears above text when you first select it, also includes commonly used text and paragraph formatting commands. **CASE** *You enhance the appearance of the memo by formatting the text using the Mini toolbar. When you are finished, you preview the memo for errors and then print it.*

STEPS

TROUBLE
If the Mini toolbar disappears, right-click the selection to display it again.

1. **Select Reason2Go**

   The Mini toolbar appears over the selected text, as shown in **FIGURE 1-9**. You click a formatting option on the Mini toolbar to apply it to the selected text. **TABLE 1-5** describes the function of the buttons on the Mini toolbar. The buttons on the Mini toolbar are also available on the Ribbon.

QUICK TIP
Click the Decrease Font Size button to decrease the font size.

2. **Click the Increase Font Size button A̦ on the Mini toolbar six times, then click the Bold button B on the Mini toolbar**

   Each time you click the Increase Font Size button the selected text is enlarged. Applying bold to the text makes it thicker.

3. **Click the Center button in the Paragraph group on the Home tab**

   The selected text is centered between the left and right margins.

4. **Select TO:, click B, select FROM:, click B, select DATE:, click B, select RE:, then click B**

   Bold is applied to the memo header labels.

5. **Click the blank line between the RE: line and the body text, then click the Bottom Border button ⊞ in the Paragraph group**

   A single-line border is added between the heading and the body text in the memo.

QUICK TIP
You can customize your Quick Access toolbar to include the Quick Print button, which prints a document using the default print settings.

6. **Save the document, click the File tab, then click Print**

   Information related to printing the document appears on the Print screen in Backstage view. Options for printing the document appear on the left side of the Print screen and a preview of the document as it will look when printed appears on the right side, as shown in **FIGURE 1-10**. Before you print a document, it's a good habit to examine it closely so you can identify and correct any problems.

7. **Click the Zoom In button ✚ on the status bar five times, then proofread your document carefully for errors**

   The document is enlarged in print preview. If you notice errors in your document, you need to correct them before you print. To do this, press [Esc] or click the Back button in Backstage view, correct any mistakes, save your changes, click the File tab, and then click the Print command again to be ready to print the document.

8. **Click the Print button on the Print screen**

   A copy of the memo prints using the default print settings. To change the current printer, change the number of copies to print, select what pages of a document to print, or modify another print setting, you simply change the appropriate setting on the Print screen before clicking the Print button.

9. **Click the File tab, then click Close**

   The document closes, but the Word program window remains open.

FIGURE 1-9: Mini toolbar

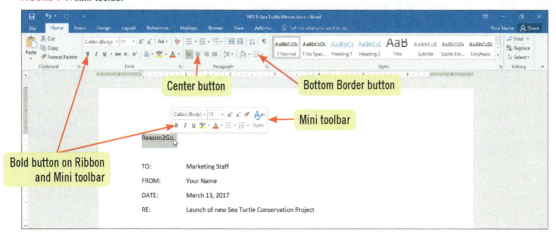

Center button

Bottom Border button

Mini toolbar

Bold button on Ribbon and Mini toolbar

FIGURE 1-10: Preview of the completed memo

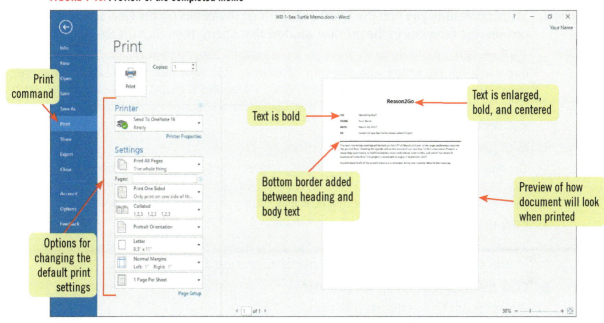

Print command

Options for changing the default print settings

Text is bold

Bottom border added between heading and body text

Text is enlarged, bold, and centered

Preview of how document will look when printed

Word 2016

TABLE 1-5: Buttons on the Mini toolbar

button	use to	button	use to
Calibri (Body) ▾	Change the font of text	B	Apply bold to text
11 ▾	Change the font size of text	I	Apply italic to text
A	Make text larger	U	Apply an underline to text
A	Make text smaller	aby ▾	Apply colored highlighting to text
✦	Copy the formats applied to selected text to other text	A ▾	Change the color of text
A Styles	Apply a style to text	☰ ▾	Apply bullets to paragraphs
		☷ ▾	Apply numbering to paragraphs

Use a Document Template

Learning Outcomes
- Search for templates
- Customize a template
- Use content controls

Word includes many templates that you can use to create letters, reports, brochures, calendars, and other professionally designed documents quickly. A **template** is a formatted document that contains place-holder text and graphics, which you replace with your own text and graphics. To create a document that is based on a template, you use the New command on the File tab in Backstage view, and then select a template to use. You can then customize the document and save it with a new filename. **CASE** ▸ *You use a template to create a cover letter for a contract you will send to the Rainforest Hotel in Tamarindo.*

STEPS

QUICK TIP
You must have an active Internet connection to search for templates.

1. **Click the File tab, then click New**

   The New screen opens in Backstage view, as shown in **FIGURE 1-11**. You can select a template from the gallery shown in this window, or use the search box and links in the Suggested Searches section to find other templates.

TROUBLE
Templates change over time. If this template is not available, select another Cover Letter template or just read the steps to understand how to work with templates.

2. **Scroll down until you find the Cover Letter (blue) thumbnail on the New screen, click it, preview the template in the preview window that opens, then click Create**

   The Cover Letter (blue) template opens as a new document in the document window. It contains placeholder text, which you can replace with your own information. Your name might appear at the top of the document. Don't be concerned if it does not. When a document is created using this template, Word automatically enters the username from the Word Options dialog box at the top of the document and in the signature block.

3. **Click [Date] in the document**

   The placeholder text is selected and appears inside a content control. A **content control** is an interactive object that you use to customize a document with your own information. A content control might include placeholder text, a drop-down list of choices, or a calendar.

4. **Click the [Date] list arrow**

   A calendar opens below the content control. You use the calendar to select the date you want to appear on your document—simply click a date on the calendar to enter that date in the document.

5. **Click the Today button on the calendar**

   The current date replaces the placeholder text.

QUICK TIP
You can delete any content control by right-clicking it, and then clicking Remove Content Control on the menu that opens.

6. **Click [Recipient Name], type Ms. Yana Roy, press [Enter], type Manager, press [Enter], type Rainforest Lodge, press [Enter], type P.O. Box 4397, press [Enter], then type Tamarindo 50309, COSTA RICA**

   You do not need to drag to select the placeholder text in a content control, you can simply click it. The text you type replaces the placeholder text.

7. **Click [Recipient], then type Ms. Roy**

   The text you type replaces the placeholder text in the greeting line.

8. **Click the File tab, click Save As, then save the document as WD 1-Rainforest Letter to the location where you store your Data Files**

   The document is saved with the filename WD 1-Rainforest Letter, as shown in **FIGURE 1-12**.

FIGURE 1-11: New screen in Backstage view

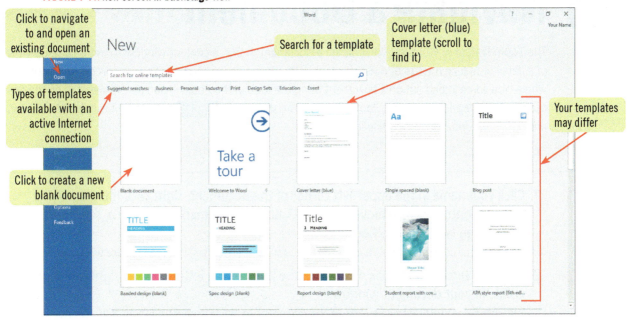

Click to navigate to and open an existing document

Search for a template

Cover letter (blue) template (scroll to find it)

Types of templates available with an active Internet connection

Your templates may differ

Click to create a new blank document

FIGURE 1-12: Document created using the Cover Letter (blue) template

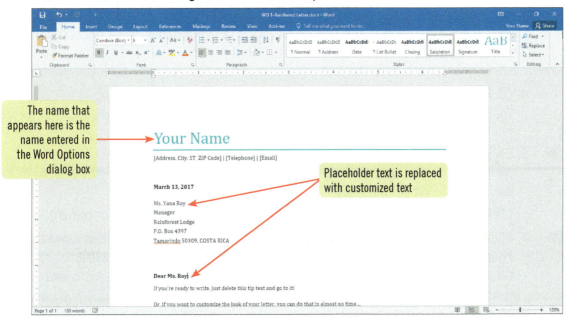

The name that appears here is the name entered in the Word Options dialog box

Placeholder text is replaced with customized text

Using the Undo, Redo, and Repeat commands

Word remembers the editing and formatting changes you make so that you can easily reverse or repeat them. You can reverse the last action you took by clicking the Undo button 🔄 on the Quick Access toolbar, or you can undo a series of actions by clicking the Undo list arrow 🔄▾ and selecting the action you want to reverse. When you undo an action using the Undo list arrow, you also undo all the actions above it in the list—that is, all actions that were performed after the action you selected. Similarly, you can keep the change you just reversed by using the Redo button 🔄

on the Quick Access toolbar. The Redo button appears only immediately after clicking the Undo button to undo a change.

If you want to repeat an action you just completed, you can use the Repeat button 🔄 on the Quick Access toolbar. For example, if you just typed "thank you," clicking 🔄 inserts "thank you" at the location of the insertion point. If you just applied bold, clicking 🔄 applies bold to the currently selected text. You also can repeat the last action you took by pressing [F4].

Navigate a Document

Learning Outcomes
- Remove a content control
- Zoom, scroll, and use Word views

The Zoom feature in Word lets you enlarge a document in the document window to get a close-up view of a detail or reduce the size of the document in the document window for an overview of the layout as a whole. You zoom in and out on a document using the tools in the Zoom group on the View tab or you can use the Zoom level buttons and Zoom slider on the status bar. **CASE** ▶ *You find it is helpful to zoom in and out on the document as you finalize the letter.*

STEPS

TROUBLE

If your name does not appear in the content control, replace the text that does.

1. **Click your name in the upper-left corner of the document, right-click the Your Name content control, click Remove Content Control on the menu that opens, select your name, then type Reason2Go**

   Removing the content control changes the text to static text that you can then replace with other text.

TROUBLE

If you do not see the vertical scroll box, move the pointer to the right side of the document window to display it.

2. **Drag the vertical scroll box down until the body of the letter and the signature block are visible in your document window**

   You **scroll** to display different parts of the document in the document window. You can also scroll by clicking the scroll arrows above and below the scroll bar, or by clicking the scroll bar.

3. **Select the four paragraphs of placeholder body text, type Enclosed please find a copy of our contract for the Sea Turtle Conservation Project. We look forward to working with you., then, if the name in the signature block is not your name, select the text in the content control and type your name**

   The text you type replaces the placeholder text, as shown in **FIGURE 1-13**.

4. **Click the View tab, then click the Page Width button in the Zoom group**

   The document is enlarged to the width of the document window. When you enlarge a document, the area where the insertion point is located appears in the document window.

QUICK TIP

You can also click the Zoom button in the Zoom group on the View tab to open the Zoom dialog box.

5. **Click the Zoom level button 154% on the status bar**

   The Zoom dialog box opens. You use the Zoom dialog box to select a zoom level for displaying the document in the document window.

6. **Click the Whole page option button, then click OK to view the entire document**

7. **Click Reason2Go to move the insertion point to the top of the page, then move the Zoom slider to the right until the Zoom percentage is approximately 230%**

QUICK TIP

You can also move the Zoom slider by clicking a point on the Zoom slide, or by clicking the Zoom Out and Zoom In buttons.

   Dragging the Zoom slider to the right enlarges the document in the document window. Dragging the zoom slider to the left allows you to see more of the page at a reduced size.

8. **Click the [Address...] content control, type Travel, click [Telephone], type Volunteer, click [Email], type www.r2g.com, then press [Tab]**

   You can replace placeholder text with information that is different from what is suggested in the content control.

9. **Click the Read Mode button 📖 on the status bar**

   The document appears in the document window in Read Mode view. Read Mode view hides the tabs and ribbon to make it easier to read documents on screen. Read Mode view is useful for reading long documents.

QUICK TIP

You can also click View on the menu bar, then click Edit Document to return to Print Layout view.

10. **Click the Print Layout view button 📄 on the status bar, click the Zoom Out button ▬ on the status bar until the zoom level is 100%, then save the document**

    The completed cover letter is displayed at 100% zoom level in Print Layout view, as shown in **FIGURE 1-14**.

11. **Submit the document to your instructor, close the file, then exit Word**

FIGURE 1-13: Replacement text and Zoom slider

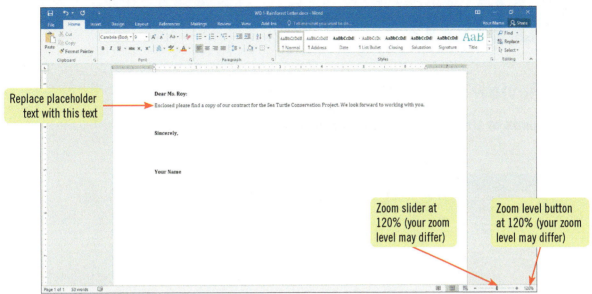

Replace placeholder text with this text

Zoom slider at 120% (your zoom level may differ)

Zoom level button at 120% (your zoom level may differ)

FIGURE 1-14: Completed letter

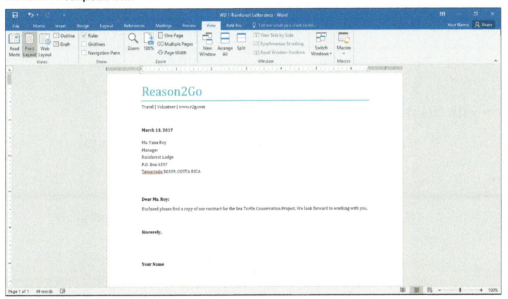

Using Word document views

Document **views** are different ways of displaying a document in the document window. Each Word view provides features that are useful for working on different types of documents. The default view, **Print Layout view**, displays a document as it will look on a printed page. Print Layout view is helpful for formatting text and pages, including adjusting document margins, creating columns of text, inserting graphics, and formatting headers and footers. Also useful is **Read Mode view**, which displays document text so that it is easy to read on screen. Other Word views are helpful for performing specialized tasks. **Web Layout view** allows you to format webpages or documents that will be viewed on a computer screen. In Web Layout view,

a document appears just as it will when viewed with a web browser. **Outline view** is useful for editing and formatting longer documents that include multiple headings. Outline view allows you to reorganize text by moving the headings. Finally, **Draft view**, shows a simplified layout of a document, without margins, headers and footers, or graphics. When you want to quickly type and edit text, it's often easiest to work in Draft View. You switch between views by clicking the view buttons on the status bar or by using the commands on the View tab. Changing views does not affect how the printed document will appear. It simply changes the way you view the document in the document window.

Practice

Concepts Review

Label the elements of the Word program window shown in FIGURE 1-15.

FIGURE 1-15

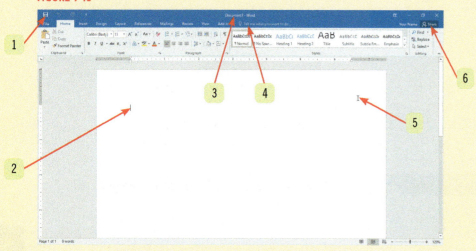

Match each term with the statement that best describes it.

7. **Ribbon**	**a.** A formatted document that contains placeholder text
8. **AutoCorrect**	**b.** Suggests text to insert into a document
9. **AutoComplete**	**c.** Fixes certain errors as you type
10. **Zoom slider**	**d.** Provides access to Word commands
11. **Status bar**	**e.** Special characters that appear on screen but do not print
12. **Horizontal ruler**	**f.** Displays tab settings and paragraph indents
13. **Template**	**g.** Enlarges and reduces the document in the document window
14. **Formatting marks**	**h.** Displays the number of pages in the current document

Select the best answer from the list of choices.

15. **Which of the following shows the number of words in the document?**

   a. The title bar   **c.** The status bar

   b. The Ribbon   **d.** The Mini toolbar

16. **Which tab includes buttons for formatting text?**

   a. View   **c.** Insert

   b. Page Layout   **d.** Home

17. **Which element of the Word window shows the top and bottom document margins settings?**

   a. Status bar   **c.** Vertical ruler

   b. View tab   **d.** Vertical scroll bar

18. **What is the default file extension for a document created in Word 2016?**

   a. .doc   **c.** .dotx

   b. .dot   **d.** .docx

19. **Which of the following is not included in a ScreenTip for a command?**
   a. Link to a help topic on the command
   b. Alternative location of the command
   c. Keyboard shortcut for the command
   d. Description of the function of the command

20. **Which view is best for reading text onscreen?**
   a. Print Layout view
   b. Outline view
   c. Read Mode view
   d. Draft view

Skills Review

1. **Explore the Word program window.**
   a. Start Word and open a new, blank document.
   b. Identify as many elements of the Word program window as you can without referring to the module material.
   c. Click the File tab, then click the Info, New, Save, Open, Save As, Print, Share, and Export commands.
   d. Click the Back button in Backstage view to return to the document window.
   e. Click each tab on the Ribbon, review the groups and buttons on each tab, then return to the Home tab.
   f. Point to each button on the Home tab and read its ScreenTip.
   g. Click the view buttons to view the blank document in each view, then return to Print Layout view.
   h. Use the Zoom slider to zoom all the way in and all the way out on the document, then return to 120%.

2. **Start a document.**
   a. In a new blank document, type **Summer of Music Festivals** at the top of the page, then press [Enter] two times.
   b. Type the following, pressing [Tab] as indicated and pressing [Enter] at the end of each line:
      To: [Tab] [Tab] **Michael Mellon**
      From: [Tab] [Tab] **Your Name**
      Date: [Tab] [Tab] **Today's date**
      Re: [Tab] [Tab] **Reservation confirmation**
      Pages: [Tab] [Tab] **1**
      Fax: [Tab] [Tab] **(603) 555-5478**
   c. Press [Enter] again, then type **Thank you for your interest in our summer music festival weekend package, which includes accommodations for three nights, continental breakfast, and a festival pass. Rooms are still available during the following festivals: International Jazz Festival, Americana Festival, Classical Fringe Festival, and the Festival of Arts. Please see the attached schedule for festival dates and details.**
   d. Press [Enter], then type **To make a reservation, please call me at (617) 555-7482 or visit our website. Payment must be received in full by the 3rd of June to hold a room. No one knows how to celebrate summer like music-lovers!**
   e. Insert **Summer Strings Festival,** before International Jazz Festival.
   f. Using the [Backspace] key, delete **1** in the Pages: line, then type **2**.
   g. Using the [Delete] key, delete **festival** in the last sentence of the first paragraph.

3. **Save a document.**
   a. Click the Save button on the Quick Access toolbar.
   b. Save the document as **WD 1-Mellon Fax** with the default file extension to the location where you store your Data Files.
   c. After your name, type a comma, press [Spacebar], then type **Reservations Manager**
   d. Save the document.

4. **Select text.**
   a. Turn on formatting marks.
   b. Select the **Re:** line, then type **Re:** [Tab] [Tab] **Summer Music Festival Weekend Package**

Skills Review (continued)

    c. Select **three** in the first sentence, then type **two**.

    d. Select **3rd of June** in the second sentence of the last paragraph, type **15th of May**, select **room**, then type **reservation**.

    e. Delete the sentence **No one knows how to celebrate summer like music-lovers!**

    f. Turn off the display of formatting marks, then save the document.

5. Format text using the Mini toolbar.

    a. Select **Summer of Music Festivals**, click the Increase Font Size button on the Mini toolbar six times, then apply bold.

    b. Center **Summer of Music Festivals** on the page.

    c. Apply a bottom border under **Summer of Music Festivals**.

    d. Apply bold to the following words in the fax heading: **To:**, **From:**, **Date:**, **Re:**, **Pages:**, and **Fax:**.

    e. Read the document using the Read Mode view.

    f. Return to Print Layout view, zoom in on the document, then proofread the fax.

    g. Correct any typing errors in your document, then save the document. Compare your document to **FIGURE 1-16**.

    h. Submit the fax to your instructor, then close the document.

FIGURE 1-16

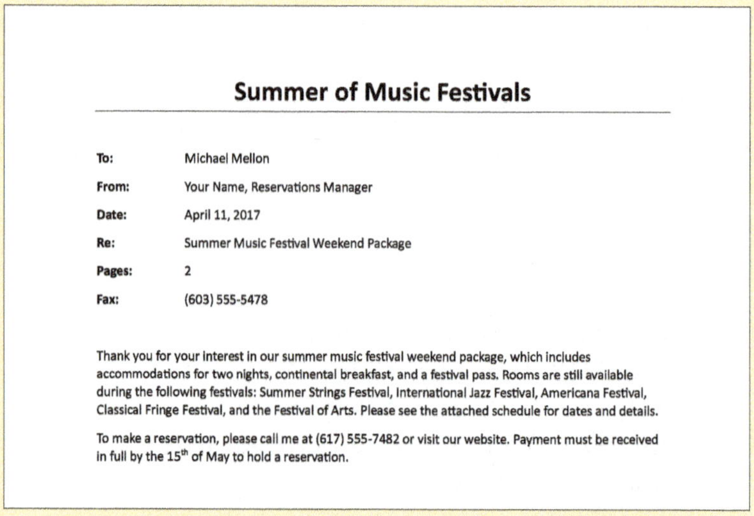

Summer of Music Festivals

To:	Michael Mellon
From:	Your Name, Reservations Manager
Date:	April 11, 2017
Re:	Summer Music Festival Weekend Package
Pages:	2
Fax:	(603) 555-5478

Thank you for your interest in our summer music festival weekend package, which includes accommodations for two nights, continental breakfast, and a festival pass. Rooms are still available during the following festivals: Summer Strings Festival, International Jazz Festival, Americana Festival, Classical Fringe Festival, and the Festival of Arts. Please see the attached schedule for dates and details.

To make a reservation, please call me at (617) 555-7482 or visit our website. Payment must be received in full by the 15th of May to hold a reservation.

6. Create a document using a template.

    a. Click the File tab, click New, then scroll the gallery of templates.

    b. Create a new document using the Fax cover sheet (Professional design) template.

    c. Click the "Company Name" placeholder text, type **Summer of Music Festivals**, delete the "Street Address" and "City..." content controls, click the "Phone number" placeholder text, type **Tel: 617-555-7482**, click the "Fax number" placeholder text, type **Fax: 617-555-1176**, click the website placeholder text, then type **www.summerofmusic.com**.

    d. Type **Jude Lennon** to replace the "To:" placeholder text; type **555-2119** to replace the "Fax:" placeholder text; click the "Phone:" placeholder text, then press [Delete]; then type **Summer of Music Festivals** to replace the "Re:" placeholder text.

    e. If your name is not on the From line, select the text in the From content control, then type your name.

    f. Insert today's date using the date content control.

    g. Delete the "Pages:" and "cc:" placeholder text.

    h. Save the document with the filename **WD 1-Lennon Fax** to the location where you store your Data Files, clicking OK if a warning box opens.

7. View and navigate a document.

    a. Scroll down until Comments is near the top of your document window.

    b. Replace the Comments placeholder text with the following text: **Packages for the following summer music festivals are sold out: Chamber Music Festival, Solstice Festival, and Dragonfly Festival. We had expected these packages to be less popular than those for the bigger festivals, but interest has been high. Next year, we will increase our bookings for these festivals by 30%.**

Skills Review (continued)

c. Use the Zoom dialog box to view the Whole Page.

d. Use the Zoom slider to set the Zoom percentage at approximately 100%.

e. Read the document using the Read Mode view.

f. Return to Print Layout view, zoom in on the document, then proofread the fax.

g. Preview the document, then correct any errors, saving changes if necessary. Compare your document to **FIGURE 1-17**. Submit the document to your instructor, close the file, then exit Word.

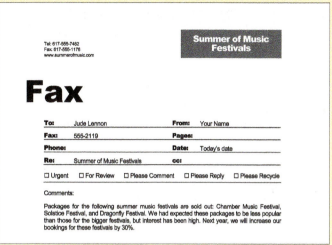

FIGURE 1-17

Independent Challenge 1

Yesterday you interviewed for a job as marketing director at Rose Design Services. You spoke with several people at the company, including Yuko Picard, chief executive officer, whose business card is shown in **FIGURE 1-18**. You need to write a follow-up letter to Ms. Picard, thanking her for the interview and expressing your interest in the company and the position. She also asked you to send her some samples of your marketing work, which you will enclose with the letter.

a. Start Word and save a new blank document as **WD 1-Picard Letter** to the location where you store your Data Files.

b. Begin the letter by clicking the No Spacing button in the Styles group. You use this button to apply the No Spacing style to the document so that your document does not include extra space between paragraphs.

c. Type a personal letterhead for the letter that includes your name, address, telephone number, and e-mail address. If Word formats your e-mail address as a hyperlink, right-click your e-mail address, then click Remove Hyperlink. (*Note: Format the letterhead after you finish typing the letter.*)

d. Three lines below the bottom of the letterhead, type today's date.

e. Four lines below the date, type the inside address, referring to **FIGURE 1-18** for the information. Include the recipient's title, company name, and full mailing address.

f. Two lines below the inside address, type **Dear Ms. Picard:** for the salutation.

g. Two lines below the salutation, type the body of the letter according to the following guidelines:

- In the first paragraph, thank her for the interview. Then restate your interest in the position and express your desire to work for the company. Add any specific details you think will enhance the power of your letter.
- In the second paragraph, note that you are enclosing three samples of your work, and explain something about the samples you are enclosing.
- Type a short final paragraph.

h. Two lines below the last body paragraph, type a closing, then four lines below the closing, type the signature block. Be sure to include your name in the signature block.

i. Two lines below the signature block, type an enclosure notation. (*Hint:* An enclosure notation usually includes the word "Enclosures" or the abbreviation "Enc." followed by the number of enclosures in parentheses.)

j. Format the letterhead with bold, centering, and a bottom border.

k. Save your changes, preview the letter, submit it to your instructor, then close the document and exit Word.

FIGURE 1-18

Rose Design Services
www.rosedesign.com

Yuko Picard
Chief Executive Officer

438 W. 23rd Street, Suite 76
New York, NY 10011
p. 212.555.7028
ypicard@rosedesign.com

Independent Challenge 2

Your company has recently installed Word 2016 on its company network. As the training manager, it's your responsibility to teach employees how to use the new software productively. Now that they have begun working with Word 2016, several employees have asked you about sharing documents with colleagues using OneDrive. In response, you wrote a memo to all employees explaining the Share feature. You now need to format the memo before distributing it.

a. Start Word, open the file **WD 1-1.docx** from the location where you store your Data Files, clicking the Enable Editing button if prompted to do so, then read the memo to get a feel for its contents. Switch to Print Layout view if the document is not already displayed in Print Layout view.

b. Save the file as **WD 1-Share Memo** to the location where you store your Data Files.

c. Replace the information in the memo header with the information shown in **FIGURE 1-19**. Make sure to include your name in the From line and the current date in the Date line.

d. Apply bold to **To:**, **From:**, **Date:**, and **Re:**.

e. Increase the size of **WORD TRAINING MEMORANDUM** to match **FIGURE 1-19**, center the text on the page, add a border below it, then save your changes.

f. Preview the memo, submit it to your instructor, then close the document and exit Word.

FIGURE 1-19

> ### WORD TRAINING MEMORANDUM
>
> | | |
> |---|---|
> | **To:** | All employees |
> | **From:** | Your Name, Training Manager |
> | **Date:** | Today's date |
> | **Re:** | Sharing documents |

Independent Challenge 3

You are an expert on climate change. The president of the National Parks Association, Isabella Meerts, has asked you to be the keynote speaker at an upcoming conference on the impact of climate change on the national parks, to be held in Grand Teton National Park. You use one of the Word letter templates to write a letter to Ms. Meerts accepting the invitation and confirming the details. Your letter to Ms. Meerts should reference the following information:

- The conference will be held September 17–19, 2017, at the Jackson Lake Lodge in the park.
- You have been asked to speak for an hour on Saturday, September 18, followed by one-half hour for questions.
- Ms. Meerts suggested the lecture topic "Melting Glaciers, Changing Ecosystems."
- Your talk will include a 45-minute slide presentation.
- The National Parks Association will make your travel arrangements.
- Your preference is to arrive at Jackson Hole Airport on the morning of Friday, September 17, and to depart on Monday, September 20. You would like to rent a car at the airport for the drive to the Jackson Lake Lodge.
- You want to fly in and out of the airport closest to your home.

a. Start Word, click the File tab, click New, and then search for and select an appropriate letter template. Save the document as **WD 1-Meerts Letter** to the location where you store your Data Files.

b. Replace the placeholders in the letterhead with your personal information. Include your name, address, phone number, and e-mail address. Delete any placeholders that do not apply. (*Hints:* Depending on the template you choose, the letterhead might be located at the top or on the side of the document. You can press [Enter] when typing in a placeholder to add an additional line of text. You can also change the format of text typed in a placeholder. If your e-mail address appears as a hyperlink, right-click the e-mail address and click Remove Hyperlink.)

Independent Challenge 3 (continued)

c. Use the [Date] content control to select the current date.

d. Replace the placeholders in the inside address. Be sure to include Ms. Meerts title and the name of the organization. Make up a street address and zip code.

e. Type **Dear Ms. Meerts:** for the salutation.

f. Using the information listed previously, type the body of the letter:

- In the first paragraph, accept the invitation to speak.
- In the second paragraph, confirm the important conference details, confirm your lecture topic, and provide any relevant details.
- In the third paragraph, state your travel preferences.
- Type a short final paragraph.

g. Type **Sincerely,** for the closing, then include your name in the signature block.

h. Adjust the formatting of the letter as necessary. For example, remove bold formatting or change the font color of text to a more appropriate color.

i. Proofread your letter, make corrections as needed, then save your changes.

j. Submit the letter to your instructor, close the document, then exit Word.

Independent Challenge 4: Explore

Word includes a wide variety of templates that can help you create professional-looking documents quickly, including business letters, business cards, résumés, calendars, faxes, memos, labels, reports, blog posts, posters, invitations, certificates, newsletters, and holiday and party cards. In this independent challenge, you will explore the variety of Word templates available to you, and use a template to make a document that is helpful to you in your business or personal life. You might create business cards for yourself, a poster for an event, a letter for a job search, a new résumé, or an invitation to a party. Choose a template that allows you to personalize the text.

a. Start Word, click the File tab, click New, then click each link after Suggested searches: (Business, Personal, Industry, Print, Design Sets, Education, Event) to explore the templates available to you.

b. Preview all the templates for the type of document you want to create, and then select one to create a new document.

c. Save the document as **WD 1-Template Document** to the location where you store your Data Files.

d. Replace the placeholders in the document with your personal information. Delete any placeholders that do not apply. (*Hints:* You can press [Enter] when typing in a placeholder to add an additional line of text. If an e-mail or web address appears as a hyperlink in your document, right-click the e-mail or web address and then click Remove Hyperlink.)

e. Use the [Pick the date] content control to select a date if your document includes a date placeholder.

f. Experiment with changing the font of the text in your document by using the Font list arrow on the Mini toolbar or in the Font group on the Home tab. (*Note:* Remember to use the Undo button immediately after you make the change if you do not like the change and want to remove it.)

g. Experiment with changing the font size of the text in your document by using the Font Size list arrow on the Mini toolbar or in the Font group on the Home tab.

h. Experiment with changing the color of text in your document using the Font Color button on the Mini toolbar or in the Font group on the Home tab.

i. Make other adjustments to the document as necessary, using the Undo button to remove a change you decide you do not want to keep.

j. Save your changes to the document, preview it, submit it to your instructor, then close the document and exit Word.

Visual Workshop

Create the cover letter shown in **FIGURE 1-20**. Before beginning to type, click the No Spacing button in the Styles group on the Home tab. Add the bottom border to the letterhead after typing the letter. Save the document as **WD 1-Davidson Cover Letter** to the location where you store your Data Files, submit the letter to your instructor, then close the document and exit Word.

FIGURE 1-20

Your Name
82 Genesee Street, Madison, WI 53701
Tel: 608-555-7283; E-mail: yourname@gmail.com

November 8, 2017

Ms. Marta Davidson
Davidson Associates
812 Jefferson Street
Suite 300
Madison, WI 53704

Dear Ms. Davidson:

I read of the opening for a public information assistant in the November 4 edition of wisconsinjobs.com, and I would like to be considered for the position. I am a recent graduate of the University of Wisconsin-Madison (UW), and I am interested in pursuing a career in public relations.

My interest in a public relations career springs from my publicly acknowledged writing and journalism abilities. For example, at UW, I was a reporter for the student newspaper and frequently wrote press releases for campus and community events.

I have a wealth of experience using Microsoft Word in professional settings. Last summer, I worked as an office assistant for the architecture firm Mason & Greenbush, where I used Word to create newsletters, brochures, and financial reports. During the school year, I also worked part-time in the UW Office of Community Relations, where I used the Word mail merge feature to create form letters and mailing labels.

My enclosed resume details my skills and experience. I welcome the opportunity to discuss the position and my qualifications with you. I can be reached at 608-555-7283.

Sincerely,

Your Name

Enc.

Editing Documents

CASE ▶ You have been asked to edit and finalize a press release for an R2G promotional lecture series. The press release should provide information about the series so that newspapers, radio stations, and other media outlets can announce it to the public. R2G press releases are disseminated via the website and by e-mail. Before distributing the file electronically to your lists of press contacts and local R2G clients, you add several hyperlinks and then strip the file of private information.

Module Objectives

After completing this module, you will be able to:

- Cut and paste text
- Copy and paste text
- Use the Office Clipboard
- Find and replace text

- Check spelling and grammar
- Research information
- Add hyperlinks
- Work with document properties

Files You Will Need

WD 2-1.docx	WD 2-5.docx
WD 2-2.docx	WD 2-6.docx
WD 2-3.docx	WD 2-7.docx
WD 2-4.docx	

Cut and Paste Text

The editing features in Word allow you to move text from one location to another in a document. Moving text is often called **cut and paste**. When you **cut** text, it is removed from the document and placed on the **Clipboard**, a temporary storage area for text and graphics that you cut or copy from a document. You can then **paste**, or insert, text that is stored on the Clipboard in the document at the location of the insertion point. You cut and paste text using the Cut and Paste buttons in the Clipboard group on the Home tab. You also can move selected text by dragging it to a new location using the mouse. This operation is called **drag and drop**. **CASE** ▶ *You open the press release, save it with a new filename, and then reorganize the information in the press release using the cut-and-paste and drag-and-drop methods.*

STEPS

1. **Start Word, click Blank document, click the File tab, click This PC on the Open screen, click Browse to open the Open dialog box, navigate to the location where you store your Data Files, click WD 2-1.docx, then click Open**

   The document opens in Print Layout view. Once you have opened a file, you can edit it and use the Save or the Save As command to save your changes. You use the **Save** command when you want to save the changes you make to a file, overwriting the stored file. You use the **Save As** command when you want to leave the original file intact and create a duplicate file with a different filename, file extension, or location.

2. **Click the File tab, click Save As, click Computer, click Browse to open the Save As dialog box, type WD 2-Lecture PR in the File name text box, then click Save**

   You can now make changes to the press release file without affecting the original file.

3. **Replace Mary Watson with your name, scroll down until the headline "Pedro Soares to Speak..." is at the top of your document window, then click the Show/Hide ¶ button ¶ in the Paragraph group on the Home tab to display formatting marks**

4. **Select Alaskan guide Michael Coonan, (including the comma and the space after it) in the third body paragraph, then click the Cut button in the Clipboard group**

   The text is removed from the document and placed on the Clipboard. Word uses two different clipboards: the **system clipboard**, which holds just one item, and the **Office Clipboard** (the Clipboard), which holds up to 24 items. The last item you cut or copy is always added to both clipboards.

5. **Place the insertion point before African (but after the space) in the first line of the third paragraph, then click the Paste button in the Clipboard group**

   The text is pasted at the location of the insertion point, as shown in **FIGURE 2-1**. The Paste Options button appears below text when you first paste it in a document. For now you can ignore the Paste Options button.

6. **Press and hold [Ctrl], click the sentence Ticket prices include lunch. in the fourth paragraph, then release [Ctrl]**

   The entire sentence is selected. You will drag the selected text to a new location using the mouse.

7. **Press and hold the mouse button over the selected text, then drag the pointer's vertical line to the end of the fifth paragraph (between the period and the paragraph mark) as shown in FIGURE 2-2**

   You drag the insertion point to where you want the text to be inserted when you release the mouse button.

8. **Release the mouse button**

   The selected text is moved to the location of the insertion point. Text is not placed on the Clipboard when you drag and drop it.

9. **Deselect the text, then click the Save button 🖫 on the Quick Access toolbar**

FIGURE 2-1: Moved text with Paste Options button

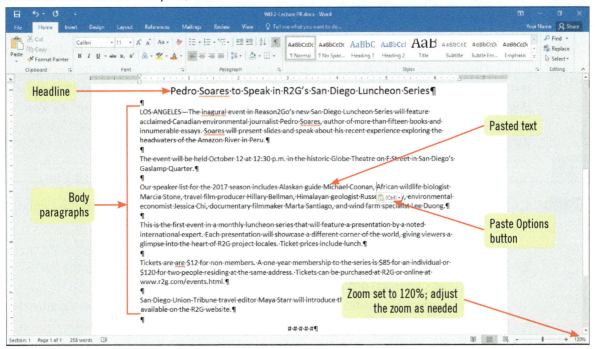

Headline → Pedro·Soares·to·Speak·in·R2G's·San·Diego·Luncheon·Series¶

Pasted text

Body paragraphs

Paste Options button

Zoom set to 120%; adjust the zoom as needed

FIGURE 2-2: Dragging and dropping text in a new location

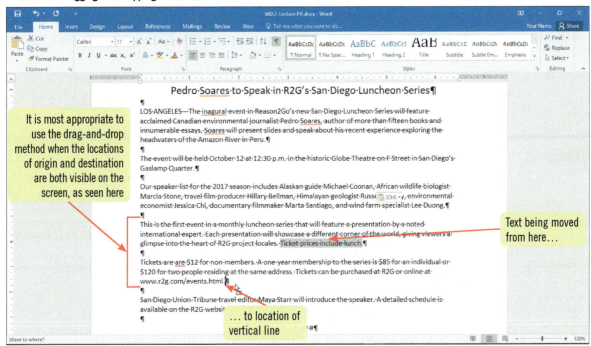

It is most appropriate to use the drag-and-drop method when the locations of origin and destination are both visible on the screen, as seen here

Text being moved from here…

… to location of vertical line

Copy and Paste Text

Copying and pasting text is similar to cutting and pasting text, except that the text you **copy** is not removed from the document. Rather, a copy of the text is placed on the Clipboard, leaving the original text in place. You can copy text to the Clipboard using the Copy button in the Clipboard group on the Home tab, or you can copy text by pressing [Ctrl] as you drag the selected text from one location to another. **CASE** *You continue to edit the press release by copying text from one location to another using the copy-and-paste and drag-and-drop methods.*

STEPS

1. **Select San Diego Luncheon in the headline, then click the Copy button in the Clipboard group on the Home tab**

   A copy of the selected text is placed on the Clipboard, leaving the original text you copied in place.

2. **Place the insertion point before season in the third paragraph, then click the Paste button in the Clipboard group**

   "San Diego Luncheon" is inserted before "season," as shown in **FIGURE 2-3**. Notice that the pasted text is formatted differently than the paragraph in which it was inserted.

3. **Click the Paste Options button, move the mouse over each button on the menu that opens to read its ScreenTip, then click the Keep Text Only (T) button**

   The formatting of "San Diego Luncheon" is changed to match the rest of the paragraph. The buttons on the Paste Options menu allow you to change the formatting of pasted text. You can choose to keep the original formatting (Keep Source Formatting), match the destination formatting (Merge Formatting), or paste as unformatted text (Keep Text Only).

4. **Select www.r2g.com in the fifth paragraph, press and hold [Ctrl], then drag the pointer's vertical line to the end of the last paragraph, placing it between site and the period**

   As you drag, the pointer changes to ⬚, indicating that the selected text is being copied and moved.

5. **Release the mouse button, then release [Ctrl]**

   The text is copied to the last paragraph. Since the formatting of the text you copied is the same as the formatting of the destination paragraph, you can ignore the Paste Options button. Text is not copied to the Clipboard when you copy it using the drag-and-drop method.

6. **Place the insertion point before www.r2g.com in the last paragraph, type at followed by a space, then save the document**

   Compare your document with **FIGURE 2-4**.

Splitting the document window to copy and move items in a long document

If you want to copy or move items between parts of a long document, it can be useful to split the document window into two panes. This allows you to display the item you want to copy or move in one pane and the destination for the item in the other pane. To split a window, click the Split button in the Window group on the View tab, and then drag the horizontal split bar that appears to the location you want to split the window. Once the document window is split into two panes, you can use the scroll bars in each pane to display different parts of the document. To copy or move an item from one pane to another, you can use the Cut, Copy, and Paste commands, or you can drag the item between the panes. When you are finished editing the document, double-click the split bar to restore the window to a single pane, or click the Remove Split button in the Window group on the View tab.

FIGURE 2-3: Text pasted in document

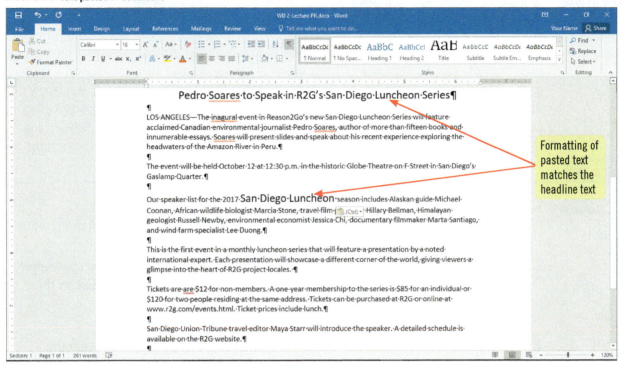

Formatting of pasted text matches the headline text

FIGURE 2-4: Copied text in document

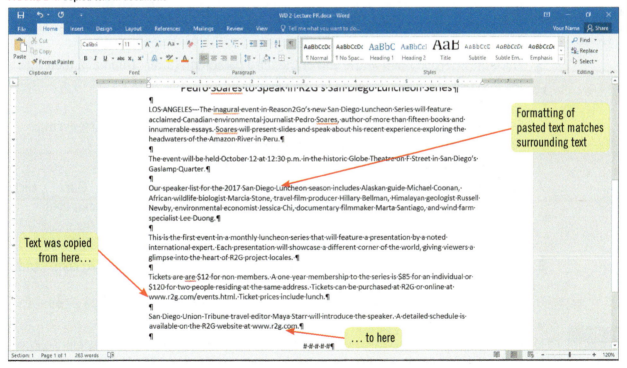

Formatting of pasted text matches surrounding text

Text was copied from here…

… to here

Use the Office Clipboard

Learning Outcomes
• Copy and cut items to the Clipboard
• Paste items from the Clipboard

The Office Clipboard allows you to collect text and graphics from files created in any Office program and insert them into your Word documents. It holds up to 24 items and, unlike the system clipboard, the items on the Office Clipboard can be viewed. To display the Office Clipboard (the Clipboard), you simply click the launcher in the Clipboard group on the Home tab. You add items to the Office Clipboard using the Cut and Copy commands. The last item you collect is always added to both the system clipboard and the Office Clipboard. **CASE** *You use the Office Clipboard to move several sentences in your press release.*

STEPS

QUICK TIP
You can set the Clipboard pane to open automatically when you cut or copy two items consecutively by clicking Options on the Clipboard pane, and then selecting Show Office Clipboard Automatically.

1. **Click the launcher 🔲 in the Clipboard group on the Home tab**
   The Office Clipboard opens in the Clipboard pane. It contains the San Diego Luncheon item you copied in the last lesson.

2. **Select the sentence San Diego Union-Tribune travel editor... (including the space after the period) in the last paragraph, right-click the selected text, then click Cut on the menu that opens**
   The sentence is cut to the Clipboard.

3. **Select the sentence A detailed schedule is... (including the ¶ mark), right-click the selected text, then click Cut**
   The Clipboard displays the items you cut or copied, as shown in **FIGURE 2-5**. The icon next to each item indicates the items are from a Word document. The last item collected is displayed at the top of the Clipboard pane. As new items are collected, the existing items move down the Clipboard.

QUICK TIP
If you add a 25th item to the Clipboard, the first item you collected is deleted.

4. **Place the insertion point at the end of the second paragraph (after "Quarter." but before the ¶ mark), then click the San Diego Union-Tribune... item on the Clipboard**
   Clicking an item on the Clipboard pastes the item in the document at the location of the insertion point. Items remain on the Clipboard until you delete them or close all open Office programs.

5. **Place the insertion point at the end of the third paragraph (after "Duong."), then click the A detailed schedule is... item on the Clipboard**
   The sentence is pasted into the document.

6. **Select the fourth paragraph, which begins with the sentence This is the first event... (including the ¶ mark), right-click the selected text, then click Cut**
   The paragraph is cut to the Clipboard.

7. **Place the insertion point at the beginning of the third paragraph (before "Our..."), click the Paste button in the Clipboard group on the Home tab, then press [Backspace]**
   The sentences from the "This is the first..." paragraph are pasted at the beginning of the "Our speaker list..." paragraph. You can paste the last item collected using either the Paste command or the Clipboard.

8. **Place the insertion point at the end of the third paragraph (after "www.r2g.com." and before the ¶ mark), then press [Delete] twice**
   Two ¶ symbols and the corresponding blank lines between the third and fourth paragraphs are deleted.

QUICK TIP
To delete an individual item from the Clipboard, click the list arrow next to the item, then click Delete.

9. **Click the Show/Hide ¶ button ¶ on in the Paragraph group**
   Compare your press release with **FIGURE 2-6**. Note that many Word users prefer to work with formatting marks on at all times. Experiment to see which method you prefer.

10. **Click the Clear All button on the Clipboard pane to remove the items from the Clipboard, click the Close button ✖ on the Clipboard pane, press [Ctrl][Home], then save the document**
    Pressing [Ctrl][Home] moves the insertion point to the top of the document.

FIGURE 2-5: Office Clipboard in Clipboard pane

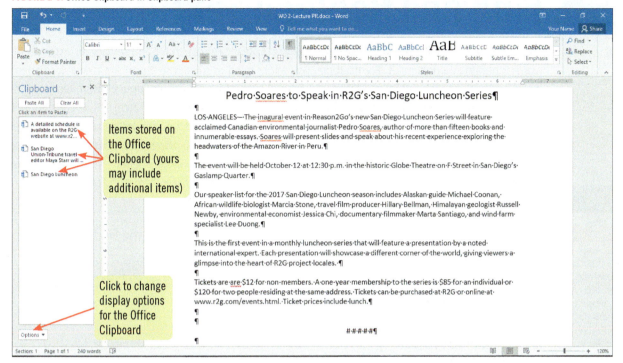

Items stored on the Office Clipboard (yours may include additional items)

Click to change display options for the Office Clipboard

FIGURE 2-6: Revised press release

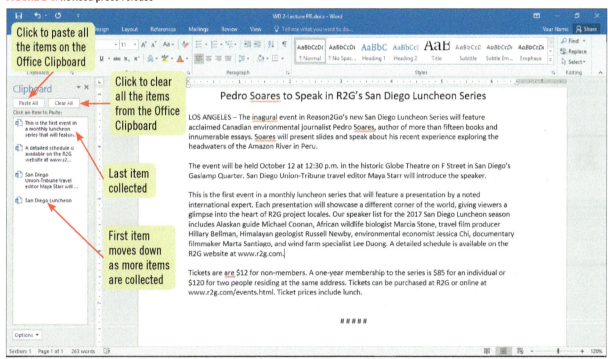

Click to paste all the items on the Office Clipboard

Click to clear all the items from the Office Clipboard

Last item collected

First item moves down as more items are collected

Copying and moving items between documents

You can also use the Clipboard to copy and move items between documents. To do this, open both documents and the Clipboard pane. With multiple documents open, copy or cut an item from one document and then switch to the other document and paste the item. To switch between open documents, point to the Word icon 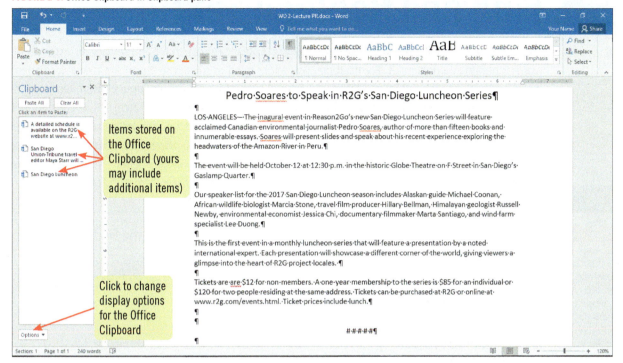 on the taskbar, and then click the document you want to appear in the document window. You can also display more than one document at the same time by clicking the Arrange All button or the View Side by Side button in the Window group on the View tab.

Word 2016

Find and Replace Text

Learning Outcomes
- Replace text
- Find text with the Navigation pane
- Navigate a document

The Find and Replace feature in Word allows you to automatically search for and replace all instances of a word or phrase in a document. For example, you might need to substitute "tour" for "trip." To manually locate and replace each instance of "trip" in a long document would be very time-consuming. Using the Replace command, you can find and replace all occurrences of specific text at once, or you can choose to find and review each occurrence individually. Using the Find command, you can locate and highlight every occurrence of a specific word or phrase in a document. **CASE** ▶ *R2G management has decided to change the name of the lecture series from "Travel Luncheon Series" to "Travel Lecture Series." You use the Replace command to search the document for all instances of "Luncheon" and replace them with "Lecture."*

STEPS

1. **Click the Replace button in the Editing group, then click More in the Find and Replace dialog box**

   The Find and Replace dialog box opens and expands, as shown in **FIGURE 2-7**.

2. **Type Luncheon in the Find what text box**

   "Luncheon" is the text that will be replaced.

3. **Press [Tab], then type Lecture in the Replace with text box**

   "Lecture" is the text that will replace "Luncheon."

4. **Click the Match case check box in the Search Options section to select it**

   Selecting the Match case check box tells Word to find only exact matches for the uppercase and lowercase characters you entered in the Find what text box. You want to replace all instances of "Luncheon" in the proper name "San Diego Luncheon Series." You do not want to replace "luncheon" when it refers to a lunchtime event.

5. **Click Replace All**

   Clicking Replace All changes all occurrences of "Luncheon" to "Lecture" in the press release. A message box reports three replacements were made.

6. **Click OK to close the message box, then click the Close button in the Find and Replace dialog box**

   Word replaced "Luncheon" with "Lecture" in three locations, but did not replace "luncheon."

7. **Click the Find button in the Editing group**

   Clicking the Find button opens the Navigation pane, which is used to browse a longer document by headings, by pages, or by specific text. The Find command allows you to quickly locate all instances of text in a document. You use it to verify that Word did not replace "luncheon."

8. **Type luncheon in the search text box in the Navigation pane, then scroll up until the headline is at the top of the document window**

   The word "luncheon" is highlighted and selected in the document, as shown in **FIGURE 2-8**.

9. **Click the Close button in the Navigation pane**

   The highlighting is removed from the text when you close the Navigation pane.

10. **Press [Ctrl][Home], then save the document**

FIGURE 2-7: Find and Replace dialog box

Replace only exact matches of uppercase and lowercase characters

Find only complete words

Use wildcards (*) in a search string

Find words that sound like the Find what text

Find and replace all forms of a word

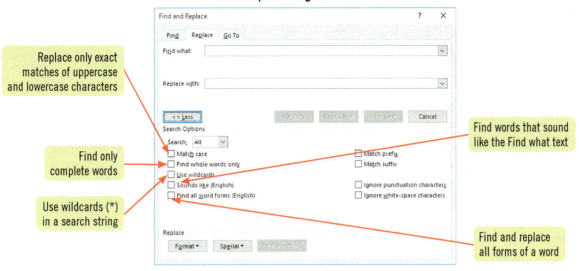

FIGURE 2-8: Found text highlighted in document

Navigation pane

Search text box

List shows each match and its surrounding text

Found text is highlighted and selected

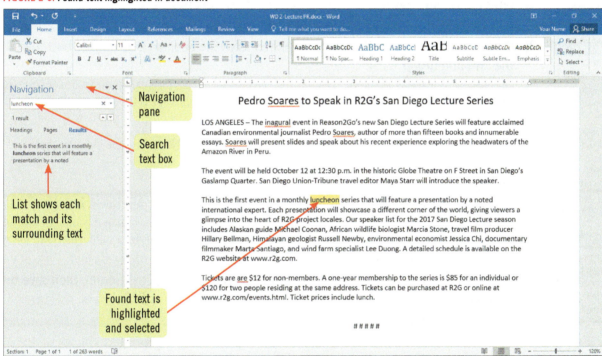

Navigating a document using the Navigation pane and the Go To command

Rather than scrolling to move to a different place in a longer document, you can use the Navigation pane to quickly move the insertion point to a specific page or a specific heading. One way to open the Navigation pane is by clicking the Page number button on the status bar, then clicking the link in the Navigation pane for the type of item you want to use to navigate the document.

To move to a specific page, section, line, table, graphic, or other item in a document, you use the Go To tab in the Find and Replace dialog box. On the Go To tab in the Find and Replace dialog box, select the type of item you want to find in the Go to what list box, enter the relevant information about that item, and then click Next to move the insertion point to the item.

Check Spelling and Grammar

When you finish typing and revising a document, you can use the Spelling and Grammar command to search the document for misspelled words and grammar errors. The Spelling and Grammar checker flags possible mistakes, suggests correct spellings, and offers remedies for grammar errors such as subject–verb agreement, repeated words, and punctuation. **CASE** *You use the Spelling and Grammar checker to search your press release for errors. Before beginning the search, you set the Spelling and Grammar checker to ignore words, such as Soares, that you know are spelled correctly.*

STEPS

1. **Right-click Soares in the headline**

   A menu that includes suggestions for correcting the spelling of "Soares" opens. You can correct individual spelling and grammar errors by right-clicking text that is underlined with a red or blue wavy line and selecting a correction. Although "Soares" is not in the Word dictionary, it is spelled correctly in the document.

2. **Click Ignore All**

   Clicking Ignore All tells Word not to flag "Soares" as misspelled.

3. **Press [Ctrl][Home], click the Review tab, then click the Spelling & Grammar button in the Proofing group**

   The Spelling pane opens, as shown in **FIGURE 2-9**. The pane identifies "inagural" as misspelled and suggests a possible correction for the error. The word selected in the suggestions box is the correct spelling.

4. **Click Change**

   Word replaces the misspelled word with the correctly spelled word. Next, the pane indicates that "are" is repeated in a sentence.

5. **Click Delete**

   Word deletes the second occurrence of the repeated word, and the Spelling pane closes. Keep in mind that the Spelling and Grammar checker identifies many common errors, but you cannot rely on it to find and correct all spelling and grammar errors in your documents, or to always suggest a valid correction. Always proofread your documents carefully.

6. **Click OK to complete the spelling and grammar check, press [Ctrl][Home], then save the document**

Using Smart Lookup

The Smart Lookup feature gives you quick access to information about document text, including definitions, images, and other material from online sources. For example, you might use Smart Lookup to see the definition of a word used in a document or to hear the word pronounced. To use Smart Lookup, select the text you want to look up in your document, then click the Smart Lookup button in the Insights group on the Review tab. The Insights pane opens and includes the Explore and Define tabs. The Explore tab includes images and web links related to the selected text. The Define tab includes a dictionary definition of the selected text and a link you can click to hear the selected text pronounced.

FIGURE 2-9: Spelling pane

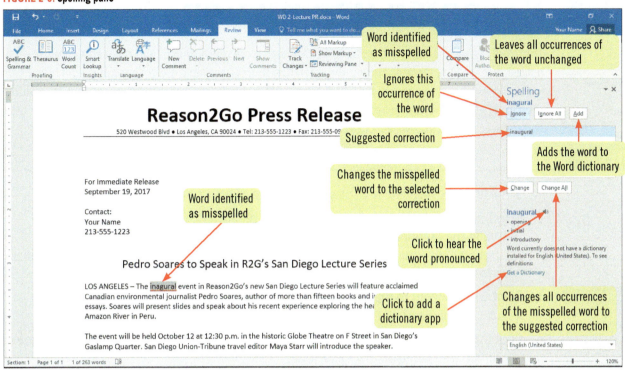

Inserting text with AutoCorrect

As you type, AutoCorrect automatically corrects many commonly misspelled words. By creating your own AutoCorrect entries, you can set Word to insert text that you type often, such as your name or contact information, or to correct words you misspell frequently. For example, you could create an AutoCorrect entry so that the name "Mary T. Watson" is automatically inserted whenever you type "mtw" followed by a space. You create AutoCorrect entries and customize other AutoCorrect and AutoFormat options using the AutoCorrect dialog box. To open the AutoCorrect dialog box, click the File tab, click Options, click Proofing in the Word Options dialog box that opens, and then click AutoCorrect Options. On the AutoCorrect tab in the AutoCorrect dialog box, type the text you want to be corrected automatically in the Replace text box (such as "mtw"), type the text you want to be inserted in its place automatically in the With text box (such as "Mary T. Watson"), and then click Add. The AutoCorrect entry is added to the list. Click OK to close the AutoCorrect dialog box, and then click OK to close the Word Options dialog box. Word inserts an AutoCorrect entry in a document when you press [Spacebar] or a punctuation mark after typing the text you want Word to correct. For example, Word inserts "Mary T. Watson" when you type "mtw" followed by a space. If you want to remove an AutoCorrect entry you created, simply open the AutoCorrect dialog box, select the AutoCorrect entry you want to remove in the list, click Delete, click OK, and then click OK to close the Word Options dialog box.

Research Information

Learning Outcomes
- Find synonyms using the Thesaurus
- Check word count

The Word research features allow you to quickly search reference sources and the web for information related to a word or phrase. Among the reference sources available are a Thesaurus, which you can use to look up synonyms for awkward or repetitive words, as well as dictionary and translation sources. **CASE** ▶ *After proofreading your document for errors, you decide the press release would read better if several adjectives were more descriptive. You use the Thesaurus to find synonyms.*

STEPS

1. **Scroll until the headline is displayed at the top of your screen**

2. **Select noted in the first sentence of the third paragraph, then click the Thesaurus button in the Proofing group on the Review tab**

   The Thesaurus pane opens, as shown in **FIGURE 2-10**. "Noted" appears in the search text box, and possible synonyms for "noted" are listed under the search text box.

QUICK TIP

To look up synonyms for a different word, type the word in the search text box, then click the search button.

3. **Point to prominent in the list of synonyms**

   A shaded box containing a list arrow appears around the word.

4. **Click the list arrow, click Insert on the menu that opens, then close the Thesaurus pane**

   "Prominent" replaces "noted" in the press release.

5. **Right-click innumerable in the first sentence of the first paragraph, point to Synonyms on the menu that opens, then click numerous**

   "Numerous" replaces "innumerable" in the press release.

6. **Select the four paragraphs of body text, then click the Word Count button in the Proofing group**

   The Word Count dialog box opens, as shown in **FIGURE 2-11**. The dialog box lists the number of pages, words, characters, paragraphs, and lines included in the selected text. Notice that the status bar also displays the number of words included in the selected text and the total number of words in the entire document. If you want to view the page, character, paragraph, and line count for the entire document, make sure nothing is selected in your document, and then click Word Count in the Proofing group.

7. **Click Close, press [Ctrl][Home], then save the document**

8. **Click the File tab, click Save As, navigate to the location where you store your files, type WD 2-Lecture PR Public in the File name text box, then click Save**

   The WD 2-Lecture PR file closes, and the WD 2-Lecture PR Public file is displayed in the document window. You will modify this file to prepare it for electronic release to the public.

Publishing a blog directly from Word

A **blog**, which is short for weblog, is an informal journal that is created by an individual or a group and available to the public on the Internet. A blog usually conveys the ideas, comments, and opinions of the blogger and is written using a strong personal voice. The person who creates and maintains a blog, the **blogger**, typically updates the blog regularly. If you have or want to start a blog, you can configure Word to link to your blog site so that you can write, format, and publish blog entries directly from Word.

To create a new blog post, click the File tab, click New, then double-click Blog post to open a predesigned blog post document that you can customize with your own text, formatting, and images. You can also publish an existing document as a blog post by opening the document, clicking the File tab, clicking Share, and then clicking Post to Blog. In either case, Word prompts you to log onto your personal blog account. To blog directly from Word, you must first obtain a blog account with a blog service provider. Resources, such as the Word Help system and online forums, provide detailed information on obtaining and registering your personal blog account with Word.

FIGURE 2-10: Thesaurus pane

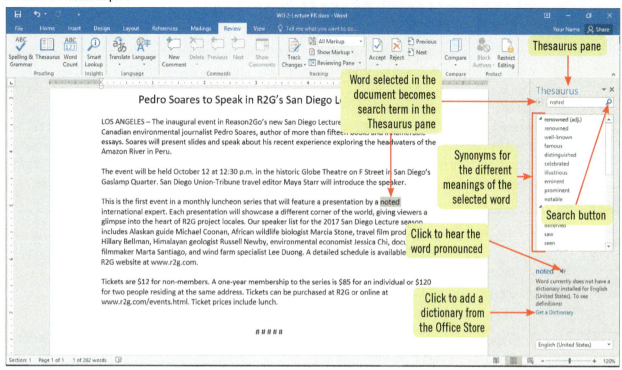

FIGURE 2-11: Word Count dialog box

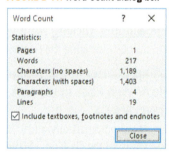

Using a dictionary and other add-ins for Word

Instead of a built-in dictionary, Word includes the ability to install a free dictionary add-in from the Office Store that you can use to see definitions of words. A dictionary add-in is just one of many add-ins that are available in Word. **Add-ins** are small programs embedded in Word that allow you to access information on the web without having to leave Word. For example, you can look up something on Wikipedia, insert an online map in one of your documents, or access dictionaries and other reference sources, all from within Word using an add-in. To install a free dictionary add-in from the Office Store, click the Thesaurus button In the Proofing group on the Review tab, click the Get a Dictionary link to open the Dictionaries pane, decide which dictionary you want, review the Terms & Conditions as well as the Privacy Policy associated with the add-in you want, and then click the Download button associated with the dictionary you want in order to install that dictionary. If you want to download other dictionaries or other add-ins, click the Store button in the Add-ins group on the Insert tab, find the add-in you want, and then follow the prompts to install the add-in. Some add-ins are free, and some require purchase. To use an add-in, click the My Add-ins button in the Add-ins group to see your list of add-ins, and then click the add-in you want to use.

Add Hyperlinks

A **hyperlink** is text or a graphic that, when clicked, "jumps" the viewer to a different location or program. When a document is viewed on screen, hyperlinks allow readers to link (or jump) to a webpage, an e-mail address, a file, or a specific location in a document. When you create a hyperlink in a document, you select the text or graphic you want to use as a hyperlink and then you specify the location you want to jump to when the hyperlink is clicked. You create a hyperlink using the Hyperlink button in the Links group on the Insert tab. Text that is formatted as a hyperlink appears as colored, underlined text. **CASE** *Hundreds of people on your lists of press and client contacts will receive the press release by e-mail or view it on your website. To make it easier for these people to access additional information about the series, you add several hyperlinks to the press release.*

STEPS

1. **Select your name, click the Insert tab, then click the Hyperlink button in the Links group**

   The Insert Hyperlink dialog box opens, as shown in **FIGURE 2-12**. You use this dialog box to specify the location you want to jump to when the hyperlink—in this case, your name—is clicked.

2. **Click E-mail Address in the Link to section**

   The Insert Hyperlink dialog box changes so you can create a hyperlink to your e-mail address.

3. **Type your e-mail address in the E-mail address text box, type San Diego Lecture Series in the Subject text box, then click OK**

   As you type, Word automatically adds mailto: in front of your e-mail address. After you close the dialog box, the hyperlink text—your name—is formatted in blue and underlined.

4. **Press and hold [Ctrl], then click the your name hyperlink**

   An e-mail message addressed to you with the subject "San Diego Lecture Series" opens in the default e-mail program. People can use this hyperlink to send you an e-mail message.

5. **Close the e-mail message window, clicking No if you are prompted to save**

   The hyperlink text changes to purple, indicating the hyperlink has been followed.

6. **Scroll down, select Gaslamp Quarter in the second paragraph, click the Hyperlink button, click Existing File or Web Page in the Link to section, type www.gaslamp.org in the Address text box, then click OK**

   As you type the web address, Word automatically adds "http://" in front of "www." The text "Gaslamp Quarter" is formatted as a hyperlink to the Gaslamp Quarter Association home page at www.gaslamp.org. When clicked, the hyperlink will open the webpage in the default browser window. If you point to a hyperlink in Word, the link to location appears in a ScreenTip. You can edit ScreenTip text to make it more descriptive.

7. **Right-click Quarter in the Gaslamp Quarter hyperlink, click Edit Hyperlink, click ScreenTip in the Edit Hyperlink dialog box, type Map, parking, and other information about the Gaslamp Quarter in the ScreenTip text box, click OK, click OK, save your changes, then point to the Gaslamp Quarter hyperlink in the document**

   The ScreenTip you created appears above the Gaslamp Quarter hyperlink, as shown in **FIGURE 2-13**.

8. **Press [Ctrl], click the Gaslamp Quarter hyperlink, verify the link opened in your browser, then click the Word icon 🔲 on the taskbar to return to the press release**

   Before distributing a document, it's important to test each hyperlink to verify it works as you intended.

FIGURE 2-12: Insert Hyperlink dialog box

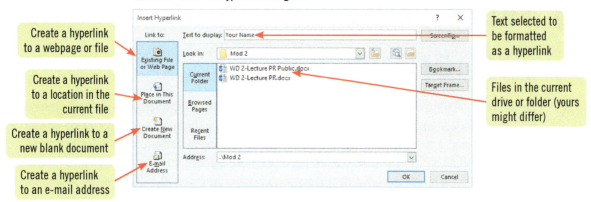

Create a hyperlink to a webpage or file

Create a hyperlink to a location in the current file

Create a hyperlink to a new blank document

Create a hyperlink to an e-mail address

Text selected to be formatted as a hyperlink

Files in the current drive or folder (yours might differ)

FIGURE 2-13: Hyperlinks in the document

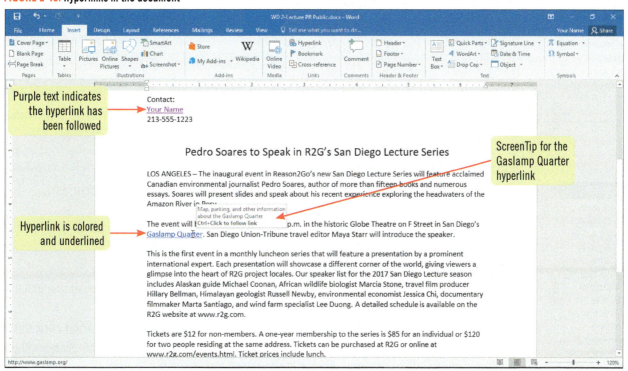

Purple text indicates the hyperlink has been followed

Hyperlink is colored and underlined

ScreenTip for the Gaslamp Quarter hyperlink

Sharing documents directly from Word, including e-mailing

Word includes several options for distributing and sharing documents over the Internet directly from within Word, including saving a document to OneDrive for others to view and edit, e-mailing a document, presenting a document online so others can view it in a web browser, sending it by Instant Message, and posting a document to a blog. To share a document, open the file in Word, click the File tab, click Share, and then click one of the Share options. You can also use the Share button on the title bar to save a document to an online location.

When you e-mail a document from within Word, the document is sent as an attachment to an e-mail message using your default e-mail program. You can choose to attach the document as a Word file, a .pdf file, or an .xps file, or to send it as an Internet fax. When you click an option, a message window opens that includes the filename of the current file as the message subject and the file as an attachment. Type the e-mail address(es) of the recipient(s) in the To and Cc text boxes, any message you want in the message window, and then click Send to send the message. The default e-mail program sends a copy of the document to each recipient. Note that faxing a document directly from Word requires registration with a third-party Internet fax service.

Work with Document Properties

Learning Outcomes
- Edit document properties
- Remove document properties
- Modify advanced document properties

Before you distribute a document electronically to people outside your organization, it's wise to make sure the file does not include embedded private or confidential information. The Info screen in Backstage view includes tools for stripping a document of sensitive information, for securing its authenticity, and for guarding it from unwanted changes once it is distributed to the public. One of these tools, the Document Inspector, detects and removes unwanted private or confidential information from a document. **CASE** *Before sending the press release to the public, you remove all identifying information from the file.*

STEPS

1. **Press [Ctrl][Home], then click the File tab**

   Backstage view opens with the Info screen displayed. The left side of the Info screen includes options related to stripping the file of private information. See **TABLE 2-1**. The right side of the Info screen displays basic information about the document. Notice that the file contains document properties. You want to remove these before you distribute the press release to the public.

2. **Click the Show All Properties link at the bottom of the Info screen**

   The Properties section expands on the Info screen. It shows the document properties for the press release. **Document properties** are user-defined details about a file that describe its contents and origin, including the name of the author, the title of the document, and keywords that you can assign to help organize and search your files. You decide to remove this information from the file before you distribute it electronically.

3. **Click the Check for Issues button on the Info screen, then click Inspect Document, clicking Yes if prompted to save changes**

   The Document Inspector dialog box opens. You use this dialog box to indicate which private or identifying information you want to search for and remove from the document.

4. **Make sure all the check boxes are selected, then click Inspect**

   After a moment, the Document Inspector dialog box indicates the file contains document properties, as shown in **FIGURE 2-14**.

5. **Click Remove All next to Document Properties and Personal Information, then click Close**

   The document property information is removed from the press release document, but the change will not be reflected on the Info screen until you close the document and reopen it.

6. **Click Save on the Info screen, close the document, open the document again in Word, then click the File tab**

   The Info screen shows the document properties have been removed from the file.

7. **Save the document, submit it to your instructor, close the file, then exit Word**

   The completed press release is shown in **FIGURE 2-15**.

TABLE 2-1: Options on the Info screen

option	use to
Protect Document	Mark a document as final so that it is read-only and cannot be edited; encrypt a document so that a password is required to open it; restrict what kinds of changes can be made to a document and by whom; restrict access to editing, copying, and printing a document and add a digital signature to a document to verify its integrity
Check for Issues	Detect and remove unwanted information from a document, including document properties and comments; check for content that people with disabilities might find difficult to read; and check the document for features that are not supported by previous versions of Microsoft Word
Manage Document	Browse and recover draft versions of unsaved files

FIGURE 2-14: Results after inspecting a document

Removes document property information from the file

FIGURE 2-15: Completed press release for electronic distribution

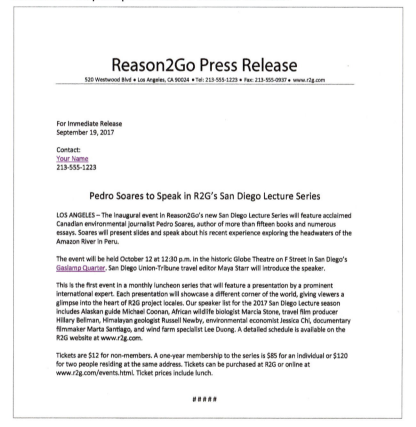

Viewing and modifying advanced document properties

The Properties section of the Info screen includes summary information about the document that you enter. To view more detailed document properties, click the Properties button on the Info screen, and then click Advanced Properties to open the Properties dialog box. The General, Statistics, and Contents tabs of the Properties dialog box display information about the file that is automatically created and updated by Word. The General tab shows the file type, location, size, and date and time the file was created and last modified; the Statistics tab displays information about revisions to the document along with the number of pages, words, lines, paragraphs, and characters in the file; and the Contents tab shows the title of the document.

You can define other document properties using the Summary and Custom tabs in the Properties dialog box. The Summary tab shows information similar to the information shown on the Info screen. The Custom tab allows you to create new document properties, such as client, project, or date completed. To create a custom property, select a property name in the Name list box on the Custom tab, use the Type list arrow to select the type of data you want for the property, type the identifying detail (such as a project name) in the Value text box, and then click Add. When you are finished viewing or modifying the document properties, click OK to close the Properties dialog box.

Practice

Concepts Review

Label the elements of the Word program window shown in FIGURE 2-16.

FIGURE 2-16

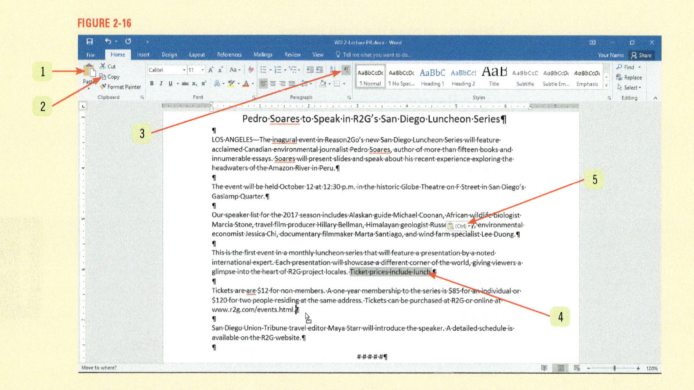

Match each term with the statement that best describes it.

6. Office Clipboard
7. Paste
8. Hyperlink
9. Thesaurus
10. Shortcut Key
11. Smart Lookup
12. Cut
13. System clipboard
14. Document properties

a. Command used to insert text stored on the Clipboard into a document
b. Temporary storage area for up to 24 items collected from Office files
c. Temporary storage area for only the last item cut or copied from a document
d. A function key or a combination of keys that perform a command when pressed
e. Text or a graphic that jumps the reader to a different location or program when clicked
f. A program that accesses information on the web from within Word
g. User-defined details about a file that describe its contents and origin
h. Feature used to suggest synonyms for words
i. Command used to remove text from a document and place it on the Clipboard

Select the best answer from the list of choices.

15. **What is the keyboard shortcut for the Cut command?**
    - **a.** [Ctrl][V]
    - **b.** [Ctrl][C]
    - **c.** [Ctrl][P]
    - **d.** [Ctrl][X]

16. **Which command is used to display a document in two panes in the document window?**
    - **a.** Split
    - **b.** New Window
    - **c.** Arrange All
    - **d.** Two pages

17. **Which of the following statements is _not_ true?**
    - **a.** You can view the contents of the Office Clipboard.
    - **b.** The last item cut or copied from a document is stored on the system clipboard.
    - **c.** The Office Clipboard can hold more than one item.
    - **d.** When you move text by dragging it, a copy of the text you move is stored on the system clipboard.

18. **To locate and select all instances of a word in a document, which command do you use?**
    - **a.** Highlight
    - **b.** Show/Hide
    - **c.** Find
    - **d.** Search

19. **Which of the following is an example of a document property?**
    - **a.** URL
    - **b.** Keyword
    - **c.** Permission
    - **d.** Language

20. **A hyperlink _cannot_ be linked to which of the following?**
    - **a.** Document
    - **b.** E-mail address
    - **c.** ScreenTip
    - **d.** Webpage

Skills Review

1. **Cut and paste text.**
    a. Start Word, click the Open Other Documents link, open the file WD 2-2.docx from the location where you store your Data File, then save the document with the filename **WD 2-MATOS 2017 PR**.
    b. Select **Your Name** and replace it with your name.
    c. Display paragraph and other formatting marks in your document if they are not already displayed.
    d. Use the Cut and Paste buttons to switch the order of the two sentences in the fourth body paragraph (which begins New group shows…).
    e. Use the drag-and-drop method to switch the order of the second and third paragraphs.
    f. Adjust the spacing if necessary so that there is one blank line between paragraphs, then save your changes.

2. **Copy and paste text.**
    a. Use the Copy and Paste buttons to copy **MATOS 2015** from the headline and paste it before the word **map** in the third paragraph.
    b. Change the formatting of the pasted text to match the formatting of the third paragraph, then insert a space between **2015** and **map** if necessary.
    c. Use the drag-and-drop method to copy **MATOS** from the third paragraph and paste it before the word **group** in the second sentence of the fourth paragraph, then save your changes.

3. **Use the Office Clipboard.**
    a. Use the launcher in the Clipboard group to open the Clipboard pane.
    b. Scroll so that the first body paragraph is displayed at the top of the document window.
    c. Select the fifth paragraph (which begins Studio location maps…) and cut it to the Clipboard.
    d. Select the third paragraph (which begins Manchester is easily accessible…) and cut it to the Clipboard.
    e. Use the Clipboard to paste the Studio location maps… item as the new fourth paragraph.
    f. Use the Clipboard to paste the Manchester is easily accessible… item as the new fifth paragraph.
    g. Adjust the spacing if necessary so there is one blank line between each of the six body paragraphs.
    h. Turn off the display of formatting marks, clear and close the Clipboard pane, then save your changes.

4. **Find and replace text.**

   a. Using the Replace command, replace all instances of **2015** with **2017**.

   b. Replace all instances of **tenth** with **twelfth**.

   c. Replace all instances of the abbreviation **st** with **street**, taking care to replace whole words only when you perform the replace. (*Hint*: Deselect Match case if it is selected.)

   d. Click the Find tab, deselect the Find whole words only check box, click the Reading Highlight button, click Highlight All, close the dialog box, then view all instances of **st** in the document to make sure no errors occurred when you replaced st with street.

   e. Click the Find button to open the Navigation pane, notice the results and the highlighted text, close the Navigation pane, then save your changes to the press release. (*Note: You can see the highlighted results using either the Reading Highlight button in the Find and Replace dialog box or the Navigation pane.*)

5. **Check spelling and grammar and research information.**

   a. Switch to the Review tab.

   b. Move the insertion point to the top of the document, then use the Spelling & Grammar command to search for and correct any spelling and grammar errors in the press release.

   c. Use the Thesaurus to replace **thriving** in the second paragraph with a different suitable word, then close the Thesaurus pane.

   d. Check the word count of the press release.

   e. Proofread your press release, correct any errors, then save your changes.

6. **Add hyperlinks.**

   a. Save the document as **WD 2-MATOS 2017 PR Public**, then switch to the Insert tab.

   b. Select your name, then open the Insert Hyperlink dialog box.

   c. Create a hyperlink to your e-mail address with the subject **MATOS 2017**.

   d. Test the your name hyperlink, then close the message window that opens and click No if a message window opens. (*Hint*: Press [Ctrl], then click the hyperlink.)

   e. Select **NEA** in the last paragraph of the press release, then create a hyperlink to the webpage with the URL **www.nea.gov**.

   f. Right-click the NEA hyperlink, then edit the hyperlink ScreenTip to become **Information on the National Endowment for the Arts**.

   g. Point to the NEA hyperlink to view the new ScreenTip, then save your changes.

   h. If you are working with an active Internet connection, press [Ctrl], click the NEA hyperlink, view the NEA home page in the browser window, then close the browser window and return to Word. The finished press release is shown in **FIGURE 2-17**.

FIGURE 2-17

PRESS RELEASE

FOR IMMEDIATE RELEASE
September 7, 2017

Contact:
Your Name
910-555-2938

MATOS 2017
Manchester Artists Open Their Studios to the Public

MANCHESTER, NH — The fall 2017 Open Studios season kicks off with Manchester Art/Tech Open Studios (MATOS) on Saturday and Sunday, October 13 and 14, from 11 a.m. to 6 p.m. More than 60 Manchester artists will open their studios and homes to the public for this annual event, now in its twelfth year.

Manchester is a historic and diverse city, long home to a flourishing community of artists. Quiet residential streets lined with charming Victorians edge a vibrant commercial and industrial zone, all peppered with the studios of printmakers, sculptors, painters, glass and jewelry makers, illustrators, potters, photographers, watercolorists, and other artists working in a wide range of digital mediums.

Internationally celebrated sculptor Mara Currier will display her new work in the rotunda of City Library. New MATOS group shows will open at the Art 5 Gallery and at the Fisher Café, both on Hanover Street.

Studio location maps will be available prior to the opening at businesses and public libraries, and on the days of the event in Victory Park. Victory Park is located at the junction of Amherst Street and Chestnut Street in downtown Manchester.

Manchester is easily accessible from all points in New England by car or bus, and from other cities by air. On Saturday, non-Manchester residents may park in permit-only areas provided they display a copy of the MATOS 2017 map on the dashboard. There are no parking restrictions on Sundays in Manchester.

MATOS 2017 receives funds from participating artists and from the Manchester Arts Council, the North Hampshire Cultural Council, and the NEA, with valuable support from local universities and businesses.

#####

Skills Review (continued)

7. Work with document properties.

    a. Click the File tab, click the Properties button on the Info screen, then click Advanced Properties to open the Properties dialog box and view the document properties for the press release on the Summary tab.

    b. Close the Properties dialog box, then use the Check for Issues command to run the Document Inspector.

    c. Remove the document property and personal information data, close the Document Inspector, save your changes, then close the file.

    d. Open the file WD 2-MATOS 2017 PR Public, then verify that the document propertes have been removed both on the Info screen and in the Properties dialog box. Save the document, submit it to your instructor, close the file, then exit Word.

Independent Challenge 1

Because of your success in revitalizing a historic theatre in Auckland, New Zealand, you were hired as the director of The Adelaide Opera House in Adelaide, Australia, to breathe life into its revitalization efforts. After a year on the job, you are launching your first major fund-raising drive. You'll create a fund-raising letter for The Adelaide Opera House by modifying a letter you wrote for the Lyric Theatre in Auckland.

    a. Start Word, open the file WD 2-3.docx from the location where you store your Data Files, then save it as **WD 2-Fundraising Letter**.

    b. Replace the theatre name and address, the date, the inside address, and the salutation with the text shown in **FIGURE 2-18**.

    c. Use the Replace command to replace all instances of **Auckland** with **Adelaide**.

    d. Use the Replace command to replace all instances of **Lyric Theatre** with **Opera House**.

    e. Use the Replace command to replace all instances of **New Zealanders** with **Australians**.

    f. Use the Find command to locate the word **considerable**, then use the Thesaurus to replace the word with a synonym.

FIGURE 2-18

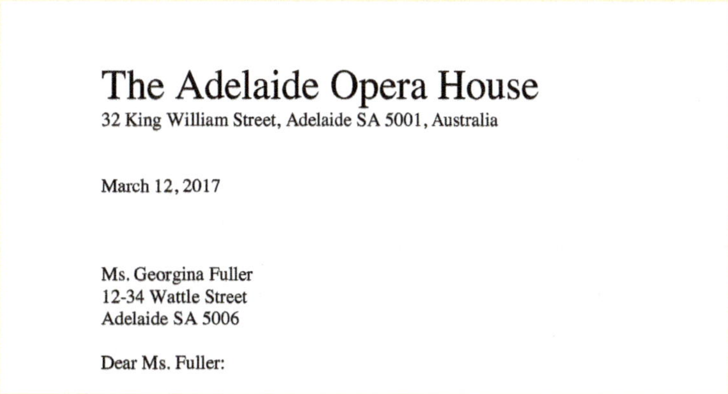

> # The Adelaide Opera House
> 32 King William Street, Adelaide SA 5001, Australia
>
> March 12, 2017
>
> Ms. Georgina Fuller
> 12-34 Wattle Street
> Adelaide SA 5006
>
> Dear Ms. Fuller:

    g. Move the fourth body paragraph so that it becomes the second body paragraph.

    h. Create an AutoCorrect entry that inserts **Executive Director** whenever you type **exd**.

    i. Replace Your Name with your name in the signature block, select Title, then type **exd** followed by a space.

    j. Use the Spelling and Grammar command to check for and correct spelling and grammar errors.

    k. Delete the AutoCorrect entry you created for exd. (*Hint*: Open the AutoCorrect dialog box, select the AutoCorrect entry you created, then click [Delete].)

    l. Open the Properties dialog box, add your name as the author, change the title to **Adelaide Opera House**, add the keyword **fund-raising**, then add the comment **Letter for the capital campaign**.

    m. Review the paragraph, line, word, and character count on the Statistics tab.

    n. On the Custom tab, add a property named **Project** with the value **Capital Campaign**, then close the dialog box.

    o. Proofread the letter, correct any errors, save your changes, submit a copy to your instructor, close the document, then exit Word.

Independent Challenge 2

An advertisement for job openings in Chicago caught your eye and you have decided to apply. The ad, shown in FIGURE 2-19, was printed in last weekend's edition of your local newspaper. Instead of writing a cover letter from scratch, you revise a draft of a cover letter you wrote several years ago for a summer internship position.

FIGURE 2-19

ThinkPoint Technologies

Career Opportunities in Detroit

ThinkPoint Technologies, an established software development firm with offices in North America, Asia, and Europe, is seeking candidates for the following positions in its Detroit facility:

Instructor

Responsible for delivering software training to our expanding Midwestern customer base. Duties include delivering hands-on training, keeping up-to-date with product development, and working with the Director of Training to ensure the high quality of course materials. Successful candidate will have excellent presentation skills and be proficient in Microsoft PowerPoint and Microsoft Word. Position B12C6

Administrative Assistant

Proficiency with Microsoft Word a must! Administrative office duties include making travel arrangements, scheduling meetings, taking notes and publishing meeting minutes, handling correspondence, and ordering office supplies. Must have superb multitasking abilities, excellent communication, organizational, and interpersonal skills, and be comfortable working with e-mail and the Internet. Position B16F5

Copywriter

The ideal candidate will have marketing or advertising writing experience in a high tech environment, including collateral, newsletters, and direct mail. Experience writing for the Web, broadcast, and multimedia is a plus. Fluency with Microsoft Word required. Position C13D4

Positions offer salary, excellent benefits, and career opportunities.

Send resume and cover letter referencing position code to:

Selena Torres
Director of Recruiting
ThinkPoint Technologies
700 Woodward Ave.
Detroit, MI 48226

a. Read the ad shown in FIGURE 2-19 and decide which position to apply for. Choose the position that most closely matches your qualifications.

b. Start Word, open WD 2-4.docx from the location where you store your Data Files, then save it as **WD 2-ThinkPoint Cover Letter**.

c. Replace the name, address, telephone number, and e-mail address in the letterhead with your own information.

d. Remove the hyperlink from the e-mail address.

e. Replace the date with today's date, then replace the inside address and the salutation with the information shown in FIGURE 2-19.

f. Read the draft cover letter to get a feel for its contents.

g. Rework the text in the body of the letter to address your qualifications for the job you have chosen to apply for in the following ways:

- Delete the third paragraph.
- Adjust the first sentence of the first paragraph as follows: specify the job you are applying for, including the position code, and indicate where you saw the position advertised.
- Move the first sentence in the last paragraph, which briefly states your qualifications and interest in the position, to the end of the first paragraph, then rework the sentence to describe your current qualifications.
- Adjust the second paragraph as follows: describe your work experience and skills. Be sure to relate your experience and qualifications to the position requirements listed in the advertisement. Add a third paragraph if your qualifications are extensive.
- Adjust the final paragraph as follows: politely request an interview for the position and provide your phone number and e-mail address.

h. Include your name in the signature block.

i. When you are finished revising the letter, check it for spelling and grammar errors, and correct any mistakes. Make sure to remove any hyperlinks.

j. Save your changes to the letter, submit the file to your instructor, close the document, then exit Word.

Independent Challenge 3

As administrative director of continuing education, you drafted a memo to instructors asking them to help you finalize the course schedule for next semester. Today, you'll examine the draft and make revisions before distributing it as an e-mail attachment.

a. Start Word, open the file WD 2-5.docx from the drive and folder where you store your Data Files, then save it as **WD 2-Business Courses Memo**.

Independent Challenge 3 (continued)

b. Replace Your Name with your name in the From line, then scroll until the first body paragraph is at the top of the screen.

c. Use the Split command on the View tab to split the window under the first body paragraph, then scroll until the last paragraph of the memo is displayed in the bottom pane.

d. Use the Cut and Paste buttons to move the sentence **If you are planning to teach...** from the first body paragraph to become the first sentence in the last paragraph of the memo.

e. Double-click the split bar to restore the window to a single pane.

f. Use the [Delete] key to merge the first two paragraphs into one paragraph.

g. Use the Clipboard to reorganize the list of twelve-week courses so that the courses are listed in alphabetical order, then clear and close the Clipboard.

h. Use drag-and-drop to reorganize the list of one-day seminars so they are in alphabetical order.

i. Select the phrase "website" in the first paragraph, then create a hyperlink to the URL **www.course.com** with the ScreenTip **Spring 2018 Business Courses**.

j. Select "e-mail me" in the last paragraph, then create a hyperlink to your e-mail address with the subject **Final Business Course Schedule**.

k. Use the Spelling and Grammar command to check for and correct spelling and grammar errors.

l. Use the Document Inspector to strip the document of document property information, ignore any other content that is flagged by the Document Inspector, then close the Document Inspector.

m. Proofread the memo, correct any errors, save your changes, submit a copy to your instructor, close the document, then exit Word.

Independent Challenge 4: Explore

Reference sources—dictionaries, thesauri, style and grammar guides, and guides to business etiquette and procedure—are essential for day-to-day use in the workplace. Much of this reference information is available on the World Wide Web. In this independent challenge, you will locate reference sources that might be useful to you, including the Office Add-ins resources that are available for Word. Your goal is to familiarize yourself with online reference sources and Office Add-ins for Word so you can use them later in your work. You will insert a screenshot of an Office Add-in webpage in your document.

a. Start Word, open the file WD 2-6.docx from the location where you store your Data Files, then save it as **WD 2-References**. This document contains the questions you will answer about the web reference sources you find and Office Add-ins. You will type your answers to the questions in the document.

b. Replace the placeholder text at the top of the WD 2-References document with your name and the date.

c. Use your favorite search engine to search the web for grammar and style guides, dictionaries, and thesauri. Use the keywords **grammar**, **usage**, **dictionary**, **glossary**, or **thesaurus** to conduct your search.

d. Complete question 1 of the WD 2-References document, making sure to format each website name as a hyperlink to that website.

e. Read question 2 of the WD 2-References document, then move the insertion point under question 2.

f. Click the Store button in the Add-ins group on the Insert tab. Explore the add-ins available through the Office Add-ins window, click one add-in to select it, then click the hyperlink for that add-in to open it in a new browser window. (*Hint:* The hyperlink for an add-in is located under the icon for the add-in.)

g. Switch to the WD 2-References document in Word. Close the Office Add-ins window if it is still open.

h. With the insertion point below question 2, click the Screenshot button in the Illustrations group on the Insert tab. The Available Windows gallery opens.

i. Read the ScreenTip for each thumbnail in the gallery, find the Add-in browser window thumbnail in the gallery, click it, then click Yes in the dialog box that opens. A screenshot of the Add-in you selected is inserted in the WD 2-References document.

j. Save the document, submit a copy to your instructor, close the document, then exit Word.

Visual Workshop

Open WD 2-7.docx from the drive and folder where you store your Data Files, then save the document as **WD 2-Visa Letter**. Replace the placeholders for the date, letterhead, inside address, salutation, and closing with the information shown in FIGURE 2-20, then use the Office Clipboard to reorganize the sentences to match FIGURE 2-20. Correct spelling and grammar errors, remove the document property information from the file, then submit a copy to your instructor.

FIGURE 2-20

Your Name

863 East 18th Street, Apt. 4, New York, NY 20211; Tel: 212-555-9384

1/12/2017

Embassy of the Republic of Korea
2320 Massachusetts Avenue NW
Washington, DC 20008

Dear Sir or Madam:

I am applying for a long-stay tourist visa to South Korea, valid for four years. I am scheduled to depart for Seoul on March 9, 2017, returning to Chicago on September 22, 2017.

During my stay in South Korea, I will be interviewing musicians and recording footage for a film I am making on contemporary Korean music. I would like a multiple entry visa valid for four years so I can return to South Korea after this trip to follow up on my initial research. I will be based in Seoul, but I will be traveling frequently to record performances and to meet with musicians and producers.

Included with this letter are my completed visa application form, my passport, a passport photo, a copy of my return air ticket, and the visa fee. Please contact me if you need further information.

Sincerely,

Your Name

Enc: 5

Formatting Text and Paragraphs

CASE You have finished drafting the text for a two-page flyer advertising last minute specials for R2G October projects. Now, you need to format the flyer so it is attractive and highlights the significant information.

Module Objectives

After completing this module, you will be able to:

- Format with fonts
- Use the Format Painter
- Change line and paragraph spacing
- Align paragraphs
- Work with tabs
- Work with indents
- Add bullets and numbering
- Add borders and shading
- Insert online pictures

Files You Will Need

WD 3-1.docx	WD 3-4.docx
WD 3-2.docx	WD 3-5.docx
WD 3-3.docx	WD 3-6.docx

Format with Fonts

Learning Outcomes
- Change font and font size
- Change font color
- Select an entire document

Formatting text with fonts is a quick and powerful way to enhance the appearance of a document. A **font** is a complete set of characters with the same typeface or design. Arial, Times New Roman, Courier, Tahoma, and Calibri are some of the more common fonts, but there are hundreds of others, each with a specific design and feel. Another way to change the appearance of text is to increase or decrease its **font size**. Font size is measured in points. A **point** is 1/72 of an inch. **CASE** *You change the font and font size of the body text, title, and headings in the flyer. You select fonts and font sizes that enhance the positive tone of the document and help to structure the flyer visually for readers.*

STEPS

1. **Start Word, open the file WD 3-1.docx from the location where you store your Data Files, save it as WD 3-October Projects, then change the zoom level to 120%**

   Notice that the name of the font used in the document, Calibri, is displayed in the Font list box in the Font group. The word "(Body)" in the Font list box indicates Calibri is the font used for body text in the current theme, the default theme. A **theme** is a related set of fonts, colors, styles, and effects that is applied to an entire document to give it a cohesive appearance. The font size, 11, appears in the Font Size list box in the Font group.

   > **QUICK TIP**
   > There are two types of fonts: **serif fonts** have a small stroke, called a serif, at the ends of characters; **sans serif fonts** do not have a serif. Garamond is a serif font. Trebuchet MS is a sans serif font.

2. **Scroll the document to get a feel for its contents, press [Ctrl][Home], press [Ctrl][A] to select the entire document, then click the Font list arrow in the Font group**

   The Font list, which shows the fonts available on your computer, opens as shown in **FIGURE 3-1**. The font names are formatted in the font. Font names can appear in more than one location on the Font list.

3. **Drag the pointer slowly down the font names in the Font list, drag the scroll box to scroll down the Font list, then click Garamond**

   As you drag the pointer over a font name, a preview of the font is applied to the selected text. Clicking a font name applies the font. The font of the flyer changes to Garamond.

   > **QUICK TIP**
   > You can also type a font size in the Font Size text box.

4. **Click the Font Size list arrow in the Font group, drag the pointer slowly up and down the Font Size list, then click 12**

   As you drag the pointer over a font size, a preview of the font size is applied to the selected text. Clicking 12 increases the font size of the selected text to 12 points.

5. **Select the title Reason2Go October Projects, click the Font list arrow, scroll to and click Trebuchet MS, click the Font Size list arrow, click 22, then click the Bold button B in the Font group**

   The title is formatted in 22-point Trebuchet MS bold.

   > **QUICK TIP**
   > To use a different set of theme colors, click the Design tab, click the Colors button in the Document Formatting group, then select a different color set.

6. **Click the Font Color list arrow [A ·] in the Font group**

   A gallery of colors opens. It includes the set of theme colors in a range of tints and shades as well as a set of standard colors. You can point to a color in the gallery to preview it applied to the selected text.

7. **Click the Green, Accent 6 color as shown in FIGURE 3-2, then deselect the text**

   The color of the title text changes to green. The active color on the Font Color button also changes to green.

   > **TROUBLE**
   > If the mini toolbar closes, select the text again.

8. **Scroll down, select the heading Animal Care Rajasthan, then, using the Mini toolbar, click the Font list arrow, click Trebuchet MS, click the Font Size list arrow, click 14, click B, click [A], then deselect the text**

   The heading is formatted in 14-point Trebuchet MS bold with a green color.

9. **Press [Ctrl][Home], then click the Save button on the Quick Access toolbar**

   Compare your document to **FIGURE 3-3**.

FIGURE 3-1: Font list

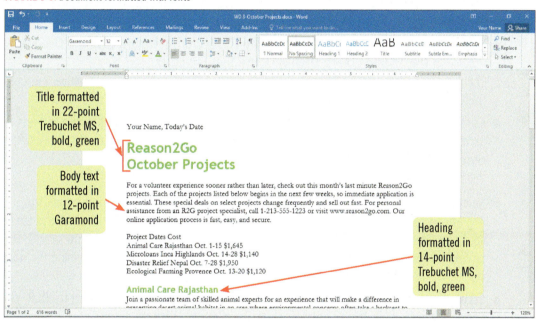

Fonts used in the default theme

List of recently used fonts (your list may differ)

Alphabetical list of all fonts on your computer (your list may differ)

Font Size list arrow

Font list arrow

FIGURE 3-2: Font Color Palette

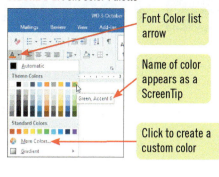

Font Color list arrow

Name of color appears as a ScreenTip

Click to create a custom color

FIGURE 3-3: Document formatted with fonts

Title formatted in 22-point Trebuchet MS, bold, green

Body text formatted in 12-point Garamond

Heading formatted in 14-point Trebuchet MS, bold, green

Adding a drop cap

A fun way to illustrate a document with fonts is to add a drop cap to a paragraph. A **drop cap** is a large initial capital letter, often used to set off the first paragraph of an article. To create a drop cap, place the insertion point in the paragraph you want to format, click the Insert tab, and then click the Drop Cap button in the Text group to open a menu of Drop cap options. Preview and select one of the options on the menu, or click Drop Cap Options to open the Drop Cap dialog box, shown in **FIGURE 3-4**. In the Drop Cap dialog box, select the position, font, number of lines to drop, and the distance you want the drop cap to be from the paragraph text, and then click OK. The drop cap is added to the paragraph as a graphic object.

Once a drop cap is inserted in a paragraph, you can modify it by selecting it and then changing the settings in the Drop Cap dialog box. For even more interesting effects, you can enhance a drop cap with font color, font styles, or font effects. You can also fill the graphic object with shading or add a border around it. To enhance a drop cap, first select it, and then experiment with the formatting options available in the Font dialog box and in the Borders and Shading dialog box.

FIGURE 3-4: Drop Cap dialog box

Use the Format Painter

You can dramatically change the appearance of text by applying different font styles, font effects, and character-spacing effects. For example, you can use the buttons in the Font group to make text darker by applying **bold** or to make text slanted by applying *italic*. When you are satisfied with the formatting of certain text, you can quickly apply the same formats to other text using the Format Painter. The **Format Painter** is a powerful Word feature that allows you to copy all the format settings applied to selected text to other text that you want to format the same way. **CASE** ▶ *You spice up the appearance of the text in the document by applying different font styles and text effects.*

STEPS

1. **Select immediate application is essential in the first body paragraph, click the Bold button B on the Mini toolbar, select the entire paragraph, then click the Italic button I**
   The phrase "immediate application is essential" is bold, and the entire paragraph is italic.

2. **Select October Projects, then click the launcher in the Font group**
   The Font dialog box opens, as shown in **FIGURE 3-5**. You can use the options on the Font tab to change the font, font style, size, and color of text, and to add an underline and apply font effects to text.

3. **Scroll down the Size list, click 48, click the Font color list arrow, click the Orange, Accent 2 color in the Theme Colors, then click the Text Effects button**
   The Format Text Effects dialog box opens with the options for Text Fill & Outline active. You can also use this dialog box to apply text effects, such as shadow, reflection, and 3-D effects to selected text.

4. **Click the white Text Effects icon in the dialog box, click Shadow, click the Presets list arrow, click Offset Diagonal Bottom Right in the Outer section, click OK, click OK, then deselect the text**
   The text is larger, orange, and has a shadow effect.

5. **Select October Projects, right-click, click Font on the menu that opens, click the Advanced tab, click the Scale list arrow, click 80%, click OK, then deselect the text**
   You use the Advanced tab in the Font dialog box to change the scale, or width, of the selected characters, to alter the spacing between characters, or to raise or lower the characters. Decreasing the scale of the characters makes them narrower and gives the text a tall, thin appearance, as shown in **FIGURE 3-6**.

6. **Scroll down, select the subheading Wildlife Refuge, then, using the Mini toolbar, click the Font list arrow, click Trebuchet MS, click B, click I, click the Font Color list arrow A ▾, click the Orange, Accent 2 color in the Theme Colors, then deselect the text**
   The subheading is formatted in Trebuchet MS, bold, italic, and orange.

7. **Select Wildlife Refuge, then click the Format Painter button in the Clipboard group**
   The pointer changes to.

8. **Scroll down, select Animal Shelter with the pointer, then deselect the text**
   The subheading is formatted in Trebuchet MS, bold, italic, and orange, as shown in **FIGURE 3-7**.

9. **Scroll up, select Animal Care Rajasthan, then double-click the Format Painter button**
   Double-clicking the Format Painter button allows the Format Painter to remain active until you turn it off. By keeping the Format Painter active, you can apply formatting to multiple items.

10. **Scroll down, select the headings Microloans Inca Highlands, Disaster Relief Nepal, and Ecological Farming Provence with the pointer, click the Format Painter button to turn off the Format Painter, then save your changes**
    The headings are formatted in 14-point Trebuchet MS bold with a green font color.

FIGURE 3-5: Font tab in Font dialog box

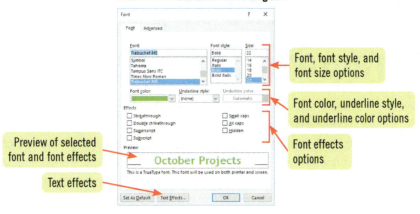

Font, font style, and font size options

Font color, underline style, and underline color options

Font effects options

Preview of selected font and font effects

Text effects

FIGURE 3-6: Font and character spacing effects applied to text

Title formatted in 48-point, orange, with a shadow effect and a character scale of 80%

Paragraph formatted in italic

FIGURE 3-7: Formats copied and applied using the Format Painter

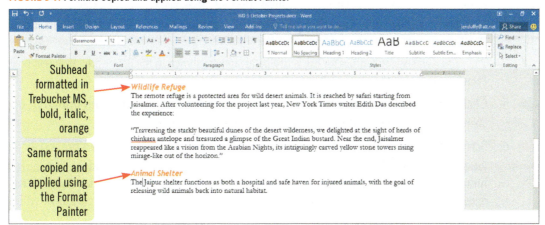

Subhead formatted in Trebuchet MS, bold, italic, orange

Same formats copied and applied using the Format Painter

Underlining text

Another creative way to call attention to text and to jazz up the appearance of a document is to apply an underline style to words you want to highlight. The Underline list arrow in the Font group displays straight, dotted, wavy, dashed, and mixed underline styles, along with a gallery of colors to choose from. To apply an underline to text, simply select it, click the Underline list arrow, and then select an underline style from the list. For a wider variety of underline styles, click More Underlines in the list, and then select an underline style in the Font dialog box. You can change the color of an underline at any time by selecting the underlined text, clicking the Underline list arrow, pointing to Underline Color, and then choosing from the options in the color gallery. If you want to remove an underline from text, select the underlined text, and then click the Underline button.

Change Line and Paragraph Spacing

Learning Outcomes
- Add spacing under paragraphs
- Change line spacing in paragraphs
- Apply styles to text

Increasing the amount of space between lines adds more white space to a document and can make it easier to read. Adding space before and after paragraphs can also open up a document and improve its appearance. You use the Line and Paragraph Spacing list arrow in the Paragraph group on the Home tab to quickly change line spacing. To change paragraph spacing, you use the Spacing options in the Paragraph group on the Layout tab. Both line and paragraph spacing are measured in points. **CASE** *You increase the line spacing of several paragraphs and add extra space under each heading to give the flyer a more open feel. You work with formatting marks turned on, so you can see the paragraph marks (¶).*

STEPS

1. **Press [Ctrl][Home], click the Show/Hide ¶ button ¶ in the Paragraph group, place the insertion point in the italicized paragraph under the title, then click the Line and Paragraph Spacing list arrow ☰ in the Paragraph group on the Home tab**

    The Line Spacing list opens. This list includes options for increasing the space between lines. The check mark on the Line Spacing list indicates the current line spacing.

2. **Click 1.15**

    The space between the lines in the paragraph increases to 1.15 lines. Notice that you do not need to select an entire paragraph to change its paragraph formatting; simply place the insertion point in the paragraph.

QUICK TIP

Word recognizes any string of text that ends with a paragraph mark as a paragraph, including titles, headings, and single lines in a list.

3. **Scroll down, select the five-line list that begins with "Project Dates Cost", click ☰, then click 1.5**

    The line spacing between the selected paragraphs changes to 1.5. To change the paragraph-formatting features of more than one paragraph, you must select the paragraphs.

4. **Scroll down, place the insertion point in the heading Animal Care Rajasthan, then click the Layout tab**

    The paragraph spacing settings for the active paragraph are shown in the Before and After text boxes in the Paragraph group on the Layout tab.

QUICK TIP

You can also type a number in the Before and After text boxes.

5. **Click the After up arrow in the Spacing section in the Paragraph group until 6 pt appears**

    Six points of space are added after the Animal Care Rajasthan heading paragraph.

TROUBLE

If your [F4] key does not work, use the After up arrow to apply 6 pts of space to the headings listed in Steps 6 and 7, then continue with Step 8.

6. **Scroll down, place the insertion point in Microloans Inca Highlands, then press [F4]**

    Pressing [F4] repeats the last action you took. In this case, six points of space are added after the Microloans Inca Highlands heading. Note that using [F4] is not the same as using the Format Painter. Pressing [F4] repeats only the last action you took, and using the Format Painter applies multiple format settings at the same time.

7. **Scroll down, select Disaster Relief Nepal, press and hold [Ctrl], select Ecological Farming Provence, release [Ctrl], then press [F4]**

    When you press [Ctrl] as you select items, you can select and format multiple items at once. Six points of space are added after each heading.

QUICK TIP

Adjusting the space between paragraphs is a more precise way to add white space to a document than inserting blank lines.

8. **Press [Ctrl][Home], place the insertion point in October Projects, then click the Before up arrow in the Spacing section in the Paragraph group twice so that 12 pt appears**

    The second line of the title has 12 points of space before it, as shown in **FIGURE 3-8**.

9. **Click the Home tab, click ¶, then save your changes**

FIGURE 3-8: Line and paragraph spacing applied to document

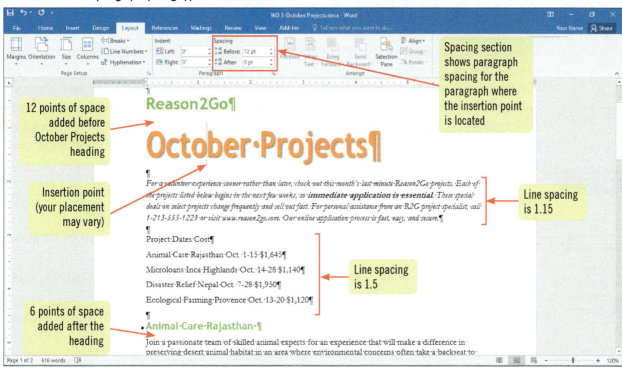

12 points of space added before October Projects heading

Spacing section shows paragraph spacing for the paragraph where the insertion point is located

Insertion point (your placement may vary)

Line spacing is 1.15

Line spacing is 1.5

6 points of space added after the heading

Formatting with Quick Styles

You can also apply multiple format settings to text in one step by applying a style. A **style** is a set of formats, such as font, font size, and paragraph alignment, that is named and stored together. Formatting a document with styles is a quick and easy way to give it a professional appearance. To make it even easier, Word includes sets of styles, called **Quick Styles**, that are designed to be used together in a document to make it attractive and readable. A Quick Style set includes styles for a title, several heading levels, body text, quotes, and lists. The styles in a Quick Style set use common fonts, colors, and formats so that using the styles together in a document gives the document a cohesive look.

To view the active set of Quick Styles, click the More button ⤓ in the Styles group on the Home tab to expand the Quick Styles gallery, shown in **FIGURE 3-9**. As you move the pointer over each style in the gallery, a preview of the style is applied to the selected text. To apply a style to the selected text, you simply click the style in the Quick Styles gallery. To remove a style from

FIGURE 3-9: Quick Styles gallery

AaBbCcDc	AaBbCcDc	AaBbC	AaBbCcD	AaB	AaBbCcD	AaBbCcDc	AaBbCcDc
¶ Normal	No Spacing	Heading 1	Heading 2	Title	Subtitle	Subtle Em...	Emphasis
AaBbCcDc	AaBbCcDc	AaBbCcDc	AaBbCcDc	AABBCCDC	AABBCCDC	AaBbCcDc	AaBbCcDc
Intense E...	Strong	Quote	Intense Q...	Subtle Ref...	Intense R...	Book Title	¶ List Para...

⭐ Create a Style
🅰 Clear Formatting
🄰 Apply Styles...

selected text, you click the Clear All Formatting button 🅰 in the Font group or the Clear Formatting command in the Quick Styles gallery.

If you want to change the active set of Quick Styles to a Quick Style set with a different design, click the Design tab, click the More button ⤓ in the Document Formatting group, and then select the Quick Style set that best suits your document's content, tone, and audience. When you change the Quick Style set, a complete set of new fonts and colors is applied to the entire document. You can also change the color scheme or font used in the active Quick Style set by clicking the Colors or Fonts buttons, and then selecting from the available color schemes or font options.

Align Paragraphs

Changing paragraph alignment is another way to enhance a document's appearance. Paragraphs are aligned relative to the left and right margins in a document. By default, text is **left-aligned**, which means it is flush with the left margin and has a ragged right edge. Using the alignment buttons in the Paragraph group, you can **right-align** a paragraph—make it flush with the right margin—or **center** a paragraph so that it is positioned evenly between the left and right margins. You can also **justify** a paragraph so that both the left and right edges of the paragraph are flush with the left and right margins. **CASE** *You change the alignment of several paragraphs at the beginning of the flyer to make it more visually interesting.*

STEPS

1. **Replace Your Name, Today's Date with your name, a comma, and the date**

2. **Select your name, the comma, and the date, then click the Align Right button ☰ in the Paragraph group**

   The text is aligned with the right margin. In Page Layout view, the place where the white and shaded sections on the horizontal ruler meet shows the left and right margins.

3. **Place the insertion point between your name and the comma, press [Delete] to delete the comma, then press [Enter]**

   The new paragraph containing the date is also right-aligned. Pressing [Enter] in the middle of a paragraph creates a new paragraph with the same text and paragraph formatting as the original paragraph.

4. **Select the two-line title, then click the Center button ☰ in the Paragraph group**

   The two paragraphs that make up the title are centered between the left and right margins.

5. **Scroll down as needed, place the insertion point in the Animal Care Rajasthan heading, then click ☰**

   The Animal Care Rajasthan heading is centered.

6. **Place the insertion point in the italicized paragraph under the title, then click the Justify button ☰ in the Paragraph group**

   The paragraph is aligned with both the left and right margins, as shown in **FIGURE 3-10**. When you justify a paragraph, Word adjusts the spacing between words so that each line in the paragraph is flush with the left and the right margins.

7. **Scroll down, place the insertion point in Animal Care Rajasthan, then click the launcher ☑ in the Paragraph group**

   The Paragraph dialog box opens, as shown in **FIGURE 3-11**. The Indents and Spacing tab shows the paragraph format settings for the paragraph where the insertion point is located. You can check or change paragraph format settings using this dialog box.

8. **Click the Alignment list arrow, click Left, click OK, then save your changes**

   The Animal Care Rajasthan heading is left-aligned.

FIGURE 3-10: Modified paragraph alignment

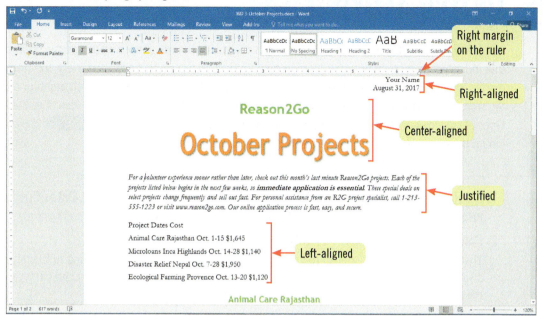

FIGURE 3-11: Indents and Spacing tab in the Paragraph dialog box

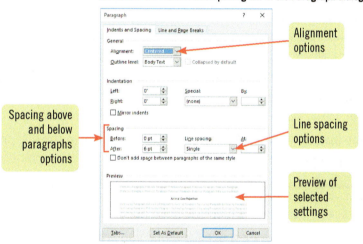

Formatting a document using themes

Changing the theme applied to a document is another powerful and efficient way to tailor a document's look and feel, particularly when a document is formatted with a Quick Style set. By default, all documents created in Word are formatted with the default Office theme—which uses Calibri as the font for the body text—but you can change the theme at any time to fit the content, tone, and purpose of a document. When you change the theme for a document, a complete set of new theme colors, fonts, and effects is applied to the whole document.

To preview how various themes look when applied to the current document, click the Themes button in the Document Formatting group on the Design tab, and then move the pointer over each theme in the gallery and notice how the document changes. When you click the theme you like, all document content that uses theme colors, all text that is formatted with a style, including default body text, and all table styles and graphic effects change to the colors, fonts, and effects used by the theme. In addition, the gallery of colors changes to display the set of theme colors, and the active Quick Style set changes to employ the theme colors and fonts. Note that changing the theme does not change the non-theme-based font formatting that has already been applied. For example, if you changed the font of text, applied bold to text, or changed the font color of text to a standard or custom color, that formatting remains in place.

If you want to tweak the document design further, you can modify it by applying a different set of theme colors, heading and body text fonts, or graphic effects. To do this, simply click the Colors, Fonts, or Effects button in the Document Formatting group, move the pointer over each option in the gallery to preview it in the document, and then click the option you like best.

Work with Tabs

Learning Outcomes
- Set tab stops and tab leaders
- Modify tabs
- Use tabs to align text

Tabs allow you to align text at a specific location in a document. A **tab stop** is a point on the horizontal ruler that indicates the location at which to align text. By default, tab stops are located every 1/2" from the left margin, but you can also set custom tab stops. Using tabs, you can align text to the left, right, or center of a tab stop, or you can align text at a decimal point or insert a bar character. TABLE 3-1 describes the different types of tab stops. You set tabs using the horizontal ruler or the Tabs dialog box. **CASE** ▶ *You use tabs to format the summary information on last minute projects so it is easy to read.*

STEPS

1. **Scroll as needed, then select the five-line list beginning with "Project Dates Cost"**
   Before you set tab stops for existing text, you must select the paragraphs for which you want to set tabs.

2. **Point to the tab indicator ⌊ at the left end of the horizontal ruler**
   The icon that appears in the tab indicator indicates the active type of tab; pointing to the tab indicator displays a ScreenTip with the name of the active tab type. By default, left tab is the active tab type. Clicking the tab indicator scrolls through the types of tabs and indents.

3. **Click the tab indicator to see each of the available tab and indent types, make Left Tab ⌊ the active tab type, click the 1" mark on the horizontal ruler, then click the 3½" mark on the horizontal ruler**
   A left tab stop is inserted at the 1" mark and the 3½" mark on the horizontal ruler. Clicking the horizontal ruler inserts a tab stop of the active type for the selected paragraph or paragraphs.

4. **Click the tab indicator twice so the Right Tab icon ⌉ is active, then click the 5" mark on the horizontal ruler**
   A right tab stop is inserted at the 5" mark on the horizontal ruler, as shown in FIGURE 3-12.

5. **Place the insertion point before Project in the first line in the list, press [Tab], place the insertion point before Dates, press [Tab], place the insertion point before Cost, then press [Tab]**
   Inserting a tab before "Project" left-aligns the text at the 1" mark, inserting a tab before "Dates" left-aligns the text at the 3½" mark, and inserting a tab before "Cost" right-aligns "Cost" at the 5" mark.

6. **Insert a tab at the beginning of each remaining line in the list**
   The paragraphs left-align at the 1" mark.

7. **Insert a tab before each Oct. in the list, then insert a tab before each $ in the list**
   The dates left-align at the 3½" mark. The prices right-align at the 5" mark.

8. **Select the five lines of tabbed text, drag the right tab stop to the 5½" mark on the horizontal ruler, then deselect the text**
   Dragging the tab stop moves it to a new location. The prices right-align at the 5½" mark.

9. **Select the last four lines of tabbed text, click the launcher ⌐ in the Paragraph group, then click the Tabs button at the bottom of the Paragraph dialog box**
   The Tabs dialog box opens, as shown in FIGURE 3-13. You can use the Tabs dialog box to set tab stops, change the position or alignment of existing tab stops, clear tab stops, and apply tab leaders to tabs. **Tab leaders** are lines that appear in front of tabbed text.

10. **Click 3.5" in the Tab stop position list box, click the 2 option button in the Leader section, click Set, click 5.5" in the Tab stop position list box, click the 2 option button in the Leader section, click Set, click OK, deselect the text, then save your changes**
    A dotted tab leader is added before each 3.5" and 5.5" tab stop in the last four lines of tabbed text, as shown in FIGURE 3-14.

Formatting Text and Paragraphs

FIGURE 3-12: Left and right tab stops on the horizontal ruler

Right Tab icon in tab indicator

Left tab stops

Right tab stop

FIGURE 3-13: Tabs dialog box

Select the tab stop you want to modify

Select Leader options

Apply the selected settings to the selected tab stop

Clears the selected tab stop

Clears all tab stops

FIGURE 3-14: Tab leaders

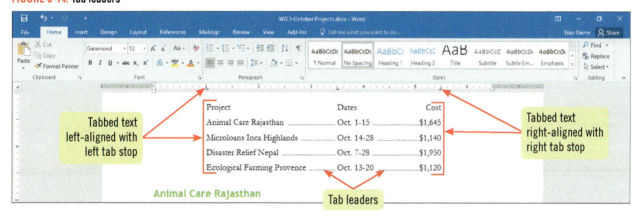

Tabbed text left-aligned with left tab stop

Tabbed text right-aligned with right tab stop

Tab leaders

TABLE 3-1: Types of tabs

tab	use to
Left tab	Set the start position of text so that text runs to the right of the tab stop as you type
Center tab	Set the center align position of text so that text stays centered on the tab stop as you type
Right tab	Set the right or end position of text so that text moves to the left of the tab stop as you type
Decimal tab	Set the position of the decimal point so that numbers align around the decimal point as you type
Bar tab	Insert a vertical bar at the tab position

Work with Indents

Learning Outcomes
- Indent a paragraph
- Indent the first line of a paragraph

When you **indent** a paragraph, you move its edge in from the left or right margin. You can indent the entire left or right edge of a paragraph, just the first line, or all lines except the first line. The **indent markers** on the horizontal ruler indicate the indent settings for the paragraph in which the insertion point is located. Dragging an indent marker to a new location on the ruler is one way to change the indentation of a paragraph; changing the indent settings in the Paragraph group on the Layout tab is another; and using the indent buttons in the Paragraph group on the Home tab is a third. **TABLE 3-2** describes different types of indents and some of the methods for creating each. **CASE** *You indent several paragraphs in the flyer.*

STEPS

1. **Press [Ctrl][Home], place the insertion point in the italicized paragraph under the title, then click the Increase Indent button 🔲 in the Paragraph group on the Home tab**
   The entire paragraph is indented ½" from the left margin, as shown in **FIGURE 3-15**. The indent marker also moves to the ½" mark on the horizontal ruler. Each time you click the Increase Indent button, the left edge of a paragraph moves another ½" to the right.

2. **Click the Decrease Indent button 🔲 in the Paragraph group**
   The left edge of the paragraph moves ½" to the left, and the indent marker moves back to the left margin.

3. **Drag the First Line Indent marker 🔽 to the ¼" mark on the horizontal ruler**
   FIGURE 3-16 shows the First Line Indent marker being dragged. The first line of the paragraph is indented ¼". Dragging the First Line Indent marker indents only the first line of a paragraph.

4. **Scroll to the bottom of page 1, place the insertion point in the quotation, click the Layout tab, click the Indent Left text box in the Paragraph group, type .5, click the Indent Right text box, type .5, then press [Enter]**
   The left and right edges of the paragraph are indented ½" from the margins, as shown in **FIGURE 3-17**.

5. **Press [Ctrl][Home], place the insertion point in the italicized paragraph, then click the launcher 🔲 in the Paragraph group**
   The Paragraph dialog box opens. You can use the Indents and Spacing tab to check or change the alignment, indentation, and paragraph and line spacing settings applied to a paragraph.

6. **Click the Special list arrow, click (none), click OK, then save your changes**
   The first line indent is removed from the paragraph.

Applying text effects and clearing formatting

The Word Text Effects and Typography feature allows you to add visual appeal to your documents by adding special text effects to text, including outlines, shadows, reflections, and glows. The feature also includes a gallery of preformatted combined text effect styles, called **WordArt**, that you can apply to your text to format it quickly and easily. To apply a WordArt style or a text effect to text, simply select the text, click the Text Effects and Typography button in the Font group on the Home tab, and select a WordArt style from the gallery or point to a type of text effect, such as reflection or shadow, to open a gallery of styles related to that type of text effect. Experiment with combining text effect styles to give your text a striking appearance.

If you are unhappy with the way text is formatted, you can use the Clear All Formatting command to return the text to the default format settings. The default format includes font and paragraph formatting: text is formatted in 11-point Calibri, and paragraphs are left-aligned with 1.08 point line spacing, 8 points of space after, and no indents. To clear formatting from text and return it to the default format, select the text you want to clear, and then click the Clear All Formatting button in the Font group on the Home tab. If you prefer to return the text to the default font and remove all paragraph formatting, making the text 11-point Calibri, left-aligned, single spaced, with no paragraph spacing or indents, select the text and then simply click the No Spacing button in the Styles group on the Home tab.

FIGURE 3-15: Indented paragraph

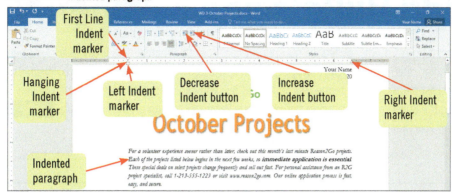

FIGURE 3-16: Dragging the First Line Indent marker

FIGURE 3-17: Paragraph indented from the left and right

TABLE 3-2: Types of indents

indent type: description	to create
Left indent: The left edge of a paragraph is moved in from the left margin	Drag the Left Indent marker ☐ on the ruler to the right to the position where you want the left edge of the paragraph to align; when you drag the left indent marker, all the indent markers move as one
Right indent: The right edge of a paragraph is moved in from the right margin	Drag the Right Indent marker △ on the ruler to the left to the position where you want the right edge of the paragraph to align
First line indent: The first line of a paragraph is indented more than the subsequent lines	Drag the First Line Indent marker ▽ on the ruler to the right to the position where you want the first line of the paragraph to begin; or activate the First Line Indent marker ▽ in the tab indicator, and then click the ruler at the position where you want the first line of the paragraph to begin
Hanging indent: The subsequent lines of a paragraph are indented more than the first line	Drag the Hanging Indent marker △ on the ruler to the right to the position where you want the hanging indent to begin; or activate the Hanging Indent marker △ in the tab indicator, and then click the ruler at the position where you want the second and remaining lines of the paragraph to begin; when you drag the hanging indent marker, the left indent marker moves with it
Negative indent (or Outdent): The left edge of a paragraph is moved to the left of the left margin	Drag the Left Indent marker ☐ on the ruler left to the position where you want the negative indent to begin; when you drag the left indent marker, all markers move as one

Add Bullets and Numbering

Learning Outcomes
- Apply bullets or numbering to lists
- Renumber a list
- Change bullet or numbering styles

Formatting a list with bullets or numbering can help to organize the ideas in a document. A **bullet** is a character, often a small circle, that appears before the items in a list to add emphasis. Formatting a list as a numbered list helps illustrate sequences and priorities. You can quickly format a list with bullets or numbering by using the Bullets and Numbering buttons in the Paragraph group on the Home tab. **CASE** *You format the lists in your flyer with numbers and bullets.*

STEPS

1. **Scroll until the Disaster Relief Nepal heading is at the top of your screen**

2. **Select the three-line list of 3-day add-ons, click the Home tab, then click the Numbering list arrow** [icon] **in the Paragraph group**

   The Numbering Library opens, as shown in **FIGURE 3-18**. You use this list to choose or change the numbering style applied to a list. You can drag the pointer over the numbering styles to preview how the selected text will look if the numbering style is applied.

3. **Click the numbering style called out in FIGURE 3-18**

   The paragraphs are formatted as a numbered list.

   QUICK TIP
   To remove a bullet or number, select the paragraph(s), then click [icon] or [icon].

4. **Place the insertion point after Pokhara — Valley of Lakes, press [Enter], then type Temples of Janakpur**

   Pressing [Enter] in the middle of the numbered list creates a new numbered paragraph and automatically renumbers the remainder of the list. Similarly, if you delete a paragraph from a numbered list, Word automatically renumbers the remaining paragraphs.

5. **Click 1 in the list**

   Clicking a number in a list selects all the numbers, as shown in **FIGURE 3-19**.

6. **Click the Bold button** [B] **in the Font group**

   The numbers are all formatted in bold. Notice that the formatting of the items in the list does not change when you change the formatting of the numbers. You can also use this technique to change the formatting of bullets in a bulleted list.

   QUICK TIP
   To use a symbol or a picture for a bullet character, click the Bullets list arrow, click Define New Bullet, and then select from the options in the Define New Bullet dialog box.

7. **Select the list of items under "Last minute participants in the Disaster Relief Nepal project...", then click the Bullets button** [icon] **in the Paragraph group**

   The four paragraphs are formatted as a bulleted list using the most recently used bullet style.

8. **Click a bullet in the list to select all the bullets, click the Bullets list arrow** [icon] **in the Paragraph group, click the check mark bullet style, click the document to deselect the text, then save your changes**

   The bullet character changes to a check mark, as shown in **FIGURE 3-20**.

Creating multilevel lists

You can create lists with hierarchical structures by applying a multilevel list style to a list. To create a **multilevel list**, also called an outline, begin by applying a multilevel list style using the Multilevel List list arrow [icon] in the Paragraph group on the Home tab, then type your outline, pressing [Enter] after each item. To demote items to a lower level of importance in the outline, place the insertion point in the item, then click the Increase Indent button [icon] in the Paragraph group on the Home tab. Each time you indent a paragraph, the item is demoted to a lower level in the outline. Similarly, you can use the Decrease Indent button [icon] to promote an item to a higher level in the outline. You can also create a hierarchical structure in any bulleted or numbered list by using [icon] and [icon] to demote and promote items in the list. To change the multilevel list style applied to a list, select the list, click [icon] and then select a new style.

FIGURE 3-18: Numbering Library

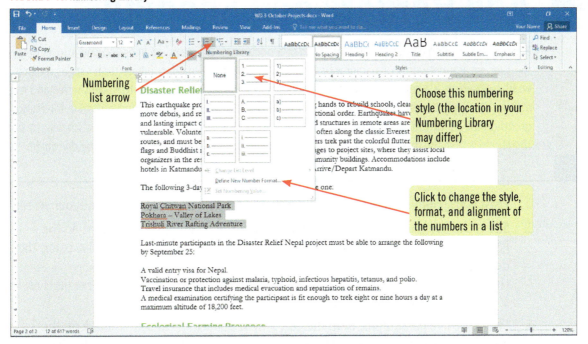

Numbering list arrow

Choose this numbering style (the location in your Numbering Library may differ)

Click to change the style, format, and alignment of the numbers in a list

FIGURE 3-19: Numbered list

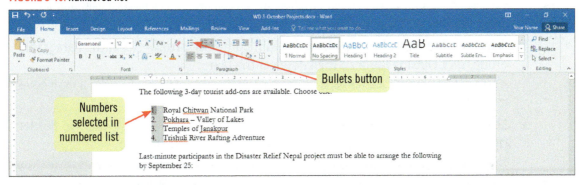

Bullets button

Numbers selected in numbered list

FIGURE 3-20: Check mark bullets applied to list

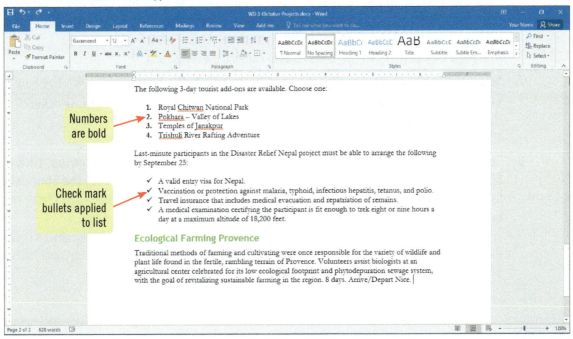

Numbers are bold

Check mark bullets applied to list

Add Borders and Shading

Borders and shading can add color and splash to a document. **Borders** are lines you add above, below, to the side, or around words or paragraphs. You can format borders using different line styles, colors, and widths. **Shading** is a color or pattern you apply behind words or paragraphs to make them stand out on a page. You apply borders and shading using the Borders button and the Shading button in the Paragraph group on the Home tab. **CASE** *You enhance the tabbed text of the last minute projects schedule by adding shading to it. You also apply a border around the tabbed text to set it off from the rest of the document.*

STEPS

1. **Press [Ctrl][Home], then scroll down until the tabbed text is at the top of your screen**

2. **Select the five paragraphs of tabbed text, click the Shading list arrow 🎨 ⋅ in the Paragraph group on the Home tab, click the Green, Accent 6, Lighter 60% color, then deselect the text**

   Light green shading is applied to the five paragraphs. Notice that the shading is applied to the entire width of the paragraphs, despite the tab settings.

3. **Select the five paragraphs, drag the Left Indent marker ▫ to the ¾" mark on the horizontal ruler, drag the Right Indent marker △ to the 5¾" mark, then deselect the text**

   The shading for the paragraphs is indented from the left and right, which makes it look more attractive, as shown in **FIGURE 3-21**.

4. **Select the five paragraphs, click the Bottom Border list arrow ⊞ ⋅ in the Paragraph group, click Outside Borders, then deselect the text**

   A black outside border is added around the selected text. The style of the border added is the most recently used border style, in this case the default, a thin black line.

5. **Select the five paragraphs, click the Outside Borders list arrow ⊞ ⋅, click No Border, click the No Border list arrow ⊟ ⋅, then click Borders and Shading**

   The Borders and Shading dialog box opens, as shown in **FIGURE 3-22**. You use the Borders tab to change the border style, color, and width, and to add boxes and lines to words or paragraphs.

6. **Click the Box icon in the Setting section, scroll down the Style list, click the double-line style, click the Color list arrow, click the Green, Accent 6, Darker 25% color, click the Width list arrow, click 1½ pt, click OK, then deselect the text**

   A 1½-point dark green double-line border is added around the tabbed text.

7. **Select the five paragraphs, click the Bold button B in the Font group, click the Font Color list arrow A ⋅ in the Font group, click the Green, Accent 6, Darker 25% color, then deselect the text**

   The text changes to bold dark green.

8. **Select the first line in the tabbed text, click the launcher ◰ in the Font group, click the Font tab if it is not the active tab, scroll and click 14 in the Size list, click the Font color list arrow, click the Orange, Accent 2, Darker 25% color, click the Small caps check box in the Effects section, click OK, deselect the text, then save your changes**

   The text in the first line of the tabbed text is enlarged and changed to orange small caps, as shown in **FIGURE 3-23**. When you change text to small caps, the lowercase letters are changed to uppercase letters in a smaller font size.

FIGURE 3-21: Shading applied to the tabbed text

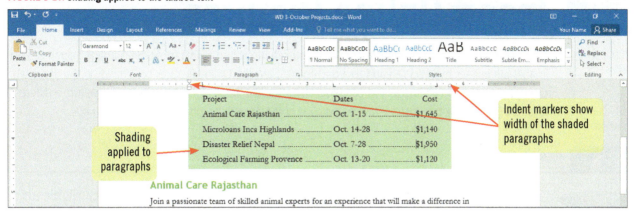

FIGURE 3-22: Borders tab in Borders and Shading dialog box

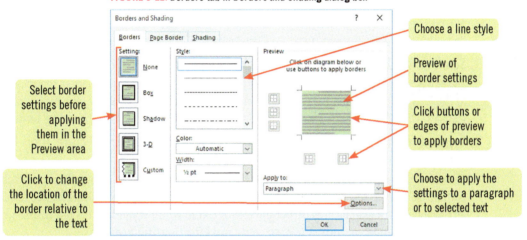

FIGURE 3-23: Borders and shading applied to the document

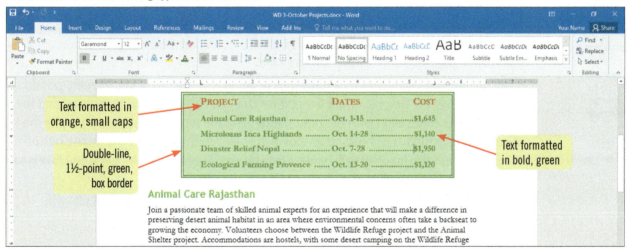

Highlighting text in a document

The Highlight tool allows you to mark and find important text in a document. **Highlighting** is transparent color that is applied to text using the Highlight pointer. To highlight text, click the Text Highlight Color list arrow in the Font group on the Home tab, select a color, then use the I-beam part of the pointer to select the text you want to highlight. Click to turn off the Highlight pointer. To remove highlighting, select the highlighted text, click then click No Color. Highlighting prints, but it is used most effectively when a document is viewed on screen.

Insert Online Pictures

**Learning
Outcomes**
- Insert images
- Resize images
- Wrap text and
  position images

Clip art is a collection of graphic images that you can insert into a document. Bing Image Search clip art images are images that you can add to a document using the Online Pictures command on the Insert tab. Once you insert a clip art image, you can wrap text around it, resize it, enhance it, and move it to a different location. **CASE** *You illustrate the second page of the document with an online clip art image.*

STEPS

1. **Scroll to the top of page 2, place the insertion point before Microloans Inca Highlands, click the Insert tab, then click the Online Pictures button in the Illustrations group**

   The Insert Pictures window opens. You can use this to search for images related to a keyword.

2. **Type Inca in the Bing Image Search text box, then press [Enter]**

   Images that have the keyword "Inca" associated with them appear in the Bing Image Search window.

3. **Scroll down the gallery of images, click the clip called out in FIGURE 3-24, then click Insert**

   The clip is inserted at the location of the insertion point. When a graphic is selected, the active tab changes to the Picture Tools Format tab. This tab contains commands used to adjust, enhance, arrange, and size graphics. The white circles that appear on the square edges of the graphic are the **sizing handles**.

4. **Type 1.8 in the Shape Height text box in the Size group on the Picture Tools Format tab, then press [Enter]**

   The size of the graphic is reduced. When you decreased the height of the graphic, the width decreased proportionally. You can also resize a graphic proportionally by dragging a corner sizing handle. Until you apply text wrapping to a graphic, it is part of the line of text in which it was inserted (an **inline graphic**). To move a graphic independently of text, you must make it a **floating graphic**.

5. **Click the Position button in the Arrange group, then click Position in Middle Center with Square Text Wrapping**

   The graphic is moved to the middle of the page and the text wraps around it. Applying text wrapping to the graphic made it a floating graphic. A floating graphic can be moved anywhere on a page. You can also wrap text around a graphic using the Layout Options button.

6. **Scroll up until the Microloans Inca Highlands heading is at the top of your screen, position the pointer over the graphic, when the pointer changes to ⁺⇖, drag the graphic up and to the right so its edges align with the right margin and the top of the paragraph under the Microloans Inca Highlands heading as shown in FIGURE 3-25, then release the mouse button**

   The graphic is moved to the upper-right corner of the page. Green alignment guides may appear to help you align the image with the margins.

7. **Click the Position button in the Arrange group, then click Position in Top Left with Square Text Wrapping**

   The graphic is moved to the upper-left corner of the page.

8. **Click the Picture Effects button in the Picture Styles group, point to Shadow, point to each style to see a preview of the style applied to the graphic, then click Offset Left**

   A shadow effect is applied to the graphic.

9. **Press [Ctrl][Home], click the View tab, then click the Multiple Pages button in the Zoom group to view the completed document as shown in FIGURE 3-26.**

10. **Save your changes, submit the document to your instructor, then close the document and exit Word**

Formatting Text and Paragraphs

FIGURE 3-24: Insert Pictures window

Select this clip (your clip might be in a different location in the gallery)

FIGURE 3-25: Graphic being moved to a new location

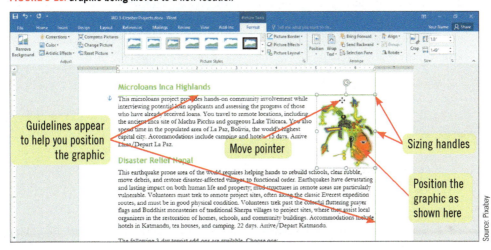

Guidelines appear to help you position the graphic

Move pointer

Sizing handles

Position the graphic as shown here

FIGURE 3-26: Completed Document

Practice

Concepts Review

Label each element of the Word program window shown in FIGURE 3-27.

FIGURE 3-27

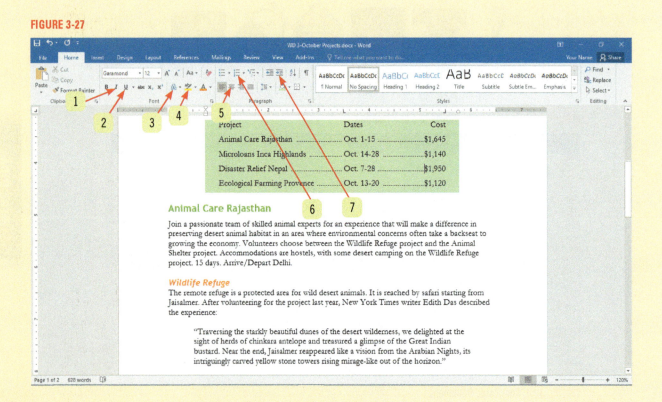

Match each term with the statement that best describes it.

8. **Inline graphic**

9. **Style**

10. **Shading**

11. **Border**

12. **Floating graphic**

13. **Highlight**

14. **Point**

15. **Bullet**

a. A graphic symbol that appears at the beginning of a paragraph in a list

b. Transparent color that is applied to text to mark it in a document

c. A set of format settings

d. An image that text wrapping has been applied to

e. An image that is inserted as part of a line of text

f. A line that can be applied above, below, or to the sides of a paragraph

g. A unit of measurement equal to $1/72$ of an inch

h. Color or pattern that is applied behind text to make it look attractive

Select the best answer from the list of choices.

16. **Which dialog box is used to change the scale of characters?**
    a. Paragraph
    b. Font
    c. Tabs
    d. Borders and Shading

17. **What is Calibri?**
    a. A font
    b. A style
    c. A text effect
    d. A character format

18. **What is the most precise way to increase the amount of white space between two paragraphs?**
    a. Indent the paragraphs
    b. Change the line spacing of the paragraphs
    c. Change the before spacing for the second paragraph
    d. Change the font size

19. **Which type of indent results in subsequent lines of a paragraph being indented more than the first line?**
    a. Right indent
    b. First line indent
    c. Negative indent
    d. Hanging indent

20. **Which command is used to add a reflection or an outline to text?**
    a. Underline
    b. Text Effects and Typography
    c. Strikethrough
    d. Change Case

Skills Review

1. **Format with fonts.**
   a. Start Word, open the file WD 3-2.docx from the location where you store your Data Files, save it as **WD 3-Manchester EDA Report**, then scroll through the document to get a feel for its contents.
   b. Press [Ctrl][A], then format the text in 12-point Californian FB. Choose a different serif font if Californian FB is not available to you.
   c. Press [Ctrl][Home], format the report title **City of Manchester** in 28-point Berlin Sans FB Demi. Choose a different sans serif font if Berlin Sans FB Demi is not available to you.
   d. Change the font color of the report title to Blue, Accent 5, Darker 25%.
   e. Format the subtitle **Economic Development Authority Report Executive Summary** in 16-point Berlin Sans FB Demi, then press [Enter] before Executive in the subtitle.
   f. Format the heading **Mission Statement** in 14-point Berlin Sans FB Demi with a Gold, Accent 4, Darker 25% font color.
   g. Press [Ctrl][Home], then save your changes to the report.

2. **Copy formats using the Format Painter.**
   a. Use the Format Painter to copy the format of the Mission Statement heading to the following headings: **Guiding Principles**, **Issues**, **Proposed Actions**.
   b. Show formatting marks, then format the paragraph under the Executive Summary heading in italic.
   c. Format **Years Population Growth**, the first line in the four-line list under the Issues heading, in bold, small caps, with a Blue, Accent 5, Darker 25% font color.
   d. Change the font color of the next two lines under Years Population Growth to Blue, Accent 5, Darker 25%.
   e. Format the line **Source: Office of State Planning** in italic, then save your changes.

3. **Change line and paragraph spacing.**
   a. Change the line spacing of the three-line list under the first body paragraph to 1.5 lines.
   b. Add 6 points of space after the title City of Manchester. Add 18 points of space before and 6 points of space after the Executive Summary line in the subtitle.
   c. Add 12 points of space after the Mission Statement heading, then add 12 points of space after each additional heading in the report (Guiding Principles, Issues, Proposed Actions).

Skills Review (continued)

    d. Add 6 points of space after each paragraph in the list under the Guiding Principles heading.

    e. Change the line spacing of the four-line list under the Issues heading that begins with Years Population Growth to 1.15.

    f. Add 6 points of space after each paragraph under the Proposed Actions heading.

    g. Press [Ctrl][Home], then save your changes to the report.

4. Align paragraphs.

    a. Press [Ctrl][A] to select the entire document, then justify all the paragraphs.

    b. Center the three-line report title.

    c. Press [Ctrl][End], press [Enter], type your name, press [Enter], type the current date, then right-align your name and the date.

    d. Save your changes to the report.

5. Work with tabs.

    a. Scroll up and select the four-line list of population information under the Issues heading.

    b. Set left tab stops at the 2" mark and the 3¾" mark.

    c. Insert a tab at the beginning of each line in the list.

    d. In the first line, insert a tab before Population. In the second line, insert a tab before 4.5%. In the third line, insert a tab before 53%.

    e. Select the first three lines, then drag the second tab stop to the 3" mark on the horizontal ruler.

    f. Press [Ctrl][Home], then save your changes to the report.

6. Work with indents.

    a. Indent the first line of the paragraph under the Mission Statement heading ½".

    b. Indent the first line of the paragraph under the Guiding Principles heading ½".

    c. Indent the first line of each of the three body paragraphs under the Issues heading ½".

    d. Press [Ctrl][Home], then save your changes to the report.

7. Add bullets and numbering.

    a. Apply bullets to the three-line list under the first body paragraph. Change the bullet style to small black circles if that is not the current bullet symbol.

    b. Change the font color of the bullets to Blue, Accent 5, Darker 25%.

    c. Scroll down until the Guiding Principles heading is at the top of your screen.

    d. Format the six-paragraph list under Guiding Principles as a numbered list.

    e. Format the numbers in 14-point Berlin Sans FB Demi, then change the font color to Blue, Accent 5, Darker 25%.

    f. Scroll down until the Proposed Actions heading is at the top of your screen, then format the paragraphs under the heading as a bulleted list using check marks as the bullet style.

    g. Change the font color of the bullets to Blue, Accent 5, Darker 25%, press [Ctrl][Home], then save your changes to the report.

8. Add borders and shading.

    a. Add a 1-point Blue, Accent 5, Darker 25% bottom border below the Mission Statement heading.

    b. Use the Format Painter or the [F4] keys to add the same border to the other headings in the report (Guiding Principles, Issues, Proposed Actions).

    c. Under the Issues heading, select the first three lines of tabbed text, which are formatted in blue, then apply Gold, Accent 4, Lighter 60% shading to the paragraphs.

    d. Select the first three lines of tabbed text again if necessary, then add a 1½ -point Blue, Accent 5, Darker 25% single line box border around the paragraphs.

    e. Indent the shading and border around the paragraphs 1¾" from the left and 1¾" from the right.

    f. Turn off formatting marks, then save your changes.

Skills Review (continued)

9. **Insert online pictures.** *(Note: To complete these steps, your computer must be connected to the Internet.)*

   a. Press [Ctrl][Home], then open the Insert Pictures window.

   b. Search using Bing Image Search to find images related to the keyword **buildings**.

   c. Insert the image shown in **FIGURE 3-28**. *(Note:* Select a different image if this one is not available to you. It is best to select an image that is similar in shape to the image shown in **FIGURE 3-28**.)

   d. Use the Shape Width text box in the Size group on the Picture Tools Format tab to change the width of the image to 1.5".

   e. Use the Position command to position the image in the top right with square text wrapping.

   f. Apply an Offset Diagonal Bottom Left shadow style to the image.

   g. View your document in two-page view and compare it to the document shown in **FIGURE 3-28**. Adjust the size or position of the image as needed to so that your document resembles the document shown in the figure.

   h. Save your changes to the document, submit it to your instructor, close the file, and then exit Word.

FIGURE 3-28

City of Manchester
Economic Development Authority Report
Executive Summary

The City of Manchester Economic Development Authority (EDA) has written an economic policy plan for the city of Manchester. The plan is intended to advance dynamic and interactive discussion. It will be used to continuously assess and foster decision-making about the following in the city of Manchester:

- Development
- Infrastructure
- Quality of life

Mission Statement

The purpose of the EDA is to foster a sustainable economy consistent with the city's planning objectives. The mix of industry, commerce, open space, residential development, and the arts in Manchester results in the city's vitality and an excellent quality of life for its citizens. Maintaining this balance is important.

Guiding Principles

Six basic principles guide Manchester's economic policy. These principles seek to safeguard the special features that give the city its character while embracing appropriate economic opportunities.

1. Manchester should remain a major economic center of the region.
2. Economic activity must respect Manchester's natural, cultural, and historic heritage.
3. A pedestrian-friendly commercial center is essential.
4. Sustained economic prosperity requires a balance between residential development, industrial/commercial development, and open space.
5. Open space in the rural district must be preserved.
6. Investing in the infrastructure is necessary to maintain and expand the existing tax and job base.

Issues

Of Manchester's approximately 64,000 acres of land, 12% is zoned for business, commercial, or industrial use, and 88% for residential development. Historically the city has relied upon business and industry to provide 35%-40% of the tax base, as well as employment opportunities. Non-residential development has traditionally been the backbone of the Manchester economy. Today, however, Manchester does not have a great deal of non-residential development potential.

The population of Manchester is expected to rise dramatically over the next few decades. The following chart shows the expected change:

Years	Population Growth
2020-2040	4.5%
2040-2060	53% (projected)

Source: Office of State Planning

At issue is the city's ability to continue to support increasing public costs (most importantly, education) with a tax base shifting toward residential taxpayers. The EDA believes Manchester should remain the market center of the region and avoid becoming a bedroom community. Manchester has maintained a sense of community in part because more than 50% of working residents are able to earn a living within the city. Jobs must be continuously created to sustain the percentage of residents who live and work in Manchester.

Proposed Actions

- Implement a business retention program that focuses on the growth and expansion of businesses already operating in Manchester.
- Build a consortium of technical and skill development resources to assist companies with educational and training needs.
- Sponsor a green business workshop.
- Allocate funds for expanded downtown parking.
- Develop a strategic open space plan.

Your Name

Today's Date

Source: Pixabay

Independent Challenge 1

You are an estimator for Sustainable Life Design | Build in Jackson, Illinois. You have drafted an estimate for a home renovation job and you need to format it. It's important that your estimate have a clean, striking design, and reflect your company's professionalism.

a. Start Word, open the file WD 3-3.docx from the drive and folder where you store your Data Files, save it as

FIGURE 3-29

SustainableLIFE Design | Build

482 North Street, Jackson, IL 62705; Tel: 217-555-3202; www.sustainablelifedesignbuild.com

WD 3-Chou Birch Estimate, then read the document to get a feel for its contents. **FIGURE 3-29** shows how you will format the letterhead.

b. Select the entire document, change the style to No Spacing, then change the font to 11-point Calibri Light.

c. In the first line of the letterhead, format **Sustainable Life** in 30-point Arial Black, then apply all caps to Life. Format **Sustainable** with the Green, Accent 6, Darker 25% font color, format **LIFE** with the Green, Accent 6 font color, then delete the space between the two words. Format **Design | Build** in 30-point Arial with a Green, Accent 6, Darker 25% font color. (*Hint*: Type 30 in the Font Size text box, then press [Enter].)

d. Format the next line in 10-point Arial with a Green, Accent 6, Darker 25% font color.

e. Center the two-line letterhead.

f. Add a 2¼-point dotted Green, Accent 6, Darker 25% border below the address line paragraph.

g. With the insertion point in the address line, open the Borders and Shading dialog box, click Options to open the Border and Shading Options dialog box, change the Bottom setting to **5** points, then click OK twice to close the dialog boxes and to adjust the location of the border relative to the line of text.

h. Format the title **Proposal of Renovation** in 14-point Arial, then center the title.

i. Format the following headings (including the colons) in 11-point Arial: **Date**, **Work to be performed for and at**, **Scope of work**, **Payment schedule**, and **Agreement**.

j. Select the 14-line list under **Scope of work** that begins with **Demo of all...**, then change the paragraph spacing to add 4 points of space after each paragraph in the list. (*Hint*: Select 0 pt in the After text box, type 4, then press Enter.)

k. With the list selected, set a right tab stop at the 6¼" mark, insert tabs before every price in the list, then apply dotted line tab leaders.

l. Format the list as a numbered list, then apply bold to the numbers.

m. Apply bold and italic to the two lines, **Total estimated job cost...** and **Approximate job time...** below the list.

n. Replace Your Name with your name in the signature block, select the signature block (Respectfully submitted through your name), set a left tab stop at the 3¼" mark, then indent the signature block using tabs.

o. Examine the document carefully for formatting errors, and make any necessary adjustments.

p. Save the document, submit it to your instructor, then close the file and exit Word.

Independent Challenge 2

Your employer, the Mission Center for Contemporary Arts in Guelph, Ontario, is launching a membership drive. Your boss has written the text for a flyer advertising Mission membership, and asks you to format it so that it is eye catching and attractive.

a. Open the file WD 3-4.docx from the drive and folder where you store your Data Files, save it as **WD 3-Mission 2017**, then read the document. **FIGURE 3-30** shows how you will format the first several paragraphs of the flyer.

FIGURE 3-30

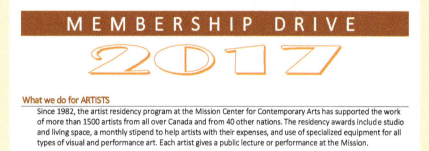

b. Select the entire document, change the style to No Spacing, then change the font to 10-point Calibri Light.

c. Center the first line, **MEMBERSHIP DRIVE**, and apply shading to the paragraph. Choose a dark custom shading color of your choice for the shading color. (*Hint*: Click More Colors, then select a color from the Standard or Custom tab.) Format the text in 24-point Calibri Light, bold, with a white font color. Expand the character spacing by 10 points. (*Hint*: Use the Advanced tab in the Font dialog box. Set the Spacing to Expanded, and then type **10** in the By text box.)

d. Format the second line, **2017**, in 48-point Broadway, bold. Apply the Fill - White, Outline - Accent 2, Hard Shadow - Accent 2 text effect style to the text. (*Hint*: Use the Text Effects and Typography button.) Expand the character spacing by 10 points, and change the character scale to 250%. Center the line.

e. Format each **What we do for...** heading in 11-point Calibri Light, bold. Change the font color to the same custom color used for shading the title. (*Note*: The color now appears in the Recent Colors section of the Font Color gallery.) Add a single-line ½-point black border under each heading.

f. Format each subheading (**Gallery**, **Lectures**, **Library**, **All members...**, and **Membership Levels**) in 10-point Calibri Light, bold. Add 3 points of spacing before each paragraph. (*Hint*: Select 0 in the Before text box, type 3, then press Enter.)

g. Indent each body paragraph ¼", except for the lines under the **What we do for YOU** heading.

h. Format the four lines under the **All members...** subheading as a bulleted list. Use a bullet symbol of your choice, and format the bullets in the custom font color.

i. Indent the five lines under the **Membership Levels** heading ¼". For these five lines, set left tab stops at the 1¼" mark and the 2¼" mark on the horizontal ruler. Insert tabs before the price and before the word All in each of the five lines.

j. Format the name of each membership level (**Artistic**, **Conceptual**, etc.) in 10-point Calibri Light, bold, italic, with the custom font color.

k. Format the **For more information...** heading in 14-point Calibri Light, bold, with the custom font color, then center the heading.

l. Center the last two lines, replace Your Name with your name, then apply bold to your name.

m. Examine the document carefully for formatting errors, and make any necessary adjustments.

n. Save the flyer, submit it to your instructor, then close the file and exit Word.

Independent Challenge 3

One of your responsibilities as program coordinator at Alpine Vistas Resort is to develop a program of winter outdoor learning and adventure workshops. You have drafted a memo to your boss to update her on your progress. You need to format the memo so it is professional looking and easy to read.

a. Start Word, open the file WD 3-5.docx from the drive and folder where you store your Data Files, then save it as **WD 3-Alpine Vistas Memo**.

b. Select the **Alpine Vistas Resort Memorandum** heading, apply the Quick Style Title to it, then center the heading. (*Hint*: Open the Quick Style gallery, then click the Title style.)

c. In the memo header, replace Today's Date and Your Name with the current date and your name.

d. Select the four-line memo header, set a left tab stop at the ¾" mark, then insert tabs before the date, the recipient's name, your name, and the subject of the memo.

e. Apply the Quick Style Strong to **Date:**, **To:**, **From:**, and **Re:**.

f. Apply the Quick Style Heading 2 to the headings **Overview**, **Workshops**, **Accommodations**, **Fees**, and **Proposed winter programming**.

g. Under the Fees heading, apply the Quick Style Emphasis to the words **Workshop fees** and **Accommodations fees**.

h. On the second page of the document, format the list under the **Proposed winter programming** heading as a multilevel list. FIGURE 3-31 shows the hierarchical structure of the outline. (*Hints*: The list is on pages 2 and 3 so be sure to select the entire list before applying the multilevel style. Apply a multilevel list style, then use the Increase Indent and Decrease Indent buttons to change the level of importance of each item.)

i. Change the outline numbering style to the bullet numbering style shown in FIGURE 3-31 if a different style is used in your outline.

j. Change the font color of each bullet level in the list to a theme font color of your choice. (*Hint*: Select one bullet of each level to select all the bullets at that level, then apply a font color.)

k. Zoom out on the memo so that two pages are displayed in the document window, then, using the Change Case button, change the title Alpine Vistas Resort Memorandum so that only the initial letter of each word is capitalized.

l. Using the Fonts button on the Design tab, change the fonts to a font set of your choice. Choose fonts that allow the document to fit on two pages.

m. Using the Colors button on the Design tab, change the colors to a color palette of your choice.

n. Apply different styles and adjust other formatting elements as necessary to make the memo attractive, eye catching, and readable. The finished memo should fit on two pages.

o. Save the document, submit it to your instructor, then close the file and exit Word.

FIGURE 3-31

Proposed winter programming

- ❖ Skiing, Snowboarding, and Snowshoeing
  - ➢ Skiing and Snowboarding
    - ▪ Cross-country skiing
      - • Cross-country skiing for beginners
      - • Intermediate cross-country skiing
      - • Inn-to-inn ski touring
      - • Moonlight cross-country skiing
    - ▪ Telemarking
      - • Basic telemark skiing
      - • Introduction to backcountry skiing
      - • Exploring on skis
    - ▪ Snowboarding
      - • Backcountry snowboarding
  - ➢ Snowshoeing
    - ▪ Beginner
      - • Snowshoeing for beginners
      - • Snowshoeing and winter ecology
    - ▪ Intermediate and Advanced
      - • Intermediate snowshoeing
      - • Guided snowshoe trek
      - • Above tree line snowshoeing
- ❖ Winter Hiking, Camping, and Survival
  - ➢ Hiking
    - ▪ Beginner
      - • Long-distance hiking
      - • Winter summits
      - • Hiking for women
  - ➢ Winter camping and survival
    - ▪ Beginner
      - • Introduction to winter camping
      - • Basic winter mountain skills
      - • Building snow shelters
    - ▪ Intermediate
      - • Basic winter mountain skills II
      - • Ice climbing
      - • Avalanche awareness and rescue

Independent Challenge 4: Explore

The fonts you choose for a document can have a major effect on the document's tone. Not all fonts are appropriate for use in a business document, and some fonts, especially those with a definite theme, are appropriate only for specific purposes. In this Independent Challenge, you will use font formatting and other formatting features to design a letterhead and a fax coversheet for yourself or your business. The letterhead and coversheet should not only look professional and attract interest, but also say something about the character of your business or your personality. **FIGURE 3-32** shows an example of a business letterhead.

a. Start Word, and save a new blank document as **WD 3-Personal Letterhead** to the drive and folder where you store your Data Files.

b. Type your name or the name of your business, your address, your phone number, your fax number, and your website or e-mail address.

c. Format your name or the name of your business in a font that expresses your personality or says something about the nature of your business. Use fonts, font colors, text effects and typography, borders, shading, paragraph formatting, and other formatting features to design a letterhead that is appealing and professional.

d. Save your changes, submit the document to your instructor, then close the file.

e. Open a new blank document, and save it as **WD 3-Personal Fax Coversheet**. Type FAX, your name or the name of your business, your address, your phone number, your fax number, and your website or e-mail address at the top of the document.

f. Type a fax header that includes the following: Date:, To:, From:, Re:, Pages:, and Comments:.

g. Format the information in the fax coversheet using fonts, font effects, borders, paragraph formatting, and other formatting features. Since a fax coversheet is designed to be faxed, all fonts and other formatting elements should be black or grey.

h. Save your changes, submit the document to your instructor, close the file, then exit Word.

FIGURE 3-32

443 Sanchez Street, 6th floor, Santa Fe, NM 87501 Tel: 505-555-9767 Fax: 505-555-2992 www.valerino.com

Visual Workshop

Open the file WD 3-6.docx from the drive and folder where you store your Data Files. Create the menu shown in FIGURE 3-33. (*Hints*: Use the sizing handles to resize the graphic to be approximately 1.4" tall and 6.5" wide. Use Californian FB or a similar font for the text. Add color, bold, and italic as shown in the figure. Change the font size of the café name to 28 points, the font size of Today's Specials to 14 points, the font size of the menu to 12 points, and the font size of the italicized text at the bottom to 10 points. Format the prices using tabs and leader lines. Use paragraph spacing to adjust the spacing between paragraphs so that all the text fits on one page. Make other adjustments as needed so your menu is similar to the one shown in FIGURE 3-33.) Save the menu as **WD 3-Todays Specials**, then submit a copy to your instructor.

FIGURE 3-33

City Beach Café

Today's Specials

Strawberry Summer Salad

Arugula and baby spinach topped with sliced strawberries, goat cheese, sunflower seeds, and croutons, served with a strawberry vinaigrette. Add shrimp or lobster. $9.00

Shrimp and Avocado Salad

Shrimp and avocado salad over mixed greens with sliced tomatoes, cucumbers, and corn salsa, served with cilantro lime vinaigrette. $12.00

Lobster Tacos

Generous chunks of lobster over ginger slaw with chipotle crema and pickled onions. Served with cilantro lime rice and beans. $15.00

Coconut Encrusted Haddock

Filet of haddock lighted breaded with panko and coconut. Oven baked and served with cilantro lime rice and beans and corn on the cob. $16.00

Tropical Grilled Swordfish

Seasoned swordfish grilled and finished with citrus pineapple salsa. Served with cilantro lime rice and beans, and ginger slaw. $18.00

Shrimp Burrito

Tender grilled shrimp served with cilantro rice, black beans, romaine lettuce, cheese, salsa verde, pico de gallo, and corn on the cob. $11.00

Scallop Kebob

Ginger lime drenched scallops grilled and served with tropical macaroni salad, citrus pineapple salsa, and corn on the cob. $15.00

We serve only fresh, local, sustainably farmed and harvested ingredients.

Chef: Your Name

Formatting Text and Paragraphs

Formatting Documents

CASE You have written and formatted the text for an informational report for Reason2Go volunteers about staying healthy while traveling. You are now ready to format the pages. You plan to organize the text in columns, to illustrate the report with a table, and to add footnotes and a bibliography.

Module Objectives

After completing this module, you will be able to:

- Set document margins
- Create sections and columns
- Insert page breaks
- Insert page numbers
- Add headers and footers
- Insert a table
- Add footnotes and endnotes
- Insert citations
- Manage sources and create a bibliography

Files You Will Need

WD 4-1.docx	WD 4-5.docx
WD 4-2.docx	WD 4-6.docx
WD 4-3.docx	WD 4-7.docx
WD 4-4.docx	

Set Document Margins

Changing a document's margins is one way to change the appearance of a document and control the amount of text that fits on a page. The **margins** of a document are the blank areas between the edge of the text and the edge of the page. When you create a document in Word, the default margins are 1" at the top, bottom, left, and right sides of the page. You can adjust the size of a document's margins using the Margins command on the Layout tab or using the rulers. **CASE** ▶ *The report should be a four-page document when finished. You begin by reducing the size of the document margins so that more text fits on each page.*

STEPS

1. **Start Word, open the file WD 4-1.docx from the location where you store your Data Files, then save it as WD 4-Travel Health 2Go**

   The report opens in Print Layout view.

2. **Scroll through the report to get a feel for its contents, then press [Ctrl][Home]**

   The report is currently five pages long. Notice that the status bar indicates the page where the insertion point is located and the total number of pages in the document.

3. **Click the Layout tab, then click the Margins button in the Page Setup group**

   The Margins menu opens. You can select predefined margin settings from this menu, or you can click Custom Margins to create different margin settings.

4. **Click Custom Margins**

   The Page Setup dialog box opens with the Margins tab displayed, as shown in **FIGURE 4-1**. You can use the Margins tab to change the top, bottom, left, or right document margin, to change the orientation of the pages from portrait to landscape, and to alter other page layout settings. **Portrait orientation** means a page is taller than it is wide; **landscape orientation** means a page is wider than it is tall. This report uses portrait orientation. You can also use the Orientation button in the Page Setup group on the Layout tab to change the orientation of a document.

5. **Click the Top down arrow three times until 0.7" appears, then click the Bottom down arrow until 0.7" appears**

   The top and bottom margins of the report will be .7".

6. **Press [Tab], type .7 in the Left text box, press [Tab], then type .7 in the Right text box**

   The left and right margins of the report will also be .7". You can change the margin settings by using the arrows or by typing a value in the appropriate text box.

7. **Click OK**

   The document margins change to .7", as shown in **FIGURE 4-2**. The location of each margin (right, left, top, and bottom) is shown on the horizontal and vertical rulers at the intersection of the white and shaded areas. You can also change a margin setting by using the ⌐ pointer to drag the intersection to a new location on the ruler.

8. **Click the View tab, then click the Multiple Pages button in the Zoom group**

   The first three pages of the document appear in the document window.

9. **Scroll down to view all five pages of the report, press [Ctrl][Home], click the 100% button in the Zoom group, then save your changes**

FIGURE 4-1: Margins tab in Page Setup dialog box

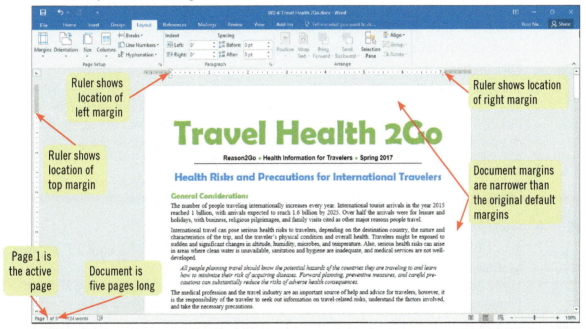

Default margin settings

Set gutter margin

Select page orientation

Select gutter position

Set mirror margins and other page layout options

Preview of margin settings

Select part of document to apply settings to

FIGURE 4-2: Report with smaller margins

Ruler shows location of left margin

Ruler shows location of right margin

Ruler shows location of top margin

Document margins are narrower than the original default margins

Page 1 is the active page

Document is five pages long

Travel Health 2Go

Reason2Go • Health Information for Travelers • Spring 2017

Health Risks and Precautions for International Travelers

General Considerations

The number of people traveling internationally increases every year. International tourist arrivals in the year 2015 reached 1 billion, with arrivals expected to reach 1.6 billion by 2025. Over half the arrivals were for leisure and holidays, with business, religious pilgrimages, and family visits cited as other major reasons people travel.

International travel can pose serious health risks to travelers, depending on the destination country, the nature and characteristics of the trip, and the traveler's physical condition and overall health. Travelers might be exposed to sudden and significant changes in altitude, humidity, microbes, and temperature. Also, serious health risks can arise in areas where clean water is unavailable, sanitation and hygiene are inadequate, and medical services are not well-developed.

All people planning travel should know the potential hazards of the countries they are traveling to and learn how to minimize their risk of acquiring diseases. Forward planning, preventive measures, and careful precautions can substantially reduce the risks of adverse health consequences.

The medical profession and the travel industry are an important source of help and advice for travelers, however, it is the responsibility of the traveler to seek out information on travel-related risks, understand the factors involved, and take the necessary precautions.

Changing orientation, margin settings, and paper size

By default, the documents you create in Word use an 8½" x 11" paper size in portrait orientation with the default margin settings. You can change the orientation, margin settings, and paper size to common settings using the Orientation, Margins, and Size buttons in the Page Setup group on the Layout tab. You can also adjust these settings and others in the Page Setup dialog box. For example, to change the layout of multiple pages, use the Multiple pages list arrow on the Margins tab to create pages that use mirror margins, that include two pages per sheet of paper, or that are formatted using a book fold. **Mirror margins** are used in a document with facing pages, such as a magazine, where the margins on the left page of the document are a mirror image of the margins on the right page. Documents with mirror margins have inside and outside margins, rather than right and left margins. Another type of margin is a gutter margin, which is used in documents that are bound, such as books. A **gutter** adds extra space to the left, top, or inside margin to allow for the binding. Add a gutter to a document by adjusting the setting in the Gutter position text box on the Margins tab. To change the size of the paper used, use the Paper size list arrow on the Paper tab to select a standard paper size, or enter custom measurements in the Width and Height text boxes.

Create Sections and Columns

Dividing a document into sections allows you to format each section of the document with different page layout settings. A **section** is a portion of a document that is separated from the rest of the document by section breaks. **Section breaks** are formatting marks that you insert in a document to show the end of a section. Once you have divided a document into sections, you can format each section with different column, margin, page orientation, header and footer, and other page layout settings. By default, a document is formatted as a single section, but you can divide a document into as many sections as you like. **CASE** *You insert a section break to divide the document into two sections, and then format the text in the second section in two columns. First, you customize the status bar to display section information.*

STEPS

1. **Right-click the status bar, click Section on the Customize Status Bar menu that opens (if it is not already checked), then click the document to close the menu**

    The status bar indicates the insertion point is located in section 1 of the document.

2. **Click the Home tab, then click the Show/Hide ¶ button ¶ in the Paragraph group**

    Turning on formatting marks allows you to see the section breaks you insert in a document.

3. **Place the insertion point before the heading General Considerations, click the Layout tab, then click the Breaks button in the Page Setup group**

    The Breaks menu opens. You use this menu to insert different types of section breaks. See **TABLE 4-1**.

4. **Click Continuous**

    Word inserts a continuous section break, shown as a dotted double line, above the heading. When you insert a section break at the beginning of a paragraph, Word inserts the break at the end of the previous paragraph. The section break stores the formatting information for the previous section. The document now has two sections. Notice that the status bar indicates the insertion point is in section 2.

5. **Click the Columns button in the Page Setup group**

    The columns menu opens. You use this menu to format text using preset column formats or to create custom columns.

6. **Click More Columns to open the Columns dialog box**

7. **Select Two in the Presets section, click the Spacing down arrow twice until 0.3" appears as shown in FIGURE 4-3, then click OK**

    Section 2 is formatted in two columns of equal width with .3" of spacing between, as shown in **FIGURE 4-4**. Formatting text in columns is another way to increase the amount of text that fits on a page.

8. **Click the View tab, click the Multiple Pages button in the Zoom group, scroll down to examine all four pages of the document, press [Ctrl][Home], then save the document**

    The text in section 2—all the text below the continuous section break—is formatted in two columns. Text in columns flows automatically from the bottom of one column to the top of the next column.

TABLE 4-1: Types of section breaks

section	function
Next page	Begins a new section and moves the text following the break to the top of the next page
Continuous	Begins a new section on the same page
Even page	Begins a new section and moves the text following the break to the top of the next even-numbered page
Odd page	Begins a new section and moves the text following the break to the top of the next odd-numbered page

FIGURE 4-3: Columns dialog box

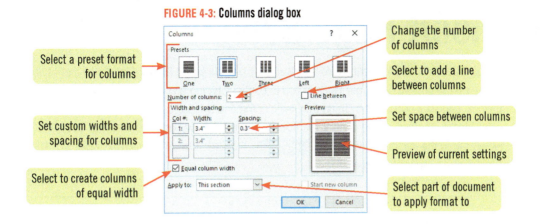

Select a preset format for columns

Change the number of columns

Select to add a line between columns

Set custom widths and spacing for columns

Set space between columns

Preview of current settings

Select to create columns of equal width

Select part of document to apply format to

FIGURE 4-4: Continuous section break and columns

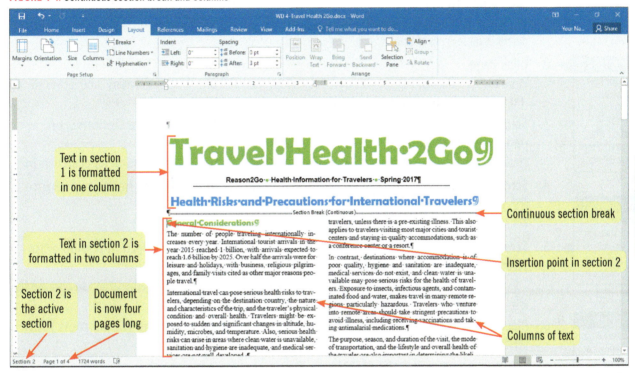

Text in section 1 is formatted in one column

Text in section 2 is formatted in two columns

Section 2 is the active section

Document is now four pages long

Continuous section break

Insertion point in section 2

Columns of text

Word 2016

Changing page layout settings for a section

Dividing a document into sections allows you to vary the layout of a document. In addition to applying different column settings to sections, you can apply different margins, page orientation, paper size, vertical alignment, header and footer, page numbering, footnotes, endnotes, and other page layout settings. For example, if you are formatting a report that includes a table with many columns, you might want to change the table's page orientation to landscape so that it is easier to read. To do this, you would insert a section break before and after the table to create a section that contains only the table, and then you would change the page orientation of the section that contains the table to landscape. If the table does not fill the page, you could also change the vertical alignment of the table so that it is centered vertically on the page. To do this, use the Vertical alignment list arrow on the Layout tab of the Page Setup dialog box.

To check or change the page layout settings for an individual section, place the insertion point in the section, then open the Page Setup dialog box. Select any options you want to change, click the Apply to list arrow, click This section, then click OK. When you select This section in the Apply to list box, the settings are applied to the current section only. When you select This point forward, the settings are applied to the current section and all sections that follow it. If you select Whole document in the Apply to list box, the settings are applied to all the sections in the document. Use the Apply to list arrow in the Columns dialog box or the Footnote and Endnote dialog box to change those settings for a section.

Insert Page Breaks

Learning Outcomes
- Insert and delete page breaks
- Insert a column break
- Balance columns

As you type text in a document, Word inserts an **automatic page break** (also called a soft page break) when you reach the bottom of a page, allowing you to continue typing on the next page. You can also force text onto the next page of a document by using the Breaks command to insert a **manual page break** (also called a hard page break). Another way to control the flow of text is to apply pagination settings using the Line and Page Breaks tab in the Paragraph dialog box. **CASE** ▶ *You insert manual page breaks where you know you want to begin each new page of the report.*

STEPS

1. **Click the 100% button, scroll to the bottom of page 1, place the insertion point before the heading Malaria: A Serious..., click the Layout tab, then click the Breaks button in the Page Setup group**

   The Breaks menu opens. You also use this menu to insert page, column, and text-wrapping breaks. TABLE 4-2 describes these types of breaks.

   QUICK TIP
   To control the flow of text between columns, insert a column break to force the text after the break to the top of the next column.

2. **Click Page**

   Word inserts a manual page break before "Malaria: A Serious Health Risk for Travelers" and moves all the text following the page break to the beginning of the next page, as shown in FIGURE 4-5.

3. **Scroll down, place the insertion point before the heading Preventive Options... on page 2, press and hold [Ctrl], then press [Enter]**

   Pressing [Ctrl][Enter] is a fast way to insert a manual page break. The heading is forced to the top of the third page.

   QUICK TIP
   You can also double-click a page break to select it, and then press [Delete] to delete it.

4. **Scroll to the bottom of page 3, place the insertion point before the heading Insurance for Travelers on page 3, then press [Ctrl][Enter]**

   The heading is forced to the top of the fourth page.

5. **Scroll up, click to the left of the page break on page 2 with the selection pointer ⍀ to select the page break, then press [Delete]**

   The manual page break is deleted and the text from pages 2 and 3 flows together. You can also use the selection pointer to click to the left of a section or a column break to select it.

   QUICK TIP
   You can balance columns of unequal length on a page by inserting a continuous section break at the end of the last column on the page.

6. **Place the insertion point before the heading Medical Kit... on page 2, then press [Ctrl] [Enter]**

   The heading is forced to the top of the third page.

7. **Click the View tab, click the Multiple Pages button in the Zoom group, scroll to view all four pages of the document, then save your changes**

   Pages 1, 2, and 3 are shown in FIGURE 4-6. Your screen might show a different number of pages.

Controlling automatic pagination

Another way to control the flow of text between pages (or between columns) is to apply pagination settings to specify where Word positions automatic page breaks. To apply automatic pagination settings, simply select the paragraphs(s) or line(s) you want to control, click the launcher in the Paragraph group on the Home or Layout tab, click the Line and Page Breaks tab in the Paragraph dialog box, and then select one or more of the following settings in the Pagination section before clicking OK.

- Keep with next: Apply to any paragraph you want to appear together with the next paragraph in order to prevent the page or column from breaking between the paragraphs.

- Keep lines together: Apply to selected paragraph or lines to prevent a page or column from breaking in the middle of a paragraph or between certain lines.

- Page break before: Apply to add an automatic page break before a specific paragraph.

- Widow/Orphan control: Turned on by default; ensures at least two lines of a paragraph appear at the top and bottom of every page or column by preventing a page or column from beginning with only the last line of a paragraph (a **widow**), or ending with only the first line of a new paragraph (an **orphan**).

FIGURE 4-5: Manual page break in document

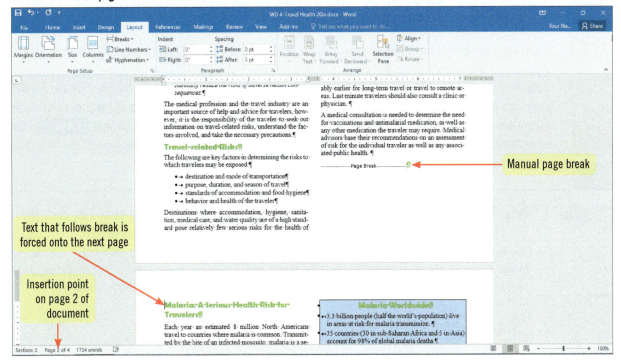

Text that follows break is forced onto the next page

Insertion point on page 2 of document

Manual page break

FIGURE 4-6: Pages 1, 2, and 3

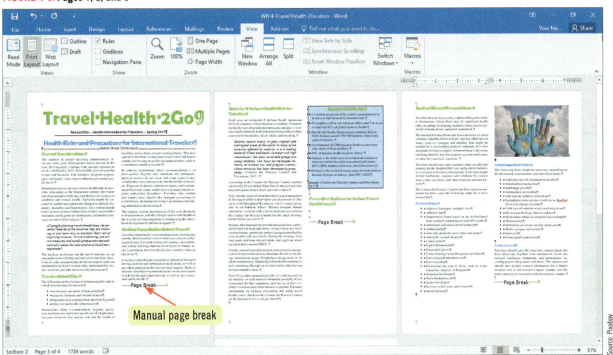

Manual page break

Manual page break

Source: Pixabay

TABLE 4-2: Types of breaks

break	function
Page	Forces the text following the break to begin at the top of the next page
Column	Forces the text following the break to begin at the top of the next column
Text Wrapping	Forces the text following the break to begin at the beginning of the next line

Insert Page Numbers

Learning Outcomes
- Insert a page number field
- Modify page numbers
- Close the footer area

If you want to number the pages of a multiple-page document, you can insert a page number field to add a page number to each page. A **field** is a code that serves as a placeholder for data that changes in a document, such as a page number or the current date. When you use the Page Number button on the Insert tab to add page numbers to a document, you insert the page number field at the top, bottom, or side of any page, and Word automatically numbers all the pages in the document for you. **CASE** ▶ *You insert a page number field so that page numbers will appear centered between the margins at the bottom of each page in the document.*

STEPS

1. **Press [Ctrl][Home], click the 100% button in the Zoom group on the View tab, click the Insert tab, then click the Page Number button in the Header & Footer group**

   The Page Number menu opens. You use this menu to select the position for the page numbers. If you choose to add a page number field to the top, bottom, or side of a document, a page number will appear on every page in the document. If you choose to insert it in the document at the location of the insertion point, the field will appear on that page only.

2. **Point to Bottom of Page**

   A gallery of formatting and alignment options for page numbers to be inserted at the bottom of a page opens, as shown in **FIGURE 4-7**.

3. **Scroll down the gallery to view the options, scroll to the top of the gallery, then click Plain Number 2 in the Simple section**

   A page number field containing the number 1 is centered in the Footer area at the bottom of page 1 of the document, as shown in **FIGURE 4-8**. The document text is gray, or dimmed, because the Footer area is open. Text that is inserted in a Footer area appears at the bottom of every page in a document.

4. **Double-click the document text**

   Double-clicking the document text closes the Footer area. The page number is now dimmed because it is located in the Footer area, which is no longer the active area. When the document is printed, the page numbers appear as normal text. You will learn more about working with the Footer area in the next lesson.

5. **Scroll down the document to see the page number at the bottom of each page**

   Word numbered each page of the report automatically, and each page number is centered at the bottom of the page. If you want to change the numbering format or start page numbering with a different number, you can simply click the Page Number button, click Format Page Numbers, and then choose from the options in the Page Number Format dialog box.

6. **Press [Ctrl][Home], click the View tab, click the Page Width button in the Zoom group, then save the document**

Moving around in a long document

Rather than scrolling to move to a different place in a long document, you can use the Navigation pane to move the insertion point to the top of a specific page. To open the Navigation pane, click the Find button in the Editing group on the Home tab, and then click Pages to display a thumbnail of each page in the document in the Navigation pane. Use the scroll box in the Navigation pane to scroll through the thumbnails. Click a thumbnail in the Navigation pane to move the insertion point to the top of that page in the document window.

FIGURE 4-7: Page Number gallery

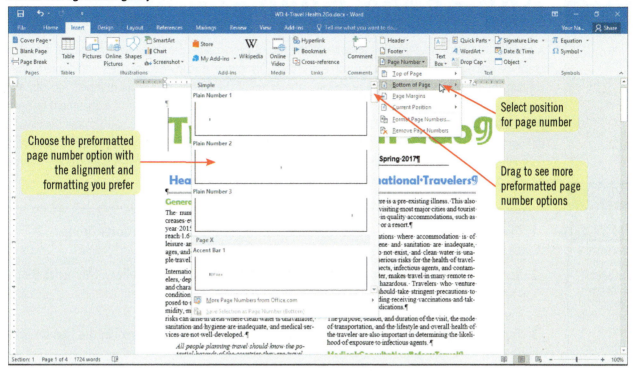

Choose the preformatted page number option with the alignment and formatting you prefer

Select position for page number

Drag to see more preformatted page number options

FIGURE 4-8: Page number in document

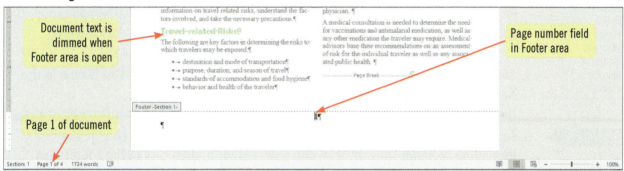

Document text is dimmed when Footer area is open

Page number field in Footer area

Page 1 of document

Inserting Quick Parts

The Word Quick Parts feature makes it easy to insert reusable pieces of content into a document quickly. The **Quick Parts** items you can insert include fields, such as for the current date or the total number of pages in a document; document property information, such as the author and title of a document; and building blocks, which are customized content that you create, format, and save for future use.

To insert a Quick Part into a document at the location of the insertion point, click the Quick Parts button in the Text group on the Insert tab (or, if headers and footers are open, click the Quick Parts button in the Insert group on the Header & Footer Tools Design tab), and then select the type of Quick Part you want to insert. To insert a field into a document, click Field on the Quick Parts menu that opens, click the name of the field you want to insert in the Field dialog box, and then click OK. Field information is updated automatically each time the document is opened or saved.

To insert a document property, point to Document Property on the Quick Parts menu, and then click the property you want to insert. The property is added to the document as a content control and contains the document property information shown in the Properties dialog box. If you did not assign a document property, the content control contains a placeholder, which you can replace with your own text. Once you replace the placeholder text—or edit the document property information that appears in the content control—this text replaces the property information in the Properties dialog box.

To insert a building block, click Building Blocks Organizer on the Quick Parts menu, select the building block you want, and then click Insert. You will learn more about working with building blocks in later lessons.

Add Headers and Footers

Learning Outcomes
- Create and format headers and footers
- Create a different first page header or footer

A **header** is text or graphics that appears at the top of every page of a document. A **footer** is text or graphics that appears at the bottom of every page. In longer documents, headers and footers often contain the title of the publication or chapter, the name of the author, or a page number. You can add headers and footers to a document by double-clicking the top or bottom margin of a document to open the Header and Footer areas, and then inserting text and graphics into them. You can also use the Header or Footer command on the Insert tab to insert predesigned headers and footers that you can modify with your information. When the header and footer areas are open, the document text is dimmed and cannot be edited. **CASE** *You create a header that includes the name of the report.*

STEPS

QUICK TIP

Unless you set different headers and footers for different sections, the information you insert in any Header or Footer area appears on every page in the document.

1. **Click the Insert tab, then click the Header button in the Header & Footer group**

   A gallery of built-in header designs opens.

2. **Scroll down the gallery to view the header designs, scroll up the gallery, then click Blank**

   The Header & Footer Tools Design tab opens and is the active tab, as shown in **FIGURE 4-9**. This tab is available whenever the Header and Footer areas are open.

3. **Type Reason2Go Health Information for Travelers in the content control in the Header area**

   This text will appear at the top of every page in the document.

QUICK TIP

You can also use the Insert Alignment Tab button in the Position group to left-, center-, and right-align text in the Header and Footer areas.

4. **Select the header text (but not the paragraph mark below it), click the Home tab, click the Font list arrow in the Font group, click Berlin Sans FB Demi, click the Font Color list arrow** ⌶ **, click Blue, Accent 5, click the Center button in the Paragraph group, click the Bottom Border button** ⊞ **, then click in the Header area to deselect the text**

   The text is formatted in blue Berlin Sans FB Demi and centered in the Header area with a bottom border.

5. **Click the Header & Footer Tools Design tab, then click the Go to Footer button in the Navigation group**

   The insertion point moves to the Footer area, where a page number field is centered in the Footer area.

QUICK TIP

To change the distance between the header and footer and the edge of the page, change the Header from Top and Footer from Bottom settings in the Position group.

6. **Select the page number field in the footer, use the Mini toolbar to change the formatting to Berlin Sans FB Demi and Blue, Accent 5, then click in the Footer area to deselect the text and field**

   The footer text is formatted in blue Berlin Sans FB Demi.

7. **Click the Close Header and Footer button in the Close group, then scroll down until the bottom of page 1 and the top of page 2 appear in the document window**

   The Header and Footer areas close, and the header and footer text is dimmed, as shown in **FIGURE 4-10**.

8. **Press [Ctrl][Home]**

   The report already includes the company information at the top of the first page, making the header information redundant. You can modify headers and footers so that the header and footer text does not appear on the first page of a document.

9. **Position the pointer over the header text at the top of page 1, then double-click**

   The Header and Footer areas open. The Options group on the Header & Footer Tools Design tab includes options for creating a different header and footer for the first page of a document, and for creating different headers and footers for odd- and even-numbered pages.

QUICK TIP

To remove headers or footers from a document, click the Header or Footer button, and then click Remove Header or Remove Footer.

10. **Click the Different First Page check box to select it, click the Close Header and Footer button, scroll to see the header and footer on pages 2, 3, and 4, then save the document**

    The header and footer text is removed from the Header and Footer areas on the first page.

FIGURE 4-9: Header area

- Header area is open
- [Type here]¶
- Header -Section 1-
- Content control
- Header & Footer Tools Design tab active
- Tab stops for the header are set for the default document margins
- Document text is dimmed

FIGURE 4-10: Header and footer in document

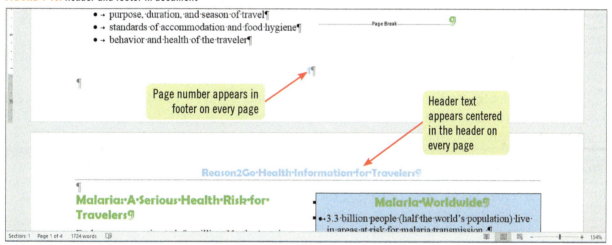

- Page number appears in footer on every page
- Header text appears centered in the header on every page

Adding a custom header or footer to the gallery

When you design a header that you want to use again in other documents, you can add it to the Header gallery by saving it as a building block. **Building blocks** are reusable pieces of formatted content or document parts, including headers and footers, page numbers, and text boxes, that are stored in galleries. Building blocks include predesigned content that comes with Word, as well as content that you create and save for future use. For example, you might create a custom header that contains your company name and logo and is formatted using the fonts, border, and colors you use in all company documents.

To add a custom header to the Header gallery, select all the text in the header, including the last paragraph mark, click the Header button, and then click Save Selection to Header Gallery.

In the Create New Building Block dialog box that opens, type a unique name for the header in the Name text box, click the Gallery list arrow and select the appropriate gallery, verify that the Category is General, and then type a brief description of the new header design in the Description text box. This description appears in a ScreenTip when you point to the custom header in the gallery. When you are finished, click OK. The new header appears in the Header gallery under the General category.

To remove a custom header from the Header gallery, right-click it, click Organize and Delete, make sure the appropriate building block is selected in the Building Blocks Organizer that opens, click Delete, click Yes, and then click Close. You can follow the same process to add or remove a custom footer to the Footer gallery.

Insert a Table

Learning Outcomes
- Create a table
- Delete a table
- Apply a table style

Adding a table to a document is a useful way to illustrate information that is intended for quick reference and analysis. A **table** is a grid of columns and rows that you can fill with text and graphics. A **cell** is the box formed by the intersection of a column and a row. The lines that divide the columns and rows of a table and help you see the grid-like structure of the table are called **borders**. A simple way to insert a table into a document is to use the Insert Table command on the Insert tab. **CASE** *You add a table to page 2 showing the preventive options for serious travel health diseases.*

STEPS

TROUBLE

If the final line in the blue shaded box on your screen wraps differently than that shown in the figure, click the References tab, click the Style list arrow in the Citations & Bibliography group, then click MLA Seventh Edition.

1. **Scroll until the heading Preventive Options... is at the top of your document window**

2. **Select the heading Preventive Options... and the two paragraph marks below it, click the Layout tab, click the Columns button in the Page Setup group, click One, click the heading to deselect the text, then scroll down to see the bottom half of page 2**

   A continuous section break is inserted before the heading and after the second paragraph mark, creating a new section, section 3, as shown in FIGURE 4-11. The document now includes four sections, with the heading Preventive Options... in Section 3. Section 3 is formatted as a single column.

3. **Place the insertion point before the first paragraph mark below the heading, click the Insert tab, click the Table button in the Tables group, then click Insert Table**

   The Insert Table dialog box opens. You use this dialog box to create a blank table.

QUICK TIP

To delete a table, click in the table, click the Table Tools Layout tab, click the Delete button in the Rows & Columns group, then click Delete Table.

4. **Type 5 in the Number of columns text box, press [Tab], type 6 in the Number of rows text box, make sure the Fixed column width option button is selected, then click OK**

   A blank table with five columns and six rows is inserted in the document. The insertion point is in the upper-left cell of the table, and the Table Tools Design tab becomes the active tab.

5. **Click the Home tab, click the Show/Hide ¶ button ¶ in the Paragraph group, type Disease in the first cell in the first row, press [Tab], type Vaccine, press [Tab], type Prophylaxis Drug, press [Tab], type Eat and Drink Safely, press [Tab], type Avoid Insects, then press [Tab]**

   Don't be concerned if the text wraps to the next line in a cell as you type. Pressing [Tab] moves the insertion point to the next cell in the row or to the first cell in the next row.

QUICK TIP

You can also click in a cell to move the insertion point to it.

6. **Type Malaria, press [Tab][Tab], click the Bullets list arrow ☰▾ in the Paragraph group, click the check mark style, press [Tab][Tab], then click the Bullets button ☰**

   The active bullet style, a check mark, is added to a cell when you click the Bullets button.

TROUBLE

If you pressed [Tab] after the last row, click the Undo button ↩ on the Quick Access toolbar to remove the blank row.

7. **Type the text shown in FIGURE 4-12 in the table cells**

8. **Click the Table Tools Layout tab, click the AutoFit button in the Cell Size group, click AutoFit Contents, click the AutoFit button again, then click AutoFit Window**

   The width of the table columns is adjusted to fit the text and then the window.

QUICK TIP

You can also format table text using the buttons on the Mini toolbar or the Home tab.

9. **Click the Select button in the Table group, click Select Table, click the Align Center button ▤ in the Alignment group, click Disease in the table, click the Select button, click Select Column, click the Align Center Left button ▤, then click in the table to deselect the column**

   The text in the table is centered in each cell, and then the text in the first column is left-aligned.

10. **Click the Table Tools Design tab, click the More button ▼ in the Table Styles group, scroll down, click the List Table 3 – Accent 5 style, then save your changes**

    The List Table 3 - Accent 5 table style is applied to the table, as shown in FIGURE 4-13. A **table style** includes format settings for the text, borders, and shading in a table.

FIGURE 4-11: New section

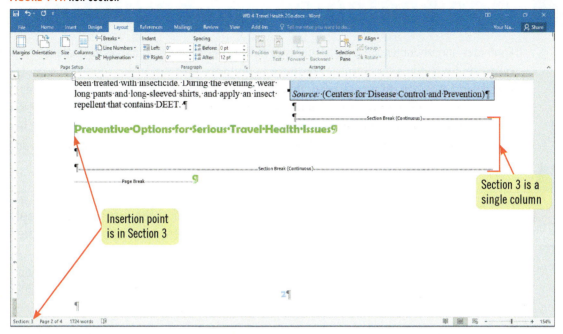

FIGURE 4-12: Text in table

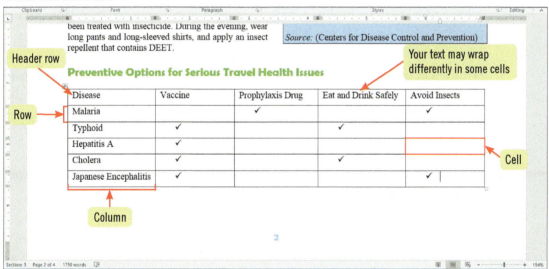

FIGURE 4-13: Completed table

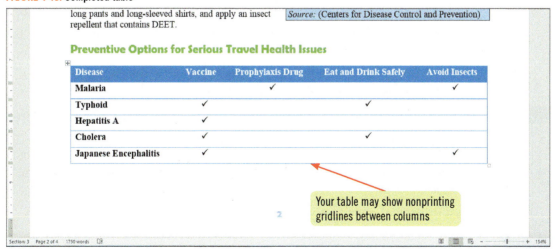

Add Footnotes and Endnotes

Learning Outcomes
- Insert and delete a footnote
- Modify note reference marks
- Convert footnotes to endnotes

Footnotes and endnotes are used in documents to provide further information, explanatory text, or references for text in a document. A **footnote** or **endnote** is an explanatory note that consists of two linked parts: the **note reference mark** that appears next to text to indicate that additional information is offered in a footnote or endnote, and the corresponding footnote or endnote text. Word places footnotes at the end of each page and endnotes at the end of the document. You insert and manage footnotes and endnotes using the tools in the Footnotes group on the References tab. **CASE** *You add several footnotes to the report.*

STEPS

1. **Press [Ctrl][Home], place the insertion point at the end of the first body paragraph in the second column of text (after "resort."), click the References tab, then click the Insert Footnote button in the Footnotes group**

   A note reference mark, in this case a superscript 1, appears after "resort.", and the insertion point moves below a separator line at the bottom of the page. A note reference mark can be a number, a symbol, a character, or a combination of characters.

2. **Type Behavior is a critical factor. For example, going outdoors in a malaria-endemic area could result in becoming infected., place the insertion point at the end of the second column of text (after "health."), click the Insert Footnote button, then type It is best to consult a travel medicine specialist.**

   The footnote text appears below the separator line at the bottom of page 1, as shown in **FIGURE 4-14**.

3. **Scroll down until the bottom half of page 3 appears in the document window, place the insertion point at the end of "Medications taken on a regular basis at home" in the second column, click the Insert Footnote button, then type All medications should be stored in carry-on luggage, in their original containers and labeled clearly.**

   The footnote text for the third footnote appears at the bottom of the first column on page 3.

4. **Place the insertion point at the end of "Sunscreen" in the bulleted list in the second column, click the Insert Footnote button, then type SPF 15 or greater.**

   The footnote text for the fourth footnote appears at the bottom of page 3.

5. **Place the insertion point after "Disposable gloves" in the first column, click the Insert Footnote button, type At least two pairs., place the insertion point after "Scissors, safety pins, and tweezers" in the first column, click the Insert Footnote button, then type Pack these items in checked luggage.**

   Notice that when you inserted new footnotes between existing footnotes, Word automatically renumbered the footnotes and wrapped the footnote text to the next column. The new footnotes appear at the bottom of the first column on page 3, as shown in **FIGURE 4-15**.

6. **Press [Ctrl][Home], then click the Next Footnote button in the Footnotes group**

   The insertion point moves to the first reference mark in the document.

7. **Click the Next Footnote button twice, press [Delete] to select the number 3 reference mark, then press [Delete] again**

   The third reference mark and associated footnote are deleted from the document and the footnotes are renumbered automatically. You must select a reference mark to delete a footnote; you can not simply delete the footnote text itself.

8. **Press [Ctrl][Home], then save your changes**

FIGURE 4-14: Footnotes in the document

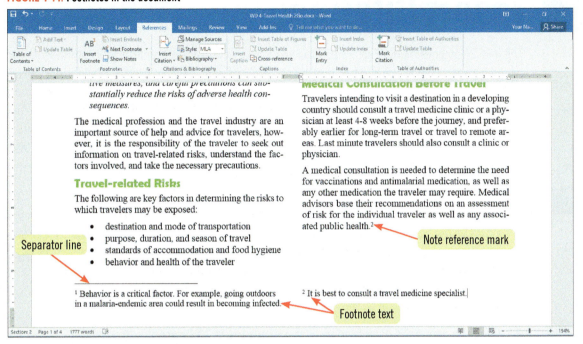

FIGURE 4-15: Renumbered footnotes in the document

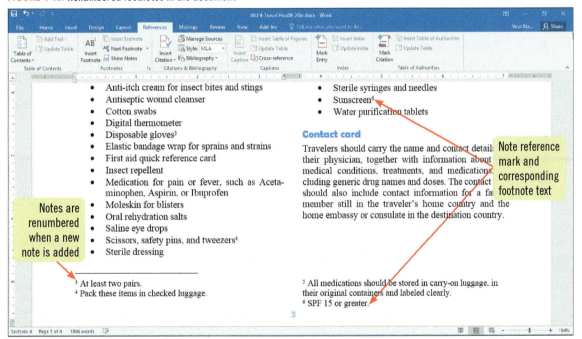

Customizing the layout and formatting of footnotes and endnotes

You can change the location, formatting, and numbering options for footnotes and endnotes in a document using the Footnote and Endnote dialog box. To open the dialog box, click the launcher in the Footnotes group on the References tab. Use the list arrows in the Location section of the dialog box to locate footnotes at the bottom of the page (the default) or directly below the text on a page, and to locate endnotes at the end of a document or at the end of a section. Use the Columns list arrow in the Footnote layout section to format footnote text in one or more columns, or to match section layout (the default). Use the options in the Format section of the dialog box to change the number format of the note reference marks, to use a symbol instead of a character, and to change the numbering of footnotes and endnotes. You can choose to apply the settings to a section or to the document as a whole. When you are finished, click Apply.

Insert Citations

Learning Outcomes
• Add a source to a document
• Insert a citation
• Edit a citation

The Word References feature allows you to keep track of the reference sources you consult when writing research papers, reports, and other documents, and makes it easy to insert a citation in a document. A **citation** is a parenthetical reference in the document text that gives credit to the source for a quotation or other information used in a document. Citations usually include the name of the author and, for print sources, a page number. When you insert a citation you can use an existing source or create a new source. Each time you create a new source, the source information is saved on your computer so that it is available for use in any document. **CASE** *The report already includes two citations. You add several more citations to the report.*

STEPS

1. **Scroll down, place the insertion point after "people travel" but before the period at the end of the first paragraph in the first column of text, click the Style list arrow in the Citations & Bibliography group, then click MLA Seventh Edition**

   You will format the sources and citations in the report using the style recommended by the Modern Language Association (MLA).

QUICK TIP
When you create a new source for a document, it appears automatically in the bibliography when you generate it.

2. **Click the Insert Citation button in the Citations & Bibliography group**

   A list of the sources already used in the document opens. You can choose to cite one of these sources, create a new source, or add a placeholder for a source. When you add a new citation to a document, the source is added to the list of master sources that is stored on the computer. The new source is also associated with the document.

QUICK TIP
Only sources that you associate with a document stay with the document when you move it to another computer. The master list of sources remains on the computer where it was created.

3. **Click Add New Source, click the Type of Source list arrow in the Create Source dialog box, scroll down to view the available source types, click Report, then click the Corporate Author check box**

   You select the type of source and enter the source information in the Create Source dialog box. The fields available in the dialog box change, depending on the type of source selected.

4. **Enter the data shown in FIGURE 4-16 in the Create Source dialog box, then click OK**

   The citation (World Tourism Organization) appears at the end of the paragraph. Because the source is a print publication, it needs to include a page number.

5. **Click the citation to select it, click the Citation Options list arrow on the right side of the citation, then click Edit Citation**

   The Edit Citation dialog box opens, as shown in FIGURE 4-17.

QUICK TIP
You can also choose to add or remove the author, year, or title from a citation.

6. **Type 19 in the Pages text box, then click OK**

   The page number 19 is added to the citation.

7. **Scroll down, place the insertion point at the end of the quotation (after ...consequences.), click the Insert Citation button, click Add New Source, enter the information shown in FIGURE 4-18, then click OK**

   A citation for the Web publication that the quotation was taken from is added to the report. No page number is used in this citation because the source is a Web site.

8. **Scroll to the bottom of page 2, click under the table, type Source:, italicize Source:, click after Source:, click the Insert Citation button, then click Johnson, Margaret in the list of sources**

   The citation (Johnson) appears under the table.

9. **Click the citation, click the Citation Options list arrow, click Edit Citation, type 55 in the Pages text box, click OK, then save your changes**

   The page number 55 is added to the citation.

FIGURE 4-16: Adding a Report source

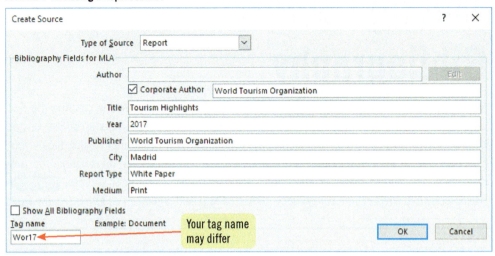

FIGURE 4-17: Edit Citation dialog box

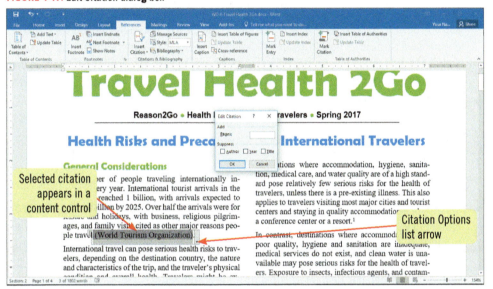

FIGURE 4-18: Adding a Web publication source

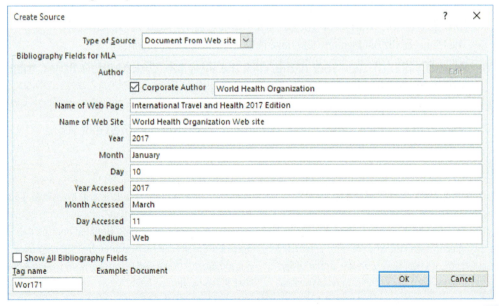

Manage Sources and Create a Bibliography

Learning Outcomes
- Add and delete sources
- Edit a source
- Insert a bibliography field

Many documents require a **bibliography**, a list of sources that you used in creating the document. The list of sources can include only the works cited in your document (a **works cited** list) or both the works cited and the works consulted (a bibliography). The Bibliography feature in Word allows you to generate a works cited list or a bibliography automatically based on the source information you provide for the document. The Source Manager dialog box helps you to organize your sources. **CASE** ▶ *You add a bibliography to the report. The bibliography is inserted as a field and it can be formatted any way you choose.*

STEPS

1. **Press [Ctrl][End] to move the insertion point to the end of the document, then click the Manage Sources button in the Citations & Bibliography group**

   The Source Manager dialog box opens, as shown in **FIGURE 4-19**. The Master List shows the two sources you added and any other sources available on your computer. The Current List shows the sources available in the current document. A check mark next to a source indicates the source is cited in the document. You use the tools in the Source Manager dialog box to add, edit, and delete sources from the lists, and to copy sources between the Master and Current Lists. The sources that appear in the Current List will appear in the bibliography.

2. **Click the Baker, Mary source in the Current List**

   A preview of the citation and bibliographical entry for the source in MLA style appears in the Preview box. You do not want this source to be included in your bibliography for the report.

3. **Click Delete**

   The source is removed from the Current List but remains on the Master List on the computer where it originated.

4. **Click Close, click the Bibliography button in the Citations & Bibliography group, click References, then scroll up to see the heading References at the top of the field**

   A Bibliography field labeled "References" is added at the location of the insertion point. The bibliography includes all the sources associated with the document, formatted in the MLA style for bibliographies. The text in the Bibliography field is formatted with the default styles.

5. **Select References; apply the following formats: Berlin Sans FB Demi and the Green, Accent 6 font color; drag down the list of sources to select the entire list and change the font size to 11; then click outside the bibliography field to deselect it**

   The format of the bibliography text now matches the rest of the report.

6. **Press [Ctrl][End], type your name, click the View tab, click Multiple Pages, then scroll up and down to view each page in the report**

   The completed report is shown in **FIGURE 4-20**.

7. **Save your changes, submit your document, close the file, then exit Word**

Working with Web sources

Publications found on the Web can be challenging to document. Many Web sites can be accessed under multiple domains, URLs change, and electronic publications are often updated frequently, making each visit to a Web site potentially unique. For these reasons, it's best to rely on the author, title, and publication information for a Web publication when citing it as a source in a research document. If possible, you can include a URL as supplementary information only, along with the date the Web site was last updated and the date you accessed the site. Since Web sites are often removed, it's also a good idea to download or print any Web source you use so that it can be verified later.

FIGURE 4-19: Source Manager dialog box

Your Master List will contain the two sources you added and either no additional sources or different additional sources

Preview of the citation and bibliography entry for the selected source in MLA style (as defined by Word)

List of sources associated with the document

Sources with a check mark have a citation in the document

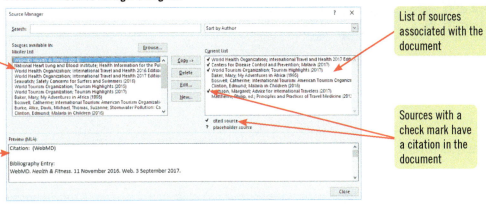

FIGURE 4-20: Completed report

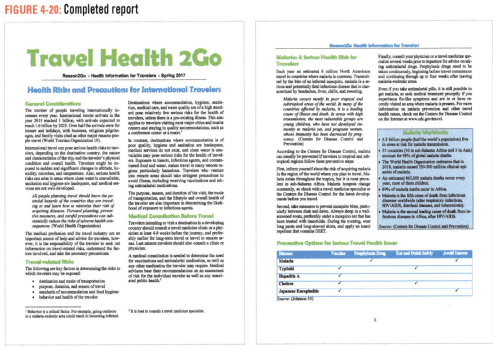

Source: Pixabay

Practice

Concepts Review

Label each element shown in FIGURE 4-21.

FIGURE 4-21

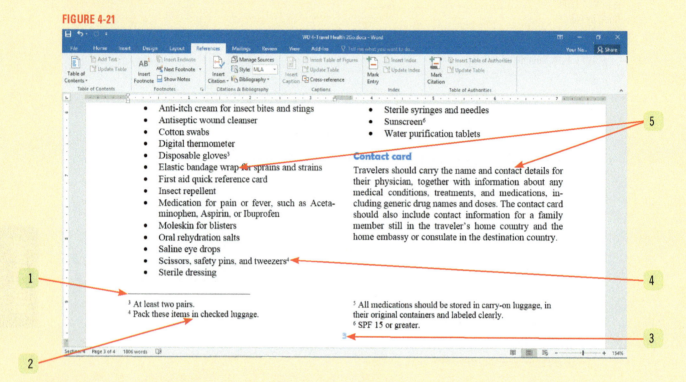

Match each term with the statement that best describes it.

6. **Bibliography**
7. **Header**
8. **Margin**
9. **Table**
10. **Citation**
11. **Manual page break**
12. **Field**
13. **Footer**
14. **Section break**

a. A grid of columns and rows that you can fill with text and graphics

b. A list of the sources used to create a document

c. Text or graphics that appear at the top of every page in a document

d. A formatting mark that forces the text following the mark to begin at the top of the next page

e. Text or graphics that appear at the bottom of every page in a document

f. A placeholder for information that changes

g. A formatting mark that divides a document into parts that can be formatted differently

h. The blank area between the edge of the text and the edge of the page

i. A parenthetical reference in the document text that gives credit to a source

Select the best answer from the list of choices.

15. **Which type of break can you insert if you want to force text to begin on the next page?**
    a. Column break
    b. Continuous section break
    c. Next page section break
    d. Text wrapping break

16. **Which type of break do you insert if you want to balance the columns in a section?**
    a. Text wrapping break
    b. Manual page break
    c. Column break
    d. Continuous section break

17. **Which of the following do documents with mirror margins always have?**
    a. Inside and outside margins
    b. Sections
    c. Portrait orientation
    d. Different first page headers and footers

18. **Which of the following cannot be inserted using the Quick Parts command?**
    a. AutoText building block
    b. Page number field
    c. Page break
    d. Document property

19. **Which appears at the end of a document?**
    a. Endnote
    b. Citation
    c. Page break
    d. Footnote

20. **What name describes formatted pieces of content that are stored in galleries?**
    a. Field
    b. Endnote
    c. Property
    d. Building Block

Skills Review

1. **Set document margins.**
   a. Start Word, open the file WD 4-2.docx from the location where you store your Data Files, then save it as **WD 4-Seaside Fitness**.
   b. Change the top and bottom margin settings to Moderate: 1" top and bottom, and .75" left and right.
   c. Save your changes to the document.

2. **Create sections and columns.**
   a. Turn on the display of formatting marks, then customize the status bar to display sections if they are not displayed already.
   b. Insert a continuous section break before the **Welcome to the Seaside Fitness Center** heading.
   c. Format the text in section 2 in two columns, then save your changes to the document.

3. **Insert page breaks.**
   a. Scroll to page 3, then insert a manual page break before the heading **Facilities and Services**. (*Hint*: The page break will appear at the bottom of page 2.)
   b. Scroll down and insert a manual page break before the heading **Membership**, then press [Ctrl][Home].
   c. On page 1, select the heading **Welcome to the Seaside Fitness Center** and the paragraph mark below it, use the Columns button to format the selected text as one column, then center the heading on the page.
   d. Follow the direction in step c to format the heading **Facilities and Services** and the paragraph mark below it on page 3, and the heading **Membership** and the paragraph mark below it on page 4, as one column, with centered text, then save your changes to the document.

4. **Insert page numbers.**
   a. Insert page numbers in the document at the bottom of the page. Select the Plain Number 2 page number style from the gallery.
   b. Close the Footer area, scroll through the document to view the page number on each page, then save your changes to the document.

Skills Review (continued)

5. **Add headers and footers.**

   a. Double-click the margin at the top of a page to open the Header and Footer areas.

   b. With the insertion point in the Header area, click the Quick Parts button in the Insert Group on the Header & Footer Tools Design tab, point to Document Property, then click Author.

   c. Replace the text in the Author content control with your name, press [End] to move the insertion point out of the content control, then press [Spacebar]. (*Note*: If your name does not appear in the header, right-click the Author content control, click Remove Content Control, then type your name in the header.)

   d. Click the Insert Alignment Tab button in the Position group, select the Right option button and keep the alignment relative to the margin, then click OK in the dialog box to close the dialog box and move the insertion point to the right margin.

   e. Use the Insert Date and Time command in the Insert group to insert the current date using a format of your choice as static text. (*Hint*: Be sure the Update automatically check box is not checked.)

   f. Apply italic to the text in the header.

   g. Move the insertion point to the Footer area.

   h. Double-click the page number to select it, then format the page number in bold and italic.

   i. Move the insertion point to the header on page 1, use the Header & Footer Tools Design tab to create a different header and footer for the first page of the document, type your name in the First Page Header area, then apply italic to your name.

   j. Close headers and footers, scroll to view the header and footer on each page, then save your changes to the document.

6. **Insert a table.**

   a. On page 4, double-click the word **Table** at the end of the Membership Rates section to select it, press [Delete], open the Insert Table dialog box, then create a table with two columns and five rows.

   b. Apply the List Table 2 table style to the table.

   c. Press [Tab] to leave the first cell in the header row blank, then type **Rate**.

   d. Press [Tab], then type the following text in the table, pressing [Tab] to move from cell to cell.

Enrollment/Individual	**$100**
Enrollment/Couple	**$150**
Monthly membership/Individual	**$125**
Monthly membership/Couple	**$200**

   e. Select the table, use the AutoFit command on the Table Tools Layout tab to select the AutoFit to Contents option, and then select the AutoFit to Window option. (*Note*: In this case, AutoFit to Window fits the table to the width of the column of text.)

   f. Save your changes to the document.

7. **Add footnotes and endnotes.**

   a. Press [Ctrl[Home], scroll down, place the insertion point at the end of the first body paragraph, insert a footnote, then type **People who are active live longer and feel better.**

   b. Place the insertion point at the end of the first paragraph under the Benefits of Exercise heading, insert a footnote, then type **There are 1,440 minutes in every day. Schedule 30 of them for physical activity.**

   c. Place the insertion point at the end of the first paragraph under the Tips for Staying Motivated heading, insert a footnote, type **Always consult your physician before beginning an exercise program.**, then save your changes.

8. **Insert citations.**

   a. Place the insertion point at the end of the second paragraph under the Benefits of Exercise heading (after "down from 52% in 2015" but before the period), then be sure the style for citations and bibliography is set to MLA Seventh Edition.

Skills Review (continued)

b. Insert a citation, add a new source, enter the source information shown in the Create Source dialog box in **FIGURE 4-22**, then click OK.

c. Place the insertion point at the end of the italicized quotation in the second column of text, insert a citation, then select Jason, Laura from the list of sources.

d. Edit the citation to include the page number **25**.

e. Scroll to page 2, place the insertion point at the end of the "Be a morning exerciser" paragraph but before the ending period, insert a citation for WebMD, then save your changes.

FIGURE 4-22

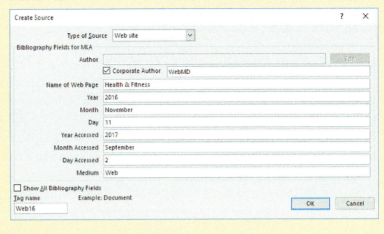

9. **Manage sources and create a bibliography.**

a. Press [Ctrl][End], then open the Source Manager dialog box.

b. Select the source Health, National Institute of: … in the Current List, click Edit, click the Corporate Author check box, edit the entry so it reads **National Institute of Health**, click OK, then click Close.

c. Insert a bibliography labeled References.

d. Select References, then change the font to 14-point Tahoma with a black font color. Pages 1 and 4 of the formatted document are shown in **FIGURE 4-23**.

e. Save your changes to the document, submit it to your instructor, then close the document and exit Word.

FIGURE 4-23

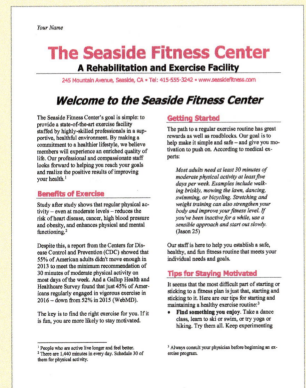

Independent Challenge 1

You are the owner of a small business called Lone Tree Catering. You have begun work on the text for a brochure advertising your business and you are now ready to lay out the pages and prepare the final copy. The brochure will be printed on both sides of an 8½" x 11" sheet of paper, and folded in thirds.

a. Start Word, open the file WD 4-3.docx from the location where you store your Data Files, then save it as **WD 4-Lone Tree Catering**. Read the document to get a feel for its contents.

b. Change the page orientation to landscape, and change all four margins to .6".

c. Format the document in three columns of equal width.

d. Insert a next page section break before the heading **Catering Services**.

e. On page 1, insert column breaks before the headings **Sample Tuscan Banquet Menu** and **Sample Indian Banquet Menu**.

f. Change the column spacing in section 1 (which is the first page) to .4", add lines between the columns on the first page, then select the text in the columns in section 1 and center it.

g. Double-click the bottom margin to open the footer area, create a different header and footer for the first page, then type **Call for custom menus designed to your taste and budget.** in the First Page Footer -Section 1- area.

h. Center the text in the footer area, format it in 20-point Papyrus, bold, with a Green, Accent 6 font color, then close headers and footers.

i. On page 2, insert a column break before Your Name, then press [Enter] 22 times to move the contact information to the bottom of the second column.

j. Replace Your Name with your name, then center the contact information in the column.

k. Press [Ctrl][End], insert a column break at the bottom of the second column. Type the text shown in **FIGURE 4-24** in the third column, then apply the No Spacing style to the text. Refer to the figure as you follow the instructions for formatting the text in the third column.

l. Format Lone Tree Catering in 28-point Papyrus, bold, with a Green, Accent 6 font color.

m. Format the remaining text in 12-point Papyrus with a Green, Accent 6 font color. Center the text in the third column.

n. Insert an online picture of a tree, similar to the tree shown in **FIGURE 4-24**. Do not be concerned if the image you select is not the same tree image as that shown in the figure. Do not wrap text around the graphic.

o. Resize the graphic and add or remove blank paragraphs in the third column of your brochure so that the spacing between elements roughly matches the spacing shown in **FIGURE 4-24**.

p. Save your changes, then submit a copy to your instructor. If possible, you can print the brochure with the two pages back to back so that the brochure can be folded in thirds.

q. Close the document and exit Word.

FIGURE 4-24

Lone Tree Catering

Complete catering services available for all types of events. Menus and estimates provided upon request.

Source: OpenClipart.org

Independent Challenge 2

You work in the Campus Safety Department at Valley State College. You have written the text for an informational flyer about parking regulations on campus, and now you need to format the flyer so it is attractive and readable.

a. Start Word, open the file WD 4-4.docx from the drive and folder where you store your Data Files, then save it as **WD 4-Valley Parking**. Read the document to get a feel for its contents.

b. Change all four margins to .7".

c. Insert a continuous section break before **1. May I bring a car to school?** (*Hint*: Place the insertion point before the word May.)

d. Scroll down and insert a next page section break before **Sample Parking Permit**.

e. Format the text in section 2 in three columns of equal width with .3" of space between the columns.

f. Hyphenate the document using the automatic hyphenation feature. (*Hint*: Use the Hyphenation button in the Page Setup group on the Layout tab.)

g. Add a 3-point dotted-line bottom border to the blank paragraph under Valley State College Department of Campus Safety. (*Hint*: Place the insertion point before the paragraph mark under Valley State College...)

h. Open the Header area, and type your name in the header. Right-align your name, and format it in 10-point Arial.

i. Add the following text to the footer, inserting symbols between words as indicated: **Parking and Shuttle Service Office • 54 Buckley Street • Valley State College • 942-555-2227**. (*Hint*: Click the Symbol command in the Symbols group on the Insert tab to insert a symbol. To find a small circle symbol, be sure the font is set to (normal text) and the subset is set to General Punctuation.)

j. Format the footer text in 9-point Arial Black, and center it in the footer.

k. Apply a 3-point dotted-line border above the footer text. Make sure to apply the border to the paragraph.

l. Add a continuous section break at the end of section 2 to balance the columns in section 2.

m. Place the insertion point on page 2 (which is section 4). Change the left and right margins in section 4 to 1". Also change the page orientation of section 4 to landscape.

n. Change the vertical alignment of section 4 to center. (*Hint*: Use the Vertical Alignment list arrow on the Layout tab in the Page Setup dialog box.)

o. Apply an appropriate table style to the table, such as the style shown in **FIGURE 4-25**. (*Hint*: Check and uncheck the options in the Table Style Options group on the Table Tools Design tab to customize the style so it enhances the table data.)

p. Save your changes, submit your work, close the document, then exit Word.

FIGURE 4-25

Sample Parking Permit

Valley State College
Office of Parking and Shuttle Service

2017-18 Student Parking Permit

License number:	VT 623 487
Make:	Subaru
Model:	Forester
Year:	2013
Color:	Silver
Permit Issue Date:	September 6, 2017
Permit Expiration Date:	June 4, 2018

Restrictions:
Parking is permitted in the Valley State College Greene Street lot 24 hours a day, 7 days a week. Shuttle service is available from the Greene Street lot to campus from 7 a.m. to 7 p.m. Monday through Friday. Parking is also permitted in any on-campus lot from 4:30 p.m. Friday to midnight Sunday.

Independent Challenge 3

A book publisher would like to publish an article you wrote on stormwater pollution in Australia as a chapter in a forthcoming book called *Environmental Issues for the New Millennium*. The publisher has requested that you format your article like a book chapter before submitting it for publication, and has provided you with a style sheet. According to the style sheet, the citations and bibliography should be formatted in Chicago style. You have already created the sources for the chapter, but you need to insert the citations.

a. Start Word, open the file WD 4-5.docx from the location where you store your Data Files, then save it as **WD 4-Chapter 8**. You will format the first page as shown in **FIGURE 4-26**.

b. Change the font of the entire document to 10-point Book Antigua. If this font is not available to you, select a different font suitable for the pages of a book. Change the alignment to justified.

c. Use the Page Setup dialog box to change the paper size to a custom setting of 6" x 9".

d. Create mirror margins. (*Hint*: Use the Multiple pages list arrow.) Change the top and bottom margins to .8", change the inside margin to .4", change the outside margin to .6", and create a .3" gutter to allow room for the book's binding.

e. Change the Zoom level to Page Width, open the Header and Footer areas, then apply the setting to create different headers and footers for odd- and even-numbered pages.

f. In the odd-page header, type **Chapter 8**, insert a symbol of your choice, type **The Silver Creek Catchment and Stormwater Pollution**, then format the header text in 9-point Book Antigua italic and right-align the text.

g. In the even-page header, type your name, then format the header text in 9-point Book Antigua italic. (*Note*: The even-page header should be left-aligned.)

h. Insert a left-aligned page number field in the even-page footer area, format it in 10-point Book Antigua, insert a right-aligned page number field in the odd-page footer area, then format it in 10-point Book Antigua.

i. Format the page numbers so that the first page of your chapter, which is Chapter 8 in the book, begins on page 167. (*Hint*: Select a page number field, click the Page Number button, then click Format Page Numbers.)

j. Go to the beginning of the document, press [Enter] 10 times, type **Chapter 8: The Silver Creek Catchment and Stormwater Pollution**, press [Enter] twice, type your name, then press [Enter] twice.

k. Format the chapter title in 16-point Book Antigua bold, format your name in 14-point Book Antigua, then left-align the title text and your name.

l. Click the References tab, make sure the citations and bibliography style is set to Chicago Sixteenth Edition, place the insertion point at the end of the first body paragraph on page 1 but before the ending period, insert a citation for Alice Burke, et. al., then add the page number **40** to the citation.

m. Add the citations listed in **TABLE 4-3** to the document using the sources already associated with the document.

FIGURE 4-26

TABLE 4-3

page	location for citation	source	page number
2	End of the first complete paragraph (after …WCSMP, but before the period)	City of Weston	3
3	End of the first complete paragraph (after …pollution, but before the colon)	Jensen	135
4	End of first paragraph (after …health effects, but before the period)	City of Weston	5
4	End of fourth bulleted list item (after 1 month.)	Seawatch	None
5	End of second paragraph (after …problem arises, but before the period)	Burke, et. al.	55
6	End of paragraph before Conclusion (after …stormwater system, but before the period)	City of Weston	7
6	End of first paragraph under Conclusion (after …include, but before the colon)	Jensen	142

Formatting Documents

Independent Challenge 3 (continued)

n. Press [Ctrl][End], insert a Works Cited list, format the Works Cited heading in 11-point Book Antigua, black font color, bold, then format the list of works cited in 10-point Book Antigua.

o. Scroll to page 4 in the document, place the insertion point at the end of the paragraph above the Potential health effects... heading, press [Enter] twice, type **Table 1: Total annual pollutant loads per year in the Silver Creek Catchment**, press [Enter] twice, then format the text you just typed as bold if it is not bold.

p. Insert a table with four columns and four rows.

q. Type the text shown in **FIGURE 4-27** in the table. Do not be concerned when the text wraps to the next line in a cell.

FIGURE 4-27

Area	Nitrogen	Phosphorus	Suspended solids
Silver Creek	9.3 tonnes	1.2 tonnes	756.4 tonnes
Durras Arm	6.2 tonnes	.9 tonnes	348.2 tonnes
Cabbage Tree Creek	9.8 tonnes	2.3 tonnes	485.7 tonnes

r. Apply the Grid Table 1 Light table style. Make sure the text in the header row is bold, then remove any bold formatting from the text in the remaining rows.

s. Use AutoFit to make the table fit the contents, then use AutoFit to make the table fit the window.

t. Save your changes, submit your work, then close the document and exit Word.

Independent Challenge 4: Explore

One of the most common opportunities to use the page layout features of Word is when formatting a research paper. The format recommended by the *MLA Handbook for Writers of Research Papers*, a style guide that includes information on preparing, writing, and formatting research papers, is the standard format used by many schools, colleges, and universities. In this independent challenge, you will research the MLA guidelines for formatting a research paper and use the guidelines you find to format the pages of a sample research report.

a. Use your favorite search engine to search the Web for information on the MLA guidelines for formatting a research report. Use the keywords **MLA Style** and **research paper format** to conduct your search.

b. Look for information on the proper formatting for the following aspects of a research paper: paper size, margins, title page or first page of the report, line spacing, paragraph indentation, and page numbers. Also find information on proper formatting for citations and a works cited page. Print the information you find.

c. Start Word, open the file WD 4-6.docx from the drive and folder where you store your Data Files, then save it as **WD 4-Research Paper**. Using the information you learned, format this document as a research report.

d. Adjust the margins, set the line spacing, and add page numbers to the document in the format recommended by the MLA. Use **The Maori History of New Zealand** as the title for your sample report, use your name as the author name, and use the name of the course you are enrolled in currently as well as the instructor's name for that course. Make sure to format the title page exactly as the MLA style dictates.

e. Format the remaining text as the body of the research report. Indent the first line of each paragraph rather than use quadruple spacing between paragraphs.

f. Create three sources, insert three citations in the document—a book, a journal article, and a Web site—and create a works cited page, following MLA style. If necessary, edit the format of the citations and works cited page to conform to MLA format. (*Note*: For this practice document, you are allowed to make up sources. Never make up sources for real research papers.)

g. Save the document, submit a copy to your instructor, close the document, then exit Word.

Visual Workshop

Open the file WD 4-7.docx from the location where you store your Data Files, then modify it to create the article shown in **FIGURE 4-28**. (*Hint*: Change all four margins to .6". Add the footnotes as shown in the figure.) Save the document with the filename **WD 4-Garden**, then print a copy.

FIGURE 4-28

GARDENER'S NOTEBOOK

Preparing a Perennial Garden for Winter

By Your Name

A sense of peace descends when a perennial garden is put to bed for the season. The plants are safely tucked in against the elements, and the garden is ready to welcome the winter. When the work is done, you can sit back and anticipate the bright blooms of spring. Many gardeners are uncertain about how to close a perennial garden. This week's column demystifies the process.

Clean up

Garden clean up can be a gradual process—plants will deteriorate at different rates, allowing you to do a little bit each week.

- Edge beds and borders and remove stakes, trellises, and other plant supports.
- Dig and divide irises, daylilies, and other early bloomers.
- Cut back plants when foliage starts to deteriorate, then rake all debris out of the garden and pull any weeds that remain.

Plant perennials

Fall is the perfect time to plant perennials.[1] The warm, sunny days and cool nights provide optimal conditions for new root growth, without the stress of summer heat.

- Dig deeply and enhance soil with organic matter.
- Use a good starter fertilizer to speed up new root growth and establish a healthy base.
- Untangle the roots of new plants before planting.

- Water after planting as the weather dictates, and keep plants moist for several days.

Add compost

Organic matter is the key ingredient to healthy garden soil. Composting adds nutrients to the soil, helps the soil retain water and nutrients, and keeps the soil well aerated. If you take care of the soil, your plants will become strong and disease resistant.[2]

Before adding compost, use an iron rake to loosen the top few inches of soil. Spread a one to two inch layer of compost over the entire garden—the best compost is made up of yard waste and kitchen scraps—and then refrain from stepping on the area and compacting the soil.

Winter mulch

Winter protection for perennial beds can only help plants survive the winter. Winter mulch prevents the freezing and thawing cycles, which cause plants to heave and eventually die. Here's what works and what doesn't:

- Always apply mulch after the ground is frozen.
- Never apply generic hay because it contains billions of weed seeds. Also, whole leaves and bark mulch hold too much moisture.[3]
- Use a loose material to allow air filtration. Straw and salt marsh hay are excellent choices for mulch.
- Remove the winter mulch in the spring as soon as new growth begins.

---

[1] Fall is also an excellent time to plant shrubs and trees.
[2] You can buy good compost, but it is easy and useful to make it at home. Composting kitchen scraps reduces household garbage by about one-third.

[3] If using leaves, use only stiff leaves, such as Oak or Beech. Soft leaves, such as Maple, make it difficult for air and water to filtrate.

Source: StockSnap

Getting Started with Excel 2016

CASE You have been hired as an assistant at Reason2Go (R2G), a company that allows travelers to make a difference in the global community through voluntourism, while having a memorable vacation experience. You report to Yolanda Lee, the vice president of finance. As Yolanda's assistant, you create worksheets to analyze data from various divisions of the company, so you can help her make sound decisions on company expansion, investments, and new voluntourism opportunities.

Module Objectives

After completing this module, you will be able to:

- Understand spreadsheet software
- Identify Excel 2016 window components
- Understand formulas
- Enter labels and values and use the AutoSum button
- Edit cell entries
- Enter and edit a simple formula
- Switch worksheet views
- Choose print options

Files You Will Need

EX 1-1.xlsx   EX 1-4.xlsx

EX 1-2.xlsx   EX 1-5.xlsx

EX 1-3.xlsx

Understand Spreadsheet Software

Learning Outcomes
- Describe the uses of Excel
- Define key spreadsheet terms

Microsoft Excel is the electronic spreadsheet program within the Microsoft Office suite. An **electronic spreadsheet** is an app you use to perform numeric calculations and to analyze and present numeric data. One advantage of a spreadsheet program over pencil and paper is that your calculations are updated automatically, so you can change entries without having to manually recalculate. **TABLE 1-1** shows some of the common business tasks people accomplish using Excel. In Excel, the electronic spreadsheet you work in is called a **worksheet**, and it is contained in a file called a **workbook**, which has the file extension .xlsx. **CASE** ▶ *At R2G, you use Excel extensively to track finances and manage corporate data.*

DETAILS

When you use Excel, you have the ability to:

- ### Enter data quickly and accurately

  With Excel, you can enter information faster and more accurately than with pencil and paper. **FIGURE 1-1** shows a payroll worksheet created using pencil and paper. **FIGURE 1-2** shows the same worksheet created using Excel. Equations were added to calculate the hours and pay. You can use Excel to recreate this information for each week by copying the worksheet's structure and the information that doesn't change from week to week, then entering unique data and formulas for each week.

- ### Recalculate data easily

  Fixing typing errors or updating data is easy in Excel. In the payroll example, if you receive updated hours for an employee, you just enter the new hours and Excel recalculates the pay.

- ### Perform what-if analysis

  The ability to change data and quickly view the recalculated results gives you the power to make informed business decisions. For instance, if you're considering raising the hourly rate for an entry-level tour guide from $12.50 to $15.00, you can enter the new value in the worksheet and immediately see the impact on the overall payroll as well as on the individual employee. Any time you use a worksheet to ask the question "What if?" you are performing **what-if analysis**. Excel also includes a Scenario Manager where you can name and save different what-if versions of your worksheet.

- ### Change the appearance of information

  Excel provides powerful features, such as the Quick Analysis tool, for making information visually appealing and easier to understand. Format text and numbers in different fonts, colors, and styles to make it stand out.

- ### Create charts

  Excel makes it easy to create charts based on worksheet information. Charts are updated automatically in Excel whenever data changes. The worksheet in **FIGURE 1-2** includes a 3-D pie chart.

- ### Share information

  It's easy for everyone at R2G to collaborate in Excel using the company intranet, the Internet, or a network storage device. For example, you can complete the weekly payroll that your boss, Yolanda Lee, started creating. You can also take advantage of collaboration tools such as shared workbooks so that multiple people can edit a workbook simultaneously.

- ### Build on previous work

  Instead of creating a new worksheet for every project, it's easy to modify an existing Excel worksheet. When you are ready to create next week's payroll, you can open the file for last week's payroll, save it with a new filename, and modify the information as necessary. You can also use predesigned, formatted files called **templates** to create new worksheets quickly. Excel comes with many templates that you can customize.

FIGURE 1-1: Traditional paper worksheet

Reason2Go
Project Leader Divison Payroll Calculator

Name	Hours	O/T Hrs	Hrly Rate	Reg Pay	O/T Pay	Gross Pay
Brucker, Pieter	40	4	16.75	670	134	804
Cucci, Lucia	35	0	12	420	0	420
Klimt, Gustave	40	2	13.25	530	53	583
Lafontaine, Jeanne	29	0	15.25	442.25	0	442.25
Martinez, Juan	37	0	13.2	488.4	0	488.4
Mioshi, Keiko	39	0	21	819	0	819
Shernwood, Burt	40	0	16.75	670	0	670
Strano, Riccardo	40	8	16.25	650	260	910
Wadsworth, Alice	40	5	13.25	530	132.5	662.5
Yamamoto, Johji	38	0	15.5	589	0	589

FIGURE 1-2: Excel worksheet

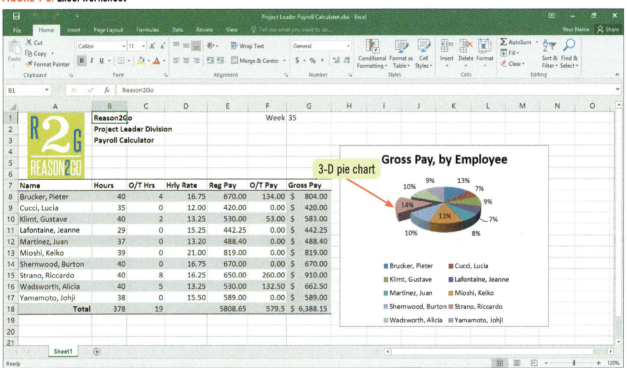

TABLE 1-1: Business tasks you can accomplish using Excel

you can use spreadsheets to	by
Perform calculations	Adding formulas and functions to worksheet data; for example, adding a list of sales results or calculating a car payment
Represent values graphically	Creating charts based on worksheet data; for example, creating a chart that displays expenses
Generate reports	Creating workbooks that combine information from multiple worksheets, such as summarized sales information from multiple stores
Organize data	Sorting data in ascending or descending order; for example, alphabetizing a list of products or customer names, or prioritizing orders by date
Analyze data	Creating data summaries and short lists using PivotTables or AutoFilters; for example, making a list of the top 10 customers based on spending habits
Create what-if data scenarios	Using variable values to investigate and sample different outcomes, such as changing the interest rate or payment schedule on a loan

Identify Excel 2016 Window Components

Learning Outcomes
• Open and save an Excel file
• Identify Excel window elements

To start Excel, Microsoft Windows must be running. Similar to starting any app in Office, you can use the Start button on the Windows taskbar, the Start button on your keyboard, or you may have a shortcut on your desktop you prefer to use. If you need additional assistance, ask your instructor or technical support person. **CASE** *You decide to start Excel and familiarize yourself with the worksheet window.*

STEPS

1. **Start Excel, click Open Other Workbooks on the navigation bar, click This PC, then click Browse to open the Open dialog box**

2. **In the Open dialog box, navigate to the location where you store your Data Files, click EX 1-1.xlsx, then click Open**

   The file opens in the Excel window.

3. **Click the File tab, click Save As on the navigation bar, then click Browse to open the Save As dialog box**

4. **In the Save As dialog box, navigate to the location where you store your Data Files if necessary, type EX 1-Project Leader Payroll Calculator in the File name text box, then click Save**

   Using **FIGURE 1-3** as a guide, identify the following items:

   • The **Name box** displays the active cell address. "A1" appears in the Name box.

   • The **formula bar** allows you to enter or edit data in the worksheet.

   • The **worksheet window** contains a grid of columns and rows. Columns are labeled alphabetically and rows are labeled numerically. The worksheet window can contain a total of 1,048,576 rows and 16,384 columns. The intersection of a column and a row is called a **cell**. Cells can contain text, numbers, formulas, or a combination of all three. Every cell has its own unique location or **cell address**, which is identified by the coordinates of the intersecting column and row. The column and row indicators are shaded to make identifying the cell address easy.

   • The **cell pointer** is a dark rectangle that outlines the cell you are working in. This cell is called the **active cell**. In **FIGURE 1-3**, the cell pointer outlines cell A1, so A1 is the active cell. The column and row headings for the active cell are highlighted, making it easier to locate.

   • **Sheet tabs** below the worksheet grid let you switch from sheet to sheet in a workbook. By default, a workbook file contains one worksheet—but you can have as many sheets as your computer's memory allows, in a workbook. The New sheet button to the right of Sheet 1 allows you to add worksheets to a workbook. **Sheet tab scrolling buttons** let you navigate to additional sheet tabs when available.

   • You can use the **scroll bars** to move around in a worksheet that is too large to fit on the screen at once.

   • The **status bar** is located at the bottom of the Excel window. It provides a brief description of the active command or task in progress. **The mode indicator** in the lower-left corner of the status bar provides additional information about certain tasks.

5. **Click cell A4**

   Cell A4 becomes the active cell. To activate a different cell, you can click the cell or press the arrow keys on your keyboard to move to it.

6. **Click cell B5, press and hold the mouse button, drag ✥ to cell B14, then release the mouse button**

   You selected a group of cells and they are highlighted, as shown in **FIGURE 1-4**. A selection of two or more cells such as B5:B14 is called a **range**; you select a range when you want to perform an action on a group of cells at once, such as moving them or formatting them. When you select a range, the status bar displays the average, count (or number of items selected), and sum of the selected cells as a quick reference.

FIGURE 1-3: Open workbook

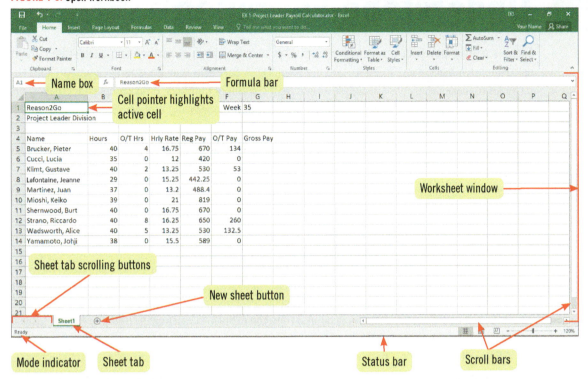

FIGURE 1-4: Selected range

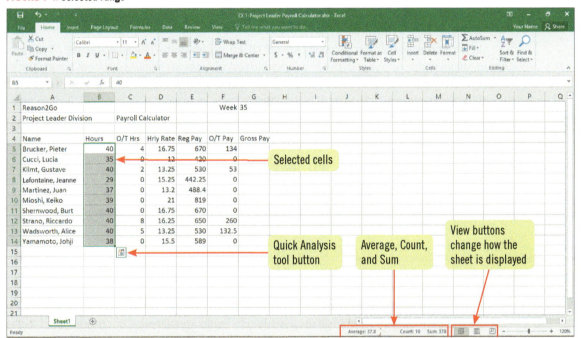

Using OneDrive and Office Online

If you have a Microsoft account, you can save your Excel files and photos in OneDrive, a cloud-based service from Microsoft. When you save files in OneDrive, you can access them on other devices—such as a tablet or smartphone. OneDrive is available as an app on smartphones and tablets, making access simple. You can open files to view them on any device, and you can even make edits to them using **Office Online**, which includes simplified versions of the apps found in the Office 2016 suite. Because Office Online is web-based, the apps take up no computer disk space and you can use them on any Internet-connected device.

Understand Formulas

Learning Outcomes
- Explain how a formula works
- Identify Excel arithmetic operators

Excel is a truly powerful program because users at every level of mathematical expertise can make calculations with accuracy. To do so, you use formulas. A **formula** is an equation in a worksheet. You use formulas to make calculations as simple as adding a column of numbers, or as complex as creating profit-and-loss projections for a global corporation. To tap into the power of Excel, you should understand how formulas work. **CASE** *Managers at R2G use the Project Leader Payroll Calculator workbook to keep track of employee hours prior to submitting them to the Payroll Department. You'll be using this workbook regularly, so you need to understand the formulas it contains and how Excel calculates the results.*

STEPS

1. **Click cell E5**

   The active cell contains a formula, which appears on the formula bar. All Excel formulas begin with the equal sign (=). If you want a cell to show the result of adding 4 plus 2, the formula in the cell would look like this: =4+2. If you want a cell to show the result of multiplying two values in your worksheet, such as the values in cells B5 and D5, the formula would look like this: =B5*D5, as shown in **FIGURE 1-5**. While you're entering a formula in a cell, the cell references and arithmetic operators appear on the formula bar. See **TABLE 1-2** for a list of commonly used arithmetic operators. When you're finished entering the formula, you can either click the Enter button on the formula bar or press [Enter].

2. **Click cell F5**

   This cell contains an example of a more complex formula, which calculates overtime pay. At R2G, overtime pay is calculated at twice the regular hourly rate times the number of overtime hours. The formula used to calculate overtime pay for the employee in row 5 is:

   O/T Hrs times (2 times Hrly Rate)

   In the worksheet cell, you would enter: =C5*(2*D5), as shown in **FIGURE 1-6**. The use of parentheses creates groups within the formula and indicates which calculations to complete first—an important consideration in complex formulas. In this formula, first the hourly rate is multiplied by 2, because that calculation is within the parentheses. Next, that value is multiplied by the number of overtime hours. Because overtime is calculated at twice the hourly rate, managers are aware that they need to closely watch this expense.

DETAILS

In creating calculations in Excel, it is important to:

- **Know where the formulas should be**

  An Excel formula is created in the cell where the formula's results should appear. This means that the formula calculating Gross Pay for the employee in row 5 will be entered in cell G5.

- **Know exactly what cells and arithmetic operations are needed**

  Don't guess; make sure you know exactly what cells are involved before creating a formula.

- **Create formulas with care**

  Make sure you know exactly what you want a formula to accomplish before it is created. An inaccurate formula may have far-reaching effects if the formula or its results are referenced by other formulas, as shown in the payroll example in **FIGURE 1-6**.

- **Use cell references rather than values**

  The beauty of Excel is that whenever you change a value in a cell, any formula containing a reference to that cell is automatically updated. For this reason, it's important that you use cell references in formulas, rather than actual values, whenever possible.

- **Determine what calculations will be needed**

  Sometimes it's difficult to predict what data will be needed within a worksheet, but you should try to anticipate what statistical information may be required. For example, if there are columns of numbers, chances are good that both column and row totals should be present.

FIGURE 1-5: Viewing a formula

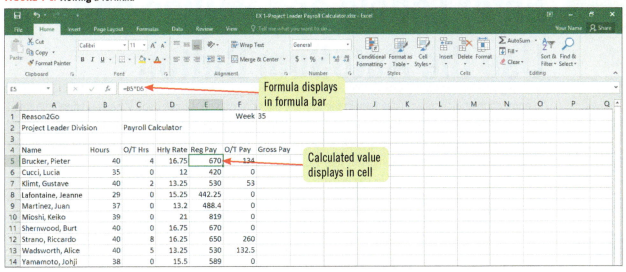

FIGURE 1-6: Formula with multiple operators

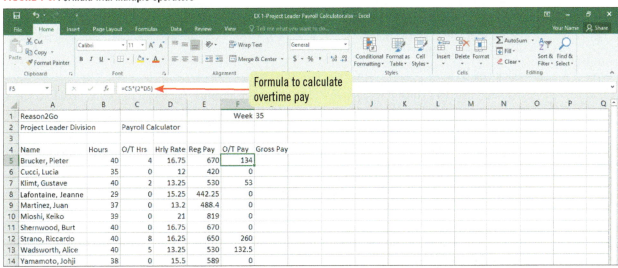

TABLE 1-2: Excel arithmetic operators

operator	purpose	example
+	Addition	=A5+A7
-	Subtraction or negation	=A5-10
*	Multiplication	=A5*A7
/	Division	=A5/A7
%	Percent	=35%
^ (caret)	Exponent	=6^2 (same as 6^2)

Enter Labels and Values and Use the AutoSum Button

Learning Outcomes
- Build formulas with the AutoSum button
- Copy formulas with the fill handle

To enter content in a cell, you can type in the formula bar or directly in the cell itself. When entering content in a worksheet, you should start by entering all the labels first. **Labels** are entries that contain text and numerical information not used in calculations, such as "2019 Sales" or "Travel Expenses". Labels help you identify data in worksheet rows and columns, making your worksheet easier to understand. **Values** are numbers, formulas, and functions that can be used in calculations. To enter a calculation, you type an equal sign (=) plus the formula for the calculation; some examples of an Excel calculation are "=2+2" and "=C5+C6". Functions are built-in formulas; you learn more about them in the next module. **CASE** ▶ *You want to enter some information in the Project Leader Payroll Calculator workbook and use a very simple function to total a range of cells.*

STEPS

1. **Click cell A15, then click in the formula bar**

   Notice that the **mode indicator** on the status bar now reads "Edit," indicating you are in Edit mode. You are in Edit mode any time you are entering or changing the contents of a cell.

   QUICK TIP
   If you change your mind and want to cancel an entry in the formula bar, click the Cancel button ☒ on the formula bar.

2. **Type Totals, then click the Enter button ✓ on the formula bar**

   Clicking the Enter button accepts the entry. The new text is left-aligned in the cell. Labels are left-aligned by default, and values are right-aligned by default. Excel recognizes an entry as a value if it is a number or it begins with one of these symbols: +, -, =, @, #, or $. When a cell contains both text and numbers, Excel recognizes it as a label.

3. **Click cell B15**

   You want this cell to total the hours worked by all the trip advisors. You might think you need to create a formula that looks like this: =B5+B6+B7+B8+B9+B10+B11+B12+B13+B14. However, there's an easier way to achieve this result.

   QUICK TIP
   The AutoSum button is also referred to as the Sum button because clicking it inserts the SUM function.

4. **Click the AutoSum button Σ in the Editing group on the Home tab on the Ribbon**

   The SUM function is inserted in the cell, and a suggested range appears in parentheses, as shown in **FIGURE 1-7**. A **function** is a built-in formula; it includes the **arguments** (the information necessary to calculate an answer) as well as cell references and other unique information. Clicking the AutoSum button sums the adjacent range (that is, the cells next to the active cell) above or to the left, although you can adjust the range if necessary by selecting a different range before accepting the cell entry. Using the SUM function is quicker than entering a formula, and using the range B5:B14 is more efficient than entering individual cell references.

   QUICK TIP
   You can create formulas in a cell even before you enter the values to be calculated.

5. **Click ✓ on the formula bar**

   Excel calculates the total contained in cells B5:B14 and displays the result, 378, in cell B15. The cell actually contains the formula =SUM(B5:B14), and the result is displayed.

6. **Click cell C13, type 6, then press [Enter]**

   The number 6 replaces the cell's contents, the cell pointer moves to cell C14, and the value in cell F13 changes.

7. **Click cell C18, type Average Gross Pay, then press [Enter]**

   The new label is entered in cell C18. The contents appear to spill into the empty cells to the right.

   QUICK TIP
   You can also press [Tab] to complete a cell entry and move the cell pointer to the right.

8. **Click cell B15, position the pointer on the lower-right corner of the cell (the fill handle) so that the pointer changes to +, drag + to cell G15, then release the mouse button**

   Dragging the fill handle across a range of cells copies the contents of the first cell into the other cells in the range. In the range B15:G15, each filled cell now contains a function that sums the range of cells above, as shown in **FIGURE 1-8**.

9. **Save your work**

FIGURE 1-7: Creating a formula using the AutoSum button

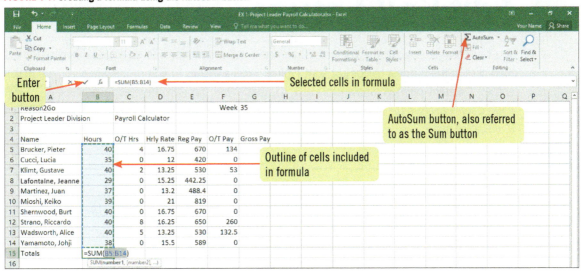

FIGURE 1-8: Results of copied SUM functions

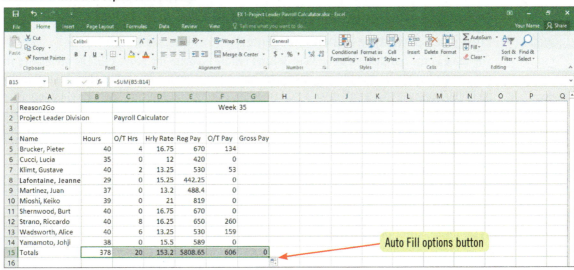

Navigating a worksheet

With over a million cells available in a worksheet, it is important to know how to move around in, or **navigate**, a worksheet. You can use the arrow keys on the keyboard ↑, ↓, →, or ← to move one cell at a time, or press [Page Up] or [Page Down] to move one screen at a time. To move one screen to the left, press [Alt][Page Up]; to move one screen to the right, press [Alt][Page Down]. You can also use the mouse pointer to click the desired cell. If the desired cell is not visible in the worksheet window, use the scroll bars or use the Go To command by clicking the Find & Select button in the Editing group on the Home tab on the Ribbon. To quickly jump to the first cell in a worksheet, press [Ctrl][Home]; to jump to the last cell, press [Ctrl][End].

Excel 2016

Edit Cell Entries

Learning Outcomes
- Edit cell entries in the formula bar
- Edit cell entries in the cell

You can change, or **edit**, the contents of an active cell at any time. To do so, double-click the cell, and then click in the formula bar or just start typing. Excel switches to Edit mode when you are making cell entries. Different pointers, shown in **TABLE 1-3**, guide you through the editing process. **CASE** *You noticed some errors in the worksheet and want to make corrections. The first error is in cell A5, which contains a misspelled name.*

STEPS

1. **Click cell A5, then click to the right of P in the formula bar**

   As soon as you click in the formula bar, a blinking vertical line called the **insertion point** appears on the formula bar at the location where new text will be inserted. See **FIGURE 1-9**. The mouse pointer changes to I when you point anywhere in the formula bar.

2. **Press [Delete], then click the Enter button ✓ on the formula bar**

   Clicking the Enter button accepts the edit, and the spelling of the employee's first name is corrected. You can also press [Enter] or [Tab] to accept an edit. Pressing [Enter] to accept an edit moves the cell pointer down one cell, and pressing [Tab] to accept an edit moves the cell pointer one cell to the right.

   QUICK TIP
   On some keyboards, you might need to press an [F-Lock] key to enable the function keys.

3. **Click cell B6, then press [F2]**

   Excel switches to Edit mode, and the insertion point blinks in the cell. Pressing [F2] activates the cell for editing directly in the cell instead of the formula bar. Whether you edit in the cell or the formula bar is simply a matter of preference; the results in the worksheet are the same.

   QUICK TIP
   The Undo button allows you to reverse up to 100 previous actions, one at a time.

4. **Press [Backspace], type 8, then press [Enter]**

   The value in the cell changes from 35 to 38, and cell B7 becomes the active cell. Did you notice that the calculations in cells B15 and E15 also changed? That's because those cells contain formulas that include cell B6 in their calculations. If you make a mistake when editing, you can click the Cancel button ✕ on the formula bar *before* pressing [Enter] to confirm the cell entry. The Enter and Cancel buttons appear only when you're in Edit mode. If you notice the mistake *after* you have confirmed the cell entry, click the Undo button � on the Quick Access toolbar.

   QUICK TIP
   You can use the keyboard to select all cell contents by clicking to the right of the cell contents in the cell or formula bar, pressing and holding [Shift], then pressing [Home].

5. **Click cell A9, then double-click the word Juan in the formula bar**

   Double-clicking a word in a cell selects it. When you selected the word, the Mini toolbar automatically displayed.

6. **Type Javier, then press [Enter]**

   When text is selected, typing deletes it and replaces it with the new text.

7. **Double-click cell C12, press [Delete], type 4, then click ✓**

   Double-clicking a cell activates it for editing directly in the cell. Compare your screen to **FIGURE 1-10**.

8. **Save your work**

Recovering unsaved changes to a workbook file

You can use Excel's AutoRecover feature to automatically save (Autosave) your work as often as you want. This means that if you suddenly lose power or if Excel closes unexpectedly while you're working, you can recover all or some of the changes you made since you saved it last. (Of course, this is no substitute for regularly saving your work: this is just added insurance.) To customize the AutoRecover settings, click the File tab, click Options, then click

Save. AutoRecover lets you decide how often and into which location it should Autosave files. When you restart Excel after losing power, a Document Recovery pane opens and provides access to the saved and Autosaved versions of the files that were open when Excel closed. You can also click the File tab, click Open on the navigation bar, then click any file in the Recover Unsaved Workbooks list to open Autosaved workbooks.

FIGURE 1-9: Worksheet in Edit mode

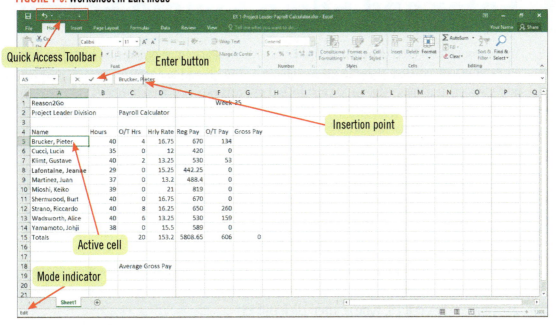

Quick Access Toolbar

Enter button

Insertion point

Active cell

Mode indicator

FIGURE 1-10: Edited worksheet

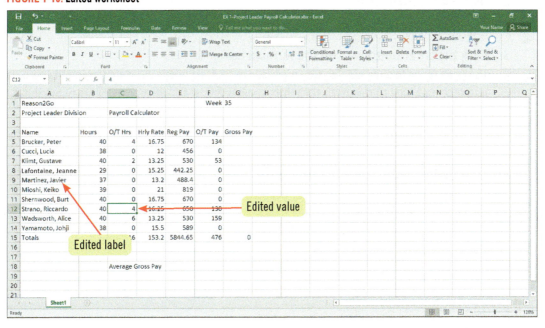

Edited value

Edited label

TABLE 1-3: Common pointers in Excel

name	pointer	use to	visible over the
Normal	⊕	Select a cell or range; indicates Ready mode	Active worksheet
Fill handle	✛	Copy cell contents to adjacent cells	Lower right corner of the active cell or range
I-beam	I	Edit cell contents in active cell or formula bar	Active cell in Edit mode or over the formula bar
Move	⊹	Change the location of the selected cell(s)	Perimeter of the active cell(s)
Copy	⊹⁺	Create a duplicate of the selected cell(s)	Perimeter of the active cell(s) when [Ctrl] is pressed
Column resize	↔	Change the width of a column	Border between column heading indicators

Enter and Edit a Simple Formula

Learning Outcomes
- Enter a formula
- Use cell references to create a formula

You use formulas in Excel to perform calculations such as adding, multiplying, and averaging. Formulas in an Excel worksheet start with the equal sign (=), also called the **formula prefix**, followed by cell addresses, range names, values, and **calculation operators**. Calculation operators indicate what type of calculation you want to perform on the cells, ranges, or values. They can include **arithmetic operators**, which perform mathematical calculations (see **TABLE 1-2** in the "Understand Formulas" lesson); **comparison operators**, which compare values for the purpose of true/false results; **text concatenation operators**, which join strings of text in different cells; and **reference operators**, which enable you to use ranges in calculations. **CASE** *You want to create a formula in the worksheet that calculates gross pay for each employee.*

STEPS

1. **Click cell G5**

   This is the first cell where you want to insert the formula. To calculate gross pay, you need to add regular pay and overtime pay. For employee Peter Brucker, regular pay appears in cell E5 and overtime pay appears in cell F5.

   QUICK TIP
   You can reference a cell in a formula either by typing the cell reference or clicking the cell in the worksheet; when you click a cell to add a reference, the Mode indicator changes to "Point."

2. **Type =, click cell E5, type +, then click cell F5**

   Compare your formula bar to **FIGURE 1-11**. The blue and red cell references in cell G5 correspond to the colored cell outlines. When entering a formula, it's a good idea to use cell references instead of values whenever you can. That way, if you later change a value in a cell (if, for example, Peter's regular pay changes to 690), any formula that includes this information reflects accurate, up-to-date results.

3. **Click the Enter button ✓ on the formula bar**

   The result of the formula =E5+F5, 804, appears in cell G5. This same value appears in cell G15 because cell G15 contains a formula that totals the values in cells G5:G14, and there are no other values at this time.

4. **Click cell F5**

   The formula in this cell calculates overtime pay by multiplying overtime hours (C5) times twice the regular hourly rate (2*D5). You want to edit this formula to reflect a new overtime pay rate.

5. **Click to the right of 2 in the formula bar, then type .5 as shown in FIGURE 1-12**

   The formula that calculates overtime pay has been edited.

6. **Click ✓ on the formula bar**

   Compare your screen to **FIGURE 1-13**. Notice that the calculated values in cells G5, F15, and G15 have all changed to reflect your edits to cell F5.

7. **Save your work**

Understanding named ranges

It can be difficult to remember the cell locations of critical information in a worksheet, but using cell names can make this task much easier. You can name a single cell or range of contiguous, or touching, cells. For example, you might name a cell that contains data on average gross pay "AVG_GP" instead of trying to remember the cell address C18. A named range must begin with a letter or an underscore. It cannot contain any spaces or be the same as a built-in name, such as a function or another object (such as a different named range) in the workbook. To name a range, select the cell(s) you want to name, click the Name box in the formula bar, type the name you want to use, then press [Enter]. You can also name a range by clicking the Formulas tab, then clicking the Define Name button in the Defined Names group. Type the new range name in the Name text box in the New Name dialog box, verify the selected range, then click OK. When you use a named range in a formula, the named range appears instead of the cell address. You can also create a named range using the contents of a cell already in the range. Select the range containing the text you want to use as a name, then click the Create from Selection button in the Defined Names group. The Create Names from Selection dialog box opens. Choose the location of the name you want to use, then click OK.

FIGURE 1-11: Simple formula in a worksheet

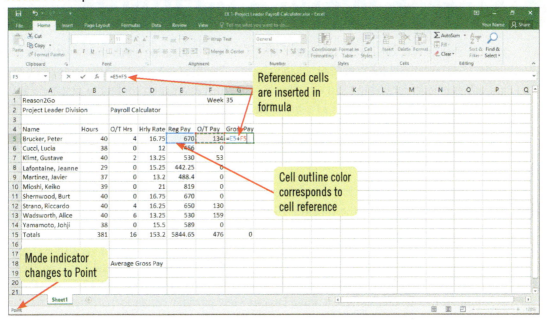

FIGURE 1-12: Edited formula in a worksheet

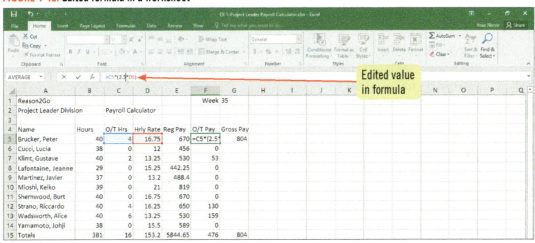

FIGURE 1-13: Edited formula with changes

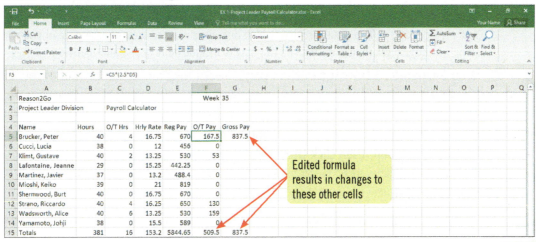

Switch Worksheet Views

Learning Outcomes
- Change worksheet views
- Create a header/footer
- Select a range

You can change your view of the worksheet window at any time, using either the View tab on the Ribbon or the View buttons on the status bar. Changing your view does not affect the contents of a worksheet; it just makes it easier for you to focus on different tasks, such as entering content or preparing a worksheet for printing. The View tab includes a variety of viewing options, such as View buttons, zoom controls, and the ability to show or hide worksheet elements such as gridlines. The status bar offers fewer View options but can be more convenient to use. **CASE** *You want to make some final adjustments to your worksheet, including adding a header so the document looks more polished.*

STEPS

> **QUICK TIP**
>
> Although a worksheet can contain more than a million rows and thousands of columns, the current document contains only as many pages as necessary for the current project.

1. **Click the View tab on the Ribbon, then click the Page Layout button in the Workbook Views group**

   The view switches from the default view, Normal, to Page Layout view. **Normal view** shows the worksheet without including certain details like headers and footers, or tools like rulers and a page number indicator; it's great for creating and editing a worksheet, but may not be detailed enough when you want to put the finishing touches on a document. **Page Layout view** provides a more accurate view of how a worksheet will look when printed, as shown in **FIGURE 1-14**. The margins of the page are displayed, along with a text box for the header. A footer text box appears at the bottom of the page, but your screen may not be large enough to view it without scrolling. Above and to the left of the page are rulers. Part of an additional page appears to the right of this page, but it is dimmed, indicating that it does not contain any data. A page number indicator on the status bar tells you the current page and the total number of pages in this worksheet.

2. **Move the pointer ⬚ over the header *without clicking***

   The header is made up of three text boxes: left, center, and right. Each text box is outlined in green as you pass over it with the pointer.

> **QUICK TIP**
>
> You can change header and footer information using the Header & Footer Tools Design tab that opens on the Ribbon when a header or footer is active. For example, you can insert the date by clicking the Current Date button in the Header & Footer Elements group, or insert the time by clicking the Current Time button.

3. **Click the left header text box, type Reason2Go, click the center header text box, type Project Leader Payroll Calculator, click the right header text box, then type Week 35**

   The new text appears in the text boxes, as shown in **FIGURE 1-15**. You can also press the [Tab] key to advance from one header box to the next.

4. **Select the range A1:G2, then press [Delete]**

   The duplicate information you just entered in the header is deleted from cells in the worksheet.

5. **Click the View tab if necessary, click the Ruler check box in the Show group, then click the Gridlines check box in the Show group**

   The rulers and the gridlines are hidden. By default, gridlines in a worksheet do not print, so hiding them gives you a more accurate image of your final document.

6. **Click the Page Break Preview button 🖫 on the status bar**

   Your view changes to Page Break Preview, which displays a reduced view of each page of your worksheet, along with page break indicators that you can drag to include more or less information on a page.

> **QUICK TIP**
>
> Once you view a worksheet in Page Break Preview, the page break indicators appear as dotted lines after you switch back to Normal view or Page Layout view.

7. **Drag the pointer ⬍ from the bottom page break indicator to the bottom of row 20**

   See **FIGURE 1-16**. When you're working on a large worksheet with multiple pages, sometimes you need to adjust where pages break; in this worksheet, however, the information all fits comfortably on one page.

8. **Click the Page Layout button in the Workbook Views group, click the Ruler check box in the Show group, then click the Gridlines check box in the Show group**

   The rulers and gridlines are no longer hidden. You can show or hide View tab items in any view.

9. **Save your work**

FIGURE 1-14: Page Layout view

Turns ruler on/off

Workbook Views group

Turns gridlines on/off

Horizontal ruler

Header text box

Additional dimmed page

Vertical ruler

Current page and total number of pages

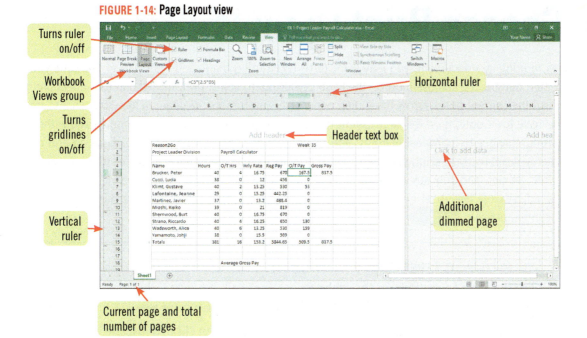

FIGURE 1-15: Header text entered

Header & Footer Tools Design tab

Header text boxes

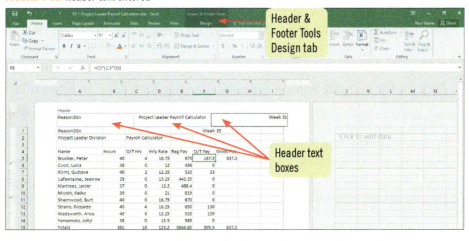

FIGURE 1-16: Page Break Preview

Blue outline indicates print area

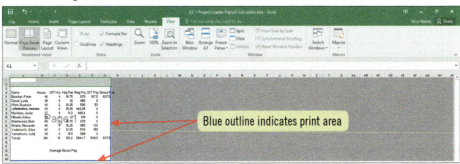

Choose Print Options

Before printing a document, you may want to review it using the Page Layout tab to fine-tune your printed output. You can use tools on the Page Layout tab to adjust print orientation (the direction in which the content prints across the page), paper size, and location of page breaks. You can also use the Scale to Fit options on the Page Layout tab to fit a large amount of data on a single page without making changes to individual margins, and to turn gridlines and column/row headings on and off. When you are ready to print, you can set print options such as the number of copies to print and the correct printer, and you can preview your document in Backstage view using the File tab. You can also adjust page layout settings from within Backstage view and immediately see the results in the document preview. **CASE** ➤ *You are ready to prepare your worksheet for printing.*

STEPS

1. **Click cell A20, type your name, then click ✓**

2. **Click the Page Layout tab on the Ribbon**
   Compare your screen to **FIGURE 1-17**. The solid outline indicates the default **print area**, the area to be printed.

3. **Click the Orientation button in the Page Setup group, then click Landscape**
   The paper orientation changes to **landscape**, so the contents will print across the length of the page instead of across the width. Notice how the margins of the worksheet adjust.

4. **Click the Orientation button in the Page Setup group, then click Portrait**
   The orientation returns to **portrait**, so the contents will print across the width of the page.

5. **Click the Gridlines View check box in the Sheet Options group on the Page Layout tab, click the Gridlines Print check box to select it if necessary, then save your work**
   Printing gridlines makes the data easier to read, but the gridlines will not print unless the Gridlines Print check box is checked.

6. **Click the File tab, click Print on the navigation bar, then select an active printer if necessary**
   The Print tab in Backstage view displays a preview of your worksheet exactly as it will look when it is printed. To the left of the worksheet preview, you can also change a number of document settings and print options. To open the Page Setup dialog box and adjust page layout options, click the Page Setup link in the Settings section. Compare your preview screen to **FIGURE 1-18**. You can print from this view by clicking the Print button, or return to the worksheet without printing by clicking the Back button ⬅. You can also print an entire workbook from the Backstage view by clicking the Print button in the Settings section, then selecting the active sheet or entire workbook.

7. **Compare your settings to FIGURE 1-18, then click the Print button**
   One copy of the worksheet prints.

8. **Submit your work to your instructor as directed, then exit Excel**

Printing worksheet formulas

Sometimes you need to keep a record of all the formulas in a worksheet. You might want to do this to see exactly how you came up with a complex calculation, so you can explain it to others. To prepare a worksheet to show formulas rather than results when printed, open the workbook containing the formulas you want to print. Click the Formulas tab, then click the Show Formulas button in the Formula Auditing group to select it. When the Show Formulas button is selected, formulas rather than resulting values are displayed in the worksheet on screen and when printed. (The Show Formulas button is a toggle: click it again to hide the formulas.)

FIGURE 1-17: Worksheet with Portrait orientation

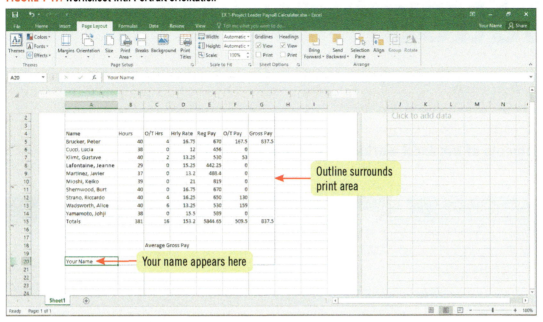

Outline surrounds print area

Your name appears here

FIGURE 1-18: Worksheet in Backstage view

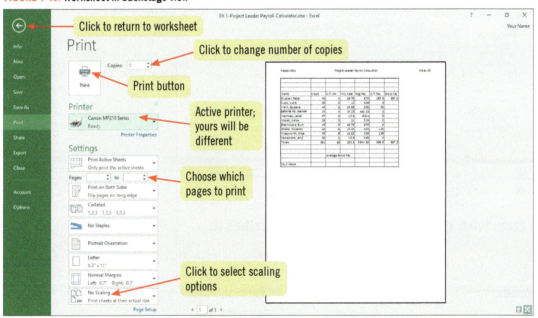

Click to return to worksheet

Click to change number of copies

Print button

Active printer; yours will be different

Choose which pages to print

Click to select scaling options

Scaling to fit

If you have a large amount of data that you want to fit to a single sheet of paper, but you don't want to spend a lot of time trying to adjust the margins and other settings, you have several options. You can easily print your work on a single sheet by clicking the No Scaling list arrow in the Settings section on the Print place in Backstage view, then clicking Fit Sheet in One Page. Another method for fitting worksheet content onto one page is to click the Page Layout tab, then change the Width and Height settings in the Scale to Fit group each to 1 Page. You can also use the Fit to option in the Page Setup dialog box to fit a worksheet on one page. To open the Page Setup dialog box, click the dialog box launcher in the Scale to Fit group on the Page Layout tab, or click the Page Setup link in the Print place in Backstage view. Make sure the Page tab is selected in the Page Setup dialog box, then click the Fit to option button.

Practice

Concepts Review

Label the elements of the Excel worksheet window shown in FIGURE 1-19.

FIGURE 1-19

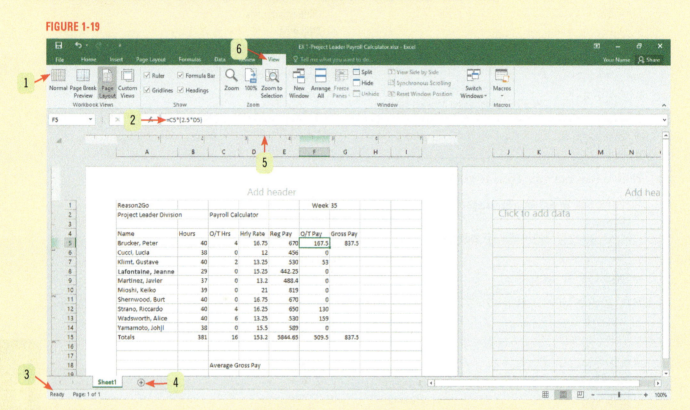

Match each term with the statement that best describes it.

7. **Name box**
8. **Workbook**
9. **Formula prefix**
10. **Orientation**
11. **Cell**
12. **Normal view**

a. Part of the Excel program window that displays the active cell address
b. Default view in Excel
c. Direction in which contents of page will print
d. Equal sign preceding a formula
e. File consisting of one or more worksheets
f. Intersection of a column and a row

Select the best answer from the list of choices.

13. **Which feature could be used to print a very long worksheet on a single sheet of paper?**
    a. Show Formulas
    b. Scale to Fit
    c. Page Break Preview
    d. Named Ranges

14. **In which area can you see a preview of your worksheet?**
    a. Page Setup
    b. Backstage view
    c. Printer Setup
    d. View tab

15. **A selection of multiple cells is called a:**
    a. Group.
    b. Range.
    c. Reference.
    d. Package.

16. **Using a cell address in a formula is known as:**
    a. Formularizing.
    b. Prefixing.
    c. Cell referencing.
    d. Cell mathematics.

17. **Which worksheet view shows how your worksheet will look when printed?**
    a. Page Layout
    b. Data
    c. Review
    d. View

18. **Which key can you press to switch to Edit mode?**
    a. [F1]
    b. [F2]
    c. [F4]
    d. [F6]

19. **In which view can you see the header and footer areas of a worksheet?**
    a. Normal view
    b. Page Layout view
    c. Page Break Preview
    d. Header/Footer view

20. **Which view shows you a reduced view of each page of your worksheet?**
    a. Normal
    b. Page Layout
    c. Thumbnail
    d. Page Break Preview

21. **The maximum number of worksheets you can include in a workbook is:**
    a. 3.
    b. 250.
    c. 255.
    d. Unlimited.

Skills Review

1. **Understand spreadsheet software.**
   a. What is the difference between a workbook and a worksheet?
   b. Identify five common business uses for electronic spreadsheets.
   c. What is what-if analysis?

2. **Identify Excel 2016 window components.**
   a. Start Excel.
   b. Open EX 1-2.xlsx from the location where you store your Data Files, then save it as **EX 1-Weather Data**.
   c. Locate the formula bar, the Sheet tabs, the mode indicator, and the cell pointer.

3. **Understand formulas.**
   a. What is the average high temperature of the listed cities? (*Hint*: Select the range B5:G5 and use the status bar.)
   b. What formula would you create to calculate the difference in altitude between Atlanta and Dallas? Enter your answer (as an equation) in cell D13.

4. Enter labels and values and use the AutoSum button.

   a. Click cell H8, then use the AutoSum button to calculate the total snowfall.

   b. Click cell H7, then use the AutoSum button to calculate the total rainfall.

   c. Save your changes to the file.

5. Edit cell entries.

   a. Use [F2] to correct the spelling of SanteFe in cell G3 (the correct spelling is Santa Fe).

   b. Click cell A17, then type your name.

   c. Save your changes.

6. Enter and edit a simple formula.

   a. Change the value 41 in cell C8 to **52**.

   b. Change the value 37 in cell D6 to **35.4**.

   c. Select cell J4, then use the fill handle to copy the formula in cell J4 to cells J5:J8.

   d. Save your changes.

7. Switch worksheet views.

   a. Click the View tab on the Ribbon, then switch to Page Layout view.

   b. Add the header **Average Annual Weather Data** to the center header text box.

   c. Add your name to the right header box.

   d. Delete the contents of cell A17.

   e. Delete the contents of cell A1.

   f. Save your changes.

8. Choose print options.

   a. Use the Page Layout tab to change the orientation to Portrait.

   b. Turn off gridlines by deselecting both the Gridlines View and Gridlines Print check boxes (if necessary) in the Sheet Options group.

   c. Scale the worksheet so all the information fits on one page. If necessary, scale the worksheet so all the information fits on one page. (*Hint*: Click the Width list arrow in the Scale to Fit group, click 1 page, click the Height list arrow in the Scale to Fit group, then click 1 page.) Compare your screen to FIGURE 1-20.

   d. Preview the worksheet in Backstage view, then print the worksheet.

   e. Save your changes, submit your work to your instructor as directed, then close the workbook and exit Excel.

FIGURE 1-20

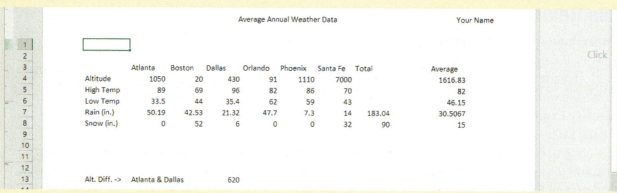

	Atlanta	Boston	Dallas	Orlando	Phoenix	Santa Fe	Total	Average
Altitude	1050	20	430	91	1110	7000		1616.83
High Temp	89	69	96	82	86	70		82
Low Temp	33.5	44	35.4	62	59	43		46.15
Rain (in.)	50.19	42.53	21.32	47.7	7.3	14	183.04	30.5067
Snow (in.)	0	52	6	0	0	32	90	15

Average Annual Weather Data   Your Name

Alt. Diff. ->   Atlanta & Dallas   620

Independent Challenge 1

A real estate development company has hired you to help them make the transition to using Excel in their office. They would like to list properties they are interested in acquiring in a workbook. You've started a worksheet for this project that contains labels but no data.

a. Open the file EX 1-3.xlsx from the location where you store your Data Files, then save it as **EX 1-Real Estate Acquisitions**.

b. Enter the data shown in **TABLE 1-4** in columns A, C, D, and E (the property address information should spill into column B).

TABLE 1-4

Property Address	Price	Bedrooms	Bathrooms	Area
1507 Pinon Lane	575000	4	2.5	NE
32 Zanzibar Way	429000	3	4	SE
60 Pottery Lane	526500	2	2	NE
902 Excelsior Drive	315000	4	3	NW

c. Use Page Layout view to create a header with the following components: the title **Real Estate Acquisitions** in the center and your name on the right.

d. Create formulas for totals in cells C6:E6.

e. Save your changes, then compare your worksheet to **FIGURE 1-21**.

f. Submit your work to your instructor as directed.

g. Close the worksheet and exit Excel.

FIGURE 1-21

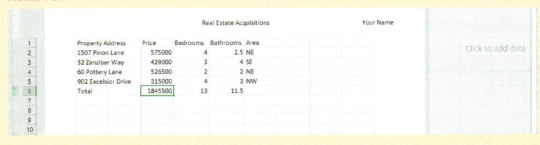

Independent Challenge 2

You are the general manager for Luxury Motors, a high-end auto reseller. Although the company is just five years old, it is expanding rapidly, and you are continually looking for ways to save time. You recently began using Excel to manage and maintain data on inventory and sales, which has greatly helped you to track information accurately and efficiently.

a. Start Excel.

b. Save a new workbook as **EX 1-Luxury Motors** in the location where you store your Data Files.

c. Switch to an appropriate view, then add a header that contains your name in the left header text box and the title **Luxury Motors** in the center header text box.

Independent Challenge 2 (continued)

d. Using **FIGURE 1-22** as a guide, create labels for at least seven car manufacturers and sales for three months. Include other labels as appropriate. The car make should be in column A and the months should be in columns B, C, and D. A Total row should be beneath the data, and a Total column should be in column E.

FIGURE 1-22

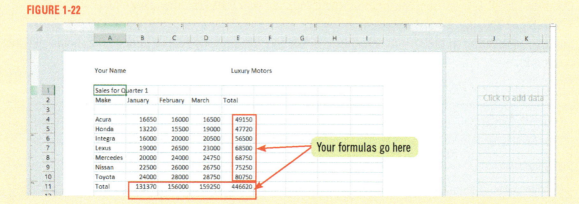

e. Enter values of your choice for the monthly sales for each make.

f. Add formulas in the Total column to calculate total quarterly sales for each make. Add formulas at the bottom of each column of values to calculate the total for that column. Remember that you can use the AutoSum button and the fill handle to save time.

g. Save your changes, preview the worksheet in Backstage view, then submit your work to your instructor as directed.

h. Close the workbook and exit Excel.

Independent Challenge 3

This Independent Challenge requires an Internet connection.

Your company, which is headquartered in Paris, is planning to open an office in New York City. You think it would be helpful to create a worksheet that can be used to convert Celsius temperatures to Fahrenheit, to help employees who are unfamiliar with this type of temperature measurement.

a. Start Excel, then save a blank workbook as **EX 1-Temperature Conversions** in the location where you store your Data Files.

b. Create column headings using **FIGURE 1-23** as a guide. (*Hint*: You can widen column B by clicking cell B1, clicking the Format button in the Cells group on the Home tab, then clicking AutoFit Column Width.)

FIGURE 1-23

c. Create row labels for each of the seasons.

d. In the appropriate cells, enter what you determine to be a reasonable indoor temperature for each season.

e. Use your web browser to find out the conversion rate for Fahrenheit to Celsius. (*Hint*: Use your favorite search engine to search on a term such as **temperature conversion formula**.)

Independent Challenge 3 (continued)

f. In the appropriate cells, create a formula that calculates the conversion of the Fahrenheit temperature you entered into a Celsius temperature.

g. In Page Layout View, add your name and the title **Temperature Conversions** to the header.

h. Save your work, then submit your work to your instructor as directed.

i. Close the file, then exit Excel.

Independent Challenge 4: Explore

You've been asked to take over a project started by a co-worker whose Excel skills are not as good as your own. The assignment was to create a sample invoice for an existing client. The invoice will include personnel hours, supplies, and sales tax. Your predecessor started the project, including layout and initial calculations, but she has not made good use of Excel features and has made errors in her calculations. Complete the worksheet by correcting the errors and improving the design. Be prepared to discuss what is wrong with each of the items in the worksheet that you change.

a. Start Excel, open the file EX 1-4.xlsx from the location where you store your Data Files, then save it as **EX 1-Improved Invoice**.

b. There is an error in cell E5: please use the Help feature to find out what is wrong. If you need additional assistance, search Help on *overview of formulas*.

c. Correct the error in the formula in cell E5, then copy the corrected formula into cells E6:E7.

d. Correct the error in the formula in cell E11, then copy the corrected formula into cells E12 and E13.

e. Cells E8 and E14 also contain incorrect formulas. Cell E8 should contain a formula that calculates the total personnel expense, and cell E14 should calculate the total supplies used.

f. Cell G17 should contain a formula that adds the Invoice subtotal (total personnel and total supplies).

g. Cell G18 should calculate the sales tax by multiplying the Subtotal (G17) and the sales tax (cell G18).

h. The Invoice Total (cell G19) should contain a formula that adds the Invoice subtotal (cell G17) and Sales tax (cell G18).

i. Add the following to cell A21: **Terms**, then add the following to cell B21: **Net 10**.

j. Switch to Page Layout view and make the following changes to the Header: Improved Invoice for Week 22 (in the left header box), Client ABC (in the center header box), and your name (in the right header box).

k. Delete the contents of A1:A2, switch to Normal view, then compare your worksheet to FIGURE 1-24.

l. Save your work.

FIGURE 1-24

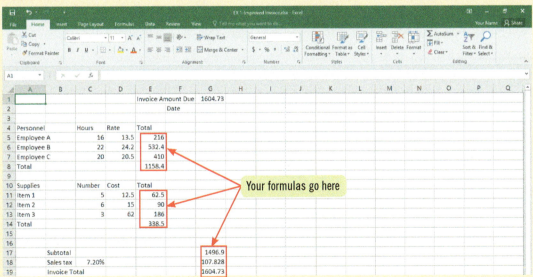

Visual Workshop

Open the file EX 1-5.xlsx from the location where you store your Data Files, then save it as **EX 1-Project Tools**. Using the skills you learned in this module, modify your worksheet so it matches FIGURE 1-25. Enter formulas in cells D4 through D13 and in cells B14 and C14. Use the AutoSum button and fill handle to make entering your formulas easier. Add your name in the left header text box, then print one copy of the worksheet with the formulas displayed.

FIGURE 1-25

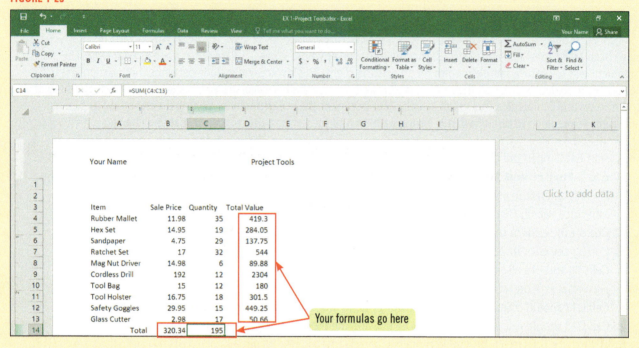

Working with Formulas and Functions

CASE   Yolanda Lee, the vice president of finance at Reason2Go, needs to analyze tour expenses for the current year. She has asked you to prepare a worksheet that summarizes this expense data and includes some statistical analysis. She would also like you to perform some what-if analysis, to see what quarterly expenses would look like with various projected increases.

Module Objectives

After completing this module, you will be able to:

- Create a complex formula
- Insert a function
- Type a function
- Copy and move cell entries
- Understand relative and absolute cell references
- Copy formulas with relative cell references
- Copy formulas with absolute cell references
- Round a value with a function

Files You Will Need

EX 2-1.xlsx   EX 2-3.xlsx

EX 2-2.xlsx   EX 2-4.xlsx

Create a Complex Formula

A **complex formula** is one that uses more than one arithmetic operator. You might, for example, need to create a formula that uses addition and multiplication. In formulas containing more than one arithmetic operator, Excel uses the standard **order of precedence** rules to determine which operation to perform first. You can change the order of precedence in a formula by using parentheses around the part you want to calculate first. For example, the formula =4+2*5 equals 14, because the order of precedence dictates that multiplication is performed before addition. However, the formula =(4+2)*5 equals 30, because the parentheses cause 4+2 to be calculated first. **CASE** *You want to create a formula that calculates a 20% increase in tour expenses.*

STEPS

1. **Start Excel, open the file EX 2-1.xlsx from the location where you store your Data Files, then save it as EX 2-R2G Tour Expense Analysis**

2. **Select the range B4:B11, click the Quick Analysis tool 📄 that appears below the selection, then click the Totals tab**

   The Totals tab in the Quick Analysis tool displays commonly used functions, as seen in **FIGURE 2-1**.

3. **Click the AutoSum button Σ in the Quick Analysis tool**

   The newly calculated value displays in cell B12 and has bold formatting automatically applied, helping to set it off as a sum. This shading is temporary, and will not appear after you click a cell.

4. **Click cell B12, then drag the fill handle to cell E12**

   The formula in cell B12, as well as the bold formatting, is copied to cells C12:E12.

5. **Click cell B14, type =, click cell B12, then type +**

   In this first part of the formula, you are inserting a reference to the cell that contains total expenses for Quarter 1.

6. **Click cell B12, then type *.2**

   The second part of this formula adds a 20% increase (B12*.2) to the original value of the cell (the total expenses for Quarter 1).

7. **Click the Enter button ✓ on the formula bar**

   The result, 42749.58, appears in cell B14.

8. **Press [Tab], type =, click cell C12, type +, click cell C12, type *.2, then click ✓**

   The result, 42323.712, appears in cell C14.

9. **Drag the fill handle from cell C14 to cell E14, then save your work**

   The calculated values appear in the selected range, as shown in **FIGURE 2-2**. Dragging the fill handle on a cell copies the cell's contents or continues a series of data (such as Quarter 1, Quarter 2, etc.) into adjacent cells. This option is called **Auto Fill**.

Using Add-ins to improve worksheet functionality

Excel has more functionality than simple and complex math computations. Using the My Add-ins feature (found in the Add-ins group in the Insert tab), you can insert an add-in into your worksheet that accesses the web and adds functionality. Many of the add-ins are free or available for a small fee and can be used to create an email, appointment, meeting, contact, or task, or be a reference source, such as the Mini Calendar or Date Picker. When you click the My Add-ins button list arrow, you'll see any Recently Used Add-ins. Click See All to display the featured Add-ins for Office and to go to the Store to view available add-ins. When you find one you want, make sure you're logged in to Office.com, click the add-in, click Trust It, and the add-in will be installed. Click the My Add-ins button and your add-in should display under Recently Used Add-ins. Click it, then click Insert. The add-in will display in the Recently Used Add-ins pane when you click the My Add-ins button.

FIGURE 2-1: Totals tab in the Quick Analysis tool

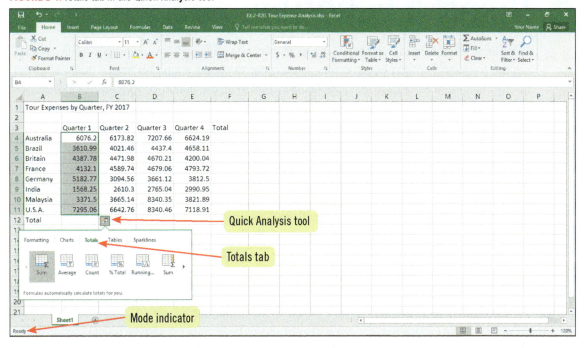

FIGURE 2-2: Results of copied formulas

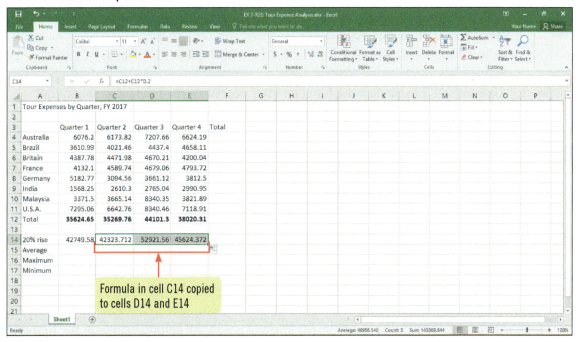

Formula in cell C14 copied to cells D14 and E14

Reviewing the order of precedence

When you work with formulas that contain more than one operator, the order of precedence is very important because it affects the final value. If a formula contains two or more operators, such as 4+.55/4000*25, Excel performs the calculations in a particular sequence based on the following rules: Operations inside parentheses are calculated before any other operations. Reference operators (such as ranges) are calculated first. Exponents are calculated next, then any multiplication and division—progressing from left to right. Finally, addition and subtraction are calculated from left to right. In the example 4+.55/4000*25, Excel performs the arithmetic operations by first dividing .55 by 4000, then multiplying the result by 25, then adding 4. You can change the order of calculations by using parentheses. For example, in the formula (4+.55)/4000*25, Excel would first add 4 and .55, then divide that amount by 4000, then finally multiply by 25.

Insert a Function

Learning Outcomes
- Use the Insert Function button
- Select a range for use in a function
- Select a function from the AutoSum list arrow

Functions are predefined worksheet formulas that enable you to perform complex calculations easily. You can use the Insert Function button on the formula bar to choose a function from a dialog box. You can quickly insert the SUM function using the AutoSum button on the Ribbon, or you can click the AutoSum list arrow to enter other frequently used functions, such as **AVERAGE**. You can also use the Quick Analysis tool to calculate commonly used functions. Functions are organized into categories, such as Financial, Date & Time, and Statistical, based on their purposes. You can insert a function on its own or as part of another formula. For example, you have used the SUM function on its own to add a range of cells. You could also use the SUM function within a formula that adds a range of cells and then multiplies the total by a decimal. If you use a function alone, it always begins with an equal sign (=) as the formula prefix. **CASE** *You need to calculate the average expenses for the first quarter of the year and decide to use a function to do so.*

STEPS

1. **Click cell B15**

   This is the cell where you want to enter a calculation that averages expenses per country for the first quarter.

2. **Click the Insert Function button** f_x **on the formula bar**

   An equal sign (=) is inserted in the active cell and in the formula bar, and the Insert Function dialog box opens, as shown in **FIGURE 2-3**. In this dialog box, you specify the function you want to use by clicking it in the Select a function list. The Select a function list initially displays recently used functions. If you don't see the function you want, you can click the Or select a category list arrow to choose the desired category. If you're not sure which category to choose, you can type the function name or a description in the Search for a function field. The AVERAGE function is a statistical function, but you don't need to open the Statistical category because this function already appears in the Most Recently Used category.

3. **Click AVERAGE in the Select a function list if necessary, read the information that appears under the list, then click OK**

   The Function Arguments dialog box opens, in which you define the range of cells you want to average.

4. **Click the Collapse button** ⊞ **in the Number1 field of the Function Arguments dialog box, select the range B4:B11 in the worksheet, then click the Expand button** ⊞ **in the Function Arguments dialog box**

   Clicking the Collapse button minimizes the dialog box so that you can select cells in the worksheet. When you click the Expand button, the dialog box is restored, as shown in **FIGURE 2-4**. You can also begin dragging in the worksheet to automatically minimize the dialog box; after you select the desired range, the dialog box is restored.

5. **Click OK**

   The Function Arguments dialog box closes, and the calculated value is displayed in cell B15. The average expenses per country for Quarter 1 is 4453.0813.

6. **Click cell C15, click the AutoSum list arrow** Σ ▾ **in the Editing group on the Home tab, then click Average**

   A ScreenTip beneath cell C15 displays the arguments needed to complete the function. The text "number1" is in boldface, telling you that the next step is to supply the first cell in the group you want to average.

7. **Select the range C4:C11 in the worksheet, then click the Enter button** ✓ **on the formula bar**

   The average expenses per country for the second quarter appear in cell C15.

8. **Drag the fill handle from cell C15 to cell E15**

   The formula in cell C15 is copied to the rest of the selected range, as shown in **FIGURE 2-5**.

9. **Save your work**

FIGURE 2-3: Insert Function dialog box

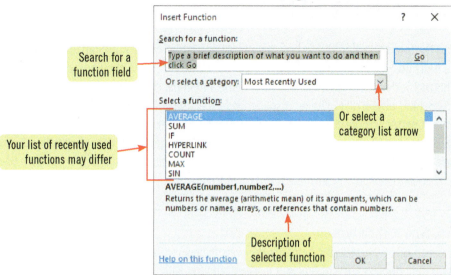

Search for a function field →

Or select a category list arrow →

Your list of recently used functions may differ →

Description of selected function

FIGURE 2-4: Expanded Function Arguments dialog box

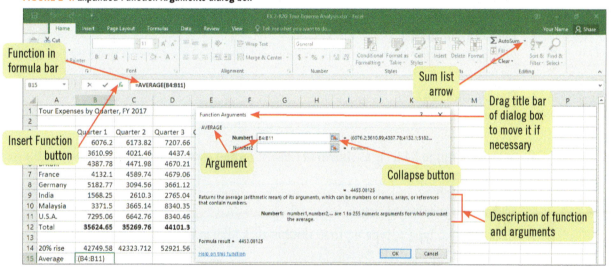

Function in formula bar

Insert Function button

Argument

Sum list arrow

Drag title bar of dialog box to move it if necessary

Collapse button

Description of function and arguments

Excel 2016

FIGURE 2-5: Average functions used in worksheet

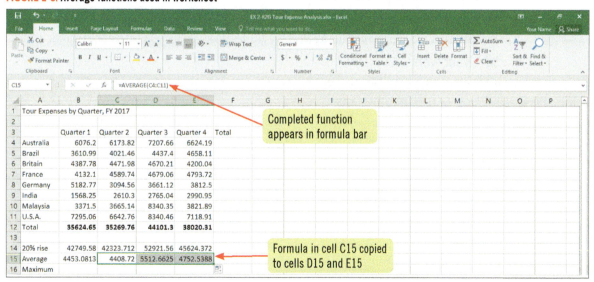

Completed function appears in formula bar

Formula in cell C15 copied to cells D15 and E15

Working with Formulas and Functions

Excel 29

Type a Function

Learning Outcomes
- Select a function by typing
- Use AutoComplete to copy formulas

In addition to using the Insert Function dialog box, the AutoSum button, or the AutoSum list arrow on the Ribbon to enter a function, you can manually type the function into a cell and then complete the arguments needed. This method requires that you know the name and initial characters of the function, but it can be faster than opening several dialog boxes. Experienced Excel users often prefer this method, but it is only an alternative, not better or more correct than any other method. The Excel **Formula AutoComplete** feature makes it easier to enter function names by typing, because it suggests functions depending on the first letters you type. **CASE** *You want to calculate the maximum and minimum quarterly expenses in your worksheet, and you decide to manually enter these statistical functions.*

STEPS

1. **Click cell B16, type =, then type m**

   Because you are manually typing this function, it is necessary to begin with the equal sign (=). The Formula AutoComplete feature displays a list of function names beginning with "M" beneath cell B16. Once you type an equal sign in a cell, each letter you type acts as a trigger to activate the Formula AutoComplete feature. This feature minimizes the amount of typing you need to do to enter a function and reduces typing and syntax errors.

2. **Click MAX in the list**

   Clicking any function in the Formula AutoComplete list opens a ScreenTip next to the list that describes the function.

3. **Double-click MAX**

   The function is inserted in the cell, and a ScreenTip appears beneath the cell to help you complete the formula. See **FIGURE 2-6**.

4. **Select the range B4:B11, as shown in FIGURE 2-7, then click the Enter button ✔ on the formula bar**

   The result, 7295.06, appears in cell B16. When you completed the entry, the closing parenthesis was automatically added to the formula.

5. **Click cell B17, type =, type m, then double-click MIN in the list of function names**

   The MIN function appears in the cell.

6. **Select the range B4:B11, then press [Enter]**

   The result, 1568.25, appears in cell B17.

7. **Select the range B16:B17, then drag the fill handle from cell B17 to cell E17**

   The maximum and minimum values for all of the quarters appear in the selected range, as shown in **FIGURE 2-8**.

8. **Save your work**

Using the COUNT and COUNTA functions

When you select a range, a count of cells in the range that are not blank appears in the status bar. You can use this information to determine things such as how many team members entered project hours in a worksheet. For example, if you select the range A1:A5 and only cells A1, A4, and A5 contain data, the status bar displays "Count: 3." To count nonblank cells more precisely, or to incorporate these calculations in a worksheet, you can use the COUNT and COUNTA functions. The COUNT function returns the number of cells in a range that contain numeric data, including numbers, dates, and formulas. The COUNTA function returns the number of cells in a range that contain any data at all, including numeric data, labels, and even a blank space. For example, the formula =COUNT(A1:A5) returns the number of cells in the range that contain numeric data, and the formula =COUNTA(A1:A5) returns the number of cells in the range that are not empty. If you use the COUNT functions in the Quick Analysis tool, the calculation is entered in the cell immediately beneath the selected range.

FIGURE 2-6: MAX function in progress

13					
14	20% rise	42749.58	42323.712	52921.56	45624.372
15	Average	4453.0813	4408.72	5512.6625	4752.5388
16	Maximum	=MAX(			
17	Minimum	MAX(**number1**, [number2], ...)			

FIGURE 2-7: Completing the MAX function

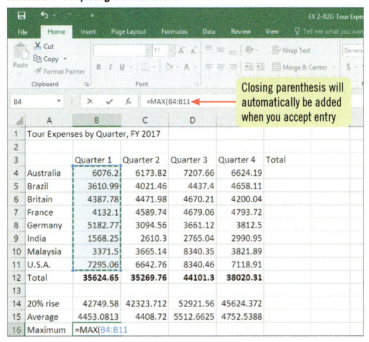

FIGURE 2-8: Completed MAX and MIN functions

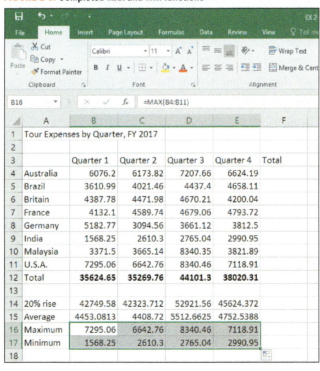

Excel 2016

Copy and Move Cell Entries

Learning
Outcomes
- Copy a range to the Clipboard
- Paste a Clipboard entry
- Empty cell contents
- Copy cell contents

There are three ways you can copy or move cells and ranges (or the contents within them) from one location to another: the Cut, Copy, and Paste buttons on the Home tab on the Ribbon; the fill handle in the lower-right corner of the active cell or range; or the drag-and-drop feature. When you copy cells, the original data remains in the original location; when you cut or move cells, the original data is deleted from its original location. You can also cut, copy, and paste cells or ranges from one worksheet to another. **CASE** *In addition to the 20% rise in tour expenses, you also want to show a 30% rise. Rather than retype this information, you copy and move selected cells.*

STEPS

QUICK TIP

To cut or copy selected cell contents, activate the cell, then select the characters within the cell that you want to cut or copy.

1. **Select the range B3:E3, then click the Copy button 📋 in the Clipboard group on the Home tab**

   The selected range (B3:E3) is copied to the **Clipboard**, a temporary Windows storage area that holds the selections you copy or cut. A moving border surrounds the selected range until you press [Esc] or copy an additional item to the Clipboard.

2. **Click the launcher 🔲 in the Clipboard group**

   The Office Clipboard opens in the Clipboard task pane, as shown in **FIGURE 2-9**. When you copy or cut an item, it is cut or copied both to the Clipboard provided by Windows and to the Office Clipboard. Unlike the Windows Clipboard, which holds just one item at a time, the Office Clipboard contains up to 24 of the most recently cut or copied items from any Office program. Your Clipboard task pane may contain more items than shown in the figure.

QUICK TIP

Once the Office Clipboard contains 24 items, the oldest existing item is automatically deleted each time you add an item.

3. **Click cell B19, then click the Paste button in the Clipboard group**

   A copy of the contents of range B3:E3 is pasted into the range B19:E19. When pasting an item from the Office Clipboard or Clipboard into a worksheet, you only need to specify the upper left cell of the range where you want to paste the selection. Notice that the information you copied remains in the original range B3:E3; if you had cut instead of copied, the information would have been deleted from its original location once it was pasted.

4. **Press [Delete]**

   The selected cells are empty. You have decided to paste the cells in a different row. You can repeatedly paste an item from the Office Clipboard as many times as you like, as long as the item remains in the Office Clipboard.

QUICK TIP

You can also close the Office Clipboard pane by clicking the launcher in the Clipboard group.

5. **Click cell B20, click the first item in the Office Clipboard, then click the Close button ✖ on the Clipboard task pane**

   Cells B20:E20 contain the copied labels.

6. **Click cell A14, press and hold [Ctrl], point to any edge of the cell until the pointer changes to ⥱, drag cell A14 to cell A21, release the mouse button, then release [Ctrl]**

   The copy pointer ⥱ continues to appear as you drag, as shown in **FIGURE 2-10**. When you release the mouse button, the contents of cell A14 are copied to cell A21.

7. **Click to the right of 2 in the formula bar, press [Backspace], type 3, then click the Enter button ✓**

8. **Click cell B21, type =, click cell B12, type *1.3, click ✓ on the formula bar, then save your work**

   This new formula calculates a 30% increase of the expenses for Quarter 1, though using a different method from what you previously used. Anything you multiply by 1.3 returns an amount that is 130% of the original amount, or a 30% increase. Compare your screen to **FIGURE 2-11**.

FIGURE 2-9: Copied data in Office Clipboard

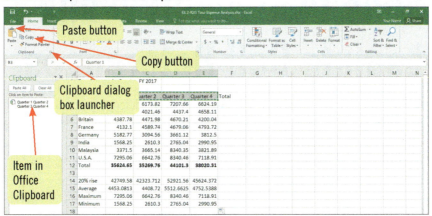

FIGURE 2-10: Copying cell contents with drag-and-drop

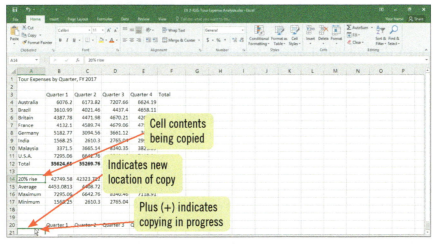

FIGURE 2-11: Formula entered to calculate a 30% increase

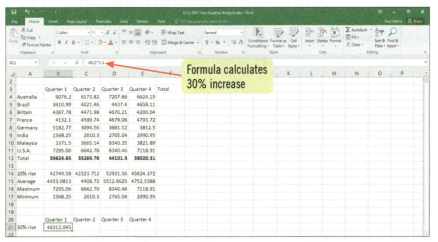

Inserting and deleting selected cells

As you add formulas to your workbook, you may need to insert or delete cells. When you do this, Excel automatically adjusts cell references to reflect their new locations. To insert cells, click the Insert list arrow in the Cells group on the Home tab, then click Insert Cells. The Insert dialog box opens, asking if you want to insert a cell and move the current active cell down or to the right of the new one. To delete one or more selected cells, click the Delete list arrow in the Cells group, click Delete Cells, and in the Delete dialog box, indicate which way you want to move the adjacent cells. When using this option, be careful not to disturb row or column alignment that may be necessary to maintain the accuracy of cell references in the worksheet. Click the Insert button or Delete button in the Cells group to insert or delete a single cell.

Learning
Outcomes
• Identify cell
  referencing
• Identify when to
  use absolute or
  relative cell
  references

Understand Relative and Absolute Cell References

As you work in Excel, you may want to reuse formulas in different parts of a worksheet to reduce the amount of data you have to retype. For example, you might want to include a what-if analysis in one part of a worksheet showing a set of sales projections if sales increase by 10%. To include another analysis in another part of the worksheet showing projections if sales increase by 50%, you can copy the formulas from one section to another and simply change the "1" to a "5". But when you copy formulas, it is important to make sure that they refer to the correct cells. To do this, you need to understand the difference between relative and absolute cell references. **CASE** *You plan to reuse formulas in different parts of your worksheets, so you want to understand relative and absolute cell references.*

DETAILS

Consider the following when using relative and absolute cell references:

• **Use relative references when you want to preserve the relationship to the formula location**

When you create a formula that references another cell, Excel normally does not "record" the exact cell address for the cell being referenced in the formula. Instead, it looks at the relationship that cell has to the cell containing the formula. For example, in **FIGURE 2-12**, cell F5 contains the formula: =SUM(B5:E5). When Excel retrieves values to calculate the formula in cell F5, it actually looks for "the four cells to the left of the formula," which in this case is cells B5:E5. This way, if you copy the cell to a new location, such as cell F6, the results will reflect the new formula location and will automatically retrieve the values in cells B6, C6, D6, and E6. These are **relative cell references**, because Excel is recording the input cells *in relation to* or *relative to* the formula cell.

In most cases, you want to use relative cell references when copying or moving, so this is the Excel default. In **FIGURE 2-12**, the formulas in cells F5:F12 and cells B13:F13 contain relative cell references. They total the "four cells to the left of" or the "eight cells above" the formulas.

• **Use absolute cell references when you want to preserve the exact cell address in a formula**

There are times when you want Excel to retrieve formula information from a specific cell, and you don't want the cell address in the formula to change when you copy it to a new location. For example, you might have a price in a specific cell that you want to use in all formulas, regardless of their location. If you use relative cell referencing, the formula results would be incorrect, because the formula would reference a different cell every time you copy it. Therefore, you need to use an **absolute cell reference**, which is a reference that does not change when you copy the formula.

You create an absolute cell reference by placing a $ (dollar sign) in front of both the column letter and the row number of the cell address. You can either type the dollar sign when typing the cell address in a formula (for example, "=C12*B16") or you can select a cell address on the formula bar and then press [F4], and the dollar signs are added automatically. **FIGURE 2-13** shows formulas containing both absolute and relative references. The formulas in cells B19 to E26 use absolute cell references to refer to a potential sales increase of 50%, shown in cell B16.

FIGURE 2-12: Formulas containing relative references

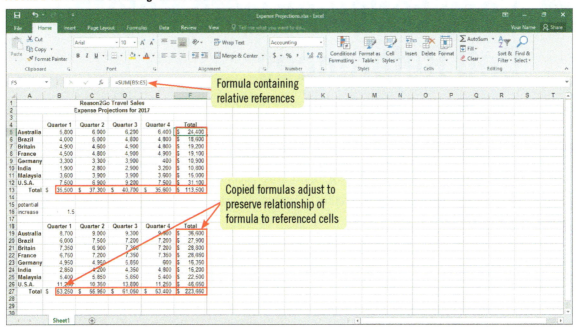

FIGURE 2-13: Formulas containing absolute and relative references

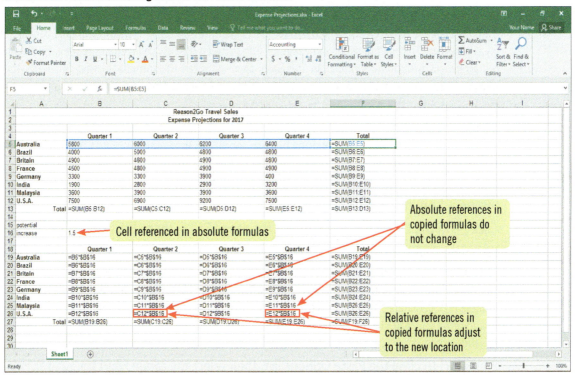

Using a mixed reference

Sometimes when you copy a formula, you want to change the row reference, but keep the column reference the same. This type of cell referencing combines elements of both absolute and relative referencing and is called a **mixed reference**. For example, when copied, a formula containing the mixed reference C$14 would change the column letter relative to its new location, but not the row number. In the mixed reference $C14, the column letter would not change, but the row number would be updated relative to its location. Like an absolute reference, a mixed reference can be created by pressing the [F4] function key with the cell reference selected. With each press of the [F4] key, you cycle through all the possible combinations of relative, absolute, and mixed references (C14, C14, C$14, and $C14).

Copy Formulas with Relative Cell References

Learning Outcomes
- Copy and Paste formulas with relative cell references
- Examine Auto Fill and Paste Options
- Use the Fill button

Copying and moving a cell allow you to reuse a formula you've already created. Copying cells is usually faster than retyping the formulas in them and helps to prevent typing errors. If the cells you are copying contain relative cell references and you want to maintain the relative referencing, you don't need to make any changes to the cells before copying them. **CASE** *You want to copy the formula in cell B21, which calculates the 30% increase in quarterly expenses for Quarter 1, to cells C21 through E21. You also want to create formulas to calculate total expenses for each tour country.*

STEPS

QUICK TIP

To paste only specific components of a copied cell or range, click the Paste list arrow in the Clipboard group, then click Paste Special. You can selectively copy formats, formulas, values, comments, and validation rules; transpose columns and rows; paste a link; or add, subtract, multiply, or divide using the Paste Special dialog box.

1. **Click cell B21 if necessary, then click the Copy button in the Clipboard group on the Home tab**

    The formula for calculating the 30% expense increase during Quarter 1 is copied to the Clipboard. Notice that the formula =B12*1.3 appears in the formula bar, and a moving border surrounds the active cell.

2. **Click cell C21, then click the Paste button** *(not the list arrow) in the Clipboard group*

    The formula from cell B21 is copied into cell C21, where the new result of 45850.688 appears. Notice in the formula bar that the cell references have changed so that cell C12 is referenced instead of B12. This formula contains a relative cell reference, which tells Excel to substitute new cell references within the copied formulas as necessary. This maintains the same relationship between the new cell containing the formula and the cell references within the formula. In this case, Excel adjusted the formula so that cell C12—the cell reference nine rows above C21—replaced cell B12, the cell reference nine rows above B21.

3. **Drag the fill handle from cell C21 to cell E21**

    A formula similar to the one in cell C21 now appears in cells D21 and E21. After you use the fill handle to copy cell contents, the **Auto Fill Options button** appears, as shown in **FIGURE 2-14**. You can use the Auto Fill Options button to fill the cells with only specific elements of the copied cell if you wish.

4. **Click cell F4, click the AutoSum button Σ in the Editing group, then click the Enter button ✓ on the formula bar**

5. **Click in the Clipboard group, select the range F5:F6, then click**

    See **FIGURE 2-15**. After you click the Paste button, the **Paste Options button** appears.

6. **Click the Paste Options button adjacent to the selected range**

    You can use the Paste options list to paste only specific elements of the copied selection if you wish. The formula for calculating total expenses for tours in Britain appears in the formula bar. You would like totals to appear in cells F7:F11. The Fill button in the Editing group can be used to copy the formula into the remaining cells.

7. **Press [Esc] to close the Paste Options list, then select the range F6:F11**

8. **Click the Fill button in the Editing group, then click Down**

    The formulas containing relative references are copied to each cell. Compare your worksheet to **FIGURE 2-16**.

9. **Save your work**

FIGURE 2-14: Formula copied using the fill handle

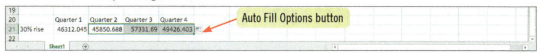

FIGURE 2-15: Formulas pasted in the range F5:F6

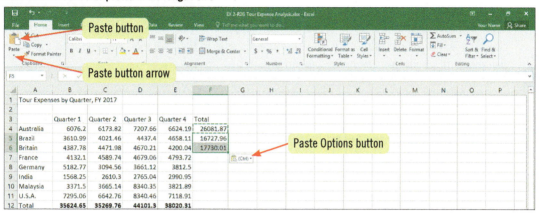

FIGURE 2-16: Formula copied using Fill Down

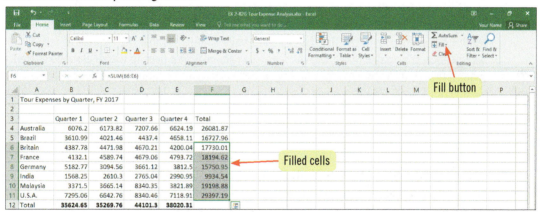

Using Paste Preview

You can selectively copy formulas, values, or other choices using the Paste list arrow, and you can see how the pasted contents will look using the Paste Preview feature. When you click the Paste list arrow, a gallery of paste option icons opens. When you point to an icon, a preview of how the content will be pasted using that option is shown in the worksheet. Options include pasting values only, pasting values with number formatting, pasting formulas only, pasting formatting only, pasting transposed data so that column data appears in rows and row data appears in columns, and pasting with no borders (to remove any borders around pasted cells).

Copy Formulas with Absolute Cell References

Learning Outcomes
- Create an absolute cell reference
- Use the fill handle to copy absolute cell references

When copying cells, you might want one or more cell references in a formula to remain unchanged. In such an instance, you need to apply an absolute cell reference before copying the formula to preserve the specific cell address when the formula is copied. You create an absolute reference by placing a dollar sign ($) before the column letter and row number of the address (for example, A1). **CASE** *You need to do some what-if analysis to see how various percentage increases might affect total expenses. You decide to add a column that calculates a possible increase in the total tour expenses, and then change the percentage to see various potential results.*

STEPS

1. **Click cell G1, type Change, then press [Enter]**

2. **Type 1.1, then press [Enter]**
   You store the increase factor that will be used in the what-if analysis in this cell (G2). The value 1.1 can be used to calculate a 10% increase: anything you multiply by 1.1 returns an amount that is 110% of the original amount.

3. **Click cell H3, type What if?, then press [Enter]**

4. **In cell H4, type =, click cell F4, type *, click cell G2, then click the Enter button ✓ on the formula bar**
   The result, 28690.1, appears in cell H4. This value represents the total annual expenses for Australia if there is a 10% increase. You want to perform a what-if analysis for all the tour countries.

> **QUICK TIP**
> Before you copy or move a formula, always check to see if you need to use an absolute cell reference.

5. **Drag the fill handle from cell H4 to cell H11**
   The resulting values in the range H5:H11 are all zeros, which is not the result you wanted. Because you used relative cell addressing in cell H4, the copied formula adjusted so that the formula in cell H5 is =F5*G3; because there is no value in cell G3, the result is 0, an error. You need to use an absolute reference in the formula to keep the formula from adjusting itself. That way, it will always reference cell G2.

> **QUICK TIP**
> When changing a cell reference to an absolute reference, make sure the reference is selected or the insertion point is next to it in the cell before pressing [F4].

6. **Click cell H4, press [F2] to change to Edit mode, then press [F4]**
   When you press [F2], the range finder outlines the arguments of the equation in blue and red. The insertion point appears next to the G2 cell reference in cell H4. When you press [F4], dollar signs are inserted in the G2 cell reference, making it an absolute reference. See **FIGURE 2-17**.

7. **Click ✓, then drag the fill handle from cell H4 to cell H11**
   Because the formula correctly contains an absolute cell reference, the correct values for a 10% increase appear in cells H4:H11. You now want to see what a 20% increase in expenses looks like.

8. **Click cell G2, type 1.2, then click ✓**
   The values in the range H4:H11 change to reflect the 20% increase. Compare your worksheet to **FIGURE 2-18**.

9. **Save your work**

FIGURE 2-17: Absolute reference created in formula

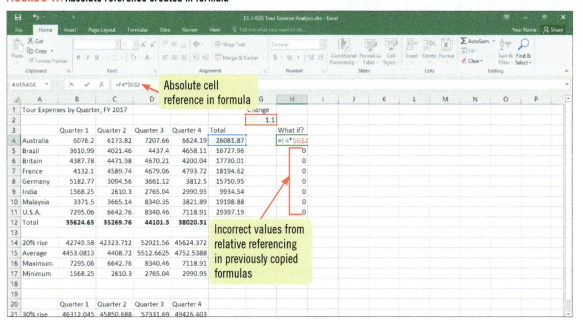

Absolute cell reference in formula

Incorrect values from relative referencing in previously copied formulas

FIGURE 2-18: What-if analysis with modified change factor

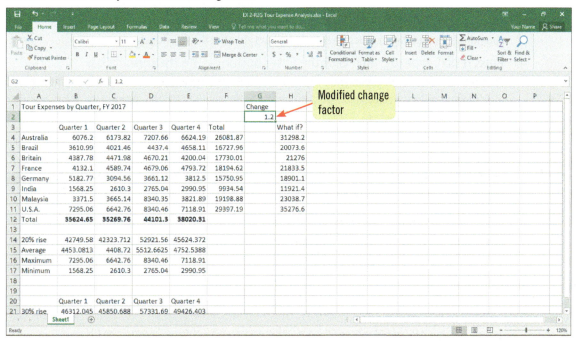

Modified change factor

Using the fill handle for sequential text or values

Often, you need to fill cells with sequential text: months of the year, days of the week, years, or text plus a number (Quarter 1, Quarter 2,...). For example, you might want to create a worksheet that calculates data for every month of the year. Using the fill handle, you can quickly and easily create labels for the months of the year just by typing "January" in a cell. Drag the fill handle from the cell containing "January" until you have all the monthly labels you need. You can also easily fill cells with a date sequence by dragging the fill handle on a single cell containing a date. You can fill cells with a number sequence (such as 1, 2, 3,...) by dragging the fill handle on a selection of two or more cells that contain the sequence. To create a number sequence using the value in a single cell, press and hold [Ctrl] as you drag the fill handle of the cell. As you drag the fill handle, Excel automatically extends the existing sequence into the additional cells. (The content of the last filled cell appears in the ScreenTip.) To choose from all the fill series options for the current selection, click the Fill button in the Editing group on the Home tab, then click Series to open the Series dialog box.

Excel 2016

Round a Value with a Function

Learning Outcomes
- Use Formula AutoComplete to insert a function
- Copy an edited formula

The more you explore features and tools in Excel, the more ways you'll find to simplify your work and convey information more efficiently. For example, cells containing financial data are often easier to read if they contain fewer decimal places than those that appear by default. You can round a value or formula result to a specific number of decimal places by using the ROUND function. **CASE** ▶ In your worksheet, you'd like to round the cells showing the 20% rise in expenses to show fewer digits; after all, it's not important to show cents in the projections, only whole dollars. You want Excel to round the calculated value to the nearest integer. You decide to edit cell B14 so it includes the ROUND function, and then copy the edited formula into the other formulas in this row.

STEPS

1. **Click cell B14, then click to the right of = in the formula bar**

   You want to position the function at the beginning of the formula, before any values or arguments.

2. **Type RO**

   Formula AutoComplete displays a list of functions beginning with RO beneath the formula bar.

3. **Double-click ROUND in the functions list**

   The new function and an opening parenthesis are added to the formula, as shown in **FIGURE 2-19**. A few additional modifications are needed to complete your edit of the formula. You need to indicate the number of decimal places to which the function should round numbers, and you also need to add a closing parenthesis around the set of arguments that comes after the ROUND function.

4. **Press [END], type ,0), then click the Enter button ✓ on the formula bar**

   The comma separates the arguments within the formula, and 0 indicates that you don't want any decimal places to appear in the calculated value. When you complete the edit, the parentheses at either end of the formula briefly become bold, indicating that the formula has the correct number of open and closed parentheses and is balanced.

5. **Drag the fill handle from cell B14 to cell E14**

   The formula in cell B14 is copied to the range C14:E14. All the values are rounded to display no decimal places. Compare your worksheet to **FIGURE 2-20**.

6. **Scroll down so row 25 is visible, click cell A25, type your name, then click ✓**

7. **Save your work, preview the worksheet in the Print place in Backstage view, then submit your work to your Instructor as directed**

8. **Exit Excel**

Using Auto Fill options

When you use the fill handle to copy cells, the Auto Fill Options button appears. Auto Fill options differ depending on what you are copying. If you had selected cells containing a series (such as "Monday" and "Tuesday") and then used the fill handle, you would see options for continuing the series (such as "Wednesday" and "Thursday") or for simply pasting the copied cells. Clicking the Auto Fill Options button opens a list that lets you choose from the following options: Copy Cells, Fill Series (if applicable), Fill Formatting Only, Fill Without Formatting, or Flash Fill. Choosing Copy Cells means that the cell's contents and its formatting will be copied. The Fill Formatting Only option copies only the formatting attributes, but not cell contents. The Fill Without Formatting option copies the cell contents, but no formatting attributes. Copy Cells is the default option when using the fill handle to copy a cell, so if you want to copy the cell's contents and its formatting, you can ignore the Auto Fill Options button. The Flash Fill option allows you to create customized fill ranges on the fly, such as 2, 4, 6, 8, 10, by entering at least two values in a pattern: Excel automatically senses the pattern.

FIGURE 2-19: ROUND function added to an existing formula

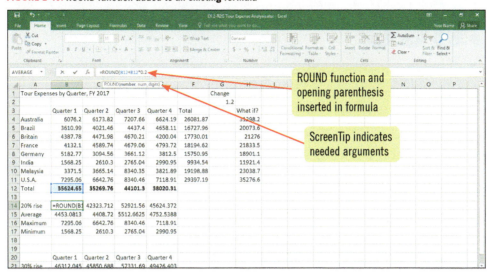

ROUND function and opening parenthesis inserted in formula

ScreenTip indicates needed arguments

FIGURE 2-20: Completed worksheet

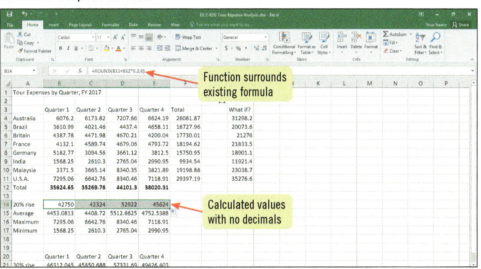

Function surrounds existing formula

Calculated values with no decimals

Creating a new workbook using a template

Excel **templates** are predesigned workbook files intended to save time when you create common documents such as balance sheets, budgets, or time cards. Templates contain labels, values, formulas, and formatting, so all you have to do is customize them with your own information. Excel comes with many templates, and you can also create your own or find additional templates on the web. Unlike a typical workbook, which has the file extension .xlsx, a template has the extension .xltx. To create a workbook using a template, click the File tab, then click New on the navigation bar. The New place in Backstage view displays thumbnails of some of the many templates available. The Blank workbook template is selected by default and is used to create a blank workbook with no content or special formatting. To select a different template, click one of the selections in the New place, view the preview, then click Create. **FIGURE 2-21** shows an example. (Your available templates may differ.) When you click

Create, a new workbook is created based on the template; when you save the new file in the default format, it has the regular .xlsx extension. To save a workbook of your own as a template, open the Save As dialog box, click the Save as type list arrow, then change the file type to Excel Template.

FIGURE 2-21: Previewing the Budget Planner template

Practice

Concepts Review

Label each element of the Excel worksheet window shown in FIGURE 2-22.

FIGURE 2-22

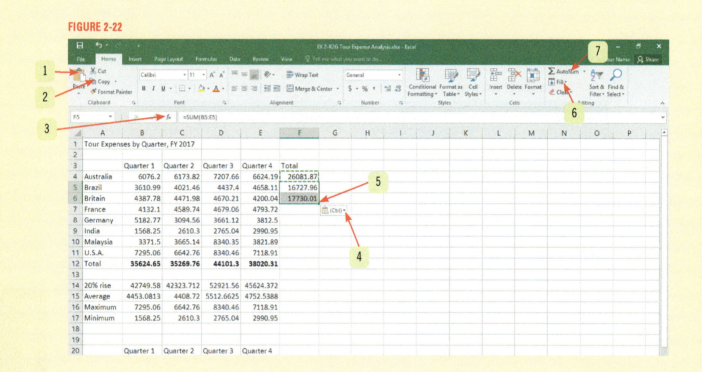

Match each term or button with the statement that best describes it.

8. **Launcher**
9. **Fill handle**
10. **Drag-and-drop method**
11. **Formula AutoComplete**
12. **[Delete] key**

a. Clears the contents of selected cells
b. Item on the Ribbon that opens a dialog box or task pane
c. Lets you move or copy data from one cell to another without using the Clipboard
d. Displays an alphabetical list of functions from which you can choose
e. Lets you copy cell contents or continue a series of data into a range of selected cells

Select the best answer from the list of choices.

13. You can use any of the following features to enter a new function *except*:

   a. Insert Function button.

   b. Formula AutoComplete.

   c. AutoSum list arrow.

   d. Clipboard.

14. Which key do you press and hold to copy while dragging and dropping selected cells?

   a. [Alt]

   b. [Ctrl]

   c. [F2]

   d. [Tab]

15. What type of cell reference is C$19?

   a. Relative

   b. Absolute

   c. Mixed

   d. Certain

16. Which key do you press to convert a relative cell reference to an absolute cell reference?

   a. [F2]

   b. [F4]

   c. [F5]

   d. [F6]

17. What type of cell reference changes when it is copied?

   a. Circular

   b. Absolute

   c. Relative

   d. Specified

Skills Review

1. Create a complex formula.

   a. Open EX 2-2.xlsx from the location where you store your Data Files, then save it as **EX 2-Construction Supply Company Inventory**.

   b. Select the range B4:B8, click the Totals tab in the Quick Analysis tool, then click the AutoSum button.

   c. Use the fill handle to copy the formula in cell B9 to cells C9:E9.

   d. In cell B11, create a complex formula that calculates a 30% decrease in the total number of cases of pylons.

   e. Use the fill handle to copy this formula into cell C11 through cell E11.

   f. Save your work.

2. Insert a function.

   a. Use the AutoSum list arrow to create a formula in cell B13 that averages the number of cases of pylons in each storage area.

   b. Use the Insert Function button to create a formula in cell B14 that calculates the maximum number of cases of pylons in a storage area.

   c. Use the AutoSum list arrow to create a formula in cell B15 that calculates the minimum number of cases of pylons in a storage area.

   d. Save your work.

3. **Type a function.**
   a. In cell C13, type a formula that includes a function to average the number of cases of bricks in each storage area. (*Hint*: Use Formula AutoComplete to enter the function.)
   b. In cell C14, type a formula that includes a function to calculate the maximum number of cases of bricks in a storage area.
   c. In cell C15, type a formula that includes a function to calculate the minimum number of cases of bricks in a storage area.
   d. Save your work.

4. **Copy and move cell entries.**
   a. Select the range B3:F3.
   b. Copy the selection to the Clipboard.
   c. Open the Clipboard task pane, then paste the selection into cell B17.
   d. Close the Clipboard task pane, then select the range A4:A9.
   e. Use the drag-and-drop method to copy the selection to cell A18. (*Hint*: The results should fill the range A18:A23.)
   f. Save your work.

5. **Understand relative and absolute cell references.**
   a. Write a brief description of the difference between relative and absolute references.
   b. List at least three situations in which you think a business might use an absolute reference in its calculations. Examples can include calculations for different types of worksheets, such as time cards, invoices, and budgets.

6. **Copy formulas with relative cell references.**
   a. Calculate the total in cell F4.
   b. Use the Fill button to copy the formula in cell F4 down to cells F5:F8.
   c. Select the range C13:C15.
   d. Use the fill handle to copy these cells to the range D13:F15.
   e. Save your work.

7. **Copy formulas with absolute cell references.**
   a. In cell H1, change the existing value to **1.575**.
   b. In cell H4, create a formula that multiplies F4 and an absolute reference to cell H1.
   c. Use the fill handle to copy the formula in cell H4 to cells H5 and H6.
   d. Use the Copy and Paste buttons to copy the formula in cell H4 to cells H7 and H8.
   e. Change the amount in cell H1 to **2.5**.
   f. Save your work.

Skills Review (continued)

8. Round a value with a function.

   a. Click cell H4.

   b. Edit this formula to include the ROUND function showing zero decimal places.

   c. Use the fill handle to copy the formula in cell H4 to the range H5:H8.

   d. Enter your name in cell A25, then compare your work to FIGURE 2-23.

   e. Save your work, preview the worksheet in Backstage view, then submit your work to your instructor as directed.

   f. Close the workbook, then exit Excel.

FIGURE 2-23

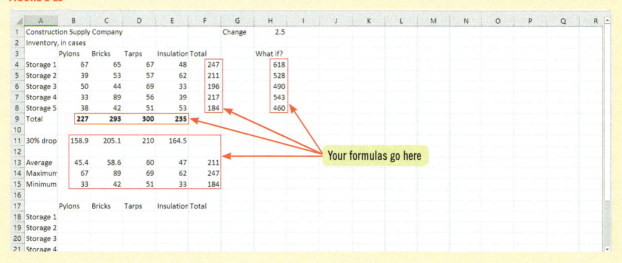

Independent Challenge 1

You are thinking of starting a small coffee shop where locals can gather. Before you begin, you need to evaluate what you think your monthly expenses will be. You've started a workbook, but need to complete the entries and add formulas.

a. Open EX 2-3.xlsx from the location where you store your Data Files, then save it as **EX 2-Coffee Shop Expenses**.

b. Make up your own expense data, and enter it in cells B4:B10. (Monthly sales are already included in the worksheet.)

c. Create a formula in cell C4 that calculates the annual rent.

d. Copy the formula in cell C4 to the range C5:C10.

e. Move the label in cell A15 to cell A14.

f. Create formulas in cells B11 and C11 that total the monthly and annual expenses.

g. Create a formula in cell C13 that calculates annual sales.

h. Create a formula in cell B14 that determines whether you will make a profit or loss, then copy the formula into cell C14.

i. Copy the labels in cells B3:C3 to cells E3:F3.

j. Type **Projected Increase** in cell G1, then type **.2** in cell H2.

k. Create a formula in cell E4 that calculates an increase in the monthly rent by the amount in cell H2. You will be copying this formula to other cells, so you'll need to use an absolute reference.

l. Create a formula in cell F4 that calculates the increased annual rent expense based on the calculation in cell E4.

m. Copy the formulas in cells E4:F4 into cells E5:F10 to calculate the remaining monthly and annual expenses.

n. Create a formula in cell E11 that calculates the total monthly expenses, then copy that formula to cell F11.

o. Copy the contents of cells B13:C13 into cells E13:F13.

p. Create formulas in cells E14 and F14 that calculate profit/loss based on the projected increase in monthly and annual expenses.

q. Change the projected increase to **.17**, then compare your work to the sample in FIGURE 2-24.

r. Enter your name in a cell in the worksheet.

s. Save your work, preview the worksheet in Backstage view, submit your work to your instructor as directed, close the workbook, and exit Excel.

FIGURE 2-24

	A	B	C	D	E	F	G	H	I
1	Estim	*Your formulas go here (your formula results will differ)*	nses				Projected Increase		
2								0.17	
3		Monthly	Annually		Monthly	Annually			
4	Rent	2500	30000		2925	35100			
5	Supplies	1600	19200		1872	22464			
6	Milk	3600	43200		4212	50544			
7	Sugar	1300	15600		1521	18252			
8	Pastries	850	10200		994.5	11934			
9	Coffee	600	7200		702	8424			
10	Utilities	750	9000		877.5	10530			
11	Total	11200	134400		13104	157248			
12									
13	Sales	24500	294000		23000	276000			
14	Profit/Loss	13300	159600		9896	118752			

Working with Formulas and Functions

Independent Challenge 2

The Office Specialists Center is a small, growing business that rents small companies space and provides limited business services. They have hired you to organize their accounting records using Excel. The owners want you to track the company's expenses. Before you were hired, one of the bookkeepers began entering last year's expenses in a workbook, but the analysis was never completed.

a. Start Excel, open EX 2-4.xlsx from the location where you store your Data Files, then save it as **EX 2-Office Specialists Center Finances**. The worksheet includes labels for functions such as the average, maximum, and minimum amounts of each of the expenses in the worksheet.

b. Think about what information would be important for the bookkeeping staff to know.

c. Using the Quick Analysis tool, create a formula in the Quarter 1 column that uses the SUM function, then copy that formula into the Total row for the remaining quarters.

d. Use the SUM function to create formulas for each expense in the Total column.

e. Create formulas for each expense and each quarter in the Average, Maximum, and Minimum columns and rows using the method of your choice.

f. Compare your worksheet to the sample shown in FIGURE 2-25.

g. Enter your name in cell A25, then save your work.

h. Preview the worksheet, then submit your work to your instructor as directed.

i. Close the workbook and exit Excel.

FIGURE 2-25

	A	B	C	D	E	F	G	H	I	J
1	Office Specialists Center									
2										
3	Operating Expenses for 2017									
4										
5	Expense	Quarter 1	Quarter 2	Quarter 3	Quarter 4	Total	Average	Maximum	Minimum	
6	Rent	10240	10240	10240	10240	40960	10240	10240	10240	
7	Utilities	9500	8482	7929	8596	34507	8626.75	9500	7929	
8	Payroll	24456	27922	26876	30415	109669	27417.3	30415	24456	
9	Insurance	9000	8594	8472	8523	34589	8647.25	9000	8472	
10	Education	4000	4081	7552	5006	20639	5159.75	7552	4000	
11	Inventory	15986	14115	14641	15465	60207	15051.8	15986	14115	
12	Total	**73182**	**73434**	**75710**	**78245**					
13										
14	Average	12197	12239	12618.3	13040.8		Your formulas go here			
15	Maximum	24456	27922	26876	30415					
16	Minimum	4000	4081	7552	5006					

Excel 2016

Independent Challenge 3

As the accounting manager of a locally owned food co-op with multiple locations, it is your responsibility to calculate accrued sales tax payments on a monthly basis and then submit the payments to the state government. You've decided to use an Excel workbook to make these calculations.

a. Start Excel, then save a new, blank workbook to the drive and folder where you store your Data Files as **EX 2-Food Co-op Sales Tax Calculations**.

b. Decide on the layout for all columns and rows. The worksheet will contain data for six stores, which you can name by store number, neighborhood, or another method of your choice. For each store, you will calculate total sales tax based on the local sales tax rate. You'll also calculate total tax owed for all six locations.

c. Make up sales data for all six stores.

d. Enter the rate to be used to calculate the sales tax, using your own local rate.

e. Create formulas to calculate the sales tax owed for each location. If you don't know the local tax rate, use **6.5%**.

f. Create a formula to total all the accrued sales tax.

g. Use the ROUND function to eliminate any decimal places in the sales tax figures for each location and in the total due.

h. Add your name to the header, then compare your work to the sample shown in FIGURE 2-26.

i. Save your work, preview the worksheet, and submit your work to your instructor as directed.

j. Close the workbook and exit Excel.

FIGURE 2-26

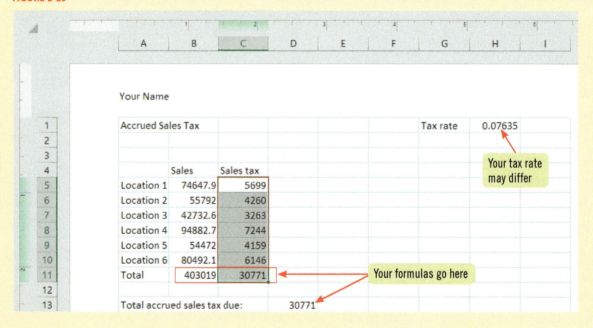

Independent Challenge 4: Explore

So many friends have come to you for help in understanding the various fees associated with purchasing a home that you've decided to create a business that specializes in helping first-time home-buyers. Your first task is to create a worksheet that clearly shows all the information a home buyer will need. Some fees are based on a percentage of the purchase price, and others are a flat fee; overall, they seem to represent a substantial amount above the purchase prices you see listed. A client has seen five houses so far that interest her; one is easily affordable, and the remaining four are all nice, but increasingly more expensive. You decide to create an Excel workbook to help her figure out the real cost of each home.

a. Find out the typical cost or percentage rate of at least three fees that are usually charged when buying a home and taking out a mortgage. (*Hint*: If you have access to the Internet, you can research the topic of home buying on the web, or you can ask friends about standard rates or percentages for items such as title insurance, credit reports, and inspection fees.)

b. Start Excel, then save a new, blank workbook to the location where you store your Data Files as **EX 2-Home Purchase Fees Worksheet**.

c. Create labels and enter data for at least five homes. If you enter this information across the columns in your worksheet, you should have one column for each house, with the purchase price in the cell below each label. Be sure to enter a different purchase price for each house.

d. Create labels for the Fees column and for an Amount or Rate column. Enter the information for each of the fees you have researched.

e. In each house column, enter formulas that calculate the fee for each item. The formulas (and use of absolute or relative referencing) will vary depending on whether the charges are a flat fee or based on a percentage of the purchase price. Make sure that the formulas for items that are based on a percentage of the purchase price (such as the fees for the Title Insurance Policy, Loan Origination, and Underwriter) contain absolute references. A sample of what your workbook might look like is shown in **FIGURE 2-27**.

f. Total the fees for each house, then create formulas that add the total fees to the purchase price.

g. Enter a title for the worksheet and include your client's name (or use Client 1) in the header.

h. Enter your name in the header, save your work, preview the worksheet, then submit your work to your instructor as directed.

i. Close the file and exit Excel.

Excel 2016

FIGURE 2-27

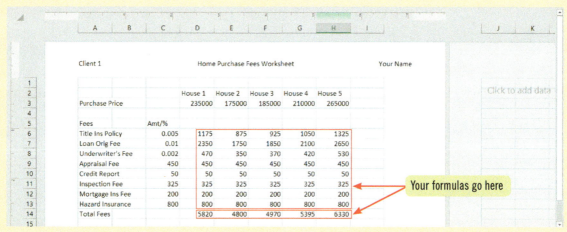

Visual Workshop

Create the worksheet shown in **FIGURE 2-28** using the skills you learned in this module. Save the workbook as **EX 2-Monthly Expenses** to the location where you store your Data Files. Enter your name and worksheet title in the header as shown, hide the gridlines, preview the worksheet, and then submit your work to your instructor as directed. (*Hint:* Change the Zoom factor to 90% by using the Zoom out button.)

FIGURE 2-28

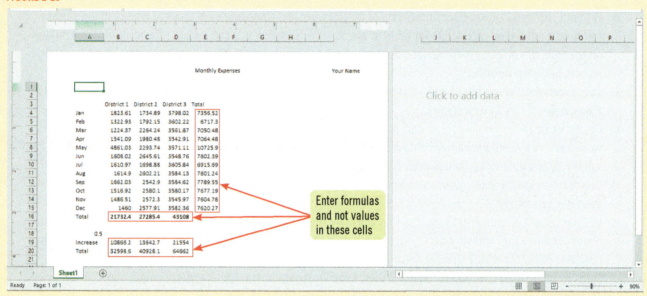

Formatting a Worksheet

CASE ▶ The marketing managers at Reason2Go have requested data from all R2G locations for advertising expenses incurred during the first quarter of this year. Mary Watson has created a worksheet listing this information. She asks you to format the worksheet to make it easier to read and to call attention to important data.

Module Objectives

After completing this module, you will be able to:

- Format values
- Change font and font size
- Change font styles and alignment
- Adjust column width
- Insert and delete rows and columns
- Apply colors, patterns, and borders
- Apply conditional formatting
- Rename and move a worksheet
- Check spelling

Files You Will Need

EX 3-1.xlsx

EX 3-2.xlsx

EX 3-3.xlsx

EX 3-4.xlsx

EX 3-5.xlsx

Format Values

The **format** of a cell determines how the labels and values look—for example, whether the contents appear boldfaced, italicized, or with dollar signs and commas. Formatting changes only the appearance of a value or label; it does not alter the actual data in any way. To format a cell or range, first you select it, then you apply the formatting using the Ribbon, Mini toolbar, or a keyboard shortcut. You can apply formatting before or after you enter data in a cell or range. **CASE** *Mary has provided you with a worksheet that details advertising expenses, and you're ready to improve its appearance and readability. You start by formatting some of the values so they are displayed as currency, percentages, and dates.*

STEPS

1. **Start Excel, open the file EX 3-1.xlsx from the location where you store your Data Files, then save it as EX 3-R2G Advertising Expenses**

   This worksheet is difficult to interpret because all the information is crowded and looks the same. In some columns, the contents appear cut off because there is too much data to fit given the current column width. You decide not to widen the columns yet, because the other changes you plan to make might affect column width and row height. The first thing you want to do is format the data showing the cost of each ad.

2. **Select the range D4:D32, then click the Accounting Number Format button $ in the Number group on the Home tab**

   The default Accounting **number format** adds dollar signs and two decimal places to the data, as shown in **FIGURE 3-1**. Formatting this data in Accounting format makes it clear that its values are monetary values. Excel automatically resizes the column to display the new formatting. The Accounting and Currency number formats are both used for monetary values, but the Accounting format aligns currency symbols and decimal points of numbers in a column.

3. **Select the range F4:H32, then click the Comma Style button ⁹ in the Number group**

   The values in columns F, G, and H display the Comma Style format, which does not include a dollar sign but can be useful for some types of accounting data.

4. **Select the range J4:J32, click the Number Format list arrow, click Percentage, then click the Increase Decimal button in the Number group**

   The data in the % of Total column is now formatted with a percent sign (%) and three decimal places. The Number Format list arrow lets you choose from popular number formats and shows an example of what the selected cell or cells would look like in each format (when multiple cells are selected, the example is based on the first cell in the range). Each time you click the Increase Decimal button, you add one decimal place; clicking the button twice would add two decimal places.

5. **Click the Decrease Decimal button in the Number group twice**

   Two decimal places are removed from the percentage values in column J.

6. **Select the range B4:B31, then click the launcher in the Number group**

   The Format Cells dialog box opens with the Date category already selected on the Number tab.

7. **Select the first 14-Mar-12 format in the Type list box as shown in FIGURE 3-2, then click OK**

   The dates in column B appear in the 14-Mar-12 format. The second 14-Mar-12 format in the list (visible if you scroll down the list) displays all days in two digits (it adds a leading zero if the day is only a single-digit number), while the one you chose displays single-digit days without a leading zero.

8. **Select the range C4:C31, right-click the range, click Format Cells on the shortcut menu, click 14-Mar in the Type list box in the Format Cells dialog box, then click OK**

   Compare your worksheet to **FIGURE 3-3**.

9. **Press [Ctrl][Home], then save your work**

FIGURE 3-1: Accounting number format applied to range

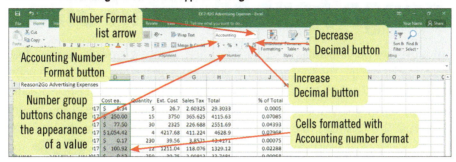

FIGURE 3-2: Format Cells dialog box

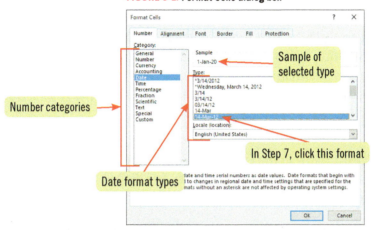

FIGURE 3-3: Worksheet with formatted values

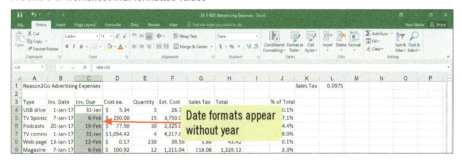

Formatting as a table

Excel includes 60 predefined **table styles** to make it easy to format selected worksheet cells as a table. You can apply table styles to any range of cells that you want to format quickly, or even to an entire worksheet, but they're especially useful for those ranges with labels in the left column and top row, and totals in the bottom row or right column. To apply a table style, select the data to be formatted or click anywhere within the intended range (Excel can automatically detect a range of cells filled with data), click the Format as Table button in the Styles group on the Home tab, then click a style in the gallery, as shown in **FIGURE 3-4.** Table styles are organized in three categories: Light, Medium, and Dark. Once you click a style, Excel asks you to confirm the range selection, then applies the style. Once you have formatted a range as a table, you can use Live Preview to preview the table in other styles by pointing to any style in the Table Styles gallery.

FIGURE 3-4: Table Styles gallery

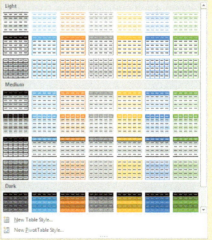

Change Font and Font Size

A **font** is the name for a collection of characters (letters, numbers, symbols, and punctuation marks) with a similar, specific design. The **font size** is the physical size of the text, measured in units called points. A **point** is equal to 1/72 of an inch. The default font and font size in Excel is 11-point Calibri. TABLE 3-1 shows several fonts in different font sizes. You can change the font and font size of any cell or range using the Font and Font Size list arrows. The Font and Font Size list arrows appear on the Home tab on the Ribbon and on the Mini toolbar, which opens when you right-click a cell or range. **CASE** *You want to change the font and font size of the labels and the worksheet title so that they stand out more from the data.*

STEPS

1. **Click the Font list arrow in the Font group on the Home tab, scroll down in the Font list to see an alphabetical listing of the fonts available on your computer, then click Times New Roman, as shown in FIGURE 3-5**

   The font in cell A1 changes to Times New Roman. Notice that the font names on the list are displayed in the font they represent.

2. **Click the Font Size list arrow in the Font group, then click 20**

   The worksheet title appears in 20-point Times New Roman, and the Font and Font Size list boxes on the Home tab display the new font and font size information.

3. **Click the Increase Font Size button A˄ in the Font group twice**

   The font size of the title increases to 24 point.

4. **Select the range A3:J3, right-click, then click the Font list arrow on the Mini toolbar**

   The Mini toolbar includes the most commonly used formatting tools, so it's great for making quick formatting changes.

5. **Scroll down in the Font list and click Times New Roman, click the Font Size list arrow on the Mini toolbar, then click 14**

   The Mini toolbar closes when you move the pointer away from the selection. Compare your worksheet to FIGURE 3-6. Notice that some of the column labels are now too wide to appear fully in the column. Excel does not automatically adjust column widths to accommodate cell formatting; you have to adjust column widths manually. You'll learn to do this in a later lesson.

6. **Save your work**

TABLE 3-1: Examples of fonts and font sizes

font	12 point	24 point
Calibri	Excel	Excel
Playbill	Excel	Excel
Comic Sans MS	Excel	Excel
Times New Roman	Excel	Excel

FIGURE 3-5: Font list

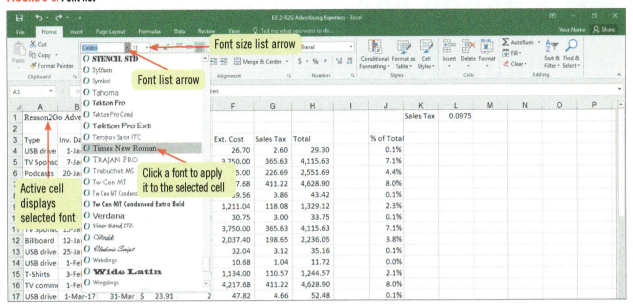

FIGURE 3-6: Worksheet with formatted title and column labels

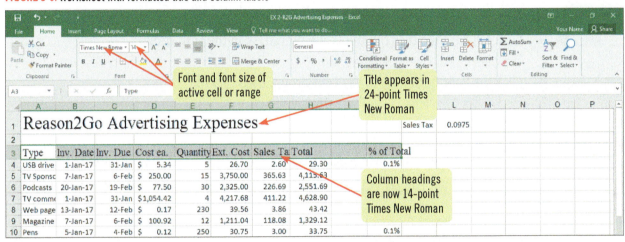

Inserting and adjusting online pictures and other images

You can illustrate your worksheets using online pictures and other images. Office.com makes many photos and animations available for your use. To add a picture to a worksheet, click the Online Pictures button in the Illustrations group on the Insert tab. The Insert Pictures window opens. Here you can search for online pictures (or Clip Art) from a variety of popular sources such as Facebook and Flickr, through the Bing search engine, or on OneDrive. To search, type one or more **keywords** (words related to your subject) in the appropriate Search text box, then press [Enter]. For example, pictures that relate to the keyword house in a search of Office.com appear in the Office.com window, as shown in **FIGURE 3-7**. When you double-click the image you want in the window, the image is inserted at the location of the active cell. To add images on your computer (or computers on your network) to a worksheet, click the Insert tab on the Ribbon, then click the Pictures button in the Illustrations group. Navigate to

the file you want, then click Insert. To resize an image, drag any corner sizing handle. To move an image, point inside the clip until the pointer changes to ⌖, then drag it to a new location.

FIGURE 3-7: Results of Online Picture search

Excel 2016

Excel 2016
Module 3

Learning
Outcomes
• Apply formatting
• Use the Format Painter
• Change cell alignment

Change Font Styles and Alignment

Font styles are formats such as bold, italic, and underlining that you can apply to affect the way text and numbers look in a worksheet. You can also change the **alignment** of labels and values in cells to position them in relation to the cells' edges—such as left-aligned, right-aligned, or centered. You can apply font styles and alignment options using the Home tab, the Format Cells dialog box, or the Mini toolbar. See **TABLE 3-2** for a description of common font style and alignment buttons that are available on the Home tab and the Mini toolbar. Once you have formatted a cell the way you want it, you can "paint" or copy the cell's formats into other cells by using the Format Painter button in the Clipboard group on the Home tab. This is similar to using copy and paste, but instead of copying cell contents, it copies only the cell's formatting. **CASE** *You want to further enhance the worksheet's appearance by adding bold and underline formatting and centering some of the labels.*

STEPS

QUICK TIP
You can use the following keyboard shortcuts to format a selected cell or range: [Ctrl][B] to bold, [Ctrl][I] to italicize, and [Ctrl][U] to underline.

1. **Press [Ctrl][Home], then click the Bold button B in the Font group on the Home tab**
   The title in cell A1 appears in bold.

2. **Click cell A3, then click the Underline button U in the Font group**
   The column label is now underlined.

3. **Click the Italic button I in the Font group, then click B**
   The heading now appears in boldface, underlined, italic type. Notice that the Bold, Italic, and Underline buttons in the Font group are all selected.

QUICK TIP
Overuse of any font style and random formatting can make a workbook difficult to read. Be consistent and add the same formatting to similar items throughout a worksheet or in related worksheets.

4. **Click the Italic button I to deselect it**
   The italic font style is removed from cell A3, but the bold and underline font styles remain.

5. **Click the Format Painter button in the Clipboard group, then select the range B3:J3**
   The formatting in cell A3 is copied to the rest of the column labels. To paint the formats on more than one selection, double-click the Format Painter button to keep it activated until you turn it off. You can turn off the Format Painter by pressing [Esc] or by clicking . You decide the title would look better if it were centered over the data columns.

6. **Select the range A1:H1, then click the Merge & Center button in the Alignment group**
   The Merge & Center button creates one cell out of the eight cells across the row, then centers the text in that newly created, merged cell. The title "Reason2Go Advertising Expenses" is centered across the eight columns you selected. To split a merged cell into its original components, select the merged cell, then click the Merge & Center button to deselect it. Occasionally, you may find that you want cell contents to wrap within a cell. You can do this by selecting the cells containing the text you want to wrap, then clicking the Wrap Text button in the Alignment group on the Home tab on the Ribbon.

QUICK TIP
To clear all formatting from a selected range, click the Clear button in the Editing group on the Home tab, then click Clear Formats.

7. **Select the range A3:J3, right-click, then click the Center button on the Mini toolbar**
   Compare your screen to **FIGURE 3-8**. Although they may be difficult to read, notice that all the headings are centered within their cells.

8. **Save your work**

FIGURE 3-8: Worksheet with font styles and alignment applied

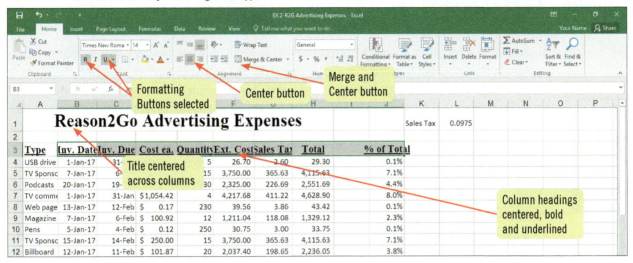

TABLE 3-2: Common font style and alignment buttons

button	description
B	Bolds text
I	Italicizes text
U	Underlines text
	Centers text across columns, and combines two or more selected, adjacent cells into one cell
	Aligns text at the left edge of the cell
	Centers text horizontally within the cell
	Aligns text at the right edge of the cell
	Wraps long text into multiple lines

Rotating and indenting cell entries

In addition to applying fonts and font styles, you can rotate or indent data within a cell to further change its appearance. You can rotate text within a cell by altering its alignment. Click the Home tab, select the cells you want to modify, then click the launcher in the Alignment group to open the Alignment tab of the Format Cells dialog box. Click a position in the Orientation box or type a number in the Degrees text box to rotate text from its default horizontal orientation, then click OK. You can indent cell contents using the Increase Indent button in the Alignment group, which moves cell contents to the right one space, or the Decrease Indent button , which moves cell contents to the left one space.

Adjust Column Width

Learning Outcomes
- Change a column width by dragging
- Resize a column with AutoFit
- Change the width of multiple columns

As you format a worksheet, you might need to adjust the width of one or more columns to accommodate changes in the amount of text, the font size, or font style. The default column width is 8.43 characters, a little less than 1". With Excel, you can adjust the width of one or more columns by using the mouse, the Format button in the Cells group on the Home tab, or the shortcut menu. Using the mouse, you can drag or double-click the right edge of a column heading. The Format button and shortcut menu include commands for making more precise width adjustments. **TABLE 3-3** describes common column formatting commands. **CASE** *You have noticed that some of the labels in columns A through J don't fit in the cells. You want to adjust the widths of the columns so that the labels appear in their entirety.*

STEPS

1. **Position the mouse pointer on the line between the column A and column B headings until it changes to ↔**

   See **FIGURE 3-9**. The **column heading** is the box at the top of each column containing a letter. Before you can adjust column width using the mouse, you need to position the pointer on the right edge of the column heading for the column you want to adjust. The cell entry "TV commercials" is the widest in the column.

2. **Click and drag the ↔ to the right until the column displays the "TV commercials" cell entries fully (approximately 15.29 characters, 1.23", or 112 pixels)**

   As you change the column width, a ScreenTip is displayed listing the column width. In Normal view, the ScreenTip lists the width in characters and pixels; in Page Layout view, the ScreenTip lists the width in inches and pixels.

3. **Position the pointer on the line between columns B and C until it changes to ↔, then double-click**

   Double-clicking the right edge of a column heading activates the **AutoFit** feature, which automatically resizes the column to accommodate the widest entry in the column. Column B automatically widens to fit the widest entry, which is the column label "Inv. Date".

4. **Use AutoFit to resize columns C, D, and J**

5. **Select the range E5:H5**

   You can change the width of multiple columns at once, by first selecting either the column headings or at least one cell in each column.

6. **Click the Format button in the Cells group, then click Column Width**

   The Column Width dialog box opens. Column width measurement is based on the number of characters that will fit in the column when formatted in the Normal font and font size (in this case, 11-point Calibri).

7. **Drag the dialog box by its title bar if its placement obscures your view of the worksheet, type 11 in the Column width text box, then click OK**

   The widths of columns E, F, G, and H change to reflect the new setting. See **FIGURE 3-10**.

8. **Save your work**

TABLE 3-3: Common column formatting commands

command	description	available using
Column Width	Sets the width to a specific number of characters	Format button; shortcut menu
AutoFit Column Width	Fits to the widest entry in a column	Format button; mouse
Hide & Unhide	Hides or displays hidden column(s)	Format button; shortcut menu
Default Width	Resets column to worksheet's default column width	Format button

FIGURE 3-9: Preparing to change the column width

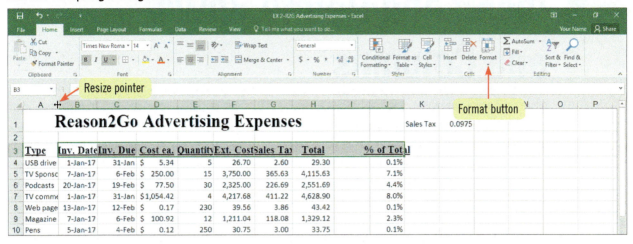

FIGURE 3-10: Worksheet with column widths adjusted

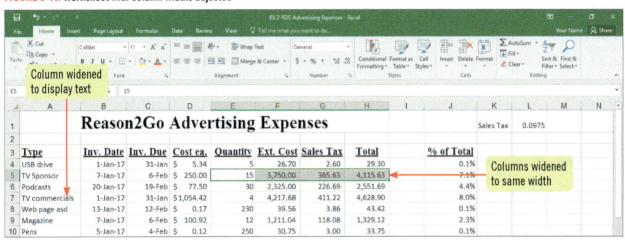

Changing row height

Changing row height is as easy as changing column width. Row height is calculated in points, the same units of measure used for fonts. The row height must exceed the size of the font you are using. Normally, you don't need to adjust row heights manually, because row heights adjust automatically to accommodate font size changes. If you format something in a row to be a larger point size, Excel adjusts the row to fit the largest point size in the row. However, you have just as many options for changing row

height as you do column width. Using the mouse, you can place the ✛ pointer on the line dividing a row heading from the heading below, and then drag to the desired height; double-clicking the line AutoFits the row height where necessary. You can also select one or more rows, then use the Row Height command on the shortcut menu, or click the Format button on the Home tab and click the Row Height or AutoFit Row Height command.

Insert and Delete Rows and Columns

Learning Outcomes
- Use the Insert dialog box
- Use column and row heading buttons to insert and delete

As you modify a worksheet, you might find it necessary to insert or delete rows and columns to keep your worksheet current. For example, you might need to insert rows to accommodate new inventory products or remove a column of yearly totals that are no longer necessary. When you insert a new row, the row is inserted above the cell pointer and the contents of the worksheet shift down from the newly inserted row. When you insert a new column, the column is inserted to the left of the cell pointer and the contents of the worksheet shift to the right of the new column. To insert multiple rows, select the same number of row headings as you want to insert before using the Insert command. **CASE** *You want to improve the overall appearance of the worksheet by inserting a row between the last row of data and the totals. Also, you have learned that row 27 and column J need to be deleted from the worksheet.*

STEPS

1. **Right-click cell A32, then click Insert on the shortcut menu**

   The Insert dialog box opens. See **FIGURE 3-11**. You can choose to insert a column or a row; insert a single cell and shift the cells in the active column to the right; or insert a single cell and shift the cells in the active row down. An additional row between the last row of data and the totals will visually separate the totals.

2. **Click the Entire row option button, then click OK**

   A blank row appears between the Billboard data and the totals, and the formula result in cell E33 has not changed. The Insert Options button 🖌 appears beside cell A33. Pointing to the button displays a list arrow, which you can click and then choose from the following options: Format Same As Above (the default setting, already selected), Format Same As Below, or Clear Formatting.

3. **Click the row 27 heading**

   All of row 27 is selected, as shown in **FIGURE 3-12**.

4. **Click the Delete button in the Cells group; *do not click the list arrow***

   Excel deletes row 27, and all rows below it shift up one row. You must use the Delete button or the Delete command on the shortcut menu to delete a row or column; pressing [Delete] on the keyboard removes only the *contents* of a selected row or column.

5. **Click the column J heading**

   The percentage information is calculated elsewhere and is no longer necessary in this worksheet.

6. **Click the Delete button in the Cells group**

   Excel deletes column J. The remaining columns to the right shift left one column.

7. **Use AutoFit to resize columns F and H, then save your work**

Hiding and unhiding columns and rows

When you don't want data in a column or row to be visible, but you don't want to delete it, you can hide the column or row. To hide a selected column, click the Format button in the Cells group on the Home tab, point to Hide & Unhide, then click Hide Columns. A hidden column is indicated by a dark green vertical line in its original position. This green line disappears when you click elsewhere in the worksheet. You can display a hidden column by selecting the columns on either side of the hidden column, clicking the Format button in the Cells group, pointing to Hide & Unhide, and then clicking Unhide Columns. (To hide or unhide one or more rows, substitute Hide Rows and Unhide Rows for the Hide Columns and Unhide Columns commands.)

FIGURE 3-11: Insert dialog box

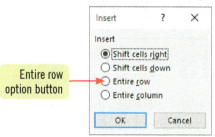

Entire row option button

FIGURE 3-12: Worksheet with row 27 selected

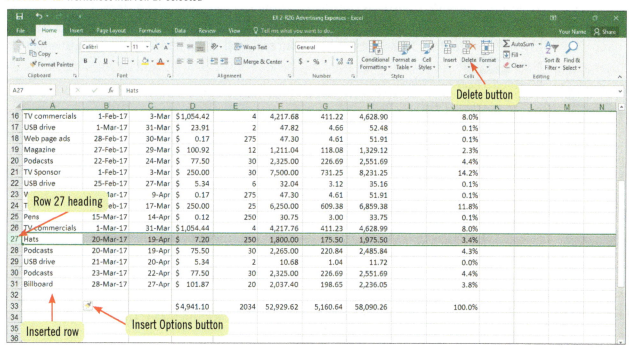

Delete button

Row 27 heading

Inserted row

Insert Options button

Adding and editing comments

Much of your work in Excel may be in collaboration with teammates with whom you share worksheets. You can share ideas with other worksheet users by adding comments within selected cells. To include a comment in a worksheet, click the cell where you want to place the comment, click the Review tab on the Ribbon, then click the New Comment button in the Comments group. You can type your comments in the resizable text box that opens containing the computer user's name. A small, red triangle appears in the upper-right corner of a cell containing a comment. If comments are not already displayed in a workbook, other users can point to the triangle to display the comment. To see all worksheet comments, as shown in FIGURE 3-13, click the Show All Comments button in the Comments group. To edit a comment, click the cell containing the comment, then click the Edit Comment button in the Comments

group. To delete a comment, click the cell containing the comment, then click the Delete button in the Comments group.

FIGURE 3-13: Comments displayed in a worksheet

	A	B	C	D
21	TV Sponsor	1-Feb-16	2-Mar	Food Network
22	Newspaper	25-Feb-16	26-Mar	Village Reader
23	Web page ads	10-Mar-16	9-Apr	Advertising Concepts
24	TV Sponsor	15-Feb-16	16-Mar	Food Network
25	Pens	15-Mar-16	14-Apr	Mass Appeal, Inc.
26	TV commercials	1-Mar-16	31-Mar	Discovery Channel
27	Podcasts	20-Mar-16	19-Apr	iPodAds
28	Newspaper	1-Apr-16	1-May	University Voice
29	Podcasts	10-Apr-16	10-May	iPodAds
30	Billboard	28-Mar-16	27-Apr	Advertising Concepts
31				
32				
33				
34				

Harriet McDonald: I think this will turn out to be a very good decision.

Will Moss: Should we continue with this market, or expand to other types of publications?

Apply Colors, Patterns, and Borders

You can use colors, patterns, and borders to enhance the overall appearance of a worksheet and make it easier to read. You can add these enhancements by using the Borders, Font Color, and Fill Color buttons in the Font group on the Home tab of the Ribbon and on the Mini toolbar, or by using the Fill tab and the Border tab in the Format Cells dialog box. You can open the Format Cells dialog box by clicking the dialog box launcher in the Font, Alignment, or Number group on the Home tab, or by right-clicking a selection, then clicking Format Cells on the shortcut menu. You can apply a color to the background of a cell or a range or to cell contents (such as letters and numbers), and you can apply a pattern to a cell or range. You can apply borders to all the cells in a worksheet or only to selected cells to call attention to selected information. To save time, you can also apply **cell styles**, predesigned combinations of formats. **CASE** *You want to add a pattern, a border, and color to the title of the worksheet to give the worksheet a more professional appearance.*

STEPS

1. **Select cell A1, click the Fill Color list arrow** 🎨 **in the Font group, then hover the pointer over the Turquoise, Accent 2 color (first row, sixth column from the left)**
   See **FIGURE 3-14**. Live Preview shows you how the color will look *before* you apply it. (Remember that cell A1 spans columns A through H because the Merge & Center command was applied.)

2. **Click the Turquoise, Accent 2 color**
   The color is applied to the background (or fill) of this cell. When you change fill or font color, the color on the Fill Color or Font Color button changes to the last color you selected.

3. **Right-click cell A1, then click Format Cells on the shortcut menu**
   The Format Cells dialog box opens.

4. **Click the Fill tab, click the Pattern Style list arrow, click the 6.25% Gray style (first row, sixth column from the left), then click OK**

5. **Click the Borders list arrow** ⊞ **in the Font group, then click Thick Bottom Border**
   Unlike underlining, which is a text-formatting tool, borders extend to the width of the cell, and can appear at the bottom of the cell, at the top, on either side, or on any combination of the four sides. It can be difficult to see a border when the cell is selected.

6. **Select the range A3:H3, click the Font Color list arrow** 𝐀 **in the Font group, then click the Blue, Accent 1 color (first Theme Colors row, fifth column from the left) on the palette**
   The new color is applied to the labels in the selected range.

7. **Select the range J1:K1, click the Cell Styles button in the Styles group, click the Neutral cell style (first row, fourth column from the left) in the gallery, then AutoFit column J**
   The font and color change in the range, as shown in **FIGURE 3-15**.

8. **Save your work**

FIGURE 3-14: Live Preview of fill color

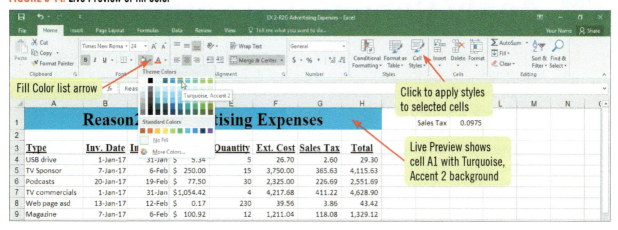

Fill Color list arrow

Click to apply styles to selected cells

Live Preview shows cell A1 with Turquoise, Accent 2 background

FIGURE 3-15: Worksheet with color, patterns, border, and style applied

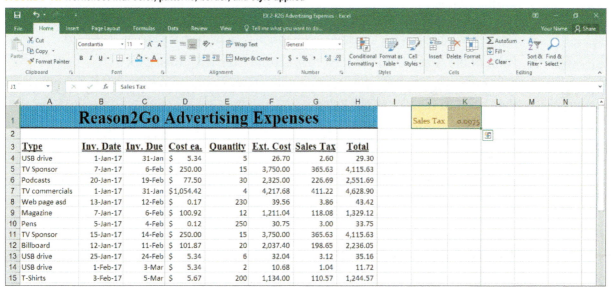

Working with themes and cell styles

Using themes and cell styles makes it easier to ensure that your worksheets are consistent. A **theme** is a predefined set of formats that gives your Excel worksheet a professional look. Formatting choices included in a theme are colors, fonts, and line and fill effects. To apply a theme, click the Themes button in the Themes group on the Page Layout tab to open the Themes gallery, as shown in **FIGURE 3-16**, then click a theme in the gallery. **Cell styles** are automatically updated if you change a theme. For example, if you apply the 20% - Accent1 cell style to cell A1 in a worksheet that has no theme applied, the fill color changes to light blue with no pattern, and the font changes to Calibri. If you change the theme of the worksheet to Ion Boardroom, cell A1's fill color changes to red and the font changes to Century Gothic, because these are the new theme's associated formats.

FIGURE 3-16: Themes gallery

Apply Conditional Formatting

So far, you've used formatting to change the appearance of different types of data, but you can also use formatting to highlight important aspects of the data itself. For example, you can apply formatting that changes the font color to red for any cells where the value is greater than $100 and to green where the value is below $50. This is called **conditional formatting** because Excel automatically applies different formats to data if the data meets conditions you specify. The formatting is updated if you change data in the worksheet. You can also copy conditional formats the same way you copy other formats. **CASE** *Mary is concerned about advertising costs exceeding the yearly budget. You decide to use conditional formatting to highlight certain trends and patterns in the data so that it's easy to spot the most expensive advertising.*

STEPS

1. **Select the range H4:H30, click the Conditional Formatting button in the Styles group on the Home tab, point to Data Bars, then point to the Light Blue Data Bar (second row, second from left)**

   Data bars are colored horizontal bars that visually illustrate differences between values in a range of cells. Live Preview shows how this formatting will appear in the worksheet, as shown in **FIGURE 3-17**.

2. **Point to the Green Data Bar (first row, second from left), then click it**

3. **Select the range F4:F30, click the Conditional Formatting button in the Styles group, then point to Highlight Cells Rules**

   The Highlight Cells Rules submenu displays choices for creating different formatting conditions. For example, you can create a rule for values that are greater than or less than a certain amount, or between two amounts.

4. **Click Between on the submenu**

   The Between dialog box opens, displaying input boxes you can use to define the condition and a default format (Light Red Fill with Dark Red Text) selected for cells that meet that condition. Depending on the condition you select in the Highlight Cells Rules submenu (such as "Greater Than" or "Less Than"), this dialog box displays different input boxes. You define the condition using the input boxes and then assign the formatting you want to use for cells that meet that condition. Values used in input boxes for a condition can be constants, formulas, cell references, or dates.

5. **Type 2000 in the first text box, type 4000 in the second text box, click the with list arrow, click Light Red Fill, compare your settings to FIGURE 3-18, then click OK**

   All cells with values between 2000 and 4000 in column F appear with a light red fill.

6. **Click cell E7, type 3, then press [Enter]**

   When the value in cell E7 changes, the formatting also changes because the new value meets the condition you set. Compare your results to **FIGURE 3-19**.

7. **Press [Ctrl][Home] to select cell A1, then save your work**

FIGURE 3-17: Previewing data bars in a range

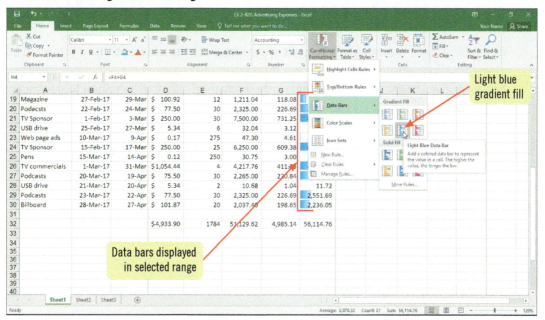

Data bars displayed in selected range

Light blue gradient fill

FIGURE 3-18: Between dialog box

Input boxes

Format for cells meeting the condition

FIGURE 3-19: Worksheet with conditional formatting

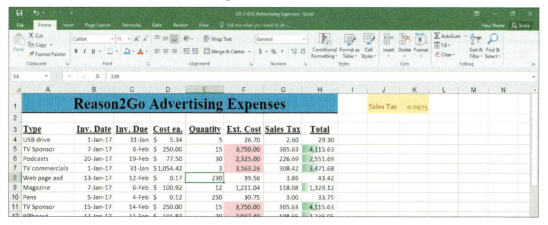

Managing conditional formatting rules

If you create a conditional formatting rule and then want to change a condition, you don't need to create a new rule; instead, you can modify the rule using the Rules Manager. Click the Conditional Formatting button in the Styles group, then click Manage Rules. The Conditional Formatting Rules Manager dialog box opens. Select the rule you want to edit, click Edit Rule, and then modify the settings in the Edit the Rule Description area in the Edit Formatting Rule dialog box. To change the formatting for

a rule, click the Format Style button in the Edit the Rule Description area, select the formatting styles you want the text to have, then click OK three times to close the Format Cells dialog box, the Edit Formatting Rule dialog box, and the Conditional Formatting Rules Manager dialog box. The rule is modified, and the new conditional formatting is applied to the selected cells. To delete a rule, select the rule in the Conditional Formatting Rules Manager dialog box, then click the Delete Rule button.

Rename and Move a Worksheet

**Learning
Outcomes**
• Rename a sheet
• Apply color to a
  sheet tab
• Reorder sheets in
  a workbook

By default, an Excel workbook initially contains one worksheet named Sheet1, although you can add sheets at any time. Each sheet name appears on a sheet tab at the bottom of the worksheet. When you open a new workbook, the first worksheet, Sheet1, is the active sheet. To move from sheet to sheet, you can click any sheet tab at the bottom of the worksheet window. The sheet tab scrolling buttons, located to the left of the sheet tabs, are useful when a workbook contains too many sheet tabs to display at once. To make it easier to identify the sheets in a workbook, you can rename each sheet and add color to the tabs. You can also organize them in a logical way. For instance, to better track performance goals, you could name each workbook sheet for an individual salesperson, and you could move the sheets so they appear in alphabetical order. **CASE** ▶ *In the current worksheet, Sheet1 contains information about actual advertising expenses. Sheet2 contains an advertising budget, and Sheet3 contains no data. You want to rename the two sheets in the workbook to reflect their contents, add color to a sheet tab to easily distinguish one from the other, and change their order.*

STEPS

1. **Click the Sheet2 tab**

   Sheet2 becomes active, appearing in front of the Sheet1 tab; this is the worksheet that contains the budgeted advertising expenses. See **FIGURE 3-20**.

2. **Click the Sheet1 tab**

   Sheet1, which contains the actual advertising expenses, becomes active again.

3. **Double-click the Sheet2 tab, type Budget, then press [Enter]**

   The new name for Sheet2 automatically replaces the default name on the tab. Worksheet names can have up to 31 characters, including spaces and punctuation.

4. **Right-click the Budget tab, point to Tab Color on the shortcut menu, then click the Bright Green, Accent 4, Lighter 40% color (fourth row, third column from the right) as shown in FIGURE 3-21**

5. **Double-click the Sheet1 tab, type Actual, then press [Enter]**

   Notice that the color of the Budget tab changes depending on whether it is the active tab; when the Actual tab is active, the color of the Budget tab changes to the green tab color you selected. You decide to rearrange the order of the sheets so that the Budget tab is to the left of the Actual tab.

6. **Click the Budget tab, hold down the mouse button, drag it to the left of the Actual tab, as shown in FIGURE 3-22, then release the mouse button**

   As you drag, the pointer changes to ▯, the sheet relocation pointer, and a small, black triangle just above the tabs shows the position the moved sheet will be in when you release the mouse button. The first sheet in the workbook is now the Budget sheet. See **FIGURE 3-23**. You can move multiple sheets by pressing and holding [Shift] while clicking the sheets you want to move, then dragging the sheets to their new location.

7. **Click the Actual sheet tab, click the Page Layout button 🔲 on the status bar to open Page Layout view, enter your name in the left header text box, then click anywhere in the worksheet to deselect the header**

8. **Click the Page Layout tab on the Ribbon, click the Orientation button in the Page Setup group, then click Landscape**

9. **Right-click the Sheet3 tab, click Delete on the shortcut menu, press [Ctrl][Home], then save your work**

FIGURE 3-20: Sheet tabs in workbook

Sheet1 tab   Sheet2 tab

FIGURE 3-21: Tab Color palette

Sheet2 renamed

FIGURE 3-22: Moving the Budget sheet

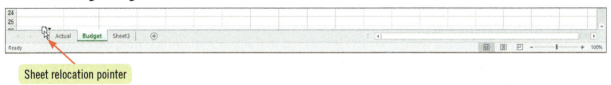

Sheet relocation pointer

FIGURE 3-23: Reordered sheets

Budget sheet comes before Actual sheet

Copying, adding, and deleting worksheets

There are times when you may want to copy a worksheet. For example, a workbook might contain a sheet with Quarter 1 expenses, and you want to use that sheet as the basis for a sheet containing Quarter 2 expenses. To copy a sheet within the same workbook, press and hold [Ctrl], drag the sheet tab to the desired tab location, release the mouse button, then release [Ctrl]. A duplicate sheet appears with the same name as the copied sheet followed by "(2)" indicating that it is a copy. You can then rename the sheet to a more meaningful name. To copy a sheet to a different workbook, both the source and destination workbooks must be open. Select the sheet to copy or move, right-click the sheet tab, then click Move or Copy in the shortcut menu. Complete the information in the Move or Copy dialog box. Be sure to click the Create a copy check box if you are copying rather than moving the worksheet. Carefully check your calculation results whenever you move or copy a worksheet. You can add multiple worksheets to a workbook by clicking the Home tab on the Ribbon, pressing and holding [Shift], then clicking the number of existing worksheet tabs that correspond with the number of sheets you want to add, clicking the Insert list arrow in the Cells group on the Home tab, then clicking Insert Sheet. You can delete multiple worksheets from a workbook by clicking the Home tab, pressing and holding [Shift], clicking the sheet tabs of the worksheets you want to delete, clicking the Delete list arrow in the Cells group on the Home tab, then clicking Delete Sheet.

Check Spelling

Excel includes a spell checker to help you ensure that the words in your worksheet are spelled correctly. The spell checker scans your worksheet, displays words it doesn't find in its built-in dictionary, and suggests replacements when they are available. To check all of the sheets in a multiple-sheet workbook, you need to display each sheet individually and run the spell checker for each one. Because the built-in dictionary cannot possibly include all the words that anyone needs, you can add words to the dictionary, such as your company name, an acronym, or an unusual technical term. Once you add a word or term, the spell checker no longer considers that word misspelled. Any words you've added to the dictionary using Word, Access, or PowerPoint are also available in Excel. **CASE** *Before you distribute this workbook to Mary, you check the spelling.*

STEPS

1. **Click the Review tab on the Ribbon, then click the Spelling button in the Proofing group**

   The Spelling: English (United States) dialog box opens, as shown in **FIGURE 3-24**, with "asd" selected as the first misspelled word in the worksheet, and with "ads" selected in the Suggestions list as a possible replacement. For any word, you have the option to Ignore this case of the flagged word, Ignore All cases of the flagged word, Change the word to the selected suggestion, Change All instances of the flagged word to the selected suggestion, or add the flagged word to the dictionary using Add to Dictionary.

2. **Click Change**

   Next, the spell checker finds the word "Podacsts" and suggests "Podcasts" as an alternative.

3. **Verify that the word Podcasts is selected in the Suggestions list, then click Change**

   When no more incorrect words are found, Excel displays a message indicating that the spell check is complete.

4. **Click OK**

5. **Click the Home tab, click Find & Select in the Editing group, then click Replace**

   The Find and Replace dialog box opens. You can use this dialog box to replace a word or phrase. It might be a misspelling of a proper name that the spell checker didn't recognize as misspelled, or it could simply be a term that you want to change throughout the worksheet. Mary has just told you that each instance of "Billboard" in the worksheet should be changed to "Sign."

6. **Type Billboard in the Find what text box, press [Tab], then type Sign in the Replace with text box**

   Compare your dialog box to **FIGURE 3-25**.

7. **Click Replace All, click OK to close the Microsoft Excel dialog box, then click Close to close the Find and Replace dialog box**

   Excel has made two replacements.

8. **Click the File tab, click Print on the navigation bar, click the No Scaling setting in the Settings section on the Print tab, then click Fit Sheet on One Page**

9. **Click the Return button ⊙ to return to your worksheet, save your work, submit it to your instructor as directed, close the workbook, then exit Excel**

   The completed worksheet is shown in **FIGURE 3-26**.

Emailing a workbook

You can send an entire workbook from within Excel using your installed email program, such as Microsoft Outlook. To send a workbook as an email message attachment, open the workbook, click the File tab, then click Share on the navigation bar. With the Email option selected in the Share section in Backstage view, click Send as Attachment in the right pane. An email message opens in your default email program with the workbook automatically attached; the filename appears in the Attached field. Complete the To and optional Cc fields, include a message if you wish, then click Send.

FIGURE 3-24: Spelling: English (United States) dialog box

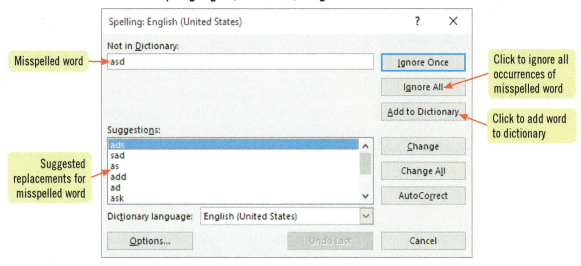

Misspelled word →

Suggested replacements for misspelled word →

Click to ignore all occurrences of misspelled word

Click to add word to dictionary

FIGURE 3-25: Find and Replace dialog box

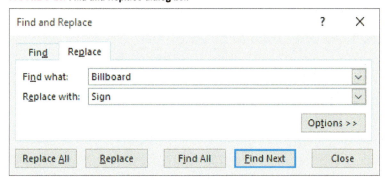

FIGURE 3-26: Completed worksheet

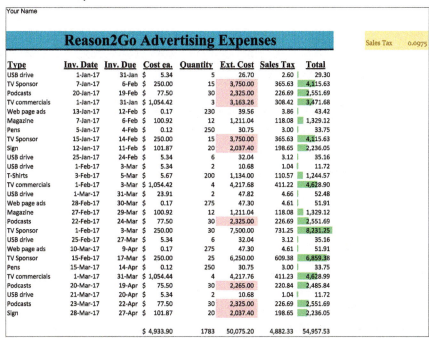

Formatting a Worksheet

Practice

Concepts Review

Label each element of the Excel worksheet window shown in FIGURE 3-27**.**

FIGURE 3-27

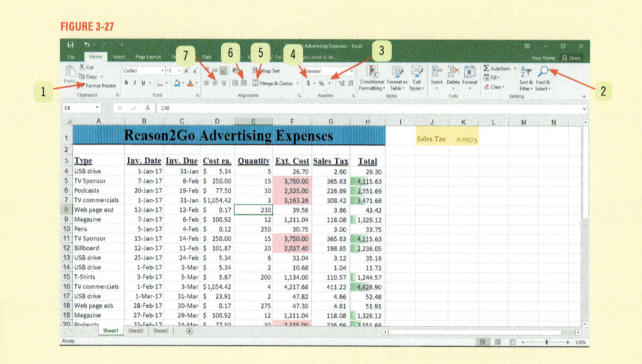

Match each command or button with the statement that best describes it.

8. **Spelling button**

9. [$]

10. [fill color icon]

11. **[Ctrl][Home]**

12. [merge icon]

13. **Conditional formatting**

a. Checks for apparent misspellings in a worksheet

b. Adds dollar signs and two decimal places to selected data

c. Displays fill color options for a cell

d. Moves cell pointer to cell A1

e. Centers cell contents across multiple cells

f. Changes formatting of a cell that meets a certain rule

Select the best answer from the list of choices.

14. **Which of the following is an example of Accounting number format?**
    - **a.** 5555
    - **b.** $5,555.55
    - **c.** 55.55%
    - **d.** 5,555.55

15. **What is the name of the feature used to resize a column to accommodate its widest entry?**
    - **a.** AutoFormat
    - **b.** AutoFit
    - **c.** AutoResize
    - **d.** AutoRefit

16. **Which button copies multiple formats from selected cells to other cells?**
    - **a.** [icon]
    - **b.** [icon]
    - **c.** [icon]
    - **d.** [icon]

17. **Which button increases the number of decimal places in selected cells?**
    - **a.** [icon]
    - **b.** [icon]
    - **c.** [icon]
    - **d.** [icon]

18. **Which button removes the italic font style from selected cells?**
    - **a.** [I icon]
    - **b.** [B icon]
    - **c.** [I icon]
    - **d.** [U icon]

19. **What feature is used to delete a conditional formatting rule?**
    - **a.** Rules Reminder
    - **b.** Conditional Formatting Rules Manager
    - **c.** Condition Manager
    - **d.** Format Manager

Skills Review

1. **Format values.**
   a. Start Excel, open the file EX 3-2.xlsx from the location where you store your Data Files, then save it as **EX 3-Health Insurance Premiums**.
   b. Use the Sum function to enter a formula in cell B10 that totals the number of employees.
   c. Create a formula in cell C5 that calculates the monthly insurance premium for the accounting department. (*Hint*: Make sure you use the correct type of cell reference in the formula. To calculate the department's monthly premium, multiply the number of employees by the monthly premium in cell B14.)
   d. Copy the formula in cell C5 to the range C6:C10.
   e. Format the range C5:C10 using Accounting number format.
   f. Change the format of the range C6:C9 to the Comma Style.
   g. Reduce the number of decimals in cell B14 to 0 using a button in the Number group on the Home tab.
   h. Save your work.

2. **Change font and font sizes.**
   a. Select the range of cells containing the column labels (in row 4).
   b. Change the font of the selection to Times New Roman.
   c. Increase the font size of the selection to 12 points.
   d. Increase the font size of the label in cell A1 to 14 points.
   e. Save your changes.

3. **Change font styles and alignment.**
   a. Apply the bold and italic font styles to the worksheet title in cell A1.
   b. Use the Merge & Center button to center the Health Insurance Premiums label over columns A–C.
   c. Apply the italic font style to the Health Insurance Premiums label.
   d. Add the bold font style to the labels in row 4.
   e. Use the Format Painter to copy the format in cell A4 to the range A5:A10.
   f. Apply the format in cell C10 to cell B14.
   g. Change the alignment of cell A10 to Align Right using a button in the Alignment group.

Skills Review (continued)

h. Select the range of cells containing the column labels, then center them.

i. Remove the italic font style from the Health Insurance Premiums label, then increase the font size to 14.

j. Move the Health Insurance Premiums label to cell A3, remove the Merge & Center format, then add the bold and underline font styles.

k. Save your changes.

4. Adjust column width.

a. Resize column C to a width of 10.71 characters.

b. Use the AutoFit feature to resize columns A and B.

c. Clear the contents of cell A13 (do not delete the cell).

d. Change the text in cell A14 to **Monthly Premium**, then change the width of the column to 25 characters.

e. Save your changes.

5. Insert and delete rows and columns.

a. Insert a new row between rows 5 and 6.

b. Add a new department, **Donations**, in the newly inserted row. Enter **6** as the number of employees in the department.

c. Copy the formula in cell C7 to C6.

d. Add the following comment to cell A6: **New department**. Display the comment, then drag to move it out of the way, if necessary.

e. Add a new column between the Department and Employees columns with the title **Family Coverage**, then resize the column using AutoFit.

f. Delete the Legal row from the worksheet.

g. Move the value in cell C14 to cell B14.

h. Save your changes.

6. Apply colors, patterns, and borders.

a. Add Outside Borders around the range A4:D10.

b. Add a Bottom Double Border to cells C9 and D9 (above the calculated employee and premium totals).

c. Apply the Aqua, Accent 5, Lighter 80% fill color to the labels in the Department column (do not include the Total label).

d. Apply the Orange, Accent 6, Lighter 60% fill color to the range A4:D4.

e. Change the color of the font in the range A4:D4 to Red, Accent 2, Darker 25%.

f. Add a 12.5% Gray pattern style to cell A1.

g. Format the range A14:B14 with a fill color of Dark Blue, Text 2, Lighter 40%, change the font color to White, Background 1, then apply the bold font style.

h. Save your changes.

7. Apply conditional formatting.

a. Select the range D5:D9, then create a conditional format that changes cell contents to green fill with dark green text if the value is between 150 and 275.

b. Select the range C5:C9, then create a conditional format that changes cell contents to red text if the number of employees exceeds 10.

c. Apply a purple gradient-filled data bar to the range C5:C9. (*Hint*: Click Purple Data Bar in the Gradient Fill section.)

d. Use the Rules Manager to modify the conditional format in cells C5:C9 to display values greater than 10 in bold dark red text.

e. Save your changes.

8. Rename and move a worksheet.

a. Name the Sheet1 tab **Insurance Data**.

b. Add a sheet to the workbook, then name the new sheet **Employee Data**.

c. Change the Insurance Data tab color to Red, Accent 2, Lighter 40%.

Skills Review (continued)

   d. Change the Employee Data tab color to Aqua, Accent 5, Lighter 40%.

   e. Move the Employee Data sheet so it comes before (to the left of) the Insurance Data sheet.

   f. Make the Insurance Data sheet active, enter your name in cell A20, then save your work.

9. Check spelling.

   a. Move the cell pointer to cell A1.

   b. Use the Find & Select feature to replace the Accounting label with **Accounting/Legal**.

   c. Check the spelling in the worksheet using the spell checker, and correct any spelling errors if necessary.

   d. Save your changes, then compare your Insurance Data sheet to **FIGURE 3-28**.

   e. Preview the Insurance Data sheet in Backstage view, submit your work to your instructor as directed, then close the workbook and exit Excel.

FIGURE 3-28

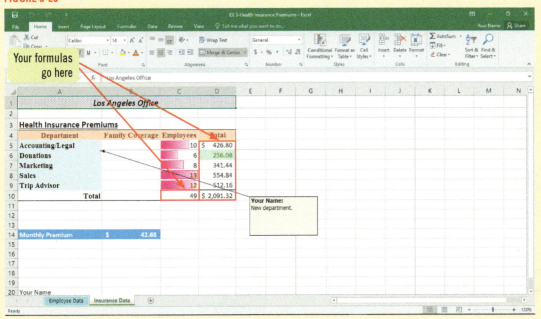

Independent Challenge 1

You run a freelance accounting business, and one of your newest clients is Fresh To You, a small local grocery store. Now that you've converted the store's accounting records to Excel, the manager would like you to work on an analysis of the inventory. Although more items will be added later, the worksheet has enough items for you to begin your modifications.

   a. Start Excel, open the file EX 3-3.xlsx from the location where you store your Data Files, then save it as **EX 3-Fresh To You Inventory**.

   b. Create a formula in cell E4 that calculates the value of the items in stock based on the price paid per item in cell B4. Format the cell in the Comma Style.

   c. In cell F4, calculate the sale value of the items in stock using an absolute reference to the markup value shown in cell H1.

   d. Copy the formulas created above into the range E5:F14; first convert any necessary cell references to absolute so that the formulas work correctly.

   e. Apply bold to the column labels, and italicize the inventory items in column A.

   f. Make sure that all columns are wide enough to display the data and labels.

   g. Format the values in the Sale Value column as Accounting number format with two decimal places.

   h. Format the values in the Price Paid column as Comma Style with two decimal places.

Independent Challenge 1 (continued)

i. Add a row under Cheddar Cheese for **Whole Wheat flour**, price paid **0.95**, sold by weight (**pound**), with **23** on hand. Copy the appropriate formulas to cells E7:F7.

j. Verify that all the data in the worksheet is visible and formulas are correct. Adjust any items as needed, and check the spelling of the entire worksheet.

k. Use conditional formatting to apply yellow fill with dark yellow text to items with a quantity of less than 25 on hand.

l. Use an icon set of your choosing in the range D4:D14 to illustrate the relative differences between values in the range.

m. Add an outside border around the data in the Item column (*do not* include the Item column label).

n. Delete the row containing the Resource Coffee - decaf entry.

o. Enter your name in an empty cell below the data, then save the file. Compare your worksheet to the sample in FIGURE 3-29.

p. Preview the worksheet in Backstage view, submit your work to your instructor as directed, close the workbook, then exit Excel.

FIGURE 3-29

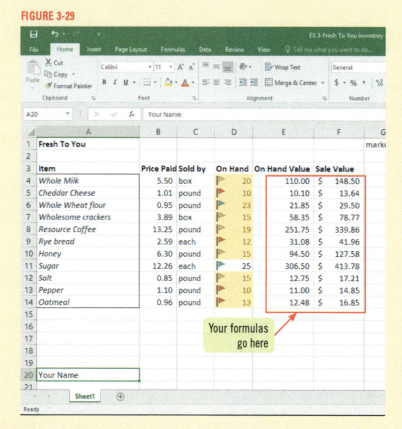

Independent Challenge 2

You volunteer several hours each week with the Assistance League of San Antonio, and you are in charge of maintaining the membership list. You're currently planning a mailing campaign to members in certain regions of the city. You also want to create renewal letters for members whose membership expires soon. You decide to format the list to enhance the appearance of the worksheet and make your upcoming tasks easier to plan.

a. Start Excel, open the file EX 3-4.xlsx from the location where you store your Data Files, then save it as **EX 3-Memphis Assistance League**.

b. Remove any blank columns.

c. Create a conditional format in the Zip Code column so that entries greater than 38249 appear in light red fill with dark red text.

d. Make all columns wide enough to fit their data and labels. (*Hint*: You can use any method to size the columns.)

e. Use formatting enhancements, such as fonts, font sizes, font styles, and fill colors, to make the worksheet more attractive.

Independent Challenge 2 (continued)

f. Center the column labels.

g. Use conditional formatting so that entries for Year of Membership Expiration that are between 2021 and 2023 appear in green fill with bold black text. (*Hint*: Create a custom format for cells that meet the condition.)

h. Adjust any items as necessary, then check the spelling.

i. Change the name of the Sheet1 tab to one that reflects the sheet's contents, then add a tab color of your choice.

j. Enter your name in an empty cell, then save your work.

k. Preview the worksheet, make any final changes you think necessary, then submit your work to your instructor as directed. Compare your work to the sample shown in FIGURE 3-30.

l. Close the workbook, then exit Excel.

FIGURE 3-30

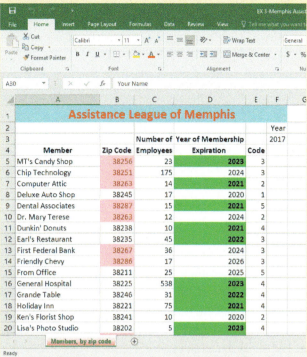

Independent Challenge 3

Advantage Calendars is a Dallas-based printer that prints and assembles calendars. As the finance manager for the company, one of your responsibilities is to analyze the monthly reports from the five district sales offices. Your boss, Joanne Bennington, has just asked you to prepare a quarterly sales report for an upcoming meeting. Because several top executives will be attending this meeting, Joanne reminds you that the report must look professional. In particular, she asks you to highlight the fact that the Northeastern district continues to outpace the other districts.

a. Plan a worksheet that shows the company's sales during the first quarter. Assume that all calendars are the same price. Make sure you include the following:

-   The number of calendars sold (units sold) and the associated revenues (total sales) for each of the five district sales offices. The five sales districts are Northeastern, Midwestern, Southeastern, Southern, and Western.
-   Calculations that show month-by-month totals for January, February, and March, and a 3-month cumulative total.
-   Calculations that show each district's share of sales (percent of Total Sales).
-   Labels that reflect the month-by-month data as well as the cumulative data.
-   Formatting enhancements such as data bars that emphasize the recent month's sales surge and the Northeastern district's sales leadership.

b. Ask yourself the following questions about the organization and formatting of the worksheet: What worksheet title and labels do you need, and where should they appear? How can you calculate the totals? What formulas can you copy to save time and keystrokes? Do any of these formulas need to use an absolute reference? How do you show dollar amounts? What information should be shown in bold? Do you need to use more than one font? Should you use more than one point size?

c. Start Excel, then save a new, blank workbook as **EX 3-Advantage Calendars** to the location where you store your Data Files.

Independent Challenge 3 (continued)

d. Build the worksheet with your own price and sales data. Enter the titles and labels first, then enter the numbers and formulas. You can use the information in TABLE 3-4 to get started.

TABLE 3-4

Advantage Calendars										
1st Quarter Sales Report										
		January		February		March		Total		
Office	Price	Units Sold	Sales	Units Sold	Sales	Units Sold	Sales	Units Sold	Sales	Total % of Sales
Northeastern										
Midwestern										
Southeastern										
Southern										
Western										

e. Add a row beneath the data containing the totals for each column.

f. Adjust the column widths as necessary.

g. Change the height of row 1 to 33 points.

h. Format labels and values to enhance the look of the worksheet, and change the font styles and alignment if necessary.

i. Resize columns and adjust the formatting as necessary.

j. Add data bars for the monthly Units Sold columns.

k. Add a column that calculates a 25% increase in total sales dollars. Use an absolute cell reference in this calculation. (*Hint*: Make sure that the current formatting is applied to the new information.)

l. Delete the contents of cells J4:K4 if necessary, then merge and center cell I4 over column I:K.

m. Add a bottom double border to cells I10:L10.

n. Enter your name in an empty cell.

o. Check the spelling in the workbook, change to a landscape orientation, save your work, then compare your work to FIGURE 3-31.

p. Preview the worksheet in Backstage view, then submit your work to your instructor as directed.

q. Close the workbook file, then exit Excel.

FIGURE 3-31

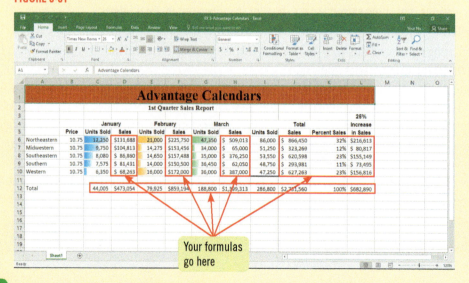

Formatting a Worksheet

Independent Challenge 4: Explore

This Independent Challenge requires an Internet connection.

Your corporate relocation company helps employees to settle quickly and easily into new cities around the world. Your latest client plans to send employees to seven different countries. All employees will receive the same weekly budget in American currency. You need to create a worksheet to help all the employees understand the currency conversion rates in the different countries so that they can plan their spending effectively.

a. Start Excel, then save a new, blank workbook as **EX 3-Foreign Currency Rates** to the location where you store your Data Files.

b. Add a title at the top of the worksheet.

c. Think of seven countries that each use a different currency, then enter column and row labels for your worksheet. (*Hint*: You may wish to include row labels for each country, plus column labels for the country, the $1 equivalent in native currency, the total amount of native currency employees will have in each country, and the name of each country's monetary unit.)

d. Decide how much money employees will bring to each country (for example, $1,000), and enter that in the worksheet.

e. Use your favorite search engine to find your own information sources on currency conversions for the countries you have listed.

f. Enter the cash equivalent to $1 in U.S. dollars for each country in your list.

g. Create an equation that calculates the amount of native currency employees will have in each country, using an absolute cell reference in the formula.

h. Format the entries in the column containing the native currency $1 equivalent as Number number format with three decimal places, and format the column containing the total native currency budget with two decimal places, using the correct currency number format for each country. (*Hint*: Use the Number tab in the Format cells dialog box; choose the appropriate currency number format from the Symbol list.)

i. Create a conditional format that changes the font style and color of the calculated amount in the $1,000 US column to light red fill with dark red text if the amount exceeds **1000** units of the local currency.

j. Merge and center the worksheet title over the column headings.

k. Add any formatting you want to the column headings, and resize the columns as necessary.

l. Add a background color to the title and change the font color if you choose.

m. Enter your name in the header of the worksheet.

n. Spell check the worksheet, save your changes, compare your work to **FIGURE 3-32**, then preview the worksheet, and submit your work to your instructor as directed.

o. Close the workbook and exit Excel.

FIGURE 3-32

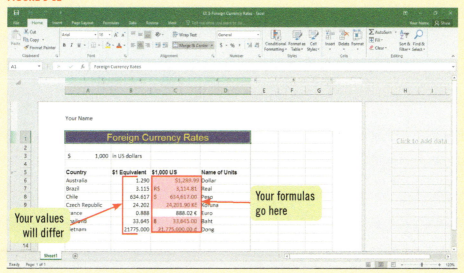

Visual Workshop

Open the file EX 3-5.xlsx from the location where you store your Data Files, then save it as **EX 3-London Employees**. Use the skills you learned in this module to format the worksheet so it looks like the one shown in FIGURE 3-33. Create a conditional format in the Level column so that entries greater than 3 appear in light red fill with dark red text. Create an additional conditional format in the Review Cycle column so that any value equal to 3 appears in black fill with white bold text. Replace the Accounting department label with **Legal**. (*Hint*: The only additional font used in this exercise is 18-point Times New Roman in row 1.) Enter your name in the upper-right part of the header, check the spelling in the worksheet, save your changes, then submit your work to your instructor as directed. (*Hint*: To match the figure exactly, remember to match the zoom level.)

FIGURE 3-33

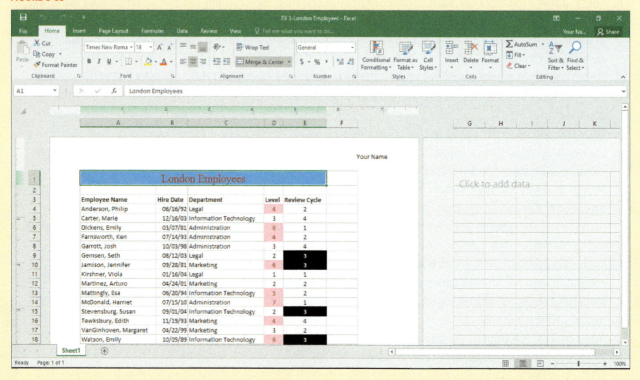

Working with Charts

CASE At the upcoming annual meeting, Yolanda Lee wants to discuss spending patterns at Reason2Go. She asks you to create a chart showing the trends in company expenses over the past four quarters.

Module Objectives

After completing this module, you will be able to:

- Plan a chart
- Create a chart
- Move and resize a chart
- Change the chart design
- Change the chart format
- Format a chart
- Annotate and draw on a chart
- Create a pie chart

Files You Will Need

EX 4-1.xlsx	EX 4-4.xlsx
EX 4-2.xlsx	EX 4-5.xlsx
EX 4-3.xlsx	EX 4-6.xlsx

Plan a Chart

Before creating a chart, you need to plan the information you want your chart to show and how you want it to look. Planning ahead helps you decide what type of chart to create and how to organize the data. Understanding the parts of a chart makes it easier to format and change specific elements so that the chart best illustrates your data. **CASE** ▶ *In preparation for creating the chart for Yolanda's presentation, you identify your goals for the chart and plan its layout.*

DETAILS

Use the following guidelines to plan the chart:

- **Determine the purpose of the chart, and identify the data relationships you want to communicate graphically**

  You want to create a chart that shows quarterly tour expenses for each country where Reason2Go provides tours. This worksheet data is shown in **FIGURE 4-1**. You also want the chart to illustrate whether the quarterly expenses for each country increased or decreased from quarter to quarter.

- **Determine the results you want to see, and decide which chart type is most appropriate**

  Different chart types display data in distinctive ways. For example, a pie chart compares parts to the whole, so it's useful for showing what proportion of a budget amount was spent on tours in one country relative to what was spent on tours in other countries. A line chart, in contrast, is best for showing trends over time. To choose the best chart type for your data, you should first decide how you want your data displayed and interpreted. **TABLE 4-1** describes several different types of charts you can create in Excel and their corresponding buttons on the Insert tab on the Ribbon. Because you want to compare R2G tour expenses in multiple countries over a period of four quarters, you decide to use a column chart.

- **Identify the worksheet data you want the chart to illustrate**

  Sometimes you use all the data in a worksheet to create a chart, while at other times you may need to select a range within the sheet. The worksheet from which you are creating your chart contains expense data for each of the past four quarters and the totals for the past year. You will need to use all the quarterly data except the quarterly totals.

- **Understand the elements of a chart**

  The chart shown in **FIGURE 4-2** contains basic elements of a chart. In the figure, R2G tour countries are on the horizontal axis (also called the **x-axis**) and expense dollar amounts are on the vertical axis (also called the **y-axis**). The horizontal axis is also called the **category axis** because it often contains the names of data groups, such as locations, months, or years. The vertical axis is also called the **value axis** because it often contains numerical values that help you interpret the size of chart elements. (3-D charts also contain a **z-axis**, for comparing data across both categories and values.) The area inside the horizontal and vertical axes is the **plot area**. The **tick marks**, on the vertical axis, and **gridlines** (extending across the plot area) create a scale of measure for each value. Each value in a cell you select for your chart is a **data point**. In any chart, a **data marker** visually represents each data point, which in this case is a column. A collection of related data points is a **data series**. In this chart, there are four data series (Quarter 1, Quarter 2, Quarter 3, and Quarter 4). Each is made up of column data markers of a different color, so a **legend** is included to make it easy to identify them.

FIGURE 4-1: Worksheet containing expense data

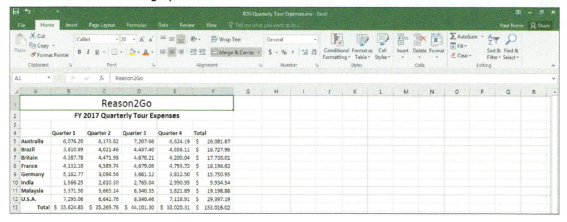

FIGURE 4-2: Chart elements

TABLE 4-1: Common chart types

type	button	description
Column		Compares data using columns; the Excel default; sometimes referred to as a bar chart in other spreadsheet programs
Line		Compares trends over even time intervals; looks similar to an area chart, but does not emphasize total
Pie		Compares sizes of pieces as part of a whole; used for a single series of numbers
Bar		Compares data using horizontal bars; sometimes referred to as a horizontal bar chart in other spreadsheet programs
Area		Shows how individual volume changes over time in relation to total volume
Scatter		Compares trends over uneven time or measurement intervals; used in scientific and engineering disciplines for trend spotting and extrapolation
Combo		Displays two or more types of data using different chart types; illustrates mixed or widely varying types of data

Create a Chart

Learning Outcomes
• Create a chart
• Switch a chart's columns/rows
• Add a chart title

To create a chart in Excel, you first select the range in a worksheet containing the data you want to chart. Once you've selected a range, you can use The Quick Analysis tool or the Insert tab on the Ribbon to create a chart based on the data in the range. **CASE** ▶ *Using the worksheet containing the quarterly expense data, you create a chart that shows how the expenses in each country varied across the quarters.*

STEPS

QUICK TIP
When charting data for a particular time period, make sure that all series are for the same time period.

1. **Start Excel, open the file EX 4-1.xlsx from the location where you store your Data Files, then save it as EX 4-R2G Quarterly Tour Expenses**

   You want the chart to include the quarterly tour expenses values, as well as quarter and country labels. You don't include the Total column and row because the figures in these cells would skew the chart.

2. **Select the range A4:E12, click the Quick Analysis tool 📰 in the lower-right corner of the range, then click Charts**

   The Charts tab on the Quick Analysis tool recommends commonly used chart types based on the range you have selected. The Charts tab also includes a More Charts button for additional chart types, such as stock charts for charting stock market data.

QUICK TIP
To base a chart on data in nonadjacent ranges, press and hold [Ctrl] while selecting each range, then use the Insert tab to create the chart.

3. **On the Charts tab, verify that Clustered Column is selected, as shown in FIGURE 4-3, then click Clustered Column**

   The chart is inserted in the center of the worksheet, and two contextual Chart Tools tabs appear on the Ribbon: Design and Format. On the Design tab, which is currently active, you can quickly change the chart type, chart layout, and chart style, and you can swap how the columns and rows of data in the worksheet are represented in the chart. When seen in the Normal view, three tools display to the right of the chart: these enable you to add, remove, or change chart elements ➕, set a style and color scheme 🖌, and filter the results shown in a chart 🔽. Currently, the countries are charted along the horizontal x-axis, with the quarterly expense dollar amounts charted along the y-axis. This lets you easily compare the quarterly expenses for each country.

4. **Click the Switch Row/Column button in the Data group on the Chart Tools Design tab**

   The quarters are now charted along the x-axis. The expense amounts per country are charted along the y-axis, as indicated by the updated legend. See FIGURE 4-4.

5. **Click the Undo button 🔄 ▾ on the Quick Access Toolbar**

   The chart returns to its original design.

QUICK TIP
You can also triple-click to select the chart title text.

6. **Click the Chart Title placeholder to show the text box, click anywhere in the Chart Title text box, press [Ctrl][A] to select the text, type R2G Quarterly Tour Expenses, then click anywhere in the chart to deselect the title**

   Adding a title helps identify the chart. The border around the chart and the **sizing handles**, the small series of dots at the corners and sides of the chart's border, indicate that the chart is selected. See FIGURE 4-5. Your chart might be in a different location on the worksheet and may look slightly different; you will move and resize it in the next lesson. Any time a chart is selected, as it is now, a blue border surrounds the worksheet data range on which the chart is based, a purple border surrounds the cells containing the category axis labels, and a red border surrounds the cells containing the data series labels. This chart is known as an **embedded chart** because it is inserted directly in the current worksheet and doesn't exist in a separate file. Embedding a chart in the current sheet is the default selection when creating a chart, but you can also embed a chart on a different sheet in the workbook, or on a newly created chart sheet. A **chart sheet** is a sheet in a workbook that contains only a chart that is linked to the workbook data.

7. **Save your work**

FIGURE 4-3: Charts tab in Quick Analysis tool

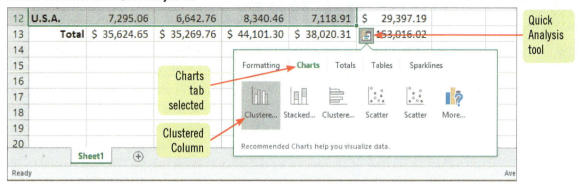

FIGURE 4-4: Clustered Column chart with different configuration of rows and columns

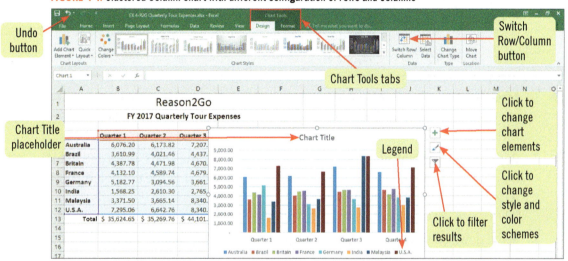

FIGURE 4-5: Chart with original configuration restored and title added

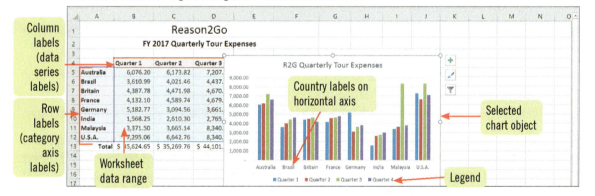

Creating sparklines

You can quickly create a miniature chart called a **sparkline** that serves as a visual indicator of data trends. You can create a sparkline by selecting a range of data, clicking the Quick Analysis tool, clicking the Sparklines tab, then clicking the type of sparkline you want. (The sparkline appears in the cell immediately adjacent to the selected range.) You can also select a range, click the Insert tab, then click the Line, Column, or Win/Loss button in the Sparklines group. In the Create Sparklines dialog box that opens, enter the cell in which you want the sparkline to appear,

then click OK. **FIGURE 4-6** shows a sparkline created in a cell. Any changes to data in the range are reflected in the sparkline. To delete a selected sparkline from a cell, click the Clear button in the Group group on the Sparkline Tools Design tab.

FIGURE 4-6: Sparklines in a cell

Move and Resize a Chart

Learning Outcomes
• Reposition a chart
• Resize a chart
• Modify a legend
• Modify chart data

A chart is an **object,** or an independent element on a worksheet, and is not located in a specific cell or range. You can select an object by clicking it; sizing handles around the object indicate it is selected. (When a chart is selected in Excel, the Name box, which normally tells you the address of the active cell, tells you the chart number.) You can move a selected chart anywhere on a worksheet without affecting formulas or data in the worksheet. Any data changed in the worksheet is automatically updated in the chart. You can even move a chart to a different sheet in the workbook, and it will still reflect the original data. You can resize a chart to improve its appearance by dragging its sizing handles. You can reposition chart objects (such as a title or legend) to predefined locations using commands using the Chart Elements button or the Add Chart Element button on the Chart Tools Design tab, or you can freely move any chart object by dragging it or by cutting and pasting it to a new location. When you point to a chart object, the name of the object appears as a ScreenTip. **CASE** *You want to resize the chart, position it below the worksheet data, and move the legend.*

STEPS

QUICK TIP
To delete a selected chart, press [Delete].

1. **Make sure the chart is still selected, then position the pointer over the chart**

   The pointer shape ⁺↖ indicates that you can move the chart. For a table of commonly used object pointers, refer to **TABLE 4-2**.

TROUBLE
Dragging a chart element instead of a blank area moves the element instead of the chart; if this happens, undo the action and try again.

2. **Position ↖ on a blank area near the upper-left edge of the chart, press and hold the left mouse button, drag the chart until its upper-left corner is at the upper-left corner of cell A16, then release the mouse button**

   When you release the mouse button, the chart appears in the new location.

3. **Scroll down so you can see the whole chart, position the pointer on the right-middle sizing handle until it changes to ⟷, then drag the right border of the chart to the right edge of column G**

   The chart is widened. See **FIGURE 4-7**.

QUICK TIP
To resize a selected chart to an exact size, click the Chart Tools Format tab, then enter the desired height and width in the Size group.

4. **Position the pointer over the upper-middle sizing handle until it changes to ↕, then drag the top border of the chart to the top edge of row 15**

5. **Position the pointer over the lower-middle sizing handle until it changes to ↕, then drag the bottom border of the chart to the bottom border of row 26**

   You can move any object on a chart. You want to align the top of the legend with the top of the plot area.

QUICK TIP
You can move a legend to the right, top, left, or bottom of a chart by clicking Legend in the Add Chart Element button in the Chart Layouts group on the Chart Tools Design tab, then clicking a location option.

6. **Click the Quick Layout button in the Chart Layouts group of the Chart Tools Design tab, click Layout 1 (in the upper-left corner of the palette), click the legend to select it, press and hold [Shift], drag the legend up using ⁺↖ so the dotted outline is approximately 1/4" above the top of the plot area, then release [Shift]**

   When you click the legend, sizing handles appear around it and "Legend" appears as a ScreenTip when the pointer hovers over the object. As you drag, a dotted outline of the legend border appears. Pressing and holding the [Shift] key holds the horizontal position of the legend as you move it vertically. Although the sizing handles on objects within a chart look different from the sizing handles that surround a chart, they function the same way.

7. **Click cell A12, type United States, click the Enter button ✓ on the formula bar, use AutoFit to resize column A, then save your work**

   The axis label changes to reflect the updated cell contents, as shown in **FIGURE 4-8**. Changing any data in the worksheet modifies corresponding text or values in the chart. Because the chart is no longer selected, the Chart Tools tabs no longer appear on the Ribbon.

FIGURE 4-7: Moved and resized chart

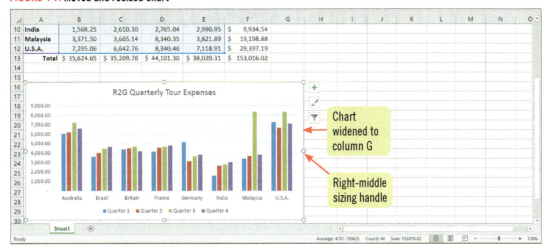

Chart widened to column G

Right-middle sizing handle

FIGURE 4-8: Worksheet with modified legend and label

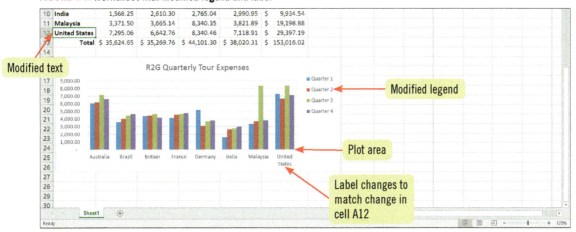

Modified text

Modified legend

Plot area

Label changes to match change in cell A12

TABLE 4-2: Common object pointers

name	pointer	use	name	pointer	use
Diagonal resizing	⬁ or ⬂	Change chart shape from corners	I-beam	I	Edit object text
Draw	+	Draw an object	Move	⊹	Move object
Horizontal resizing	⟺	Change object width	Vertical resizing	↕	Change object height

Moving an embedded chart to a sheet

Suppose you have created an embedded chart that you decide would look better on a chart sheet or in a different worksheet. You can make this change without recreating the entire chart. To do so, first select the chart, click the Chart Tools Design tab, then click the Move Chart button in the Location group. The Move Chart dialog box opens. To move the chart to its own chart sheet, click the New sheet option button, type a name for the new sheet if desired, then click OK. If the chart is already on its own sheet or you want to move it to a different existing sheet, click the Object in option button, click the desired worksheet, then click OK.

Change the Chart Design

Learning Outcomes
- Change the chart design
- Change the chart type
- Apply a chart style

Once you've created a chart, you can change the chart type, modify the data range and column/row configuration, apply a different chart style, and change the layout of objects in the chart. The layouts in the Chart Layouts group on the Chart Tools Design tab offer arrangements of objects in your chart, such as its legend, title, or gridlines; choosing one of these layouts is an alternative to manually changing how objects are arranged in a chart. **CASE** ▶ *You discovered that the data for Malaysia and the United States in Quarter 3 is incorrect. After the correction, you want to see how the data looks using different chart layouts and types.*

STEPS

1. **Click cell D11, type 5568.92, press [Enter], type 7107.09, then press [Enter]**

   In the chart, the Quarter 3 data markers for Malaysia and the United States reflect the adjusted expense figures. See **FIGURE 4-9**.

2. **Select the chart by clicking a blank area within the chart border, click the Chart Tools Design tab on the Ribbon, click the Quick Layout button in the Chart Layouts group, then click Layout 3**

   The legend moves to the bottom of the chart. You prefer the original layout.

3. **Click the Undo button ↺▾ on the Quick Access Toolbar, then click the Change Chart Type button in the Type group**

   The Change Chart Type dialog box opens, as shown in **FIGURE 4-10**. The left pane of the dialog box lists the available categories, and the right pane shows the individual chart types. A pale gray border surrounds the currently selected chart type.

4. **Click Bar in the left pane of the Change Chart Type dialog box, confirm that the first Clustered Bar chart type is selected in the right pane, then click OK**

   The column chart changes to a clustered bar chart. See **FIGURE 4-11**. You decide to see how the data looks in a three-dimensional column chart.

5. **Click the Change Chart Type button in the Type group, click Column in the left pane of the Change Chart Type dialog box, click 3-D Clustered Column (fourth from the left in the top row) in the right pane, verify that the left-most 3-D chart is selected, then click OK**

   A three-dimensional column chart appears. You notice that the three-dimensional column format gives you a sense of volume, but it is more crowded than the two-dimensional column format.

6. **Click the Change Chart Type button in the Type group, click Clustered Column (first from the left in the top row) in the right pane of the Change Chart Type dialog box, then click OK**

7. **Click the Style 3 chart style in the Chart Styles group**

   The columns change to lighter shades of color. You prefer the previous chart style's color scheme.

8. **Click ↺▾ on the Quick Access Toolbar, then save your work**

Creating a combo chart

A **combo chart** presents two or more charts in one; a column chart with a line chart, for example. This type of chart is helpful when charting dissimilar but related data. For example, you can create a combo chart based on home price and home size data, showing home prices in a column chart and related home sizes in a line chart. Here a **secondary axis** (such as a vertical axis on the right side of the chart) would supply the scale for the home sizes.

To create a combo chart, select all the data you want to plot, click the Combo chart button 📊▾ in the Charts group in the Insert tab, click a suggested type or Create Custom Combo Chart, supply additional series information if necessary, then click OK. To change an existing chart to a combo chart, select the chart, click Change Chart Type in the Type group on the Chart Tools Design tab, then follow the same procedure.

FIGURE 4-9: Worksheet with modified data

Modified data

Adjusted data points

FIGURE 4-10: Change Chart Type dialog box

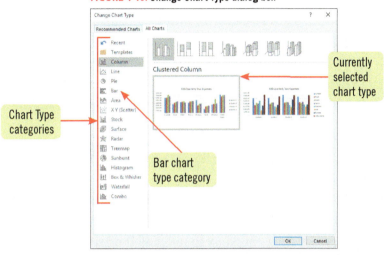

Chart Type categories

Bar chart type category

Currently selected chart type

FIGURE 4-11: Column chart changed to bar chart

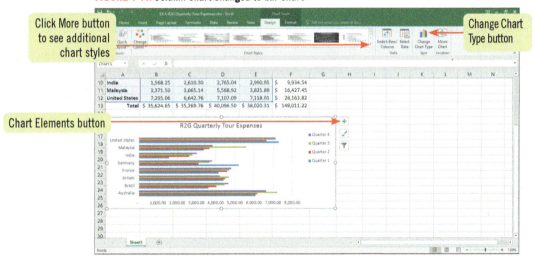

Click More button to see additional chart styles

Change Chart Type button

Chart Elements button

Working with a 3-D chart

Excel includes two kinds of 3-D chart types. In a true 3-D chart, a third axis, called the **z-axis**, lets you compare data points across both categories and values. The z-axis runs along the depth of the chart, so it appears to advance from the back of the chart. To create a true 3-D chart, look for chart types that begin with "3-D," such as 3-D Column. In a 3-D chart, data series can sometimes obscure other columns or bars in the same chart, but you can rotate the chart to obtain a better view. Right-click the chart, then click 3-D Rotation. The Format Chart Area pane opens with the 3-D Rotation category active. The 3-D Rotation options let you change the orientation and perspective of the chart area, plot area, walls, and floor. The 3-D Format category lets you apply three-dimensional effects to selected chart objects. (Not all 3-D Rotation and 3-D Format options are available on all charts.)

Change the Chart Format

Learning Outcomes
- Change the gridlines display
- Add axis titles
- Change the border color
- Add a shadow to an object

While the Chart Tools Design tab contains preconfigured chart layouts you can apply to a chart, the Chart Elements button makes it easy to add, remove, and modify individual chart objects such as a chart title or legend. Using options on this shortcut menu (or using the Add Chart Element button on the Chart Tools Design tab), you can also add text to a chart, add and modify labels, change the display of axes, modify the fill behind the plot area, create titles for the horizontal and vertical axes, and eliminate or change the look of gridlines. You can format the text in a chart object using the Home tab or the Mini toolbar, just as you would the text in a worksheet. **CASE** *You want to change the layout of the chart by creating titles for the horizontal and vertical axes. To improve the chart's appearance, you'll add a drop shadow to the chart title.*

STEPS

1. **With the chart still selected, click the Add Chart Element button in the Chart Layouts group on the Chart Tools Design tab, point to Gridlines, then click Primary Major Horizontal to deselect it**

   The gridlines that extend from the value axis tick marks across the chart's plot area are removed as shown in **FIGURE 4-12**.

2. **Click the Chart Elements button** ⊞ **in the upper-right corner** *outside* **the chart border, click the Gridlines arrow, click Primary Major Horizontal, click Primary Minor Horizontal, then click** ⊞ **to close the Chart Elements fly-out menu**

   Both major and minor gridlines now appear in the chart. **Major gridlines** represent the values at the value axis tick marks, and **minor gridlines** represent the values between the tick marks.

3. **Click** ⊞ **, click the Axis Titles checkbox to select all the axis titles options, triple-click the vertical axis title on the chart, then type Expenses (in $)**

   Descriptive text on the category axis helps readers understand the chart.

4. **Triple-click the horizontal axis title on the chart, then type Tour Countries**

   The text "Tour Countries" appears on the horizontal axis, as shown in **FIGURE 4-13**.

5. **Right-click the horizontal axis labels ("Australia", "Brazil", etc.), click Font on the shortcut menu, click the Latin text font list arrow in the Font dialog box, click Times New Roman, click the Size down arrow until 8 is displayed, then click OK**

   The font of the horizontal axis labels changes to Times New Roman, and the font size decreases, making more of the plot area visible.

6. **Right-click the vertical axis labels, then click Reset to Match**

7. **Right-click the Chart Title ("R2G Quarterly Tour Expenses"), click Format Chart Title on the shortcut menu, click the Border arrow** ▶ **in the Format Chart Title pane to display the options if necessary, then click the Solid line option button in the pane**

   A solid border appears around the chart title with the default blue color.

8. **Click the Effects button** ◻ **in the Format Chart Title pane, click Shadow, click the Presets list arrow, click Offset Diagonal Bottom Right in the Outer group (first row, first from the left), click the Format Chart Title pane Close button** ✕ **, then save your work**

   A blue border with a drop shadow surrounds the title. Compare your work to **FIGURE 4-14**.

FIGURE 4-12: Gridlines removed from chart

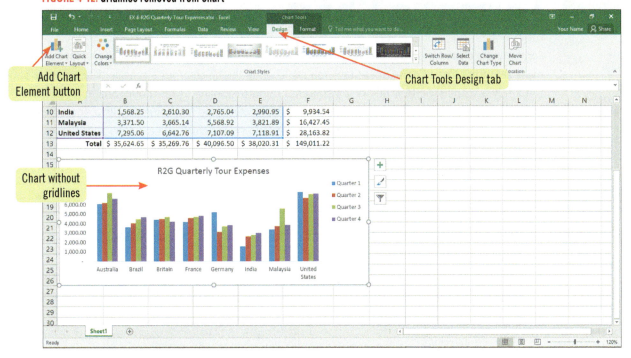

Add Chart Element button

Chart Tools Design tab

Chart without gridlines

FIGURE 4-13: Axis titles added to chart

Chart title

Vertical axis title

Vertical axis labels

Horizontal axis title

Horizontal axis labels

FIGURE 4-14: Enhanced chart

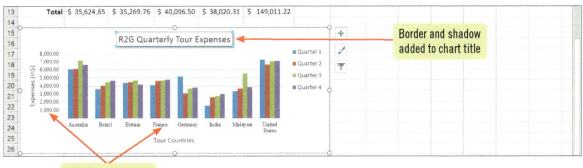

Border and shadow added to chart title

Modified axis labels

Adding data labels to a chart

There are times when your audience might benefit by seeing data labels on a chart. These labels appear next to the data markers in the chart and can indicate the series name, category name, and/or the value of one or more data points. Once your chart is selected, you can add this information to your chart by clicking the Chart Elements button in the upper-right corner outside the selected chart, clicking the Data Labels arrow, and then clicking a display option for the data labels. Once you have added the data labels, you can format them or delete individual data labels. To delete a data label, select it and then press [Delete].

Format a Chart

Learning Outcomes
- Change the fill of a data series
- Use Live Preview to see a new data series color
- Apply a style to a data series

Formatting a chart can make it easier to read and understand. Many formatting enhancements can be made using the Chart Tools Format tab. You can change the fill color for a specific data series, or you can apply a shape style to a title or a data series using the Shape Styles group. Shape styles make it possible to apply multiple formats, such as an outline, fill color, and text color, all with a single click. You can also apply different fill colors, outlines, and effects to chart objects using arrows and buttons in the Shape Styles group. **CASE** *You want to use a different color for one data series in the chart and apply a shape style to another, to enhance the look of the chart.*

STEPS

QUICK TIP

You can change the chart type of a selected data series by clicking the Chart Tools Design tab on the Ribbon, clicking the Change Chart Type button in the Type group, selecting a chart type for that data series, then clicking OK.

1. **With the chart selected, click the Chart Tools Format tab on the Ribbon, then click any column in the Quarter 4 data series**

   Handles appear on each column in the Quarter 4 data series, indicating that the entire series is selected.

2. **Click the Shape Fill list arrow in the Shape Styles group on the Chart Tools Format tab**

3. **Click Orange, Accent 6 (first row, 10th from the left) as shown in FIGURE 4-15**

   All the columns for the series become orange, and the legend changes to match the new color. You can also change the color of selected objects by applying a shape style.

4. **Click any column in the Quarter 3 data series**

   Handles appear on each column in the Quarter 3 data series.

QUICK TIP

To apply a WordArt style to a text object (such as the chart title), select the object, then click a style in the WordArt Styles group on the Chart Tools Format tab.

5. **Click the More button ▼ on the Shape Styles gallery, then *hover the pointer* over the Moderate Effect – Olive Green, Accent 3 shape style (fifth row, fourth from the left) in the gallery, as shown in FIGURE 4-16**

   Live Preview shows the data series in the chart with the shape style applied.

6. **Click the Subtle Effect – Olive Green, Accent 3 shape style**

   The style for the data series changes, as shown in FIGURE 4-17.

7. **Save your work**

Previewing a chart

To print or preview just a chart, select the chart (or make the chart sheet active), click the File tab, then click Print on the navigation bar. To reposition a chart by changing the page's margins, click the Show Margins button ⊞ in the lower-right corner of the Print tab to display the margins in the preview. You can drag the margin lines to the exact settings you want; as the margins change, the size and placement of the chart on the page change too.

FIGURE 4-15: New shape fill applied to data series

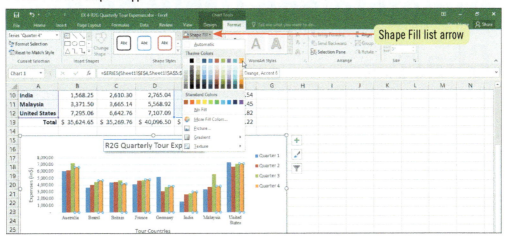

FIGURE 4-16: Live Preview of new style applied to data series

FIGURE 4-17: Style of data series changed

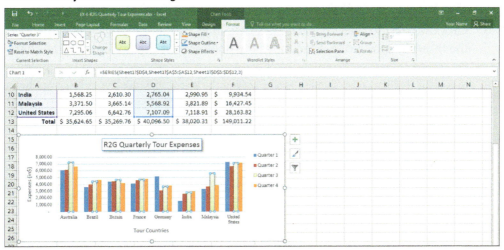

Changing alignment and angle in axis labels and titles

The buttons on the Chart Tools Design tab provide a few options for positioning axis labels and titles, but you can customize their position and rotation to exact specifications using the Format Axis pane or Format Axis Title pane. With a chart selected, right-click the axis text you want to modify, then click Format Axis or Format Axis Title on the shortcut menu. In the pane that opens, click the Size & Properties button, then select the appropriate option. You can also create a custom angle by clicking the Custom angle up and down arrows. When you have made the desired changes, close the pane.

Excel 2016

Annotate and Draw on a Chart

Learning Outcomes
- Type text in a text box
- Draw an arrow on a chart
- Modify a drawn object

You can use text annotations and graphics to point out critical information in a chart. **Text annotations** are labels that further describe your data. You can also draw lines and arrows that point to the exact locations you want to emphasize. Shapes such as arrows and boxes can be added from the Illustrations group on the Insert tab or from the Insert Shapes group on the Chart Tools Format tab on the Ribbon. The Insert group is also used to insert pictures into worksheets and charts. **CASE** *You want to call attention to the Germany tour expense decrease, so you decide to add a text annotation and an arrow to this information in the chart.*

STEPS

1. **With the chart selected and the Chart Tools Format tab active, click the Text Box button** ⊞ **in the Insert Shapes group, then move the pointer over the worksheet**
   The pointer changes to ↓, indicating that you will insert a text box where you next click.

> **QUICK TIP**
> You can also insert a text box by clicking the Text Box button in the Text group in the Insert tab, then clicking in the worksheet.

2. **Click to the right of the chart (anywhere *outside* the chart boundary)**
   A text box is added to the worksheet, and the Drawing Tools Format tab appears on the Ribbon so that you can format the new object. First you need to type the text.

3. **Type Great Improvement**
   The text appears in a selected text box on the worksheet, and the chart is no longer selected, as shown in **FIGURE 4-18**. Your text box may be in a different location; this is not important because you'll move the annotation in the next step.

4. **Point to an edge of the text box so that the pointer changes to** 🔖**, drag the text box into the chart to the left of the chart title, as shown in FIGURE 4-19, then release the mouse button**
   The text box is a text annotation for the chart. You also want to add a simple arrow shape in the chart.

> **QUICK TIP**
> To annotate a chart using a callout, click the Shapes button in the Illustrations group on the Insert tab or the More button on the Insert Shapes group on the Chart Tools Format tab, then click a shape in the Callouts category of the Shapes gallery.

5. **Click the chart to select it, click the Chart Tools Format tab, click the Arrow button** ◥ **in the Insert Shapes group, then move the pointer over the text box on the chart**
   The pointer changes to ✚, and the status bar displays "Click and drag to insert an AutoShape." When ✚ is over the text box, black handles appear around the text in the text box. A black handle can act as an anchor for the arrow.

6. **Position ✚ on the black handle to the right of the "t" in the word "improvement" (in the text box), press and hold the left mouse button, drag the line to the Quarter 2 column for the Germany category in the chart, then release the mouse button**
   An arrow points to the Quarter 2 expense for Germany, and the Drawing Tools Format tab displays options for working with the new arrow object. You can resize, format, or delete it just like any other object in a chart.

7. **Click the Shape Outline list arrow in the Shape Styles group, click the Automatic color, click the Shape Outline list arrow again, point to Weight, then click 1½ pt**
   Compare your finished chart to **FIGURE 4-20**.

8. **Save your work**

FIGURE 4-18: Text box added

Drawing Tools Format tab

Text annotation

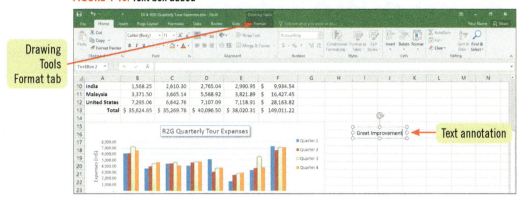

FIGURE 4-19: Text annotation on the chart

Text annotation

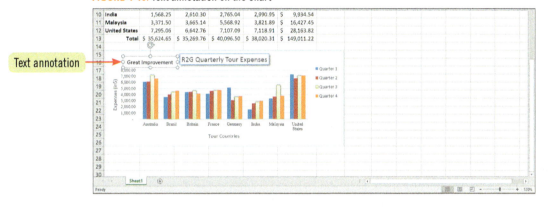

FIGURE 4-20: Arrow shape added to chart

Arrow drawn and formatted

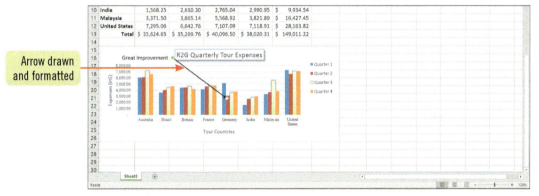

Adding SmartArt graphics

In addition to charts, annotations, and drawn objects, you can create a variety of diagrams using SmartArt graphics. **SmartArt graphics** are available in List, Process, Cycle, Hierarchy, Relationship, Matrix, Pyramid, Picture, and Office.com categories. To insert SmartArt, click the Insert a SmartArt Graphic button in the Illustrations group on the Insert tab to open the Choose a SmartArt Graphic dialog box. Click a SmartArt category in the left pane, then click a layout for the graphic in the right pane. The right pane shows sample layouts for the selected SmartArt, as shown in **FIGURE 4-21**. The SmartArt graphic appears in the worksheet as an embedded object with sizing handles. Depending on the type of SmartArt graphic you selected, a text pane opens next to the graphic; you can enter text into the graphic using the text pane or by typing directly in the shapes in the diagram.

FIGURE 4-21: Choose a SmartArt Graphic dialog box

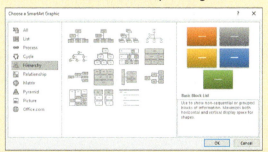

Excel 2016

Create a Pie Chart

Learning Outcomes
• Create a pie chart
• Explode a pie chart slice

You can create multiple charts based on the same worksheet data. While a column chart may illustrate certain important aspects of your worksheet data, you may find that you want to create an additional chart to emphasize a different point. Depending on the type of chart you create, you have additional options for calling attention to trends and patterns. For example, if you create a pie chart, you can emphasize one data point by **exploding**, or pulling that slice away from, the pie chart. When you're ready to print a chart, you can preview it just as you do a worksheet to check the output before committing it to paper. You can print a chart by itself or as part of the worksheet. **CASE** ▶ *At an upcoming meeting, Yolanda plans to discuss the total tour expenses and which countries need improvement. You want to create a pie chart she can use to illustrate total expenses. Finally, you want to fit the worksheet and the charts onto one worksheet page.*

STEPS

1. **Select the range A5:A12, press and hold [Ctrl], select the range F5:F12, click the Insert tab, click the Insert Pie or Doughnut Chart button in the Charts group, then click 3-D Pie in the chart gallery**

   The new chart appears in the center of the worksheet. You can move the chart and quickly format it using a chart layout.

2. **Drag the chart so its upper-left corner is at the upper-left corner of cell G1, click the Quick Layout button in the Chart Layouts group of the Chart Tools Design tab, then click Layout 2**

   The chart is repositioned on the page, and its layout changes so that a chart title is added, the percentages display on each slice, and the legend appears just below the chart title.

3. **Select the Chart Title text, then type R2G Total Expenses, by Country**

TROUBLE
If the Format Data Series command appears on the shortcut menu instead of Format Data Point, double-click the slice you want to explode to make sure it is selected by itself, then right-click it again.

4. **Click the slice for the India data point, click it again so it is the only slice selected, right-click it, then click Format Data Point**

   The Format Data Point pane opens, as shown in **FIGURE 4-22**. You can use the Point Explosion slider to control the distance a pie slice moves away from the pie, or you can type a value in the Point Explosion text box.

5. **Double-click 0 in the Point Explosion text box, type 40, then click the Close button [✕]**

   Compare your chart to **FIGURE 4-23**. You decide to preview the chart and data before you print.

6. **Click cell A1, switch to Page Layout view, type your name in the left header text box, then click cell A1**

   You decide the chart and data would fit better on the page if they were printed in landscape orientation.

7. **Click the Page Layout tab, click the Orientation button in the Page Setup group, then click Landscape**

8. **Click the File tab, click Print on the navigation bar, verify that the correct printer is selected, click the No Scaling setting in the Settings section on the Print tab, then click Fit Sheet on One Page**

   The data and chart are positioned horizontally on a single page, as shown in **FIGURE 4-24**. The printer you have selected may affect the appearance of your preview screen.

9. **Save and close the workbook, submit your work to your instructor as directed, then exit Excel**

FIGURE 4-22: Format Data Point pane

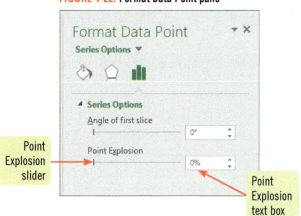

Point Explosion slider

Point Explosion text box

FIGURE 4-23: Exploded pie slice

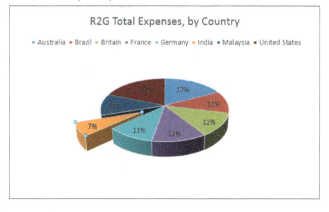

FIGURE 4-24: Preview of worksheet with charts in Backstage view

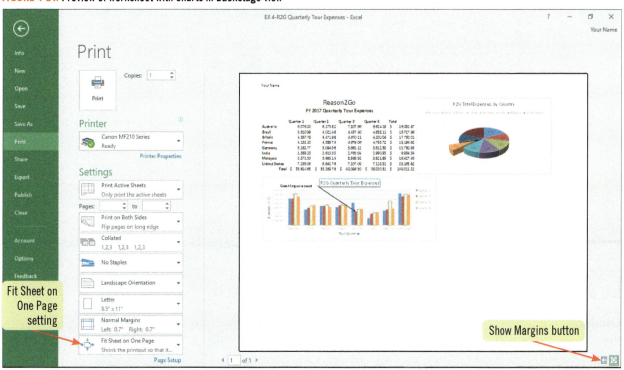

Fit Sheet on One Page setting

Show Margins button

Using the Insert Chart dialog box to discover new chart types

Excel 2016 includes five new chart types. You can explore these charts by clicking the Insert tab on the Ribbon, clicking Recommended Charts, then clicking the All Charts tab in the Insert Chart dialog box. Near the bottom of the list in the left panel are the new chart types: Treemap (which has nine variations), Sunburst, Histogram, Box & Whisker, and Waterfall. If cells are selected prior to opening the Insert Chart dialog box, you will see a sample of the chart type when you click

each chart type; the sample will be magnified when you hover the mouse over the sample. The Treemap and Sunburst charts both offer visual comparisons of relative sizes. The Histogram looks like a column chart, but each column (or bin) represents a range of values. The Box & Whisker chart shows distribution details as well as the mean, quartiles, and outliers. The Waterfall chart shows results above and below an imaginary line.

Practice

Concepts Review

Label each element of the Excel chart shown in FIGURE 4-25.

FIGURE 4-25

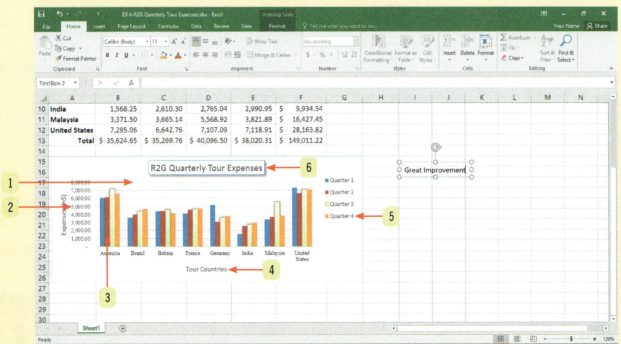

Match each chart type with the statement that best describes it.

7. **Combo**   a. Displays different chart types within one chart
8. **Pie**   b. Compares trends over even time intervals
9. **Area**   c. Compares data using columns
10. **Column**   d. Compares data as parts of a whole
11. **Line**   e. Shows how volume changes over time

Select the best answer from the list of choices.

12. Which tab on the Ribbon do you use to create a chart?

a. Design

b. Insert

c. Page Layout

d. Format

13. A collection of related data points in a chart is called a:

a. Data series.

b. Data tick.

c. Cell address.

d. Value title.

14. The object in a chart that identifies the colors used for each data series is a(n):

a. Data marker.

b. Data point.

c. Organizer.

d. Legend.

15. How do you move an embedded chart to a chart sheet?

a. Click a button on the Chart Tools Design tab.

b. Drag the chart to the sheet tab.

c. Delete the chart, switch to a different sheet, then create a new chart.

d. Use the Copy and Paste buttons on the Ribbon.

16. Which is *not* an example of a SmartArt graphic?

a. Sparkline

b. Basic Matrix

c. Organization Chart

d. Basic Pyramid

17. Which tab appears only when a chart is selected?

a. Insert

b. Chart Tools Format

c. Review

d. Page Layout

Skills Review

1. Plan a chart.

a. Start Excel, open the Data File EX 4-2.xlsx from the location where you store your Data Files, then save it as **EX 4-Software Usage Polling Results**.

b. Describe the type of chart you would use to plot this data.

c. What chart type would you use to compare the number of Excel users in each type of business?

2. Create a chart.

a. In the worksheet, select the range containing all the data and headings.

b. Click the Quick Analysis tool.

c. Create a Clustered Column chart, then add the chart title **Software Usage, by Business** above the chart.

d. If necessary, click the Switch Row/Column button so the business type (Accounting, Advertising, etc.) appears as the x-axis.

e. Save your work.

Skills Review (continued)

3. Move and resize a chart.

   a. Make sure the chart is still selected, and close any open panes if necessary.

   b. Move the chart beneath the worksheet data.

   c. Widen the chart so it extends to the right edge of column H.

   d. Use the Quick Layout button in the Chart Tools Design tab to move the legend to the right of the charted data. (*Hint*: Use Layout 1.)

   e. Resize the chart so its bottom edge is at the top of row 25.

   f. Save your work.

4. Change the chart design.

   a. Change the value in cell B3 to **8**. Observe the change in the chart.

   b. Select the chart.

   c. Use the Quick Layout button in the Chart Layouts group on the Chart Tools Design tab to apply the Layout 10 layout to the chart, then undo the change.

   d. Use the Change Chart Type button on the Chart Tools Design tab to change the chart to a Clustered Bar chart.

   e. Change the chart to a 3-D Clustered Column chart, then change it back to a Clustered Column chart.

   f. Save your work.

5. Change the chart layout.

   a. Use the Chart Elements button to turn off the primary major horizontal gridlines in the chart.

   b. Change the font used in the horizontal and vertical axis labels to Times New Roman.

   c. Turn on the primary major gridlines for both the horizontal and vertical axes.

   d. Change the chart title's font to Times New Roman if necessary, with a font size of 20.

   e. Insert **Business** as the primary horizontal axis title.

   f. Insert **Number of Users** as the primary vertical axis title.

   g. Change the font size of the horizontal and vertical axis titles to 10 and the font to Times New Roman, if necessary.

   h. Change "Personnel" in the worksheet column heading to **Human Resources**, then AutoFit column D, and any other columns as necessary.

   i. Change the font size of the legend to 14.

   j. Add a solid line border in the default color and a (preset) Offset Diagonal Bottom Right shadow to the chart title.

   k. Save your work.

6. Format a chart.

   a. Make sure the chart is selected, then select the Chart Tools Format tab, if necessary.

   b. Change the shape fill of the Excel data series to Dark Blue, Text 2.

   c. Change the shape style of the Excel data series to Subtle Effect – Orange, Accent 6.

   d. Save your work.

7. Annotate and draw on a chart.

   a. Make sure the chart is selected, then create the text annotation **Needs more users**.

   b. Position the text annotation so the word "Needs" is just below the word "Software" in the chart title.

   c. Select the chart, then use the Chart Tools Format tab to create a 1½ pt weight dark blue arrow that points from the bottom center of the text box to the Excel users in the Human Resources category.

   d. Deselect the chart.

   e. Save your work.

Skills Review (continued)

8. Create a pie chart.

a. Select the range A1:F2, then create a 3-D Pie chart.

b. Drag the 3-D pie chart beneath the existing chart.

c. Change the chart title to **Excel Users**.

d. Apply the Style 7 chart style to the chart, then apply Layout 6 using the Quick Layout button.

e. Explode the Law Firm slice from the pie chart at **25%**.

f. In Page Layout view, enter your name in the left section of the worksheet header.

g. Preview the worksheet and charts in Backstage view, make sure all the contents fit on one page, then submit your work to your instructor as directed. When printed, the worksheet should look like **FIGURE 4-26**. (Note that certain elements such as the title may look slightly different when printed.)

h. Save your work, close the workbook, then exit Excel.

FIGURE 4-26

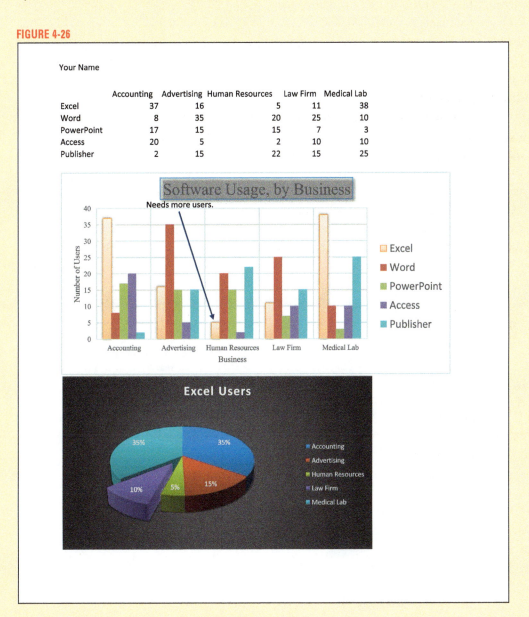

Independent Challenge 1

You are the operations manager for the Chicago Arts Alliance. Each year the group revisits the number and types of activities they support to better manage their budgets. For this year's budget, you need to create charts to document the number of events in previous years.

a. Start Excel, open the file EX 4-3.xlsx from the location where you store your Data Files, then save it as **EX 4-Chicago Arts Alliance**.

b. Take some time to plan your charts. Which type of chart or charts might best illustrate the information you need to display? What kind of chart enhancements do you want to use? Will a 3-D effect make your chart easier to understand?

c. Create a Clustered Column chart for the data.

d. Change at least one of the colors used in a data series.

e. Make the appropriate modifications to the chart to make it visually attractive and easier to read and understand. Include a legend to the right of the chart, and add chart titles and horizontal and vertical axis titles using the text shown in **TABLE 4-3**.

TABLE 4-3

title	text
Chart title	Chicago Arts Alliance Events
Vertical axis title	Number of Events
Horizontal axis title	Types of Events

f. Create at least two additional charts for the same data to show how different chart types display the same data. Reposition each new chart so that all charts are visible in the worksheet. One of the additional charts should be a pie chart for an appropriate data set; the other is up to you.

g. Modify each new chart as necessary to improve its appearance and effectiveness. A sample worksheet containing three charts based on the worksheet data is shown in **FIGURE 4-27**.

h. Enter your name in the worksheet header.

i. Save your work. Before printing, preview the worksheet in Backstage view, then adjust any settings as necessary so that all the worksheet data and charts will print on a single page.

j. Submit your work to your instructor as directed.

k. Close the workbook, then exit Excel.

FIGURE 4-27

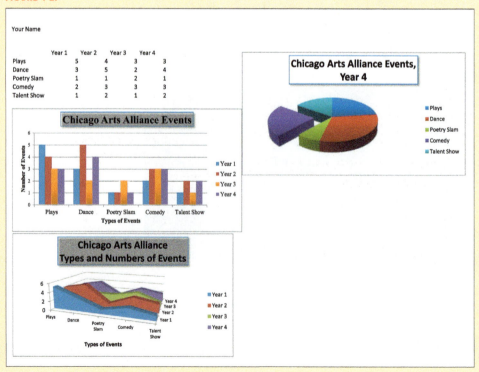

Independent Challenge 2

You work at Canine Companions, a locally owned dog obedience school. One of your responsibilities at the school is to manage the company's sales and expenses using Excel. As part of your efforts, you want to help the staff better understand and manage the school's largest sources of both expenses and sales. To do this, you've decided to create charts using current operating expenses including rent, utilities, and payroll. The manager will use these charts at the next monthly meeting.

a. Start Excel, open EX 4-4.xlsx from the location where you store your Data Files, then save it as **EX 4-Canine Companions Expense Analysis**.

b. Decide which data in the worksheet should be charted. What chart types are best suited for the information you need to show? What kinds of chart enhancements are necessary?

c. Create a 3-D Clustered Column chart in the worksheet showing the expense data for all four quarters. (*Hint*: The expense categories should appear on the x-axis. Do not include the totals.)

d. Change the vertical axis labels (Expenses data) so that no decimals are displayed. (*Hint*: Use the Number category in the Format Axis pane.)

e. Using the sales data, create two charts on this worksheet that compare the sales amounts. (*Hint*: Move each chart to a new location on the worksheet, then deselect it before creating the next one.)

f. In one chart of the sales data, add data labels, then add chart titles as you see fit.

g. Make any necessary formatting changes to make the charts look more attractive, then enter your name in a worksheet cell.

h. Save your work.

i. Preview each chart in Backstage view, and adjust any items as needed. Fit the worksheet to a single page, then submit your work to your instructor as directed. A sample of a printed worksheet is shown in FIGURE 4-28.

j. Close the workbook, then exit Excel.

FIGURE 4-28

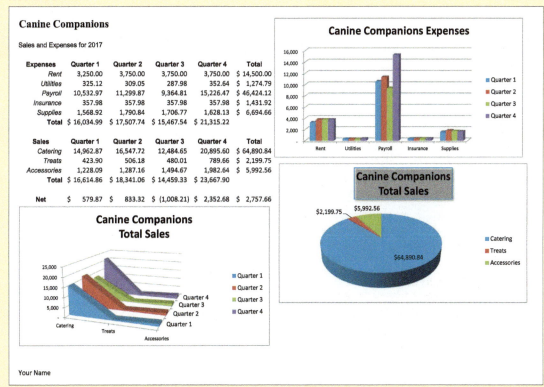

Excel 2016

Independent Challenge 3

You are working as an account representative at a clothing store called Zanzibar. You have been examining the advertising expenses incurred recently. The CEO wants to examine expenses designed to increase sales and has asked you to prepare charts that can be used in this evaluation. In particular, you want to see how dollar amounts compare among the different expenses, and you also want to see how expenses compare with each other proportional to the total budget.

a. Start Excel, open the Data File EX 4-5.xlsx from the location where you store your Data Files, then save it as **EX 4-Zanzibar Advertising Expenses**.

b. Identify three types of charts that seem best suited to illustrate the data in the range A16:B24. What kinds of chart enhancements are necessary?

c. Create at least two different types of charts that show the distribution of advertising expenses. (*Hint*: Move each chart to a new location on the same worksheet.) One of the charts should be a 3-D pie chart.

d. In at least one of the charts, add annotated text and arrows highlighting important data, such as the largest expense.

e. Change the color of at least one data series in at least one of the charts.

f. Add chart titles and category and value axis titles where appropriate. Format the titles with a font of your choice. Apply a shadow to the chart title in at least one chart.

g. Add your name to a section of the header, then save your work.

h. Explode a slice from the 3-D pie chart.

i. Add a data label to the exploded pie slice.

j. Preview the worksheet in Backstage view. Adjust any items as needed. Be sure the charts are all visible on one page. Compare your work to the sample in FIGURE 4-29.

k. Submit your work to your instructor as directed, close the workbook, then exit Excel.

FIGURE 4-29

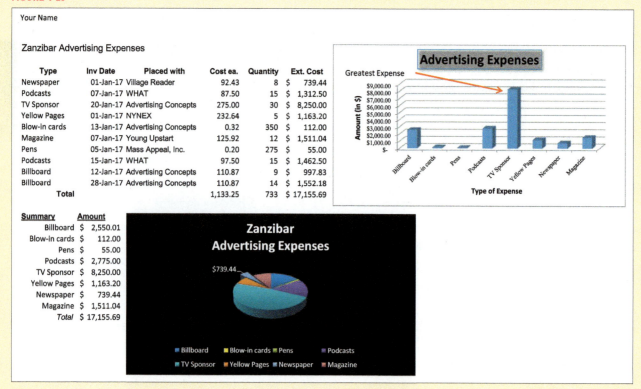

Independent Challenge 4: Explore

This Independent Challenge requires an Internet connection.

All the years of hard work and saving money have paid off, and you have decided to purchase a home. You know where you'd like to live, and you decide to use the web to find out more about houses that are currently available. A worksheet would be a great place to compare the features and prices of potential homes.

a. Start Excel, then save a new, blank workbook as **EX 4-My New House** to the location where you save your Data Files.

b. Decide on where you would like to live, and use your favorite search engine to find information sources on homes for sale in that area. (*Hint*: Try using realtor.com or other realtor-sponsored sites.)

c. Determine a price range and features within the home. Find data for at least five homes that meet your location and price requirements, and enter them in the worksheet. See **TABLE 4-4** for a suggested data layout.

d. Format the data so it looks attractive and professional.

e. Create any type of column chart using only the House and Asking Price data. Place it on the same worksheet as the data. Include a descriptive title.

f. Change the colors in the chart using the chart style of your choice.

g. Enter your name in a section of the header.

h. Create an additional chart: a combo chart that plots the asking price on one axis and the size of the home on the other axis. (*Hint*: Use the Tell me what you want to do text box above the Ribbon to get more guidance on creating a Combo Chart.)

i. Save the workbook. Preview the worksheet in Backstage view and make adjustments if necessary to fit all of the information on one page. See **FIGURE 4-30** for an example of what your worksheet might look like.

j. Submit your work to your instructor as directed.

k. Close the workbook, then exit Excel.

TABLE 4-4

suggested data layout					
Location					
Price range					
	House 1	House 2	House 3	House 4	House 5
Asking price					
Bedrooms					
Bathrooms					
Year built					
Size (in sq. ft.)					

FIGURE 4-30

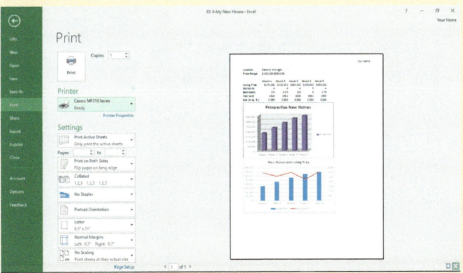

Visual Workshop

Open the Data File EX 4-6.xlsx from the location where you store your Data Files, then save it as **EX 4-Estimated Cost Center Expenses**. Format the worksheet data so it looks like FIGURE 4-31, then create and modify two charts to match the ones shown in the figure. You will need to make formatting, layout, and design changes once you create the charts. (*Hint:* The shadow used in the 3-D pie chart title is made using the Outer Offset Diagonal Top Right shadow.) Enter your name in the left text box of the header, then save and preview the worksheet. Submit your work to your instructor as directed, then close the workbook and exit Excel.

FIGURE 4-31

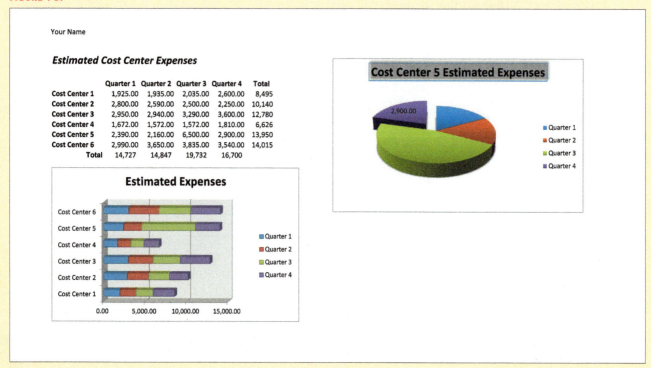

Integrating Word and Excel

CASE You are working as an operations assistant to Kevin Lawrence, the vice president of Operations for R2G. Kevin has asked you to explore the integration capabilities of Office 2016. First, you create a report in Word that includes values and a chart created in Excel, and then you embed a paragraph of text created in Word into an Excel worksheet.

Module Objectives

After completing this module, you will be able to:

- Integrate data between Word and Excel
- Copy data from Excel to Word
- Copy a chart from Excel to Word
- Create linked objects
- Embed a Word file in Excel

Files You Will Need

INT 1-1.xlsx	INT 1-9.docx
INT 1-2.docx	INT 1-10.xlsx
INT 1-3.xlsx	INT 1-11.xlsx
INT 1-4.docx	INT 1-12.docx
INT 1-5.xlsx	INT 1-13.xlsx
INT 1-6.docx	INT 1-14.docx
INT 1-7.xlsx	INT 1-15.xlsx
INT 1-8.docx	INT 1-16.docx

Integrate Data Between Word and Excel

Microsoft Office programs are designed to work together through a process called **integration**. When you integrate data from multiple Office programs, you work with both a source file and a destination file. The **source file** is the file from which the information is copied or used. The **destination file** is the file that receives the copied information. You can choose from three integration methods: pasting, linking, and embedding. **CASE** ▶ *As an operations assistant, you often create documents such as reports and price lists that include data from both Word and Excel. You decide to review some of the ways in which you integrate data between the two programs.*

DETAILS

You can integrate Word and Excel by:

• **Copying and pasting data from the Clipboard**

You use the Copy and Paste commands to duplicate **objects** such as text selections, numbers (called values in Excel), and pictures from one program and place them into another program. After you copy and paste an object, changes that you make to the object in the source file do not appear in the destination file. The report shown in **FIGURE 1-1** was created in Word and includes two objects that were copied from Excel—the photograph that appears to the right of the document title and the shaded table under the document subtitle.

• **Linking data**

Sometimes you want to connect the data that is included in two or more files. For example, suppose you copy the contents of a cell containing a formula from an Excel worksheet and paste it into a Word document. When you change the formula values in Excel, you want the corresponding values to change in the Word document. To create a **link** between data in two files, you select one of the link options that appears when you either click the Paste button list arrow or view options in the Paste Special dialog box. You use the term **linked object** to refer to the connected data. In the report shown in **FIGURE 1-1**, the value "90" is a linked object. If this percentage changes in the Excel worksheet, the linked percentage in the Word document also changes.

• **Copying and pasting charts**

When you copy a chart from Excel and paste it into Word using the Paste command, Word automatically creates a link between the pasted chart and the original chart. In the report shown in **FIGURE 1-1**, the column chart was copied from Excel and pasted into the Word document. When the chart values are updated in Excel, the same chart values are updated in the chart copied to Word. You can also copy a chart from the source file and then paste it into the destination file as an object that is not linked.

• **Embedding a Word file in Excel**

You can **embed**, or place an unlinked copy of, the contents of a Word file into an Excel worksheet. You edit the embedded object by double-clicking it and using Word program tools to change text and formatting. This process changes the embedded copy of the Word object in Excel, but does not affect the original source document you created in Word. Similarly, any changes to the source Word document are not reflected in the embedded copy in Excel. In the price list shown in **FIGURE 1-2**, the text that describes the R2G tours was inserted in Excel as an embedded Word file.

FIGURE 1-1: Word report with objects copied from Excel

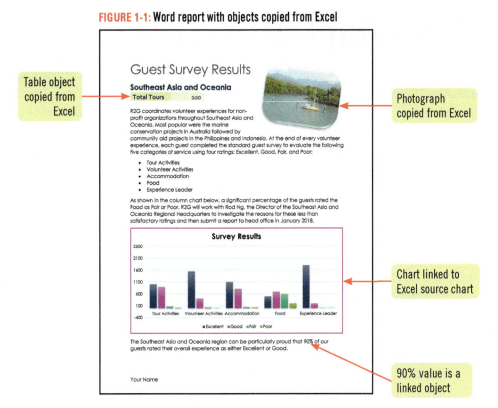

Table object copied from Excel

Photograph copied from Excel

Chart linked to Excel source chart

90% value is a linked object

FIGURE 1-2: Price list with embedded Word file

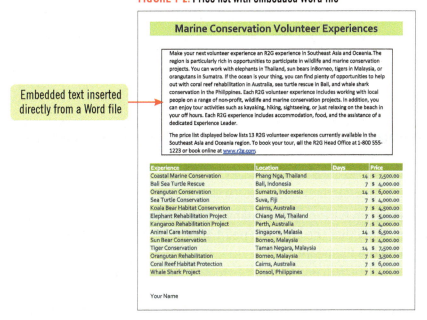

Embedded text inserted directly from a Word file

Understanding object linking and embedding (OLE)

The term **object linking and embedding (OLE)** refers to the technology that Microsoft uses to let you integrate data between programs. You create an object in one program, and then you can choose to either link the object to or embed it in another program. The difference between linking and embedding relates to where the object is stored and how you update the object after you place it in a document. A linked object in a destination file is an image of an object contained in a source file, not a copy of it. Both objects share a single source, which means you make changes to an object only in the source file.

When you embed an object that you created in another program, you include a copy of the object in a destination file. To update the object, you double-click it in the destination file and then use the tools of the source program to make changes. You cannot edit the source object using the tools of the destination program.

Copy Data from Excel to Word

Learning Outcomes
• Switch between Word and Excel
• Copy objects to the clipboard
• Paste Excel objects into Word

You use the Copy and Paste commands when you want to copy an item from one program to another program. The item might be a line of text, a selection of cells, or an object such as a chart or a picture. The procedure is the same as the one you use to copy and paste an object from one location in a document to another location in the same document. By default, an object copied from one program to another program retains the formatting of the original object and is not linked to the original object. The exception occurs when you copy and paste a chart, which you will learn about in the next lesson. **CASE** ▸ *Kevin Lawrence, the vice president of Operations at R2G, has provided you with an Excel worksheet containing survey data from the Southeast Asia and Oceania Regional Headquarters and created a report in Word that describes the survey results. He asks you to copy two objects from the Excel worksheet and paste them into the Word report.*

STEPS

1. **Start Excel, open the file INT 1-1.xlsx from the location where you store your Data Files, then save it as INT 1-Customer Survey Data**

   The values in the range B7:F10 represent the total number of responses in each of the four rating categories for the volunteer experiences that R2G operated in Southeast Asia and Oceania.

2. **Start Word, open the file INT 1-2.docx from the location where you store your Data Files, then save it as INT 1-Customer Survey Report**

   The Word report contains text that describes the results of the survey.

3. **Move the mouse pointer over the Excel program button on the taskbar, as shown in FIGURE 1-3, then click the Excel program button to switch to Excel**

   When you point to the Excel program button, a picture of the worksheet and the filename appear.

4. **On the Home tab, click the dialog box launcher 🔲 in the Clipboard group**

   The Clipboard task pane opens to the left of the worksheet window. You use the Clipboard when you want to copy and paste more than one item from one program to another program. You can "collect" up to 24 items on the Clipboard and then switch to the other program to paste them.

5. **Click the photograph, click the Copy button in the Clipboard group, select the range A4:B4, then click the Copy button**

   Both items now appear on the Clipboard, as shown in **FIGURE 1-4**. When you place multiple items on the Clipboard, newer items appear at the top of the list and older items move down.

6. **Click the Word program button on the taskbar, click the dialog box launcher 🔲 in the Clipboard group, verify that the Insertion point appears to the left of the title, then click the photograph on the Clipboard**

7. **Click in the blank space below the subtitle Southeast Asia and Oceania, click Total Tours 100 on the Clipboard, then click the Close button ✖ on the Clipboard task pane**

   You pasted the object as a table below the document subtitle. When you use the Copy and Paste commands, the default setting is for the copied object to retain the formatting applied to it in the source file.

8. **Click the photograph in the Word document, click the Layout Options button 🖼 in the upper-right corner of the photograph, click the Square option 🔲, then drag the photograph to the right of the first paragraph using the green alignment guides, as shown in FIGURE 1-5**

9. **Click anywhere in the document to deselect the photograph, then save the document**

FIGURE 1-3: Word and Excel on the taskbar

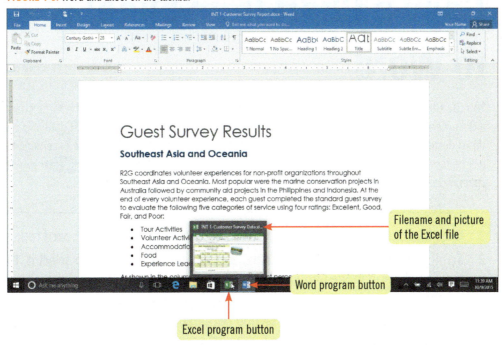

Filename and picture of the Excel file

Word program button

Excel program button

FIGURE 1-4: Two items collected on the Clipboard

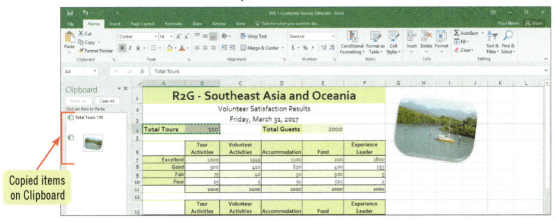

Copied items on Clipboard

FIGURE 1-5: Picture positioned in the Word report

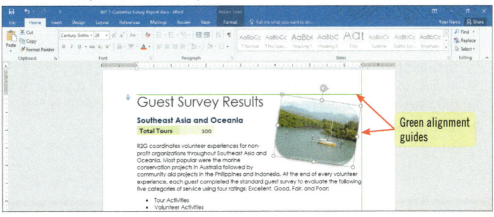

Green alignment guides

Copy a Chart from Excel to Word

Learning Outcomes
- Copy a chart
- View Paste options
- Update a linked chart

You use the Copy and Paste tools to create a link between a chart in Excel and the same chart pasted into a document in Word. When you change the data in the Excel source file, the linked data also changes in the Word destination file. By default, the copied chart will be linked to the chart in the Excel report. However, it will be formatted with the same theme applied to the destination document. **CASE** ▶ *You need to copy a column chart representing survey results from Excel and paste it into the Word report.*

STEPS

1. **Click the Excel program button on the taskbar, then close the Clipboard task pane**

2. **Scroll down to view the column chart, click an edge of the chart to select it, then click the Copy button in the Clipboard group**
   The chart in Excel is formatted with the colors of the Banded theme.

3. **Switch to Word, click below the second paragraph (which ends with "January 2018"), then click the Paste button in the Clipboard group**
   The chart appears in the Word document formatted with the colors of the Slice theme, because this theme was already applied to the Word document. The Paste Options button appears in the lower-right corner of the chart.

4. **Click the Paste Options button [🗐 (Ctrl) ▾] outside the lower-right corner of the pasted chart, as shown in FIGURE 1-6**
   A selection of paste options appears. By default, the option Use Destination Theme & Link Data is selected. The Word document is the destination file and is formatted with the Slice theme. The Excel document is the source file and is formatted with the Banded theme. As a result, the Slice theme applied to the Word file is applied to the chart. **TABLE 1-1** describes the five options available for pasting a copied chart.

5. **Move the mouse over each of the five Paste Options buttons to view how the formatting of the chart changes depending on which button is selected, then click the Use Destination Theme & Link Data button [🗐]**

6. **Switch to Excel, then note the position of the bars for the Food category in the column chart**
   At present, the Poor column (pink) is quite high compared to the Poor columns for the other categories.

7. **Scroll up, click cell E8, type 700, press [Enter], click cell E10, type 200, then press [Enter] and scroll down to the chart**
   In the chart, the Good column (lime green) in the Food category has grown, and the Poor column has shrunk.

TROUBLE
You may not need to refresh the chart data.

8. **Switch to Word, click the chart, click the Chart Tools Design tab, then click the Refresh Data button in the Data group**
   As shown in **FIGURE 1-7**, the bars for the Food category in the column chart change in the linked chart to reflect the changes you made to the chart in Excel.

9. **Save the document, switch to Excel, then save the workbook**

FIGURE 1-6: Paste Options

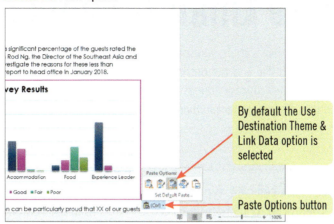

By default the Use Destination Theme & Link Data option is selected

Paste Options button

FIGURE 1-7: Linked chart updated in Word

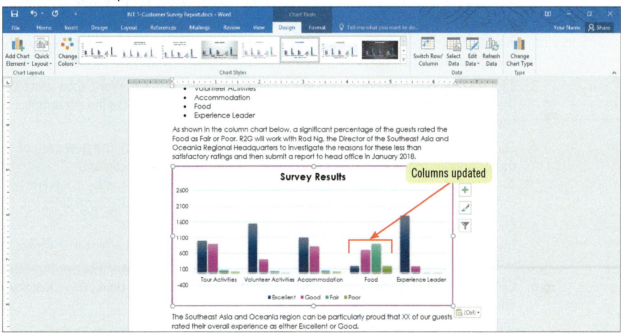

TABLE 1-1: Paste options for charts

Paste Options button	button name	description
	Use Destination Theme & Embed Workbook	The pasted chart is not linked to the source document, and the pasted chart assumes the formatting of the destination document
	Keep Source Formatting & Embed Workbook	The pasted chart is not linked to the source document, and the pasted chart keeps the same formatting as the source document
	Use Destination Theme & Link Data	This button is selected by default when a chart is pasted into the destination document; the theme of the destination document is applied to the chart, and the chart is linked to the object in the source document
	Keep Source Formatting & Link Data	The pasted chart is linked to the source document, so any changes made to the chart in the source document will be made to the copied chart in the Word document; in addition, the formatting of the source document is retained
	Picture	The chart is pasted as a picture that cannot be modified, and uses the same formatting as the chart in the source document

Create Linked Objects

To link data other than a chart, you use the Copy button and the Paste Special command to create a link between the source file and the destination file. **CASE** ▶ *You need your report to include a value that represents the average customer ratings. You decide to link the report to the source file data so you can update the data in both files when new information becomes available.*

STEPS

1. **In Excel, click cell G14, type the formula =AVERAGE(B14:F14), press [Enter], click cell G14, then drag its fill handle to cell G17 to enter the remaining three percentages**
   The value "56%" appears in cell G14. This value indicates that, on average, 56% of the responses were Excellent. Only 3% of the responses were Poor.

2. **Click cell F18, type Good/Excellent, press [Tab], type the formula =G14+G15 in cell G18, then press [Enter]**
   The value "87%" appears in cell G18, indicating that 87% of guests rated their R2G volunteer experience as Good or Excellent.

3. **Click cell G18, click the Copy button in the Clipboard group, switch to Word, then select XX that appears following the phrase "can be particularly proud that" in the last paragraph**
   You will paste the contents of cell G18 from Excel over the "XX" in Word.

4. **Click the Paste list arrow in the Clipboard group, then move your mouse over each of the six options to view how the pasted object will appear in the document**
   Two options allow linking—Link & Keep Source Formatting and Link & Merge Formatting. However, both options also insert a line break, so you look for additional paste options in the Paste Special dialog box.

5. **Click Paste Special**
   The Paste Special dialog box opens, as shown in **FIGURE 1-8**. In this dialog box, you have more options for pasting the value and for controlling its appearance in the destination file.

6. **Click the Paste link option button, click Unformatted Text, click OK, then press [Spacebar] once to add a space after "87%" if necessary**
   The percentage, 87%, appears in the Word document. You decide to test the link.

7. **Switch to Excel, click cell E7, type 500, press [Enter], click cell E9, type 600, then press [Enter]**
   The Good/Excellent rating in cell G18 is now 90%.

8. **Switch to Word, right-click 87%, then click Update Link**
   The value 90% appears. The final document is shown in **FIGURE 1-9**.

9. **Type your name where indicated in the Word footer, save the document, switch to Excel, type your name where indicated in cell A37, save the workbook, submit your files to your instructor, then close the files**
   If you print the Excel workbook, make sure you fit it on one page.

FIGURE 1-8: Paste Special dialog box

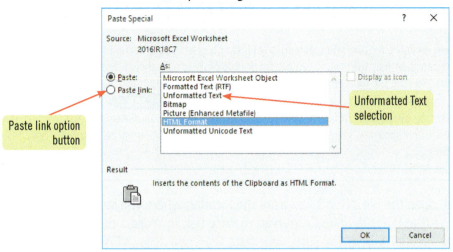

FIGURE 1-9: Completed report

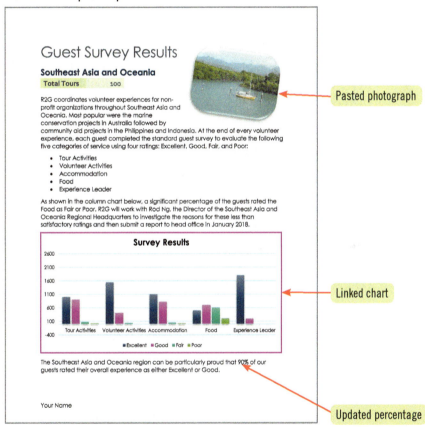

Opening linked files and reestablishing links to charts

When you open a Word file that contains links from an Excel file, a dialog box opens with a message telling you that the document contains links that may refer to other files. The message also asks if you want to update this document with the data from the linked file. Click Yes to update the document with data from the linked file. If you want to change information in both the Excel file and the Word file, you need to open the Excel workbook first, followed by the Word document.

If you make a change to a linked chart in the Excel file, you need to refresh the chart data in Word. To do so, click the chart in Word, click the Chart Tools Design tab, then click the Refresh Data button in the Data group. You also need to manually update any other links by right-clicking the link in Word and then clicking Update Link.

Embed a Word File in Excel

Learning Outcomes
- Insert a Word file as an object
- Edit the Word file in Excel

You can embed an entire file that you create in one Office program into a document created in another Office program. You can then edit the embedded file by double-clicking it in the destination program to open the source program. You use the tools of the source program to make changes. **TABLE 1-2** summarizes the four ways in which you integrated data between Word and Excel in this module. **CASE** *You have created a price list in Excel that lists the wildlife and marine conservation experiences offered in Southeast Asia and Oceania, but before you distribute it at an upcoming meeting, you decide to include some explanatory text that you have stored in a Word document.*

STEPS

1. **In Excel, open the file INT 1-3.xlsx from the location where you store your Data Files, then save it as INT 1-Wildlife Conservation Price List; in Word, open the file INT 1-4.docx from the location where you store your Data Files, save it as INT 1-Wildlife Conservation, then close the document**

2. **In Excel, click cell G3, click the Insert tab, then click the Object button ☐ in the Text group**

   The Object dialog box opens. Here you can choose to either create a new object or insert an object from a file.

TROUBLE
If the Object button is not visible on the Ribbon, click the down arrow in the Text group.

3. **Click the Create from File tab, click Browse, navigate to where you stored the INT 1-Wildlife Conservation file if necessary, double-click INT 1-Wildlife Conservation, then click OK**

   The text from the Word document appears in a box that starts in cell G3. When you insert an object from another program such as Word, you sometimes need to reposition the current worksheet contents to accommodate the inserted object.

4. **Select the range A4:D20, move the mouse pointer over any border of the selection to show the ⬚, then drag the selection down to cell A18**

5. **Move the mouse pointer over the border of the box containing the Word text to show the ⬚ pointer, drag the selection to cell A3, click a blank cell, then compare your screen to FIGURE 1-10**

6. **Double-click the box containing the Word text**

   Because the object is embedded, the Word Ribbon and tabs appear within the Excel window. As a result, you can use the tools from the source program (Word) to edit the text. The title bar shows "Document in INT 1-Wildlife Conservation Price List.xlsx - Excel" because you are working within the destination file to edit the embedded object.

7. **Click the Select button in the Editing group, click Select All, click the dialog box launcher ⬚ in the Paragraph group, select the contents of the Left text box in the Indentation section, type .2, press [Tab], type .2 in the Right text box, then click OK**

8. **Select 10 in the first line of paragraph 2, type 13, compare the edited object to FIGURE 1-11, then click outside the object to return to Excel**

   The embedded object is updated in Excel. The text in the source file is not updated because the source file is not linked to the destination file.

9. **Click the File tab, click Print, click Page Setup, click the Margins tab, click the Horizontally check box, click OK, then click ⬅ to return to the workbook**

   The embedded Word object and Excel data are centered between the left and right margins of the page.

10. **Type your name where indicated in cell A34, save the workbook, submit your files to your instructor, then close the workbook and exit Word and Excel**

FIGURE 1-10: Embedded Word file positioned in Excel

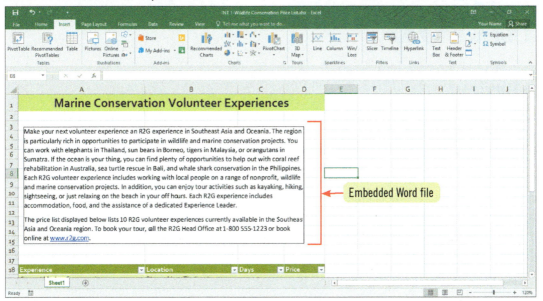

FIGURE 1-11: Embedded object updated in Excel

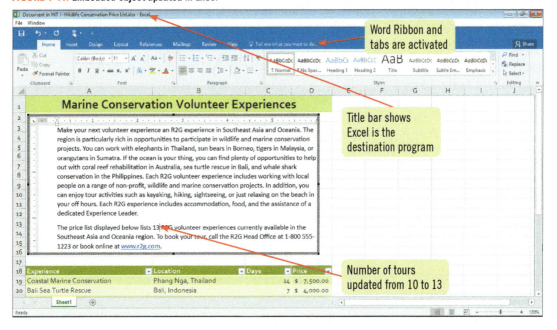

TABLE 1-2: Module 1 integration tasks

object	command	source program	destination program	result	connection	page no.
Cells	Copy/Paste	Excel	Word	Object with Excel formatting	Pasted: no link	4
Chart	Copy/Paste	Excel	Word	Object with Word formatting	Linked	6
Cell	Copy/Paste Special/Paste link	Excel	Word	Formatting varies depending on the formatting option chosen in the Paste Special dialog box	Linked	8
File	Insert/Object/ Create from File	Word	Excel	Text box containing the Word file: to update, double-click and use Word tools within the Excel destination file	Embedded: no link	10

Practice

Concepts Review

Match each term with the statement that best describes it.

1. Embedded file
2. Paste Special
3. Destination file
4. Source file
5. Linked object

a. An unlinked copy of a file placed into another file and then activated by double-clicking

b. The file containing information that is copied and often linked to a different file

c. Within a document, an element that maintains a connection to a different file

d. Used to create and format a connection between objects copied from one file to another file

e. The file that receives the information copied from a different file

Select the best answer from the list of choices.

6. Which of the following objects is, by default, pasted as a link in the destination file?
   - **a.** Excel chart pasted into Word
   - **b.** Word text pasted into Excel
   - **c.** Excel values pasted into Word
   - **d.** Picture pasted from Excel to Word

7. Use the Keep Source Formatting & _____ Data option to paste a chart that you wish to connect with the source document.
   - **a.** Embed
   - **b.** Paste
   - **c.** Link File
   - **d.** Link

8. By default, what theme is applied to a chart when it is copied from Excel and pasted into Word?
   - **a.** The theme used in the source file (Excel)
   - **b.** The Word 2016 theme
   - **c.** The theme used in the destination file (Word)
   - **d.** No theme is applied.

9. In which group on the Excel Ribbon do you find the option to embed an entire file?
   - **a.** Insert
   - **b.** Clipboard
   - **c.** Text
   - **d.** Links

Skills Review

1. **Copy data from Excel to Word.**
   a. Start Excel, open the file INT 1-5.xlsx from the location where you store your Data Files, then save it as **INT 1-Humanities Data**.
   b. Start Word, open the file INT 1-6.docx from the location where you store your Data Files, then save it as **INT 1-Humanities Report**.
   c. Switch to Excel, open the Clipboard task pane, then, if there are items on the Clipboard, click Clear All.
   d. Copy the contents of cell A1 to the Clipboard.
   e. Select the range A4:A7, then copy the contents to the Clipboard.
   f. Switch to Word, open the Clipboard task pane, paste the Humanities object at the top of the document (at the current position of the insertion point), then press [Enter] to add an additional blank line.
   g. Paste the subject areas object on the blank line below the first paragraph.
   h. Close the Clipboard task pane, then save the document.

Skills Review (continued)

2. Copy a chart from Excel to Word.

a. Switch to Excel, close the Clipboard task pane, then copy the bar chart.

b. Switch to Word, then paste the bar chart below the second paragraph of text (which ends with "and State scores").

c. Switch to Excel, then note the position of the bars for Literature.

d. Change the value in cell C4 to **70**, then switch to Word.

e. Click the chart, refresh the data, if necessary, then save the document.

f. Switch to Excel, then save the workbook.

3. Create linked objects.

a. In Excel, enter the formula **=B4-C4** in cell D4.

b. Use the Fill handle to copy the formula to the range D5:D7.

c. Select the range A3:D7, copy it, switch to Word, then use the Paste Special command to paste the cells as a link below paragraph 3 (which ends with "state-wide"), using the Formatted Text (RTF) selection in the Paste Special dialog box.

d. In Excel, copy cell D7, switch to Word, then use Paste Special to paste the cell over "XX" in the last paragraph as a link using the Unformatted Text option in the Paste Special dialog box. Add a space after the linked object if necessary.

e. In Excel, change the value in cell B7 to **90**.

f. In Word, refresh the chart if necessary.

g. Update the link in the table and the link in the last paragraph so that "20" appears in both places.

h. Enter your name where indicated in the footer in Word, save the Word report, compare your document to **FIGURE 1-12**, submit your file to your instructor, then close the document.

i. In Excel, enter your name in cell A26, save the workbook, submit the file to your instructor, then close the workbook.

4. Embed a Word file in Excel.

a. In Excel, open the file INT 1-7.xlsx from the location where you store your Data Files, then save it as **INT 1-Art Course Revenue**.

b. In Word, open the file INT 1-8.docx from the location where you store your Data Files, save it as **INT 1-Art Courses**, then close it.

c. In Excel, in cell H4, insert the Word file INT 1-Art Courses.docx as an embedded file.

d. Select the range A6:F16, then move it to cell A14.

e. Position the box containing the Word text so its upper-left corner is in cell A3.

f. Change "XX" to **$65** in paragraph 1, then change "ZZ" in paragraph 1 to **80%**.

g. Click outside the embedded object to return to Excel, compare your screen to **FIGURE 1-13**, enter your name in cell A24, save the workbook, submit the file to your instructor, then close the workbook and exit Word and Excel.

FIGURE 1-12

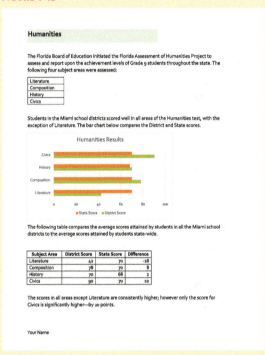

FIGURE 1-13

Independent Challenge 1

As a member of the Wolf Island Arts Commission in Alaska, you are responsible for compiling the minutes of the commission's quarterly meetings. You have already written most of the text required for the minutes. Now you need to insert data from Excel that shows how much money was raised from various fund-raising activities.

   a. Start Word, open the file INT 1-9.docx from the location where you store your Data Files, save it as **INT 1-Wolf Island Arts Commission Minutes**, start Excel, open the file INT 1-10.xlsx from the location where you store your Data Files, then save it as **INT 1-Wolf Island Data**.

   b. In Excel, open the Clipboard task pane, clear all items if necessary, then copy the photograph and cell A2.

   c. In Word, open the Clipboard task pane, paste the photograph at the top of the Word document, change the text wrapping of the picture to Square, then position the photograph to the right of the first paragraph.

   d. Click to the left of "Approval of Minutes," then paste cell A2.

   e. Copy the Fundraising Revenue chart from Excel, then paste it in the appropriate area in the Word document.

   f. In Excel, change the number of participants in the plant sale to **1000**; then in Word, refresh the data in the chart if necessary. The Plant Sale slice should be 60%.

   g. In Excel, copy the contents of cell E7, switch to Word, select "XX" in the paragraph below the chart, view the paste options, then paste the value as a link using the Unformatted Text selection in the Paste Special dialog box. Add a space if necessary.

   h. In Excel, click cell G7, then calculate the total funds raised by adding the contents of the range B7:F7.

   i. In cell B8, enter the formula **=B7/G7**, use [F4] to make cell G7 absolute, then copy the formula to the range C8:F8.

   j. Copy cell E8, switch to Word, select "ZZ" in the paragraph below the chart, then paste the value as a link using the Unformatted Text selection, adding a space if necessary.

   k. In Excel, change the number of participants in the plant sale to **1200**; then in Word, verify the Plant Sale slice changed to 64% and the links updated to $60,000 and 64%. If the links do not update automatically, right-click them and click Update Link in the Word document.

   l. Type your name in the Word footer, then save the Word document and Excel workbook, submit the files to your instructor, then close them.

Independent Challenge 2

You work at a summer camp in Montana that provides teens with training programs in digital literacy and community service. You have collected data about the camp enrollment from 2014 to 2019 in an Excel workbook. Now you need to prepare the workbook for distribution at an upcoming meeting with local businesspeople who are interested in sponsoring the camp. You want to include text in the workbook that you have stored in a Word document.

   a. Start Excel, open the file INT 1-11.xlsx from the location where you store your Data Files, then save it as **INT 1-High Plains Camp Data**.

   b. Start Word, open the file INT 1-12.docx from the location where you store your Data Files, save it as **INT 1-High Plains Camp Information**, then close it.

   c. In a blank area of the Excel worksheet, insert the Camp Information file as an embedded object.

   d. Adjust the positions of the Excel data and the box containing the Word text so the Word text appears above the Excel data and below the title.

   e. In Excel, calculate the total enrollment for the Digital Literacy and Community Service programs in the appropriate cells.

   f. To the right of "Community Service," enter and format **Total** to match the formatting for "Digital Literacy" and "Community Service," then calculate the total enrollment for both programs for each year and the total for all programs in all years.

Independent Challenge 2 (continued)

g. Copy the Total enrollment value, edit the embedded Word document so the text is indented by .3" from the left and right margins, then paste the correct total enrollment figure to replace "XX" using the Keep Text Only paste option.

h. Enter your name in cell A22 in Excel, save the Excel workbook, submit the file to your instructor, then close the workbook and exit Excel.

Independent Challenge 3

You own Garden Artist, a landscaping business in Portland, Oregon. You have entered your projected income and expenses in Excel. Now you need to link objects to the company's sales summary in Word.

a. Start Excel, open the file INT 1-13.xlsx from the location where you store your Data Files, then save it as **INT 1-Garden Artist Sales Data**.

b. In cell B14, calculate the Cost of Sales by multiplying the Sales Amount by 60%. (*Hint*: In your formula, multiply the value in cell B6 times .6.) Copy the formula to the range C14:E14.

c. In cell B16, calculate the total profit or loss by subtracting the total expenses from the total income for the month, then copy the formula to the range C16:F16. You should see $66,800 in cell F16.

d. Save the workbook, start Word, open the file INT 1-14.docx from the location where you store your Data Files, then save it as **INT 1-Garden Artist Sales Report**.

e. Select EXPENSES in the paragraph under Projected Expenses, switch to Excel, then copy the value in cell F15 and paste it as a link and as Unformatted Text in Word.

f. Use the same procedure to copy the INCOME and PROFIT amounts from Excel to the appropriate locations in the Word document. Make sure you paste the copied values as links in Unformatted Text.

g. Copy the pie chart from Excel, and paste it into the Word document below the first paragraph after Projected Expenses. Center the pie chart.

h. In Excel, note the percentages in the pie chart (for example, the April slice is 35%), then increase the salaries expense for June to **15,000** and for July to **12,000**.

i. Change the salaries for both April and May to **20,000**. Note how the April slice is now 32%.

j. In Word, update all three links, and verify that the April slice is now 32%.

k. In Excel, open the Clipboard task pane, then copy the heading in cell A1 to the Clipboard.

l. In Word, open the Clipboard task pane, paste the heading at the top of the page and center it, then change the font to Arial Black, the font size to 22 point, and the font color to Dark Green, Accent 2, Darker 25%.

m. Add your name to the document footer, compare the completed sales report to **FIGURE 1-14**, save the Word file, submit the file to your instructor, then close the Word file.

n. In Excel, enter your name in cell A35, save the workbook, submit the file to your instructor, then close the workbook.

FIGURE 1-14

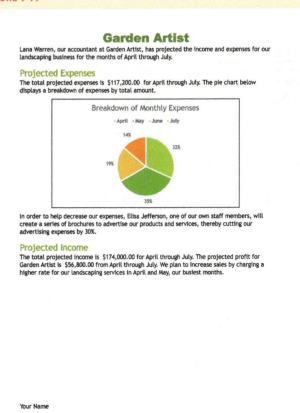

Visual Workshop

Using the Data Files INT 1-15.xlsx and INT 1-16.docx, create the price list shown in **FIGURE 1-15**. Use formulas to calculate the prices for two-packs and four-packs. Save the workbook as **INT 1-Great Organics Price List**, and save the Word document as **INT 1-Great Organics Information**. Embed the Word document into the Excel worksheet, position the inserted file and the price list in Excel as shown in **FIGURE 1-15**, then format the embedded Word object as shown in **FIGURE 1-15**. (*Hint*: The indentation on both sides of the text is .3, and the font size is 12 point.) Add your name to the Excel worksheet, save all files, submit them to your instructor, then close all files.

FIGURE 1-15

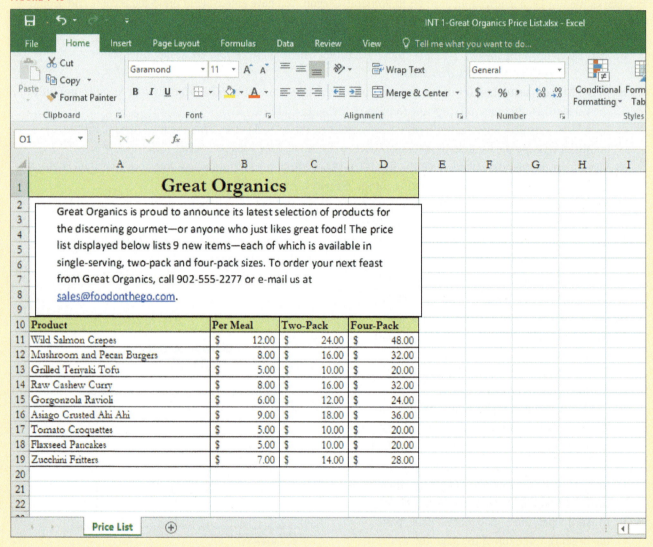

Getting Started with Access 2016

CASE ▶ Julia Rice is the developer for a new initiative at Reason 2 Go (R2G), a specialized type of travel company that combines volunteer opportunities and tourism into meaningful experiences for its customers. Julia has been asked to create products to meet a market demand for shorter experiences in the United States. Julia uses Microsoft Access 2016 to store, maintain, and analyze customer and trip information.

Module Objectives

After completing this module, you will be able to:

- Understand relational databases
- Explore a database
- Create a database
- Create a table

- Create primary keys
- Relate two tables
- Enter data
- Edit data

Files You Will Need

R2G-1.accdb
LakeHomes-1.accdb
Salvage-1.accdb

Contacts-1.accdb
Basketball-1.accdb

Access 2016
Module 1

Learning
Outcomes
• Describe relational
database concepts
• Explain when to
use a database
• Compare a
relational database
to a spreadsheet

Understand Relational Databases

Microsoft Access 2016 is relational database software that runs on the Windows operating system. You use **relational database software** to manage data that is organized into lists, such as information about customers, products, vendors, employees, projects, or sales. Many small companies track customer, inventory, and sales information in a spreadsheet program such as Microsoft Excel. Although Excel offers some list management features, Access provides many more tools and advantages for managing data. Some advantages are due to Access using a relational database model whereas Excel manages data as a single list. **TABLE 1-1** compares the two programs. **CASE** *You and Julia review the advantages of database software over spreadsheets for managing lists of information.*

DETAILS

The advantages of using Access for database management include the following:

- **Duplicate data is minimized**

  FIGURES 1-1 and **1-2** compare how you might store sales data in a single Excel spreadsheet list versus three related Access tables. With Access, you do not have to reenter information such as a customer's name and address or trip name every time a sale is made, because lists can be linked, or "related," in relational database software.

- **Information is more accurate, reliable, and consistent because duplicate data is minimized**

  The relational nature of data stored in an Access database allows you to minimize duplicate data entry, which creates more accurate, reliable, and consistent information. For example, customer data in a Customers table is entered only once, not every time a customer makes a purchase.

- **Data entry is faster and easier using Access forms**

  Data entry forms (screen layouts) make data entry faster, easier, and more accurate than entering data in a spreadsheet.

- **Information can be viewed and sorted in many ways using Access queries, forms, and reports**

  In Access, you can save multiple queries (questions about the data), data entry forms, and reports, allowing you to use them over and over without performing extra work to re-create a particular view of the data.

- **Information is more secure using Access passwords and security features**

  Access databases can be encrypted and password protected.

- **Several users can share and edit information at the same time**

  Unlike spreadsheets or word-processing documents, more than one person can enter, update, and analyze data in an Access database at the same time.

FIGURE 1-1: Using a spreadsheet to organize sales data

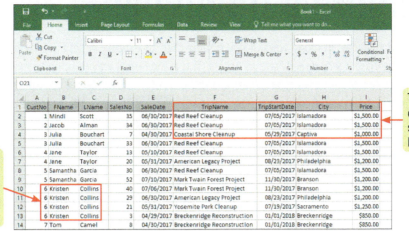

Customer information is duplicated when the same customer purchases multiple trips

Trip information is duplicated when the same trip is purchased by multiple customers

FIGURE 1-2: Using a relational database to organize sales data

TABLE 1-1: Comparing Excel with Access

feature	Excel	Access
Layout	Provides only a tabular spreadsheet layout	Provides tabular layouts as well as the ability to create customized data entry screens called forms
Storage	Restricted to a file's limitations	Virtually unlimited when coupled with the ability to use Microsoft SQL Server to store data
Linked tables	Manages single lists of information—no relational database capabilities	Relates lists of information to reduce data redundancy and create a powerful relational database
Reporting	Limited	Provides the ability to create an unlimited number of reports
Security	Limited to file security options such as marking the file "read-only" or protecting a range of cells	When used with SQL Server, provides extensive security down to the user and data level
Multiuser capabilities	Not allowed	Allows multiple users to simultaneously enter and update data
Data entry	Provides only one spreadsheet layout	Provides the ability to create an unlimited number of data entry forms

Explore a Database

Learning Outcomes
- Start Access and open a database
- Open and define Access objects

You can start Access in many ways. If you double-click an existing Access database icon or shortcut, that specific database opens directly within Access. This is the fastest way to open an existing Access database. If you start Access on its own, however, you see a window that requires you to make a choice between opening a database and creating a new database. **CASE** ▶ *Julia Rice has developed a database called R2G-1, which contains trip information. She asks you to start Access 2016 and review this database.*

STEPS

1. **Start Access**

   Access starts, as shown in **FIGURE 1-3**. This window allows you to open an existing database, create a new database from a template, or create a new blank database.

   TROUBLE
   If a yellow Security Warning bar appears below the Ribbon, click Enable Content.

2. **Click the Open Other Files link, navigate to the location where you store your Data Files, click the R2G-1.accdb database, click Open, then click the Maximize button ▣ if the Access window is not already maximized**

   The R2G-1.accdb Access database application contains five tables of data named Categories, Customers, Sales, States, and Trips. It also includes five queries, six forms, and four reports. Each of these items (table, query, form, and report) is a different type of **object** in an Access database application and is displayed in the **Navigation Pane**. The purpose of each object is defined in **TABLE 1-2**. To learn about an Access database application, you explore its objects.

   TROUBLE
   If the Navigation Pane is not open, click the Shutter Bar Open/Close Button ⏵⏵ to open it and view the database objects.

3. **In the Navigation Pane, double-click the Trips table to open it, then double-click the Customers table to open it**

   The Trips and Customers tables open in Datasheet View to display the data they store. A **table** is the fundamental building block of a relational database because it stores all of the data.

4. **In the Navigation Pane, double-click the TripSales query to open it, double-click any occurrence of Heritage in "American Heritage Tour," type Legacy, then click any other row**

   A **query** selects a subset of data from one or more tables. In this case, the TripSales query selects data from the Trips, Sales, and Customers tables. Entering or editing data in one object changes that information in every other object of the database, because all objects build on the same data stored only in the tables.

5. **Double-click the CustomerRoster form to open it, double-click Tour in "American Legacy Tour," type Project, then click any name in the middle part of the window**

   An Access **form** is a data entry screen. Users prefer forms for data entry (rather than editing and entering data in tables and queries) because forms can present information in any layout and include command buttons to make common tasks easy to perform.

6. **Double-click the TripSales report to open it**

   An Access **report** is a professional printout that can be distributed electronically or on paper. As shown in **FIGURE 1-4**, the edits made to the American Legacy Project name have carried through to the report, demonstrating the power and productivity of a relational database.

7. **Click the Close button ☒ in the upper-right corner of the window**

   Clicking the Close button in the upper-right corner of the window closes Access as well as the database on which you are working. Changes to data, such as the edits you made to the American Legacy Project record, are automatically saved as you work. Access will prompt you to save design changes to objects before it closes.

FIGURE 1-3: Opening the Microsoft Access 2016 window

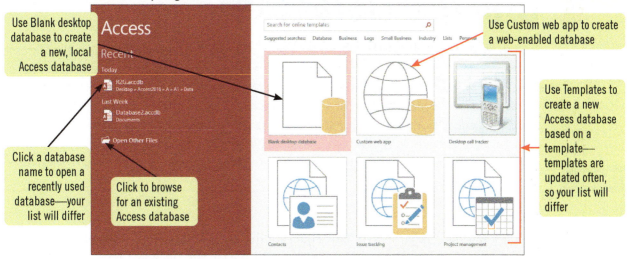

Use Blank desktop database to create a new, local Access database

Use Custom web app to create a web-enabled database

Use Templates to create a new Access database based on a template—templates are updated often, so your list will differ

Click a database name to open a recently used database—your list will differ

Click to browse for an existing Access database

FIGURE 1-4: Objects in the R2G-1 database

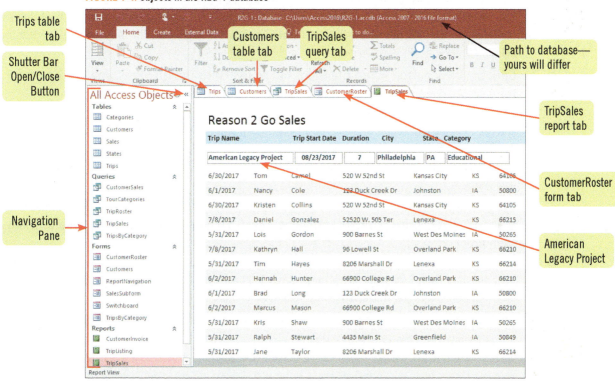

Trips table tab

Shutter Bar Open/Close Button

Customers table tab

TripSales query tab

Path to database—yours will differ

TripSales report tab

CustomerRoster form tab

American Legacy Project

Navigation Pane

TABLE 1-2: Access objects and their purpose

object	icon	purpose
Table		Contains all of the data within the database in a spreadsheet-like view called Datasheet View; tables are linked with a common field to create a relational database, which minimizes redundant data
Query		Allows you to select a subset of fields or records from one or more tables; create a query when you have a question about the data
Form		Provides an easy-to-use data entry screen
Report		Provides a professional presentation of data with headers, footers, graphics, and calculations on groups of records

Create a Database

Learning Outcomes
- Create a database
- Create a table
- Define key database terms

You can create a database using an Access **template**, a sample database provided within the Microsoft Access program, or you can start with a blank database to create a database from scratch. Your decision depends on whether Access has a template that closely resembles the type of data you plan to manage. If it does, building your own database from a template might be faster than creating the database from scratch. Regardless of which method you use, you can always modify the database later, tailoring it to meet your specific needs. **CASE** *Julia Rice reasons that the best way for you to learn Access is to start a new database from scratch, so she asks you to create a new database that will track customer communication.*

STEPS

1. **Start Access**

2. **Click the Blank desktop database icon, click the Browse button [image], navigate to the location where you store your Data Files, type R2G in the File name box, click OK, then click the Create button**

   A new database file with a single table named Table1 is created, as shown in **FIGURE 1-5**. Although you might be tempted to start entering data into the table, a better way to build a table is to first define the columns, or **fields**, of data that the table will store. **Table Design View** provides the most options for defining fields.

3. **Click the View button [image] on the Fields tab to switch to Design View, type Customers in the Save As dialog box as the new table name, then click OK**

   The table name changes from Table1 to Customers, and you are positioned in Table Design View, a window you use to name and define the fields of a table. Access automatically created a field named ID with an AutoNumber data type. The **data type** is a significant characteristic of a field because it determines what type of data the field can store such as text, dates, or numbers. See **TABLE 1-3** for more information about data types.

4. **Type CustID to rename ID to CustID, press [↓] to move to the first blank Field Name cell, type FirstName, press [↓], type LastName, press [↓], type Phone, press [↓], type Birthday, then press [↓]**

   Be sure to always separate a person's first and last names into two fields so that you can easily sort, find, and filter on either part of the name later. The Birthday field will only contain dates, so you should change its data type from Short Text (the default data type) to Date/Time.

5. **Click Short Text in the Birthday row, click the list arrow, then click Date/Time**

   With these five fields properly defined for the new Customers table, as shown in **FIGURE 1-6**, you're ready to enter data. You switch back to Datasheet View to enter or edit data. **Datasheet View** is a spreadsheet-like view of the data in a table. A **datasheet** is a grid that displays fields as columns and records as rows. The new **field names** you just defined are listed at the top of each column.

6. **Click the View button [image] to switch to Datasheet View, click Yes when prompted to save the table, press [Tab] to move to the FirstName field, type *your* first name, press [Tab] to move to the LastName field, type *your* last name, press [Tab] to move to the Phone field, type 555-666-7777, press [Tab], type 1/32/1990, then press [Tab]**

   Because 1/32/1990 is not a valid date, Access does not allow you to make that entry and displays an error message, as shown in **FIGURE 1-7**. This shows that selecting the best data type for each field in Table Design View before entering data in Datasheet View helps prevent data entry errors.

7. **Press [Esc], edit the Birthday entry for the first record to 1/31/1990, press [Tab], enter two more sample records using realistic data, right-click the Customers table tab, then click Close to close the Customers table**

Getting Started with Access 2016

FIGURE 1-5: Creating a database with a new table

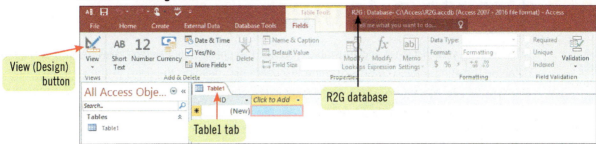

FIGURE 1-6: Defining field names and data types for the Customers table in Table Design View

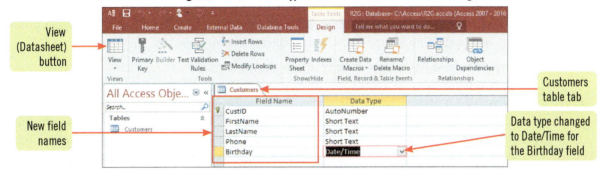

FIGURE 1-7: Entering your first record in the Customers table

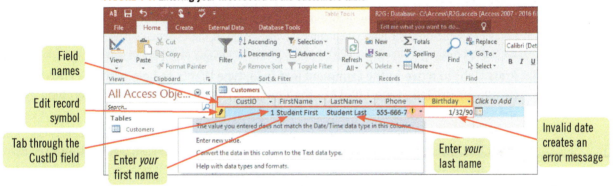

TABLE 1-3: Data types

data type	description of data
Short Text	Text or numbers not used in calculations such as a name, zip code, or phone number less than 255 characters
Long Text	Lengthy text greater than 255 characters, such as comments or notes
Number	Numeric data that can be used in calculations, such as quantities
Date/Time	Dates and times
Currency	Monetary values
AutoNumber	Sequential integers controlled by Access
Yes/No	Only two values: Yes or No
OLE Object	OLE (Object Linking and Embedding) objects such as an Excel spreadsheet or Word document
Hyperlink	Web and email addresses or links to local files
Attachment	Files such as .jpg images, spreadsheets, and documents
Calculated	Result of a calculation based on other fields in the table
Lookup Wizard	The Lookup Wizard helps you set Lookup properties, which display a drop-down list of values for the field; after using the Lookup Wizard, the final data type for the field is either Short Text or Number depending on the values in the drop-down list

Create a Table

Learning Outcomes
- Create a table in Table Design View
- Set appropriate data types for fields

After creating your database and first table, you need to create new, related tables to build a relational database. Creating a table consists of these essential tasks: defining the fields in the table, selecting an appropriate data type for each field, naming the table, and determining how the table will participate in the relational database. **CASE** ▶ *Julia Rice asks you to create another table to store customer comments. The new table will eventually be connected to the Customers table so each customer record in the Customers table may be related to many records in the Comments table.*

STEPS

1. **Click the Create tab on the Ribbon, then click the Table Design button in the Tables group**

   You create and manipulate the structure of an object in **Design View**.

2. **Enter the field names and data types, as shown in FIGURE 1-8**

   The Comments table will contain four fields. CommentID is set with an AutoNumber data type so each record is automatically numbered by Access. The CommentText field has a Long Text data type so a long comment can be recorded. CommentDate is a Date/Time field to identify the date of the comment. CustID has a Number data type and will be used to link the Comments table to the Customers table later.

   TROUBLE

   To rename an object, close it, right-click it in the Navigation Pane, and then click Rename.

3. **Click the View button 📊 to switch to Datasheet View, click Yes when prompted to save the table, type Comments as the table name, click OK, then click No when prompted to create a primary key**

   A **primary key field** contains unique data for each record. You'll identify a primary key field for the Comments table later. For now, you'll enter the first record in the Comments table in Datasheet View. A **record** is a row of data in a table. Refer to **TABLE 1-4** for a summary of important database terminology.

4. **Press [Tab] to move to the CommentText field, type Wants to help with the Rose Bowl Parade, press [Tab], type 1/7/17 in the CommentDate field, press [Tab], then type 1 in the CustID field**

   You entered 1 in the CustID field to connect this comment with the customer in the Customers table that has a CustID value of 1. Knowing which CustID value to enter for each comment is difficult. After you relate the tables properly (a task you have not yet performed), Access can make it easier to link each comment to the correct customer.

   TROUBLE

   The CommentID field is an AutoNumber field, which will automatically increment to provide a unique value. If the number has already incremented beyond 1 for the first record, AutoNumber still works as intended.

5. **Point to the divider line between the CommentText and CommentDate field names, and then double-click the ◀▶ pointer to widen the CommentText field to read the entire comment, as shown in FIGURE 1-9**

6. **Right-click the Comments table tab, click Close, then click Yes if prompted to save the table**

Creating a table in Datasheet View

You can also create a new table in Datasheet View using the commands on the Fields tab of the Ribbon. However, if you use Design View to design your table before entering data, you will probably avoid some common data entry errors. Design View helps you focus on the appropriate data type for each field.

Selecting the best data type for each field before entering any data into that field helps prevent incorrect data and unintended typos. For example, if a field has a Number, Currency, or Date/Time data type, you will not be able to enter text into that field by mistake.

FIGURE 1-8: Creating the Comments table

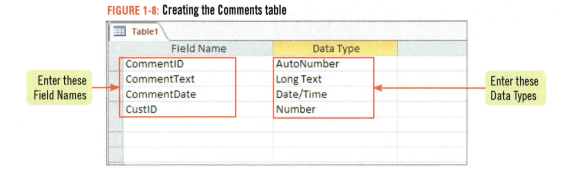

Enter these Field Names

Enter these Data Types

FIGURE 1-9: Entering a record in the Comments table

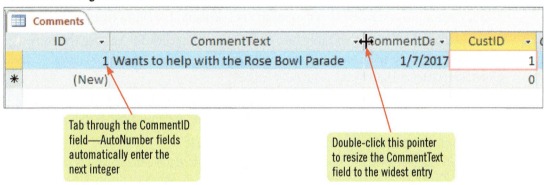

Tab through the CommentID field—AutoNumber fields automatically enter the next integer

Double-click this pointer to resize the CommentText field to the widest entry

TABLE 1-4: Important database terminology

term	description
Field	A specific piece or category of data such as a first name, last name, city, state, or phone number
Record	A group of related fields that describes a person, place, thing, or transaction such as a customer, location, product, or sale
Key field	A field that contains unique information for each record, such as a customer number for a customer
Table	A collection of records for a single subject such as Customers, Products, or Sales
Relational database	Multiple tables that are linked together to address a business process such as managing trips, sales, and customers at Reason 2 Go
Objects	The parts of an Access database that help you view, edit, manage, and analyze the data: tables, queries, forms, reports, macros, and modules

Create Primary Keys

Learning
Outcomes
• Set the primary
  key field
• Define one-to-
  many relationships

The **primary key field** of a table serves two important purposes. First, it contains data that uniquely identifies each record. No two records can have the exact same entry in the field designated as the primary key field. Second, the primary key field helps relate one table to another in a **one-to-many relationship**, where one record from one table may be related to many records in the second table. For example, one record in the Customers table may be related to many records in the Comments table. (One customer may have many comments.) The primary key field is always on the "one" side of a one-to-many relationship between two tables. **CASE** ▶ *Julia Rice asks you to check that a primary key field has been appropriately identified for each table in the new R2G database.*

STEPS

1. **Right-click the Comments table in the Navigation Pane, then click Design View**

   Table Design View for the Comments table opens. The field with the AutoNumber data type is generally the best candidate for the primary key field in a table because it automatically contains a unique number for each record.

   TROUBLE
   Make sure the Design tab is selected on the Ribbon.

2. **Click the CommentID field if it is not already selected, then click the Primary Key button in the Tools group on the Design tab**

   The CommentID field is now set as the primary key field for the Comments table, as shown in **FIGURE 1-10**.

   QUICK TIP
   You can also click the Save button 🖫 on the Quick Access Toolbar to save a table.

3. **Right-click the Comments table tab, click Close, then click Yes to save the table**

   Any time you must save design changes to an Access object such as a table, Access displays a dialog box to remind you to save the object.

4. **Right-click the Customers table in the Navigation Pane, then click Design View**

   Access has already set CustID as the primary key field for the Customers table, as shown in **FIGURE 1-11**.

5. **Right-click the Customers table tab, then click Close**

   You were not prompted to save the Customers table because you did not make any design changes. Now that you're sure that each table in the R2G database has an appropriate primary key field, you're ready to link the tables. The primary key field plays a critical role in this relationship.

Object views

Each object has a number of **views** that allow you to complete different tasks. For example, to enter and edit data into the database, use **Datasheet View** for tables and queries and **Form View** for forms. To change the structure of an object, you most often work in **Design View**. Use **Print Preview** to see how a report will appear on a physical piece of paper. Click the arrow at the bottom of the View button on the Design tab of the Ribbon to see all of the available views for an object.

Learning about field properties

Properties are the characteristics that define the field. Two properties are required for every field: Field Name and Data Type. Many other properties, such as Field Size, Format, Caption, and Default Value, are defined in the Field Properties pane in the lower half of a table's Design View. As you add more property entries, you are generally restricting the amount or type of data that can be entered in the field, which increases data entry accuracy. For example, you might change the Field Size property for a State field to 2 to eliminate an incorrect entry such as FLL. Field properties change depending on the data type of the selected field. For example, date fields do not have a Field Size property because Access controls the size of fields with a Date/Time data type.

FIGURE 1-10: Creating a primary key field for the Comments table

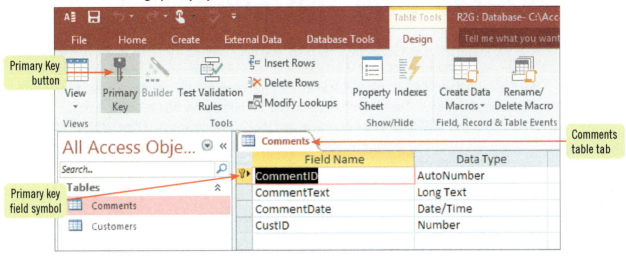

FIGURE 1-11: Confirming the primary key field for the Customers table

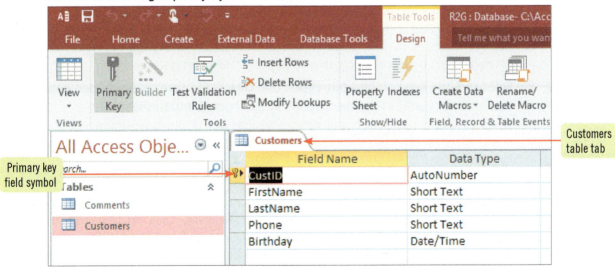

Relate Two Tables

Learning Outcomes
• Define foreign key field
• Create one-to-many relationships
• Set referential integrity

After you create tables and set primary key fields, you must connect the tables in one-to-many relationships to enjoy the benefits of a relational database. A one-to-many relationship between two tables means that one record from the first table is related to many records in the second table. You use a common field to make this connection. The common field is always the primary key field in the table on the "one" side of the relationship. **CASE** *Julia Rice explains that she has new comments to enter into the R2G database. To identify which customer is related to each comment, you define a one-to-many relationship between the Customers and Comments tables.*

STEPS

1. **Click the Database Tools tab on the Ribbon, then click the Relationships button**

TROUBLE
If the Show Table dialog box doesn't appear, click the Show Table button on the Design tab.

2. **In the Show Table dialog box, double-click Customers, double-click Comments, then click Close**

   Each table is represented by a small **field list** window that displays the table's field names. A **key symbol** identifies the primary key field in each table. To relate the two tables in a one-to-many relationship, you connect them using a common field, which is always the primary key field on the "one" side of the relationship.

QUICK TIP
Drag a table's title bar to move the field list.

3. **Drag CustID in the Customers field list to the CustID field in the Comments field list**

   The Edit Relationships dialog box opens, as shown in **FIGURE 1-12**. **Referential integrity**, a set of Access rules that governs data entry, helps ensure data accuracy.

TROUBLE
If you need to delete an incorrect relationship, right-click a relationship line, then click Delete.

4. **Click the Enforce Referential Integrity check box in the Edit Relationships dialog box, then click Create**

   The **one-to-many line** shows the link between the CustID field of the Customers table (the "one" side) and the CustID field of the Comments table (the "many" side, indicated by the **infinity symbol**), as shown in **FIGURE 1-13**. The linking field on the "many" side is called the **foreign key field**. Now that these tables are related, it is much easier to enter comments for the correct customer.

QUICK TIP
To print the Relationships window, click the Relationship Report button on the Design tab, then click Print.

5. **Right-click the Relationships tab, click Close, click Yes to save changes, then double-click the Customers table in the Navigation Pane to open it in Datasheet View**

   When you relate two tables in a one-to-many relationship, expand buttons appear to the left of each record in the table on the "one" side of the relationship. In this case, the Customers table is on the "one" side of the relationship.

6. **Click the expand button + to the left of the first record**

   A **subdatasheet** shows the related comment records for each customer. In other words, the subdatasheet shows the records on the "many" side of a one-to-many relationship. The expand button + also changed to the collapse button − for the first customer. Widening the CommentText field allows you to see the entire entry in the Comments subdatasheet. Now the task of entering comments for the correct customer is much more straightforward.

TROUBLE
Be careful to enter complete comments for the correct customer, as shown in **FIGURE 1-14**.

7. **Enter two more comments, as shown in FIGURE 1-14**

   Interestingly, the CustID field in the Comments table (the foreign key field) is not displayed in the subdatasheet. Behind the scenes, Access is entering the correct CustID value in the Comments table, which is the glue that ties each comment to the correct customer.

8. **Close the Customers table, then click Yes if prompted to save changes**

FIGURE 1-12: Edit Relationships dialog box

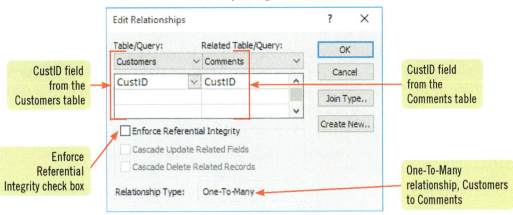

CustID field from the Customers table

CustID field from the Comments table

Enforce Referential Integrity check box

One-To-Many relationship, Customers to Comments

FIGURE 1-13: Linking the Customers and Comments tables

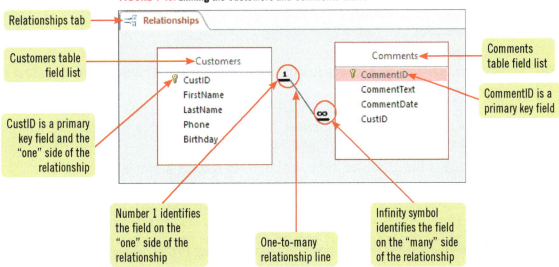

Relationships tab

Customers table field list

CustID is a primary key field and the "one" side of the relationship

Number 1 identifies the field on the "one" side of the relationship

One-to-many relationship line

Infinity symbol identifies the field on the "many" side of the relationship

Comments table field list

CommentID is a primary key field

FIGURE 1-14: Entering comments using the subdatasheet

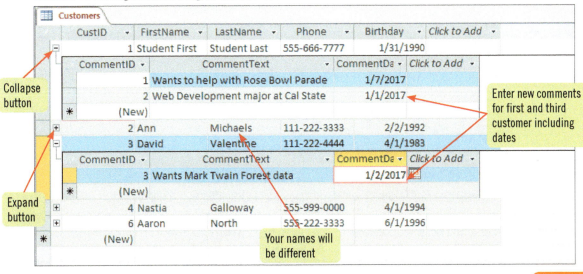

Collapse button

Expand button

Enter new comments for first and third customer including dates

Your names will be different

Enter Data

Learning Outcomes
- Navigate records in a datasheet
- Enter records in a datasheet

Your skill in navigating and entering new records is a key to your success with a relational database. You can use many techniques to navigate through the records in the table's datasheet. **CASE** *Even though you have already successfully entered some records, Julia Rice asks you to master this essential skill by entering several more customers in the R2G database.*

STEPS

1. **Double-click the Customers table in the Navigation Pane to open it, press [Tab] three times, then press [Enter] three times**

   The Customers table reopens. The Comments subdatasheets are collapsed. Both the [Tab] and [Enter] keys move the focus to the next field. The **focus** refers to which data you would edit if you started typing. When you navigate to the last field of the record, pressing [Tab] or [Enter] advances the focus to the first field of the next record. You can also use the Next record ▶ and Previous record ◀ **navigation buttons** on the navigation bar in the lower-left corner of the datasheet to navigate through the records. The **Current record** text box on the navigation bar tells you the number of the current record as well as the total number of records in the datasheet.

   > **QUICK TIP**
   > Press [Tab] in the CustID AutoNumber field.

2. **Click the FirstName field of the fourth record to position the insertion point to enter a new record**

   You can also use the New (blank) record button ▶꙰ on the navigation bar to move to a new record. You enter new records at the end of the datasheet. You learn how to sort and reorder records later. A complete list of navigation keystrokes is shown in **TABLE 1-5**.

   > **QUICK TIP**
   > Access databases are multiuser with one important limitation: Two users cannot edit the same record at the same time. In that case, a message explains that the second user must wait until the first user moves to a different record.

3. **At the end of the datasheet, enter the last three records shown in FIGURE 1-15**

   The **edit record symbol** 🖉 appears to the left of the record you are currently editing. When you move to a different record, Access saves the data. Therefore, Access never prompts you to save data because it performs that task automatically. Saving data automatically allows Access databases to be **multiuser** databases, which means that more than one person can enter and edit data in the same database at the same time.

   Your CustID values might differ from those in **FIGURE 1-15**. Because the CustID field is an **AutoNumber** field, Access automatically enters the next consecutive number into the field as it creates the record. If you delete a record or are interrupted when entering a record, Access discards the value in the AutoNumber field and does not reuse it. Therefore, AutoNumber values do not represent the number of records in your table. Instead, they provide a unique value per record, similar to check numbers.

Changing from Navigation mode to Edit mode

If you navigate to another area of the datasheet by clicking with the mouse pointer instead of pressing [Tab] or [Enter], you change from **Navigation mode** to Edit mode. In **Edit mode**, Access assumes that you are trying to make changes to the current field value, so keystrokes such as [Ctrl][End], [Ctrl][Home], [←], and [→] move the insertion point within the field. To return to Navigation mode, press [Tab] or [Enter] (thus moving the focus to the next field), or press [↑] or [↓] (thus moving the focus to a different record).

FIGURE 1-15: New records in the Customers table

FIGURE 1-15: New records in the Customers table

	CustID ▾	FirstName ▾	LastName ▾	Phone ▾	Birthday ▾	Click to Add ▾
⊞	1	Student First	Student Last	555-666-7777	1/31/1990	
⊞	2	Ann	Michaels	555-777-8888	2/1/1991	
⊞	3	David	Valentine	555-888-9999	3/1/1993	
⊞	4	Nastia	Galloway	555-999-0000	4/1/1994	
⊞	5	Sean	Lincoln	555-111-2222	5/1/1995	
⊞	6	Aaron	North	555-222-3333	6/1/1996	
✱	(New)					

Your first three names will be different

Your CustID values may vary

Enter the last three Customer records as shown

Previous record button

First record button

Record: ◄ ◄ 7 of 7 ► ►◄ ► No Filter Search

Current record box — Next record button — Last record button — New (blank) record button

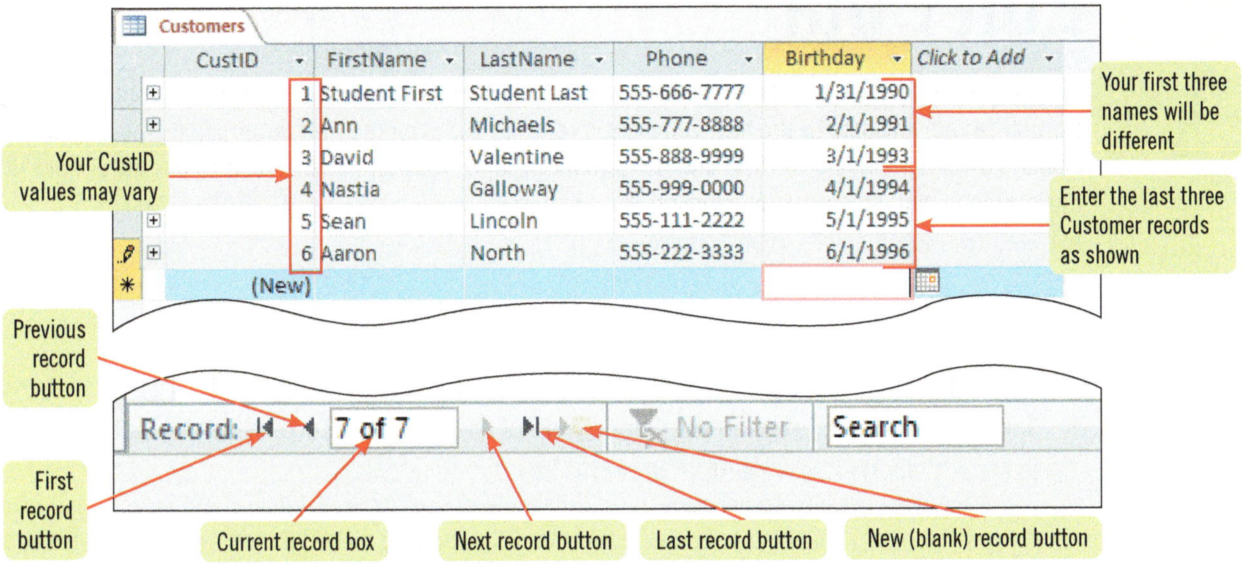

TABLE 1-5: Navigation mode keyboard shortcuts

shortcut key	moves to the
[Tab], [Enter], or [→]	Next field of the current record
[Shift][Tab] or [←]	Previous field of the current record
[Home]	First field of the current record
[End]	Last field of the current record
[Ctrl][Home] or [F5]	First field of the first record
[Ctrl][End]	Last field of the last record
[↑]	Current field of the previous record
[↓]	Current field of the next record

Cloud computing

Using **OneDrive**, a free service from Microsoft, you can store files in the "cloud" and retrieve them anytime you are connected to the Internet. Saving your files to the OneDrive is one example of cloud computing. **Cloud computing** means you are using an Internet resource to complete your work.

Edit Data

Learning Outcomes
- Edit data in a datasheet
- Delete records in a datasheet
- Preview and print a datasheet

Updating existing data in a database is another critical database task. To change the contents of an existing record, navigate to the field you want to change and type the new information. You can delete unwanted data by clicking the field and using [Backspace] or [Delete] to delete text to the left or right of the insertion point. Other data entry keystrokes are summarized in **TABLE 1-6.** **CASE** *Julia Rice asks you to correct two records in the Customers table.*

STEPS

1. **Select the phone number in the Phone field of the second record, type 111-222-3333, press [Enter], type 2/2/92, then press [Enter]**

   You changed the telephone number and birth date of the second customer. When you entered the last two digits of the year value, Access inserted the first two digits after you pressed [Enter]. You'll also update the third customer.

QUICK TIP
The ScreenTip for the Undo button displays the action you can undo.

2. **Press [Enter] enough times to move to the Phone field of the third record, type 111-222-4444, then press [Esc]**

   Pressing [Esc] once removes the current field's editing changes, so the Phone value changes back to the previous entry. Pressing [Esc] twice removes all changes to the current record. When you move to another record, Access saves your edits, so you can no longer use [Esc] to remove editing changes to the current record. You can, however, click the Undo button on the Quick Access Toolbar to undo changes to a previous record.

3. **Retype 111-222-4444, press [Enter], type 3/1/83 in the Birthday field, press [Enter], click the 3/1/83 date you just entered, click the Calendar icon , then click April 1, 1983, as shown in FIGURE 1-16**

   When you are working in the Birthday field, which has a Date/Time data type, you can enter a date from the keyboard or use the **Calendar Picker**, a pop-up calendar, to find and select a date.

4. **Click the record selector for the fifth record (Sean Lincoln), click the Delete button in the Records group on the Home tab, then click Yes**

   A message warns that you cannot undo a record deletion. The Undo button is dimmed, indicating that you cannot use it. The Customers table now has five records, as shown in **FIGURE 1-17.** Keep in mind that your CustID values might differ from those in the figure because they are controlled by Access.

QUICK TIP
If requested to print the Customers datasheet by your instructor, click the Print button, then click OK.

5. **Click the File tab, click Print, then click Print Preview to review the printout of the Customers table before printing**

6. **Click the Close Print Preview button, then click the Close button in the upper-right corner of the window to close the R2G.accdb database and Access 2016**

FIGURE 1-16: Editing customer records

Quick Access Toolbar—your buttons might be different

Edit record symbol

Record selector button for Sean Lincoln record

Delete button

Calendar icon

April 1, 1983

Click the left or right arrow to change the month

FIGURE 1-17: Final Customers datasheet

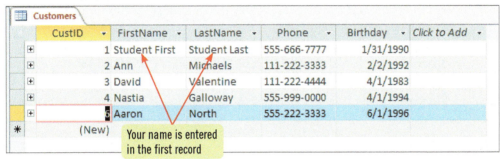

Your name is entered in the first record

TABLE 1-6: Edit mode keyboard shortcuts

editing keystroke	action
[Backspace]	Deletes one character to the left of the insertion point
[Delete]	Deletes one character to the right of the insertion point
[F2]	Switches between Edit and Navigation mode
[Esc]	Undoes the change to the current field
[Esc][Esc]	Undoes all changes to the current record
[F7]	Starts the spell-check feature
[Ctrl][']	Inserts the value from the same field in the previous record into the current field
[Ctrl][;]	Inserts the current date in a Date field

Resizing and moving datasheet columns

You can resize the width of a field in a datasheet by dragging the column separator, the thin line that separates the field names to the left or right. The pointer changes to ✛ as you make the field wider or narrower. Release the mouse button when you have resized the field. To adjust the column width to accommodate the widest entry in the field, double-click the column separator. To move a column, click the field name to select the entire column, then drag the field name left or right.

Practice

Concepts Review

Label each element of the Access window shown in FIGURE 1-18.

FIGURE 1-18

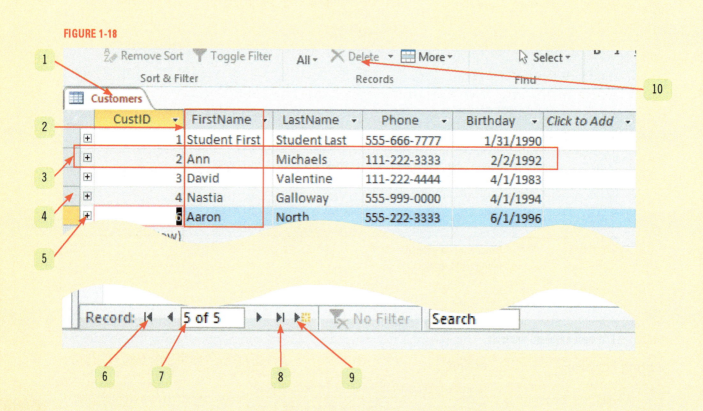

Match each term with the statement that best describes it.

11. **Field**
12. **Record**
13. **Table**
14. **Datasheet**
15. **Query**
16. **Form**
17. **Report**

a. A subset of data from one or more tables

b. A collection of records for a single subject, such as all the customer records

c. A professional printout of database information

d. A spreadsheet-like grid that displays fields as columns and records as rows

e. A group of related fields for one item, such as all of the information for one customer

f. A category of information in a table, such as a company name, city, or state

g. An easy-to-use data entry screen

Select the best answer from the list of choices.

18. When you create a new database, which object is created first?
    a. Module
    b. Query
    c. Table
    d. Form

19. Which of the following is *not* a typical benefit of relational databases?
    a. Minimized duplicate data entry
    b. More accurate data
    c. Tables automatically create needed relationships
    d. More consistent data

20. Which of the following is *not* an advantage of managing data with relational database software such as Access versus spreadsheet software such as Excel?
    a. Allows multiple users to enter data simultaneously
    b. Uses a single table to store all data
    c. Provides data entry forms
    d. Reduces duplicate data entry

Skills Review

1. **Understand relational databases.**
    a. Write down five advantages of managing database information in Access versus using a spreadsheet.
    b. Write a sentence to explain how the terms field, record, table, and relational database relate to one another.

2. **Explore a database.**
    a. Start Access.
    b. Open the LakeHomes-1.accdb database from the location where you store your Data Files. Click Enable Content if a yellow Security Warning message appears.
    c. Open each of the four tables to study the data they contain. Complete the following table:

table name	number of records	number of fields

    d. Double-click the ListingsByRealtor query in the Navigation Pane to open it. Change any occurrence of Gordon Bono to *your* name. Move to another record to save your changes.
    e. Double-click the RealtorsMainForm in the Navigation Pane to open it. Use the navigation buttons to navigate through the 13 realtors to observe each realtor's listings.
    f. Double-click the RealtorListingReport in the Navigation Pane to open it. The records are listed in ascending order by realtor last name. Scroll through the report to make sure your name is positioned correctly.
    g. Close the LakeHomes-1 database, then close Access 2016.

3. **Create a database.**
    a. Start Access, click the Blank desktop database icon, use the Browse button to navigate to the location where you store your Data Files, type **LakeHomeMarketing** as the filename, click OK, and then click Create to create a new database named LakeHomeMarketing.accdb.

Skills Review (continued)

b. Switch to Table Design View, name the table **Prospects**, then enter the following fields and data types:

field name	data type
ProspectID	AutoNumber
ProspectFirst	Short Text
ProspectLast	Short Text
Phone	Short Text
Email	Hyperlink
Street	Short Text
City	Short Text
State	Short Text
Zip	Short Text

c. Save the table, switch to Datasheet View, and enter two records using your name in the first record and your instructor's name in the second. Tab through the ProspectID field, an AutoNumber field.

d. Enter **TN** (Tennessee) as the value in the State field for both records. Use school or fictitious (rather than personal) data for all other field data, and be sure to fill out each record completely.

e. Widen each column in the Prospects table so that all data is visible, then save and close the Prospects table.

4. Create a table.

a. Click the Create tab on the Ribbon, click the Table Design button in the Tables group, then create a new table with the following two fields and data types:

field name	data type
State2	Short Text
StateName	Short Text

b. Save the table with the name **States**. Click No when asked if you want Access to create the primary key field.

5. Create primary keys.

a. In Table Design View of the States table, set the State2 field as the primary key field.

b. Save the States table and open it in Datasheet View.

c. Enter one state record, using **TN** for the State2 value and **Tennessee** for the StateName value to match the State value of TN that you entered for both records in the Prospects table.

d. Close the States table.

6. Relate two tables.

a. From the Database Tools tab, open the Relationships window.

b. Add the States, then the Prospects table to the Relationships window.

c. Drag the bottom edge of the Prospects table to expand the field list to display all of the fields.

d. Drag the State2 field from the States table to the State field of the Prospects table.

e. In the Edit Relationships dialog box, click the Enforce Referential Integrity check box, then click Create. Your Relationships window should look like **FIGURE 1-19**. If you connect the wrong fields by mistake, right-click the line connecting the two fields, click Delete, then try again.

f. Close the Relationships window, and save changes when prompted.

FIGURE 1-19

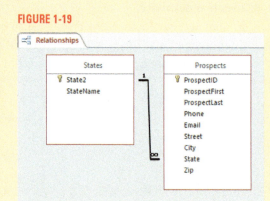

Skills Review (continued)

7. Enter data.

   a. Open the States table and enter the following records:

State2 field	StateName field
CO	Colorado
IA	Iowa
KS	Kansas
MO	Missouri
NE	Nebraska
OK	Oklahoma
WI	Wisconsin
TX	Texas

   b. Add three more state records of your choice for a total of 12 records in the States table using the correct two-character abbreviation for the state and the correctly spelled state name.

   c. Close and reopen the States table. Notice that Access automatically sorts the records by the values in the primary key field, the State2 field.

8. Edit data.

   a. Click the Expand button for the TN record to see the two related records from the Prospects table.

   b. Enter two more prospects in the TN subdatasheet using any fictitious but realistic data, as shown in **FIGURE 1-20**. Notice that you are not required to enter a value for the State field, the foreign key field in the subdatasheet.

   c. If required by your instructor, print the States datasheet and the Prospects datasheet.

   d. Click the Close button in the upper-right corner of the Access window to close all open objects as well as the LakeHomeMarketing.accdb database and Access 2016. If prompted to save any design changes, click Yes.

FIGURE 1-20

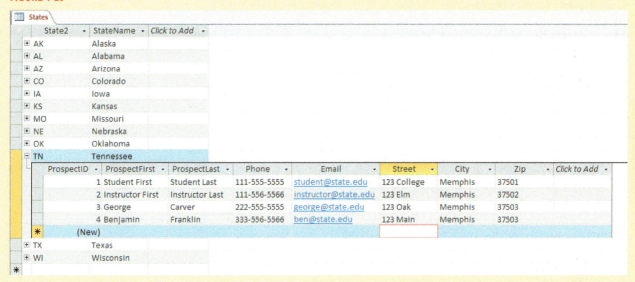

Independent Challenge 1

Consider the following twelve subject areas:

- Telephone directory
- Islands of the Caribbean
- Members of the U.S. House of Representatives
- College course offerings
- Physical activities
- Ancient wonders of the world
- Restaurant menu
- Shopping catalog items
- Vehicles
- Conventions
- Party guest list
- Movie listings

a. For each subject, build a Word table with 4–7 columns and three rows. In the first row, enter field names that you would expect to see in a table used to manage that subject.

b. In the second and third rows of each table, enter two realistic records. The first table, Telephone Directory, is completed as an example to follow.

TABLE: Telephone Directory

FirstName	LastName	Street	Zip	Phone
Marco	Lopez	100 Main Street	88715	555-612-3312
Christopher	Stafford	253 Maple Lane	77824	555-612-1179

c. Consider the following guidelines as you build the table:

Make sure each record represents one item in that table. For example, in the Restaurant Menu table, the following table is a random list of categories of food. The records do not represent one item in a restaurant menu.

Beverage	Appetizer	Meat	Vegetable	Dessert
Milk	Chicken wings	Steak	Carrots	Chocolate cake
Tea	Onion rings	Salmon	Potato	Cheesecake

A better example of records that describe an item in the restaurant menu would be the following:

Category	Description	Price	Calories	Spicy
Appetizer	Chicken wings	$10	800	Yes
Beverage	Milk	$2	250	No

Do not put first and last names in the same field. This prevents you from easily sorting, filtering, or searching on either part of the name later.

For the same reasons, break street, city, state, zip, and country data into separate fields as well.

Do not put values and units of measure such as 5 minutes, 4 lbs, or 6 sq. miles in the same field. This also prevents you from sorting and calculating on the numeric part of the information. Make your field names descriptive such as TimeInMinutes or AreaInSquareMiles so that each record's entries are consistent.

Do not put these tables in one Access database. Putting all of these tables in one Access database would be analogous to putting a letter to your Congressman, a creative poem, and a cover letter to a future employer all in the same Word file. Just as that wouldn't make organizational sense, these tables do not belong together in the same Access database either. Create your sample tables in a Word document to stay focused on proper field and record construction versus the task of building Access tables.

Independent Challenge 2

You are working with several civic groups to coordinate a community-wide recycling effort. You have started a database called Salvage-1, which tracks the clubs, their recyclable material deposits, and the collection centers that are participating.

a. Start Access, then open the Salvage-1.accdb database from the location where you store your Data Files. Enable content if prompted.

b. Open each table's datasheet to study the number of fields and records per table. Notice that there are no expand buttons to the left of any records because relationships have not yet been established between these tables.

c. In a Word document, re-create the following table and fill in the blanks:

table name	number of records	number of fields

d. Close all table datasheets, then open the Relationships window and create the following one-to-many relationships. Drag the tables from the Navigation Pane to the Relationships window, and drag the title bars and borders of the field lists to position them as shown in **FIGURE 1-21**.

field on the "one" side of the relationship	field on the "many" side of the relationship
ClubNumber in Clubs table	ClubNumber in Deposits table
CenterNumber in Centers table	CenterNumber in Deposits table

e. Be sure to enforce referential integrity on all relationships. If you create an incorrect relationship, right-click the line linking the fields, click Delete, and try again. Your final Relationships window should look like **FIGURE 1-21**.

f. Click the Relationship Report button on the Design tab, and if required by your instructor, click Print to print a copy of the Relationships for Salvage-1 report. To close the report, right-click the Relationships for Salvage-1 tab and click Close. Click Yes when prompted to save changes to the report with the name **Relationships for Salvage-1**. Save and close the Relationships window.

g. Open the Clubs table and add a new record with fictitious but realistic data in all of the fields. Enter **8** as the ClubNumber value and your name in the FName (first name) and LName (last name) fields.

h. Expand the subdatasheets for each record in the Clubs table to see the related records from the Deposits table. Which club made the most deposits? Be ready to answer in class. Close the Clubs table.

i. Open the Centers table and add a new record with fictitious but realistic data in all of the fields. Enter your first and last names in the CenterName field and enter **5** as the CenterNumber.

j. Expand the subdatasheets for each record in the Centers table to see the related records from the Deposits table. Which center made the most deposits? Be ready to answer in class. Close the Centers table.

k. Close the Salvage-1.accdb database, then exit Access 2016.

FIGURE 1-21

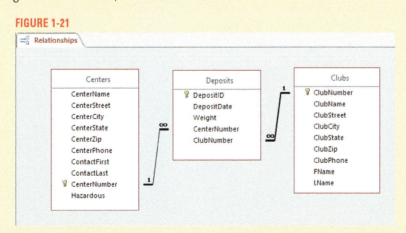

Independent Challenge 3

You are working for an advertising agency that provides social media consulting for small and large businesses in the mid-western United States. You have started a database called Contacts-1, which tracks your company's customers. (*Note*: To complete this Independent Challenge, make sure you are connected to the Internet.)

a. Start Access and open the Contacts-1.accdb database from the location where you store your Data Files. Enable content if prompted.

b. Add a new record to the Customers table, using any local business name, your first and last names, **$10,500** in the YTDSales field, and fictitious but reasonable entries for the rest of the fields.

c. Edit the Sprint Systems record (ID 1). Change the Company name to **A1 Cellular**, and change the Street value to **4455 Mastin St**.

d. Delete the record for EBC (ID 18), then close the Customers table.

e. Create a new table with two fields, **State2** and **StateName**. Assign both fields a Short Text data type. The State2 field will contain the two-letter abbreviation for state names. The StateName field will contain the Set the State2 field as the primary key field, then save the table as **States**.

f. Enter at least three records into the States table, making sure that all of the states used in the Customers datasheet are entered in the States table. This includes **KS Kansas**, **MO Missouri**, and any other state you entered in Step b when you added a new record to the Customers table.

g. Close all open tables. Open the Relationships window, add both the States and Customers field lists to the window, then expand the size of the Customers field list so that all fields are visible. (*Hint*: The field list will not show a vertical scroll bar when all fields in the list are visible.)

h. Build a one-to-many relationship between the States and Customers tables by dragging the State2 field from the States table to the State field of the Customers table to create a one-to-many relationship between the two tables. Enforce referential integrity on the relationship. If you are unable to enforce referential integrity, it means that a value in the State field of the Customers table doesn't have a perfect match in the State2 field of the States table. Open both table datasheets, making sure every state in the State field of the Customers table is also represented in the State2 field of the States table, close all datasheets, then reestablish the one-to-many relationship between the two tables with referential integrity.

i. Click the Relationship Report button on the Design tab, then if requested by your instructor, click Print to print the report.

j. Right-click the Relationships for Contacts-1 tab, then click Close. Click Yes when prompted to save the report with the name **Relationships for Contacts-1**.

k. Close the Relationships window, saving changes as prompted.

l. Close the Contacts-1.accdb database, then exit Access 2016.

Independent Challenge 4: Explore

Now that you've learned about Microsoft Access and relational databases, brainstorm how you might use an Access database in your daily life or career. Start by visiting the Microsoft website, and explore what's new in Access 2016.

(*Note*: To complete this Independent Challenge, make sure you are connected to the Internet.)

a. Using your favorite search engine, look up the keywords *benefits of a relational database* or *benefits of Microsoft Access* to find articles that discuss the benefits of organizing data in a relational database.

b. Read several articles about the benefits of organizing data in a relational database such as Access, identifying three distinct benefits. Use a Word document to record those three benefits. Also, copy and paste the website address of the article you are referencing for each benefit you have identified.

c. In addition, as you read the articles that describe relational database benefits, list any terminology unfamiliar to you, identifying at least five new terms.

d. Using a search engine or a website that provides a computer glossary such as www.whatis.com or www.webopedia.com, look up the definition of the new terms, and enter both the term and the definition of the term in your document as well as the website address where your definition was found.

e. Finally, based on your research and growing understanding of Access 2016, list three ways you could use an Access database to organize, enhance, or support the activities and responsibilities of your daily life or career. Type your name at the top of the document, and submit it to your instructor as requested.

Visual Workshop

Open the Basketball-1.accdb database from the location where you store your Data Files, then enable content if prompted. Open the Offense query datasheet, which lists offensive statistics by player by game. Modify any of the Matthew Douglas records to contain your first and last names, then move to a different record, observing the power of a relational database to modify every occurrence of that name throughout the database. Close the Offense query, then open the Players table. Note that there are no expand buttons to the left of the records, indicating that this table does not participate on the "one" side of a one-to-many relationship. Close the Players table and open the Relationships window. Drag the tables from the Navigation Pane and create the relationships with referential integrity, as shown in FIGURE 1-22. Note the one-to-many relationship between the Players and Stats table. Print the Relationships report if requested by your instructor and save it with the name **Relationships for Basketball-1**. Close the report and close and save the Relationships window. Now reopen the Players table noting the expand buttons to the left of each record. Expand the subdatasheet for your name and for several other players to observe the "many" records from the Stats table that are now related to each record in the Players table.

FIGURE 1-22

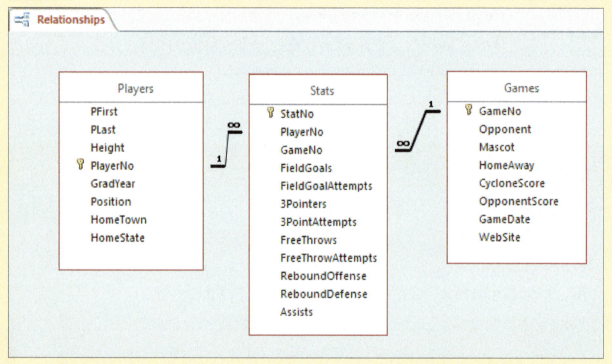

Building and Using Queries

CASE Julia Rice, trip developer for U.S. group travel at Reason 2 Go, has several questions about the customer and trip information in the R2G database. You'll develop queries to provide Julia with up-to-date answers.

Module Objectives

After completing this module, you will be able to:

- Use the Query Wizard
- Work with data in a query
- Use Query Design View
- Sort and find data
- Filter data
- Apply AND criteria
- Apply OR criteria
- Format a datasheet

Files You Will Need

R2G-2.accdb	HouseOfReps-2.accdb
Salvage-2.accdb	VetClinic-2.accdb
Service-2.accdb	Baseball-2.accdb

Use the Query Wizard

Learning Outcomes
- Describe the purpose for a query
- Create a query with the Simple Query Wizard

A **query** answers a question about the information in the database. A query allows you to select a subset of fields and records from one or more tables and then present the selected data as a single datasheet. A major benefit of working with data through a query is that you can focus on only the specific information you need, rather than navigating through all the fields and records from one or more large tables. You can enter, edit, and navigate data in a query datasheet just like a table datasheet. However, keep in mind that Access data is physically stored only in tables, even though you can select, view, and edit it through other Access objects such as queries and forms. Because a query doesn't physically store the data, a query data-sheet is sometimes called a **logical view** of the data. A query stores a set of **SQL (Structured Query Language)** instructions, but because you can use Access query tools such as Query Design View to create and modify the query, you are not required to write SQL statements to build or use Access queries. Access provides several tools to create a new query, one of which is the Simple Query Wizard. **CASE** *Julia Rice suggests that you use the Simple Query Wizard to create a query that displays fields from the Trips and Customers tables in one datasheet.*

STEPS

1. **Start Access, open the R2G-2.accdb database, enable content if prompted, then maximize the window**

   Access provides several tools to create a new query. One way is to use the **Simple Query Wizard**, which prompts you for the information it needs to create the query.

2. **Click the Create tab on the Ribbon, click the Query Wizard button in the Queries group, then click OK to start the Simple Query Wizard**

   The first Simple Query Wizard dialog box opens, prompting you to select the fields you want to view in the new query. You can select fields from one or more existing tables or queries.

3. **Click the Tables/Queries list arrow, click Table: Trips, double-click TripName, double-click City, double-click Category, then double-click Price**

   So far, you've selected four fields from the Trips table to display basic trip information in this query. You also want to add the first and last name information from the Customers table so you know which customers purchased each trip.

4. **Click the Tables/Queries list arrow, click Table: Customers, double-click FName, then double-click LName**

   You've selected four fields from the Trips table and two from the Customers table for your new query, as shown in **FIGURE 2-1**.

5. **Click Next, click Next to select Detail, select Trips Query in the title text box, type TripCustomerList as the name of the query, then click Finish**

   The TripCustomerList datasheet opens, displaying four fields from the Trips table and two from the Customers table, as shown in **FIGURE 2-2**. The query can show which customers have purchased which Trips because of the one-to-many table relationships established in the Relationships window.

Simple Query Wizard

The **Simple Query Wizard** is a series of dialog boxes that prompt you for the information needed to create a Select query. A **Select query** selects fields from one or more tables in your database and is by far the most common type of query. The other query wizards—Crosstab, Find Duplicates, and Find Unmatched—are used to create queries that do specialized types of data analysis and are covered in Module 10 on advanced queries.

FIGURE 2-1: Selecting fields using the Simple Query Wizard

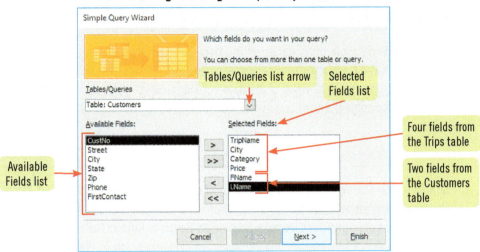

FIGURE 2-2: TripCustomerList datasheet

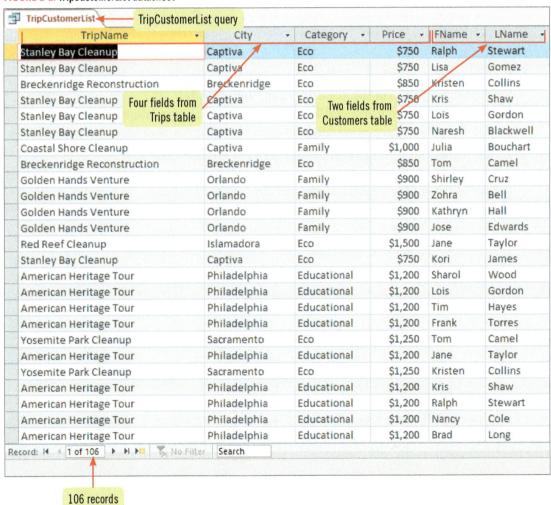

Work with Data in a Query

Learning Outcomes
- Edit records in a query
- Delete records in a query

You enter and edit data in a query datasheet the same way you do in a table datasheet. Because all data is stored in tables, any edits you make to data in a query datasheet are actually stored in the underlying tables and are automatically updated in all views of the data in other queries, forms, and reports. **CASE** ▶ *Julia Rice wants to change the name of one trip and update a city name. You can use the TripCustomerList query datasheet to make these edits.*

STEPS

TROUBLE
Be sure the final TripName is *Captiva Bay Cleanup*, not just *Captiva*.

1. **Double-click Stanley in the TripName field of the first or second record, type Captiva, then click any other record**

   All occurrences of Stanley Bay Cleanup automatically update to Captiva Bay Cleanup because this TripName field value is stored only once in the Trips table. See **FIGURE 2-3**. The TripName is selected from the Trips table and displayed in the TripCustomerList query for each customer who purchased this trip.

2. **Double-click Orlando in the City field of any record for the Golden Hands Venture trip, type College Park, then click any other record**

   All occurrences of Orlando automatically update to College Park for the Golden Hands Venture trip because this value is stored only once in the City field of the Trips table for the Golden Hands Venture record. The Golden Hands Venture trip is displayed in the TripCustomerList query for each customer who purchased that trip.

3. **Click the record selector button to the left of the first record, click the Home tab, click the Delete button in the Records group, then click Yes**

   You can delete records from a query datasheet the same way you delete them from a table datasheet. Notice that the navigation bar now indicates you have 105 records in the datasheet, as shown in **FIGURE 2-4**.

4. **Right-click the TripCustomerList query tab, then click Close**

   Each time a query is opened, it shows a current view of the data. This means that as new trips, customers, or sales are recorded in the database, the next time you open this query, the information will include all updates.

Hiding and unhiding fields in a datasheet

To hide a field in a datasheet, right-click the field name at the top of the datasheet and click the Hide Fields option on the shortcut menu. To unhide a field, right-click any field name, click Unhide Fields, and check the hidden field's check box in the Unhide Columns dialog box.

Freezing and unfreezing fields in a datasheet

In large datasheets, you may want to freeze certain fields so that they remain on the screen at all times. To freeze a field, right-click its field name in the datasheet, and then click Freeze Fields. To unfreeze a field, right-click any field name and click Unfreeze All Fields.

FIGURE 2-3: Working with data in a query datasheet

Record selector button for first record

TripName	City	Category	Price	FName	LName
Captiva Bay Cleanup	Captiva	Eco	$750	Ralph	Stewart
Captiva Bay Cleanup	Captiva	Eco	$750	Lisa	Gomez
Breckenridge Reconstruction	Breckenridge	Eco	$850	Kristen	Collins
Captiva Bay Cleanup	Captiva		$750	Kris	Shaw
Captiva Bay Cleanup	Captiva		$750	Lois	Gordon
Captiva Bay Cleanup	Captiva		$750	Naresh	Blackwell
Coastal Shore Cleanup	Captiva		$1,000	Julia	Bouchart
Breckenridge Reconstruction	Brecken		$850	Tom	Camel
Golden Hands Venture	Orlando	Family	$900	Shirley	Cruz
Golden Hands Venture	Orlando	Family	$900	Zohra	Bell
Golden Hands Venture	Orlando	Family	$900	Kathryn	Hall
Golden Hands Venture	Orlando	Family	$900	Jose	Edwards
Red Reef Cleanup	Islamadora	Eco	$1,500	Jane	Taylor
Captiva Bay Cleanup	Captiva	Eco	$750	Kori	James
American Heritage Tour	Philadelphia	Educational	$1,200	Sharol	Wood

Updating Stanley to Captiva in one record updates all records with that TripName

FIGURE 2-4: Final TripCustomerList datasheet

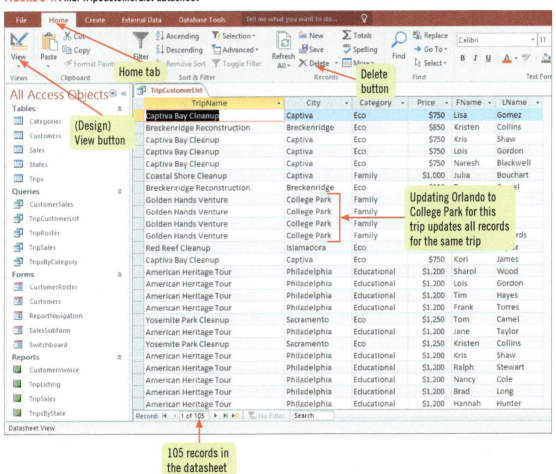

Home tab

(Design) View button

Delete button

Updating Orlando to College Park for this trip updates all records for the same trip

105 records in the datasheet

Access 2016

Use Query Design View

Learning
Outcomes
• Work in Query
  Design View
• Add criteria to a
  query

You use **Query Design View** to add, delete, or move the fields in an existing query; to specify sort orders; or to add **criteria** to limit the number of records shown in the resulting datasheet. You can also use Query Design View to create a new query from scratch. In the upper pane, Query Design View presents the fields you can use for that query in small windows called **field lists**. If you use the fields of two or more related tables in the query, the relationship between two tables is displayed with a **join line** (also called a **link line**) identifying which fields are used to establish the relationship. **CASE** *Julia Rice asks you to produce a list of trips in California. You use Query Design View to modify the existing TripsByState query to meet her request.*

STEPS

1. **Double-click the TripsByState query in the Navigation Pane to review the datasheet, then click the View button ☒ on the Home tab to switch to Query Design View**

   The TripsByState query contains the StateName field from the States table and the TripName, TripStartDate, and Price fields from the Trips table. This query contains two ascending sort orders: StateName and TripName. All records in California, for example, are further sorted by the TripName value.

QUICK TIP

Drag the lower edge of the field list to resize it to view all fields.

2. **Click the File tab, click Save As, click Save Object As, click the Save As button, type CATrips to replace Copy of TripsByState, then click OK**

   If you want to build a new query starting from an existing query, use the Save As command and give the new query a new name before you start working on it. This will prevent you from accidentally changing the original query.

   In Access, the **Save As command** on the File tab allows you to save the *entire database* (the entire database includes all objects within it) or just the *current object* with a new name. Recall that Access saves *data* automatically as you move from record to record.

   Query Design View displays the tables used in the upper pane of the window. The link line shows that one record in the States table may be related to many records in the Trips table. The lower pane of the window, called the **query design grid** (or **query grid** for short), displays the field names, sort orders, and criteria used within the query.

QUICK TIP

Query criteria are not case sensitive, so "California" equals "CALIFORNIA" equals "california".

3. **Click the first Criteria cell for the StateName field, type California, then click any other cell in the query grid as shown in FIGURE 2-5**

   Criteria are limiting conditions you set in the query design grid. In this case, the condition limits the selected records to only those with "California" in the StateName field. Criteria for a field with a Short Text data type are surrounded by "quotation marks" though you do not need to type the quotation marks. Access automatically adds them for you.

4. **Click the View button 🖩 in the Results group to switch to Datasheet View**

   Now only 15 records are selected, because only 15 of the trips have "California" in the StateName field, as shown in **FIGURE 2-6**.

5. **Right-click the CATrips query tab, click Close, then click Yes when prompted to save changes**

Adding or deleting a table in a query

You might want to add a table's field list to the upper pane of Query Design View to select fields from that table for the query. To add a new table to Query Design View, drag it from the Navigation Pane to Query Design View, or click the Show Table button on the Design tab, then add the desired table(s). To delete an unneeded table from Query Design View, click its title bar, then press [Delete].

FIGURE 2-5: CATrips query in Design View

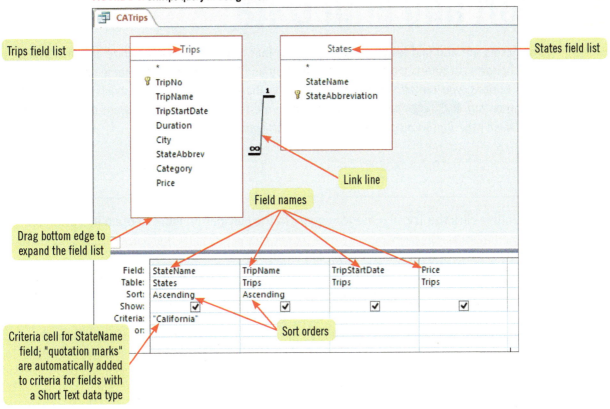

Trips field list

States field list

Trips

*
🔑 TripNo
TripName
TripStartDate
Duration
City
StateAbbrev
Category
Price

States

*
StateName
🔑 StateAbbreviation

Link line

Field names

Drag bottom edge to expand the field list

Field:	StateName	TripName	TripStartDate	Price
Table:	States	Trips	Trips	Trips
Sort:	Ascending	Ascending		
Show:	✓	✓	✓	✓
Criteria:	"California"			
or:				

Criteria cell for StateName field; "quotation marks" are automatically added to criteria for fields with a Short Text data type

Sort orders

FIGURE 2-6: CATrips query with California criterion

CATrips

StateName	TripName	TripStartDate	Price
California	Bear Valley Adventures	08/18/2017	$800
California	Bigfoot Rafting Club	09/12/2017	$850
California	Black Sheep Hikers	08/25/2017	$3,000
California	Cactus Ecosystem	09/13/2017	$800
California	Golden State Trips	07/19/2017	$2,300
California	Japanese California Connection	08/18/2017	$900
California	Kings Canyon Bridge Builders	07/12/2017	$2,800
California	Langguth Environment	10/18/2017	$2,900
California	Monterey Mysteries	07/13/2017	$1,800
California	Oakland Museum of Science	07/19/2017	$1,000
California	Perfect Waves Project	06/26/2017	$800
California	Redwood Forest Lab	09/28/2017	$1,500
California	Silver Country Venture	07/12/2017	$3,500
California	Water Education Foundation	09/20/2017	$1,300
California	Yosemite Park Cleanup	07/19/2017	$1,250

TripName values are in ascending order

Only 15 California records are selected

Sort and Find Data

Learning Outcomes
• Apply sort orders to a query
• Add fields to a query
• Find and replace data
• Undo edits

The Access sort and find features are handy tools that help you quickly organize and find data in a table or query datasheet. **TABLE 2-1** describes the Sort and Find buttons on the Home tab. Besides using these buttons, you can also click the list arrow on the field name in a datasheet, and then click a sorting option. **CASE** ▶ *Julia asks you to provide a list of trips sorted by Category, and then by Price. You'll modify the TripsByCategory query to answer this request.*

STEPS

1. **Double-click the TripsByCategory query in the Navigation Pane to open its datasheet**

   The TripsByCategory query currently sorts Trips by Category, then by TripName. You'll add the Duration field to this query, then change the sort order for the records.

QUICK TIP

Drag a selected field selector right or left to move the column to a new position in the query grid.

2. **Click the View button ☑ in the Views group to switch to Design View, then double-click the Duration field in the Trips field list**

   When you double-click a field in a field list, Access inserts it in the next available column in the query grid. You can also drag a field from a field list to a specific column of the query grid. To select a field in the query grid, you click its field selector. The **field selector** is the thin gray bar above each field in the query grid. To delete a field from a query, click its field selector, then press [Delete]. Deleting a field from a query does not delete it from the underlying table; the field is only deleted from the query.

   Currently, the TripsByCategory query is sorted by Category and then by TripName. Access evaluates sort orders from left to right. You want to change the sort order so that the records sort first by Category then by Price.

3. **Click Ascending in the TripName Sort cell, click the list arrow, click (not sorted), double-click the Price Sort cell, click the list arrow, then click Descending**

   The records are now set to be sorted in ascending order by Category, and within each Category, in a descending order by the Price field, as shown in **FIGURE 2-7**. Because sort orders always work from left to right, you might need to rearrange the fields before applying a sort order that uses more than one field. To move a field in the query design grid, click its field selector, then drag it left or right.

4. **Click the View button ▦ in the Results group to switch to Datasheet View**

   The new datasheet shows the Duration field in the fifth column. The records are now sorted in ascending order by the Category field, but for records in the same Category, they are further sorted in descending order by Price. Your next task is to replace all occurrences of "Tour" with "Trip" in the TripName field.

5. **Click in any TripName field, click the Replace button on the Home tab, type Tour in the Find What box, click in the Replace With box, type Trip, click the Match arrow button, then click Any Part of Field**

   The Find and Replace dialog box is shown in **FIGURE 2-8**.

TROUBLE

If your find-and-replace effort did not work correctly, click the Undo button ↺ and repeat Steps 5 and 6.

6. **Click the Replace All button in the Find and Replace dialog box, click Yes to continue, then click Cancel to close the Find and Replace dialog box**

   Access replaced both occurrences of "Tour" with "Trip" in the TripName field, as shown in **FIGURE 2-9**.

7. **Right-click the TripsByCategory query tab, click Close, then click Yes if prompted to save changes**

FIGURE 2-7: Changing sort orders for the TripsByCategory query

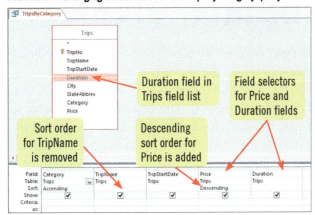

Duration field in Trips field list

Field selectors for Price and Duration fields

Sort order for TripName is removed

Descending sort order for Price is added

FIGURE 2-8: Find and Replace dialog box

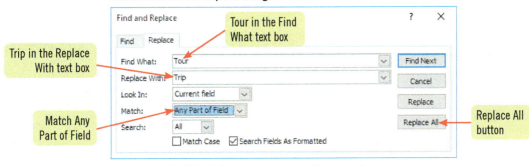

Tour in the Find What text box

Trip in the Replace With text box

Match Any Part of Field

Replace All button

FIGURE 2-9: Final TripsByCategory datasheet with new sort orders

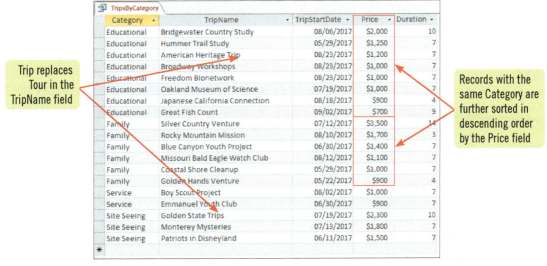

Category	TripName	TripStartDate	Price	Duration
Educational	Bridgewater Country Study	08/06/2017	$2,000	10
Educational	Hummer Trail Study	05/29/2017	$1,250	7
Educational	American Heritage Trip	08/23/2017	$1,200	7
Educational	Broadway Workshops	08/23/2017	$1,000	7
Educational	Freedom Bionetwork	08/23/2017	$1,000	7
Educational	Oakland Museum of Science	07/19/2017	$1,000	7
Educational	Japanese California Connection	08/18/2017	$900	4
Educational	Great Fish Count	09/02/2017	$700	9
Family	Silver Country Venture	07/12/2017	$3,500	14
Family	Rocky Mountain Mission	08/10/2017	$1,700	3
Family	Blue Canyon Youth Project	06/30/2017	$1,400	7
Family	Missouri Bald Eagle Watch Club	08/12/2017	$1,100	7
Family	Coastal Shore Cleanup	05/29/2017	$1,000	7
Family	Golden Hands Venture	05/22/2017	$900	4
Service	Boy Scout Project	08/02/2017	$1,000	7
Service	Emmanuel Youth Club	06/30/2017	$900	7
Site Seeing	Golden State Trips	07/19/2017	$2,300	10
Site Seeing	Monterey Mysteries	07/13/2017	$1,800	7
Site Seeing	Patriots in Disneyland	06/11/2017	$1,500	7

Trip replaces Tour in the TripName field

Records with the same Category are further sorted in descending order by the Price field

TABLE 2-1: Sort and Find buttons

name	button	purpose
Ascending		Sorts records based on the selected field in ascending order (0 to 9, A to Z)
Descending		Sorts records based on the selected field in descending order (Z to A, 9 to 0)
Remove Sort		Removes the current sort order
Find		Opens the Find and Replace dialog box to find data
Replace		Opens the Find and Replace dialog box to find and replace data
Go To		Helps you navigate to the first, previous, next, last, or new record
Select		Helps you select a single record or all records in a datasheet

Filter Data

Learning Outcomes
- Apply and remove filters in a query
- Use wildcards in criteria

Filtering a table or query datasheet temporarily displays only those records that match given criteria. Recall that criteria are limiting conditions you set. For example, you might want to show only trips in the state of Missouri, or only trips with a duration of fewer than 14 days. Although filters provide a quick and easy way to display a temporary subset of records in the current datasheet, they are not as powerful or flexible as queries. Most important, a query is a saved object within the database, whereas filters are temporary. Access removes all filters when you close the datasheet. TABLE 2-2 compares filters and queries. **CASE** *Julia asks you to find all Family trips offered in the month of August. You can filter the Trips table datasheet to provide this information.*

STEPS

QUICK TIP

You can also apply a sort or filter by clicking the Sort and filter arrow to the right of the field name and choosing the sort order or filter values you want.

1. **Double-click the Trips table to open it, click any occurrence of Family in the Category field, click the Selection button in the Sort & Filter group on the Home tab, then click Equals "Family"**

   Six records are selected as shown in FIGURE 2-10. A filter icon appears to the right of the Category field. Filtering by the selected field value, called **Filter By Selection**, is a fast and easy way to filter the records for an exact match. To filter for comparative data (for example, where TripStartDate is equal to or greater than 7/1/2017), you must use the **Filter By Form** feature. Filter buttons are summarized in TABLE 2-3.

QUICK TIP

To clear previous criteria, click the Advanced button, then click Clear All Filters.

2. **Click the Advanced button in the Sort & Filter group, then click Filter By Form**

   The Filter by Form window opens. The previous Filter By Selection criterion, "Family" in the Category field, is still in the grid. Access places "quotation marks" around text criteria.

3. **Click the TripStartDate cell, then type 8/*/2017 as shown in FIGURE 2-11**

   Filter By Form also allows you to apply two or more criteria at the same time. An asterisk (*) in the day position of the date criterion works as a wildcard, selecting any date in the month of August in the year 2017.

QUICK TIP

Be sure to remove existing filters before applying a new filter, or the new filter will apply to the current subset of records instead of the entire datasheet.

4. **Click the Toggle Filter button in the Sort & Filter group**

   The datasheet selects one record that matches both filter criteria, as shown in FIGURE 2-12. Note that filter icons appear next to the TripStartDate and Category field names as both fields are involved in the filter.

5. **Close the Trips datasheet, then click Yes when prompted to save the changes**

   Saving changes to the datasheet saves the last sort order and column width changes. *Filters are not saved.*

Using wildcard characters

To search for a pattern, you can use a **wildcard** character to represent any character in the condition entry. Use a question mark (?) to search for any single character and an asterisk (*) to search for any number of characters. Wildcard characters are often used with the **Like** operator. For example, the criterion Like "12/*/17" would find all dates in December of 2017, and the criterion Like "F*" would find all entries that start with the letter F.

FIGURE 2-10: Filtering the Trips table

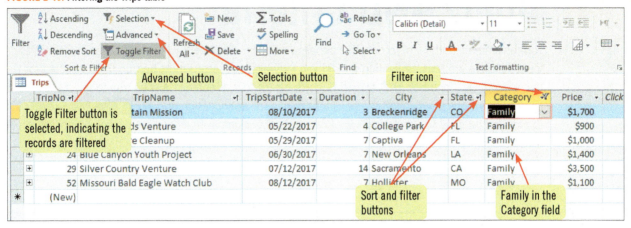

FIGURE 2-11: Filtering by Form criteria

FIGURE 2-12: Results of filtering by form

TABLE 2-2: Filters vs. queries

characteristics	filters	queries
Are saved as an object in the database		•
Can be used to select a subset of records in a datasheet	•	•
Can be used to select a subset of fields in a datasheet		•
Resulting datasheet used to enter and edit data	•	•
Resulting datasheet used to sort, filter, and find records	•	•
Commonly used as the source of data for a form or report		•
Can calculate sums, averages, counts, and other types of summary statistics across records		•
Can be used to create calculated fields		•

TABLE 2-3: Filter buttons

name	button	purpose
Filter		Provides a list of values in the selected field that can be used to customize a filter
Selection		Filters records that equal, do not equal, or are otherwise compared with the current value
Advanced		Provides advanced filter features such as Filter By Form, Save As Query, and Clear All Filters
Toggle Filter		Applies or removes the current filter

Apply AND Criteria

You can limit the number of records that appear on a query datasheet by entering criteria in Query Design View. **Criteria** are tests, or limiting conditions, for which the record must be true to be selected for the query datasheet. To create **AND criteria**, which means that *all* criteria must be true to select the record, enter two or more criteria on the *same* Criteria row of the query design grid. **CASE** *Julia Rice asks you to provide a list of all Eco (ecological) trips in the state of Colorado with a duration of seven days or more. Use Query Design View to create the query with AND criteria to meet her request.*

STEPS

1. **Click the Create tab on the Ribbon, click the Query Design button, double-click Trips, then click Close in the Show Table dialog box**

   You want four fields from the Trips table in this query.

2. **Drag the bottom edge of the Trips field list down to display all of the fields, double-click TripName, double-click Duration, double-click StateAbbrev, then double-click Category to add these fields to the query grid**

   First add criteria to select only those records in Colorado. Because you are using the StateAbbrev field, you need to use the two-letter state abbreviation for Colorado, CO, as the Criteria entry.

3. **Click the first Criteria cell for the StateAbbrev field, type CO, then click the View button 🔲 to display the results**

   Querying for only those trips in the state of Colorado selects seven records. Next, you add criteria to select only the trips in the Eco category.

4. **Click the View button 🔲, click the first Criteria cell for the Category field, type Eco, then click the View button 🔲 in the Results group**

   Criteria added to the same line of the query design grid are AND criteria. When entered on the same line, each criterion must be true for the record to appear in the resulting datasheet. Querying for both CO and Eco trips narrows the selection to three records. Every time you add AND criteria, you narrow the number of records that are selected because the record must be true for all criteria.

5. **Click the View button 🔲, click the first Criteria cell for the Duration field, then type >=7, as shown in FIGURE 2-13**

   Access assists you with **criteria syntax**, rules that specify how to enter criteria. Access automatically adds "quotation marks" around text criteria in Short Text and Long Text fields ("CO" and "Eco") and pound signs (#) around date criteria in Date/Time fields. The criteria in the Number, Currency, and Yes/No fields are not surrounded by any characters. See **TABLE 2-4** for more information about comparison operators such as >= (greater than or equal to).

6. **Click the View button 🔲 in the Results group**

   The third AND criterion further narrows the number of records selected to two, as shown in **FIGURE 2-14**.

7. **Click the Save button 🖫 on the Quick Access Toolbar, type EcoCO7 as the query name, click OK, then close the query**

   The query is saved with the new name, EcoCO7, as a new object in the R2G-2 database. Criteria entered in Query Design View are permanently saved with the query (as compared to filters in the previous lesson, which are temporary and not saved with the object).

FIGURE 2-13: Query Design View with AND criteria

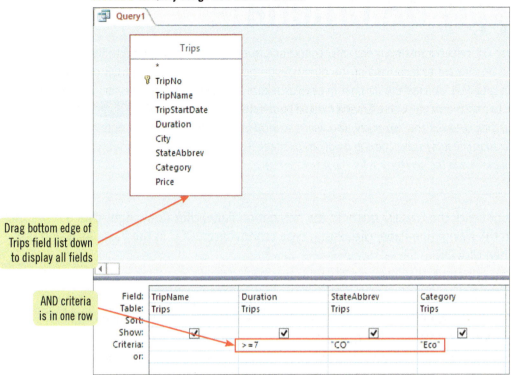

Drag bottom edge of Trips field list down to display all fields

AND criteria is in one row

FIGURE 2-14: Final datasheet of EcoCO7 query

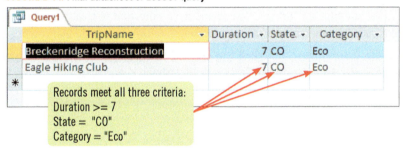

Records meet all three criteria:
Duration >= 7
State = "CO"
Category = "Eco"

TABLE 2-4: Comparison operators

operator	description	expression	meaning
>	Greater than	>500	Numbers greater than 500
>=	Greater than or equal to	>=500	Numbers greater than or equal to 500
<	Less than	<"Elder"	Names from A to Elder, but not Elder
<=	Less than or equal to	<="Buehler"	Names from A through Buehler, inclusive
<>	Not equal to	<>"Bridgewater"	Any name except for Bridgewater

Searching for blank fields

Is Null and Is Not Null are two other types of common criteria. The **Is Null** criterion finds all records where no entry has been made in the field. **Is Not Null** finds all records where there is any entry in the field, even if the entry is 0. Primary key fields cannot have a null entry.

Apply OR Criteria

You use **OR criteria** when *any one criterion* must be true in order for the record to be selected. Enter OR criteria on *different* Criteria rows of the query design grid. As you add rows of OR criteria to the query design grid, you increase the number of records selected for the resulting datasheet because the record needs to match only one of the Criteria rows to be selected for the datasheet. **CASE** ▶ *Julia Rice asks you to add criteria to the previous query. She wants to include Adventure trips in the state of Colorado that are greater than or equal to seven days in duration. To do this, you make a copy of the EcoCO7 query to modify with OR criteria to add the new records for the Adventure trips.*

STEPS

1. **Right-click the EcoCO7 query in the Navigation Pane, click Copy, right-click a blank spot in the Navigation Pane, click Paste, type EcoAdventureCO7 in the Paste As dialog box, then click OK**

   By copying the EcoCO7 query before starting your modifications, you avoid changing the EcoCO7 query by mistake.

2. **Right-click the EcoAdventureCO7 query in the Navigation Pane, click Design View, click the second Criteria cell in the Category field, type Adventure, then click the View button 🔲 to display the query datasheet**

   The query selected 11 records including all of the trips with Adventure in the Category field. Note that some of the Duration values are less than seven and some of the StateAbbrev values are not CO. Because each row of the query grid is evaluated separately, *all* Adventure trips are selected regardless of criteria in any other row. In other words, the criteria in one row have no effect on the criteria of other rows. To make sure that the Adventure trips are also in Colorado and have a duration of greater than or equal to seven days, you need to modify the second row of the query grid (the "or" row) to add that criteria.

3. **Click the View button 📝, click the second Criteria cell in the Duration field, type >=7, click the second Criteria cell in the StateAbbrev field, type CO, then click in any other cell of the grid**

   Query Design View should look like **FIGURE 2-15**.

4. **Click the View button 🔲**

   Three records are selected that meet all three criteria as entered in row one or row two of the query grid, as shown in **FIGURE 2-16**.

5. **Right-click the EcoAdventureCO7 query tab, click Close, then click Yes to save and close the query datasheet**

FIGURE 2-15: Query Design View with OR criteria

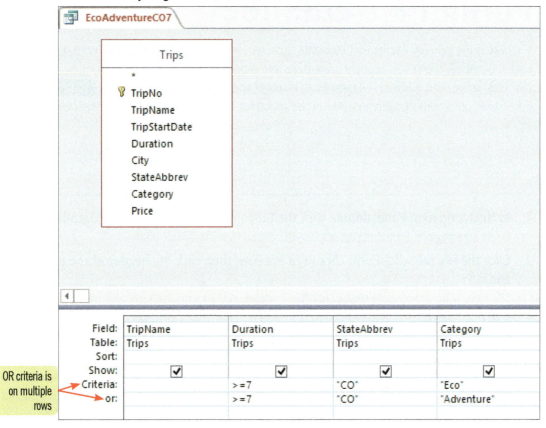

OR criteria is on multiple rows

FIGURE 2-16: Final datasheet of EcoAdventureCO7 query

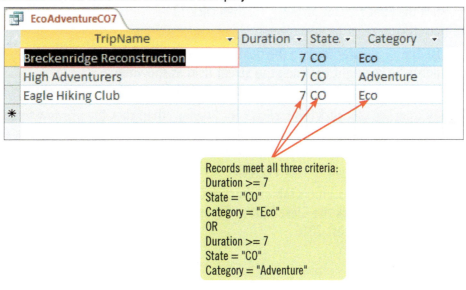

Records meet all three criteria:
Duration >= 7
State = "CO"
Category = "Eco"
OR
Duration >= 7
State = "CO"
Category = "Adventure"

Format a Datasheet

A report is the primary Access tool to create a professional printout, but you can print a datasheet as well. A datasheet allows you to apply some basic formatting modifications such as changing the font size, font face, colors, and gridlines. All formatting changes apply to the entire datasheet. **CASE** *Julia Rice asks you to print a list of customers. You decide to format the Customers table datasheet before printing it for her.*

STEPS

1. **In the Navigation Pane, double-click the Customers table to open it in Datasheet View**
   Before applying new formatting enhancements, you preview the default printout.

2. **Click the File tab, click Print, click Print Preview, then click the header of the printout to zoom in**
   The preview window displays the layout of the printout, as shown in **FIGURE 2-17**. By default, the printout of a datasheet contains the object name and current date in the header. The page number is in the footer.

3. **Click the Next Page button ▶ in the navigation bar to move to the next page of the printout**
   The last two fields, Phone and FirstContact, print on the second page because the first is not wide enough to accommodate them. You decide to switch the report to landscape orientation so that all of the fields print on one page, and then increase the size of the font before printing to make the text easier to read.

4. **Click the Landscape button on the Print Preview tab to switch the report to landscape orientation, then click the Close Print Preview button**
   You return to Datasheet View where you can make font face, font size, font color, gridline color, and background color choices.

5. **Click the Font list arrow** `Calibri (Detail)` **in the Text Formatting group, click Arial Narrow, click the Font Size list arrow** `11` **, then click 12**
   You decide to widen the Street column.

6. **Use the ⇹ pointer to drag the field separator between the Street and City field names slightly to the right to widen the Street field as shown in FIGURE 2-18**
   Double-clicking the field separators widens the columns as needed to display every entry in those fields.

7. **Click the File tab, click Print, click Print Preview, then click the preview to zoom in and out to review the information**
   All of the fields now fit across a page in landscape orientation. The preview of the printout is two pages, and in landscape orientation, it is easier to read.

8. **Right-click the Customers table tab, click Close, click Yes when prompted to save changes, then click the Close button ✕ on the title bar to close the R2G-2.accdb database and Access 2016**

FIGURE 2-17: Preview of Customers datasheet

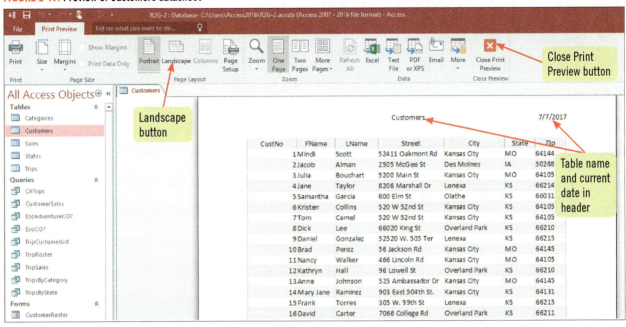

Landscape button

Close Print Preview button

Table name and current date in header

FIGURE 2-18: Formatting the Customers datasheet

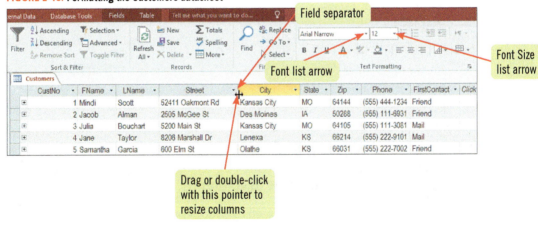

Field separator

Font Size list arrow

Font list arrow

Drag or double-click with this pointer to resize columns

Practice

Concepts Review

Label each element of the Access window shown in FIGURE 2-19.

FIGURE 2-19

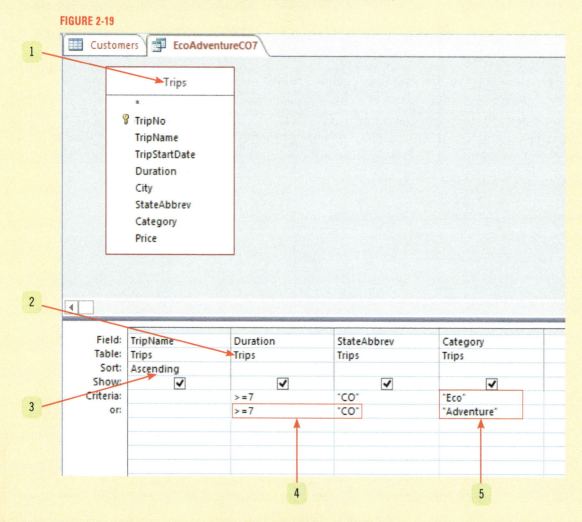

Match each term with the statement that best describes it.

6. **Query grid**

7. **Field selector**

8. **Filter**

9. **Filter By Selection**

10. **Field lists**

11. **Sorting**

12. **Join line**

13. **Criteria**

14. **Syntax**

15. **Wildcard**

a. Putting records in ascending or descending order based on the values of a field

b. Limiting conditions used to restrict the number of records that are selected in a query

c. The thin gray bar above each field in the query grid

d. Creates a temporary subset of records

e. Small windows that display field names

f. Rules that determine how criteria are entered

g. Used to search for a pattern of characters

h. The lower pane in Query Design View

i. Identifies which fields are used to establish a relationship between two tables

j. A fast and easy way to filter the records for an exact match

Select the best answer from the list of choices.

16. AND criteria:

    a. determine sort orders.

    b. must all be true for the record to be selected.

    c. determine fields selected for a query.

    d. help set link lines between tables in a query.

17. SQL stands for which of the following?

    a. Structured Query Language

    b. Standard Query Language

    c. Special Query Listing

    d. Simple Query Listing

18. A query is sometimes called a logical view of data because:

    a. you can create queries with the Logical Query Wizard.

    b. queries contain logical criteria.

    c. query naming conventions are logical.

    d. queries do not store data—they only display a view of data.

19. Which of the following describes OR criteria?

    a. Selecting a subset of fields and/or records to view as a datasheet from one or more tables

    b. Using two or more rows of the query grid to select only those records that meet given criteria

    c. Reorganizing the records in either ascending or descending order based on the contents of one or more fields

    d. Using multiple fields in the query design grid

20. Which of the following is *not* true about a query?

    a. A query is the same thing as a filter.

    b. A query can select fields from one or more tables in a relational database.

    c. A query can be created using different tools.

    d. An existing query can be modified in Query Design View.

Skills Review

1. **Use the Query Wizard.**
   a. Open the Salvage-2.accdb database from the location where you store your Data Files. Enable content if prompted.
   b. Create a new query using the Simple Query Wizard. Select the CenterName field from the Centers table, the DepositDate and Weight fields from the Deposits table, and the ClubName field from the Clubs table. Select Detail, and enter **CenterDeposits** as the name of the query.
   c. Open the query in Datasheet View, then change any record with the Johnson Recycling value to a center name that includes your last name.

2. **Work with data in a query.**
   a. Delete the first record (A1 Salvage Center with a DepositDate value of 2/4/2014).
   b. Change any occurrence of JavaScript KC in the ClubName field to **Bootstrap Club**.
   c. Click any value in the DepositDate field, then click the Descending button on the Home tab to sort the records in descending order on the DepositDate field.
   d. Use the Calendar Picker to choose the date of **1/30/17** for the first record.
   e. Save and close the CenterDeposits query.

3. **Use Query Design View.**
   a. Click the Create tab, click the Query Design button, double-click Clubs, double-click Deposits, and then click Close to add the Clubs and Deposits tables to Query Design View.
   b. Drag the bottom edge of both field lists down as needed to display all of the field names in both tables.
   c. Add the following fields from the Clubs table to the query design grid in the following order: FName, LName, ClubName. Add the following fields from the Deposits table in the following order: DepositDate, Weight. View the results in Datasheet View, observing the number of records that are selected in the record navigation bar at the bottom of the datasheet.
   d. In Design View, enter criteria to display only those records with a Weight value of **>=100**, then observe the number of records that are selected in Datasheet View.
   e. Save the query with the name **100PlusDeposits**.

4. **Sort and find data.**
   a. In Query Design View of the 100PlusDeposits query, choose an ascending sort order for the ClubName field and a descending sort order for the Weight field.
   b. Display the query in Datasheet View, noting how the records have been resorted.
   c. In the ClubName field, change any occurrence of Boy Scout Troop 324 to Boy Scout Troop **6**.
   d. In the FName field, change any occurrence of Trey to *your* initials and save the query.

5. **Filter data.**
   a. Filter the 100PlusDeposits datasheet for only those records where the ClubName equals **Access Users Group**.
   b. Apply an advanced Filter By Form and use the >= operator to further narrow the records so that only the deposits with a DepositDate value on or after 1/1/2015 are selected.
   c. Apply the filter to see the datasheet and, if requested by your instructor, print the filtered 100PlusDeposits datasheet.
   d. Save and close the 100PlusDeposits query. Reopen the 100PlusDeposits query to confirm that filters are temporary (not saved), and then close the 100PlusDeposits query again.

6. **Apply AND criteria.**

   a. Right-click the 100PlusDeposits query, copy it, and then paste it as **100PlusDeposits2016**.

   b. Open the 100PlusDeposits2016 query in Query Design View.

   c. Modify the criteria to select all of the records with a DepositDate in **2016** and a Weight value **greater than or equal to 100**. (*Hint*: To select all records with a DepositDate in 2016, use a wildcard character for the month and day positions of the date criterion.)

   d. Display the results in Datasheet View. If requested by your instructor, print the 100PlusDeposits2016 datasheet, then save and close it.

7. **Apply OR criteria.**

   a. Right-click the 100PlusDeposits query, copy it, then paste it as **100PlusDeposits2Clubs**.

   b. Open the 100PlusDeposits2Clubs query in Design View, then add criteria to select the records with a ClubName of **Social Media Club** and a Weight value **greater than or equal to 100**.

   c. Add criteria to also include the records with a ClubName of **Access Users Group** with a Weight value **greater than or equal to 100**. FIGURE 2-20 shows the results.

   d. If requested by your instructor, print the 100PlusDeposits2Clubs datasheet, then save and close it.

FIGURE 2-20

Your initials will be in the FName field

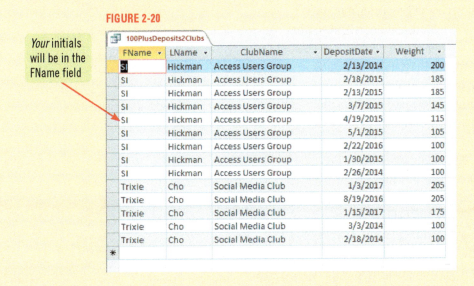

8. **Format a datasheet.**

   a. In the Centers table datasheet, apply the Times New Roman font and a 14-point font size.

   b. Resize all columns so that all data and field names are visible.

   c. Display the Centers datasheet in Print Preview, switch the orientation to landscape, click the Margins button in the Page Size group, then click Narrow.

   d. If requested by your instructor, print the Centers datasheet.

   e. Save and close the Centers table, then close Access 2016.

Independent Challenge 1

You have built an Access database to track membership in a community service club. The database tracks member names and addresses as well as their community service hours.

a. Open the Service-2.accdb database from the location where you store your Data Files, enable content if prompted, then open the Activities, Members, and Zips tables to review their datasheets.

b. In the Zips table, click the expand button to the left of the 64111, Kansas City, MO record to display the two members linked to that zip code. Click the expand button to the left of the Jeremiah Hopper record to display the three activity records linked to Jeremiah.

c. Close all three datasheets, click the Database Tools tab, then click the Relationships button. The Relationships window shows you that one record in the Zips table is related to many records in the Members table through the common ZipCode field, and that one record in the Members table is related to many records in the Activities table through the common MemberNo field.

d. Click the Relationship Report button, then if requested by your instructor, print the Relationship report. Close and save the report with the default name **Relationships for Service-2**. Close the Relationships window.

e. Using Query Design View, build a query with the following fields: FirstName and LastName from the Members table and ActivityDate and HoursWorked from the Activities table.

f. View the datasheet, observe the number of records selected, then return to Query Design View.

g. Add criteria to select only those records where the ActivityDate is in March of 2017.

h. In Query Design View, apply an ascending sort order to the LastName and a descending sort order to the ActivityDate field, then view the datasheet.

i. Change the name Quentin Garden to your name, widen all columns so that all data and field names are visible, and save the query with the name **March2017**, as shown in FIGURE 2-21.

j. If requested by your instructor, print the March2017 datasheet, then close the March2017 query and close Access 2016.

FIGURE 2-21

FirstName	LastName	ActivityDate	HoursWorked
Rhea	Alman	3/23/2017	4
Micah	Ati	3/23/2017	4
Evan	Bouchart	3/24/2017	8
Forrest	Browning	3/23/2017	5
Patch	Bullock	3/21/2017	4
Angela	Cabriella	3/23/2017	5
Andrea	Collins	3/25/2017	8
Student First	Student Last	3/25/2017	8
Student First	Student Last	3/23/2017	4
Gabriel	Hammer	3/23/2017	5
Jeremiah	Hopper	3/21/2017	4
Heidi	Kalvert	3/23/2017	4
Karla	Larson	3/23/2017	5
Katrina	Margolis	3/23/2017	4
Jose	Martin	3/24/2017	8
Jon	Maxim	3/24/2017	4
Harvey	McCord	3/24/2017	4
Mallory	Olson	3/25/2017	8
Jana	Pence	3/24/2017	10
Allie	Pitt	3/23/2017	4
Su	Vogue	3/24/2017	8
Taney	Wilson	3/24/2017	8

Record: 23 of 23   No Filter   Search

Independent Challenge 2

You work for a nonprofit agency that tracks voting patterns. You have developed an Access database with contact information for members of the House of Representatives. The director of the agency has asked you to create several state lists of representatives. You will use queries to extract this information.

a. Open the HouseOfReps-2.accdb database from the location where you store your Data Files, then enable content if prompted.

b. Open the Representatives and the States tables. Notice that one state is related to many representatives as evidenced by the expand buttons to the left of the records in the States tables.

c. Close both datasheets, then using Query Design View, create a query with the StateAbbrev, StateName, and Capital fields from the States table (in that order) as well as the FName and LName fields from the Representatives table.

d. Sort the records in ascending order on the StateName field, then in ascending order on the LName field.

e. Add criteria to select the representatives from Ohio or Pennsylvania. Use the StateAbbrev field to enter your criteria, using the two-character state abbreviations of **OH** and **PA**.

f. Save the query with the name **OhioAndPenn**, view the results, shown in FIGURE 2-22, then change the last name of Butterfield in the second record to *your* last name. Resize the columns as needed to view all the data and field names.

g. Print the OhioAndPenn datasheet if requested by your instructor, then close it and exit Access 2016.

FIGURE 2-22

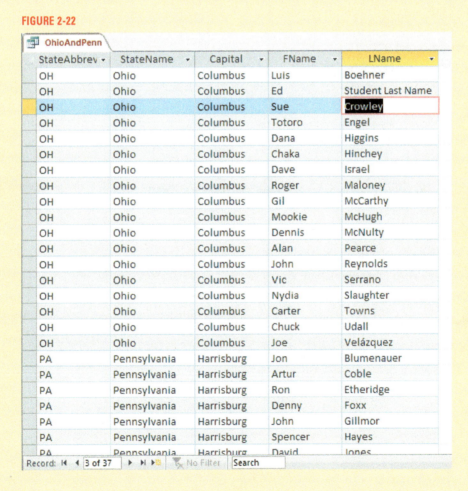

Access 2016

Independent Challenge 3

You have built an Access database to track the veterinarian clinics in your area.

a. Open the VetClinic-2.accdb database from the location where you store your Data Files, then enable content if prompted.

b. Open the Vets table and then the Clinics table to review the data in both datasheets.

c. Click the expand button next to the Animal Haven record in the Clinics table, then add your name as a new record to the Vets subdatasheet.

d. Close both datasheets.

e. Using the Simple Query Wizard, select the VetLast and VetFirst fields from the Vets table, and select the ClinicName and Phone fields from the Clinics table. Title the query **ClinicVetListing**, then view the datasheet.

f. Update any occurrence of Animal Haven in the ClinicName field to **Animal Emergency Shelter**.

g. In Query Design View, add criteria to select only **Animal Emergency Shelter** or **Veterinary Specialists** in the ClinicName field, then view the datasheet.

h. In Query Design View, move the ClinicName field to the first column, then add an ascending sort order on the ClinicName and VetLast fields.

i. Display the ClinicVetListing query in Datasheet View, resize the fields as shown in FIGURE 2-23, then print the datasheet if requested by your instructor.

j. Save and close the ClinicVetListing datasheet, then exit Access 2016.

FIGURE 2-23

Independent Challenge 4: Explore

An Access database is an excellent tool to help record and track job opportunities. For this exercise, you'll create a database from scratch that you can use to enter, edit, and query data in pursuit of a new job or career.

a. Create a new desktop database named **Jobs.accdb**.

b. Create a table named **Positions** with the following field names, data types, and descriptions:

Field name	Data type	Description
PositionID	AutoNumber	Primary key field
Title	Short Text	Title of position such as Accountant, Assistant Court Clerk, or Web Developer
CareerArea	Short Text	Area of the career field such as Accounting, Government, or Information Systems
AnnualSalary	Currency	Annual salary
Desirability	Number	Desirability rating of 1 = low to 5 = high to show how desirable the position is to you
EmployerID	Number	Foreign key field to the Employers table

c. Create a table named **Employers** with the following field names, data types, and descriptions:

Field name	Data type	Description
EmployerID	AutoNumber	Primary key field
CompanyName	Short Text	Company name of the employer
EmpStreet	Short Text	Employer's street address
EmpCity	Short Text	Employer's city
EmpState	Short Text	Employer's state
EmpZip	Short Text	Employer's zip code
EmpPhone	Short Text	Employer's phone, such as 111-222-3333

d. Be sure to set EmployerID as the primary key field in the Employers table and the PositionID as the primary key field in the Positions table.

e. Link the Employers and Positions tables together in a one-to-many relationship using the common EmployerID field. One employer record will be linked to many position records. Be sure to enforce referential integrity.

f. Using any valid source of potential employer data, enter five records into the Employers table.

g. Using any valid source of job information, enter five records into the Positions table by using the subdatasheets from within the Employers datasheet.

Because one employer may have many positions, all five of your Positions records may be linked to the same employer, you may have one position record per employer, or any other combination.

h. Build a query that selects CompanyName from the Employers table, and the Title, CareerArea, AnnualSalary, and Desirability fields from the Positions table. Sort the records in descending order based on Desirability. Save the query as **JobList**, and print it if requested by your instructor.

i. Close the JobList datasheet, then exit Access 2016.

Visual Workshop

Open the Baseball-2.accdb database from the location where you store your Data Files, and enable content if prompted. Create a query in Query Design View based on the Players and Teams tables, as shown in **FIGURE 2-24**. Add criteria to select only those records where the PlayerPosition field values are equal to 1 or 2 (representing pitchers and catchers). In Query Design View, set an ascending sort order on the TeamName and PlayerPosition fields. In the results, change the name of Aaron Campanella to your name. Save the query with the name **PitchersAndCatchers**, then compare the results with **FIGURE 2-24**, making changes and widening columns to display all of the data. Print the datasheet if requested by your instructor. Save and close the query and the Baseball-2.accdb database, then exit Access 2016.

FIGURE 2-24

PitchersAndCatchers			
TeamName	PlayerFirst	PlayerLast	Positi
Brooklyn Beetles	Student First	Student Last	1
Brooklyn Beetles	Cy	Young	2
Mayfair Monarchs	Luis	Durocher	1
Mayfair Monarchs	Carl	Mathewson	2
Rocky's Rockets	Andrew	Spalding	1
Rocky's Rockets	Sanford	Koufax	2
Snapping Turtles	Charles	Ford	1
Snapping Turtles	Greg	Perry	2

Using Forms

CASE Julia Rice, a trip developer at Reason 2 Go, asks you to create forms to make trip information easier to access, enter, and update.

Module Objectives

After completing this module, you will be able to:

- Use the Form Wizard
- Create a split form
- Use Form Layout View
- Add fields to a form
- Modify form controls
- Create calculations
- Modify tab order
- Insert an image

Files You Will Need

R2G-3.accdb

R2GLogo.jpg

LakeHomes-3.accdb

LakeHome.jpg

Scuba-3.accdb

Service-3.accdb

Salvage-3.accdb

Jobs-3.accdb

Baseball-3.accdb

Use the Form Wizard

Learning Outcomes
- Create a form with the Form Wizard
- Sort data in a form
- Describe form terminology and views

A **form** is an easy-to-use data entry and navigation screen. A form allows you to arrange the fields of a record in any layout so a database **user** can quickly and easily find, enter, edit, and analyze data. The database **designer** or **application developer** is the person responsible for building and maintaining tables, queries, forms, and reports for all of the users. **CASE** *Julia Rice asks you to build a form to enter and maintain trip information.*

STEPS

1. **Start Access, open the R2G-3.accdb database from the location where you store your Data Files, then enable content if prompted**

   You can use many methods to create a new form, but the Form Wizard is a fast and popular tool that helps you get started. The **Form Wizard** prompts you for information it needs to create a form, such as the fields, layout, and title for the form.

2. **Click the Create tab on the Ribbon, then click the Form Wizard button in the Forms group**

   The Form Wizard starts, prompting you to select the fields for this form. You want to create a form to enter and update data in the Trips table.

3. **Click the Tables/Queries list arrow, click Table: Trips, then click the Select All Fields button** >>

   You could now select fields from other tables, if necessary, but in this case, you have all of the fields you need.

4. **Click Next, click the Columnar option button, click Next, type Trips Entry Form as the title, then click Finish**

   The Trips Entry Form opens in **Form View**, as shown in **FIGURE 3-1**. Access provides three different views of forms, as summarized in **TABLE 3-1**. Each item on the form is called a **control**. A **label control** is used to describe the data shown in other controls such as text boxes. A label is also used for the title of the form, Trips Entry Form. A **text box** is used to display the data as well as enter, edit, find, sort, and filter the data. A **combo box** is a combination of two controls: a text box and a list. The Category data is displayed in a combo box control. You click the arrow button on a combo box control to display a list of values, or you can edit data directly in the combo box itself.

QUICK TIP
Click in the text box of the field you want to sort before clicking a sort button.

5. **Click Stanley Bay Cleanup in the TripName text box, click the Ascending button in the Sort & Filter group, then click the Next record button ▶ in the navigation bar to move to the second record**

   The Bass Habitat Project trip is the second record when the records are sorted in ascending order on the TripName data. Information about the current record number and total number of records appears in the navigation bar, just as it does in a datasheet.

6. **Click the Previous record button ◀ in the navigation bar to move back to the first record, click the TripName text box, then change American Legacy Project to American Heritage Project**

   Your screen should look like **FIGURE 3-2**. Forms displayed in Form View are the primary tool for database users to enter, edit, and delete data in an Access database.

7. **Right-click the Trips Entry Form tab, then click Close**

   When a form is closed, Access automatically saves any edits made to the current record.

FIGURE 3-1: Trips Entry Form in Form View

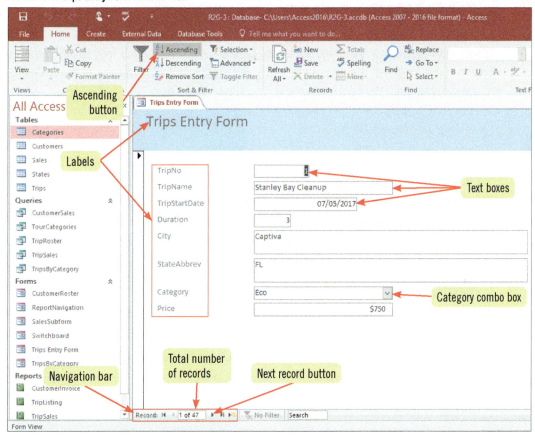

FIGURE 3-2: Editing data in Form View

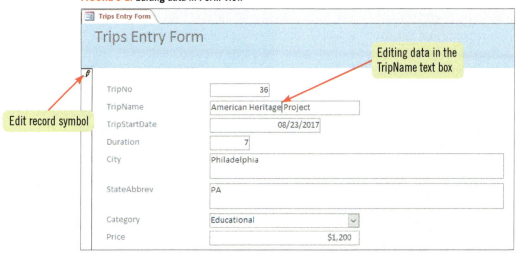

TABLE 3-1: Form views

view	primary purpose
Form	To find, sort, enter, and edit data
Layout	To modify the size, position, or formatting of controls; shows data as you modify the form, making it the tool of choice when you want to change the appearance and usability of the form while viewing data
Design	To modify the Form Header, Detail, and Footer section, or to access the complete range of controls and form properties; Design View does not display data

Create a Split Form

Learning Outcomes
• Create a split form
• Enter and edit data in a form

In addition to the Form Wizard, you should be familiar with several other form creation tools. **TABLE 3-2** identifies those tools and the purpose for each. **CASE** ▸ *Julia Rice asks you to create another form to manage customer data. You'll work with the Split Form tool for this task.*

STEPS

QUICK TIP
Layout View allows you to view and filter the data, but not edit it.

1. **Click the Customers table in the Navigation Pane, click the Create tab, click the More Forms button, click Split Form, then click the Add Existing Fields button in the Tools group on the Design tab to close the Field List if it opens**

   The Customers data appears in a split form with the top half in **Layout View**. The benefit of a **split form** is that the upper pane allows you to display the fields of one record in any arrangement, and the lower pane maintains a datasheet view of the first few records. If you edit, sort, or filter records in the upper pane, the lower pane is automatically updated, and vice versa.

2. **Click MO in the State text box in the upper pane, click the Home tab, click the Selection button in the Sort & Filter group, then click Does Not Equal "MO"**

   Thirty-seven records are filtered where the State field is not equal to MO. You also need to change a value in the Jacob Alman record.

TROUBLE
Make sure you edit the record in the datasheet in the lower pane.

3. **In the lower pane, select Des Moines in the City field of the first record, edit the entry to read Waukee, then press [Enter]**

   Note that "Waukee" is now the entry in the City field in both the upper and lower panes, as shown in **FIGURE 3-3**.

4. **Click the record selector for the Kristen Collins record in the lower pane as shown in FIGURE 3-4, then click the Delete button in the Records group on the Home tab**

   You cannot delete this record because it contains related records in the Sales table. This is a benefit of referential integrity on the one-to-many relationship between the Customers and Sales tables. Referential integrity prevents the creation of **orphan records**, records on the many side of a relationship that do not have a match on the one side.

5. **Click OK, right-click the Customers form tab, click Close, click Yes when prompted to save changes, then click OK to save the form with Customers as the name**

TABLE 3-2: Form creation tools

tool	icon	creates a form
Form		with one click based on the selected table or query
Form Design		from scratch in Form Design View
Blank Form		from scratch in Form Layout View
Form Wizard		by answering a series of questions provided by the Form Wizard dialog boxes
Navigation		used to navigate or move between different areas of the database
More Forms		based on Multiple Items, Datasheet, Split Form, or Modal Dialog arrangements
Split Form		with two panes, the upper showing one record at a time and the lower displaying a datasheet of many records

FIGURE 3-3: Customers table in a split form

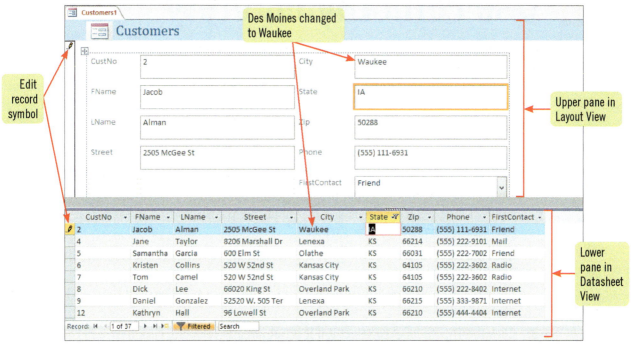

Edit record symbol

Des Moines changed to Waukee

Upper pane in Layout View

Lower pane in Datasheet View

FIGURE 3-4: Editing data in a split form

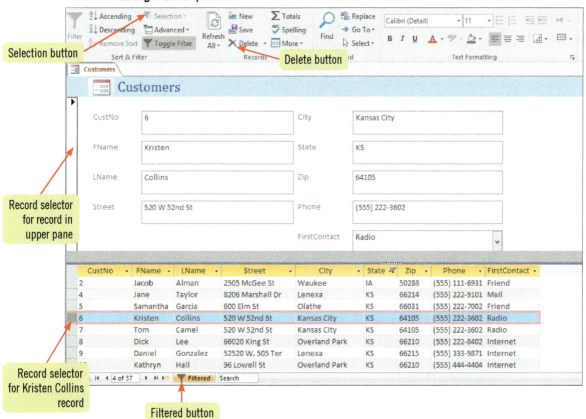

Selection button

Delete button

Record selector for record in upper pane

Record selector for Kristen Collins record

Filtered button

Use Form Layout View

Learning Outcomes
- Resize controls in Layout View
- Format controls in Layout View

Layout View lets you make some design changes to a form while you are browsing the data. For example, you can move and resize controls, add or delete a field on the form, filter and sort data, or change formatting characteristics, such as fonts and colors. **TABLE 3-4** lists several of the most popular formatting commands found on the Format tab when you are working in Layout or Form Design View. **CASE** *Julia Rice asks you to make several design changes to the Trips Entry Form. You can make these changes in Layout View.*

STEPS

1. **Right-click Trips Entry Form in the Navigation Pane, then click Layout View**

   In Layout View, you can move through the records, but you cannot enter or edit the data as you can in Form View.

   TROUBLE
   If your third record is not Bear Valley Adventures, sort the records in ascending order on the TripName field.

2. **Click the Next record button ▶ in the navigation bar twice to move to the third record, Bear Valley Adventures**

   You often use Layout View to make minor design changes, such as editing labels and changing formatting characteristics.

3. **Click the TripNo label to select it if it is not already selected, click between the words Trip and No, then press [Spacebar]**

   You also want to edit a few more labels.

   TROUBLE
   Be sure to modify the labels in the left column instead of the text boxes on the right.

4. **Continue editing the labels, as shown in FIGURE 3-5**

   You also want to change the text color of the labels to black to make them more noticeable.

5. **Click the Trip No label, press and hold [Shift] while clicking all of the other labels in the first column to select them together, release [Shift], click the Format tab, click the Font Color list arrow ![A] in the Font group, then click Automatic at the top of the list**

   You also decide to narrow the City and StateAbbrev text boxes.

   TROUBLE
   Be sure to modify the text boxes in the right column instead of the labels on the left.

6. **Click Sacramento in the City text box, press and hold [Shift], click CA in the StateAbbrev text box to select the two text boxes at the same time, release [Shift], then use the ↔ pointer to drag the right edge of the selection to the left to make the text boxes approximately half as wide**

   Layout View for the Trips Entry Form should look like **FIGURE 3-5**. Mouse pointers in Form Layout and Form Design View are very important as they indicate what happens when you drag the mouse. Mouse pointers are described in **TABLE 3-3**.

TABLE 3-3: Mouse pointer shapes

shape	when does this shape appear?	action
⌖	When you point to any unselected control on the form (the default mouse pointer)	Single-clicking with this mouse pointer selects a control
✥	When you point to the upper-left corner or edge of a selected control in Form Design View or the middle of the control in Form Layout View	Dragging with this mouse pointer moves the selected control(s)
↕ ↔ ⤡ ⤢	When you point to any sizing handle (except the larger one in the upper-left corner in Form Design View)	Dragging with one of these mouse pointers resizes the control

FIGURE 3-5: Using Layout View to modify controls on the Trips Entry Form

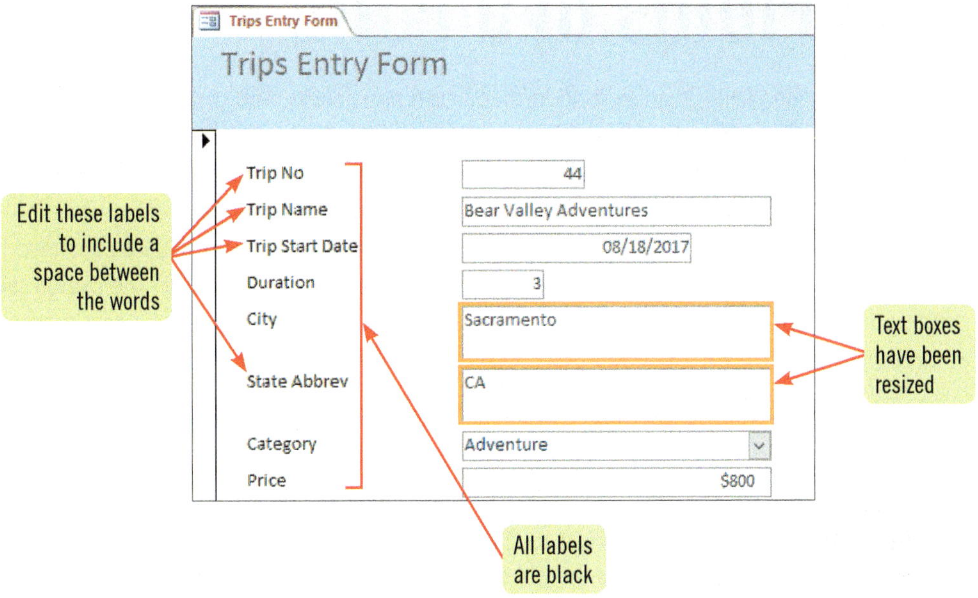

TABLE 3-4: Useful formatting commands

button	button name	description
B	Bold	Toggles bold on or off for the selected control(s)
I	Italic	Toggles italic on or off for the selected control(s)
U	Underline	Toggles underline on or off for the selected control(s)
A	Font Color	Changes the text color of the selected control(s)
	Background Color or Shape Fill	Changes the background color of the selected control(s)
	Align Left	Left-aligns the selected control(s) within its own border
	Center	Centers the selected control(s) within its own border
	Align Right	Right-aligns the selected control(s) within its own border
	Alternate Row Color	Changes the background color of alternate records in the selected section
	Shape Outline	Changes the border color, thickness, or style of the selected control(s)
	Shape Effects	Changes the special visual effect of the selected control(s)

Table layouts

Layouts provide a way to group several controls together on a form or report to more quickly add, delete, rearrange, resize, or align controls. To insert a layout into a form or report, select the controls you want to group together, then choose the Stacked or Tabular button on the Arrange tab in Layout View. Each option applies a table layout to the controls so that you can insert, delete, merge, or split the cells in the layout to quickly rearrange or edit the controls in the layout. To remove a layout, use the Remove Layout button on the Arrange tab in Form Design View.

Access 2016

Add Fields to a Form

Learning Outcomes
• Add fields to a form
• Define bound and unbound controls

Adding and deleting fields in an existing form is a common activity. You can add or delete fields in a form in either Layout View or Design View using the Field List. The **Field List** lists the database tables and the fields they contain. To add a field to the form, drag it from the Field List to the desired location on the form. To delete a field on a form, click the field to select it, then press the [Delete] key. Deleting a field from a form does not delete it from the underlying table or have any effect on the data contained in the field. You can toggle the Field List on and off using the Add Existing Fields button on the Design tab in Layout or Design View. **CASE** *Julia Rice asks you to add the Trip description from the Categories table to the Trips Entry Form. You can use Layout View and the Field List to accomplish this goal.*

STEPS

1. **Click the Design tab on the Ribbon, click the Add Existing Fields button in the Tools group, then click the Show all tables link in the Field List**

   The Field List opens in Layout View, as shown in **FIGURE 3-6**. Notice that the Field List is divided into sections. The upper section shows the tables currently used by the form, the middle section shows directly related tables, and the lower section shows other tables in the database. The expand/collapse button to the left of the table names allows you to expand (show) the fields within the table or collapse (hide) them. The Description field is in the Categories table in the middle section.

   To move the Field List, drag its title bar. Double-click the title bar of the Field List to dock it to the right.

2. **Click the expand button ⊞ to the left of the Categories table, drag the Description field to the form, then use the ⬧ pointer to drag the new Description combo box and label below the Price text box**

   When you add a new field to a form, two controls are usually created: a label and a text box. The label contains the field name and the text box displays the data in the field. The Categories table moved from the middle to the top section of the Field List. You also want to align and format the new controls with others already on the form.

3. **Click the Description label, click the Format tab on the Ribbon, then click the Font color button A⋅ to change the text color from gray to black**

   With the new controls in position and formatted, you want to enter a new record. You must switch to Form View to edit, enter, or delete data.

4. **Click the Home tab, click the View button ▦ to switch to Form View, click the New (blank) record button ▶▦ in the navigation bar, click the TripName text box, then enter a new record in the updated form, as shown in FIGURE 3-7**

   Be sure to enter the correct value for each field and note that when you select a value in the Category combo box, the Description is automatically updated. This is due to the one-to-many relationship between the Categories and Trips tables in the Relationships window.

FIGURE 3-6: Field List in Form Layout View

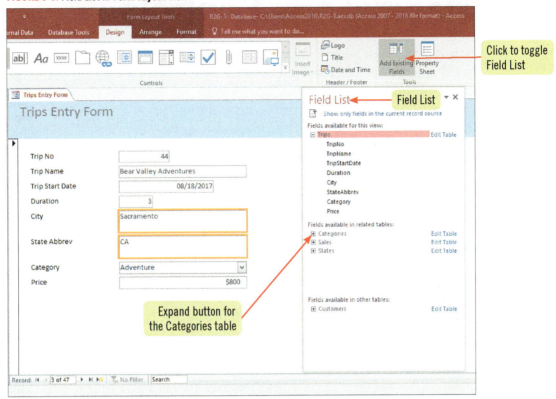

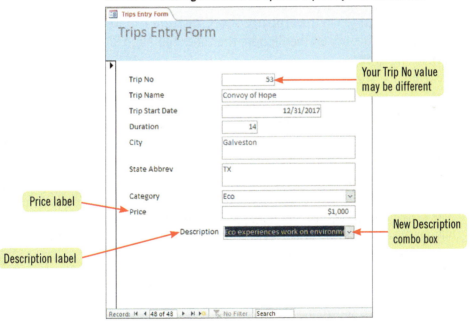

FIGURE 3-7: Entering a record in the updated Trips Entry Form in Form View

Bound versus unbound controls

Controls are either bound or unbound. **Bound controls** display values from a field such as text boxes and combo boxes. **Unbound controls** do not display data; unbound controls describe data or enhance the appearance of the form. Labels are the most common type of unbound control, but other types include lines, images, tabs, and command buttons. Another way to distinguish bound from unbound controls is to observe the form as you move from record to record. Because bound controls display data, their contents change as you move through the records, displaying data from the field of the current record. Unbound controls such as labels and lines do not change as you move through the records in a form.

Modify Form Controls

You have already made many modifications to form controls, such as changing the font color of labels and the size of text boxes. Labels and text boxes are the two most popular form controls. Other common controls are listed in TABLE 3-5. When you modify controls, you change their **properties** (characteristics). All of the control characteristics you can modify are stored in the control's **Property Sheet**. CASE ▶ *Because R2G is now focused on Eco (ecological) trips, you decide to use the Property Sheet of the Category field to modify the default value to be "Eco." Julia asks you to use the Property Sheet to make other control modifications to better size and align the controls.*

STEPS

1. **Right-click the Trips Entry Form tab, click Layout View, then click the Property Sheet button in the Tools group**

   The Property Sheet opens, replacing the Field List and showing you all of the properties for the selected item. Drag the title bar of the Property Sheet to move it. Double-click the title bar to dock it to the right.

2. **Click the Category combo box on the form, click the Data tab in the Property Sheet (if it is not already selected), click the Default Value box, type Eco, then press [Enter]**

   The Property Sheet should look like FIGURE 3-8. Access often helps you with the **syntax** (rules) of entering property values. In this case, Access added quotation marks around "Eco" to indicate that the default entry is text. Properties are categorized in the Property Sheet with the Format, Data, Event, and Other tabs. The All tab is a complete list of all the control's properties. You can use the Property Sheet to make all control modifications, although you'll probably find that some changes are easier to make using the Ribbon. The property values change in the Property Sheet as you modify a control using the Ribbon and vice versa.

TROUBLE
Be sure to click the
Trip No label on the
left, not the TripNo
text box on the right.

3. **Click the Format tab in the Property Sheet, click the Trip No label in the form to select it, click the Home tab on the Ribbon, then click the Align Right button ≡ in the Text Formatting group**

   Notice that the **Text Align property** on the Format tab in the Property Sheet is automatically updated from Left to Right even though you changed the property using the Ribbon instead of the Property Sheet.

4. **Click the Trip Name label, press and hold [Shift], then click each other label in the first column on the form**

   With all the labels selected, you can modify their Text Align property at the same time.

5. **Click ≡ in the Text Formatting group**

   Don't be overwhelmed by the number of properties available for each control on the form or the number of ways to modify each property. Over time, you will learn about most of these properties. At this point, it's only important to know the purpose of the Property Sheet and understand that properties are modified in various ways.

TROUBLE
Your Trip No value
might not match
FIGURE 3-9. It is an
AutoNumber value,
controlled by Access.

6. **Click the Save button 🖫 on the Quick Access Toolbar, click the Form View button to switch to Form View, click the New (blank) record button in the navigation bar, then enter the record shown in FIGURE 3-9**

   For new records, "Eco" is provided as the default value for the Category combo box, but you can change it by typing a new value or selecting one from the list. With the labels right-aligned, they are much closer to the data in the text boxes that they describe.

FIGURE 3-8: Using the Property Sheet

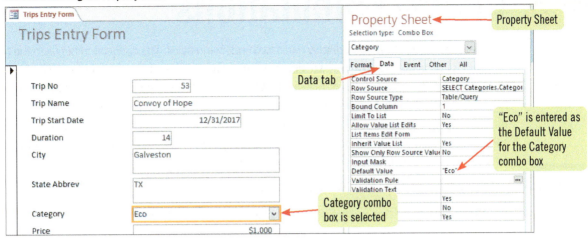

FIGURE 3-9: Modified Trips Entry Form

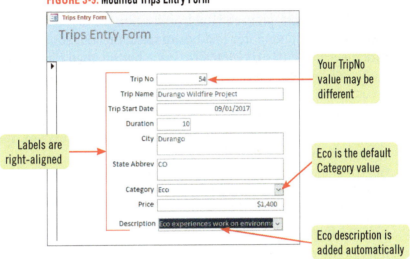

TABLE 3-5: Common form controls

name	used to	bound	unbound
Label	Provide consistent descriptive text as you navigate from record to record; the label is the most common type of unbound control and can also be used as a hyperlink to another database object, external file, or webpage		•
Text box	Display, edit, or enter data for each record from an underlying record source; the text box is the most common type of bound control	•	
List box	Display a list of possible data entries	•	
Combo box	Display a list of possible data entries for a field, and provide a text box for an entry from the keyboard; combines the list box and text box controls	•	
Tab control	Create a three-dimensional aspect on a form		•
Check box	Display "yes" or "no" answers for a field; if the box is checked, it means "yes"	•	
Toggle button	Display "yes" or "no" answers for a field; if the button is pressed, it means "yes"	•	
Option button	Display a choice for a field	•	
Option group	Display and organize choices (usually presented as option buttons) for a field	•	
Line and Rectangle	Draw lines and rectangles on the form		•
Command button	Provide an easy way to initiate a command or run a macro		•

Create Calculations

**Learning
Outcomes**
• Build calculations
on a form
• Move controls on
a form

Text boxes are generally used to display data from underlying fields. The connection between the text box and field is defined by the **Control Source property** on the Data tab of the Property Sheet for that text box. A text box control can also display a calculation. To create a calculation in a text box, you enter an expression instead of a field name in the Control Source property. An **expression** is a combination of field names, operators (such as +, −, /, and *), and functions (such as Sum, Count, or Avg) that results in a single value. Sample expressions are shown in TABLE 3-6. **CASE** *Julia Rice asks you to add a text box to the Trips Entry Form to calculate the trip end date. You can add a text box in Form Design View to accomplish this.*

STEPS

1. **Right-click the Trips Entry Form tab, then click Design View**

   You want to add the trip end date calculation just below the Duration text box. First, you'll resize the City and State Abbrev fields.

2. **Click the City label, press and hold [Shift], click the City text box, click the State Abbrev label, click the StateAbbrev text box to select the four controls together, release [Shift], click the Arrange tab, click the Size/Space button, then click To Shortest**

   With the City and StateAbbrev fields resized, you're ready to move them to make room for the new control to calculate the tour end date.

3. **Click a blank spot on the form to deselect the four controls, click the StateAbbrev text box, use the 🖑 pointer to move it down, click the City text box, then use the 🖑 pointer to move it down**

   To add the calculation to determine the trip end date (the trip start date plus the duration), start by adding a new text box to the form between the Duration and City text boxes.

4. **Click the Design tab, click the Text Box button [abl] in the Controls group, then click between the Duration and City text boxes to insert the new text box**

   Adding a new text box automatically adds a new label to the left of the text box.

5. **Double-click Text23, type Trip End Date, click the Home tab, click the Font Color button [A ▾], then press [Enter]**

   With the label updated to correctly identify the text box to the right, you're ready to enter the expression to calculate the tour end date.

6. **Click the new text box to select it, click the Data tab in the Property Sheet, click the Control Source property, type =[TripStartDate]+[Duration], then press [Enter] to update the form as shown in FIGURE 3-10**

   All expressions entered in a control must start with an equal sign (=). When referencing a field name within an expression, [square brackets]—(not parentheses) and not {curly braces}—surround the field name. In an expression, you must type the field name exactly as it was created in Table Design View, but you do not need to match the capitalization.

7. **Click the View button [▦] to switch to Form View, tab three times to the Duration field, type 5, then press [Enter]**

   Note that the trip end date, calculated by an expression, automatically changed to five days after the trip start date to reflect the new duration value. The updated Trips Entry Form with the trip end date calculation for the Bikers for Ecology is shown in FIGURE 3-11.

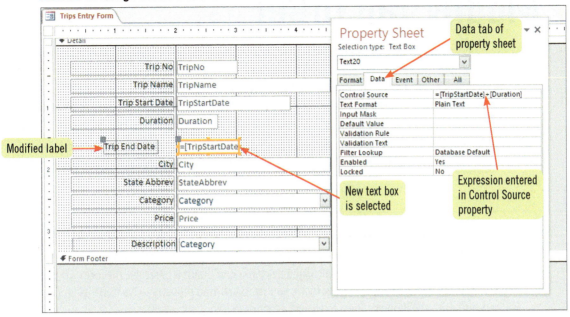

FIGURE 3-10: Adding a text box to calculate a value

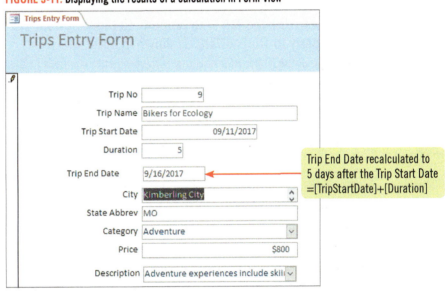

FIGURE 3-11: Displaying the results of a calculation in Form View

TABLE 3-6: Sample expressions

sample expression	description
=Sum([Salary])	Uses the **Sum** function to add the values in the Salary field
=[Price] * 1.05	Multiplies the Price field by 1.05 (adds 5% to the Price field)
=[Subtotal] + [Shipping]	Adds the value of the Subtotal field to the value of the Shipping field
=Avg([Freight])	Uses the **Avg** function to display an average of the values in the Freight field
=Date()	Uses the **Date** function to display the current date in the form of mm-dd-yy
="Page " &[Page]	Displays the word Page, a space, and the result of the [Page] field, an Access field that contains the current page number
=[FirstName]& " " &[LastName]	Displays the value of the FirstName and LastName fields in one control, separated by a space
=Left([ProductNumber],2)	Uses the **Left** function to display the first two characters in the ProductNumber field

Modify Tab Order

After positioning all of the controls on the form, you should check the tab order and tab stops. **Tab order** is the order the focus moves as you press [Tab] in Form View. A **tab stop** refers to whether a control can receive the focus in the first place. By default, the Tab Stop property for all text boxes and combo boxes is set to Yes, but some text boxes, such as those that contain expressions, will not be used for data entry. Therefore, the Tab Stop property for a text box that contains a calculation should be set to No. Unbound controls such as labels and lines do not have a Tab Stop property because they cannot be used to enter or edit data. **CASE** *Julia suggests that you check the tab order of the Trips Entry Form, then change tab stops and tab order as necessary.*

STEPS

1. **Press [Tab] enough times to move through several records, watching the focus move through the bound controls of the form**

   Because the Trip End Date text box is a calculated field, you don't want it to receive the focus. To prevent the Trip End Date text box from receiving the focus, you set its Tab Stop property to No using its Property Sheet. You can work with the Property Sheet in either Layout or Design View.

2. **Right-click the Trips Entry Form tab, click Design View, click the text box with the Trip End Date calculation if it is not already selected, click the Other tab in the Property Sheet, double-click the Tab Stop property to toggle it from Yes to No, then change the Name property to TripEndDate, as shown in FIGURE 3-12**

   The Other tab of the Property Sheet contains the properties you need to change the tab stop and tab order. The **Tab Stop property** determines whether the field accepts focus, and the **Tab Index property** indicates the numeric tab order for all controls on the form that have the Tab Stop property set to Yes. The **Name property** on the Other tab is also important as it identifies the name of the control, which is used in other areas of the database. To review your tab stop changes, return to Form View.

3. **Click the View button 📋 to switch to Form View, then press [Tab] nine times to move to the next record**

   Now that the tab stop has been removed from the TripEndDate text box, the tab order flows correctly from the top to the bottom of the form, skipping the calculated field. To review the tab order for the entire form in one dialog box, you must switch to Form Design View.

4. **Right-click the Trips Entry Form tab, click Design View, then click the Tab Order button in the Tools group to open the Tab Order dialog box**

   The Tab Order dialog box allows you to view and change the tab order by dragging fields up or down using the **field selector** to the left of the field name. Moving fields up and down in this list also renumbers the Tab Index property for the controls in their respective Property Sheets. If you want Access to create a top-to-bottom and left-to-right tab order, click **Auto Order**.

5. **Click the Auto Order button to make sure your tab order goes top to bottom as shown in FIGURE 3-13, click OK to close the Tab Order dialog box, click the Property Sheet button to toggle it off, click the Save button 💾 on the Quick Access Toolbar to save your work, then click a blank spot on the form to deselect the text box**

FIGURE 3-12: Using the Property Sheet to set tab properties

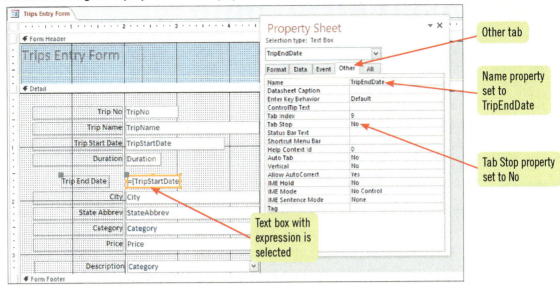

FIGURE 3-13: Tab Order dialog box

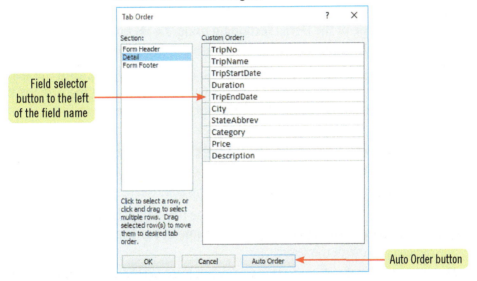

Form layouts

A **layout** helps you keep the controls on a form organized as a group. You can apply a stacked or tabular layout to the controls on your form by clicking the Stacked or Tabular buttons on the Arrange tab in Form Design View. Remove a layout by clicking the Remove Layout button. You can also modify a layout by modifying the margins, padding, and anchoring options of the layout using buttons found in the Position group on the

Arrange tab in Form Design View. **Margin** refers to the space between the outer edge of the control and the data displayed inside the control. **Padding** is the space between the controls. **Anchoring** allows you to tie controls together so you can work with them as a group. Some of the Form Wizards automatically apply a layout to the controls that you can modify or remove as needed.

Insert an Image

Graphic images, such as pictures, logos, or clip art, can add style and professionalism to a form. The form section in which you place the images is significant. **Form sections** determine where controls are displayed and printed; they are described in **TABLE 3-7**. For example, if you add a company logo to the Form Header section, the image appears at the top of the form in Form View as well as at the top of a printout. If you add the same image to the Detail section, it prints next to each record in the printout because the Detail section is printed for every record. **CASE** ▶ *Julia Rice suggests that you add the R2G logo to the top of the Trips Entry Form. You can add the control in either Layout or Design View, but if you want to place it in the Form Header section, you have to work in Design View.*

STEPS

1. **Click the Insert Image button in the Controls group, click Browse, then navigate to the location where you store your Data Files**

   The Insert Picture dialog box opens, prompting you for the location of the image.

2. **Click the Web-Ready Image Files button, click All Files, double-click R2GLogo.jpg, then click at the top of the Form Header section at about the 3" mark on the ruler**

   The R2GLogo image is added to the right side of the Form Header section. When an image or control is selected in Design View, you can use **sizing handles**, which are small squares at the corners of the selection box. Drag a handle to resize the image or control. You use the ⌖ pointer to move a control.

3. **Use the ⌖ pointer to move the logo to the top edge of the Form Header section, then drag the top edge of the Detail section up using the ╬ pointer**

   You also want to align the Trip End Date label with the other labels in the first column.

4. **Click the Trip End Date label, click the Home tab on the Ribbon, click the Align Right button ▤, press and hold [Shift], click the Duration label, click the Arrange tab on the Ribbon, click the Align button, then click Right as shown in FIGURE 3-14**

   With the form completed, you open it in Form View to observe the changes.

5. **Click the Save button 🖫 on the Quick Access Toolbar, click the Home tab, then click the View button ▦ to switch to Form View**

   You decide to add one more record with your final Trips Entry Form.

6. **Click the New (blank) record button ▶⊞ in the navigation bar, then enter the new record shown in FIGURE 3-15, using your last name in the Trip Name field**

   Now print only this single new record.

7. **Click the File tab, click Print in the navigation bar, click Print, click the Selected Record(s) option button, then click OK**

8. **Close the Trips Entry Form, click Yes if prompted to save it, close the R2G-3.accdb database, then exit Access 2016**

FIGURE 3-14: Adding an image to the Form Header section

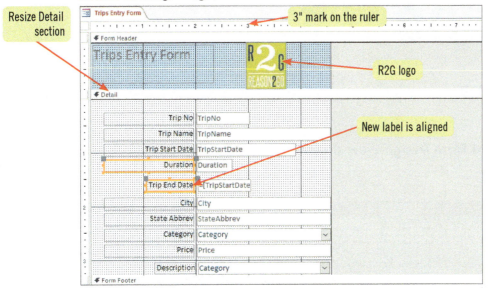

FIGURE 3-15: Final Trips Entry Form with new record

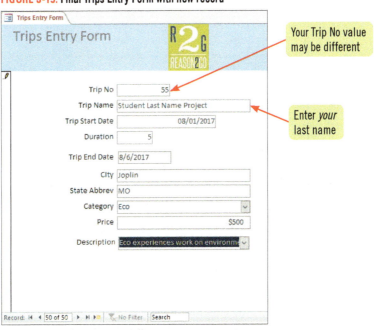

TABLE 3-7: Form sections

section	controls placed in this section print
Form Header	Only once at the top of the first page of the printout
Detail	Once for every record
Form Footer	Only once at the end of the last page of the printout

Applying a background image

A **background image** is an image that fills the entire form or report, appearing "behind" the other controls. A background image is sometimes called a watermark image. To add a background image, use the Picture property for the form or report to browse for the image that you want to use in the background.

Practice

Concepts Review

Label each element of Form Design View shown in FIGURE 3-16.

FIGURE 3-16

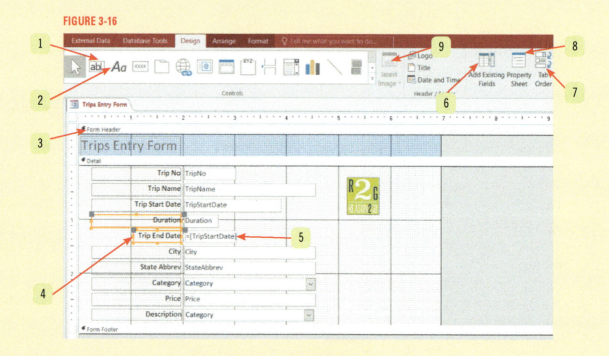

Match each term with the statement that best describes it.

10. Tab order
11. Calculated control
12. Detail section
13. Form Footer section
14. Bound control
15. Database designer

a. Created by entering an expression in a text box
b. Controls placed here print once for every record in the underlying record source
c. Used on a form to display data from a field
d. Controls placed here print only once at the end of the printout
e. The way the focus moves from one bound control to the next in Form View
f. Responsible for building and maintaining tables, queries, forms, and reports

Select the best answer from the list of choices.

16. Every element on a form is called a(n):
    a. property.
    b. item.
    c. control.
    d. tool.

17. Which of the following is probably *not* a graphic image?
    a. Logo
    b. Clip art
    c. Calculation
    d. Picture

18. The most common bound control is the:

a. combo box.

b. label.

c. list box.

d. text box.

19. The most common unbound control is the:

a. text box.

b. combo box.

c. label.

d. command button.

20. Which form view cannot be used to view data?

a. Layout

b. Design

c. Datasheet

d. Preview

Skills Review

1. Use the Form Wizard.

a. Start Access and open the LakeHomes-3.accdb database from the location where you store your Data Files. Enable content if prompted.

b. Click the Create tab, then use the Form Wizard to create a form based on all of the fields in the Realtors table. Use a Columnar layout and type **Realtor Entry Form** to title the form.

c. Add a *new record* with your name in the RFirst and RLast text boxes. Note that the RealtorNo field is an AutoNumber field that is automatically incremented as you enter your first and last names. Enter your school's telephone number for the RPhone field value, and enter **4** as the AgencyNo field value.

d. Save and close the Realtor Entry Form.

2. Create a split form.

a. Click the Agencies table in the Navigation Pane, click the Create tab, click the More Forms button, then click Split Form.

b. Close the Property Sheet if it opens then switch to Form View.

c. Click the record selector in the lower pane for AgencyNo 3, Green Mountain Realty, then click the Delete button in the Records group to delete this realtor. Click OK when prompted that you cannot delete this record because there are related records in the Realtors table.

d. Navigate to the AgencyNo 4 record, Shepherd of the Hills Realtors, in either the upper or lower pane of the split form. Change 7744 Pokeberry Lane to **800 Lake Shore Drive**.

e. Right-click the Agencies form tab, click Close, click Yes when prompted to save changes, type **Agencies Split Form** as the name of the form, then click OK.

3. Use Form Layout View.

a. Open the Realtor Entry Form in Layout View.

b. Modify the labels on the left to read: **Realtor Number**, **Realtor First Name**, **Realtor Last Name**, **Realtor Cell**, **Agency Number**.

c. Modify the text color of the labels to be black.

d. Resize all of the text boxes on the right to be the same width as the RealtorNo text box.

e. Save the Realtor Entry Form.

4. Add fields to a form.

a. Open the Field List, show all the tables, then expand the Agencies table to display its fields.

b. Drag the AgencyName field to the form, then move the AgencyName label and combo box below the Agency Number controls.

c. Modify the AgencyName label to read **Agency Name**.

d. Modify the text color of the Agency Name label to black.

e. Close the Field List and save and close the Realtor Entry Form.

Skills Review (continued)

5. Modify form controls.

a. Reopen the Realtor Entry Form in Layout View, then select all of the labels in the left column and use the Align Right button on the Home tab to right-align them.

b. Save the form, switch to Form View, navigate to Realtor No 5 (Jane Ann Welch), then use the Agency Name combo box to change the Agency Name to **Big Cedar Realtors**.

c. In Layout View, resize and align all controls so that the labels are lined up on the left and the text boxes are lined up on the right, as shown in **FIGURE 3-17**.

FIGURE 3-17

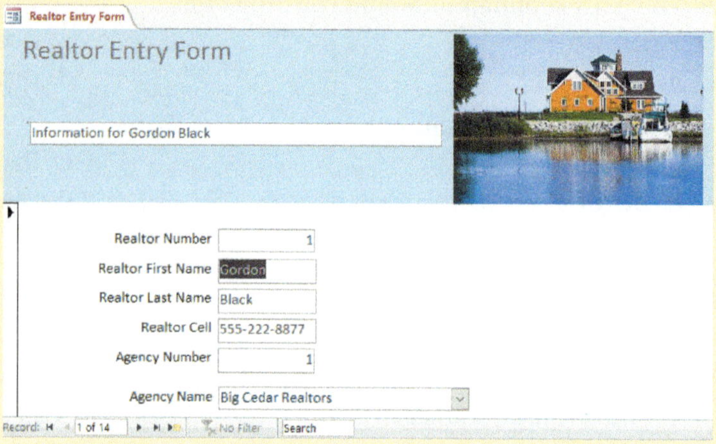

6. Create calculations.

a. Switch to Form Design View, expand the size of the Form Header section by dragging the top edge of the Detail section down about 0.5", then add a text box at about the 1" mark below the Realtor Entry Form label in the Form Header section.

b. Delete the Text14 label that is created when you add a new text box. The number in your label is based on previous work done to the form, so it might vary.

c. Widen the text box to be almost as wide as the entire form, then enter the following expression into the text box, which will add the words *Information for* to the realtor's first name, a space, and then the realtor's last name.

="Information for "&[RFirst]&" "&[RLast]

d. Save the form, then view it in Form View. Be sure the new text box correctly displays a space before and after the realtor's first name. If #Name? appears, which indicates that the expression was entered incorrectly, return to Design View to correct the expression.

e. In Form View, change the Realtor Last Name for Realtor Number 1 from Bono to **Black**. Tab to the RPhone text box to observe how the expression in the Form Header automatically updates.

f. Tab through several records, observing the expression in the Form Header section.

7. Modify tab order.

a. Switch to Form Design View, then open the Property Sheet.

b. Select the new text box with the expression in the Form Header section, then change the Tab Stop property from Yes to **No**.

c. Select the RealtorNo text box in the Detail section, then change the Tab Stop property from Yes to **No**. (AutoNumber fields cannot be edited, so they do not need to have a tab stop.)

d. Close the Property Sheet.

e. Open the Tab Order dialog box and click the Auto Order button to make sure the focus moves from top to bottom through the form.

f. Save the form and view it in Form View. Tab through the form to make sure that the tab order is sequential and skips the expression in the Form Header as well as the Realtor Number text box. Use the Tab Order button on the Design tab in Form Design View to modify the tab order, if necessary.

Skills Review (continued)

8. Insert an image.

   a. Switch to Design View, then click the Form Header section bar.

   b. Add the LakeHome.jpg image to the right side of the Form Header, then resize the image to be about 2.5" × 1.5". Remember to search for All files.

   c. Remove the extra blank space in the Form Header section by dragging the top edge of the Detail section up as far as possible.

   d. Drag the right edge of the form as far as possible to the left.

   e. Save the form, then switch to Form View as shown in **FIGURE 3-17**. Move through the records, observing the calculated field from record to record to make sure it is calculating correctly.

   f. Find the record with your name, and if requested by your instructor, print only that record.

   g. Close the Realtor Entry Form, close the LakeHomes-3.accdb database, then exit Access.

Independent Challenge 1

As a volunteer for a scuba divers' club, you have developed a database to help manage scuba dives. In this exercise, you'll create a data entry form to manage the dive trips.

   a. Start Access, then open the Scuba-3.accdb database from the location where you store your Data Files. Enable content if prompted.

   b. Using the Form Wizard, create a form that includes all the fields in the DiveTrips table and uses the Columnar layout, then type **Dive Trip Entry** as the title of the form.

   c. Switch to Layout View, then delete the ID text box and label.

   d. Using Form Design View, use the [Shift] key to select all of the text boxes except the last one for TripReport, then resize them to the shortest size using the To Shortest option on the Size/Space button on the Arrange tab.

   e. Using Form Design View, resize the Location, City, State/Province, Country, and Lodging text boxes to be no wider than the Rating text box.

   f. Using Form Design View, move and resize the controls, as shown in **FIGURE 3-18**. This will require several steps. Once the controls are resized, drag the top of the Form Footer section up to remove the extra blank space in the Detail section.

   g. Using Form Layout View, modify the labels and alignment of the labels, as shown in **FIGURE 3-18**. Note that there are spaces between the words in the labels, the labels are right-aligned, and the text boxes are left-aligned.

   h. In Form View, sort the records in ascending order on the Dive Master ID field, which will order the Great Barrier Reef tour as the first record. Edit the Certification Diving and Trip Report fields, as shown in **FIGURE 3-18** for the TripReport field using your name.

   i. Save the form, then if requested by your instructor, print only the record with your name.

   j. Close the Dive Trip Entry form, close the Scuba-3.accdb database, then exit Access 2016.

FIGURE 3-18

Independent Challenge 2

You have built an Access database to track membership in a community service club. The database tracks member names and addresses as well as their status in the club.

a. Start Access, then open the Service-3.accdb database from the location where you store your Data Files. Enable content if prompted.

b. Using the Form Wizard, create a form based on all of the fields of the Members table and the DuesOwed field in the Status table.

c. View the data by Members, use a Columnar layout, then enter **Member Information** as the title of the form.

d. Enter a new record with your name and the school name, and address of your school for the Company and address fields. Give yourself a StatusNo entry of **1**. In the DuesPaid field, enter **50**. The DuesOwed field automatically displays 100 because that value is pulled from the Status table and is based on the entry in the StatusNo field, which links the Members table to the Status table.

e. In Layout View, add a text box to the form and move it below the DuesOwed text box.

f. Open the Property Sheet for the new text box, display the Data tab, and in the Control Source property of the new text box, enter **=[DuesOwed]-[DuesPaid]**, the expression that calculates the balance between DuesOwed and DuesPaid.

g. Open the Property Sheet for the new label, and change the Caption property on the Format tab for the new label to **Balance**. Resize the label to be as wide as the labels above it.

h. Right-align all of the labels in the first column.

i. Set the Tab Stop property for the text box that contains the calculated Balance to **No**.

j. In Layout or Design View, resize DuesPaid and DuesOwed text boxes to be the same width as the new Balance text box, then right-align all data within the three text boxes because numbers are clearer when they align on the decimal point.

k. Make sure that the Format property on the Format tab is Currency for the DuesPaid, DuesOwed, and Balance expression text boxes. Close the Property Sheet.

l. In Form Design View, make sure that the right edge of the form is at or less than the 7" mark on the horizontal ruler. The horizontal ruler is located just above the Form Header section.

m. Save the form, find the record with your name, change the DuesPaid value to **60**, then move and resize controls as necessary to match **FIGURE 3-19**.

n. If requested by your instructor, print only the record with your name.

o. Save and close the Member Information form, then close the Service-3.accdb database and exit Access 2016.

FIGURE 3-19

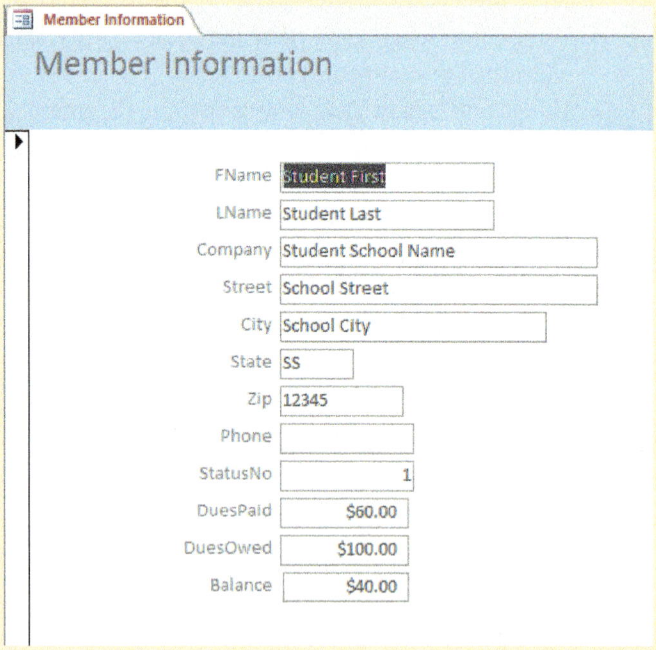

Independent Challenge 3

You have built an Access database to organize the deposits at a salvage and recycling center. Various clubs regularly deposit recyclable material, which is measured in pounds when the deposits are made.

a. Open the Salvage-3.accdb database from the location where you store your Data Files. Enable content if prompted.

b. Using the Form Wizard, create a form based on all of the fields in the CenterDeposits query. View the data by Deposits, use the Columnar layout, and title the form **Deposit Listing**.

c. Switch to Layout View, then make each label bold.

d. Modify the labels so that CenterName is **Center Name**, DepositDate is **Deposit Date**, and ClubName is **Club Name**.

e. Switch to Form Design View and resize the CenterName and ClubName text boxes so they are the same height and width as the Weight text box, as shown in **FIGURE 3-20**.

f. Switch to Form View, find and change any entry of A1 Salvage Center to *your* last name, then print one record with your name if requested by your instructor.

g. Using Form View of the Deposit Listing form, filter for all records with your last name in the CenterName field.

h. Using Form View of the Deposit Listing form, sort the filtered records in descending order on the DepositDate field.

i. In Form Design View, narrow the form by dragging the right edge as far left as possible.

j. Preview the first record, as shown in **FIGURE 3-20**. If requested by your instructor, print the first record.

k. Save and close the Deposit Listing form, close the Salvage-3.accdb database, then exit Access.

FIGURE 3-20

Independent Challenge 4: Explore

One way you can use an Access database on your own is to record and track your job search efforts. In this exercise, you will develop a form to help you enter data into your job-tracking database.

a. Start Access and open the Jobs-3.accdb database from the location where you store your Data Files. Enable content if prompted.

b. Click the Create tab, then use the Form Wizard to create a new form based on all the fields of both the Employers and Positions tables.

c. View the data by Employers, use a Datasheet layout for the subform, accept the default names for the form and subform, then open the form to view information.

d. Use Layout View and Design View to modify the form labels, text box positions, alignment, and sizes, as shown in **FIGURE 3-21**. Also note that the columns within the subform have been resized to display all of the data in the subform.

FIGURE 3-21

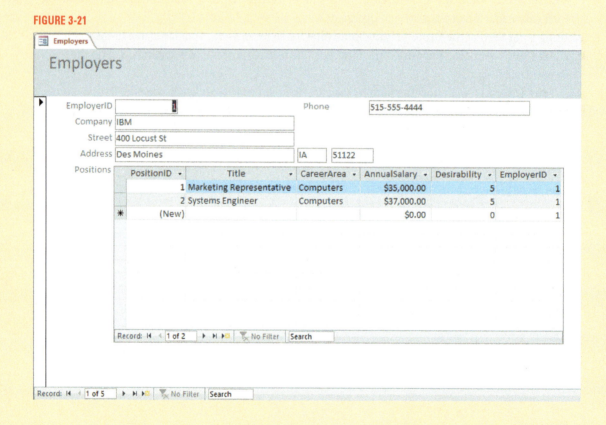

Independent Challenge 4: Explore (continued)

e. Change the CompanyName of IBM in the first record to *Your* **Last Name Software**, and if instructed to create a printout, print only that record. Close the Employers form.

f. Click the Employers table in the Navigation Pane, then use the Split Form option on the More Forms button of the Create tab to create a split form on the Employers table. Close and save the split form with the name **Employers Split Form**.

g. Open the Employers Split Form in Form View, change the address and phone number information for EmployerID 1 to your school's address and phone information, as shown in **FIGURE 3-22**.

h. Navigate through all five records, then back to EmployerID 1, observing both the upper and lower panes of the split form as you move from record to record.

i. Open the Employers form and navigate forward and backward through all five records to study the difference between the Employers form, which uses a form/subform versus the Employers Split Form. Even though both the Employers form and Employers Split Form show datasheets in the bottom halves of the forms, they are fundamentally very different. The split form is displaying the records of only the Employers table, whereas the Employers form is using a subform to display related records from the Positions table in the lower datasheet. You will learn more about forms and subforms in later modules.

j. Close the Jobs-3.accdb database, then exit Access.

FIGURE 3-22

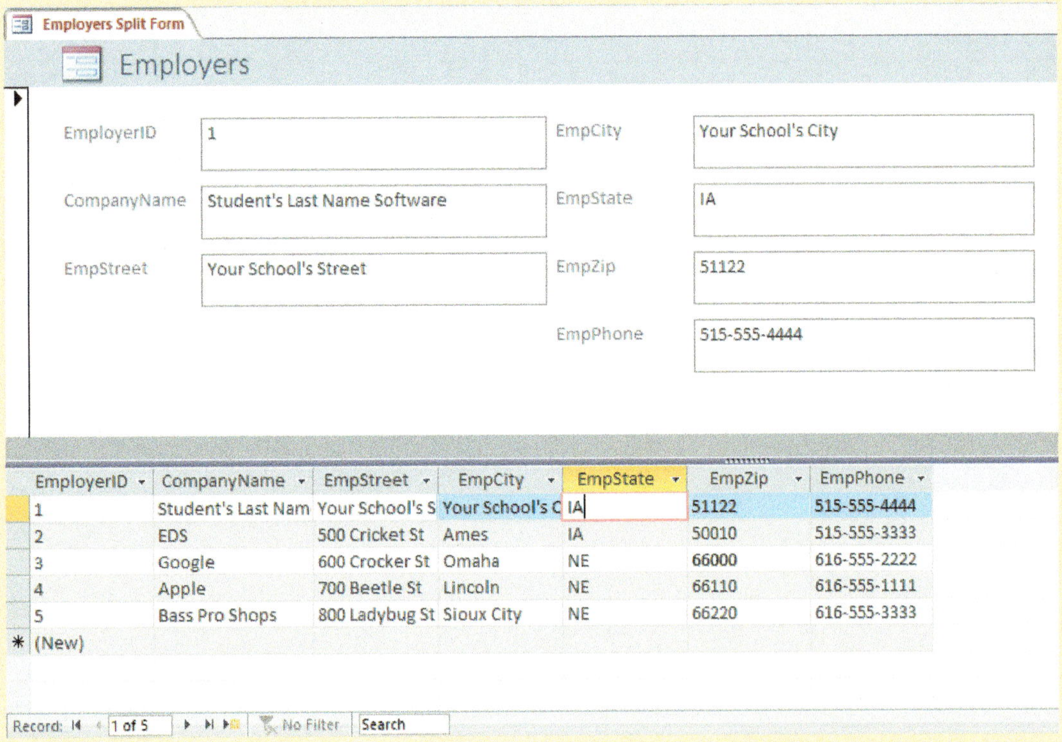

Visual Workshop

Open the Baseball-3.accdb database, enable content if prompted, then use the Split Form tool to create a form named **Players**, as shown in FIGURE 3-23, based on the Players table. Switch to Form Design View, remove the layout, and resize the controls as shown. Modify the labels as shown and note that they are all right-aligned. View the data in Form View, and sort the records in ascending order by last name. Change the first, last, and nickname of the John Bench record in the first record to your name, and if instructed to create a printout, print only that record. Save and close the Players form, close the Baseball-3.accdb database, then exit Access.

FIGURE 3-23

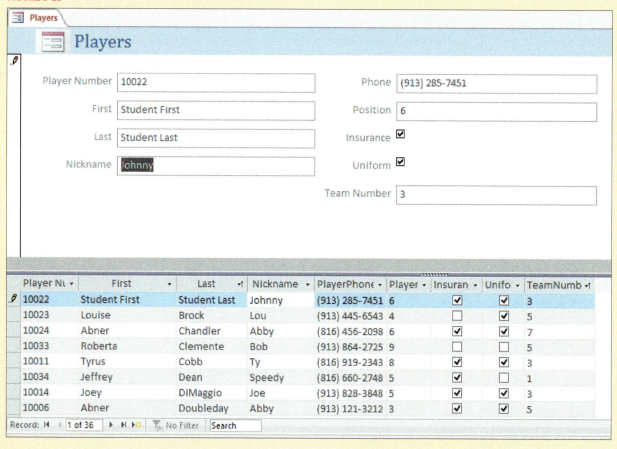

Using Reports

CASE Julia Rice, a trip developer at Reason 2 Go, asks you to produce some reports to help her share and analyze data. A report is an Access object that creates a professional-looking printout.

Module Objectives

After completing this module, you will be able to:

- Use the Report Wizard
- Use Report Layout View
- Review report sections
- Apply group and sort orders
- Add subtotals and counts
- Resize and align controls
- Format a report
- Create mailing labels

Files You Will Need

R2G-4.accdb
LakeHomes-4.accdb
Conventions-4.accdb
Service-4.accdb

Salvage-4.accdb
JobSearch-4.accdb
Basketball-4.accdb

Use the Report Wizard

Learning Outcomes
• Create a report with the Report Wizard
• Change page orientation

A **report** is the primary object you use to print database content because it provides the most formatting, layout, and summary options. A report may include various fonts and colors, clip art and lines, and multiple headers and footers. A report can also calculate subtotals, averages, counts, and other statistics for groups of records. You can create reports in Access by using the **Report Wizard**, a tool that asks questions to guide you through the initial development of the report. Your responses to the Report Wizard determine the record source, style, and layout of the report. The **record source** is the table or query that defines the fields and records displayed on the report. The Report Wizard also helps you sort, group, and analyze the records. **CASE** ▶ *Julia Rice asks you to use the Report Wizard to create a report to display the trips within each state.*

STEPS

1. **Start Access, open the R2G-4.accdb database, enable content if prompted, click the Create tab on the Ribbon, then click the Report Wizard button in the Reports group**

   The Report Wizard starts, prompting you to select the fields you want on the report. You can select fields from one or more tables or queries.

2. **Click the Tables/Queries list arrow, click Table: States, double-click the StateName field, click the Tables/Queries list arrow, click Table: Trips, click the Select All Fields button `>>` , click StateAbbrev in the Selected Fields list, then click the Remove Field button `<`**

   By selecting the StateName field from the States table, and all fields from the Trips table except the StateAbbrev field, you have all of the fields you need for the report, as shown in **FIGURE 4-1**.

3. **Click Next, then click by States if it is not already selected**

   Choosing "by States" groups the records for each state. In addition to record-grouping options, the Report Wizard later asks if you want to sort the records within each group. You can use the Report Wizard to specify up to four fields to sort in either ascending or descending order.

4. **Click Next, click Next again to include no additional grouping levels, click the first sort list arrow, click TripName, then click Next**

   The last questions in the Report Wizard deal with report appearance and the report title.

5. **Click the Stepped option button, click the Landscape option button, click Next, type State Trips for the report title, then click Finish**

   The State Trips report opens in **Print Preview**, which displays the report as it appears when printed, as shown in **FIGURE 4-2**. The records are grouped by state, the first state being California, and then sorted in ascending order by the TripName field within each state. Reports are **read-only** objects, meaning you can use them to read and display data but not to change (write to) data. As you change data using tables, queries, or forms, reports constantly display those up-to-date edits just like all of the other Access objects.

6. **Scroll down to see the second grouping section on the report for the state of Colorado, then click the Next Page button `▶` in the navigation bar to see the second page of the report**

   Even in **landscape orientation** (11" wide by 8.5" tall as opposed to **portrait orientation**, which is 8.5" wide by 11" tall), the fields on the State Trips report may not fit on one sheet of paper. The labels in the column headings and the data in the columns need to be resized to improve the layout. Depending on your monitor, you might need to scroll to the right to display all the fields on this page.

FIGURE 4-1: Selecting fields for a report using the Report Wizard

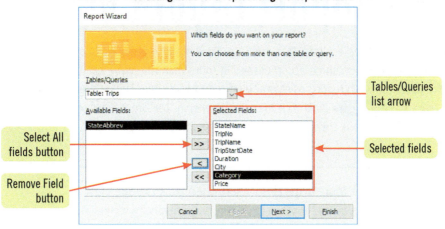

Tables/Queries list arrow

Select All fields button

Remove Field button

Selected fields

FIGURE 4-2: State Trips report in Print Preview

Some information is cut off and needs to be resized

Trips are grouped by the StateName field

Trips sorted by the TripName field within each state

Depending on your monitor and resolution, the format of your report may vary

Changing page orientation

To change page orientation from Portrait (8.5" wide by 11" tall) to Landscape (11" wide by 8.5" tall) and vice versa, click the Portrait or Landscape button on the Print Preview tab when viewing the report in Print Preview. To switch to Print Preview, right-click the report in the Navigation Pane, and then choose Print Preview on the shortcut menu.

Use Report Layout View

Reports have multiple views that you use for various report-building and report-viewing activities. Although some tasks can be accomplished in more than one view, each view has a primary purpose to make your work with reports as easy and efficient as possible. The different report views are summarized in TABLE 4-1. **CASE** ▸ *Julia Rice asks you to modify the State Trips report so that all of the fields fit comfortably across one sheet of paper in landscape orientation.*

STEPS

TROUBLE

If the Field List or Property Sheet window opens, close it.

1. **Right-click the State Trips report tab, then click Layout View**

   Layout View opens and applies a grid to the report that helps you resize, move, and position controls. You decide to narrow the City column to make room for the Price data.

2. **Click Sacramento (or any value in the City column), then use the ↔ pointer to drag the left edge of the City column to the right to narrow it to about half of its current size, as shown in FIGURE 4-3**

   By narrowing the City column, you create extra space in the report.

QUICK TIP

If you select the entire row, just click again directly on the label to select it.

3. **Click the City label, then use ↔ to drag the left edge to the right to position it above the column of City data**

   You use the extra room to better display the data on the report.

QUICK TIP

You can use the Undo button ↺ to undo multiple actions in Layout View.

4. **Continue to use ↔ to resize the columns of data and labels so that the entire trip name in the TripName column is visible**

   The TripName column now has more space to completely display the trip names.

5. **Click the StateName label, click between the words State and Name, press the [Spacebar] so that the label reads State Name, then modify the TripName, TripNo, and TripStartDate labels to contain spaces as well**

6. **Click the StateName label, press and hold [Shift], click each of the other seven labels to select them as a group, release [Shift], click the Format tab, click the Font Color drop-down list arrow A ▾, then click Automatic**

7. **Continue working with the columns so that all of the data is visible and your report looks like FIGURE 4-4**

FIGURE 4-3: Modifying the column width in Report Layout View

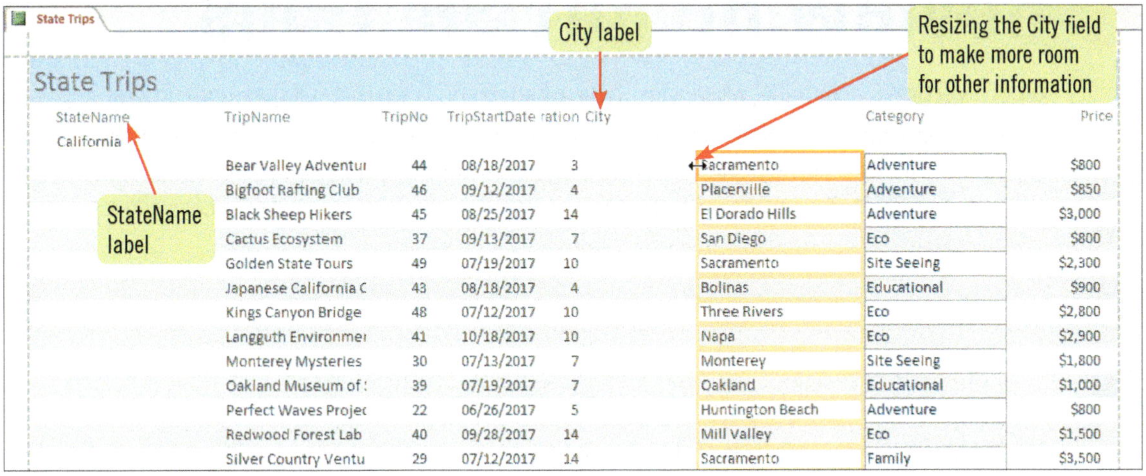

City label

Resizing the City field to make more room for other information

StateName label

FIGURE 4-4: Final State Trips report in Report Layout View

Duration label is completely displayed

Labels have spaces and are black

Longest tour name is clearly displayed

TABLE 4-1: Report views

view	primary purpose
Report View	To quickly review the report without page breaks
Print Preview	To review each page of an entire report as it will appear if printed
Layout View	To modify the size, position, or formatting of controls; shows live data as you modify the report, making it the tool of choice when you want to change the appearance and positioning of controls on a report while also reviewing live data
Design View	To work with report sections or to access the complete range of controls and report properties; Design View does not display data

Review Report Sections

Learning
Outcomes
• Navigate through
  report sections
  and pages
• Resize the width of
  the report
• Work with error
  indicators

Report **sections** determine where and how often controls in that section print in the final report. For example, controls in the Report Header section print only once at the beginning of the report, but controls in the Detail section print once for every record the report displays. **TABLE 4-2** describes report sections. **CASE** ▷ *You and Julia Rice preview the State Trips report to review and understand report sections.*

STEPS

1. **Right-click the State Trips tab, click Print Preview, then scroll up as needed and click the light blue bar at the top of the report above the Trip Start Date label until you display the first page of the report, as shown in FIGURE 4-5**

   The first page shows four report sections: Report Header, Page Header, StateAbbreviation Header, and Detail.

2. **Click the Next Page button ▶ on the navigation bar to move to the second page of the report**

   If the second page of the report does not contain data, it means that the report may be too wide to fit on a single sheet of paper. You fix that problem in Report Design View.

QUICK TIP
If your report is too
wide, you will see a
green error indicator
in the upper-left
corner of the report.
Pointing to the
error icon ![error icon] ▼
displays a message
about the error.

3. **Right-click the State Trips tab, click Design View, scroll to the far right using the bottom horizontal scroll bar, then use the ↔ pointer to drag the right edge of the report as far as you can to the left, as shown in FIGURE 4-6**

   In Report Design View, you can work with the report sections and make modifications to the report that you cannot make in other views, such as narrowing the width. Report Design View does not display any data, however. For your report to fit on one page in landscape orientation, you need to move all of the controls to the left of the 10.5" mark on the horizontal **ruler** using the default 0.25" left and right margins. You will practice fixing this problem by moving the page calculation in the Page Footer section.

4. **Use the ⁺ₖ pointer to drag the page calculation text box about 0.5" to the left**

   To review your modifications, show the report in Print Preview.

QUICK TIP
You can also use the
View buttons in the
lower-right corner
of a report to
switch views.

5. **Right-click the State Trips tab, click Print Preview, click the Last Page button ▶❘ to navigate to the last page of the report, then click the report to zoom in and out to examine the page, as shown in FIGURE 4-7**

   Previewing each page of the report helps you confirm that no blank pages are created and allows you to examine how the different report sections print on each page.

TABLE 4-2: Report sections

section	where does this section print?
Report Header	At the top of the first page
Page Header	At the top of every page (but below the Report Header on the first page)
Group Header	Before every group of records
Detail	Once for every record
Group Footer	After every group of records
Page Footer	At the bottom of every page
Report Footer	At the end of the report

FIGURE 4-5: State Trips in Print Preview

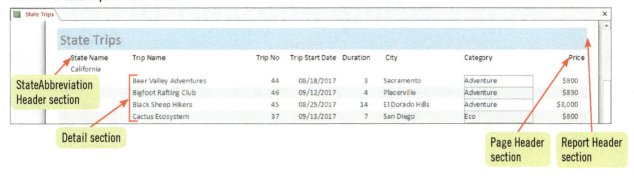

FIGURE 4-6: State Trips report in Design View

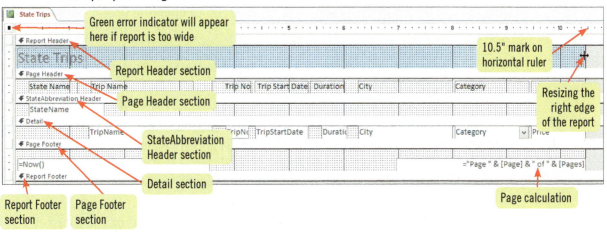

FIGURE 4-7: Last page of State Trips report in Print Preview

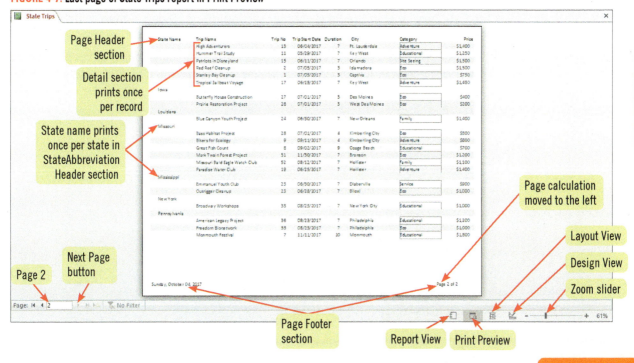

Apply Group and Sort Orders

Grouping means to sort records by a particular field plus provide a header and/or footer section before or after each group of sorted records. For example, if you group records by the StateAbbreviation field, the Group Header is called the StateAbbreviation Header and the Group Footer is called the StateAbbreviation Footer. The StateAbbreviation Header section appears once for each state in the report, immediately before the records in that state. The StateAbbreviation Footer section also appears once for each state in the report, immediately after the records for that state. **CASE** *The records in the State Trips report are currently grouped by the StateAbbreviation field. Julia Rice asks you to further group the records by the Category field (Adventure, Eco, Educational, and Family, for example) within each state.*

STEPS

1. **Click the Close Print Preview button to return to Report Design View, then click the Group & Sort button in the Grouping & Totals group to open the Group, Sort, and Total pane**

   Currently, the records are grouped by the StateAbbreviation field and further sorted by the TripName field. To add the Category field as a grouping field within each state, you work with the Group, Sort, and Total pane in Report Design View.

2. **Click the Add a group button in the Group, Sort, and Total pane, click Category, then click the Move up button 🔼 on the right side of the Group, Sort, and Total pane so that Category is positioned between StateAbbreviation and TripName**

   A Category Header section is added to Report Design View just below the StateAbbreviation Header section. You move the Category control from the Detail section to the Category Header section so it prints only once for each new Category instead of once for each record in the Detail section.

3. **Right-click the Category combo box in the Detail section, click Cut on the shortcut menu, right-click the Category Header section, click Paste, then use the ⬚ pointer to drag the Category combo box to the right to position it as shown in FIGURE 4-8**

   Now that you've moved the Category combo box to the Category Header, it will print only once per category within each state. You no longer need the Category label in the Page Header section.

4. **Click the Category label in the Page Header section, press [Delete], then switch to Print Preview and zoom to 100%**

   The State Trips report should look like **FIGURE 4-9**. Notice that the records are now grouped by category within state. Detail records are further sorted in ascending order by the TripName field value.

FIGURE 4-8: Group, Sort, and Total pane and new Category Header section

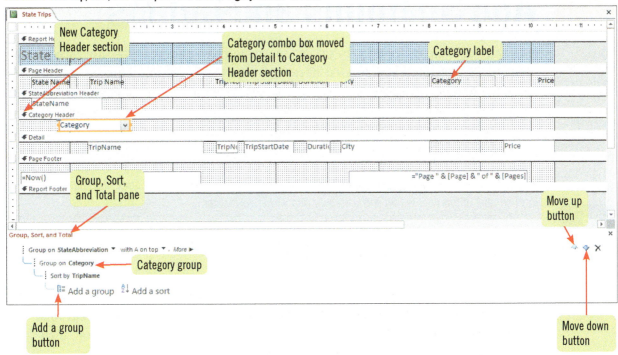

FIGURE 4-9: State Trips report grouped by category within state

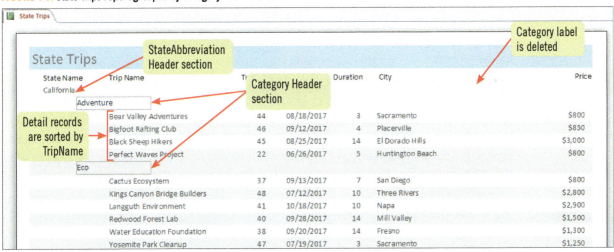

Record Source Property

The **Record Source property** of a report or form determines what fields and records that report or form will display. It is the first property on the Data tab of the Property Sheet for a report or form. The value of the Record Source property may be the name of a table or query. The Record Source property can also be a SELECT statement, which is SQL (Structured Query Language) code. In the Property Sheet for a report, click the Record Source property, and then click the Build button [**...**] to enter Query Design View, where you can change the Record Source property or save it as a query object within the database.

Add Subtotals and Counts

Learning Outcomes
• Create calculations to subtotal and count records
• Copy and paste controls

In a report, you create a **calculation** by entering an expression into a text box. When a report is previewed or printed, the expression is evaluated and the resulting calculation is placed on the report. An **expression** is a combination of field names, operators (such as +, –, /, and *), and functions that results in a single value. A **function** is a built-in formula, such as Sum or Count, that helps you quickly create a calculation. Notice that every expression starts with an equal sign (=), and when it uses a function, the arguments for the function are placed in (parentheses). **Arguments** are the pieces of information that the function needs to create the final answer. When an argument is a field name, the field name must be surrounded by [square brackets]. **CASE** *Julia Rice asks you to add a calculation to the State Trips report to sum the total number of trip days within each category and within each state.*

STEPS

1. **Switch to Report Design View**

   A logical place to add subtotals for each group is right after that group of records prints, in the Group Footer section. You use the Group, Sort, and Total pane to open Group Footer sections.

   TROUBLE
   Click Category in the Group, Sort, and Total pane to display the grouping options.

2. **Click the More button for the StateAbbreviation field in the Group, Sort, and Total pane, click the without a footer section list arrow, click with a footer section, then do the same for the Category field, as shown in FIGURE 4-10**

   With the StateAbbreviation Footer and Category Footer sections open, you're ready to add controls to calculate the total number of trip days within each category and within each state. You use a text box control with an expression to make this calculation.

3. **Click the Text Box button** 🔲 **in the Controls group, then click just below the Duration text box in the Category Footer section**

   Adding a new text box automatically adds a new label to its left. First, you modify the label to identify the information; then you modify the text box to contain the correct expression to sum the number of trip days for that category.

   TROUBLE
   Depending on your activity, you may see a different number in the Text##: label.

4. **Click the Text20 label to select it, double-click Text20, type Total days:, click the Unbound text box to select it, click Unbound again, type =Sum([Duration]), press [Enter], then widen the text box to view the entire expression**

   The expression =Sum([Duration]) uses the Sum function to add the days in the Duration field. Because the expression is entered in the Category Footer section, it will sum all Duration values for that category within that state. To sum the Duration values for each state, the expression also needs to be inserted in the StateAbbreviation Footer.

   QUICK TIP
   An expression in the Report Footer section would subtotal values for the entire report.

5. **Right-click the =Sum([Duration]) text box, click Copy, right-click the StateAbbreviation Footer section, click Paste, then press [→] enough times to position the controls in the StateAbbreviation Footer section just below those in the Category Footer section, as shown in FIGURE 4-11**

   With the expression copied to the StateAbbreviation Footer section, you're ready to preview your work.

   TROUBLE
   If your pages are different, it's probably due to extra white space. In Design View, drag the top edge of all section bars up to eliminate extra blank space.

6. **Switch to Print Preview, navigate to the last page of the report, then click to zoom so you can see all of the Pennsylvania trips**

   As shown in FIGURE 4-12, seven trip days are totaled for the Eco category, and 17 for the Educational category, which is a total of 24 trip days for the state of Pennsylvania. The summary data would look better if it were aligned more directly under the trip Duration values. You resize and align controls in the next lesson.

FIGURE 4-10: Opening group footer sections

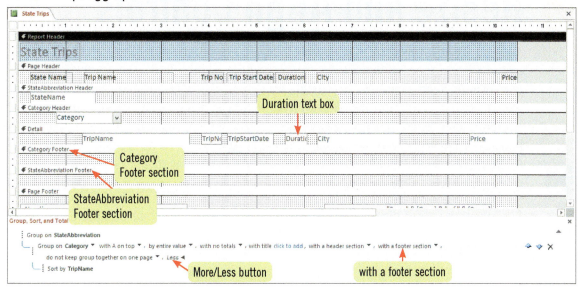

FIGURE 4-11: Adding subtotals to group footer sections

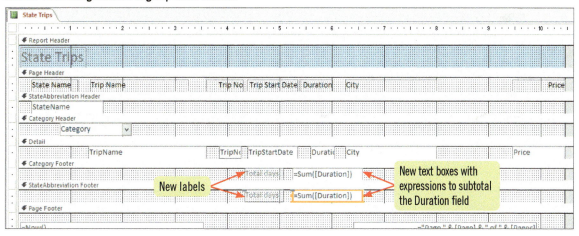

FIGURE 4-12: Previewing the new group footer calculations

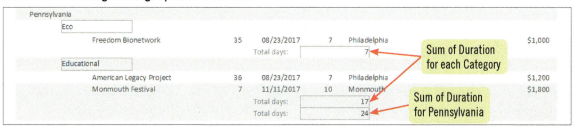

Resize and Align Controls

Learning Outcomes
• Align data within a control
• Align the borders of controls

After you add information to the appropriate section of a report, you might also want to align the data in precise columns and rows to make the information easier to read. To do so, you can use two different types of **alignment** commands. You can left-, right-, or center-align a control within its own border using the Align Left ≣, Center ≣, and Align Right ≣ buttons on the Home tab. You can also align the edges of controls with respect to one another using the Left, Right, Top, and Bottom commands on the Align button of the Arrange tab in Report Design View. **CASE** *You decide to resize and align several controls to improve the readability of the State Trips report. Layout View is a good choice for these tasks.*

STEPS

QUICK TIP
You can also use the buttons on the Format tab to align and format text, including applying number formats and increasing or decreasing decimals.

1. **Switch to Layout View, click the Design tab on the Ribbon, then click the Group & Sort button to toggle off the Group, Sort, and Total pane**

    You decide to align the expressions that subtotal the number of trip days for each category within the Duration column to make the report easier to read and more professional.

2. **Click the Total days text box in the Category Footer, then use the ↔ pointer to resize the text box so that the data is aligned in the Duration column, as shown in FIGURE 4-13**

    If the value in your Total days text box is not right-aligned, click the Align Right button (shown in FIGURE 4-13). With the calculation formatted as desired in the Category Footer, you can quickly apply those modifications to the calculation in the StateAbbreviation Footer as well.

TROUBLE
If you make a mistake, click the Undo button ↶ on the Quick Access toolbar. You can click ↶ multiple times in Report or Form Design View.

3. **Scroll down the report far enough to find and then click the Total days text box in the StateAbbreviation Footer, then use the ↔ pointer to resize the text box so that it is the same width as the text box in the Category Footer section**

    With both expressions resized so they line up under the Duration values in the Detail section, they are easier to read on the report.

4. **Scroll the report so you can see all of the Colorado trips, as shown in FIGURE 4-14**

    You can apply resize, alignment, or formatting commands to more than one control at a time. TABLE 4-3 provides techniques for selecting more than one control at a time in Report Design View.

Precisely moving and resizing controls

You can move and resize controls using the mouse or other pointing device, but you can move controls more precisely using the keyboard. Pressing the arrow keys while holding [Ctrl] moves selected controls one **pixel** (picture element) at a time in the direction of the arrow. Pressing the arrow keys while holding [Shift] resizes selected controls one pixel at a time.

FIGURE 4-13: Resizing controls in Layout View

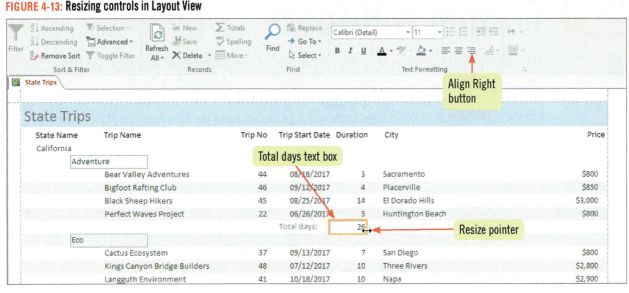

FIGURE 4-14: Reviewing the aligned and resized controls

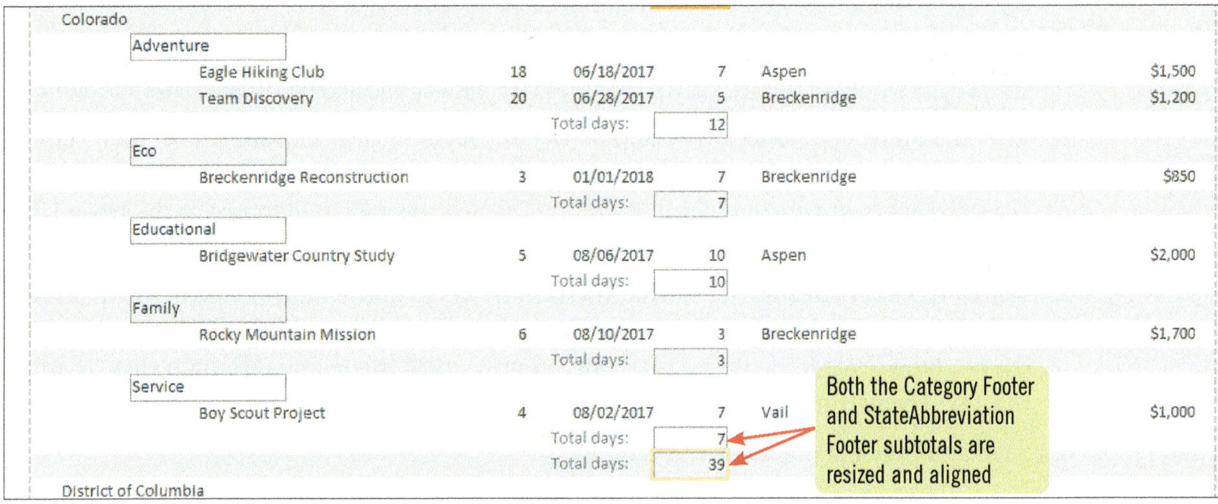

TABLE 4-3: Selecting more than one control at a time in Report Design View

technique	description
Click, [Shift]+click	Click a control, and then press and hold [Shift] while clicking other controls; each one is selected
Drag a selection box	Drag a selection box (an outline box you create by dragging the pointer in Report Design View); every control that is in or is touched by the edges of the box is selected
Click in the ruler	Click in either the horizontal or vertical ruler to select all controls that intersect the selection line
Drag in the ruler	Drag through either the horizontal or vertical ruler to select all controls that intersect the selection line as it is dragged through the ruler

Format a Report

Learning Outcomes
- Format controls and sections of a report
- Add labels to a report

Formatting refers to enhancing the appearance of the information. Although the Report Wizard automatically applies many formatting embellishments, you often want to change the appearance of the report to fit your particular needs. **CASE** *When reviewing the State Trips report with Julia, you decide to change the background color of some of the report sections to make the data easier to read. The Report Wizard applied alternating formats, which you want to change. You want to shade each Category Header and Category Footer section using the same color. To make changes to entire report sections, you work in Report Design View.*

STEPS

QUICK TIP

The quick keystroke for Undo is [Ctrl][Z]. The quick keystroke for Redo is [Ctrl][Y].

1. **Switch to Design View, click the Category Header section bar, click the Format tab on the Ribbon, click the Alternate Row Color button arrow, click the Maroon 2 color square as shown in FIGURE 4-15, click the Shape Fill button, then click the Maroon 2 color square**

   Make a similar modification by applying a different fill color to the Category Footer section.

2. **Click the Category Footer section bar, click the Alternate Row Color button arrow, click the Maroon 1 color square (just above Maroon 2 in the Standard Colors section), click the Shape Fill button, then click the Maroon 1 color square**

   When you use the Alternate Row Color and Shape Fill buttons, you're actually modifying the **Back Color** and **Alternate Back Color** properties in the Property Sheet of the section or control you selected. Background shades can help differentiate parts of the report, but be careful with dark colors, as they may print as solid black on some printers and fax machines.

3. **Switch to Layout View to review your modifications**

   The category sections are clearer, but you decide to make one more modification to emphasize the report title.

4. **Click the State Trips label in the Report Header section, click the Home tab, then click the Bold button B in the Text Formatting group**

   The report in Layout View should look like FIGURE 4-16. You also want to add a label to the Report Footer section to identify yourself.

5. **Switch to Report Design View, drag the bottom edge of the Report Footer down about 0.5", click the Label button Aa in the Controls group, click at the 1" mark in the Report Footer, type Created by *your* name, press [Enter], click the Home tab, then click B in the Text Formatting group**

6. **Save and preview the State Trips report**

7. **If required by your instructor, print the report, and then close it**

FIGURE 4-15: Formatting section backgrounds

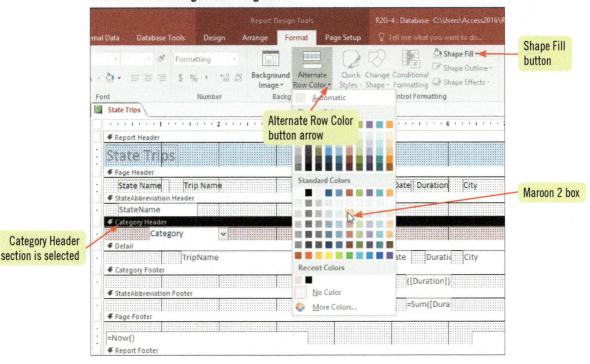

Shape Fill button

Alternate Row Color button arrow

Maroon 2 box

Category Header section is selected

FIGURE 4-16: Final formatted State Trips report

State Trips label is bold

CategoryHeader has Maroon 2 shade

CategoryFooter has Maroon 1 shade

Create Mailing Labels

Learning Outcomes
- Create a report of labels
- Print specific pages of a report

Mailing labels are often created to apply to envelopes, postcards, or letters when assembling a mass mailing. They have many other business purposes too, such as labels for paper file folders or name tags. Any data in your Access database can be converted into labels using the **Label Wizard**, a special report wizard that precisely positions and sizes information for hundreds of standard business labels. **CASE** *Julia Rice asks you to create mailing labels for all of the addresses in the Customers table. You use the Label Wizard to handle this request.*

STEPS

1. **Click the Customers table in the Navigation Pane, click the Create tab, then click the Labels button in the Reports group**

   The first Label Wizard dialog box opens. The Filter by manufacturer list box provides over 30 manufacturers of labels. Avery is the default choice. With the manufacturer selected, your next task is to choose the product number of the labels you will feed through the printer. The cover on the box of labels you are using provides this information. In this case, you'll be using Avery 5160 labels, a common type of sheet labels used for mailings and other purposes.

2. **Scroll through the Product number list, then click 5160 as shown in FIGURE 4-17**

   Note that by selecting a product number, you also specify the dimensions of the label and number of columns.

3. **Click Next, then click Next again to accept the default font and color choices**

   The third question of the Label Wizard asks how you want to construct your label. You'll add the fields from the Customers table with spaces and line breaks to pattern a standard mailing format.

4. **Double-click FName, press [Spacebar], double-click LName, press [Enter], double-click Street, press [Enter], double-click City, type a comma (,) and press [Spacebar], double-click State, press [Spacebar], then double-click Zip**

   If your prototype label doesn't look exactly like **FIGURE 4-18**, delete the fields in the Prototype label box and try again. Be careful to put a space between the FName and LName fields in the first row, a comma and a space between the City and State fields, and a space between the State and Zip fields.

   QUICK TIP
   In this case, all data is displayed. This message reminds you to carefully preview the data to make sure long names and addresses are fully displayed within the constraints of the 5160 label dimensions.

5. **Click Next, double-click LName to select it as a sorting field, click Next, click Finish to accept the name Labels Customers for the new report, then click OK if prompted that some data may not be displayed**

   A portion of the new report is shown in **FIGURE 4-19**. It is generally a good idea to print the first page of the report on standard paper to make sure everything is aligned correctly before printing on labels.

   QUICK TIP
   To include your name on the printout, change Jacob Alman to your own name in the Customers table, and then close and reopen the Labels Customers report.

6. **If requested by your instructor, click the Print button on the Print Preview tab, click the From box, type 1, click the To box, type 1, then click OK to print the first page of the report**

7. **Close the Labels Customers report, close the R2G-4.accdb database, then exit Access 2016**

FIGURE 4-17: Label Wizard dialog box

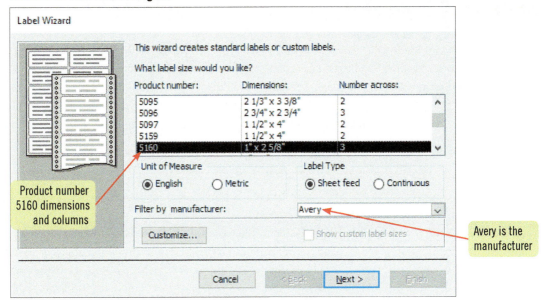

Product number 5160 dimensions and columns

Avery is the manufacturer

FIGURE 4-18: Building a prototype label

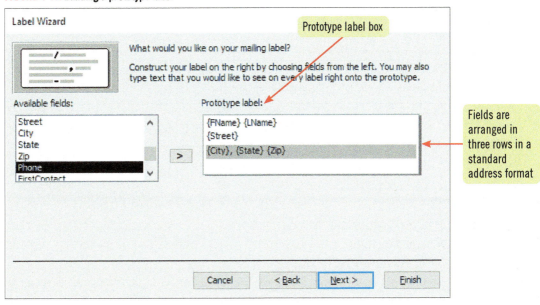

Prototype label box

Fields are arranged in three rows in a standard address format

FIGURE 4-19: Labels Customers report

Data is merged to a 3-column Avery 5160 label format

Practice

Concepts Review

Label each element of the Report Design View window shown in FIGURE 4-20.

FIGURE 4-20

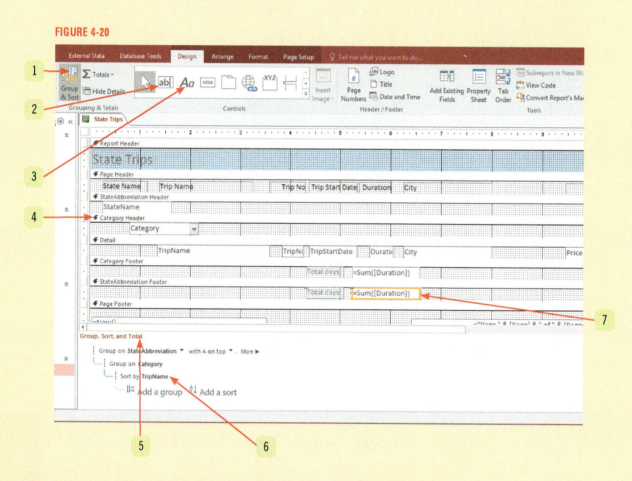

Match each term with the statement that best describes it.

8. **Record source**
9. **Alignment**
10. **Detail section**
11. **Expression**
12. **Grouping**
13. **Section**
14. **Formatting**

a. Left, center, or right are common choices
b. Prints once for every record
c. Used to identify which fields and records are passed to the report
d. Sorting records *plus* providing a header or footer section
e. Determines how controls are positioned on the report
f. A combination of field names, operators, and functions that results in a single value
g. Enhancing the appearance of information displayed in the report

Select the best answer from the list of choices.

15. **Which type of control is most commonly placed in the Detail section?**
    - **a.** Image
    - **b.** Line
    - **c.** Text box
    - **d.** Label

16. **Which of the following is not a valid report view?**
    - **a.** Print Preview
    - **b.** Section View
    - **c.** Layout View
    - **d.** Design View

17. **A title for a report would most commonly be placed in which report section?**
    - **a.** Group Footer
    - **b.** Detail
    - **c.** Report Header
    - **d.** Report Footer

18. **A calculated expression that presents page numbering information would probably be placed in which report section?**
    - **a.** Report Header
    - **b.** Detail
    - **c.** Group Footer
    - **d.** Page Footer

19. **To align the edges of several controls with each other, you use the alignment commands on the:**
    - **a.** Formatting tab.
    - **b.** Design tab.
    - **c.** Print Preview tab.
    - **d.** Arrange tab.

20. **Which of the following expressions counts the number of records using the FirstName field?**
    - **a.** =Count([FirstName])
    - **b.** =Count[FirstName]
    - **c.** =Count((FirstName))
    - **d.** =Count{FirstName}

21. **What is the difference between grouping and sorting in a report?**
    - **a.** Grouping allows you to add a Group Header and/or Group Footer section to a report.
    - **b.** Grouping means to sort in ascending order.
    - **c.** Grouping means to sort by more than one field.
    - **d.** You can have more than one grouping field, but you can only have one sorting field.

Skills Review

1. **Use the Report Wizard.**
   - **a.** Start Access and open the LakeHomes-4.accdb database from the location where you store your Data Files. Enable content if prompted.
   - **b.** Use the Report Wizard to create a report based on the RLast and RPhone fields from the Realtors table and the Type, SqFt, BR, Bath, and Asking fields from the Listings table. (*Hint*: Make sure your fields are added in the order listed.)
   - **c.** View the data by Realtors, do not add any more grouping levels, and sort the records in descending order by the Asking field. (*Hint*: Click the Ascending button to toggle it to Descending.)
   - **d.** Use a Stepped layout and a Landscape orientation. Title the report **Listings by Realtor**.
   - **e.** Preview the first and second pages of the new report.

2. **Use Report Layout View.**
   - **a.** Switch to Layout View and close the Field List and Property Sheet if they are open.
   - **b.** Drag the right edge of the Asking column and label to the left to provide a little more space between the Asking column and Type column.
   - **c.** Modify the RLast label to read **Realtor**, the RPhone label to read **Cell**, the SqFt label to read **Square Ft**, the BR label to read **Bedrooms**, and the Bath label to read **Baths**.
   - **d.** Switch to Print Preview to review your changes.

Skills Review (continued)

3. **Review report sections.**
   a. Switch to Report Design View.
   b. Drag the text box that contains the Page calculation in the lower-right corner of the Page Footer section to the left so that it is to the left of the 9" mark on the horizontal ruler.
   c. Drag the right edge of the entire report to the left as far as possible.
   d. Preview the report and make sure there are no blank pages between printed pages. You may need to move or narrow more controls and narrow the report again in order to accomplish this.

4. **Apply group and sort orders.**
   a. Open the Group, Sort, and Total pane.
   b. Add the Type field as a grouping field between the RealtorNo grouping field and Asking sort field. Make sure the sort order on the Asking field is in descending order (from largest to smallest). (*Hint*: Use the Move up button to move the Type field between the RealtorNo and Asking fields in the Group, Sort, and Total pane.)
   c. Cut and paste the Type combo box from its current position in the Detail section to the Type Header section.
   d. Move the Type combo box in the Type Header section so its left edge is at about the 1" mark on the horizontal ruler.
   e. Delete the Type label in the Page Header section.
   f. Switch to Layout View, and resize the Asking, Square Ft, Bedrooms, and Baths columns as needed so they are more evenly spaced across the page.

5. **Add subtotals and counts.**
   a. Switch to Report Design View, then open the RealtorNo Footer section. (*Hint*: Use the More button on the RealtorNo field in the Group, Sort, and Total pane.)
   b. Add a text box control to the RealtorNo Footer section, just below the Asking text box in the Detail section. Change the label to read **Subtotal:**, and enter the expression **=Sum([Asking])** in the text box.
   c. Drag the bottom edge of the Report Footer section down about 0.25" to add space to the Report Footer.
   d. Copy and paste the new expression in the RealtorNo Footer section to the Report Footer section. Position the new controls in the Report Footer section directly below the controls in the RealtorNo Footer section.
   e. Modify the Subtotal: label in the Report Footer section to read **Grand Total:**.
   f. Preview the last page of the report to view the new subtotals in the RealtorNo Footer and Report Footer sections.

6. **Resize and align controls.**
   a. Switch to Design View, then click the Group & Sort button on the Design tab to close the Group, Sort, and Total pane if it is open.
   b. Click the Asking text box in the Detail section, press and hold [Shift], and then click the expression in the RealtorNo Footer as well as the Report Footer sections to select the three text boxes at the same time. Click the Arrange tab on the Ribbon, click the Align button, then click Right to right-align the edges of the three text boxes.
   c. With all three text boxes still selected, click the Format tab on the Ribbon, click the Apply Comma Number Format button, and click the Decrease Decimals button twice so that the values appear as whole dollar amounts without cents.
   d. Preview the report to view the alignment and format on the Asking data and subtotals.

7. **Format a report.**
   a. In Report Design View, change the Alternate Row Color of the Detail section to No Color.
   b. Change the Alternate Row Color of the Type Header, the RealtorNo Header, and the RealtorNo Footer sections to No Color.
   c. Change the Shape Fill color of the RealtorNo Header section to Green 2. (*Hint*: The Shape Fill button will change the Back Color property in the Property Sheet.)

d. Select the RLast and RPhone text boxes in the RealtorNo Header section, and change the Shape Fill color to Green 2 to match the RealtorNo Header section.

e. Bold the title of the report, which is the **Listings by Realtor** label in the Report Header, and resize it to make it a little wider to accommodate the bold text.

f. Change the font color of each label in the Page Header section to Automatic (black).

g. Save and preview the report in Print Preview. It should look like FIGURE 4-21. The report should fit on three pages, and the grand total for all Asking values should be 7,957,993. If there are blank pages between printed pages, return to Report Design View and drag the right edge of the report to the left.

FIGURE 4-21

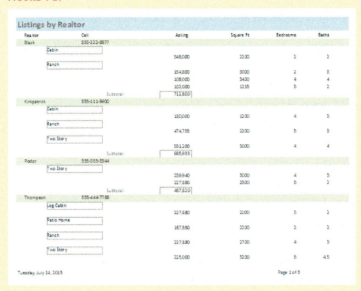

h. In Report Design View, add a label to the left side of the Report Footer section with your name. Be sure to add a label and not a text box control. Make sure that your name is displayed clearly on the last page only in Print Preview.

i. Print the report if requested by your instructor, then save and close the Listings by Realtor report.

8. Create mailing labels.

a. Click the Agencies table in the Navigation Pane, then start the Label Wizard.

b. Choose Avery 5160 labels and the default text appearance choices.

c. Build a prototype label with the AgencyName on the first line, Street on the second line, and City, State, and Zip on the third line with a comma and space between City and State, and a space between State and Zip.

d. Sort by AgencyName, and name the report **Labels Agencies**.

e. Preview then save and close the report. Click OK if a warning dialog box appears regarding horizontal space. The data in your label report does not exceed the dimensions of the labels.

f. Open the Agencies table and change the name of Big Cedar Realtors to *Your Last Name* **Realtors**. Close the Agencies table, reopen the Labels Agencies report, then print it if requested by your instructor.

g. Close the Labels Agencies report, close the LakeHomes-4.accdb database, then exit Access 2016.

Independent Challenge 1

As the office manager of an international convention planning company, you have created a database to track convention, enrollment, and company data. Your goal is to create a report of up-to-date attendee enrollments.

a. Start Access, then open the Conventions-4.accdb database from the location where you store your Data Files. Enable content if prompted.

b. Use the Report Wizard to create a report with the AttendeeLast and AttendeeFirst fields from the Attendees table, the CompanyName field from the Companies table, and the ConventionName and CountryName from the Conventions table. Add the fields in the order listed.

c. View your data by Conventions, add the CompanyName as a second grouping field, then sort in ascending order by AttendeeLast.

d. Use the Block layout and Portrait orientation, then name the report **Convention Attendees**.

e. In Layout View, change the labels in the Page Header section from ConventionName to **Convention** and CompanyName to **Company**. Delete the CountryName, AttendeeLast, and AttendeeFirst labels in the Page Header section.

f. In Report Design View, open the Group, Sort, and Total pane, then open the ConventionNo Footer section.

g. In Report Design View, add a text box to the ConventionNo Footer section just below the AttendeeLast text box in the Detail section. The purpose of the text box is to count the number of people enrolled for each convention. The label should read **Count of Attendees:**, and the expression in the text box should be **=Count([AttendeeLast])**.

h. Resize the new label and text box as needed to make their contents clearly visible.

i. Copy and paste the new label and expression to the Report Footer section. Move and align the controls so they are at the same horizontal position on the page.

j. Change the text color of all labels to Automatic (black). (*Hint*: There are labels in the Report Header, Page Header, ConventionNo Footer, and Report Footer sections.)

k. Preview the report and make sure there are no blank pages between pages. Resize controls in Layout View and narrow the report in Report Design view as needed to remove blank pages.

l. Preview the last page of the report to make sure the subtotal count for each convention and grand total count for the report are aligned as shown in FIGURE 4-22.

m. Add a label with your name to the left side of the Report Footer section, change the text color to Automatic (black), and then print the last page if required by your instructor.

n. Save and close the Convention Attendees report, close the Conventions-4.accdb database, then exit Access 2016.

FIGURE 4-22

Independent Challenge 2

You have built an Access database to track membership in a community service club. The database tracks member names and addresses as well as their status and rank in the club and their hours of service to the community.

a. Start Access and open the Service-4.accdb database from the location where you store your Data Files. Enable content if prompted.

b. Open the Members table, find and change the name of Micah Ati to *your* name, then close the Members table.

c. Use the Report Wizard to create a report using the FirstName, LastName, and Dues fields from the Members table and the ActivityDate and HoursWorked fields from the Activities table, all in that order.

d. View the data by Members. Do not add any more grouping fields, and sort the records in ascending order by ActivityDate.

e. Use a Stepped layout and Portrait orientation, title the report **Activity Log**, then preview the report.

f. Use Report Layout View to resize the controls to fit the available space and display all data clearly.

g. Change the FirstName label to **First Name**. Change the LastName label to **Last Name**. Change the ActivityDate label to **Date**. Change the HoursWorked label to **Hours**.

h. Switch to Report Design View, then use the Group, Sort, and Total pane to open the MemberNo Footer section.

i. Add a text box to the MemberNo Footer section, just below the HoursWorked text box in the Detail section. Change the label to **Total:** and the expression in the text box to **=Sum([HoursWorked])**.

j. Open the Report Footer section, then copy and paste the **=Sum([HoursWorked])** text box to the Report Footer section. Change the label in the Report Footer section to read **Grand Total:**.

k. Align the HoursWorked text box in the Detail section and the two expressions in the MemberNo Footer and Report Footer sections so that the numbers are perfectly aligned. Be sure to preview the last page of the report to make sure all three controls are aligned as shown in FIGURE 4-23.

l. Add a label to the left edge of the Report Footer section with your name.

m. Preview each page of the report to make sure there are no blank pages. If there are, narrow the controls and the right edge of the report in Report Design View to fix this problem.

n. Print the last page of the report if requested to do so by your instructor.

o. Close the Activity Log report, close the Service-4.accdb database, then exit Access.

FIGURE 4-23

Total:	13
Grand Total:	476

Independent Challenge 3

You have built an Access database to organize the deposits at a salvage center. Various clubs regularly deposit material, which is measured in pounds when the deposits are made.

a. Start Access and open the Salvage-4.accdb database from the location where you store your Data Files. Enable content if prompted.

b. Open the Centers table, change **A1 Salvage Center** to **Your Last Name Salvage**, then close the table.

c. Use the Report Wizard to create a report with the CenterName field from the Centers table, the DepositDate and Weight fields from the Deposits table, and the ClubName field from the Clubs table.

d. View the data by Centers, do not add any more grouping levels, and sort the records in ascending order by DepositDate.

e. Use a Stepped layout and a Portrait orientation, then title the report **Deposit Log**.

f. In Layout View, resize the Weight label and Weight data to better position the data across the report. Rename the DepositDate label to **Date**.

g. Add spaces to the labels so that CenterName becomes **Center Name**, and ClubName becomes **Club Name**.

h. In Report Design View, open the Group, Sort, and Total pane and then open the CenterNumber Footer section.

i. Add a text box to the CenterNumber Footer section just below the Weight text box with the expression **=Sum([Weight])**.

j. Rename the new label to be **Subtotal:**.

k. Copy the new text box and paste it back to the CenterNumber Footer section. Change the new label to **Count:** and the expression to **=Count([Weight])**. Align the new controls directly below the Subtotal and =Sum([Weight]) expression.

l. Paste the controls a second time to the CenterNumber Footer section, and change the new label to **Average:** and the expression to **=Avg([Weight])**.

m. Change the Format property of the =Avg([Weight]) expression to **Standard**, and change the Decimal Places property to **0**. (*Hint:* Open the Property Sheet for the text box and click the Format tab to find the Format and Decimal Places properties.)

n. Expand the Report Footer section, then copy and paste the three text boxes from the CenterNumber Footer section to the Report Footer section.

o. Move and align the text boxes in the CenterNumber Footer and Report Footer sections to be positioned directly under the Weight text box in the Detail section. (*Hint:* You may need to both right-align the text boxes as well as align the right edges of the text boxes.)

p. Change the Subtotal label in the Report Footer section to **Total Sum:**. Change the Count label in the Report Footer section to **Total Count:** and also left-align the labels in the CenterNumber Footer and Report Footer sections.

q. Add a label to the left edge of the Report Footer section with your name and preview the last page of the report, a portion of which is shown in FIGURE 4-24. Your numbers should match.

r. Continue to improve the report as needed to align all numbers and labels and to remove any extra blank space in the report by making your sections as vertically short as possible in Report Design View.

s. Save and close the Deposit Log report, close the Salvage-4.accdb database, then exit Access.

FIGURE 4-24

	1/16/2017	85	Access Users Group
	1/21/2017	150	Boy Scout Troop 324
	Subtotal:	3315	
	Count:	36	
	Average:	92	
Student Name	Total Sum:	11360	
	Total Count:	118	
	Average:	96	

Independent Challenge 4: Explore

One way you can use an Access database on your own is to record and track your job search efforts. In this exercise, you create a report to help read and analyze data in your job-tracking database.

a. Start Access and open the JobSearch-4.accdb database from the location where you store your Data Files. Enable content if prompted.

b. Open the Employers table, and enter five more records to identify five more potential employers.

c. Use subdatasheets in the Employers table to enter five more potential jobs. You may enter all five jobs for one employer, one job for five different employers, or any combination thereof. Be sure to check the spelling of all data entered. For the Desirability field, enter a value from **1** to **5**, 1 being the least desirable and 5 being the most desirable. Close the Employers table.

d. Use the Report Wizard to create a report that lists the CompanyName, EmpCity, and EmpState fields from the Employers table, and the Title, AnnualSalary, and Desirability fields from the Positions table.

e. View the data by Employers, do not add any more grouping levels, and sort the records in descending order by Desirability.

f. Use an Outline layout and a Portrait orientation, then title the report **Jobs**.

g. In Design View, revise the labels in the EmployerID Header section from CompanyName to **Company**, EmpCity to **City**, EmpState to **State**, and AnnualSalary to **Salary**.

h. Right-align the text within the Company, City, and State labels so they are closer to the text boxes they describe.

i. In Report Layout View, resize the Desirability, Title, and Salary labels and text boxes to space the controls evenly across the report.

j. Preview the report, then switch to Report Design View to remove any extra space in the report sections. This will involve moving the controls in the EmployerID Header section as far to the top of that section as possible, then dragging the top edge of the Detail section up.

k. Preview the report, making sure all controls fit within the width of portrait orientation. If not, switch to Report Design View and fix this problem.

l. Print the first page if requested by your instructor.

m. Close the Jobs report, close the JobSearch-4.accdb database, then exit Access 2016.

Visual Workshop

Open the Basketball-4.accdb database from the location where you store your Data Files and enable content if prompted. Open the Players table, change the name of Matthew Douglas to *your* name, then close the table. Your goal is to create the report shown in FIGURE 4-25. Use the Report Wizard, and select the PFirst, PLast, HomeTown, and HomeState fields from the Players table. Select the FieldGoals, 3Pointers, and FreeThrows fields from the Stats table. View the data by Players, do not add any more grouping levels, and do not add any more sorting levels. Use a Block layout and a Portrait orientation, then title the report **Scoring Report**. In Layout View, resize all of the columns so that they fit on a single piece of portrait paper, and change the labels in the Page Header section as shown. In Design View, open the PlayerNo Footer section and add text boxes with expressions to sum the FieldGoals, 3Pointers, and FreeThrows fields and bold those controls. Drag the top edge of the Page Footer section down a little to add a little space between the subtotals in the PlayerNo Footer section and the next set of records for the next player. Move, modify, align, and resize all controls as needed to match FIGURE 4-25. (*Hint*: Change the Shape Outline of the text boxes in the PlayerNo Footer section to Transparent to remove the outline.) Be sure to print preview the report to make sure that it fits within the width of one sheet of paper. Modify the report to narrow it in Report Design View if needed.

FIGURE 4-25

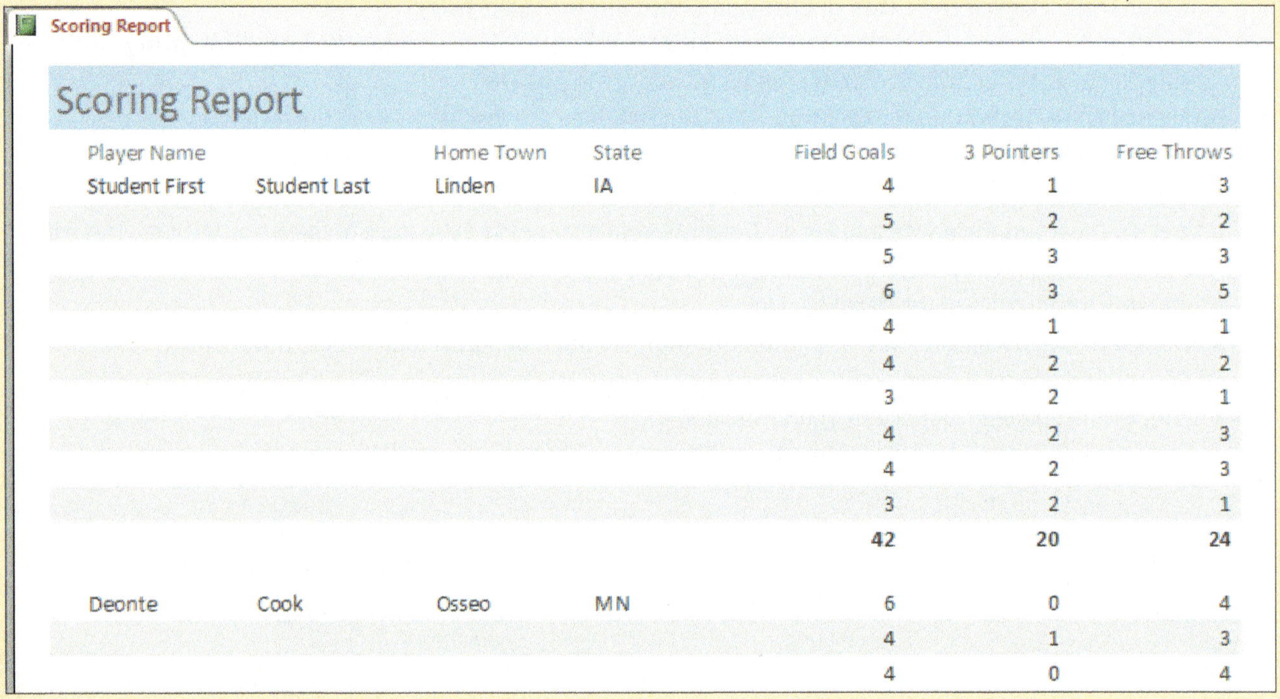

Scoring Report						
Player Name		**Home Town**	**State**	**Field Goals**	**3 Pointers**	**Free Throws**
Student First	Student Last	Linden	IA	4	1	3
				5	2	2
				5	3	3
				6	3	5
				4	1	1
				4	2	2
				3	2	1
				4	2	3
				4	2	3
				3	2	1
				42	20	24
Deonte	Cook	Osseo	MN	6	0	4
				4	1	3
				4	0	4

Integrating Word, Excel, and Access

CASE ▶ Kevin Lawrence, vice president of Operations for R2G uses Word, Excel, and Access in Office 2016 to organize and process data related to the coordination of the Regional offices. He stores volunteer experiences data in Access, financial and numerical data in Excel, and documents in Word. He asks you to help him combine data from all three applications into a Word report.

Module Objectives

After completing this module, you will be able to:

- Integrate data among Word, Excel, and Access
- Import an Excel worksheet into Access
- Copy a Word table to Access
- Link an Access table to Excel and Word
- Link an Access table to Word

Files You Will Need

INT 2-1.xlsx	INT 2-7.xlsx
INT 2-2.docx	INT 2-8.docx
INT 2-3.docx	INT 2-9.docx
INT 2-4.xlsx	INT 2-10.xlsx
INT 2-5.docx	INT 2-11.docx
INT 2-6.docx	INT 2-12.docx

Integration
Module 2

Learning
Outcomes
• Identify integration
  options for Word,
  Excel, and Access

Integrate Data Among Word, Excel, and Access

You can increase efficiency by integrating the information you create in Word, Excel, and Access so it works together. For example, you can enter data into an Access database, make calculations using that data in Excel, and then create a report in Word that incorporates the Excel data and the Access table. You can also import data from an Excel spreadsheet into Access and copy a table created in Word into an Access table. **CASE** *Kevin Lawrence needs to create a database containing information about the conservation experiences that R2G runs in the Southeast Asia and Oceania region. He then needs to include this information in a report that he creates in Word. Before you create this report, you decide to review some of the ways in which information can be shared among Word, Excel, and Access.*

DETAILS

You can integrate Word, Excel, and Access by:

• **Importing an Excel worksheet into Access**

You can enter data directly into an Access database table, or you can import data from other sources such as an Excel workbook, another Access database, or even a text file. You use the Get External Data command in Access to import data from an outside source. **FIGURE 2-1** shows how data entered in an Excel file appears when imported into a new table in an Access database. During the import process, you can change the field names and the data types of selected fields.

• **Copying a Word table into Access**

You can also create a table in Word that contains data you want to include in an Access database. To save time, you can copy the table from Word and paste it into a new or existing Access table. By doing so, you save typing time and minimize errors.

• **Linking an Access table to Excel and Word**

You link an Access table to Excel and then to Word when you want the data in all three applications to always remain current. First, you use the Copy and Paste Special commands to copy an Access table and paste it into Excel as a link. You can then make calculations using Excel tools that are not available in Access. Any changes you make to the data in Access are also reflected in the linked Excel copy. However, you cannot change the structure of the linked Access table in Excel. For example, you cannot delete any of the columns or rows that contain copied data. The data used in the Excel calculations is linked to the source file in Access. When the data in Access is changed, the results of the formulas in Excel also change.

Once you have made calculations based on the data in Excel, you can then copy the data from Excel and paste it as a link into Word. When you change the data in Access, the data in both the Excel and the Word files also changes. **FIGURE 2-2** shows a Word document that contains two tables. The top table is linked to both Excel and Access. The table was copied from Access and pasted as a link into Excel, additional calculations were made in Excel, and then the table was copied to the Word report and pasted as a link.

• **Linking an Access table to Word**

You can use the Copy and Paste Special commands to copy a table from Access and then paste it as a link into a Word document. You can then format the linked table attractively. In **FIGURE 2-2**, the bottom table was copied from Access, pasted as a link in Word, and then reformatted.

FIGURE 2-1: Excel data imported to an Access table

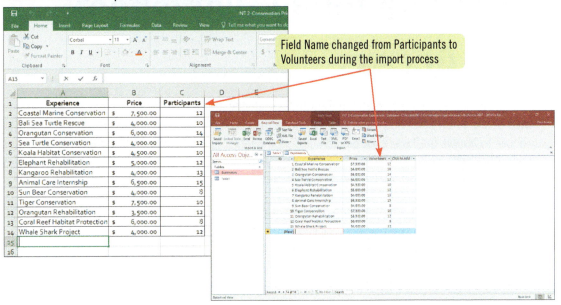

Field Name changed from Participants to Volunteers during the import process

FIGURE 2-2: Word report with links to Excel and Access

Conservation Volunteer Experiences
Southeast Asia and Oceania Region

Overview

Leaders for the conservation volunteer experiences are based in Australia, the Philippines, Thailand, Indonesia, and Malaysia. In 2017, R2G's Southeast Asia and Oceania region offered thirteen conservation experiences. The two most popular experiences were the Animal Care Internship in Malaysia and the Orangutan Conservation experiences in Indonesia. Here's a list of the conservation experiences:

Experience	Price	Volunteers	Start Location	Days	Revenue
Coastal Marine Conservation	$ 5,500.00	12	Phang Nga, Thailand	14	$ 66,000.00
Bali Sea Turtle Rescue	$ 4,000.00	10	Bali, Indonesia	7	$ 40,000.00
Orangutan Conservation	$ 6,000.00	14	Sumatra, Indonesia	14	$ 84,000.00
Sea Turtle Conservation	$ 4,000.00	12	Suva, Fiji	7	$ 48,000.00
Koala Habitat Conservation	$ 4,500.00	10	Cairns, Australia	7	$ 45,000.00
Elephant Rehabilitation	$ 5,000.00	12	Chiang Mai, Thailand	7	$ 60,000.00
Kangaroo Rehabilitation	$ 4,000.00	13	Perth, Australia	7	$ 52,000.00
Animal Care Internship	$ 6,500.00	15	Singapore, Malaysia	14	$ 97,500.00
Sun Bear Conservation	$ 4,000.00	8	Borneo, Malaysia	7	$ 32,000.00
Tiger Conservation	$ 7,500.00	10	Taman Negara, Malaysia	14	$ 75,000.00
Orangutan Rehabilitation	$ 3,500.00	12	Borneo, Malaysia	7	$ 42,000.00
Coral Reef Habitat Protection	$ 6,000.00	8	Cairns, Australia	7	$ 48,000.00
Whale Shark Project	$ 4,000.00	12	Donsol, Philippines	7	$ 48,000.00

Table linked to Excel and to Access

Experience Leaders

The overwhelming success of the conservation experiences operated in the Southeast Asia and Oceania region is a direct result of the outstanding efforts of our team of dedicated, personable, and skilled experience leaders. Shown below is the list of leaders who led our 2017 conservation experiences.

Leader ID	Last Name	First Name	Home Country	E-mail
1	Chow	Jane	Australia	jchan@r2gasia.com
2	Andaya	Tala	Philippines	tandaya@r2gasia.com
3	Darmadi	Hendra	Indonesia	hdarmadi@r2gasia.com
4	Suttikul	Solada	Thailand	ssuttikul@r2gasia.com
5	Naruma	Maki	Malaysia	mnaruma@r2gasia.com

Table copied from Access and pasted as a link

In every survey of every conservation experience operated in 2017, the Experience Leaders category received the highest ranking. In addition, the head office of Reason2Go has confirmed that these rankings exceed the rankings from all other surveys generated by all other regional headquarters company-wide.

Your Name

**Learning
Outcomes**
• Prepare an Excel
  table for export
  to Access
• Import an Excel
  table to Access
• Rename imported
  field names

Import an Excel Worksheet into Access

You can minimize typing time by importing data directly into a table in an Access database. You can then delete field names and data you do not need and add additional records to the table. You can choose to import the Excel data directly into a new table, or you can append the data to an existing table. **CASE** ▸ *Kevin Lawrence has already entered data about the 13 conservation experiences run from the Southeast Asia and Oceania Regional Headquarters. He asks you to import this table into a new Access database.*

STEPS

1. **Start Excel, open the file INT 2-1.xlsx from the location where you store your Data Files, then save it as INT 2-Conservation Prices**

   The Experiences sheet of the Excel workbook contains a list of the conservation experiences available in the Southeast Asia and Oceania region. A workbook that you plan to export from Excel into Access must contain only the data that you want to appear in the Access table; you need to remove titles, subtitles, charts, and any other extraneous data.

2. **Move the mouse pointer to the left of row 1, click and drag to select rows 1 and 2, click the right mouse button, click Delete, then save and close the workbook**

3. **Start Access, click Blank desktop database, replace the current filename with INT 2-Conservation Experiences in the File Name box, click the Browse button 📁, navigate to the location where you store your Data Files, click OK, then click Create**

   A new database opens in Access.

TROUBLE
Be sure to click the
Excel button in the
Import & Link
group, not the
Export group.

4. **Click the External Data tab, click the Excel button in the Import & Link group, click Browse, then navigate to the location where you stored the INT 2-Conservation Prices file**

5. **Click INT 2-Conservation Prices, then click Open**

   In the Get External Data - Excel Spreadsheet dialog box shown in **FIGURE 2-3**, you can choose from among three options. When you select the first or second option, any change you make to the data in the Excel source file will not be made to the data imported to Access. If you choose the third option, the imported Excel source file is linked to the data imported to Access. You want to import, rather than link, the data.

TROUBLE
If a security dialog
box opens, click
Open.

6. **Click OK to accept the default option and start the Import Spreadsheet Wizard, then verify the First Row Contains Column Headings check box is selected**

   The column headings in the Excel spreadsheet become field names in the Access table. A preview of the Access table appears, with the column names shown in gray header boxes.

QUICK TIP
In this dialog box,
you can also change
the data types of
imported data using
the Data Type list
arrow.

7. **Click Next, click the Participants column to select it, then type Volunteers as shown in FIGURE 2-4**

   The field name changes in the Field Name text box and in the table preview.

8. **Click Next, click Next to let Access add the primary key, verify that Experiences appears as the table name, click Finish, then click Close**

   Access creates a new table called Experiences. You can work with this table in the same way you work with any table you create in Access.

9. **Double-click Experiences in the list of tables, widen the Experience column, click below "Whale Shark Project", then compare the table to FIGURE 2-5**

   The imported Excel data now appears in a new Access table. You chose to import the data without links, so any changes you make to the Excel source data will not be reflected in the Access table.

FIGURE 2-3: Selecting a data source in the Get External Data dialog box

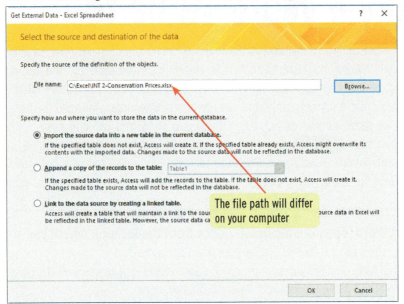

FIGURE 2-4: Changing a field name in an imported table

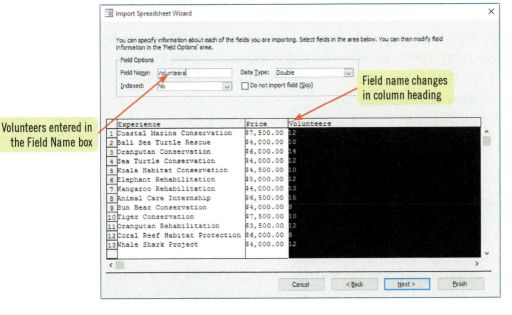

FIGURE 2-5: Excel data imported to an Access table

Copy a Word Table to Access

**Learning
Outcomes**
• Copy a Word table
  to an existing
  Access table
• Copy a Word
  table to a new
  Access table

When you have entered data into a Word table and then want to make it part of a database, you can copy the table from Word and paste it into Access. The source Word table and the destination Access table are not linked, so any change you make to one table does not affect the other table. If you want to paste a Word table into an Access table that already contains records, you need to make sure the Word table contains the same number of records as the Access table. You can also paste a Word table into a new, blank Access table. **CASE** ▶ *Kevin has given you a Word document containing two tables that he wants you to incorporate into the Word report. One table contains information that was not included in the price list you imported into Access from Excel, and the other table contains information about the experience leaders.*

STEPS

1. **Start Word, open the file INT 2-2.docx from the location where you store your Data Files, then save it as INT 2-Conservation Information**

   The top table contains information about conservation experiences, and the bottom table lists the tour leaders who work in the Southeast Asia and Oceania region.

2. **Move the mouse pointer over the upper-left corner of the top table, click the table select button ⊕, then click the Copy button in the Clipboard group**

   You copied the selected table to the Clipboard.

QUICK TIP
If you want to
import additional
records to an exist-
ing database, make
sure the imported
Excel data contains
the same number of
fields (columns) as
the database.

3. **Click the Access program button on the taskbar, then click Click to Add at the top of the blank column in the Experiences table as shown in FIGURE 2-6**

   You want the Word table columns inserted as new fields in the Access table.

4. **Click Paste as Fields, then click Yes**

   Additional data for the 13 records is pasted into the Experiences table in Access. You do not need the names of the volunteer experiences to appear twice in the database table. When you copy data from another source and paste it into an Access table, you can delete fields and records in the same way you normally do in Access.

5. **Click anywhere in the table, right-click Experience1, click Delete Field, click Yes, widen the Start Location field so all the records are visible, then click in the blank field below "Whale Shark Project"**

   The Experiences table appears as shown in FIGURE 2-7.

6. **Close the Experiences table, then click Yes to save it**

   You can copy a table directly from Word into a new blank table in Access. A blank table called Table1 was automatically created when you created the database, so you can place the copied information there.

7. **Switch to Word, scroll down and select the table containing the list of experience leaders, click the Copy button in the Clipboard group, switch to Access, click the Home tab, click Click to Add in Table 1, click Paste as Fields, then click Yes**

   The five records are pasted into a new Access table.

8. **Double-click ID, type Leader ID, press [Enter], widen the E-Mail column, click below Record 5 in the Last Name field, then compare the table to FIGURE 2-8**

9. **Close the table, click Yes to save your changes, type Leaders, click OK, then switch to Word and close the INT 2-Conservation Information file**

   You created a new table using data imported from a Word table and named it Leaders.

FIGURE 2-6: Selecting the location for copied data

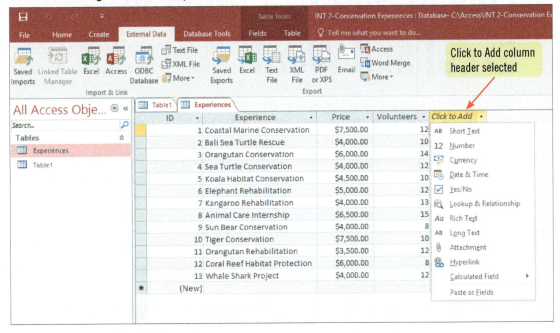

FIGURE 2-7: Table containing data copied from Word

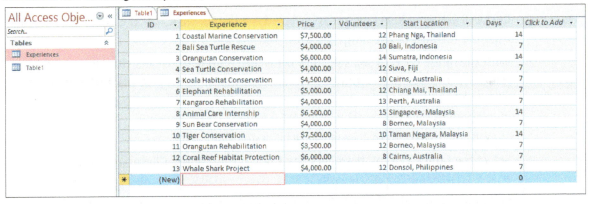

FIGURE 2-8: Renaming the ID field

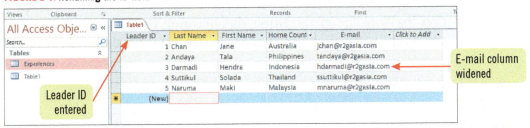

Link an Access Table to Excel and Word

**Learning
Outcomes**
• Use Copy and
Paste Special to
create links
• Update linked data

You can link data among three programs to increase efficiency and to reduce the need to enter the same data more than once. To do this, you can use the Copy and Paste Special commands to create a link between an Access database object and an Excel destination file, where you can perform calculations and create charts. You can then copy the Excel data, calculations, and charts to a Word document. When you change the data in the source Access database, the linked data in both Excel and Word are updated to reflect the new information. **CASE** ➤ *You want your report to include revenue information. You link the Access Tours table to an Excel worksheet, calculate the revenue using Excel tools, then link the calculation results to the report in Word.*

STEPS

1. In Access, click the Experiences table in the list of tables if necessary, then click the Copy button in the Clipboard group

2. In Excel, create a new blank workbook, click the Paste list arrow in the Clipboard group, then click the Paste Link button 📋 (the second of the three Paste options)

   The Experiences table appears in Excel. You cannot delete any of the rows or columns in the pasted data in Excel because it is linked to the Access source table. However, you can modify cell formatting, and you can perform calculations based on the pasted data.

3. With all the data still selected, click the Format button in the Cells group, then click AutoFit Column Width

   In the copied table, you can make calculations based on the linked data.

4. Click cell G1, type Revenue, press [Enter], type the formula =C2*D2, press [Enter], then copy the formula to the range G3:G14

5. With the range G2:G14 still selected, press and hold [Ctrl], select the range C2:C14, release [Ctrl], click the Accounting Number Format button $ in the Number group, click cell A15, increase the Zoom percentage to 120% and increase column widths as needed, then save the workbook as INT 2-Conservation Revenue

   The values in columns C and G are formatted in the Accounting format as shown in **FIGURE 2-9**.

6. Select the range B1:G14, then click the Copy button in the Clipboard group

7. Switch to Word, open the file INT 2-3.docx from the location where you store your Data Files, then save it as INT 2-Conservation Report

   The report contains information about the conservation experiences run from the Southeast Asia and Oceania region. Placeholders show where you will paste two tables.

8. Select the text EXPERIENCES TABLE, click the Paste list arrow, move the mouse over the paste icons to view paste options, then click Paste Special

   None of the Paste options provide you with appropriate formatting, so you select an option from the Paste Special dialog box.

9. Click the Paste link option button, click Microsoft Excel Worksheet Object, click OK, add a blank line below the object if necessary, then save the document

   The table appears as shown in **FIGURE 2-10**. This table is linked to the table you copied from Excel, which, in turn, is linked to the table you copied from Access. **TABLE 2-1** describes the differences between the three Paste options you have used in these lessons.

FIGURE 2-9: Copied data formatted in Excel

Accounting style applied

FIGURE 2-10: Excel data pasted and linked in Word

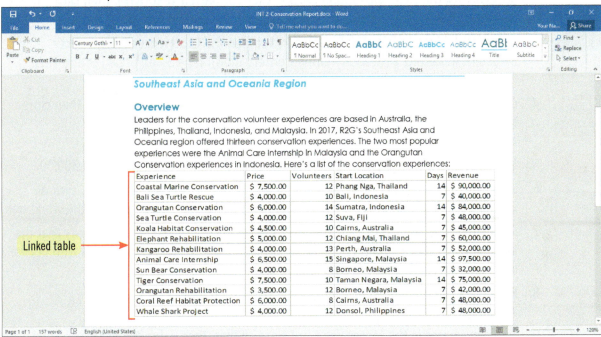

Linked table

TABLE 2-1: Paste options

command	location	use to
Paste	Paste button in Word and Excel	Paste an object without creating a link; the exception is a chart—when you copy a chart from Excel and paste it into Word, the chart is, by default, linked to the source file in Excel
Paste Special	Paste button list shows Paste Special selection in Word and Excel	Paste an object when you want to create a link or you want to select from a variety of formatting options for the pasted object, whether linked or not
Paste Link	Paste button list shows Paste Link button in Excel	Paste an object such as a copied table from Access into Excel as a link

Integrating Word, Excel, and Access

Link an Access Table to Word

If you don't need to use Excel to make calculations based on Access data, you can copy an Access table and paste it directly into Word as a link. When you update the source Access table, the linked data is also updated in Word. You can also use Word tools to modify the formatting of the pasted table so the table communicates the data clearly. **TABLE 2-2** summarizes the integration tasks you performed in this module. **CASE** ▶ *The Word report needs to contain a list of the experience leaders. You copy the Leaders table from Access and paste it into Word as a link, then test the links.*

STEPS

1. Switch to Access, click **Leaders** in the list of tables to select it, click the **Copy button** in the Clipboard group, then switch to Word

2. Select the text **LEADERS TABLE** below paragraph 2, click the **Paste list arrow**, click **Paste Special**, click the **Paste link option button**, click **Formatted Text (RTF)**, then click **OK**
   The Leaders table is pasted as formatted text in Word. You decide to test the links you created.

3. Switch to Access, double-click **Experiences** to open the Experiences table, select **$7,500.00** in Record 1 (Coastal Marine Conservation), type **5500**, press **[Enter]**, then close the table

4. Open the Leaders table, select **Chan** in Record 1, type **Chow**, press **[Enter]**, then close the table
   When you modify data in Access, the data in the linked Excel and Word files also changes.

5. Switch to Excel, then verify the price for Coastal Marine Conservation is $5,500.00

6. Select the range **A1:G14**, click the **Borders list arrow** in the Font group, click **All Borders**, select the range **A1:G1**, apply bold and center the data, then save the workbook

7. Switch to Word, right-click the **Experiences table**, click **Update Link**, then verify that the Coastal Marine Conservation revenue is now $66,000, the table is formatted with border lines, and the text in row 1 is bold and centered

8. Right-click the **Leaders table**, click **Update Field**, then deselect the table
   As shown in **FIGURE 2-11**, the last name of the first leader changes from "Chan" to "Chow".

9. Type your name in the footer, save and close all files, then submit your files to your instructor

---

Opening linked files and enabling content

When you open files created in different applications, you need to create them on the same computer logged in as the same user. Open them in the order in which they were created. For example, if you want to change the Word report and need to maintain links, open the Access database first, followed by the Excel workbook. When you open a linked Excel file, click Enable Content if prompted, click Update in response to the message, then, if prompted, click Yes. The exact order of these steps varies depending on how often you have opened the files. In Word, click Yes in response to the message. If all the files were created on the same computer by the same user, the links will all update.

When you email your files to another user, such as your instructor, the links will not work. However, the new user may view the files. After opening the workbook in Excel, they click No, close the workbook without saving it, then reopen the workbook and click Don't Update. In Word, they click No to update links.

FIGURE 2-11: Completed Word report

Conservation Volunteer Experiences
Southeast Asia and Oceania Region

Overview

Leaders for the conservation volunteer experiences are based in Australia, the Philippines, Thailand, Indonesia, and Malaysia. In 2017, R2G's Southeast Asia and Oceania region offered thirteen conservation experiences. The two most popular experiences were the Animal Care Internship in Malaysia and the Orangutan Conservation experiences in Indonesia. Here's a list of the conservation experiences:

Experience	Price	Volunteers	Start Location	Days	Revenue
Coastal Marine Conservation	$ 5,500.00	12	Phang Nga, Thailand	14	$ 66,000.00
Bali Sea Turtle Rescue	$ 4,000.00	10	Bali, Indonesia	7	$ 40,000.00
Orangutan Conservation	$ 6,000.00	14	Sumatra, Indonesia	14	$ 84,000.00
Sea Turtle Conservation	$ 4,000.00	12	Suva, Fiji	7	$ 48,000.00
Koala Habitat Conservation	$ 4,500.00	10	Cairns, Australia	7	$ 45,000.00
Elephant Rehabilitation	$ 5,000.00	12	Chiang Mai, Thailand	7	$ 60,000.00
Kangaroo Rehabilitation	$ 4,000.00	13	Perth, Australia	7	$ 52,000.00
Animal Care Internship	$ 6,500.00	15	Singapore, Malaysia	14	$ 97,500.00
Sun Bear Conservation	$ 4,000.00	8	Borneo, Malaysia	7	$ 32,000.00
Tiger Conservation	$ 7,500.00	10	Taman Negara, Malaysia	14	$ 75,000.00
Orangutan Rehabilitation	$ 3,500.00	12	Borneo, Malaysia	7	$ 42,000.00
Coral Reef Habitat Protection	$ 6,000.00	8	Cairns, Australia	7	$ 48,000.00
Whale Shark Project	$ 4,000.00	12	Donsol, Philippines	7	$ 48,000.00

Revenue updated to $66,000

Experience Leaders

The overwhelming success of the conservation experiences operated in the Southeast Asia and Oceania region is a direct result of the outstanding efforts of our team of dedicated, personable, and skilled experience leaders. Shown below is the list of leaders who led our 2017 conservation experiences.

Leader ID	Last Name	First Name	Home Country	E-mail
1	Chow	Jane	Australia	jchan@r2gasia.com
2	Andaya	Tala	Philippines	tandaya@r2gasia.com
3	Darmadi	Hendra	Indonesia	hdarmadi@r2gasia.com
4	Suttikul	Solada	Thailand	ssuttikul@r2gasia.com
5	Naruma	Maki	Malaysia	mnaruma@r2gasia.com

Chan changed to Chow

In every survey of every conservation experience operated in 2017, the Experience Leaders category received the highest ranking. In addition, the head office of Reason2Go has confirmed that these rankings exceed the rankings from all other surveys generated by all other regional headquarters company-wide.

Your Name

TABLE 2-2: Module 2 integration tasks

object	commands	source program(s)	destination program	result	connection	page no.
Excel file	External Data/Excel	Excel	Access	Excel spreadsheet is imported into a new table in Access; the spreadsheet must contain only the rows and columns required for the Access table	None	20
Word table	Copy/Paste	Word	Access	Word table is pasted in a new or existing table in Access; if an existing table, the Word table should contain the same number of records as the Access table	None	22
Access table	Copy/Paste Special/ Paste Link	Access	Excel	Access table is pasted into Excel as a link; the linked data can be formatted in Excel and included in formulas but cannot be modified or deleted	Linked	24
Linked Access table in Excel	Copy/Paste Link in Excel Copy/Paste Special/ Paste Link in Word	Access and Excel	Word	Access table is linked to Excel and then to Word; changes made in Access appear in Excel and Word	Linked	24
Access table	Copy/Paste Special/ Paste Link	Access	Word	Access table is pasted in Word and can be formatted using Word tools	Linked	26

Integration

Practice

Concepts Review

Match each term with the statement that best describes it.

1. Update
2. External Data
3. Formatted Text (RTF)
4. Paste Link
5. Column headings

a. Option to select in Excel to maintain a connection with a pasted Access table
b. To change linked data in a destination file to match data in the source file
c. Excel labels that become field names in an Access table
d. Selection used to retain divisions of columns and rows in a pasted table
e. In Access, click to import data into an existing Access table

Select the best answer from the list of choices.

6. In Access, which of the following options do you click when you want to paste data into an Access table?
   a. Insert
   b. Click to Add
   c. Paste
   d. Paste Link
7. Why would you copy a table from Access and paste it as a link in Excel?
   a. To remove selected columns
   b. To change selected data
   c. To use pasted data in calculations
   d. To modify the number of records
8. Which command(s) do you use to copy a table from Access and paste it into Excel as a link?
   a. Import
   b. Copy/Paste
   c. Copy/Paste Link
   d. Copy/Link
9. In Word, which option do you select to paste a copied table so that the structure of the table is maintained?
   a. Unformatted Text
   b. HTML Text
   c. Formatted Text
   d. Formatted Text (RTF)

Skills Review

1. **Import an Excel worksheet into Access.**
   a. Start Excel, open the file INT 2-4.xlsx from the location where you store your Data Files, then save it as **INT 2-Isle View Gallery Postcards**.
   b. Delete rows 1 and 2, then save and close the workbook.
   c. Start Access, then create a new desktop database called **INT 2-Isle View Gallery Inventory** in the location where you store your Data Files.
   d. In Access, import the file **INT 2-Isle View Gallery Postcards.xlsx** file from Excel as external data. In the Import Spreadsheet wizard, change the name of the Title field to **Image Title**, then name the new table **Images**.
   e. Close the wizard, open the Images table, then widen columns as necessary.
2. **Copy a Word table to Access.**
   a. Start Word, open the file INT 2-5.docx from the location where you store your Data Files, then save it as **INT 2-Isle View Gallery Information**.
   b. Select the top table (which contains the list of images), copy it, then switch to Access.
   c. Paste the table in the Images table, delete the duplicate column, widen columns as needed, then save and close the table. *Note*: Don't worry if no data appears in the duplicate column.
   d. In Word, select the table containing the list of gift shop products, copy the table, then paste it as a new table in Access.

Skills Review (continued)

e. Change the ID field to **Product ID**, then close the table and name it **Gift Shop Products**.

f. In Word, close the Isle View Gallery Information file.

3. Link an Access table to Excel and Word.

a. In Access, copy the Images table.

b. Create a new Excel workbook, paste the Images table as a link in cell A1, save the workbook as **INT 2-Isle View Gallery Inventory Data**, then adjust column widths where necessary.

c. Enter **Total Value** in cell G1, adjust the column width, then in cell G2, enter a formula to multiply the Price by the Print Run.

d. Copy the formula to the range G3:G16, then format the values in columns C and G in the Accounting Number format if necessary.

e. Copy the range B1:G16, switch to Word, open the file INT 2-6.docx from the location where you store your Data Files, then save it as **INT 2-Isle View Gallery Report**.

f. In the Word document, select the text POSTCARD LIST, paste the copied data as a linked Microsoft Excel Worksheet Object, add a blank line below the table if necessary, then save the document.

4. Link an Access table to Word.

a. In Access, copy the Gift Shop Products table, switch to Word, then select the PRICE LIST placeholder.

b. Paste the copied table as a linked Formatted Text (RTF) object, then modify column widths so none of the lines wrap.

c. In Access, open the Images table, change the print run for Forest Path (Record 4) to **75** units, then close the table.

d. Open the Gift Shop Products table, change the title Wave Action to **Whitecaps at Sunset**, widen columns as needed, then close and save the table.

e. In Excel, verify the total inventory value for Forest Path is $450. You may need to wait a few minutes.

f. Select the range A1:G16, add border lines to all cells, select the range A1:G1, then apply bold and centering.

g. In Word, update the link to the table that lists the postcard images, then verify the Forest Path total changes to $450.00 and the header formats change to the new format.

h. Update the data in the Gift Shop Product table.

i. Compare the completed report to **FIGURE 2-12**, type your name where indicated in the footer, save and close all open files and programs, then submit your files to your instructor.

FIGURE 2-12

Isle View Gallery

Art Postcard Sales

Isle View Gallery recently began selling postcard reproductions of work by some of its gallery artists. Sales have been brisk, particularly to tourists during the summer months. The table below lists the current stock of postcard images by the top-selling artists in each of five categories. The top-selling category is Ocean.

Image Title	Price	Print Run	Category	Artist	Total Value
Two Dolphins	$ 4.00	50	Animals	Kevin Donahue	$ 200.00
Leaping Orca	$ 5.00	75	Animals	Carola Lee	$ 375.00
Cedar Trees in Mist	$ 5.00	75	Forest	Carlos Sanchez	$ 375.00
Forest Path	$ 6.00	75	Forest	Robin Knutson	$ 450.00
Mountain Mists	$ 5.00	100	Mountains	Jasjit Singh	$ 500.00
Mountain Clouds	$ 4.00	50	Mountains	Olivia Jones	$ 200.00
Moonlight on the Beach	$ 7.00	50	Ocean	Mary Renfrew	$ 350.00
Islands in the Sound	$ 6.00	75	Ocean	Pierre Lalonde	$ 450.00
Crashing Waves	$ 5.00	100	Ocean	Gary Schwein	$ 500.00
Beachcombing	$ 7.00	100	Ocean	Janice Essex	$ 700.00
Sailboats at Sunset	$ 5.00	50	Ocean	Rory Seaton	$ 250.00
Islands in the Mist	$ 6.00	50	Ocean	Patty Martin	$ 300.00
Driftwood	$ 6.00	75	Ocean	Sook-Yin Chow	$ 450.00
Rock Pools	$ 7.00	100	Ocean	Jen Kowalski	$ 700.00
Sand Dunes	$ 4.00	50	Ocean	Ellen Rowe	$ 200.00

Price List

The price list shown below lists the top five products sold by Isle View Gallery. Three product categories are represented: Clothing, Posters, and Sundry. The Sundry category includes such items as mouse pads, mugs, tote bags, pens, and jigsaw puzzles.

Product ID	Title	Description	Category	Price
1	Ocean Swells	Mouse Pad	Sundry	$12.00
2	Whitecaps at Sunset	Mouse pad	Sundry	$12.00
3	Misty Mountains	Mug	Sundry	$20.00
4	Leaping Dolphin	Sweatshirt	Clothing	$55.00
5	Suspended Raindrop	Framed Poster	Poster	$60.00

Your Name

Independent Challenge 1

Red Rock Marketing provides online marketing services to small business owners in Arizona. You have been asked to build a database that the owner can use to keep track of contracts. The owner would also like you to create a report that analyzes sales trends.

a. Start Excel, open the file INT 2-7.xlsx from the location where you store your Data Files, widen columns if necessary, then save it as **INT 2-Red Rock Sales Data**.

b. Delete any rows and objects that cannot be imported into Access, then save and close the workbook.

Independent Challenge 1 (continued)

c. Create a database in Access called **INT 2-Red Rock Marketing**, and save it in the location where you store your Data Files.

d. Import the Excel file INT 2-Red Rock Sales Data into the Access database, change the Category field name to **Service**, and name the new table **Clients**.

e. Start Word, open the file INT 2-8.docx from the location where you store your Data Files, save it as **INT 2-Red Rock Consultants**, copy the table, close the document, then paste the table into the Clients table in Access.

f. Delete the Client Name1 column from the pasted information, widen columns as needed, then save and close the table.

g. Copy the Clients table, paste it as a linked file into cell A1 of a new Excel workbook, then adjust the column widths.

h. Format the data in column B with the Short Date style. (*Hint*: Select the range B2:B11, click the Number Format list arrow in the Number group, then click Short Date).

i. Calculate the total revenue from each contract total based on an hourly rate of $90. (*Hint*: Add two new columns—one called "Rate" with "90" entered for each record and one called "Total" with the formula entered for each record.)

j. Format the values in columns H and I with the Accounting Number format, then save the Excel workbook as **INT 2-Red Rock Client Revenue**.

k. In Word, open a new document and enter the text shown in FIGURE 2-13, then save it as **INT 2-Red Rock Clients**. Format the title in 22 point, bold and the subtitle in 14 point, bold.

FIGURE 2-13

> ### Red Rock Marketing
>
> **Spring Contracts**
>
> Red Rock Marketing provides small businesses with a one-stop shop for Web marketing services. The table below lists the clients serviced by Red Rock Marketing in March and April.

l. Copy cells B1 to I11 from Excel, paste them as a link using the Microsoft Excel Worksheet Object option in the Paste Special dialog box below the text paragraph in the INT 2-Red Rock Clients document, resize the object so it fits into the Word document (*Hint*: Drag the bottom left corner sizing handle up), then save the document.

m. In the Clients table in Access, change the number of hours for the March 6 client to **20**, close the table, then verify the March 6th revenue has changed from $1,080 to $1,800 in the Excel file. Remember, you may need to wait a few minutes for the values to update.

n. Format the range A1:I11 with border lines around all cells, and bold and center column titles.

o. Update the worksheet object in the Word file.

p. Add your name below the worksheet object, save all files and close all programs, then submit your files to your instructor.

Independent Challenge 2

Health First Apps sells tablet and computer applications related to health and well-being. The business is growing rapidly, and you need to develop a system for keeping track of inventory. You have a price list saved in a Word document. You transfer the price list into an Access database, then add some new records. You then perform calculations on the data in Excel and verify that when you update data in the Access database, the data in Excel also changes.

a. Start Word, open the file INT 2-9.docx from the location where you store your Data Files, then save it as **INT 2-Health First Apps Price List**.

b. Copy the table, create a new database in Access called **INT 2-Health First Apps** in the location where you store your Data Files, then paste the copied table into a new table named **Products**.

c. Add two new records to the Products table with the following information:

Product	Category	Price
Happy Yoga	Fitness	$3.00
Organize for Success	Career	$2.00

d. Close the table, copy it and link it into a new Excel workbook, then add a new column in Excel called **Sales**.

e. Enter **200** as the number of sales for the first four products and **300** as the number of sales for the last eight products.

Independent Challenge 2 (continued)

f. Add a new column called **Revenue**, calculate the total revenue for each product, then save the workbook as **INT 2-Health First Apps Sales**.

g. Format the Price and Revenue values with the Accounting Number format, then adjust column widths as necessary.

h. Note the current revenue amount for the Job Talk and Fitness Buddy apps ($800 and $1,650).

i. In the Access Products table, change the price of the Job Talk app to $5.00 and the price of the Fitness Buddy app to $4.00, then close the table.

j. In Excel, verify the values have been updated to $1,000 and $1,200. You may need to wait a few minutes.

k. Bold and center the labels in row 1, insert a new row 1, enter **Health First Apps Sales**, center it across the range A1:F1, increase the font size to 16 point, apply bold formatting, then apply the fill color of your choice.

l. Type your name in cell A16, save and close all open files and programs, then submit your files to your instructor.

Independent Challenge 3

Pacific Crest Surfing sells surfboards from retail outlets in Hawai'i and along the west coast of North America. You need to create a memo that analyzes the summer sales posted by resort. The memo contains data copied from Excel and Access.

a. Start Access, create a new database called **INT 2-Pacific Crest Surfing Inventory** in the location where you store your Data Files, then import the Excel file INT 2-10.xlsx. In the Import Spreadsheet wizard, change the name of the Hawaii field to **Oahu**, the California field to **Santa Monica**, and the British Columbia field to **Tofino**.

b. Name the new table **Boards**, then open the table and widen columns as necessary.

c. Close and save the Boards table, copy it, paste it into a new Excel workbook as a link, adjust the widths of columns as necessary, then save the workbook as **INT 2-Pacific Crest Surfing Sales**.

d. Enter **Total** in cell H1, then, in the appropriate cell, enter a formula to add the values for the first product (Crester RS4) sales for the three locations. Calculate the totals for the remaining products.

e. Enter **Revenue** in cell I1, then enter and copy a formula to calculate total revenue for all products.

f. In cell I15, use AutoSum to calculate the total revenue from all products. Verify that 1767000 appears in cell I15.

g. Enter **Crester Sales** in cell B16, then in cell C16 enter the formula to add the total revenue from only the three Crester products. Repeat the process to enter the brands and total sales for the remaining three brands in cells B17:C19, then verify that the Big Surf brand revenue is 569200.

h. Format all dollar amounts in the Accounting Number format, if necessary, then save the workbook.

i. Copy the range B1:H14, start Word, open the file INT 2-11.docx from the location where you store your Data Files, then save it as **INT 2-Pacific Crest Surfing Summer Sales**.

j. Replace the word "SALES" with the copied data as a linked object in the Microsoft Excel Worksheet Object format.

k. In Excel, copy the value for the total revenue, then paste it as a linked object into the appropriate area of paragraph 1 in the Word document using the Formatted Text (RTF) format from the Paste Special dialog box.

l. In Excel, copy the Big Surf amount in cell C17, then paste it as a linked object into the appropriate area of paragraph 2 in Word using the Formatted Text (RTF) format.

m. Verify the total revenue is $1,767,000.00 and the total Big Surf sales are $569,200.00.

n. In Access, change the price of the Rainman 230 surfboard to **$1,000**, then close the table.

o. In Excel, click the File tab, click Edit Links to Files, click Update Values, then click Close. Return to the worksheet, and verify that the values are updated in Excel.

p. Switch to Word, then use the same procedure as you did for Excel to access the Edit Links to Files dialog box, update each link, close the dialog box, then verify that all links are updated.

q. In Excel, bold the values in row 1 and the totals in cells I15 and C17, fill the range A1:I1 with a fill color of your choice, then add border lines to the range A1: I14.

r. Verify that the formatting is updated in Word or update the link manually, type your name where indicated in the memo footer, save and close all open files and programs, then submit your files to your instructor.

Visual Workshop

Create a new database called **INT 2-Markham Insurance** in the location where you store your Data Files, then copy the table from the Word file INT 2-12.docx into the database as a new table. Name the table **Consultant Travel**. Copy the table, then paste it as linked data in a new Excel workbook. Save the workbook as **INT 2-Markham Insurance Travel Expenses**. Refer to FIGURE 2-14 to add two new columns, enter a per diem rate of **$300**, and calculate the total expenses for each staff person. Calculate the total expenses in cell G12. In the Access source table, change the number of days that Jason Renfrew was away to **10** and the number of days that Gail Parrish was away to **12**, then close the table. In Excel, verify that the appropriate values are updated, then as shown in FIGURE 2-14, add and format a title and subtitle. (*Hint*: The font size of the title is 20 point, and the font size of the subtitle is 16 point.) Format data as shown in the figure. Include your name under the table, save and close all open files and programs, then submit your files to your instructor.

FIGURE 2-14

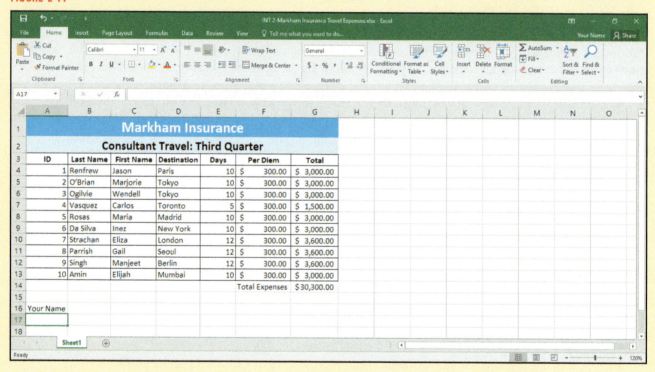

Creating a Presentation in PowerPoint 2016

CASE ▶ Reason2Go (R2G) is a voluntourism company that provides customers a unique experience of traveling to different countries and performing volunteer work. As a marketing representative for R2G, one of your responsibilities is to develop materials that describe the company vision, philosophy, and services. You have been asked to create a presentation using PowerPoint 2016 that describes projects R2G is currently developing in Kenya Africa.

Module Objectives

After completing this module, you will be able to:

- Define presentation software
- Plan an effective presentation
- Examine the PowerPoint window
- Enter slide text
- Add a new slide
- Apply a design theme
- Compare presentation views
- Print a PowerPoint presentation

Files You Will Need

No files needed.

Define Presentation Software

Presentation software (also called presentation graphics software) is a computer program you use to organize and present information to others. Presentations are typically in the form of a slide show. Whether you are explaining a new product or moderating a meeting, presentation software can help you effectively communicate your ideas. You can use PowerPoint to create informational slides that you print or display on a monitor, share in real time on the web, or save as a video for others to watch. **CASE** ▸ *You need to start working on your Kenya presentation. Because you are only somewhat familiar with PowerPoint, you get to work exploring its capabilities.* **FIGURE 1-1** *shows how a presentation looks printed as handouts.* **FIGURE 1-2** *shows how the same presentation might look shared on the Internet with others.*

DETAILS

You can easily complete the following tasks using PowerPoint:

• **Enter and edit text easily**

Text editing and formatting commands in PowerPoint are organized by the task you are performing at the time, so you can enter, edit, and format text information simply and efficiently to produce the best results in the least amount of time.

• **Change the appearance of information**

PowerPoint has many effects that can transform the way text, graphics, and slides appear. By exploring some of these capabilities, you discover how easy it is to change the appearance of your presentation.

• **Organize and arrange information**

Once you start using PowerPoint, you won't have to spend much time making sure your information is correct and in the right order. With PowerPoint, you can quickly and easily rearrange and modify text, graphics, and slides in your presentation.

• **Include information from other sources**

Often, when you create presentations, you use information from a variety of sources. With PowerPoint, you can import text, photographs, videos, numerical data, and other information from files created in programs such as Adobe Photoshop, Microsoft Word, Microsoft Excel, and Microsoft Access. You can also import information from other PowerPoint presentations as well as graphic images from a variety of sources such as the Internet, other computers, a digital camera, or other graphics programs. Always be sure you have permission to use any work that you did not create yourself.

• **Present information in a variety of ways**

With PowerPoint, you can present information using a variety of methods. For example, you can print handout pages or an outline of your presentation for audience members. You can display your presentation as an on-screen slide show using your computer, or if you are presenting to a large group, you can use a video projector and a large screen. If you want to reach an even wider audience, you can broadcast the presentation or upload it as a video to the Internet so people anywhere in the world can use a web browser to view your presentation.

• **Collaborate with others on a presentation**

PowerPoint makes it easy to collaborate or share a presentation with colleagues and coworkers using the Internet. You can use your email program to send a presentation as an attachment to a colleague for feedback. If you have a number of people that need to work together on a presentation, you can save the presentation to a shared workspace such as a network drive or OneDrive so authorized users in your group with an Internet connection can access the presentation.

FIGURE 1-1: PowerPoint handout

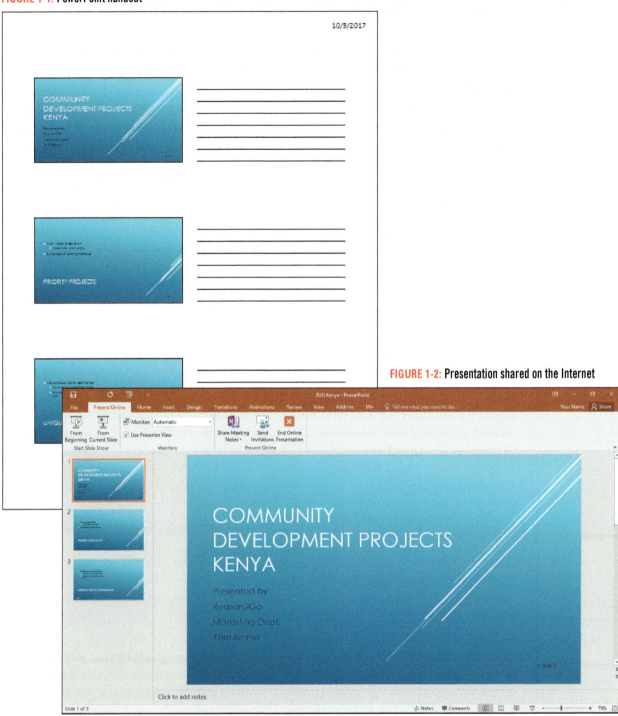

FIGURE 1-2: Presentation shared on the Internet

Using PowerPoint on a touch screen

You can use PowerPoint 2016 on a Windows computer with a touch-enabled monitor or any other compatible touch screen, such as a tablet computer. Using your fingers, you can use typical touch gestures to create, modify, and navigate presentations. To enable touch mode capabilities in PowerPoint, you need to add the Touch Mode button to the Quick Access toolbar. Click the Customize Quick Access Toolbar button, click

Touch/Mouse Mode, click the on the Quick Access toolbar then click Touch. In Touch mode, additional space is added around all of the buttons and icons in the Ribbon and the status bar to make them easier to touch. Common gestures that you can use in PowerPoint include double-tapping text to edit it and tapping a slide then dragging it to rearrange it in the presentation.

Plan an Effective Presentation

Before you create a presentation, you need to have a general idea of the information you want to communicate. PowerPoint is a powerful and flexible program that gives you the ability to start a presentation simply by entering the text of your message. If you have a specific design in mind that you want to use, you can start the presentation by working on the design. In most cases you'll probably enter the text of your presentation into PowerPoint first and then tailor the design to the message and audience. When preparing your presentation, you need to keep in mind not only who you are giving it to, but also how you are presenting it. For example, if you are giving a presentation using a projector, you need to know what other equipment you will need, such as a sound system and a projector. **CASE** *Use the planning guidelines below to help plan an effective presentation.* **FIGURE 1-3** *illustrates a storyboard for a well-planned presentation.*

DETAILS

In planning a presentation, it is important to:

• **Determine and outline the message you want to communicate**

The more time you take developing the message and outline of your presentation, the better your presentation will be in the end. A presentation with a clear message that reads like a story and is illustrated with appropriate visual aids will have the greatest impact on your audience. Start the presentation by providing a general description of the Kenyan projects currently being developed. See **FIGURE 1-3**.

• **Identify your audience and where and how you are giving the presentation**

Audience and delivery location are major factors in the type of presentation you create. For example, a presentation you develop for a staff meeting that is held in a conference room would not necessarily need to be as sophisticated or detailed as a presentation that you develop for a large audience held in an auditorium. Room lighting, natural light, screen position, and room layout all affect how the audience responds to your presentation. You might also broadcast your presentation over the Internet to several people who view the presentation on their computers in real time. This presentation will be broadcast over the Internet.

• **Determine the type of output**

Output choices for a presentation include black-and-white or color handouts for audience members, on-screen slide show, a video, or an online broadcast. Consider the time demands and computer equipment availability as you decide which output types to produce. Because this presentation will be broadcast over the Internet, the default output settings work just fine.

• **Determine the design**

Visual appeal, graphics, and presentation design work together to communicate your message. You can choose one of the professionally designed themes that come with PowerPoint, modify one of these themes, or create one of your own. You decide to choose one of PowerPoint's design themes for your presentation.

FIGURE 1-3: Storyboard of the presentation

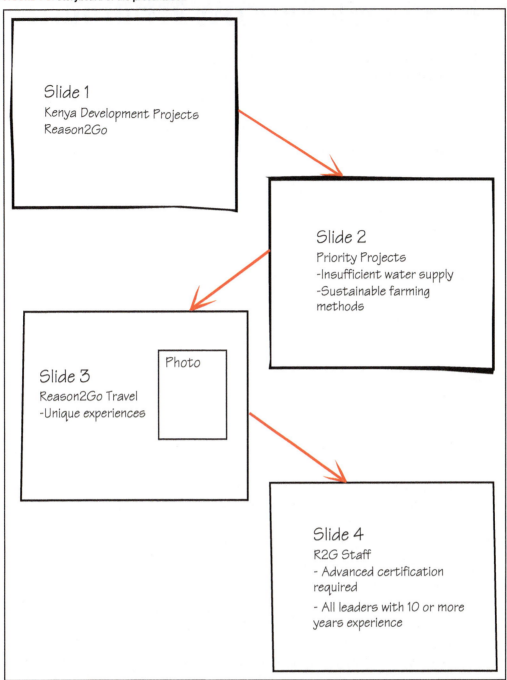

Understanding copyright

Intellectual property is any idea or creation of the human mind. Copyright law is a type of intellectual property law that protects works of authorship, including books, webpages, computer games, music, artwork, and photographs. Copyright protects the expression of an idea, but not the underlying facts or concepts. In other words, the general subject matter is not protected, but how you express it is, such as when several people photograph the same sunset. Copyright attaches to any original work of authorship as soon as it is created, you do not have to register it with the Copyright Office or display the copyright symbol, ©. Fair use is an exception to copyright and permits the public to use copyrighted material for certain purposes without obtaining prior consent from the owner. Determining whether fair use applies to a work depends on its purpose, the nature of the work, how much of the work you want to copy, and the effect on the work's value. Unauthorized use of protected work (such as downloading a photo or a song from the web) is known as copyright infringement and can lead to legal action.

Learning Outcomes
• Explain PowerPoint window elements

Examine the PowerPoint Window

When you first start PowerPoint, you have the ability to choose what kind of presentation you want to use to start—a blank one, or one with a preformatted design. You can also open and work on an existing presentation. PowerPoint has different **views** that allow you to see your presentation in different forms. By default, the PowerPoint window opens in **Normal view**, which is the primary view that you use to write, edit, and design your presentation. Normal view is divided into areas called **panes**: the pane on the left, called the **Slides tab**, displays the slides of your presentation as small images, called **slide thumbnails**. The large pane is the Slide pane where you do most of your work on the slide. **CASE** *The PowerPoint window and the specific parts of Normal view are described below.*

STEPS

1. **Start PowerPoint 2016**
   PowerPoint starts and the PowerPoint start screen opens, as shown in **FIGURE 1-4**.

2. **Click the Blank Presentation slide thumbnail**
   The PowerPoint window opens in Normal view, as shown in **FIGURE 1-5**.

DETAILS

TROUBLE
If you are unsure how to start PowerPoint, refer to the "Getting Started with Office 2016" Module in this book for specific instructions on how to start the application.

Using Figure 1-5 as a guide, examine the elements of the PowerPoint window, then find and compare the elements described below:

• The **Ribbon** is a wide band spanning the top of the PowerPoint window that organizes all of PowerPoint's primary commands. Each set of primary commands is identified by a **tab**; for example, the Home tab is selected by default, as shown in **FIGURE 1-5**. Commands are further arranged into **groups** on the Ribbon based on their function. So, for example, text formatting commands such as Bold, Underline, and Italic are located on the Home tab, in the Font group.

• The **Slides tab** is to the left. You can navigate through the slides in your presentation by clicking the slide thumbnails. You can also add, delete, or rearrange slides using this pane.

• The **Slide pane** displays the current slide in your presentation.

• The **Quick Access toolbar** provides access to common commands such as Save, Undo, Redo, and Start From Beginning. The Quick Access toolbar is always visible no matter which Ribbon tab you select. Click the Customize Quick Access Toolbar button to add or remove buttons.

• The **View Shortcuts** buttons on the status bar allow you to switch quickly between PowerPoint views.

• The **Notes button** on the status bar opens the Notes pane and is used to enter text that references a slide's content. You can print these notes and refer to them when you make a presentation or use them as audience handouts. The Notes pane is not visible in Slide Show view.

• The **Comments button** on the status bar opens the Comments pane. In the Comments pane you can create, edit, select, and delete comments.

• The **status bar**, located at the bottom of the PowerPoint window, shows messages about what you are doing and seeing in PowerPoint, including which slide you are viewing and the total number of slides. In addition, the status bar displays the Zoom slider controls, the Fit slide to current window button ⊞, and other functionality information.

• The **Zoom slider** on the lower-right corner of the status bar is used to zoom the slide in and out.

FIGURE 1-4: PowerPoint start screen

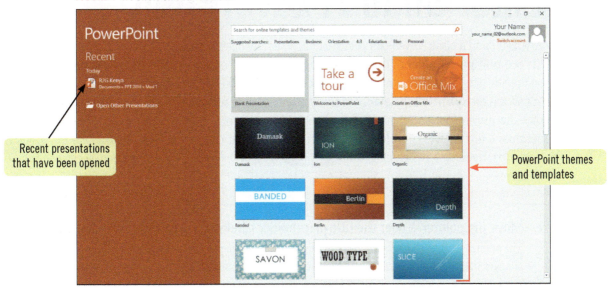

Recent presentations that have been opened

PowerPoint themes and templates

FIGURE 1-5: PowerPoint window in Normal view

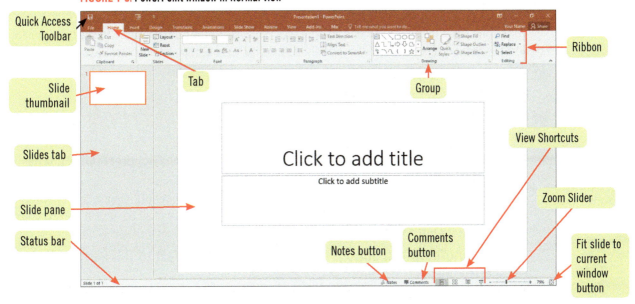

Quick Access Toolbar

Ribbon

Slide thumbnail

Tab

Group

Slides tab

View Shortcuts

Slide pane

Zoom Slider

Status bar

Notes button

Comments button

Fit slide to current window button

Viewing your presentation in gray scale or black and white

Viewing your presentation in gray scale (using shades of gray) or pure black and white is very useful when you are printing a presentation on a black-and-white printer and you want to make sure your presentation prints correctly. To see how your color presentation looks in gray scale or black and white, click the View tab, then click either the Grayscale or Black and White button in the Color/Grayscale group. Depending on which button you select, the Grayscale or the Black and White tab appears, and the Ribbon displays different settings that you can customize. If you don't like the way an individual object looks in black and white or gray scale, you can change its color. Click the object while still in Grayscale or Black and White view, then choose an option in the Change Selected Object group on the Ribbon.

Enter Slide Text

When you start a blank PowerPoint presentation, an empty title slide appears in Normal view. The title slide has two **text placeholders**—boxes with dotted borders—where you enter text. The top text placeholder on the title slide is the **title placeholder**, labeled "Click to add title". The bottom text placeholder on the title slide is the **subtitle text placeholder**, labeled "Click to add subtitle". To enter text in a placeholder, click the placeholder and then type your text. After you enter text in a placeholder, the placeholder becomes a text object. An **object** is any item on a slide that can be modified. Objects are the building blocks that make up a presentation slide. **CASE** ▸ *Begin working on your presentation by entering text on the title slide.*

STEPS

1. **Move the pointer ▷ over the title placeholder labeled** Click to add title **in the Slide pane**

   The pointer changes to I when you move the pointer over the placeholder. In PowerPoint, the pointer often changes shape, depending on the task you are trying to accomplish.

2. **Click the** title placeholder **in the Slide pane**

   The **insertion point**, a blinking vertical line, indicates where your text appears when you type in the placeholder. A **selection box** with a dashed line border and **sizing handles** appears around the placeholder, indicating that it is selected and ready to accept text. When a placeholder or object is selected, you can change its shape or size by dragging one of the sizing handles. See **FIGURE 1-6**.

3. **Type** Community Development Projects Kenya

   PowerPoint wraps the text to a second line and then center-aligns the title text within the title placeholder, which is now a text object. Notice the text also appears on the slide thumbnail on the Slides tab.

4. **Click the** subtitle text placeholder **in the Slide pane**

   The subtitle text placeholder is ready to accept text.

5. **Type** Presented by, **then press** [Enter]

   The insertion point moves to the next line in the text object.

6. **Type** Community Health Education, **press** [Enter], **type** Reason2Go, **press** [Enter], **type** Marketing Dept., **press** [Enter], **then type** your name

   Notice the AutoFit Options button ⊞ appears near the text object. The AutoFit Options button on your screen indicates that PowerPoint has automatically decreased the font size of all the text in the text object so it fits inside the text object.

7. **Click the** AutoFit Options button ⊞, **then click** Stop Fitting Text to This Placeholder **on the shortcut menu**

   The text in the text object changes back to its original size and no longer fits inside the text object.

8. **In the subtitle text object, position** I **to the right of** Education, **drag left to select the entire line of text, press** [Backspace], **then click outside the text object in a blank area of the slide**

   The Community Health Education line of text is deleted and the AutoFit Options button menu closes, as shown in **FIGURE 1-7**. Clicking a blank area of the slide deselects all selected objects on the slide.

9. **Click the** Save button 🖫 **on the Quick Access toolbar to open Backstage view, then save the presentation as** PPT 1-R2G **in the location where you store your Data Files**

   In Backstage view, you have the option of saving your presentation to your computer or OneDrive. Notice that PowerPoint automatically entered the title of the presentation as the filename in the Save As dialog box.

FIGURE 1-6: Title text placeholder selected

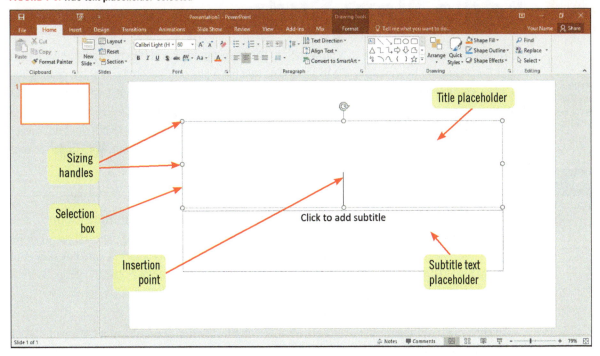

FIGURE 1-7: Text on title slide

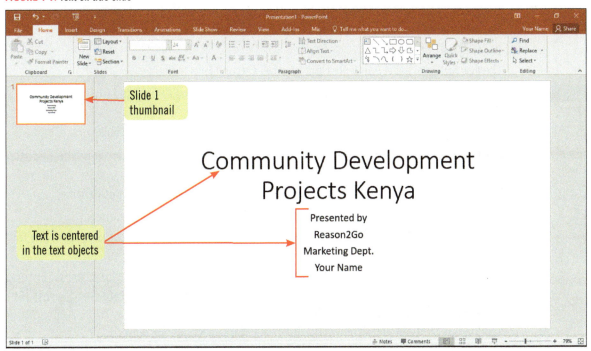

Inking a slide

In Slide View, you can add freehand pen and highlighter marks, also known as **inking**, to the slides of your presentation to emphasize information. To begin inking, go to the slide you want mark up, click the Review tab, then click the Start Inking button in the Ink group. The Pens tab appears on the Ribbon and the Pen tool appears on the slide ready for you to draw using your mouse. To customize your pen, select a different pen color, style, or thickness from options in the Pens group. Click the Highlighter button in the Write group to insert highlighter strokes on your slide. To erase inking on the slide, click the Eraser button in the Write group.

Add a New Slide

Learning Outcomes
• Add a new slide
• Indent text levels
• Modify slide layout

Usually when you add a new slide to a presentation, you have a pretty good idea of what you want the slide to look like. For example, you may want to add a slide that has a title over bulleted text and a picture. To help you add a slide like this quickly and easily, PowerPoint provides many standard slide layouts. A **slide layout** contains text and object placeholders that are arranged in a specific way on the slide. You have already worked with the Title Slide layout in the previous lesson. In the event that a standard slide layout does not meet your needs, you can modify an existing slide layout or create a new, custom slide layout. **CASE** *To continue developing the presentation, you create a slide that explains the needs in Kenya.*

STEPS

1. **Click the New Slide button in the Slides group on the Home tab on the Ribbon**

   A new blank slide (now the current slide) appears as the second slide in your presentation, as shown in **FIGURE 1-8**. The new slide contains a title placeholder and a content placeholder. A **content placeholder** can be used to insert text or objects such as tables, charts, videos, or pictures. Notice the status bar indicates Slide 2 of 2 and the Slides tab now contains two slide thumbnails.

2. **Type Priority Projects, then click the bottom content placeholder**

   The text you typed appears in the title placeholder, and the insertion point is now at the top of the bottom content placeholder.

3. **Type Well water production, then press [Enter]**

   The insertion point appears directly below the text when you press [Enter], and a new first-level bullet automatically appears.

4. **Press [Tab]**

   The new first-level bullet is indented and becomes a second-level bullet.

QUICK TIP
You can also press [Shift][Tab] to decrease the indent level.

5. **Type Inadequate water supply, press [Enter], then click the Decrease List Level button ⇤ in the Paragraph group**

   The Decrease List Level button changes the second-level bullet into a first-level bullet.

6. **Type Sustainable farming methods, then click the New Slide list arrow in the Slides group**

   The Office Theme layout gallery opens. Each slide layout is identified by a descriptive name.

7. **Click the Two Content slide layout, then type Unique Travel Experience**

   A new slide with a title placeholder and two content placeholders appears as the third slide. The text you typed is the title text for the slide.

8. **Click the left content placeholder, type Adventurous travel destinations, press [Enter], click the Increase List Level button ⇥, type Serve others in desperate need, press [Enter], then type Satisfaction of helping your fellow man**

   The Increase List Level button moves the insertion point one level to the right.

9. **Click a blank area of the slide, then click the Save button 🖫 on the Quick Access toolbar**

   The Save button saves all of the changes to the file. Compare your screen with **FIGURE 1-9**.

FIGURE 1-8: New blank slide in Normal view

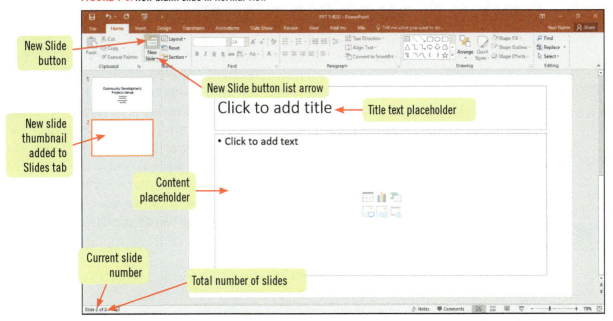

New Slide button

New Slide button list arrow

Title text placeholder

New slide thumbnail added to Slides tab

Content placeholder

Current slide number

Total number of slides

FIGURE 1-9: New slide with Two Content slide layout

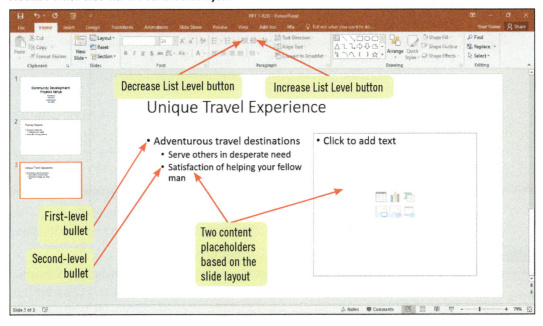

Decrease List Level button

Increase List Level button

First-level bullet

Second-level bullet

Two content placeholders based on the slide layout

Entering and printing notes

You can add notes to your slides when there are certain facts you want to remember during a presentation or when there is additional information you want to hand out to your audience. Notes do not appear on the slides when you run a slide show. Use the Notes pane in Normal view or Notes Page view to enter notes for your slides. To open or close the Notes pane, click the Notes button on the status bar. To enter text notes on a slide, click in the Notes pane, then type. If you want to insert graphics as notes, you must use Notes Page view. To open Notes Page view, click the View tab on the Ribbon, then click the Notes Page button in the Presentation Views group. You can print your notes by clicking the File tab on the Ribbon to open Backstage view. Click Print, click the Full Page Slides list arrow in the Settings group (this button retains the last setting for what was printed previously so it might differ) to open the gallery, and then click Notes Pages. Once you verify your print settings, click the Print button. If you don't enter any notes in the Notes pane, and print the notes pages, the slides print as large thumbnails with blank space below the thumbnails to hand write notes.

Apply a Design Theme

PowerPoint provides many design themes to help you quickly create a professional and contemporary looking presentation. A **theme** includes a set of 12 coordinated colors for text, fill, line, and shadow, called **theme colors**; a set of fonts for titles and other text, called **theme fonts**; and a set of effects for lines and fills, called **theme effects** to create a cohesive look. Each theme has at least four custom coordinated variants that provides you with additional color options. In most cases, you would apply one theme to an entire presentation; you can, however, apply multiple themes to the same presentation. You can use a design theme as is, or you can alter individual elements of the theme as needed. Unless you need to use a specific design theme, such as a company theme or product design theme, it is faster and easier to use one of the themes supplied with PowerPoint. If you design a custom theme, you can save it to use in the future. **CASE** ▶ *You decide to change the default design theme in the presentation to a new one.*

STEPS

1. **Click the Slide 1 thumbnail on the Slides tab**

   Slide 1, the title slide, appears in the Slide pane.

2. **Click the Design tab on the Ribbon, then point to the Integral theme in the Themes group, as shown in FIGURE 1-10**

   The Design tab appears, and a Live Preview of the Integral theme is displayed on the selected slide. A **Live Preview** allows you to see how your changes affect the slides before actually making the change. The Live Preview lasts about 1 minute, and then your slide reverts back to its original state. The first (far left) theme thumbnail identifies the current theme applied to the presentation, in this case, the default design theme called the Office Theme. The number of themes you can see in the Themes group depends on your monitor resolution and screen size.

3. **Slowly move your pointer ᐅ over the other design themes, then click the Themes group down scroll arrow**

   A Live Preview of the theme appears on the slide each time you pass your pointer over the theme thumbnails, and a ScreenTip identifies the theme names.

4. **Move ᐅ over the design themes, then click the Wisp theme**

   The Wisp design theme is applied to all the slides in the presentation. Notice the new slide background color, graphic elements, fonts, and text color. You decide this theme isn't right for this presentation.

5. **Click the More button ⬇ in the Themes group**

   The Themes gallery window opens. At the top of the gallery window in the This Presentation section is the current theme applied to the presentation. Notice that just the Wisp theme is listed here because when you changed the theme in the last step, you replaced the default theme with the Wisp theme. The Office section identifies all of the standard themes that come with PowerPoint.

6. **Right-click the Slice theme in the Office section, then click Apply to Selected Slides**

   The Slice theme is applied only to Slide 1. You like the Slice theme better, and decide to apply it to all slides.

7. **Right-click the Slice theme in the Themes group, then click Apply to All Slides**

   The Slice theme is applied to all three slides. Preview the next slides in the presentation to see how it looks.

8. **Click the Next Slide button ⬇ at the bottom of the vertical scroll bar**

   Compare your screen to FIGURE 1-11.

9. **Click the Previous Slide button ⬆ at the bottom of the vertical scroll bar, then save your changes**

FIGURE 1-10: Slide showing a different design theme

Current theme applied

Office theme

Design tab

Screentip

Integral theme

More button

Themes group down scroll arrow

Variants

New font type

New graphic elements

FIGURE 1-11: Presentation with Slice theme applied

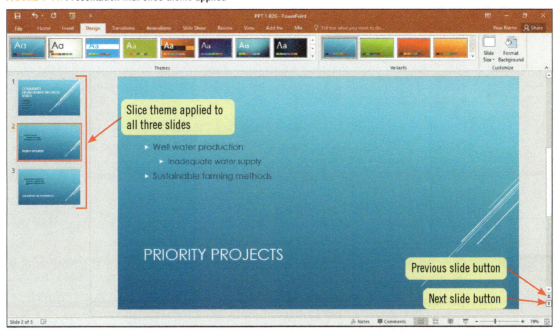

Slice theme applied to all three slides

▸ Well water production
  ▸ Inadequate water supply
▸ Sustainable farming methods

PRIORITY PROJECTS

Previous slide button

Next slide button

Customizing themes

You are not limited to using the standard themes PowerPoint provides; you can also modify a theme to create your own custom theme. For example, you might want to incorporate your school's or company's colors on the slide background of the presentation or be able to type using fonts your company uses for brand recognition. To change an existing theme, click the View tab on the Ribbon, then click one of the Master buttons in the Master Views group. Click the Theme Colors button, the Theme Fonts button, or the Theme Effects button in the Background group to make changes to the theme, save this new theme for future use by clicking the Themes button in the Edit Themes group, then click Save Current Theme. You also have the ability to create a new font theme or color theme from scratch by clicking the Theme Fonts button or the Theme Colors button and then clicking Customize Fonts or Customize Colors. You work in the Create New Theme Fonts or Create New Theme Colors dialog box to define the custom theme fonts or colors.

Compare Presentation Views

PowerPoint has six primary views: Normal view, Outline view, Slide Sorter view, Notes Page view, Slide Show view, and Reading view. Each PowerPoint view displays your presentation in a different way and is used for different purposes. Normal view is the primary editing view where you add text, graphics, and other elements to the slides. Outline view is the view you use to focus on the text of your presentation. Slide Sorter view is primarily used to rearrange slides; however, you can also add slide effects and design themes in this view. You use Notes Page view to type notes that are important for each slide. Slide Show view displays your presentation over the whole computer screen and is designed to show your presentation to an audience. Similar to Slide Show view, Reading view is designed to view your presentation on a computer screen. To move easily among the PowerPoint views, use the View Shortcuts buttons located on the status bar and the View tab on the Ribbon. **TABLE 1-1** provides a brief description of the PowerPoint views. **CASE** ▶ *Examine each of the PowerPoint views, starting with Normal view.*

STEPS

1. **Click the View tab on the Ribbon, then click the Outline View button in the Presentation Views group**

   The presentation text is in the Outline pane on the left side of the window, as shown in **FIGURE 1-12**. Notice the status bar identifies the number of the slide you are viewing and the total number of slides in the presentation.

2. **Click the small slide icon ▢ next to Slide 2 in the Outline pane, then click the Slide Sorter button ▦ on the status bar**

   Slide Sorter View opens to display a thumbnail of each slide in the presentation in the window. You can examine the flow of your slides and drag any slide or group of slides to rearrange the order of the slides in the presentation.

3. **Double-click the Slide 1 thumbnail, then click the Reading View button ▤ on the status bar**

   The first slide fills the screen, as shown in **FIGURE 1-13**. Use Reading view to review your presentation or to show your presentation to someone directly on your computer. The status bar controls at the bottom of the window make it easy to move between slides in this view.

4. **Click the Slide Show button ▭ on the status bar**

   The first slide fills the entire screen now without the title bar and status bar. In this view, you can practice running through your slides as they would appear in a slide show.

5. **Click the left mouse button to advance through the slides one at a time until you see a black slide, then click once more to return to Outline view**

   The black slide at the end of the slide show indicates the slide show is finished. At the end of a slide show, you return to the slide and PowerPoint view you were in before you ran the slide show, in this case, Slide 1 in Outline view.

6. **Click the Notes Page button in the Presentation Views group**

   Notes Page view appears, showing a reduced image of the current slide above a large text placeholder. You can enter text in this placeholder and then print the notes page for your own use.

7. **Click the Normal button in the Presentation Views group, then click the Home tab on the Ribbon**

FIGURE 1-12: Outline view

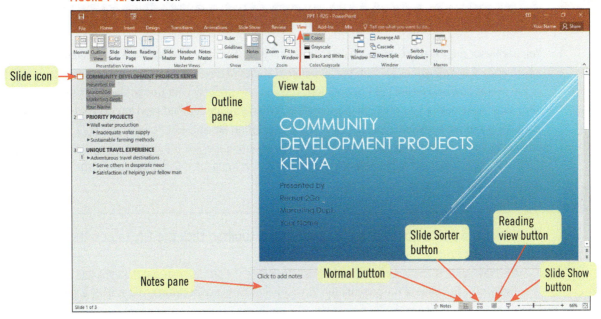

FIGURE 1-13: Reading view

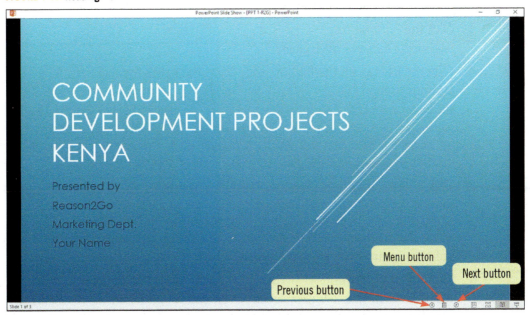

TABLE 1-1: PowerPoint views

view name	button	button name	displays
Normal	回	Normal	The Slide pane and the Slides tab at the same time
Outline View	(no View Shortcuts button)		An outline of the presentation and the Slide pane at the same time
Slide Sorter	88	Slide Sorter	Thumbnails of all slides
Slide Show	⬚	Slide Show	Your presentation on the whole computer screen
Reading View	📖	Reading View	Your presentation in a large window on your computer screen
Notes Page	(no View Shortcuts button)		A reduced image of the current slide above a large text box

Print a PowerPoint Presentation

Learning Outcomes
- Print a presentation
- Set print settings
- Modify color settings

You print your presentation when you want to review your work or when you have completed it and want a hard copy. Reviewing your presentation at different stages of development gives you a better perspective of the overall flow and feel of the presentation. You can also preview your presentation to see exactly how each slide looks before you print the presentation. When you are finished working on your presentation, even if it is not yet complete, you can close the presentation file and exit PowerPoint. **CASE** ➤ *You are done working on the Kenya presentation for now. You save and preview the presentation, then you print the slides and notes pages of the presentation so you can review them later. Before leaving for the day, you close the file and exit PowerPoint.*

STEPS

1. **Click the Save button 🖫 on the Quick Access toolbar, click the File tab on the Ribbon, then click Print**

   The Print window opens, as shown in **FIGURE 1-14**. Notice the preview pane on the right side of the window displays the first slide of the presentation. If you do not have a color printer, you will see a grayscale image of the slide.

QUICK TIP

To quickly print the presentation with the current Print options, add the Quick Print button to the Quick Access toolbar.

2. **Click the Next Page button ▶ at the bottom of the Preview pane, then click ▶ again**

   Each slide in the presentation appears in the preview pane.

3. **Click the Print button**

   Each slide in the presentation prints.

4. **Click the File tab on the Ribbon, click Print, then click the Full Page Slides button in the Settings group**

   The Print Layout gallery opens. In this gallery you can specify what you want to print (slides, handouts, notes pages, or outline), as well as other print options. To save paper when you are reviewing your slides, you can print in handout format, which lets you print up to nine slides per page. The options you choose in the Print window remain there until you change them or close the presentation.

QUICK TIP

To print slides appropriate in size for overhead transparencies, click the Design tab, click the Slide Size button in the Customize group, click Customize Slide Size, click the Slides sized for list arrow, then click Overhead.

5. **Click 3 Slides, click the Color button in the Settings group, then click Pure Black and White**

   PowerPoint removes the color and displays the slides as thumbnails next to blank lines, as shown in **FIGURE 1-15**. Using the Handouts with three slides per page printing option is a great way to print your presentation when you want to provide a way for audience members to take notes. Printing pure black-and-white prints without any gray tones can save printer toner.

6. **Click the Print button**

   The presentation prints one page showing all the slides of the presentation as thumbnails next to blank lines.

7. **Click the File tab on the Ribbon, then click Close**

   If you have made changes to your presentation, a Microsoft PowerPoint alert box opens asking you if you want to save changes you have made to your presentation file.

8. **Click Save, if necessary, to close the alert box**

   Your presentation closes.

9. **Click the Close button ☒ in the Title bar**

   The PowerPoint program closes, and you return to the Windows desktop.

FIGURE 1-14: Print window

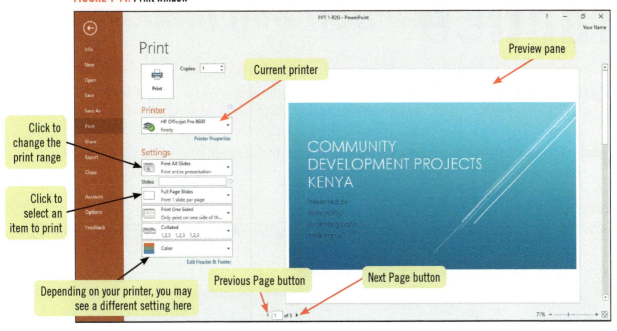

Preview pane

Current printer

Click to change the print range

Click to select an item to print

Depending on your printer, you may see a different setting here

Previous Page button

Next Page button

FIGURE 1-15: Print window with changed settings

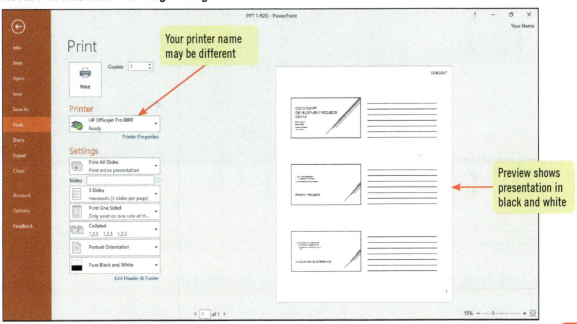

Your printer name may be different

Preview shows presentation in black and white

Microsoft Office Online Apps

Some Office programs, PowerPoint for example, include the capability to incorporate feedback—called online collaboration—across the Internet or a company network. Using **cloud computing** (work done in a virtual environment), you can take advantage of web programs called Microsoft Office Online Apps, which are simplified versions of the programs found in the Microsoft Office 2016 suite. Because these programs are online,

they take up no computer disk space and are accessed using Microsoft OneDrive, a free service from Microsoft. Using Microsoft OneDrive, you and your colleagues can create and store documents in the "cloud" and make the documents available to whomever you grant access. To use Microsoft OneDrive, you need to create a free Microsoft account, which you obtain at the Microsoft website.

Practice

Concepts Review

Label each element of the PowerPoint window shown in FIGURE 1-16.

FIGURE 1-16

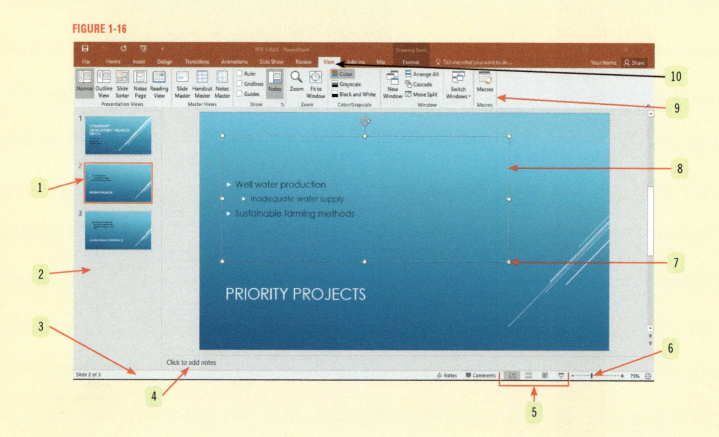

Match each term with the statement that best describes it.

11. Slide Show view
12. Slide Layout
13. Inking
14. Theme
15. Zoom slider
16. Text placeholder

a. Freehand pen and highlighter marks on a slide
b. A view that displays a presentation to show to an audience
c. Allows you to change the size of the slide in the window
d. Set of coordinated colors, fonts, and effects
e. Placeholders arranged in a specific way on the slide
f. Box with dotted border where you enter text

Select the best answer from the list of choices.

17. **The view that fills the entire computer screen with each slide in the presentation is called:**
    - **a.** Outline view.
    - **b.** Normal view.
    - **c.** Slide Show view.
    - **d.** Fit to window view.

18. **You can enter slide text in the Slide Pane and in the _____.**
    - **a.** Reading pane
    - **b.** Notes Page view
    - **c.** Outline view
    - **d.** Slides tab

19. **What is the function of the slide layout?**
    - **a.** Defines how all the elements on a slide are arranged.
    - **b.** Enables you to apply a template to the presentation.
    - **c.** Puts all your slides in order.
    - **d.** Shows you which themes you can apply.

20. **Which of the following is not included in a design theme?**
    - **a.** Pictures
    - **b.** Normal view
    - **c.** Fonts
    - **d.** Colors

21. **Which button indents the insertion point to the right?**
    - **a.** Right Indent Level
    - **b.** Increase List Level
    - **c.** Decrease Indent Level
    - **d.** Move Margin

22. **Which status bar feature allows you to quickly switch between views?**
    - **a.** Zoom Slider
    - **b.** View Shortcuts
    - **c.** Fit slide to current window button
    - **d.** Switch view button

23. **What can you drag to adjust the size of an object?**
    - **a.** Rotate handle
    - **b.** Object border point
    - **c.** Sizing handle
    - **d.** Selection box

24. **What are the basic building blocks of any presentation?**
    - **a.** Placeholders
    - **b.** Objects
    - **c.** Slides
    - **d.** Graphics

Skills Review

1. **Examine the PowerPoint window.**
   - **a.** Start PowerPoint, if necessary then open a new blank presentation.
   - **b.** Identify as many elements of the PowerPoint window as you can without referring to the lessons in this module.
   - **c.** Be able to describe the purpose or function of each element.
   - **d.** For any elements you cannot identify, refer to the lessons in this module.

2. **Enter slide text.**
   - **a.** In the Slide pane in Normal view, enter the text **Nelsonville** in the title placeholder.
   - **b.** In the subtitle text placeholder, enter **Wyoming Ghost Town Preservation Society**.
   - **c.** On the next line of the placeholder, enter your name.
   - **d.** Deselect the text object.
   - **e.** Save the presentation using the filename **PPT 1-Nelsonville** to location where you store your Data Files.

Skills Review (continued)

3. **Add a new slide.**

   a. Create a new slide.

   b. Using **FIGURE 1-17**, enter text on the slide.

   c. Create another new slide.

   d. Using **FIGURE 1-18**, enter text on the slide.

   e. Save your changes.

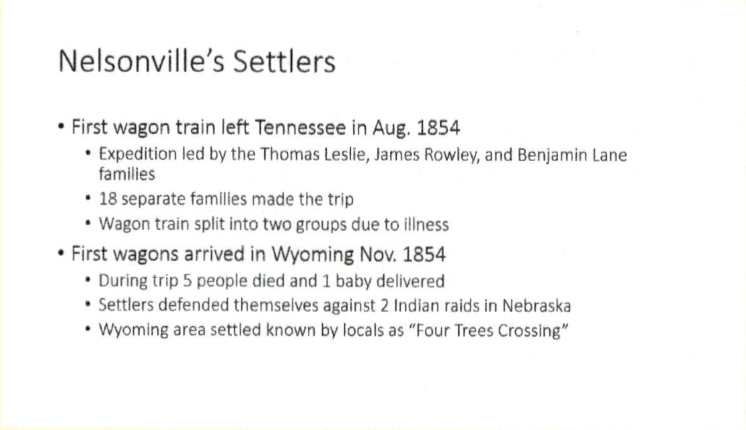

4. **Apply a design theme.**

   a. Click the Design tab.

   b. Click the Themes group More button, then point to all of the themes.

   c. Locate the Ion Boardroom theme, then apply it to the selected slide.

   d. Select Slide 1.

   e. Locate the Wisp theme, then apply it to Slide 1.

   f. Apply the Wisp theme to all of the slides in the presentation.

   g. Use the Next Slide button to move to Slide 3, then save your changes.

5. **Compare presentation views.**

   a. Click the View tab, then click the Outline View button in the Presentation Views group.

   b. Click the Slide Sorter button in the Presentation Views group.

   c. Click the Notes Page button in the Presentation Views group, then click the Previous Slide button twice.

   d. Click the Reading View button in the Presentation Views group, then click the Next button on the status bar.

   e. Click the Normal button on the status bar, then click the Slide Show button.

   f. Advance the slides until a black screen appears, then click to end the presentation.

   g. Save your changes.

6. **Print a PowerPoint presentation.**

   a. Print all the slides as handouts, 3 Slides, in color.

   b. Print the presentation outline.

   c. Close the file, saving your changes.

   d. Exit PowerPoint.

FIGURE 1-17

Nelsonville's Settlers

- First wagon train left Tennessee in Aug. 1854
  - Expedition led by the Thomas Leslie, James Rowley, and Benjamin Lane families
  - 18 separate families made the trip
  - Wagon train split into two groups due to illness
- First wagons arrived in Wyoming Nov. 1854
  - During trip 5 people died and 1 baby delivered
  - Settlers defended themselves against 2 Indian raids in Nebraska
  - Wyoming area settled known by locals as "Four Trees Crossing"

FIGURE 1-18

Nelsonville Hotel & Bar History

- Built by John Nelson in 1868
  - Constructed from local lodgepole and ponderosa pine
  - Sold cattle and land for construction capital
- Continuously operated from 1870 to 1929
  - Featured 14 double rooms and 1 bridal suite
  - Restaurant, bath house, and barber shop eventually added to property
  - Featured gambling tables until 1911

Independent Challenge 1

You work for RuraLink Systems, a business that offers rural broadband Internet service and network server management. One of your jobs at the company is to present the company's services to local government and community meetings. Your boss has asked you to create a company profile presentation that describes company goals and services.

a. Start PowerPoint then open a new blank presentation.

b. In the title placeholder on Slide 1, type **RuraLink Systems**.

c. In the subtitle placeholder, type your name, press [Enter], then type today's date.

d. Apply the Ion Boardroom design theme to the presentation.

e. Save your presentation with the filename **PPT 1-RuraLink** to the location where you store your Data Files.

f. Use FIGURE 1-19 and FIGURE 1-20 to add two more slides to your presentation. (*Hint*: Slide 3 uses the Comparison layout.)

g. Use the buttons on the View tab to switch between all of PowerPoint's views.

h. Print the presentation using handouts, 3 Slides, in black and white.

i. Save and close the file, then exit PowerPoint.

FIGURE 1-19

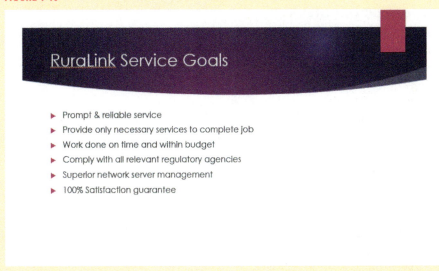

FIGURE 1-20

Independent Challenge 2

You have recently been promoted to sales manager at General Hardwood Industries, which sells and distributes specialty hardwood products used in flooring, cabinets, and furniture. Part of your job is to present company sales figures at a yearly sales meeting. Use the following information as the basis for units of wood sold nationally in your presentation: 501 units cherry, 429 units birch, 95 units hickory, 742 units mahogany, 182 units Brazilian walnut, 401 units American walnut, and 269 units pine. Assume that General Hardwood has five sales regions throughout the country: Pacific Northwest, West, South, Midwest, and Northeast. Also, assume the sales in each region rose between 1.2% and 3.6% over last year, and gross sales reached $31 million. The presentation should have at least five slides.

a. Spend some time planning the slides of your presentation. What is the best way to show the information provided? What other information could you add that might be useful for this presentation?

b. Start PowerPoint.

c. Give the presentation an appropriate title on the title slide, and enter today's date and your name in the subtitle placeholder.

d. Add slides and enter appropriate slide text.

e. On the last slide of the presentation, include the following information:
   General Hardwood Industries
   "Your specialty hardwood store"

f. Apply a design theme. A typical slide might look like the one shown in **FIGURE 1-21**.

g. Switch views. Run through the slide show at least once.

h. Save your presentation with the filename **PPT 1-General** where you store your Data Files.

i. Close the presentation and exit PowerPoint.

FIGURE 1-21

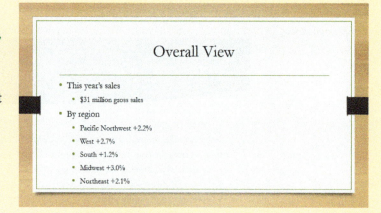

Independent Challenge 3

You work for Janic Corporation, an international trade company that distributes products made in the Midwest. The marketing manager has asked you to plan and create a PowerPoint presentation that describes the primary products Janic exports and the top 3 importing countries; Saudi Arabia, Mexico, and Japan. Describe the top exports, which include tractors, fresh and frozen pork meat, soybeans, corn, and aircraft engine parts. Use the Internet, if possible, to research information that will help you formulate your ideas. The presentation should have at least five slides.

a. Spend some time planning the slides of your presentation.

b. Start PowerPoint then open a new blank presentation.

c. Give the presentation an appropriate title on the title slide, and enter today's date and your name in the subtitle placeholder.

d. Add slides and enter appropriate slide text.

e. On the last slide of the presentation, type the following information:
   Janic Corp.
   Est. 1948
   Headquarters: Independence, MO

f. Apply a design theme.

g. Switch views. Run through the slide show at least once.

h. Save your presentation with the filename **PPT 1-Janic** to the location where you store your Data Files.

i. Close the presentation and exit PowerPoint.

Independent Challenge 4: Explore

You are a member of the Chattanooga Service Organization (CSO), a non profit organization in Chattanooga, TN. This organization raises money throughout the year to support community needs such as schools, youth organizations, and other worthy causes. This year CSO has decided to support the Penhale Youth Center by hosting a regional barbeque cook-off, called the Ultimate BBQ Cook-Off. The competition includes over 20 cooking teams from a five-state region. Create a presentation that describes the event.

a. Spend some time planning the slides of your presentation. Assume the following: the competition is a 2-day event; event advertising will be multistate wide; musical groups will be invited; there will be events and games for kids; the event will be held at the county fairgrounds. Use the Internet, if possible, to research information that will help you formulate your ideas.

b. Start PowerPoint then open a new blank presentation.

c. Give the presentation an appropriate title on the title slide, and enter your name and today's date in the subtitle placeholder.

d. Add slides and enter appropriate slide text. You must create at least three slides.

e. Apply a Design Theme. Typical slides might look like the ones shown in **FIGURE 1-22** and **FIGURE 1-23**.

f. View the presentation.

g. Save your presentation with the filename **PPT 1-CSO** to the location where you store your Data Files.

h. Close the presentation and exit PowerPoint.

FIGURE 1-22

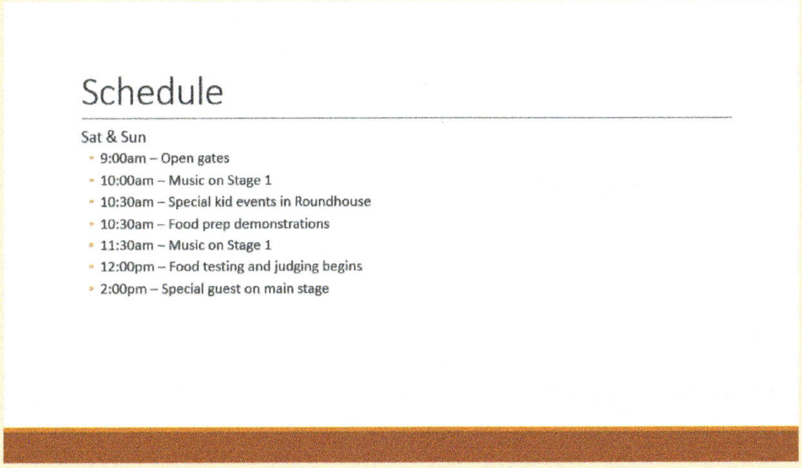

FIGURE 1-23

Visual Workshop

Create the presentation shown in **FIGURE 1-24** and **FIGURE 1-25**. Make sure you include your name on the title slide. Save the presentation as **PPT 1-Neptune** to the location where you store your Data Files. Print the slides.

FIGURE 1-24

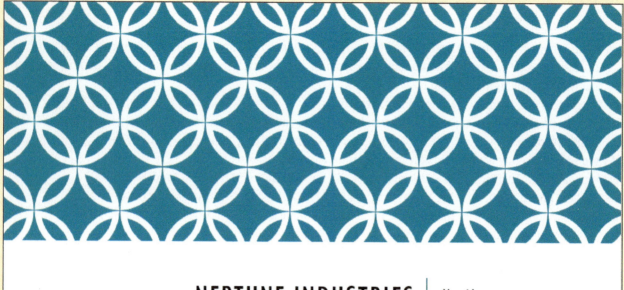

NEPTUNE INDUSTRIES

Your Name
Senior Project Manager

FIGURE 1-25

PRODUCT OVERVIEW

Product designation: Genford XDS-2000
- Turf reduction device
- Primary guidance system: global positioning system

Systems tested
- Integrated on-board computer system
- Engine and hydraulics
- Turf reduction components
- Obstacle detection system

Modifying a Presentation

CASE You continue working on your Kenya Africa projects presentation. In this module, you'll enter text using Outline view, then you'll format text, create a SmartArt graphic, draw and modify objects, and add slide footer information in the presentation.

Module Objectives

After completing this module, you will be able to:

- Enter text in Outline view
- Format text
- Convert text to SmartArt
- Insert and modify shapes
- Rearrange and merge shapes
- Edit and duplicate shapes
- Align and group objects
- Add slide footers

Files You Will Need

PPT 2-1.pptx   PPT 2-4.pptx

PPT 2-2.pptx   PPT 2-5.pptx

PPT 2-3.pptx

Enter Text in Outline View

You can enter presentation text by typing directly on the slide in the Slide pane, or, if you need to focus on the text of the presentation, you can enter text in Outline view. Text in Outline view is organized so the headings, or slide titles, appear at the top of the outline. Each subpoint, or each line of bulleted text, appears as one or more indented lines under the title. Each indent in the outline creates another level of bulleted text on the slide. **CASE** ▶ *You switch to Outline view to enter text for two more slides for your presentation.*

STEPS

1. **Start PowerPoint, open the presentation PPT 2-1.pptx from the location where you store your Data Files, then save it as PPT 2-R2G.pptx**

   A presentation with the new name appears in the PowerPoint window.

2. **Click the Slide 2 thumbnail in the Slides tab, click the New Slide button list arrow in the Slides group, then click Title and Content**

   A new slide, Slide 3, with the Title and Content layout appears as the current slide below Slide 2.

3. **Click the View tab on the Ribbon, then click the Outline View button in the Presentation Views group**

   The text of the presentation appears in the Outline pane next to the Slide pane. The slide icon and the insertion point for Slide 3 are highlighted, indicating it is selected and ready to accept text. Text that you enter next to a slide icon becomes the title for that slide.

4. **Type Water: The Strategic Commodity, press [Enter], then press [Tab]**

   When you pressed [Enter] after typing the slide title, you created a new slide. However, because you want to enter bulleted text on Slide 3, you then pressed [Tab] so the text you type will be entered as bullet text on Slide 3. See **FIGURE 2-1**.

5. **Type Economic efficiency, press [Enter], type Social fairness, press [Enter], type Sustainability, press [Enter], type Population demands, then press [Enter]**

   Each time you press [Enter], the insertion point moves down one line.

6. **Press [Shift][Tab]**

   Because you are working in Outline view, a new slide with the same layout, Slide 4, is created when you press [Shift][Tab].

7. **Type Water: Developmental Essentials, press [Ctrl][Enter], type Household water safety, press [Enter], type Catchment area, press [Enter], type Water quality, press [Enter], then type Conflict resolution**

   Pressing [Ctrl][Enter] while the insertion point is in the title text object moves the cursor into the content placeholder.

8. **Position the pointer on the Slide 3 icon ▢ in the Outline pane**

   The pointer changes to ✥. The Water: The Strategic Commodity slide, Slide 3, is out of order.

9. **Drag ▢ down until a horizontal indicator line appears above the Slide 5 icon, then release the mouse button**

   The third slide moves down and switches places with the fourth slide, as shown in **FIGURE 2-2**.

10. **Click the Normal button ▣ on the status bar, then save your work**

    The Outline pane closes, and the Slides tab is now visible in the window.

FIGURE 2-1: Outline view showing new slide

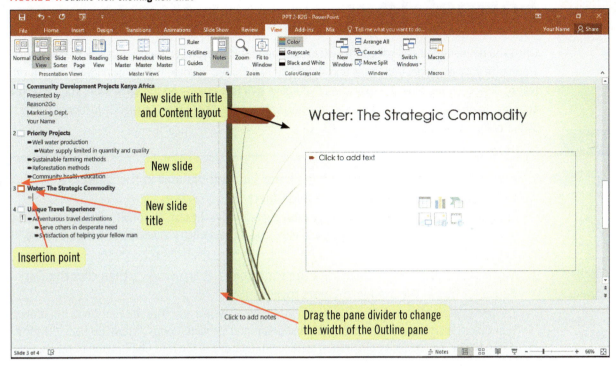

FIGURE 2-2: Outline view showing moved slide

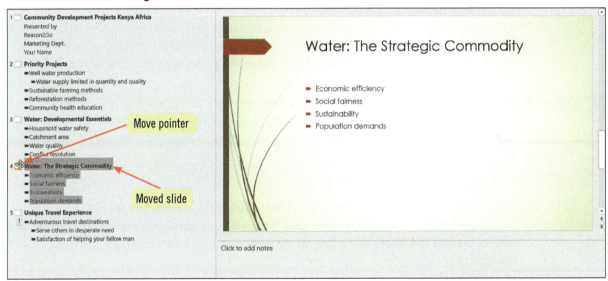

Using proofing tools for other languages

If you have a presentation in another language, how would you check the spelling and grammar of that presentation? Every version of PowerPoint contains a language pack with a primary language, such as English, Italian, or Arabic. Each language pack includes additional languages other than the primary language. For example, the English language pack also includes French and Spanish. So, let's say you have an English version of PowerPoint and you want to check the spelling of a presentation that is written in French. To check the spelling of a French presentation, click a text object on a slide, click the Review tab on the Ribbon, click the Language button in the Language group, then click Set Proofing Language to open the Language dialog box. Click one of the French options from the list, then click OK. Only languages in the list with a spelling symbol are available to use for checking spelling and grammar. Now when you check the spelling, PowerPoint will do so in French. If your version of PowerPoint does not have the language you want to use, you can purchase additional language packs from Microsoft.

Format Text

Once you have entered and edited the text in your presentation, you can modify the way the text looks to emphasize your message. Important text should be highlighted in some way to distinguish it from other text or objects on the slide. For example, if you have two text objects on the same slide, you could draw attention to one text object by changing its color, font, or size. **CASE** *You decide to format the text on Slide 5 of the presentation.*

STEPS

1. **Click the Home tab on the Ribbon, click the Slide 5 thumbnail in the Slides tab, then double-click Travel in the title text object**

   The word "Travel" is selected, and a Mini toolbar appears above the text. The **Mini toolbar** contains basic text-formatting commands, such as bold and italic, and appears when you select text using the mouse. This toolbar makes it quick and easy to format text, especially when the Home tab is closed.

2. **Move ⬚ over the Mini toolbar, click the Font Color list arrow A⁻, then click the Dark Red color box in the Standard Colors row**

   The text changes color to dark red, as shown in **FIGURE 2-3**. When you click the Font Color list arrow, the Font Color gallery appears showing the Theme Colors and Standard Colors. ScreenTips help identify font colors. Notice that the Font Color button on the Mini toolbar and the Font Color button in the Font group on the Home tab change color to reflect the new color choice, which is now the active color.

3. **Move the pointer over the title text object border until the pointer changes to ⬚, then click the border**

   The border changes from a dashed to a solid line as you move the pointer over the text object border. The entire title text object is selected, and changes you make now affect all of the text in the text object. When the whole text object is selected, you can change its size, shape, and other attributes. Changing the color of the text helps emphasize it.

4. **Click the Font Color button A⁻ in the Font group**

   All of the text in the title text object changes to the current active color, dark red.

5. **Click the Font list arrow in the Font group**

   A list of available fonts opens with Century Gothic, the current font used in the title text object, selected at the top of the list in the Theme Fonts section.

6. **Scroll down the alphabetical list, then click Goudy Old Style in the All Fonts section**

   The Goudy Old Style font replaces the original font in the title text object. Notice that as you move the pointer over the font names in the font list the selected text on the slide displays a Live Preview of the available fonts.

7. **Click the Underline button U in the Font group, then click the Increase Font Size button A˄ in the Font group**

   All of the text now displays an underline and increases in size to 40.

8. **Click the Character Spacing button AV⁻ in the Font group, then click Tight**

   The spacing between the letters in the title decreases. Compare your screen to **FIGURE 2-4**.

9. **Click a blank area of the slide outside the text object to deselect it, then save your work**

   Clicking a blank area of the slide deselects all objects that are selected.

FIGURE 2-3: Selected word with Mini toolbar open

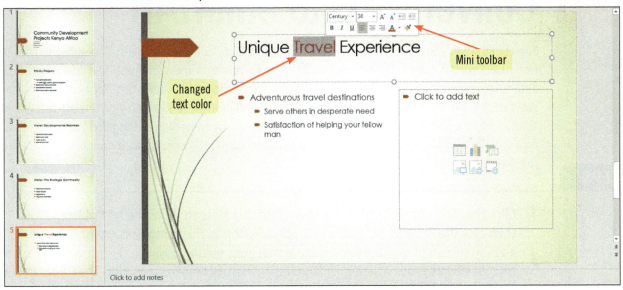

FIGURE 2-4: Formatted text

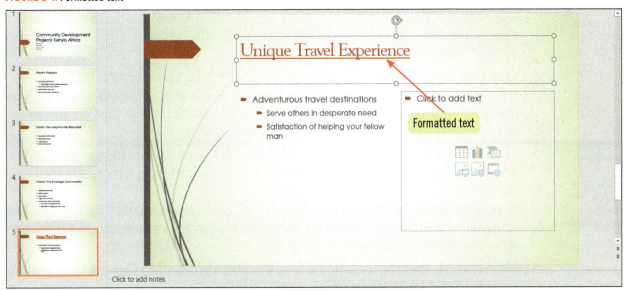

Replacing text and fonts

As you review your presentation, you may decide to replace certain text or fonts throughout the entire presentation using the Replace command. Text can be a word, phrase, or sentence. To replace specific text, click the Home tab on the Ribbon, then click the Replace button in the Editing group. In the Replace dialog box, enter the text you want to replace, then enter the text you want to use as its replacement. You can also use the Replace command to replace one font for another. Simply click the Replace button list arrow in the Editing group, then click Replace Fonts to open the Replace Font dialog box.

Convert Text to SmartArt

Learning Outcomes
• Create a SmartArt graphic
• Modify the SmartArt design

Sometimes when you are working with text it just doesn't capture your attention. The ability to convert text to a SmartArt graphic provides a creative way to convey a message using text and graphics. A **SmartArt** graphic is a professional-quality diagram that graphically illustrates text. For example, you can show steps in a process or timeline, show proportional relationships, or show how parts relate to a whole. You can create a SmartArt graphic from scratch or create one by converting existing text you have entered on a slide. **CASE** ▸ *You want the presentation to appear visually dynamic, so you convert the text on Slide 3 to a SmartArt graphic.*

STEPS

1. **Click the Slide 3 thumbnail in the Slides tab, click Household in the text object, then click the Convert to SmartArt Graphic button in the Paragraph group**

   A gallery of SmartArt graphic layouts opens. As with many features in PowerPoint, you can preview how your text will look prior to applying the SmartArt graphic layout by using PowerPoint's Live Preview feature. You can review each SmartArt graphic layout and see how it changes the appearance of the text.

2. **Move ⥮ over the SmartArt graphic layouts in the gallery**

   Notice how the text becomes part of the graphic and the color and font changes each time you move the pointer over a different graphic layout. SmartArt graphic names appear in ScreenTips.

   TROUBLE
   If the Text pane is not open as shown in Figure 2-5, click the Text pane control on the SmartArt graphic.

3. **Click the Basic Process layout in the SmartArt graphics gallery**

   A SmartArt graphic appears on the slide in place of the text object, and the SmartArt Tools Design tab opens on the Ribbon, as shown in **FIGURE 2-5**. A SmartArt graphic consists of two parts: the SmartArt graphic and a Text pane where you type and edit text. This graphic also has placeholders where you can add pictures to the SmartArt graphic.

4. **Click each bullet point in the Text pane, then click the Text pane control button ▷**

   Notice that each time you select a bullet point in the text pane, a selection box appears around the text objects in the SmartArt graphic. The Text pane control opens and closes the Text pane. You can also open and close the Text pane using the Text Pane button in the Create Graphic group.

   QUICK TIP
   Text objects in the SmartArt graphic can be moved and edited like any other text object in PowerPoint.

5. **Click the More button ⯆ in the Layouts group, click More Layouts to open the Choose a SmartArt Graphic dialog box, click Matrix, click the Basic Matrix layout icon, then click OK**

   The SmartArt graphic changes to the new graphic layout. You can change how the SmartArt graphic looks by applying a SmartArt Style. A **SmartArt Style** is a preset combination of simple and 3-D formatting options that follows the presentation theme.

6. **Move ⥮ slowly over the styles in the SmartArt Styles group, then click the More button ⯆ in the SmartArt Styles group**

   A Live Preview of each style is displayed on the SmartArt graphic. The SmartArt styles are organized into sections; the top group offers suggestions for the best match for the document, and the bottom group shows you all of the possible 3-D styles that are available.

   QUICK TIP
   Click the Convert button in the Reset group, then click Convert to Text to revert the SmartArt graphic to a standard text object.

7. **Move ⥮ over the styles in the gallery, click Intense Effect in the Best Match for Document section, then click in a blank area of the slide outside the SmartArt graphic**

   Notice how this new style adds a shadow to each object to achieve a dimensional effect. Compare your screen to **FIGURE 2-6**.

8. **Click the Slide 4 thumbnail in the Slides tab, then save your work**

   Slide 4 appears in the Slide pane.

FIGURE 2-5: Text converted to a SmartArt graphic

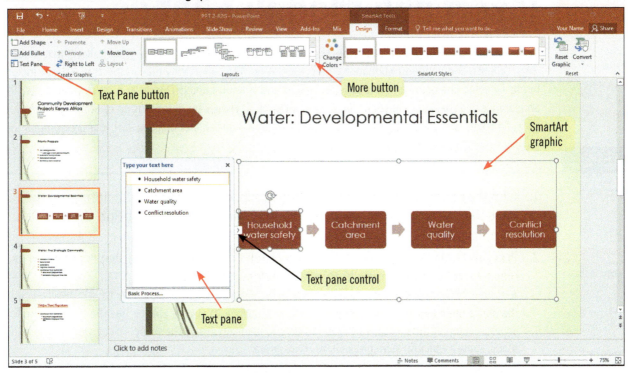

FIGURE 2-5: Text converted to a SmartArt graphic

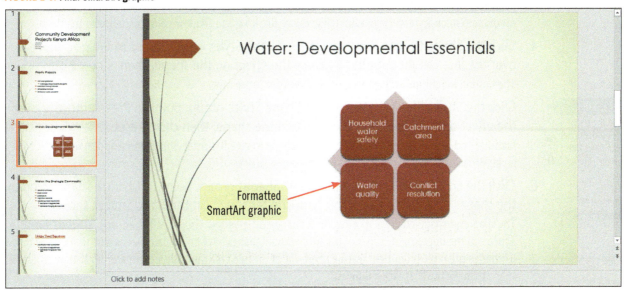

FIGURE 2-6: Final SmartArt graphic

Choosing SmartArt graphics

When choosing a SmartArt graphic to use on your slide, remember that you want the SmartArt graphic to communicate the message of the text effectively; not every SmartArt graphic layout achieves that goal. You must consider the type of text you want to illustrate. For example, does the text show steps in a process, does it show a continual process, or does it show nonsequential information? The answer to this question will dictate the type of SmartArt graphic layout you should choose. Also, the amount of text you want to illustrate will have an effect on the SmartArt graphic layout you choose. Most of the time key points will be the text you use in a SmartArt graphic. Finally, some SmartArt graphic layouts are limited by the number of shapes they can accommodate, so be sure to choose a graphic layout that can illustrate your text appropriately. Experiment with the SmartArt graphic layouts until you find the right one, and have fun in the process!

Insert and Modify Shapes

Learning Outcomes
- Create a shape
- Modify a shape's style

In PowerPoint you can insert many different types of shapes including lines, geometric figures, arrows, stars, callouts, and banners to enhance your presentation. You can modify many aspects of a shape including its fill color, line color, and line style, as well as add shadows and 3-D effects. A quick way to alter the appearance of a shape is to apply a Quick Style. A **Quick Style** is a set of formatting options, including line style, fill color, and effects. **CASE** *You decide to draw some shapes on Slide 4 of your presentation that identify strategies for increasing water supply.*

STEPS

1. **Click the More button ▾ in the Drawing group, click the Diamond button ◇ in the Basic Shapes section, then position ╂ in the blank area of Slide 4 below the slide title**
   ScreenTips help you identify the shapes.

TROUBLE
If your shape is not approximately the same size as the one shown in Figure 2-7, press [Shift], then drag one of the corner sizing handles to resize the object.

2. **Press and hold [Shift], drag ╂ down and to the right to create the shape, as shown in FIGURE 2-7, release the mouse button, then release [Shift]**
   A diamond shape appears on the slide, filled with the default theme color. Pressing [Shift] while you create the object maintains the object proportions as you change its size. A **rotate handle**—circular arrow—appears on top of the shape, which you can drag to manually rotate the shape. To change the style of the shape, apply a Quick Style from the Shape Styles group.

3. **Click the Drawing Tools Format tab on the Ribbon, click the ▾ in the Shape Styles group, move ⇖ over the styles in the gallery to review the effects on the shape, then click Moderate Effect - Orange, Accent 2**
   An orange Quick Style with coordinated gradient fill, line, and shadow color is applied to the shape.

4. **Click the Shape Outline list arrow in the Shape Styles group, point to Weight, move ⇖ over the line weight options to review the effect on the shape, then click 4½ pt**
   The outline weight (or width) increases and is easier to see now.

QUICK TIP
To change the transparency of a shape or text object filled with a color, right-click the object, click Format Shape, click Fill, then move the Transparency slider.

5. **Click the Shape Effects button in the Shape Styles group, point to Preset, move ⇖ over the effect options to review the effect on the shape, then click Preset 7**
   Lighting and shadow effects are added to the shape to give it a three-dimensional appearance. It is easy to change the shape to any other shape in the shapes gallery.

6. **Click the Edit Shape button in the Insert Shapes group, point to Change Shape to open the shapes gallery, then click the Teardrop button ◯ in the Basic Shapes section**
   The diamond shape changes to a teardrop shape and a yellow circle—called an **adjustment handle**—appears in the upper-right corner of the shape. Some shapes have an adjustment handle that can be moved to change the most prominent feature of an object, in this case the end of the teardrop. You can rotate the shape to make the shape look different.

7. **Click the Rotate button in the Arrange group, move ⇖ over the rotation options to review the effect on the shape, then click Flip Horizontal**
   Notice that the adjustment handle is now on the top left of the shape, indicating that the shape has flipped horizontally, or rotated 180 degrees, as shown in FIGURE 2-8. You prefer the diamond shape, and you decide the shape looks better rotated back the way it was before.

8. **Click the Undo button list arrow ↺▾ in the Quick Access Toolbar, click Change Shape, click a blank area of the slide, then save your work**
   The last two commands you performed are undone, and the shape changes back to a diamond and is flipped back to its original position. Clicking a blank area of the slide deselects all selected objects.

FIGURE 2-7: Diamond shape added to slide

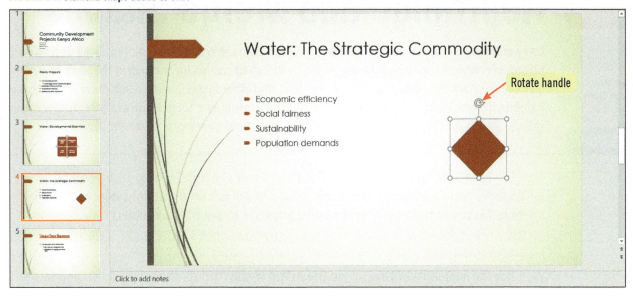

FIGURE 2-8: Rotated teardrop shape

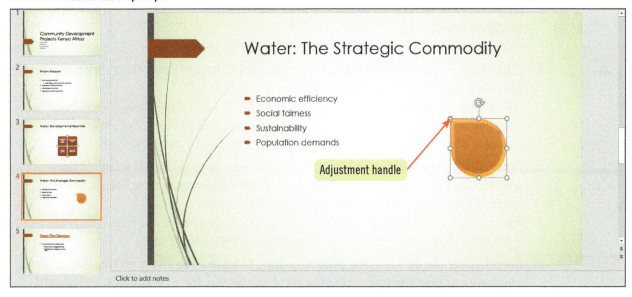

Using the Eyedropper to match colors

As you develop your presentation and work with different shapes and pictures, sometimes from other sources, there may be a certain color that is not in the theme colors of the presentation that you want to capture and apply to objects in your presentation. To capture a color on a specific slide, select any object on the slide, click any button list arrow with a color feature, such as the Shape Fill button or the Shape Outline button on the Drawing Tools Format tab, then click Eyedropper. Move the over the

color you want to capture and pause, or hover. As you hover over a color, a Live Preview of the color appears and the RGB (Red Green Blue) values, called coordinates, appear in a ScreenTip. Click when you see the color you want to capture. The new color now appears in any color gallery under Recent Colors. If you decide not to capture a new color, press [Esc] to close the Eyedropper without making any change.

Rearrange and Merge Shapes

Every object on a slide is placed, or stacked, on the slide in the order it was created, like a deck of cards placed one on top of another. Each object on a slide can be moved up or down in the stack depending on how you want the objects to look on the slide. **Merging** shapes, which combines multiple shapes together, provides you the potential to create unique geometric shapes not available in the Shapes gallery. **CASE** *You create a rectangle shape on Slide 4 and then merge it with the diamond shape.*

STEPS

1. **Click Economic in the text object, position ⌖ over the right-middle sizing handle, ⌖ changes to ⟷, then drag the sizing handle to the left until the right border of the text object is under the middle of the word Strategic in the title text object**

   The width of the text object decreases. When you position ⌖ over a sizing handle, it changes to ⟷. This pointer points in different directions depending on which sizing handle it is over.

2. **Click the Rectangle button ▭ in the Insert Shapes group, then drag down and to the right to create the shape**

   Compare your screen to **FIGURE 2-9**. A rectangle shape appears on the slide, filled with the default theme color. You can move shapes by dragging them on the slide.

TROUBLE
If Smart Guides do not appear, right-click a blank area of the slide, point to Grid and Guides, then click Smart Guides.

3. **Drag the rectangle shape over the diamond shape, then use the Smart Guides that appear to position the rectangle shape in the center of the diamond shape where the guides intersect**

   Smart Guides help you position objects relative to each other and determine equal distances between objects.

4. **Click the Select button in the Editing group, click Selection Pane, then click the Send Backward button ▼ in the Selection pane once**

   The Selection pane opens on the right side of the window showing the four objects on the slide and the order they are stacked on the slide. The Send Backward and Bring Forward buttons let you change the stacking order. The rectangle shape moves back one position in the stack behind the diamond shape.

5. **Press [SHIFT], click the diamond shape on the slide, release [SHIFT] to select both shapes, click the Drawing Tools Format tab on the Ribbon, click the Merge Shapes button in the Insert Shapes group, then point to Union**

   The two shapes appear to merge, or combine, together to form one shape. The merged shape assumes the theme and formatting style of the rectangle shape because it was selected first.

QUICK TIP
To move an object to the top of the stack, click the Bring Forward arrow, then click Bring to Front. To move an object to the bottom of the stack, click the Send Backward arrow, then click Send to Back.

6. **Move ⌖ over the other merge shapes options to review the effect on the shape, click a blank area of the slide twice, click the rectangle shape, then click the Bring Forward button in the Arrange group on the Drawing Tools Format tab once**

   Each merge option produces a different result. The rectangle shape moves back to the top of the stack. Now, you want to see what happens when you select the diamond shape first before you merge the two shapes together.

7. **Click the diamond shape, press [SHIFT], click the rectangle shape, release [SHIFT], click the Merge Shapes button in the Insert Shapes group, then point to Union**

   The merged shape adopts the theme and formatting style of the diamond shape.

8. **Point to each of the merge shapes options, then click Subtract**

   The two shapes merge into one shape. This merge option deletes the area of all shapes from the first shape you selected, so in this case the area of the rectangle shape is deleted from the diamond shape. The merged shape is identified as Freeform 5 in the Selection pane. See **FIGURE 2-10**.

9. **Click the Selection Pane button in the Arrange group, click a blank area of the slide, then save your work**

FIGURE 2-9: Rectangle shape added to slide

FIGURE 2-10: New Merged shape

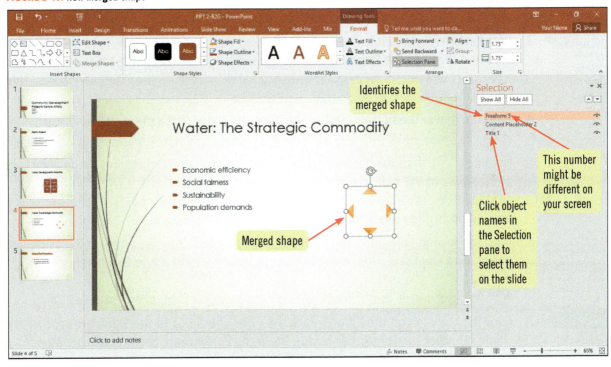

Changing the size and position of shapes

Usually when you resize a shape you can simply drag one of the sizing handles around the outside of the shape, but sometimes you may need to resize a shape more precisely. When you select a shape, the Drawing Tools Format tab appears on the Ribbon, offering you many different formatting options including some sizing commands located in the Size group. The Width and Height commands in the Size group allow you to change the width and height of a shape. You also have the option to open the Format Shape pane, which allows you to change the size of a shape, as well as the rotation, scale, and position of a shape on the slide.

Edit and Duplicate Shapes

Once you have created a shape you still have the ability to refine its basic characteristics, which helps change the size and appearance of the shape. For example, if you create a shape and it is too large, you can reduce its size by dragging any of its sizing handles. Most PowerPoint shapes can have text attached to them. All shapes can be moved and copied. To help you resize and move shapes and other objects precisely, PowerPoint has rulers you can add to the Slide pane. Rulers display the measurement system your computer uses, either inches or metric measurements. **CASE** ▶ *You want three identical diamond shapes on Slide 4. You first add the ruler to the slide to help you change the size of the diamond shape you've already created, and then you make copies of it.*

STEPS

1. **Right-click a blank area of Slide 4, click Ruler on the shortcut menu, then click the bottom part of the diamond shape to select it**

   Rulers appear on the left and top of the Slide pane. Unless the ruler has been changed to metric measurements, it is divided into inches with half-inch and eighth-inch marks. Notice the current location of the ⌖ is identified on both rulers by a small dotted red line in the ruler.

2. **Drag the middle left sizing handle on the diamond shape to the left approximately ½", then release the mouse button**

   The diamond shape is now slightly larger in diameter.

3. **Position ⌖ over the selected diamond shape so that it changes to ⬧, then drag the diamond shape to the Smart Guides on the slide, as shown in FIGURE 2-11**

   PowerPoint uses a series of evenly spaced horizontal and vertical lines—called **gridlines**—to align objects, which force objects to "snap" to the grid.

4. **Position ⬧ over the bottom part of the diamond shape, then press and hold [Ctrl]**

   The pointer changes to ⬧, indicating that PowerPoint makes a copy of the shape when you drag the mouse.

5. **Holding [Ctrl], drag the diamond shape to the right until the diamond shape copy is in a blank area of the slide, release the mouse button, then release [Ctrl]**

   An identical copy of the diamond shape appears on the slide and Smart Guides appear above and below the shape as you drag the new shape to the right, which helps you align shapes.

6. **With the second diamond shape still selected, click the Copy list arrow in the Clipboard group, click Duplicate, then move the duplicated diamond shape to a blank area of the slide**

   You have duplicated the diamond shape twice and now have three identical shapes on the slide.

7. **Click the View tab on the Ribbon, click the Ruler check box in the Show group, click the Home tab, click the Font Color button 🅐 in the Font group, then type Rainwater Harvesting**

   The ruler closes, and the text you type appears in the selected diamond shape and becomes a part of the shape. Now if you move or rotate the shape, the text moves with it. Compare your screen with **FIGURE 2-12**.

8. **Click the left diamond shape, click 🅐, type Salt Removal, click the right diamond shape, click 🅐, type Continuous Water Use, click in a blank area of the slide, then save your work**

   All three diamond shapes include text.

FIGURE 2-11: Merged shape moved on slide

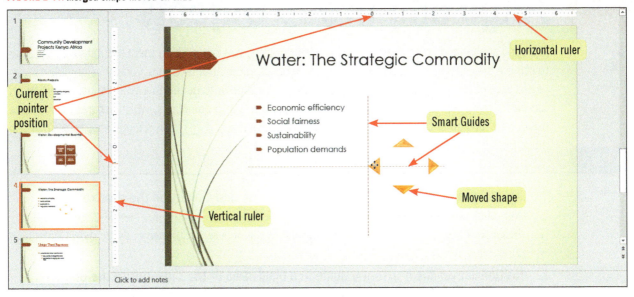

FIGURE 2-12: Duplicated shapes

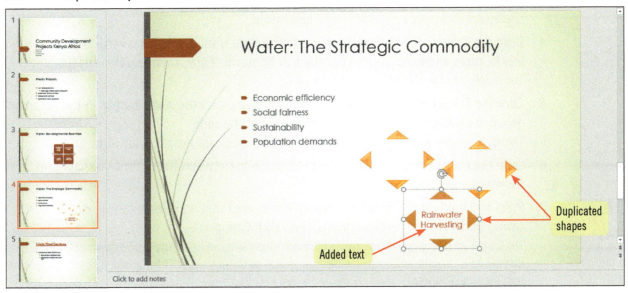

Editing points of a shape

If you want to customize the form (or outline) of any shape in the shapes gallery, you can modify its edit points. To display a shape's edit points, select the shape you want to modify, click the Drawing Tools Format tab on the Ribbon, click the Edit Shape button in the Insert Shapes group, then click Edit Points. Black edit points appear on the shape. To change the form of a shape, drag a black edit point. When you click a black edit point, white square edit points appear on either side of the black edit point, which allow you to change the curvature of a line between two black edit points. When you are finished with your custom shape, you can save it as picture and reuse it in other presentations or other files. To save the shape as a picture, right-click the shape, then click Save as Picture.

Align and Group Objects

Learning Outcomes
• Move shapes using guides
• Align and group shapes

After you are finished creating and modifying your objects, you can position them accurately on the slide to achieve the look you want. Using the Align commands in the Arrange group, you can align objects relative to each other by snapping them to the gridlines on a slide or to guides that you manually position on the slide. The Group command groups two or more objects into one object, which secures their relative position to each other and makes it easy to edit and move them. **CASE** ▶ *You are ready to position and group the diamond shapes on Slide 4 to finish the slide.*

STEPS

1. **Right-click a blank area of the slide, point to Grid and Guides on the shortcut menu, then click Guides**

   The guides appear as dotted lines on the slide and usually intersect at the center of the slide. Guides help you position objects precisely on the slide.

2. **Position ⬚ over the horizontal guide in a blank area of the slide, notice the pointer change to ⬍, press and hold the mouse button until the pointer changes to a measurement guide box, then drag the guide up until the guide position box reads 1.33**

3. **Drag the vertical guide to the left until the guide position box reads .33, then drag the Salt Removal shape so that the top and left edges of the shape touch the guides, as shown in FIGURE 2-13**

   The Salt Removal shape attaches or "snaps" to the guides.

4. **Drag the Continuous Water Use shape to the right until it touches a vertical Smart Guide, press and hold [Shift], click the Salt Removal shape, then release [Shift]**

   Two shapes are now selected.

5. **Click the Drawing Tools Format tab on the Ribbon, click the Align button in the Arrange group, click Align Top, then click a blank area of the slide**

   The right diamond shape moves up and aligns with the other shape along their top edges.

6. **Drag the Rainwater Harvesting diamond shape in between the other two shapes, as shown in FIGURE 2-14**

7. **Press and hold [Shift], click the other two diamond shapes, release [Shift], click the Group button in the Arrange group, then click Group**

   The shapes are now grouped together to form one object without losing their individual attributes. Notice that the sizing handles and rotate handle now appear on the outer edge of the grouped object, not around each individual object.

8. **Drag the horizontal guide to the middle of the slide until its guide position box reads 0.00, then drag the vertical guide to the middle of the slide until its guide position box reads 0.00**

9. **Click the View tab on the Ribbon, click the Guides check box in the Show group, click a blank area of the slide, then save your work**

   The guides are no longer displayed on the slide.

FIGURE 2-13: Repositioned shape

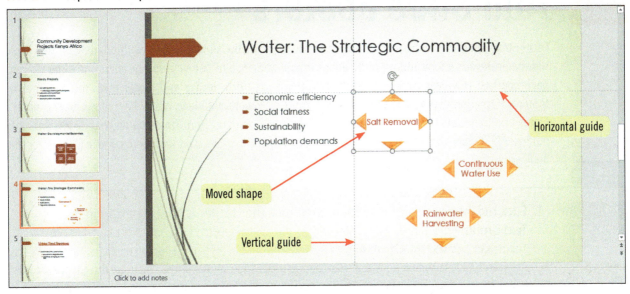

FIGURE 2-14: Repositioned shapes

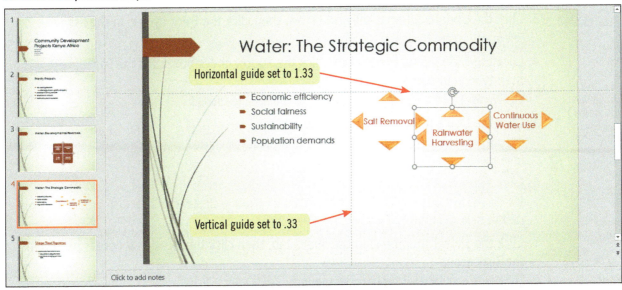

Distributing objects

There are two ways to distribute objects in PowerPoint: relative to each other and relative to the slide edge. If you choose to distribute objects relative to each other, PowerPoint evenly divides the empty space between all of the selected objects. When distributing objects in relation to the slide, PowerPoint evenly splits the empty space from slide edge to slide edge between the selected objects. To distribute objects relative to each other, click the Align button in the Arrange group on the Drawing Tools Format tab, then click Align Selected Objects. To distribute objects relative to the slide, click the Align button in the Arrange group on the Drawing Tools Format tab, then click Align to Slide.

Add Slide Footers

Learning Outcomes
• Add footer text to slides

Footer text, such as a company, school, or product name, the slide number, or the date, can give your slides a professional look and make it easier for your audience to follow your presentation. Slides do not have headers. However, notes or handouts can include both header and footer text. You can review footer information that you apply to the slides in the PowerPoint views and when you print the slides. Notes and handouts header and footer text is visible when you print notes pages, handouts, and the outline. **CASE** *You add footer text to the slides of the Kenya Africa presentation to make it easier for the audience to follow.*

STEPS

QUICK TIP
The placement of the footer text objects on the slide is dependent on the presentation theme.

1. **Click the Insert tab on the Ribbon, then click the Header & Footer button in the Text group**

   The Header and Footer dialog box opens, as shown in **FIGURE 2-15**. The Header and Footer dialog box has two tabs: a Slide tab and a Notes and Handouts tab. The Slide tab is selected. There are three types of footer text, Date and time, Slide number, and Footer. The bold rectangles in the Preview box identify the default position of the three types of footer text placeholders on the slides.

2. **Click the Date and time check box to select it**

   The date and time options are now available to select. The Update automatically date and time option button is selected by default. This option updates the date and time to the date and time set by your computer every time you open or print the file.

QUICK TIP
If you want a specific date to appear every time you view or print the presentation, click the Fixed date option button, then type the date in the Fixed text box.

3. **Click the Update automatically list arrow, then click the third option in the list**

   The month is spelled out in this option.

4. **Click the Slide number check box, click the Footer check box, click the Footer text box, then type your name**

   The Preview box now shows all three footer placeholders are selected.

5. **Click the Don't show on title slide check box**

   Selecting this check box prevents the footer information you entered in the Header and Footer dialog box from appearing on the title slide.

6. **Click Apply to All**

   The dialog box closes, and the footer information is applied to all of the slides in your presentation except the title slide. Compare your screen to **FIGURE 2-16**.

7. **Click the Slide 1 thumbnail in the Slides tab, then click the Header & Footer button in the Text group**

   The Header and Footer dialog box opens again.

8. **Click the Don't show on title slide check box to deselect it, click the Footer check box, then select the text in the Footer text box**

TROUBLE
If you click Apply to All in Step 9, click the Undo button on the Quick Access toolbar and repeat Steps 7, 8, and 9.

9. **Type Striving Toward a Sustainable Future, click Apply, then save your work**

   Only the text in the Footer text box appears on the title slide. Clicking Apply applies this footer information to just the current slide.

10. **Submit your presentation to your instructor, then exit PowerPoint**

FIGURE 2-15: Header and Footer dialog box

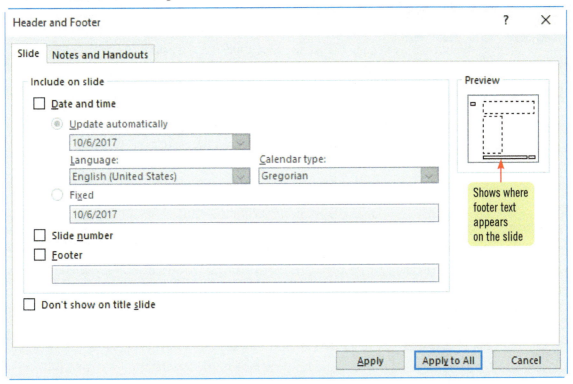

FIGURE 2-16: Footer information added to presentation

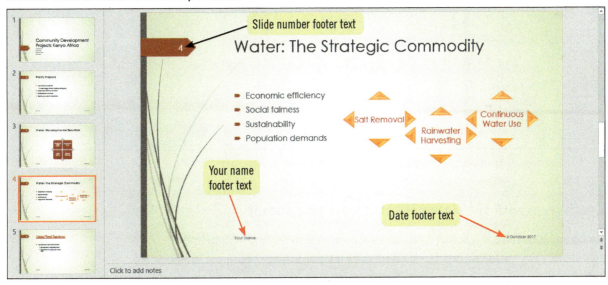

Creating superscript and subscript text

Superscript or subscript text is a number, figure, symbol, or letter that appears smaller than other text and is positioned above or below the normal line of text. A common superscript in the English language is the sign indicator next to number, such as 1st or 3rd. Other examples of superscripts are the trademark symbol™ and the copyright symbol©. To create superscript text in PowerPoint, select the text, number, or symbol, then press [CTRL] [SHIFT] [+] at the same time. Probably the most familiar subscript text are the numerals in chemical compounds and formulas, for example, H_2O and CO_2. To create subscript text, select the text, number, or symbol, then press [CTRL] [=] at the same time. To change superscript or subscript text back to normal text, select the text, then press [CTRL] [Spacebar].

Practice

Concepts Review

Label each element of the PowerPoint window shown in FIGURE 2-17.

FIGURE 2-17

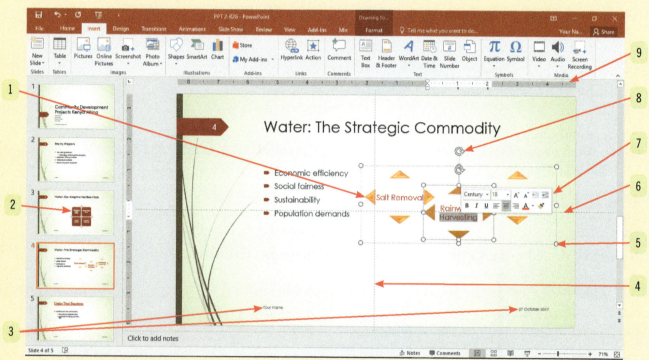

Match each term with the statement that best describes it.

10. **Adjustment handle**
11. **Quick Style**
12. **Rotate handle**
13. **Gridlines**
14. **Merge**
15. **Smart Guides**

a. Evenly spaced horizontal and vertical lines
b. A set of formatting options you apply to an object
c. Combines multiple shapes to create a unique geometric shape
d. Changes the most prominent feature of an object
e. Helps you determine equal distances between objects
f. Drag to turn an object

Select the best answer from the list of choices.

16. **What is *not* true about grouped objects?**
    a. Grouped objects have one rotate handle.
    b. Grouped objects act as one object but maintain their individual attributes.
    c. Sizing handles appear around the grouped object.
    d. Each object is distributed relative to the slide edges.

17. **A professional-quality diagram that visually illustrates text best describes which of the following?**
    a. A SmartArt Style
    b. A merged shape
    c. A subscript
    d. A SmartArt graphic

18. **Which of the following statements is *not* true about Outline view?**
    a. Pressing [Enter] moves the insertion point down one line.
    b. Text you enter next to the slide icon becomes a bullet point for that slide.
    c. Headings are the same as slide titles.
    d. Added slides use the same layout as the previous slide.

19. **What do you have to drag to customize the form or outline of a shape?**
    a. Anchor points
    b. Edit points
    c. Slide edges
    d. Shape area

20. **Why would you use the Eyedropper tool?**
    a. To format an object with a new style
    b. To soften the edges of a shape
    c. To capture and apply a new color to an object
    d. To change the fill color of an object

21. **What appears just above text when it is selected?**
    a. Mini toolbar
    b. QuickStyles
    c. Adjustment handle
    d. AutoFit Options button

22. **Which of the following statements about merged shapes is *not* true?**
    a. Merged shapes can be added to the shapes gallery.
    b. A merged shape assumes the theme of the shape that is selected first.
    c. The stacking order of shapes changes the way a merged shape looks.
    d. A merged shape is a combination of multiple shapes.

Skills Review

FIGURE 2-18

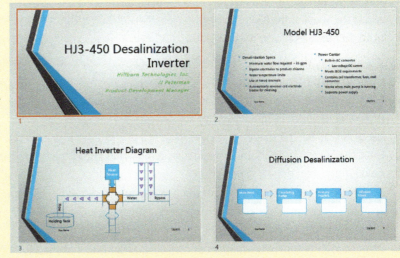

1. **Enter text in Outline view.**
   a. Open the presentation PPT 2-2.pptx from the location where you store your Data Files, then save it as **PPT 2-Inverter**. The completed presentation is shown in **FIGURE 2-18**.
   b. Create a new slide after Slide 2 with the Title and Content layout.
   c. Open Outline view, then type **Diffusion Desalinization**.
   d. Press [Enter], press [Tab], type **Main Feed**, press [Enter], type **Circulating Pump**, press [Enter], type **Primary Heaters**, press [Enter], then type **Diffusion Tower**.

Skills Review (continued)

    e. Move Slide 3 below Slide 4, then switch back to Normal view.

    f. Click the Home tab, then save your changes.

2. Format text.

    a. Go to Slide 1, select the name JJ Peterman, then move the pointer over the Mini Toolbar.

    b. Click the Font Color list arrow, then click Green under Standard Colors.

    c. Select the text object, then change all of the text to the color Green.

    d. Click the Font Size list arrow, click 24, then click the Italic button.

    e. Click the Character Spacing button, click Loose, then save your changes.

3. Convert text to SmartArt.

    a. Click the text object on Slide 4.

    b. Click the Convert to SmartArt Graphic button, then apply the Basic Matrix graphic layout to the text object.

    c. Click the More button in the Layouts group, click More Layouts, click Process in the Choose a SmartArt Graphic dialog box, click Accent Process, then click OK.

    d. Click the More button in the SmartArt Styles group, then apply the Intense Effect style from the Best Match for Document group to the graphic.

    e. Close the text pane if necessary, then click outside the SmartArt graphic in a blank part of the slide.

    f. Save your changes.

4. Insert and modify shapes.

    a. Go to Slide 3, then add rulers to the Slide pane.

    b. Click the More button in the Drawing group to open the Shapes gallery, click the Plus button in the Equation Shapes section, press [Shift], then draw a two-inch shape in a blank area of the slide.

    c. On the Drawing Tools Format tab, click the More button in the Shape Styles group, then click Colored Fill – Orange, Accent 3.

    d. Click the Shape Effects button, point to Shadow, then click Offset Diagonal Bottom Left.

    e. Click the Shape Outline list arrow, then click Black, Text 1, Lighter 15% in the Theme Colors section.

    f. Drag the Plus shape to the small open area in the middle of the diagram, adjust the shape if needed to make it fit in the space as shown in **FIGURE 2-19**, then save your changes.

FIGURE 2-19

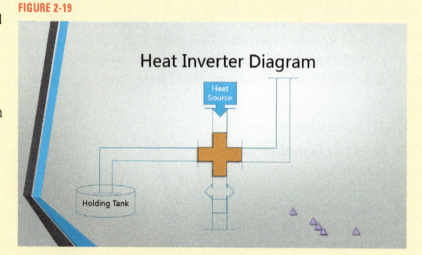

5. Rearrange and merge shapes.

    a. Click the title text object on Slide 3, then drag the bottom-middle sizing handle up above the shapes.

    b. Click the More button in the Insert Shapes group, click the Hexagon button in the Basic Shapes section, press and hold [Shift], then draw a 1-inch shape.

    c. Drag the hexagon shape over top of the plus shape and center it, then open the Selection pane.

    d. Send the hexagon shape back one level, press [Shift], click the plus shape, then click the Merge Shapes button in the Insert Shapes group on the Drawing Tools Format tab.

    e. Point to each of the merge shapes options, click a blank area of the slide twice, then click the plus shape.

Skills Review (continued)

   f. Send the plus shape back one level, press [Shift], click the hexagon shape, click the Merge Shapes button, then click Combine.

   g. Close the Selection pane, then save your work.

6. Edit and duplicate shapes.

   a. Select the up-angled shape to the right of the merged shape, then using [Ctrl] make one copy of the shape.

   b. Use Smart Guides to align the new up-angled shape just to the right of the original shape.

   c. Click the Rotate button in the Arrange group, click Flip Vertical, click the Undo button, click the Rotate button, then click Flip Horizontal.

   d. Type **Bypass**, click the up-angled shape to the right of the merged shape, type **Water**, click the down-angled shape to the left of the merged shape, then type **Flow**.

   e. Click the Heat Source arrow shape above the merged shape, then drag the bottom-middle sizing handle down until the arrow touches the merged shape.

   f. Click a blank area of the slide, add the guides to the Slide pane, then save your changes.

7. Align and group objects.

   a. Move the vertical guide to the left until 3.42 appears, drag a selection box to select the five small purple triangle shapes at the bottom of the slide, then click the Drawing Tools Format tab.

   b. Click the Align button in the Arrange group, click Align Middle, click the Align button, then click Distribute Horizontally.

   c. Click the Rotate button in the Arrange group, click Rotate Left 90º, click the Group button in the Arrange group, then click Group.

   d. Move the grouped triangle shape object to the guide in the blank space on the down-angled shape to the left of the merged shape.

   e. Duplicate the grouped triangle shape object, then rotate the new object to the left 90º.

   f. Duplicate the rotated grouped triangle shape object, then move the two new triangle shape objects on the slide as shown in **FIGURE 2-20**.

   g. Set the guides back to 0.00, remove the guides from your screen, remove the rulers, then save your work.

FIGURE 2-20

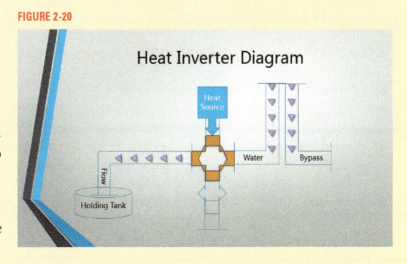

8. Add slide footers.

   a. Open the Header and Footer dialog box.

   b. On the Slide tab, click the Date and time check box to select it, then click the Fixed option button.

   c. Add the slide number to the footer, then type your name in the Footer text box.

   d. Apply the footer to all of the slides except the title slide.

   e. Open the Header and Footer dialog box again, then click the Notes and Handouts tab.

   f. Click the Date and time check box, then type today's date in the Fixed text box.

   g. Type the name of your class in the Header text box, then click the Page number check box.

   h. Type your name in the Footer text box.

   i. Apply the header and footer information to all the notes and handouts, then save your changes.

   j. Submit your presentation to your instructor, close the presentation, then exit PowerPoint.

Independent Challenge 1

You are the director of the Center for the Arts in Rapid City, South Dakota, and one of your many duties is to raise funds to cover operation costs. One of the primary ways you do this is by speaking to businesses, community clubs, and other organizations throughout the region. Every year you speak to many organizations, where you give a short presentation detailing what the theater center plans to do for the coming season. You need to continue working on the presentation you started already.

a. Start PowerPoint, open the presentation PPT 2-3.pptx from the location where you store your Data Files, and save it as **PPT 2-Arts**.

b. Use Outline view to enter the following as bulleted text on the Commitment to Excellence slide:
   Excellence
   Testing
   Study
   Diligence

c. Apply the Ion design theme to the presentation.

d. Change the font color of each play name on Slide 3 to Gold, Accent 3.

e. Change the bulleted text on Slide 5 to the Trapezoid List SmartArt Graphic, then apply the Polished SmartArt style.

f. Add your name and slide number as a footer on the slides, then save your changes.

g. Submit your presentation to your instructor, close your presentation, then exit PowerPoint.

Independent Challenge 2

You are a manager for J Barrett Inc., a financial services company. You have been asked by your boss to develop a presentation outlining important details and aspects of the mortgage process to be used at a financial seminar.

a. Start PowerPoint, open the presentation PPT 2-4.pptx from the location where you store your Data Files, and save it as **PPT 2-Broker**.

b. Apply the Facet design theme to the presentation.

c. On Slide 3, press [Shift], select the three shapes, Banks, Mortgage Bankers, and Private Investors, release [Shift], then using the Align command align them to their left edges.

d. Select the blank shape, type **Borrower**, press [Shift], select the Mortgage Broker and Mortgage Bankers shapes, release [Shift], then using the Align command distribute them horizontally and align them to the middle.

e. Select all of the shapes, then apply Intense Effect – Orange, Accent 4 from the Shape Styles group.

f. Create a diamond shape, then merge it with the Borrower shape as shown in **FIGURE 2-21**. (*Hint*: Use the Fragment Merge option.)

g. Using the Arrow shape from the Shapes gallery, draw a 6-pt arrow between all of the shapes. (*Hint*: Draw one arrow shape, change the line weight using the Shape Outline list arrow, then duplicate the shape.)

h. Group all the shapes together.

i. Add the page number and your name as a footer on the notes and handouts, then save your changes.

j. Submit your presentation to your instructor, close your presentation, then exit PowerPoint.

FIGURE 2-21

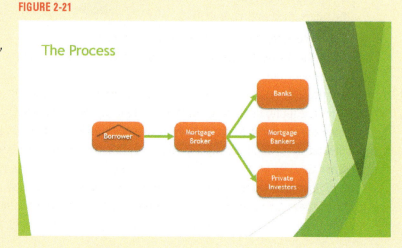

Independent Challenge 3

You are an independent distributor of natural foods in Birmingham, Alabama. Your business, Southern Whole Foods, has grown progressively since its inception 5 years ago, but sales have leveled off over the last 9 months. In an effort to increase your market share, you decide to purchase J&R Foods, a natural food dealer, which would allow your company to expand into surrounding states. Use PowerPoint to develop a presentation you can use to gain a financial backer for the acquisition. Create your own information for the presentation.

a. Start PowerPoint, create a new presentation, then apply the Wood Type design theme to the presentation.

b. Type **A Plan for Growth** as the main title on the title slide, and **Southern Whole Foods** as the subtitle.

c. Save the presentation as **PPT 2-Southern** to the location where you store your Data Files.

d. Add five more slides with the following titles: Slide 2, **Trends**; Slide 3, **Growth**; Slide 4, **Funding**; Slide 5, **History**; Slide 6, **Management Team**.

e. Enter appropriate text into the text placeholders of the slides. Use both the Slide pane and Outline view to enter text.

f. Convert text on one slide to a SmartArt graphic, then apply the SmartArt graphic style Inset Effect.

g. Create two shapes, format the shapes, then merge the shapes together.

h. View the presentation as a slide show, then view the slides in Slide Sorter view.

i. Add the slide number and your name as a footer on the slides, then save your changes.

j. Submit your presentation to your instructor, close your presentation, then exit PowerPoint.

Independent Challenge 4: Explore

Your computer instructor at Basset City College has been asked by the department head to convert her Computer Basics 101 course into an accelerated night course designed for adult students. Your instructor has asked you to help her create a presentation for the class that she can post on the Internet. Most of the basic text information is already on the slides, you primarily need to add a theme and other object formatting.

a. Start PowerPoint, open the presentation PPT 2-5.pptx from the location where you store your Data Files, and save it as **PPT 2-Basset**.

b. Add a new slide after the Course Facts slide with the same layout, type **Course Details** in the title text placeholder, then enter the following as bulleted text in Outline view:
Information systems
Networking
Applied methods
Technology solutions
Software design
Applications

c. Apply the Retrospect design theme to the presentation.

d. Select the title text object on Slide 1 (*Hint*: Press [Shift] to select the whole object), then change the text color to Orange.

e. Change the font of the title text object to Biondi, then decrease the font size to 48.

f. Click the subtitle text object on Slide 1, then change the character spacing to Very Loose.

g. Change the text on Slide 4 to a SmartArt graphic. Use an appropriate diagram type for a list.

h. Change the style of the SmartArt diagram using one of the SmartArt Styles, then view the presentation in Slide Show view.

i. Add the slide number and your name as a footer on the notes and handouts, then save your changes.

j. Submit your presentation to your instructor, close your presentation, then exit PowerPoint.

Visual Workshop

Create the presentation shown in **FIGURE 2-22** and **FIGURE 2-23**. Add today's date as the date on the title slide. Save the presentation as **PPT 2-Nebraska Trade** to the location where you store your Data Files. (*Hint*: The SmartArt style used for the SmartArt is a 3D style.) Review your slides in Slide Show view, then add your name as a footer to the notes and handouts. Submit your presentation to your instructor, save your changes, close the presentation, then exit PowerPoint.

FIGURE 2-22

FIGURE 2-23

Inserting Objects into a Presentation

CASE ▶ In this module, you continue working on the presentation by inserting text from Microsoft Word. You also add visual elements into the presentation including a photograph, a table, and a chart. You format these objects using PowerPoint's powerful object-editing features.

Module Objectives

After completing this module, you will be able to:

- Insert text from Microsoft Word
- Insert and style a picture
- Insert a text box
- Insert a chart

- Enter and edit chart data
- Insert slides from other presentations
- Insert a table
- Insert and format WordArt

Files You Will Need

PPT 3-1.pptx	PPT 3-10.pptx
PPT 3-2.docx	PPT 3-11.pptx
PPT 3-3.jpg	PPT 3-12.jpg
PPT 3-4.pptx	PPT 3-13.pptx
PPT 3-5.pptx	PPT 3-14.docx
PPT 3-6.docx	PPT 3-15.jpg
PPT 3-7.jpg	PPT 3-16.jpg
PPT 3-8.pptx	PPT 3-17.jpg
PPT 3-9.pptx	PPT 3-18.jpg

Insert Text from Microsoft Word

Learning Outcomes
- Create slides using Outline view
- Move and delete slides

It is easy to insert documents saved in Microsoft Word format (.docx), Rich Text Format (.rtf), plain text format (.txt), and HTML format (.htm) into a PowerPoint presentation. If you have an outline saved in a document file, you can import it into PowerPoint to create a new presentation or create additional slides in an existing presentation. When you import a document into a presentation, PowerPoint creates an outline structure based on the styles in the document. For example, a Heading 1 style in the Word document becomes a slide title and a Heading 2 style becomes the first level of text in a bulleted list. If you insert a plain text format document into a presentation, PowerPoint creates an outline based on the tabs at the beginning of the document's paragraphs. Paragraphs without tabs become slide titles, and paragraphs with one tab indent become first-level text in bulleted lists. **CASE** *You have a Microsoft Word document with information about the new Kenyan well project tour that you want to insert into your presentation.*

STEPS

QUICK TIP
While in Normal view you can click the Normal button in the status bar to go to Outline view.

1. **Start PowerPoint, open the presentation PPT 3-1.pptx from the location where you store your Data Files, save it as PPT 3-R2G, click the View tab on the Ribbon, then click the Outline View button in the Presentation Views group**

2. **Click the Slide 6 icon ▭ in the Outline pane, click the Home tab on the Ribbon, click the New Slide button list arrow in the Slides group, then click Slides from Outline**

   Slide 6 appears in the Slide pane. The Insert Outline dialog box opens. Before you insert an outline into a presentation, you need to determine where you want the new slides to be placed. You want the text from the Word document inserted as new slides after Slide 6.

3. **Navigate to the location where you store your Data Files, click the Word document file PPT 3-2.docx, then click Insert**

   Six new slides (7, 8, 9, 10, 11, and 12) are added to the presentation, and the new Slide 7 appears in the Slide pane. See **FIGURE 3-1**.

4. **Click the down scroll arrow ▾ in the Outline pane and read the text for all the new slides, then click the Normal button ▣ on the status bar**

   The information on Slides 7 and 12 refer to information not needed for this presentation.

5. **Click the Slide 7 thumbnail in the Slides tab, press [Ctrl], click the Slide 12 thumbnail, then click the Cut button in the Clipboard group**

   Slides 7 and 12 are deleted, and the next slide down (Suggested Itinerary) becomes the new Slide 10 and appears in the Slide pane.

6. **Drag the Slide 10 thumbnail in the Slides tab above Slide 8**

   Slide 10 becomes Slide 8. The inserted slides have a different slide layout and font style than the other slides. You want the text of the inserted outline to adopt the theme fonts of the presentation.

QUICK TIP
You can also use Slide Sorter view to move slides around in the presentation.

7. **Click the Slide 7 thumbnail in the Slides tab, press [Shift], click the Slide 10 thumbnail, release [Shift], click the Reset button in the Slides group, click the Layout button in the Slides group, then click the Title and Content slide layout**

   The new slides now follow the presentation design and font themes. Compare your screen to **FIGURE 3-2**.

8. **Click the Save button 🖫 on the Quick Access toolbar**

FIGURE 3-1: Outline pane showing imported text

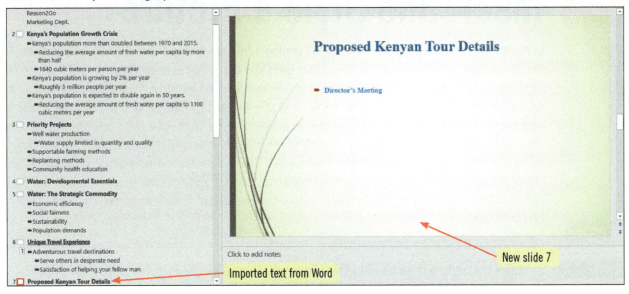

FIGURE 3-2: Slides reset to Wisp theme default settings

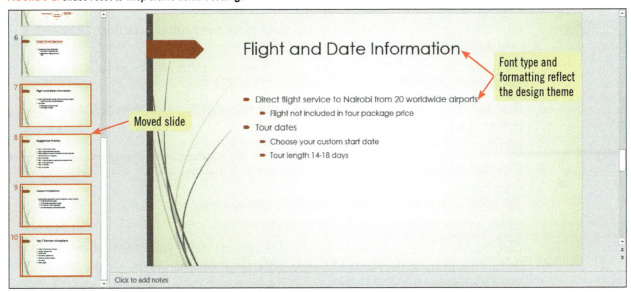

Insert and Style a Picture

In PowerPoint, a **picture** is defined as a digital photograph, a piece of line art or clip art, or other artwork that is created in another program. PowerPoint gives you the ability to insert different types of pictures including JPEG File Interchange Format and BMP Windows Bitmap files into a PowerPoint presentation. As with all objects in PowerPoint, you can format and style inserted pictures to help them fit the theme of your presentation. You can also hide a portion of the picture you don't want to be seen by **cropping** it. The cropped portion of a picture is still available to you if you ever want to show that part of picture again. To reduce the size of the file you can permanently delete the cropped portion by applying picture compression settings in the Compress Pictures dialog box. **CASE** ▶ *In this lesson you insert a JPG file picture taken by an R2G staff member that is saved on your computer. Once inserted, you crop and style it to best fit the slide.*

STEPS

1. **Click the Slide 6 thumbnail in the Slides tab, then click the Pictures icon 🖼 in the content placeholder on the slide**

   The Insert Picture dialog box opens displaying the pictures available in the default Pictures folder.

2. **Navigate to location where you store your Data Files, select the picture file PPT 3-3.jpg, then click Insert**

   The picture fills the content placeholder on the slide, and the Picture Tools Format tab opens on the Ribbon. The picture would look better if you cropped some of the image.

3. **Click the Crop button in the Size group, then place the pointer over the middle-left cropping handle on the picture**

   The pointer changes to ⌐. When the Crop button is active, cropping handles appear next to the sizing handles on the selected object.

4. **Drag the middle of the picture to the right as shown in FIGURE 3-3, release the mouse button, then press [Esc]**

   The picture would look better on the slide if it were larger.

5. **Click the number (3.08) in the Width text box in the Size group to select it, type 4, then press [Enter]**

   The picture height and width increase proportionally. PowerPoint has a number of picture formatting options, and you decide to experiment with some of them.

6. **Click the More button ▼ in the Picture Styles group, move your pointer over the style thumbnails in the gallery to see how the different styles change the picture, then click Bevel Rectangle (3rd row)**

   The picture now has rounded corners and a background shadow.

7. **Click the Corrections button in the Adjust group, move your pointer over the thumbnails to see how the picture changes, then click Sharpen: 25% in the Sharpen/Soften section**

   The picture clarity is better.

8. **Click the Artistic Effects button in the Adjust group, move your pointer over the thumbnails to see how the picture changes, then click a blank area of the slide**

   The artistic effects are all interesting, but none of them will work well for this picture.

9. **Drag the picture to the center of the blank area of the slide to the right of the text object, click a blank area on the slide, then save your changes**

   Compare your screen to **FIGURE 3-4**.

FIGURE 3-3: Using the cropping pointer to crop a picture

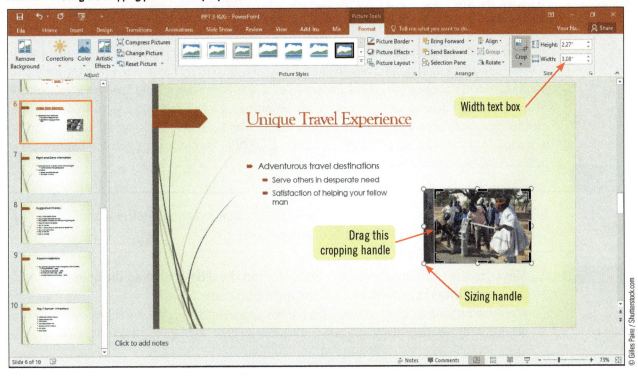

FIGURE 3-4: Cropped and styled picture

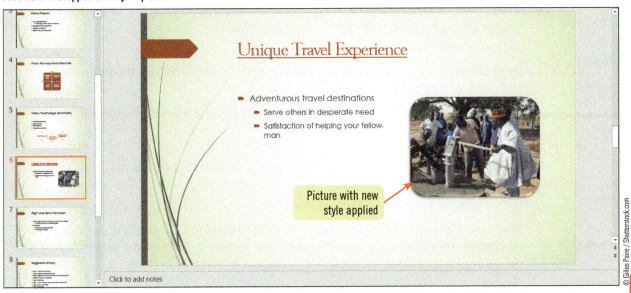

Inserting a screen recording

Using the Screen Recording button in the Media group on the Insert tab, you can record your computer screen with audio and insert the recording to a slide. For example, if you want to make a recording of an Internet video, locate and display the video on your computer screen. In PowerPoint on the slide where you want to insert the recording, click the Screen Recording button.

On the toolbar, click the Select Area button, drag a selection box around the video, click the Audio button if necessary, then click the Record button on the toolbar. Click the video play button. When finished recording, click Windows Logo+[Shift]+Q to stop recording. PowerPoint opens and the recording appears on your slide. Click the Play button to review your recording.

Insert a Text Box

As you've already learned, you enter text on a slide using a title or content placeholder that is arranged on the slide based on a slide layout. Every so often you need additional text on a slide where the traditional placeholder does not place text. There are two types of text boxes: a text label, used for a small phrase where text doesn't automatically wrap inside the boundaries of a text box, and a word-processing box, used for a sentence or paragraph where the text wraps inside a text box. Either type of text box can be formatted and edited just like any other text object. **CASE** *You decide to create a text box next to the picture on Slide 6 and then edit and format the text.*

STEPS

1. **Click the Slide 6 thumbnail in the Slides tab, click the Insert tab on the Ribbon, then click the Text Box button in the Text group**

   The pointer changes to ↓.

2. **Move ↓ to the blank area below the text object on the slide, then drag the pointer + down and toward the right about 3" to create a text box**

   When you begin dragging, an outline of the text box appears, indicating the size of the text box you are drawing. After you release the mouse button, a blinking insertion point appears inside the text box, in this case a word-processing box, indicating that you can enter text.

3. **Type Village chief in March 2017 inaugurates new hand pump**

   Notice the text box increases in size as your text wraps to additional lines inside the text box. Your screen should look similar to **FIGURE 3-5**. After entering the text, you decide to edit the sentence.

4. **Drag I over the phrase in March 2017 to select it, position ⬚ on top of the selected phrase, then press and hold the left mouse button**

   The pointer changes to ⬚.

5. **Drag the selected words to the right of the word "pump", release the mouse button, then click outside the text box**

   A grey insertion line appears as you drag, indicating where PowerPoint places the text when you release the mouse button. The phrase "in March 2017" moves after the word "pump". Notice there is no space between the words "pump" and "in" and the spelling error is identified by a red wavy underline.

6. **Right-click the red underlined words in the text box, then click "pump in" on the shortcut menu**

   Space is added between the two words in the text box.

7. **Move I to the edge of the text box, which changes to ⬚, click the text box border (it changes to a solid line), then click the Italic button I in the Font group**

   All of the text in the text box is italicized.

8. **Click the Shape Fill list arrow in the Drawing group, click the Light Green, Background 2, Darker 10% color box, click the Shape Outline list arrow in the Drawing group, then click the Dark Red, Accent 1, Lighter 40% color box**

   The text object is now filled with a light green color and has a red outline.

9. **Position ⬚ over the text box edge, drag the text box to the Smart Guide on the slide as shown in FIGURE 3-6, then save your changes**

FIGURE 3-5: New text object

© Gilles Paire / Shutterstock.com

FIGURE 3-6: Formatted text object

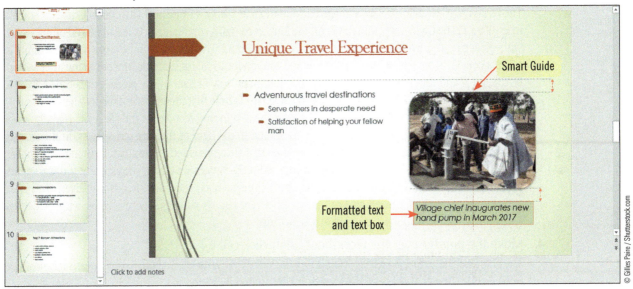
© Gilles Paire / Shutterstock.com

PowerPoint 2016

Changing text box defaults

You can change the default formatting characteristics of text boxes you create using the Text Box button on the Insert tab. To change the formatting defaults for text boxes, select an existing formatted text box, or create a new one and format it using any of PowerPoint's formatting commands. When you are ready to change the text box defaults of a text box that is not selected, press [Shift], right-click the formatted text box, release [Shift], then click Set as Default Text Box on the shortcut menu. Any new text boxes you create now will display the formatting characteristics of this formatted text box.

Insert a Chart

Learning
Outcomes
• Insert a new chart
  on a slide

Frequently, the best way to communicate numerical information is with a visual aid such as a chart. A **chart** is the graphical representation of numerical data. PowerPoint uses Excel to create charts. Every chart has a corresponding **worksheet** that contains the numerical data displayed by the chart. When you insert a chart object into PowerPoint, you are embedding it. An **embedded object** is one that is a part of your presentation (just like any other object you insert into PowerPoint) except that an embedded object's data source can be opened, in this case using Excel, for editing purposes. Changes you make to an embedded object in PowerPoint using the features in PowerPoint do not affect the data source for the data. **CASE** ▶ *You insert a chart on a new slide.*

STEPS

QUICK TIP
Right-click a slide in the Slides tab, then click Duplicate Slide to create an exact copy of the slide.

1. **Click the Slide 2 thumbnail in the Slides tab, then press [Enter]**
   Pressing [Enter] adds a new slide to your presentation with the slide layout of the selected slide, in this case the Title and Content slide layout.

2. **Click the Title placeholder, type Population Growth Comparison, then click the Insert Chart icon** 📊 **in the Content placeholder**
   The Insert Chart dialog box opens as shown in **FIGURE 3-7**. Each chart type includes a number of 2D and 3D styles. The Clustered Column chart is the default 2D chart style. For a brief explanation of common chart types, refer to **TABLE 3-1**.

QUICK TIP
You can also add a chart to a slide by clicking the Chart button in the Illustrations group on the Insert tab.

3. **Click OK**
   The PowerPoint window displays a clustered column chart below a worksheet with sample data, as shown in **FIGURE 3-8**. The Chart Tools Design tab on the Ribbon contains commands you use in PowerPoint to work with the chart. The worksheet consists of rows and columns. The intersection of a row and a column is called a **cell**. Cells are referred to by their row and column location; for example, the cell at the intersection of column A and row 1 is called cell A1. Each column and row of data in the worksheet is called a **data series**. Cells in column A and row 1 contain **data series labels** that identify the data or values in the column and row. "Category 1" is the data series label for the data in the second row, and "Series 1" is a data series label for the data in the second column. Cells below and to the right of the data series labels, in the shaded blue portion of the worksheet, contain the data values that are represented in the chart. Cells in row 1 appear in the chart **legend** and describe the data in the series. Each data series has corresponding **data series markers** in the chart, which are graphical representations such as bars, columns, or pie wedges. The boxes with the numbers along the left side of the worksheet are **row headings**, and the boxes with the letters along the top of the worksheet are **column headings**.

4. **Move the pointer over the worksheet, then click cell C4**
   The pointer changes to ⊹. Cell C4, containing the value 1.8, is the selected cell, which means it is now the **active cell**. The active cell has a thick green border around it.

5. **Click the Close button** ✕ **on the worksheet title bar, then click the Quick Layout button in the Chart Layouts group**
   The worksheet window closes, and the Quick Layout gallery opens.

6. **Move** ⌖ **over the layouts in the gallery, then click Layout 1**
   This new layout moves the legend to the right side of the chart and increases the size of the data series markers.

7. **Click in a blank area of the slide to deselect the chart, then save your changes**
   The Chart Tools Design tab is no longer active.

FIGURE 3-7: Insert Chart dialog box

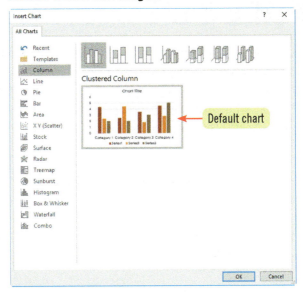

FIGURE 3-8: Worksheet open showing chart data

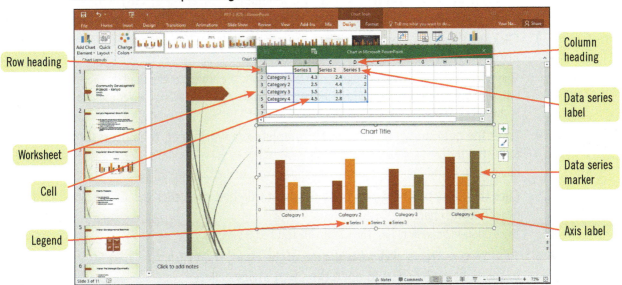

TABLE 3-1: Chart types

chart type	icon looks like	use to
Column		Track values over time or across categories
Line		Track values over time
Pie		Compare individual values to the whole
Bar		Compare values in categories or over time
Area		Show contribution of each data series to the total over time
X Y (Scatter)		Compare pairs of values
Stock		Show stock market information or scientific data
Surface		Show value trends across two dimensions
Radar		Show changes in values in relation to a center point
Combo		Use multiple types of data markers to compare values

Enter and Edit Chart Data

After you insert a chart into your presentation, you need to replace the sample information with the correct data. If you have the data you want to chart in an Excel worksheet, you can import it from Excel; otherwise, you can type your own data into the worksheet on the slide. As you enter data and make other changes in the worksheet, the chart on the slide automatically reflects the new changes. **CASE** *You enter and format population data you have gathered comparing the growth trends of three African countries.*

STEPS

1. **Click the chart on Slide 3, click the Chart Tools Design tab on the Ribbon, then click the Edit Data button in the Data group**

   The chart is selected and the worksheet opens in a separate window. The information in the worksheet needs to be replaced with the correct data.

2. **Click the Series 1 cell, type Kenya, press [Tab], type Uganda, press [Tab], then type S. Africa**

   The data series labels you enter in the worksheet are displayed in the legend on the chart. Pressing [Tab] moves the active cell from left to right one cell at a time in a row. Pressing [Enter] in the worksheet moves the active cell down one cell at a time in a column.

3. **Click the Category 1 cell, type 1990, press [Enter], type 2000, press [Enter], type 2010, press [Enter], type 2015, then press [Enter]**

   These data series labels appear in the worksheet and along the bottom of the chart on the *x*-axis. The *x*-axis is the horizontal axis also referred to as the **category axis**, and the *y*-axis is the vertical axis also referred to as the **value axis**.

4. **Enter the data shown in FIGURE 3-9 to complete the worksheet, then press [Enter]**

   Notice that the height of each column in the chart, as well as the values along the *y*-axis, adjust to reflect the numbers you typed. You have finished entering the data in the Excel worksheet.

5. **Click the Close button ☒ on the worksheet title bar, then click the Chart Title text box object in the chart**

   The worksheet window closes. The Chart Title text box is selected.

6. **Type 25 Year Trend, click a blank area of the chart, then click the Chart Styles button 🖌 to the right of the chart to open the Chart Styles gallery**

   The Chart Styles gallery opens on the left side of the chart with Style selected.

7. **Scroll down the gallery, click Style 6, click Color at the top of the Chart Styles gallery, then click the Color 3 palette in the Colorful section**

   The new chart style and color gives the column data markers a professional look as shown in FIGURE 3-10.

8. **Click a blank area on the slide, then save the presentation**

   The Chart Styles gallery closes.

FIGURE 3-9: Worksheet data for the chart

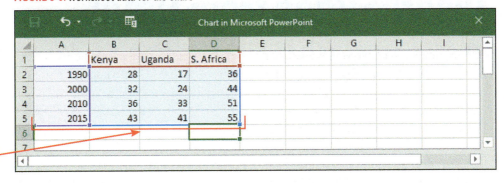

New data

FIGURE 3-10: Formatted chart

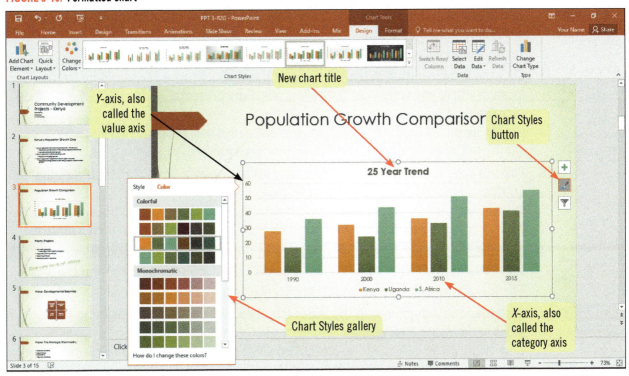

Y-axis, also called the value axis

New chart title

Chart Styles button

Chart Styles gallery

X-axis, also called the category axis

Adding a hyperlink to a chart

You can add a hyperlink to any object in PowerPoint, including a chart. Select that chart, click the Insert tab on the Ribbon, then click the Hyperlink button in the Links group. If you are linking to another file, click the Existing File or Web Page button, locate the file you want to link to the chart, then click OK. Or, if you want to link to another slide in the presentation, click the Place in This Document button, click the slide in the list, then click OK. Now, during a slide show you can click the chart to open the linked object. To remove the link, click the chart, click the Hyperlink button in the Links group, then click Remove Link.

Insert Slides from Other Presentations

To save time and energy, you can insert one or more slides you already created in other presentations into an existing presentation or one you are currently working on. One way to share slides between presentations is to open an existing presentation, copy the slides you want to the Clipboard, and then paste them into your open presentation. However, PowerPoint offers a simpler way to transfer slides directly between presentations. By using the Reuse Slides pane, you can insert slides from another presentation or a network location called a Slide Library. A **Slide Library** is folder that you and others can access to open, modify, and review presentation slides. Newly inserted slides automatically take on the theme of the open presentation, unless you decide to use slide formatting from the original source presentation. **CASE** ▶ *You decide to insert slides you created for another presentation into the Kenya presentation.*

STEPS

QUICK TIP
You can also open a second presentation window and work on the same presentation in different places at the same time. Click the View tab, then click the New Window button in the Window group.

1. **Click the Slide 6 thumbnail in the Slides tab, click the New Slide list arrow in the Slides group, then click Reuse Slides**

   The Reuse Slides pane opens on the right side of the pre sentation window.

2. **Click the Browse button in the Reuse Slides pane, click Browse File, navigate to the location where you store your Data Files, select the presentation file PPT 3-4.pptx, then click Open**

   Five slide thumbnails are displayed in the pane with the first slide thumbnail selected as shown in **FIGURE 3-11**. The slide thumbnails identify the slides in the **source presentation**, PPT 3-4.pptx.

3. **Point to each slide in the Reuse Slides pane list to display a ScreenTip, then click the Strategies for Managing Water Demand slide**

   The new slide appears in the Slides tab and Slide pane as the new Slide 7. Notice the title new slide assumes the design style and formatting of your presentation, which is called the **destination presentation**.

4. **Click the Keep source formatting check box at the bottom of the Reuse Slides pane, click the Water Restructuring Policies slide, then click the Keep source formatting check box**

   This new slide keeps the design style and formatting of the source presentation.

QUICK TIP
To copy noncontiguous slides, open Slide Sorter view, click the first slide thumbnail, press and hold [Ctrl], click each additional slide thumbnail, release [Ctrl], then click the Copy button.

5. **Click the Slide 7 thumbnail in the Slides tab, then click each of the remaining three slides in the Reuse Slides pane**

   Three more slides are inserted into the presentation with the design style and formatting of the destination presentation. You realize that Slides 7 and 11 are not needed for this presentation.

6. **Click the Slide 11 thumbnail in the Slides tab, press [Ctrl], click the Slide 7 thumbnail, release [Ctrl], right-click the Slide 7 thumbnail, then click Delete Slide in the shortcut menu**

   Slides 7 and 11 are deleted.

7. **Click the Reuse Slides pane Close button ✖, click a blank area of the slide, then save the presentation**

   The Reuse Slides pane closes. Compare your screen to **FIGURE 3-12**.

FIGURE 3-11: Presentation window with Reuse Slides pane open

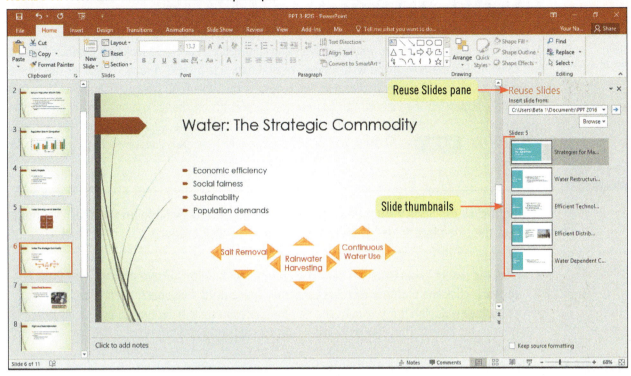

FIGURE 3-12: New slides added to presentation

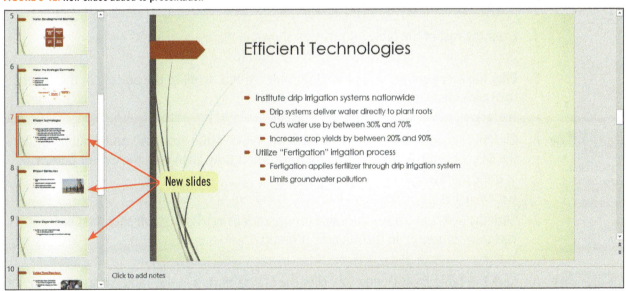

Working with multiple windows

Another way to work with information in multiple presentations is to arrange the presentation windows on your monitor so you see each window side by side. Open each presentation, click the View tab on the Ribbon in any presentation window, then click the Arrange All button in the Window group. Each presentation you have open is placed next to each other so you can easily drag, or transfer, information between the presentations.

If you are working with more than two open presentations, you can overlap the presentation windows on top of one another. Open all the presentations you want, then click the Cascade Windows button in the Window group. Now you can easily jump from one presentation to another by clicking on the presentation title bar or any part of the presentation window.

Inserting Objects into a Presentation

Insert a Table

As you create your presentation, you may have some information that would look best organized in rows and columns. For example, if you want to view related data side by side, a table is ideal for this type of information. Once you have created a table, two new tabs, the Table Tools Design tab and the Table Tools Layout tab, appear on the Ribbon. You can use the commands on the table tabs to apply color styles, change cell borders, add cell effects, add rows and columns to your table, adjust the size of cells, and align text in the cells. **CASE** *You decide a table best illustrates the technology considerations for building a well in Kenya.*

STEPS

1. **Right-click the Slide 9 thumbnail in the Slides tab, click New Slide on the shortcut menu, click the title placeholder, then type Technology Considerations**
   A new slide with the Title and Content layout appears.

2. **Click the Insert Table icon ▦, click the Number of columns down arrow twice until 3 appears, click the Number of rows up arrow twice until 4 appears, then click OK**
   A formatted table with three columns and four rows appears on the slide, and the Table Tools Design tab opens on the Ribbon. The table has 12 cells. The insertion point is in the first cell of the table and is ready to accept text.

3. **Type Financial, press [Tab], type Maintenance, press [Tab], type Population, then press [Tab]**
   The text you typed appears in the top three cells of the table. Pressing [Tab] moves the insertion point to the next cell; pressing [Enter] moves the insertion point to the next line in the same cell.

4. **Enter the rest of the table information shown in FIGURE 3-13**
   The table would look better if it were formatted differently.

5. **Click the More button ▼ in the Table Styles group, scroll to the bottom of the gallery, then click Medium Style 3**
   The background and text color change to reflect the table style you applied.

6. **Click the Financial cell in the table, click the Table Tools Layout tab on the Ribbon, click the Select button in the Table group, click Select Row, then click the Center button ▤ in the Alignment group**
   The text in the top row is centered horizontally in each cell.

7. **Click the Select button in the Table group, click Select Table, then click the Center Vertically button ▤ in the Alignment group**
   The text in the entire table is aligned in the center of each cell.

8. **Click the Table Tools Design tab, click the Effects button in the Table Styles group, point to Cell Bevel, then click Soft Round (2nd row)**
   The 3D effect makes the cells of the table stand out. The table would look better in a different place on the slide.

9. **Place the pointer ⟨ over the top edge of the table, drag the table straight down so it is placed as shown in FIGURE 3-14, click a blank area of the slide, then save the presentation**
   The slide looks better with more space between the table and the slide title.

FIGURE 3-13: Inserted table with data

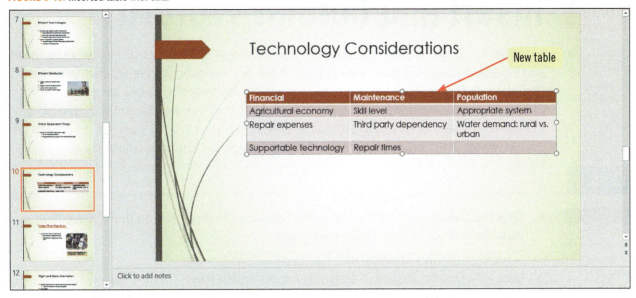

FIGURE 3-14: Formatted table

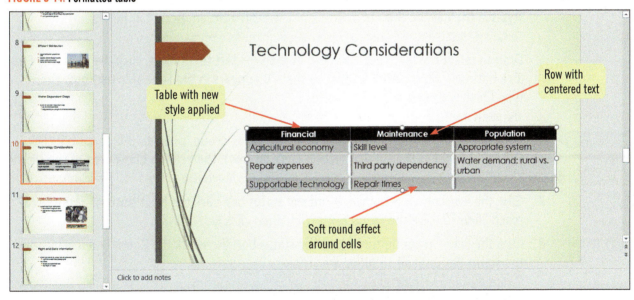

Setting permissions

In PowerPoint, you can set specific access permissions for people who review or edit your work so you have better control over your content. For example, you may want to give a user permission to edit or change your presentation but not allow them to print it. You can also restrict a user by permitting them to view the presentation without the ability to edit or print the presentation, or you can give the user full access or control of the presentation. To use this feature, you first must have access to an information rights management company. Then, to set user access permissions, click the File tab, click the Protect Presentation button, point to Restrict Access, then click an appropriate option.

Insert and Format WordArt

Learning Outcomes
- Create, format, and resize WordArt

As you work to create an interesting presentation, your goal should include making your slides visually appealing. Sometimes plain text can come across as dull and unexciting in a presentation. **WordArt** is a set of decorative text styles, or text effects, you can apply to any text object to help direct the attention of your audience to a certain piece of information. You can use WordArt in two different ways: you can apply a WordArt text style to an existing text object that converts the text into WordArt, or you can create a new WordArt object. The WordArt text styles and effects include text shadows, reflections, glows, bevels, 3D rotations, and transformations. **CASE** *Create a new WordArt text object on Slide 4.*

STEPS

QUICK TIP

To format any text with a WordArt style, select the text, click the Drawing Tools Format tab on the Ribbon, then click a WordArt style option in the WordArt Styles group.

1. **Click the Slide 4 thumbnail in the Slides tab, click the Insert tab on the Ribbon, then click the WordArt button in the Text group**

   The WordArt gallery appears displaying 20 WordArt text styles.

2. **Click Fill – Orange, Accent 2, Outline – Accent 2 (first row)**

   A text object appears in the middle of the slide displaying sample text with the WordArt style you just selected. The Drawing Tools Format tab is open on the Ribbon.

3. **Click the edge of the WordArt text object, then when the pointer changes to ⇱, drag the text object to the blank area of the slide**

4. **Click the More button ⬇ in the WordArt Styles group, move ⬚ over all of the WordArt styles in the gallery, then click Gradient Fill – Olive Green, Accent 1, Reflection**

   The sample text in the WordArt text object changes to the new WordArt style.

5. **Drag to select the text Your text here in the WordArt text object, click the Decrease Font Size button A⬇ in the Mini toolbar so that 48 appears in the Font Size text box, then type Clean water equals self-reliance**

   The text is smaller.

QUICK TIP

To convert a WordArt object to a SmartArt object, right-click the WordArt object, point to Convert to SmartArt on the shortcut menu, then click a SmartArt layout.

6. **Click the Text Effects button in the WordArt Styles group, point to 3-D Rotation, click Off Axis 1 Right in the Parallel section (second row), then click a blank area of the slide**

   The off-axis effect is applied to the text object. Compare your screen to **FIGURE 3-15**.

7. **Click the Reading View button 📖 on the status bar, click the Next button ⏵ until you reach Slide 15, click the Menu button 🗈, then click End Show**

8. **Click the Slide Sorter button ⊞ on the status bar, then click the Zoom Out icon ⊟ on the status bar until all 15 slides are visible**

   Compare your screen with **FIGURE 3-16**.

9. **Click the Normal button 🗔 on the status bar, add your name, the slide number and the date as a footer to the slides, save your changes, submit your presentation to your instructor, then exit PowerPoint**

FIGURE 3-15: WordArt inserted on slide

FIGURE 3-15: WordArt inserted on slide

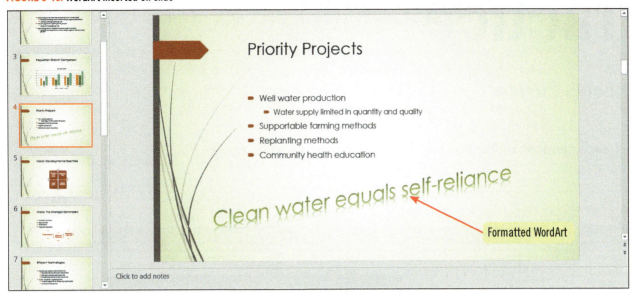

FIGURE 3-16: Completed presentation in Slide Sorter view

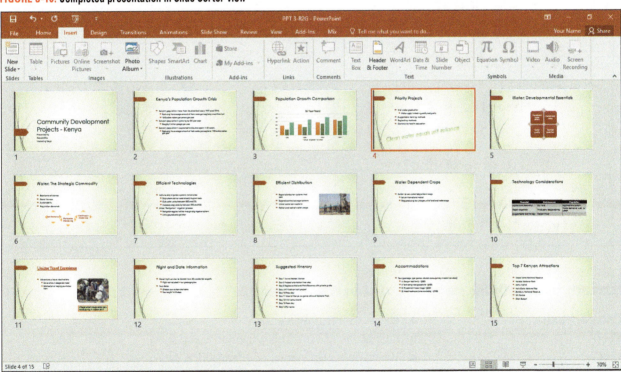

Saving a presentation as a video

You can save your PowerPoint presentation as a full-fidelity video, which incorporates all slide timings, transitions, animations, and narrations. The video can be distributed using a disc, the web, or email. Depending on how you want to display your video, you have three resolution settings from which to choose: Presentation Quality, Internet Quality, and Low Quality. The Large setting, Presentation Quality (1920 X 1080), is used for viewing on a computer monitor, projector, or other high-definition displays. The Medium setting, Internet Quality (1280 X 720), is used for uploading to the web or copying to a standard DVD. The Small setting, Low Quality (852 X 480), is used on portable media players. To save your presentation as a video, click the File tab, click Export, click Create a Video, choose your settings, then click the Create Video button.

Practice

Concepts Review

Label each element of the PowerPoint window shown in FIGURE 3-17.

FIGURE 3-17

FIGURE 3-17

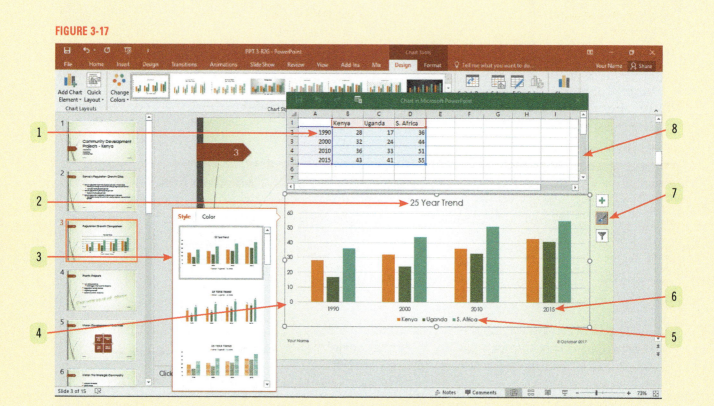

Match each term with the statement that best describes it.

9. **Category axis**

10. **Crop**

11. **Cell**

12. **Value axis**

13. **Chart**

a. The *y*-axis (vertical) in a chart

b. Intersection of a row and column in a worksheet

c. The graphical representation of numerical data

d. The *x*-axis (horizontal) in a chart

e. Hide a portion of a picture

Select the best answer from the list of choices.

14. _____ is the network folder that you can open in the Reuse Slides pane to insert slides from other presentations.
   a. Slide Library
   b. Slide Exchange
   c. Export Exchange
   d. Slide Room

15. Use a(n) _____ object to best illustrate information you want to compare side by side.
   a. WordArt
   b. Table
   c. SmartArt
   d. Equation

16. An object that has its own data source and becomes a part of your presentation after you insert it best describes which of the following?
   a. Embedded object
   b. WordArt
   c. Table
   d. Screenshot

17. Each column and row of data in a worksheet are _____.
   a. Data series labels
   b. Headings
   c. Data series
   d. Data markers

18. The slide thumbnails in the Reuse Slides pane identify the slides of the _____ presentation.
   a. destination
   b. default
   c. source
   d. open

19. _____ to permanently delete a cropped portion of a picture.
   a. Use the Crop to Fit feature
   b. Change the aspect ratio
   c. Change the picture's artistic effect
   d. Apply picture compression

20. _____ is created by inserting text from Word document that does not have tabs.
   a. A new presentation
   b. A slide title
   c. A first level text in a bulleted list
   d. A Heading 1 style

Skills Review

1. **Insert text from Microsoft Word.**
   a. Open PPT 3-5.pptx from the location where you store your Data Files, then save it as **PPT 3-Tsar Tour**. You will work to create the completed presentation as shown in FIGURE 3-18.
   b. Click Slide 2 in the Slides tab, then use the Slides from Outline command to insert the file PPT 3-6.docx from the location where you store your Data Files.
   c. In the Slides tab, drag Slide 7 above Slide 6, then delete Slide 9, "Budapest, Hungary".
   d. Select Slides 3, 4, 5, 6, 7, and 8 in the Slides tab, reset the slides to the default theme settings, then save your work.

FIGURE 3-18

Skills Review (continued)

2. **Insert and style a picture.**

   a. Select Slide 2 in the Slides tab, then insert the picture PPT 3-7.jpg from the location where you store your Data Files.

   b. Crop the right side of the picture up to the building, then increase the size of the picture so it is 5" wide.

   c. Drag the picture to the right so it is in the center of the blank area of the slide.

   d. Click the Color button, change the color tone to Temperature: 11200 K, then save your changes.

3. **Insert a text box.**

   a. On Slide 2, insert a text box below the picture.

   b. Type **Catherine palace**.

   c. Select the text object, then click the More button in the Shape Styles group on the Drawing Tools Format tab.

   d. Click Moderate Effect – Orange, Accent 5, then fit the text box to the text by dragging its sizing handles.

   e. Center the text object under the picture using Smart Guides.

   f. In the main text object, type the word **on** before the word **Volga**, then move the word **cruise** before the word **on**.

4. **Insert a chart.**

   a. Create a new slide after Slide 8 with a Title Only layout and title it **Sales by Quarter**.

   b. On the Insert tab, click the Chart button in the Illustrations group, click Pie in the left column, then insert a Pie chart.

   c. Close the worksheet, drag the top-middle sizing handle of the chart down under the slide title, then apply the Layout 1 quick layout to the chart.

5. **Enter and edit chart data.**

   a. Show the worksheet, enter the data shown in TABLE 3-2 into the worksheet, then close the worksheet.

   b. Type **Tsar River Tour Sales** in the chart title text object.

   c. Click the Chart Styles button next to the chart, then change the chart style to Style 12.

   d. Click Color in the Charts Styles gallery, then change the color to Color 3 in the Colorful section.

   e. Close the Charts Styles gallery, then save your changes.

TABLE 3-2

	Sales
1st Qtr	11
2nd Qtr	31
3rd Qtr	37
4th Qtr	21

6. **Insert slides from other presentations.**

   a. Go to Slide 8, then open the Reuse Slides pane.

   b. Open PPT 3-8.pptx from the location where you store your Data Files.

   c. Insert the fourth slide thumbnail, insert the second slide thumbnail, and then insert the third slide thumbnail.

   d. Close the Reuse Slides pane, then save your work.

7. **Insert a table.**

   a. Add a new slide after Slide 11 with the Title and Content layout.

   b. Add the slide title **Stateroom Special Features**.

   c. Insert a table with three columns and four rows.

   d. Enter the information shown in TABLE 3-3, then change the table style to Light Style 2 – Accent 2.

   e. In the Table Tools Layout tab, center the text in the top row.

   f. Open the Table Tools Design tab, click the Effects button, point to Cell Bevel, then apply the Convex effect.

   g. Move the table to the center of the blank area of the slide, then save your changes.

TABLE 3-3

Deluxe Stateroom	Veranda Suite	Master Suite
160 sq. ft.	225 sq. ft.	400 sq. ft.
Private bathroom	Glass sliding door	Queen bed
Large picture window	Walk-in closet	Panoramic veranda

Skills Review (continued)

8. **Insert and format WordArt.**

   a. Go to Slide 5, then, insert a WordArt text object using the style Fill – Yellow, Accent 3, Sharp Bevel.

   b. Type **A Golden Ring City**, apply the Triangle Down Transform text effect (first row in the Warp section) to the text object, then move the text object to the middle of the blank area of the slide.

   c. View the presentation in Slide Show view, add your name as a footer to all the slides, then save your changes.

   d. Submit your presentation to your instructor, close your presentation, and exit PowerPoint.

Independent Challenge 1

You are a financial management consultant for Pitlock, Bryer & Mansouetti, located in Bradenton, Florida. One of your responsibilities is to create standardized presentations on different financial investments for use on the company website. As part of the presentation for this meeting, you insert a chart, add a WordArt object, and insert slides from another presentation.

   a. Open PPT 3-9.pptx from the location where you store your Data Files, then save it as **PPT 3-BIP**.

   b. Add your name as the footer on all of the slides, then apply the Frame Design Theme.

   c. Insert a clustered column chart on Slide 2, then enter the data in TABLE 3-4 into the worksheet.

   d. Close the worksheet, format the chart using Style 14, then resize and move the chart to the blank area beside the text object.

   e. Type **Annualized Return** in the chart title text object.

   f. Open the Reuse Slides pane, open PPT 3-10.pptx from the location where you store your Data Files, then insert Slides 2, 3, and 4.

   g. Close the Reuse Slides pane, move Slide 5 above Slide 4, then select Slide 3.

   h. Insert a WordArt object using the Fill - Orange, Accent 4, Soft Bevel style, type **Invest early**, press [Enter], type **for**, press [Enter], then type **the long haul**.

   i. Click the Text Effects button, point to Transform, then apply the Button text effect from the Follow Path section.

   j. Move the WordArt object to a blank area of the slide, click the Text Effects button, point to Shadow, then apply an Outer shadow effect.

   k. View the presentation slide show, make any necessary changes, then save your work. See FIGURE 3-19.

   l. Submit the presentation to your instructor, then close the presentation, and exit PowerPoint.

TABLE 3-4

	Stocks	**Bonds**	**Mutual funds**
1 Year	5.3%	1.9%	3.8%
3 Year	4.8%	3.7%	6.7%
5 Year	3.2%	2.2%	8.3%
10 Year	2.6%	3.4%	7.2%

FIGURE 3-19

PowerPoint 2016

Independent Challenge 2

You work for the Boston Port Group in the commercial container division. You have been asked to enhance a marketing presentation that is going to promote the port facilities. You work on completing a presentation by inserting a picture, a text box, and a table.

a. Start PowerPoint, open PPT 3-11.pptx from the location where you store your Data Files, and save it as **PPT 3-Port**.

b. Add your name and today's date to Slide 1 in the Subtitle text box.

c. Apply the Droplet theme to the presentation.

d. On Slide 5, click the Pictures icon in the content placeholder, then insert the file PPT 3-12.jpg from the location where you store your Data Files.

e. Apply the Simple Frame, Black picture style to the picture, click the Color button, then change the color saturation to Saturation: 0%.

f. Change the size of the picture so its width is 5.2" using the Width text box in the Size group.

g. Insert a text box on the slide below the picture, type **Largest volume port on East Coast**, then format the text and text box with three formatting commands.

h. Go to Slide 2, select the picture, click the Picture Effects button, point to Soft Edges, then click 5 Point.

i. Open the Artistic Effects gallery, then apply the Cement effect to the picture.

j. Go to Slide 4, create a new table, then enter the data in **TABLE 3-5**. Format the table using at least two formatting commands. Be able to identify which formatting commands you applied to the table.

k. View the final presentation in Slide Show view. Make any necessary changes (refer to **FIGURE 3-20**).

l. Save the presentation, submit the presentation to your instructor, close the file, and exit PowerPoint.

TABLE 3-5

Total	August	September
Total containers	25,524.0	22,417.0
Loaded containers	15,283.0	14,016.0
Empty containers	10,241.0	8,401.0
Total tons	375,240	334,180

FIGURE 3-20

© tcly/Shutterstock; © Prasit Rodphan/Shutterstock

Independent Challenge 3

You work for World Partners Inc., a company that produces instructional software to help people learn foreign languages. Once a year, World Partners holds a meeting with their biggest client, the United States Department of Homeland Security, to brief the government on new products and to receive feedback on existing products. Your supervisor has started a presentation and has asked you to look it over and add other elements to make it look better.

a. Start PowerPoint, open PPT 3-13.pptx from the location where you store your Data Files, and save it as **PPT 3-World**.

b. Add an appropriate design theme to the presentation.

c. Insert the Word outline PPT 3-14.docx after the Product Revisions slide, then reset the new slides to the design theme.

d. Insert and format a text object and a WordArt object.

e. Insert an appropriate table on a slide of your choice. Use your own information, or use text from a bulleted list on one of the slides.

f. Add your name as footer text on the slides, then save the presentation.

g. Submit your presentation to your instructor, close the file, then exit PowerPoint.

Independent Challenge 4: Explore

As an international exchange student at your college, one of your assignments in your Intercultural Communication Studies class is to present information on a student exchange you took last semester. You need to create a pictorial presentation that highlights a trip to a different country. Create a presentation using your own pictures. If you don't have access to any appropriate pictures, use the three pictures provided in the Data Files for this unit: PPT 3-15.jpg, PPT 3-16.jpg, and PPT 3-17.jpg. *(NOTE: To complete steps below, your computer must be connected to the Internet.)*

a. Start PowerPoint, create a new blank presentation, and save it as **PPT 3-Exchange** to the location where you store your Data Files.

b. Locate and insert the pictures you want to use. Place one picture on each slide using the Content with Caption slide layout, then apply a picture style to each picture.

c. Click the Crop list arrow, and use one of the other cropping options to crop a picture.

d. Add information about each picture in the text placeholder, and enter a slide title. If you use the pictures provided, research Costa Rica, using the Internet for relevant information to place on the slides.

e. Apply an appropriate design theme, then apply an appropriate title and your name to the title slide.

FIGURE 3-21

© Tami Freed/Shutterstock; © Ruth Choi/Shutterstock; © Mihai-Bogdan Lazar/Shutterstock

f. View the final presentation slide show (refer to **FIGURE 3-21**).

g. Add a slide number and your class name as footer text to all of the slides, save your work, then submit your presentation to your instructor.

h. Close the file, and exit PowerPoint.

Visual Workshop

Create a one-slide presentation that looks like **FIGURE 3-22**. The slide layout used is a specific layout designed for pictures. Insert the picture file PPT 3-18.jpg to complete this presentation. Add your name as footer text to the slide, save the presentation as **PPT 3-TCM** to the location where you store your Data Files, then submit your presentation to your instructor.

FIGURE 3-22

Finishing a Presentation

CASE You have reviewed your work and are pleased with the slides you created so far for the Reason2Go presentation. Now you are ready to add some final enhancements to the slides to make the PowerPoint presentation interesting to watch.

Module Objectives

After completing this module, you will be able to:

- Modify masters
- Customize the background and theme
- Use slide show commands
- Set slide transitions and timings
- Animate objects
- Use proofing and language tools
- Inspect a presentation
- Create an Office Mix

Files You Will Need

PPT 4-1.pptx	PPT 4-6.jpg
PPT 4-2.jpg	PPT 4-7.pptx
PPT 4-3.pptx	PPT 4-8.pptx
PPT 4-4.jpg	PPT 4-9.jpg
PPT 4-5.pptx	PPT 4-10.jpg

Modify Masters

Learning Outcomes
• Navigate Slide Master view
• Add and modify a picture

Each presentation in PowerPoint has a set of **masters** that store information about the theme and slide layouts. Masters determine the position and size of text and content placeholders, fonts, slide background, color, and effects. There are three Master views: Slide Master view, Notes Master view, and Handout Master view. Changes made in Slide Master view are reflected on the slides in Normal view; changes made in Notes Master view are reflected in Notes Page view, and changes made in Handout Master view appear when you print your presentation using a handout printing option. The primary benefit to modifying a master is that you can make universal changes to your whole presentation instead of making individual repetitive changes to each of your slides. **CASE** ▶ *You want to add the R2G company logo to every slide in your presentation, so you open your presentation and insert the logo on the slide master.*

STEPS

1. **Start PowerPoint, open the presentation PPT 4-1.pptx from the location where you store your Data Files, save the presentation as PPT 4-R2G, then click the View tab on the Ribbon**
   The title slide for the presentation appears.

QUICK TIP
You can press and hold [Shift] and click the Normal button on the status bar to display the slide master.

2. **Click the Slide Master button in the Master Views group, scroll to the top of the Master Thumbnails pane, then click the Wisp Slide Master thumbnail (first thumbnail)**
   The Slide Master view appears with the slide master displayed in the Slide pane as shown in **FIGURE 4-1**. A new tab, the Slide Master tab, appears next to the Home tab on the Ribbon. The slide master is the Wisp theme slide master. Each theme comes with its own slide master. Each master text placeholder on the slide master identifies the font size, style, color, and position of text placeholders on the slides in Normal view. For example, for the Wisp theme, the Master title placeholder positioned at the top of the slide uses a black, 36 pt, Century Gothic font. Slide titles use this font style and formatting. Each slide master comes with associated slide layouts located below the slide master in the Master Thumbnails pane. Slide layouts follow the information on the slide master, and changes you make are reflected in all of the slide layouts.

QUICK TIP
You can make sure the current master remains with the presentation by clicking the Preserve button in the Edit Master group.

3. **Point to each of the slide layouts in the Master Thumbnails pane, then click the Title and Content Layout thumbnail**
   As you point to each slide layout, a ScreenTip appears identifying each slide layout by name and lists if any slides in the presentation are using the layout. Slides 2–9 and 12–15 are using the Title and Content Layout.

4. **Click the Wisp Slide Master thumbnail, click the Insert tab on the Ribbon, then click the Pictures button in the Images group**
   The Insert Picture dialog box opens.

5. **Select the picture file PPT 4-2.jpg from the location where you store your Data Files, then click Insert**
   The R2G logo picture is placed on the slide master and will now appear on all slides in the presentation. The picture is too large and would look better with a transparent background.

6. **Click 2.45" in the Width text box in the Size group, type 1.75, press [Enter], click the Color button in the Adjust group, then click Set Transparent Color**
   The pointer changes to ⬉.

QUICK TIP
To reset the background color of a picture to its original state, click the Reset Picture button in the Adjust group.

7. **Click the lime green color in the logo picture, drag the logo as shown in FIGURE 4-2, then click a blank area of the slide**
   The picture background color is now transparent.

8. **Click the Normal button ▣ on the status bar, then save your changes**

FIGURE 4-1: Slide Master view

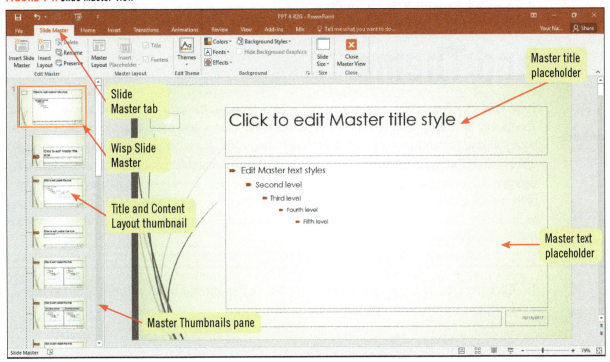

FIGURE 4-2: Picture added to slide master

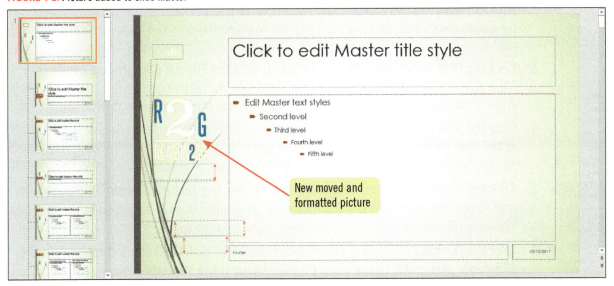

Create custom slide layouts

As you work with PowerPoint, you may find that you need to develop a customized slide layout. For example, you may need to create a presentation for a client that has a slide that displays four pictures with a caption underneath each picture. To make everyone's job easier, you can create a custom slide layout that includes only the placeholders you need. To create a custom slide layout, open Slide Master view, and then click the Insert Layout button in the Edit Master group. A new slide layout appears below the last layout for the selected master in the Master Thumbnails pane.

You can choose to add several different placeholders including Content, Text, Picture, Chart, Table, SmartArt, Media, and Online Image. Click the Insert Placeholder list arrow in the Master Layout group, click the placeholder you want to add, drag + to create the placeholder, then position the placeholder on the slide. In Slide Master view, you can add or delete placeholders in any of the slide layouts. You can rename a custom slide layout by clicking the Rename button in the Edit Master group and entering a descriptive name to better identify the layout.

Customize the Background and Theme

Learning Outcomes
- Apply a slide background and change the style
- Modify presentation theme

Every slide in a PowerPoint presentation has a **background**, the area behind the text and graphics. You modify the background to enhance the slides using images and color. You can quickly change the background appearance by applying a background style, which is a set of color variations derived from the theme colors. Theme colors determine the colors for all slide elements in your presentation, including slide background, text and lines, shadows, fills, accents, and hyperlinks. Every PowerPoint theme has its own set of theme colors. See **TABLE 4-1** for a description of the theme colors. **CASE** *The R2G presentation can be improved with some design enhancements. You decide to modify the background of the slides by changing the theme colors and fonts.*

STEPS

1. **Click the Design tab on the Ribbon, then click the Format Background button in the Customize group**

   The Format Background pane opens displaying the Fill options. The gradient option button is selected indicating the slide has a gradient background.

QUICK TIP

To add artistic effects, picture corrections, or picture color changes to a slide background, click the Effects or Picture icons in the Format Background pane, then click one of the options.

2. **Click the Solid fill option button, review the slide, click the Pattern fill option button, then click the Dotted diamond pattern (seventh row)**

   FIGURE 4-3 shows the new background on Slide 1 of the presentation. The new background style covers the slide behind the text and background graphics. **Background graphics** are objects placed on the slide master.

3. **Click the Hide background graphics check box in the Format Background pane**

   All of the background objects, which include the R2G logo, the red pentagon shape, and the other colored shapes, are hidden from view, and only the text objects and slide number remain visible.

4. **Click the Hide background graphics check box, then click the Reset Background button at the bottom of the Format Background pane**

   All of the background objects and the gradient fill slide background appear again as specified by the theme.

QUICK TIP

To create a custom theme, click the View tab, click the Slide Master button in the Master Views group, then click the Colors button, the Fonts button, or the Effects button in the Background group.

5. **Click the Picture or texture fill option button, click the Texture button 🖾, click Woven mat (top row), then drag the Transparency slider until 40% is displayed in the text box**

   The new texture fills the slide background behind the background items.

6. **Click the Format Background pane Close button ✕, click the Slide 3 thumbnail in the Slides tab, then point to the black theme variant in the Variants group**

   The new theme variant changes the color of the shapes on the slide and the background texture. A **variant** is a custom variation of the applied theme, in this case the Wisp theme. Theme variants are similar to the original theme, but they are made up of different complementary colors, slide backgrounds, such as textures and patterns, and background elements, such as shapes and pictures.

7. **Point to the other variants in the Variants group, click the second variant from the left, then save your work**

   The new variant is applied to the slide master and to all the slides in the presentation. Compare your screen to **FIGURE 4-4**.

FIGURE 4-3: New background style applied

FIGURE 4-4: New theme variant

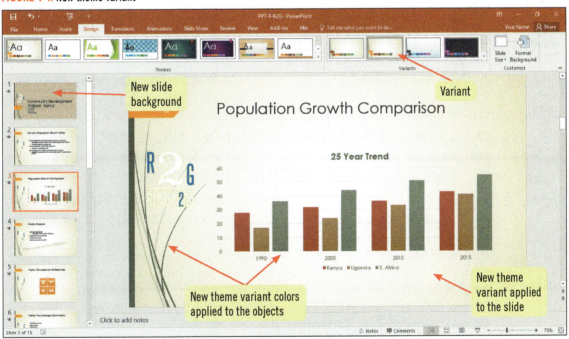

TABLE 4-1: Theme colors

color element	description
Text/Background colors	Contrasting colors for typed characters and the slide background
Accent colors	There are six accent colors used for shapes, drawn lines, and text; the shadow color for text and objects and the fill and outline color for shapes are all accent colors; all of these colors contrast appropriately with background and text colors
Hyperlink color	Colors used for hyperlinks you insert
Followed Hyperlink color	Color used for hyperlinks after they have been clicked

Use Slide Show Commands

Learning
Outcomes
• Preview a slide show
• Navigate a slide
  show
• Use slide show tools

With PowerPoint, Slide Show view is used primarily to deliver a presentation to an audience, either over the Internet using your computer or through a projector connected to your computer. As you've seen, Slide Show view fills your computer screen with the slides of the presentation, showing them one at a time. In Slide Show view, you can draw freehand pen or highlighter strokes, also known as **ink annotations**, on the slide or jump to other slides in the presentation. **CASE** *You run the slide show of the presentation and practice using some of the custom slide show options.*

STEPS

1. **Click the Slide Show button ⬚ on the status bar, then press [Spacebar]**

   Slide 3 filled the screen first, and then Slide 4 appears. Pressing [Spacebar] or clicking the left mouse button is an easy way to move through a slide show. See **TABLE 4-2** for other basic slide show keyboard commands. You can easily navigate to other slides in the presentation during the slide show.

2. **Move ⬚ to the lower-left corner of the screen to display the Slide Show toolbar, click the See all slides button ⬚, then click the Slide 2 thumbnail**

   Slide 2 appears on the screen. With the Slide Show toolbar you can emphasize points in your presentation by drawing highlighter strokes on the slide during a slide show.

3. **Click the Pen and laser pointer tools button ⬚, on the Slide Show toolbar, then click Highlighter**

   The pointer changes to the highlighter pointer ▌. You can use the highlighter anywhere on the slide.

4. **Drag ▌, to highlight doubled between 1970 and 2015 and double again in 50 years in the text object, then press [Esc]**

   Two lines of text are highlighted as shown in **FIGURE 4-5**. While the ▌ is visible, mouse clicks do not advance the slide show; however, you can still move to the next slide by pressing [Spacebar] or [Enter]. Pressing [Esc] or [Ctrl][A] while drawing with the highlighter or pen switches the pointer back to ⬚.

5. **Right-click anywhere on the screen, point to Pointer Options, click Eraser, the pointer changes to ⬚, then click the lower highlight annotation in the text object**

   The highlight annotation on the "double again in 50 years" text is erased.

6. **Press [Esc], click the More slide show options button ⬚ on the Slide Show toolbar, click Show Presenter View, then click the Pause the timer button ⏸ above the slide as shown in FIGURE 4-6**

   Presenter view is a view that you can use when showing a presentation through two monitors; one that you see as the presenter and one that your audience sees. The current slide appears on the left of your screen (which is the only object your audience sees), the next slide in the presentation appears in the upper-right corner of the screen. Speaker notes, if you have any, appear in the lower-right corner. The timer you paused identifies how long the slide has been viewed by the audience.

7. **Click ⬚, click Hide Presenter View, then click the Advance to the next slide button ⬚ on the Slide Show toolbar**

   Slide 3 appears.

8. **Press [Enter] to advance through the entire slide show until you see a black slide, then press [Spacebar]**

   If there are ink annotations on your slides, you have the option of saving them when you quit the slide show. Saved ink annotations appear as drawn objects in Normal view.

9. **Click Discard, then save the presentation**

   The highlight ink annotation is deleted on Slide 2, and Slide 3 appears in Normal view.

FIGURE 4-5: Slide 2 in Slide Show view with highlighter drawings

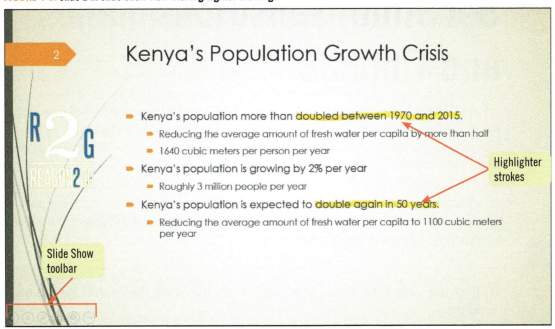

FIGURE 4-6: Slide 2 in Presenter view

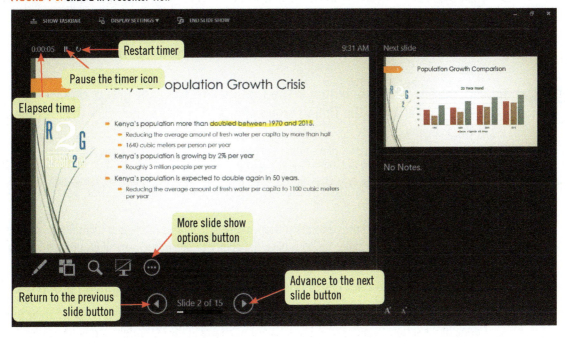

TABLE 4-2: Basic Slide Show view keyboard commands

keyboard commands	description
[Enter], [Spacebar], [PgDn], [N], [down arrow], or [right arrow]	Advances to the next slide
[E]	Erases the ink annotation drawing
[Home], [End]	Moves to the first or last slide in the slide show
[up arrow], [PgUp], or [left arrow]	Returns to the previous slide
[S]	Pauses the slide show when using automatic timings; press again to continue
[B]	Changes the screen to black; press again to return
[Esc]	Stops the slide show

Set Slide Transitions and Timings

Learning Outcomes
• Apply and modify a transition
• Modify slide timings

In a slide show, you can determine how each slide advances in and out of view and how long each slide appears on the screen. **Slide transitions** are the visual and audio effects you apply to a slide that determine how each slide moves on and off the screen during the slide show. **Slide timing** refers to the amount of time a slide is visible on the screen. Typically, you set slide timings only if you want the presentation to automatically progress through the slides during a slide show. Setting the correct slide timing, in this case, is important because it determines how much time your audience has to view each slide. Each slide can have a different slide transition and different slide timing. **CASE** ▶ *You decide to set slide transitions and 7-second slide timings for all the slides.*

STEPS

1. **Click the Slide 1 thumbnail in the Slides tab, then click the Transitions tab on the Ribbon**

   Transitions are organized by type into three groups: Subtle, Exciting, and Dynamic Content.

2. **Click the More button ▼ in the Transition to This Slide group, then click Drape in the Exciting section**

   The new slide transition plays on the slide, and a transition icon ⭐ appears next to the slide thumbnail in the Slides tab as shown in **FIGURE 4-7**. You can customize the slide transition by changing its direction and speed.

   QUICK TIP
   You can add a sound that plays with the transition from the Sound list arrow in the Timing group.

3. **Click the Effect Options button in the Transition to This Slide group, click Right, click the Duration up arrow in the Timing group until 3.00 appears, then click the Preview button in the Preview group**

   The Drape slide transition now plays from the right on the slide for 3.00 seconds. You can apply this transition with the custom settings to all of the slides in the presentation.

4. **Click the Apply To All button in the Timing group, then click the Slide Sorter button ▦ on the status bar**

   All of the slides now have the customized Drape transition applied to them as identified by the transition icons located below each slide. You also have the ability to determine how slides progress during a slide show—either manually by mouse click or automatically by slide timing.

5. **Click the On Mouse Click check box under Advance Slide in the Timing group to clear the check mark**

   When this option is selected, you would have to click to manually advance slides during a slide show. Now, with this option disabled, you can set the slides to advance automatically after a specified amount of time.

   QUICK TIP
   Click the transition icon under any slide in Slide Sorter view to see its transition play.

6. **Click the After up arrow in the Timing group, until 00:07.00 appears in the text box, then click the Apply To All button**

   The timing between slides is 7 seconds as indicated by the time under each slide thumbnail in **FIGURE 4-8**. When you run the slide show, each slide will remain on the screen for 7 seconds. You can override a slide's timing and speed up the slide show by using any of the manual advance slide commands.

7. **Click the Slide Show button ⬛ on the status bar**

   The slide show advances automatically. A new slide appears every 7 seconds using the Drape transition.

8. **When you see the black slide, press [Spacebar], then save your changes**

   The slide show ends and returns to Slide Sorter view with Slide 1 selected.

FIGURE 4-7: Applied slide transition

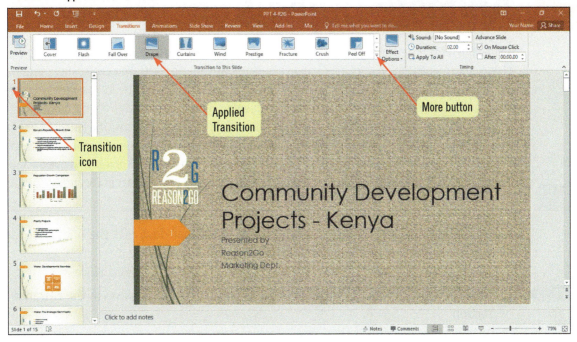

FIGURE 4-8: Slide sorter view showing applied transition and timing

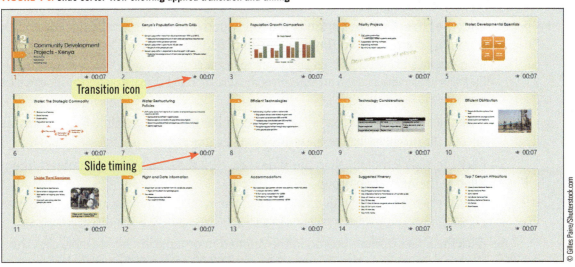

© Gilles Paire/Shutterstock.com

Rehearsing slide show timings

You can set different slide timings for each slide; for example, the title slide can appear for 20 seconds and the second slide for 1 minute. To set timings click the Rehearse Timings button in the Set Up group on the Slide Show tab. Slide Show view opens and the Recording toolbar shown in **FIGURE 4-9** opens. It contains buttons to pause between slides and to advance to the next slide. After opening the Recording toolbar, you can practice giving your presentation by manually advancing each slide in the presentation. When you are finished, PowerPoint displays the total recorded time for the presentation and you have the option to save the recorded timings. The next time you run the slide show, you can use the timings you rehearsed.

FIGURE 4-9: Recording toolbar

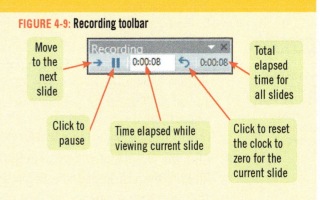

Animate Objects

Learning Outcomes
• Animate objects
• Modify animation effects

Animations let you control how objects and text appear and move on the screen during a slide show and allow you to manage the flow of information and emphasize specific facts. You can animate text, pictures, sounds, hyperlinks, SmartArt diagrams, charts, and individual chart elements. For example, you can apply a Fade animation to bulleted text so each paragraph enters the slide separately from the others. Animations are organized into four categories, Entrance, Emphasis, Exit, and Motion Paths. The Entrance and Exit animations cause an object to enter or exit the slide with an effect. An Emphasis animation causes an object visible on the slide to have an effect and a Motion Path animation causes an object to move on a specified path on the slide. **CASE** ▶ *You animate the text and graphics of several slides in the presentation.*

STEPS

1. **Double-click the Slide 5 thumbnail to return to Normal view, click the Animations tab on the Ribbon, then click the SmartArt object**

   Text as well as other objects, such as a shape or picture, can be animated during a slide show.

   QUICK TIP
   There are additional animation options for each animation category located at the bottom of the animations gallery.

2. **Click the More button ⮟ in the Animation group, then click Swivel in the Entrance section**

   Animations can be serious and business-like, or humorous, so be sure to choose appropriate effects for your presentation. A small numeral 1, called an animation tag ⬛, appears near the object. **Animation tags** identify the order in which objects are animated during slide show.

3. **Click the Effect Options button in the Animation group, click All at Once, then click the Duration up arrow in the Timing group until 03.00 appears**

   Effect options are different for every animation, and some animations don't have effect options. Changing the animation timing increases the duration of the animation and gives it a more dramatic effect. Compare your screen to **FIGURE 4-10**.

4. **Click the Slide Show button 🖵 on the status bar until you see Slide 6, then press [Esc]**

   After the slide transition finishes, the shapes object spins twice for a total of three seconds.

5. **Click the Slide 2 thumbnail in the Slides tab, click the bulleted list text object, then click Wipe in the Animation group**

   The text object is animated with the Wipe animation. Each line of text has an animation tag with each paragraph displaying a different number. Accordingly, each paragraph is animated separately.

6. **Click the Effect Options button in the Animation group, click All at Once, click the Duration up arrow in the Timing group until 02.00 appears, then click the Preview button in the Preview group**

   Notice the animation tags for each line of text in the text object now have the same numeral (1), indicating that each line of text animates at the same time.

   QUICK TIP
   If you want to individually animate the parts of a grouped object, then you must ungroup the objects before you animate them.

7. **Click Population in the title text object, click ⮟ in the Animation group, scroll down, then click Shapes in the Motion Paths section**

   A motion path object appears over the shapes object and identifies the direction and shape, or path, of the animation. When needed, you can move, resize, and change the direction of the motion path. Notice the numeral 2 animation tag next to the title text object indicating that it is animated *after* the bulleted list text object. Compare your screen to **FIGURE 4-11**.

8. **Click the Move Earlier button in the Timing group, click the Slide Show tab on the Ribbon, then click the From Beginning button in the Start Slide Show group**

   The slide show begins from Slide 1. The animations make the presentation more interesting to view.

9. **When you see the black slide, press [Enter], then save your changes**

FIGURE 4-10: Animation applied to SmartArt object

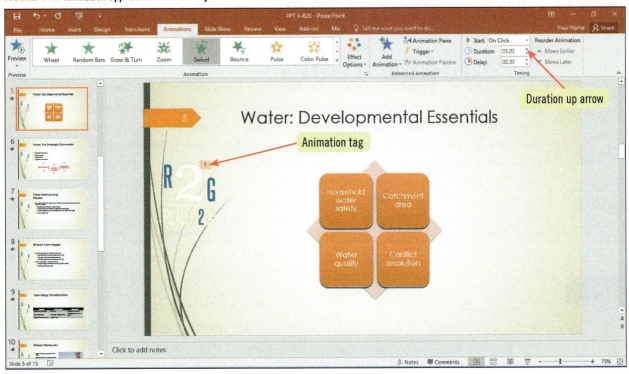

FIGURE 4-11: Motion path applied to title text object

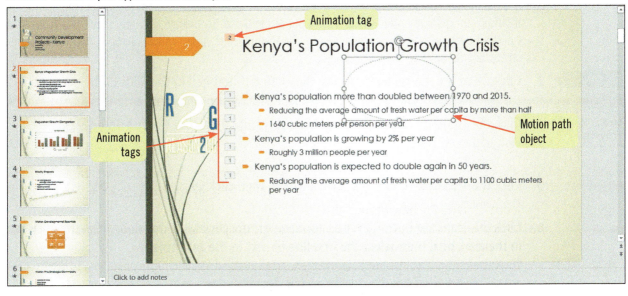

Attaching a sound to an animation

Text or objects that have animation applied can be customized further by attaching a sound for extra emphasis. First, select the animated object, then on the Animations tab, click the Animation Pane button in the Advanced Animation group. In the Animation Pane, click the animation you want to apply the sound to, click the Animation list arrow, then click Effect Options to open the animation effect's dialog box. In the Enhancements section, click the Sound list arrow, then choose a sound. Click OK when you are finished. Now, when you run the slide show, the sound you applied will play with the animation.

Use Proofing and Language Tools

As your work on the presentation file nears completion, you need to review and proofread your slides thoroughly for errors. You can use the Spell Checker feature in PowerPoint to check for and correct spelling errors. This feature compares the spelling of all the words in your presentation against the words contained in the dictionary. You still must proofread your presentation for punctuation, grammar, and word-usage errors because the Spell Checker recognizes only misspelled and unknown words, not misused words. For example, the spell checker would not identify the word "last" as an error, even if you had intended to type the word "past." PowerPoint also includes language tools that translate words or phrases from your default language into another language using the Microsoft Translator. **CASE** ▶ *You're finished working on the presentation for now, so it's a good time to check spelling. You then experiment with language translation because the final presentation will be translated into different languages.*

STEPS

1. **Click the Review tab on the Ribbon, then click the Spelling button in the Proofing group**

   PowerPoint begins to check the spelling in your presentation. When PowerPoint finds a misspelled word or a word that is not in its dictionary, the Spelling pane opens, as shown in **FIGURE 4-12**. In this case, the Spell Checker identifies a word on Slide 13, but it does not recognize that is spelled correctly and suggests some replacement words.

2. **Click Ignore All in the Spelling pane**

   PowerPoint ignores all instances of this word and continues to check the rest of the presentation for errors. If PowerPoint finds any other words it does not recognize, either change or ignore them. When the Spell Checker finishes checking your presentation, the Spelling pane closes, and an alert box opens with a message stating the spelling check is complete.

3. **Click OK in the Alert box, then click the Slide 4 thumbnail in the Slides tab**

   The alert box closes. Now you experiment with the language translation feature.

4. **Click the Translate button in the Language group, then click Choose Translation Language**

   The Translation Language Options dialog box opens.

5. **Click the Translate to list arrow, click Czech, then click OK**

   The Translation Language Options dialog box closes.

6. **Click the Translate button in the Language group, click Mini Translator [Czech], click Yes in the alert box, then select the first line of text in the text object**

   The Microsoft Translator begins to analyze the selected text, and a semitransparent Microsoft Translator box appears below the text. The Mini toolbar may also appear above the text.

7. **Move the pointer over the Microsoft Translator box**

   A Czech translation of the text appears as shown in **FIGURE 4-13**. The translation language setting remains in effect until you reset it.

8. **Click the Translate button in the Language group, click Choose Translation Language, click the Translate to list arrow, click English (United States), click OK, click the Translate button again, then click Mini Translator [English (United States)]**

   The Mini Translator is turned off, and the translation language is restored to the default setting.

FIGURE 4-12: Spelling pane

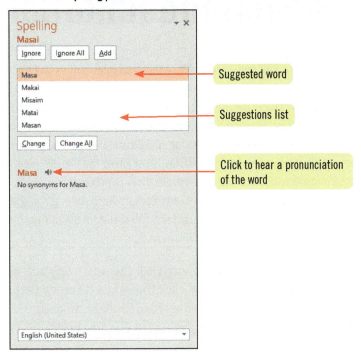

FIGURE 4-13: Translated text in the Microsoft Translator box

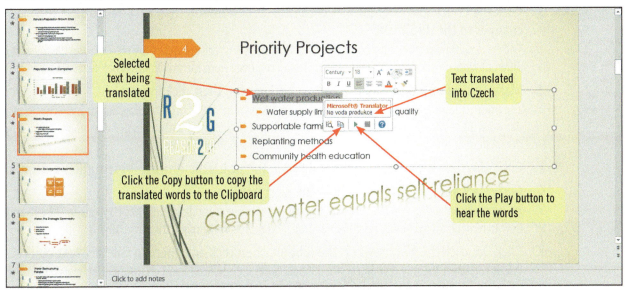

Checking spelling as you type

By default, PowerPoint checks your spelling as you type. If you type a word that is not in the dictionary, a wavy red line appears under it. To correct an error, right-click the misspelled word, then review the suggestions, which appear in the shortcut menu. You can select a suggestion, add the word you typed to your custom dictionary, or ignore it. To turn off automatic spell checking, click the File tab, then click Options to open the PowerPoint Options dialog box. Click Proofing in the left column, then click the Check spelling as you type check box to deselect it. To temporarily hide the wavy red lines, click the Hide spelling and grammar errors check box to select it. Contextual spelling in PowerPoint identifies common grammatically misused words, for example, if you type the word "their" and the correct word is "there," PowerPoint will identify the mistake and place a wavy red line under the word. To turn contextual spelling on or off, click Proofing in the PowerPoint Options dialog box, then click the Check grammar with spelling check box.

Inspect a Presentation

Learning Outcomes
- Modify document properties
- Inspect and remove unwanted data

Reviewing your presentation can be an important step. You should not only find and fix errors, but also locate and delete confidential company or personal information and document properties you do not want to share with others. If you share presentations with others, especially over the Internet, it is a good idea to inspect the presentation file using the Document Inspector. The **Document Inspector** looks for hidden data and personal information that is stored in the file itself or in the document properties. Document properties, also known as **metadata**, include specific data about the presentation, such as the author's name, subject matter, title, who saved the file last, and when the file was created. Other types of information the Document Inspector can locate and remove include presentation notes, comments, ink annotations, invisible on-slide content, off-slide content, and custom XML data. **CASE** *You decide to view and add some document properties, inspect your presentation file, and learn about the Mark as Final command.*

STEPS

QUICK TIP

Click the Properties list button, then click Advanced Properties to open the Properties dialog box to see or change more document properties.

1. **Click the File tab on the Ribbon, click the Add a tag text box in the Properties section, type Kenya, water well, then click the Add a category text box**

   This data provides some descriptive keywords for the presentation.

2. **Type Proposal, then click the Show All Properties link**

   The information you enter here about the presentation file can be used to identify and organize your file. The Show All Properties link displays all of the file properties and those you can change. You now use the Document Inspector to search for information you might want to delete in the presentation.

QUICK TIP

If you need to save a presentation to run in an earlier version of PowerPoint, check for unsupported features using the Check Compatibility feature.

3. **Click the Check for Issues button, click Inspect Document, then click Yes to save the changes to the document**

   The Document Inspector dialog box opens. The Document Inspector searches the presentation file for seven different types of information that you might want removed from the presentation before sharing it.

4. **Make sure all of the check boxes have check marks, then click Inspect**

   The presentation file is reviewed, and the results are shown in **FIGURE 4-14**. The Document Inspector found items having to do with document properties, which you just entered, and embedded documents which are the pictures in the file. You decide to leave all the document properties alone.

5. **Click Close, click the File tab on the Ribbon, then click the Protect Presentation button**

6. **Click Mark as Final, then click OK in the alert box**

   An information alert box opens. Be sure to read the message to understand what happens to the file and how to recognize a marked-as-final presentation. You decide to complete this procedure.

7. **Click OK, click the Home tab on the Ribbon, then click anywhere in the title text object**

   When you select the title text object, the Ribbon closes automatically and an information alert box at the top of the window notes that the presentation is marked as final, making it a read-only file. Compare your screen to **FIGURE 4-15**. A **read-only** file is one that can't be edited or modified in any way. Anyone who has received a read-only presentation can only edit the presentation by changing its marked-as-final status. You still want to work on the presentation, so you remove the marked-as-final status.

8. **Click the Edit Anyway button in the information alert box, then save your changes**

   The Ribbon and all commands are active again, and the file can now be modified.

FIGURE 4-14: Document Inspector dialog box

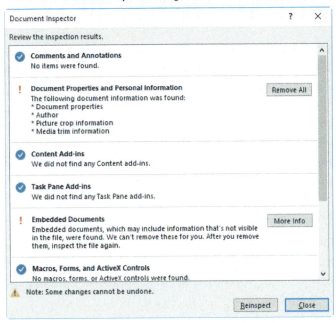

FIGURE 4-15: Marked as final presentation

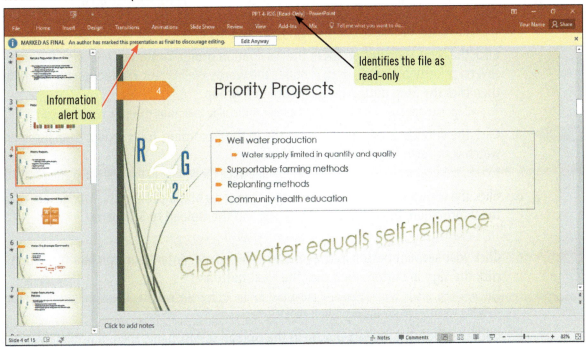

Digitally sign a presentation

What is a digital signature, and why would you want to use one in PowerPoint? A **digital signature** is similar to a handwritten signature in that it authenticates your document; however, a digital signature, unlike a handwritten signature, is created using computer cryptography and is not visible within the presentation itself. There are three primary reasons you would add a digital signature to a presentation: one, to authenticate the signer of the document; two, to ensure that the content of the presentation has not been changed since it was signed; and three, to assure the reader of the origin of the signed document. To add a digital signature, click the File tab on the Ribbon, click the Protect Presentation button, click Add a Digital Signature, then follow the dialog boxes.

PowerPoint 2016

Create an Office Mix

Learning
Outcomes
• Create and insert
  an Office Mix
• Publish an Office
  Mix

Office Mix is a free add-in application developed by Microsoft which, once downloaded from the web, is integrated directly on the PowerPoint Ribbon with its own set of tools located on the Mix tab. Using Office Mix, you create and then insert interactive content onto the slides of your presentation. Content such as a video recording of you giving a presentation, video clips from the web, and interactive quizzes or polls are easy to create. Once you are finished creating your Office Mix, you can publish it to the Office Mix website or the cloud to be shared with others. **CASE** *You decide to create a short recording explaining the chart and introducing a priority project. You then publish the Mix to the Office Mix website. (Note: The Office Mix add-in must be installed from the Office Mix website prior to performing the steps of this lesson.)*

STEPS

1. **Click the Slide 3 thumbnail in the Slides tab, click the Mix tab on the Ribbon, look over the commands on the Mix tab, then click the Slide Recording button in the Record group**
   The Screen Recording view opens as shown in **FIGURE 4-16**. The Screen Recording view displays the current slide with navigation, recording, and inking tools.

2. **When you are ready to begin recording, click the Record button in the Record group, look into your computer's camera, then speak these words into your microphone "This chart shows the population trends for Kenya, Uganda, and South Africa"**
   Your Office Mix recording begins as soon as you click the Record button. If a slide has animations, each animation must be advanced manually during the recording in order to see the animation.

3. **Click the Next Slide button ➡ in the Navigation group, continue speaking "R2G has several priority projects", drag ✏ under the words Well Water Production on the slide, then click the Stop button in the Navigation group**
   A small speaker appears in the upper right corner of the slide indicating there is a recording on the slide.

4. **Click the Preview Slide Recording button in the Recording Tools group, then listen and watch your recording**
   You can move to any slide and preview its recording using the buttons in the Navigation group.

5. **Click the window Close button, click the Upload to Mix button in the Mix group, read the information, then click the Next button in the Upload to Mix pane**
   The Upload to Mix pane displays sign in account methods.

6. **Click your account button in the Upload to Mix pane, enter your sign in information, click the Sign in button, then click the Next button**
   The new Office Mix is uploaded and published to the Office Mix website. There is a percentage counter showing you the upload and publishing progress.

7. **Click the Show me my Mix button in the Upload to Mix pane, then, if necessary, click the Sign in button on the webpage that appears**
   The Office Mix webpage appears with the new Office Mix you just created as shown in **FIGURE 4-17**. On this page you can provide a content description, a category, or a tag, as well as set permissions.

8. **Click My Mixes at the top of the window, click the PPT 4-R2G Play button, then follow the directions on the screen to watch the Office Mix**
   Each slide in the presentation, including the Office Mix recordings you made on Slide 3 and 4, appears.

9. **Click Your Name at the top of the window, click sign out, click your web browser Close button, click the Close button in the Upload to Mix pane, save your changes, submit your presentation to your instructor, then exit PowerPoint**

FIGURE 4-16: Office Mix screen recording view

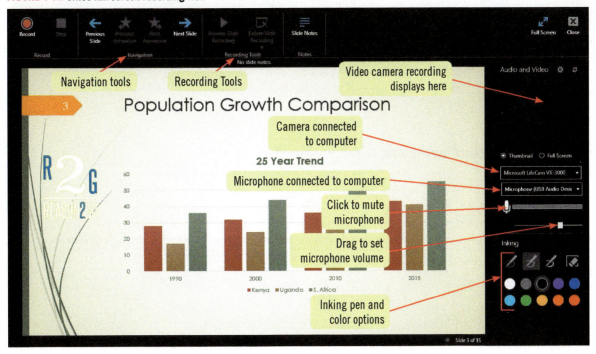

FIGURE 4-16: Office Mix screen recording view

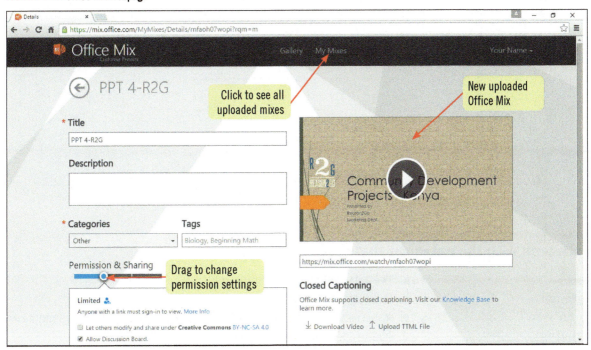

FIGURE 4-17: Office Mix webpage

Inserting a multiple choice interactive quiz

Using the Mix tab, you can create a custom interactive quiz that can be presented in Slide Show view or uploaded to the Office Mix website to share with others. On the Mix tab, click the Quizzes Videos Apps button in the Insert group. In the Lab Office Add-ins dialog box, click Multiple Choice Quiz, then click Trust It. A multiple choice quiz object appears on your slide with blank text boxes that you fill out with a quiz question and answers. Be sure to enter the correct answer in the light green answer text box, then add as many other possible answers as you like. You can customize your question by shuffling the answer every time the question is opened, limiting the number of answer attempts, and allowing more than one right answer.

Practice

Concepts Review

Label each element of the PowerPoint window shown in FIGURE 4-18.

FIGURE 4-18

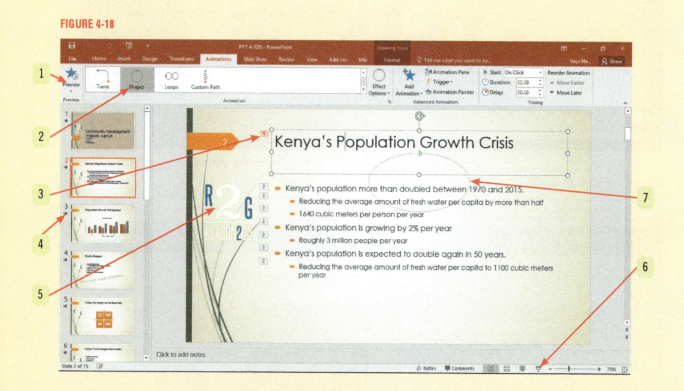

Match each term with the statement that best describes it.

8. Masters
9. Background
10. Presenter view
11. Slide timing
12. Office Mix
13. Ink annotations

a. The area behind the text and graphics
b. Drawings on slide created during slide show
c. A special view that you use when showing a presentation on two monitors
d. Add-in application you use to create interactive content
e. Determines how long slide is visible on screen
f. Slides that store theme and placeholder information

Select the best answer from the list of choices.

14. What determines the position and size of text and content placeholders and the slide background of a presentation?

    a. Home tab   **c.** Master

    b. Background   **d.** Normal view

15. Apply this to your presentation to quickly modify the applied theme.

    a. Office Mix   **c.** Animation

    b. Background   **d.** Variant

16. Freehand pen and highlighter strokes are also known as _____.

    a. ink annotations   **c.** markings

    b. pictures   **d.** scribbles

17. A slide _____ is a special visual effect that determines how a slide moves during a slide show.

    a. annotation   **c.** background

    b. view   **d.** transition

18. Set slide _____ to make your presentation automatically progress through the slides during a slide show.

    a. animations   **c.** hyperlinks

    b. timings   **d.** recordings

19. Animation _____ identify the order in which objects are animated during a slide show.

    a. tags   **c.** thumbnails

    b. paths   **d.** schemes

20. A _____ file is one that can't be edited or modified in any way.

    a. signed   **c.** read-only

    b. final   **d.** saved

Skills Review

1. **Modify masters.**

    a. Open the presentation PPT 4-3.pptx from the location where you store your Data Files, then save the presentation as **PPT 4-Dual Arm**.

    b. Open Slide Master view using the View tab, then click the Circuit Slide Master thumbnail.

    c. Insert the picture PPT 4-4.jpg, then set the background color to transparent.

    d. Resize the picture so it is 1.0" wide.

    e. Drag the picture to the upper-right corner of the slide to align with the top of the Title text object, then deselect the picture.

    f. Switch to Normal view, then save your changes.

2. **Customize the background and theme.**

    a. Click the Design tab, then click the second variant from the left.

    b. Go to Slide 4, then open the Format Background pane.

    c. Click the Solid fill option button, then click Gold, Accent 1, Darker 25%.

    d. Set the Transparency to 30%, close the Format Background pane then save your changes.

Skills Review (continued)

3. **Use slide show commands.**
   a. Open Slide Show view, then go to Slide 1 using the See all slides button on the Slide Show toolbar.
   b. Use the Pen ink annotation tool to circle the slide title.
   c. Go to Slide 2, then use the Highlighter to highlight four points in the bulleted text on the slide.
   d. Erase two highlight annotations on the bulleted text, then press [Esc].
   e. Open Presenter view, then stop the timer.
   f. Advance the slides to Slide 5, then click the Zoom into the slide button (now called the Zoom out button) on the Slide Show toolbar, then click in the center of the graph.
   g. Click the Zoom into the slide button, then return to Slide 1.
   h. Hide Presenter view, advance through the slide show, save your ink and highlight annotations, then save your work.

4. **Set slide transitions and timings.**
   a. Go to Slide Sorter view, click the Slide 1 thumbnail, then apply the Fall Over transition to the slide.
   b. Change the effect option to Right, change the duration to 2.50, then apply to all the slides.
   c. Change the slide timing to 5 seconds, then apply to all of the slides.
   d. Switch to Normal view, view the slide show, then save your work.

5. **Animate objects.**
   a. Go to Slide 3, click the Animations tab, then select both arrows on the slide. (*Hint*: Use SHIFT to select both arrows.)
   b. Apply the Wipe effect to the objects, click the Effect Options button, then apply the From Top effect.
   c. Select the lower two box shapes, apply the Random Bars animation, then preview the animations.
   d. Change the effect options to Vertical, then preview the animations.
   e. Select the top two box shapes, apply the Shape animation, click the Effect Options button, then click Box.
   f. Click the Move Earlier button in the Timing group until the two top box shape animation tags display 1.
   g. Preview the animations, then save your work.

6. **Use proofing and language tools.**
   a. Check the spelling of the document, and change any misspelled words. Ignore any words that are correctly spelled but that the spell checker doesn't recognize. There is one misspelled word in the presentation.
   b. Go to Slide 6, then set the Mini Translator language to Thai.
   c. View the Thai translation of text on Slide 6.
   d. Choose one other language (or as many as you want), translate words or phrases on the slide, reset the default language to English (United States), turn off the Mini Translator, then save your changes.

7. **Inspect a presentation.**
   a. On the File tab in the Properties section, type information of your choosing in the Tags and Categories text fields.
   b. Open the Document Inspector dialog box.
   c. Make sure the Off-Slide Content check box is selected, then inspect the presentation.
   d. Delete the off-slide content, then close the dialog box. Save your changes.

8. **Create an Office Mix.**
   a. Go to Slide 2, open the Mix tab, then click the Slide Recording button.
   b. Click the Record button, speak these words into your microphone, "Here you see the typical applications for the new R2G series dual robotic arm," use your pen to underline the slide title, then click the Stop button.
   c. Preview your slide recording, then close the window.
   d. Click the Upload to Mix button, sign in to your account, then upload your new mix to the Office Mix website.
   e. Watch the Office Mix, sign out of your account, then close the webpage window.
   f. Close the Upload to Mix pane, then save your work.

Skills Review (continued)

    g. Switch to Slide Sorter view, then compare your presentation to FIGURE 4-19.

    h. Submit your presentation to your instructor, then close the presentation.

FIGURE 4-19

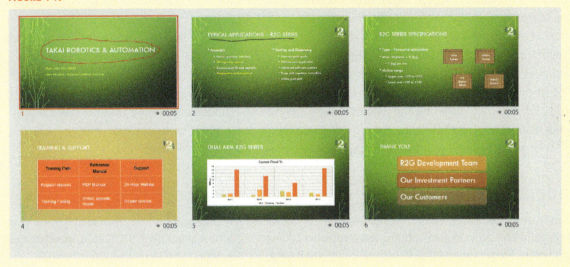

Independent Challenge 1

You work for World International Studies Program (WISP) as a study consultant. You have been working on a presentation that describes a new study program developed in Russia. You need to finish up what you have been working on by adding transitions, timings, and animation effects to the presentation.

    a. Open the file PPT 4-5.pptx from the location where you store your Data Files, and save the presentation as **PPT 4-WISP**.

    b. Add the slide number and your name as the footer on all slides, except the title slide.

    c. Open Slide Master view, click the Celestial Slide Master thumbnail, insert the picture PPT 4-6.jpg, then resize the picture so it is 1.5" wide.

    d. Click the Color button, then click the Purple, Accent color 1 Dark in the Recolor section.

    e. Move the picture to the top left corner of the slide, then close Slide Master view.

    f. Apply the Shape animation to the title text on each slide.

    g. Apply the Float In animation to the bulleted text objects on each slide.

    h. Apply the Shape animation to the picture on Slide 3, then change the effect option to Box.

    i. Apply the Vortex slide transition, apply a 5-second slide timing, then apply to all of the slides.

    j. Check the spelling of the presentation, save your changes, then view the presentation in Slide Show view.

    k. Submit your presentation to your instructor, close the presentation, then exit PowerPoint.

Independent Challenge 2

You are a development engineer at Adtec Global Systems, Inc., a manufacturer of civilian drone technology located in Phoenix, Arizona. Adtec designs and manufactures personal drone systems largely used in the movie industry and in commercial agricultural business. You need to finish the work on a quarterly presentation that outlines the progress of the company's newest technologies by adding animations, customizing the background, and using the Document Inspector.

    a. Open the file PPT 4-7.pptx from the location where you store your Data Files, and save the presentation as **PPT 4-Adtec**.

Independent Challenge 2 (continued)

b. Apply an appropriate design theme, then apply a gradient fill slide background to the title slide using the Format Background pane.

c. Apply the Airplane slide transition to all slides, apply the Shape animation to the following objects: the bulleted text on Slide 2 and the table on Slide 4, then change the Effect options on the table to a box shape with an out direction.

d. Use the Microsoft Translator to translate the bulleted text on Slide 2 using two different languages.

e. Run the Document Inspector with all options selected, identify what items the Document Inspector finds, close the Document Inspector dialog box, then review the slides to find the items.

f. Add a slide at the end of the presentation that identifies the items the Document Inspector found.

g. Run the Document Inspector again, and remove all items except the document properties.

h. View the slide show, and make ink annotations to the slides. Save the annotations at the end of the slide show.

i. Add your name as a footer to all slides, check the spelling, fix any misspellings, then save your work.

j. Submit your presentation to your instructor, then close the presentation and exit PowerPoint.

Independent Challenge 3

You work for Buffington, Genung, O'Lynn & Associates, a full-service investment and pension firm. Your manager wants you to create a presentation on pension plan options. You completed adding the information to the presentation, now you need to add a design theme, format information to highlight important facts, add animation effects, and add slide timings.

a. Open the file PPT 4-8.pptx from the location where you store your Data Files, and save the presentation as **PPT 4-Invest**.

b. Apply an appropriate design theme, then apply a theme variant.

c. Apply animation effects to the following objects: the shapes on Slide 3 and the bulleted text on Slide 4. View the slide show to evaluate the effects you added, and make adjustments as necessary.

d. Convert the text on Slide 5 to a Circle Relationship SmartArt graphic (found in the Relationship category).

e. Apply the Inset SmartArt style to the SmartArt graphic, then change its color to Dark 2 Fill.

f. Go to Slide 3, align the Sector and Quality arrow shapes to their bottoms, then align the Allocation and Maturity arrow shapes to their right edges.

g. On Slides 6 and 7, change the table style format to Themed Style 1 - Accent 2, and adjust the tables.

h. Apply a 7-second timing to Slides 3–7 and a 5-second timing to Slides 1 and 2.

i. Add your name as a footer to the slides, check the spelling, then save your work. An example of a finished presentation is shown in FIGURE 4-20.

j. Submit your presentation to your instructor, then close the presentation and exit PowerPoint.

FIGURE 4-20

Independent Challenge 4: Explore

You work for the Office of Veterans Affairs at your college. Create a basic presentation that you can publish to the Office Mix website that describes the basic services offered by the school to service members. (*Note: To complete this Independent Challenge, you may need to be connected to the Internet.*)

a. Plan and create the slide presentation that describes the veteran services provided by the college. To help create content, use your school's website or use the Internet to locate information at another college. The presentation should contain at least six slides.

b. Use an appropriate design theme then change the theme variant.

c. Add one or more photographs to the presentation, then style and customize at least one photo.

d. Save the presentation as **PPT 4-Vet** to the location where you store your Data Files.

e. Add slide transitions and animation effects to the presentation. View the slide show to evaluate the effects you added.

f. Go to Slide 5, translate the last line of text in the bulleted text box into Greek, then click the Copy button on the Microsoft Translator box.

g. Insert a new text box on Slide 5, paste the Greek text into the text box, then drag the Greek text box below the bulleted text box.

h. Change the language in the Microsoft translator back to English, then turn off the Microsoft Translator.

i. Add the slide number and your name as a footer to the slides, check the spelling, inspect the presentation, then save your work.

j. Make an Office Mix of this presentation, then upload it to the Office Mix website. Make sure to include information in your recording on at least 2 slides and use the pen to make ink annotations on your slides.

k. Submit your presentation to your instructor, then exit PowerPoint. An example of a finished presentation is shown in FIGURE 4-21.

FIGURE 4-21

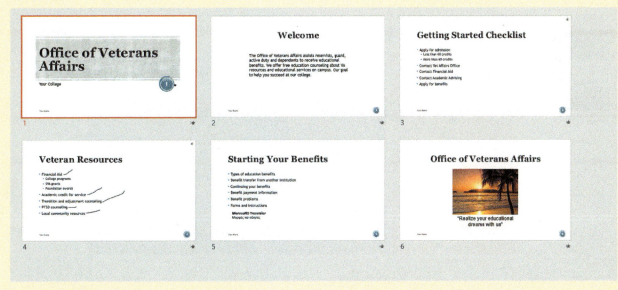

Visual Workshop

Create a presentation that looks like **FIGURE 4-22**, and **FIGURE 4-23**, which shows two slides with a specific slide layout, slide background, theme, and theme variant. Insert pictures **PPT 4-9** and **PPT 4-10** to the slides, then insert the picture **PPT 4-6** to the presentation slide master. (*Hint*: the slide master picture background is transparent.) Add your name as footer text to the slide, save the presentation as **PPT 4-Corp** to the location where you store your Data Files, then submit your presentation to your instructor.

FIGURE 4-22

© Prasit Rodphan/Shutterstock.com

FIGURE 4-23

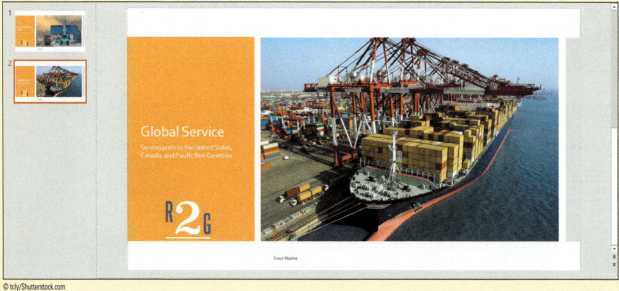

© tcly/Shutterstock.com

Integrating Word, Excel, Access, and PowerPoint

CASE ▶ Kevin Lawrence, vice president of Operations for R2G, creates presentations for clients that often include objects from Word, Excel, and Access. He asks you to explore how to use linking and embedding in Office 2016 and then how to insert linked objects from Word, Excel, and Access into a PowerPoint presentation.

Module Objectives

After completing this module, you will be able to:

- Integrate data among Word, Excel, Access, and PowerPoint
- Import a Word outline into PowerPoint
- Embed an Excel worksheet in PowerPoint
- Link Access and Excel objects to PowerPoint
- Manage links

Files You Will Need

INT 3-1.docx	INT 3-6.accdb
INT 3-2.accdb	INT 3-7.docx
INT 3-3.docx	INT 3-8.accdb
INT 3-4.accdb	INT 3-9.accdb
INT 3-5.docx	

Learning
Outcomes
• Identify integration
options for Word,
Excel, Access, and
PowerPoint

Integrate Data Among Word, Excel, Access, and PowerPoint

You can integrate information into a PowerPoint presentation using the linking and embedding techniques you learned with Word, Excel, and Access. As with those programs, you embed data created in other programs in PowerPoint when you want to be able to edit the data from within the destination file. You use linking when you want the linked data in the destination file to be updated when you change the data in the source file. In addition, you can import a Word outline into PowerPoint to automatically create slides without having to reenter information. The PowerPoint presentation in **FIGURE 3-1** includes information originally created in Word, Excel, and Access. **CASE** *Before you create the presentation, you review some of the ways you can integrate information among Word, Excel, Access, and PowerPoint.*

DETAILS

You can integrate Word, Excel, Access, and PowerPoint by:

• **Importing a Word outline into PowerPoint**

In the course of your work, you may create Word documents that contain information that you also want to use in a PowerPoint presentation. Instead of retyping the information in PowerPoint, you can save time by importing it directly from Word into PowerPoint. **FIGURE 3-1** shows how a Word outline appears before and after it is imported into a PowerPoint presentation. Each Level 1 heading in the outline becomes a slide, and the Level 2 headings become bullets on the slides. Before you import a Word outline, you need to make sure all the headings and subheadings are formatted with heading styles. When you import an outline from Word to PowerPoint, you cannot create a link between the two files.

• **Embedding objects**

Recall that when you embed an object, you do not create a link to the source file. However, you can use the source program tools to edit the embedded object within the destination file. An embedded object becomes a part of the PowerPoint file, which means that the file size of the PowerPoint presentation increases relative to the file size of the embedded object; a large embedded object, such as a graphic, will increase the size of the PowerPoint presentation considerably. To embed an object in a PowerPoint presentation, you use the Object command in the Text group on the Insert tab. In **FIGURE 3-1**, the table on Slide 3 is an embedded Excel worksheet object.

To edit an embedded object, you double-click it. The source program starts, and the Ribbon and tabs of the source program appear inside the PowerPoint window.

• **Linking objects**

When you link an object to a PowerPoint slide, a picture of the object is placed on the slide instead of the actual object. This representation of the object is connected, or linked, to the original file. The object is still stored in the source file in the source program, unlike an embedded object, which is stored directly on the PowerPoint slide. Any change you make to a linked object's source file is reflected in the linked object. The pie chart shown on Slide 4 of the presentation in **FIGURE 3-1** is linked to values entered in an Excel worksheet, which is, in turn, linked to data entered in an Access database. The differences between embedding and linking are summarized in **TABLE 3-1**.

You can open the source file and make changes to the linked object as long as all files remain on your computer. When you move files among machines or transmit files to other people, the links will not be maintained. However, recipients can open and view the linked files. After opening the workbook in Excel, they need to click No, close the workbook without saving it, then reopen the workbook and click Don't Update. In Word, they click No to update links.

FIGURE 3-1: PowerPoint presentation with integrated objects

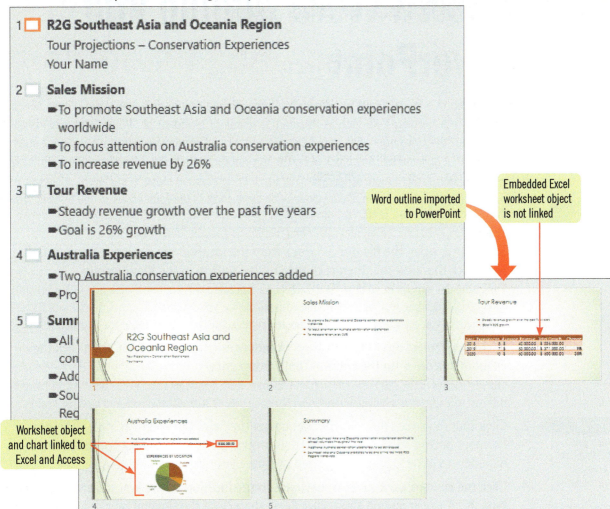

TABLE 3-1: Embedding vs. linking

	Embed	**Link**
User	You are the only user of an object and you want the object to be a part of your presentation	The object's source file is shared on a network or other users have access to the file and can change it.
Availability	You want to open the object in its source program, even when the source file is not available	You are able to open the source file
Timeliness	Information does not change over time	You always want the object to include the latest information
Updating	You want to update the object manually while working in PowerPoint	You want the object to update automatically
File size	File size is not an issue	You want to keep the file size of the presentation small

Import a Word Outline into PowerPoint

Learning Outcomes
- Prepare a Word outline for PowerPoint
- Import a Word outline into PowerPoint

Before you import a Word outline into PowerPoint, you should ensure that each Word outline heading is formatted with a heading style such as Heading 1, Heading 2, and so on. PowerPoint imports all text formatted with the Heading 1 style as a slide title and all text formatted with the Heading 2 style as a Level 1 item in a bulleted list. Any block of text that is not formatted with a heading style is not included in the PowerPoint presentation. **CASE** *You use tour information included in a Word document as the basis of a PowerPoint presentation about conservation experiences in the Southeast Asia and Oceania region.*

STEPS

1. **Start Word, open the file INT 3-1.docx from the location where you store your Data Files, click the View tab, then click the Outline button in the Views group**

   The document appears in Outline view. Each Level 1 heading will become a slide title in PowerPoint, and each Level 2 heading will become a bulleted item. Before you import a Word outline into a PowerPoint presentation, you check that all the headings and subheadings are positioned at the correct levels.

2. **Click Tour Projections - Conservation Experiences (the second line), then click the Demote button ➡ in the Outline Tools group once**

   The text moves to the right one tab stop and changes from body text to a Level 2 heading. In PowerPoint, this text will appear as a bulleted item under the slide title "R2G Southeast Asia and Oceania Region."

3. **Click Tour Revenue (the fourth bullet below the Sales Mission heading), click the Promote button ⬅ in the Outline Tools group, click Two Australia conservation experiences added, press [Tab], then compare your Word outline to FIGURE 3-2**

4. **Click the File tab, click Save As, navigate to the location where you store your Data Files, type INT 3-Conservation Sales, click Save, then close the document**

5. **Start PowerPoint, create a blank presentation, then save it as INT 3-Conservation Sales Presentation in the location where you store your Data Files**

6. **Click the New Slide list arrow in the Slides group, click Slides from Outline, navigate to the location where you stored INT 3-Conservation Sales, then double-click INT 3-Conservation Sales**

   The Thumbnails pane and the status bar indicate the presentation now contains six slides. Slide 1 is blank, and Slides 2 through 6 represent the Level 1 headings in the Word outline.

7. **Click Slide 1 in the Thumbnails pane, press [Delete], click the Layout button in the Slides group, click Title Slide, click the View tab, click the Outline View button in the Presentation Views group, click after Conservation Experiences on Slide 1, press [Enter], then type your name**

   You change the slide layout for the first slide so the title of the presentation and your name appear in the middle of the slide.

8. **Click the Design tab, click the More button ⬇ in the Themes group, then click the Wisp theme**

9. **Click the View tab, click the Slide Sorter button in the Presentation Views group, press [Ctrl][A] to select all the slides, click the Home tab, click the Reset button in the Slides group, then save the presentation**

   The formatted presentation appears as shown in **FIGURE 3-3**.

FIGURE 3-2: Edited outline in Word Outline view

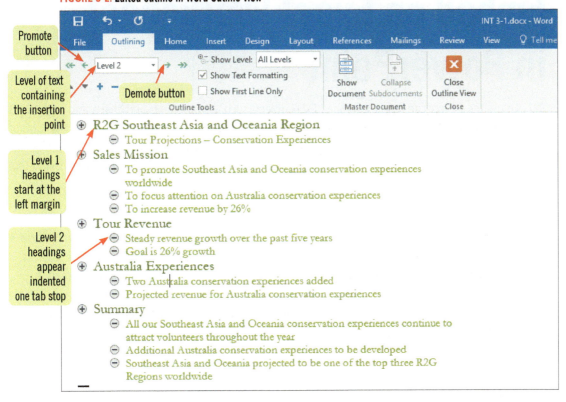

- Promote button
- Level of text containing the insertion point
- Demote button
- Level 1 headings start at the left margin
- Level 2 headings appear indented one tab stop

FIGURE 3-3: Formatted presentation in Slide Sorter view

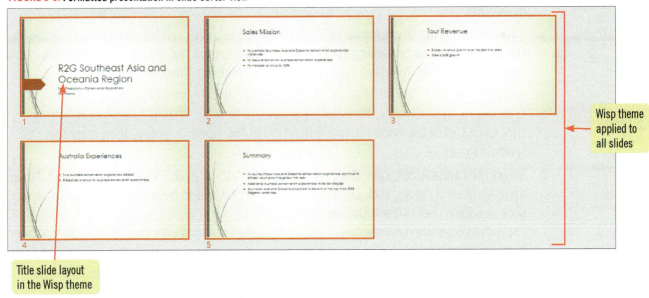

- Wisp theme applied to all slides
- Title slide layout in the Wisp theme

Embed an Excel Worksheet in PowerPoint

Learning Outcomes
- Embed a Worksheet object in PowerPoint
- Edit an embedded worksheet

You can use the Object command to embed Excel objects such as worksheets and charts into both Word and PowerPoint documents. When you double-click the embedded object, you can then use the tools of the source program to edit the object. **CASE** *You want Slide 3 to include a worksheet with calculations that you can edit from within PowerPoint when you obtain new data. You create an Excel worksheet on the slide, and then edit it using Excel tools.*

STEPS

1. **Click the View tab, click the Normal button in the Presentation Views group, click Slide 3 in the Thumbnails pane to move to Slide 3, click the Insert tab, click the Object button in the Text group, verify the Create new option button is selected, scroll to and click Microsoft Excel Worksheet, then click OK**

   An Excel worksheet appears on the PowerPoint slide, and the Excel Ribbon and tabs appear. The PowerPoint title bar and menu bar, above the Excel tools, indicate that Excel is operating within PowerPoint. When you embed a worksheet object in a PowerPoint slide, you generally want to show only the cells that contain data.

2. **Drag the lower-right corner handle of the worksheet object up so only columns A to E and rows 1 to 4 are visible, as shown in FIGURE 3-4**

   You want to clearly see the data you need to enter into the worksheet object.

3. **Click the Select All button in the upper-left corner of the embedded worksheet to select all the worksheet cells, change the font size to 24 point, then click cell A1**

4. **Enter the labels and values in the range A1:D4 as shown in FIGURE 3-5, widening columns as needed**

5. **Click cell D2, enter the formula =B2*C2, press [Enter], click cell D2, drag its fill handle to cell D4 to enter the remaining two formulas, then format the values in the Average Revenue and Total Growth columns with the Accounting Number format**

   You need to calculate the percentage change in revenue over the past two years.

6. **Click cell E1, type Change, click cell E3, enter the formula =(D3-D2)/D3, press [Enter], click cell E3, click the Percent Style button % in the Number group, then copy the formula to cell E4**

7. **Select the range A1:E4, click the Format as Table button in the Styles group, select Table Style Medium 2 (blue), click OK, click the Convert to Range button in the Tools group, click Yes, then click outside the worksheet object**

   The embedded worksheet uses the default Office theme, and you want the fonts and colors of the worksheet to use the Wisp theme you applied to the PowerPoint slide.

8. **Double-click the worksheet object to show the Excel Ribbon and tabs again, click the Page Layout tab, click the Themes button in the Themes group, then click Wisp**

9. **Change 9 in cell B3 to 7, press [Tab], click outside the worksheet object, drag the object below the text as shown in FIGURE 3-6, then save the presentation**

   The percentage growth for 2016 is now 38%.

FIGURE 3-4: Resizing the worksheet object

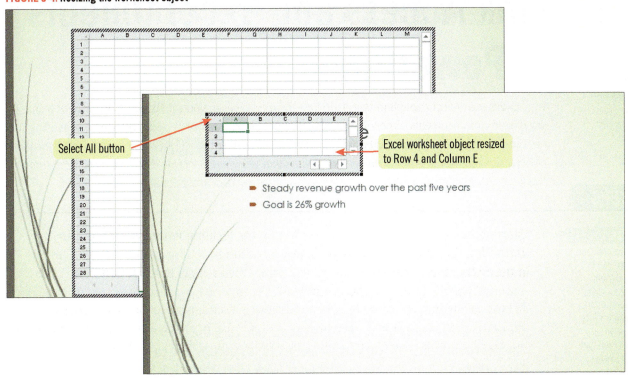

Select All button

Excel worksheet object resized to Row 4 and Column E

➡ Steady revenue growth over the past five years
➡ Goal is 26% growth

FIGURE 3-5: Labels and values entered in the Excel worksheet object

Year	Experiences	Average Revenue	Total Growth	
2014	8	42000		
2015	9	53000		
2016	10	60000		

Sheet1

Double-click column dividers to widen columns

FIGURE 3-6: Completed Excel worksheet object

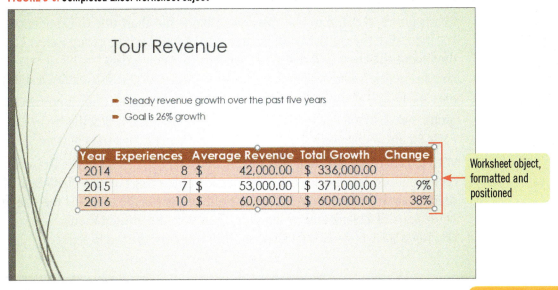

Tour Revenue

➡ Steady revenue growth over the past five years
➡ Goal is 26% growth

Year	Experiences	Average Revenue	Total Growth	Change
2014	8	$ 42,000.00	$ 336,000.00	
2015	7	$ 53,000.00	$ 371,000.00	9%
2016	10	$ 60,000.00	$ 600,000.00	38%

Worksheet object, formatted and positioned

Integration

Link Access and Excel Objects to PowerPoint

Learning Outcomes
• Link an Access table to Excel
• Link an Excel chart to PowerPoint

You can copy an Access table from Access to PowerPoint; however, you cannot paste the table as a link. To link data from an Access database to a PowerPoint presentation, you first copy the data to Excel as a link and then copy the data from Excel and paste it as a link into PowerPoint. **CASE** *You already have data about conservation experiences stored in an Access database that you want to include in the PowerPoint presentation. You want any changes you make to the table in Access also to appear in the PowerPoint presentation.*

STEPS

1. **Start Access, open the file INT 3-2.accdb from the location where you store your Data Files, save the database as INT 3-Conservation Experiences, click Enable Content if necessary, double-click the Experiences table, then review the Location field**
   You need to sort the Experiences table alphabetically by Location so you can use the data in a chart you create in Excel. You create a query to sort the data so the sorting is maintained when you copy the data to Excel.

2. **Close the Experiences table, click the Create tab, click the Query Wizard button in the Queries group, click OK, click the Select All Fields button >> to add all the fields in the Experiences table to the query, click Next, click Next, then click Finish**

3. **Click the Home tab, click the View button in the Views group to go to Design view, click the blank line below "Experiences" in the [Location] column, click the Location Sort list arrow, then select Ascending as shown in FIGURE 3-7**

4. **Close and save the Experiences query, click Experiences Query in the Navigation Pane, then click the Copy button in the Clipboard group**

5. **Create a new blank workbook in Excel, click cell A1, click the Paste list arrow in the Clipboard group, click the Paste Link button , click cell F1, type Total, click cell F2, enter the formula =C2*D2, copy the formula to the range F3:F11, format the values in columns C and F with the Accounting Number format, then widen columns as necessary**

6. **Save the file as INT 3-Conservation Locations in the location where you store your Data Files, click cell C14, then enter the labels and formulas as shown in FIGURE 3-8**

7. **Select the range C14:G15, click the Insert tab, click the Insert Pie button in the Charts group, click the top-left pie style, change the chart title to Experiences by Location, click the Quick Layout button in the Chart Layouts group, select Layout 6, then move the chart so it doesn't cover cells containing data**
   Australia experiences generated 16% of revenue, Fiji 9%, Indonesia 19%, Malaysia 32%, and Thailand 24%.

8. **Click the border of the pie chart, click the Home tab, click the Copy button in the Clipboard group, switch to the PowerPoint presentation, show Slide 4, click the Home tab, click the Paste list arrow, then click the Use Destination Theme & Link Data button **

9. **With the chart still selected, click the Shape Outline list arrow in the Drawing group, click the Black, Text 1 color box, click outside of the chart, click a blank area of the chart, drag it below the text, drag the lower right corner handle to adjust the size as shown in FIGURE 3-9, click a blank area of the slide, then save the presentation**
   The chart is linked to the Excel worksheet and the Tours Query datasheet in Access.

FIGURE 3-7: Sorting the Season field in Query Design view

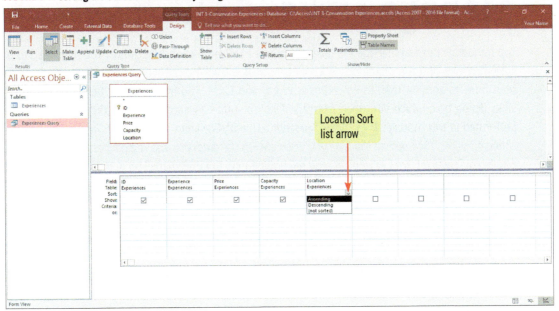

FIGURE 3-8: Formulas to calculate total tours by Category

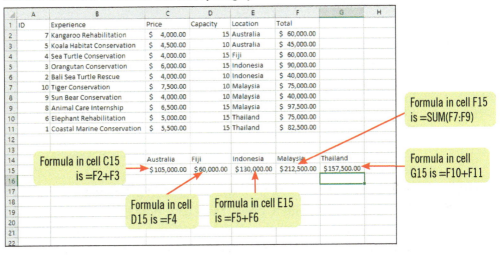

FIGURE 3-9: Linking a copied chart to PowerPoint

Manage Links

Learning
Outcomes
• Manually update
  links
• Break links

You frequently need to manage the links you create between files and programs. You may need to update links manually, find the source of a link, or even break a link. You normally break a link when you need to send a file to another user. In PowerPoint, Word, and Excel, you manage links between files in the Edit Links dialog box, which you open from the File tab. TABLE 3-2 summarizes all the integration tasks you performed in this module. CASE ▸ *You want to modify the chart on Slide 4 of the presentation to reflect changing prices, then update the links you've created in the database, the spreadsheet, and the presentation. Finally, you break the links so you can send the presentation to R2G's marketing department.*

STEPS

1. Switch to Access, open the Experiences Query datasheet, change the price of the Kangaroo Rehabilitation tour to $7,000, press [Enter], then close the Experiences Query datasheet

   When you change data in the Experiences Query datasheet, the corresponding data in the Experiences table also changes.

2. Switch to Excel, click the File tab, then click Edit Links to Files in the lower-right corner of the screen, as shown in FIGURE 3-10

   The Edit Links dialog box opens.

QUICK TIP
The linked values will automatically be updated in Excel if you wait a few minutes, but you can speed up the updating process by updating the values manually in the Edit Links dialog box.

3. Click Update Values, click Close, click ⬅ to return to the worksheet, verify that Australia experiences now account for 21% of projected tour revenue, then save the workbook

4. Switch to PowerPoint, then verify that the Australia experiences slice is now 21%

5. Click the pie chart, click the Chart Tools Design tab, click the More button ⬇ in the Chart Styles group, then select Style 9

   When you insert an Excel chart into a PowerPoint presentation, you usually need to select a new chart style so the data is easy to read on a slide.

QUICK TIP
A value you copy from Excel and paste into PowerPoint as a link is formatted as an object that you can move and resize the same as you would any object.

6. Switch to Excel, copy cell C15, switch back to PowerPoint, click after "experiences" in the second bulleted item, press [Spacebar], type is, click the Paste list arrow, click Paste Special, click the Paste link option button, click OK to paste the link as a Microsoft Excel Worksheet Object, then position the worksheet object to the right of "is" and increase its size slightly

   The copied object appears as $150,000.00.

7. Switch to Access, open the Experiences Query datasheet, change the cost of each of the two Australia experiences to $8,000, close the datasheet, switch to Excel and open the Edit Links dialog box on the File tab, update the link in Excel, switch to PowerPoint, then verify the worksheet object in PowerPoint is now $200,000.00 and the Australia pie slice is 26%

8. In PowerPoint, click the File tab, click Edit Links to Files, click the top link, click Break Link, confirm the deletion if necessary, click the remaining link, click Break Link, click Close, then repeat the process in Excel to break the link to Access

   Now when you change data in the Access file, the linked Excel chart in PowerPoint will not be updated.

9. Click ⬅ to return to PowerPoint, click the View tab, click the Slide Sorter button in the Presentation Views group, compare the completed presentation to FIGURE 3-11, save and close all open files and programs, then submit your files to your instructor

FIGURE 3-10: Updating links using the FILE tab

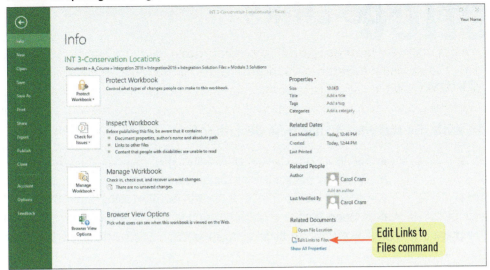

FIGURE 3-11: Completed presentation in Slide Sorter view

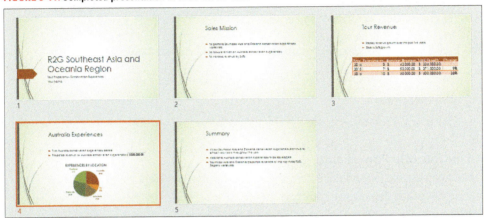

TABLE 3-2: Module 3 integration tasks

object	commands	source program(s)	destination program	result	connection	page no.
Word outline	In PowerPoint: New Slide/Slides from Outline	Word	PowerPoint	Word outline inserted into PowerPoint; Level 1 headings are slide titles, and Level 2 headings are text items	None	36
Excel worksheet	In PowerPoint: Insert/Object/ Create New	Excel	PowerPoint	Excel worksheet created in PowerPoint, then updated by double-clicking and using Excel tools	Embedded	38
Access query	Copy/Paste Link button	Access	Excel	Access query is pasted into Excel as a link; linked data can only be formatted in Excel	Linked	40
Excel chart	Copy/Paste Link using the Use Destination Themes and Link Data button	Access/Excel	PowerPoint	Chart created from linked Access query is pasted into PowerPoint as a link; when Access data changes, Excel and PowerPoint data is updated	Linked	40

Practice

Concepts Review

Match each term with the statement that best describes it.

1. Link
2. Linked object
3. Embedded object
4. Edit Links
5. Destination program

a. Edit by making changes in the source file
b. The dialog box containing commands to manage connections between files
c. Contains embedded objects that can be edited using the tools of source programs
d. Increases the size of the destination file
e. The best way to share information when the file size should remain small

Select the best answer from the list of choices.

6. In Word, which view do you work in to prepare text to import into a PowerPoint presentation?
   a. Outline
   b. Print
   c. Full Screen Reading
   d. Draft

7. In Excel, which Paste option do you choose to paste a linked Access table?
   a. Import
   b. Paste Link
   c. Paste
   d. Link

Skills Review

1. **Import a Word outline into PowerPoint.**
   a. Start Word, then open the file INT 3-3.docx from the location where you store your Data Files.
   b. Switch to Outline view, then demote the body text "Maui, HI" to Level 2.
   c. Demote the three subheadings: "Townhouses," "Houses," and "Estates" to Level 3.
   d. Promote the Property Values subheading to Level 1, save the document as **INT 3-Paradise Realty Outline**, then close the document.
   e. Open a blank presentation in PowerPoint, then save it as **INT 3-Paradise Realty Presentation** in the location where you store your Data Files.
   f. Import the INT 3-Paradise Realty Outline document as slides into PowerPoint.
   g. Delete the blank Slide 1, apply the Title Slide layout to the new Slide 1, then add your name after the subtitle on Slide 1.
   h. Apply the Droplet slide design.
   i. Switch to Slide Sorter view, select all the slides, reset the layout, then save the presentation.

2. **Embed an Excel worksheet in PowerPoint.**
   a. Switch to Outline view, move to Slide 4, delete the blank text placeholder, then insert a Microsoft Excel Worksheet object.
   b. Resize the object so only columns A to D and rows 1 to 5 are visible.
   c. Change the font size of all the cells to 28 point, enter labels and values as shown in **FIGURE 3-12**, then adjust column widths and the size of the worksheet object as needed.

FIGURE 3-12

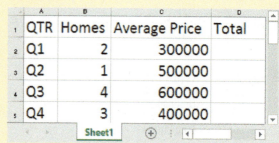

	A	B	C	D
1	QTR	Homes	Average Price	Total
2	Q1	2	300000	
3	Q2	1	500000	
4	Q3	4	600000	
5	Q4	3	400000	

Sheet1

d. Enter a formula in cell D2 to multiply the number of homes by the average price for the first quarter, then copy the formula to the range D3:D5 and widen columns as needed. Note that you may see E+ notations until you widen the columns.

e. Apply the Droplet theme to the embedded workbook, apply the Table Style Medium 3 style, convert the table to a range, format the dollar values in columns C and D with the Accounting Number format, then widen columns as needed. (*Hint*: To widen column D, resize the object to show column E, widen Column D, then reduce the object size again.)

f. Center the worksheet object below the slide title.

g. In the worksheet object, change the number of homes sold in the third quarter to **6**, then save the presentation.

3. Link Access and Excel objects to PowerPoint.

a. Start Access, open the file INT 3-4.accdb from the location where you store your Data Files, save it as **INT 3-Paradise Realty Properties**, then enable the content.

b. Create a query called **Properties Query** from the Properties table, that contains all fields and that sorts the contents of the Category field in ascending order. (*Hint*: Remember to sort the Category field in Design view.)

c. Close and save the query, copy it, create a new workbook in Excel, then paste the query datasheet as a link into cell A1.

d. Format the values in column E using the Accounting Number format, then widen columns as necessary.

e. In the range B16:D17, enter labels and formulas to calculate the total value of all the houses in each of the three categories: Estate, House, and Townhouse, then save the workbook as **INT 3-Paradise Realty Property Values**.

f. Create a pie chart in the first 2D style from the range B16:D17, then apply Layout 1.

g. Change the chart title to **Breakdown of Property Values**, copy the chart, then paste it on Slide 5 in the PowerPoint presentation using the Use Destination Theme & Link Data option.

h. Move the worksheet object below the bullet point, then add a black outline.

4. Manage links.

a. In the Access query, change the price of the Kapalua estate to **$4,500,000**, then close the query.

b. Switch to Excel, then update the link in the Edit Links dialog box if the value in cell E2 does not automatically update to 4,500,000.

c. Switch to PowerPoint, then update the link, if necessary, and verify that the Estate wedge is now 61%.

d. Size and position the pie chart so it fills the blank area on the slide attractively, then apply Chart Style 11.

e. In Excel, copy cell B17, then paste it as a linked worksheet object on Slide 5 in PowerPoint.

f. Position the Excel object after "is" and resize it so its font size is comparable to the bullet text.

g. In the Properties Query datasheet in Access, change the price of the Lahaina Estate to **$2,000,000**, then close the datasheet.

h. Update the link in Excel, switch to PowerPoint, then, if necessary, update the links to the chart and the worksheet object. The worksheet object is now $8,900,000.00 and the Estate slice is 59%.

i. Break the links to the Excel chart and worksheet, view the presentation in Slide Sorter view, compare the presentation to **FIGURE 3-13**, save and close all open files and programs, then submit your files to your instructor.

FIGURE 3-13

Integration

Independent Challenge 1

You work at Best Friends, a boutique pet store that sells purebred puppies and dog accessories. You have collected data about recent sales in an Access database, and now you need to create a presentation in PowerPoint that contains links to the sales figures. You also need to import some of the slides needed for the presentation from a Word outline.

a. In Word, open the file INT 3-5.docx from the location where you store your Data Files.

b. In Outline view, demote the Dog Breed Information text to Level 2, then demote the list of the four breeds under the Promotions Level 1 heading to Level 3.

c. Save the document as **INT 3-Best Friends Outline**, then close the document.

d. Start a blank presentation in PowerPoint, then save it as **INT 3-Best Friends Presentation** in the location where you store your Data Files.

e. Insert the Best Friends Outline document into PowerPoint, delete Slide 1, apply the Title Slide layout to the new Slide 1, then add your name after the subtitle on Slide 1.

f. In Slide Sorter view, reset the layout of all the slides, then apply the Facet slide design.

g. On the new Slide 2 (Top Sellers), embed an Excel Worksheet object resized to column B and row 5 with a 22 pt font size and containing the information and formatted as shown in **FIGURE 3-14**.

h. Calculate the total revenue in cell B5.

i. Apply Table Style Medium 13, convert the table to a range, apply the Facet theme, then position the worksheet object attractively on the slide.

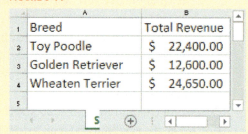

FIGURE 3-14

	A	B
1	Breed	Total Revenue
2	Toy Poodle	$ 22,400.00
3	Golden Retriever	$ 12,600.00
4	Wheaten Terrier	$ 24,650.00
5		

j. Start Access, open the file INT 3-6.accdb from the location where you store your Data Files, then save the database as **INT 3-Best Friends Inventory** and enable content.

k. Add two new records to the Breeds table (records 16 and 17) as follows: a Newfoundland and a Saint Bernard. Describe each breed as Large, with sales of 5 dogs and a price of $500.

l. Create a query called **Breeds Query** from the Breeds table, using all fields, that sorts the contents of the Size field in ascending order. Save and close the query, copy the query, paste it as a link into a new Excel workbook, then save the workbook as **INT 3-Best Friends Breed Information** in the location where you save your Data Files.

m. Calculate the total revenue for each breed in column F, then starting in cell D20, enter labels and formulas to calculate the total revenue from each of the three sizes of dogs. (*Hint:* Enter **Small** in cell D20, **Medium** in cell E20, and **Large** in cell F20, then enter the required calculations in cells D21:F21.)

n. Format all dollar amounts with the Accounting Number format, then use the data in the range D20:F21 to create a 2D pie chart entitled **Sales by Dog Size** using Quick Layout 6 and Chart Style 3.

o. Move the chart to the right of the data, copy the pie chart, then paste it on the appropriate slide in the presentation using the Use Destination Theme & Link Data option.

p. In Excel, copy the total revenue from Medium dogs, then paste it as a linked worksheet object in the appropriate location on the slide containing the chart.

q. Size and position the worksheet object attractively, then enclose the chart in a black outline.

r. In Access, change the Collie sale price to **900** and the quantity sold to **10**, then update the links in Excel and PowerPoint.

s. Break the links in Excel and PowerPoint, view the presentation in Slide Sorter view, save and close all open files and programs, then submit your files to your instructor.

Independent Challenge 2

You are the Assistant Manager at Peak Times, a store in Boulder, Colorado, that sells camping, hiking, and mountaineering equipment. To assist your customers, you have created a database of trail information they can access online. You have also decided to create a short PowerPoint presentation from information you have stored in Word. The presentation will include data from the database, an embedded worksheet, and a linked chart.

a. Start Word, open the file INT 3-7.docx from the location where you store your Data Files, demote the subtitle and the line "All skill levels are accommodated" to Level 2 and promote "Distances" to Level 1.

b. Save the document as **INT 3-Peak Times Outline**, and close the document.

c. Start a new PowerPoint presentation, save it as **INT 3-Peak Times Presentation**, then import the INT 3-Peak Times Outline document into the presentation.

d. Delete the blank Slide 1, apply the Title Slide layout to the new Slide 1, add your name below the subtitle on Slide 1, then apply the Ion slide design. Select the blue variant in the Variants group to change the colors of the slide design.

e. In Slide Sorter view, reset the layout of all the slides.

f. On Slide 2, embed an Excel Worksheet object displaying three columns and five rows, apply the 22-point font size so the cells are visible, then enter the information shown in **FIGURE 3-15** and adjust column widths.

FIGURE 3-15

g. Calculate the total sales in cell B5, then, in cell C2, enter **=B2/B5** to calculate the average percent of sales of Backpacking/Hiking products.

h. Copy the formula to the other two product categories, format values with the Accounting Number and Percent formats, reduce the decimals to 0 for the values in both Column B and C, then widen columns, as necessary.

i. Apply the Ion theme, apply Table Style Medium 10, convert the table to a range, right-align and bold "Total Sales" and bold the total, then position the worksheet object on the slide.

j. Replace XX in the bulleted item by typing the appropriate value from the embedded worksheet.

k. Start Access, open the file INT 3-8.accdb from the location where you store your Data Files, save the database as **INT 3-Peak Times Trails Database**, then enable content.

l. Create a query called **Colorado Trails Query** from all the fields in the Colorado Trails table that sorts the contents of the Type field in ascending order.

m. Close and save the query, copy it, then paste it as a link into a new Excel workbook saved as **INT 3-Peak Times Trails Information** in the location where you store your Data Files. Widen columns as needed.

n. Starting in cell C15 of the worksheet, enter labels and formulas to calculate the total miles covered in each of the three trip types: Backpacking, Hiking, and Walking.

o. Create a pie chart of the totals, apply Quick Layout 1, and add a chart title: **Total Distances by Trail Type**.

p. Copy the chart, then paste it using the Use Destination Theme & Link Data paste option on the appropriate slide in the presentation. Resize and reposition it to fit the space attractively.

q. Apply Chart Style 12 to the chart and remove the legend. (*Hint:* Click the Add Chart Element button in the Chart Layouts group, point to Legend, then click None.)

r. Copy cell C16 in the source workbook, then paste it as a linked worksheet object so it replaces the YY placeholder. (*Hint:* Move "miles" to the right using the Spacebar, then size and position the object so it fits.) Change the font color of the value to yellow in Excel, then in PowerPoint, resize the object so it is easy to read.

s. In the Access query, change the distance of the Capitol Creek Trail to **12** miles and the Mount Sopris Summit Trail to **18** miles, then close the query.

t. Update links in Excel and PowerPoint. Note that you will need to adjust the position of the worksheet object. Verify that the value is now 77.3.

u. In Excel and PowerPoint, break the links, view the presentation, save and close all open files and programs, then submit your files to your instructor.

Visual Workshop

For a course on tourism in Canada, you have decided to create a presentation that focuses on popular hotels in various locations. The presentation will contain one slide displaying a pie chart showing the breakdown of hotel guests by location. In Access, open the file INT 3-9.accdb from the location where you store your Data Files, then save the database as **INT 3-Canada Hotels**. Create a query called **Locations** that includes all fields and that sorts the Hotels table in ascending order by Location. Copy the query, and paste it as a link into Excel, then create the 3D pie chart similar to the one shown in **FIGURE 3-16**, and save the Excel workbook as **INT 3-Canada Hotels Data**. As shown in the figure, create a one-slide PowerPoint presentation called **INT 3-Canada Hotels Presentation**, apply the Title Only slide layout, then copy the pie chart from Excel and paste it onto the slide using the Use Destination Theme & Link Data option. Format the slide as shown: add the slide title, apply the Quotable slide design with the Red variant, and format the chart with Quick Layout 1 and Style 8, and remove the chart title from the chart. Switch to Access, open the Locations query, change the number of guests who stayed at the Glacier Lake Resort in Banff to **150**, close the query, update the links in Excel and PowerPoint, then enter your name in the slide footer. Break the link to the Excel workbook and PowerPoint presentation, save and close all open files and programs, then submit your files to your instructor.

FIGURE 3-16

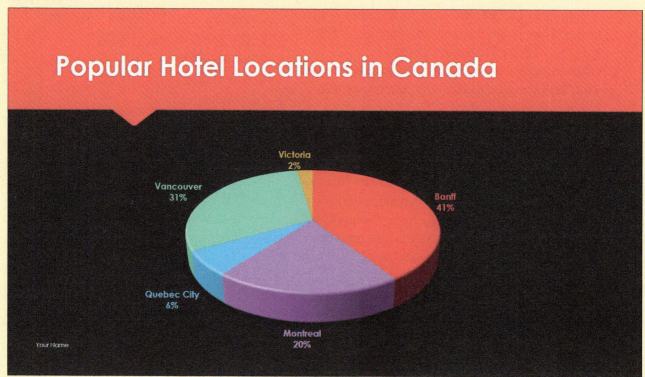

Getting Started with Email

CASE ▶ Email is a communication tool that is used for business and personal correspondence. You can use a desktop information management program like Microsoft Outlook 2016, an email program, or any of several web-based email programs to send and receive email. Reason2Go provides adventurous travelers with meaningful opportunities to give back to the global community. You are an Experience Leader working at Reason2Go in the New York office. Your supervisor, Lance Reichman, wants you to learn the basics of email.

Module Objectives

After completing this module, you will be able to:

- Communicate with email
- Use email addresses
- Create and send emails
- Understand email folders

- Receive and reply to emails
- Forward emails
- Send email attachments
- Employ good email practices

Files You Will Need

photo1.jpg   Branch Offices.docx

Communicate with Email

Electronic mail (email) is the technology that lets you send and receive written messages through the Internet. The messages sent using email technology are known as **email messages**, or **email** for short. **Email software**, such as Mail in Microsoft Outlook shown in FIGURE 1-1, enables you to send and receive email messages over a computer network. A **computer network** is the hardware and software that enables two or more computers to share information and resources. CASE ▶ *Reason2Go employees use email to communicate with each other and with clients around the world because it is fast, reliable, and easy.*

DETAILS

Email enables you to:

- **Communicate conveniently and efficiently**

  Email is an effective way to correspond with coworkers or colleagues. Email can be sent from one person to another person or to a group of people anywhere in the world. You can send and receive messages directly from any computer with an Internet or network connection. You can also send and receive email from wireless devices such as smartphones or tablet computers with email capability. Unlike mail sent using the postal service, email can be delivered almost instantaneously. But like mail sent using the postal service, a person receiving an email does not have to be at his or her computer at the same time that a message is sent in order to receive the message.

- **Organize your emails**

  Organizing your email messages lets you keep a record of communications to help you manage a project or business. You can organize the messages you send and receive in a way that best suits your working style. For example, you can store email messages in folders to help you locate them again in the future. You can also flag messages or categorize messages by color to give instant visual cues that distinguish those that require immediate attention from those that can wait. You can download email to your computer or keep it on the provider's web server.

- **Send images, video, and computer files as well as text information**

  Message text can be formatted so the message is easy to read and appears professional, attractive, or even amusing. Messages can include graphics in the body of the message to convey visual information. See FIGURE 1-2. In addition, you can attach files to a message, such as photographs, graphics, spreadsheets, word-processing documents, and even short sound or video files.

- **Communicate with numerous people at once, and never forget an address**

  You can create your own electronic address book that stores the names and email addresses of people with whom you frequently communicate. You can send the same message to more than one person at the same time. You can also create named groups of email addresses, and then send messages to that group of people by entering only the group name.

- **Ensure the delivery of information**

  With some email software, you have the option of receiving a delivery confirmation message when a recipient receives your email. In addition, if you are away and unable to access email because of a vacation or other plans, you can set up an automatic message that is delivered to senders so they are alerted to the fact that you might not receive your email for a specified time period.

- **Correspond from a remote place**

  If you have an Internet connection and communications software, you can use your computer or handheld device to send and receive messages from any location. If you are using a web-based email program, such as Outlook.com shown in FIGURE 1-3, you can access your email from any computer that is connected to the Internet from anywhere in the world.

FIGURE 1-1: Mail window in Microsoft Outlook

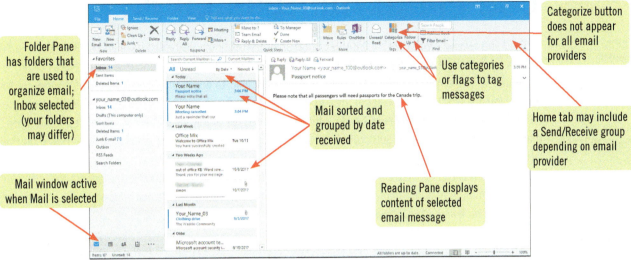

Folder Pane has folders that are used to organize email; Inbox selected (your folders may differ)

Mail window active when Mail is selected

Mail sorted and grouped by date received

Reading Pane displays content of selected email message

Use categories or flags to tag messages

Categorize button does not appear for all email providers

Home tab may include a Send/Receive group depending on email provider

FIGURE 1-2: Messages can include formatted text and graphics

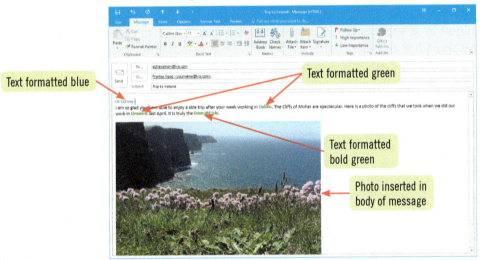

Text formatted blue

Text formatted green

Text formatted bold green

Photo inserted in body of message

FIGURE 1-3: Web-based email website Outlook.com

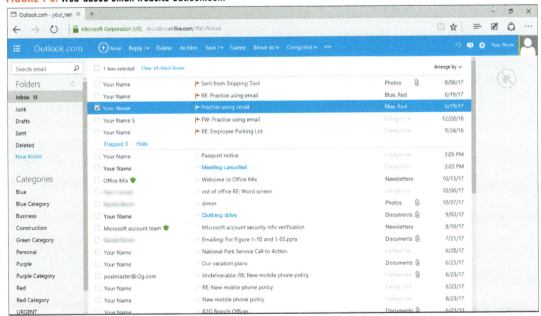

Use Email Addresses

Learning Outcomes
• Know the four parts of an email address
• Explain the benefits of an email address book

To send and receive email over the Internet using an email program, you must have an email address. Each person has a unique email address. To log in to an email program, a user enters a password in order to send and receive email. To send an email message, you need to know the email address of the person to whom you are sending the message. Instead of having to remember an email address, you can select the name you want from an **address book**, which is a stored list of names and email addresses. In addition, many email programs use an autocomplete feature, which provides a list of email addresses based on the letters as you type. **CASE** *At Reason2Go, each employee is assigned an email address. The company maintains a list of all employee email addresses in an electronic address book as well as a client list and volunteer list. Most communication is handled through email. You review the parts of an email address and the benefits of maintaining an email address book.*

DETAILS

An email address has several parts (see FIGURE 1-4):

- **Username**

  The first part of an email address is the username. The **username** identifies the person who receives the email. At Reason2Go, as in many companies, universities, or organizations, usernames are assigned and are based on a specified format. At R2G, a username is the first initial of the person's first name and his or her last name. In many email systems, such as those used primarily for personal email, you get to create your username. Username formats can vary based on the requirements of the email service provider, for example, a username might be a person's initial of his or her first name, an underscore or period, and the last name or it might be a combination of letters and numbers.

- **@ sign**

  The middle part of an email address is the @ sign, called an "at sign." It separates the username from the email service provider. Every email address includes an @ sign.

- **Email service provider**

  The next part of the email address is the email service provider, which actually contains two parts: the service provider and the top-level domain. There are many different service providers. The service provider generally is a company or organization that provides the connection to the Internet and provides email services. The service provider can also be the website name for a web-based email program. The name of the service provider is followed by a dot or period, and then a top-level domain, such as org, com, or edu. Top-level domains help identify the type of service provider. **TABLE 1-1** provides some examples of email address formats that are used with different service providers.

The benefits of an email address book include the following:

- **Stores the names and email addresses of people to whom you send email messages**

  Outlook and several other email programs refer to the address book entries as "contacts" and place them in a folder called Contacts. When you create a new contact, you enter the person's full name and email address. You might also have the option to enter additional information about that person, including his or her personal and business mailing address, telephone number, cell phone number, webpage, instant message address, social networking contact information, and even a picture.

- **Reduces errors and makes using email quicker and more convenient**

  Being able to select a contact from your address book not only saves time but also reduces errors. Selecting the email address from an address book reduces the chance that your message will not be delivered because you typed the email address incorrectly. In most email programs, if someone sends you a message, you can add the sender's address as well as other recipients' addresses in the message header directly to your address book without making any errors. **FIGURE 1-5** shows a sample address book from Outlook.

FIGURE 1-4: Parts of an email address

FIGURE 1-5: Outlook 2016 address book with sample contacts

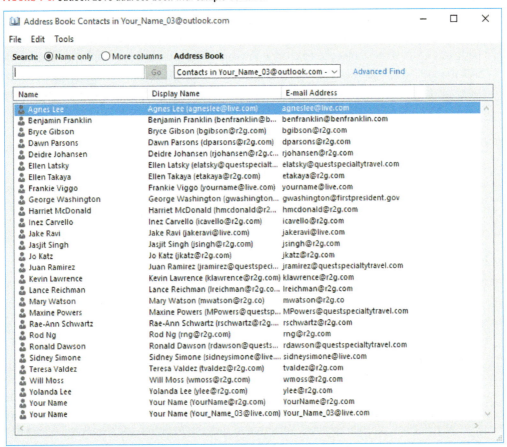

TABLE 1-1: Examples of email providers and addresses

email service provider	examples of email service providers	description of email services	where email is stored	sample email addresses
Corporate or company email	Reason2Go	Email for employees	Company server or downloaded to a user's computer	username@r2g.com
Commercial provider: Cable TV, voice, and data communications companies	Comcast Cablevision ATT Verizon	Web space and several email addresses	ISP server, until downloaded to a user's computer	username@comcast.net username@optimum.net username@att.net username@verizon.net
Web-based email	Outlook.com (Microsoft) Live.com (Microsoft) Gmail (Google) Yahoo! Mail (Yahoo!)	Free email addresses and service	Website email server	username@outlook.com username@live.com username@gmail.com username@yahoo.com
Educational institution	Wesleyan University University of Delaware	Email for faculty, staff, and students	University email server	username@wesleyan.edu username@udel.edu
Organization	American Museum of Natural History	Email for staff	Organization email server	username@amnh.org

Outlook 2016

Create and Send Emails

Learning Outcomes
• Enter email addresses in the To and Cc text boxes
• Write and send an email message

When you create an email message, you enter the email addresses of the people you want to receive the message in the To or Cc text boxes in the **message header**. You also type a meaningful subject in the **Subject line** so the recipients will have an idea of the message content. You write the text of your message in the **message body**. You can add graphics, format the message text, and attach files. Outlook uses Microsoft Word as the default text editor in email messages, which means that you have access to the same text-formatting features in Outlook that you use when you create Word documents. Most email programs use a basic text editor that enables you to change the color of text, use different fonts, create a bulleted list, and check the spelling of your message. After you create the message, you send it. **CASE** ▶ *You write and send a message using Outlook to several employees about an upcoming trip to help build a much needed new school.*

STEPS

1. **Start Microsoft Outlook 2016, then click Mail (or click ✉) on the Navigation Pane in the lower-left corner of the Outlook window if it is not already selected**

   If you are using Outlook, you can start the program and then create a message without connecting to the Internet. If your email program is web-based, such as Outlook, Live.com, Yahoo! Mail, or Gmail, you have to be connected to the Internet to create an email message. Although you can write and read messages in Outlook when you are not online, you must be connected to the Internet to send or receive messages.

2. **Click the New Email button in the New group on the Home tab**

   All email programs provide a button or link that opens a new email window so you can begin writing a new message. All email programs have some basic similarities, such as a new message window that provides text boxes or spaces to enter address information, subject, and message content, as shown in **FIGURE 1-6**.

3. **Click the To text box, then type the email address of a friend or an associate or you can type your email address**

   Your email message will go to the person at this email address after you send the message. You can send an email message to more than one person at one time; as shown in **FIGURE 1-7**, just enter each email address in the To text box or Cc text box and separate the addresses with a semicolon or comma (depending on what your email program requires). You can also click the To button in the message header or the Address Book button in the Names group on the Message tab to open the Select Names: Contacts dialog box and select each email address from the address book.

4. **Click the Cc text box, then type another friend's email address**

   Cc stands for carbon or courtesy copy. Courtesy copies are typically sent to message recipients who need to be aware of the correspondence between the sender and the recipients. Bcc, or blind courtesy copy, is used when the sender does not want to reveal who he or she has sent courtesy copies to. Bcc is available in the Select Names: Contacts dialog box.

5. **Click the Subject text box, then type Escuela Libertad project - Villa Nueva**

   The subject should be a brief statement that indicates the purpose of your message. The subject line becomes the title of the message.

6. **Type your message in the message window**

   FIGURE 1-7 shows a sample completed message. Many email programs provide a spell-checking program that alerts you to spelling errors in your message. Messages should be concise and polite. If you want to send a lengthy message, consider attaching a file to the message. (You will learn about attaching files later in this module.)

7. **Click the Send button to send your email message**

   Once the message is sent, the message window closes. Most email programs store a copy of the message in your Sent or Sent Items folder or give you the option to do so.

FIGURE 1-6: New message window

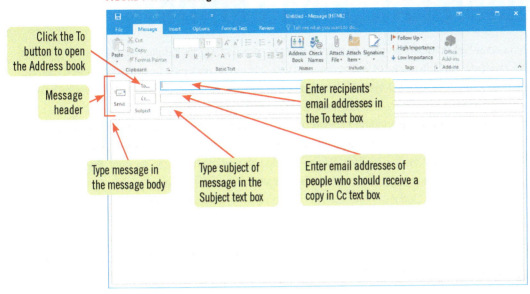

Click the To button to open the Address book

Message header

Enter recipients' email addresses in the To text box

Type message in the message body

Type subject of message in the Subject text box

Enter email addresses of people who should receive a copy in Cc text box

FIGURE 1-7: A sample message

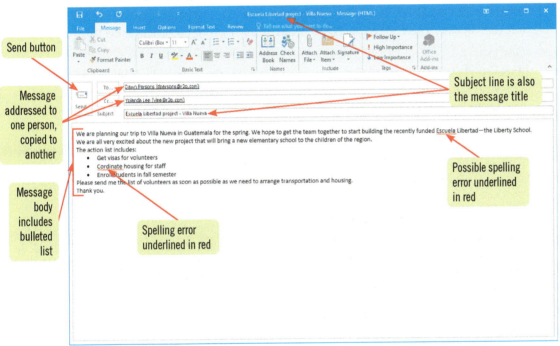

Send button

Message addressed to one person, copied to another

Message body includes bulleted list

Subject line is also the message title

Possible spelling error underlined in red

Spelling error underlined in red

Understanding message headers in emails you receive

The message header is the first information that you see when you retrieve your email. The message header contains the basic information about the message. It includes the sender's name and email address, the names and email addresses of recipients and Cc recipients, a date and time stamp, and the subject of the message. Bcc recipients are not shown in the message header. Email programs date- and time-stamp email messages when they are received at the recipient's computer, using the current date and time.

Understand Email Folders

Just as you save files in folders on your computer, you save email messages in folders in your email program. All email programs provide a way for you to organize and save email messages. You save messages so you can refer to them again in the future. Most email programs come with several default folders. These folders include Inbox, Drafts, Sent Items, Deleted Items, Junk E-mail, and Outbox, (or folders with similar names). See **FIGURE 1-8**. Also, you can create additional folders as well as manage folders by using the commands on the Folder tab. You can move or copy messages into folders, and you can search messages based on keywords. You can also sort and filter messages within folders to help you find the message you want. **CASE** ▶ *As an employee of Reason2Go, you send and receive lots of messages on several topics. Before organizing your email, you review the default folders in Outlook.*

DETAILS

Most email programs come with default folders, such as the following:

- **Inbox**

  An Inbox is a mail folder that receives all incoming email as it arrives. You know who sent the email message because the username or email address and subject line appear in the list of emails in your Inbox, as shown in **FIGURE 1-9**. You will also know when the message came in because your computer puts a date on it, which you can see along with the username and subject line. A dark blue bar along the left side of the message info means the message has not been read. A blue highlighted message means the message is selected. If the Reading Pane is open, you can preview the selected message before opening it. You can organize email by date, sender, subject, and other header data by selecting the options at the top of the column.

- **Drafts**

  If you want to finish writing a message later, you can save it to the Drafts folder. Many programs automatically save unsent messages at regular intervals in the Drafts folder as a safety measure. Depending on how your system is set up, drafts are saved either remotely to a server or locally to your computer.

- **Sent Items**

  When you send a message, a copy of it is stored in the Sent Items folder unless you change the default setting. This folder helps you track the messages that you send out. You can change the settings on most email programs so you do not save messages to the Sent Items folder.

- **Deleted Items**

  When you delete a message from any folder, it is placed in the Deleted Items folder, sometimes called the Trash folder. The Deleted Items folder keeps items from being immediately and permanently deleted. To empty the Deleted Items folder, select the folder, click the Folder tab on the Ribbon, then click the Empty Folder button in the Clean Up group.

- **Junk E-mail**

  Junk email, or **spam**, is unwanted email that arrives from unsolicited sources. Most junk email is advertising or offensive messages. Many email programs have filters that identify this type of email and place it in a special folder. In Outlook, this folder is called Junk E-mail. This makes it easy for you to delete the email you don't want. It is possible that a message that you do want might get caught by the spam filter. It is good practice to look at the headers in the Junk E-mail folder before deleting the messages stored there.

- **Outbox**

  The Outbox is a temporary storage folder for messages that have not been sent. If you are working offline or if you set your email program so messages do not get sent immediately after you click the Send button, the messages are placed in the Outbox. When you connect to the Internet or click the Send/Receive All Folders button in the Send & Receive group on the Send/Receive tab, the messages in the Outbox are sent.

FIGURE 1-8: Default mail folders

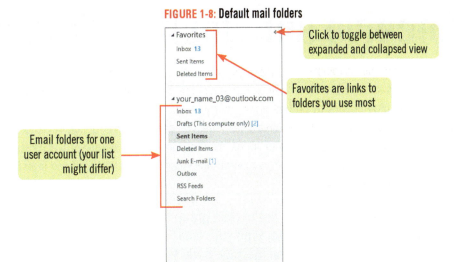

Click to toggle between expanded and collapsed view

Favorites are links to folders you use most

Email folders for one user account (your list might differ)

FIGURE 1-9: Outlook Mail window

Mail in Inbox folder organized by date with newest on top

Number of unread messages in each folder

Read messages do not have a blue bar

Icon for replied to message

Dark blue bars indicate unread messages

Icon for forwarded message

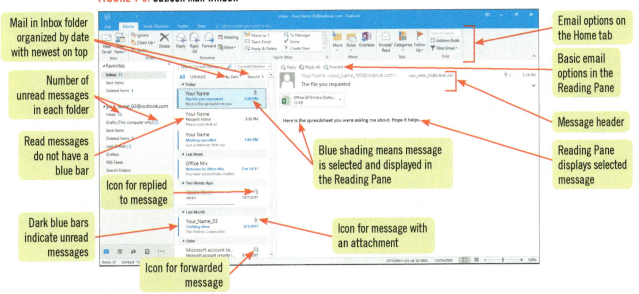

Email options on the Home tab

Basic email options in the Reading Pane

Message header

Reading Pane displays selected message

Blue shading means message is selected and displayed in the Reading Pane

Icon for message with an attachment

Outlook 2016

Receive and Reply to Emails

Outlook and many other email software programs let you preview a selected message in the Reading Pane. To open the message in its own window, you can double-click the message header. The default in Outlook is to hide images to protect your privacy so you might have to click a link or button to display inserted graphics or video. After reading a message, you can reply to it, delete it, move it to another folder, flag it for follow-up, or keep it in your Inbox. You respond to the sender of the message by clicking the Reply button. **CASE** *You often reply to email messages from the R2G staff and from clients.*

STEPS

1. Click the New Email button in the New group on the Home tab to open a new message window, click the To text box, type your email address, click the Subject text box, type Practice using email, click the message body text box, then type I am sending this message to myself to learn how to send and reply to messages with Outlook.

TROUBLE

Depending on your email provider, you may have a Sent Mail folder, rather than Sent Items and you may have to wait a few moments before the email message comes in.

2. Click the Send button in the message window, click the Send/Receive tab, click the Send/Receive All Folders button in the Send & Receive group, click the Sent Items folder to verify that the message was sent, then click the Inbox folder

    Clicking Send sends the message out unless you have changed the default setting to place the message in the Outbox but not send it. Clicking the Send/Receive All Folders or Send All buttons tells your email program to send messages in the Outbox and to deliver incoming messages to your Inbox. Many email programs deliver email to your Inbox when you sign in with your username and password. Outlook plays an alert tune and displays the unread message in the Inbox with a blue bar on the left side.

QUICK TIP

Outlook may display the message header in a pop-up window when the message arrives.

3. Click the Practice using email message in the Inbox to select it and view the message

    You read the message header to identify the message by subject, date, and sender. The selected message appears in the Reading Pane in the Outlook window.

4. Double-click the Practice using email message in the center pane to open it

    See **FIGURE 1-10**. The Message window has several options. Reply lets you reply to the original sender. The Reply All option lets you reply to the original sender and all the Cc recipients of the original message. Bcc recipients are not included in Reply or Reply All messages. The Quick Steps group offers commands frequently used to manage email.

5. Click the File tab, then click Close

    The email message window closes. The Practice using email message is selected in the Outlook window.

QUICK TIP

You can also click the Reply button in the Reading Pane.

6. Click the Home tab, then click the Reply button in the Respond group

    Clicking the Reply button automatically opened a message addressed to the original sender in the Reading Pane. The subject line is preceded by "RE:", indicating that the message is a reply. The header from the original message appears above the original message. The insertion point is at the top of the message body. The Compose Tools Message tab is active.

7. Type I can type a reply in the Reading Pane or click the Pop Out button to reply in a window. in the message body

    Include the original message in a reply to help the recipient recall the topic. Outlook saves a draft of your message automatically. See **FIGURE 1-11**. Depending on how you set up your email program, you can automatically include or exclude the text of the original sender's message, and the message header and body.

8. Click the Send button in the Reading Pane

    The message is sent, and a copy of it is stored in your Sent Items folder. Most email programs add a Replied to Message icon 🖻 next to the original message in the Inbox, indicating that you have replied to the message.

FIGURE 1-10: Message open in new window

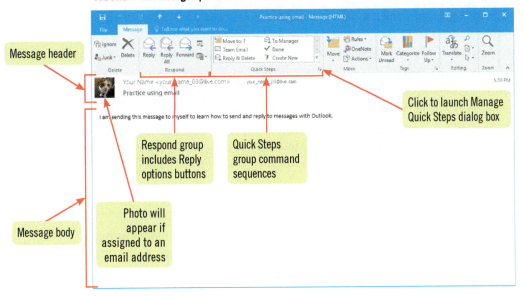

Message header

Click to launch Manage
Quick Steps dialog box

Respond group
includes Reply
options buttons

Quick Steps
group command
sequences

Message body

Photo will
appear if
assigned to an
email address

FIGURE 1-11: Replying to a message

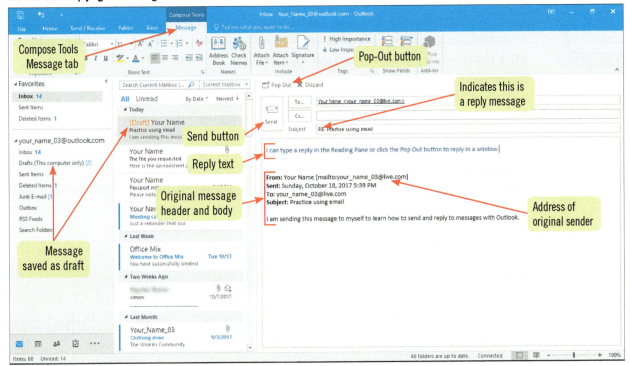

Compose Tools
Message tab

Pop-Out button

Indicates this is
a reply message

Send button

Reply text

Original message
header and body

Message
saved as draft

Address of
original sender

Setting up vacation responses

Most email programs allow you to set up an automatic response or vacation message if you are not going to be able to receive your email for a specified period of time. This is a helpful way to let people know that you are not ignoring any email they send, but rather that you are not reading your email. When vacation mode is active, your email program automatically sends out a reply when a message comes in. You determine the content of the reply message. A typical message might be "Thank you for your message. I am on vacation from July 1 to July 10 and will respond to your message when I return." Most email programs only send one automatic response to each sender each day or within a specified period of time.

Forward Emails

You might receive an email that you need to send to someone else. Sending a message you have received from one person to someone else is called **forwarding**. When you forward a message, you send it to people who have not already received it—that is, people not in the To or Cc text boxes of the original message. You can include an additional message about the forwarded message in the message body. The subject of the forwarded message is preceded by FW:, but the subject stays the same so you can organize it by subject as a conversation with any other messages on the same topic. In most email programs, you forward a message that you have received to another person by clicking the Forward button. **CASE** ▶ *Working at R2G, you get email from and volunteers that you forward to the teams and staff.*

STEPS

QUICK TIP
You can also click the Send/Receive All Folders button on the Quick Access toolbar.

1. **Click the Send/Receive tab, then click the Send/Receive All Folders button**

   Outlook sends messages in the Outbox and delivers any incoming messages to your Inbox.

2. **Click the Home tab, click the Inbox, then click the newest Practice using email message in the center pane if it is not selected**

   You read the message header to identify the message. You can see the original recipients of the message by reviewing the header. You can see who received the message by reviewing the email addresses in the To and Cc areas of the header (if there were courtesy copies). You will not know who might have received a Bcc on the message. When you view a message, you see buttons in the Reading Pane that provide several options for responding to the message. One of the options is to click the Forward button to forward the message.

QUICK TIP
The Forward button is also in the Respond group on the Home tab.

3. **Click the Forward button in the Reading Pane**

   A New Message window opens in the Reading Pane. Clicking the Forward button does not automatically address the email to anyone; the To, Cc, and Bcc address fields are blank. The entire original message is included in the body of the message. The subject line is preceded by "FW:", indicating that the message is a forwarded one. Most email software includes the message header from the original message in the Message window above the original message. The insertion point is at the top of the message window in the To field. You can address this message as you would any new email and include multiple Cc and Bcc recipients.

4. **Type a friend's email address in the To text box, place the insertion point in the message body above the forwarded message, then type I am forwarding this message to you as a test for class. Please let me know if you received it. as shown in FIGURE 1-12**

   If you have Contacts in your address book, you can click the To button to open the Select Names: Contacts dialog box and click to select the email address for your recipients. You can also click the Address book button in the Names group on the Message tab to open the Select Names: Contacts dialog box.

5. **Click the Send button in the message window**

   The message is sent, and a copy of it is stored in your Sent Items folder. Most email programs add a Forwarded Message icon next to the original message, indicating that you have forwarded the message.

Controlling your message

When you communicate with email, take extra care in what you say and how you say it. The recipient of an email message cannot see body language or hear the tone of voice to interpret the meaning of the message. For example, using all capital letters in the text of a message is the email equivalent of shouting and is not appropriate. Carefully consider the content of a message before you send it, and don't send confidential or sensitive material. Remember, once you send a message, you might not be able to prevent it from being

delivered. Email is not private; you cannot control who might read the message once it has been sent. Do not write anything in an email that you would not write on a postcard that you send through the postal service. If your email account is a company account, be sure you know the policy on whether or not your company permits the sending of personal messages. All messages you send through an employer's email system legally belong to the company for which you work, so don't assume that your messages are private.

FIGURE 1-12: Forwarding a message

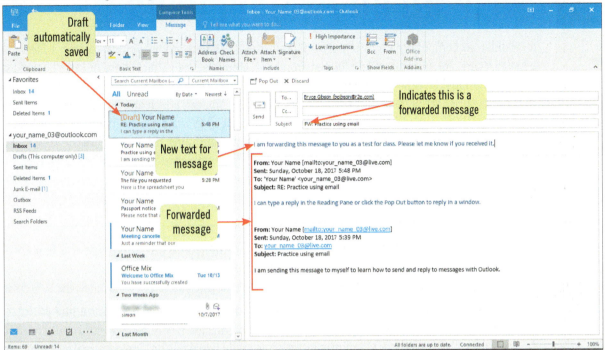

Flagging or labeling messages

Most email programs provide a way to identify or categorize email. If you use email for business, school, or personal communication, you will find that you receive many email messages. Some can be read and discarded. Others require additional attention or follow-up. Organizing your email can help you keep up with the many messages you are likely to receive. If you are using Outlook, flags can assist you in your effort to manage your email. If you point to a message and click the flag icon ![flag] that appears, it is marked by default with a red Quick Flag. However, you can use flags of different shades of red to mark messages for different categories of follow-up.

To apply a flag, click the flag in the message you want to flag. To select from a list of flag actions and specify a due date, right-click a message in the center pane, point to Follow Up, then click Add Reminder to open the Custom dialog box. Depending on your email provider, you may not have this feature.

Outlook also allows you to color-code messages for categories. See **FIGURE 1-13**. If you are using web-based email, you might have other options for categorizing, labeling, or flagging email.

FIGURE 1-13: Flagging and using colors to categorize messages

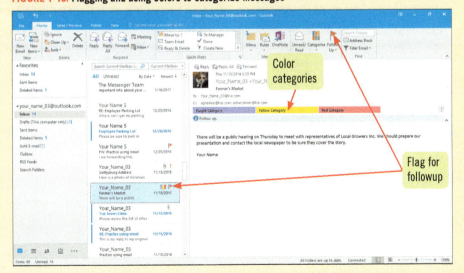

Send Email Attachments

In addition to composing a message by typing in the Message window, you can attach a file to an email message. For example, in an office environment, employees can attach Word or Excel documents to email messages so other employees can open them, make changes to them, and then return them to the original sender or forward them to others for review. You can attach any type of computer file to an email message, including pictures, video, and audio. Keep in mind that to open an **attachment** created using a particular software program, such as Adobe Illustrator, the recipient of the attachment will need that software to open the attached file. **CASE** *You often send trip photos from clients to people in the office. You also have to send documents to employees throughout the year. Attaching files, such as a document listing the branch offices, is a common task in your job at Reason2Go.*

STEPS

1. **Click the New Email button in the New group on the Home tab, then type the first three letters of your email address in the To text box**

   Notice as you start to type, a list of email addresses based on the letters you typed opens under the To text box.

2. **Point to the address you want to enter in the To text box, then click your email address**

   The email address you clicked is entered in the To text box. You can send a message with an attachment to more than one person at one time; just enter each email address in the To text box, separated by a semicolon or comma. You can also click the Cc text box or Bcc text box, and then enter email addresses for recipients who are to receive a Cc or Bcc.

3. **Click the Subject text box, type R2G Branch Offices, click the message body, then type Please review the attached document and add the branch offices to your contact list.**

4. **Click the Attach File button in the Include group on the Message tab**

   The Recent Items list opens. This is helpful if you want to attach any files you have recently worked on.

5. **Click Browse This PC at the bottom of the Recent Items list**

   The Insert File dialog box opens, as shown in **FIGURE 1-14**. You might have to navigate to the file or files you want to attach. Often you can use the icons or Thumbnails view in the dialog box to see what the files look like before you attach them to a message.

6. **Navigate to the location where you store your Data Files, click Branch Offices.docx, then click Insert**

   Once attached, files appear in the Attached text box, as shown in **FIGURE 1-15**. You can click the arrow next to the filename to display additional options. Often, an icon next to each filename indicates the type of file it is. The numbers next to the filenames specify the size of each file. Most programs will allow you to attach more than one file to a message. Some Internet service providers will limit message size or the number of attachments for one email. Attachments such as movies might be too large for some email systems to handle. As a general rule, try to keep the total size of attachments below 10 MB. Also, consider the Internet connection speed of the recipient's computer. If a recipient does not have a fast Internet connection, a large file could take a long time to download.

7. **Click the Send button to send the message**

FIGURE 1-14: Attaching a file in Outlook

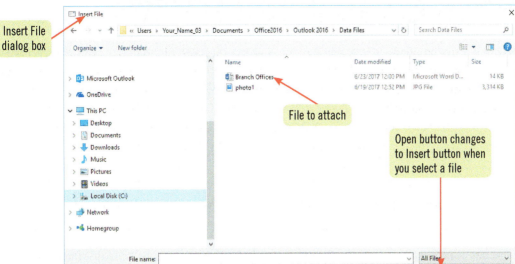

Insert File dialog box

File to attach

Open button changes to Insert button when you select a file

FIGURE 1-15: Message with attached file

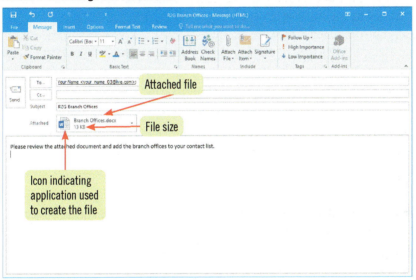

Attached file

File size

Icon indicating application used to create the file

Reviewing options when sending messages

Email programs can have several options that affect how messages are delivered. To change these message options in Outlook, click the Options tab in a Message window to view the Message Options, then click the launcher in the More Options group to open the Properties dialog box shown in **FIGURE 1-16**. You can, for example, assign a level of importance and a level of sensitivity so the reader can prioritize messages. You can also encrypt the message for privacy. If both the sender and recipient are using Outlook, you can add Voting buttons to your message for recipients to use when replying. In addition, when you want to know when a message has been received or read, you can select the Request a delivery receipt for this message check box or the Request a read receipt for this message check box. You can also specify a future date for delivering a message if the timing of the message is important.

FIGURE 1-16: Message options

Employ Good Email Practices

Email has become an accepted standard for business correspondence. It is also widely used for personal communication as well as communication between students and teachers. Although it is an easy and a fast way to communicate, there are many considerations to keep in mind before sending email. **CASE** *Working in a company that interacts with clients and volunteers around the world, you are responsible to follow the corporate policy relating to email. You review the company policy for email.*

DETAILS

The following are good practices to follow when sending and receiving email:

- **Be considerate**

  Always be polite and use proper spelling and grammar in email messages. Be sure to use the spelling checker as a last step before sending messages. See **FIGURE 1-17**.

- **Consider file size**

  Unless you have consulted with the recipient and know that he or she can receive large file attachments, avoid sending any attachment that exceeds 10 MB.

- **Be safe**

  Never open an email message unless you know who sent it to you. Keep your spam filter, spyware software, and virus software up to date. Be sure to run the virus checker through all emails you receive. Keeping computers safe from viruses and spyware is very important.

- **Think before forwarding**

  Before you forward a message, consider the contents of the message and the privacy of the person who sent the message. A joke, a story, or anything that is not personal usually can be forwarded without invading the sender's privacy. When you are certain the sender would not mind having his or her message forwarded, you can forward the message to others.

- **Be professional**

  In very casual correspondence, you can present an informal message by using shortcuts like "LOL" for "laughing out loud", LMK for "Let me know", and "BRB!" for "be right back!" However, limit this technique to personal messages. Any email that is intended for professional use or is a reflection on a professional organization should not use shortcuts.

- **Limit emoticons**

  You can use **emoticons** in your text to show how you are feeling. You create an emoticon by combining more than one keyboard character to make a graphic. For example, type a colon and a closing parenthesis to make a smiley face.

- **Maintain your account**

  Outlook offers Clean Up tools. Most programs offer similar tools for maintaining your folders. When you are finished using an email program, it is good practice to delete or archive email messages that you no longer need. If working for a company, you should comply with corporate policy. For personal email, you should periodically delete unneeded messages from the Sent Items to help manage storage space on your computer. It is also good practice to empty the Deleted Items folder. To delete a message, first you select it. Then you can do one of the following: click the Delete button in the Delete group on the Home tab, press the [Delete] key, or click the Delete button to the right of the message when you mouse over it. To empty the Deleted Items folder, right-click the folder, then click Empty Folder. You can also click the Folder tab, then click the Empty Folder button in the Clean Up group. When you see a confirmation message, as shown in **FIGURE 1-18**, click Yes.

FIGURE 1-17: Spell Checker

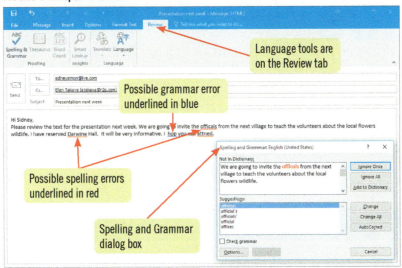

Language tools are on the Review tab

Possible grammar error underlined in blue

Possible spelling errors underlined in red

Spelling and Grammar dialog box

FIGURE 1-18: Deleting items

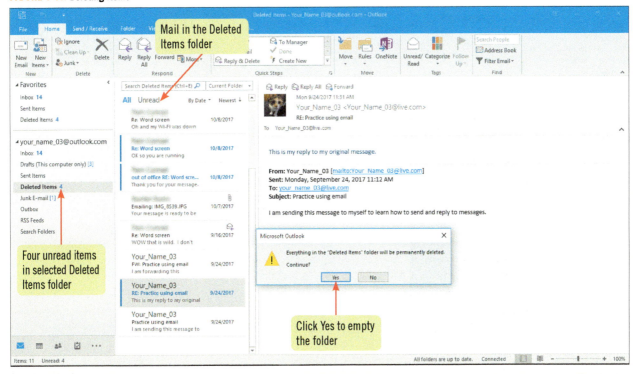

Mail in the Deleted Items folder

Four unread items in selected Deleted Items folder

Click Yes to empty the folder

Practice

Concepts Review

Label each element of the Message window shown in FIGURE 1-19.

FIGURE 1-19

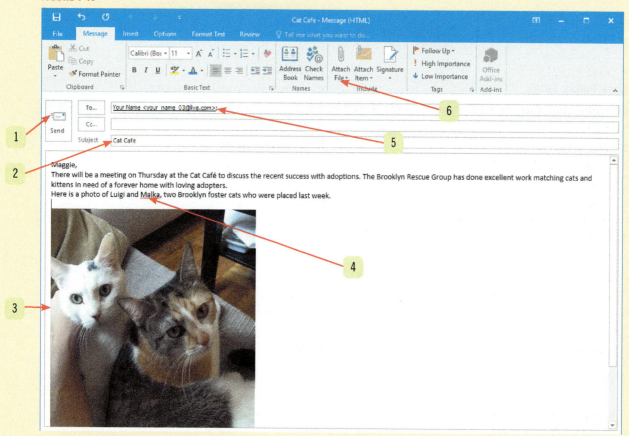

Match each term with the statement that best describes it.

7. Outbox folder   **a.** Contains unsent messages

8. Attachment   **b.** An email address

9. Bcc feature   **c.** Identifies a forwarded message

10. Your_Name@live.com   **d.** File sent with an email

11. Inbox   **e.** Folder that receives arriving email

12. FW: **f.** Hides email address of recipient to all others

Select the best answer from the list of choices.

13. The _____ of a message also appears in the title bar of the message window.
    a. addressee
    b. subject
    c. flags
    d. date

14. The _____ folder is NOT a default mail folder in Outlook.
    a. My Mail
    b. Deleted Items
    c. Inbox
    d. Junk E-Mail

15. When you forward a selected message to another person, the email addresses for the original recipients of the message:
    a. Appear only in the Cc text box in the message header.
    b. Do not appear in any text box in the message header.
    c. Appear in the To and the Cc text boxes in the message header.
    d. Appear only in the To text box in the message header.

16. To ensure that you send the same message to the same group of multiple recipients, set up a(n) _____.
    a. Address book
    b. Quick Step
    c. Draft folder
    d. Contact group or distribution list

17. An email that you are still working on is stored in the _____.
    a. Inbox
    b. New Mail folder
    c. Drafts folder
    d. Sent Items folder

18. Files you send along with your email messages are called _____.
    a. attachments
    b. headers
    c. drafts
    d. flags

19. If you do not want the recipients of your message to see the others you also sent the message to, you should use the _____ feature.
    a. Cc
    b. Flag
    c. Hide
    d. Bcc

20. When you can't view or respond to email messages right away, you should set up a(n) _____ to alert people who send an email message that you are not currently available.
    a. Contact list
    b. Vacation response
    c. Attachment
    d. Bcc

Skills Review

Note: To complete this Skills Review, your computer must be connected to the Internet.

1. **Communicate with email.**
    a. Start Outlook.
    b. Click Mail if it is not selected.
    c. Click the Send/Receive All Folders button to get new email delivered to the Inbox.
    d. Open the Inbox to view any new messages.

2. **Use email addresses.**
    a. Open a new message window.
    b. Click the To text box, then type your **email address**.
    c. Type a friend's **email address** in the Cc text box.

3. **Create and send emails.**
    a. Type **New mobile phone policy** as the subject of the message.
    b. Place the insertion point in the message body, type **As of January 1 all employees will be given new cellular phones that include a 100GB data plan. Please pick up your new mobile device in the Darwin Conference Room ASAP. Thank you.**
    c. Send the message.

Skills Review (continued)

4. Understand email folders.

    a. Review the mail folders in your email program. *(Note: your folder names may differ slightly from those in the following steps.)*

    b. Look in the Sent Items folder for the New mobile phone policy message.

    c. Open the Deleted Items folder. See if any email is in that folder.

    d. Review the Spam or Junk E-mail folder.

5. Receive and reply to emails.

    a. Click the Send/Receive All Folders button to deliver messages to your Inbox.

    b. Display the contents of the Inbox folder.

    c. Read the message from yourself.

    d. Click the Reply All button.

    e. Place the insertion point in the message body, type **Will our cellular numbers change?**, then send the message.

6. Forward emails.

    a. Forward the message you received to another friend. See **FIGURE 1-20**.

    b. Place the insertion point on the top of the forwarded message body, type **This important message came from HR.**

FIGURE 1-20

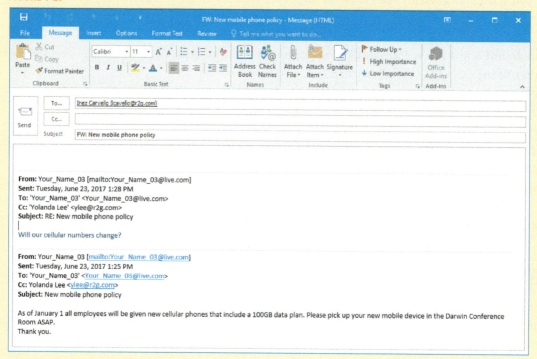

    c. Send the message.

    d. Close the original message if you opened it in a new window.

7. Send email attachments.

    a. Create a new email message.

    b. Enter your email address as the message recipient.

    c. Enter a friend's email address in the Cc text box.

    d. Enter **Travel photo** as the subject of the message.

    e. In the message body, type **Here is the photo from my trip to Ireland.**

Skills Review (continued)

   f. Click the Attach File button in the Include group on the Message tab.

   g. Click Browse This PC, then navigate to the location where you store your Data Files.

   h. Select the file **photo1.jpg**, then click Insert. See FIGURE 1-21.

   i. Send the message.

FIGURE 1-21

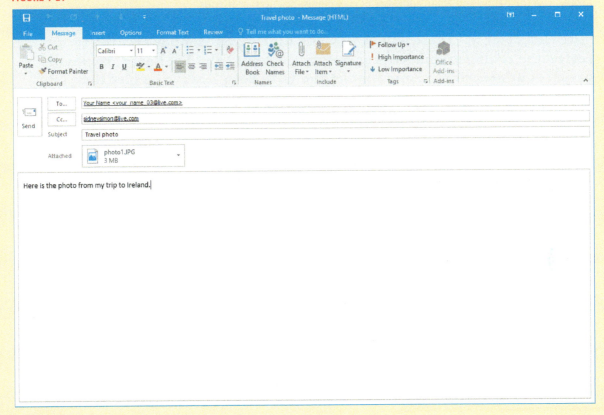

8. Delete items.

   a. Delete all of the messages received in this exercise from the Inbox folder.

   b. Delete all of the messages sent in this exercise from the Sent Items.

   c. Empty the Deleted Items folder.

   d. Exit Outlook.

Independent Challenge 1

You have been appointed to chair the committee to address land-use in your municipality. You decide to use email to communicate with the other members of the committee as well as the town council and the mayor. *Note: To complete the Independent Challenge, your computer must be connected to the Internet.*

a. Start Outlook.

b. Create a new message, and address it to yourself, then use the Cc field to send this message to two other people. Use the names and email addresses of classmates, teachers, or friends.

c. Type **Mayor and Council meeting** as the subject of the message.

d. In the message body, type **There will be a public hearing on Monday evening to review the zoning ordinance proposed by the Joint Land Use Board. We should prepare our presentation and contact the Twin Boro News to be sure they cover the story.**

e. Press [Enter] two times, then type your name. See **FIGURE 1-22**.

FIGURE 1-22

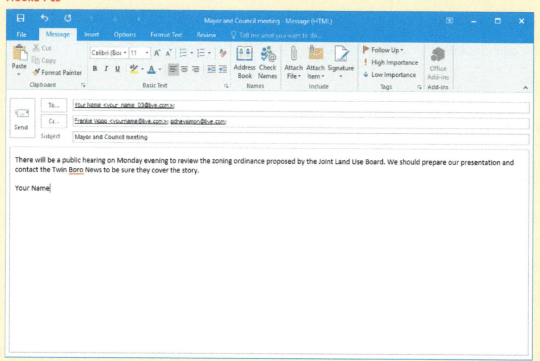

f. Send the message, then click the Send/Receive All Folders button.

g. Open the message in the Inbox, then print it.

h. Forward the message to another person you did not include in the original mailing.

i. In the message body, type **Forgot to include you in this mailing! Please read the message; hope you can be there.**

j. Send the message.

k. Delete all of the messages related to this Independent Challenge from the Inbox folder. Delete all of the messages related to this Independent Challenge from the Sent Items.

l. Empty the Deleted Items folder.

m. Exit Outlook.

Independent Challenge 2: Explore

You are planning a vacation with a group of friends. Think about a trip you would like to take, and consider this destination as you work on this Independent Challenge. You have to send email messages with an attachment as you organize this trip. *Note: To complete the Independent Challenge, your computer must be connected to the Internet.*

a. Start Outlook, then create a new message and address it to a contact, such as a friend, family member, or classmate.

b. Enter your email address in the Cc text box.

c. Type **Our vacation plans** in the Subject text box.

d. Start your word processor and write a brief letter to your friends to encourage them to join you on the adventure. Briefly detail your plans and reasons for selecting the destination. For example, if you are planning a trip to New York City, you might explain that you want to learn more about how the city developed over the past 200 years. If you are planning a trip to Orlando, Florida, you can say how much fun it is to go to the theme parks. Save the document file to the location where you store your Data Files, using a filename you will remember.

e. Type a short note in the message body of the email to the recipients of the message, telling them you hope they would like to join you on this trip and you are looking forward to them coming along.

f. Attach the document you created in your word processing program to the message.

g. Send the message, then click the Send/Receive All Folders button.

h. Print a copy of the message you receive in response.

i. Click the message Forward button and then enter the email address for you and another friend in the To: box. You will see that this message also includes the attachment.

j. Click the Insert tab on the Message Ribbon. In the Illustrations group, click the Online Pictures button, then search for a photo using Bing Image Search by typing a relevant keyword in the box and then pressing Enter.

k. Insert an image that best represents the message. Use **FIGURE 1-23** as a guide.

l. Send the message.

m. When the message arrives in your inbox, read the message, view the image, and open the attachment.

n. Delete all of the messages received for this Independent Challenge from your Inbox.

o. Delete all of the messages sent for this Independent Challenge from the Sent Items.

p. Empty the Deleted Items folder, then exit Outlook.

FIGURE 1-23

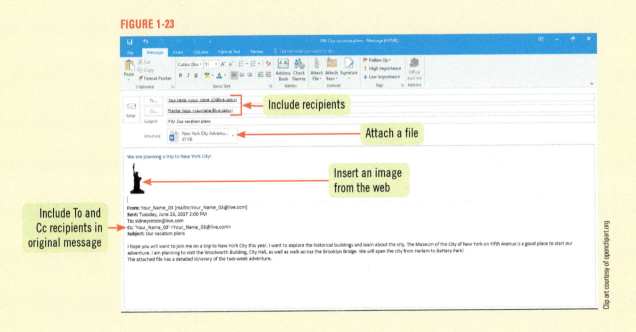

Visual Workshop

Refer to the email message in **FIGURE 1-24** to complete this Visual Workshop. Use Outlook to create and then send this message. Be sure to send the message to at least one recipient. Attach a file that you created on your computer. It can be a document, worksheet, image, or database file. *Note: To complete the Visual Workshop, your computer must be connected to the Internet.*

FIGURE 1-24

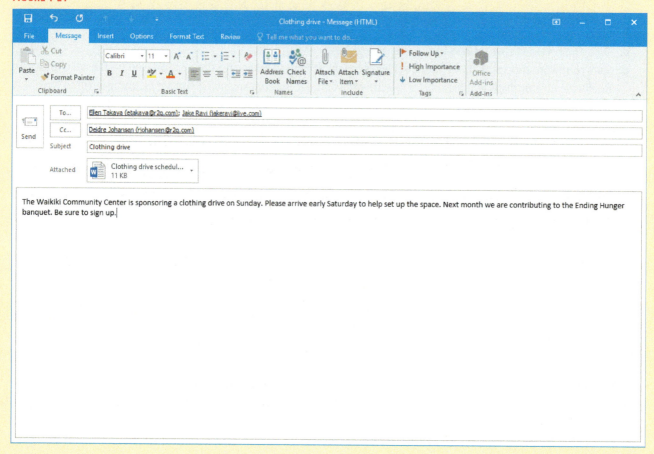

Managing Information Using Outlook

CASE ▶ Outlook is a complete personal information and time management program you can use for all your business and personal data. Outlook integrates Mail, Calendar, People, Tasks, and Notes that let you manage your mail, appointments and activities, contacts and address book, to-do list, and notes all in one program.

Module Objectives

After completing this module, you will be able to:

- Describe Outlook
- Organize email
- Manage your contacts
- Manage your calendar
- Manage tasks
- Create notes
- Connect Mail to Contacts
- Apply categories

Files You Will Need

No files needed.

Describe Outlook

The Outlook screen is fully customizable to let you personalize how you view and find the information about the people you interact with, your appointments and schedule, or mail, with different levels of detail. The first time you start Outlook, you will be prompted to set up a **personal account** that identifies you as a user. If you want to use Outlook for email, you must set up your email account. You can set up more than one account in a single installation of Outlook. Each account requires a username and password. **CASE** *Working in the human resources department, you learn Outlook so you can use it for communication and scheduling.*

STEPS

TROUBLE
Because Outlook is fully customizable and depends on the accounts that have been set up, your screen will look different than the figures in this book. You might also see some differences in the tabs and options.

1. **Start Microsoft Outlook 2016**

   When you start Outlook, you will see Mail. You use the **Navigation Pane** by clicking the Mail, Calendar, People, or Tasks buttons to switch from one to another. When Mail is selected, the Navigation Pane shows the Folder List, which you can minimize or expand. The information on the status bar varies depending on what you are working on. When Mail is active, the status bar includes the number of items and unread messages in the Inbox, the mail server connection status, and zoom percentage of the window.

2. **Click the View tab on the Ribbon, click the Message Preview button in the Arrangement group, then click 1 Line even if it is already checked**

   The options on the View tab let you customize each view in Outlook. The Message Preview option determines how many lines of each email in the center pane you see, which helps you review your messages.

3. **Click the To-Do Bar button in the Layout group, click Calendar, click the To-Do Bar button, click Tasks, click the Reading Pane button, then click Right**

   Refer to **FIGURE 2-1**. The To-Do Bar, which opens on the right side of the window, includes the Date Navigator (calendar) and tasks (including appointments). The **Date Navigator** gives you an overview of the month.

TROUBLE
If you do not see the People Pane button, you may need to enable the Outlook Social Connector 2016 add-in.

4. **Click an email message in the center pane, click the People Pane button in the People Pane group, then click Normal**

   The People Pane opens at the bottom of the Reading Pane. The People Pane shows relevant information for people who were included in the header of the message in the Reading Pane, such as attachments, appointments, and notes related to those people.

5. **In the People pane, click the People Pane Close button ⊠, click the Home tab, click the More button ⊽ in the Quick Steps group, review the menu that opens, then click anywhere outside the menu to close the Quick Steps menu**

   Quick Steps are shortcuts that help you complete basic Outlook tasks with one click.

TROUBLE
If you see words instead of buttons, click each word; your setting for the Navigation Pane is not compact.

6. **Click each button in the Navigation Pane: Calendar ▦, People ▨, and Tasks ▨, reviewing each window as it opens**

   Mail, Calendar, People, and Tasks are all in Outlook. As you place the mouse on each button, a Peek appears showing you a brief view of each window. The Mail button is ✉.

7. **Click ⋯ in the Navigation Pane, click Notes, review the window that opens, click ⋯, click Folders, then review the pane that opens**

   The Folder Pane in Folders view shows you the folders for storing your email, calendar, and contacts.

TROUBLE
Drag the border between the different panes to expand or shrink each one.

8. **Click ⋯, click Navigation Options, then click the Compact Navigation check box to remove the check mark if there is one**

   FIGURE 2-2 shows the Navigation Options dialog box. You can customize the Navigation Pane to your personal preferences. The Navigation Pane can be compact or expanded.

9. **Click OK**

FIGURE 2-1: Outlook Mail

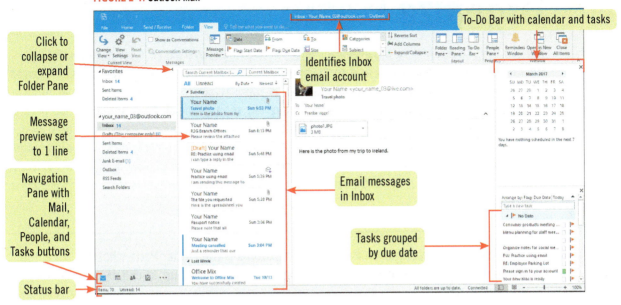

Click to collapse or expand Folder Pane

To-Do Bar with calendar and tasks

Identifies Inbox email account

Message preview set to 1 line

Navigation Pane with Mail, Calendar, People, and Tasks buttons

Status bar

Email messages in Inbox

Tasks grouped by due date

FIGURE 2-2: Navigation Options dialog box

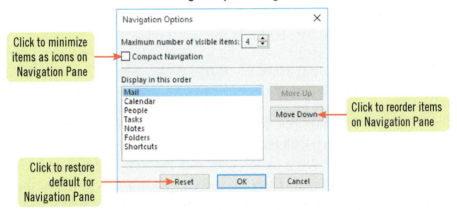

Click to minimize items as icons on Navigation Pane

Click to reorder items on Navigation Pane

Click to restore default for Navigation Pane

Weather in Calendar view

What you do during a day may change depending on the local weather. You cannot ski if there's no snow, and a trip to the beach can be disrupted by thunderstorms. When you display the Calendar, weather information for the next 3 days appears above the calendar. The weather location is the default city for the account in which Outlook was installed. This city name appears to the left of the weather information. To change the weather location displayed, click the arrow next to the city name in Calendar view, then click Add Location from the menu. You can type a city name, country, or zip code, and then select from the suggested list. To customize the Weather options, click the File tab, click Options, click Calendar, scroll down to Weather, click the Show weather on the calendar check box to turn the feature on or off, then click the Show temperature in: Celsius or Fahrenheit option button. Weather settings are saved for each user profile, and you must be connected to the Internet for this feature to work.

Organize Email

You can use Outlook Mail to organize your email, such as by conversation, view, or folder. By default, Outlook groups the mail by date, and **sorts**, or orders, the email in descending order by date received. You can use People to store your email addresses as contacts, see relevant contact information for all included in an email message, and get meeting requests through email. These requests then become appointments on your Calendar. You can search messages for specific content, dates, or senders. All new email arrives in the Inbox folder unless you set up rules to deliver email to other folders. A **rule** is an action you can create to have Outlook automatically handle messages in a certain way. **CASE** *You receive email from clients, voluteers, and R2G employees. You set up Outlook to view and manage the email using its organizational features.*

STEPS

TROUBLE
If you use Outlook for some web-based email, such as Gmail, you may not have access to all features, such as flags.

1. **Click Mail in the Navigation Pane, click the Inbox in the Folder Pane, click the View tab on the Ribbon, click the To-Do Bar button in the Layout group, click Off, then click the Home tab**

   Mail is active. The People Pane and the To-Do Bar are closed. See **FIGURE 2-3**. A list of all mail folders is in the Folder Pane, divided into sections. The Favorites section at the top of the Folder Pane is available for you to create shortcuts to folders you use most often. The Mail Folders section under the Favorites section contains the folders associated with each user account. It includes the default mail folders and any folders the user has created. When you click a folder in the Folder Pane, the contents of the folder appears in the center pane. Color-coding and icons associated with the messages in the center pane help you identify mail that is read, unread, has been forwarded or replied to, or has attachments. You can move your mouse pointer over a message in the center pane for additional options, such as a delete button or Follow-Up flags for messages.

QUICK TIP
A Personal Mail folder is a good option to add as a link in the Favorites list in the Folder Pane.

2. **Click the Arrange By Date button in the center pane**

   The menu opens as shown in **FIGURE 2-4**. You see the ways you can use filtering, sorting, and grouping, to arrange email messages. If you show the messages as **conversations**, all emails that discuss a common subject or thread will be grouped together. The Subject of a message defines the conversation. **Message threading** allows you to navigate through a group of messages, seeing all replies and forwards from all recipients about a particular topic. You can search your messages using keywords.

3. **Click the File tab on the Ribbon, verify that Info is selected in the Navigation Pane, click the Manage Rules & Alerts button, then click the New Rule button**

   The Rules and Alerts dialog box opens, and then the Rules Wizard opens, as shown in **FIGURE 2-5**. You can specify how you want your mail from specific senders—or other criteria—to be sorted as it arrives. The Rules Wizard provides templates to help you create rules. The rules help you **filter** your email messages based on specific criteria, such as who sent you a message.

4. **Click Cancel to close the Rules Wizard, click Cancel to close the Rules and Alerts dialog box, click Options in the Navigation Pane, then click Mail in the left pane**

   Mail options set up the way you compose, send, receive, organize, track, view, save, and format messages.

QUICK TIP
If email comes in that you know is offensive, add the source address to the Blocked Senders list.

5. **Scroll through the list of options, click Cancel, click the Home tab, then click the Junk button in the Delete group**

   By specifying safe senders (Never Block Sender) and blocked senders from whom you do not want mail (Block Sender), you can help ensure that the email you get is the email you want to receive.

6. **Click the Inbox for your account in the Folder Pane, click the View tab, click the Reset View button in the Current View group if necessary, then click Yes if a warning message opens**

   You can control how the email appears in any folder by using the View options.

FIGURE 2-3: Mail in Outlook

Number of unread messages in the Inbox; Inbox selected

Default mail folders

Draft message not sent yet

Unread messages

Status bar provides up-to-date information about Inbox

Mail sorted by Newest on top; click to reverse sort order

Replied message icon

Message with attachment icon

Forwarded message icon

Message has a file attached

Email message coded with three color categories

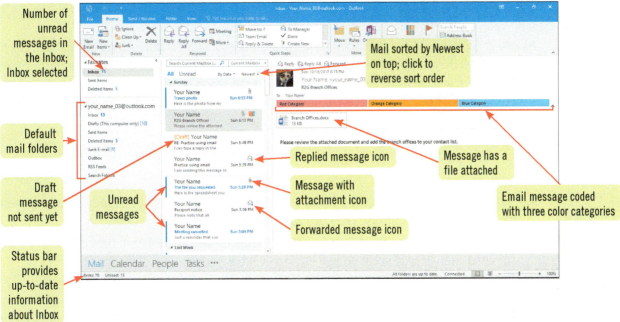

FIGURE 2-4: Arrange By options

Enter text in Search box to filter for mail based on keywords

All mail is selected

Click Unread to show only mail you haven't opened

Arrange By button; By Date is the default option

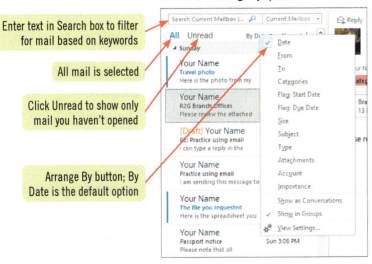

FIGURE 2-5: Setting up Rules and Alerts

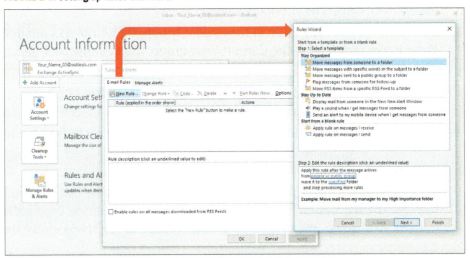

Manage Your Contacts

Learning Outcomes
- Explain how fields are used to define contacts
- Enter data to create a new contact

People or Contacts in Microsoft Outlook lets you manage all your business and personal contact information. When you enter the information for a contact, you store general and detailed data about that person. Once you create a contact, you can locate a phone number, make a call, send a meeting request, assign a task, or email a message. **CASE** ▸ *You learn about Contacts so you can store all the contact information for employees and clients.*

STEPS

1. **Click People in the Navigation Pane, click the Home tab if it is not already selected, then click People in the Current View group**

   Outlook displays People using the People view, which shows several contacts in the Contacts folder. See **FIGURE 2-6**. The other options in the Current View group let you view contacts in different ways.

2. **Click the New Contact button in the New group**

   A new, untitled contact card opens. You enter information for a new contact in each field. A **field** is an area that stores one piece of information. If you do not enter a first and last name in the Full Name text box, the Check Full Name dialog box opens so you can enter the full name for the contact.

3. **Type your name as the contact name in the Full Name text box, press [Tab], type Reason2Go in the Company text box, press [Tab], type Volunteer Coordinator in the Job title text box, type your email address in the E-mail text box, type www.r2g.com as the Web page address, type telephone numbers in the appropriate text boxes, click the Addresses Business arrow, click Home, then enter your street number and street name**

4. **Notice that the This is the mailing address check box is selected, type your city below the street name in the Address text box, then click any other field**

   If Outlook can't identify an address component that you type in the Address text box or if the address is incomplete, the Check Address dialog box opens for you to verify the component. You can store up to three addresses in the Address text box. Choose Business, Home, or Other, then type the address in the Address text box.

5. **Complete your address by filling in the remaining fields in the Check Address dialog box, click OK, click the Home address list arrow, click Business, click the This is the mailing address check box, type 750 West 56th Street, press Enter, type New York City, NY 10024, click the Business list arrow, then click Home**

   The completed contact card should look similar to **FIGURE 2-7**.

6. **Click the Save & Close button in the Actions group, click Business Card in the Current View group, click Card in the Current View group, then double-click the contact with your name to open the Contact with information for that contact**

7. **Click the Picture icon to open the Add Contact Picture dialog box**

   The information on any card can be changed, and new data added at any time for any contact.

8. **Add a photo of yourself or click Cancel, then click the Details button in the Show group**

   You can enter more detailed information about the contact. Any birthday or anniversary dates entered in the contact card will appear on the Calendar as a recurring event.

9. **Click the Birthday calendar icon [▦], click today's date on the calendar that opens, click the Save & Close button in the Actions group, click the Business Card button in the Current View group, then click the Calendar button in the Navigation Pane**

   The birthday entry appears in the Calendar.

Managing Information Using Outlook

FIGURE 2-6: Contacts in People view

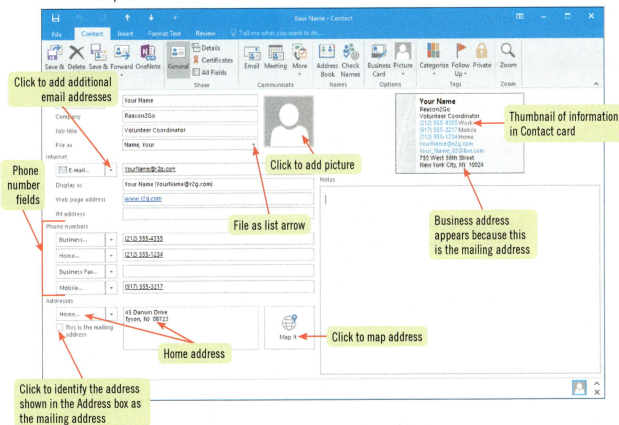

New Contact button

Selected contact

Current View options

Contacts folder selected

Click a letter to quickly jump to contacts whose last name begins with that letter

Person icon displays photo of person if photo is added to Contact information

People selected

Information about selected contact in Reading Pane

FIGURE 2-7: Completed new Contact card

Click to add additional email addresses

Phone number fields

Thumbnail of information in Contact card

Click to add picture

File as list arrow

Business address appears because this is the mailing address

Home address

Click to map address

Click to identify the address shown in the Address box as the mailing address

Manage Your Calendar

Learning Outcomes
• Describe the features of Calendar
• Create a recurring appointment

Calendar in Microsoft Outlook provides a convenient, effective way to manage your appointments and remember events. See FIGURE 2-8. Outlook defines an **appointment** as an activity that does not involve inviting other people or scheduling resources, a **meeting** as an activity you invite people to or reserve resources for, and an **event** as an activity that lasts 24 hours or longer. You can specify the subject and location of an activity and its start and end times. Outlook can sound and display a reminder for you before the start of the activity. You can set up recurring activities by specifying the recurrence parameters, such as every week, month, or any period of time, and specify when the recurrence ends. People in your group or company can each have their own calendars. **CASE** *You will use Outlook to manage the schedule for the human resources department.*

STEPS

TROUBLE
If more than one calendar is open, and they appear side-by-side, remove the check marks to close all but your calendar.

1. **Click Calendar in the Navigation Pane if it is not already selected, click the Week button in the Arrange group, then click the Month button in the Arrange group**

   The calendar can be viewed by day, work week, week, or month. The Folder Pane, if open, shows the current and next month in the Date Navigator. You can click the arrows in the Date Navigator to move forward or backward month by month, or you can click the month to select from a list. Dates with appointments or events appear in bold in the Date Navigator. You can click the Next Appointment or Previous Appointment buttons on the right or left side of the Calendar view if no appointment appears in the current time period to view your appointments. If you place the tip of the pointer on any activity, the **Peek** feature opens to show details, including reminder notices and the recurring icon for recurring events.

2. **Click any date next week in your calendar, click the Home tab if it is not selected, then click the New Appointment button in the New group**

   An untitled Appointment window opens. You use this window to specify the subject, location, reminders, and start and end times of an event. You can choose how you want to display your time associated with a scheduled appointment, such as Busy or Out of Office. You can add meeting notes and invite other people who are connected to your calendar. You can even categorize the appointment with a color.

QUICK TIP
To see upcoming tasks using the Calendar, click the View tab, click the To-Do Bar button, then click Tasks.

3. **Type Experience Leaders meeting in the Subject text box, type Conference Room A in the Location text box, click the Start time calendar icon 📅, click the date that is one week from the date you clicked in Step 2, click the Start time list arrow, click 9:00 AM, click the End time list arrow, click 10:00 AM (1 hour), click the Reminder list arrow in the Options group, then click 1 day**

   See FIGURE 2-9. If this was a one-time meeting, you could click the Save & Close button in the Actions group and the appointment would be set. However, since this is a monthly meeting, you set a recurrence pattern.

4. **Click the Recurrence button in the Options group, review the default recurrence options shown in FIGURE 2-10, click the Monthly option button, notice the change in the patterns, click the End after option button, type 12 in the occurrences text box, click OK, click OK if a warning box opens, then click the Save & Close button in the Actions group**

   The Appointment window closes. This is a recurring appointment that will be displayed on your calendar each month for a year. Recurring events or appointments appear in the Peek window.

QUICK TIP
To quickly enter an appointment, click the time slot in the calendar, then type the information.

5. **Click any date the week before the scheduled appointment, click the Home tab, click the Day button in the Arrange group, click the Work Week button, click the Week button, then click the Forward button ▶ in the calendar three times**

   You can view the calendar by day, week, or month. In all calendar views, you can click the Time Scale button in the Arrangement group on the View tab to change the level of detail of the days shown.

6. **On the Home tab, click the Today button in the Go To group to return to today's date**

FIGURE 2-8: Calendar for a month

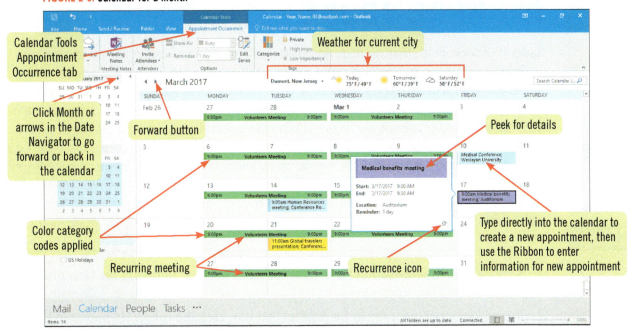

Calendar Tools Appointment Occurrence tab

Click Month or arrows in the Date Navigator to go forward or back in the calendar

Forward button

Color category codes applied

Recurring meeting

Weather for current city

Peek for details

Recurrence icon

Type directly into the calendar to create a new appointment, then use the Ribbon to enter information for new appointment

FIGURE 2-9: New Appointment window

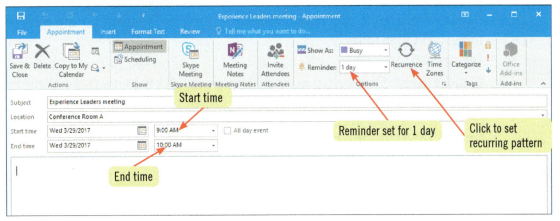

Start time

End time

Reminder set for 1 day

Click to set recurring pattern

FIGURE 2-10: Appointment Recurrence dialog box

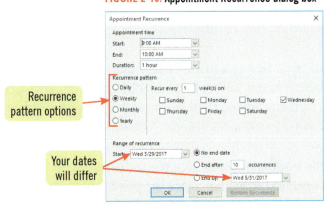

Recurrence pattern options

Your dates will differ

Outlook 2016

Manage Tasks

Learning Outcomes
- Explain the features of Tasks
- Create a new Task and set the Date, Priority, and Reminder fields

Tasks in Outlook are an electronic to-do list. When you have something you need to do, you can enter it in **Tasks**. Each task has a subject, a start and due date, and a description. You can also assign a priority to a task. You can mark your progress on tasks by percentage complete, and you can have Outlook create status summary reports in email messages and then send the summary to anyone on a task update list. Tasks can also have reminders. If you **flag** an email message, it appears as a task in your task list to remind you to follow-up. When you are using Outlook, your tasks appear at the bottom of the To-Do Bar if it is open. You can also view the tasks that are due on each date in the Calendar. Similar to meetings and events, tasks can recur. You can also assign a flag and category to each task to help you organize your tasks. **CASE** *A month from today, the Sydney office is hosting a webinar on water systems. You have to make sure the employees sign up and prepare for this important event. You enter the task in Outlook to keep track of it.*

STEPS

1. Click Tasks in the Navigation Pane, then click the New Task button in the New group

   The new untitled Task window opens.

2. Type Sydney webinar prep in the Subject text box, click the Follow Up button in the Tags group, click Flag Message, click the Start date calendar icon 📅, click the date that is one month from today, click the Priority list arrow, click High, click the Reminder check box to select it, click the Reminder calendar icon 📅, then click the date that is three weeks from today

   The completed task looks like FIGURE 2-11.

3. Click the Save & Close button in the Actions group, click the View tab, click the Reading Pane button in the Layout group, then click Right

   FIGURE 2-12 shows Tasks as a To-Do List with a ScreenTip (a Peek) displaying additional task information about one task. Existing tasks may appear in the window (your screen will be different).

4. Click the Change View button in the Current View group

   A gallery opens with different options for viewing tasks.

5. Click the Home tab, click the New Task button in the New group to open the Untitled Task window, click the Subject text box, type Organize notes social media campaign in the Subject text box, then click the Assign Task button in the Manage Task group

   You can assign tasks to another person and have Outlook automatically update you on the status of the task completion.

6. Click the To text box, type your or a friend's email address, verify that Organize notes for social media campaign is in the Subject text box, click the Status arrow, click In Progress as shown in FIGURE 2-13, then click the Send button in the message window

   The assigned task you created appears in the To-Do List for No Date. You may need to scroll to see the task. Notice the task icon has a person icon with an arrow to indicate this task is assigned to another person.

7. Click Calendar in the Navigation Pane, click the Today button in the Go To group if the calendar does not open to today, then place the pointer over Tasks in the Navigation Pane to see the tasks list

8. Click the View tab, click the To-Do Bar button in the Layout group, then click Tasks

   To schedule time to complete a task, you can drag a task from the To-Do Bar to a time block in the Calendar. When you check your mail, you will see that you have the option to Accept or Decline the task from the Inbox.

FIGURE 2-11: Task information entered

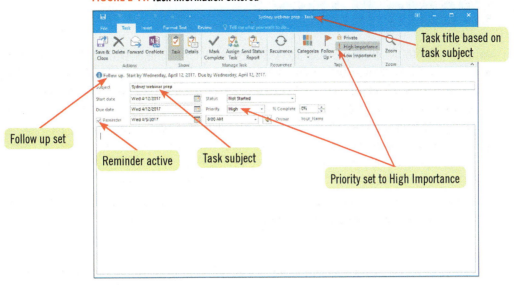

Task title based on task subject

Follow up set

Reminder active

Task subject

Priority set to High Importance

FIGURE 2-12: Tasks in To-Do List view

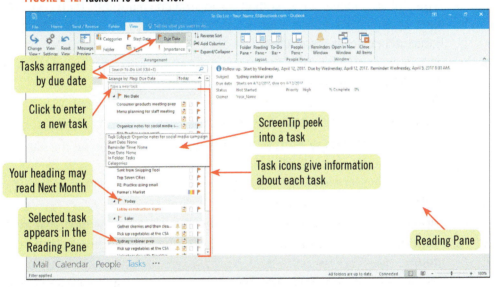

Tasks arranged by due date

Click to enter a new task

Your heading may read Next Month

Selected task appears in the Reading Pane

ScreenTip peek into a task

Task icons give information about each task

Reading Pane

FIGURE 2-13: Assigning a task

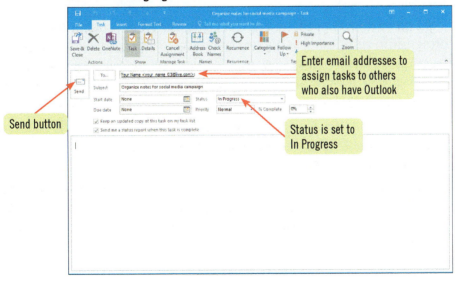

Enter email addresses to assign tasks to others who also have Outlook

Send button

Status is set to In Progress

Create Notes

Learning Outcomes
- Create a new Note in Outlook
- Create an event from a note

Notes in Microsoft Outlook provides access to notes, which are the electronic version of the sticky notes you buy at your local stationery store. Notes created in Outlook are a convenient way to quickly jot down a reminder or an idea. You can group and organize notes, like tasks and appointments, and you can assign categories, contacts, or colors to them. You can also forward a note to share an idea with a colleague. **CASE** *You use Notes in Outlook to quickly write down notes concerning a new phone plan and expense reports at Reason2Go.*

STEPS

TROUBLE
If the new note fills the screen, double-click the title bar to create a thumbnail version of the note.

1. **Click ⋯ in the Navigation Pane, click Notes on the menu, then click the New Note button in the New group on the Home tab**

   A blank new Note opens. See FIGURE 2-14. You type your note directly in the Note window, which is a separate window that you can move by dragging the title bar. The icon in the upper-left corner of the note opens a menu. The note should begin with a meaningful phrase so the Notes list displays a clear descriptive title for it.

2. **Type Mobile phone plans changing for Australian volunteers, then click the Note Close button ✕**

   The note appears in the Notes window.

QUICK TIP
If a note is covering an area of the window you want to view, click the title bar of the note and drag it to a new location.

3. **Click the New Note button, type Review expense reports, click the Note Close button ✕, then click the Notes List button in the Current View group**

   All new notes appear next to any existing notes that have been created previously. See FIGURE 2-15. Notes are date- and time-stamped at the time they are created.

4. **Drag the Mobile phone plans note over the Calendar button on the Navigation Pane, then release the mouse button**

   A new Appointment window opens with the details from the note entered in the Subject line and the notes area.

5. **Click the Start time calendar icon 🔲, click August 15 for the next year, click the All day event check box, refer to FIGURE 2-16, then click the Save & Close button in the Actions group**

   You now have an event to remind you about the contents in the note. In a similar way, you can drag a note to the Tasks button in the Navigation Pane to create a task based on the note. When you drag a note to the Tasks button, a new task window opens so you can specify a due date and other details for the task.

QUICK TIP
To quickly copy a note, drag the closed note while you press [Ctrl].

6. **Right-click a note to open the shortcut menu, review the options on the menu, then press [ESC]**

   You can use the shortcut menu to copy, print, forward, categorize, or delete notes. In addition, the Current View group on the Home tab and the View tab provide many options for viewing notes so you can organize them the way you want.

FIGURE 2-14: New note

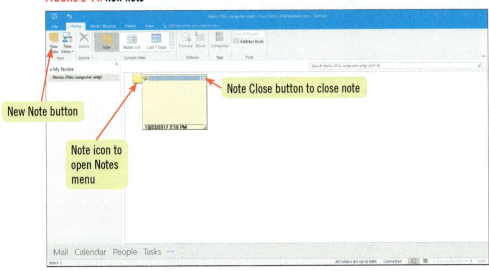

FIGURE 2-15: Two new completed notes

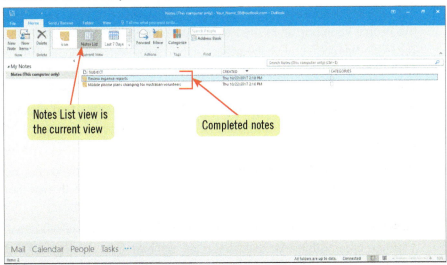

FIGURE 2-16: Creating an event from a note

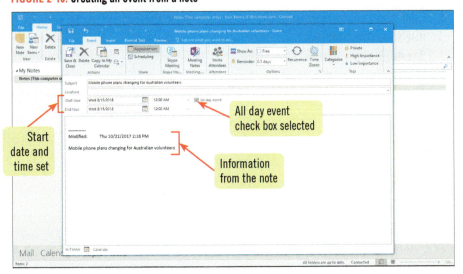

Connect Mail to Contacts

Learning Outcomes
• Describe how to use contacts to connect

When email arrives in your inbox, you may or may not already have the senders name, address, email, phone numbers, and other information stored in your contacts. Some email senders will be people you hear from once. However, you will usually be working and corresponding with people who send you email over a period of time. You can access a contact's information through Mail and use it to send a letter, make a phone call, or schedule a meeting. **CASE** *When email comes in to the R2G office, you sometimes need to call or correspond with the sender to clarify a tour. You explore the mail contact manager feature to better understand how to connect mail to contacts.*

STEPS

TROUBLE
If you cannot find your message, select any message in the Inbox.

1. **Click Mail in the Navigation pane, then locate the most recent message that you sent to yourself and a friend in Module 1 or any message with more than one recipient**

2. **Click the message to select it, then place the pointer over each email address in the header to display the screentip**

   A screentip displays the information about the person assigned to that email. See **FIGURE 2-17**.

QUICK TIP
The first time you get a message from a person, you can easily add their information to a new contact card.

3. **Click the email address in the message header, click the View tab on the Ribbon, click the People Pane button in the People Pane group, then click Normal**

   The People Pane opens beneath the message in the Preview Pane. You can see all the mail, attachments, and meetings assigned to any selected email address in a message. You can use this feature in any mail folder to find out if you have meetings or previous correspondence with any mail recipient. See **FIGURE 2-18**.

4. **In the People Pane, click All, click Mail, click Attachments, then click Meetings**

   You see the different types of information for the selected recipient.

5. **Double-click the selected email address in the header**

   That person's contact information, such as their name, phone numbers, addresses, and company name that is stored in your Contacts folder, appears in a dialog box. You can directly view the Contact card through this and review the source of the information by clicking Outlook (Contacts).

6. **Click the Schedule a meeting link in the Calendar section**

   A calendar opens with the Meeting tab selected, as shown in **FIGURE 2-19**, with a schedule and any other recipients on the original email message. You can add or select attendees for the meeting as well as specify various meeting characteristics. For example, you can scroll through the calendar to select a date and time for a meeting. You can then see who accepts, declines, or doesn't respond to your meeting request.

7. **Click the Delete button in the Actions group, then click Yes to cancel the meeting and not save the changes**

   You return to the Inbox in Mail.

FIGURE 2-17: Email with contact selected

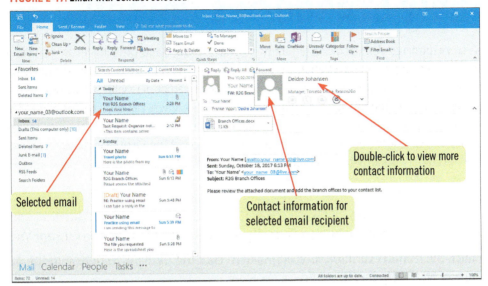

Selected email

Double-click to view more contact information

Contact information for selected email recipient

FIGURE 2-18: People Pane open Normal view

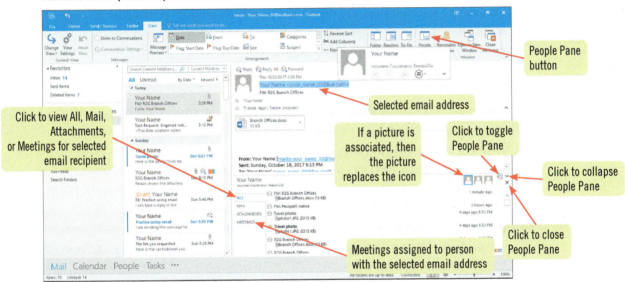

Click to view All, Mail, Attachments, or Meetings for selected email recipient

People Pane button

Selected email address

If a picture is associated, then the picture replaces the icon

Click to toggle People Pane

Click to collapse People Pane

Click to close People Pane

Meetings assigned to person with the selected email address

FIGURE 2-19: People Pane open Normal view

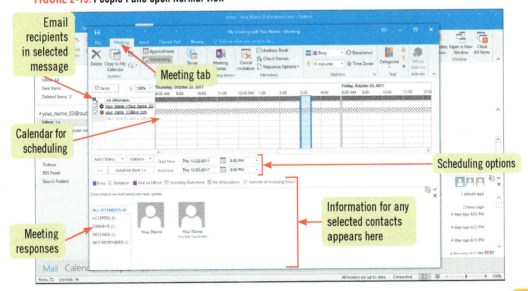

Email recipients in selected message

Meeting tab

Calendar for scheduling

Scheduling options

Information for any selected contacts appears here

Meeting responses

Apply Categories

You use **categories** in Outlook to tag items so you can track and organize them by specific criteria. Outlook comes with color categories that are set by default. You can rename the categories as needed. For example, red can be urgent, blue can be business, and green can be personal. By assigning color categories to contacts, tasks, appointments, notes, or any item in Outlook, you can quickly filter and sort by color to review all items assigned to a specific color category. If you change your Contacts view to List view and then click the Categories button in the Arrangement section of the View tab, you can see your contacts clearly by category. **CASE** *You want to use color to help organize information about volunteers and staff. Eventually, you will set up a system to assign colors to contacts.*

STEPS

1. **Click People in the Navigation Pane, then click Business Card in the Current View group**

2. **Click the Contact card for your name, then click the Categorize button in the Tags group on the Home tab**

   Outlook comes with six predefined color categories: Orange, Green, Purple, Blue, Red, and Yellow.

3. **Click Green Category (or the name of the green category if its name has been changed)**

   Your Contact card is now assigned the color green.

4. **Double click the Contact card for your name**

   You can see the green color bar. You can also see the color categories assigned to contacts if you view your contacts as a list.

5. **Click the Close button ☒ to close your contact card, click the View tab, click the Change View button in the Current View group, then click the List button**

   The contacts are grouped by category. **FIGURE 2-20** shows a sample of contacts with categories applied. Your contact information is listed with the other contacts in the green category.

6. **Click Calendar in the Navigation Pane, verify that the Week button is selected in the Arrange group, click the Forward arrow to scroll to next week, click the Tuesday 10 AM time slot on the Calendar, type Regional planning meeting, then press [Enter]**

   The Regional planning meeting is entered in the calendar as an appointment and the Calendar Tools Appointment tab is active.

7. **Click the Categorize button in the Tags group, click Green Category (or the category's name), click the Categorize button in the Tags group again, then click Purple Category (or the category's name)**

   The appointment is assigned the colors purple and green. If you view the calendar as a list and group by color category, the meeting will appear in both the purple and the green category groups.

8. **Click People in the Navigation Pane, click any Contact, click the Categorize button in the Tags group, then click All Categories to open the Color Categories dialog box, as shown in FIGURE 2-21**

9. **Click Green Category (or the category's name), click Rename, type Personal as the new name, then click OK**

   The name of the green category changes to "Personal". To display the list of color categories and the name associated with each, click the Home tab, then click the Categorize list arrow in the Tags group.

10. **Click the File tab, then click Exit to exit Outlook**

    As you work on other applications at your computer, you can leave Outlook open so you can refer to your contacts, be reminded of appointments, and see new email from any friends or colleagues.

FIGURE 2-20: Contacts grouped by color category

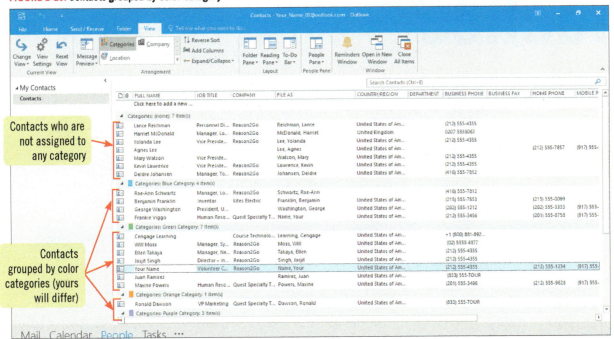

Contacts who are not assigned to any category

Contacts grouped by color categories (yours will differ)

FIGURE 2-21: Color Categories dialog box

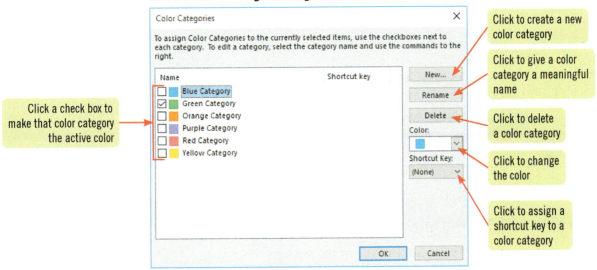

Click to create a new color category

Click to give a color category a meaningful name

Click to delete a color category

Click to change the color

Click to assign a shortcut key to a color category

Click a check box to make that color category the active color

Coordinating calendars

Calendar can check the availability of all the people and resources for the meetings you want to set up. Once you select a meeting time and location, you can send invitations as meeting requests by entering contact names in the To text box, then clicking the Send button. The meeting request arrives in the invitee's Inbox with buttons to Accept, Reject, or Request a change directly in the email message. If an invitee accepts the invitation, a positive email reply is sent back to you, and Outlook posts the meeting to the invitee's calendar. If you share calendars through a network, you can click the Open Calendar button in the Manage Calendars group on the Home tab, then click Open Shared Calendar to view the calendars of your colleagues. To send a copy of a time period in your calendar to someone through email, click the E-mail Calendar button in the Share group on the Home tab, adjust the options in the Send a Calendar via Email dialog box, click OK, then address and send the email.

Practice

Concepts Review

Label each element of the Calendar window shown in FIGURE 2-22

FIGURE 2-22

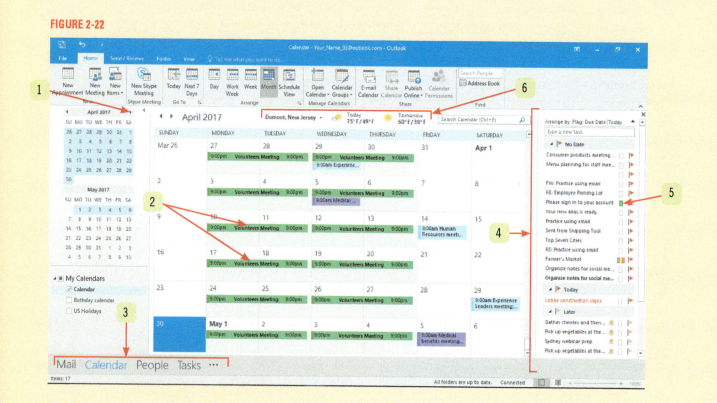

Match each term with the statement that best describes it.

7. People   a. Send and receive messages
8. Calendar   b. Keep and track appointments
9. Mail   c. Manage a to-do list
10. Tasks   d. Organize contacts
11. Notes   e. Jot down ideas or reminders

Select the best answer from the list of choices.

12. **If you want to quickly know the weather in your current city, use _____.**
    - **a.** Mail
    - **b.** Calendar
    - **c.** People
    - **d.** Notes

13. **If you have a weekly meeting, create a(n) _____.**
    - **a.** recurring event
    - **b.** appointment reminder
    - **c.** event that lasts 24 hours or more
    - **d.** seven-day event

14. **When you enter an address that doesn't meet the field requirements in a new Contact card, Outlook _____.**
    - **a.** cancels the contact
    - **b.** offers a list of possible suggestions
    - **c.** leaves the entry as is
    - **d.** opens the Check Address dialog box

15. **If you enter a contact's birthday using the Details page, the date appears as a(n) _____ on the calendar.**
    - **a.** recurring event
    - **b.** appointment for today
    - **c.** repeating task
    - **d.** email in the Inbox

16. **To color-code your appointments, meetings, contacts, and events, use _____.**
    - **a.** flags
    - **b.** paint
    - **c.** categories
    - **d.** notes

17. **Set a _____ when you enter an appointment in the Calendar and you want to invite others.**
    - **a.** date
    - **b.** flag
    - **c.** note
    - **d.** meeting

18. **Which of the following is *not* in Outlook?**
    - **a.** Mail
    - **b.** OneNote
    - **c.** Calendar
    - **d.** Notes

19. **Which of these fields is only available when you click Details as you create a new Contact card?**
    - **a.** Birthday
    - **b.** Company
    - **c.** Business address
    - **d.** Web page

20. **If you want to be alerted when a task is due, you should set and use a _____.**
    - **a.** category
    - **b.** reminder
    - **c.** flag
    - **d.** signal

Skills Review

1. **Describe Outlook.**
    - **a.** Start Outlook and view Mail.
    - **b.** Arrange the Outlook window so the Folder Pane is set to Normal, the Reading Pane is on the right, and the People Pane is set to Normal.
    - **c.** If there is any mail in the Inbox, click a message and view the message in the Reading Pane.
    - **d.** Click each tab on the Ribbon, and view the different command buttons.
    - **e.** Click Calendar, click People, click Tasks, then click Mail in the Navigation Pane.
    - **f.** Click the Home tab on the Ribbon.

2. **Organize email.**
    - **a.** View the Inbox.
    - **b.** View the email in the Inbox by Date, with the most recent on top.
    - **c.** Select a message, review the People Pane, review the contents, then collapse the People Pane.

d. Open a new Message window, and write an email message to your instructor and at least one friend so there are two email addresses in the To box. Include an address in the Cc box, then type **National Park Service Call to Action** as the subject of the message. As the body of the message, enter the message shown in **FIGURE 2-23**.

e. Send the message.

f. Open the Sent Items folder, review the emails, then return to the Inbox.

FIGURE 2-23

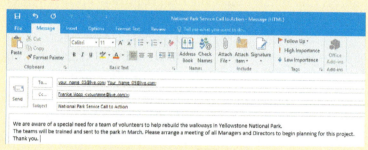

3. **Manage your contacts.**

    a. Click People and view the Contacts.

    b. Open a new untitled Contact window.

    c. Create a new contact using the information in **FIGURE 2-24**. Assign the categories as shown.

    d. If you have a photo or any picture, add it to the Contact card.

    e. Click the Details button in the Show group, enter February 22nd as the birthday, then click OK if a message dialog box opens.

    f. Save and close the contact.

FIGURE 2-24

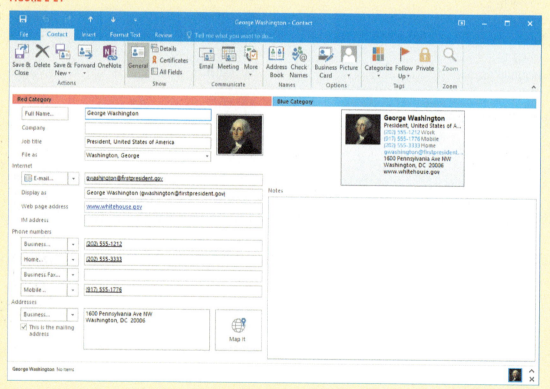

Skills Review (continued)

4. Manage your calendar.

   a. Open the Calendar.

   b. View the calendar by Week.

   c. Go to today.

   d. Scroll to February and view George Washington's birthday.

   e. Return to any day next week, create a new appointment for next week for a 3-hour lecture with **Jennifer, Emily, and Michael** starting at 12:30 at **Museum of Natural History**. Set a reminder for **2 days**. This appointment should be labeled **Out of Office**. (*Hint*: click the Show As list arrow, then click Out of Office.)

   f. Assign the Orange Category. Refer to **FIGURE 2-25**.

   g. Save and close the appointment.

FIGURE 2-25

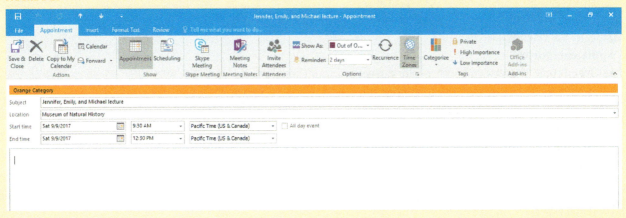

5. Manage tasks.

   a. Open Tasks.

   b. Create a new task with the subject of the task **Volunteer day with Brooklyn Bridge Animal Rescue Team**.

   c. Start the new task any day next month.

   d. Set the reminder for 8 a.m. the day before you have to volunteer.

   e. Set this task as a high-priority task. See **FIGURE 2-26**.

   f. Save and close the task.

   g. View the task list in Simple List and Detailed views.

FIGURE 2-26

Skills Review (continued)

6. Create notes.

  a. Open Notes.

  b. Create a new note with the following text: **Post fliers in town hall about the new recruitment campaign.** See FIGURE 2-27.

  c. Close the note.

7. Connect Mail to Contacts

  a. Locate an email in your Sent Items folder.

  b. Double-click an email address in the header to view the contact information.

  c. Click the Schedule a meeting link to view the meeting options.

  d. Close the meeting window, discarding any changes.

  e. Click the Click to expand the People Pane arrow in the lower-right corner of the message window to open the People Pane.

  f. View all information for at least two email recipients from your inbox or sent folder.

  g. Close the People Pane.

8. Apply categories.

  a. Open People, then assign another color category to your Contact card.

  b. Assign a second category to the appointment that you created in Step 4.

  c. Assign a category to the task you created in Step 5.

  d. View Contacts as a list grouped by category.

  e. View the Tasks as a list grouped by category.

  f. Exit Outlook.

FIGURE 2-27

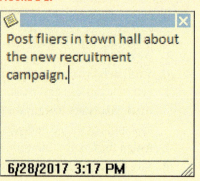

Post fliers in town hall about the new recruitment campaign.

6/28/2017 3:17 PM

Independent Challenge 1

As manager of a local travel agency for families with special needs travelers, your job is to develop contacts for all customers that come into the agency and set the schedule for the trips. The contacts will also be used to send direct mail for future promotions. You created a form for customers to complete so you can gather their contact information. The information includes first and last name, mailing address, email address, and at least one phone number. Each week, you select one customer from the list of new names to receive a small prize package. You need to create the contacts in Outlook and use Outlook to schedule the weekly prize giveaway.

  a. Open Contacts in Outlook, and then create five new Contact cards. Use your friends' information or make up fictitious names and contact information.

  b. Create two notes, each in the Blue category, that remind you about two different events that take place in the agency.

  c. Create a recurring appointment on each Thursday for the next 2 months to select a winner from the list of new names.

  d. Enter two new tasks in the task list. One task is for you to review the lectures and special events in the area and contact them to participate, and the other task is for you to review the changes to laws regarding travel outside the country. Each task should have a start date of next week, a high priority, and be in the Yellow category.

  e. View the Calendar with the To-Do Bar open.

  f. Exit Outlook.

Independent Challenge 2: Explore

Outlook is an integrated information management system that stores information in folders specific to the type of information stored. You can create new folders for specific types of information and view them in the folders list. You can also transfer one type of item to another. For example, you can drag a task to the Calendar to create an appointment. The integration of the different types of information is what makes Outlook so powerful. You are going to move items within Outlook to see how easily you can integrate information. New tasks and messages will be created as you go through this exercise; save and close each one before moving to the next step.

a. Open Mail in Outlook, then drag an email message from the Inbox to Tasks in the Navigation Pane to create a new task. In a note in Outlook, explain what happens. What elements of the email message are entered in which task fields?

b. Drag an email message from the Inbox to Calendar in the Navigation Pane, then write a brief paragraph that explain what happens.

c. Create a new Note, then drag the note to Calendar in the Navigation Pane, then explain what happens.

d. Open the Calendar, drag an existing appointment from the Calendar to Tasks in the Navigation Pane, then explain what happens.

e. Drag the same appointment you dragged in Step d to Mail in the Navigation Pane, then explain what happens.

f. Find the location for the Weather in the Calendar. Select another part of the country for the location. Did you notice a change in the weather information that is displayed? (If you are using a computer that is not connected to the Internet, skip this step.)

g. View the Contacts list in two different views.

h. Drag a Contact card from the Contacts list to Calendar in the Navigation Pane, then explain what happens.

i. Open an existing contact, click the Categorize button, then click All Categories.

j. Rename the Purple and Red categories to names of your choice, close the Color Categories dialog box, then assign the contact to both categories.

k. Save and close the contact.

l. Drag a Contact card from the Contacts list to Mail in the Navigation Pane, then explain what happens.

m. Create a new contact for yourself using the name of a celebrity and your personal information, add two categories, then click the Email button in the Communicate group to send an email to yourself.

n. Open the Contact card for your name. Click the Map It button, print the screen that appears in a web browser. (If you are using a computer that is not connected to the Internet, skip this step.)

o. Find a photo of yourself, and add it to your new contact card.

p. Print your contact card as directed by your instructor.

q. Exit Outlook.

Visual Workshop

Start Outlook. First, create a new contact, as shown in **FIGURE 2-28**, using any photo you want. Create an appointment as shown in **FIGURE 2-29**, using a weekday in the next 2 weeks as the date for the appointment. Finally, create a task, as shown in **FIGURE 2-30**. Note that the dates in the figures will differ from those on your screen.

FIGURE 2-28

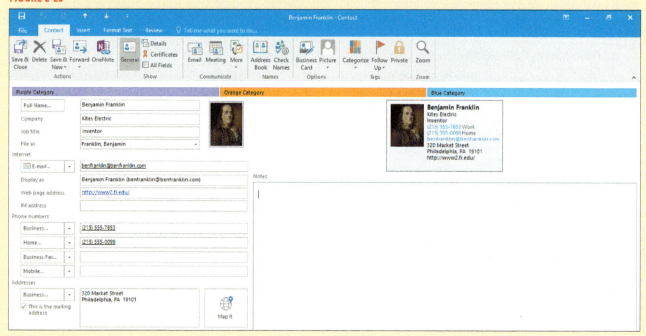

FIGURE 2-29

FIGURE 2-30

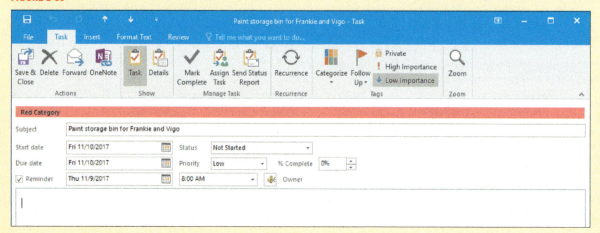

Glossary

3D graphics software Provides a set of tools for creating wireframe drawings that represent three-dimensional objects.

3D printer Deposits multiple layers of material (typically heated plastic) onto a surface. To achieve the desired shape, the tool head may travel in a different direction as each layer is applied.

Absolute cell reference In a formula, a cell address that refers to a specific cell and does not change when you copy the formula; indicated by a dollar sign before the column letter and/or row number. *See also* Relative cell reference.

Access time The estimated time for a storage device to locate data on a disk, usually measured in milliseconds.

Accessories Simple Windows application programs (apps) that perform specific tasks, such as the Calculator accessory for performing calculations. *Also called* Windows accessories.

Account Log-on information including ISP, email address, and password for each person using Outlook; used to create folders in Outlook for contacts, email, and schedules. *See also* Personal account.

Accounting software A category of software that helps you keep a record of monetary transactions and investments.

Action Center Opened by clicking the Notifications button on the right side of the taskbar; shows notifications, tips, and reminders. Contains Quick Actions buttons for commonly-used Windows settings.

Active The currently available document, program, or object; on the taskbar, when more than one program is open, the button for the active program appears slightly lighter.

Active cell The cell in which you are currently working.

Active window The window you are currently using; if multiple windows are open, the window in front of other open windows.

Add-in Software that works with an installed app to extend its features.

Add-ins Small programs available from the online Office Store that allow you to access information on the web without having to leave the main application or program.

Address A sequence of drive and folder names that describes a folder's or file's location in the file hierarchy; the highest hierarchy level is on the left, with lower hierarchy levels separated by the ⟩ symbol to its right.

Address bar In a window, the area just below the Ribbon that shows the file hierarchy, or address of the files that appear in the file list below it; the address appears as a series of links you can click to navigate to other locations on your computer.

Address book A stored list of names and email addresses that you can access through an email program such as Outlook to address messages.

Adjustment handle A small yellow handle that changes the appearance of an object's most prominent feature.

Align To place objects' edges or centers on the same plane.

Alignment The placement of cell contents in relation to a cell's edges; for example, left-aligned, centered, or right-aligned.

Alignment command A command used in Layout or Design View for a form or report to left-, center-, or right-align a value within its control using the Align Left, Center, or Align Right buttons on the Home tab. In Design View, you can also align the top, bottom, right, or left edge of selected controls using the Align button.

Alternate Back Color property A property that determines the alternating background color of the selected section in a form or report.

ALU (Arithmetic Logic Unit) The part of the processor that performs mathematical and logical operations.

Analog data Data that is represented using an infinite scale of values, in contrast to digital data, which is represented as discrete digits, such as 0s and 1s.

Anchoring A layout positioning option that allows you to tie controls together so you can work with them as a group.

AND criteria Criteria placed in the same row of the query design grid. All criteria on the same row must be true for a record to appear on the resulting datasheet.

Android A mobile operating system that is a popular platform for tablet computers, smartphones, and ebook readers.

Animation emphasis effect In Sway, a special effect you can apply to an object to animate it.

Animation tag Identifies the order in which an object is animated on a slide during a slide show.

App A program such as a game, flashlight, calendar, stock market tracker, traffic or weather monitor, or news feed designed to run on mobile devices such as smartphones and tablet computers. *Also called* mobile app and mobile application.

App window The window that opens after you start an app, showing you the tools you need to use the program and any open program documents.

Application developer The person responsible for building and maintaining tables, queries, forms, and reports for all of the database users.

Application program Any program that lets you work with files or create and edit files such as graphics, letters, financial summaries, and other useful documents, as well as view webpages on the Internet and send and receive e-mail. *Also called* an app.

Application software Computer programs that help you perform a specific task such as word processing. *Also called* application programs, applications, or programs.

Appointment In the Outlook Calendar, an activity that does not involve inviting other people or scheduling resources.

Argument Information that a function uses to create the final answer. Multiple arguments are separated by commas. All of the arguments for a function are surrounded by a single set of parentheses.

Arithmetic operators In a formula, symbols that perform mathematical calculations, such as addition (+), subtraction (–), multiplication (*), division (/), or exponentiation (^).

ASCII (American Standard Code for Information Interchange) A code that represents characters as a series of 1s and 0s, making it possible to transfer data between computers.

Aspect ratio The relationship between height and width of a display; typically 16:9 for a widescreen monitor.

Attachment A file, such as a picture, audio clip, video clip, document, worksheet, or presentation, that is sent in addition to the email message composed by typing in the message window.

Audio editing software A category of software that includes sound playback as well as recording capabilities. Menus provide additional digital editing features, such as speed control, volume adjustments, clipping, and mixing of sounds.

AutoComplete A feature that automatically suggests text to insert.

AutoCorrect A feature that automatically detects and corrects typing errors, minor spelling errors, and capitalization, and inserts certain typographical symbols as you type.

AutoFill Feature activated by dragging the fill handle; copies a cell's contents or continues a series of entries into adjacent cells.

AutoFill Options button Button that appears after using the fill handle to copy cell contents; enables you to choose to fill cells with specific elements (such as formatting) of the copied cell if desired.

AutoFit A feature that automatically adjusts the width of a column or the height of a row to accommodate its widest or tallest entry.

Automatic page break A page break that is inserted automatically at the bottom of a page.

AutoNumber A field data type in which Access enters a sequential integer for each record added into the datasheet. Numbers cannot be reused even if the record is deleted.

Avg function A built-in function used to calculate the average of the values in a given field or cell range.

Background The area behind the text and graphics on a slide.

Background graphic An object placed on the slide master.

Background image An image that fills an entire form or report, appearing "behind" the other controls; also sometimes called a watermark.

Backstage view View that appears when the File tab is clicked as shown. The navigation bar on the left side contains commands to perform actions common to most Office programs, such as opening a file, saving a file, and closing the file.

Backup A duplicate copy of a file that is stored in another location.

Backward-compatible Software feature that enables documents saved in an older version of a program to be opened in a newer version of the program.

BD (Blu-ray Disc) A high-capacity disc for storing large quantities of digital content, such as high-definition video.

BD drive A drive that plays Blu-ray discs.

Benchmark A test used to measure computer hardware or software performance.

Bibliography A list of sources that you consulted or cited while creating a document.

Binary digit The smallest unit of information handled by a computer; can hold one of two values, either a 0 or a 1. Eight bits make up a byte, which can represent a letter or number. *See also* Bit.

Binary number system A method for representing numbers using only two digits, 0 and 1; as compared with the decimal system, which uses ten digits: 0, 1, 2, 3, 4, 5, 6, 7, 8, and 9.

Bit The smallest unit of information handled by a computer; can hold one of two values, either a 0 or a 1. Eight bits make up a byte, which can represent a letter or number; short for binary digit.

Bit depth The number of bits that determines the range of possible colors that can be assigned to each pixel. For example, an 8-bit color depth can create 256 colors. *Also called* color depth.

Blind courtesy copy (Bcc) A way to send an email message to recipients when the sender does not want to reveal who has received courtesy copies.

Blog Derived from the phrase "weB LOG," refers to a personal journal focusing on a single topic or covering a variety of issues posted on the web for access by the general public.

Blogger The person who creates and maintains a blog.

Blu-ray disc *See* BD.

Blu-ray drive *See* BD drive.

Bluetooth A type of wireless technology that uses short range radio waves. A Bluetooth device must first be "paired" with a computer so that it knows to trust that particular device.

Bold Formatting applied to text to make it thicker and darker.

Boot process The sequence of events that occurs within a computer system between the time the user starts the computer and the time it is ready to process commands.

Bootstrap A program stored in ROM that loads and initializes the operating system on a computer.

Border A line that can be added above, below, or to the sides of a paragraph, text, or table cell; a line that divides the columns and rows of a table.

Bound control A control used in either a form or report to display data from the underlying field; used to edit and enter new data in a form.

Browser A program that communicates with a web server and displays webpages.

BSD license (Berkeley Software Distribution) One of two of the most common open source and free software licenses for a server operating system.

Buffer The area of computer memory that holds data from one device while it is waiting to be transferred to another device.

Building block Reusable piece of formatted content or document part that is stored in a gallery.

Bullet A small graphic symbol used to identify an item in a list.

Bus An electronic pathway that carries the electronic signals between the electronic parts of a computer.

Business Intelligence tools Excel features for gathering and analyzing data to answer sophisticated business questions.

Button A small rectangle you can click in order to issue a command to an application program.

Byte An 8-bit unit of information that represents a single character.

Cable A wire used to connect a peripheral device to a computer through a port.

Cable modem A communications device that can be used to connect a computer to the Internet via the cable TV infrastructure.

Cache Special high-speed memory that gives the CPU rapid access to data that would otherwise be accessed from memory elsewhere on the motherboard. *Also called* RAM cache or cache memory.

Cache memory *See* Cache.

CAD software A special type of 3D graphics software designed for architects and engineers who use computers to create blueprints and product specifications. *Also called* computer-aided design software.

Calculation A new value that is created by an expression in a text box on a form or report.

Calculation operators Symbols in a formula that indicate what type of calculation to perform on the cells, ranges, or values.

Calendar In Outlook, provides a convenient way to manage appointments and events.

Calendar Picker A pop-up calendar from which you can choose dates for a date field.

Canvas In the Paint accessory, the area in the center of the app window that you use to create drawings.

Capacitor The electronic parts in a chip that hold the bits that represent data.

Card A section for a particular type of content in a Sway presentation.

Card reader A device that transfers data to or from a computer.

Case sensitive An application program's (app's) ability to differentiate between uppercase and lowercase letters; usually used to describe how an operating system evaluates passwords that users type to gain entry to user accounts.

Categories In Outlook, a feature used to tag items so you can track and organize them by specific criteria.

Category axis Horizontal axis in a chart, usually containing the names of data categories; in a 2-dimensional chart, also known as the x-axis.

CD (compact disc) An optical storage medium that can store up to 700 MB of data. There are a variety of CDs including CD-ROM, CD-R, and CD-RW.

CD drive A storage device that uses laser technology to read data from a CD-ROM.

CD writer A general term for recordable CD technologies such as CD-R and CD-RW.

CD-R disc An acronym for compact disc-recordable; a CD disc using optical disc technology that allows the user to create CD-ROMs and audio CDs.

CD-ROM disc An optical storage media that is read only and that can store up to 700 MB of data.

CD-RW disc An acronym for compact disc-rewritable; a CD disc using optical disc technology that allows the user to write data onto a CD, then change that data.

Cell The box formed by the intersection of a table row and table column.

Cell address The location of a cell, expressed by cell coordinates; for example, the cell address of the cell in column A, row 1 is A1.

Cell pointer Dark rectangle that outlines the active cell.

Cell styles Predesigned combinations of formats based on themes that can be applied to selected cells to enhance the look of a worksheet.

Center Alignment in which an item is centered between the margins.

Central processing unit *See* CPU.

Character data Letters, symbols, or numerals that will not be used in arithmetic operations (name, social security number, etc.).

Character spacing Formatting that changes the width or scale of characters, expands or condenses the amount of space between characters, raises or lowers characters relative to the line of text, and adjusts kerning (the space between standard combinations of letters).

Chart A graphical representation of numerical data from a worksheet. Chart types include 2-D and 3-D column, bar, pie, area, and line charts.

Chart sheet A separate sheet in a workbook that contains only a chart, which is linked to the workbook data.

Charts Pictorial representations of worksheet data that make it easier to see patterns, trends, and relationships; *also called* graphs.

Chat group A discussion in which a group of people communicates by typing messages to each other online simultaneously.

Check box A box that turns an option on when checked or off when unchecked.

Chip *See* Computer chip.

Citation A parenthetical reference in the document text that gives credit to the source for a quotation or other information used in a document.

Click To quickly press and release the left button on the pointing device; *also called* single-click. The touch-screen equivalent is a tap on the screen.

Click and Type A feature that allows you to automatically apply the necessary paragraph formatting to a table, graphic, or text when you insert the item in a blank area of a document in Print Layout or Web Layout view.

Click and Type pointer A pointer used to move the insertion point and automatically apply the paragraph formatting necessary to insert text at that location in the document.

Clip A media file, such as a graphic, sound, animation, or movie.

Clip art A collection of graphic images that can be inserted into documents, presentations, webpages, spreadsheets, and other Office files.

Clipboard A temporary storage area for items that are cut or copied from any Office file and are available for pasting. *See also* Office Clipboard and System Clipboard.

Clock speed The pace for executing instructions as set by the processor clock specified in megahertz (MHz) or gigahertz (GHz).

Close button In a Windows title bar, the rightmost button; closes the open window, app, and/or document.

Cloud Mass storage for programs and data on remote computers connected to the Internet or other network.

Cloud computing A method of offering Internet-accessible computing services ranging from office productivity applications to complex corporate data processing.

Cloud Storage *See* Cloud.

Cloud storage location File storage locations on the World Wide Web, such as Windows OneDrive or Dropbox.

Cloudware Software applications that are not installed locally on your computer but rather installed on the web and used while online through a browser. *Also called* web apps.

Color depth The number of bits that determines the range of possible colors that can be assigned to each pixel. For example, an 8-bit color depth can create 256 colors. *Also called* bit depth.

Column break A break that forces text following the break to begin at the top of the next column.

Column heading The box containing the column letter on top of the columns in the worksheet.

Column separator The thin line that separates field names to the left or right in a datasheet or the query design grid.

Combination chart Two charts in one, such as a column chart combined with a line chart, that together graph related but dissimilar data.

Combo box In Access, a bound control used to display a drop-down list of possible entries for a field. You can also type an entry from the keyboard into the control so it is a "combination" of the list box and text box controls.

Command An instruction to perform a task, such as opening a file or emptying the Recycle Bin.

Comments button A button on the PowerPoint status bar in Normal view allows you to open the Comments pane where you can create, edit, select, and delete comments.

Commercial software Copyrighted computer applications sold to consumers for profit.

CompactFlash (CF) card A solid-state storage device that is about the size of a matchbook and provides high storage capacities and access speeds; includes a built-in controller that reads and writes data within the solid-state grid.

Comparison operators In a formula, symbols that compare values for the purpose of true/false results.

Compatibility The ability of different programs to work together and exchange data.

Compiler Software that translates a program written in a high-level language into low-level instructions before the program is executed.

Complex formula A formula that uses more than one arithmetic operator.

Compression utility Software that reduces file size for quick transmission or efficient storage.

Computer An electronic device that accepts input, processes data, stores data, and produces output.

Computer chip A very thin slice of semiconducting material, such as silicon and germanium. *Also called* integrated circuit or chip.

Computer file A named collection of data (such as a computer program, document, or graphic) that exists on a storage medium, such as a hard drive, flash drive, CD, or DVD. *Also called* file or data file.

Computer network A collection of computers and related devices, connected in a way that allows them to share resources including data, hardware, and software.

Computer platform A computer system's underlying hardware and software, in particular, its processor and operating system; such as the Windows platform, by Microsoft Corp. and Mac, by Apple Computer, Inc.

Computer program Detailed, step-by-step instructions that tell a computer how to solve a problem or carry out a task. *Also called* program.

Computer programmer A person who codes or writes computer programs.

Computer system The hardware, peripheral devices, and software working together to input data, process data, store data, and produce output.

Computer-aided design software (CAD) *See* CAD software.

Computer-aided music software Helps musicians compose, edit, and print the notes for compositions.

Concurrent-use license A software license agreement that is priced per copy and allows a specific number of copies to be used simultaneously.

Conditional formatting A type of cell formatting that changes based on the cell's value or the outcome of a formula.

Contact Group A named subset of the people in your Outlook Contacts folder, the named group includes the email addresses for all people in the group so you can send a message or invitation to everyone in the group at once. *See also* Distribution list.

Contacts In Outlook, all information related to people, such as business associates and personal friends.

Content control An interactive object that is embedded in a document you create from a template and that expedites your ability to customize the document with your own information.

Content placeholder A placeholder that is used to enter text or objects such as clip art, charts, or pictures.

Contextual tab A tab that appears only when a specific task can be performed; contextual tabs appear in an accent color and close when no longer needed.

Continuous section break A break that begins a new section on the same page.

Control Any element on a form or report such as a label, text box, line, or combo box. Controls can be bound, unbound, or calculated.

Control Source property A property of a bound control in a form or report that determines the field to which the control is connected.

Control Unit The part of the processor that fetches each instruction.

Conversations Emails that discuss a common subject or thread.

Copy To make a duplicate copy of a file, folder, or other object that you want to store in another location.

Copy and paste To move text or graphics using the Copy and Paste commands.

Copyright A form of legal protection that grants certain exclusive rights to the author of a program or the owner of the copyright.

Copyright notice A line such as "Copyright 2017 ACME Co." that identifies a copyright holder.

Cortana The digital personal assistant that comes with Windows 10 and Windows phones; can search, give you reminders, alarms, directions, news, weather, and more.

Courtesy copy (Cc) In email, a way to send a message to a recipient who needs to be aware of the correspondence between the sender and the recipients but who is not the primary recipient of the message.

CPU (central processing unit) The main processing unit in a computer, consisting of circuits that processes data. *Also called* the "brain" of a computer.

Creative Commons license A public copyright license that allows the free distribution of an otherwise copyrighted work.

Criteria Entries (rules and limiting conditions) that determine which records are displayed when finding or filtering records in a datasheet or form, or when building a query.

Criteria syntax Rules by which criteria need to be entered. For example, text criteria syntax requires that the criteria are surrounded by quotation marks (" "). Date criteria are surrounded by pound signs (#).

Crop To hide part of an object by using the Cropping tool or to delete a part of a picture.

Current record The database record that has the focus or is being edited.

Cursor A symbol that marks the user's place on the screen and shows where typing will appear. *Also called* insertion point.

Cut To remove an item from a document and place it on the Clipboard.

Cut and paste To move text or graphics using the Cut and Paste commands.

Cycle The smallest unit of time a processor can recognize. For example, 2.8 GHz means that the processor's clock operates at a speed of 2.8 billion cycles per second.

Data In the context of computing and data management, the symbols that a computer uses to represent facts and ideas.

Data bus An electronic pathway or circuit that connects the electronic components (such as the processor and RAM) on a computer's motherboard.

Data file A named collection of data (such as a computer program, document, or graphic) that exists on a storage medium, such as a hard drive, flash drive, CD, or DVD. *Also called* computer file or file.

Data marker A graphical representation of a data point in a chart, such as a bar or column.

Data point Individual piece of data plotted in a chart.

Data representation The use of electrical signals, marks, or binary digits to represent character, numeric, visual, or audio data.

Data series The selected range in a worksheet whose related data points Excel converts into a chart.

Data series label Text in the first row and column of a worksheet that identifies data in a chart.

Data series marker A graphical representation of a data series, such as a bar or column.

Data transfer rate The amount of data that a storage device can move from a storage medium to computer memory in one second.

Data type A required property for each field that defines the type of data that can be entered in each field. Valid data types include AutoNumber, Short Text, Long Text, Number, Currency, Yes/No, Date/Time, and Hyperlink.

Database A collection of data that is stored electronically as a series of records in tables.

Database designer The person responsible for building and maintaining tables, queries, forms, and reports.

Database software A category of software designed for tasks associated with maintaining and accessing data stored in data files.

Database user The person primarily interested in entering, editing, and analyzing the data in the database.

Datasheet A spreadsheet-like grid that displays fields as columns and records as rows.

Datasheet View A view that lists the records of an object in a datasheet. Tables, queries, and most form objects have a Datasheet View.

Date function A built-in Access function used to display the current date on a form or report; enter the Date function as Date().

Date Navigator A monthly calendar in the To-Do Bar that gives you an overview of the month.

Default In an app window or dialog box, a value that is automatically set; you can change the default to any valid value.

Delete To permanently remove an item from a document.

Deleted Items The folder that stores items when you delete or erase a message from any email folder, which means a deleted item, such as an email or contact card, is actually stored rather than being immediately and permanently deleted. *Also called* Trash folder.

Demoware Commercial software available as a trial version and distributed for free. Often comes preinstalled on new computers, but it is limited in some way until paid for.

Design View A view in which the structure of an object can be manipulated. Every Access object (table, query, form, report, macro, and module) has a Design View.

Desktop apps Application programs (apps), such as Microsoft Word, that are full-featured and that are often purchased, either from the Windows Store or from a software developer; *also called* traditional apps.

Desktop computer A category of computer small enough to fit on a desk but is too big to carry around and has attached, rather than built-in, keyboard, display, and pointing device.

Desktop publishing software (DPT) A category of software used to create high-quality output suitable for commercial printing. DPT software provides precise control over layout.

Destination file In integration, the file that receives the copied information. A Word file that contains an Excel file is the destination file.

Destination presentation The presentation you insert slides to when you reuse slides from another presentation.

Development software Software that includes programming and scripting languages to create applications, utilities, and webpages.

Device A hardware component that is part of your computer system, such as a disk drive, a pointing device, or a touch screen device.

Device driver The software that provides the computer with the means to control a peripheral device.

Dialog box A window with controls that lets you tell Windows how you want to complete an application program's (app's) command.

Dialog box launcher An icon you can click to open a dialog box or task pane from which to choose related commands.

Digital Any system that works with discrete data, such as 0s and 1s, in contrast to analog.

Digital camera A peripheral input device that records photographic images in digital format.

Digital content Any text, graphics, video, audio, or any data and information stored in a file and available for transmission, viewing or playing, and storage via a computer.

Digital convergence The trend to blend several technologies that have distinct functionalities into a single product, such as smartphones that combine voice communication, text messaging, email, web browsing, cameras, and GPS.

Digital data Text, numbers, graphics, sound, and video that have been converted into discrete digits, such as 0s and 1s.

Digital device A device that works with discrete (distinct or separate) numbers or digits.

Digital electronics Circuitry that is designed to work with digital signals.

Digital media player A peripheral device that can be attached to a personal computer system to transfer and play music and photo files.

Digital revolution An ongoing process of social, political, and economic change brought about by digital technology, such as computers and the Internet.

Digital signature A way to authenticate presentation files using computer cryptography. A digital signature is not visible in a presentation.

Digital technology Technologies that work using digital electronics such as computers, communications networks, the web, and digitization.

Digital versatile disc *See* DVD.

Digitization *See* Digitize.

Digitize To convert text, numbers, sound, photos, and video to a digital format that can be processed by a computer, through the use of a scanner, camera, or other input device.

DIMM (dual in-line memory module) A long, slim memory chip package that has gold pins that provide the electronic connection between the chip and other computer parts.

DIP (dual in-line package) A chip configuration characterized by a rectangular body with numerous plugs along its edge.

Direct access The ability of a storage device (such as a hard drive) to go directly to a specific storage location without having to search sequentially from a beginning location. *Also called* random access.

Directory A list of files contained on a computer storage device.

Display device The main output device for a computer; presents visual information on a screen such as a computer monitor.

Distribute To evenly divide the space horizontally or vertically between objects relative to each other or the document or slide edges.

Distribution list A collection of contacts to whom you want to send the same messages; makes it possible for you to send a message to the same group without having to select each contact in the group. *See also* Contact Group.

Distribution media One or more discs, CDs, or other storage media that contain programs and data, which can be installed on a hard drive.

DMG Mac software downloads are typically supplied as a disk image package which has has a .dmg extension.

Docs.com A Microsoft website designed for sharing Sway sites.

Document The electronic file you create using Word.

Document Inspector A PowerPoint feature that examines a presentation for hidden data or personal information.

Document properties Details about a file, such as author name or the date the file was created, that are used to describe, organize, and search for files.

Document reader utility Computer program, such as Adobe Reader, that transforms files into a portable format that can be created and read by any computer on which it is installed.

Document window The portion of a application program's (app's) window in which you create the document; displays all or part of an open document.

Documents folder The folder on your hard drive used to store most of the files you create or receive from others; might contain subfolders to organize the files into smaller groups.

DOS (disk operating system) The operating system software shipped with the first IBM PCs until the introduction of Microsoft Windows.

Dot pitch The diagonal distance between colored dots on a display screen. Measured in millimeters, dot pitch helps to determine the quality of an image displayed on a monitor. A smaller dot pitch means a crisper image.

Dots per inch (dpi) A measure of screen resolution and printer quality. A higher number of dots per inch indicates a higher resolution and better-quality output.

Double-click To quickly press and release or click the left button on the pointing device twice. The touch-screen equivalent is a double-tap on the screen.

Download To transfer a copy of a file from a remote computer to a local computer's hard drive.

Dpi (dots per inch) *See* Dots per inch (dpi).

Drafts The folder that stores unfinished messages that you can finish writing at a later time; many email programs automatically save unsent messages at regular intervals in the Drafts folder as a safety measure.

Draft view A view that shows a document without margins, headers and footers, or graphics.

Drag To point to an object, press and hold the left button on the pointing device, move the object to a new location, and then release the left button. Touch-screen users can press and hold a location, then move along the screen with a finger or stylus.

Drag and drop To move text or a graphic by dragging it to a new location using the mouse.

Drawing canvas In OneNote, a container for shapes and lines.

Drawing software Provides tools to draw lines, shapes, and colors that can be assembled into diagrams, corporate logos, and schematics that tend to have a flat cartoon-like quality, but are very easy to modify.

Drive A physical location on your computer where you can store files.

Drive bay Storage device "parking spaces" on the system unit case for a desktop computer; until these are used, they are typically hidden from view with a faceplate. *Also called* expansion bay.

Drive name A name for a drive that consists of a letter followed by a colon, such as C: for the hard disk drive.

Drop cap A large dropped initial capital letter that is often used to set off the first paragraph of an article.

Dropbox An online storage site that lets you transfer files that can be retrieved by other people you invite. *See also* Cloud storage location.

Duplex printer A printer that has the capability of printing on both sides of a page in a single pass.

Duty cycle Determines how many pages a printer is able to print out; is usually measured in pages per month.

DVD (digital video disc or digital versatile disc) An optical storage medium similar in appearance and technology to a CD but with higher storage capacity.

DVD authoring software Provides tools for transferring video footage from a digital video camera to a computer, deleting unwanted footage, assembling video segments in any sequence, adding special visual effects, adding a sound track, and creating a DVD.

DVD drive An optical storage device that reads data from CD-ROM and DVD discs.

DVD writer A device that can be used to create and copy CDs and DVDs.

DVD-R (digital versatile disc recordable) disc A type of DVD disc that stores data using recordable optical disc technology.

DVD-ROM (digital versatile disc read-only memory) disc A type of DVD disc that stores data that has been permanently stamped on the disc surface.

DVD-RW (digital versatile disc rewritable) disc A type of DVD disc that stores data using rewritable optical disc technology.

DVD+R (digital versatile disc recordable) disc A type of DVD disc that stores data using recordable optical disc technology.

DVD+RW (digital versatile disc rewritable) disc A type of DVD disc that stores data using rewritable optical disc technology.

Edit To make a change to the contents of an active cell.

Edit mode The mode in which Access assumes you are trying to edit a particular field, so keystrokes such as [Ctrl][End], [Ctrl][Home], [↓], and [↑] move the insertion point within the field.

Edit record symbol A pencil-like symbol that appears in the record selector box to the left of the record that is currently being edited in either a datasheet or a form.

Educational software A category of software that helps you learn and practice new skills.

Edutainment software A category of software that is both educational and entertaining.

Electronic mail *See* Email.

Electronic spreadsheet A computer program used to perform calculations and analyze and present numeric data.

Email (electronic mail) A single electronic message, or the entire system of computers and software that handles electronic messages transmitted between computers over a communications network.

Email account A service that provides an email address and mailbox.

Email address The unique address for each mailbox on the Internet, which typically consists of a user ID, an @ symbol, and the name of the computer that maintains the mailbox.

Email attachment A separate file that is transmitted along with an email message.

Email message A message, letter, or memo that is transmitted electronically via a network.

Email software Computer program that is used to compose, send, and read email messages. Usually includes an address book to help you maintain contact information.

Embed Placement of an object such as a text selection, value, or picture created in a source file into a destination file. An embedded object is edited by opening it in the destination file and then using the tools of the source file to make changes. These changes appear only in the embedded object in the destination file.

Embedded chart A chart displayed as an object in a worksheet.

Embedded object An object that is created in one application and inserted to another; can be edited using the original program file in which they were created.

Emoticon A symbol created by combining keyboard characters; used to communicate feelings in emails.

Endnote Text that provides additional information or acknowledges sources for text in a document and that appears at the end of a document.

Error indicator In Access, an icon that automatically appears in Design View to indicate some type of error. For example, a green error indicator appears in the upper-left corner of a text box in Form Design View if the text box Control Source property is set to a field name that doesn't exist.

EULA (end-user license agreement) License agreement that is displayed on the screen when you first install software; you accept the terms of the license by clicking a designated button.

Even page section break A break that begins a new section on the next even-numbered page.

Event In the Outlook Calendar, an activity that lasts 24 hours or longer.

Exa- A prefix for quintillion.

Exabyte Used to identify vast amounts of data; approximately equal to 1 billion gigabytes.

Executable file A file, usually with an .exe extension, containing instructions that tell a computer how to perform a specific task.

Expansion bay Storage device "parking spaces" on the system unit case for a desktop computer; until used these are typically hidden from view with a faceplate. *Also called* drive bays.

Expansion bus The segment of the data bus that transports data between RAM and peripheral devices.

Expansion card A circuit board that is plugged into a slot on a motherboard to add extra functions, devices, or ports.

Expansion port A socket into which the user plugs a cable from a peripheral device, allowing data to pass between the computer and the peripheral device.

Expansion slot A socket or slot on a motherboard designed to hold a circuit board called an expansion card.

Exploding Visually pulling a slice of a pie chart away from the whole pie chart in order to add emphasis to the pie slice.

Expression A combination of values, functions, and operators that calculates to a single value. Access expressions start with an equal sign and are placed in a text box in either Form Design View or Report Design View.

Field A code that serves as a placeholder for data that changes in a document, such as a page number.

Field list A list of the available fields in the table or query that the field list represents. Also, a pane that opens in Access and lists the database tables and the fields they contain.

Field name The name given to each field in a table.

Field selector The button to the left of a field in Table Design View that indicates the currently selected field. Also the thin gray bar above each field in the query grid.

File A named collection of data (such as a computer program, document, or graphic) that exists on a storage medium, such as a hard drive, flash drive, CD, or DVD. *Also called* computer file and data file.

File date Saved as part of the file information, the date on which a file was created or last modified; useful if you have created several versions of a file and want to make sure that you know which version is the most recent.

File Explorer A file management utility included with most Windows operating systems that helps users manage their files.

File extension A three- or four-letter sequence, preceded by a period, at the end of a filename that identifies the file as a particular type of document; for example, documents in the Rich Text Format have the file extension .rtf.

File format The method of organization used to encode and store data in a computer. Text formats include DOCX and TXT. Graphics formats include BMP, TIFF, and GIF.

File hierarchy The tree-like structure of folders and files on your computer.

File list A section of a window that shows the contents of the folder or drive currently selected in the Navigation pane.

File management The ability to organize folders and files on your computer.

File management program Software, such as File Explorer or Mac OS Finder, that helps users find files and folders on their hard drives or other storage media, as well as, rename, move, copy, and delete files.

File path *See* File specification.

File size The physical size of a file on a storage medium, usually measured in kilobytes (KB) or megabytes (MB).

File specification A combination of the drive letter, subdirectory, filename, and extension that identifies a file (for example, C:\ Documents\filename.docx). *Also called* path or file path.

File syncing Changes to files stored in the Cloud are automatically synced to all devices.

File tab Provides access to Backstage view and the Options dialog box.

File tag Information that helps describe the contents of a file; for example the location, camera settings, and people pictured in a photograph.

Filename A set of letters or numbers that identifies a file. Consists of a name followed by a period, followed by a file extension. *See also* File extension.

Filename extension *See* File extension.

Filenaming conventions A set of rules established by the operating system that must be followed to create a valid filename.

Filter A way to temporarily display only those records that match given criteria.

Filter By Form A way to filter data that allows two or more criteria to be specified at the same time.

Filter By Selection A way to filter records for an exact match.

Finance software Category of software to help you keep a record of monetary transactions and investments.

First line indent A type of indent in which the first line of a paragraph is indented more than the subsequent lines.

Flag A method of coding email messages by assigning different flags to the messages to categorize them or indicate their level of importance for follow up.

Flash Fill A feature that lets you fill a range of text based on samples existing in the current worksheet.

Floating graphic A graphic to which text wrapping has been applied, making the graphic independent of text and able to be moved anywhere on a page.

Focus The property that indicates which field would be edited if you were to start typing.

Folder An electronic container that helps you organize your computer files, like a cardboard folder on your desk; it can contain subfolders for organizing files into smaller groups.

Folder name A unique, descriptive name for a folder that helps identify the folder's contents.

Font The typeface or design of a set of characters (letters, numbers, symbols, and punctuation marks).

Font effect Font formatting that applies a special effect to text, such as small caps or superscript.

Font size The size of characters, measured in units called points.

Font style Format such as bold, italic, and underlining that can be applied to change the way characters look in a worksheet or chart.

Footer Information, such as text, a page number, or a graphic, that appears at the bottom of every page in a document or a section.

Footnote Text that provides additional information or acknowledges sources for text in a document and that appears at the bottom of the page on which the note reference mark appears.

Foreign key field In a one-to-many relationship between two tables, the foreign key field is the field in the "many" table that links the table to the primary key field in the "one" table.

Form An Access object that provides an easy-to-use data entry screen that generally shows only one record at a time.

Form factor The size, shape, and dimensions of a personal computer system including standard equipment or devices.

Form section A location in a form that contains controls. The section in which a control is placed determines where and how often the control prints.

Form View View of a form object that displays data from the underlying recordset and allows you to enter and update data.

Form Wizard An Access wizard that helps you create a form.

Format Painter A feature used to copy the format settings applied to the selected text to other text you want to format the same way.

Format The appearance of a cell and its contents, including font, font styles, font color, fill color, borders, and shading. *See also* Number format.

Formatting Enhancing the appearance of information through font, size, and color changes.

Formatting marks Nonprinting characters that appear on screen to indicate the ends of paragraphs, tabs, and other formatting elements.

Formula A set of instructions used to perform one or more numeric calculations, such as adding, multiplying, or averaging, on values or cells.

Formula bar The area above the worksheet grid where you enter or edit data in the active cell.

Formula prefix An arithmetic symbol, such as the equal sign (=), used to start a formula.

Forwarding Sending an email message you have received to someone else.

Free response quiz A type of Office Mix quiz containing questions that require short answers.

Freeware Copyrighted software that is given away by the author or owner.

Front Side Bus (FSB) Refers to the circuitry that transports data to and from the processor.

Function A special, predefined formula that provides a shortcut for a commonly used or complex calculation, such as SUM (for calculating a sum) or FV (for calculating the future value of an investment).

Gallery A collection of choices you can browse through to make a selection. Often available with Live Preview.

General Public License (GPL) Software created under this licensing policy allows people to make copies of software for their own use, to give it to others, or to sell it.

Gesture On touch screen displays, a touch event such as a tap, drag, swipe, and pinch.

Giga– Prefix for a billion.

Gigabit (Gb) Approximately one billion bits.

Gigabyte (GB) Approximately one billion bytes; typically used to refer to RAM and hard drive capacity.

Gigahertz (GHz) A measure of frequency equivalent to one billion cycles per second; usually used to measure speed.

Graphic image *See* Image.

Graphical user interface (GUI) A type of user interface that features on-screen objects, such as menus and icons, manipulated by a mouse. The GUI acronym is pronounced "gooey."

Graphics Any pictures, photographs, or images that can be manipulated or viewed on a computer.

Graphics card A circuit board inserted into a computer to handle the display of text, graphics, animation, and videos. *Also called* a video card.

Graphics software Computer programs for creating, editing, and manipulating images.

Graphics tablet A device that accepts input from a pressure-sensitive stylus and converts strokes into images on the screen.

Gridlines Evenly spaced horizontal and vertical lines on the slide that help you align objects.

Group A PowerPoint feature in which you combine multiple objects into one object.

Grouping A way to sort records in a particular order, as well as provide a section before and after each group of records.

Groups Areas of the Ribbon that arrange commands based on their function, for example, text formatting commands such as Bold, Underline, and Italic are located on the Home tab, in the Font group.

Gutter Extra space left for a binding at the top, left, or inside margin of a document.

Hacker A person who creates malicious computer programs sometimes to steal or damage your data or hardware or to assume your identity for financial gain.

Handheld computer A small, pocket-sized computer designed to run on its own power supply and provide users with basic applications.

Hanging indent A type of indent in which the second and subsequent lines of a paragraph are indented more than the first.

Hard copy The results of printing, typically on paper or some other medium.

Hard disk A built-in, high-capacity, high-speed storage medium for all the software, folders, and files on a computer. *Also called* a hard drive.

Hard disk drive *See* Hard drive.

Hard drive A computer storage device that contains a large-capacity hard disk sealed inside the drive case.

Hard page break *See* Manual page break.

Hardware The electronic and mechanical devices in a computer system.

Head crash A collision between the read-write head and the surface of the hard drive platter, resulting in damage to some of the data on the disk.

Header Information, such as text, a page number, or a graphic, that appears at the top of every page in a document or a section.

Highlighted Describes the changed appearance of an item or other object, usually a change in its color, background color, and/or border; often used for an object on which you will perform an action, such as a desktop icon.

Highlighting Transparent color that can be applied to text to call attention to it.

Home page On a website, the page that is the first page you see when you go to the site. On an individual computer, the webpage that a browser displays each time it is started.

Horizontal ruler In Word, a ruler that appears at the top of the document window in Print Layout, Draft, and Web Layout view. In PowerPoint, rulers appear above and to the left of the slide pane.

Horizontal scroll bar *See* Scroll bar.

HTML (Hypertext Markup Language) A standardized programming language used to specify the format for webpage documents.

HTTP (Hypertext Transfer Protocol) A communications standard that is used to transport webpages over the Internet.

Hub A pane in Microsoft Edge that provides access to favorite websites, a reading list, browsing history, and downloaded files.

Hyperlink Provides the fundamental tool for navigating webpages. Click a hyperlink to jump to a location in the same webpage, open a different webpage, or go to a different website. *Also called* a link.

Hypertext A way of linking information through the use of text and multimedia.

Hypertext Transfer Protocol (HTTP) *See* HTTP.

I-beam pointer The pointer used to move the insertion point and select text.

Icon A small image that represents an item, such as the Recycle Bin on your Windows desktop; you can rearrange, add, and delete desktop icons.

Image A nontextual piece of information such as a picture, piece of clip art, drawn object, or graph. Because images are graphical (and not numbers or letters), they are sometimes referred to as graphical images.

Image editing software Software that provides a set of electronic pens, brushes, and paints for drawing, creating, or editing graphics such as drawings and photographs. *Also called* paint software.

Inactive window An open window you are not currently using; if multiple windows are open, the window(s) behind the active window.

Inbox An email folder that stores all incoming email.

Indent The space between the edge of a line of text or a paragraph and the margin.

Indent marker A marker on the horizontal ruler that shows the indent settings for the active paragraph.

Infinity symbol The symbol that indicates the "many" side of a one-to-many relationship.

Information The words, numbers, and graphics used as the basis for human actions and decisions.

Ink annotations A freehand drawing on the screen in Slide Show view made by using the pen or highlighter tool.

Ink to Math tool The OneNote tool that converts handwritten mathematical formulas to formatted equations or expressions.

Ink to Text tool The OneNote tool that converts inked handwriting to typed text.

Ink-jet printer A nonimpact printer that creates characters or graphics by spraying liquid ink onto paper or other media.

Inked handwriting In OneNote, writing produced when using a pen tool to enter text.

Inking Freehand pen and highlighter marks you can draw on a slide in Normal view to emphasize information.

Inking toolbar In Microsoft Edge, a collection of tools for annotating a webpage.

Inline graphic A graphic that is part of a line of text.

Input As a noun, "input" means the information that is conveyed to a computer. As a verb, "input" means to enter data into a computer.

Input device A device, such as a keyboard or mouse, that gathers input and transforms it into a series of electronic signals for the computer.

Insertion point Appears on the screen as a flashing vertical bar or flashing underline and indicates where the characters you type will appear on the screen. *Also called* cursor.

Install The process by which programs and data are copied to the hard drive of a computer system and otherwise prepared for access and use.

Installation agreement A version of the license agreement that appears on the computer screen when software is being installed and prompts the user to accept or decline.

Instant messaging (IM) A private chat in which users can communicate with each other using the computer to type messages in real time.

Integrate To incorporate a document and parts of a document created in one program into another program; for example, to incorporate an Excel chart into a PowerPoint slide, or an Access table into a Word document.

Integrated circuit (IC) A thin slice of silicon crystal containing microscopic circuit elements, such as transistors, wires, capacitors, and resistors. *Also called* chip, computer chip, and microchip.

Integration Term used to describe the process of combining objects and data from two or more applications. For example, a report created in Word can include a chart copied from Excel, or a presentation created in PowerPoint can include a table copied from Access.

Intellectual property Refers to the ownership of certain types of information, ideas, or representations. Includes patents, trademarks, and copyrighted material, such as music, photos, software, books, and films.

Interface The look and feel of a program; for example, the appearance of commands and the way they are organized in the program window.

Internet The worldwide communication infrastructure made up of connected computer networks using TCP/IP protocol.

Internet forum A website where people post comments to discussion threads (topics) which can be read at any time by others who visit the forum.

Internet of Things The concept and technology that enables everyday objects to send and receive data over the Internet.

Internet Service Provider (ISP) A company that maintains Internet computers and telecommunications equipment in order to provide Internet access to businesses, organizations, and individuals.

Internet telephony A set of hardware and software that allows users to make phone-style calls over the Internet, usually without a long-distance charge. *Also called* Voice over IP (VoIP).

Interpreter A program that converts high-level instructions in a computer program into machine language instructions, one instruction at a time.

IP address A unique identifying number assigned to each computer connected to the Internet.

Is Not Null A criterion that finds all records in which any entry has been made in the field.

Is Null A criterion that finds all records in which no entry has been made in the field.

ISP (Internet Service Provider) *See* Internet Service Provider.

Italic Formatting applied to text to make the characters slant to the right.

Join line The line identifying which fields establish the relationship between two related tables. *Also called* a link line.

Joystick A pointing input device often used in gaming as an alternative to a mouse.

Junk email Unwanted email that arrives from unsolicited sources. *Also called* spam. Also a default folder in Outlook for junk email.

Justify Alignment in which an item is flush with both the left and right margins.

Key symbol The symbol that identifies the primary key field in each table.

Keyboard An arrangement of letter, number, and special function keys that acts as the primary input device to the computer.

Keyboard shortcut A combination of keys or a function key that can be pressed to perform a command.

Keyword A descriptive word or phrase you enter to obtain a list of results that include that word or phrase. *Also called* shortcut key.

Kilo- A prefix for a thousand.

Kilobit (Kbit or **Kb)** Approximately 1,000 bits; exactly 1,024 bits.

Kilobyte (KB) Approximately 1,000 bytes; exactly 1,024 bytes.

L

Label control An unbound control that displays text to describe and clarify other information on a form or report.

Label Wizard A report wizard that precisely positions and sizes information to print on a vast number of standard business label specifications.

Labels Descriptive text or other information that identifies data in rows, columns, or charts, but is not included in calculations.

LAN (local area network) An interconnected group of computers and peripherals located within a relatively limited geographic area, such as a home office, building, or campus.

Landscape Page orientation in which the contents of a page span the length of a page rather than its width, making the page wider than it is tall.

Landscape orientation Page orientation in which the page is wider than it is tall.

Laptop computer A type of portable computer that is small and light enough to be carried from one location to another. *See also* Notebook computer.

Laptop *See* Notebook computer.

Laser mouse A pointing device that uses a laser as the light source to track movement.

Laser printer A printer that uses laser-based technology, similar to that used by photocopiers, to produce text and graphics.

Launch To open or start a program on your computer.

Launcher An icon you click to open a dialog box or task pane.

Layout A way to group several controls together on a form or report to more quickly add, delete, rearrange, resize, or align controls.

Layout View An Access view that lets you make some design changes to a form or report while you are browsing the data.

LCD (liquid crystal display) A type of flat panel computer screen that produces an image by manipulating light within a layer of liquid crystal cells.

LCD screen *See* LCD.

LED (light emitting diodes) A technology used on electronic device screens that features a crisp image and a faster response rate than a standard LCD screen; it also uses less power.

Left function An Access function that returns a specified number of characters, starting with the left side of a value in a Text field.

Left indent A type of indent in which the left edge of a paragraph is moved in from the left margin.

Left-align Alignment in which the item is flush with the left margin.

Legend Text box feature in a chart that provides an explanation about the data presented in a chart.

LGA (land-grid array) A type of chip package.

License agreement A legal contract that defines the ways in which you may use a computer program. For personal computer software, you will find the license on the outside of the package, on a separate card inside the package, on the CD/DVD packaging, or in one of the program files.

Like operator An operator used in a query to find values in a field that match the pattern you specify.

Line spacing The amount of space between lines of text.

Link A connection created between a source file and a destination file. When an object created in a source file is inserted into or copied to a destination file, any changes made to the object in the source file also appear in the object contained in the destination file.

Link line The line identifying which fields establish the relationship between two related tables.

Linked object An object such as a text selection, value, or picture that is contained in a destination file and linked to a source file. When a change is made to the linked object in the source file, the change also occurs in the linked object in the destination file.

Linux An operating system that is a derivative of UNIX and available as freeware.

List box A box that displays a list of options from which you can choose (you may need to scroll and adjust your view to see additional options in the list).

Live Preview A feature that lets you point to a choice in a gallery or palette and see the results in the document or object without actually clicking the choice.

Live tile Updated, "live" content that appears on some apps' tiles on the Windows Start menu, including the Weather app and the News app.

Local application Software that is intended to be installed on a computer's hard drive.

Lock screen The screen that appears when you first start your computer, or after you leave it unattended for a period of time, before the sign-in screen.

Log in To select a user account name when a computer starts up, giving access to that user's files. *Also called* sign in.

Logical view The datasheet of a query is sometimes called a logical view of the data because it is not a copy of the data, but rather, a selected view of data from the underlying tables.

M

Mac (Macintosh computer) A personal computer platform designed and manufactured by Apple Computer.

Mac OS The operating system software designed for use on Apple Macintosh computers.

Macro An Access object that stores a collection of keystrokes or commands such as those for printing several reports in a row or providing a toolbar when a form opens.

Magnetic storage The recording of data onto disks or tape by magnetizing particles of an oxide-based surface coating.

Mail In Outlook, lets you manage all email.

Mailbox Any storage location for email such as the Inbox or Outbox.

Mainframe computer A large, fast, and expensive computer used by businesses or government agencies to provide centralized storage processing and management for large amounts of data.

Major gridlines In a chart, the gridlines that represent the values at the tick marks on the value axis.

Malicious software A type of software that can do harm to your computer data, such as viruses, worms, Trojan horses, and spyware. *Also called* malware.

Malware *See* Malicious software.

Manual page break A page break inserted to force the text following the break to begin at the top of the next page.

Map It An Outlook feature on a Contact card that lets you view a contact's address on a map.

Margin The blank area between the edge of the text and the edge of a page.

Masters One of three views that stores information about the presentation theme, fonts, placeholders, and other background objects. The three master views are Slide Master view, Handout Master view, and Notes Master view.

Mathematical modeling software A category of software that provides tools for solving a wide range of math, science, and engineering problems.

Maximize button On the right side of a window's title bar, the center button of three buttons; used to expand a window so that it fills the entire screen. In a maximized window, this button changes to a Restore button.

Maximized window A window that fills the desktop.

Media player *See* Digital media player.

Meeting In the Outlook Calendar, an activity you invite people to or reserve resources for.

Mega- Prefix for a million.

Megabit (Mb or Mbit) Approximately 1 million bits; exactly 1,048,576 bits.

Megabyte (MB) Approximately 1 million bytes; exactly 1,048,576 bytes.

Megahertz (MHz) A measure of frequency equivalent to 1 million cycles per second.

Memory The computer circuitry that holds data waiting to be processed, stored, or output.

Menu A list of related commands.

Merge A feature in PowerPoint used to combine multiple shapes together; provides you a way to create a variety of unique geometric shapes that are not available in the Shapes gallery.

Message body In an email message, where you write the text of your message.

Message header Contains the basic information about a message including the sender's name and email address, the names and email addresses of recipients and Cc recipients, a date and time stamp, and the subject of the message.

Message threading Allows you to navigate through a group of messages, seeing all replies and forwards from all recipients; includes all emails that discuss a common subject.

Metadata Another name for document properties that includes the author name, the document subject, the document title, and other personal information.

Microcomputer A category of computer that is built around one processor chip.

Microprocessor *See* Processor.

Microsoft account A web service that lets users sign on to one web address so they can use Windows computers as well as Outlook.com.

Microsoft Edge New in Windows 10, the Microsoft web browser that is intended to replace Internet Explorer.

Microsoft OneDrive A Microsoft website where you can obtain file storage space, using your own account, that you can share with others; you can access OneDrive from a laptop, tablet computer, or smartphone.

Microsoft OneNote Mobile app The lightweight version of Microsoft OneNote designed for phones, tablets, and other mobile devices.

Microsoft Store A website, accessible from the Store icon in the Windows 10 taskbar, where you can purchase and download apps, including games, productivity tools, and media software.

Microsoft Windows An operating system developed by Microsoft Corporation that provides a graphical interface.

Microsoft Windows 10 An operating system.

Millisecond (ms) A thousandth of a second; used to measure access time, the time it takes a computer to find data on a storage medium and read it.

Mini toolbar A small toolbar that appears next to selected text that contains basic text-formatting commands.

Minimize button On the right side of a window's title bar, the leftmost button of three buttons; use to reduce a window so that it only appears as an icon on the taskbar.

Minimized window A window that is visible only as an icon on the taskbar.

Minor gridlines In a chart, the gridlines that represent the values between the tick marks on the value axis.

Mirror margins Margins used in documents with facing pages, where the inside and outside margins are mirror images of each other.

Mixed reference Cell reference that combines both absolute and relative cell addressing.

Mobile app A program such as a game, calendar, stock market tracker, traffic or weather monitor, or news feed designed to run on mobile devices such as smartphones and tablet computers. *Also called* mobile application or app.

Mode indicator An area on the left end of the status bar that indicates the program's status. For example, when you are changing the contents of a cell, the word 'Edit' appears in the mode indicator.

Modem A device that sends and receives data to and from computers over cable, satellite, or telephone lines.

Module An Access object that stores Visual Basic programming code that extends the functions of automated Access processes.

Monitor A display device that forms an image by converting electrical signals from the computer into points of colored light on the screen; usually a computer's primary output device.

Motherboard The main circuit board in a computer that houses chips and other electronic components.

Mouse An input device that allows the user to select and move objects on the screen by moving it on a surface. *Also called* pointing device.

Mouse pointer A small arrow or other symbol on the screen that you move by manipulating the pointing device; *also called* a pointer.

Move To change the location of a file, folder, or other object by physically placing it in another location.

MP3 A file format that provides highly compressed audio files with very little loss of sound quality.

MP3 player Software and/or hardware that plays MP3 music files.

ms *See* Millisecond (ms).

Multi-core processor A single chip containing the circuitry for multiple processors; faster than a processor with a single core.

Multilevel list A list with a hierarchical structure; an outline.

Multimedia Messaging Service (MMS) Messages sent using a smartphone or mobile device that can include text characters, video, audio, and graphics.

Multiple-user license A software license that allows more than one person to use the software; priced per user and allows the allocated number of people to use the software at any time.

Multitasking Provides processor and memory-management services that allow two or more tasks, jobs, or programs to run simultaneously. Most of today's operating systems offer multitasking services.

Multiuser A characteristic that means more than one person can enter and edit data in the same Access database at the same time.

Name box Box to the left of the formula bar that shows the cell reference or name of the active cell.

Name property A property that uniquely identifies each object and control on a form or report.

Nanosecond A unit of time representing 1 billionth of a second.

Native file format A file format that is unique to a program or group of programs and has a unique file extension.

Navigate To move around in a worksheet; for example, you can use the arrow keys on the keyboard to navigate from cell to cell, or press [Page Up] or [Page Down] to move one screen at a time.

Navigate down To move to a lower level in your computer's file hierarchy.

Navigate up To move to a higher level in your computer's file hierarchy.

Navigation buttons Buttons in the lower-left corner of a datasheet or form that allow you to quickly navigate between the records in the underlying object as well as add a new record.

Navigation keypad On a keyboard, the keypad with the Home, End, and arrow keys; used to efficiently move the screen-based insertion point or cursor.

Navigation mode A mode in which Access assumes that you are trying to move between the fields and records of the datasheet (rather than edit a specific field's contents), so keystrokes such as [Ctrl][Home] and [Ctrl][End] move you to the first and last field of the datasheet.

Navigation pane A pane in the Access program window that provides a way to move between objects (tables, queries, forms, reports, macros, and modules) in the database.

Negative indent A type of indent in which the left edge of a paragraph is moved to the left of the left margin. *Also called* outdent.

Nested *See* Nested folders.

Nested folders A method of file management whereby folders are created within folders to hold folders as well as files. *Also called* subfolders.

Netbook A type of portable computer that is smaller than a notebook or a laptop computer.

Network *See* Computer network.

Network card An expansion board mounted inside a computer to allow access to a local area network.

Network-enabled printer A printer that connects directly to the network, rather than to one of the computers on a network.

Next page section break A break that begins a new section on the next page.

Normal style The default style for text and paragraphs in Word.

Normal view In Excel, the default worksheet view that shows the worksheet without features such as headers and footers; ideal for creating and editing a worksheet, but may not be detailed enough when formatting a document. In PowerPoint, the view that shows the Slide pane, Navigation pane, and optionally the Notes pane.

Note In OneNote, a small window that contains text or other types of information.

Note reference mark A mark (such as a letter or a number) that appears next to text to indicate that additional information is offered in a footnote or endnote.

Notebook In OneNote, the container for notes, drawings, and other content.

Notebook computer Small, lightweight, portable computer that can run on batteries. *Also called* laptop or laptop computer.

Notes In Outlook, the electronic version of the sticky notes you buy at your local stationery store; a convenient way to quickly jot down a reminder or an idea.

Notes button A button on the status bar in PowerPoint that opens the Notes pane.

Notes Page view A presentation view that displays a reduced image of the current slide above a large text box where you can type notes.

Notes pane The area in Normal view that shows speaker notes for the current slide; also in Notes Page view, the area below the slide image that contains speaker notes.

Notification area An area on the right side of the Windows taskbar that displays the current time as well as icons representing selected information; the Notifications button displays pop-up messages when a program on your computer needs your attention. Click the Notifications button to display the Action Center. *See also* Action Center.

Number format A format applied to values to express numeric concepts, such as currency, date, and percentage.

Numeric data Numbers that represent quantities and can be used in arithmetic operations.

Object A table, query, form, report, macro, or module in an Access database.

Object code The low-level instructions that result from compiling source code.

Object Linking and Embedding (OLE) The term used to refer to the technology Microsoft uses to allow the integration of data between programs. The difference between linking and embedding relates to where the object is stored and how the object is updated after placement in a document. A linked object in a destination file is an image of an object contained in a source file. Both objects share a single source, which means the object is updated only in the source file.

Odd page section break A break that begins a new section on the next odd-numbered page.

Off-site backup Duplicate storage of computer data at a remote location other than your home or office. The backup may be stored on a removable hard drive or sent over the Internet to a Cloud service.

Office Clipboard A temporary storage area shared by all Office programs that can be used to cut, copy, and paste multiple items within and between Office programs. The Office Clipboard can hold up to 24 items collected from any Office program. *See also* System Clipboard.

Office Mix A free add-in application integrated to the PowerPoint Ribbon that allows you to create interactive content.

Office Online Apps Versions of the Microsoft Office applications with limited functionality that are available online from Microsoft OneDrive. Users can view documents online and then edit them in the browser using a selection of functions.

Office productivity software Software that integrates word processing, spreadsheet, database, drawing, and presentation capabilities.

One-to-many line The line that appears in the Relationships window and shows which field is duplicated between two tables to serve as the linking field. The one-to-many line displays a "1" next to the field that serves as the "one" side of the relationship and displays an infinity symbol next to the field that serves as the "many" side of the relationship when referential integrity is specified for the relationship. *Also called* the one-to-many join line.

One-to-many relationship The relationship between two tables in an Access database in which a common field links the tables together. The linking field is called the primary key field in the "one" table of the relationship and the foreign key field in the "many" table of the relationship.

OneDrive An online storage and file sharing service. Access to OneDrive is through a Microsoft account.

Online collaboration The ability to incorporate feedback or share information across the Internet or a company network or intranet.

Open To use one of the methods for opening a document to retrieve it and display it in the document window.

Open source software A category of software, such as Linux, that includes its uncompiled source code, which can be modified and distributed by programmers.

Operating system (OS) System software that controls the computer's use of its hardware resources, such as memory and disk storage space.

Optical drive A CD drive, a DVD drive, a Blu-ray Disc (BD) drive, or a combination drive that is usually mounted inside the system unit.

Optical mouse Pointing device that uses an LED light and computer chip to track a light beam as it moves on a surface, such as a desk or mouse pad.

Optical storage A means of recording data as light and dark spots on a CD, DVD, BD, or other optical media.

Option button A small circle in a dialog box that you click to select only one of two or more related options.

OR criteria Criteria placed on different rows of the query design grid. A record will be selected for the resulting datasheet if it is true for any single row.

Order of precedence Rules that determine the order in which operations are performed within a formula containing more than one arithmetic operator.

Orphan record A record in the "many" table of a one-to-many relationship that doesn't have a matching entry in the linking field of the "one" table. Orphan records cannot be created if referential integrity is enforced on a relationship.

Orphan The first line of a paragraph when it appears alone at the bottom of a page.

Outbox A temporary storage folder for email messages that have not yet been sent.

Outdent *See* Negative indent.

Outline view A view in PowerPoint where you can enter text on slides in outline form. Includes three areas. The Outline pane where you enter text, the Slide pane for the main slide, and the Notes pane where you enter notes.

Outlook Today A feature in Outlook that shows your day at a glance, like an electronic version of a daily planner book; when it is open, you can see what is happening in the Calendar, Tasks, and Messages for the day.

Output The results produced by a computer (for example, reports, graphs, documents, pictures, and music).

Output device A device, such as a monitor or printer, that displays, prints, or transmits the results of processing from the computer memory.

Padding The space between controls.

Page In OneNote, a workspace for inserting notes and other content, similar to a page in a physical notebook.

Page break *See* Automatic page break or Manual page break.

Page Break Preview A worksheet view that displays a reduced view of each page in your worksheet, along with page break indicators that you can drag to include more or less information on a page.

Page Layout view Provides an accurate view of how a worksheet will look when printed, including headers and footers.

Pages per minute (ppm) A measure of printer speed; most personal or small business printers are rated 15–30 ppm.

Paint software A category of software that provides a set of electronic pens, brushes, and paints for painting images on the screen. *Also called* image editing software.

Pane A section of a window, such as the Navigation pane in the File Explorer window.

Paragraph spacing The amount of space between paragraphs.

Password A special sequence of numbers and letters that users can employ to control who can access the files in their user account area; keeping the password private helps keep users' computer information secure.

Paste Options button Button that appears onscreen after pasting content; enables you to choose to paste only specific elements of the copied selection, such as the formatting or values, if desired.

Paste To place a copied item from the Clipboard to a location in a document.

Patch Small program or programs designed to correct, secure, or enhance an existing program.

Path An address that describes the exact location of a file in a file hierarchy; shows the folder with the highest hierarchy level on the left and steps through each hierarchy level toward the right. Locations are separated by small triangles or by backslashes.

PC A microcomputer that uses Windows software and contains an Intel-compatible processor. *See also* Personal computer (PC).

PDF (Portable Document Format) A universal file format that enables a document to be read on all types of computers using Adobe Acrobat Reader.

Peek A feature in Outlook that opens a small window when you mouse over an event, task, or some activity and shows you a snapshot of the details for the item.

People In Outlook, where you manage all your business and personal contact information.

People Pane Available in several Outlook views; shows you any social media information available for the person sending the current message and included files, appointments, and notes related to that person.

Peripheral device A component or equipment, such as a printer or scanner, that expands a computer's input, output, or storage capabilities.

Personal account In Outlook, identifies you as a user with information such as your email address and password, the type of Internet service provider (ISP) you are using, and the incoming and outgoing email server address for your ISP. *See also* Account.

Personal computer (PC) A microcomputer designed for use by an individual user for applications such as Internet browsing, graphics, email, and word processing; PC often used to refer to personal computers running the Windows platform.

Personal finance software A category of software designed to help manage individual finances.

Peta- Prefix for thousand trillion.

Petabyte (PB) Used to identify vast amounts of data; approximately equal to 1,000 terabytes.

PGA (pin-grid array) A common chip design used for processors.

Photo editing software A category of software that provides tools that simplify common photo editing tasks; includes features specially designed to fix poor-quality photos by modifying contrast and brightness, cropping out unwanted objects, and removing red eye.

Photo printer Uses inkjet technology to produce photographic quality images.

Photos app A Windows 10 app that lets you view and organize your pictures.

Picture A digital photograph, piece of line art, or other graphic that is created in another program and is inserted into a document, spreadsheet, or presentation.

Pin A feature that allows you to create links to folders in File Explorer for Quick Access.

Pirated software Illegal copies of software.

Pixel (picture element) One pixel is the measurement of one picture element on the screen.

Platform A family or category of computers based on the same underlying software and hardware.

Plot area In a chart, the area inside the horizontal and vertical axes.

Point A unit of measure used for font size and row height. One point is equal to 1/72nd of an inch.

Pointer *See* Mouse pointer.

Pointing device A device that lets you interact with your computer by controlling the movement of the mouse pointer on your computer screen; examples include a mouse, trackball, touchpad, pointing stick, on-screen touch pointer, or a tablet.

Pointing device action A movement you execute with your computer's pointing device to communicate with the computer; the five basic pointing device actions are point, click, double-click, drag, and right-click.

Portable application Software designed to run from removable storage such as a CD, DVD, or a USB flash drive.

Portable computer A computer that is small and light enough to be carried from one place to another, including notebook computers, laptop computers, netbooks, and tablet computers.

Portable media player *See* Digital media player.

Portable software *See* Portable application.

Portrait orientation Page orientation in which the page is taller than it is wide.

Portrait Page orientation in which the contents of a page span the width of a page, so the page is taller than it is wide.

Power button The physical button on your computer that turns your computer on.

PowerPoint window A window that contains the running PowerPoint application including the Ribbon, panes, and tabs.

Ppm *See* Pages per minute.

Presentation software A category of software that provides tools to combine text, graphics, graphs, animation, and sound into a series of electronic slides that can be output on a projector, or as overhead transparencies, paper copies, or made available on the Internet.

Presenter view A PowerPoint view you access while in Slide Show view. Typically you use this view when showing a presentation through two monitors, one that you see as the presenter and one that the audience sees.

Preview pane A pane on the right side of a File Explorer window that shows the actual contents of a selected file without opening an app; might not work for some types of files, such as databases.

Previewing Prior to printing, seeing onscreen exactly how the printed document will look.

Primary key field A field that contains unique information for each record. A primary key field cannot contain a null entry.

primary recipient of the message.

Print area The portion of a worksheet that will be printed; can be defined by selecting a range and then using the Print Area button on the Page Layout tab.

Print Layout view A view that shows a document as it will look on a printed page.

Print Preview An Access view that shows you how a report or other object will print on a sheet of paper.

Printer A peripheral output device that creates hard copy output, including text, photographs, and graphic images.

Printer resolution The density of the ink on the printed page, determines the quality or sharpness of printed images and text.

Process To manipulate data (symbols that represent facts, objects, and ideas) using a systematic series of actions.

Processor An integrated circuit that contains the circuitry for processing data. It is a single-chip version of the central processing unit (CPU) found in all computers. *Also called* a microprocessor.

Processor clock A device on the motherboard of a computer responsible for setting the pace of executing instructions.

Productivity software Any type of application software that has the potential to help people do their work more efficiently.

Program The instructions that tell a computer how to perform a specific task such as word processing, graphics, or email. *Also called* application software or software.

Programming language Provides the tools that a programmer uses to create software. *Also called* computer language.

Project management software A category of software specifically designed as a tool for planning, scheduling, and tracking projects and their costs.

Property A characteristic that further defines a field (if field properties), control (if control properties), section (if section properties), or object (if object properties).

Property Sheet A window that displays an exhaustive list of properties for the chosen control, section, or object on a form or report.

Proprietary software Software program that has restrictions on its use that are delineated by copyright, patents, or license agreements. Might be free or distributed commercially and includes commercial software, demoware, shareware, freeware, and open source software.

Public domain software Any software that is available for use by the public without restriction, except that it cannot be copyrighted.

Query An Access object that provides a spreadsheet-like view of the data, similar to that in tables. It may provide the user with a subset of fields and/or records from one or more tables. Queries are created when the user has a "question" about the data in the database.

Query design grid The bottom pane of the Query Design View window in which you specify the fields, sort order, and limiting criteria for the query.

Query Design View The window in which you develop queries by specifying the fields, sort order, and limiting criteria that determine which fields and records are displayed in the resulting datasheet.

Quick Access Part of File Explorer that has links or pinned folders that you create to quickly find folders on your storage device.

Quick Access buttons Buttons that appear at the bottom of the Windows Action Center; single-click to perform common actions such as turning WiFi on or off.

Quick Access toolbar A customizable toolbar that contains buttons you can click to perform frequently used commands.

Quick Access view A list of frequently-used folders and recently used files that appears when you first open File Explorer.

Quick Analysis tool An icon that is displayed below and to the right of a range that lets you easily create charts and other elements.

Quick Part A reusable piece of content that can be inserted into a document, including a field, document property, or a preformatted building block.

Quick Style Determines how fonts, colors, and effects of the theme are combined and which color, font, and effect is dominant. A Quick Style can be applied to shapes or text.

RAM (Random Access Memory) The storage location that is part of every computer, that temporarily stores open apps and document data while a computer is on.

RAM cache Special high-speed memory that gives the CPU rapid access to data that would otherwise be accessed from memory elsewhere on the motherboard. *Also called* cache.

Random access The ability of a storage device (such as a hard drive) to go directly to a specific storage location without having to search sequentially from a beginning location. *Also called* direct access.

Range In Excel, a selection of two or more cells, such as B5:B14.

Read Mode view A document view that hides the tabs and Ribbon and is useful for reading long documents.

Read-only An object property that indicates whether the object can read and display data, but cannot be used to change (write to) data.

Read-only (ROM) technology Data stamped on the CD or DVD surface when it was manufactured, such as commercial software, music, and movies.

Read-write head The mechanism in a hard drive that magnetizes particles on the storage disk surface to write data, or senses the bits that are present to read data.

Reading view In Microsoft Edge, the display of a webpage that removes ads and most graphics and uses a simple format for the text.

Record In the context of database management, a record is the set of fields of data that pertain to a single entity in a database.

Record source The table or query that defines the field and records displayed in a form or report.

Recordable technology Optical storage technology used to create CDs, DVDs, and BDs.

Recycle Bin A desktop object that stores folders and files you delete from your hard drive(s) and enables you to restore them.

Reference operators In a formula, symbols which enable you to use ranges in calculations.

Reference software A category of software that provides a collection of information and a way to access that information.

Referential integrity A set of Access rules that govern data entry and help ensure data accuracy. Setting referential integrity on a relationship prevents the creation of orphan records.

Register Used by the ALU in a processor to hold data that is being processed.

Relational database software Software such as Access that is used to manage data organized in a relational database.

Relative cell reference In a formula, a cell address that refers to a cell's location in relation to the cell containing the formula and that automatically changes to reflect the new location when the formula is copied or moved; default type of referencing used in Excel worksheets. *See also* Absolute cell reference.

Remote storage Data storage that is not on a local computer.

Removable storage Storage media that you can easily transfer from one computer to another, such as DVDs, CDs, or USB flash drives.

Report An Access object that creates a professional printout of data that may contain such enhancements as headers, footers, and calculations on groups of records.

Report Wizard An Access wizard that helps you create a report.

Resolution The density of the grid used to display or print text and graphics, usually expressed in pixels; the greater the horizontal and vertical density, the higher the resolution.

Resource In the context of a computer system, refers to any component that is required to perform work such as the processor, RAM, storage space, and peripherals.

Response rate In the context of display device technology, response rate is how fast a screen updates the information being displayed.

Responsive design A way to provide content so that it adapts appropriately to the size of the display on any device.

Restore Down button On the right side of a maximized window's title bar, the center of three buttons; use to reduce a window to its last non-maximized size. In a restored window, this button changes to a Maximize button.

Restore point A snapshot of your computer settings created by a Windows utility either automatically when you install new software, or manually that you can use if you have a hard drive failure or instability.

Rewritable technology (RW) An optical storage technology that uses phase change technology to alter a crystal structure on the disc surface to create patterns of light and dark spots, making it possible for stored data to be recorded and erased or modified multiple times.

Ribbon In many Microsoft app windows, a horizontal strip near the top of the window that contains tabs (pages) of grouped command buttons that you click to interact with the app.

Ribbon Display Options button A button on the title bar that is used to use to hide or show the Ribbon and the Ribbon tabs and commands.

Rich Text Format (RTF) The file format that the WordPad app uses to save files.

Right indent A type of indent in which the right edge of a paragraph is moved in from the right margin.

Right-align Alignment in which an item is flush with the right margin.

Right-click To press and release the right button on the pointing device; use to display a shortcut menu with commands you issue by left-clicking them.

ROM (read-only memory) One or more integrated circuits that contain permanent instructions the computer uses during the boot process.

ROM BIOS (basic input/output system) A small set of basic input/output system instructions stored in ROM that causes the computer system to load critical operating files when the user turns on the computer.

Root directory The main directory of a disk or other storage medium.

Rotate handle A small round arrow at the top of a selected object that you can drag to turn the selected object.

Router The hardware device that connects a computer to the Internet.

Row heading The box containing the row number to the left of the row in a worksheet.

RTF *See* Rich Text Format.

Rule In Outlook, enables you to organize your email by setting parameters for incoming email; for example, you can specify that all email from a certain person goes into the folder for a specific project.

Ruler A vertical or horizontal guide that appears in Form and Report Design View to help you position controls.

Sandbox A computer security mechanism that helps to prevent attackers from gaining control of a computer.

Sans serif font A font (such as Calibri) whose characters do not include serifs, which are small strokes at the ends of letters.

Save To store a file permanently on a disk or to overwrite the copy of a file that is stored on a disk with the changes made to the file.

Save As Command used to save a file for the first time or to create a new file with a different filename, leaving the original file intact.

Save As command A command on the File tab that saves the entire database (and all objects it contains) or only the current object with a new name.

Scanner An input device that converts a printed page of text or images into a digital format.

Screen capture An electronic snapshot of your screen, as if you took a picture of it with a camera, which you can paste into a document.

Screen clipping An image copied from any part of a computer screen.

Screen recording In Office Mix, a video you create by capturing your desktop and any actions performed on it.

Screen size On a display device, the measurement in inches from one corner of the screen diagonally across to the opposite corner.

ScreenTip A label that identifies the name of the button or feature, briefly describes its function, conveys any keyboard shortcut for the command, and includes a link to associated help topics, if any.

Scroll To use the scroll bars or the arrow keys to display different parts of a document in the document window.

Scroll arrow A button at each end of a scroll bar for adjusting your view in a window in small increments in that direction.

Scroll bars Bars on the right edge (vertical scroll bar) and bottom edge (horizontal scroll bar) of a window that allow you to move around in a window with information that is too large to fit on the screen at once.

Scroll box A box in a scroll bar that you can drag to display a different part of a window.

Search criteria Descriptive text that helps identify the application program (app), folder, file, or website you want to locate when conducting a search.

Search engine Program that uses keywords to find information on the Internet and return a list of relevant documents.

Search site A website that provides a variety of tools to help you find information on the web based on keyword searches.

Search Tools tab A tab that appears in the File Explorer window after you click the Search text box; lets you specify a specific search location, limit your search, repeat previous searches, save searches, and open a folder containing a found file.

Secondary axis In a combination chart, an additional axis that supplies the scale for one of the chart types used.

Section A location of a form or report that contains controls. The section in which a control is placed determines where and how often the control prints.

Section break A formatting mark inserted to divide a document into sections.

Section tab In OneNote, a divider for organizing a notebook.

SecureDigital (SD) card Solid state storage popular for MP3 and digital imaging storage featuring fast data transfer rates.

Security utility Program that protects and secures the computer. Helps control nuisance ads, intrusion attempts, and spam; also provides file-encryption and antivirus software.

Select To change the appearance of an item by clicking, double-clicking, or dragging across it, to indicate that you want to perform an action on it.

Select pointer The mouse pointer shape that looks like a white arrow pointing toward the upper-left corner of the screen.

Selection box A dashed border that appears around a text object or placeholder, indicating that it is ready to accept text.

Selection pointer A pointer used to click a button or another element of the Word program window.

Semiconducting material Materials such as silicon and germanium that are used to make chips. The conductive properties create miniature electronic pathways and components, such as transistors. *Also called* semiconductors.

Sent Items When you send an email message, a copy of the message is stored in this folder to help you track the messages you send out.

Serif font A font (such as Times New Roman) whose characters include serifs, which are small strokes at the ends of letters.

Server A computer on a network that supplies the network with shared data and storage.

Server operating system Provides communications and routing services that allow computers to share data, programs, and peripheral devices by routing data and programs to each user's local computer, where the actual processing takes place.

Server software The software used by servers to locate and distribute data requested by a network or Internet users.

Service pack A collection of updates, fixes, and/or enhancements to a software program delivered in the form of a single installable package usually distributed over the Internet.

Service provider The organization or company that provides email or Internet access.

Setup program A program module supplied with a software package for the purpose of installing the software.

Shading A background color or pattern that can be applied to text, tables, or graphics.

Share button A button on the Ribbon that is used to save a document to the Cloud.

Shareware Copyrighted software marketed under a license that allows users to use the software for a trial period and then send in a registration fee if they wish to continue to use it.

Sheet tab scrolling buttons Allow you to navigate to additional sheet tabs when available; located to the left of the sheet tabs.

Sheet tabs Identify the sheets in a workbook and let you switch between sheets; located below the worksheet grid.

Shortcut An icon that acts as a link to an app, file, folder, or device that you use frequently.

Shortcut key *See* Keyboard shortcut.

Shortcut menu A menu of context-appropriate commands for an object that opens when you right-click that object.

Shrink-wrap license A software license usually sealed in an envelope, plastic box, or shrink wrapping that goes into effect as soon as you open the packaging.

Shut down To exit the operating system and turn off your computer.

Sign in To select a user account name when a computer starts up, giving access to that user's files. *Also called* log in.

Simple Query Wizard An Access wizard that prompts you for information it needs to create a new query.

Single-click *See* Click.

Single-factor authentication Security protocol in which an individual provides only one credential, such as a password, to verify their identity.

Single-user license A license that limits use of the software to only one person at a time.

Site license A software license generally priced at a flat rate and allows software to be used on all computers at a specific location.

Sizing handles Small series of dots at the corners and edges of a chart indicating that the chart is selected; drag to resize the chart.

Slide A component of presentation software that combines text, graphics, graphs, animations, and sound into a series of electronic slides for display on a monitor for a one-on-one presentation or on a computer projection device for group presentations.

Slide layout This determines how all of the elements on a slide are arranged, including text and content placeholders.

Slide Library A folder that you and others can access to open, modify, and review presentation slides.

Slide Notes In Office Mix, the written and displayed version of notes typically used to recite narration while creating a slide recording.

Slide pane The main section of Normal view that displays the current slide.

Slide recording In Office Mix, a video you create by recording action with a webcam, a camera attached or built into a computer.

Slide Show view A view that shows a presentation as an electronic slide show; each slide fills the screen.

Slide Sorter view A view that displays a thumbnail of all slides in the order in which they appear in a presentation; used to rearrange slides and slide transitions.

Slide thumbnail *See* Thumbnail.

Slide timing The amount of time each slide is visible on the screen during a slide show.

Slide transition The special effect that moves one slide off the screen and the next slide on the screen during a slide show. Each slide can have its own transition effect.

Slides tab On the left side of the Normal view, displays the slides in the presentation as thumbnails.

Smart Guides A feature in PowerPoint used to help position objects relative to each other and determine equal distances between objects.

SmartArt A professional quality graphic diagram that visually illustrates text.

SmartArt graphics Predesigned diagram types for the following types of data: List, Process, Cycle, Hierarchy, Relationship, Matrix, and Pyramid.

SmartArt Style A pre-set combination of formatting options that follows the design theme that you can apply to a SmartArt graphic.

Smartphone A handheld digital communications device that usually has many features such as removable storage, email, web access, voice communications, built-in camera, and GPS.

SMS (Short Message Service) System used to send short text messages using your smartphone or mobile device. *See also* Text message.

Snap assist feature The Windows 10 feature that lets you drag a window to the left or right side of the screen, where it "snaps" to fill that half of the screen and displays remaining open windows as thumbnails you click to fill the other half.

Social networking An online networking activity that allows registered members to communicate with others in the network such as LinkedIn, Twitter, and Facebook.

Soft copy The output on a display device.

Soft page break *See* Automatic page break.

Software The instructions that tell a computer how to perform tasks, such as system software and application software.

Software license A legal contract that defines the ways in which you may use a computer program. For personal computer software, the license is on the outside of the package, on a separate card inside the package, on the CD packaging, or in one of the program files. *Also called* license agreement.

Software pirate A person who evades copyright law and illegally copies, distributes, or modifies software.

Software suite A collection of application software sold as a single package.

Software upgrade Improvements or enhancements to existing installed software that is available to consumers who already have a software program installed.

Solid-state drive (SSD) A storage device that can be internal or external to a computer that has no moving parts.

Solid-state storage A variety of compact storage cards, pens, drives, and sticks that stores data in a nonvolatile, erasable, low-power chip in a microscopic grid of cells.

Solid-state technology Data storage technology that stores data in a durable, erasable, low-power chip with no moving parts.

Sort Change the order of, such as the order of files or folders in a window, based on criteria such as date, file size, or alphabetical by filename.

Sound card A small circuit board that gives the computer the ability to accept audio input from a microphone, play sound files, and produce audio output through speakers or headphones. Required for high-quality music, narration, and sound effects.

Sound system Speakers and a circuit board (sound card) used to create high-quality music, narration, and sound effects using a computer.

Source code Computer instructions written in a high-level language.

Source file In integration, the file from which the information is copied or used. An Excel file that is inserted into a file that contains a Word report is the source file.

Source presentation The presentation you insert slides from when you reuse slides from another presentation.

Spam Unwanted email that arrives from unsolicited sources. *Also called* junk email.

Spam filter Software that automatically routes advertisements and other junk mail to the Deleted Items folder maintained by your email client; can be effective for blocking unwanted emails.

Spamming The sending of identical or near-identical unsolicited messages to a large number of recipients. Many email programs have filters that identify this email and place it in a special folder.

Sparkline A quick, simple chart located within a cell that serves as a visual indicator of data trends.

Speakers Output devices that receive signals for the computer's sound card to play music, narration, or sound effects.

Spin box A text box with up and down arrows; you can type a setting in the text box or click the arrows to increase or decrease the setting.

Split form A form split into two panes; the upper pane allows you to display the fields of one record in any arrangement, and the lower pane maintains a datasheet view of the first few records.

Spreadsheet An electronic worksheet for numerical calculations presented in the form of a grid of columns and rows. Each cell in the grid has a unique cell reference, or address, that is based on its column and row location. *Also called* worksheet.

Spreadsheet software The software for creating electronic worksheets that hold data in cells and perform calculations based on that data.

SQL (Structured Query Language) A language that provides a standardized way to request information from a relational database system.

Start button A clickable button at in the lower left corner of the Windows screen that you click to open the Start menu.

Start menu Appears after you click the Start button; provides access to all programs, documents, and settings on the computer.

Statistical software A category of software that helps you analyze large sets of data to discover relationships and patterns, summarize survey results, test scores, experiment results, or population data.

Status bar The bar at the bottom of an Office program window that shows information about the document, workbook, database, or presentation, such as its zoom level or the current view.

Storage The area in a computer that holds data on a permanent basis when it is not immediately needed for processing.

Storage capacity The amount of data that can be stored on a storage medium.

Storage device A mechanical apparatus that records data to and retrieves data from a storage medium.

Storage medium The physical material used to store computer data, such as a flash drive, a hard drive, USB flash drive, or an optical disc.

Storage technology Defines the data storage systems (storage media and storage devices) used by computers to store data and program files.

Stored program A set of instructions that resides on a storage device, such as a hard drive, and can be loaded into memory and executed.

Storyline In Sway, the workspace for assembling a presentation.

Style A named collection of character and paragraph formats that are stored together and can be applied to text to format it quickly.

Subdatasheet A datasheet that is nested within another datasheet to show related records. The subdatasheet shows the records on the "many" side of a one-to-many relationship.

Subdirectory A directory found under the root directory.

Subfolder A method of file management whereby folders are created within folder to hold folders. *Also called* nested folders.

Subject line Meaningful text in the subject text box of an email message providing recipients with an idea of the message content.

Subscript A font effect in which text is formatted in a smaller font size and placed below the line of text.

Subtitle text placeholder A box on the title slide reserved for subpoint text.

Suite A group of programs that are bundled together and share a similar interface, making it easy to transfer skills and program content among them.

Sum function A mathematical function that totals values in a field.

Supercomputer The fastest and most expensive type of computer. At the time it is built, one of the fastest computers in the world; can tackle tasks, such as breaking codes and modeling worldwide weather systems, that would not be practical for other computers.

Superscript A font effect in which text is formatted in a smaller font size and placed above the line of text.

Swap file The data on the hard drive that has been moved from RAM to virtual memory.

Sway site A website Sway creates to share and display a Sway presentation.

Symbol A special character that can be inserted into a document using the Symbol command.

Sync In OneNote, to save a new or updated notebook so that all versions of the notebook, such as a notebook on OneDrive and a copy on a hard drive, have the same contents.

Syntax Rules for entering information such as query criteria or property values.

System Clipboard A clipboard that stores only the last item cut or copied from a document. *See also* Clipboard and Office Clipboard.

System on a Chip (SoC) Consolidates the functions of the CPU, graphics and sound cards, memory, and more onto a single silicon chip. This miniaturization allows devices to become increasingly compact.

System requirements Specifications for the operating system and hardware configuration necessary for a software product to work correctly.

System software Computer programs that help the computer carry out essential operating tasks, such as an operating system.

System unit The case or box that contains the computer's power supply, storage devices, main circuit board, processor, and memory.

Tab A page in an application program's Ribbon, or in a dialog box, that contains a group of related commands and settings.

Tab Index property A form property that indicates the numeric tab order for all controls on the form that have the Tab Stop property set to Yes.

Tab leader A line that appears in front of tabbed text.

Tab order property A form property that determines the sequence in which the controls on the form receive the focus when the user presses [Tab] or [Enter] in Form view.

Tab stop A location on the horizontal ruler that indicates where to align text.

Tab Stop property A form property that determines whether a field accepts focus.

Table (database) An arrangement of data in a grid of rows and columns. In a relational database, a collection of record types with their data.

Table (layout) In Word or PowerPoint, a gridlike structure that can hold text or pictures. In Excel, a list of columnar data with the same structure that can be manipulated as a single collection of data.

Table Design View A view of a table that provides the most options for defining fields.

Table styles Predesigned formatting that can be applied to a range of cells or even to an entire worksheet; especially useful for those ranges with labels in the left column and top row, and totals in the bottom row or right column. *See also* Table.

Tablet computer A portable computing device featuring a touch-sensitive screen that can be used as a writing or a drawing pad.

Task In Outlook, an item in Tasks.

Task view A Windows 10 area, accessible from the Task view button on the taskbar, that lets you switch applications and create multiple desktops (*also called* virtual desktops).

Taskbar The horizontal bar at the bottom of the Windows desktop; displays icons representing apps, folders, and/or files on the left, and the Notification area, containing the date and time and special program messages, on the right.

Tasks In Outlook, the electronic to-do list, whereby each task has a subject, a start and end date, priority, and a description.

Tax preparation software A specialized type of personal finance software designed to help gather annual income and expense data, identify deductions, and calculate tax payments.

TCP/IP (Transmission Control Protocol/Internet Protocol) A standard set of communication rules used by every computer that connects to the Internet.

Tell Me box A text box on the Ribbon that is used to find a command or access an Office program's Help system.

Template A predesigned, formatted file that serves as the basis for a new document, workbook, database, or presentation.

Tera- Prefix for a trillion.

Terabyte Used to identify a large amount of data; approximately equal to a trillion bytes.

Text Align property A control property that determines the alignment of text within the control.

Text annotations Labels added to a chart to draw attention to or describe a particular area.

Text box An area in a Windows program that you click to enter text.

Text concatenation operators In a formula, symbols used to join strings of text in different cells.

Text effect Formatting that applies a visual effect to text, such as a shadow, glow, outline, or reflection.

Text message A system used to send character messages using a smartphone, or mobile device. *See also* SMS (Short Message Service).

Text placeholder A box with a dotted border and text that you replace with your own text.

Text wrapping break Forces the text following the break to begin at the beginning of the next line.

Text wrapping Formatting applied to a graphic to make it a floating graphic.

Theme A predefined set of colors, fonts, line and fill effects, and other formats that can be applied to an Access database and give it a consistent, professional look.

Theme colors The set of 12 coordinated colors that make up a PowerPoint presentation; a theme assigns colors for text, lines, fills, accents, hyperlinks, and background.

Theme effects The set of effects for lines and fills.

Theme fonts The set of fonts for titles and other text.

Thumbnail A small image of a slide. Thumbnails are visible on the Slides tab and in Slide Sorter view.

Tick marks Notations of a scale of measure on a chart axis.

Tile A shaded rectangle on the Windows 10 Start menu that represents an app. *See also* App and Application program.

Title bar Appears at the top of every Office program window; displays the document name and program name.

Title placeholder A box on a slide reserved for the title of a presentation or slide.

Title slide The first slide in a presentation.

To Do tag In OneNote, an icon that helps you keep track of your assignments and other tasks.

Toggle button A button that turns a feature on and off.

Toner The fine powder in the cartridges used in laser printers that creates the image on the page.

Toolbar In an application program, a set of buttons, lists, and menus you can use to issue program commands.

Touch screen technology Display device technology that makes it possible for a single touch or handwriting to be used to input data.

Touchpad An alternative input device often found on notebook computers. *Also called* trackpad.

Trackball Pointing input device used as an alternative to a mouse.

Trackpad An alternative input device often found on notebook computers. *Also called* touchpad.

Trash folder *See* Deleted Items folder.

Two-factor authentication (2FA) Security protocol in which an individual provides two credentials (often a pre-established password plus a one-time, randomly-generated code sent to a mobile phone) to verify their identity.

Ultraportable computer A type of laptop that is generally smaller and less powerful.

Unbound control A control that does not change from record to record and exists only to clarify or enhance the appearance of the form, using elements such as labels, lines, and clip art.

Unicode A 16-bit character representation code that can represent more than 65,000 characters.

Uninstall To remove software files, references, and Windows Registry entries from a computer's hard drive.

Universal apps *See* Windows 10 apps.

Unzipped Refers to files that have been uncompressed.

Uploading The process of sending a copy of a file from a local computer to a remote computer.

URL (Uniform Resource Locator) The unique address of a webpage.

USB (Universal Serial Bus) Data communications standard designed to replace the need for earlier interfaces such as parallel and serial ports.

USB (Universal Serial Bus) port Popular ports for connecting peripheral devices including mice, cameras, mp3 players, scanners, and printers that have USB connections.

USB drive *See* USB flash drive.

USB flash drive A portable solid state storage device featuring a built-in connector that plugs directly into a computer's USB port. *Also called* USB drive.

USB hub A device used to add USB ports to a computer.

User account A special area in a computer's operating system where users can store their own files and preferences.

User ID A combination of letters and numbers that identifies a user on a computer. *Also called* a username.

User interface A collective term for all the ways you interact with a software program.

Username The first part of an email address that identifies the person who receives the email that is sent to this email address.

Utility software A subcategory of system software that augments the operating system by providing ways for a user to control the allocation and use of hardware resources. *Also called* utilities.

Vacation response An automatically-generated email message you can have sent in response to received emails when you are away; most email programs allow you to create a vacation response.

Validation code Series of alphanumeric characters supplied by the software publisher that is required to complete the installation of software.

Value axis In a chart, the axis that contains numerical values; in a 2-dimensional chart, also known as the y-axis.

Values Numbers, formulas, and functions used in calculations.

Variant A custom variation of the applied theme that uses different colors, fonts, and effects.

Vertical alignment The position of text in a document relative to the top and bottom margins.

Vertical ruler A ruler that appears on the left side of the document window in Print Layout view.

Vertical scroll bar *See* scroll bar.

Video card *See* Graphics card.

Video editing software Category of software that provides a set of tools for transferring video footage from a digital video camera to a computer, clipping out unwanted footage, assembling video segments in any sequence, adding special visual effects, and adding a sound track.

View Each Office program has different views for different purposes. Change views by clicking the View buttons on the right side of the taskbar in any Office program.

View buttons Buttons on the status bar that are used to change document, workbook, database, or presentation views. *Also called* view shortcuts.

Viewing angle width Measurement of a monitor or display device that indicates how far to the side you can still clearly see the screen image.

Virtual keyboard An onscreen keyboard.

Virtual memory A computer's use of hard drive storage to simulate RAM.

Voice Over IP (VOIP) Technology used to send and receive voice conversations over the Internet. *Also called* Internet telephony.

Volatile data Data that can exist only with a constant power supply.

Wearables Computer devices that may be worn on a person's wrist or incorporated into clothing.

Wearable computers Devices, such as fitness trackers, smartwatches, smartglasses, that are portable and have specific functions.

Web (World Wide Web) An Internet service that links documents and information from computers distributed all over the world using the HTTP protocol.

Web application (Web app) Software that, instead of being installed on a local computer, is accessed with a web browser; runs on a remote computer connected to the Internet.

Web authoring software Category of software that provides easy-to-use tools for composing, assembling, and generating HTML to develop webpages.

Web browser A program such as Internet Explorer, Firefox, or Safari that communicates with a web server and displays webpages.

Web cam A camera that captures digital video images using a computer.

Web Layout view A view that shows a document as it will look when viewed with a web browser.

Web Note In Microsoft Edge, an annotation on a webpage.

Web server A computer and software that stores and transmits webpages to computers connected to the Internet.

Web-based email An email account that stores, sends, and receives email on a website rather than a program on a user's computer.

Webpage A document on the World Wide Web that consists of a specially coded HTML file with associated text, audio, video, graphics, and links to other webpages.

Website Location on the World Wide Web that contains information stored in webpages relating to specific topics.

What-if analysis A decision-making tool in which data is changed and formulas are recalculated, in order to predict various possible outcomes.

Widow The last line of a paragraph when it is carried over to the top of the following page, separate from the rest of the paragraph.

Wiki A collaborative website that allows people to add to and modify material posted by others.

Wildcard A special character used in criteria to find, filter, and query data. The asterisk (*) stands for any group of characters. For example, the criteria I* in a State field criterion cell would find all records where the state entry was IA, ID, IL, IN, or Iowa. The question mark (?) wildcard stands for only one character.

Window A rectangular-shaped work area that displays an app or a collection of files, folders, and Windows tools.

Window control buttons The set of three buttons on the right side of a window's title bar that let you control the window's state, such as minimized, maximized, restored to its previous open size, or closed.

Windows *See* Microsoft Windows.

Windows 10 apps Apps (application programs) for Windows 10 that often have a single purpose, such as Photos, News, or OneDrive.

Windows 10 desktop An electronic work area that lets you organize and manage your information, much like your own physical desktop.

Windows 10 UI The Windows 10 user interface. *See also* User interface.

Windows accessories Application programs (apps), such as Paint or WordPad, that come with the Windows operating system.

Windows Action Center A pane that appears in the lower right corner of the Windows 10 screen that lets you quickly view system notifications and selected settings; also has Quick Action buttons to perform common actions in one click.

Windows app Small program available for free or for purchase in the Windows Store; can run on Windows desktops, laptops, tablets, and phones.

Windows Mobile A version of the Windows operating system designed for portable or mobile computers and smartphones.

Windows Search The Windows feature that lets you look for files and folders on your computer storage devices; to search, type text in the Search text box in the title bar of any open window, or click the Start button and type text in the search text box.

Word processing software A category of software that assists the user in producing documents, such as reports, letters, papers, and manuscripts. Includes tools for entering, editing, and formatting text and graphics.

Word program window The window that contains the Word program elements, including the document window, Quick Access toolbar, Ribbon, and status bar.

Word size The number of bits a CPU can manipulate at one time, which is dependent on the size of the registers in the CPU and the number of data lines in the bus.

Word wrap A feature that automatically moves the insertion point to the next line as you type.

WordArt A set of decorative styles or text effects that is applied to text.

Workbook A collection of related worksheets contained within a single file which has the file extension xlsx.

Works cited A list of sources that you cited while creating a document.

Worksheet A single sheet within a workbook file; also, the entire area within an electronic spreadsheet that contains a grid of columns and rows.

Worksheet window Area of the program window that displays part of the current worksheet; the worksheet window displays only a small fraction of the worksheet, which can contain a total of 1,048,576 rows and 16,384 columns.

Workstation (1) A computer connected to a local area network. (2) A powerful desktop computer designed for specific tasks.

X-axis The horizontal axis in a chart; because it often shows data categories, such as months or locations, *also called* Category axis.

XML Acronym that stands for eXtensible Markup Language, which is a language used to structure, store, and send information.

Y-axis The vertical axis in a chart; because it often shows numerical values, *also called* Value axis.

Z-axis The third axis in a true 3-D chart, lets you compare data points across both categories and values.

Zetta- Prefix for sextillion.

Zettabyte Used to identify vast amounts of data; approximately equal to 1,000 exabytes (2^{70} bytes).

Zoom level button A button on the status bar that is used to change the zoom level of content in a document, spreadsheet, or presentation.

Zoom slider A slider on the status bar that is dragged to enlarge or decrease the display size of content in a document, spreadsheet, or presentation.

Zooming A feature that makes screen information appear larger but shows less of it on screen at once, or shows more of a document, spreadsheet, or slide on screen at once but at a reduced size; does not affect actual document, workbook, or slide size.

Zooming in A feature that makes screen content appear larger but shows less of it on screen at once; does not affect the actual size of the content.

Zooming out A feature that shows more content on screen at once but at a reduced size; does not affect the actual size of the content.

Index

SPECIAL CHARACTERS

– (minus sign), EX 7
/ (forward slash), EX 7
* (asterisk), AC 36
? (question mark), AC 36
= (equal sign), AC 36
"" (quotation marks), AC 38
(pound sign), AC 38
[] (square brackets), AC 64
= (equal sign), AC 64
+ (plus sign), EX 7
* (asterisk), EX 7
% (percent sign), EX 7
^ (caret), EX 7
= (equal sign), EX 12, EX 28, EX 30
% (percent sign), EX 52
# (number sign), EX 58
@ (at sign), OUT 3
¶ (paragraph symbol), WD 10, WD 54, WD 55
↑ (arrow symbol), WD 10
< (left angle bracket), AC 39
> (right angle bracket), AC 39

A

absolute cell references, EX 34, EX 35
  copying formulas, EX 38–39
accent colors, PPT 77
Access. *See* Microsoft Access 2016
access time, data storage systems, CC 32
accessibility, video recordings, PA 11
accounting software, CC 63
active cell, EX 4, EX 5
  charts, PPT 56
active window, WIN 12
add-ins, PA 10, WD 37. *See also specific add-ins*
  improving worksheet functionality, EX 26
addition operator (+), EX 7
address(es), WIN 26
Address bar, WIN 6, WIN 26
address books, OUT 4, OUT 5
adjustment handles, PPT 32
Advanced button, AC 36
advanced document properties, WD 41
Advanced Micro Devices (AMD), CC 81
aligning
  objects, PPT 38, PPT 39
  paragraphs, WD 56–57

alignment
  axis labels and titles, changing, EX 91
  labels and values, changing, EX 56, EX 57
alignment commands, AC 90
Alternate Back Color, AC 92
ALU (arithmetic logic unit), CC 83
AMD (Advanced Micro Devices), CC 81
anchoring controls, AC 67
AND criteria, AC 38–39
Android, CC 55
angle, axis labels and titles, changing, EX 91
animation(s), PPT 82–83
  attaching sounds, PPT 83
animation emphasis effects, PA 8
annotating
  charts, EX 92, EX 93
  webpages, PA 15
app(s), CC 11, CC 47, WIN 4
  desktop, WIN 8
  inserting in slides, PA 12
  launching, OFF 4–5
  starting, WIN 8–9
  universal, WIN 8
application programs. *See* app(s)
application software, CC 11, CC 46. *See also* app(s); *specific types of application software*
appointments, OUT 32, OUT 33
area charts, EX 81, PPT 57
arguments, AC 88, EX 8
arithmetic logic unit (ALU), CC 83
arithmetic operators, EX 7, EX 12
ARM technology, CC 81
arrow symbol (↑), WD 10
Ascending button, AC 35
aspect ratio, CC 27
asterisk (*)
  multiplication operator, EX 7
  wildcard, AC 36
at sign (@), email addresses, OUT 4
attachment(s), email messages, OUT 14–15, OUT 16, WD 39
Attachment data type, AC 7
audience, presentations, PPT 4
audio editing software, CC 62
Auto Fill Options button, EX 36
Auto Order, AC 66

AutoComplete, WD 6, WD 7
AutoCorrect, WD 6, WD 7, WD 35
AutoFit Column Width command, EX 58
automatic page breaks, WD 82
AutoNumber data type, AC 7
AutoNumber fields, AC 8, AC 14
AutoRecover feature, EX 10
AutoSum button, EX 8, EX 9
axes, charts, EX 80, EX 81, EX 86, EX 87
axis labels, changing alignment and angle, EX 91

B

Back button, Save As dialog box, WD 9
background
   colors, PPT 77
   customizing, PPT 76, PPT 77
background images
   forms, AC 69
   graphics, PPT 76
Backstage view, OFF 6, OFF 7, WD 4, WD 14, WD 15
backups, CC 77
backward compatibility, OFF 11
bar charts, EX 81, PPT 57
bar tabs, WD 59
basic input/output system. *See* ROM BIOS
   (basic input/output system)
basic input/output system (ROM BIOS), CC 87
BD(s) (Blu-ray discs), CC 34, CC 35
BD drives, CC 35
benchmarks, CC 83
binary digits. *See* bit(s)
binary number system, CC 78
bit(s), CC 78, CC 79
bit depth, CC 27
black and white presentations, PPT 7
blank fields, finding, AC 39
Blank Form tool, AC 56
blog(s), CC 15
   publishing directly from Word, WD 36
bloggers, WD 36
Blu-ray discs (BDs), CC 34, CC 35
bold text, WD 52
boot process, CC 52, CC 86–87
borders
   chart objects, EX 88
   documents, WD 64, WD 65
   tables, WD 88
   windows, WIN 12
   worksheets, EX 62, EX 63
bound controls, AC 61
Box & Whisker charts, EX 95
BSD license, CC 49

buffers, CC 52
building blocks, WD 87
bulleted lists, WD 62, WD 63
business cards, electronic, sending, OUT 33
Business Intelligence tools, EX 2
button(s), WIN 14. *See also specific button names*
   adding to taskbar, WIN 4
   dialog boxes, WIN 15
   font style and alignment, EX 57
   groups, WIN 10
   Mini toolbar, WD 13
bytes, CC 78, CC 79

C

cache, CC 83
cache memory, CC 83
CAD (computer-aided design), CC 61
Calculated data type, AC 7
calculation(s), EX 2, EX 3
   forms, AC 64–65
   reports, AC 88–89
calculation operators, EX 12
Calendar Picker, AC 16
Calendar view, OUT 32–33
   coordinating calendars, OUT 41
   weather, OUT 27
callouts, charts, EX 92
Cancel button, EX 8
capacitors, CC 84
carbon copy (Cc), OUT 6
card readers, CC 37
cards, Sway, PA 6
caret (^), exponent operator, EX 7
case, text, changing, WD 52
categories, OUT 40–41
category axis, EX 80, EX 81
CD(s) (compact discs), CC 34, CC 35
CD drives, CC 35
cell(s), EX 4, EX 5
   active, EX 4, EX 5, PPT 56
   changing color behind text, PPT 62
   changing height or width, PPT 62
   charts, PPT 56, PPT 57
   editing entries, EX 10–11
   selected, inserting and deleting, EX 33
   tables, WD 88
cell addresses, EX 4
cell contents
   copying, EX 32, EX 33
   copying using fill handle, EX 36, EX 37
   indenting, EX 57
   moving, EX 32, EX 33
   rotating, EX 57
   selecting using keyboard, EX 10

cell pointer, EX 4, EX 5
cell references
   absolute. *See* absolute cell references
   mixed, EX 35
   relative. *See* relative cell references
cell styles, EX 62, EX 63
center tabs, WD 59
centering paragraphs, WD 56
central processing unit (CPU), CC 5, CC81. *See also*
   microprocessors; processor(s)
CF (CompactFlash) cards, CC 37
Change Case button, WD 52
Change Chart Type dialog box, EX 86–87
Change your view button, Save As dialog box, WD 9
character data, processing, CC 78
chart(s), EX 2, EX 3, EX 79–95
   adding data labels, EX 89
   adding to documents, WD 2
   annotating, EX 92–93
   borders, EX 88
   changing design, EX 86–87
   changing format, EX 88–89
   changing style, PPT 58
   combo, EX 86
   copying from Excel to Word, INT 6–7
   creating, EX 82–83, EX 94–95
   data entry, PPT 58, PPT 59
   data labels, EX 89
   drawing on, EX 92–93
   editing data, PPT 58, PPT 59
   elements, EX 80, EX 81
   embedded. *See* embedded charts
   formatting. *See* formatting charts
   hyperlinks, PPT 59
   inserting in presentations, PPT 56–57
   moving, EX 84, EX 85
   planning, EX 80–81
   previewing, EX 90
   reestablishing links, INT 9
   resizing, EX 84, EX 85
   shadows, EX 88
   text boxes, EX 92
   3-D, EX 87
   types, EX 81, PPT 57
chart sheets, EX 82
chat groups, CC 14
check boxes, WIN 15
   forms, AC 63
Check for Issues option, Info screen, WD 40
chips, CC 37. *See also* integrated circuits (ICs)
Chrome OS, CC 55
citations, WD 92–93
clicking, WIN 7
clip(s), PA 11
clip art, CC 60–61, WD 66–67
clipboard. *See* Office Clipboard;
   system clipboard
clock speed, CC 82

Close button, WIN 10
closing, Start menu, WIN 4
cloud, CC 5, CC 13
   syncing notebooks to, PA 2–3
cloud computing, AC 15, CC 5, CC 13, OFF 9, PPT 17
cloud storage
   locations, WIN 35
   remote storage compared, CC 86
cloudware. *See* web applications (web apps)
co-authoring, OFF 15
collaboration
   online, OFF 2, OFF 9
   presentations, PPT 2
color(s)
   background, resetting to original state, PPT 74
   behind text, changing, PPT 62
   matching using Eyedropper, PPT 33
   recoloring pictures, PPT 52
   themes, PPT 12, PPT 77
   worksheets, EX 62, EX 63
Color button, Adjust group, PPT 52
color categories, OUT 40, OUT 41
color depth, CC 27
column(s)
   adjusting width, EX 58–59
   datasheets, resizing and moving, AC 17
   deleting, EX 60, EX 61
   documents, WD 80, WD 81
   formatting, EX 58
   hiding and unhiding, EX 60
   inserting, EX 60, EX 61
   too narrow to display values, EX 58
   of unequal length, balancing on page, WD 82
column breaks, WD 82, WD 83
column charts, EX 81
column headings, charts, PPT 56, PPT 57
Column resize pointer, EX 11
Column Width command, EX 58
combo boxes, AC 54
   forms, AC 63
combo charts, EX 81, EX 86, PPT 57
Comma Style format, EX 52
command(s), WIN 6. *See also specific commands*
   Help, OFF 14
   Slide Show view, PPT 78–79
command buttons. *See also specific buttons*
   forms, AC 63
comments, EX 61
Comments button, PowerPoint window, PPT 6, PPT 7
commercial software, CC 48
compact discs. *See* CD(s) (compact discs)
compact discs (CDs), CC 34, CC 35
CompactFlash (CF) cards, CC 37
comparison operators, AC 38, AC 39, EX 12
compatibility
   backward, OFF 11
   Office documents, OFF 2

compatibility mode, OFF 11

compilers, CC 83

complex formulas, EX 26–27

compression utilities, CC 57

computer(s). *See also specific types of computers*
  adding devices, CC 38–39
  basic functions, CC 4
  defined, CC 2
  interacting with, CC 4
  protecting, CC 16–17
  turning off, CC 5
  turning on, CC 4
  types, CC 6–7
  uses, CC 2
  wearable, CC 25

computer chips. *See* chips; integrated circuits (ICs)

computer games, CC 62

computer networks, CC 9, OUT 2

computer platforms, CC 10

computer program(s). *See* program(s); software

computer programmers, CC 83

computer systems, CC 2

computer-aided design (CAD), CC 61

computer-aided music software, CC 62

concurrent-use licenses, CC 49

conditional formatting, EX 64–65

contact(s), OUT 30–31
  connecting mail to, OUT 38–39
  sending business cards, OUT 33

contact cards, OUT 30, OUT 31

contact groups, OUT 17

content, adding to build story, PA 7

content controls, WD 14
  deleting, WD 14

content placeholders, PPT 10

Contents tab, Properties dialog box, WD 41

continuous section breaks, WD 80, WD 82

control(s), forms, AC 54
  bound and unbound, AC 61
  list, AC 63
  modifying, AC 62–63

control(s), reports
  moving and resizing, AC 90
  multiple, selecting at same time, AC 91

Control Source property, AC 64

control unit, CC 83

conversations, OUT 28

Copy command, CC 76

Copy pointer, EX 11

copying. *See also* copying and pasting; cutting and
  copying; duplicating
  cell contents, EX 32, EX 33
  files, CC 76, WIN 36–37
  folders, CC 72–73, CC 76
  formulas. *See* copying formulas
  items between documents, WD 31

  items in long documents, WD 28
  noncontiguous slides, PPT 60
  text, PPT 8, WD 2 . *See also* copying and pasting, text
  Word tables to Access, INT 18, INT 22–23
  worksheets, EX 67

copying and pasting
  data from Excel to Word, INT 4–5
  Excel charts into Word documents, INT 2,
    INT 3, INT 6–7
  objects from Clipboard, INT 2
  text, WD 28–29

copying formulas
  with absolute cell references, EX 38–39
  with relative cell references, EX 36–37

copyright, CC 48, PPT 5

copyright notice, CC 48

Cortana, PA 14–15, WIN 16, WIN 17

COUNT function, EX 30

COUNTA function, EX 30

courtesy copy (Cc), OUT 6

CPU (central processing unit), CC 5, CC 81. *See also*
  microprocessors; processor(s)

Creative Commons license, PA 7

criteria, AC 32, AC 38

criteria syntax, AC 38

Crop button list arrow, PPT 52

cropping, pictures, PPT 52, PPT 53

Currency data type, AC 7

Current Date button, EX 14

Current record text box, AC 14

custom formatting, EX 64

custom slide layouts, PPT 75

Custom tab, Properties dialog box, WD 41

Customize Status Bar menu, WD 80

customizing
  background, PPT 76, PPT 77
  desktop, CC 57
  footers, WD 87
  headers, WD 87
  layout and formatting of footnotes and endnotes, WD 91
  Quick Access toolbar, OFF 12
  theme, PPT 76, PPT 77

cutting and copying, using Office Clipboard, OFF 5

cutting and pasting text, WD 26

cutting files, WIN 38, WIN 39

cycles, CC 82

D

data
  copying and pasting from Excel to Word, INT 4–5
  responsible use, CC 61

data analysis, EX 3

data buses, CC 38, CC 82

data entry, AC 14–15
  Excel and Access compared, AC 3
  query datasheets, AC 30, AC 31
data labels, charts, EX 89
data markers, EX 80, EX 81
data organization, EX 3
data points, EX 80
data representation, CC 78–79
  character data, CC 78
  digital data, CC 78
  digital sound files, CC 79
  images, CC 79
  numbers to be used in calculations, CC 79
data series, EX 80, EX 81
data series labels, charts, PPT 56, PPT 57
data series markers, charts, PPT 56, PPT 57
data storage, CC 30–31
data storage systems, CC 30–37
  capacity, CC 32
  durability, CC 32
  magnetic, CC 32
  optical, CC 33, CC 34–35
  solid-state, CC 33, CC 36–37
  speed, CC 32
  terminology, CC 33
  versatility, CC 32
  viewing using File Explorer, CC 35
data transfer rate, CC 32
data types, AC 6, AC 7
database(s)
  creating, AC 6–7
  data entry, AC 14–15
  editing data, AC 16–17
  multiuser, AC 14
  objects, AC 4–5
  primary keys, AC 10–11
  queries. *See* queries
  relational, AC 2–3
  tables. *See* table(s)
  terminology, AC 9
  users, AC 54
database software, CC 59. *See also* Microsoft Access
datasheet(s), AC 6
  data entry, AC 30, AC 31
  editing data, AC 30, AC 31
  filtering data, AC 36–37
  finding data, AC 34, AC 35
  formatting, AC 42–43
  freezing and unfreezing fields, AC 30
  hiding and unhiding fields, AC 30
  resizing and moving columns, AC 17
  sorting data, AC 34, AC 35
Datasheet View, AC 6, AC 10
  creating tables, AC 8
date(s)
  Fixed date option button, PPT 40
  inserting in headers or footers, EX 14
Date Navigator, OUT 26, OUT 32

Date/Time data type, AC 7
decimal tabs, WD 59
default(s)
  file extensions, OFF 8
  number of copies, WIN 14
  setting formatting of shape as, PPT 38
  storage locations, WIN 28
  text boxes, changing, PPT 55
Default Width command, EX 58
Delete command, CC 76
Deleted Items folder, OUT 8, OUT 9
deleting. *See also* removing
  cells, EX 33
  columns, EX 60, EX 61
  content controls, WD 14
  email messages, OUT 16, OUT 17
  files, CC76, CC 77, WIN 42, WIN 43
  folders, CC 76, CC 77
  items from Clipboard, WD 30
  page breaks, WD 82
  rows, EX 60, EX 61
  section breaks, WD 80
  slide recordings, PPT 88
  tables, WD 88
  tables in queries, AC 32
  worksheets, EX 66, EX 67
demoware, CC 48
Descending button, AC 35
deselecting text, WD 10
design, presentations, PPT 4
design themes. *See* theme(s)
Design View, AC 10, AC 55
  reports, AC 83
desktop(s)
  customizing, CC 57
  multiple, creating using Task View button, WIN 38
  navigating, WIN 4, WIN 5
desktop apps, WIN 8
desktop computers, CC 6, CC 9
desktop publishing software, CC 59
destination file, INT 2
destination presentation, PPT 60
Detail section, AC 69, AC 84
Details view, WIN 33
development software, CC 46
device drivers, CC 39, CC 57
diagonal resizing pointer, EX 85
dialog boxes, WIN 14. *See also specific dialog boxes*
  controls, WIN 15
dictionaries, WD 37
digital audio players, solid-state memory cards, CC 36
digital cameras, CC 9, CC 25
  solid-state memory cards, CC 36
digital content, CC 48
digital convergence, CC 3
digital data, CC 78

digital media players, CC 9
digital revolution, CC 2
digital signatures, PPT 76
digital technology, CC 2
digital video discs or digital versatile discs (DVDs), CC 34, CC 35
digitizing, CC 3, CC 79
DIMM (dual inline memory module) chip package, CC 80
DIP (dual inline package) chip package, CC 80
direct access, CC 32
directories, folders vs., CC 73
disabilities, computer accessibility. *See* accessibility
display devices, CC 8, CC 26–27. *See also* monitors
   aspect ratio, CC 27
displaying. *See also* unhiding; viewing
   grid of clickable letters, WIN 4
   information in status bar, WD 80
   Mini toolbar, PPT 28
   minimizing buttons and commands on tabs, OFF 12
   rulers, WD 56, WD 78
   taskbar, WIN 4
distributing objects, PPT 39
distribution lists, OUT 17
division operator (/), EX 7
Docs.com public gallery, PA 8
document(s), WD 2. *See also* file(s)
   copying items between, WD 31
   editing. *See* editing documents
   enhancing, WD 2, WD 88–89
   formatting. *See* formatting documents
   long. *See* long documents
   moving items between, WD 31
   navigating. *See* navigating documents
   planning, WD 3
   recovering, OFF 15
   saving, WD 8–9, WD 26
   sharing. *See* sharing documents
   starting, WD 6–7
   templates, WD 14–15
Document Inspector, PPT 86, PPT 87, WD 40
document production software. *See* desktop publishing software; Microsoft Word 2016; word-processing software
document properties, WD 40–41
   advanced, WD 41
document window, WD 4, WD 5
   Microsoft Office 2016, OFF 6, OFF 7
   splitting, WD 28
dot pitch (dp), CC 27
double-clicking, WIN 6, WIN 7
download links, CC 50
draft(s), email messages, OUT 8, OUT 9
Draft view, WD 17
Drafts folder, OUT 8
dragging, WIN 7
dragging and dropping, WIN 43
   text, WD 26
draw pointer, EX 85
drawing canvas, PA 3

drawing on charts, EX 92, EX 93
drawing software, CC 60
drive bays, CC 31
drivers. *See* device drivers
drop cap(s), WD 51
Drop Cap dialog box, WD 51
dual inline memory module (DIMM) chip package, CC 80
dual inline package (DIP) chip package, CC 80
duplex printers, CC 29
duplicating. *See also* copying
   shapes, PPT 36, PPT 37
duty cycle, CC 29
DVD(s) (digital video discs or digital versatile discs), CC 34, CC 35
DVD authoring software, CC 62–63
DVD drives, CC 35

E

Edge. *See* Microsoft Edge
Edit Citation dialog box, WD 92, WD 93
Edit mode, AC 14
   keyboard shortcuts, AC 17
edit record symbol, AC 14
Edit Relationships dialog box, AC 12, AC 13
editing
   cell entries, EX 10–11
   comments, EX 61
   data. *See* editing data
   documents. *See* editing documents
   files, WIN 34, WIN 35
   formulas, EX 12, EX 13
   points of shapes, PPT 37
   shapes, PPT 36, PPT 37
   text, PPT 2, WD 2 . *See also* editing documents
   text objects in SmartArt graphics, PPT 30
editing data
   charts, PPT 58, PPT 59
   databases, AC 16–17
   query datasheets, AC 30, AC 31
editing documents, WD 25–41
   checking spelling and grammar, WD 34–35
   copying and pasting text, WD 28–29
   cutting and pasting text, WD 26–27
   document properties, WD 40–41
   finding and replacing text, WD 32–33
   hyperlinks, WD 38–39
   Office Clipboard, WD 30–31
   researching information, WD 36–37
educational software, CC 63
edutainment software, CC 63
electronic mail. *See* email
electronic spreadsheets, EX 2. *See also* Microsoft Excel 2016
email, CC 14. *See also* email messages; Microsoft Outlook 2016
   addresses, OUT 4–5
   communication using, OUT 2
   good practices, OUT 16–17

sending presentations, PPT 51
web-based, OUT 2, OUT 3, OUT 5, OUT 6
email accounts, CC 14
email addresses, CC 14
email attachments, CC 14
email folders, OUT 8–9
creating, OUT 9
default, OUT 8, OUT 9
maintaining, OUT 16
email messages, CC 14, OUT 2
attachments, OUT 14–15, OUT 16, WD 39
care in composing, OUT 12
connecting to contacts, OUT 38–39
creating, OUT 6, OUT 7
deleting, OUT 16, OUT 17
drafts, OUT 8, OUT 9
emoticons, OUT 16
filtering, OUT 28
flagging, OUT 13, OUT 34
forwarding, OUT 12–13, OUT 16
headers, OUT 7
images, video, and computer files, OUT 2
labeling, OUT 13
managing, OUT 9
organizing, OUT 2, OUT 28–29
professionalism, OUT 16
receiving, OUT 10, OUT 11
replying to, OUT 10, OUT 11
sending, OUT 6, OUT 7, OUT 15
sorting, OUT 9
email service providers, OUT 4, OUT 5
email software, OUT 2
emailing workbooks, EX 68
embedded charts, EX 82
moving to sheets, EX 85
embedded objects, PPT 56
embedding, INT 34
charts in presentations, PPT 56–57
Excel worksheets in PowerPoint, INT 38–39
linking vs., INT 35
Word files in Excel, INT 2, INT 3, INT 10–11
emoticons, OUT 16
endnotes, WD 90, WD 91
customizing layout and formatting, WD 91
end-user license agreement (EULA), CC 49
equal sign (=)
comparison operators, AC 36
expressions entered in controls, AC 64
formula prefix, EX 12, EX 28, EX 30
EULA (end-user license agreement), CC 49
even page section breaks, WD 80
events, OUT 32
exa-, CC 79
exabytes, CC 79
Excel. *See* Microsoft Excel 2016
exiting. *See* shutting down
expansion bays, CC 31
expansion bus, CC 38

expansion cards, CC 38–39
installing, CC 38–39
expansion ports, CC 38
expansion slots, CC 38
exploding pie charts, EX 94
exponent operator (^), EX 7
expressions
forms, AC 64, AC 65
reports, AC 88
Eyedropper, matching colors using, PPT 33

F

field(s), AC 9, WD 84
adding to forms, AC 60–61
blank, finding, AC 36
contact cards, OUT 30
databases, AC 6
datasheets, freezing and unfreezing, AC 30
datasheets, hiding and unhiding, AC 30
properties, AC 10
removing from Selected Fields list, AC 28
Field List, AC 60, AC 61
field list(s), AC 12, AC 32
field names, AC 6
field selector, AC 66
file(s), OFF 8, WIN 4. *See also* document(s)
changing view, WIN 32–33
converting format, CC 76
copying, CC 76, WIN 36–37
creating, OFF 8, OFF 9, WIN 28, WIN 29
cutting, WIN 38, WIN 39
deleting, CC 77, WIN 42, WIN 43
destination, INT 2
editing, WIN 34, WIN 35
filtering, WIN 33
moving, CC 76, WIN 38, WIN 39
opening. *See* opening files
organizing in folders, CC 70
pasting, WIN 38, WIN 39
planning organization, WIN 27
renaming, WIN 38, WIN 39
restoring, WIN 42, WIN 43
saving. *See* saving files
saving documents as, WD 8–9
sorting, WIN 33
source, INT 2
storage, CC 70–71
swap, CC 86
file dates, CC 75
File Explorer, CC 70–71
viewing file extensions, CC 75
File Explorer, Search Tools tab, WIN 40
viewing data storage systems, CC 35
File Explorer button, WIN 5, WIN 26, WIN 27
file extensions, CC 5, CC 74–75, WIN 28
default, OFF 8

file formats, CC 74
   native, CC 74
file hierarchies, WIN 26, WIN 27
   navigating, WIN 31
File list, WIN 26
file management, CC 70–71, CC 76–77
   guidelines, CC 77
file management programs, CC 71
file path, CC 70
file size, email attachments, CC 75, OUT 16
file specification, CC 70
file syncing, WIN 35
File tab, WD 4, WD 5
filename extensions, CC 74–75
filenames, CC 5, CC 74–75, OFF 8, WD 8
filenaming conventions, CC 74
files
   copying and moving, CC 76
   deleting, CC 76
   renaming, CC 76
   unable to be opened, CC 75
fill handle
   copying cell contents, EX 36, EX 37
   sequential text or values, EX 39
Fill Handle pointer, EX 11
Filter button, AC 37
Filter By Form, AC 36, AC 37
Filter By Selection, AC 36
filtering
   data. See filtering data
   email messages, OUT 28
   files, WIN 33
filtering data, AC 36–37
   queries compared, AC 37
finance software, CC 63
Find and Replace dialog box, AC 34, AC 35, EX 68,
   EX 69, WD 32, WD 33
Find button, AC 35
finding
   data in tables or query datasheets, AC 34, AC 35
   text, WD 32–33
first line indents, WD 61
Fixed date option button, PPT 40
flagging, email messages, OUT 13, OUT 34
flash drives. See USB flash drives
flash fill feature, EX 2
floating graphics, WD 66
folder(s), CC 70, CC 72–73, WIN 4, WIN 26, WIN 30, WIN 31
   changing view, WIN 32–33
   copying, CC 72–73, CC 76
   deleting, CC 76, CC 77
   email. See email folders
   moving, CC 72–73, CC 76
   nested, CC 72
   reasons to use, CC 72–73

   renaming, CC 76
   sorting, WIN 33
Folder Pane, OUT 32
Folder tab, OUT 9
font(s), EX 54, WD 50–51
   changing, EX 54, EX 55
   replacing, PPT 29
   sans serif, WD 50
   serif, WD 50
Font dialog box, WD 52, WD 53
Font list, WD 50, WD 51
font sizes, WD 50
   changing, EX 54, EX 55
font styles, changing, EX 56, EX 57
footer(s), WD 86, WD 87
   changing, EX 14
   slides, PPT 40–41
Footer gallery, adding custom footers, WD 87
footnotes, WD 90, WD 91
   converting to endnotes, WD 90
   customizing layout and formatting, WD 91
foreign key field, AC 12
foreign languages, proofing tools, PPT 27
form(s), 53–69, AC 4, AC 5
   adding fields, AC 60–61
   calculations, AC 64–65
   controls, AC 54, AC 61
   Form Wizard, AC 54–55
   inserting images, AC 68–69
   Layout View, AC 58–59
   modifying controls, AC 62–63
   modifying tab order, AC 66–67
   split, AC 56–57
Form Design tool, AC 56
Form Footer section, AC 69
Form Header section, AC 69
form sections, AC 68, AC 69
Form tool, AC 56
Form View, AC 10, AC 54, AC 55
Form Wizard, AC 54–55
Form Wizard tool, AC 56
Format Painter, WD 52–53
formatting
   charts. See formatting charts
   columns, EX 58
   datasheets, AC 42–43
   documents. See formatting documents
   footnotes and endnotes, customizing, WD 91
   page numbers, WD 84
   pages, WD 2
   paragraphs, WD 2
   reports, AC 92–93
   text. See formatting text
   values, EX 52–53
   WordArt, PPT 64, PPT 65
   worksheets. See formatting worksheets

formatting charts, EX 90–91
  changing, EX 88
formatting documents, WD 77–95
  citations, WD 92–93
  columns, WD 80, WD 81
  endnotes, WD 90, WD 91
  footers, WD 86, WD 87
  footnotes, WD 90, WD 91
  headers, WD 86, WD 87
  margins, WD 78–79
  page breaks, WD 82–83
  page numbers, WD 84–85
  sections, WD 80, WD 81
  tables, WD 88–89
  themes, WD 50, WD 57
formatting marks, WD 10
formatting text, PPT 28–29, WD 2, WD 49–67
  aligning paragraphs, WD 56–57
  borders, WD 64, WD 65
  bulleted lists, WD 62, WD 63
  fonts, WD 50–51
  Format Painter, WD 52–53
  indents, WD 60–61
  inserting online pictures, WD 66–67
  line and paragraph spacing, WD 54–55
  Mini toolbar, WD 12–13
  numbered lists, WD 62, WD 63
  Quick Styles, WD 55
  replacing text and fonts, PPT 29
  Ribbon, WD 12
  shading, WD 64, WD 65
  tab stops, WD 58–59
formatting worksheets, EX 51–69
  borders, EX 62, EX 63
  clearing formatting, EX 56
  colors, EX 62, EX 63
  column width, EX 58–59
  conditional formatting, EX 64–65
  custom formatting, EX 64
  font styles and alignment, EX 56–57
  fonts and font size, EX 54–55
  inserting and deleting rows and columns, EX 60–61
  keyboard shortcuts, EX 56
  moving worksheets, EX 66, EX 67
  patterns, EX 62, EX 63
  renaming worksheets, EX 66, EX 67
  spell checking, EX 68–69
  as tables, EX 53
  values, EX 52–53
formula(s), EX 6–7
  complex, EX 26–27
  copying. *See* copying formulas
  editing, EX 12, EX 13
  entering, EX 12, EX 13
Formula AutoComplete feature, EX 30
formula bar, EX 4, EX 5
formula prefix (=), EX 12, EX 28, EX 30
formulas, copying. *See* copying formulas
Forward button, Save As dialog box, WD 9
Forward Contact button, OUT 33

forward slash (/), division operator, EX 7
forwarding email messages, OUT 12–13, OUT 16
free-response quizzes, inserting in slides, PA 12
freeware, CC 49
freezing fields in datasheets, AC 30
FSB (front side bus), CC 82
function(s), AC 88, EX 8, EX 9
  inserting, EX 28–29
  rounding values with, EX 40–41
  typing, EX 30–31
Function Arguments dialog box, EX 28, EX 29

G

galleries, OFF 6
General Public License (GPL), CC 49
General tab, Properties dialog box, WD 41
gestures, CC 25, WIN 2
Get External Data - Excel Spreadsheet dialog box, INT 20, INT 21
giga-, CC 79
gigabits, CC 79
gigabytes, CC 79
Go To button, AC 35
Go To command, WD 33
GPL (General Public License), CC 49
grammar, email messages, OUT 16
graphical user interfaces (GUIs), CC 10–11, CC 46, CC 54
graphics. *See also* **pictures**
  adding to documents, WD 2
  background, PPT 76
  floating, WD 66
  inline, WD 66
  inserting and adjusting, EX 55
  inserting in forms, AC 68–69
  positioning using precise measurements, WD 66
  reducing size, WD 66
  SmartArt. *See* SmartArt graphics
graphics cards, CC 26–27
graphics software, CC 60–61
gray scale, presentations, PPT 7
greater than operator (>), AC 36
greater than or equal to operator (>=), AC 36
gridlines, EX 80, EX 81, EX 88
group(s), WD 4, WD 5
  buttons and tool palettes, WIN 10
  PowerPoint window, PPT 6
Group Footer section, AC 84
Group Header section, AC 84
grouping
  objects, PPT 38, PPT 39
  records in reports, AC 86–87
  tasks, OUT 34
GUIs. *See* graphical user interfaces (GUIs)
gutter, WD 79

H

hackers, CC 16

handheld computers, CC 7

handwriting, converting to text, PA 3–4

hanging indents, WD 61

hard disk drives, CC 8, CC 30, CC 31
  partitions, CC 34

hard page breaks, WD 82, WD 83

hardware, CC 23–44. *See also specific hardware devices*
  defined, CC 2
  maintenance, CC 31

head crashes, CC 31

header(s), WD 86, WD 87
  changing, EX 14
  email messages, OUT 7

Header and Footer dialog box, PPT 40, PPT 41

Header & Footer Tolls Design tab, EX 14

Header gallery, adding custom headers, WD 87

Help system, OFF 14, OFF 15, WIN 16–17

Hide & Unhide command, EX 58

hiding
  columns, EX 60
  fields in datasheets, AC 30
  Mini toolbar, PPT 28
  rows, EX 60
  slides, temporarily, PPT 78

highlighting, WD 65, WIN 6

Histogram charts, EX 95

home pages, CC 13

horizontal axis, EX 80, EX 81

horizontal resizing pointer, EX 85

horizontal ruler, WD 4, WD 5

horizontal scroll bar, WD 4

HTTP (Hypertext Transfer Protocol), CC 13

Hub, Edge, PA 14

hyperlink(s), CC 12, WD 38–39
  charts, PPT 59
  color, PPT 77
  followed, color, PPT 77
  removing, WD 38

Hyperlink data type, AC 7

hypertext, CC 12

Hypertext Transfer Protocol (HTTP), CC 13

I

I-beam pointer, EX 11

IC(s). *See* integrated circuits (ICs)

Icon Sets, EX 64

identity theft, CC 16

IM (instant messaging), CC 15

image editing software, CC 60

images. *See* graphics; pictures

importing Excel worksheets into Access, INT 18, INT 19, INT 20–21

inactive windows, WIN 12

Inbox, OUT 8

indent(s), WD 60–61

indent markers, WD 60

indenting cell contents, EX 57

infinity symbol, AC 12

Info screen, WD 40

ink annotations, PPT 78

Ink to Text button, PA 3

Ink Tools Pen tab, PPT 78

inked handwriting, PA 3

inking slides, PPT 9

Inking toolbar, PA 15

ink-jet printers, CC 28

inline graphics, WD 66

input devices, CC 3, CC 24–25. *See also specific input devices*

Insert Chart dialog box, EX 95, PPT 56, PPT 57

Insert dialog box, EX 60, EX 61

Insert Function dialog box, EX 28, EX 29

Insert Hyperlink dialog box, WD 38, WD 39

Insert Pictures window, WD 66, WD 67

insertion point, CC 24, EX 10, OFF 8, PPT 8, WD 4, WD 5

installation agreements, CC 49

installing
  expansion cards, CC 38–39
  software, CC 50–51

installing updates when you exit Windows, WIN 19

instant messaging (IM), CC 15

integrated circuits (ICs), CC 80–81
  companies producing, CC 81
  connection to motherboard, CC 80–81
  identifying, CC 81
  locations, CC 80
  processors, CC 81
  protection from damage, CC 80
  upgrading, CC 81

integrating Word, Excel, Access, and PowerPoint, INT 33–43
  embedding Excel worksheets in PowerPoint, INT 38–39
  importing Word outlines into PowerPoint, INT 34, INT 36–37
  linking Access and Excel objects to PowerPoint, INT 40–41
  managing links, INT 42–43
  methods, INT 34, INT 43

integrating Word, Excel, and Access, INT 17–27
  copying Word tables to Access, INT 18, INT 22–23
  importing Excel worksheets into Access, INT 18, INT 19, INT 20–21
  linking Access tables to Excel and Word, INT 18, INT 19, INT 24–25
  linking Access tables to Word, INT 18, INT 26–27
  methods, INT 18, INT 19, INT 27

integrating Word and Excel, INT 1–11
  copying charts from Excel to Word, INT 2, INT 3, INT 6–7
  copying data from Excel to Word, INT 4–5
  creating linked objects, INT 8–9
  destination file, INT 2
  embedding Word files in Excel, INT 2, INT 3, INT 10–11
  methods, INT 2, INT 11

object linking and embedding, INT 3
source file, INT 2
integration, INT 2, OFF 2
Intel, CC 81
intellectual property, CC 49, PPT 5
interactive quizzes, inserting, PPT 89
interface(s), OFF 2. *See also* graphical user interfaces (GUIs);
user interfaces (UIs)
Internet, CC 12–13
access, CC 5, CC 12
defined, CC 12
reasons to use, CC 12
web vs., CC 12
Internet forums, CC 15
Internet telephony, CC 15
interpreters, CC 83
Is Not Null criterion, AC 39
Is Null criterion, AC 39
italic text, WD 52

J

join lines, AC 32
Junk E-mail folder, OUT 8, OUT 9
justifying paragraphs, WD 56

K

key fields, AC 9
key symbols, AC 12
keyboard(s), selecting cell contents, EX 10
keyboard shortcuts, WD 27
Edit mode, AC 17
formatting selected cells or ranges, EX 56
Navigation mode, AC 15
keyboards, CC 8, CC 24, CC 25
keywords, CC 13, EX 55
kilo-, CC 79
kilobits, CC 79
kilobytes, CC 79

L

label(s), EX 8
changing alignment, EX 56, EX 57
forms, AC 63
label controls, AC 54
Label Wizard, AC 94, AC 95
labeling, email messages, OUT 13
LAN(s) (local area networks), CC 9
land grid array (LGA) chip package, CC 80

landscape orientation, AC 80, AC 81, EX 16, WD 78
language tools, PPT 84, PPT 85
laptop computers, CC 6
laser mice, CC 24
laser printers, CC 28
launchers, OFF 6
layout(s), WIN 32
Excel and Access compared, AC 3
footnotes and endnotes, customizing, WD 91
forms, AC 67
Print Layout view, WD 17
sections, changing settings, WD 81
tables, AC 59
Web Layout view, WD 17
Layout View
Field List, AC 60, AC 61
forms, AC 55, AC 56
reports, AC 82–83
tables, AC 58–59
LCD (liquid crystal display), CC 26
lectures, recording, PA 4
LED (light emitting diode), CC 26
left angle bracket (<), comparison operators, AC 36
left indents, WD 61
left tabs, WD 59
left-aligned text, WD 56
legends, EX 80
charts, PPT 56, PPT 57
less than operator (<), AC 39
less than or equal to operator (<=), AC 39
LGA (land grid array) chip package, CC 80
license agreements, CC 48, CC 49
light emitting diode (LED), CC 26
Like operator, AC 36
line and rectangle controls, forms, AC 63
line charts, EX 81, PPT 57
link(s), CC 12, INT 2. *See also* hyperlink(s)
link lines, AC 32
linked files
enabling content, INT 26
opening, INT 26
linked objects, INT 2
creating, INT 8–9
opening linked files, INT 9
reestablishing links to charts, INT 9
linked tables, Excel and Access compared, AC 3
linking, INT 34
Access and Excel objects to PowerPoint, INT 40–41
Access tables to Excel and Word, INT 18, INT 19, INT 24–25
Access tables to Word, INT 18, INT 26–27
data between Word and Excel, INT 2
embedding vs., INT 35
managing links, INT 42–43
Linux, CC 54, CC 55
liquid crystal display (LCD), CC 26

list(s)
    bulleted, WD 62, WD 63
    multilevel, WD 62
    numbered, WD 62, WD 63
list boxes, WIN 15
    forms, AC 63
Live Preview feature, OFF 6
Live Previews, PPT 12
live tile feature, WIN 4
local applications, CC 47
local areal networks (LANs). *See* LAN(s) (local area networks)
lock screens, WIN 2, WIN 3
logging in (on), WIN 2
logging out, WIN 18
logical view, AC 28
long documents
    copying and moving items, WD 28
    moving around in, WD 84
Long Text data type, AC 7
Lookup Wizard data type, AC 7

M

Mac computers, installing software, CC 51
Mac OS, CC 54
Mac OS X, CC 54–55
magnetic storage, CC 32
Mail, OUT 2, OUT 3, OUT 28, OUT 29
mailing labels, AC 94
mainframe computers, CC 7
major gridlines, EX 88
malware (malicious software), CC 16–17
manual page breaks, WD 82, WD 83
margins, WD 78–79
    forms, AC 67
    minimum allowable setting, WD 78
    mirror, WD 79
masters, PPT 74–75
mathematical modeling software, CC 63
meetings, OUT 32
mega-, CC 79
megabits, CC 79
megabytes, CC 79
memory
    cache, CC 83
    RAM. *See* RAM (random access memory)
    ROM, CC 86–87
    storage vs., CC 5
    virtual, CC 86
memory cards, solid-state, CC 36
menus, WIN 10, WIN 14, WIN 15
Merge Document option, Info screen, WD 40
merging shapes, PPT 34, PPT 35
message, presentations, PPT 4

message threading, OUT 28
mice, CC 8, CC 24
microchips. *See* integrated circuits (ICs)
microprocessors, CC 81. *See also* processor(s)
Microsoft Access 2016, OFF 2, OFF 3
    Excel compared, AC 3
    filenames and default file extension, OFF 8
    integrating. *See* integrating Word, Excel, Access, and PowerPoint;
        integrating Word, Excel, and Access
    starting, AC 4, AC 5
    uses, AC 2
Microsoft accounts, WIN 2
Microsoft Edge, PA 14–16, WIN 6, WIN 41
    annotating webpages, PA 15
    browsing the web, PA 14
    locating information with Cortana, PA 14–15
Microsoft Edge button, WIN 5
Microsoft Excel 2016, OFF 2, OFF 3
    Access compared, AC 3
    filenames and default file extension, OFF 8
    integrating. *See* integrating Word, Excel, Access, and PowerPoint;
        integrating Word, Excel, and Access; integrating Word and Excel
    uses, EX 2, EX 3
    window components, EX 4–5
Microsoft Office Mix, PA 10–13
    adding to PowerPoint, PA 10
    capturing video clips, PA 11
    inserting quizzes, live webpages, and apps, PA 12
    sharing presentations, PA 12
Microsoft Office Online Apps, PPT 17
Microsoft Office 365, OFF 3
Microsoft Office 2016, OFF 2, OFF 3
    apps included, OFF 2, OFF 3
    benefits, OFF 2
    screen elements, OFF 6–7
    starting apps, OFF 4–5
Microsoft OneDrive, AC 15, EX 5, OFF 8, PPT 17, WIN 35
    sharing files, OFF 15
Microsoft OneNote 2016, PA 2–5
    converting handwriting to text, PA 3–4
    creating notebooks, PA 2
    recording lectures, PA 4
    syncing notebooks to cloud, PA 2–3
    taking notes, PA 3
Microsoft OneNote Mobile app, PA 2
Microsoft Outlook 2016. *See also* email; email messages
    starting, OUT 26
Microsoft PowerPoint 2016, OFF 2, OFF 3
    filenames and default file extension, OFF 8
    integrating. *See* integrating Word, Excel, Access, and PowerPoint
Microsoft Sway, PA 6–9
    adding content, PA 7
    creating presentations, PA 6–7
    designing presentations, PA 8
    publishing presentations, PA 8
    sharing presentations, PA 8
Microsoft Translator box, PPT 84, PPT 85
Microsoft Windows 10, CC 54

shutting down (exiting), WIN 18–19
  starting, WIN 2–3
Microsoft Windows 10 desktop. *See* desktop(s)
Microsoft Windows 10 UI, WIN 4
Microsoft Word 2016
  documents. *See* document(s)
  filenames and default file extension, OFF 8
  inserting text from, PPT 50–51
  integrating. *See* integrating Word, Excel, Access, and PowerPoint;
    integrating Word, Excel, and Access; integrating Word and Excel
  start screen, OFF 4, OFF 5
  uses, WD 2
milliseconds, CC 32
Mini toolbar, PPT 28
  buttons, WD 13
  formatting text, WD 12–13
  showing/hiding, PPT 28
Minimize button, WIN 10
minor gridlines, EX 88
minus sign (–), subtraction or negation operator, EX 7
mirror margins, WD 79
mixed cell references, EX 35
mobile applications, CC 47
mobile apps, CC 11
mobile devices. *See also* smartphones; tablet computers
  operating systems, CC 11
mode indicator, EX 4, EX 5
monitors, CC 8
  screens vs., CC 26
More Forms tool, AC 56
motherboard, CC 80
motion path objects, PPT 82, PPT 83
mouse pointer(s), WD 5
mouse pointer shapes, AC 58
Move command, CC 76
Move pointer, EX 11
movies, graphics software, CC 61
moving. *See also* navigating; positioning
  cell contents, EX 32, EX 33
  charts, EX 84, EX 85
  controls, AC 90
  datasheet columns, AC 17
  embedded charts to sheets, EX 85
  files, CC 76, WIN 38, WIN 39
  folders, CC 72–73, CC 76
  items between documents, WD 31
  items in long documents, WD 28
  items using touch-screen devices, WIN 7
  page numbers, WD 84
  text, WD 2
  text objects in SmartArt graphics, PPT 30
  titles, EX 88
  worksheets, EX 66
  between worksheets, EX 66
multi-core processors, CC 82
multilevel lists, WD 62
multiple-user licenses, CC 49

multiplication operator (*), EX 7
multitasking, CC 53
multiuser capabilities, Excel and Access compared, AC 3
multiuser databases, AC 14
My Add-ins feature, EX 26

N

Name box, EX 4, EX 5
Name property, AC 66
named ranges, EX 12
naming files, CC 76
nanoseconds (ns), CC 85
native file format, CC 74
navigating
  desktop, WIN 4, WIN 5
  documents. *See* navigating documents
  file hierarchy, WIN 31
  between Office programs, OFF 4
  in Open dialog box, WIN 34, WIN 35
  Start menu, WIN 4, WIN 5
  up and down, WIN 26
  websites, CC 13
  worksheets, EX 9
navigating documents, WD 16–17
  Go To command, WD 33
  long documents, WD 84
  Navigation pane, WD 33
navigation buttons, AC 14
Navigation mode, AC 14
  keyboard shortcuts, AC 15
Navigation Options dialog box, OUT 26, OUT 27
Navigation pane, WD 33, WIN 26
  File Explorer, CC 70–71
Navigation Pane, AC 4, OUT 26, OUT 27
Navigation tool, AC 56
negation operator (–), EX 7
negative indents, WD 61
nested folders, CC 72
netbooks, CC 6, CC 7
network-enabled printers, CC 29
networks, access, CC 5
New Appointment button, OUT 32
New folder button, Save As dialog box, WD 9
new message window, OUT 6, OUT 7
next page section breaks, WD 80
No Spacing style, WD 6
noncontiguous slides, copying, PPT 60
Normal pointer, EX 11
Normal style, WD 6
Normal view, EX 14, PPT 15
  PowerPoint, PPT 6, PPT 7
not equal to operator (<>), AC 39

note(s), OUT 36–37, PA 2. *See also* Microsoft OneNote 2016
   slides, PPT 11
   taking, PA 3
note reference marks, WD 90, WD 91
notebook(s), CC 9, PA 2. *See also* Microsoft OneNote 2016
notebook computers, CC 6
Notes button, PowerPoint window, PPT 6, PPT 7
Notes Page view, PPT 11, PPT 15
Notes pane, PPT 11
Notification area, WIN 4
ns (nanoseconds), CC 85
Number data type, AC 7
number format, EX 52
number sign (#), column too narrow to display values, EX 58
numbered lists, WD 62, WD 63
Numbering Library, WD 62, WD 63
numbering pages, WD 84–85
numbers, processing, CC 79

O

object(s), AC 4, AC 5, AC 9, EX 84, PPT 8. *See also specific objects*
   aligning, PPT 38, PPT 39
   copying and pasting, INT 2
   distributing, PPT 39
   embedded, PPT 56
   grouping, PPT 38, PPT 39
   read-only, AC 80
   renaming, AC 8
   SmartArt. *See* SmartArt graphics
   text, applying WordArt styles, EX 90
   text, changing outline width or style, PPT 54
   views, AC 10
object code, CC 83
object linking and embedding (OLE), INT 3
object pointers, EX 85
odd page section breaks, WD 80
Office 2016 suite, OFF 2–3. *See also* Microsoft Office 2016
Office Clipboard, EX 32, OFF 5, OFF 13, WD 26, WD 30–31
   copying and pasting data from Excel to Word, INT 4–5
   copying and pasting objects, INT 2
Office Mix, PPT 88–89
Office Online, EX 5
office productivity software, CC 58–59
   database, CC 59
   desktop publishing, CC 59
   presentation, CC 59
   software suites, CC 58
   spreadsheet, CC 58
   web authoring, CC 59
   word processing, CC 58
OLE Object data type, AC 7
OneDrive. *See* Microsoft OneDrive
OneNote. *See* Microsoft OneNote 2016

one-time meetings, OUT 32
one-to-many line, AC 12
one-to-many relationships, AC 10, AC 12–13
online collaboration, OFF 2, OFF 9
online pictures, inserting and adjusting, EX 55
Open dialog box, OFF 10, OFF 11
   navigating in, WIN 34, WIN 35
   opening, WD 26
Open Source Initiative, CC 49
open source software, CC 49
opening
   files. *See* opening files
   Open dialog box, WD 26
   PowerPoint 97-2007 presentations in PowerPoint 2016, PPT 26
   Start menu, WIN 4
opening files, OFF 10, OFF 11
   as copies, OFF 10
   documents created in older Office versions, OFF 11
   linked files, INT 26
   read-only files, OFF 10
operating systems (OSs), CC 10, CC 52–53
   comparison, CC 54–55
   functions, CC 52
   multiple versions, CC 54
   resources, CC 52–53
   starting, CC 52
   using, CC 53
   utilities included, CC 56
   warning messages, CC 53
optical data storage systems, CC 34–36
optical drives, CC 9, CC 35
   operation, CC 35
optical mice, CC 24
optical storage, CC 33
option boxes, WIN 15
option buttons, forms, AC 63
option groups, forms, AC 63
OR criteria, AC 40–41
order of precedence, EX 26, EX 27
Organize button, Save As dialog box, WD 9
organizing information, PowerPoint, PPT 2
orphan(s), WD 82
orphan records, AC 56
Outbox, OUT 8, OUT 9
outdents, WD 61
outline(s), WD 62
   Word, importing into PowerPoint, INT 34, INT 36–37
Outline view, PPT 14, PPT 15, WD 17
   text entry, PPT 26–27
Outlook. *See* Microsoft Outlook
output, CC 5
output type, presentations, PPT 4
overhead transparencies, printing slides in size for, PPT 16

P

padding, forms, AC 67

page(s), formatting, WD 2

page break(s), WD 82–83
    automatic (soft), WD 82
    deleting, WD 82
    manual (hard), WD 82, WD 83

Page Break Preview, EX 14, EX 15

Page Footer section, AC 84

Page Header section, AC 84

page layout, sections, changing settings, WD 81

Page Layout view, EX 14, EX 15

page number(s), WD 84–85

Page Number gallery, WD 85

page orientation, AC 80, AC 81

Page Setup dialog box, WD 78, WD 79

pages per minute (ppm), CC 29

paint software, CC 60

panes, WIN 26
    Normal view in PowerPoint, PPT 6

paragraph(s)
    aligning, WD 56–57
    formatting, WD 2
    indenting, WD 60–61
    spacing, changing, WD 54–55

Paragraph dialog box, WD 56, WD 57

paragraph symbol (¶), WD 10
    paragraph spacing, WD 54, WD 55

partitions, hard drives, CC 34

passwords, CC 4, CC 16, WIN 2, WIN 3

Paste command, INT 25
    options for copying charts from Excel to Word, INT 6, INT 7

Paste Link command, INT 25

Paste Options button, WD 26, WD 27

Paste Preview feature, EX 37

Paste Special command, INT 25

Paste Special dialog box, EX 36, INT 8, INT 9

pasting. *See also* copying and pasting; cutting and pasting text
    files, WIN 38, WIN 39

patches, CC 51

paths, WIN 26

patterns, worksheets, EX 62, EX 63

PCs. *See* personal computers (PCs)

PDF (Portable Document File), CC 57

Peek feature, OUT 32

people. *See* contact(s)

People Pane, OUT 38

People view, OUT 30, OUT 31

percent sign (%)
    formatting values, EX 52
    percent operator, EX 7

peripheral devices, CC 3, CC 9
    unplugging, CC 39

permissions, setting, PPT 63

personal accounts, OUT 26

personal computers (PCs), CC 2, CC 8–9
    new, installed software that comes with, CC 47

personal finance software, CC 63

peta-, CC 79

petabytes, CC 79

photo editing software, CC 60

photo printers, CC 29

photos, printing, CC 29

physical impairments, computer accessibility. *See* accessibility

picture elements (pixels), CC 26

pictures. *See also* graphics
    inserting and adjusting, EX 55
    inserting and styling, PPT 52–53
    recoloring, PPT 52

pie charts, EX 81, EX 94–95, PPT 57

pirated software, CC 48

pixels (picture elements), CC 26, CC 79

placeholders
    content, PPT 10
    text, PPT 8, PPT 9
    title, PPT 8, PPT 9

plot area, EX 80, EX 81

plus sign (+), addition operator, EX 7

pointers, EX 10, EX 11, WIN 6

pointing devices, CC 24, WIN 6, WIN 7
    actions, WIN 6, WIN 7

portable applications, CC 47

portable audio players, solid-state memory cards, CC 36

portable computers, CC 6, CC 9

Portable Document File (PDF), CC 57

portrait orientation, AC 80, AC 81, EX 16, EX 17, WD 78

positioning. *See also* moving
    graphics, using precise measurements, WD 66
    shapes, PPT 35

pound sign (#), criteria, AC 38

power options, WIN 19

PowerPoint. *See also* Microsoft PowerPoint 2016;
    presentation(s); slides
    adding Office Mix, PA 10
    opening PowerPoint 97-2007 presentations in PowerPoint 2016, PPT 26
    presentation views, PPT 6, PPT 7, PPT 14–15
    start screen, PPT 6, PPT 7
    touch screen, PPT 3
    uses, PPT 2

PowerPoint window, PPT 6–7

ppm. *See* pages per minute (ppm)

presentation(s)
    adding slides, PPT 10–11
    design themes, PPT 12–13
    destination, PPT 60
    digital signatures, PPT 76
    inserting charts, PPT 56–57
    inserting slides from other presentations, PPT 60–61
    inserting tables, PPT 62–63
    masters, PPT 74–75
    Office Mix, sharing, PA 12

planning, PPT 4–5
PowerPoint 97-2007, opening in PowerPoint 2016, PPT 26
printing, PPT 16–17
reviewing, PPT 86–87
saving as videos, PPT 65
sending using email, PPT 51
source, PPT 60
storyboard, PPT 5
Sway. *See* Microsoft Sway
text entry, PPT 8–9
viewing in gray scale or black and white, PPT 7
presentation graphics software. *See* Microsoft PowerPoint 2016;
  presentation software
presentation software, CC 59, PPT 2–3. *See also* Microsoft
  PowerPoint; PowerPoint
Presenter view, PPT 78
previewing, OFF 12
  charts, EX 90
primary key(s), creating, AC 10–11
primary key fields, AC 8
Print Layout gallery, PPT 16
Print Layout view, WD 17
Print Preview, AC 10
  reports, AC 80, AC 81
printer(s), CC 9, CC 28–29
  active, changing, EX 16
  connecting, CC 29
  multiple computers, CC 29
  speed, CC 28–29
  types, CC 28
printer resolution, CC 28
printing
  notes, PPT 11
  photos, CC 29
  print options, EX 16–17
  scaling to fit, EX 17
  slides in size for overhead transparencies, PPT 16
privacy, protecting, CC 17
processes, CC 53
processing, CC 5
processor(s), CC 5, CC 81, CC 82–83
  benchmarking, CC 83
  bus speed, CC 82–83
  cache, CC 83
  clock speed, CC 82
  factors affecting performance, CC 82
  multi-core, CC 82
  operation, CC 83
  word size, CC 83
processor clock, CC 82
productivity software. *See* office productivity software
professionalism, email messages, OUT 16
program(s), CC 4, WIN 2. *See also* software
  application. *See* app(s)
  stored, CC 5
project management software, CC 63
proofing tools, PPT 84, PPT 85
  foreign languages, PPT 27

properties, AC 62
  fields, AC 10
Properties dialog box, OUT 15, WD 41
Property Sheet, AC 62, AC 63
proprietary software, CC 48
Protect Document option, Info screen, WD 40
public domain software, CC 48
publishing Sways, PA 8

Q

queries, AC 4, AC 5, AC 27–41
  adding/deleting tables, AC 32
  AND criteria, AC 38–39
  data entry, AC 30, AC 31
  editing data, AC 30, AC 31
  filtering compared, AC 37
  filtering data, AC 36–37
  finding data, AC 34, AC 35
  OR criteria, AC 40–41
  Query Design view, AC 32–33
  Simple Query Wizard, AC 28–29
  sorting data, AC 34, AC 35
query design grid (query grid), AC 32
Query Design View, AC 32–33
question mark (?), wildcard, AC 36
Quick Access toolbar, CC 70–71, OFF 6, OFF 7, WD 4, WD 5,
  WIN 10, WIN 11
  customizing, OFF 12
  PowerPoint window, PPT 6, PPT 7
Quick Access view, WIN 31
Quick Analysis tool, EX 2, EX 64, EX 82, EX 83
Quick Parts, WD 85
Quick Print button, EX 16, OFF 12
Quick Styles, PPT 32, WD 55
Quick Styles gallery, WD 55
quizzes
  inserting in slides, PA 12
  interactive, inserting, PPT 89
quotation marks (""), criteria, AC 38

R

radar charts, PPT 57
RAM (random access memory), CC 32, CC 38, CC 84–85, WIN 28
  amount, CC 85
  effect on performance, CC 84
  hard drive storage compared, CC 84–85
  operation, CC 84
  64 GB specs, CC 85
  speed, CC 85
RAM cache, CC 83
random access memory. *See* RAM (random access memory)
ranges, EX 4
  named, EX 12

Read Mode view, OFF 12, OFF 13, WD 17
Reading view, PA 14, PPT 14, PPT 15
read-only files, PPT 86
    opening, OFF 10
read-only memory. *See* ROM (read-only memory)
read-only objects, AC 80
recalculation, EX 2
record(s), AC 8, AC 9
    orphan, AC 56
record source, AC 80
Record Source property, AC 87
recordable technology, CC 34
recording(s)
    screen, PA 11
    slide, PA 11
recording lectures, PA 4
Recording toolbar, PPT 81
recovering
    documents, OFF 15
    unsaved changes, to workbook file, EX 10
recurring appointments, OUT 32
Recycle Bin, WIN 4, WIN 6, WIN 7, WIN 42, WIN 43
Redo button, WD 15
reference operators, EX 12
reference software, CC 63
referential integrity, AC 12
registers, CC 83
rehearsing slide timing, PPT 81
relational database(s), AC 9
relational database software, AC 2. *See also* database(s);
    Microsoft Access 2016
relative cell references, EX 34, EX 35
    copying formulas, EX 36–37
remote storage, cloud storage compared, CC 86
Remove Sort button, AC 35
removing. *See also* deleting
    bullets, WD 62
    fields from Selected Fields list, AC 28
    hyperlinks, WD 38
    numbers from lists, WD 62
    page numbers, WD 84
Rename command, CC 76
renaming
    files, WIN 38, WIN 39
    files or folders, CC 76
    objects, AC 8
    worksheets, EX 66
Repeat button, WD 15
Replace button, AC 35
Replace command, PPT 29
replacing text, 10
replying to email messages, OUT 10, OUT 11
report(s), 79–93, AC 4, AC 5, EX 3
    calculations, AC 88–89
    Excel and Access compared, AC 3
    formatting, AC 92–93

    grouping records, AC 86–87
    page orientation, AC 81
    Report Layout View, AC 82–83
    Report Wizard, AC 80–81
    resizing and aligning controls, AC 90–91
    sections, AC 84–85
Report Footer section, AC 84
Report Header section, AC 84
Report View, AC 83
Report Wizard, AC 80–81
researching information, WD 36–37
resizing
    charts, EX 84, EX 85
    controls, AC 90
    datasheet columns, AC 17
    graphics, WD 66
    shapes, PPT 35
resolution
    display devices, CC 26–27
    printers, CC 28
    videos, PPT 65
resources, CC 52–53
response rate, CC 27
responsive design, PA 6
Restart option, WIN 19
Restore Down button, WIN 10
restore point, CC 56
restoring files, WIN 42, WIN 43
Reuse Slides pane, presentation window, PPT 60, PPT 61
rewritable technology, CC 34
Ribbon, OFF 6, OFF 7, WD 4, WD 5, WIN 6, WIN 30
    formatting text, WD 12
    PowerPoint window, PPT 6, PPT 7
Ribbon Display Options button, WD 4, WD 5
Rich Text Format, WIN 28
right angle bracket (>), comparison operators, AC 39
right indents, WD 61
right tabs, WD 59
right-aligned text, WD 56
right-clicking, WIN 7
ROM (read-only memory), CC 86–87
    changing contents, CC 87
ROM BIOS (basic input/output system), CC 87
root directory, CC 71
rotate handles, PPT 32
rotating cell contents, EX 57
ROUND function, EX 40, EX 41
rounding values, EX 40–41
row(s)
    blank, removing, WD 88
    changing height, EX 59
    deleting, EX 60, EX 61
    hiding, EX 60
    inserting, EX 60, EX 61
    new, creating, PPT 62
    unhiding, EX 60

row headings, charts, PPT 56, PPT 57
rule(s), organizing email messages, OUT 28, OUT 29
rulers, AC 84
  displaying, WD 56, WD 78
Rules Manager, EX 65

S

sandbox, PA 15
sans serif fonts, WD 50
Save As command, AC 32, WD 26
  Save command compared, CC 75, WIN 34
Save As dialog box, OFF 8, OFF 9, OFF 10, OFF 11, WD 8, WD 9, WIN 28
Save command, WD 26
  Save As command compared, CC 75, WIN 34
Save place, Backstage view, OFF 8, OFF 9
saving
  documents, WD 8–9, WD 26
  files. *See* saving files
  presentations as videos, PPT 65
saving files, OFF 8, OFF 9, WIN 28, WIN 29
  with new name, OFF 10, OFF 11
  OneDrive, OFF 9
scaling to fit, EX 17
scanners, CC 25
scatter charts, EX 81, PPT 57
screen(s). *See also* monitors
  monitors vs., CC 26
screen captures, OFF 13
screen clippings, PA 2
Screen Recording button, PPT 53
screen recordings, PA 11
  inserting in slides, PPT 53
screen size, CC 27
screenshots, adding to documents, WD 2
ScreenTips, EX 30, WD 4, WIN 6
scroll arrows, WD 4, WD 5, WIN 11
scroll bar, EX 4, EX 5, WIN 10
  parts, WIN 11
scroll boxes, WD 4, WD 5, WIN 11
SD (SecureDigital) cards, CC 37
search criteria, WIN 40
search engines, CC 13
Search folder, OUT 9
search sites, CC 13
Search Tools tab, WIN 40
secondary axis, EX 86
section(s)
  changing page layout settings, WD 81
  documents, WD 80, WD 81
  forms, AC 68, AC 69
  reports, AC 84–85

section breaks, WD 80, WD 81, WD 82
  deleting, WD 80
SecureDigital (SD) cards, CC 37
security, CC 16–17
  Excel and Access compared, AC 3
security utilities, CC 57
Select button, AC 35
Select queries, AC 28
selecting, WIN 6, WIN 7
  cell contents using keyboard, EX 10
  items using touch-screen devices, WIN 7
  multiple controls at same time, AC 91
  text, WD 10–11
selection boxes, PPT 8
Selection button, AC 35
Send to command, copying files, WIN 36
Send to menu commands, WIN 37
sending
  electronic business cards, OUT 33
  email messages, OUT 15
Sent Items folder, OUT 8, OUT 9
sequential text or values, fill handle, EX 39
serif fonts, WD 50
servers, CC 7
service packs, CC 51
setup programs, CC 50
shading, WD 64, WD 65
shadows, chart objects, EX 88
shapes
  changing size and position, PPT 35
  duplicating, PPT 36, PPT 37
  editing, PPT 36, PPT 37
  editing points, PPT 37
  inserting, PPT 32, PPT 33
  merging, PPT 34, PPT 35
  modifying, PPT 32, PPT 33
  rearranging, PPT 34, PPT 35
  setting formatting as default, PPT 38
Share button, OFF 6, OFF 7, WD 4, WD 5
Share feature, OFF 15
shareware, CC 49
sharing
  documents. *See* sharing documents
  information, EX 2
  Office Mix presentations, PA 12
  Sways, PA 8
sharing documents, WD 2
  directly from Word, WD 39
sheet tab(s), EX 4, EX 5
sheet tab scrolling buttons, EX 4, EX 5
Short Text data type, AC 7
shortcut keys, WD 27
  moving between Office programs, OFF 4
showing. *See* displaying; viewing
shrink-wrap licenses, CC 49

Shut down option, WIN 19
shutting down Windows 10, WIN 18–19
signatures, digital, PPT 76
signing out, WIN 18
Simple Query Wizard, AC 28–29
single-user licenses, CC 49
site licenses, CC 49
size
    fonts. See font sizes
    graphics, reducing, WD 66
    worksheets, EX 14
sizing, shapes, PPT 35
sizing handles, AC 68, EX 82, PPT 8, WD 66
Sleep option, WIN 19
slide(s)
    adding notes, PPT 11
    adding to presentations, PPT 10–11
    footers, PPT 40–41
    hiding temporarily, PPT 78
    inking, PPT 9
    inserting screen recordings, PPT 53
    noncontiguous, copying, PPT 60
    from other presentations, inserting, PPT 60–61
    printing in size for overhead transparencies, PPT 16
slide layouts, PPT 10
    custom, PPT 75
Slide Libraries, PPT 60
slide master(s), PPT 74, PPT 75
Slide Master view, PPT 74, PPT 75
Slide Notes feature, PA 11
Slide pane, PowerPoint window, PPT 6, PPT 7
slide recordings, PA 11
    deleting, PPT 88
slide show(s), advancing, PPT 14
Slide Show view, PPT 15
    commands, PPT 78–79
Slide Sorter view, PPT 15
slide thumbnails, PPT 6, PPT 7
slide timing, PPT 80, PPT 81
    rehearsing, PPT 81
slide transitions, PPT 80, PPT 81
    sounds, PPT 80
Slides tab, PowerPoint window, PPT 6, PPT 7
slots. See expansion slots
Smart Guides, PPT 34
Smart Lookup feature, WD 34
SmartArt graphics
    animation, PPT 82, PPT 83
    charts, EX 93
    choosing, PPT 31
    converting text to, PPT 30–31
    converting WordArt objects to, PPT 64,
        PPT 65
    reverting to standard text objects, PPT 30
SmartArt Styles, PPT 30

smartphones, CC 3
    operating systems, CC 55
    64 GB specs, CC 85
    solid-state memory cards, CC 36
Snap Assist feature, WIN 12
snap-to-grid feature, temporarily turning off, PPT 36
social networking, CC 15
soft page breaks, WD 82
software, CC 10–11, CC 45–68
    accounting, CC 63
    activating, CC 51
    application. See application software; specific types of application software
    audio editing, CC 62
    choosing, CC 72
    computer games, CC 62
    computer-aided music, CC 62
    copying and moving, CC 72–73
    database management. See database software; Microsoft Access
    defined, CC 3
    directories vs., CC 73
    document production. See desktop publishing software; Microsoft Word;
        word-processing software
    DVD authoring, CC 62–63
    educational, CC 63
    email, OUT 2
    file management programs, CC 71
    finance, CC 63
    graphics, CC 60–61
    installed on new computers, CC 47
    installing, CC 50–51
    licenses and copyrights, CC 48–49
    listing currently running programs, CC 53
    malicious. See malware
    mathematical modeling, CC 63
    new, creating, CC 72
    office productivity, CC 58–59
    options, CC 73
    personal finance, CC 63
    presentation. See Microsoft PowerPoint
    project management, CC 63
    properties, CC 73
    proprietary, CC 48
    public domain, CC 48
    reference, CC 63
    removing, CC 51
    starting programs, CC 51
    statistical, CC 63
    system. See system software
    tax preparation, CC 63
    types, CC 45–68 . See also application software; development software;
        system software
    utility. See utility software
    video editing, CC 62–63
    word-processing. See Microsoft Word; word-processing software
software licenses, CC 48, CC 49
software pirates, CC 48
software registration, CC 51
software suites, CC 58
software updates, CC 51

software upgrades, CC 51

solid-state data storage systems, CC 36–37

solid-state drives (SSDs), CC 30

solid-state memory cards
   choosing, CC 37
   popularity, CC 37

solid-state storage, CC 33

solid-state technology, CC 30

Sort buttons, AC 35

sorting
   data in tables or query datasheets, AC 34, AC 35
   email messages, OUT 9
   files and folders, WIN 32, WIN 33
   tasks, OUT 34

sound(s)
   animations, PPT 83
   slide transitions, PPT 80

sound cards, CC 9

sound systems, CC 9

source(s)
   bibliographies, WD 94, WD 95
   citations, WD 92–93
   found on Web, WD 94

source code, CC 83

source file, INT 2

Source Manager dialog box, WD 94, WD 95

source presentation, PPT 60

spacing
   lines, changing, WD 54–55
   paragraphs, changing, WD 54–55
   uniform, WD 6

spam filters, CC 14

sparklines, EX 83

spell checking, EX 68–69
   checking as you type, PPT 85
   email messages, OUT 16

Spelling and Grammar checker, WD 7, WD 34–35

Spelling: English (United States) dialog box, EX 68, EX 69

Spelling pane, PPT 84, PPT 85, WD 34, WD 35

spin boxes, WIN 15

Split Form tool, AC 56

split forms, AC 56–57

splitting, document window, WD 28

spreadsheet software, CC 58

SQL (Structured Query Language), AC 28

square brackets [], referencing fields names within expressions, AC 64

SSDs. See solid-state drives (SSDs)

SSDs (solid-state drives), CC 30

Start button, WIN 4

Start menu, WIN 4, WIN 5
   navigating, WIN 4, WIN 5
   opening and closing, WIN 4

start screen
   Microsoft Word 2016, OFF 4, OFF 5
   PowerPoint, PPT 6, PPT 7

starting
   apps, WIN 8–9
   documents, WD 6–7
   Microsoft Access 2016, AC 4, AC 5
   Microsoft Outlook 2016, OUT 26
   Windows 10, WIN 2–3

statistical software, CC 63

Statistics tab, Properties dialog box, WD 41

status bar, EX 4, EX 5, WD 4, WD 5
   PowerPoint window, PPT 6, PPT 7

stock charts, PPT 57

storage
   data, CC 30–31 . See also data storage systems
   Excel and Access compared, AC 3
   increasing capacity, CC 31
   memory vs., CC 5

storage capacity, CC 32

storage devices, CC 8, CC 30–31

storage media, CC 5, CC 30. See also specific types of storage media

Store button, WIN 5

store-and-forward technology, OUT 2

stored programs, CC 5

Storylines, PA 6

styles, WD 55
   cell, EX 62, EX 63
   Comma Style format, EX 52
   font, changing, EX 56, EX 57
   table, EX 53

subdatasheets, AC 12

subdirectories, subfolders vs., CC 72

subfolders, CC 72, WIN 26
   subdirectories vs., CC 72

subscript text, PPT 41

subtitle text placeholders, PPT 8

subtraction operator (–), EX 7

suites, OFF 2

Sum button, EX 8, EX 9

Summary tab, Properties dialog box, WD 41

Sunburst charts, EX 95

superscript text, PPT 41

surface charts, PPT 57

swap files, CC 86

Sway. See Microsoft Sway

Sway sites, PA 6

switching views, AC 66, EX 14–15

symbols, using for bullets, WD 62

syncing notebooks to cloud, PA 2–3

synonyms, WD 36, WD 37

syntax, entering property values, AC 62

system clipboard, WD 26, WIN 36

system requirements, CC 47

system software, CC 10, CC 46

system unit, CC 2, CC 8

T

tab(s), OFF 6, OFF 7, WD 4, WD 5
   PowerPoint window, PPT 6
tab controls, forms, AC 63
Tab Index property, AC 66
tab leaders, WD 58, WD 59
tab order, AC 66–67
Tab Order dialog box, AC 67
tab stop(s), AC 66, WD 58–59
Tab Stop property, AC 66
table(s), AC 4, AC 5, AC 9
   Access, linking to Excel and Word, INT 18, INT 19, INT 24–25
   Access, linking to Word, INT 18, INT 26–27
   adding to documents, WD 2
   creating, AC 8–9
   deleting, WD 88
   filtering data, AC 36–37
   finding data, AC 34, AC 35
   formatting worksheets as, EX 53
   inserting, PPT 62–63
   inserting in documents, WD 88–89
   layouts, AC 59
   one-to-many relationships, AC 12–13
   queries, adding or deleting, AC 32
   sorting data, AC 34, AC 35
   Word, copying to Access, INT 18, INT 22–23
Table Design View, AC 6, AC 7
table styles, EX 53
tablet computers, CC 6, CC 7
   operating systems, CC 55
Tabs, WIN 6
Tabs dialog box, WD 58, WD 59
task(s), OUT 34–35
Task View button, WIN 5, WIN 38
taskbar, WIN 4, WIN 5, WIN 11
   buttons, WIN 5
   displaying, WIN 4
   using, WIN 13
tax preparation software, CC 63
Tell Me box, WD 4, WD 5
templates, AC 6, EX 2, EX 41, OFF 4, PA 2, WD 14–15
tera-, CC 79
terabytes, CC 79
text
   bold, WD 52
   changing case, WD 52
   colors, PPT 77
   converting handwriting to, PA 3–4
   converting to SmartArt, PPT 30–31
   copying, PPT 8, WD 2
   copying and pasting, WD 28–29
   cutting and pasting, WD 26
   deselecting, WD 10
   documents. See document(s)
   dragging and dropping, WD 26
   editing, WD 2
   entering. See text entry
   finding, WD 32–33
   formatting. See formatting text
   highlighting, WD 65
   inserting with AutoCorrect, WD 6, WD 7, WD 35
   italic, WD 52
   from Microsoft Word, inserting, PPT 50–51
   moving, WD 2
   paragraphs. See paragraph(s)
   replacing, WD 32–33
   selecting, WD 10–11
   superscript and subscript, PPT 41
   typing, WD 2
   underlining, WD 53
Text Align property, AC 62
text annotations, charts, EX 92, EX 93
text boxes, WIN 15
   changing defaults, PPT 55
   forms, AC 54, AC 63
   inserting in charts, EX 92
   inserting in slides, PPT 54–55
text concatenation operators, EX 12
Text Effects and Typography button, WD 52
text entry
   Outline view, PPT 26–27
   PowerPoint, PPT 2
   slides, PPT 8–9
text messages, CC 15
text objects
   applying WordArt styles, EX 90
   changing outline width or style, PPT 54
text placeholders, PPT 8, PPT 9
text wrapping, WD 83
theft, of computer, CC 16
theme(s), EX 63, PPT 12–13, WD 50, WD 57
   colors, PPT 77
   customizing, PPT 13, PPT 76, PPT 77
   multiple, applying to same presentation, PPT 12
theme colors, PPT 12
theme effects, PPT 12
Themes gallery, EX 63
Thesaurus pane, WD 36, WD 37
3-D charts, EX 87
3-D graphics software, CC 61
3-D printers, CC 29
thumbnails, slide, PPT 6, PPT 7
tick marks, EX 80, EX 81
tiles, WIN 4
title(s)
   changing alignment and angle, EX 91
   moving, EX 88
title bar, OFF 6, WD 4, WD 5, WIN 10
title placeholders, PPT 8, PPT 9
To Do Tags, PA 2
To-Do Bar button, OUT 26, OUT 27
to-do lists, electronic, OUT 34–35

toggle buttons, WD 10
  forms, AC 63
Toggle Filter button, AC 35
toner, CC 28
tool palettes, groups, WIN 10
toolbars, WIN 10, WIN 28. *See also specific toolbars*
Totals tab, Quick Analysis tool, EX 26, EX 27
touch screen technology, CC 25
touch screens, WIN 2
  Office 2016 apps, OFF 4
  PowerPoint, PPT 3
touchpads, CC 25
touch-screen devices, selecting and moving items, WIN 7
trackballs, CC 25
trackpads, CC 25
Treemap charts, EX 95

U

UIs. *See* user interfaces (UIs)
unbound controls, AC 61
underlining text, WD 53
Undo button, EX 10, WD 10, WD 15
unfreezing fields in datasheets, AC 30
unhiding
  columns, EX 60
  fields in datasheets, AC 30
  rows, EX 60
Uniform Resource Locators (URLs), CC 12–13
uniform spacing, WD 6
universal apps, WIN 8
universal serial bus (USB) ports, CC 39
unplugging peripheral devices, CC 39
Up to button, Save As dialog box, WD 9
updates, installing when you exit Windows, WIN 19
  software, CC 51
upgrades, software, CC 51
upgrading, processors, CC 81
URLs (Uniform Resource Locators), CC 12–13
USB flash drives (USB drives), CC 8, CC 37, WIN 28
USB hubs, CC 31
USB ports, WIN 28
USB (universal serial bus) ports, CC 39
user(s), databases, AC 54
user IDs, CC 4
user interfaces (UIs), CC 54, OFF 6, WIN 4. *See also* graphical user
  interfaces (GUIs)
usernames, OUT 4
utility software, CC 56–57
  alternatives, CC 56
  customizing desktop, CC 56
  device drivers, CC 56

  included with operating system, CC 56
  need, CC 56
  PDF files, CC 56
  running in background, CC 56

V

vacation responses, OUT 11
value(s), EX 8
  changing alignment, EX 56, EX 57
  column too narrow to display, EX 58
  formatting, EX 52–53
  rounding, EX 40–41
value axis, EX 80, EX 81
vertical axis, EX 80, EX 81
vertical ruler, WD 4, WD 5
vertical scroll bar, WD 4
video(s)
  adding to documents, WD 2
  saving presentations as, PPT 65
video clips, capturing, PA 11
video editing software, CC 62–63
video game consoles, CC 7
view(s), OFF 12, OFF 13, WD 17. *See also specific views*
  files and folders, changing, WIN 32–33
  objects, AC 10
  PowerPoint, PPT 6, PPT 7, PPT 14–15
  reports, AC 83
  switching between, AC 66, EX 14–15
view buttons, WD 4, WD 5
View Shortcuts buttons, PowerPoint window, PPT 6, PPT 7
viewing. *See also* displaying; unhiding
  tasks, OUT 34
  webpages, CC 12
viewing angle width, CC 27
virtual assistant, Edge, PA 14–15
virtual keyboards, CC 25
virtual memory, CC 86
Voice over IP (VoIP), CC 15

W

Waterfall charts, EX 95
wearable computers, CC 25
weather, Calendar view, OUT 27
Web. *See* World Wide Web (Web or WWW)
web applications (web apps), CC 13, CC 47
web authoring software, CC 59
web browsers, CC 12, CC 13. *See also* Microsoft Edge
web cams, CC 9
Web Layout view, WD 17
Web Note tools, PA 15

web-based email, OUT 5, OUT 6
webpages, CC 12
    annotating, PA 15
    live, inserting in slides, PA 12
    viewing, CC 12
websites, CC 13
    navigating, CC 13
what-if analysis, EX 2, EX 3
white space, paragraph spacing, WD 54
widows, WD 82
wikis, CC 15
wildcards, AC 36
window(s), WIN 10–11
    active, WIN 12
    borders, WIN 12
    elements, WIN 10, WIN 11
    inactive, WIN 12
    multiple, PPT 61, WIN 12–13
Window control buttons, WIN 10, WIN 11
Windows, CC 54
    versions, CC 54
Windows 10. *See* Microsoft Windows 10
Windows accessories, WIN 8
Windows Action Center, WIN 32
Windows Search, WIN 40–41
Windows software, CC 10
Windows Store, WIN 8
Word. *See* Microsoft Word 2016
Word Count dialog box, WD 36, WD 37
word processing software, CC 58, WD 2.
    See also Microsoft Word 2016
Word program window, WD 4–5
word size, CC 83
word wrap, WD 6
WordArt, WD 60
    applying styles to text objects, EX 90
    converting to SmartArt objects, PPT 64, PPT 65
    formatting, PPT 64, PPT 65
    inserting, PPT 64, PPT 65
word-processing software, CC 58
workbooks, EX 2
    emailing, EX 68
    new, creating using templates, EX 41
    recovering unsaved changes, EX 10

worksheet(s), CC 58, EX 2, EX 3, PPT 56
    adding, EX 67
    add-ins to improve functionality, EX 26
    copying, EX 67
    deleting, EX 66, EX 67
    formatting. *See* formatting worksheets
    importing into Access, INT 18, INT 19, INT 20–21
    moving between, EX 66
    navigating, EX 9
    renaming, EX 66
    size, EX 14
    switching views, EX 14–15
worksheet window, EX 4, EX 5
workstations, CC 7
World Wide Web (Web or WWW), Internet vs., CC 12
WWW. *See* World Wide Web (Web or WWW)

X

X Y charts, PPT 57
x-axis, EX 80, EX 81

Y

y-axis, EX 80, EX 81
Yes/No data type, AC 7

Z

z-axis, EX 80, EX 87
zetta-, CC 79
zettabytes, CC 79
Zoom In button, Microsoft Office 2016, OFF 6, OFF 7
Zoom level button, WD 4, WD 5
Zoom Out button, Microsoft Office 2016, OFF 6, OFF 7
Zoom slider, EX 16, WD 4, WD 5
    PowerPoint window, PPT 6, PPT 7